SEVENTH EDITION

Literature for Composition

Essays, Fiction, Poetry, and Drama

Edited by

Sylvan Barnet
Tufts University

William Burto
University of Lowell

William E. Cain
Wellesley College

PEARSON
Longman

New York   San Francisco   Boston
London   Toronto   Sydney   Tokyo   Singapore   Madrid
Mexico City   Munich   Paris   Cape Town   Hong Kong   Montreal

Vice President and Editor-in-Chief: Joseph Terry
Managing Editor: Erika Berg
Development Manager: Janet Lanphier
Development Editor: Katharine Glynn
Executive Marketing Manager: Ann Stypuloski
Senior Supplements Editor: Donna Campion
Managing Editor: Bob Ginsberg
Production Manager: Joseph Vella
Project Coordination, Text Design, and Electronic Page Makeup:
   Pre-Press Company, Inc.
Cover Designer/Manager: John Callahan
Cover Illustration/Photo: Matisse, Henri (French, 1869–1954) *Open Window, Collioure,*
   Collection of Mr. and Mrs. John Hay Whitney. Photograph © 2004 Board of
   Trustees, National Gallery of Art, Washington, D.C., 1905, oil on canvas.
Photo Researcher: Photosearch, Inc.
Manufacturing Manager: Mary Fischer
Manufacturing Buyer: Roy L. Pickering, Jr.
Printer and Binder: Quebecor World Taunton
Cover Printer: The Lehigh Press, Inc.

For permission to use copyrighted material, grateful acknowledgment is made to the
copyright holders on pp. 1385–1394, which are hereby made part of this copyright
page.

Library of Congress Cataloging-in-Publication Data
Literature for composition: essays, fiction, poetry, and drama/edited by Sylvan Barnet,
William Burto, William E. Cain.–7th ed.
   p. cm.
Includes index.
ISBN 0-321-28034-2
   1. College readers. 2. English language-Rhetoric-Problems, exercises, etc. 3.
Criticism-Authorship-Problems, exercises, etc. 4. Academic writing-Problems,
exercises, etc. I. Barnet, Sylvan. II. Burto, William. III. Cain, William E., 1952
PE1417.L633 2005
808'.0427-dc22   2004053535

Please visit us at http://www.ablongman.com

ISBN 0-321-28034-2

2 3 4 5 6 7 8 9 10—QWT—07 06 05

Contents

PART I
Getting Started: From Response to Argument   1

CHAPTER 1   The Writer as Reader   3

CHAPTER 2   The Reader as Writer   13

CHAPTER 3   Reading Literature Closely: Explication   42

CHAPTER 4   Reading Literature Closely: Analysis   61

CHAPTER **5**   **Other Kinds of Writing about Literature**   **130**

CHAPTER **6**   Reading and Writing about Visual Culture   **150**

PART II

*Up Close: Thinking Critically about Literary Works
and Literary Forms*   **187**

CHAPTER **7**   Critical Thinking: Asking Questions
                   and Making Comparisons   **189**

CHAPTER **8** Reading and Writing about Essays **207**

CHAPTER **9** Reading and Writing about Fiction **225**

CHAPTER **10** Thinking and Writing Critically about
                  Short Stories: Two Case Studies **254**

CHAPTER 11   Fiction into Film   308

CHAPTER 12   Reading and Writing about Drama   333

CHAPTER **13**   **Thinking Critically about Drama**   420

CHAPTER **14**   **Reading and Writing about Poetry**   473

CHAPTER **15** Thinking Critically about Poetry: Three Case Studies

PART III

Standing Back: Arguing Interpretations and Evaluations, and Understanding Critical Strategies   581

PART IV
A Thematic Anthology

C H A P T E R **23** Studying America in Crisis: Responding to Literature of the Civil War, the Great Depression, the Vietnam War, and September 11, 2001 1054

CHAPTER 25   Law and Disorder   1208

APPENDIX **A**   **Remarks about Manuscript Form**   **1320**

APPENDIX **B**   **Writing a Research Paper**   **1325**

Contents by Genre

Essays

Fiction

Poetry

Drama

List of Illustrations

Preface to Instructors

This book is based on the assumption that students in composition or literature courses should encounter first-rate writing—not simply competent prose but the powerful reports of experience that have been recorded by highly skilled writers of the past and present—reports of experiences that *must* be shared. Our view is not original—a thousand years ago, in Japan, Lady Murasaki (978?–1026) in *The Tale of Genji* wrote a scene in which some of her characters talk about reading fiction, and one of them offers his opinion as to why an author writes:

> Again and again writers find something in their experience, or see something in the life around them, that seems so important they cannot bear to let it pass into oblivion. There must never come a time, the writer feels, when people do not know about this.

We assume that you share our belief that the study of such writing offers pleasure and insight into life and also leads to increased skill in communicating.

If we were asked to give, very briefly, the key features of *Literature for Composition,* Seventh Edition, here is what we would say:

KEY FEATURES

Extensive Instruction in Composition. Students are guided through the entire process of writing, beginning with generating ideas (for instance, by listing or by annotating a text), developing a thesis, and on through the final stages of documenting and editing. Many examples of student writing are included.

Strategies for Writing Effective Arguments. The seventh edition focuses on argument and evaluation, not only in the case studies but also in the "Topics for Critical Thinking and Writing" that follow most of the readings. We emphasize the importance of questioning your own assumptions—a key principle in critical thinking—and we also emphasize the importance of setting forth thoughtful responses in the form of coherent, readable arguments.

Wide Range of Literary Selections. The book includes some three hundred texts, ranging from such classic material as Sophocles's *Antigonê* to a story and a poem about the attack on the World Trade Center in 2001. Almost one-third of the selections are new to this edition.

Abundant Visual Material. The book is rich in photographs, paintings, and facsimiles of manuscripts. The images are chosen to enhance the reader's understanding of particular works of literature. For example, we include photos of Buffalo Bill and a facsimile of a draft of E. E. Cummings's poem about Buffalo Bill (to our knowledge, never before published in a textbook). Similarly, we include previously unpublished typescript pages of John Updike's "A&P," thereby helping students to think about the kinds of changes that a serious writer makes.

Introductory Genre Anthology. After preliminary chapters on getting ideas and thinking critically, students encounter chapters devoted to essays, fiction, drama, and poetry.

Thematic Anthology. Works are arranged under seven themes (two are new): Journeys; Love and Hate; Making Men and Women; Innocence and Experience; Studying America in Crisis: the Civil War, the Great Depression, the Vietnam War, and September 11, 2001; Identity in America; and Law and Disorder.

Case Studies. Nine case studies are included to give a variety of perspectives for writing and research: Flannery O'Connor, John Updike, Emily Dickinson, America Sings the Blues, Literary Visions (Word and Image), Raymond Carver, *Hamlet*, American Indian Identity, and Ralph Ellison.

Extensive Material on Research and the Internet. Because instructors are increasingly assigning research papers, the seventh edition includes material on short, medium-length, and long research papers on literature and history, and it provides up-to-date instruction on evaluating, using, and citing electronic sources.

Emphasis on Critical Thinking. Connected to reading and writing, critical thinking is at the heart of the first four chapters and is kept in view throughout the book, most visibly in the "Topics for Critical Thinking and Writing" that follow each literary selection, and in Chapters 16 and 17, "Arguing an Interpretation" and "Arguing an Evaluation."

Word and Image. The visual material includes a color insert, which is a case study featuring eleven paintings that are the subjects of poems. Students analyze the poems and paintings and offer evidence to support their arguments.

Checklists. Sixteen checklists on such topics as "Writing with a Word Processor," "Revising Paragraphs," "Editing a Draft," and "Citing Sources on the World Wide Web" help students to become in effect peer readers of their own writing.

ORGANIZATION

Literature for Composition, Seventh Edition, is in large part an anthology of literature, but it is more—it also offers instruction in writing.

Part I, "Getting Started: From Response to Argument," consists of six chapters with thirty-two short works of literature. The aim of all the chapters in Part I is to help students read and respond—in writing—to literature. The first two chapters discuss annotating, free writing, and listing; the third and fourth chapters discuss writing explications and analyses; and the fifth chapter discusses other kinds of writing, including parody, stories based on stories, and poems based on poems. These chapters include eight examples of student writing, all of which are accompanied by the preliminary journal entries or drafts that helped produce them. Chapter 6, "Reading and Writing about Visual Culture," includes two essays by students and a generous group of photographs for analysis.

Part II, "Up Close: Thinking Critically about Literary Works and Literary Forms," begins with a discussion of critical thinking (Chapter 7). This chapter invites students to analyze, especially by means of comparison, (1) a photograph of Buffalo Bill and Sitting Bull; (2) E. E. Cummings's poem "Buffalo Bill 's," and (3) the manuscript draft of the poem. The next eight chapters introduce the students to four genres: the essay (Chapter 8), fiction (Chapters 9–11), drama (Chapters 12 and 13), and poetry (Chapters 14 and 15). The chapter on the essay includes four essays, and additional essays appear in the later thematic chapters. The three chapters on fiction, which include a chapter on filmed fiction, present twelve stories, with case studies on Flannery O'Connor and John Updike. The two chapters on drama include three plays; the two chapters on poetry include twenty-eight poems followed by case studies on Emily Dickinson (ten poems), on the blues (thirteen songs and poems), and on poems about pictures (twelve poems). Suggested topics for discussion and examples of student writing (annotations, journal entries, drafts, and final essays) help students think critically and develop arguments about the material. Part II, then, offers a small anthology of literature organized by genre, as well as abundant guidance in thinking and writing about literature.

Part III, "Standing Back: Arguing Interpretations and Evaluations, and Understanding Critical Strategies," consists of three chapters: "Arguing an Interpretation" (Chapter 16), "Arguing an Evaluation" (Chapter 17), and "Writing about Literature: An Overview of Critical Strategies" (Chapter 18). Our idea is this: If instructors begin the course by assigning some or all of the chapters in Parts I and II, by now the students have read enough literature to be in a good position to think further about the assumptions underlying the analytic interpretations and evaluations they are writing.

About 120 literary texts appear in Parts I, II, and III; another 160 appear in Part IV, "A Thematic Anthology," where they are grouped into seven themes: Journeys, Love and Hate, Making Men and Women, Innocence and Experience, Studying America in Crisis, Identity in America, and Law and Disorder. Here, as earlier, almost all of the essays, stories, plays, and poems are followed by questions to stimulate critical thinking and writing.

The book concludes with four appendices: "Remarks about Manuscript Form," "Writing a Research Paper," "New Approaches to the Research Paper: Literature, History, and the World Wide Web," and "Glossary of Literary Terms." The material on manuscript form may seem to be yet another discussion of writing, and some readers may wonder why it is put near the back of the book. But manuscript form is less a matter of drafting and revising than it is of editing. It is, so to speak, the final packaging of a product that develops during a complicated process, a process that begins with reading, responding, and finding a topic, a thesis (supported by evidence), and a voice, not with worrying about the width of margins or the form of citations. The last thing done in writing an essay, and therefore almost the last thing presented in our book, is to set it forth in a physical form fit for human consumption.

WHAT IS NEW IN THE SEVENTH EDITION?

Instructors familiar with earlier editions will notice that we retain our emphasis on critical thinking and argument, but we have made many substitutions in the literary works. Here, for the convenience of instructors who have used an earlier edition, we will list the major changes:

New Case Studies

We now have nine case studies. These are varied and do not simply consist of a literary work followed by a number of critical interpretations. Rather, we include previously unpublished manuscripts, comments by the authors, and visual material. We have retained case studies on Ralph Ellison's "Battle Royal," Flannery

O'Connor, Raymond Carver, Emily Dickinson, *Hamlet,* American Indian Identity, and Literary Visions (Word and Image), and we have added the following:

- *Writing about John Updike* includes four stories (two with typescript pages showing Updike's revisions) and a mini-anthology of Updike's comments about short fiction.
- *America Sings the Blues: A Collection of Songs and Poems* includes not only such classics as *St. Louis Blues* and *Thinking Blues* but also poems by Auden and Pastan.

New Thematic Units

Two of the seven thematic chapters are new:

- *Journeys* includes material ranging from Joan Didion's classic essay "On Going Home" to relatively unfamiliar material such as a Japanese folk tale and Montesquieu's *Persian Letters.* (Students are invited to adopt Montesquieu's device of adopting the persona of an outsider in order to write an innocent-eye account of an aspect of contemporary society.)
- *Studying America in Crisis* contains four parts: Literature of the Civil War, the Great Depression, the Vietnam War, and September 11, 2001.

Each of the seven thematic units now begin with *Short Views,* a dozen or so brief statements, ranging from epigrammatic sentences to a paragraph. These memorable and provocative comments are followed by topics for writing, and they can also be juxtaposed with the readings in the chapter.

We have also made many changes in the literary selections presented within those themes that we have retained.

Increased Emphasis on Film

Chapter 11, "Fiction into Film," now includes Joyce Carol Oates's essay on the film version of "Where Are You Going, Where Have You Been?" and Chapter 12, "Reading and Writing about Drama," now includes an amplified discussion of "Thinking about a Filmed Version of a Play."

RESOURCES FOR STUDENTS AND INSTRUCTORS

Literature for Composition CD-ROM.   A dedicated CD-ROM allows students to learn the skills of writing and argumentation interactively through writing activities and assignments. Paintings, photographs, and audio and film clips support the chapters on visual literacy and film as well as spark student interest in the literary selections. All media are supported with apparatus and assignments. This CD-ROM is available free when value-packed with *Literature for Composition,* Seventh Edition. ISBN 0-321-27720-1.

Instructor's Manual.   An instructor's manual with detailed comments and suggestions for teaching each selection is available. This important resource, entirely written by the authors of the text, also contains references to critical articles and books that we have found to be most useful. ISBN 0-321-27721-X.

My *LiteratureLab*.   MyLiteratureLab offers students a rich source of guidance in the key areas of reading, interpreting, writing, and research. It includes audio lectures, visuals, interactive readings, student papers, many writing prompts, access to Research Navigator, and numerous tools useful for your literature course. Of special note are the distinctive Longman Lectures, given by many of Longman's prestigious authors, which provide students with insights and support about reading and interpreting the most popular works of literature.

Video Program.   For qualified adopters, an impressive selection of videotapes is available to enrich students' experience of literature. Contact your sales representative to learn how to qualify.

MLA Documentation Style: A Concise Guide for Students, Second Edition, by Michael Greer.   Replete with examples and clear explanations, this straightforward and accessible manual helps students understand and properly use the basic principles of MLA Documentation. This brief guide includes a section on Frequently Asked Questions about MLA documentation style, provides all of the information students need to properly cite works and avoid plagiarism, and offers helpful guidelines on formatting papers. FREE when packaged with *Literature for Composition*. ISBN 0-321-24357-9 (Sample through Socrates).

Responding to Literature: A Writer's Journal.   This journal provides students with their own personal space for writing. Helpful prompts for responding to fiction, poetry, and drama are also included. Available free when value-packed with *Literature for Composition*.

Evaluating a Performance.   Perfect for the student assigned to review a local production, this supplement offers students a convenient place to record their evaluation. Useful tips and suggestions of things to consider when evaluating a production are included. Available free when value-packed with *Literature for Composition*. Seventh Edition. ISBN 0-321-09541-3.

Literature Timeline by Heidi Jacobs.   This accessible and visually appealing timeline provides students with a chronological overview of the major literary works that have been written throughout history. In addition, the timeline also lists the major sociocultural and political events that had occurred contemporaneously with these major works of literature to provide students with historical and contextual insights into the impact historical events have had on writers and their works . . . and vice versa. FREE when packaged with *Literature for Composition*. ISBN 0-321-14315-9.

Take Note!   A complete information management tool for students who are working on research papers or other projects that require the use of outside sources. This cross-platform CD-ROM integrates note taking, outlining, and bibliography management into one easy-to-use package. Available at a discount when value-packed with *Literature for Composition,* Seventh Edition. ISBN 0-321-08232-X.

Merriam-Webster's Reader's Handbook: Your Complete Guide to Literary Terms.
Includes nearly 2,000 entries, including Greek and Latin terminology, and descrip-

tions for every major genre, style, and era of writing. Assured authority from the combined resources of Merriam-Webster and Encyclopaedia Britannica. Available at a significant discount when value-packed with *Literature for Composition,* Seventh Edition. ISBN 0-321-10541-9.

Penguin Discount Novel Program. In cooperation with Penguin Putnam, Inc., one of our sibling companies, Longman is proud to offer a variety of Penguin paperbacks at a significant discount when packaged with any Longman title. The available titles include works by authors as diverse as Toni Morrison, Julia Alvarez, Mary Shelley, and Shakespeare. To review the complete list of titles available, visit the Longman-Penguin-Putnam Website *<http://www.ablongman.com/ penguin>.* Discounted prices of individual Penguin novels are available on the Web site.

Acknowledgments

In preparing the first six editions of *Literature for Composition,* we were indebted to Elizabeth Addison, James Allen, Kathleen Anderson-Wyman, Mary J. Balkun, Daniel Barwick, David Beach, Phyllis Betz, Margaret Blayney, Bertha Norman Booker, John P. Boots, Pam Bourgeois, Carol Ann Britt, Jennifer Bruer, Robin W. Bryant, Sharon Buzzard, Kathleen Shine Cain, Diana Cardenas, William Carpenter, Mike Chu, Dennis Ciesielski, Arlene Clift-Pellow, Walter B. Connolly, Stanley Corkin, Linda Cravens, Bruce Danner, Donald A. Daiker, Phebe Davidson, Beth DeMeo, John Desjarlais, Emily Dial-Driver, Ren Draya, James Dubinsky, Gail Duffy, Bill Elliott, Leonard W. Engel, William Epperson, Martin J. Fertig, Elinor C. Flewellen, Kay Fortson, Marie Foster, Donna Friedman, Larry Frost, Loris Galford, Chris Grieco, Jessica Beth Gordon, Debbie Hanson, Dorothy Hardman, Sandra H. Harris, Syndey Harrison, Sally Harrold, Michael Hennessey, Mary Herbert, Ana B. Hernandez, Maureen Hoag, Clayton Hudnall, Joyce A. Ingram, Craig Johnson, Michael Johnson, Angela Jones, Rodney Keller, Beth Kemper, Alison Kuehner, Regina Lebowitz, Margaret Lindgren, Robert Lynch, Maria Makowiecka, Phil Martin, Sara McKnight Boone, Delma McLeod-Porter, Linda McPherson, Bill McWilliams, Martin Meszaros, Zack Miller, JoAnna S. Mink, Dorothy Minor, Charles Moran, Patricia G. Morgan, Nancy Morris, Jonathan Morrow, Christina Murphy, Richard Nielson, David Norlin, Marsha Nourse, John O'Connor, Chris Orchard, Eric Otto, Suzanne Owens, Janet Palmer, James R. Payne, Stephanie Pelkowski, Don K. Pierstorff, Gerald Pike, Louis H. Pratt, Michael Punches, Bruce A. Reid, Linda Robertson, Lois Sampson, Terry Santos, Jim Schwartz, Robert Schwegler, Linda Scott, Herbert Shapiro, William Shelley, Janice Slaughter, Martha Ann Smith, Tiga Spitsberg, Judith Stanford, Darlene Strawser, Geri Strecker, Jim Streeter, David Sudol, Beverly Swan, Leesther Thomas, Raymond L. Thomas, Susan D. Tilka, Mary Trachsel, Dorothy Trusock, Billie Varnum, John H. Venne, Mickey Wadia, Nancy Walker, Arthur Wohlgemuth, Cary Wolfe, Sallie Woolf, Linda Woodson, Kathy J. Wright, Carlson Yost, Dennis Young, and Gary Zacharias.

For the seventh edition, we want to thank the following reviewers: Jonathan Alexander, University of Cincinnati; Patricia Baldwin, Pittsburgh Community College; Noelle Brada-Williams, San Jose State University; Carol Ann Britt, San Antonio College; Alan P. Church, University of Texas at Brownsville; John Dobelbower, Ball State University; Susan Grimland, Collin County Community College; Tom Hayes, John Carroll University; Keith Haynes, Yavapai Community College; Michael Hennessy, Texas State University; Allen Hoey, Bucks County Community College; Diane Houston, Edmonds Community College; Kristianne

Kalata, Duquesne University; Alison Kuehner, Ohlone College; Sonya Lancaster, University of Kansas; John Loftis, University of Northern Colorado; Dennis McDonald, Iowa Lakes Community College; Wayne Moore, University of Texas at Brownsville; Torria Norman, Black Hawk College; Phyllis Orlicek, Phillips Community College; Suzanne Owens, Lorain County Community College; John Prince, Ball State University; Thomas Reynolds, Northwestern State University; Sigmar J. Schwarz, California Lutheran University; David Slater, Northwest Missouri State University; Pam Stinson, Northern Oklahoma College; Anthony Stubbs, Iowa Lakes Community College; Betty Weldon, Jefferson Community College-Southwest; Patrick White, University of Delaware; and Bertha Wise, Oklahoma City Community College.

For assistance in locating manuscripts by John Updike, we want to thank Elizabeth Falsey, of Houghton Library, Harvard University, and we wish also to thank Mr. Updike for kindly letting us reprint these pages.

For many e-mails and conversations about the seventh edition, and for help with its preparation, we are grateful to Erika Berg and Katharine Glynn at Longman. We wish also to thank Virginia Creeden, who secured copyright permission for the texts, and Peter Sanfilippo, who secured permission for the images. Katy Faria at Pre-Press Company and Joe Vella at Longman expertly coordinated the efforts of publisher, authors, copyeditor, proofreader, and compositor. In short, we have been fortunate in our associates.

Bill Cain would like to thank his wife Barbara and his daughters Julia and Isabel for their love and support.

SYLVAN BARNET
WILLIAM BURTO
WILLIAM E. CAIN

Letter to Students

We hope that you already enjoy reading literature and that *Literature for Composition* will help you enjoy it even more. But as you begin your course this semester with our book, we would like to say a little more to you about why we wrote it, how we believe it can help you, and in what ways we think it can deepen and enrich your pleasure in studying literature.

Throughout the process of writing and rewriting *Literature for Composition,* we saw ourselves as teachers, bringing to you the kinds of suggestions and strategies that, over many years, we have shared with the students we have taught.

As you can tell from a glance at the Contents, *Literature for Composition* includes a great deal of practical advice about reading and responding to literature and about writing analytical papers, advice that comes directly from our experience not only as readers and writers but also as teachers. This experience derives from classrooms, from conferences with students, and from assignments we have given, read, responded to, and graded. We have learned from our experiences (we have revised this book six times, each time fairly extensively) and have done our best to give you the tools that will help you make yourself a more perceptive reader and a more careful, cogent writer.

Speaking of making and remaking, we are reminded of a short poem by William Butler Yeats, who was a persistent reviser of his work. (You can find three versions of his poem "Leda and the Swan" on pages 140–141.)

> The friends that have it I do wrong
> Whenever I remake a song,
> Should know what issue is at stake:
> It is myself that I remake.

Like Yeats, you will develop throughout your life: you will find you have new things to say, and you may even come to find that the tools you acquired in college—and that suited you for a while—are not fully adequate to the new self that you have become. We can't claim to equip you for the rest of your life—though some of these works of literature surely will remain in your mind for years—but we do claim that, with your instructor, we are helping you develop skills that are important for your mental progress. We have in mind skills useful not merely in the course in which you are now enrolled, or other literature courses, or even courses in the humanities in general that you may take. We go further. We think that these skills in reading and writing are important for your development as an educated adult. Becoming an alert reader and an effective writer should be among the central goals of your education, and they are goals that *Literature for Composition* is designed to help you reach.

The skills we stress in *Literature for Composition* will enable you to gain confidence as a reader of literary works so that you will increase your understanding of what literature offers. You need not enjoy all authors equally. You'll have your favorites—and also some authors whom you do not like much at all. There's nothing wrong with that; reading literature is very much a personal encounter. But, at the same time, the skills we highlight in *Literature for Composition* can help you know and explain why one author means much to you and another does not. In this respect, reading and studying literature is more than personal; as we share our responses and try to express them effectively in writing, the work that we perform becomes cooperative and communal, a type of cultural conversation among fellow students, teachers, and friends.

As you proceed through *Literature for Composition* and gain further experience as a reader and writer, you will start to see features of poems, stories, and plays that you had not noticed before, or that you had noticed but not really understood, or that you had understood but not, so to speak, fully experienced. You may even find yourself enjoying an author you thought you disliked and would never be able to understand. The study of literature calls for concentration, commitment, and discipline. It's work—sometimes hard, challenging work. But it is rewarding work, and we believe that it will lead you to find literature more engaging and more pleasurable.

We hope that *Literature for Composition* will have this effect for you. Feel free to contact us with your comments and suggestions. We are eager to know what in this book has served you well, and what we might do better. You can write to us in care of Literature Editor, Longman Publishers, 1185 Avenue of the Americas, New York, NY 10036.

SYLVAN BARNET
WILLIAM BURTO
WILLIAM E. CAIN

PART I

Getting Started

From Response to Argument

1

The Writer as Reader

Interviewer: Did you know as a child you wanted to be a writer?
Toni Morrison: No. I wanted to be a reader.

READING AND RESPONDING

Learning to write is in large measure learning to read. The text you must read most carefully is the one you write, an essay you will ask someone else to read. It may start as a jotting in the margin of a book you are reading or as a brief note in a journal, and it will go through several drafts before it becomes an essay. To produce something that another person will find worth reading, you must read each draft with care, trying to imagine the effect your words are likely to have on your reader. In writing about literature, you will apply some of the same critical skills to your reading; that is, you will examine your responses to what you are reading and will try to account for them.

Let's begin by looking at a very short story by Kate Chopin (1851–1904). (The name is pronounced in the French way, something like "show pan.") Kate O'Flaherty, born into a prosperous family in St. Louis, in 1870 married Oscar Chopin, a French-Creole businessman from Louisiana. They lived in New Orleans, where they had six children. Oscar died of malaria in 1882, and in 1884 Kate returned to St. Louis, where, living with her mother and children, she began to write fiction.

KATE CHOPIN
Ripe Figs

Maman-Nainaine said that when the figs were ripe Babette might go to visit her cousins down on the Bayou-Lafourche where the sugar cane grows. Not that the ripening of figs had the least thing to do with it, but that is the way Maman-Nainaine was.

It seemed to Babette a very long time to wait; for the leaves upon the trees were tender yet, and the figs were like little hard, green marbles.

But warm rains came along and plenty of strong sunshine, and though Maman-Nainaine was as patient as the statue of la Madone, and Babette as restless as a humming-bird, the first thing they both knew it was hot summertime. Every day Babette danced out to where the fig-trees were in a long line against the fence. She walked slowly beneath them, carefully peering between the gnarled, spreading branches. But each time she came disconsolate away again. What she saw there finally was something that made her sing and dance the whole long day.

When Maman-Nainaine sat down in her stately way to breakfast, the following morning, her muslin cap standing like an aureole about her white, placid face, Babette approached. She bore a dainty porcelain platter, which she set down before her godmother. It contained a dozen purple figs, fringed around with their rich, green leaves.

"Ah," said Maman-Nainaine arching her eyebrows, "how early the figs have ripened this year!"

"Oh," said Babette. "I think they have ripened very late."

"Babette," continued Maman-Nainaine, as she peeled the very plumpest figs with her pointed silver fruit-knife, "you will carry my love to them all down on Bayou-Lafourche. And tell your Tante Frosine I shall look for her at Toussaint— when the chrysanthemums are in bloom."

[1893]

Reading as Re-creation

If we had been Chopin's contemporaries, we might have read this sketch in *Vogue* in 1893 or in an early collection of her works, *A Night in Acadie* (1897). But we are not Chopin's original readers, and, since we live more than a century later, we inevitably read "Ripe Figs" in a somewhat different way. And this gets us to an important truth about writing and reading. A writer writes, sets forth his or her meaning, and attempts to guide the reader's responses, as we all do when we write a letter home saying that we're thinking of dropping a course or asking for news or money. To this extent, the writer creates the written work and puts a meaning in it.

But the reader, whether reading that written work as a requirement or for recreation, *re-creates* it according to his or her experience and understanding. For instance, if the letter-writer's appeal for money is too indirect, the reader may miss it entirely or may sense it but feel that the need is not urgent. If, on the other hand, the appeal is direct or demanding, the reader may feel imposed upon, even assaulted. "Oh, but I didn't mean it that way," the writer later protests. Nevertheless, that's the way the reader took it. The letter is "out there," a physical reality standing between the writer and the reader, but its *meaning* is something the reader as well as the writer makes.

Since all readers bring themselves to a written work, they each bring something individual. Although many of Chopin's original readers knew that she wrote chiefly about the people of Louisiana, especially Creoles (descendants of the early French and Spanish settlers), Cajuns (descendants of the French whom the British had expelled from Canada in the eighteenth century), African Americans, and mulattoes, those readers must have varied in their attitudes about such people. And many of today's readers do *not* (before they read a work by Chopin) know anything about her subject. Some readers may know where Bayou-Lafourche is, and they may have notions about what it looks like, but most readers will not; indeed, many readers will not know that a bayou is a sluggish, marshy inlet or outlet of a river or lake. Moreover, even if a present-day reader in Chicago, Seattle, or Juneau knows what a bayou is, he or she may assume that "Ripe Figs" depicts a way of life still current, whereas a reader from Louisiana may see in the work a depiction of a lost way of life, a depiction of the good old days (or perhaps of the bad old days, depending on the reader's point of view). Much depends, we can say, on the reader's storehouse of experience.

To repeat: Reading is a *re*-creation; the author has tried to guide our responses, but inevitably our own experiences, as well as our ethnic background and education, contribute to our responses. You may find useful a distinction that E. D. Hirsch makes in *Validity in Interpretation* (1967). For Hirsch,

- the *meaning* in a text is the author's intended meaning;
- the *significance* is the particular relevance for each reader.

In this view, when you think about meaning you are thinking about what the author was trying to say and to do—for instance, to take an old theme and treat it in a new way. When you think about significance, you are thinking about what the work does for you—it enlarges your mind, deepens your understanding of love or grief, offends you by its depiction of women, or produces some other effect.

Making Reasonable Inferences

Does this mean, then, that there is no use talking (or writing) about literature, since all of us perceive it in our relatively private ways, rather like the seven blind men in the fable? One man, you will recall, touched the elephant's tail (or was it his trunk?) and said that the elephant is like a snake; another touched the elephant's side and said the elephant is like a wall; a third touched the elephant's leg and said the elephant is like a tree, and so on. This familiar story is usually told in order to illustrate human limitations, but notice, too, that each of the blind men *did* perceive an aspect of the elephant—an elephant is massive, like a wall or a tree, and an elephant is (in its way) remarkably supple, as you know if you have given peanuts to one.

As readers we can and should make an effort to understand what an author seems to be getting at. For instance, we should make an effort to understand unfamiliar words. Perhaps we shouldn't look up every word that we don't know, at least on the first reading, but if certain unfamiliar words are repeated and thus seem especially important, we will want to look them up. It happens that in "Ripe Figs" a French word appears: "*Tante* Frosine" means "*Aunt* Frosine." Fortunately, the meaning of the word is not crucial, and the context probably makes it clear that Frosine is an adult, which is all that we really need to know about her. But a reader who does not know that chrysanthemums bloom in late summer or early autumn will miss part of Chopin's meaning. The point is this: The writer is pitching, and she expects the reader to catch.

On the other hand, although writers tell us a good deal, they cannot tell us everything. We know that Maman-Nainaine is Babette's godmother, but we don't know exactly how old Maman-Nainaine and Babette are. Further, Chopin tells us nothing of Babette's parents. It *sounds* as though Babette and her godmother live alone, but readers' opinions may differ. One reader may argue that Babette's parents must be dead or ill, whereas another may say that the status of her parents is irrelevant and that what counts is that Babette is supervised by only one person, a mature woman. In short, a text includes **indeterminacies** (passages that careful readers agree are open to various interpretations) and **gaps** (things left unsaid in the story, such as why a godmother rather than a mother takes care of Babette).

As we work our way through a text, we keep reevaluating what we have read, pulling the details together to make sense of them, in a process called **consistency building**.

Whatever the gaps, careful readers are able to draw many reasonable inferences about Maman-Nainaine. What are some of these? We can list them:

She is older than Babette.
She has a "stately way," and she is "patient as the statue of la Madone."
She has an odd way (is it exasperating, or engaging, or a little of each?) of
   connecting actions with the seasons.
Given this last point, she seems to act slowly, to be very patient.
She apparently is used to being obeyed.

You may at this point want to go back and reread "Ripe Figs," to see what else you can say about Maman-Nainaine.

And now what of Babette?

She is young.
She is active and impatient ("restless as a humming-bird").
She is obedient.

And at this point, too, you may want to add to the list.

If you do add to the list, you might compare your additions with those of a classmate. The two of you may find that you disagree about what may reasonably be inferred from Chopin's words. Suppose, for instance, that your classmate said that although Babette is outwardly obedient, inwardly she probably hates Maman-Nainaine. Would you agree that this assertion is an acceptable inference? If you don't agree, how might you go about trying to convince your classmate that such a response is not justified? We are speaking here of an activity of mind called **critical thinking**, a topic discussed in the next chapter.

Reading with Pen in Hand

It's probably best to read a work of literature straight through, enjoying it and letting yourself be carried along to the end. But then, when you have an overall view, you'll want to read it again, noticing (for example) how certain innocent-seeming details given early in the work prove to be important later.

Perhaps the best way to read attentively is, after a first reading, to mark the text, underlining or highlighting passages that seem especially interesting, and to jot notes or queries in the margins. (*Caution:* Annotate and highlight, but don't get so carried away that you highlight whole pages.) Here is "Ripe Figs" once more, this time with the marks that a student added to it during and after a second reading.

KATE CHOPIN
Ripe Figs

Maman-Nainaine said that when the (figs) were ripe Babette might go to visit her cousins down on the <u>Bayou-</u>   **?**
Lafourche where the sugar cane grows. Not that the ripening of figs had the least thing to do with it, but that is the
way Maman-Nainaine was.   *strange*

It seemed to Babette a very long time to wait; for the
leaves upon the <u>trees were tender yet</u>, and the figs were like
little hard, (green marbles.)

But warm rains came along and plenty of strong sunshine, and though Maman-Nainaine was as <u>patient as the
statue of la Madone</u>, and Babette as <u>restless as a humming-
bird</u>, the first thing they both knew it was hot summertime.
Every day Babette <u>danced out to where</u> the fig-trees were in
a long line against the fence. She walked slowly beneath
them, carefully peering between the gnarled, spreading
branches. But each time she came disconsolate away again.
What she saw there finally was something that made her
sing and (dance) the whole long day.   *contrast between M-N and B*

When Maman-Nainaine (sat) down in her stately way to
breakfast, the following morning, her muslin cap standing   *another contrast*
like an <u>aureole</u> about her white, placid face, Babette approached. <u>She bore a dainty porcelain platter</u>, which she set   *ceremonious*
down before her godmother. It contained a dozen (purple)
(figs) fringed around with their rich, green leaves.   *Check? this*

"Ah," said Maman-Nainaine arching her eyebrows, "how   *nice echo.
(early) the figs have ripened this year!"   contrast
"Oh," said Babette. "I <u>think they have ripened very</u> (late.)"   like a
song*

"Babette," continued (Maman-Nainaine) as she peeled the   *time passes
very plumpest figs with her pointed silver fruit-knife, "<u>you   fast for M-N
will carry my love to them</u> all down on Bayou-Lafourche.   slowly for B*
And tell your Tante Frosine I shall look for her at Toussaint—when the (chrysanthemums) are in bloom."   *is M-N
herself
like a
plump   *B entrusted
fig?*   with a
message
of love*

*opens with figs; ends
with chrys. (autumn)*   *fulfillment?
Equivalent to figs
ripening?*

Recording Your First Responses

Another useful way of getting at the meaning of a work of literature is to jot down
your initial responses to it, recording your impressions as they come to you in any
order—almost as though you're talking to yourself. Since no one else is going to
read your notes, you can be entirely free and at ease. You can write in sentences
or not; it's up to you. You can jot down these responses either before or after you
annotate the text. Some readers find that annotating the text helps to produce
ideas for further jottings, but others prefer to jot down a few thoughts immediately
after a first reading, and then, stimulated by these thoughts, they reread and annotate the text.

Write whatever comes into your mind, whatever the literary work triggers in
your own imagination, whatever you think are the important ideas or values of
your own experience.

Here is a student's first response to "Ripe Figs":

This is a very short story. I didn't know stories were this short, but I like it because you can get it all quickly and it's no trouble to reread it carefully. The shortness, though, leaves a lot of gaps for the reader to fill in. So much is not said. Your imagination is put to work.

But I can see Maman-N sitting at her table--pleasantly powerful--no one you would want to argue with. She's formal and distant--and definitely has quirks. She wants to postpone Babette's trip, but we don't know why. And you can sense B's frustration. But maybe she's teaching her that something really good is worth waiting for and that anticipation is as much fun as the trip. Maybe I can develop this idea.

Another thing. I can tell they are not poor--from two things. The pointed silver fruit knife and the porcelain platter, and the fact that Maman sits down to breakfast in a "stately" way. They are the leisure class. But I don't know enough about life on the bayous to go into this. Their life is different from mine; no one I know has that kind of peaceful rural life.

Identifying Your Audience and Purpose

Now, suppose that you are beginning the process of writing about "Ripe Figs" for someone else, not for yourself. The first question to ask yourself is: "For whom am I writing?" That is, who is your *audience?* (Of course you probably are writing because an instructor has asked you to do so, but you must still imagine an audience. Your instructor may tell you, for instance, to write for your classmates, or to write for the readers of the college newspaper.)

- If you are writing for people who already are familiar with some of Chopin's work, you won't have to say much about the author, but
- if you are writing for an audience that perhaps has never heard of Chopin, you may want to include a brief biographical note of the sort we gave.
- If you are writing for an audience that, you have reason to believe, has read several works by Chopin, you may want to make some comparisons, explaining how "Ripe Figs" resembles or differs from Chopin's other work.

In a sense, the audience is your collaborator; it helps you to decide what you will say. You are also helped by your sense of *purpose.* If your aim is to introduce readers to Chopin, you will make certain points that reflect this purpose. If your aim is to tell people what you think "Ripe Figs" means to say about human relationships, or about time, you will say some different things. If your aim is to have a little fun and to entertain an audience that is already familiar with "Ripe Figs," you may decide to write a parody (a humorous imitation) of the story.

YOUR TURN: A WRITING ASSIGNMENT

Let's assume that you want to describe "Ripe Figs" to someone who has not read it. You will briefly summarize the action, such as it is, and will mention where it takes place; who the characters are, including what their relationship is; and what, if anything, happens to them. Beyond that, you'll try to explain as honestly as you can what makes "Ripe Figs" appealing or interesting—or trifling, or boring, or whatever. That is, you will *argue* a thesis, even though you almost surely will not say anything as formal as "In this essay I will argue that . . . " or "This essay will attempt to prove that . . ." Your essay nevertheless will essentially be an argument because (perhaps after a brief summary of the work) you will be pointing to the evidence that has caused you to respond as you did.

A Sample Essay by a Student

Here is an essay that a student, Antonia Tenori, wrote for this assignment.

Tenori 1

Antonia Tenori

Professor Lee

English 102

11 Feburary 2004

Images of Ripening in Kate Chopin's "Ripe Figs"

Very little happens in Kate Chopin's one-page story, "Ripe Figs." Maman-Nainaine tells her goddaughter Babette that she may "visit her cousins down on the Bayou-Lafourche" "when the figs were ripe"; the figs ripen, and Babette is given permission to go. So little happens in "Ripe Figs" that the story at first appears merely to be a character sketch that illustrates, through Babette and her godmother, the contrast between youth and age. But by means of the natural imagery of the tale, Chopin suggests more than this: She asks her readers to see the relationship of human time to nature's seasons, and she suggests that, try as we may to push the process of maturity, growth or "ripening" happens in its own time.

The story clearly contrasts the impatience of youth with the patience and dignity that come with age. Babette, whose name suggests she is still a "little baby," is "restless as a humming-bird." Each day when she eagerly goes to see if the figs have ripened,

---

she doesn't simply walk but she dances. By contrast, Maman-Nainaine has a "stately way," she is "patient as the statue of la Madone," and there is an "aureole"--a radiance--"about her white, placid face." The brief dialog near the end of the story also emphasizes the difference between the two characters. When the figs finally ripen, Maman-Nainaine is surprised (she arches her eyebrows), and she exclaims, "how early the figs have ripened this year!" Babette replies, "I think they have ripened very late."

Chopin is not simply remarking here that time passes slowly for young people, and quickly for old people. She suggests that nature moves at its own pace regardless of human wishes. Babette, young and "tender" as the fig leaves, can't wait to "ripen." Her visit to Bayou-Lafourche is not a mere pleasure trip, but represents her coming into her own season of maturity. Babette's desire to rush this process is tempered by a condition that her godmother sets: Babette must wait until the figs ripen, since everything comes in its own season. Maman-Nainaine recognizes the patterns of the natural world, the rhythms of life. By asking Babette to await the ripening, the young girl is asked to pay attention to the patterns as well.

Chopin further suggests that if we pay attention and wait with patience, the fruits of our own growth will be sweet, plump, and beautiful, like the "dozen purple figs, fringed around with their rich, green leaves," that Babette finally offers her godmother. Chopin uses natural imagery effectively, interweaving the young girl's growth with the rhythms of the seasons. In this way, the

reader is connected with both processes in an intimate and

inviting way.

The Argument Analyzed

- The title of the essay is informative; it clearly indicates the focus of the analysis. Notice, too, that it is much more interesting than "An Analysis of a Story" or "An Analysis of Kate Chopin's 'Ripe Figs'" or "'Ripe Figs': A Study" or "An Analysis of Imagery." In your own essays, construct titles that inform and interest.

- The first sentence names the author and title. Strictly speaking, this information is redundant, since it appears in the title, but it is customary to give the author's full name and the title of the work early in the essay, and it is essential to give such information if it is not in the title.

- The second sentence offers enough plot summary to enable the reader to follow the discussion. But notice that the essay as a whole is much more than a summary of the plot. Summary here is offered early, merely to make the analysis intelligible. Chiefly, the opening paragraph presents one view (the view that Antonia believes is inadequate); then, after a transitional "but," offers a second view and presents a thesis—the point that Antonia will argue. Perhaps the most common error students make in writing about literature is to confuse a summary of the plot with a thoughtful analysis of the work. A little plot-telling is acceptable, to remind your reader of what happens, but normally your essay will be devoted to setting forth a thesis about a work, and supporting the thesis with evidence. Your readers do not want to know what happens in the work; they want to know what you make out of the work—how you interpret it, or why you like or dislike it.

- In the second paragraph, Antonia supports her thesis by providing brief quotations. These quotations are not padding; rather, they are evidence supporting her assertion that Chopin "contrasts the impatience of youth with the patience and dignity that come with age."

- In the third paragraph Antonia develops her thesis ("Chopin is not simply . . . She suggests . . .")

- The final paragraph begins with a helpful transition ("Chopin *further* suggests"), offers additional evidence, and ends with a new idea (about the reader's response to the story) that takes the discussion a step further. The essay avoids the deadliest kind of conclusion, a mere summary of the essay ("Thus we have seen," or some such words). Antonia's effective final sentence nicely draws the reader into the essay. (Effective final sentences are hard to write, but we give advice about them on pages 87–88.)

Antonia Tenori wrote this paper for an assignment early in the semester, and it's worth noting that students were told to write "about 500 words (two double-spaced typed pages)." If

- the first question to ask is "To whom am I writing?"
- the second question to ask is, "What is the length of the assignment?"

The answer to this second question will provide two sorts of guidance: It will give you some sense of how much time you should devote to preparing the paper—obviously an instructor expects you to spend more time on a ten-page paper than on a one-page paper—and, second, it will give you a sense of how much detail you can include. For a short paper—say, 1–2 pages—you will need to make your main point with a special kind of directness; you will not have space for lots of details, just those that support the main point. This is what Antonia aims to achieve in her second and third paragraphs, where she highlights the term "ripens" and briefly, but effectively, develops its implications. For a longer paper, 3–5 pages, or one that is longer still, you can examine the characters, setting, and central themes in greater depth, and can focus on more details in the text to strengthen your analysis.

Other Possibilities for Writing

You might write a paper of a very different sort. Consider the following possibilities:

1. Write a sequel, moving from fall to spring.
2. Write a letter from Babette, at Bayou-Lafourche, to Maman-Nainaine.
3. Imagine that Babette is now an old woman, writing her memoirs. What does she say about Maman-Nainaine?
4. Write a narrative based on your own experience of learning a lesson in patience.

2

The Reader as Writer

All there is to writing is having ideas. To learn
to write is to learn to have ideas.

ROBERT FROST

DEVELOPING A THESIS, DRAFTING, AND WRITING AN ARGUMENT

Pre-writing: Getting Ideas

How do writers "learn to have ideas"? Among the methods are these: reading with a pen or pencil in hand, so that (as we have already seen) you can annotate the text; keeping a journal, in which you jot down reflections about your reading; talking with others (including your instructor) about the reading. Let's take another look at the first of these, annotating.

Annotating a Text

In reading, if you own the book don't hesitate to mark it up, indicating (by highlighting or underlining or by making marginal notes) what puzzles you, what pleases or interests you, and what displeases or bores you. Later you'll want to think further about these responses, asking yourself, on rereading, if you still feel that way, and if not, why not; but these first responses will get you started.

Annotations of the sort given on page 7, which chiefly call attention to contrasts, indicate that the student is thinking about writing an analysis of the story. That is, she is thinking of writing an essay in which she will examine the parts of a literary work either in an effort to see how they relate to each other or in an effort to see how one part relates to the whole.

More about Getting Ideas: A Second Story by Kate Chopin

Let's look at a story that is a little longer than "Ripe Figs," and then we'll discuss how in addition to annotating you might get ideas for writing about it.

The Story of an Hour

Knowing that Mrs. Mallard was afflicted with a heart trouble, great care was taken to break to her as gently as possible the news of her husband's death.

It was her sister Josephine who told her, in broken sentences, veiled hints that revealed in half concealing. Her husband's friend Richards was there, too, near her. It was he who had been in the newspaper office when intelligence of the railroad disaster was received, with Brently Mallard's name leading the list of "killed." He had only taken the time to assure himself of its truth by a second telegram, and had hastened to forestall any less careful, less tender friend in bearing the sad message.

She did not hear the story as many women have heard the same, with a paralyzed inability to accept its significance. She wept at once, with sudden, wild abandonment, in her sister's arms. When the storm of grief had spent itself she went away to her room alone. She would have no one follow her.

There stood, facing the open window, a comfortable, roomy armchair. Into this she sank, pressed down by a physical exhaustion that haunted her body and seemed to reach into her soul.

5   She could see in the open square before her house the tops of trees that were all aquiver with the new spring life. The delicious breath of rain was in the air. In the street below a peddler was crying his wares. The notes of a distant song which some one was singing reached her faintly, and countless sparrows were twittering in the eaves.

There were patches of blue sky showing here and there through the clouds that had met and piled above the other in the west facing her window. She sat with her head thrown back upon the cushion of the chair quite motionless, except when a sob came up into her throat and shook her, as a child who has cried itself to sleep continues to sob in its dreams.

She was young, with a fair, calm face, whose lines bespoke repression and even a certain strength. But now there was a dull stare in her eyes, whose gaze was fixed away off yonder on one of those patches of blue sky. It was not a glance of reflection, but rather indicated a suspension of intelligent thought.

There was something coming to her and she was waiting for it, fearfully. What was it? She did not know; it was too subtle and elusive to name. But she felt it, creeping out of the sky, reaching toward her through the sounds, the scents, the color that filled the air.

Now her bosom rose and fell tumultuously. She was beginning to recognize this thing that was approaching to possess her, and she was striving to beat it back with her will—as powerless as her two white slender hands would have been.

10   When she abandoned herself a little whispered word escaped her slightly parted lips. She said it over and over under her breath: "Free, free, free!" The vacant stare and the look of terror that had followed it went from her eyes. They stayed keen and bright. Her pulses beat fast, and the coursing blood warmed and relaxed every inch of her body.

She did not stop to ask if it were not a monstrous joy that held her. A clear and exalted perception enabled her to dismiss the suggestion as trivial.

She knew that she would weep again when she saw the kind, tender hands folded in death; the face that had never looked save with love upon her, fixed and gray and dead. But she saw beyond that bitter moment a long procession of years to come that would belong to her absolutely. And she opened and spread her arms out to them in welcome.

There would be no one to live for her during those coming years; she would live for herself. There would be no powerful will bending her in that blind persistence with which men and women believe they have a right to impose a private will upon a fellow creature. A kind intention or a cruel intention made the act seem no less a crime as she looked upon it in that brief moment of illumination.

And yet she had loved him—sometimes. Often she had not. What did it matter! What could love, the unsolved mystery, count for in face of this possession of self-assertion which she suddenly recognized as the strongest impulse of her being.

15   "Free! Body and soul free!" she kept whispering.

Josephine was kneeling before the closed door with her lips to the keyhole, imploring for admission. "Louise, open the door! I beg; open the door—you will make yourself ill. What are you doing, Louise? For heaven's sake open the door."

"Go away. I am not making myself ill." No; she was drinking in a very elixir of life through that open window.

Her fancy was running riot along those days ahead of her. Spring days, and summer days, and all sorts of days that would be her own. She breathed a quick prayer that life might be long. It was only yesterday she had thought with a shudder that life might be long.

She arose at length and opened the door to her sister's importunities. There was a feverish triumph in her eyes, and she carried herself unwittingly like a goddess of Victory. She clasped her sister's waist, and together they descended the stairs. Richards stood waiting for them at the bottom.

20   Some one was opening the front door with a latchkey. It was Brently Mallard who entered, a little travel-stained, composedly carrying his gripsack and umbrella. He had been far from the scene of accident, and did not even know there had been one. He stood amazed at Josephine's piercing cry; at Richards' quick motion to screen him from the view of his wife.

But Richards was too late.

When the doctors came they said she had died of heart disease—of joy that kills.

[1894]

Brainstorming for Ideas for Writing

Unlike annotating, which consists of making brief notes and small marks on the printed page, "brainstorming"—the free jotting down of ideas—asks that you jot down whatever comes to mind, without inhibition. Don't worry about spelling, about writing complete sentences, or about unifying your thoughts; just let one thought lead to another. Later you can review your jottings, deleting some, connecting with arrows others that are related, expanding still others, but for now you want to get going, and so there is no reason to look back. Thus you might jot down something about the title:

> Title speaks of an hour, and story covers an hour, but maybe takes five minutes to read.

And then, perhaps prompted by "an hour," you might happen to add something to this effect:

> Doubt that a woman who got news of the death of her husband could move from grief to joy within an hour.

Your next jotting might have little or nothing to do with this issue; it might simply say

> Enjoyed "Hour" more than "Ripe Figs" partly because "Hour" is so shocking.

And then you might ask yourself

> By shocking, do I mean "improbable," or what? Come to think of it, maybe it's not so improbable. A lot depends on what the marriage was like.

Focused Free Writing

Focused, or directed, free writing is a method related to brainstorming that some writers use to uncover ideas they may want to write about. Concentrating on one issue—for instance, a question that strikes them as worth puzzling over (What kind of person is Mrs. Mallard?)—they write at length, nonstop, for perhaps five or ten minutes.

Writers who find free writing helpful put down everything they can think of that bears on the one issue or question they are examining. They do not stop at this stage to evaluate the results, and they do not worry about niceties of sentence structure or of spelling. They just pour out their ideas in a steady stream of writing, drawing on whatever associations come to mind. If they pause in their writing, it is only to refer to the text, to search for more detail—perhaps a quotation—that will help them answer their question.

After the free-writing session, these writers usually go back and reread what they have written, highlighting or underlining what seems to be of value. Of course they find much that is of little or no use, but they also usually find that some strong ideas have surfaced and have received some development. At this point the writers are often able to make a rough outline and then begin a draft.

Here is an example of one student's focused free writing:

> What do I know about Mrs. Mallard? Let me put everything down here I know about her or can figure out from what Kate Chopin tells me. When she finds herself alone after the death of her husband, she says, "Free. Body and soul free" and before that she said, "Free, free, free" three times. So she has suddenly perceived that she has not been free; she has been under the influence of a "powerful will." In this case it has been her husband, but she says no one, man nor woman, should impose their will on anyone else. So it's not a feminist issue--it's a power issue. No one should push anyone else around is what I guess Chopin means, force someone to do what the other person wants. I used to have a friend that did that to me all the time; he had to run everything. They say that fathers--before the women's movement--used to run things, with the father in charge of all the decisions, so maybe this is an honest reaction to having been pushed around by a husband. I think Mrs. Mallard is a believable character, even if the plot is not all that believable--all those things happening in such quick succession.

Listing

In your preliminary thinking you may find it useful to make lists. In the previous chapter we saw that listing the traits of the two characters was helpful in thinking about Chopin's "Ripe Figs":

> Maman-Nainaine
>   older than Babette
>   "stately way"

"patient as the statue of la Madone"
connects actions with seasons
expects to be obeyed
Babette
    young
    active and impatient
    obedient

For "The Story of an Hour" you might list Mrs. Mallard's traits; or you might list the stages in her development. (Such a list is not the same as a summary of the plot. The list helps the writer to see the sequence of psychological changes.)

weeps (when she gets the news)
goes to room, alone
"pressed down by a physical exhaustion"
"dull stare"
"something coming to her"
strives to beat back "this thing"
"Free, free, free!" The "vacant stare went . . . from her eyes"
"A clear and exalted perception"
rejects Josephine
"she was drinking in a very elixir of life"
gets up, opens door, "a feverish triumph in her eyes"
sees B., and dies

Unlike brainstorming and annotating, which let you go in all directions, listing requires that you first make a decision about what you will be listing—traits of character, images, puns, or whatever. Once you make the decision, you can then construct the list, and with a list in front of you, you will probably see patterns that you were not fully conscious of earlier.

Asking Questions

If you feel stuck, ask yourself questions. (You'll recall that the assignment on "Ripe Figs" in effect asked the students to ask themselves questions about the work—for instance, questions about the relationship between the characters—and about their responses to it: "You'll try to explain as honestly as you can what makes 'Ripe Figs' appealing or interesting—or trifling, or boring."

If you are thinking about a work of fiction, ask yourself questions about the plot and the characters—are they believable, are they interesting, and what does it all add up to? What does the story mean to *you*? One student found it helpful to jot down the following questions:

Plot
    Ending false? Unconvincing? Or prepared for?
Character?
    Mrs. M. unfeeling? Immoral?
    Mrs. M. unbelievable character?
    What might her marriage have been like? Many gaps.
    (Can we tell what her husband was like?)
    "And yet she loved him--sometimes" Fickle? Realistic?
    What is "this thing that was approaching to possess her"?

Symbolism
   Set on spring day = symbolic of new life?

You don't have to be as tidy as this student. You may begin by jotting down notes and queries about what you like or dislike and about what puzzles or amuses you. What follows are the jottings of another student, Janet Vong. They are, obviously, in no particular order—the student is "brainstorming," putting down whatever occurs to her—though it is equally obvious that one note sometimes led to the next:

Title nothing special. What might be a better title?
Could a woman who loved her husband be so heartless?
Is she heartless? Did she love him?
What are (were) Louise's feelings about her husband?
Did she want too much? What did she want?
Could this story happen today? Feminist interpretation?
Sister (Josephine)--a busybody?
Tricky ending--but maybe it could be true.
"And yet she had loved him--sometimes. Often she had not."
   Why does one love someone "sometimes"?
Irony: plot has reversal. Are characters ironic too?

These jottings will help the reader-writer think about the story, find a special point of interest, and develop a thoughtful argument about it.

Keeping a Journal

A journal is not a diary, a record of what the writer did during the day ("today I read Chopin's 'Hour'"). Rather, a journal is a place to store some of the thoughts you may have inscribed on a scrap of paper or in the margin of the text, such as your initial response to the title of a work or to the ending. It is also a place to jot down further reflections, such as thoughts about what the work means to you, and what was said in the classroom about writing in general or specific works.

You will get something out of your journal if you write an entry at least once a week, but you will get much more if you write entries after reading each assignment and after each class meeting. You may, for instance, want to reflect on why your opinion is so different from that of another student, or you may want to apply a concept such as *character* or *irony* or *plausibility* to a story that later you may write about in an essay. Comparisons are especially helpful: How does this work (or this character, or this rhyme scheme) differ from last week's reading?

You might even make an entry in the form of a letter to the author or from one character to another. You might write a dialogue between characters in two works or between two authors, or you might record an experience of your own that is comparable to something in the work.

A student who wrote about "The Story of an Hour" began with the following entry in his journal. In reading this entry, notice that one idea stimulates another. The student was, quite rightly, concerned with getting and exploring ideas, not with writing a unified paragraph.

Apparently a "well-made" story, but seems clever rather than moving or real. Doesn't seem plausible. Mrs. M's change comes out of the blue--maybe some women might respond like this, but probably not most.

Does literature deal with unusual people, or with usual (typical?) people? Shouldn't it deal with typical? Maybe not. (Anyway, how can I know?) Is "typical" same as "plausible"? Come to think of it, prob. not.

Anyway, whether Mrs. M is typical or not, is her change plausible, believable? Think more about this.

Why did she change? Her husband dominated her life and controlled her actions; he did "impose a private will upon a fellow creature." She calls this a crime, even if well-intentioned. Is it a crime?

Arguing with Yourself: Critical Thinking

In our discussion of annotating, brainstorming, free writing, listing, asking questions, and keeping a journal, the emphasis has been on responding freely rather than in any highly systematic or disciplined way. Something strikes us (perhaps an idea, perhaps an uncertainty), and we jot it down. Even before we finish jotting it down we may go on to question it, but probably not; at this early stage it is enough to put onto paper some thoughts, rooted in our first responses, and to keep going.

The almost random play of mind that is evident in brainstorming and in the other activities already discussed is of course a kind of thinking, but the term **critical thinking** (which we addressed briefly in our first chapter) is reserved for something different. When we think critically, we skeptically scrutinize our own ideas—for example, by searching out our underlying assumptions, or by evaluating what we have quickly jotted down as evidence. We have already seen some examples of this sort of analysis of one's own thinking in the journal entries, where, for instance, a student wrote that literature should probably deal with "typical" people, then wondered if "typical" and "plausible" were the same, and then added "probably not."

Speaking broadly, critical thinking is rational, logical thinking. In thinking critically, writers

- scrutinize their assumptions;
- test the evidence they have collected, even to the extent of looking for counterevidence; and
- revise their thesis when necessary, in order to make the argument as complete and convincing as possible.

Let's start with assumptions. If I say that a story is weak because it is improbable, I ought to think about my assumption that improbability is a fault. I can begin by asking myself if all good stories—or all the stories that I value highly—are probable. I may recall that among my favorites is *Alice in Wonderland* (or *Gulliver's Travels* or *Animal Farm*)—so I probably have to withdraw my assumption that improbability in itself makes a story less than good. I may go on to refine the idea and decide that improbability is not a fault in satiric stories but is a fault in other kinds, but that is not the same as saying bluntly that improbability is a fault.

The second aspect of critical thinking that we have isolated—searching for counterevidence within the literary work—especially involves rereading the work to see if we have overlooked material or have taken a particular detail out of context. If, for instance, we say that in "The Story of an Hour" Josephine is a busybody, we should reexamine the work to make sure that she indeed is meddling needlessly and is not offering welcome or necessary assistance. Perhaps the original observation will stand up, but perhaps on rereading the story we may come to feel, as we examine each of Josephine's actions, that she cannot reasonably be characterized as a busybody.

Different readers may come to different conclusions; the important thing is that all readers should subject their initial responses to critical thinking, testing their responses against all of the evidence. Remember, your instructor probably expects you to hand in an essay that is essentially an **argument**, a paper that advances a thesis of your own, and therefore you will revise your drafts if you find counterevidence. The **thesis** (the point) might be that

- the story is improbable, or
- the story is typical of Chopin, or
- the story is anti-woman, or
- the story is a remarkable anticipation of contemporary feminist thinking.

Whatever your thesis, it should be able to withstand scrutiny. You may not convince every reader that you are unquestionably right, but you should make every reader feel that your argument is thoughtful. If you read your notes and then your drafts critically, you probably will write a paper that meets this standard.

One last point, or maybe it's two. Just as your first jottings probably won't be the products of critical thinking, your first reading of the literary work probably *won't* be a critical reading. It is entirely appropriate to begin by reading simply for enjoyment. After all, the reason we read literature (or listen to music, or go to an art museum, or watch dancers) is to derive pleasure. It happens, however, that in this course you are trying (among other things) to deepen your understanding of literature, so you are *studying* literature. On subsequent readings, therefore, you will read the work critically, carefully noting the writer's view of human nature and the writer's ways of achieving certain effects.

This business of critical thinking is important. We will discuss it yet again, on pages 583–586, in talking about interpretations of literature.

Arguing a Thesis

If you think critically about your early jottings and about the literary work itself, you probably will find that some of your jottings lead to dead ends, but some will lead to further ideas that hold up under scrutiny. What the thesis of the essay will be—the idea that will be asserted and *argued* (supported with evidence)—is still in doubt, but there is no doubt about one thing: A good essay will have a thesis, a point, an argument. You ought to be able to state your point in a **thesis sentence**.

Consider these candidates as possible thesis sentences:

1. Mrs. Mallard dies soon after hearing that her husband has died.

True, but scarcely a point that can be argued or even developed. About the most the essayist can do with this sentence is amplify it by summarizing the plot of the story, a task not worth doing unless the plot is unusually obscure. An essay may include a sentence or two of summary to give readers their bearings, but a summary is not an essay.

2. The story is a libel on women.

In contrast to the first statement, this one can be developed into an argument. Probably the writer will try to demonstrate that Mrs. Mallard's behavior is despicable. Whether this point can be convincingly argued is another matter; the thesis may be untenable, but it is a thesis. A second problem, however, is this: Even if the writer demonstrates that Mrs. Mallard's behavior is despicable, he or she will have to go on to demonstrate that the presentation of one despicable woman constitutes a libel on women in general. That's a pretty big order.

> 3. The story is clever but superficial because it is based on an unreal character.

Here, too, is a thesis—a point of view that can be argued. Whether this thesis is true is another matter. The writer's job will be to support it by presenting evidence. Probably the writer will have no difficulty in finding evidence that the story is "clever"; the difficulty will be in establishing a case that the characterization of Mrs. Mallard is "unreal." The writer will have to set forth some ideas about what makes a character real and then will have to show that Mrs. Mallard is an unreal (unbelievable) figure.

> 4. The irony of the ending is believable partly because it is consistent with earlier ironies in the story.

It happens that the student who wrote the essay printed on page 27 began by drafting an essay based on the third of these thesis topics, but as she worked on a draft she found that she couldn't support her assertion that the character was unconvincing. In fact, she came to believe that although Mrs. Mallard's joy was the reverse of what a reader might expect, several early reversals in the story helped to make Mrs. Mallard's shift from grief to joy acceptable.

DRAFTING YOUR ARGUMENT

After jotting down notes and then adding more notes stimulated by rereading and further thinking, you should be able to formulate a tentative thesis. At this point most writers find it useful to clear the air by glancing over their preliminary notes and by jotting down the thesis and a few especially promising notes—brief statements of what they think their key points may be. These notes may include some brief key quotations that the writer thinks will help to support the thesis.

Here are the selected notes (not the original brainstorming notes, but a later selection from them, with additions) and a draft (p. 22) that makes use of them.

> title? Ironies in an Hour (?) An Hour of Irony (?) Kate Chopin's
>   Irony (?)
> thesis: irony at end is prepared for by earlier ironies
> chief irony: Mrs. M. dies just as she is beginning to enjoy life
> smaller ironies: 1. "sad message" brings her joy
>   2. Richards is "too late" at end
>   3. Richards is too early at start

These notes are in effect a very brief **outline**. Some writers at this point like to develop a fuller outline, but most writers begin with only a brief outline, knowing that in the process of developing a draft from these few notes additional ideas will arise. For these writers, the time to jot down a detailed outline is *after* they have written a first or second draft. The outline of the written draft will, as we shall see, help them to make sure that their draft has an adequate organization, and that main points are developed.

A Sample Draft: "Ironies in an Hour"

Now for the student's draft—not the first version, but a revised draft with some of the irrelevancies of the first draft omitted and some evidence added.

The numbers in parentheses refer to the page numbers from which the quotations are drawn, though with so short a work as "The Story of an Hour," page references are hardly necessary. Check with your instructor to find out if you must always give citations. (Detailed information about how to document a paper is given on pages 1333–1342.)

Bridas 1

Jennifer Bridas

Professor Lester

English 1102

3 March 2004

Ironies in an Hour

After we know how the story turns out, if we reread it we find irony at the very start, as is true of many other stories. Mrs. Mallard's friends assume, mistakenly, that Mrs. Mallard was deeply in love with her husband, Brently Mallard. They take great care to tell her gently of his death. The friends mean well, and in fact they do well. They bring her an hour of life, an hour of freedom. They think their news is sad. Mrs. Mallard at first expresses grief when she hears the news, but soon she finds joy in it. So Richards's "sad message" (14), though sad in Richards's eyes, is in fact a happy message.

Among the ironic details is the statement that when Mallard entered the house, Richards tried to conceal him from Mrs. Mallard, but "Richards was too late" (15). This is ironic because earlier Richards "hastened" (14) to bring his sad message; if he had at the start been "too late" (15), Brently Mallard would have arrived at home first, and Mrs. Mallard's life would not

Bridas 2

have ended an hour later but would simply have gone on as it had

before. Yet another irony at the end of the story is the diagnosis

of the doctors. The doctors say she died of "heart disease--of joy

that kills" (15). In one sense the doctors are right: Mrs. Mallard

has experienced a great joy. But of course the doctors totally

misunderstand the joy that kills her.

The central irony resides not in the well-intentioned but

ironic actions of Richards, or in the unconsciously ironic words

of the doctors, but in her own life. In a way she has been dead.

She "sometimes" (15) loved her husband, but in a way she has

been dead. Now, his apparent death brings her new life. This new

life comes to her at the season of the year when "the tops of trees

. . . were all aquiver with the new spring life" (14). But, ironically,

her new life will last only an hour. She looks forward to "summer

days" (15) but she will not see even the end of this spring day. Her

years of marriage were ironic. They brought her a sort of living

death instead of joy. Her new life is ironic too. It grows out of her

moment of grief for her supposedly dead husband, and her vision

of a new life is cut short.

[New page]

Bridas 3

Work Cited

Chopin, Kate. "The Story of an Hour." Literature for Composition. Ed.

Sylvan Barnet et al. 7th ed. New York: Longman, 2005, 13–15.

Revising an Argument

The draft, although thoughtful and clear, is not yet a finished essay. The student went on to improve it in many small but important ways.

First, the draft needs a good introductory paragraph, a paragraph that will let the **audience**—the readers—know where the writer will be taking them. (In Chapter 4 we discuss introductory paragraphs.) Doubtless you know from your own experience as a reader that readers can follow an argument more easily—and with more pleasure—if early in the discussion the writer alerts them to the gist of the argument. (The title, too, can strongly suggest the thesis.) Second, some of the paragraphs could be clearer.

In revising paragraphs—or, for that matter, in revising an entire draft—writers unify, organize, clarify, and polish.

1. **Unity** is achieved partly by eliminating irrelevancies. Notice that in the final version, printed on pages 27 and 28, the writer has deleted "as is true of many other stories."
2. **Organization** is largely a matter of arranging material into a sequence that will assist the reader to grasp the point.
3. **Clarity** is achieved largely by providing concrete details and quotations—these provide evidence—to support generalizations and by providing helpful transitions ("for instance," "furthermore," "on the other hand," "however").
4. **Polish** is small-scale revision. For instance, the writer deletes unnecessary repetitions. In the second paragraph of the draft, the phrase "the doctors" appears four times, but it appears only three times in the final version of the paragraph. Similarly, in polishing, a writer combines choppy sentences into longer ones and breaks overly long sentences into shorter ones.

Later, after producing a draft that seems close to a finished essay, writers engage in yet another activity. They edit.

5. **Editing** includes checking the accuracy of quotations by comparing them with the original, checking a dictionary for the spelling of doubtful words, and checking a handbook for doubtful punctuation—for instance, whether a comma or a semicolon is needed in a particular sentence.

Outlining an Argument

Whether or not you draw up an outline as a preliminary guide to writing a draft, you will be able to improve your draft if you prepare an outline of what you have written. (If you write on a word processor it is probably especially important that you make an outline of your written draft. Writing on a word processor is—or seems—so easy, so effortless, that often we just tap away, filling screen after screen with loosely structured material.) For each paragraph in your draft, jot down the gist of the topic sentence or topic idea. Under each of these sentences, indented, jot down key words for the idea(s) developed in the paragraph. Thus, in an outline of the draft we have just looked at, for the first two paragraphs you might make these jottings:

> story ironic from start
>> friends think news is sad
>> Ms. M. finds joy
> some ironic details
>> Richards hastened, but "too late"
>> doctors right and also wrong

An outline of what you have written will help you to see if your draft is adequate in three important ways. The outline will show you:

1. the sequence of major topics
2. the degree of development of these topics
3. the argument, the thesis

By studying your outline you may see (for instance) that your first major point (probably after an introductory paragraph) would be more effective as your third point, and that your second point needs to be further developed.

An outline of this sort is essentially a brief version of your draft, perhaps even using some phrases from the draft. But consider making yet another sort of outline, an outline indicating not what each paragraph says but what each paragraph *does*. An attempt at such an outline of the three-paragraph draft of the essay on "The Story of an Hour" might look something like this:

1. The action of the friends is ironic.
2. Gives some specific (minor) details about ironies.
3. Explains "central irony."

We ought to see a red flag here. The aim of this sort of outline is to indicate what each paragraph *does*, but the jotting for the first paragraph does not tell us what the paragraph does; rather, it more or less summarizes the content of the paragraph. Why? Because the paragraph doesn't *do* much of anything. It does not clearly introduce the thesis, or define a crucial term, or set the story in the context of Chopin's other work. An outline indicating the function of each paragraph will force you to see if your essay has an effective structure. We will see that the student later wrote a new opening paragraph for the essay on "The Story of an Hour."

Soliciting Peer Review

Your instructor may encourage (or even require) you to discuss your draft with another student or with a small group of students. That is, you may be asked to get a review from your peers. Such a procedure is helpful in several ways. First, it gives the writer a real audience, readers who can point to what pleases or puzzles them, who make suggestions, who may often disagree (with the writer or with each other), and who frequently, though not intentionally, *misread*. Though writers don't necessarily like everything they hear (they seldom hear "This is perfect. Don't change a word!"), reading and discussing their work with others almost always gives them a fresh perspective on their work, and a fresh perspective may stimulate thoughtful revision. (Having your intentions misread because your writing isn't clear enough can be particularly stimulating.)

The writer whose work is being reviewed is not the sole beneficiary. When students regularly serve as readers for each other, they become better readers of their own work and consequently better revisers. As we said in Chapter 1, learning to write is in large measure learning to read.

If peer review is a part of the writing process in your course, the instructor may distribute a sheet with some suggestions and questions. Here is an example of such a sheet.

QUESTIONS FOR PEER REVIEW   ENGLISH 125A

Read each draft once, quickly. Then read it again, with the following questions in mind.

1. What is the essay's topic? Is it one of the assigned topics, or a variation from it? Does the draft show promise of fulfilling the assignment?
2. Looking at the essay as a whole, what thesis (main idea) is stated or implied? If implied, state it in your own words.
3. Is the thesis plausible? How might the argument be strengthened?
4. Looking at each paragraph separately:
   a. What is the basic point? (If it isn't clear to you, ask for clarification.)
   b. How does the paragraph relate to the essay's main idea or to the previous paragraph?
   c. Should some paragraphs be deleted? Be divided into two or more paragraphs? Be combined? Be put elsewhere? (If you outline the essay by jotting down the gist of each paragraph, it will help you to answer these questions.)
   d. Is each sentence clearly related to the sentence that precedes and to the sentence that follows?
   e. Is each paragraph adequately developed?
   f. Are there sufficient details—perhaps brief, supporting quotations from the text?
5. What are the paper's chief strengths?
6. Make at least two specific suggestions that you think will assist the author to improve the paper.

Final Version of the Sample Essay: "Ironies of Life in Kate Chopin's 'The Story of an Hour'"

Here is the final version of the student's essay. The essay submitted to the instructor had been retyped; but here, so that you can easily see how the draft has been revised, we print the draft with the final changes written in by hand.

Bridas 1

Jennifer Bridas

Professor Lester

English 1102

3 March 2004

Ironies of Life in Kate Chopin's "The Story of an Hour"

~~Ironies in an Hour~~

Despite its title, Kate Chopin's "The Story of an Hour" ironically takes only a few minutes to read. In addition, the story turns out to have an ironic ending, but on rereading it one sees that the irony is not concentrated only in the outcome of the plot--Mrs. Mallard dies just when she is beginning to live--but is also present in many details.

After we know how the story turns out, if we reread it we find irony at the very start. /~~as is true of many other stories.~~ *Because* Mrs. Mallard's friends *and her sister* assume, mistakenly, that ~~Mrs. Mallard~~ *she* was

deeply in love with her husband, Brently Mallard./, *T*hey take great care to tell her gently of his death. ~~The friends~~ *They* mean well, and in fact they do well./, ~~They~~ bring *ing* her an hour of life, an hour of *joyous* freedom./, *but it is ironic that* ~~They~~ think their news is sad. *True,* Mrs. Mallard at first *(unknown to her friends)* expresses grief when she hears the news, but soon she finds joy in

it. So Richards's "sad message" (14), though sad in Richards's

eyes, is in fact a happy message.

Among the ironic details is the statement *small but significant* that when Mallard *near the end of the story*

entered the house, Richards tried to conceal him from Mrs.

Mallard, but "Richards was too late" (15). This is ironic because *almost at the start of the story, in the second paragraph,*

~~earlier~~ Richards "hastened" (14) to bring his sad message; if he

had at the start been "too late" (15), Brently Mallard would have

arrived at home first, and Mrs. Mallard's life would not have ended

an hour later but would simply have gone on as it had before. Yet

another irony at the end of the story is the diagnosis of the

doctors. The doctors say she died of "heart disease--of joy that

kills" (15). In one sense ~~the doctors~~ *they* are right: Mrs. Mallard *for the last hour*

Bridas 2

experienced a great joy. But of course the doctors totally

misunderstand the joy that kills her. *It is not joy at seeing her husband alive, but her realization that the great joy she experienced during the last hour is over.*

All of these ironic details add richness to the story, but
∧ The central irony resides not in the well-intentioned but

ironic actions of Richards, or in the unconsciously ironic words of
the doctors, but in ~~her~~ *Mrs. Mallard's* own life. ~~In a way she has been dead.~~ She

"sometimes" (15) loved her husband, but in a way she has been
a body subjected to her husband's will
dead./ Now, his apparent death brings her new life. *Appropriately* ∧his new

life comes to her at the season of the year when "the tops of

trees . . . were all aquiver with the new spring life" (14). But,
She is "free, free, free"--but only until her husband walks through the
ironically, her new life will last only an hour. She looks *doorway.*
∧

forward to "summer days" (15) but she will not see even the
If
end of this spring day. ∧er years of marriage were ironic./,
bringing
~~They brought~~ her a sort of living death instead of joy./, ∧er
not only because
new life is ironic too/, ∧t grows out of her moment of grief for
but also because her vision of "a long progression of years"
her supposedly dead husband, ~~and her vision of a new life~~ is

cut short./ *within an hour on a spring day.*

[New page]

Bridas 3

Work Cited

Chopin, Kate. "The Story of an Hour." Literature for Composition. Ed.

Sylvan Barnet et al. 7th ed. New York: Longman, 2005, 13–15.

A Brief Overview of the Final Version

Finally, as a quick review, let's look at several principles illustrated by this essay.

- The **title of the essay** is not merely the title of the work discussed; rather, it should give the reader a clue, a small idea of the essayist's topic. Because your title will create a crucial first impression, make sure that it is interesting.

- The **opening or introductory paragraph** does not begin by saying "In this story . . . " Rather, by naming the author and the title, it lets the reader know exactly what story is being discussed. It also develops the writer's thesis so readers know where they will be going.

- The **organization** is effective. The smaller ironies are discussed in the second and third paragraphs, the central (chief) irony in the last paragraph. That is, the essay does not dwindle or become anticlimactic; rather, it builds up from the least important to the most important point. Again, if you outline your draft you will see if it has an effective organization.

- Some **brief quotations** are used, both to provide evidence and to let the reader hear—even if only fleetingly—Kate Chopin's writing.

- The essay is chiefly devoted to **analysis** (how the parts relate to each other), not to summary (a brief restatement of the happenings). The writer, properly assuming that the reader has read the work, does not tell the plot in great detail. But, aware that the reader has not memorized the story, the writer gives helpful reminders.

- The **present tense** is used in narrating the action: "Mrs. Mallard dies"; "Mrs. Mallard's friends and relatives all assume."

- Although a **concluding paragraph** is often useful—if it does more than merely summarize what has already been clearly said—it is not essential in a short analysis. In this essay, the last sentence explains the chief irony and therefore makes an acceptable ending.

- Documentation is given according to the form set forth in Appendix B.

- There are no typographical errors. The author has proofread the paper carefully.

WRITING WITH A WORD PROCESSOR

In the preceding chapter we talked about "reading with pen in hand," and we really meant a pen—or a pencil—with which, in your early stage of interacting with the text, you will underline or circle or connect with arrows words and phrases. But when it comes to jotting down ideas, or sketching an outline, or drafting an essay, many students use a computer or a word processor. Further, you can receive valuable help from reference books and handbooks on style and usage, from computer programs (which check the spelling and grammar of documents), and from Internet resources. Although no computer program or Internet site can write and revise a paper for you, it can help you to detect mistakes and weak spots in your work that you can then proceed to remedy.

✓ CHECKLIST: *Writing with a Word Processor*

Pre-writing

❑ Take notes. Try listing, then linking and clustering your ideas. Use an outline if you find it helpful.
❑ Check that your transcriptions are accurate if you quote.
❑ Keep your notes together in one file.
❑ Organize your sources in a bibliography.
❑ *Always back up your material.*
❑ Print out your notes.

Preparing a First Draft

❑ Use your notes—move them around in blocks. Expand on your ideas.
❑ Incorporate notes to yourself in your first draft.
❑ Read your draft on the screen to check for errors.
❑ Print out a copy of your first draft.

Working with Your Draft

❑ Revise your printed draft with pen or pencil. Incorporate these changes into your computer file.
❑ Read your corrected draft on the screen; then print out a fresh copy.
❑ Repeat these steps as many times as necessary.

Responding to Peer Review

❑ Give a copy to a peer for comments and suggestions.
❑ Respond appropriately to your reviewer, making changes in your computer file.
❑ Print out your revised version and reread it.

Preparing a Final Copy

❑ If there are only a few changes, make them on your printed copy. Otherwise, incorporate your changes in your computer file and print out your final copy.

Your Turn: Three Additional Stories

Kate Chopin

Désirée's Baby

As the day was pleasant, Madame Valmondé drove over to L'Abri to see Désirée and the baby.

It made her laugh to think of Désirée with a baby. Why, it seemed but yesterday that Désirée was little more than a baby herself; when Monsieur in riding through the gateway of Valmondé had found her lying asleep in the shadow of the big stone pillar.

The little one awoke in his arms and began to cry for "Dada." That was as much as she could do or say. Some people thought she might have strayed there of her own accord, for she was of the toddling age. The prevailing belief was that she had been purposely left by a party of Texans, whose canvas-covered wagon, late in the day, had crossed the ferry that Coton Maïs kept, just below the plantation. In time Madame Valmondé abandoned every speculation but the one that Désirée had been sent to her by a beneficent Providence to be the child of her affection, seeing that she was without child of the flesh. For the girl grew to be beautiful and gentle, affectionate and sincere—the idol of Valmondé.

It was no wonder, when she stood one day against the stone pillar in whose shadow she had lain asleep, eighteen years before, that Armand Aubigny riding by and seeing her there, had fallen in love with her. That was the way all the Aubignys fell in love, as if struck by a pistol shot. The wonder was that he had not loved her before; for he had known her since his father brought him home from Paris, a boy of eight, after his mother died there. The passion that awoke in him that day, when he saw her at the gate, swept along like an avalanche, or like a prairie fire, or like anything that drives headlong over all obstacles.

5   Monsieur Valmondé grew practical and wanted things well considered: that is, the girl's obscure origin. Armand looked into her eyes and did not care. He was reminded that she was nameless. What did it matter about a name when he could give her one of the oldest and proudest in Louisiana? He ordered the *corbeille*[1] from Paris, and contained himself with what patience he could until it arrived; then they were married.

Madame Valmondé had not seen Désirée and the baby for four weeks. When she reached L'Abri she shuddered at the first sight of it, as she always did. It was a sad looking place, which for many years had not known the gentle presence of a mistress, old Monsieur Aubigny having married and buried his wife in France, and she having loved her own land too well ever to leave it. The roof came down steep and black like a cowl, reaching out beyond the wide galleries that encircled the yellow stuccoed house. Big, solemn oaks grew close to it, and their thick-leaved, far-reaching branches shadowed it like a pall. Young Aubigny's rule was a strict one, too, and under it his negroes had forgotten how to be gay, as they had been during the old master's easy-going and indulgent lifetime.

The young mother was recovering slowly, and lay full length, in her soft white muslins and laces, upon a couch. The baby was beside her, upon her arm, where he had fallen asleep, at her breast. The yellow nurse woman sat beside a window fanning herself.

Madame Valmondé bent her portly figure over Désirée and kissed her, holding her an instant tenderly in her arms. Then she turned to the child.

"This is not the baby!" she exclaimed, in startled tones. French was the language spoken at Valmondé in those days.

10   "I knew you would be astonished," laughed Désirée, "at the way he has grown. The little *cochon de lait!*[2] Look at his legs, mamma, and his hands and fingernails,—real fingernails. Zandrine had to cut them this morning. Isn't it true, Zandrine?"

The woman bowed her turbaned head majestically, "Mais si,[3] Madame."

"And the way he cries," went on Désirée, "is deafening. Armand heard him the other day as far away as La Blanche's cabin."

Madame Valmondé had never removed her eyes from the child. She lifted it and walked with it over to the window that was lightest. She scanned the baby

---

[1]*corbeille* wedding gifts from the groom to the bride. [2]*cochon de lait* suckling pig (French).
[3]*Mais si* certainly (French).

narrowly, then looked as searchingly at Zandrine, whose face was turned to gaze across the fields.

"Yes, the child has grown, has changed," said Madame Valmondé, slowly, as she replaced it beside its mother. "What does Armand say?"

15   Désirée's face became suffused with a glow that was happiness itself.

"Oh, Armand is the proudest father in the parish, I believe, chiefly because it is a boy, to bear his name; though he says not—that he would have loved a girl as well. But I know it isn't true. I know he says that to please me. And mamma," she added, drawing Madame Valmondé's head down to her, and speaking in a whisper, "he hasn't punished one of them—not one of them—since baby is born. Even Négrillon, who pretended to have burnt his leg that he might rest from work—he only laughed, and said Négrillon was a great scamp. Oh, mamma, I'm so happy; it frightens me."

What Désirée said was true. Marriage, and later the birth of his son had softened Armand Aubigny's imperious and exacting nature greatly. This was what made the gentle Désirée so happy, for she loved him desperately. When he frowned she trembled, but loved him. When he smiled, she asked no greater blessing of God. But Armand's dark, handsome face had not often been disfigured by frowns since the day he fell in love with her.

When the baby was about three months old, Désirée awoke one day to the conviction that there was something in the air menacing her peace. It was at first too subtle to grasp. It had only been a disquieting suggestion; an air of mystery among the blacks; unexpected visits from far-off neighbors who could hardly account for their coming. Then a strange, an awful change in her husband's manner, which she dared not ask him to explain. When he spoke to her, it was with averted eyes, from which the old love-light seemed to have gone out. He absented himself from home; and when there, avoided her presence and that of her child, without excuse. And the very spirit of Satan seemed suddenly to take hold of him in his dealings with the slaves. Désirée was miserable enough to die.

She sat in her room, one hot afternoon, in her *peignoir*, listlessly drawing through her fingers the strands of her long, silky brown hair that hung about her shoulders. The baby, half naked, lay asleep upon her own great mahogany bed, that was like a sumptuous throne, with its satin-lined half-canopy. One of La Blanche's little quadroon boys—half naked too—stood fanning the child slowly with a fan of peacock feathers. Désirée's eyes had been fixed absently and sadly upon the baby, while she was striving to penetrate the threatening mist that she felt closing about her. She looked from her child to the boy who stood beside him, and back again; over and over. "Ah!" It was a cry that she could not help; which she was not conscious of having uttered. The blood turned like ice in her veins, and a clammy moisture gathered upon her face.

20   She tried to speak to the little quadroon boy; but no sound would come, at first. When he heard his name uttered, he looked up, and his mistress was pointing to the door. He laid aside the great, soft fan, and obediently stole away, over the polished floor, on his bare tiptoes.

She stayed motionless, with gaze riveted upon her child, and her face the picture of fright.

Presently her husband entered the room, and without noticing her, went to a table and began to search among some papers which covered it.

"Armand," she called to him, in a voice which must have stabbed him, if he was human. But he did not notice. "Armand," she said again. Then she rose and tottered towards him. "Armand," she panted once more, clutching his arm, "look at our child. What does it mean? tell me."

He coldly but gently loosened her fingers from about his arm and thrust the hand away from him. "Tell me what it means!" she cried despairingly.

25   "It means," he answered lightly, "that the child is not white; it means that you are not white."

A quick conception of all that this accusation meant for her nerved her with unwonted courage to deny it. "It is a lie; it is not true, I am white! Look at my hair, it is brown; and my eyes are gray, Armand, you know they are gray. And my skin is fair," seizing his wrist. "Look at my hand; whiter than yours, Armand," she laughed hysterically.

"As white as La Blanche's," he returned cruelly; and went away leaving her alone with their child.

When she could hold a pen in her hand, she sent a despairing letter to Madame Valmondé.

"My mother, they tell me I am not white. Armand has told me I am not white. For God's sake tell them it is not true. You must know it is not true. I shall die. I must die. I cannot be so unhappy, and live."

30   The answer that came was as brief:

"My own Désirée: Come home to Valmondé; back to your mother who loves you. Come with your child."

When the letter reached Désirée she went with it to her husband's study, and laid it open upon the desk before which he sat. She was like a stone image: silent, white, motionless after she placed it there.

In silence he ran his cold eyes over the written words. He said nothing. "Shall I go, Armand?" she asked in tones sharp with agonized suspense.

"Yes, go."

35   "Do you want me to go?"

"Yes, I want you to go."

He thought Almighty God had dealt cruelly and unjustly with him; and felt, somehow, that he was paying Him back in kind when he stabbed thus into his wife's soul. Moreover he no longer loved her, because of the unconscious injury she had brought upon his home and his name.

She turned away like one stunned by a blow, and walked slowly towards the door, hoping he would call her back.

"Good-by, Armand," she moaned.

40   He did not answer her. That was his last blow at fate.

Désirée went in search of her child. Zandrine was pacing the sombre gallery with it. She took the little one from the nurse's arms with no word of explanation, and descending the steps, walked away, under the live-oak branches.

It was an October afternoon; the sun was just sinking. Out in the still fields the negroes were picking cotton.

Désirée had not changed the thin white garment nor the slippers which she wore. Her hair was uncovered and the sun's rays brought a golden gleam from its brown meshes. She did not take the broad, beaten road which led to the far-off plantation of Valmondé. She walked across a deserted field, where the stubble bruised her tender feet, so delicately shod, and tore her thin gown to shreds.

She disappeared among the reeds and willows that grew thick along the banks of the deep, sluggish bayou; and she did not come back again.

45   Some weeks later there was a curious scene enacted at L'Abri. In the centre of the smoothly swept back yard was a great bonfire. Armand Aubigny sat in the wide hallway that commanded a view of the spectacle; and it was he who dealt out to a half dozen negroes the material which kept this fire ablaze.

A graceful cradle of willow, with all its dainty furbishings, was laid upon the pyre, which had already been fed with the richness of a priceless *layette*. Then there were silk gowns, and velvet and satin ones added to these; laces, too, and embroideries; bonnets and gloves; for the *corbeille* had been of rare quality.

The last thing to go was a tiny bundle of letters; innocent little scribblings that Désirée had sent to him during the days of their espousal. There was the remnant of one back in the drawer from which he took them. But it was not Désirée's; it was part of an old letter from his mother to his father. He read it. She was thanking God for the blessing of her husband's love:—

> "But, above all," she wrote, "night and day, I thank the good God for having so arranged our lives that our dear Armand will never know that his mother, who adores him, belongs to the race that is cursed with the brand of slavery."

[1892]

Topics for Critical Thinking and Writing

1. Let's start with the ending. Readers find the ending powerful, but they differ in their interpretations of it. Do you think that when Armand reads the letter he learns something he had never suspected, or, instead, something that he had sensed about himself all along? Find evidence in the text to support your view.
2. Describe Désirée's feelings toward Armand. Do you agree with the student who told us, "She makes him into a god"?
3. Chopin writes economically: Each word counts, each phrase and sentence is significant. What is she revealing about Armand (and perhaps about the discovery he has made) when she writes, "And the very spirit of Satan seemed suddenly to take hold of him in his dealings with the slaves"?
4. Is this story primarily a character study, or is Chopin seeking to make larger points in it about race, slavery, and gender?

KATE CHOPIN

The Storm

I

The leaves were so still that even Bibi thought it was going to rain. Bobinôt, who was accustomed to converse on terms of perfect equality with his little son, called the child's attention to certain sombre clouds that were rolling with sinister intention from the west, accompanied by a sullen, threatening roar. They were at Friedheimer's store and decided to remain there till the storm had passed. They sat within the door on two empty kegs. Bibi was four years old and looked very wise.

"Mama'll be 'fraid, yes," he suggested with blinking eyes.

"She'll shut the house. Maybe she got Sylvie helpin' her this evenin'," Bobinôt responded reassuringly.

"No; she ent got Sylvie. Sylvie was helpin' her yistiday," piped Bibi.

5   Bobinôt arose and going across to the counter purchased a can of shrimps, of which Calixta was very fond. Then he returned to his perch on the keg and sat stolidly holding the can of shrimps while the storm burst. It shook the wooden store and seemed to be ripping great furrows in the distant field. Bibi laid his little hand on his father's knee and was not afraid.

II

Calixta, at home, felt no uneasiness for their safety. She sat at a side window sewing furiously on a sewing machine. She was greatly occupied and did not notice the approaching storm. But she felt very warm and often stopped to mop her face on which the perspiration gathered in beads. She unfastened her white sacque at the throat. It began to grow dark, and suddenly realizing the situation she got up hurriedly and went about closing windows and doors.

Out on the small front gallery[1] she had hung Bobinôt's Sunday clothes to air and she hastened out to gather them before the rain fell. As she stepped outside, Alcée Laballière rode in at the gate. She had not seen him very often since her marriage, and never alone. She stood there with Bobinôt's coat in her hands, and the big rain drops began to fall. Alcée rode his horse under the shelter of a side projection where the chickens had huddled and there were plows and a harrow piled up in the corner.

"May I come and wait on your gallery till the storm is over, Calixta?" he asked.

"Come 'long in, M'sieur Alcée."

His voice and her own startled her as if from a trance, and she seized Bobinôt's vest. Alcée, mounting to the porch, grabbed the trousers and snatched Bibi's braided jacket that was about to be carried away by a sudden gust of wind. He expressed an intention to remain outside, but it was soon apparent that he might as well have been out in the open: the water beat in upon the boards in driving sheets, and he went inside, closing the door after him. It was even necessary to put something beneath the door to keep the water out.

"My! what a rain! It's good two years since it rain' like that," exclaimed Calixta as she rolled up a piece of bagging and Alcée helped her to thrust it beneath the crack.

She was a little fuller of figure than five years before when she married; but she had lost nothing of her vivacity. Her blue eyes still retained their melting quality; and her yellow hair, dishevelled by the wind and rain, kinked more stubbornly than ever about her ears and temples.

The rain beat upon the low, shingled roof with a force and clatter that threatened to break an entrance and deluge them there. They were in the dining room—the sitting room—the general utility room. Adjoining was her bed room, with Bibi's couch along side her own. The door stood open, and the room with its white, monumental bed, its closed shutters, looked dim and mysterious.

Alcée flung himself into a rocker and Calixta nervously began to gather up from the floor the lengths of a cotton sheet which she had been sewing.

"If this keeps up, *Dieu sait*[2] if the levees goin' to stan' it!" she exclaimed.

"What have you got to do with the levees?"

"I got enough to do! An' there's Bobinôt with Bibi out in that storm—if he only didn' left Friedheimer's!"

"Let us hope, Calixta, that Bobinôt's got sense enough to come in out of a cyclone."

She went and stood at the window with a greatly disturbed look on her face. She wiped the frame that was clouded with moisture. It was stiflingly hot. Alcée got up and joined her at the window, looking over her shoulder. The rain was coming down in sheets obscuring the view of far-off cabins and enveloping the distant wood in a gray mist. The playing of the lightning was incessant. A bolt

---

[1]**gallery** porch, or passageway along a wall, open to the air but protected by a roof supported by columns. [2]*Dieu sait* God only knows.

struck a tall chinaberry tree at the edge of the field. It filled all visible space with a blinding glare and the crash seemed to invade the very boards they stood upon.

20 Calixta put her hands to her eyes, and with a cry, staggered backward. Alcée's arm encircled her, and for an instant he drew her close and spasmodically to him.

"Bonté!"[3] she cried, releasing herself from his encircling arm and retreating from the window, "the house'll go next! If I only knew w'ere Bibi was!" She would not compose herself; she would not be seated. Alcée clasped her shoulders and looked into her face. The contact of her warm, palpitating body when he had unthinkingly drawn her into his arms, had aroused all the old-time infatuation and desire for her flesh.

"Calixta," he said, "don't be frightened. Nothing can happen. The house is too low to be struck, with so many tall trees standing about. There! aren't you going to be quiet? say, aren't you?" He pushed her hair back from her face that was warm and steaming. Her lips were as red and moist as pomegranate seed. Her white neck and a glimpse of her full, firm bosom disturbed him powerfully. As she glanced up at him the fear in her liquid blue eyes had given place to a drowsy gleam that unconsciously betrayed a sensuous desire. He looked down into her eyes and there was nothing for him to do but to gather her lips in a kiss. It reminded him of Assumption.[4]

"Do you remember—in Assumption, Calixta?" he asked in a low voice broken by passion. Oh! she remembered; for in Assumption he had kissed her and kissed and kissed her; until his senses would well nigh fail, and to save her he would resort to a desperate flight. If she was not an immaculate dove in those days, she was still inviolate; a passionate creature whose very defenselessness had made her defense, against which his honor forbade him to prevail. Now—well, now— her lips seemed in a manner free to be tasted, as well as her round, white throat and her whiter breasts.

They did not heed the crashing torrents, and the roar of the elements made her laugh as she lay in his arms. She was a revelation in that dim, mysterious chamber; as white as the couch she lay upon. Her firm, elastic flesh that was knowing for the first time its birthright, was like a creamy lily that the sun invites to contribute its breath and perfume to the undying life of the world.

25 The generous abundance of her passion, without guile or trickery, was like a white flame which penetrated and found response in depths of his own sensuous nature that had never yet been reached.

When he touched her breasts they gave themselves up in quivering ecstasy, inviting his lips. Her mouth was a fountain of delight. And when he possessed her, they seemed to swoon together at the very borderland of life's mystery.

He stayed cushioned upon her, breathless, dazed, enervated, with his heart beating like a hammer upon her. With one hand she clasped his head, her lips lightly touching his forehead. The other hand stroked with a soothing rhythm his muscular shoulders.

The growl of the thunder was distant and passing away. The rain beat softly upon the shingles, inviting them to drowsiness and sleep. But they dared not yield.

The rain was over; and the sun was turning the glistening green world into a place of gems. Calixta, on the gallery, watched Alcée ride away. He turned and

[3]*Bonté!* Heavens! [4]**Assumption** a parish (i.e., a county) in southeast Louisiana.

smiled at her with a beaming face; and she lifted her pretty chin in the air and laughed aloud.

III

30   Bobinôt and Bibi, trudging home, stopped without at the cistern to make themselves presentable.

"My! Bibi, w'at will yo' mama say! You ought to be ashame'. You oughtn' put on those good pants. Look at 'em! An' that mud on yo' collar! How you got that mud on yo' collar, Bibi? I never saw such a boy!" Bibi was the picture of pathetic resignation. Bobinôt was the embodiment of serious solicitude as he strove to remove from his own person and his son's the signs of their tramp over heavy roads and through wet fields. He scraped the mud off Bibi's bare legs and feet with a stick and carefully removed all traces from his heavy brogans. Then, prepared for the worst—the meeting with an over-scrupulous housewife, they entered cautiously at the back door.

Calixta was preparing supper. She had set the table and was dripping coffee at the hearth. She sprang up as they came in.

"Oh, Bobinôt! You back! My! but I was uneasy. W'ere you been during the rain? An' Bibi? he ain't wet? he ain't hurt?" She had clasped Bibi and was kissing him effusively. Bobinôt's explanations and apologies which he had been composing all along the way, died on his lips as Calixta felt him to see if he were dry, and seemed to express nothing but satisfaction at their safe return.

"I brought you some shrimps, Calixta," offered Bobinôt, hauling the can from his ample side pocket and laying it on the table.

35   "Shrimps! Oh, Bobinôt! you too good fo' anything!" and she gave him a smacking kiss on the cheek that resounded. "*J'vous reponds,*[5] we'll have a feas' to night! umph-umph!"

Bobinôt and Bibi began to relax and enjoy themselves, and when the three seated themselves at table they laughed much and so loud that anyone might have heard them as far away as Laballière's.

IV

Alcée Laballière wrote to his wife, Clarisse, that night. It was a loving letter, full of tender solicitude. He told her not to hurry back, but if she and the babies liked it at Biloxi, to stay a month longer. He was getting on nicely; and though he missed them, he was willing to bear the separation a while longer—realizing that their health and pleasure were the first things to be considered.

V

As for Clarisse, she was charmed upon receiving her husband's letter. She and the babies were doing well. The society was agreeable; many of her old friends and acquaintances were at the bay. And the first free breath since her marriage seemed to restore the pleasant liberty of her maiden days. Devoted as she was to her husband, their intimate conjugal life was something which she was more than willing to forego for a while.

So the storm passed and everyone was happy.

[1898]

[5]*J'vous reponds* Take my word; let me tell you.

Writing about "The Storm"

As we said earlier, what you write will depend partly on your audience and on your purpose, as well as on your responses (for instance, pleasure or irritation). Consider the *differences* among these assignments:

1. Assume that you are trying to describe "The Storm" to someone who has not read it. Briefly summarize the action, and then explain why you think "The Storm" is (or is not) worth reading.
2. Assume that your readers are familiar with "The Story of an Hour." Compare the implied attitudes, as you see them, toward marriage in that story and "The Storm."
3. Write an essay arguing that "The Storm" is (or is not) immoral, or (a different thing) amoral. (By the way, because one of her slightly earlier works, a short novel called *The Awakening*, was widely condemned as sordid, Chopin was unable to find a publisher for "The Storm.")
4. In Part IV we are told that Alcée wrote a letter to Clarisse. Write his letter (500 words). Or write Clarisse's response (500 words).
5. You are writing to a high school teacher, urging that one of the four stories by Chopin be taught in high school. Which one do you recommend, and why?
6. Do you think "The Storm" would make a good film? Why? (And while you are thinking about Chopin and film, think about what devices you might use to turn "Ripe Figs," "The Story of an Hour," or "Désirée's Baby" into an interesting film.)

TOBIAS WOLFF

*Tobias Wolff was born in Alabama in 1945, but he grew up in the state of Washington. He left high school before graduating, served as an apprentice seaman and as a weight-guesser in a carnival, and then joined the army, where he served four years as a paratrooper. After his discharge from the army, he hired private tutors to enable him to pass the entrance examination to Oxford University. At Oxford he did spectacularly well, graduating with First Class Honors in English. Wolff has written stories, novels, and an autobiography (*This Boy's Life*); he now teaches writing at Syracuse University.*

Powder

Just before Christmas my father took me skiing at Mount Baker. He'd had to fight for the privilege of my company, because my mother was still angry with him for sneaking me into a nightclub during his last visit, to see Thelonius Monk.

He wouldn't give up. He promised, hand on heart, to take good care of me and have me home for dinner on Christmas Eve, and she relented. But as we were checking out of the lodge that morning it began to snow, and in this snow he observed some quality that made it necessary for us to get in one last run. We got in several last runs. He was indifferent to my fretting. Snow whirled around us in bitter, blinding squalls, hissing like sand, and still we skied. As the lift bore us to the peak yet again, my father looked at his watch and said: "Criminey. This'll have to be a fast one."

By now I couldn't see the trail. There was no point in trying. I stuck to him like white on rice and did what he did and somehow made it to the bottom without sailing off a cliff. We returned our skis and my father put chains on the Austin-Healy while I swayed from foot to foot, clapping my mittens and wishing I were home. I could see everything. The green tablecloth, the plates with the holly pattern, the red candles waiting to be lit.

We passed a diner on our way out. "You want some soup?" my father asked. I shook my head. "Buck up," he said. "I'll get you there. Right, doctor?"

5   I was supposed to say, "Right, doctor," but I didn't say anything.

A state trooper waved us down outside the resort. A pair of sawhorses were blocking the road. The trooper came up to our car and bent down to my father's window. His face was bleached by the cold. Snowflakes clung to his eyebrows and to the fur trim of his jacket and cap.

"Don't tell me," my father said.

The trooper told him. The road was closed. It might get cleared, it might not. Storm took everyone by surprise. So much, so fast. Hard to get people moving. Christmas Eve. What can you do?

My father said: "Look. We're talking about four, five inches. I've taken this car through worse than that."

10   The trooper straightened up, boots creaking. His face was out of sight but I could hear him. "The road is closed."

My father sat with both hands on the wheel, rubbing the wood with his thumbs. He looked at the barricade for a long time. He seemed to be trying to master the idea of it. Then he thanked the trooper, and with a weird, old-maidy show of caution turned the car around. "Your mother will never forgive me for this," he said.

"We should have left before," I said. "Doctor."

He didn't speak to me again until we were both in a booth at the dinner, waiting for our burgers. "She won't forgive me," he said. "Do you understand? Never."

"I guess," I said, but no guesswork was required; she wouldn't forgive him.

15   "I can't let that happen." He bent toward me. "I'll tell you what I want. I want us to be all together again. Is that what you want?"

"Yes, sir."

He bumped my chin with his knuckles. "That's all I needed to hear."

When we finished eating he went to the pay phone in the back of the dinner, then joined me in the booth again. I figured he'd called my mother, but he didn't give a report. He sipped at his coffee and stared out the window at the empty road. "Come on, come on," he said. A little while later he said, "Come on!" When the trooper's car went past, lights flashing, he got up and dropped some money on the check. "O.K. Vámanos."

The wind had died. The snow was falling straight down, less of it now; lighter. We drove away from the resort, right up to the barricade. "Move it," my father told me. When I looked at him he said, "What are you waiting for?" I got out and dragged one of the sawhorses aside, then put it back after he drove through. He pushed the door open for me. "Now you're an accomplice," he said. "We go down together." He put the car into gear and gave me a look. "Joke, doctor."

20   "Funny, doctor."

Down the first long stretch I watched the road behind us, to see if the trooper was on our tail. The barricade vanished. Then there was nothing but snow: snow on the road, snow kicking up from the chains, snow on the trees, snow in the sky; and our trail in the snow. I faced around and had a shock. The lie of the road behind us had been marked by our own tracks, but there were no tracks ahead of us. My father was breaking virgin snow between a line of tall trees. He was humming "Stars Fell on Alabama." I felt snow brush along the floorboards under my feet. To keep my hands from shaking, I clamped them between my knees.

My father grunted in a thoughtful way and said, "Don't ever try this yourself."

"I won't."

"That's what you say now, but someday you'll get your license and then you'll think you can do anything. Only you won't be able to do this. You need, I don't know—a certain instinct."

25   "Maybe I have it."

"You don't. You have your strong points, but not . . . his. I only mention it, because I don't want you to get the idea this is something just anybody can do. I'm a great driver. That's not a virtue, O.K.? It's just a fact, and one you should be aware of. Of course you have to give the old heap some credit, too—there aren't many cars I'd try this with. Listen!"

I listened. I heard the slap of the chains, the stiff, jerky rasps of the wipers, the purr of the engine. It really did purr. The car was almost new. My father couldn't afford it, and kept promising to sell it, but here it was.

I said, "Where do you think that policeman went to?"

"Are you warm enough?" He reached over and cranked up the blower. Then he turned off the wipers. We didn't need them. The clouds had brightened. A few sparse, feathery flakes drifted into our slipstream and were swept away. We left the trees and entered a broad field of snow that ran level for a while and then tilted sharply downward. Orange stakes had been planted at intervals in two parallel lines and my father steered a course between them, though they were far enough apart to leave considerable doubt in my mind as to where exactly the road lay. He was humming again, doing little scat riffs around the melody.

30   "O.K. then. What are my strong points?"

"Don't get me started," he said. "It'd take all day."

"Oh, right. Name one."

"Easy. You always think ahead."

True. I always thought ahead. I was a boy who kept his clothes on numbered hangers to insure proper rotation. I bothered my teachers for homework assignments far ahead of their due dates so I could make up schedules. I thought ahead, and that was why I knew that there would be other troopers waiting for us at the end of our ride, if we got there. What I did not know was that my father would wheedle and plead his way past them—he didn't sing "O Tannenbaum" but just about—and get me home for dinner, buying a little more time before my mother decided to make the split final. I knew we'd get caught; I was resigned to it. And maybe for this reason I stopped moping and began to enjoy myself.

35   Why not? This was one for the books. Like being in a speedboat, but better. You can't go downhill in a boat. And it was all ours. And it kept coming, the laden trees, the unbroken surface of snow, the sudden white vistas. Here and there I saw hints of the road, ditches, fences, stakes, but not so many that I could have found my way. But then I didn't have to. My father was driving. My father in his 48th year, rumpled, kind, bankrupt of honor, flushed with certainty. He was a great driver. All persuasion, no coercion. Such subtlety at the wheel, such tactful pedalwork. I actually trusted him. And the best was yet to come—the switchbacks and hairpins. Impossible to describe. Except maybe to say this: If you haven't driven fresh powder, you haven't driven.

[1992]

Topics for Critical Thinking and Writing

1. How would you characterize the father?
2. How does the boy feel about his father?

A NOTE ABOUT LITERARY EVALUATIONS

One other point—and it is a big one. Until a decade or two ago, Chopin was regarded as a minor writer who worked in a minor field. She was called a "local colorist," that is, a writer who emphasizes the unique speech, mannerisms, and ways of thinking of the charming and somewhat eccentric characters associated with a particular locale. Other late-nineteenth-century writers who are widely regarded as local colorists are Bret Harte (California), Sarah Orne Jewett and Mary E. Wilkins Freeman (New England), and Joel Chandler Harris (the old South). Because of the writer's alleged emphasis on the uniqueness and charm of a region, the reader's response is likely to be "How quaint" rather than "This is life as I feel it, or at least as I can imagine it."

Probably part of the reason for the relatively low value attributed to Chopin's work was that she was a woman, and it was widely believed that "serious and important literature" was (with a very few exceptions) written by men. In short, judgments, including literary evaluations, depend partly on cultural traditions.

A question: On the basis of the four stories by Chopin, do you think Chopin's interest went beyond presenting quaint folk for our entertainment? You might set forth your response in an essay of 500 words—after you have done some brainstorming, some thinking in a journal, and some drafting, revising, and editing.

3

Reading Literature Closely: Explication

WHAT IS LITERATURE?

Perhaps the first thing to say is that it is impossible to define *literature* in a way that will satisfy everyone. And perhaps the second thing to say is that in the last twenty years or so, some serious thinkers have argued that it is impossible to set off certain verbal works from all others, and on some basis or other to designate them as literature. For one thing, it is argued, a work is just marks on paper or sounds in the air. The audience (reader or listener) turns these marks or sounds into something with meaning, and different audiences will construct different meanings out of what they read or hear. There are *texts* (birthday cards, sermons, political speeches, magazines, novels that sell by the millions and novels that don't sell at all, poems, popular songs, editorials, and so forth), but there is nothing that should be given the special title of literature.

Although there is something to be said for the idea that *literature* is just an honorific word and not a body of work embodying eternal truths and eternal beauty, let's make the opposite assumption, at least for a start. Let's assume that certain verbal works are of a distinct sort—whether because the author shapes them, or because a reader perceives them a certain way—and that we can call these works literature. But what are these works like?

Literature and Form

We all know why we value a newspaper (for instance) or a textbook or an atlas, but why do we value a verbal work that doesn't give us the latest news or important information about business cycles or the names of the capitals of nations? About a thousand years ago a Japanese woman, Shikibu Murasaki, or Lady Murasaki (978?–1026), offered an answer in *The Tale of Genji*, a book often called the world's first novel. During a discussion about reading fiction, one of the characters gives an opinion as to why a writer tells a story:

> Again and again writers find something in their experience, or see something in the life around them, that seems so important they cannot bear to let it pass into oblivion. There must never come a time, the writer feels, when people do not know about this.

Literature is about human experiences, but the experiences embodied in literature are not simply the shapeless experiences—the chaotic passing scene—captured by a mindless, unselective video camera. Poets, dramatists, and storytellers find or impose a shape on scenes (for instance, the history of two lovers), giving readers things to value—written or spoken accounts that are memorable not only for their content but also for their *form*—the shape of the speeches, of the scenes, of the plots. (In a little while we will see that form and content are inseparable, but for the moment, for our purposes, we can talk about them separately.)

Because this discussion of literature is brief, we will illustrate the point by looking at one of the briefest literary forms, the proverb. Consider this statement:

> A rolling stone gathers no moss.

Now let's compare it with a **paraphrase** (a restatement, a translation into other words):

> If a stone is always moving around, vegetation won't have a chance to grow on it.

What makes the original version more powerful, more memorable? Surely much of the answer is that the original is more concrete and its form is more shapely. At the risk of being heavy-handed, we can analyze the shapeliness thus: *Stone* and *moss* (the two nouns in the sentence) each contain one syllable; *rolling* and *gathers* (the two words of motion) each contain two syllables, with the accent on the first syllable. Notice, too, the nice contrast between stone (hard) and moss (soft).

The reader probably *feels* this shapeliness unconsciously rather than perceives it consciously. That is, these connections become apparent when one starts to analyze, but the literary work can make its effect on a reader even before the reader analyzes. As T. S. Eliot said in his essay on Dante (1929), "Genuine poetry can communicate before it is understood." Indeed, our *first* reading of a work, when, so to speak, we are all eyes and ears (and the mind is highly receptive rather than sifting for evidence), is sometimes the most important reading. Experience proves that we can feel the effects of a work without yet understanding *how* the effects are achieved.

Probably most readers will agree that

- the words in the proverb are paired interestingly and meaningfully;
- the sentence is not simply some information but is also (to quote one of Robert Frost's definitions of literature) "a performance in words";
- what the sentence *is*, we might say, is no less significant than what the sentence *says*;
- the sentence as a whole forms a memorable picture, a small but complete world, hard and soft, inorganic and organic, inert and moving;
- the idea set forth is simple—partly because it is highly focused and therefore it leaves out a lot—but it is also complex;
- by virtue of the contrasts, and, again, even by the pairing of monosyllabic nouns and of disyllabic words of motion, it is unified into a pleasing whole.

For all of its specificity and its compactness—the proverb contains only six words—it expands our minds.

A Brief Exercise: Take a minute to think about some other proverb, for instance "Look before you leap," "Finders keepers," "Haste makes waste," or "Absence makes the heart grow fonder." Paraphrase it, and then ask yourself why the original is more interesting, more memorable, than your paraphrase.

Form and Meaning

Let's turn now to a work not much longer than a proverb—a very short poem by Robert Frost (1874–1963).

The Span of Life

The old dog barks backward without getting up.
I can remember when he was a pup.

Read the poem aloud once or twice, physically experiencing Frost's "perfor-mance in words." Notice that the first line is harder to say than the second line, which more or less rolls off the tongue. Why? Because in the first line we must pause between *old* and *dog*, between *backward* and *without*, and between *without* and *getting*—and in fact between *back* and *ward*. Further, when we read the poem aloud, or with the mind's ear, in the first line we hear four consecutive stresses in "old dog barks back," a noticeable contrast to the rather jingling "when he was a pup" in the second line. No two readers will read the lines in exactly the same way, but it is probably safe to say that most readers will agree that in the first line they may stress fairly heavily as many as eight syllables, whereas in the second line they may stress only three or four:

The óld dóg bárks báckward withoút gétting úp.
Í can remémber when hé was a púp.

And so we can say that the form (a relatively effortful, hard-to-speak line fol-lowed by a bouncy line) shapes and indeed is part of the content (a description of a dog that no longer has the energy or the strength to leap up, followed by a memory of the dog as a puppy).

Thinking further about Frost's poem, we notice something else about the form. The first line is about a dog, but the second line is about a dog *and* a hu-man being ("*I* can remember"). The speaker must be getting on, too. And al-though nothing is said about the dog as a *symbol* of human life, surely the reader, prompted by the title of the poem, makes a connection between the life span of a dog and that of a human being. Part of what makes the poem effective is that this point is *not* stated explicitly, not belabored. Readers have the pleasure of making the connection for themselves—under Frost's careful guidance.

Everyone knows that puppies are frisky and that old dogs are not—though perhaps not until we encountered this poem did we think twice about the fact that "the old dog barks backward without getting up." Or let's put it this way:

- Many people may have noticed this behavior, but
- perhaps only Frost thought (to use Lady Murasaki's words), "There must never come a time . . . when people do not know about this." And,
- fortunately for all of us, Frost had the ability to put his perception into memorable words.

Part of what makes this performance in words especially memorable is, of course, the *relationship* between the two lines. Neither line in itself is anything very special, but because of the counterpoint the whole is more than the sum of the parts. Skill in handling language, obviously, is indispensable if the writer is to produce literature. A person may know a great deal about dogs and may be a great lover of dogs, but knowledge and love are not enough equipment to write even a two-line poem about a dog (or the span of life, or both). Poems, like other kinds of literature, are produced by people who know how to delight us with ver-bal performances.

The chief reason for opposing pornography is that it exerts a bad influence on those who consume it. If indeed books and pictures can exert a bad influence, it seems reasonable to think that other books and pictures can exert a good influence. Fairness requires us to mention, however, that many thoughtful people disagree and argue that literature and art entertain us but do not really influence us in any significant way. In trying to solve this debate, perhaps we can rely only on our own experience.

We can easily see that Robert Frost's "The Span of Life" is a work of literature—a work that uses language in a special way—if we contrast it with another short work in rhyme:

> Thirty days hath September,
> April, June, and November;
> All the rest have thirty-one
> Excepting February alone,
> Which has twenty-eight in fine,
> Till leap year gives it twenty-nine.

This information is important, but it is only information. The lines rhyme, giving the work some form, but there is nothing very interesting about it. (This is a matter of opinion; perhaps you will want to take issue.) It is true and therefore useful, but it is not of compelling interest, probably because it only *tells* us facts rather than *shows* or *presents* human experience. We all remember the lines, but they do not hold our interest. "Thirty days" offers neither the pleasure of an insight nor the pleasure of an interesting tune. It has nothing of what the poet Thomas Gray said characterizes literature: "Thoughts that breathe, and words that burn."

READING IN SLOW MOTION

In this chapter, and in the next, we focus on the skills that careful study of literary language requires. "Close reading" is perhaps the most familiar name for this technique of heightened responsiveness to the words on the page. But another, employed by the literary critics Reuben A. Brower and Richard Poirier, may be even better. They refer to "reading in slow motion." Brower, for example, speaks of "slowing down the process of reading to observe what is happening, in order to attend very closely to the words, their uses, and their meanings." This sort of reading, he explains, involves looking and listening with special alertness, slowly, without rushing or feeling impatient if a work puzzles us at first encounter.[1]

As Brower and Poirier point out, sometimes we are so intrigued or moved by a writer's operations with words that we are led to "slow down" in our reading, lingering over verbal details and vivid images—"a watersmooth-silver / stallion" in Cummings's poem about Buffalo Bill (p. 193), or "Babette danced out to where the fig-trees were," in Chopin's "Ripe Figs" (p. 3). Or else, we find that we want to return to a poem, or to a key section of a story or scene in a play, to articulate— "slow motion" style—why it has affected us as powerfully as it did.

"Close" or slow-motion reading can help you to understand and enjoy a work that at first seems strange or obscure. When we examine a piece of literature with care and intensity, we are not taking it apart in a destructive way but, instead, are

---

[1] The quotation is taken from Brower's introduction to *In Defense of Reading: A Reader's Approach to Literary Criticism*, ed. Reuben A. Brower and Richard Poirier (1962). See also Brower, *The Fields of Light: An Experiment in Critical Reading* (1951); and Poirier, *Poetry and Pragmatism* (1992).

seeking to satisfy our curiosity about how the writer organized it. And almost always, our increased *understanding* of the work results in increased *enjoyment*. Very few poems have been made worse by close reading, and many have been made better—made, that is, more accessible and interesting, deeper, and more rewarding.

This point is clarified when we recall what it's like to watch a scene from a movie in slow motion, or a TV replay in slow motion of a touchdown run in a football game. In slow-motion film we perceive details we might otherwise miss—the subtle changes in expression on an actress's face, for example, or the interplay of gestures among several performers at a climactic moment in the action. Similarly, seeing a touchdown multiple times in slow motion, and perhaps from a half-dozen camera angles, reveals to us how the play developed, who made the crucial blocks, where the defense failed. The touchdown was exciting when it took place; and it remains exciting—and frequently it becomes more so—when we slow it down in order to study and talk about it.

This chapter deals with explication, and the next with analysis. Both are based on the principle that responding well to literature means:

- acquiring the ability to read it closely;
- practicing this skill to become better and better at it;
- explaining and demonstrating in critical essays what we have learned.

But the two terms, while related to one another, differ in emphasis. An **explication** moves from beginning to end of an entire work (if it is fairly short) or of a section of a work; it is sustained, meticulous, thorough, systematic. An analysis builds upon the habits of attention that we have gained from explicating texts and passages of texts.

When we engage in analysis of literature, we are doing so as part of presenting an argument, a thesis, about a work. What is the central theme in this short story by Welty or that one by Updike? What is the most compelling insight into the nature of love that Rich offers in this or that group of poems about men and women? Does Hamlet delay—and if he does, why? To deal with questions like these, we have to read the text closely and study its language carefully, but we must be selective in the pieces of textual evidence that we offer. To be sure, we can explicate a single speech in Hamlet, or an exchange between characters. But it would be a daunting assignment in a short critical essay to explicate an entire scene, and impossible to explicate the entire play from start to finish.

Analysis goes hand in hand with the job of presenting and proving a thesis; it goes hand in hand with explication as well, taking that form of close reading, of reading in slow motion, as its foundation. But rather than say more about analysis here, let's turn to explication first and learn what we can discover about literature through it. As you'll see, one of the things we quickly realize is that close reading of literary works makes us not only better readers but also better writers attuned more sharply and sensitively to the organization of the language in our own prose.

EXPLICATION

A line-by-line or episode-by-episode commentary on what is going on in a text is an explication (literally, unfolding or spreading out). An explication does not deal with the writer's life and times, and it is not a paraphrase, a rewording—though it may include paraphrase. Rather, it is a commentary that reveals your sense of the meaning of the work and its structure. When we explicate a text, we ask questions about the meanings of words, the implications of metaphors and images, the speaker's tone of voice as we initially hear it and it develops and perhaps changes. How is this literary work put together? How did the writer organize it to prompt from me the response I had (and am having) to it? How does it begin, and what happens next, and next after that? And so on, through to the end.

It takes some skill to work your way along in an explication without saying, "In line one . . . In the second line . . . In the third line . . . " This sounds mechanical and formulaic. Make good use of transitional words and phrases, so that your commentary will feel to your reader more natural, with a better pace and rhythm. For example: "The speaker begins by suggesting . . . The poem then shifts in direction . . . In the next paragraph, however, the narrator implies . . . "

A Sample Explication

The following short poem is by Langston Hughes (1902–1967), an African American writer. Hughes was born in Joplin, Missouri, lived part of his youth in Mexico, spent a year at Columbia University, served as a merchant seaman, and worked in a Paris nightclub, where he showed some of his poems to Alain Locke, an influential critic, educator, and strong advocate of African American literature. When he returned to the United States, Hughes went on to publish fiction, plays, essays, and biographies; he also founded theaters, gave public readings, and was, in short, an important force.

Harlem

What happens to a dream deferred?

> Does it dry up
> like a raisin in the sun?
> Or fester like a sore—   4
> And then run?
> Does it stink like rotten meat?
> Or crust and sugar over—
> like a syrupy sweet?   8
>
> Maybe it just sags
> like a heavy load.
>
> *Or does it explode?*

[1951]

Different readers will respond at least somewhat differently to any work. On the other hand, since writers want to communicate, they try to control their readers' responses, and they count on their readers to understand the denotations of words as they understand them. Thus, Hughes assumed that his readers knew that Harlem was the site of a large African American community in New York City. A reader who confuses the title of the poem with Haarlem in the Netherlands will wonder what this poem is saying about the tulip-growing center in northern Holland. Explication is based on the assumption that the poem contains a meaning and that by studying the work thoughtfully we can unfold the meaning or meanings.

Let's assume that the reader understands Hughes is talking about Harlem, New York, and that the "dream deferred" refers to the unfulfilled hopes of African Americans who live in a society dominated by whites. But Hughes does not say "hopes," he says "dream," and he does not say "unfulfilled," he says "deferred." You might ask yourself exactly what differences there are between these words. Next, after you have read the poem several times, you might think about which expression is better in the context, "unfulfilled hopes" or "dream deferred," and why.

Working Toward an Explication

In preparing to write an explication, first write on a computer, or type or hand-write, the complete text of the work that you will explicate—usually a poem but sometimes a short passage of prose. *Don't* photocopy it; the act of typing or writing it will help you to get into the piece, word by word, comma by comma. Type or write it *double-spaced*, so that you will have plenty of room for annotations as you study the piece. It's advisable to make a few photocopies (or to print a few copies, if you are using a word processor) before you start annotating, so that if one page gets too cluttered you can continue working on a clean copy. Or you may want to use one copy for a certain kind of annotations—let's say those concerning imagery—and other copies for other kinds of notes—let's say those concerning meter or wordplay. If you are writing on a word processor, you can highlight words, boldface them, put them in capitals (for instance, to indicate accented syllables), and so forth.

Let's turn to an explication of the poem, a detailed examination of the whole. Here are the preliminary jottings of a student, Bill Horner.

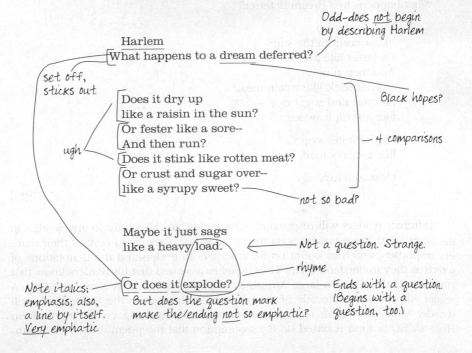

These annotations chiefly get at the structure of the poem, the relationship of the parts. Horner notices that the poem begins with a line set off by itself and ends with a line set off by itself, and he also notices that each of these lines is a question. Further, he indicates that each of these two lines is emphasized in other ways: The first begins farther to the left than any of the other lines—as though the other lines are subheadings or are in some way subordinate—and the last is italicized.

Some Journal Entries

Bill Horner later wrote entries in his journal:

Feb. 18. Since the title is "Harlem," it's obvious that the "dream" is by African American people. Also, obvious that Hughes thinks that if the "dream" doesn't become real there may be riots ("explode"). I like "raisin in the sun" (maybe because I like the play), and I like the business about "a syrupy sweet"--much more pleasant than the festering sore and the rotten meat. But if the dream becomes "sweet," what's wrong with that? Why should something "sweet" explode?

Feb. 21. Prof. McCabe said to think of structure or form of a poem as a sort of architecture, a building with a foundation, floors, etc., topped by a roof--but since we read a poem from top to bottom, it's like a building upside down. Title is foundation (even though it's at top); last line is roof, capping the whole. As you read, you add layers. Foundation of "Harlem" is a question (first line). Then, set back a bit from foundation, or built on it by white space, a tall room (7 lines high, with 4 questions); then, on top of this room, another room (lines, statement, not a question). Funny; I thought that in poems all stanzas are the same number of lines. Then--more white space, so another unit--the roof. Man, this roof is going to fall in-- "explodes." Not just the roof, maybe the whole house.

Feb. 21, p.m. I get it; one line at start, one line at end; both are questions, but the last sort of says (because it is in italics) that it is the most likely answer to the question of the first line. The last line is also a question, but it's still an answer. The big stanza (7 lines) has 4 questions: 2 lines, 2 lines, 1 line, 2 lines. Maybe the switch to 1 line is to give some variety, so as not to be dull? It's exactly in the middle of the poem. I get the progress from raisin in the sun (dried, but not so terrible), to festering sore and to stinking meat, but I still don't see what's so bad about "a syrupy sweet." Is Hughes saying that after things are very bad they will get better? But why, then, the explosion at the end?

Feb. 23. "Heavy load" and "sags" in next-to-last stanza seem to me to suggest slaves with bales of cotton, or maybe poor cotton pickers dragging big sacks of cotton. Or maybe people doing heavy labor in Harlem. Anyway, very tired. Different from running sore and stinking meat earlier; not disgusting, but pressing down, deadening. Maybe worse than a sore or rotten meat--a hard, hopeless life. And then the last line. Just one line, no fancy (and disgusting) simile. In fact, no simile at all. This is a metaphor, not a simile. Boom! Not just pressed down and tired, like maybe some racist whites think (hope?) blacks will be. Bang! Will there be survivors?

Drawing chiefly on these notes, Horner jotted down some key ideas to guide him through a draft of an analysis. (The organization of the draft posed no problem; the writer simply followed the organization of the poem.)

ll lines; short, but powerful; explosive
Question (first line)
answers (set off by space and also indented)
"raisin in the sun": shrinking
"sore"   *} disgusting*
"rotten meat"
"syrupy sweet": relief from disgusting comparisons
final question (last line): explosion?
   explosive (powerful) because:
      short, condensed, packed
      in italics
      stands by self-like first line
      no fancy comparison; very direct

A Sample Essay by a Student (Final Version): "Langston Hughes's 'Harlem'"

Here is Bill Horner's final essay:

Horner 1

Bill Horner

Professor Todd

English 122

10 March 2004

Langston Hughes's "Harlem"

"Harlem" is a poem that is only eleven lines long, but it is

charged with power. It explodes. Hughes sets the stage, so to

speak, by telling us in the title that he is talking about Harlem,

and then he begins by asking, "What happens to a dream

deferred?" The rest of the poem is set off by being indented, as

though it is the answer to his question. This answer is in three

parts (three stanzas, of different lengths).

In a way, it's wrong to speak of the answer, since the rest of

the poem consists of questions, but I think Hughes means that

each question (for instance, does a "deferred" hope "dry up / like a

raisin in the sun?") really is an answer, something that really has

happened and that will happen again. The first question, "Does it

dry up / like a raisin in the sun?," is a famous line. To compare

hope to a raisin dried in the sun is to suggest a terrible

shrinking. The next two comparisons are to a "sore" and to

"rotten meat." These comparisons are less clever, but they are very

effective because they are disgusting. Then, maybe because of the

disgusting comparisons, he gives a comparison that is not at all

disgusting. In this comparison he says that maybe the "dream

deferred" will "crust over-- / like a syrupy sweet."

The seven lines with four comparisons are followed by a

stanza of two lines with just one comparison:

> Maybe it just sags
>
> like a heavy load.

So if we thought that this postponed dream might finally turn

into something "sweet," we were kidding ourselves. Hughes comes

down to earth, in a short stanza, with an image of a heavy load,

which probably also calls to mind images of people bent under

heavy loads, maybe of cotton, or maybe just any sort of heavy load

carried by African Americans in Harlem and elsewhere.

The opening question ("What happens to a dream deferred?")

was followed by four questions in seven lines, but now, with

Horner 3

"Maybe it just sags / like a heavy load," we get a statement, as

though the poet at last has found an answer. But at the end we

get one more question, set off by itself and in italics: "Or does it

explode?" This line itself is explosive for three reasons: It is short,

it is italicized, and it is a stanza in itself. It's also interesting that

this line, unlike the earlier lines, does not use a simile. It uses a

metaphor. It's almost as though Hughes is saying, "O.K., we've

had enough fancy ways of talking about this terrible situation;

here it is, 'boom.'"

Topics for Critical Thinking and Writing

1. The student's explication suggests that the comparison with "a syrupy sweet" deliberately misleads the reader into thinking the ending will be happy, and it thus serves to make the real ending even more powerful. In class another student suggested that Hughes may be referring to African Americans who play Uncle Tom, people who adopt a smiling manner in order to cope with an oppressive society. Which explanation do you prefer, and why? What do you think of combining the two?

   Does some method or principle help us decide which interpretation is correct? Can we, in fact, talk about a "correct" interpretation, or only about a plausible or implausible interpretation and an interesting or uninteresting interpretation?

2. In *The Collected Poems of Langston Hughes* (1994), the editors title this poem "Harlem." But in the *Selected Poems of Langston Hughes* (1959), published when the poet was still alive, the poem is titled "Dream Deferred." Which title do you think is more effective? Do you interpret the poem differently depending on how it is titled? How might a reader—who knew nothing about Hughes—respond to the poem if he or she came upon it with the title "Dream Deferred"?

Note: Another explication (of W. B. Yeats's "The Balloon of the Mind") appears in Chapter 14.

Explication as Argument

We have said that an explication unfolds or opens up or interprets a work by calling attention to such things as the speaker's tone of voice and the implications in images. It might seem, then, to be an objective report, the sort of explanatory writing that is called expository rather than argumentative.

But in fact, because literature makes considerable use of connotations and symbolic meanings—"A rolling stone gathers no moss" is not essentially a statement about stones and moss but about something else—readers may differ in what they take the words to mean. The writer of an explication not only examines the meanings of specific words and images but also, having come to a conclusion about what the details add up to, argues an interpretation, supports a thesis.

What distinguishes argument from exposition is this: In argument, some statements are offered as *reasons* for others. Because writers of arguments assume that their readers may not at the outset share their views, in their writing they offer evidence to support their assertions.

If you reread Bill Horner's explication of "Harlem," you will notice, for instance, that in speaking of the line "Or does it explode?", Horner says, "This line is explosive for three reasons." He then specifies the three reasons. That is, he argues his case, presenting three pieces of supporting evidence: Hughes's line is short, it is italicized, and it is a stanza in itself.

True, much of Horner's explication does consist of expository writing, for instance when he says that the poem consists of "three parts (three stanzas, of different lengths)." There can be little disagreement between writer and reader here—although, come to think of it, a reader might respond, "No, the title is also part of the poem, so the poem consists of four parts." A reader who is looking for an argument—in the sense of a quarrel, not in the sense of a reasoned discussion—can find it with almost any piece of writing. But, again, our point is that because expository writing does not assume a difference of opinion, it chiefly sets forth information rather than seeks to make a case. Argumentative writing, on the other hand, assumes that it must set forth information in a way that persuades the reader of its truth, which means that it must give evidence.

Pure exposition—let's say, information about how to register for classes, or information about what is likely to be on the next examination—is not concerned with persuading readers to accept a thesis. But an explication, even though it might seem only to clarify the meanings of the words in a poem, essentially argues a thesis about the work as a whole. Notice Bill Horner's opening sentence:

> "Harlem" is a poem that is only eleven lines long, but it is charged with power.

What is Horner's thesis? Certainly not that the poem is "only eleven lines long"—a writer hardly needs to argue a reader into believing this assertion. Rather, Horner's thesis is that the poem "is charged with power." In the rest of the explication he offers evidence that supports this assertion. To persuade us, he points out that certain lines are indented, that certain figures of speech have certain implications, and that the last stanza is italicized and consists of only one line.

You may disagree: You may not think the poem "is charged with power," and you may think that Horner has misread certain lines. We have already mentioned, in our first "Topic for Critical Thinking and Writing," that when Horner offered this interpretation in class, another student saw a different meaning in "syrupy sweet" (line 8). But if you disagree, whether with the reading as a whole or with the interpretation of a single image, it's not enough to assert that you disagree. You will have to offer an argument, which is to say you will have to set forth reasons in your effort to persuade your readers.

Your goal, in an explication, is to present your insights about the details of the poem's language. But even more, you want these insights to add up to something as a whole. When related to one another, they should enable your reader to understand the poem, overall, more clearly, and to enjoy it more fully. Ask yourself, as you study the poem and develop your draft of the paper,

> What is my thesis (my central point, my argument)?

This question will help you to make your essay coherent and unified. It is a reminder that an explication is more than a set of observations about this and that detail. The best explications make use of the details to teach the reader something new about the poem as a whole.

✔ CHECKLIST: *Drafting an Explication*

Overall Considerations

❑ Does the poem imply a story of some sort, for instance the speaker's report of a love affair, or of a response to nature? If so, what is its beginning, middle, and end?

❑ If you detect a story in the speaker's mind, a change of mood—for instance a shift from bitterness that a love affair has ended to hope for its renewal—is this change communicated in part by the connotations of certain words? By syntax? By metrical shifts?

❑ Do the details all cohere into a meaningful whole? If so, your explication will largely be an argument on behalf of this thesis.

Detailed Considerations

❑ If the poem has a title other than the first line, what are the implications of the title?

❑ Are there clusters or patterns of imagery, for instance religious images, economic images, or images drawn from nature? If so, how do they contribute to the meaning of the poem?

❑ Is irony (understatement or overstatement) used? To what effect?

❑ How do the connotations of certain words (for instance, *dad* rather than *father*) help to establish the meaning?

❑ What are the implications of the syntax—for instance, of notably simple or notably complex sentences? What do such sentences tell us about the speaker?

❑ Do metrical variations occur, and if so, what is their significance?

❑ Do rhyming words have some meaningful connection, as in the clichés *moon* and *June, dove* and *love*?

❑ What are the implications of the poem's appearance on the page—for example, of an indented line, or of the stanzaic pattern? (For instance, if the poem consists of two stanzas of four lines each, does the second stanza offer a reversal of the first?)

WHY WRITE? PURPOSE AND AUDIENCE

In Chapter 1 we briefly talked about audience and purpose, but a few further words may be useful. People write explications (as well as other essays on literature) not only to communicate with others but also to clarify and to account for their responses to material that interests or excites or frustrates them. In putting words on paper you will have to take a second and a third look at what is in front of you and at what is within you. And so the process of writing is a way of learning. The last word is never said about complex thoughts and feelings, but when we write we hope to make at least a little progress in the difficult but rewarding job of talking about our responses. We learn, and then we hope to interest our reader because we are communicating our responses to material that for one reason or another is worth talking about.

When you write, you transform your responses into words that will let your reader share your perceptions, your enthusiasms, and even your doubts. This sharing is, in effect, teaching. Students often think that they are writing for the teacher, but this is a misconception. When you write, *you* are the teacher. An essay on literature is an attempt to help someone to see something as you see it.

If you are not writing for the teacher, for whom are you writing? For yourself, of course, but also for others. Occasionally, in an effort to help you develop an awareness that what you write depends partly on your audience, your instructor may specify an audience, suggesting that you write for high school students or for the readers of *The Atlantic* or *Ms*. But if an audience is not specified, write for your classmates.

- If you keep your classmates in mind as your audience, you will *not* write, "William Shakespeare, England's most famous playwright," because such a remark seems to imply that your reader does not know Shakespeare's nationality or trade.
- On the other hand, you *will* write, "Sei Shōnagon, a lady of the court in medieval Japan," because you can reasonably assume that your classmates do not know who she is.

YOUR TURN: POEMS FOR EXPLICATION

The basic assignment is to explicate the poems, but your instructor may also ask you to respond to some or all of the questions that follow each poem.

WILLIAM SHAKESPEARE

William Shakespeare (1564–1616), born in Stratford-upon-Avon in England, is chiefly known as a dramatic poet, but he also wrote nondramatic poetry. In 1609 a volume of 154 of his sonnets was published, apparently without his permission. Probably he chose to keep his sonnets unpublished not because he thought that they were of little value but because it was more prestigious to be an amateur (unpublished) poet than a professional (published) poet. Although the sonnets were published in 1609, they were probably written in the mid-1590s, when there was a vogue for sonneteering. A contemporary writer in 1598 said that Shakespeare's "sugred Sonnets [circulate] among his private friends."

Sonnet 73

That time of year thou mayst in me behold A
When yellow leaves, or none, or few, do hang B
Upon those boughs which shake against the cold, A
Bare ruined choirs[1] where late the sweet birds sang. B   4
In me thou see'st the twilight of such day C
As after sunset fadeth in the west, D
Which by-and-by black night doth take away, C
Death's second self that seals up all in rest, D   8
In me thou see'st the glowing of such fire E
That on the ashes of his youth doth lie, F
As the deathbed whereon it must expire, E
Consumed with that which it was nourished by. F   12
This thou perceiv'st, which makes thy love more strong, G
To love that well which thou must leave ere long. G

[1] **choir** the part of the church where services were sung.

Topics for Critical Thinking and Writing

1. In the first quatrain (the first four lines) to what "time of year" does Shakespeare compare himself? In the second quatrain (lines 5–8) to what does he compare himself? In the third? If the sequence of the three quatrains were reversed, what would be gained or lost?
2. In line 8, what is "Death's second self"? What implications do you perceive in "seals up all in rest," as opposed, for instance, to "brings most welcome rest"?
3. In line 13, exactly what is "This"?
4. In line 14, suppose in place of "To love that well which thou must leave ere long," Shakespeare had written "To love me well whom thou must leave ere long." What if anything would have been gained or lost?

John Donne

John Donne (1572–1631) was born into a Roman Catholic family in England, but in the 1590s he abandoned that faith. In 1615 he became an Anglican priest and soon was known as a great preacher. One hundred sixty of his sermons survive, including one with the famous line "No man is an island, entire of itself; every man is a piece of the continent, a part of the main; if a clod be washed away by the sea, Europe is the less . . . . ; and therefore never send to know for whom the bell tolls; it tolls for thee." From 1621 until his death he was dean of St. Paul's Cathedral in London. His love poems (often bawdy and cynical) are said to be his early work, and his "Holy Sonnets" (among the greatest religious poems written in English) his later work.

Holy Sonnet XIV

Batter my heart, three-personed God; for you
As yet but knock, breathe, shine, and seek to mend;
That I may rise and stand, o'erthrow me, and bend
Your force, to break, blow, burn, and make me new.   4
I, like an usurped town, to another due,
Labor to admit you, but oh, to no end.
Reason, your viceroy in me, me should defend,
But is captived, and proves weak or untrue   8
Yet dearly I love you, and would be loved fain,
But am betrothed unto your enemy:
Divorce me, untie, or break that knot again,
Take me to you, imprison me, for I   12
Except you enthrall me, never shall be free,
Nor ever chaste, except you ravish me.

[1633]

Topics for Critical Thinking and Writing

1. Explain the paradoxes (apparent contradictions) in lines 2, 3, 13, and 14.
   Explain the double meanings of "enthrall" (line 13) and "ravish" (line 14).
2. In lines 1–4, what is God implicitly compared to (considering especially lines 2
   and 4)? How does this comparison lead into the comparison that dominates
   lines 5–8? What words in lines 9–12 are especially related to the earlier lines?
3. What is gained by piling up verbs in lines 2–4?
4. Are sexual references necessarily irreverent in a religious poem?

WILLIAM BLAKE

*William Blake (1757–1827) was born in London and at 14 was apprenticed for
seven years to an engraver. A Christian visionary poet, he made his living by giving
drawing lessons and by illustrating books, including his own* Songs of Innocence
(1789) and Songs of Experience *(1794). These two books represent, he said, "two
contrary states of the human soul." "London" comes from* Experience.*) In 1809
Blake exhibited his art, but the show was a failure. Not until he was in his sixties,
when he stopped writing poetry, did he achieve any public recognition—and then
it was as a painter.*

London

I wander through each chartered street,
Near where the chartered Thames does flow,
And mark in every face I meet
Marks of weakness, marks of woe.   4

In every cry of every man,
In every Infant's cry of fear,
In every voice, in every ban,
The mind-forged manacles I hear.   8

How the Chimney-sweeper's cry
Every black'ning Church appalls;
And the hapless Soldier's sigh
Runs in blood down Palace walls.   12

But most through midnight streets I hear
How the youthful Harlot's curse
Blasts the new-born Infant's tear,
And blights with plagues the Marriage hearse.   16

[1794]

Topics for Critical Thinking and Writing

1. What do you think Blake means by "mind-forged manacles" (line 8)? What might be some modern examples?
2. Paraphrase the second stanza.
3. Read the poem aloud, several times. How would you characterize the *tone—* sad, angry, or what? Of course the tone may vary from line to line, but what is the prevailing tone, if any?
4. An earlier version of the last stanza ran thus:

   > But most the midnight harlot's curse
   > From every dismal street I hear,
   > Weaves around the marriage hearse
   > And blasts the new-born infant's tear.

   Compare the two versions closely. Then consider which you think is more effective, and explain why.
5. Write a poem or a paragraph setting forth your response to a city or town that you know well.

EMILY BRONTË

Emily Brontë (1818–1848) spent most of her short life (she died of tuberculosis) in an English village on the Yorkshire moors. The sister of Charlotte Brontë (author of Jane Eyre*) and of Anne Brontë, Emily is best known for her novel* Wuthering Heights *(1847), but she was a considerable poet, and her first significant publication (1846) was in a volume of poems by the three sisters.*

Spellbound

The night is darkening round me,
The wild winds coldly blow;

But a tyrant spell has bound me
And I cannot, cannot go.

4

The giant trees are bending
Their bare boughs weighed with snow.
And the storm is fast descending,
And yet I cannot go.

8

Clouds beyond clouds above me,
Wastes beyond wastes below;
But nothing drear can move me;
I will not, cannot go.

12

[1837]

Topics for Critical Thinking and Writing

1. What exactly is a "spell," and what does it mean to be "spellbound"?
2. What difference, if any, would it make if the first line said "has darkened" instead of "is darkening"?
3. What difference would it make, if any, if lines 4 and 12 were switched?
4. What does "drear" (line 11) mean? Is this word too unusual? Should the poet have used a more familiar word?
5. Describe the speaker's state of mind. Have you ever experienced anything like this yourself? What was the situation and how did you move beyond it?

LI-YOUNG LEE

Li-Young Lee was born in 1957 in Jakarta, Indonesia, of Chinese parents. In 1964 his family brought him to the United States. He was educated at the University of Pittsburgh, the University of Arizona, and the State University of New York, Brockport. He now lives in Illinois, where he works as an artist.

I Ask My Mother to Sing

She begins, and my grandmother joins her.
Mother and daughter sing like young girls.
If my father were alive, he would play
his accordion and sway like a boat.

4

I've never been in Peking, or the Summer Palace,
nor stood on the great Stone Boat to watch
the rain begin on Kuen Ming Lake, the picnickers
running away in the grass.

8

But I love to hear it sung;
how the waterlilies fill with rain until
they overturn, spilling water into water,
then rock back, and fill with more.   12

Both women have begun to cry.
But neither stops her song.

[1986]

Topics for Critical Thinking and Writing

1. Why might the speaker ask the women to sing?
2. Why do the women cry? Why do they continue to sing?

RANDALL JARRELL

Randall Jarrell (1914–1965)—in the second name the accent is on the second syllable—was educated at Vanderbilt, where he majored in psychology. After serving with the air force in World War II, he taught in several colleges and universities, meanwhile establishing a reputation as a poet and as a literary critic.

The Death of the Ball Turret Gunner

From my mother's sleep I fell into the State,
And I hunched in its belly till my wet fur froze.
Six miles from earth, loosed from its dream of life,
I woke to black flak and the nightmare fighters.
When I died they washed me out of the turret with a hose.

[1955]

Jarrell has furnished an explanatory note: "A ball turret was a plexiglass sphere set into the belly of a B-17 or B-24, and inhabited by two .50 caliber machine-guns and one man, a short small man. When this gunner tracked with his machine-guns a fighter attacking his bomber from below, he revolved with the turret; hunched upside-down in his little sphere, he looked like the fetus in the womb. The fighters which attacked him were armed with cannon firing explosive shells. The hose was a steam hose."

Topics for Critical Thinking and Writing

1. What is implied in the first line? In "I woke to . . . nightmare"? Taking account of the title, do you think "wet fur" is literal or metaphoric or both? Do you find the simplicity of the last line anticlimactic? How does it continue the metaphor of birth?
2. Why do you think Jarrell ended each line with punctuation?

4

Reading Literature Closely:
Analysis

ANALYSIS

Explication is a method used chiefly in the study of fairly short poems or brief extracts from essays, stories, novels, and plays. Of course, if a writer has world enough and time, he or she can set out to explicate all of *The Color Purple* or *Hamlet;* more likely, the writer will explicate only a paragraph or at most a page of the novel or a speech or two of the play. In writing about works longer than a page or two, a more common approach than explicating is **analyzing** (literally, separating into parts in order to better understand the whole). An analysis of, say, *The Color Purple* may consider the functions of the setting or the uses that certain minor characters serve; an analysis of *Hamlet* may consider the comic passages or the reasons for Hamlet's delay; an analysis of *Death of a Salesman* may consider the depiction of women or the causes of Willy Loman's failure.

Most of the writing that you will do in college—not only in your English courses but in courses in history, sociology, economics, fine arts, and philosophy—will be analytic. **Analysis** is a method we commonly use in thinking about complex matters and in attempting to account for our responses. Watching Steffi Graf play tennis, we may admire her serve, or her backhand, or the execution of several brilliant plays, and then think more generally about the concentration and flexibility that allow her to capitalize on her opponent's momentary weakness. And of course when we want to improve our own game, we try to analyze our performance. When writing is our game, we analyze our responses to a work, trying to name them and account for them. We analyze our notes, looking for ideas that connect, searching for significant patterns, and later we analyze our drafts, looking for strengths and weaknesses. Similarly, in peer review we analyze the draft of a fellow student, seeing how the parts (individual words, sentences, whole paragraphs, the tentative title, and so on) relate to one another and fit together as a whole.

To develop an analysis of a work, we tend, whether consciously or not, to formulate questions and then to answer them. We ask such questions as:

- What is the function of the setting in this story or play?
- Why has this character been introduced?
- What is the author trying to tell us?
- How exactly can I describe the tone?
- What is the difference in assumptions between this essay and that one?

This book contains an anthology of literary works for you to respond to and then write about, and after most of the works we pose some questions. We also pose general questions on essays, fiction, drama, and poetry. These questions may stimulate your thinking and thus help you write. Our concern as teachers of writing is not so much with the answers to these questions; we believe and we ask you to believe that there are in fact no "right answers," only more or less persuasive ones, to most questions about literature—as about life. Our aim is to help you to pose questions that will stimulate your thinking.

ANALYZING A STORY FROM THE HEBREW BIBLE: THE JUDGMENT OF SOLOMON

A brief analysis of a very short story about King Solomon, from the Hebrew Bible, may be useful here. Because the story is short, the analysis can consider all or almost all of the story's parts, and therefore the analysis can seem relatively complete. ("*Seem* relatively complete" because the analysis will in fact be far from complete, since the number of reasonable things that can be said about a work is almost as great as the number of readers. And a given reader might, at a later date, offer a different reading from what the reader offers today.)

The following story about King Solomon, customarily called the Judgment of Solomon, appears in the Hebrew Bible, in the latter part of the third chapter of the book called 1 Kings or First Kings, probably written in the mid-sixth century B.C. The translation is from the King James Version of the Bible (1611).

Two expressions in the story need clarification: (1) The woman who "overlaid" her child in her sleep rolled over on the child and suffocated it; and (2) it is said of a woman that her "bowels yearned upon her son," that is, her heart longed for her son. (In Hebrew psychology, the bowels were thought to be the seat of emotion.)

The Judgment of Solomon

Then came there two women, that were harlots, unto the king, and stood before him. And the one woman said, "O my lord, I and this woman dwell in one house, and I was delivered of a child with her in the house. And it came to pass the third day after that I was delivered, that this woman was delivered also: and we were together; there was no stranger in the house, save we two in the house. And this woman's child died in the night; because she overlaid it. And she arose at midnight, and took my son from beside me, while thine handmaid slept, and laid it in her bosom, and laid her dead child in my bosom. And when I rose in the morning to give my child suck, behold, it was dead: but when I considered it in the morning, behold, it was not my son, which I did bear."

And the other woman said, "Nay; but the living is my son, and the dead is thy son." And this said, "No; but the dead is thy son, and the living is my son." Thus they spake before the king.

Then said the king, "The one saith, 'This is my son that liveth, and thy son is dead': and the other saith, 'Nay; but thy son is the dead, and my son is the living.'" And the king said, "Bring me a sword." And they brought a sword before the king. And the king said, "Divide the living child in two, and give half to the one, and half to the other."

Then spake the woman whose the living child was unto the king, for her bowels yearned upon her son, and she said, "O my lord, give her the living child, and in no wise slay it." But the other said, "Let it be neither mine nor thine, but divide it."

5   Then the king answered and said, "Give her the living child, and in no wise slay it: she is the mother thereof."

And all Israel heard of the judgment which the king had judged; and they feared the king, for they saw that the wisdom of God was in him to do judgment.

Analyzing the Story

Let's begin by analyzing the **form** or the shape of the story. One form or shape that we notice is this:

The story moves from a problem to a solution.

We can also say, still speaking of the overall form, that

the story moves from quarreling and talk of death to unity and talk of life.

In short, it has a happy ending, a form that (because it provides an optimistic view of life and also a sense of completeness) gives most people pleasure.

In thinking about a work of literature, it is always useful to take notice of the basic form of the whole, the overall structural pattern. Doubtless you are already familiar with many basic patterns, for example,

tragedy (joy yielding to sorrow) and
romantic comedy (angry conflict yielding to joyful union).

If you think even briefly about verbal works, you'll notice the structures or patterns that govern songs, episodes in soap operas, political speeches (beginning with the candidate's expression of pleasure at being in Duluth, and ending with "God bless you all"), detective stories, westerns, and so on. And just as viewers of a western film experience one western in the context of others, so readers experience one story in the context of similar stories, and one poem in the context of others.

Second, we can say that the Judgment of Solomon is a sort of detective story: There is a death, followed by a conflict in the testimony of the witnesses, and then a solution by a shrewd outsider. Consider Solomon's predicament. Ordinarily in literature characters are sharply defined and individualized, yet the essence of a detective story is that the culprit should *not* be easily recognized as wicked, and here nothing seems to distinguish the two petitioners. Solomon is confronted by "two women, that were harlots." Until late in the story—that is, up to the time Solomon suggests dividing the child—they are described only as "the one woman," "the other woman," "the one," "the other."

Does the story suffer from weak characterization? If we think analytically about this issue, we realize that the point surely is *not* to make each woman distinct. Rather, the point is (until late in the story) to make the women as alike as possible, so that we cannot tell which of the two is speaking the truth. Like Solomon, we have nothing to go on; neither witness is known to be more honest than the other, and there are no other witnesses to support or refute either woman.

Analysis is concerned with

- seeing the relationships between the parts of a work, but it is also concerned with
- taking notice of what is *not* in the work.

A witness would destroy the story, or turn it into an utterly different story. Another thing missing from this story is an explicit editorial comment or interpretation, except for the brief remark at the end that the people "feared the king." If we had read the story in the so-called Geneva Bible (1557–1560), which is the translation of the Bible that Shakespeare was familiar with, we would have found a marginal comment: "Her motherly affection herein appeareth that she had rather endure the rigour of the lawe, than see her child cruelly slaine." Would you agree that it is better, at least in this story, for the reader to draw conclusions than for the storyteller explicitly to point them out?

Solomon wisely contrives a situation in which these two claimants, who seem so similar, will reveal their true natures: The mother will reveal her love, and the liar will reveal her hard heart. The early symmetry (the identity of the two women) pleases the reader, and so does the device by which we can at last distinguish between the two women.

But even near the end there is a further symmetry. To save the child's life, the true mother gives up her claim, crying out, "Give her the living child, and in no wise slay it." The author (or, rather, the translator who produced this part of the King James Version) takes these very words, with no change whatsoever, and puts them into Solomon's mouth as the king's final judgment. Solomon too says, "Give her the living child, and in no wise slay it," but now the sentence takes on a new meaning. In the first sentence, "her" refers to the liar (the true mother says to give the child to "her"); in Solomon's sentence, "her" refers to the true mother: "Give her the living child. . . ." Surely we take pleasure in the fact that the very words by which the mother renounces her child are the words that (1) reveal to Solomon the truth, and that (2) Solomon uses to restore the child to his mother.

This analysis has chiefly talked about the relations of parts, and especially it has tried to explain why the two women in this story are *not* distinct until Solomon finds a way to reveal their distinctive natures: If the story is to demonstrate Solomon's wisdom, the women must seem identical until Solomon can show that they differ. But the analysis could have gone into some other topic. Let's consider several possibilities.

A student might begin by asking this question: "Although it is important for the women to be highly similar, why are they harlots?" (It is too simple to say that the women in the story are harlots because the author is faithfully reporting a historical episode in Solomon's career. The story is widely recognized as a folktale, found also in other ancient cultures.) One possible reason for making the women harlots is that the story demands that there be no witnesses; by using harlots, the author disposed of husbands, parents, and siblings who might otherwise be expected to live with the women. A second possible reason is that the author wanted to show that Solomon's justice extended to all, not only to respectable folk. Third, perhaps the author wished to reject or to complicate the stereotype of the harlot as a thoroughly disreputable person. The author rejected or complicated the harlot by introducing another (and truer?) stereotype, the mother as motivated by overwhelming maternal love.

Other Possible Topics for Analysis

1. Another possible kind of analytic essay might go beyond the structure of the individual work, to the relation of the work to some larger whole. For instance, the writer might approach the Judgment of Solomon from the point of view of gender criticism (discussed in Chapter 18): In this story, it might be ar-

gued, wisdom is an attribute only of a male; women are either deceitful or emotional. From this point the writer might set out to create a research essay on gender in a larger whole, certain books of the Hebrew Bible.

2. We might also analyze the story in the context of other examples of what scholars call Wisdom Literature (the Book of Proverbs, and Ecclesiastes, for instance). Notice that Solomon's judgment leads the people to *fear* him—because his wisdom is great, formidable, and God-inspired.

It happens that we do not know who wrote the Judgment of Solomon, but the authors of most later works of literature are known, and therefore some critics seek to analyze a given work within the context of the author's life. For some other critics, the larger context would be the reading process, which includes the psychology of the reader. (Biographical criticism and reader-response criticism are discussed in Chapter 18.)

3. Still another analysis—again, remember that a work can be analyzed from many points of view—might examine two or more translations of the story. You do not need to know Hebrew in order to compare this early seventeenth-century translation with a twentieth-century version such as the New Jerusalem Bible or the Revised English Bible. You might argue that one version is, on literary grounds, more effective. Such an essay might include an attempt, by means of a comparison, to analyze the effect of the archaic language of the King James Version. Does the somewhat unfamiliar language turn a reader off, or does it add mystery or dignity or authority to the tale, valuable qualities perhaps not found in the modern version? (By the way, in the Revised English Bible, Solomon does *not* exactly repeat the mother's plea. The mother says, "Let her have the baby," and Solomon then says, "Give the living baby to the first woman." In the New Jerusalem Bible, after the mother says, "Let them give her the live child," Solomon says, "Give the live child to the first woman." If you prefer one version to the other two, why not try to analyze your preference?)

Finally, it should be mentioned that an analysis of the structure of a work, in which the relationships of the parts to the whole are considered, allows the work to be regarded as independent of the external world. If we insist, say, that literature should in all respects reflect life, and we want to analyze the work against reality as we see it, we may find ourselves severely judging the Judgment of Solomon. We might ask if it is likely that a great king would bother to hear the case of two prostitutes quarreling over a child, or if it is likely that the false claimant would really call for the killing of the child. Similarly, to take an absurd example, an analysis of this story in terms of its ability to evoke laughter would be laughable. The point: An analysis will be interesting and useful to a reader only insofar as the aim of the analysis seems reasonable.

ANALYZING A STORY FROM THE NEW TESTAMENT: THE PARABLE OF THE PRODIGAL SON

Let's now look at another brief story from the Bible, this one from the Gospel according to St. Luke, in the New Testament. Luke, the author of the third of the four Gospels, was a second-generation Christian. He probably was a Roman, though some early accounts refer to him as a Syrian; in any case, he wrote in

Greek, probably composing the Gospel about A.D. 80–85. In Chapter 15, verses 11–32, Luke reports a story that Jesus told. This story, which occurs only in Luke's Gospel, is of a type called a **parable**, an extremely brief narrative from which a moral may be drawn.

The Parable of the Prodigal Son

And he said, "A certain man had two sons: and the younger of them said to his father, 'Father, give me a portion of goods that falleth to me.' And he divided unto them his living. And not many days after, the younger son gathered all together, and took his journey into a far country, and there wasted his substance with riotous living.

"And when he had spent all, there arose a mighty famine in that land, and he began to be in want. And he went and joined himself to a citizen of that country, and he sent him into his fields to feed swine. And he would fain have filled his belly with the husks that the swine did eat: and no man gave unto him. And when he came to himself, he said, 'How many hired servants of my father's have bread enough and to spare, and I perish with hunger? I will arise and go to my father, and will say unto him, "Father, I have sinned against heaven, and before thee, and am no more worthy to be called thy son: make me as one of thy hired servants."'

"And he arose, and came to his father. But when he was yet a great way off, his father saw him, and had compassion, and ran, and fell on his neck, and kissed him. And the son said unto him, 'Father, I have sinned against heaven, and in thy sight, and am no more worthy to be called thy son.' But the father said to his servants, 'Bring forth the best robe, and put it on him, and put a ring on his hand, and shoes on his feet. And bring hither the fatted calf, and kill it, and let us eat, and be merry. For this my son was dead, and is alive again; he was lost, and is found.' And they began to be merry.

"Now his elder son was in the field, and as he came and drew nigh to the house, he heard music and dancing. And he called one of the servants, and asked what these things meant. And he said unto him 'Thy brother is come, and thy father hath killed the fatted calf, because he hath received him safe and sound.' And he was angry, and would not go in: therefore came his father out, and entreated him. And he answering said to his father 'Lo, these many years do I serve thee, neither transgressed I at any time thy commandment, and yet thou never gavest me a kid, that I might make merry with friends: but as soon as this thy son was come, which hath devoured thy living with harlots, thou hast killed for him the fatted calf.' And he said unto him, 'Son, thou art ever with me, and all that I have is thine. It was meet that we should make merry, and be glad: for this thy brother was dead, and is alive again: and was lost, and is found.'"

Topics for Critical Thinking and Writing

1. In talking about the Judgment of Solomon we commented on certain repetitions (e.g., *two* women) and contrasts (e.g., troubled beginning, happy ending), which help to give shape to the story. What parallels or contrasts (or

both) do you find in the parable of the prodigal son? What *function* does the older brother serve? If he were omitted, what if anything would be lost? (Characterize him, partly by comparing him with the younger brother and with the father.)

2. Is the father foolish and sentimental? Do you approve or disapprove of his behavior at the end? Why?

3. Jesus told the story, so it must have had a meaning consistent with his other teachings. Christians customarily interpret the story as meaning that God (like the father in the parable) rejoices in the return of a sinner. What meaning, if any, can it have for readers who are not Christians? Explain.

COMPARISON: AN ANALYTIC TOOL

Analysis frequently involves comparing. A moment ago we asked you to compare the older brother with the younger brother and the father in the parable of the prodigal son. When we compare, we examine things for their resemblances to and differences from other things. Strictly speaking, if you emphasize the differences rather than the similarities, you are contrasting rather than comparing, but we need not preserve this distinction: we can call both processes **comparing.**

Although your instructor may ask you to write a comparison of two works of literature, the *subject* of the essay is the works; comparison is simply an effective analytic technique to show some of the qualities in the works. You might compare Chopin's use of nature in "The Story of an Hour" (p. 13) with the use of nature in another story, in order to reveal the subtle differences between the stories, but a comparison of works utterly unlike can hardly tell the reader or the writer anything.

Something should be said about organizing a comparison, say between the settings in two stories, between two characters in a novel (or even between a character at the end of a novel and the same character at the beginning), or between the symbolism of two poems. Probably, a student's first thought after making some jottings is to discuss one half of the comparison and then go on to the second half. Instructors and textbooks (though not this one) usually condemn such an organization, arguing that the essay breaks into two parts and that the second part involves a good deal of repetition of categories set up in the first part. Usually, they recommend that the students organize their thoughts differently, somewhat along these lines:

1. First similarity
   a. First work (or character, or characteristic)
   b. Second work
2. Second similarity
   a. First work
   b. Second work
3. First difference
   a. First work
   b. Second work
4. Second difference
   a. First work
   b. Second work

and so on, for as many additional differences as seem relevant. If you wish to compare *Huckleberry Finn* with *The Catcher in the Rye*, you might organize the material thus:

1. First similarity: the narrator and his quest
    a. Huck
    b. Holden
2. Second similarity: the corrupt world surrounding the narrator
    a. Society in *Huck*
    b. Society in *Catcher*
3. First difference: degree to which the narrator fulfills his quest and escapes from society
    a. Huck's plan to "light out" to the frontier
    b. Holden's breakdown

Another way of organizing a comparison and contrast:

1. First point: the narrator and his quest
    a. Similarities between Huck and Holden
    b. Differences between Huck and Holden
2. Second point: the corrupt world
    a. Similarities between the worlds in *Huck* and *Catcher*
    b. Differences between the worlds in *Huck* and *Catcher*
3. Third point: degree of success
    a. Similarities between Huck and Holden
    b. Differences between Huck and Holden

A comparison need not employ either of these structures. There is even the danger that an essay employing either of them may not come into focus until the essayist stands back from the seven-layer cake and announces in the concluding paragraph that the odd layers taste better. In your preparatory thinking, you may want to make comparisons in pairs:

- good-natured humor: the clown in *Othello*, the clownish grave-digger in *Hamlet*
- social satire: the clown in *Othello*, the grave-digger in *Hamlet*
- relevance to main theme: —
- length of role: —

But before writing the final version, you must come to some conclusions about what these add up to.

This final version should not duplicate the thought processes; rather, it should be organized so as to make the point—the thesis—clearly and effectively. After reflection, you may believe that

- although there are superficial similarities between the clown in *Othello* and the clownish grave-digger in *Hamlet*,
- there are essential differences.

In the finished essay, a writer will not wish to obscure the main point by jumping back and forth from play to play, working through a series of similarities and differences. It may be better to discuss the clown in *Othello* and then to point out that although the grave-digger in *Hamlet* resembles him in A, B, and C, the grave-digger also has other functions (D, E, and F) and is of greater consequence to *Hamlet* than the clown is to *Othello*. Some repetition in the second half of the essay ("The grave-digger's puns come even faster than the clown's . . . ") will bind the two halves into a meaningful whole, making clear the degree of similarity or difference. The point of the essay is not to list pairs of similarities or differences but to illuminate a work or works by making thoughtful comparisons.

Although in a long essay the writer cannot postpone until page 30 a discussion of the second half of the comparison, in an essay of fewer than ten pages nothing is wrong with setting forth one half of the comparison and then, in light of it, the second half. The essay will break into two unrelated parts if the second half makes no use of the first or if it fails to modify the first half, but not if the second half looks back to the first half and calls attention to differences that the new material reveals. Students ought to learn how to write an essay with interwoven comparisons, but they ought also to know that a comparison may be written in another, simpler and clearer way.

Finally, a reminder: **The purpose of a comparison is to call attention to the unique features of something by holding it up against something similar but significantly different**. You can compare Macbeth with Banquo (two men who hear a prophecy but who respond differently), or Macbeth with Lady Macbeth (a husband and wife, both eager to be monarchs but differing in their sense of the consequences), or Hamlet and Holden Caulfield (two people who see themselves as surrounded by a corrupt world), but you can hardly compare Holden with Macbeth or with Lady Macbeth—there simply aren't enough points of resemblance to make it worth your effort to call attention to subtle differences.

If the differences are great and apparent, a comparison is a waste of effort. ("Blueberries are different from elephants. Blueberries do not have trunks. And elephants do not grow on bushes.") Indeed, a comparison between essentially and evidently unlike things can only obscure, for by making the comparison the writer implies that significant similarities do exist, and readers can only wonder why they do not see them. The essays that do break into two halves are essays that make uninstructive comparisons: the first half tells the reader about five qualities in Alice Walker, the second half tells the reader about five different qualities in Toni Morrison.

A Sample Essay by a Student: "Two New Women"

A student in an introductory class was asked to compare any two of the three stories by Kate Chopin ("Ripe Figs," p. 3; "The Story of an Hour," p. 13; "The Storm," p. 34). She settled on "The Story of an Hour" and "The Storm." We print the final version of her essay, preceded by a page of notes (a synthesis of earlier notes) that she prepared shortly before she wrote her first draft.

> Resemblances or differences greater?
>
> Resemblances
> Theme: release from marital bonds; liberated women
> Setting: nature plays a role in both; springtime in "Hour," storm in "Storm"
> Characterization: in both stories, no villains
> forces of nature compel;
> Clarisse presumably happier without husband
> both seem to emphasize roles of women
>
> Differences
> Ending: "Hour" sad (LM unfulfilled); "Storm" happy; all characters seem content

But endings different in that "Hour" ends suddenly, surprise; "Storm" not surprising at very end.

Overall view (theme?)

"Hour" very restricted view; only one person is of much interest (LM); Josephine interesting only in terms of LM (contrast).

In "Storm," Cal. and Alc. interesting; but also interesting are simple Bobinot and even the child, and also even Clarisse, who sort of has the last word

Possible titles

Two Women

New Women

Tragic Louise, Comic Calixta

Louise, Calixta, and Clarisse

Hernandez 1

Linda Hernandez

Professor Welsh

English 102

2 November 2004

Two New Women

It is not surprising that two stories by an author somewhat resemble each other. What is especially interesting about Kate Chopin's "The Story of an Hour" and "The Storm" is that although they both deal with women who achieve a sense of new life or growth outside of the bonds of marriage, the stories differ greatly in what we call tone. "The Story of an Hour" is bittersweet, or perhaps even bitter and tragic, whereas "The Storm" is romantic and in some ways comic.

The chief similarity is that Louise Mallard in "The Story of an Hour" and Calixta in "The Storm" both experience valuable, affirming, liberating sensations that a traditional moral view would condemn. Mrs. Mallard, after some moments of deep grief, feels a great sense of liberation when she learns of the death of her husband. She dies almost immediately after this experience, but even though she is never physically unfaithful to her husband, there is a sort of mental disloyalty, at least from a traditional point of view. Calixta's disloyalty is physical, not merely mental. Unlike Louise Mallard, Calixta does go to bed with a man who is not her husband. But Calixta, as we will see, is treated just about as sympathetically as is Mrs. Mallard.

Louise Mallard is sympathetic because she does grieve for her husband, and because Chopin suggests that Mallard's sense of freedom is natural, something associated with the spring, the "delicious breath of rain," and "the tops of trees that were all aquiver with the new spring life" (14). Furthermore, Chopin explicitly says that Mallard loved her husband. But Chopin also tells us that one aspect of the marriage was a "powerful will bending her" (14). For all of these reasons, then--Mrs. Mallard's genuine grief, the association of her new feeling with the power of nature, and the assertion that Mrs. Mallard loved her husband but was at least in some degree subject to his will--the reader sympathizes with Mrs. Mallard.

In her presentation of Calixta, too, Chopin takes care to make the unfaithful woman a sympathetic figure. As in "The Story of an Hour," nature plays a role. Here, instead of nature or the outside world being a parallel to the woman's emotions, nature in the form of a storm exerts pressure on the woman. We are told that "the water beat in upon the boards in driving sheets" (35), and a bolt of lightning causes Calixta to stagger backward, into Alcée's arms. These forces of outside nature are parallel to a force of nature within Calixta. Chopin tells us that during the sexual union Calixta's "firm, elastic flesh . . . was knowing for the first time its birthright" (36). And in one additional way, too, Chopin guards against the reader condemning Calixta. We learn, at the end of the story, that Alcée's wife, Clarisse, is quite pleased to be free from her husband for a while:

> And the first free breath since her marriage seemed to
> restore the pleasant liberty of her maiden days. Devoted as
> she was to her husband, their intimate conjugal life was
> something which she was more than willing to forego for
> a while. (37)

Since Clarisse is portrayed as somewhat pleased to be relieved of her husband for a while, we probably do not see Alcée as a villainous betrayer of his wife. The story seems to end pleasantly, like a comedy, with everybody happy.

In Louise Mallard and in Calixta we see two women who achieve new lives, although in the case of Louise Mallard the reader is surprised to learn in the last sentence that the achievement lasts only a few moments. By "new lives" I mean emancipation from their husbands, but what is especially interesting is that in both cases Chopin guides the reader to feel

Hernandez 4

that although in fact both women behave in ways that would be
strongly condemned by the codes of Chopin's day, and even by
many people today, neither woman (as Chopin presents her) is
blameworthy. Mrs. Mallard is presented almost as a tragic victim,
and Calixta is presented almost as a figure in a very pleasant
comedy.

[New page]

Hernandez 5

Work Cited

Barnet, Sylvan, et al., eds. <u>Literature for Composition</u>. 7th ed. New
York: Longman, 2005, 13–15, 34–37.

Looking at the Essay

A few comments on this student's essay may be useful.

- The title announces the *topic*.
- The first paragraph announces the *thesis*, the point that will be argued.
- The second paragraph begins by getting directly to the point: "The chief similarity is . . ."
- The third paragraph clearly advances the argument by giving *evidence*, introduced by a word that implies reasoning, "because."
- The writer provides further evidence by using short relevant quotations from the story.
- The final paragraph summarizes but does not boringly repeat; i.e., it does not merely say "Thus we see, . . ." Rather, it presents the material freshly.

Topic for Critical Thinking and Writing

We like this essay, but perhaps you have a different view. In any case, what grade would you give this essay? Why? Be as specfic as possible in calling attention to what you see as its strengths and weaknesses.

✔ **CHECKLIST:** *Revising a Comparison*

❑ Does it makes sense to compare these things? (What question will the comparison help to answer? What do you hope your reader will learn?)
❑ Is the point of the comparison—the reason for making it—clear?
❑ Does the comparison cover all significant similarities and differences?
❑ Is the comparison readable; that is, is it clear and yet not tediously mechanical?
❑ Is the organization that is used—perhaps treating one text first and then the other, or perhaps shifting back and forth between texts—the best way to make this comparison?
❑ If the essay offers a value judgment, is the judgment fair? Does the essay offer enough evidence to bring a reader into at least partial agreement?

EVALUATION IN EXPLICATION AND ANALYSIS

When we evaluate, we say how good, how successful, how worthwhile, something is. If you reread the student's essay on "Harlem," you'll notice that he implies that the poem is worth reading. He doesn't say "In this excellent poem," but a reader of the essay probably comes away with the impression that the student thinks the poem is excellent. The writer might, of course, have included a more explicit evaluation, along these lines:

> In "Harlem," every word counts, and every word is effective. The image of the "heavy load" that "sags" is not as unusual as the image of the raisin in the sun, but it nevertheless is just right, adding a simple, powerful touch just before the explosive ending.

In any case, if an essay argues that the parts fit together effectively, it almost surely is implying a favorable evaluation. But only "*almost* surely." We might argue, for instance, that the parts fit, and so on, but that the work is immoral, or trivial, or unpleasant, or untrue to life. Even though it might be granted that the work is carefully constructed, the final evaluation of the work might be low. Evaluations are based on standards. If you offer an evaluation, make certain that your standards are clear to the reader.

Notice in the following three examples of evaluations of J. D. Salinger's *The Catcher in the Rye* that the writers let their readers know what their standards are. Each excerpt is from a review that was published when the book first appeared. In the first, Anne L. Goodman, writing in *The New Republic* (16 July 1951), began by praising Salinger's earlier short stories and then said of the novel:

> But the book as a whole is disappointing, and not merely because it is a reworking of a theme that one begins to suspect must obsess the author. Holden Caulfield, the main character who tells his own story, is an extraordinary portrait, but there is too much of him. He describes himself early on and, with the sureness of a wire recording, he remains strictly in character throughout.

Goodman then quotes a longish passage from *The Catcher*, and says,

> In the course of 277 pages the reader wearies of this kind of explicitness, repetition, and adolescence, exactly as one would weary of Holden himself.

Goodman lets us know that, in her opinion, (1) a book ought not simply to repeat a writer's earlier books, and that, again in her opinion, (2) it's not enough to give a highly realistic portrait of a character; if the character is not a sufficiently interesting person, in the long run the book will be dull.

Another reviewer, Virgilia Peterson, writing in the *New York Herald Tribune Book Review* (15 July 1951), found the book realistic in some ways, but unrealistic and therefore defective because its abundant profanity becomes unconvincing:

> There is probably not one phrase in the whole book that Holden Caulfield would not have used upon occasion, but when they are piled upon each other in cumulative monotony, the car refuses to believe.

Ms. Peterson concluded her review, however, by confessing that she did not think she was in a position to evaluate a book about an adolescent, or at least *this* adolescent.

> . . . it would be interesting and highly enlightening to know what Holden Caulfield's contemporaries, male and female, think of him. Their opinion would constitute the real test of Mr. Salinger's validity. The question of authenticity is one to which no parent can really guess the reply.

Here again the standard is clear—authenticity—but the writer confesses that she isn't sure about authenticity in this matter, and she defers to her juniors. Peterson's review is a rare example of an analysis offered by a writer who confesses an inability to evaluate.

Finally, here is a brief extract from a more favorable review, written by Paul Engle and published in the *Chicago Sunday Tribune Magazine of Books* (15 July 1951):

> The book ends with Holden in a mental institution, for which the earlier events have hardly prepared the reader. But the story is an engaging and believable one for the most part, full of right observations and sharp insight, and a wonderful sort of grasp of how a boy can create his own world of fantasy and live form.

The first sentence implies that a good book prepares the reader for the end, and that in this respect *The Catcher* is deficient. The rest of the paragraph sets forth other standards that *The Catcher* meets (it is "engaging and believable," "full of right observations and sharp insight"), though one of the standards in Engle's last sentence ("live form") strikes us as obscure.

CHOOSING A TOPIC AND DEVELOPING A THESIS IN AN ANALYTIC PAPER

Because Hughes's "Harlem" is very short, the analysis may discuss the entire poem. But a short essay, or even a long one, can hardly discuss all aspects of a play or a novel or even of a long story. If you are writing about a long work, you'll have to single out an appropriate topic.

What is an appropriate topic? First, it must be a topic that you can work up some interest in or your writing will be mechanical and dull. (We say "work up some interest" because interest is commonly the result of some effort.) Second, an appropriate topic is compassable—that is, it is something you can cover with reasonable attention to detail in the few pages (and few days) you have to devote to it. If a work is fairly long, almost surely you will write an analysis of some part.

Unless you have an enormous amount of time for reflection and revision, you cannot write a meaningful essay of 500 words or even 1,000 words on "Shakespeare's *Hamlet*" or "The Fiction of Alice Walker." You cannot even write on "Character in *Hamlet*" or "Symbolism in Walker's *The Color Purple*." And probably you won't really want to write on such topics anyway. Probably *one* character or *one* symbol has caught your interest. Think of something in your annotations or "response" notes (described in Chapter 1) that has caught your attention. Trust your feelings; you are likely onto something interesting.

In Chapter 2 we talked about the value of asking yourself questions. To find an appropriate topic, ask yourself such questions as the following:

1. *What purpose does this serve?* For instance, why is this scene in the novel or play? Why is there a comic grave-digger in *Hamlet?* Why are these lines unrhymed? Why did the author call the work by this title?
2. *Why do I have this response?* Why do I feel that this work is more profound (or amusing, or puzzling) than that work? How did the author make this character funny or dignified or pathetic? How did the author communicate the idea that this character is a bore without boring me?

The first of these questions, "What purpose does this serve?" requires that you identify yourself with the author, wondering, for example, whether this opening scene is the best possible for this story. The second question, "Why do I have this response?" requires that you trust your feelings. If you are amused or puzzled or annoyed, assume that these responses are appropriate and follow them up, at least until a rereading of the work provides other responses. If you jot down notes reporting your responses and later think about them, you will probably find that you can select a topic.

A third valuable way to find a thesis is to test a published comment against your response to a particular work. Perhaps somewhere you have seen—for instance, in a textbook—a statement about the nature of fiction, poetry, or drama. Maybe you have heard that a tragic hero has a "flaw." Don't simply accept the remark. Test it against your reading of the work. And interpret the word *published* broadly. Students and instructors publish their opinions—offer them to a public—when they utter them in class. Think about something said in class; students who pay close attention to their peers learn a great deal.

Given an appropriate topic, you will find your essay easier to write and the finished version of it clearer and more persuasive if, at some point in your preparation, in note taking or in writing a first draft, you have converted your topic into a *thesis* (a proposition, a point, an argument) and constructed a *thesis statement* (a sentence stating your overall point).

Let's dwell a moment on the distinction between a topic and a thesis. It may be useful to think of it this way: A topic is a subject (for example, "The Role of Providence in *Hamlet*"); to arrive at a thesis, you have to make an arguable assertion (for example, "The role of Providence in *Hamlet* is not obvious, but it is crucial").

Of course some theses are more promising than others. Consider this thesis:

> The role of Providence in <u>Hamlet</u> is interesting.

This sentence indeed asserts a thesis, but it is vague and provides little direction, little help in generating ideas and in shaping your essay. Let's try again. It's almost always necessary to try again and again, for the process of writing is in large part a process of trial and error, of generating better and better ideas by evaluating—selecting or rejecting—ideas and options.

> The role of Providence is evident in the Ghost.

This is much better, and it could stimulate ideas for an interesting essay. Let's assume the writer rereads the play, looking for further evidence, and comes to believe that the Ghost is only one of several manifestations of Providence. The writer may stay with the Ghost or may (especially if the paper is long enough to allow for such a thesis to be developed) alter the thesis thus:

> The role of Providence is not confined to the Ghost but is found also in the killing of Polonius, in the surprising appearance of the pirate ship, and in the presence of the poisoned chalice.

Strictly speaking, the thesis here is given in the first part of the sentence ("The role of Providence is not confined to the Ghost"); the rest of the sentence provides an indication of how the argument will be supported.

Every literary work suggests its own topics for analysis to an active reader, and all essayists must set forth their own theses, but if you begin by seeking to examine one of your responses, you will soon be able to stake out a topic and to formulate a thesis.

A suggestion: With two or three other students, formulate a thesis about Kate Chopin's "The Storm" (in Chapter 2). By practicing with a group you will develop a skill that you will use when you have to formulate a thesis on your own.

ANALYZING A STORY

If a story is short enough, you may be able to examine everything in it that you think is worth commenting on, but even if it is short you may nevertheless decide to focus on one element, such as the setting, or the construction of the plot, or the connection between two characters, or the degree of plausibility. Here is a story by James Thurber (1894–1961), the American humorist. It was first published in 1939.

JAMES THURBER
The Secret Life of Walter Mitty

"We're going through!" The Commander's voice was like thin ice breaking. He wore his full-dress uniform, with the heavily braided white cap pulled down rakishly over one cold gray eye. "We can't make it, sir. It's spoiling for a hurricane, if you ask me." "I'm not asking you, Lieutenant Berg," said the Commander. "Throw on the power lights! Rev her up to 8,500! We're going through!" The pounding of the cylinders increased: ta-pocketa-pocketa-pocketa-*pocketa-pocketa*. The Commander stared at the ice forming on the pilot window. He walked over and twisted a row of complicated dials. "Switch on No. 8 auxiliary!" he shouted. "Switch on No. 8 auxiliary!" repeated Lieutenant Berg. "Full strength in No. 3 turret!" shouted the Commander. "Full strength in No. 3 turret!" The crew, bending to their various tasks in the huge, hurtling eight-engined Navy hydroplane, looked at each other and grinned. "The Old Man'll get us through," they said to one another. "The Old Man ain't afraid of Hell!" . . .

"Not so fast! You're driving too fast!" said Mrs. Mitty. "What are you driving so fast for?"

"Hmm?" said Walter Mitty. He looked at his wife, in the seat beside him, with shocked astonishment. She seemed grossly unfamiliar, like a strange woman who had yelled at him in a crowd. "You were up to fifty-five," she said. "You know I don't like to go more than forty. You were up to fifty-five." Walter Mitty drove on toward Waterbury in silence, the roaring of the SN202 through the worst storm in twenty years of Navy flying fading in the remote, intimate airways of his mind. "You're tensed up again," said Mrs. Mitty. "It's one of your days. I wish you'd let Dr. Renshaw look you over."

Walter Mitty stopped the car in front of the building where his wife went to have her hair done. "Remember to get those overshoes while I'm having my hair done," she said. "I don't need overshoes," said Mitty. She put her mirror back into her bag. "We've been all through that," she said, getting out of the car. "You're not a young man any longer." He raced the engine a little. "Why don't you wear your gloves? Have you lost your gloves?" Walter Mitty reached in a pocket and brought out the gloves. He put them on, but after she had turned and gone into the building and he had driven on to a red light, he took them off again. "Pick it up, brother!" snapped a cop as the light changed, and Mitty hastily pulled on his gloves and lurched ahead. He drove around the streets aimlessly for a time, and then he drove past the hospital on his way to the parking lot.

5   . . . "It's the millionaire banker, Wellington McMillan," said the pretty nurse. "Yes?" said Walter Mitty, removing his gloves slowly. "Who has the case?" "Dr. Renshaw and Dr. Benbow, but there are two specialists here, Dr. Remington from New York and Dr. Pritchard-Mitford from London. He flew over." A door opened down a long, cool corridor and Dr. Renshaw came out. He looked distraught and haggard. "Hello, Mitty," he said. "We're having the devil's own time with McMillan, the millionaire banker and close personal friend of Roosevelt. Obstreosis of the ductal tract. Tertiary. Wish you'd take a look at him." "Glad to," said Mitty.

In the operating room there were whispered introductions: "Dr. Remington, Dr. Mitty, Mr. Pritchard-Mitford, Dr. Mitty." "I've read your book on streptothricosis," said Pritchard-Mitford, shaking hands. "A brilliant performance, sir." "Thank you," said Walter Mitty. "Didn't know you were in the States, Mitty," grumbled Remington. "Coals to Newcastle, bringing Mitford and me up here for a tertiary." "You are very kind," said Mitty. A huge, complicated machine, connected to the operating table, with many tubes and wires, began at this moment to go pocketa-pocketa-pocketa. "The new anesthetizer is giving way!" shouted an interne. "There is no one in the East who knows how to fix it!" "Quiet, man!" said Mitty, in a low, cool voice. He sprang to the machine, which was now going pocketa-pocketa-queep-pocketa-queep. He began fingering delicately a row of glistening dials. "Give me a fountain pen!" he snapped. Someone handed him a fountain pen. He pulled a faulty piston out of the machine and inserted the pen in its place. "That will hold for ten minutes," he said. "Get on with the operation." A nurse hurried over and whispered to Renshaw, and Mitty saw the man turn pale. "Coreopsis has set in," said Renshaw nervously. "If you would take over, Mitty?" Mitty looked at him and at the craven figure of Benbow, who drank, and at the grave, uncertain faces of the two great specialists. "If you wish," he said. They slipped a white gown on him: he adjusted a mask and drew on thin gloves; nurses handed him shining . . .

"Back it up, Mac! Look out for that Buick!" Walter Mitty jammed on the brakes. "Wrong lane, Mac," said the parking-lot attendant, looking at Mitty closely. "Gee. Yeh," muttered Mitty. He began cautiously to back out of the lane marked "Exit Only." "Leave her sit there," said the attendant. "I'll put her away." Mitty got out of the car. "Hey, better leave the key." "Oh," said Mitty, handing the man the ignition key. The attendant vaulted into the car, backed it up with insolent skill, and put it where it belonged.

They're so damn cocky, thought Walter Mitty, walking along Main Street; they think they know everything. Once he had tried to take his chains off, outside New Milford, and he had got them wound around the axles. A man had had to come out in a wrecking car and unwind them, a young, grinning garageman. Since then Mrs. Mitty always made him drive to the garage to have the chains taken off. The next time, he thought, I'll wear my right arm in a sling; they won't grin at me then. I'll have my right arm in a sling and they'll see I couldn't possibly take the chains off myself. He kicked at the slush on the sidewalk. "Overshoes," he said to himself, and he began looking for a shoe store.

When he came out into the street again, with the overshoes in a box under his arm, Walter Mitty began to wonder what the other thing was his wife had told him to get. She had told him, twice, before they set out from their house for Waterbury. In a way he hated these weekly trips to town—he was always getting something wrong. Kleenex, he thought, Squibb's, razor blades? No. Toothpaste, toothbrush, bicarbonate, carborundum, initiative and referendum? He gave it up. But she would remember it. "Where's the what's-its-name?" she would ask. "Don't tell me you forgot the what's-its-name." A newsboy went by shouting something about the Waterbury trial.

10   . . . "Perhaps this will refresh your memory." The District Attorney suddenly thrust a heavy automatic at the quiet figure on the witness stand. "Have you ever seen this before?" Walter Mitty took the gun and examined it expertly. "This is my Webley-Vickers 50.80," he said calmly. An excited buzz ran around the courtroom. The Judge rapped for order. "You are a crack shot with any sort of firearms, I believe?" said the District Attorney, insinuatingly. "Objection!" shouted Mitty's attorney. "We have shown that the defendant could not have fired the shot. We have shown that he wore his right arm in a sling on the night of the fourteenth of July." Walter Mitty raised his hand briefly and the bickering attorneys were stilled. "With any known make of gun," he said evenly, "I could have killed Gregory Fitzhurst at three hundred feet *with my left hand*." Pandemonium broke loose in the courtroom. A woman's scream rose above the bedlam and suddenly a lovely, dark-haired girl was in Walter Mitty's arms. The District Attorney struck at her savagely. Without rising from his chair, Mitty let the man have it on the point of the chin. "You miserable cur!" . . .

"Puppy biscuit," said Walter Mitty. He stopped walking and the buildings of Waterbury rose up out of the misty courtroom and surrounded him again. A woman who was passing laughed. "He said 'Puppy biscuit,'" she said to her companion. "That man said 'Puppy biscuit' to himself." Walter Mitty hurried on. He went into an A. & P., not the first one he came to but a smaller one farther up the street. "I want some biscuit for small, young dogs," he said to the clerk. "Any special brand, sir?" The greatest pistol shot in the world thought a moment. "It says 'Puppies Bark for It' on the box," said Walter Mitty.

His wife would be through at the hairdresser's in fifteen minutes, Mitty saw in looking at his watch, unless they had trouble drying it; sometimes they had trouble drying it. She didn't like to get to the hotel first; she would want him to be there waiting for her as usual. He found a big leather chair in the lobby, facing a window, and he put the overshoes and the puppy biscuit on the floor beside it. He picked up an old copy of *Liberty* and sank down into the chair. "Can Germany Conquer the World through the Air?" Walter Mitty looked at the pictures of bombing planes and of ruined streets.

. . . "The cannonading has got the wind up in young Raleigh, sir," said the sergeant. Captain Mitty looked up at him through tousled hair. "Get him to bed," he said wearily. "With the others. I'll fly alone." "But you can't, sir," said the sergeant anxiously. "It takes two men to handle that bomber and the Archies are pounding hell out of the air. Von Richtman's circus is between here and Saulier." "Somebody's got to get that ammunition dump," said Mitty. "I'm going over. Spot of brandy?" He poured a drink for the sergeant and one for himself. War thundered and whined around the dugout and battered at the door. There was a rending of wood and splinters flew through the room. "A bit of a near thing," said Captain Mitty carelessly. "The box barrage is closing in," said the sergeant. "We only live once, Sergeant," said Mitty, with his faint, fleeting smile. "Or do we?" He poured another brandy and tossed it off. "I never see a man could hold his brandy like you, sir," said the sergeant. "Begging your pardon, sir." Captain Mitty stood up and strapped on his huge Webley-Vickers automatic. "It's forty kilometers through hell, sir," said the sergeant. Mitty finished one last brandy. "After all," he said softly, "what isn't?" The pounding of the cannon increased; there was the rat-tat-tatting of machine guns, and from somewhere came the menacing pocket-pocket-eta-pocketa of the new flame-throwers. Walter Mitty walked to the door of the dugout humming "Auprès de Ma Blonde." He turned and waved to the sergeant. "Cheerio!" he said. . . .

Something struck his shoulder. "I've been looking all over this hotel for you," said Mrs. Mitty. "Why do you have to hide in this old chair? How did you expect me to find you?" "Things close in," said Walter Mitty vaguely. "What?" Mrs. Mitty said. "Did you get the what's-its-name? The puppy biscuit? What's in that box?" "Overshoes," said Mitty. "Couldn't you have put them on in the store?" "I was thinking," said Walter Mitty. "Does it ever occur to you that I am sometimes thinking?" She looked at him. "I'm going to take your temperature when I get you home," she said.

15   They went out through the revolving doors that made a faintly derisive whistling sound when you pushed them. It was two blocks to the parking lot. At the drugstore on the corner she said, "Wait here for me. I forgot something. I won't be a minute." She was more than a minute. Walter Mitty lighted a cigarette. It began to rain, rain with sleet in it. He stood up against the wall of the drugstore, smoking. . . . He put his shoulders back and his heels together. "To hell with the handkerchief," said Walter Mitty scornfully. He took one last drag on his cigarette and snapped it away. Then, with that faint, fleeting smile playing about his lips, he faced the firing squad; erect and motionless, proud and disdainful, Walter Mitty the Undefeated, inscrutable to the last.

[1939]

Working Toward a Thesis: Journal Entries

Before reading the following entries about "The Secret Life of Walter Mitty," write some of your own. You may want to think about what (if anything) you found amusing in the story, or about whether the story is dated, or about some aspect of Mitty's character or of his wife's. But the choice is yours.

A student wrote the following entry in her journal after the story was discussed in class.

> March 21. Funny, I guess, especially the business about him as a doctor performing an operation. And that "pocketa-pocketa," but I don't think that it's as hysterical as everyone else seems to think it is. And how could anyone stand being married to a man like that? In fact, it's a good thing he has her to look after him. He ought to be locked up, driving into the "Exit Only" lane, talking to himself in the street, and having those crazy daydreams. No wonder the woman in the street laughs at him.

> March 24. He's certainly a case, and she's not nearly as bad as everyone was saying. So she tells him to put his overshoes on; well, he ought to put them on, since Thurber says there is slush in the street, and he's no kid anymore. About the worst I can say of her is that she seems a little unreasonable in always wanting him to wait for her, rather than sometimes the other way around, but probably she's really telling him not to wander off, because if he ever drifts away there'll be no finding him. The joke, I guess, is that he's supposed to have these daydreams because he's henpecked, and henpecked men are supposed to be funny. Would people find the story just as funny if she had the daydreams, and he bullied her?

Developing the Thesis: List Notes

In preparation for writing a draft, the student reread the story and jotted down some tentative notes based on her journal and on material that she had highlighted in the text. (At this point you may want to make your own list, based on your notes.)

Mitty helpless: he *needs* her
chains on tires
enters Exit Only
~~Waterbury~~
cop tells him to get going
fantasies

wife a nag? causes his daydreams? Evidence?
makes him get to hotel first
overshoes
backseat driver?

"Does it ever occur to you that I am sometimes *thinking*?" Is he thinking, or just having dreams?

M. confuses Richthoven with someone called Richtman.

Funny--or anti-woman? Would it be funny if he nagged her, and *she* had daydreams?

Next, the student wrote a draft; then she revised the draft and submitted the revision (printed here) to some classmates for peer review. (The number enclosed within parentheses cites the source of a quotation.) Before reading the student's draft, you may want to write a draft based on your own notes and lists.

Sample Draft by a Student: "Walter Mitty Is No Joke"

Lee 1

Susan Lee

Professor Markus

English 102

5 April 2004

Walter Mitty Is No Joke

James Thurber's "The Secret Life of Walter Mitty" seems to be highly regarded as a comic story about a man who is so dominated by his wife that he has to escape through fantasies. In my high school course in English, everyone found Mitty's dreams and his wife's bullying funny, and everyone seems to find them funny in college, too. Everyone except me.

If we look closely at the story, we see that Mitty is a pitiful man who <u>needs</u> to be told what to do. The slightest glimpse of reality sets him off on a daydream, as when he passes a hospital and immediately begins to imagine that he is a famous surgeon, or when he hears a newsboy shouting a headline about a crime and he imagines himself in a courtroom. The point seems to be that his wife nags him, so he escapes into daydreams. But the fact is that she <u>needs</u> to keep after him, because he <u>needs</u>

Lee 2

someone to tell him what to do. It depends on what one considers

nagging. She tells him he is driving too fast, and (given the date

of the story, 1939) he probably is, since he is going 55 on a

slushy or snowy road. She tells him to wear overshoes, and he

probably ought to, since the weather is bad. He resents all of

these orders, but he clearly is incompetent, since he delays when

the traffic light turns from red to green, and he enters an "Exit

Only" lane in a parking lot. We are also told that he can't put

chains on tires.

In fact, he can't do anything right. All he can do is

daydream, and the dreams, though they <u>are</u> funny, are proof of

his inability to live in the real world. When his wife asks him

why he didn't put the overshoes on in the store, instead of

carrying them in a box, he says, "Does it ever occur to you that I

am sometimes thinking?" (80). But he doesn't "think," he just

daydreams. Furthermore, he can't even get things straight in his

daydreams, since he gets everything mixed up, confusing

Richthoven with Richtman, for example.

Is "The Secret Life of Walter Mitty" really a funny story

about a man who daydreams because he is henpecked? Probably

it is supposed to be so, but it's also a story about a man who is

lucky to have a wife who can put up with him and keep him from

getting killed on the road or lost in town.

[New page]

Lee 3

Work Cited

Thurber, James. "The Secret Life of Walter Mitty." Literature for

Composition. Ed. Sylvan Barnet et al. 7th ed. New York:

Longman, 2005, 77–80.

Developing an Argument
Introductory Paragraphs

As the poet Byron said, at the beginning of a long part of a long poem, "Nothing so difficult as a beginning." Woody Allen thinks so, too. In an interview he said that the toughest part of writing is "to go from nothing to the first draft."

We can give two pieces of advice:

1. *The opening paragraph is unimportant.* It's great if you can write a paragraph that will engage your readers and let them know where the essay will be taking them, but if you can't come up with such a paragraph, just put down anything in order to prime the pump.
2. *The opening paragraph is extremely important.* It must engage your readers, and probably by means of a thesis sentence it should let the readers know where the essay will be taking them.

The contradiction is, however, only apparent, not real. The first point is relevant to the opening paragraph of a *draft*; the second point is relevant to the opening paragraph of the *final version*. Almost all writers—professionals as well as amateurs—find that the first paragraphs in their drafts are false starts. Don't worry too much about the opening paragraphs of your draft; you'll want to revise your opening later anyway. (Surprisingly often your first paragraph may simply be deleted; your second, you may find, is where your essay truly begins.)

When writing a first draft you merely need something—almost anything may do—to break the ice. But in your finished paper the opening cannot be mere throat-clearing. The opening should be interesting.

Among the commonest *un*interesting openings are these:

1. A dictionary definition ("Webster says . . . ").
2. A restatement of your title. The title is (let's assume) "Romeo's Maturation," and the first sentence says, "This essay will study Romeo's maturation." True, there is an attempt at a thesis statement here, but no information beyond what has already been given in the title. There is no information about you, either, that is, no sense of your response to the topic, such as is present in, say, "*Romeo and Juliet* covers less than one week, but within this short period Romeo is impressively transformed from a somewhat comic infatuated boy to a thoughtful tragic hero."

3. A platitude, such as "Ever since the beginning of time men and women have fallen in love." Again, such a sentence may be fine if it helps you to start drafting, but because it sounds canned and because it is insufficiently interesting, it should not remain in your final version.

What is left? What *is* a good way for a final version to begin? Your introductory paragraph will be interesting if it gives information, and it will be pleasing if the information provides a focus—that is, if it goes beyond the title in letting the reader know exactly what your topic is and where you are headed.

Let's assume that you agree: An opening paragraph should be *interesting* and *focused*. Doubtless you will find your own ways of fulfilling these goals, but you might consider using one of the following time-tested methods.

1. *Establish a connection between life and literature.* We have already suggested that a platitude (for instance, "Ever since the beginning of time men and women have fallen in love") usually makes a poor beginning because it is dull, but you may find some other way of relating the work to daily experience. For instance:

> Doubtless the popularity of Romeo and Juliet (the play has been with us for more than four hundred years) is partly due to the fact that it deals with a universal experience. Still, no other play about love is so much a part of our culture that the mere mention of the names of the lovers immediately calls up an image. But when we say that So-and-so is "a regular Romeo," exactly what do we mean? And exactly what sort of lover is Romeo?

2. *Give an overview.* Here is an example:

> Langston Hughes's "Harlem" is about the destruction of the hopes of African Americans. More precisely, Hughes begins by asking "What happens to a dream deferred?" and then offers several possibilities, the last of which is that it may "explode."

3. *Include a quotation.* The previous example illustrates this approach, also. Here is another example:

> One line from Langston Hughes's poem "Harlem" has become famous, "A raisin in the sun," but its fame is, in a sense, accidental; Lorraine Hansberry happened to use it for the title of a play. Doubtless she used it because it is impressive, but in fact the entire poem is worthy of its most famous line.

4. *Use a definition*. We have already suggested that a definition such as "Webster says . . . " is boring and therefore unusable, but consider the following:

> When we say that a character is the hero of a story, we usually
>
> mean that he is the central figure, and we probably imply that he is
>
> manly. But in Kafka's "The Metamorphosis" the hero is most <u>unmanly</u>.

5. *Introduce a critical stance.* If your approach is feminist, or psychoanalytic, or Marxist, or whatever, you may want to say so at the start. Example:

> Feminists have called our attention to the unfunny sexism of
>
> mother-in-law jokes, comments about women hooking men into
>
> marriage, and so forth. We can now see that the stories of James
>
> Thurber, long thought to be wholesome fun, are unpleasantly sexist.

Caution: We are not saying that these are the only ways to begin, and we certainly are not suggesting that you pack all five into the opening paragraph. We are saying only that after you have done some brainstorming and written some drafts, you may want to think about using one of these methods for your opening paragraph.

An Exercise: Write (either by yourself or in collaboration with one or two other students) an opening paragraph for an essay on one of Kate Chopin's stories and another for an essay on Hughes's "Harlem." (To write a useful opening paragraph you will, of course, first have to settle on the essay's thesis.)

Middle Paragraphs

The middle, or body, of your essay will develop your thesis by offering supporting evidence. Ideas for the body should emerge from the sketchy outline that you made after you reviewed your brainstorming notes or journal.

1. *Be sure that each paragraph makes a specific point* and that the point is sufficiently developed with evidence (a brief quotation is often the best evidence).
2. *Be sure that each paragraph is coherent.* Read each sentence, starting with the second sentence, to see how it relates to the preceding sentence. Does it clarify, extend, reinforce, add an example? If you can't find the relationship, the sentence probably does not belong where it is. Rewrite it, move it, or strike it out.
3. *Be sure that the connections between paragraphs are clear.* Transitional words and phrases, such as "Furthermore," "On the other hand," and "In the next stanza," will often give readers all the help they need in seeing how your points are connected.
4. *Be sure that the paragraphs are in the best possible order.* A good way to test the organization is to jot down the topic sentence or topic idea of each paragraph, and then to see if your jottings are in a reasonable sequence.

Concluding Paragraphs

Concluding paragraphs, like opening paragraphs, are especially difficult, if only because they are so conspicuous. Readers often skim first paragraphs and last paragraphs to see if an essay is worth reading. With conclusions, as with openings, say something interesting. It is not interesting to say, "Thus we see that Mrs. Mitty . . ." (and here you go on to echo your title or your first sentence).

What to do? When you are revising a draft, you might keep in mind the following widely practiced principles. They are not inflexible rules, but they often work.

1. *Hint that the end is near.* Expressions such as "Finally," "One other point must be discussed," and "In short," alert the reader that the end is nigh and help to prevent the reader from feeling that the essay ends abruptly.
2. *Perhaps reassert the thesis, but put it in a slightly new light.* Not, "I have shown that Romeo and Hamlet are similar in some ways," but:

> These similarities suggest that in some respects Romeo is an early study for Hamlet. Both are young men in love, both seek by the force of their passion to shape the world according to their own desires, and both die in the attempt. But compared with Hamlet, who at the end of the play understands everything that has happened, Romeo dies in happy ignorance; Romeo is spared the pain of knowing that his own actions will destroy Juliet, whereas Hamlet dies with the painful knowledge that his kingdom has been conquered by Norwegian invaders.

3. *Perhaps offer an evaluation.* You may find it appropriate to conclude your analysis with an evaluation, such as this:

> Romeo is as convincing as he needs to be in a play about young lovers, but from first to last he is a relatively uncomplicated figure, the ardent lover. Hamlet is a lover, but he is also a good deal more, a figure whose complexity reveals a more sophisticated or a more mature author. Only five or six years separate Romeo and Juliet from Hamlet, but one feels that in those few years Shakespeare made a quantum leap in his grasp of human nature.

4. *Perhaps include a brief significant quotation from the work.* Example:

> Romeo has won the hearts of audiences for almost four centuries, but, for all his charm, he is in the last analysis concerned only with

fulfilling his own passion. Hamlet, on the other hand, at last fulfills not only his own wish but that of the Ghost, his father. "Remember me," the Ghost says, when he first appears to Hamlet and asks for revenge. Throughout the play Hamlet does remember the Ghost, and finally, at the cost of his own life, Hamlet succeeds in avenging his dead father.

Coherence in Paragraphs: Using Transitions

In addition to having a unified point and a reasonable organization, a good paragraph is **coherent;** that is, the connections between ideas in the paragraph are clear. Coherence can often be achieved by inserting the right transitional words or by taking care to repeat key words.

Richard Wagner, commenting on his work as a composer of operas, once said "The art of composition is the art of transition," for his art moved from note to note, measure to measure, scene to scene. **Transitions** establish connections between ideas; they alert readers to the way in which you are conducting your argument. Here are some of the most common transitional words and phrases.

1. **Amplification or likeness:** similarly, likewise, and, also, again, second, third, in addition, furthermore, moreover, finally
2. **Emphasis:** chiefly, equally, indeed, even more important
3. **Contrast or concession:** but, on the contrary, on the other hand, by contrast, of course, however, still, doubtless, no doubt, nevertheless, granted that, conversely, although, admittedly
4. **Example:** for example, for instance, as an example, specifically, consider as an illustration, that is, such as, like
5. **Consequence or cause and effect:** thus, so, then, it follows, as a result, therefore, hence
6. **Restatement:** in short, that is, in effect, in other words
7. **Place:** in the foreground, further back, in the distance
8. **Time:** afterward, next, then, as soon as, later, until, when, finally, last, at last
9. **Conclusion:** finally, therefore, thus, to sum up

✔ CHECKLIST: *Revising Paragraphs*

❏ Does the paragraph *say* anything? Does it have substance?
❏ Does the paragraph have a topic sentence? If so, is it in the best place? If the paragraph doesn't have a topic sentence, might adding one improve the paragraph? Or does it have a clear topic idea?
❏ If the paragraph is an opening paragraph, is it interesting enough to attract and to hold a reader's attention? If it is a later paragraph, does it easily evolve out of the previous paragraph, and lead into the next paragraph?
❏ Does the paragraph contain some principle of development, for instance from general to particular?

❑ Does each sentence clearly follow from the preceding sentence? Have you provided transitional words or cues to guide your reader? Would it be useful to repeat certain key words, for clarity?

❑ What is the purpose of the paragraph? Do you want to summarize, or tell a story, or give an illustration, or concede a point, or what? Is your purpose clear to you, and does the paragraph fulfill your purpose?

❑ Is the closing paragraph effective, and not an unnecessary restatement of the obvious?

REVIEW: WRITING AN ANALYSIS

Each writing assignment will require its own kind of thinking, but here are a few principles that usually are relevant:

1. Assume that your reader has already read the work you are discussing but is not thoroughly familiar with it—and of course does not know what you think and how you feel about the work. Early in your essay name the author, the work, and your thesis.

2. Do not tell the plot (or, at most, summarize it very briefly); instead, tell your reader what the work is about (not what happens, but what the happenings add up to).

3. Whether you are writing about character or plot or meter or anything else, you will probably be telling your reader something about *how* the work works, that is, how it develops. The stages by which a work advances may sometimes be marked fairly clearly. For instance (to oversimplify), a poem of two stanzas may ask a question in the first and give an answer in the second, or it may express a hope in the first and reveal a doubt in the second. Novels, of course, are customarily divided into chapters, and even a short story may be printed with numbered parts. Virtually all works are built up out of parts, whether or not the parts are labeled.

4. In telling the reader how each part leads to the next, or how each part arises out of what has come before, you will probably be commenting on such things as (in a story) changes in a character's state of mind—marked perhaps by a change in the setting—or (in a poem) changes in the speaker's tone of voice—for instance from eager to resigned, or from cautious to enthusiastic. Probably you will in fact not only be describing the development of character or of tone or of plot, but also (and more important) you will be advancing your own thesis.

A Note on Technical Terminology

Literature—like the law, medicine, the dance, and for that matter, cooking and baseball—has given rise to technical terminology. A cookbook will tell you to boil, or bake, or blend, and it will speak of a "slow" oven (300 degrees), a "moderate" oven (350 degrees), or a "hot" oven (450 degrees). These are technical terms in the world of cookery. In watching a baseball game we find ourselves saying, "I think the hit-and-run is on," or "He'll probably bunt." We use these terms because they convey a good deal in a few words; they are clear and precise. Further, although we don't use them in order to impress our hearer, in fact they do indicate that we have more than a superficial acquaintance with the game. That is, the better we know our subject, the more likely we are to use the technical language of the subject. Why? *Because such language enables us to talk precisely and in considerable depth about the subject.* Technical language, unlike jargon (pretentious diction that needlessly complicates or obscures), is illuminating—provided that the reader is familiar with the terms.

In writing about literature you will, for the most part, use the same language that you use in your other courses, and you will not needlessly introduce the technical vocabulary of literary study—but you *will* use this vocabulary when it enables you to be clear, concise, and accurate.

A Lyric Poem and a Student's Essay

APHRA BEHN

Aphra Behn (1640–1689) is regarded as the first English woman to have made a living by writing. Not much is known of her life, but she seems to have married a London merchant of Dutch descent, and after his death to have served as a spy in the Dutch Wars (1665–1667). After her return to England she took up playwrighting, and she gained fame with The Rover *(1677). Behn also wrote novels, the most important of which is* Oroonoko, or The Royal Slave *(1688), which is among the first works in English to express pity for enslaved Africans.*

Song: Love Armed

> Love in fantastic triumph sate,
>   Whilst bleeding hearts around him flowed,
> For whom fresh pains he did create,
>   And strange tyrannic power he showed:
> From thy bright eyes he took his fire,   5
>   Which round about in sport he hurled;
> But 'twas from mine he took desire,
>   Enough to undo the amorous world.
> From me he took his sighs and tears:
>   From thee, his pride and cruelty;   10
> From me, his languishments and fears;
>   And every killing dart from thee.
> Thus thou and I the god have armed
>   And set him up a deity;
> But my poor heart alone is harmed,   15
>   Whilst thine the victor is, and free.

[1676]

Topics for Critical Thinking and Writing

1. The speaker (a man, although the author is a woman) talks of the suffering he is undergoing. Can we nevertheless feel that he enjoys his plight? *Why*, by the way, do we often enjoy songs of unhappy love?
2. The woman ("thee") is said to exhibit "pride and cruelty" (line 10). Is the poem sexist? Is it therefore offensive?
3. Do you suppose that men can enjoy the poem more than women? Explain.

Journal Entries

The subject is Aphra Behn's "song." We begin with two entries in a journal, kept by a first-year student, Geoffrey Sullivan, and we follow these entries with Sullivan's completed essay.

October 10. The title "Love Armed" puzzled me at first; funny, I somehow was thinking of the expression "strong-armed" and at first I didn't understand that "Love" in this poem is a human--no, not a human, but the god Cupid, who has a human form--and that he is shown as armed, with darts and so forth.

October 13. This god of "Love" is Cupid, and so he is something like what is on a valentine card--Cupid with his bow and arrow. But valentine cards just show cute little Cupids, and in this poem Cupid is a real menace. He causes lots of pain ("bleeding hearts," "tears," "killing dart," etc.). So what is Aphra Behn telling us about the god of love, or love? That love hurts? And she is <u>singing</u> about it! But we <u>do</u> sing songs about how hard life is. But do we sing them when we are really hurting, or only when we are pretty well off and just thinking about being hurt?

When you love someone and they don't return your love, it hurts, but even when love isn't returned it still gives some intense pleasure. Strange, but I think true. I wouldn't say that love always has this two-sided nature, but I do see the idea that love <u>can</u> have two sides, pleasure and pain. And love takes two kinds of people, male and female. Well, for most people, anyway. Maybe there's also something to the idea that "opposites attract." Anyway, Aphra Behn seems to be talking about men vs. women, pain vs. pleasure, power vs. weakness, etc. Pairs, opposites. And in two stanzas (a pair of stanzas?).

A Sample Essay by a Student: "The Double Nature of Love"

The final essay makes use of some, but not of all, of the preliminary jottings, and it includes much that Sullivan did not think of until he reread his jottings, reread the poem, and began drafting the essay.

Geoffrey Sullivan

Professor Morawski

English 2G

15 October 2004

The Double Nature of Love

Aphra Behn's "Love Armed" is in two stanzas, and it is about

two people, "me" and "thee," that is, you and I, the lover and the

woman he loves. I think the speaker is a man, since according to

the usual code men are supposed to be the active lovers and

women are the (relatively) passive people who are loved. In this

poem, the beloved--the woman, I think--has "bright eyes" (line 5)

that provide the god of Love with fire, and she also provides the

god with "pride and cruelty" (10). This of course is the way the

man sees it if a woman doesn't respond to him; if she doesn't love

him in return, she is (he thinks) arrogant and cruel. What does

the man give to Love? He provides "desire" (7), "sighs and tears"

(9), "languishments and fears" (11). None of this sounds very

manly, but the joke is that the god of love--which means love--can

turn a strong man into a crybaby when a woman does not

respond to him.

Although both stanzas are clever descriptions of the god of

love, the poem is not just a description. Of course there is not a

plot in the way that a short story has a plot, but there is a sort of

a switch at the end, giving the story something of a plot. The

poem is, say, ninety percent expression of feeling and description

Sullivan 2

of love, but during the course of expressing feelings and describing love something happens, so there is a tiny story. The first stanza sets the scene ("Love in fantastic triumph sate" [1]) and tells of some of the things that the speaker and the woman contributed to the god of Love. The woman's eyes provided Love with fire, and the man's feelings provided Love with "desire" (7). The second stanza goes on to mention other things that Love got from the speaker ("sighs and tears," etc. [9]), and other things that Love got from the beloved ("pride and cruelty," etc. [10]), and in line 13 the poet says, "Thus thou and I the god have armed," so the two humans share something. They have both given Love his weapons. But--and this is the story I spoke of--the poem ends by emphasizing their difference: Only the man is "harmed," and the woman is the "victor" because her heart is not captured, as the man's heart is. In the battle that Love presides over, the woman is the winner; the man's heart has fallen for the woman, but, according to the last line, the woman's heart remains "free."

We have all seen the god of Love on valentine cards, a cute little Cupid armed with a bow and arrow. But despite the bow and arrow that the Valentine Day Cupid carries, I think that until I read Aphra Behn's "Love Armed" I had never really thought about Cupid as powerful and as capable of causing real pain. On valentine cards, he is just cute, but when I think about it, I realize the truth of Aphra Behn's concept of love. Love is (or can be) two-sided, whereas the valentine cards show only the sweet side.

Sullivan 3

I think it is interesting to notice that although the poem is about the destructive power of love, it is fun to read. I am not bothered by the fact that the lover is miserable. Why? I think I enjoy the poem, rather than am bothered by it, because he is enjoying his misery. After all, he is singing about it, sort of singing in the rain, telling anyone who will listen about how miserable he is, and he is having a very good time doing it.

[New page]

Sullivan 4

Work Cited

Behn, Aphra. "Love Armed." Literature and Composition. Ed. Sylvan Barnet et al. 7th ed. New York: Longman, 2005, 90.

Topics for Critical Thinking and Writing

1. What do you think of the title? Is it sufficiently interesting and focused?
2. What are the writer's chief points? Are they clear, and are they adequately developed?
3. Do you think the writer is too concerned with himself, and that he loses sight of the poem? Or do you find it interesting that he connects the poem with life?
4. Focus on the writer's use of quotations. Does he effectively introduce and examine quoted lines and phrases?
5. What grade would you give the essay? Why?

✔ CHECKLIST: *Editing a Draft*

❏ Is the title of my essay at least moderately informative and interesting?
❏ Do I identify the subject of my essay (author and title) early?
❏ What is my thesis? Do I state it soon enough (perhaps even in the title) and keep it in view?
❏ Is the organization reasonable? Does each point lead into the next without irrelevancies and without anticlimaxes?
❏ Is each paragraph unified by a topic sentence or a topic idea? Are there adequate transitions from one paragraph to the next?
❏ Are generalizations supported by appropriate concrete details, especially by brief quotations from the text?
❏ Is the opening paragraph interesting and, by its end, focused on the topic? Is the final paragraph conclusive without being repetitive?
❏ Is the tone appropriate? No sarcasm, no apologies, no condescension?
❏ If there is a summary, is it as brief as possible, given its purpose?
❏ Are the quotations adequately introduced, and are they accurate? Do they provide evidence and let the reader hear the author's voice, or do they merely add words to the essay?
❏ Is the present tense used to describe the author's work and the action of the work ("Shakespeare *shows*," "Hamlet *dies*")?
❏ Have I kept in mind the needs of my audience, for instance, by defining unfamiliar terms or by briefly summarizing works or opinions with which the reader may be unfamiliar?
❏ Is documentation provided where necessary?
❏ Are the spelling and punctuation correct? Are other mechanical matters (such as margins, spacing, and citations) in correct form? Have I proofread carefully?
❏ Is the paper properly identified—author's name, instructor's name, course number, and date?

YOUR TURN: SHORT STORIES AND POEMS FOR ANALYSIS

EDGAR ALLAN POE

Edgar Allan Poe (1809–1849) was the son of traveling actors. His father abandoned the family almost immediately, and his mother died when he was 2. The child was adopted—though never legally—by a prosperous merchant and his wife in Richmond. The tensions were great, aggravated by Poe's drinking and heavy gambling, and in 1827 Poe left Richmond for Boston. He wrote, served briefly in the army, attended West Point but left within a year, and became an editor for the remaining eighteen years of his life. It was during these years, too, that he wrote the poems, essays, and fiction—especially detective stories and horror stories—that have made him famous.

The Cask of Amontillado

The thousand injuries of Fortunato I had borne as I best could, but when he ventured upon insult, I vowed revenge. You, who so well know the nature of my soul, will not suppose, however, that I gave utterance to a threat. At *length* I would be avenged; this was a point definitely settled—but the very definitiveness with which it was resolved precluded the idea of risk. I must not only punish, but punish with impunity. A wrong is unredressed when retribution overtakes its redresser. It is equally unredressed when the avenger fails to make himself felt as such to him who has done the wrong.

It must be understood that neither by word nor deed had I given Fortunato cause to doubt my good will. I continued, as was my wont, to smile in his face, and he did not perceive that my smile *now* was at the thought of his immolation.

He had a weak point—this Fortunato—although in other regards he was a man to be respected and even feared. He prided himself on his connoisseurship in wine. Few Italians have the true virtuoso spirit. For the most part their enthusiasm is adopted to suit the time and opportunity to practice imposture upon the British and Austrian *millionaires,* In painting and gemmary Fortunato, like his countrymen, was a quack, but in the matter of old wines he was sincere. In this respect I did not differ from him materially;—I was skillful in the Italian vintages myself, and bought largely whenever I could.

It was about dusk, one evening during the supreme madness of the carnival season, that I encountered my friend. He accosted me with excessive warmth, for he had been drinking much. The man wore motley. He had on a tight-fitting parti-striped dress, and his head was surmounted by the conical cap and bells. I was so pleased to see him, that I thought I should never have done wringing his hand.

5   I said to him—"My dear Fortunato, you are luckily met. How remarkably well you are looking to-day! But I have received a pipe[1] of what passes for Amontillado, and I have my doubts."

"How?" said he, "Amontillado? A pipe? Impossible! And in the middle of the carnival?"

"I have my doubts," I replied; "and I was silly enough to pay the full Amontillado price without consulting you in the matter. You were not to be found, and I was fearful of losing a bargain."

"Amontillado!"

"I have my doubts."

10   "Amontillado!"

"And I must satisfy them."

"Amontillado!"

"As you are engaged, I am on my way to Luchesi. If any one has a critical turn, it is he. He will tell me—"

"Luchesi cannot tell Amontillado from Sherry."

15   "And yet some fools will have it that his taste is a match for your own."

"Come, let us go."

"Whither?"

"To your vaults."

"My friend, no; I will not impose upon your good nature. I perceive you have an engagement. Luchesi—"

20   "I have no engagement; come."

---

[1]**pipe** wine cask.

"My friend, no. It is not the engagement, but the severe cold with which I perceive you are afflicted. The vaults are insufferably damp. They are encrusted with nitre."

"Let us go, nevertheless. The cold is merely nothing. Amontillado! You have been imposed upon; and as for Luchesi, he cannot distinguish Sherry from Amontillado."

Thus speaking, Fortunato possessed himself of my arm. Putting on a mask of black silk, and drawing a *roquelaure*[2] closely about my person, I suffered him to hurry me to my palazzo.

There were no attendants at home; they had absconded to make merry in honor of the time. I had told them that I should not return until the morning, and had given them explicit orders not to stir from the house. These orders were sufficient, I well knew, to insure their immediate disappearance, one and all, as soon as my back was turned.

25   I took from their sconces two flambeaux, and giving one to Fortunato, bowed him through several suites of rooms to the archway that led into the vaults. I passed down a long and winding staircase, requesting him to be cautious as he followed. We came at length to the foot of the descent, and stood together on the damp ground of the catacombs of the Montresors.

The gait of my friend was unsteady, and the bells upon his cap jingled as he strode.

"The pipe," said he.

"It is farther on," said I; "but observe the white web-work which gleams from these cavern walls."

He turned towards me, and looked into my eyes with two filmy orbs that distilled the rheum of intoxication.

30   "Nitre?" he asked, at length.

"Nitre," I replied, "How long have you had that cough?"

"Ugh! ugh! ugh!—ugh! ugh! ugh!—ugh! ugh! ugh!—ugh! ugh! ugh!—ugh! ugh! ugh!"

My poor friend found it impossible to reply for many minutes.

"It is nothing," he said, at last.

35   "Come," I said, with decision, "we will go back; your health is precious. You are rich, respected, admired, beloved; you are happy, as once I was. You are a man to be missed. For me it is no matter. We will go back; you will be ill, and I cannot be responsible. Besides, there is Luchesi—"

"Enough," he said; "the cough is a mere nothing: it will not kill me. I shall not die of a cough."

"True—true," I replied; "and, indeed, I had no intention of alarming you unnecessarily—but you should use all proper caution. A draught of this Medoc will defend us from the damps."

Here I knocked off the neck of a bottle which I drew from a long row of its fellows that lay upon the mould.

"Drink," I said, presenting him the wine.

40   He raised it to his lips with a leer: He paused and nodded to me familiarly, while his bells jingled.

"I drink," he said, "to the buried that repose around us."

"And I to your long life."

He again took my arm, and we proceeded.

---

[2]*roquelaure* short cloak.

"These vaults," he said, "are extensive."

45   "The Montresors," I replied, "were a great and numerous family."

"I forget your arms."

"A huge human foot d'or, in a field azure; the foot crushes a serpent rampant whose fangs are imbedded in the heel."

"And the motto?"

"Nemo me impune lacessit.[3]

50   "Good!" he said.

The wine sparkled in his eyes and the bells jingled. My own fancy grew warm with the Medoc. We had passed through walls of piled bones, with casks and puncheons intermingling, into the inmost recesses of the catacombs. I paused again, and this time I made bold to seize Fortunato by an arm above the elbow.

"The nitre!" I said; "see, it increases. It hangs like moss upon the vaults. We are below the river's bed. The drops of moisture tickle among the bones. Come, we will go back ere it is too late. Your cough—"

"It is nothing," he said; "let us go on. But first, another draught of the Medoc."

I broke and reached him a flagon of De Grâve. He emptied it at a breath. His eyes flashed with a fierce light. He laughed and threw the bottle upwards with a gesticulation I did not understand.

55   I looked at him in surprise. He repeated the movement—a grotesque one.

"You do not comprehend?" he said.

"Not I," I replied.

"Then you are not of the brotherhood."

"How?"

60   "You are not of the masons."[4]

"Yes, yes," I said, "yes, yes."

"You? Impossible! A mason?"

"A mason," I replied.

"A sign," he said.

65   It is this," I answered, producing a trowel from beneath the folds of my *roquelaure.*

"You jest," he exclaimed, recoiling a few paces. "But let us proceed to the Amontillado."

"Be it so," I said, replacing the tool beneath the cloak, and again offering him my arm. He leaned upon it heavily. We continued our route in search of the Amontillado. We passed through a range of low arches, descended, passed on, and descending again, arrived at a deep crypt, in which the foulness of the air caused our flambeaux rather to glow than flame.

At the most remote end of the crypt there appeared another less spacious. Its walls had been lined with human remains piled to the vault overhead, in the fashion of the great catacombs of Paris. Three sides of this interior crypt were still ornamented in this manner. From the fourth the bones had been thrown down, and lay promiscuously upon the earth, forming at one point a mound of some size. Within the wall thus exposed by the displacing of the bones, we perceived a still interior recess, in depth about four feet, in width three, in height six or seven. It seemed to have been constructed for no especial use within itself, but formed merely the interval between two of the colossal supports of the roof of the catacombs, and was backed by one of their circumscribing walls of solid granite.

---

[3]*Nemo me impune lacessit* No one dare attack me with impunity (the motto of Scotland).
[4]**of the masons** i.e., a member of the Freemasons, an international secret fraternity.

It was in vain that Fortunato, uplifting his dull torch, endeavored to pry into the depths of the recess. Its termination the feeble light did not enable us to see.

70 "Proceed," I said; "herein is the Amontillado. As for Luchesi—"

"He is an ignoramus," interrupted my friend, as he stepped unsteadily forward, while I followed immediately at his heels. In an instant he had reached the extremity of the niche, and finding his progress arrested by the rock, stood stupidly bewildered. A moment more and I had fettered him to the granite. In its surface were two iron staples, distant from each other about two feet, horizontally. From one of these depended a short chain, from the other a padlock. Throwing the links about his waist, it was but the work of a few seconds to secure it. He was too much astounded to resist. Withdrawing the key I stepped back from the recess.

"Pass your hand," I said, "over the wall; you cannot help feeling the nitre. Indeed it is very damp. Once more let me *implore* you to return. No? Then I must positively leave you. But I must first render you all the little attentions in my power."

"The Amontillado!" ejaculated my friend, not yet recovered from his astonishment.

"True," I replied; "the Amontillado."

75 As I said these words I busied myself among the pile of bones of which I have before spoken. Throwing them aside, I soon uncovered a quantity of building-stone and mortar. With these materials and with the aid of my trowel, I began vigorously to wall up the entrance of the niche.

I had scarcely laid the first tier of masonry when I discovered that the intoxication of Fortunato had in a great measure worn off. The earliest indication I had of this was a low moaning cry from the depth of the recess. It was *not* the cry of a drunken man. There was then a long and obstinate silence. I laid the second tier, and the third, and the fourth; and then I heard the furious vibrations of the chain. The noise lasted for several minutes, during which, that I might hearken to it with the more satisfaction, I ceased my labors and sat down upon the bones. When at last the clanking subsided, I resumed the trowel, and finished without interruption the fifth, the sixth, and the seventh tier. The wall was now nearly upon a level with my breast. I again paused, and holding the flambeaux over the masonwork, threw a few feeble rays upon the figure within.

A succession of loud and shrill screams, bursting suddenly from the throat of the chained form, seemed to thrust me violently back. For a brief moment I hesitated—I trembled. Unsheathing my rapier, I began to grope with it about the recess; but the thought of an instant reassured me. I placed my hand upon the solid fabric of the catacombs, and felt satisfied. I reapproached the wall. I replied to the yells of him who clamored. I re-echoed—I aided—I surpassed them in volume and in strength. I did this, and the clamorer grew still.

It was now midnight, and my task was drawing to a close. I had completed the eight, the ninth, and the tenth tier. I had finished a portion of the last and the eleventh; there remained but a single stone to be fitted and plastered in. I struggled with its weight; I placed it partially in its destined position. But now there came from out the niche a low laugh that erected the hairs upon my head. It was succeeded by a sad voice, which I had difficulty in recognizing as that of the noble Fortunato. The voice said—

"Ha! ha! ha!—he! he! he!——a very good joke indeed—an excellent jest. We will have many a rich laugh about it at the palazzo—he! he! he!—over our wine—he! he! he!"

80 "The Amontillado!" I said.

"He! he! he!—he! he! he!—yes, the Amontillado. But is it not getting late? Will not they be awaiting us at the palazzo, the Lady Fortunato and the rest? Let us be gone."

"Yes," I said, "let us be gone."

"For the love of God, Montresor!"

"Yes," I said, "for the love of God!"

85   But to these words I hearkened in vain for a reply. I grew impatient. I called aloud;

"Fortunato!"

No answer. I called again;

"Fortunato!"

No answer still. I thrust a torch through the remaining aperture and let it fall within. There came forth in return only a jingling of the bells. My heart grew sick—on account of the dampness of the catacombs. I hastened to make an end of my labor. I forced the last stone into its position; I plastered it up. Against the new masonry I reerected the old rampart of bones. For the half of a century no mortal has disturbed them. *In pace requiescat!*[5]

[1846]

[5]*In pace requiescat!* May he rest in peace!

Topics for Critical Thinking and Writing

1. To whom does Montresor tell his story? The story he tells happened fifty years earlier. Do we have any clues as to why he tells it now?

2. At the end of the story we learn that the murder occurred fifty years ago. Would the story be equally effective if Poe had had Montresor reveal that fact at the outset? Why, or why not?

3. Poe sets Montresor's story at dusk, "during the supreme madness of the carnival season." What is the "carnival season"? (If you are uncertain as to the meaning of "carnival," consult a dictionary.) What details of the story derive from the setting?

4. In the justifiably famous first line Montresor declares. "The thousand injuries of Fortunato I had borne as I best could, but when he ventured upon insult, I vowed revenge." Do we ever learn what those injuries and that insult were? What do we learn about Montresor from this declaration?

5. How does Montresor characterize Fortunato? What details of his portrait unwittingly enlist our sympathy for Fortunato? Does Montresor betray any sympathy for his victim?

6. "The Cask of Amontillado" is sometimes referred to as a "horror tale." Do you think it has anything in common with horror movies? If so, what? (You might begin by making a list of the characteristics of horror movies.) Why do people take pleasure in horror movies? Does this story offer any of the same sorts of pleasure? In any case, why might a reader take pleasure in this story?

7. Construct a definition of madness (you may want to do a little research, but if you make use of your findings, be sure to give credit to your sources) and write an essay of 500–750 words arguing whether or not Montresor is mad. (*Note:* You may want to distinguish between Montresor at the time of the killing and Montresor at the present.)

GUY DE MAUPASSANT

Born and raised in Normandy, the French novelist and short-story writer Guy de Maupassant (1850–1893) studied law in Paris, then served in the Franco-Prussian War. Afterwards he worked for a time as a clerk for the government until, with the support of the novelist Gustave Flaubert (a friend of Maupassant's mother) and later Emile Zola, he decided to pursue a career as a writer. Ironic and pointed, detached yet compassionate, Maupassant explores human folly and its both grim and comic consequences. His first great success came in April 1880, with the publication of the story "Boule de Suif" ("Ball of Fat"), about a prostitute traveling by coach, with a number of bourgeois companions, through Prussian-occupied France during wartime. Maupassant published six novels, including Bel-Ami *(1885) and* Pierre et Jean *(1888), and a number of collections of stories, before his untimely death from the effects of syphilis, a month short of his forty-third birthday. Like many of his stories, "The Necklace" uses realistic observation and keenly chosen detail to tell its story of a misunderstanding and the years of hard labor that follow from it.*

The Necklace

Translated by Marjorie Laurie

She was one of those pretty and charming girls who are sometimes, as if by a mistake of destiny, born in a family of clerks. She had no dowry, no expectations, no means of being known, understood, loved, wedded by any rich and distinguished man; and she let herself be married to a little clerk at the Ministry of Public Instruction.

She dressed plainly because she could not dress well, but she was as unhappy as though she had really fallen from her proper station, since with women there is neither caste nor rank: and beauty, grace and charm act instead of family and birth. Natural fineness, instinct for what is elegant, suppleness of wit, are the sole hierarchy, and make from women of the people the equals of the very greatest ladies.

She suffered ceaselessly, feeling herself born for all the delicacies and all the luxuries. She suffered from the poverty of her dwelling, from the wretched look of the walls, from the worn-out chairs, from the ugliness of the curtains. All those things, of which another woman of her rank would never even have been conscious, tortured her and made her angry. The sight of the little Breton peasant who did her humble housework aroused in her regrets which were despairing, and distracted dreams. She thought of the silent antechambers hung with Oriental tapestry, lit by tall bronze candelabra, and of the two great footmen in knee breeches who sleep in the big armchairs, made drowsy by the heavy warmth of the hot-air stove. She thought of the long *salons*[1] fitted up with ancient silk, of the delicate furniture carrying priceless curiosities, and of the coquettish perfumed boudoirs made for talks at five o'clock with intimate friends, with men famous and sought after, whom all women envy and whose attention they all desire.

When she sat down to dinner, before the round table covered with a tablecloth three days old, opposite her husband, who uncovered the soup tureen and

---

[1]*salons* drawing-rooms.

declared with an enchanted air, "Ah, the good *pot-au-feu!*[2] I don't know anything better than that," she thought of dainty dinners, of shining silverware, of tapestry which peopled the walls with ancient personages and with strange birds flying in the midst of a fairy forest; and she thought of delicious dishes served on marvelous plates, and of the whispered gallantries which you listen to with a sphinx-like smile, while you are eating the pink flesh of a trout or the wings of a quail.

5   She had no dresses, no jewels, nothing. And she loved nothing but that; she felt made for that. She would so have liked to please, to be envied, to be charming, to be sought after.

She had a friend, a former schoolmate at the convent, who was rich, and whom she did not like to go and see any more, because she suffered so much when she came back.

But one evening, her husband returned home with a triumphant air, and holding a large envelope in his hand.

"There," said he. "Here is something for you."

She tore the paper sharply, and drew out a printed card which bore these words:

10   "The Minister of Public Instruction and Mme. Georges Ramponneau request the honor of M. and Mme. Loisel's company at the palace of the Ministry on Monday evening, January eighteenth."

Instead of being delighted, as her husband hoped, she threw the invitation on the table with disdain, murmuring:

"What do you want me to do with that?"

"But, my dear, I thought you would be glad. You never go out, and this is such a fine opportunity. I had awful trouble to get it. Everyone wants to go; it is very select, and they are not giving many invitations to clerks. The whole official world will be there."

She looked at him with an irritated glance, and said, impatiently:

15   "And what do you want me to put on my back?"

He had not thought of that; he stammered:

"Why, the dress you go to the theater in. It looks very well, to me."

He stopped, distracted, seeing his wife was crying. Two great tears descended slowly from the corners of her eyes toward the corners of her mouth. He stuttered:

"What's the matter? What's the matter?"

20   But, by violent effort, she had conquered her grief, and she replied, with a calm voice, while she wiped her wet cheeks:

"Nothing. Only I have no dress and therefore I can't go to this ball. Give your card to some colleague whose wife is better equipped than I."

He was in despair. He resumed:

"Come, let us see, Mathilde. How much would it cost, a suitable dress, which you could use on other occasions, something very simple?"

She reflected several seconds, making her calculations and wondering also what sum she could ask without drawing on herself an immediate refusal and a frightened exclamation from the economical clerk.

25   Finally, she replied, hesitatingly:

[2]*pot-au-feu* stew.

"I don't know exactly, but I think I could manage it with four hundred francs."

He had grown a little pale, because he was laying aside just that amount to buy a gun and treat himself to a little shooting next summer on the plain of Nanterre, with several friends who went to shoot larks down there, of a Sunday.

But he said:

"All right. I will give you four hundred francs. And try to have a pretty dress."

30   The day of the ball drew near, and Mme. Loisel seemed sad, uneasy, anxious. Her dress was ready, however. Her husband said to her one evening:

"What is the matter? Come, you've been so queer these last three days."

And she answered:

"It annoys me not to have a single jewel, not a single stone, nothing to put on. I shall look like distress. I should almost rather not go at all."

He resumed:

35   "You might wear natural flowers. It's very stylish at this time of the year. For ten francs you can get two or three magnificent roses."

She was not convinced.

"No; there's nothing more humiliating than to look poor among other women who are rich."

But her husband cried:

"How stupid you are! Go look up your friend Mme. Forestier, and ask her to lend you some jewels. You're quite thick enough with her to do that."

40   She uttered a cry of joy:

"It's true. I never thought of it."

The next day she went to her friend and told of her distress.

Mme. Forestier went to a wardrobe with a glass door, took out a large jewel-box, brought it back, opened it, and said to Mme. Loisel:

"Choose, my dear."

45   She saw first of all some bracelets, then a pearl necklace, then a Venetian cross, gold and precious stones of admirable workmanship. She tried on the ornaments before the glass, hesitated, could not make up her mind to part with them, to give them back. She kept asking:

"Haven't you any more?"

"Why, yes. Look. I don't know what you like."

All of a sudden she discovered, in a black satin box, a superb necklace of diamonds, and her heart began to beat with an immoderate desire. Her hands trembled as she took it. She fastened it around her throat, outside her high-necked dress, and remained lost in ecstasy at the sight of herself.

Then she asked, hesitating, filled with anguish:

50   "Can you lend me that, only that?"

"Why, yes, certainly."

She sprang upon the neck of her friend, kissed her passionately, then fled with her treasure.

The day of the ball arrived. Mme. Loisel made a great success. She was prettier than them all, elegant, gracious, smiling, and crazy with joy. All the men looked at her, asked her name, endeavored to be introduced. All the attachés of the Cabinet wanted to waltz with her. She was remarked by the minister himself.

She danced with intoxication, with passion, made drunk by pleasure, forgetting all, in the triumph of her beauty, in the glory of her success, in a sort of cloud of happiness composed of all this homage, of all this admiration, of all these awakened desires, and of that sense of complete victory which is so sweet to a woman's heart.

55   She went away about four o'clock in the morning. Her husband had been sleeping since midnight, in a little deserted anteroom, with three other gentlemen whose wives were having a very good time. He threw over her shoulders the wraps which he had brought, modest wraps of common life, whose poverty contrasted with the elegance of the ball dress. She felt this, and wanted to escape so as not to be remarked by the other women, who were enveloping themselves in costly furs.

Loisel held her back.

"Wait a bit. You will catch cold outside. I will go and call a cab."

But she did not listen to him, and rapidly descended the stairs. When they were in the street they did not find a carriage; and they began to look for one, shouting after the cabmen whom they saw passing by at a distance.

They went down toward the Seine, in despair, shivering with cold. At last they found on the quay one of those ancient noctambulant coupés which, exactly as if they were ashamed to show their misery during the day, are never seen round Paris until after nightfall.

60   It took them to their door in the Rue des Martyrs, and once more, sadly, they climbed up homeward. All was ended, for her. And as to him, he reflected that he must be at the Ministry at ten o'clock.

She removed the wraps which covered her shoulders, before the glass, so as once more to see herself in all her glory. But suddenly she uttered a cry. She no longer had the necklace around her neck!

Her husband, already half undressed, demanded:

"What is the matter with you?"

She turned madly toward him:

65   "I have—I have—I've lost Mme. Forestier's necklace."

He stood up, distracted.

"What!—how?—impossible!"

And they looked in the folds of her dress, in the folds of her cloak, in her pockets, everywhere. They did not find it.

He asked:

70   "You're sure you had it on when you left the ball?"

"Yes, I felt it in the vestibule of the palace."

"But if you had lost it in the street we should have heard it fall. It must be in the cab."

"Yes. Probably. Did you take his number?"

"No. And you, didn't you notice it?"

75   "No."

They looked, thunderstruck, at one another. At last Loisel put on his clothes.

"I shall go back on foot," said he, "over the whole route which we have taken to see if I can find it."

And he went out. She sat waiting on a chair in her ball dress, without strength to go to bed, overwhelmed, without fire, without a thought.

Her husband came back about seven o'clock. He had found nothing.

80   He went to Police Headquarters, to the newspaper offices, to offer a reward; he went to the cab companies—everywhere, in fact, whither he was urged by the least suspicion of hope.

She waited all day, in the same condition of mad fear before this terrible calamity.

Loisel returned at night with a hollow, pale face; he had discovered nothing.

"You must write to your friend," said he, "that you have broken the clasp of her necklace and that you are having it mended. That will give us time to turn round."

She wrote at his dictation.

At the end of a week they had lost all hope.

And Loisel, who had aged five years, declared:

"We must consider how to replace that ornament."

The next day they took the box which had contained it, and they went to the jeweler whose name was found within. He consulted his books.

"It was not I, madame, who sold that necklace; I must simply have furnished the case."

Then they went from jeweler to jeweler, searching for a necklace like the other, consulting their memories, sick both of them with chagrin and anguish.

They found, in a shop at the Palais Royal, a string of diamonds which seemed to them exactly like the one they looked for. It was worth forty thousand francs. They could have it for thirty-six.

So they begged the jeweler not to sell it for three days yet. And they made a bargain that he should buy it back for thirty-four thousand francs, in case they found the other one before the end of February.

Loisel possessed eighteen thousand francs which his father had left him. He would borrow the rest.

He did borrow, asking a thousand francs of one, five hundred of another, five louis here, three louis[3] there. He gave notes, took up ruinous obligations, dealt with usurers and all the race of lenders. He compromised all the rest of his life, risked his signature without even knowing if he could meet it; and, frightened by the pains yet to come, by the black misery which was about to fall upon him, by the prospect of all the physical privation and of all the moral tortures which he was to suffer, he went to get the new necklace, putting down upon the merchant's counter thirty-six thousand francs.

When Mme. Loisel took back the necklace, Mme. Forestier said to her, with a chilly manner:

"You should have returned it sooner; I might have needed it."

She did not open the case, as her friend had so much feared. If she had detected the substitution, what would she have thought, what would she have said? Would she not have taken Mme. Loisel for a thief?

Mme. Loisel now knew the horrible existence of the needy. She took her part, moreover, all of a sudden, with heroism. That dreadful debt must be paid. She would pay it. They dismissed their servant; they changed their lodgings; they rented a garret under the roof.

She came to know what heavy housework meant and the odious cares of the kitchen. She washed the dishes, using her rosy nails on the greasy pots and pans. She washed the dirty linen, the shirts, and the dishcloths, which she dried upon a line; she carried the slops down to the street every morning, and carried up the water, stopping for breath at every landing. And, dressed like a woman of the people, she went to the fruiterer, the grocer, the butcher, her basket on her arm, bargaining, insulted, defending her miserable money sou by sou.

---

[3]**louis** a gold coin worth 20 francs.

100   Each month they had to meet some notes, renew others, obtain more time.

Her husband worked in the evening making a fair copy of some tradesman's accounts, and late at night he often copied manuscript for five sous a page.

And this life lasted for ten years.

At the end of ten years, they had paid everything, everything, with the rates of usury, and the accumulations of the compound interest.

Mme. Loisel looked old now. She had become the woman of impoverished households—strong and hard and rough. With frowsy hair, skirts askew, and red hands, she talked loud while washing the floor with great swishes of water. But sometimes, when her husband was at the office, she sat down near the window, and she thought of that gay evening of long ago, of the ball where she had been so beautiful and so fêted.

105   What would have happened if she had not lost that necklace? Who knows? Who knows? How life is strange and changeful! How little a thing is needed for us to be lost or to be saved!

But, one Sunday, having gone to take a walk in the Champs Elysées to refresh herself from the labor of the week, she suddenly perceived a woman who was leading a child. It was Mme. Forestier, still young, still beautiful, still charming.

Mme. Loisel felt moved. Was she going to speak to her? Yes, certainly. And now that she had paid, she was going to tell her all about it. Why not?

She went up.

"Good day, Jeanne."

110   The other, astonished to be familiarly addressed by this plain goodwife, did not recognize her at all, and stammered:

"But—madam!—I do not know—You must be mistaken."

"No. I am Mathilde Loisel."

Her friend uttered a cry.

"Oh, my poor Mathilde! How you are changed!"

115   "Yes, I have had days hard enough, since I have seen you, days wretched enough—and that because of you!"

"Of me! How so?"

"Do you remember that diamond necklace which you lent me to wear at the ministerial ball?"

"Yes. Well?"

"Well, I lost it."

120   "What do you mean? You brought it back."

"I brought you back another just like it. And for this we have been ten years paying. You can understand that it was not easy for us, us who had nothing. At last it is ended, and I am very glad."

Mme. Forestier had stopped.

"You say that you bought a necklace of diamonds to replace mine?"

"Yes. You never noticed it, then! They were very like."

125   And she smiled with a joy which was proud and naïve at once.

Mme. Forestier, strongly moved, took her two hands.

"Oh, my poor Mathilde! Why, my necklace was paste. It was worth at most five hundred francs!"

[1885]

Topics for Critical Thinking and Writing

1. What do we learn about Mme. Loisel from the first six paragraphs of the story? What is your response to the narrator's generalizations about women in paragraph 2?
2. Is Maupassant's point that Mme. Loisel is justly punished for her vanity and pride? What about her husband, and the impact of the apparent loss of the necklace on his life?
3. In paragraph 98, as Mme. Loisel decides she must pay the debt, Maupassant writes: "She took her part, moreover, all of a sudden, with heroism." Why the word "heroism"? Isn't this a strange way to characterize Mme. Loisel's behavior?
4. Maupassant, in a discussion of fiction, said that a serious writer's goal

   > is not to tell a story to entertain us, or to appeal to our feelings, but to make us to think, and to make us understand the hidden meaning of events. By dint of having observed and having meditated, the writer sees the world, facts, people, and things in a distinctive way, a way that is the result of all of his thoughtful observation. It is this personal view of the world that a writer strives to communicate to us. . . . To make the spectacle of life as moving to us as it has been to him, he must bring life before our eyes with scrupulous accuracy. He must construct his work with great skill—his art must seem artless—so that we cannot detect his contrivance or see his intentions.

   Among the big ideas in these few sentences are these: (a) The purpose of fiction is "to make us understand the hidden meaning of events"; (b) writers give us a "personal view"; (c) readers should be moved by the story but should not be aware that the artist has imposed a personal view on them. Do you agree with some or with all of these assertions? And do you think that "The Necklace" effectively illustrates Maupassant's points? What might be "the hidden meaning of events"? What would you guess is Maupassant's "personal view"? Would you agree that the story is so skillfully constructed that we are unaware of the author's methods and of his intentions?
5. Have you ever done something, tried to make up for it, and then discovered later that you had not done what you thought you did after all? How did this make you feel?

KATHERINE ANNE PORTER

Katherine Anne Porter (1890–1980) had the curious habit of inventing details in her life, but it is true that she was born in a log cabin in Indian Creek, Texas, that she was originally named Callie Russell Porter, that her mother died when the child was 2 years old, and that Callie was brought up by her maternal grandmother in Kyle, Texas. She was sent to convent schools, where, in her words, she received a "strangely useless and ornamental education." When she was 16 she left school, married (and soon divorced), and worked as a reporter, first in Texas and later in Denver and Chicago. She moved around a

good deal, both within the United States and abroad; she lived for a while in Mexico, Belgium, Switzerland, France, and Germany.

Even as a child she was interested in writing, but she did not publish her first story until she was 33. She wrote essays and one novel (Ship of Fools), *but she is best known for her stories. Porter's* Collected Stories *won the Pulitzer Prize and the National Book Award in 1965.*

The Jilting of Granny Weatherall

She flicked her wrist neatly out of Doctor Harry's pudgy careful fingers and pulled the sheet up to her chin. The brat ought to be in knee breeches. Doctoring around the country with spectacles on his nose! "Get along now, take your schoolbooks and go. There's nothing wrong with me."

Doctor Harry spread a warm paw like a cushion on her forehead where the forked green vein danced and made her eyelids twitch. "Now, now, be a good girl, and we'll have you up in no time."

"That's no way to speak to a woman nearly eighty years old just because she's down. I'd have you respect your elders, young man."

"Well, Missy, excuse me." Doctor Harry patted her cheek. "But I've got to warn you, haven't I? You're a marvel, but you must be careful or you're going to be good and sorry."

5   "Don't tell me what I'm going to be. I'm on my feet now, morally speaking. It's Cornelia. I had to go to bed to get rid of her."

Her bones felt loose, and floated around in her skin, and Doctor Harry floated like a balloon around the foot of the bed. He floated and pulled down his waistcoat and swung his glasses on a cord. "Well, stay where you are, it certainly can't hurt you."

"Get along and doctor your sick," said Granny Weatherall. "Leave a well woman alone. I'll call for you when I want you . . . .Where were you forty years ago when I pulled through milk-leg and double pneumonia? You weren't even born. Don't let Cornelia lead you on," she shouted, because Doctor Harry appeared to float up to the ceiling and out. "I pay my own bills, and I don't throw my money away on nonsense!"

She meant to wave good-by, but it was too much trouble. Her eyes closed of themselves, it was like a dark curtain drawn around the bed. The pillow rose and floated under her, pleasant as a hammock in a light wind. She listened to the leaves rustling outside the window. No, somebody was swishing newspapers: no, Cornelia and Doctor Harry were whispering together. She leaped broad awake, thinking they whispered in her ear.

"She was *never* like this, never like this!" "Well, what can we expect?" "Yes, eighty years old . . . ."

10   Well, and what if she was? She still had ears. It was like Cornelia to whisper around doors. She always kept things secret in such a public way. She was always being tactful and kind. Cornelia was dutiful; that was the trouble with her. Dutiful and good: "So good and dutiful," said Granny, "that I'd like to spank her." She saw herself spanking Cornelia and making a fine job of it.

"What'd you say, Mother?"

Granny felt her face tying up in hard knots.

"Can't a body think, I'd like to know?"

"I thought you might want something."

15   "I do. I want a lot of things. First off, go away and don't whisper."

She lay and drowsed, hoping in her sleep that the children would keep out and let her rest a minute. It had been a long day. Not that she was tired. It was always pleasant to snatch a minute now and then. There was always so much to be done, let me see: tomorrow.

Tomorrow was far away and there was nothing to trouble about. Things were finished somehow when the time came; thank God there was always a little margin over for peace: then a person could spread out the plan of life and tuck in the edges orderly. It was good to have everything clean and folded away, with the hair brushes and tonic bottles sitting straight on the white embroidered linen: the day started without fuss and the pantry shelves laid out with rows of jelly glasses and brown jugs and white stone-china jars with blue whirligigs and words painted on them: coffee, tea, sugar, ginger, cinnamon, allspice: and the bronze clock with the lion on top nicely dusted off. The dust that lion could collect in twenty-four hours! The box in the attic with all those letters tied up, well, she'd have to go through that tomorrow. All those letters—George's letters and John's letters and her letters to them both—lying around for the children to find afterwards made her uneasy. Yes, that would be tomorrow's business. No use to let them know how silly she had been once.

While she was rummaging around she found death in her mind and it felt clammy and unfamiliar. She had spent so much time preparing for death there was no need for bringing it up again. Let it take care of itself now. When she was sixty she had felt very old, finished, and went around making farewell trips to see her children and grandchildren, with a secret in her mind: This is the very last of your mother, children! Then she made her will and came down with a long fever. That was all just a notion like a lot of other things, but it was lucky too, for she had once for all got over the idea of dying for a long time. Now she couldn't be worried. She hoped she had better sense now. Her father had lived to be one hundred and two years old and had drunk a noggin of strong hot toddy on his last birthday. He told the reporters it was his daily habit, and he owed his long life to that. He had made quite a scandal and was very pleased about it. She believed she'd just plague Cornelia a little.

"Cornelia! Cornelia!" No footsteps, but a sudden hand on her cheek. "Bless you, where have you been?"

20 "Here, Mother."

"Well, Cornelia, I want a noggin of hot toddy."

"Are you cold, darling?"

"I'm chilly, Cornelia. Lying in bed stops the circulation. I must have told you that a thousand times."

Well, she could just hear Cornelia telling her husband that Mother was getting a little childish and they'd have to humor her. The thing that most annoyed her was that Cornelia thought she was deaf, dumb, and blind. Little hasty glances and tiny gestures tossed around her and over her head saying, "Don't cross her, let her have her way, she's eighty years old," and she sitting there as if she lived in a thin glass cage. Sometimes Granny almost made up her mind to pack up and move back to her own house where nobody could remind her every minute that she was old. Wait, wait, Cornelia, till your own children whisper behind your back!

25 In her day she had kept a better house and had got more work done. She wasn't too old yet for Lydia to be driving eighty miles for advice when one of the children jumped the track, and Jimmy still dropped in and talked things over: "Now, Mammy, you've a good business head, I want to know what you think of this? . . . " Old. Cornelia couldn't change the furniture around without asking.

Little things, little things! They had been so sweet when they were little. Granny wished the old days were back again with the children young and everything to be done over. It had been a hard pull, but not too much for her. When she thought of all the food she had cooked, and all the clothes she had cut and sewed, and all the gardens she had made—well, the children showed it. There they were, made out of her, and they couldn't get away from that. Sometimes she wanted to see John again and point to them and say, Well, I didn't do so badly, did I? But that would have to wait. That was for tomorrow. She used to think of him as a man, but now all the children were older than their father, and he would be a child beside her if she saw him now. It seemed strange and there was something wrong in the idea. Why, he couldn't possibly recognize her. She had fenced in a hundred acres once, digging the post holes herself and clamping the wires with just a negro boy to help. That changed a woman. John would be looking for a young woman with the peaked Spanish comb in her hair and the painted fan. Digging post holes changed a woman. Riding country roads in the winter when women had their babies was another thing: sitting up nights with sick horses and sick negroes and sick children and hardly ever losing one. John, I hardly ever lost one of them! John would see that in a minute, that would be something he could understand, she wouldn't have to explain anything!

It made her feel like rolling up her sleeves and putting the whole place to rights again. No matter if Cornelia was determined to be everywhere at once, there were a great many things left undone on this place. She would start tomorrow and do them. It was good to be strong enough for everything, even if all you made melted and changed and slipped under your hands, so that by the time you finished you almost forgot what you were working for. What was it I set out to do? she asked herself intently, but she could not remember. A fog rose over the valley, she saw it marching across the creek swallowing the trees and moving up the hill like an army of ghosts. Soon it would be at the near edge of the orchard, and then it was time to go in and light the lamps. Come in, children, don't stay out in the night air.

Lighting the lamps had been beautiful. The children huddled up to her and breathed like little calves waiting at the bars in the twilight. Their eyes followed the match and watched the flame rise and settle in a blue curve, then they moved away from her. The lamp was lit, they didn't have to be scared and hang on to mother any more. Never, never, never more. God, for all my life I thank Thee. Without Thee, my God, I could never have done it. Hail, Mary, full of grace.

I want you to pick all the fruit this year and see that nothing is wasted. There's always someone who can use it. Don't let good things rot for want of using. You waste life when you waste good food. Don't let things get lost. It's bitter to lose things. Now, don't let me get to thinking, not when I am tired and taking a little nap before supper . . . .

The pillow rose about her shoulders and pressed against her heart and the memory was being squeezed out of it: oh, push down that pillow, somebody: it would smother her if she tried to hold it. Such a fresh breeze blowing and such a green day with no threats in it. But he had not come, just the same. What does a woman do when she has put on the white veil and set out the white cake for a man and he doesn't come? She tried to remember. No, I swear he never harmed me but in that. He never harmed me but in that . . . and what if he did? There was the day, the day, but a whirl of dark smoke rose and covered it, crept up and over into the bright field where everything was planted so carefully in orderly rows. That was hell, she knew hell when she saw it. For sixty years she had prayed against remembering him and against losing her soul in the deep pit of hell, and now the two things were mingled in one and the thought of him was a smoky cloud from hell that moved and crept in her head when she had just got rid of Doctor Harry and was trying to rest a minute. Wounded vanity, Ellen, said a sharp voice in the top of her mind. Don't let your wounded vanity get the upper hand of you. Plenty of girls get jilted. You were jilted, weren't you? Then stand up to it. Her eyelids wavered and let in streamers of blue-gray light like tissue paper over her eyes. She must get up and pull the shades down or she'd never sleep. She was in bed again and the shades were not down. How could that happen? Better turn over, hide from the light, sleeping in the light gave you nightmares. "Mother, how do you feel now?" and a stinging wetness on her forehead. But I don't like having my face washed in cold water!

30   Hapsy? George? Lydia? Jimmy? No, Cornelia, and her features were swollen and full of little puddles. "They're coming, darling, they'll all be here soon." Go wash your face, child, you look funny.

    Instead of obeying, Cornelia knelt down and put her head on the pillow. She seemed to be talking but there was no sound. "Well, are you tongue-tied? Whose birthday is it? Are you going to give a party?"

    Cornelia's mouth moved urgently in strange shapes. "Don't do that, you bother me, daughter."

    "Oh, no, Mother. Oh, no . . . ."

    Nonsense. It was strange about children. They disputed your every word. "No what, Cornelia?"

35   "Here's Doctor Harry."

    "I won't see that boy again. He just left five minutes ago."

    "That was this morning, Mother. It's night now. Here's the nurse."

    "This is Doctor Harry, Mrs. Weatherall. I never saw you look so young and happy!"

    "Ah, I'll never be young again—but I'd be happy if they'd let me lie in peace and get rested."

40   She thought she spoke up loudly, but no one answered. A warm weight on her forehead, a warm bracelet on her wrist, and a breeze went on whispering, trying to tell her something. A shuffle of leaves in the everlasting hand of God. He blew on them and they danced and rattled. "Mother, don't mind, we're going to give you a little hypodermic." "Look here, daughter, how do ants get in this bed? I saw sugar ants yesterday." Did you send for Hapsy too?

    It was Hapsy she really wanted. She had to go a long way back through a great many rooms to find Hapsy standing with a baby on her arm. She seemed to herself to be Hapsy also, and the baby on Hapsy's arm was Hapsy and himself and herself, all at once, and there was no surprise in the meeting. Then Hapsy melted from within and turned flimsy as gray gauze and the baby was a gauzy shadow, and Hapsy came up close and said, "I thought you'd never come," and looked at her very searchingly and said, "You haven't changed a bit!" They leaned forward to kiss, when Cornelia began whispering from a long way off, "Oh, is there anything you want to tell me? Is there anything I can do for you?"

    Yes, she had changed her mind after sixty years and she would like to see George. I want you to find George. Find him and be sure to tell him I forgot him. I want him to know I had my husband just the same and my children and my house like any other woman. A good house too and a good husband that I loved and fine children out of him. Better than I hoped for even. Tell him I was given back everything he took away and more. Oh, no, oh, God, no, there was something else besides the house and the man and the children. Oh, surely they were not all? What was it? Something not given back . . . .Her breath crowded down under her ribs and grew into a monstrous frightening shape with cutting edges; it bored up into her head, and the agony was unbelievable: Yes, John, get the doctor now, no more talk, my time has come.

When this one was born it should be the last. The last. It should have been born first, for it was the one she had truly wanted. Everything came in good time. Nothing left out, left over. She was strong, in three days she would be as well as ever. Better. A woman needed milk in her to have her full health.

"Mother, do you hear me?"

45   "I've been telling you—"

"Mother, Father Connolly's here."

"I went to Holy Communion only last week. Tell him I'm not so sinful as all that."

"Father just wants to speak to you."

He could speak as much as he pleased. It was like him to drop in and inquire about her soul as if it were a teething baby, and then stay on for a cup of tea and a round of cards and gossip. He always had a funny story of some sort, usually about an Irishman who made his little mistakes and confessed them, and the point lay in some absurd thing he would blurt out in the confessional showing his struggles between native piety and original sin. Granny felt easy about her soul. Cornelia, where are your manners? Give Father Connolly a chair. She had her secret comfortable understanding with a few favorite saints who cleared a straight road to God for her. All as surely signed and sealed as the papers for the new Forty Acres. Forever . . . heirs and assigns forever. Since the day the wedding cake was not cut, but thrown out and wasted. The whole bottom dropped out of the world, and there she was blind and sweating with nothing under her feet and the walls falling away. His hand had caught her under the breast, she had not fallen, there was the freshly polished floor with the green rug on it, just as before. he had cursed like a sailor's parrot and said, "I'll kill him for you." Don't lay a hand on him, for my sake leave something to God. "Now, Ellen, you must believe what I tell you . . . ."

50   So there was nothing, nothing to worry about any more, except sometimes in the night one of the children screamed in a nightmare, and they both hustled out shaking and hunting for the matches and calling, "There, wait a minute, here we are!" John, get the doctor now, Hapsy's time has come. But there was Hapsy standing by the bed in a white cap. "Cornelia, tell Hapsy to take off her cap. I can't see her plain."

Her eyes opened very wide and the room stood out like a picture she had seen somewhere. Dark colors with the shadows rising toward the ceiling in long angles. The tall black dresser gleamed with nothing on it but John's picture, enlarged from a little one, with John's eyes very black when they should have been blue. You never saw him, so how do you know how he looked? But the man insisted the copy was perfect, it was very rich and handsome. For a picture, yes, but it's not my husband. The table by the bed had a linen cover and a candle and a crucifix. The light was blue from Cornelia's silk lampshades. No sort of light at all, just frippery. You had to live forty years with kerosene lamps to appreciate honest electricity. She felt very strong and she saw Doctor Harry with a rosy nimbus around him.

"You look like a saint, Doctor Harry, and I vow that's as near as you'll ever come to it."

"She's saying something."

"I heard you, Cornelia. What's all this carrying on?"

55 "Father Connolly's saying—"

Cornelia's voice staggered and bumped like a cart in a bad road. It rounded corners and turned back again and arrived nowhere. Granny stepped up in the cart very lightly and reached for the reins, but a man sat beside her and she knew him by his hands, driving the cart. She did not look in his face, for she knew without seeing, but looked instead down the road where the trees leaned over and bowed to each other and a thousand birds were singing a Mass. She felt like singing too, but she put her hand in the bosom of her dress and pulled out a rosary, and Father Connolly murmured Latin in a very solemn voice and tickled her feet. My God, will you stop that nonsense? I'm a married woman. What if he did run away and leave me to face the priest by myself? I found another a whole world better. I wouldn't have exchanged my husband for anybody except St. Michael himself, and you may tell him that for me with a thank you in the bargain.

Light flashed on her closed eyelids, and a deep roaring shook her. Cornelia, is that lightning? I hear thunder. There's going to be a storm. Close all the windows. Call the children in . . . ."Mother, here we are, all of us." "Is that you, Hapsy?" "Oh, no, I'm Lydia. We drove as fast as we could." Their faces drifted above her, drifted away. The rosary fell out of her hands and Lydia put it back. Jimmy tried to help, their hands fumbled together, and Granny closed two fingers around Jimmy's thumb. Beads wouldn't do, it must be something alive. She was so amazed her thoughts ran round and round. So, my dear Lord, this is my death and I wasn't even thinking about it. My children have come to see me die. But I can't, it's not time. Oh, I always hated surprises. I wanted to give Cornelia the amethyst set—Cornelia, you're to have the amethyst set, but Hapsy's to wear it when she wants, and, Doctor Harry, do shut up. Nobody sent for you. Oh, my dear Lord, do wait a minute. I meant to do something about the Forty Acres, Jimmy doesn't need it and Lydia will later on, with that worthless husband of hers. I meant to finish the altar cloth and send six bottles of wine to Sister Borgia for her dyspepsia. I want to send six bottles of wine to Sister Borgia, Father Connolly, now don't let me forget.

Cornelia's voice made short turns and tilted over and crashed. "Oh, Mother, oh, Mother, oh, Mother . . . ."

60 "I'm not going, Cornelia. I'm taken by surprise. I can't go."

You'll see Hapsy again. What about her? "I thought you'd never come." Granny made a long journey outward, looking for Hapsy. What if I don't find her? What then? Her heart sank down and down, there was no bottom to death, she couldn't come to the end of it. The blue light from Cornelia's lampshade drew into a tiny point in the center of her brain, it flickered and winked like an eye, quietly it fluttered and dwindled. Granny lay curled down within herself, amazed and watchful, starting at the point of light that was herself; her body was now only a deeper mass of shadow in an endless darkness and this darkness would curl around the light and swallow it up. God, give a sign!

For the second time there was no sign. Again no bridegroom and the priest in the house. She could not remember any other sorrow because this grief wiped them all away. Oh, no, there's nothing more cruel than this—I'll never forgive it. She stretched herself with a deep breath and blew out the light.

[1929]

Topics for Critical Thinking and Writing

1. In a paragraph characterize Granny Weatherall. In another paragraph evaluate her claim that the anguish of the jilting has been compensated for by her subsequent life.
2. The final paragraph alludes to Christ's parable of the bridegroom (Matthew 25.1–13). With this allusion in mind, write a paragraph explaining the title of the story.

JOSÉ ARMAS

Born in 1944, José Armas has been a teacher (at the University of New Mexico and at the University of Albuquerque), publisher, critic, and community organizer. His interest in community affairs won him a fellowship, which in 1974–1975 brought him into association with the Urban Planning Department at the Massachusetts Institute of Technology. In 1980 he was awarded a writing fellowship by the National Endowment for the Arts, and he now writes a column on Hispanic affairs for The Albuquerque Journal.

El Tonto del Barrio[1]

Romero Estrado was called "El Cotorro"[2] because he was always whistling and singing. He made nice music even though his songs were spontaneous compositions made up of words with sounds that he liked but which seldom made any sense. But that didn't seem to bother either Romero or anyone else in the Golden Heights Centro where he lived. Not even the kids made fun of him. It just was not permitted.

Romero had a ritual that he followed almost every day. After breakfast he would get his broom and go up and down the main street of the Golden Heights Centro whistling and singing and sweeping the sidewalks for all the businesses. He would sweep in front of the Tortillería America,[3] the XXX Liquor Store, the Tres Milpas[4] Bar run by Tino Gabaldon, Barelas' Barber Shop, the used furniture store owned by Goldstein, El Centro Market of the Avila family, the Model Cities Office, and Lourdes Printing Store. Then, in the afternoons, he would come back and sit in Barelas' Barber Shop and spend the day looking at magazines and watching and waving to the passing people as he sang and composed his songs without a care in the world.

When business was slow, Barelas would let him sit in the barber's chair. Romero loved it. It was a routine that Romero kept every day except Sundays and Mondays when Barelas' Barber Shop was closed. After a period of years, people

---

[1]**El Tonto del Barrio** the barrio dummy (in the United States, a barrio is a Spanish-speaking community) (all notes are by the editors).   [2]**El Cotorro** The Parrot.   [3]**Tortillería America** Tortilla Factory.   [4]**Tres Milpas** Three Cornfields.

in the barrio got used to seeing Romero do his little task of sweeping the sidewalks and sitting in Barelas' Barber Shop. If he didn't show up one day someone assumed the responsibility to go to his house to see if he was ill. People would stop to say hello to Romero on the street and although he never initiated a conversation while he was sober, he always smiled and responded cheerfully to everyone. People passing the barber shop in the afternoons made it a point to wave even though they couldn't see him; they knew he was in there and was expecting some salutation.

When he was feeling real good, Romero would sweep in front of the houses on both sides of the block also. He took his job seriously and took great care to sweep cleanly, between the cracks and even between the sides of buildings. The dirt and small scraps went into the gutter. The bottles and bigger pieces of litter were put carefully in cardboard boxes, ready for the garbage man.

5   If he did it the way he wanted, the work took him the whole morning. And always cheerful—always with some song.

Only once did someone call attention to his work. Frank Avila told him in jest that Romero had forgotten to pick up an empty bottle of wine from his door. Romero was so offended and made such a commotion that it got around very quickly that no one should criticize his work. There was, in fact, no reason to.

Although it had been long acknowledged that Romero was a little "touched," he fit very well into the community. He was a respected citizen.

He could be found at the Tres Milpas Bar drinking his occasional beer in the evenings. Romero had a rivalry going with the Ranchera songs on the jukebox. He would try to outsing the songs using the same melody but inserting his own selection of random words. Sometimes, like all people, he would "bust out" and get drunk.

One could always tell when Romero was getting drunk because he would begin telling everyone that he loved them.

10   "I looov youuu," he would sing to someone and offer to compose them a song.

"Ta bueno, Romero. Ta bueno, ya bete,"[5] they would tell him.

Sometimes when he got too drunk he would crap in his pants and then Tino would make him go home.

Romero received some money from Social Security but it wasn't much. None of the merchants gave him any credit because he would always forget to pay his bills. He didn't do it on purpose, he just forgot and spent his money on something else. So instead, the businessmen preferred to do little things for him occasionally. Barelas would trim his hair when things were slow. The Tortillería America would give him menudo[6] and fresh-made tortillas at noon when he was finished with his sweeping. El Centro Market would give him the overripe fruit and broken boxes of food that no one else would buy. Although it was unspoken and unwritten, there was an agreement that existed between Romero and the Golden Heights Centro. Romero kept the sidewalks clean and the barrio looked after him. It was a contract that worked well for a long time.

Then, when Seferino, Barelas' oldest son, graduated from high school he went to work in the barber shop for the summer. Seferino was a conscientious

---

[5]**Ta bueno, ya bete** OK, now go away.   [6]**menudo** tripe soup.

and sensitive young man and it wasn't long before he took notice of Romero and came to feel sorry for him.

15   One day when Romero was in the shop Seferino decided to act.

"Mira, Romero. Yo te doy 50 centavos por cada día que me barres la banqueta. Fifty cents for every day you sweep the sidewalk for us. Qué te parece?"[7]

Romero thought about it carefully.

"Hecho! Done!" he exclaimed. He started for home right away to get his broom.

"Why did you do that for, m'ijo?"[8] asked Barelas.

20   "It don't seem right, Dad. The man works and no one pays him for his work. Everyone should get paid for what they do."

"He don't need no pay. Romero has everything he needs."

"It's not the same, Dad. How would you like to do what he does and be treated the same way? It's degrading the way he has to go around getting scraps and handouts."

"I'm not Romero. Besides you don't know about these things, m'ijo. Romero would be unhappy if his schedule was upset. Right now everyone likes him and takes care of him. He sweeps the sidewalks because he wants something to do, not because he wants money."

"I'll pay him out of my money, don't worry about it then."

25   "The money is not the point. The point is that money will not help Romero. Don't you understand that?"

"Look, Dad. Just put yourself in his place. Would you do it? Would you cut hair for nothing?"

Barelas just knew his son was putting something over on him but he didn't know how to answer. It seemed to make sense the way Seferino explained it. But it still went against his "instinct." On the other hand, Seferino had gone and finished high school. He must know something. There were few kids who had finished high school in the barrio, and fewer who had gone to college. Barelas knew them all. He noted (with some pride) that Seferino was going to be enrolled at Harvard University this year. That must count for something, he thought. Barelas himself had never gone to school. So maybe his son had something there. On the other hand . . . it upset Barelas that he wasn't able to get Seferino to see the issue. How can we be so far apart on something so simple, he thought. But he decided not to say anything else about it.

Romero came back right away and swept the front of Barelas' shop again and put what little dirt he found into the curb. He swept up the gutter, put the trash in a shoe box and threw it in a garbage can.

Seferino watched with pride as Romero went about his job and when he was finished he went outside and shook Romero's hand. Seferino told him he had done a good job. Romero beamed.

30   Manolo was coming into the shop to get his hair cut as Seferino was giving Romero his wages. He noticed Romero with his broom.

"What's going on?" he asked. Barelas shrugged his shoulders. "Qué tiene Romero?[9] Is he sick or something?"

"No, he's not sick," explained Seferino, who had now come inside. He told Manolo the story.

---

[7]**Qué te parece?** How does that strike you?   [8]**m'ijo** (mi hijo), my son.   [9]**Qué tiene Romero?** What's with Romero?

"We're going to make Romero a businessman," said Seferino. "Do you realize how much money Romero would make if everyone paid him just fifty cents a day? Like my dad says, 'Everyone should be able to keep his dignity, no matter how poor.' And he does a job, you know."

"Well, it makes sense," said Manolo.

35 "Hey, maybe I'll ask people to do that," said Seferino. "That way the poor old man could make a decent wage. Do you want to help, Manolo? You can go with me to ask people to pay him."

"Well," said Manolo as he glanced at Barelas, "I'm not too good at asking people for money."

This did not discourage Seferino. He went out and contacted all the businesses on his own, but no one else wanted to contribute. This didn't discourage Seferino either. He went on giving Romero fifty cents a day.

After a while, Seferino heard that Romero had asked for credit at the grocery store. "See, Dad. What did I tell you? Things are getting better for him already. He's becoming his own man. And look. It's only been a couple of weeks." Barelas did not reply.

But then the next week Romero did not show up to sweep any sidewalks. He was around but he didn't do any work for anybody the entire week. He walked around Golden Heights Centro in his best gray work pants and his slouch hat, looking important and making it a point to walk right past the barber shop every little while.

40 Of course, the people in the Golden Heights Centro noticed the change immediately, and since they saw Romero in the street, they knew he wasn't ill. But the change was clearly disturbing the community. They discussed him in the Tortillería America where people got together for coffee, and at the Tres Milpas Bar. Everywhere the topic of conversation was the great change that had come over Romero. Only Barelas did not talk about it.

The following week Romero came into the barber shop and asked to talk with Seferino in private. Barelas knew immediately something was wrong. Romero never initiated a conversation unless he was drunk.

They went into the back room where Barelas could not hear and then Romero informed Seferino, "I want a raise."

"What? What do you mean, a raise? You haven't been around for a week. You only worked a few weeks and now you want a raise?" Seferino was clearly angry but Romero was calm and insistent.

Romero correctly pointed out that he had been sweeping the sidewalks for a long time. Even before Seferino finished high school.

45 "I deserve a raise," he repeated after an eloquent presentation.

Seferino looked coldly at Romero. It was clearly a stand-off.

Then Seferino said, "Look, maybe we should forget the whole thing. I was just trying to help you out and look at what you do."

Romero held his ground. "I helped you out too. No one told me to do it and I did it anyway. I helped you many years."

"Well, let's forget about the whole thing then," said Seferino.

50 "I quit then," said Romero.

"Quit?" exclaimed Seferino as he laughed at Romero.

"Quit! I quit!" said Romero as he walked out the front of the shop past Barelas, who was cutting a customer's hair.

Seferino came out shaking his head and laughing.

"Can you imagine that old guy?"

55   Barelas did not seem too amused. He felt he could have predicted that something bad like this would happen.

Romero began sweeping the sidewalks again the next day with the exception
that when he came to the barber shop he would go around it and continue
sweeping the rest of the sidewalks. He did this for the rest of the week. And the
following Tuesday he began sweeping the sidewalk all the way up to the shop
and then pushing the trash to the sidewalk in front of the barber shop. Romero
then stopped coming to the barber shop in the afternoon.

The barrio buzzed with fact and rumor about Romero. Tino commented that
Romero was not singing anymore. Even if someone offered to buy him a beer he
wouldn't sing. Frank Avila said the neighbors were complaining because he was
leaving his TV on loud the whole day and night. He still greeted people but seldom smiled. He had run up a big bill at the liquor store and when the manager
stopped his credit, he caught Romero stealing bottles of whiskey. He was also getting careless about his dress. He didn't shave and clean like he used to. Women
complained that he walked around in soiled pants, that he smelled bad. Even one
of the little kids complained that Romero had kicked his puppy, but that seemed
hard to believe.

Barelas felt terrible. He felt responsible. But he couldn't convince Seferino
that what he had done was wrong. Barelas himself stopped going to the Tres
Milpas Bar after work to avoid hearing about Romero. Once he came across
Romero on the street and Barelas said hello but with a sense of guilt. Romero responded, avoiding Barelas' eyes and moving past him awkwardly and quickly.
Romero's behavior continued to get erratic and some people started talking about
having Romero committed.

"You can't do that," said Barelas when he was presented with a petition.

60   "He's flipped," said Tino, who made up part of the delegation circulating the
petition. "No one likes Romero more than I do, you know that Barelas."

"But he's really crazy," said Frank Avila.

"He was crazy before. No one noticed," pleaded Barelas.

"But it was a crazy we could depend on. Now he just wants to sit on the curb
and pull up the women's skirts. It's terrible. The women are going crazy. He's also
running into the street stopping the traffic. You see how he is. What choice do we
have?"

"It's for his own good," put in one of the workers from the Model Cities
Office. Barelas dismissed them as outsiders. Seferino was there and wanted to say
something but a look from Barelas stopped him.

65   "We just can't do that," insisted Barelas. "Let's wait. Maybe he's just going
through a cycle. Look. We've had a full moon recently, qué no?[10] That must be it.
You know how the moon affects people in his condition."

"I don't know," said Tino. "What if he hurts. . . ."

"He's not going to hurt anyone," cut in Barelas.

"No, Barelas. I was going to say, what if he hurts himself. He has no one at
home. I'd say, let him come home with me for a while but you know how stubborn he is. You can't even talk to him any more."

"He gives everyone the finger when they try to pull him out of the traffic,"
said Frank Avila. "The cops have missed him, but it won't be long before they see
him doing some of his antics and arrest him. Then what? Then the poor guy is in
real trouble."

---

[10]**qué no?** right?

70   "Well, look," said Barelas. "How many names you got on the list?"

Tino responded slowly, "Well, we sort of wanted you to start off the list."

"Let's wait a while longer," said Barelas. "I just know that Romero will come around. Let's wait just a while, okay?"

No one had the heart to fight the issue and so they postponed the petition.

There was no dramatic change in Romero even though the full moon had completed its cycle. Still, no one initiated the petition again and then in the middle of August Seferino left for Cambridge to look for housing and to register early for school. Suddenly everything began to change again. One day Romero began sweeping the entire sidewalk again. His spirits began to pick up and his strange antics began to disappear.

75   At the Tortillería America the original committee met for coffee and the talk turned to Romero.

"He's going to be all right now," said a jubilant Barelas. "I guarantee it."

"Well, don't hold your breath yet," said Tino. "The full moon is coming up again."

"Yeah," said Frank Avila dejectedly.

When the next full moon was in force the group was together again drinking coffee and Tino asked, "Well, how's Romero doing?"

80   Barelas smiled and said, "Well. Singing songs like crazy."

[1982]

Topics for Critical Thinking and Writing

1. What sort of man do you think Barelas is? In your response take account of the fact that the townspeople "sort of want" Barelas "to start off the list" of petitioners seeking to commit Romero.
2. The narrator, introducing the reader to Seferino, tells us that "Seferino was a conscientious and sensitive young man." Do you agree? Why, or why not?
3. What do you make of the last line of the story?
4. Do you think this story could take place in almost any community? If you did not grow up in a barrio, could it take place in your community?

LESLIE MARMON SILKO

Leslie Marmon Silko was born in 1948 in Albuquerque, New Mexico, and grew up on the Laguna Pueblo Reservation some fifty miles to the west. Of her family she says,

> *We are mixed blood—Laguna, Mexican, white. . . . All those languages, all those ways of living are combined, and we live somewhere on the fringes of all three. But I don't apologize for this any more—not to whites, not to full bloods—our origin is unlike any other. My poetry, my storytelling rise out of this source.*

After graduating from the University of New Mexico in 1969, Silko entered law school but soon left to become a writer. She taught for two years at Navajo Community College at Many Farms, Arizona, and then went to Alaska for two years where she studied Eskimo-Aleut culture and worked on a novel, Ceremony. *After returning to the Southwest, she taught at the University of Arizona and then at the University of New Mexico.*

In addition to writing stories, a novel, and poems, Silko has written the screenplay for Marlon Brando's film Black Elk. *In 1981 she was awarded one of the so-called "genius grants" from the MacArthur Foundation, which supports "exceptionally talented individuals."*

The Man to Send Rain Clouds

One

They found him under a big cottonwood tree. His Levi jacket and pants were faded light-blue so that he had been easy to find. The big cottonwood tree stood apart from a small grove of winterbare cottonwoods which grew in the wide, sandy arroyo. He had been dead for a day or more, and the sheep had wandered and scattered up and down the arroyo. Leon and his brother-in-law, Ken, gathered the sheep and left them in the pen at the sheep camp before they returned to the cottonwood tree. Leon waited under the tree while Ken drove the truck through the deep sand to the edge of the arroyo. He squinted up at the sun and unzipped his jacket—it sure was hot for this time of year. But high and northwest the blue mountains were still deep in snow. Ken came sliding down the low, crumbling bank about fifty yards down, and he was bringing the red blanket.

Before they wrapped the old man, Leon took a piece of string out of his pocket and tied a small gray feather in the old man's long white hair. Ken gave him the paint. Across the brown wrinkled forehead he drew a streak of white and along the high cheekbones he drew a strip of blue paint. He paused and watched Ken throw pinches of corn meal and pollen into the wind that fluttered the small gray feather. Then Leon painted with yellow under the old man's broad nose, and finally, when he had painted green across the chin, he smiled.

"Send us rain clouds, Grandfather." They laid the bundle in the back of the pickup and covered it with a heavy tarp before they started back to the pueblo.

They turned off the highway onto the sandy pueblo road. Not long after they passed the store and post office they saw Father Paul's car coming toward them. When he recognized their faces he slowed his car and waved for them to stop. The young priest rolled down the car window.

5   "Did you find old Teofilo?" he asked loudly.

Leon stopped the truck. "Good morning, Father. We were just out to the sheep camp. Everything is O.K. now."

"Thank God for that. Teofilo is a very old man. You really shouldn't allow him to stay at the sheep camp alone."

"No, he won't do that any more now."

"Well, I'm glad you understand. I hope I'll be seeing you at Mass this week—we missed you last Sunday. See if you can get old Teofilo to come with you." The priest smiled and waved at them as they drove away.

Two

10 Louise and Teresa were waiting. The table was set for lunch, and the coffee was boiling on the black iron stove. Leon looked at Louise and then at Teresa.

"We found him under a cottonwood tree in the big arroyo near sheep camp. I guess he sat down to rest in the shade and never got up again." Leon walked toward the old man's head. The red plaid shawl had been shaken and spread carefully over the bed, and a new brown flannel shirt and pair of stiff new Levis were arranged neatly beside the pillow. Louise held the screen door open while Leon and Ken carried in the red blanket. He looked small and shriveled, and after they dressed him in the new shirt and pants he seemed more shrunken.

It was noontime now because the church bells rang the Angelus.[1] They ate the beans with hot bread, and nobody said anything until after Teresa poured the coffee.

Ken stood up and put on his jacket. "I'll see about the grave-diggers. Only the top layer of soil is frozen. I think it can be ready before dark."

Leon nodded his head and finished his coffee. After Ken had been gone for a while, the neighbors and clanspeople came quietly to embrace Teofilo's family and to leave food on the table because the grave-diggers would come to eat when they were finished.

Three

15 The sky in the west was full of pale-yellow light. Louise stood outside with her hands in the pockets of Leon's green army jacket that was too big for her. The funeral was over, and the old men had taken their candles and medicine bags and were gone. She waited until the body was laid into the pickup before she said anything to Leon. She touched his arm, and he noticed that her hands were still dusty from the corn meal that she had sprinkled around the old man. When she spoke, Leon could not hear her.

"What did you say? I didn't hear you."

"I said that I had been thinking about something."

"About what?"

"About the priest sprinkling holy water for Grandpa. So he won't be thirsty."

20 Leon stared at the new moccasins that Teofilo had made for the ceremonial dances in the summer. They were nearly hidden by the red blanket. It was getting colder, and the wind pushed gray dust down the narrow pueblo road. The sun was approaching the long mesa where it disappeared during the winter. Louise stood there shivering and watching his face. Then he zipped up his jacket and opened the truck door. "I'll see if he's there."

Ken stopped the pickup at the church, and Leon got out; and then Ken drove down the hill to the graveyard where people were waiting. Leon knocked at the old carved door with its symbols of the Lamb. While he waited he looked up at the twin bells from the king of Spain with the last sunlight pouring around them in their tower.

The priest opened the door and smiled when he saw who it was. "Come in! What brings you here this evening?"

---

[1]**Angelus** a devotional prayer commemorating the Annunciation (the angel Gabriel's announcement of the Incarnation of God in the human form of Jesus).

The priest walked toward the kitchen, and Leon stood with his cap in his hand, playing with the earflaps and examining the living room—the brown sofa, the green armchair, and the brass lamp that hung down from the ceiling by links of chain. The priest dragged a chair out of the kitchen and offered it to Leon.

"No thank you, Father. I only came to ask you if you would bring your holy water to the graveyard."

25   The priest turned away from Leon and looked out the window at the patio full of shadows and the dining-room windows of the nuns' cloister across the patio. The curtains were heavy, and the light from within faintly penetrated; it was impossible to see the nuns inside eating supper. "Why didn't you tell me he was dead? I could have brought the Last Rites anyway."

Leon smiled. "It wasn't necessary, Father."

The priest stared down at his scuffed brown loafers and the worn hem of his cassock. "For a Christian burial it was necessary."

His voice was distant, and Leon thought that his blue eyes looked tired.

"It's O.K., Father, we just want him to have plenty of water."

30   The priest sank down in the green chair and picked up a glossy missionary magazine. He turned the colored pages full of lepers and pagans without looking at them.

"You know I can't do that, Leon. There should have been the Last Rites and a funeral Mass at the very least."

Leon put on his green cap and pulled the flaps down over his ears. "It's getting late, Father. I've got to go."

When Leon opened the door Father Paul stood up and said, "Wait." He left the room and came back wearing a long brown overcoat. He followed Leon out the door and across the dim churchyard to the adobe steps in front of the church. They both stooped to fit through the low adobe entrance. And when they started down the hill to the graveyard only half of the sun was visible above the mesa.

The priest approached the grave slowly, wondering how they had managed to dig into the frozen ground, and then he remembered that this was New Mexico, and saw the pile of cold loose sand beside the hole. The people stood close to each other with little clouds of steam puffing from their faces. The priest looked at them and saw a pile of jackets, gloves, and scarves in the yellow, dry tumbleweeds that grew in the graveyard. He looked at the red blanket, not sure that Teofilo was so small, wondering if it wasn't some perverse Indian trick—something they did in March to ensure a good harvest—wondering if maybe old Teofilo was actually at sheep camp corraling the sheep for the night. But there he was, facing into a cold dry wind and squinting at the last sunlight, ready to bury a red wool blanket while the faces of the parishioners were in shadow with the last warmth of the sun on their backs.

35   His fingers were stiff, and it took them a long time to twist the lid off the holy water. Drops of water fell on the red blanket and soaked into dark icy spots. He sprinkled the grave and the water disappeared almost before it touched the dim, cold sand; it reminded him of something—he tried to remember what it was, because he thought if he could remember he might understand this. He sprinkled more water; he shook the container until it was empty, and the water fell through the light from sundown like August rain that fell while the sun was still shining, almost evaporating before it touched the wilted squash flowers.

The wind pulled at the priest's brown Franciscan robe and swirled away the corn meal and pollen that had been sprinkled on the blanket. They lowered the bundle into the ground, and they didn't bother to untie the stiff pieces of new rope that were tied around the ends of the blanket. The sun was gone, and over on the highway the eastbound lane was full of headlights. The priest walked away slowly. Leon watched him climb the hill, and when he had disappeared within the tall, thick walls, Leon turned to look up at the high blue mountains in the deep snow that reflected a faint red light from the west. He felt good because it was finished, and he was happy about the sprinkling of the holy water, now the old man could send them big thunderclouds for sure.

[1969]

Topics for Critical Thinking and Writing

1. How would you describe the response of Leon, Ken, Louise, and Teresa to Teofilo's death? To what degree does it resemble or differ from responses to death that you are familiar with?
2. How do the funeral rites resemble or differ from those of your community?
3. How well does Leon understand the priest? How well does the priest understand Leon?
4. At the end of the story we are told that Leon "felt good." Do you assume that the priest also felt good? Why, or why not?
5. From what point of view is the story told? Mark the passages where the narrator enters a character's mind, and then explain what, in your opinion, Silko gains (or loses) by doing so.

ROBERT FROST

Robert Frost (1874–1963) was born in California. After his father's death in 1885, Frost's mother brought the family to New England, where she taught in high schools in Massachusetts and New Hampshire. Frost studied for part of one term at Dartmouth College in New Hampshire, then did odd jobs (including teaching), and from 1897 to 1899 was enrolled as a special student at Harvard. He later farmed in New Hampshire, published a few poems in local newspapers, left the farm and taught again, and in 1912 left for England, where he hoped to achieve more popular success as a writer. By 1915 he had won a considerable reputation, and he returned to the United States, settling on a farm in New Hampshire and cultivating the image of the country-wise farmer-poet. In fact he was well read in the classics, in the Bible, and in English and American literature.

Among Frost's many comments about literature, here are three: "Writing is unboring to the extent that it is dramatic"; "Every poem is . . . a figure of the will braving alien entanglements"; and, finally, a poem "begins in delight and ends in wisdom. . . . It runs a course of lucky events, and ends in a clarification of life— not necessarily a great clarification, such as sects and cults are founded on, but in a momentary stay against confusion."

Come In

As I came to the edge of the woods,
Thrush music—hark!
Now if it was dusk outside,
Inside it was dark.

Too dark in the woods for a bird   5
By sleight of wing
To better its perch for the night,
Though it still could sing.

The last of the light of the sun
That had died in the west   10
Still lived for one song more
In a thrush's breast.

Far in the pillared dark
Thrush music went—
Almost like a call to come in   15
To the dark and lament.

But no, I was out for stars:
I would not come in.
I meant not even if asked,
And I hadn't been.   20

[1942]

Topic for Critical Thinking and Writing

In our headnote we quote Frost's comment that a poem is "a figure of the will braving alien entanglements." What "alien entanglements" are implied in this poem? One way to begin is to think about the words suggesting light and those suggesting dark. Is it too simple to say that in this poem darkness stands for evil? Explain.

ELIZABETH BISHOP

Elizabeth Bishop (1911–1979) was born in Worcester, Massachusetts. Because her father died when she was 8 months old and her mother was confined to a sanitarium four years later, Bishop was raised by relatives in New England and Nova Scotia. After graduating from Vassar College in 1934, where she was co-editor of the student literary magazine, she lived (on a small private income) for a while in Key West, France, and Mexico, and then for much of her adult life in Brazil, before returning to the United States to teach at Harvard. Her financial independence enabled her to write without worrying about the sales of her books and without having to devote energy to distracting jobs.

Filling Station

Oh, but it is dirty!
—this little filling station,
oil-soaked, oil-permeated
to a disturbing, over-all
black translucency.   5
Be careful with that match!

Father wears a dirty,
oil-soaked monkey suit
that cuts him under the arms,
and several quick and saucy   10
and greasy sons assist him
(it's a family filling station),
all quite thoroughly dirty.

Do they live in the station?
It has a cement porch   15
behind the pumps, and on it
a set of crushed and grease-
impregnated wickerwork;
on the wicker sofa
a dirty dog, quite comfy.   20

Some comic books provide
the only note of color—
of certain color. They lie
upon a big dim doily
draping a taboret   25
(part of the set), beside
a big hirsute begonia.

Why the extraneous plant?
Why the taboret?
Why, oh why, the doily?   30
(Embroidered in daisy stitch
with marguerites, I think,
and heavy with gray crochet.)

Somebody embroidered the doily.
Somebody waters the plant,   35
or oils it, maybe. Somebody
arranges the rows of cans
so that they softly say:
ESSO[1]—so—so—so
to high-strung automobiles.   40
Somebody loves us all.

[1965]

---

[1]ESSO a brand of gasoline, now Exxon (editors' note).

Topics for Critical Thinking and Writing

1. Taking into account only the first 14 lines, how would you characterize the speaker?
2. Robert Lowell, a poet and a friend of Elizabeth Bishop, said of her poems that they have "a tone of . . . grave tenderness and sorrowing amusement." Do you agree? If so, illustrate his comment by calling attention to specific passages in "Filling Station." If you disagree, how would you describe the tone?
3. In lines 21–30, what evidence suggests that the speaker feels that her taste is superior to the taste of the family? Does she change her mind by the end of the poem, or not?
4. "High-strung" in the last stanza *is* a rather odd way to characterize automobiles. What else strikes you as odd in the last stanza?
5. In two or three paragraphs, characterize a store, or stand, or territory that you know. Focus on an aspect of it (as Bishop focuses on the dirt and oil) so that readers can see what you find odd, or interesting, or striking about it.

ROBERT HERRICK

Robert Herrick (1591–1674) was born in London, the son of a goldsmith. After taking an MA at Cambridge, he was ordained in the Church of England, and later he was sent to the country parish of Dean Prior in Devonshire, where he wrote most of this poetry. A loyal supporter of the king, he was expelled in 1647 from his parish by the Puritans, though in 1662 he was restored to Dean Prior.

To the Virgins, to Make Much of Time

Gather ye rosebuds while ye may,
    Old Time is still a-flying;
And this same flower that smiles today,
    Tomorrow will be dying.   4

The glorious lamp of heaven, the sun,
    The higher he's a-getting,
The sooner will his race be run,
    And nearer he's to setting.   8

That age is best which is the first,
    When youth and blood are warmer;
But being spent, the worse, and worst
    Times still succeed the former.   12

Then be not coy, but use your time;
    And while ye may, go marry;
For having lost but once your prime,
    You may for ever tarry.   16

[1648]

Topics for Critical Thinking and Writing

1. Why "rosebuds" rather than "roses" in the first line?
2. What sort of person seems to be speaking? Young or old? How do you know?
3. Doubtless this advice has something to commend it but it cannot tell the whole truth, more or less, as proverbs can be both true and limited. (Proverbs in fact are often contradictory: "Look before you leap" is pretty good advice, but so is "He who hesitates is lost"; "Birds of a feather flock together" is true—sometimes—but so is "Opposites attract.") In short, does the value of this poem depend on the soundness of its advice? Explain.

LYN LIFSHIN

Born in Burlington, Vermont, in 1944 and educated at Syracuse University and the University of Vermont, Lyn Lifshin has written many books of poetry on a range of topics, from Shaker communities of early America to Eskimo culture in the Arctic. Much of her work shows a strong feminist concern.

My Mother and the Bed

No, not that way she'd
say when I was 7, pulling
the bottom sheet smooth,
you've got to   saying
hospital corners,   5

I wet the bed much later
than I should, until
just writing this I
hadn't thought of
the connection   10

My mother would never
sleep on sheets someone
else had   I never
saw any stains on hers
tho her bedroom was   15

a maze of powder   hair
pins   black dresses
Sometimes she brings her
own sheets to my house,
carries toilet seat covers   20

Did anybody sleep
in my   she always asks
Her sheets   her hair
she says the rooms here
smell funny   25

We drive at 3 am
slowly into Boston and
strip what looks like
two clean beds as the
sky gets light   I   30

smooth on the form
fitted flower bottom,
she redoes it

She thinks of my life
as a bed only she   35
can make right

[1999]

Topics for Critical Thinking and Writing

1. What do you make of the extra spaces—for instance, the space between "to" and "saying" in line 4? In reading the poem aloud, how do you "read" the spaces?
2. Would you agree that the poem is humorous and, on the whole, genial? Or do you think that bitterness overshadows the humor? Explain.
3. One student made the suggestion that the final stanza, perhaps because it seems to "explain" the poem to the reader, is the least effective part of the poem. Do you agree? If you do, write a new final stanza.

MARTÍN ESPADA

Martin Espada was born in Brooklyn in 1957. He received a bachelor's degree from the University of Wisconsin and a law degree from Northeastern University. A poet who publishes regularly, Espada is also Outreach Coordinator and Supervisor of Lawyers of the Arts at the Artists' Foundation in Boston.

Bully

Boston, Massachusetts, 1987

In the school auditorium,
the Theodore Roosevelt statue;
is nostalgic
for the Spanish-American War,
each fist lonely for a saber,   5
or the reins of anguish-eyed horses,
or a podium to clatter with speeches
glorying in the malaria of conquest.

But now the Roosevelt school
is pronounced *Hernández*.   10
Puerto Rico has invaded Roosevelt

with its army of Spanish-singing children
in the hallways,
brown children devouring
the stockpiles of the cafeteria,   15
children painting *Taíno* ancestors
that leap naked across murals.

Roosevelt is surrounded
by all the faces
he ever shoved in eugenic spite   20
and cursed as mongrels, skin of one race,
hair and cheekbones of another.

Once Marines tramped
from the newsreel of his imagination;
now children plot to spray graffiti   25
in parrot-brilliant colors across the Victorian mustache
and monocle.

[1990]

Topics for Critical Thinking and Writing

1. If you are not sure what Theodore Roosevelt was famous for, consult an encyclopedia. What *was* he famous for? In the first stanza, what words best express
   Espada's attitude toward him?
2. In the second stanza, what does Espada means when he says "Puerto Rico has
   invaded Roosevelt"? What does he mean by an "*army* of Spanish-singing children"? What are the *Taíno?*
3. What does "bully" mean as a noun? As an adjective?
4. Roosevelt was a great believer in what is called The Melting Pot Theory of
   America. What is this theory? do you think there is a great deal to it, something
   to it, or nothing to it? Why?
5. Here is a quotation from one of Roosevelt's speeches:

   > Every immigrant who comes here should be required within five years to
   > learn English or leave the country.

   What do you think of this idea? Why? Suppose that for some reason (perhaps
   political, perhaps economic) you decided to spend the rest of your life in, say,
   Argentina, or Germany, or Israel, or Nigeria. Do you think the government
   might reasonably require you to learn the language? Why?

5

Other Kinds of Writing about Literature

SUMMARY

The essay on "The Story of an Hour" in Chapter 2 does not include a *summary* because the writer knew that all of her readers were thoroughly familiar with Chopin's story. Sometimes, however, it is advisable to summarize the work you are writing about, thus reminding a reader who has not read the work recently, or even informing a reader who may never have read the work. A review of a new work of literature or of a new film, for instance, usually includes a summary, on the assumption that readers are unfamiliar with it.

A summary is a brief restatement or condensation of the plot. Consider this **summary** of Chopin's "The Story of an Hour."

> A newspaper office reports that Brently Mallard has been killed in a railroad accident. When the news is gently broken to Mrs. Mallard by her sister Josephine, Mrs. Mallard weeps wildly and then shuts herself up in her room, where she sinks into an armchair. Staring dully through the window, she sees the signs of spring, and then an unnameable sensation possesses her. She tries to reject it but finally abandons herself to it. Renewed, she exults in her freedom, in the thought that at last the days will be her own. She finally comes out of the room, embraces her sister, and descends the stairs. A moment later her husband--who in fact had not been in the accident--enters. Mrs. Mallard dies--of the joy that kills, according to the doctors' diagnosis.

Here are a few principles that govern summaries:

1. A summary is **much briefer than the original**. It is not a paraphrase—a word-by-word translation of someone's words into your own. A paraphrase is usually at least as long as the original, whereas a summary is rarely longer than one-fourth of the original and is usually much shorter. A novel may be summarized in a few paragraphs, or even in one paragraph.
2. A summary **usually achieves its brevity by omitting almost all of the concrete details of the original** and by omitting minor characters and episodes. Notice that the summary of "The Story of an Hour" omits the friend of the family, omits specifying the signs of spring, and omits the business of the sister imploring Mrs. Mallard to open the door.
3. A summary is **as accurate as possible**, given the limits of space. It has no value if it misrepresents the point of the original.
4. A summary is **normally written in the present tense**. Thus "A newspaper office reports . . . , Mrs. Mallard weeps. . . ."

5. If the summary is brief (say, fewer than 250 words), it **may be given as a single paragraph**. If you are summarizing a long work, you may feel that a longer summary is needed. In this case your reader will be grateful to you if you divide the summary into paragraphs. As you draft your summary, you may find **natural divisions**. For instance, the scene of the story may change midway, giving you the opportunity to use two paragraphs. Or you may want to summarize a five-act play in five paragraphs.

6. The writer of a summary **need not make the points in the same order as that of the original**. If the writer of an essay has delayed revealing the main point until the end of the essay, the summary may rearrange the order, stating the main point first. Occasionally, for instance, if the original author has presented an argument in a disorderly or confusing sequence, a summary is written to disengage the author's argument from its confusing structure.

7. Because a summary is openly based on someone else's views, it is usually **not necessary to use quotation marks** around key words or phrases from the original. Nor is it necessary to repeat "he says" or "she goes on to prove." From the opening sentence of a summary it should be clear that what follows is what the original author says.

Summaries have their place in essays, but remember that a summary is not an analysis; it is only a summary.

PARAPHRASE
What Paraphrase Is

A **paraphrase** is a restatement—a sort of translation in the same language—of material that may in its original form be somewhat obscure to a reader. A native speaker of English will not need a paraphrase of "Thirty days hath September," though a nonnative speaker might be puzzled by two things, the meaning of *hath* and the inverted word order. For such a reader, "September has thirty days" would be a helpful paraphrase.

Although a paraphrase seeks to make clear the gist of the original, if the original is even a little more complex than "Thirty days hath September" the paraphrase will—in the process of clarifying something—lose something, since the substitution of one word for another will change the meaning. For instance, "Shut up" and "Be quiet" do not say exactly the same thing; the former (in addition to asking for quiet) says that the speaker is rude, or perhaps it says that the speaker feels little respect for the auditor, but the paraphrase loses all of this.

The Value of Paraphrase

Still, a paraphrase can be a first step in helping a reader to understand a line that includes an obsolete word or phrase, or a word or phrase that is current only in one region. In a poem by Emily Dickinson (1830–1886), the following line appears:

The sun engrossed the East. . . .

"Engrossed" here has (perhaps among other meanings) a special commercial meaning, "to acquire most or all of a commodity; to monopolize the market," so a paraphrase of the line might go thus:

The sun took over all of the east.

(It's worth mentioning, parenthetically, that you should have at your elbow a good desk dictionary, such as *The American Heritage Dictionary of the English Language*, fourth edition. Writers—especially poets—expect you to pay close attention to every word. If a word puzzles you, look it up.)

Idioms, as well as words, may puzzle a reader. The Anglo-Irish poet William Butler Yeats (1865–1939) begins one poem with

The friends that have it I do wrong. . . .

Because the idiom "to have it" (meaning "to believe that," "to think that") is unfamiliar to many American readers today, a discussion of the poem might include a **paraphrase**—a rewording, a translation into more familiar language, such as

The friends who think that I am doing the wrong thing. . . .

Perhaps the rest of the poem is immediately clear, but in any case here is the entire poem, followed by a paraphrase:

The friends that have it I do wrong
When ever I remake a song,
Should know what issue is at stake:
It is myself that I remake.

Now for the paraphrase:

The friends who think that I am doing the wrong thing when I revise one of my poems should be informed what the important issue is: I'm not just revising a poem—rather, I am revising myself (my thoughts, feelings).

Here, as with any paraphrase, the meaning is not translated exactly; there is some distortion. For instance, if "song" in the original is clarified by "poem" in the paraphrase, it is also altered; the paraphrase loses the sense of lyricism that is implicit in "song." Further, "Should know what issue is at stake" (in the original) is ambiguous. Does "should" mean "ought," as in "You should know better than to speak so rudely," or does it mean "deserve to be informed," as in "You ought to know that I am thinking about quitting"?

Granted that a paraphrase may miss a great deal, a paraphrase often helps you, or your reader, to understand at least the surface meaning, and the act of paraphrasing will usually help you to understand at least some of the implicit meaning. Furthermore, a paraphrase makes you see that the original writer's words (if the work is a good one) are exactly right, better than any words we might substitute. It becomes clear that the thing said in the original—not only the rough "idea" expressed but the precise tone with which it is expressed—is a sharply defined experience.

LITERARY RESPONSE

Anything that you write about a work of literature is a response, even if it seems to be as matter-of-fact as a summary. It's sometimes useful to compare your summary with that of a classmate. You may be surprised to find that the two summaries differ considerably—though when you think about it, it isn't really surprising. Two different people are saying what they think is the gist of the work, and their views are shaped, to some degree, by such things as their gender, their ethnicity, and their experience (including, of course, their *literary* experience).

But when we talk about writing a response, we usually mean something more avowedly personal, something like an entry in a journal, where the writer may set forth an emotional response, perhaps relating the work to one of his or her own experiences. (On journals, see pages 18–19.)

Writing a Literary Response

You may want to rewrite a literary work, for instance by giving it a different ending or by writing an epilogue in which you show the characters 20 years later. (We have already talked about the possibility of writing a sequel to Chopin's "Ripe Figs," or writing a letter from Babette to Maman-Nainaine, or writing Babette's memoirs.) Or you might want to rewrite the work by presenting the characters from a different point of view. The student who in an essay on Thurber's "The Secret Life of Walter Mitty" argued that Mitty *needed* someone very much like Mrs. Mitty might well have rewritten Thurber's story along those lines. The fun for the reader would of course reside largely in hearing the story reinterpreted, in seeing the story turned inside out.

A Story by a Student: "The Ticket (A Different View of 'The Story of an Hour')"

Here is an example, written by Lola Lee Loveall for a course taught by Diana Muir at Solano Community College. Ms. Loveall's story is a response to Kate Chopin's "The Story of an Hour" (p. 13). Notice that Loveall's first sentence is close to her source—a good way to get started, but by no means the only way; notice, too, that elsewhere in her story she occasionally echoes Chopin—for instance, in the references to the treetops, the sparrows, and the latchkey. A reader enjoys detecting these echoes.

What is especially interesting, however, is that before she conceived her story Loveall presumably said to herself something like, "Well, Chopin's story is superb, but suppose we shift the focus a bit. Suppose we think about what it would be like, *from the husband's point of view,* to live with a woman who suffered from 'heart trouble,' a person whom one had to treat with 'great care'" (Chopin's words, in the first sentence of "The Story of an Hour"). "And what about Mrs. Mallard's sister, Josephine—so considerate of Mrs. Mallard? What, exactly, would *Mr.* Mallard think of her? Wouldn't he see her as a pain in the neck? And what might he be prompted to do? That is, how might this character in this situation respond?" And so Loveall's characters and her plot began to take shape. As part of the game, she committed herself to writing a plot that, in its broad outline, resembled Chopin's by being highly ironic. But read it yourself.

Loveall 1

Lola Lee Loveall

Professor Thatcher

English 102

15 March 2004

The Ticket

(A Different View of "The Story of an Hour")

Knowing full well his wife was afflicted with heart trouble,

Brently Mallard wondered how he was going to break the news

about the jacket. As he strode along his boots broke through the

shallow crust from the recent rain, and dust kicked up from the

well-worn wagon road came up to flavor his breathing. At least,

the gentle spring rain had settled the dusty powder even as it had

sprinkled his stiffly starched shirt which was already dampened

from the exertion of stamping along. The strenuous pace he set

himself to cover the intervening miles home helped him regain

his composure. Mr. Brently Mallard was always calm, cool, and

confident.

However, he hadn't been this morning when he stepped

aboard the train, took off his jacket and folded it neatly beside him,

and settled in his seat on the westbound train. He had been wildly

excited. Freedom was his. He was Free! He was off for California,

devil take the consequences! He would be his old self again, let the

chips fall where they may. And he would have been well on his

way, too, if that accursed ticket agent hadn't come bawling out,

"Mr. Mallard, you left your ticket on the counter!" just when

Mallard himself had spied that nosy Jan Ardan bidding her sister

goodbye several car lengths down the depot. How could he be so

unfortunate as to run into them both twice this morning? Earlier,

they had come into the bank just as the banker had extended the

thick envelope.

"You understand, this is just an advance against the estate for

a while?"

Only Mallard's persuasiveness could have extracted that

amount from the cagey old moneybags. Mallard had carefully

tucked it into his inside pocket.

This was the kind of spring day to fall in love--or lure an

adventurer to the top of the next hill. Sparrows hovered about

making happy sounds. Something about their movements

reminded Mallard of his wife--quick, fluttering, then darting away.

He had loved her at first for her delicate ways. They had

made a dashing pair--he so dark and worldly, she so fragile and

fair--but her delicacy was a trap, for it disguised the heart trouble,

bane of his life. Oh, he still took her a sip of brandy in bed in the

morning as the doctor had suggested, although, of course, it

wasn't his bed anymore. He had moved farther down the hall not

long after her sister, Josephine, came to help, quick to come when

Mrs. Mallard called, even in the middle of the night. After one

such sudden appearance one night--"I thought I heard you call"--

he had given up even sharing the same bed with his wife,

although there had been little real sharing there for some time.

"No children!" the doctor had cautioned.

Mallard concentrated harder on the problem of the missing jacket. What to say? She would notice. Maybe not right away, but she would be aware. Oh, he knew Louise's reaction. She would apparently take the news calmly, then make a sudden stab toward her side with her delicate hands, then straighten and walk away-- but not before he observed. A new jacket would cost money. Discussing money made the little drama happen more often, so now Mr. Mallard handled all the financial affairs, protecting her the best he could. After all, it was her inheritance, and he took great care with it, but there were the added costs: doctors, Josephine living with them, the medications, even his wife's brandy. Why, he checked it daily to be sure it was the proper strength. Of course, a man had to have a few pleasures, even if the cards did seem to fall against him more often than not. He manfully kept trying.

Everyone has a limit, though, and Mr. Mallard had reached his several days ago when the doctor had cautioned him again.

"She may go on like she is for years, or she may just keel over any time. However, the chances are she will gradually go downhill and need continual care. It is impossible to tell."

Mallard could not face "gradually go downhill." His manhood revolted against it. He was young, full of life. Let Josephine carry the chamber pot! After Louise's demise (whenever that occurred!)

Loveall 4

the simple estate which she had inherited reverted to Josephine.

Let her earn it. Also, good old friend Richards was always about

with a suggestion here or a word of comfort there for Louise.

They'd really not care too much if Mallard were a long time

absent.

As he drew nearer his home, Mallard continued to try to

calm his composure, which was difficult for he kept hearing the

sound of the train wheels as it pulled away, jacket, envelope, and

all, right before his panic-stricken eyes: CALIFORNIA; California;

california; california.

DUTY! It was his duty not to excite Louise. As he thought of

duty he unconsciously squared his drooping shoulders, and the

image of Sir Galahad flitted across his mind.

The treetops were aglow in the strange afterlight of the

storm. A shaft of sunlight shot through the leaves and fell upon

his face. He had come home.

He opened the front door with the latchkey. Fortunately, it

had been in his pants pocket.

Later, the doctors did not think Mr. Mallard's reaction

unusual, even when a slight smile appeared on the bereaved

husband's face. Grief causes strange reactions.

"He took it like a man," they said.

Only later, when the full significance of his loss reached

him, did he weep.

A Poem Based on a Poem

We begin with a poem by William Blake (1757–1827), an English Christian visionary poet.

The Tyger

Tyger! Tyger! burning bright
In the forests of the night,
What immortal hand or eye
Could frame thy fearful symmetry?   4

In what distant deeps or skies
Burnt the fire of thine eyes?
On what wings dare he aspire?
What the hand dare seize the fire?   8

And what shoulder, and what art,
Could twist the sinews of thy heart?
And, when thy heart began to beat,
What dread hand? and what dread feet?   12

What the hammer? what the chain?
In what furnace was thy brain?
What the anvil? What dread grasp
Dare its deadly terrors clasp?   16

When the stars threw down their spears,
And watered heaven with their tears,
Did he smile his work to see?
Did he who made the lamb make thee?   20

Tyger! Tyger! burning bright
In the forests of the night,
What immortal hand or eye,
Dare frame thy fearful symmetry?   24

[1794]

William Blake was the favorite poet of Allen Ginsberg (1926–1997). Ginsberg, a New Yorker who established his fame in San Francisco, was noted for his declamatory poetry and his celebration of outsiders, especially protestors against the wars in Korea and Vietnam. He often chanted Blake's poems at his own poetry readings. In the following poem X. J. Kennedy pays homage to Ginsberg by adopting the form of one of Ginsberg's favorite poems. Kennedy alludes, in his poem, to Ginsberg's left-wing activities ("Taunter of the ultra right"), his view that his hearers should drop out of a corrupt and repressive society, his interest in Buddhist mantras (syllables laden with mystic power), his antiwar activity ("Mantra-minded flower child"), his homosexuality ("Queer," "Queen"), and his use of finger cymbals in some of his readings. *Om* (line 9) is a syllable that begins several mantras. Ginsberg often had his audience utter the sound.

X. J. Kennedy

For Allen Ginsberg

Ginsberg, Ginsberg, burning bright,
Taunter of the ultra right,
What blink of the Buddha's eye
Chose the day for you to die?   4

Queer pied piper, howling wild,
Mantra-minded flower child,
Queen of Maytime, misrule's lord
Bawling, *Drop out! All aboard!*   8

Finger-cymbaled, chanting *Om*,
Foe of fascist, bane of bomb,
Proper poets' thorn-in-side,
Turner of a whole time's tide,   12

Who can fill your sloppy shoes?
What a catch for Death. We lose
Glee and sweetness, freaky light,
Ginsberg, Ginsberg, burning bright.   16

[1997]

Rewriting a Poem

William Butler Yeats: "Leda and the Swan"

William Butler Yeats (1865–1939) was born in Dublin, Ireland. The early Yeats was much interested in highly lyrical, romantic poetry, often drawing on Irish mythology. The later poems, from about 1910 (and especially after Yeats met Ezra Pound in 1911), are usually more colloquial. Although these later poems often employ mythological references, too, one feels that the poems are more down-to-earth. Yeats was awarded the Nobel Prize in Literature in 1923.

According to Greek mythology, Zeus fell in love with Leda, disguised himself as a swan, and raped her. Among the offspring of this union were Helen and Clytemnestra. Paris abducted Helen, causing the Greeks to raze Troy; Clytemnestra, wife of Agamemnon, murdered her husband on his triumphant return to Greece. Yeats saw political significance in the myth of beauty and war engendered by a god, but, as he tells us, when he was composing "Leda and the Swan" the political significance evaporated:

> *After the individualistic, demagogic movements, founded by Hobbes and popularized by the Encyclopaedists and the French Revolution, we have a soil so exhausted that it cannot grow that crop again for centuries. Then I thought "Nothing is now possible but some movement, or birth from above, preceded by some violent annunciation." My fancy began to play with Leda and the Swan for metaphor, and I began this poem, but as I wrote, bird and lady took such possession of the scene that all politics went out of it.*

The first version, "Annunciation," is from a manuscript dated September 18, 1923; the second was printed in a magazine, June 1924; the third, first published in his Collected Poems *of 1933, is Yeats's final one. But this third version had been almost fully achieved by 1925; the 1933 version differs from the 1925 version only in two punctuation marks: The question marks at the ends of lines 6 and 8 in the latest version were, in 1925, respectively, a comma and a semicolon.*

Annunciation

Now can the swooping Godhead have his will
Yet hovers, though her helpless thighs are pressed
By the webbed toes; and that all powerful bill
Has suddenly bowed her face upon his breast,   4
How can those terrified vague fingers push
The feathered glory from her loosening thighs?
All the stretched body's laid on that white rush
And feels the strange heart beating where it lies   8
A shudder in the loins engenders there
The broken wall, the burning roof and tower
And Agamemnon dead . . .
                              Being so caught up   12
Did nothing pass before her in the air?
Did she put on his knowledge with his power
Before the indifferent beak could let her drop.   [1923]

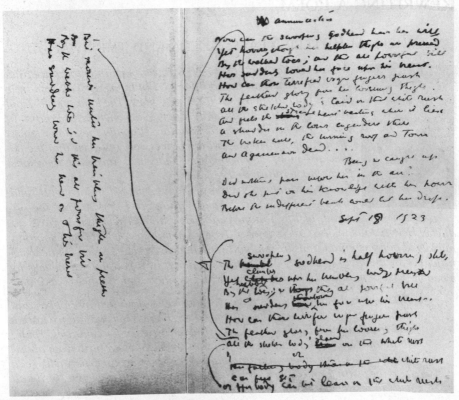

Yeats's first drafts of "Leda and the Swan" (1923).

Leda and the Swan

A rush, a sudden wheel, and hovering still
The bird descends, and her frail thighs are pressed
By the webbed toes, and that all-powerful bill
Has laid her helpless face upon his breast   4
How can those terrified vague fingers push
The feathered glory from her loosening thighs!
All the stretched body's laid on the white rush
And feels the strange heart beating where it lies;   8
A shudder in the loins engenders there
The broken wall, the burning roof and tower
And Agamemnon dead.
                            Being so caught up,   12
So mastered by the brute blood of the air,
Did she put on his knowledge with his power
Before the indifferent beak could let her drop?

                                                        [1924]

Leda and the Swan

A sudden blow: the great wings beating still
Above the staggering girl, her thighs caressed
By the dark webs, her nape caught in his bill,
He holds her helpless breast upon his breast.   4

How can those terrified vague fingers push
The feathered glory from her loosening thighs?
And how can body, laid in that white rush,
But feel the strange heart beating where it lies?   8

A shudder in the loins engenders there
The broken wall, the burning roof and tower
And Agamemnon dead.
                            Being so caught up,   12
So mastered by the brute blood of the air,
Did she put on his knowledge with his power
Before the indifferent beak could let her drop?

                                                        [1933]

MONA VAN DUYN

The first woman poet laureate of the United States (1992–1993), Mona Van Duyn was born in Waterloo, Iowa, in 1921, and educated at the University of Northern Iowa and the University of Iowa. Her first books, Valentines to the Wide World *(1959) and* A Time of Bees *(1964), were praised for their "simple, human subjects" and adroit handling of traditional forms. In 1971, Van Duyn received the National Book Award for* To See, To Take *(1970), and she has since then published a number of other books, including* Letters from a Father, and Other Poems *(1982) and* Near Changes *(1990). Much of her work has been gathered in* If It Be Not I: Collected Poems 1959–1982 *(1993).*

The following poem, "Leda," was first published in To See, To Take. *This same book includes another, longer poem, titled "Leda Reconsidered." Both can be understood as poetic responses to Yeats's "Leda and the Swan."*

Leda

> *"Did she put on his knowledge with his power*
> *Before the indifferent beak could let her drop?"*

Not even for a moment. He knew, for one thing, what he was.
When he saw the swan in her eyes he could let her drop.
In the first look of love men find their great disguise,
and collecting these rare pictures of himself was his life.   4

Her body became the consequence of his juice,
while her mind closed on a bird and went to sleep.
Later, with the children in school, she opened her eyes
and saw her own openness, and felt relief.   8

In men's stories her life ended with his loss.
She stiffened under the storm of his wings to a glassy shape,
stricken and mysterious and immortal. But the fact is,
she was not, for such an ending, abstract enough.   12

She tried for a while to understand what it was
that had happened, and then decided to let it drop.
She married a smaller man with a beaky nose,
and melted away in the storm of everyday life.   16

[1971]

Topics for Critical Thinking and Writing

1. Van Duyn uses as an epigraph, in quotation marks and italicized, the last lines of Yeats's poem. How do you understand these lines? Why do you think that Van Duyn chose to use them as an epigraph, in quotation marks and italicized? What does her poem gain (or lose) from this epigraph?
2. In line 2 Van Duyn writes, "When he saw the swan in her eyes." Is Van Duyn talking about Zeus's reflection in Leda's eyes, or about something else? And in line 3 she writes of "the first look of love." Is she talking about Zeus's "look of love" or Leda's?

3. The poem begins with its focus, in stanza 1, on the swan; but then in stanza 2 the focus, the point of view, shifts to Leda. Do you find this to be awkward? Or does it strike you as effective—and if so, in what ways?
4. In the second stanza, line 7, we read of "the children in school." Who are Leda's children? What does it tell you about Leda to find that the children are "in school"?
5. Can you explain lines 5–6? And what does it mean to say, in lines 11–12, that Leda was not "abstract enough"?
6. Consider the phrases "to let it drop" and "with a beaky nose": What is the tone of each of these phrases, and of the final stanza as a whole?
7. Can Van Duyn's poem stand alone and be effective? Or do you think that it is truly meaningful only for a reader who knows Yeats's poem?
8. Yeats's "Leda and the Swan" is a sonnet. Try to describe the form of Van Duyn's poems. Where do you find rhymes, or off-rhymes (also called "half-rhymes" or "imperfect rhymes," such as "come" and "home," or "mirth" and "forth")?
9. Which poem, Yeats's or Van Duyn's, do you like better? Why is that?

PARODY

One special kind of response is the **parody**, a comic form that imitates the original in a humorous way. It is a caricature in words. A parody may imitate the style of the original—let's say, short, punchy sentences—but apply this style to a subject that the original author would not be concerned with. Thus, because Ernest Hemingway often wrote short, simple sentences about tough guys engaged in activities such as hunting, fishing, and boxing, parodists of Hemingway are likely to use the same style, but for their subject they may choose something like opening the mail or preparing a cup of tea.

We once heard on the radio a parody of an announcer doing a baseball game. It went something like this:

> Well, here's Bill Shakespeare now, approaching the desk. Like so many other writers, Bill likes to work at a desk. In fact, just about every writer we know writes at a desk, but every writer has a particular way of approaching the desk and sitting at it. Bill is sitting down now; now he's adjusting the chair, moving it forward a little. Oh, he's just pushed the chair back an inch or two. He likes his chair to be just right. Now he's picking up a pen. It's a gray quill. I think it's the pen he uses when he writes a tragedy, and he's due for a tragedy—of his last five plays, only one was a tragedy, and two were comedies and two were history plays. But you never can tell with Bill, or "The Bard" as his fans call him. Some people call him "The Swan of Avon," but I'm told that he really hates that. Well, he's at the desk, and, you know, in circumstances like these, he might even sneak in a sonnet or two. Oh, he's put down the gray quill, and now he's trying a white one. Oh boy, oh boy, he's written a *word*. No, he's going for *a whole sentence!*

Parodies are, in a way, critical, but they are usually affectionate too. In the best parodies the reader feels that the writer admires the author being parodied. The distinguished sociologist Daniel Bell wrote a deliberate parody of sociological writing. It begins thus:

The purpose of this scene is to present a taxonomic dichotomization which would allow for unilinear comparison. In this fashion we could hope to distinguish the relevant variables which determine the functional specificities of social movements.

The journalist H. L. Mencken (1880–1956), who had a love-hate relationship with what he called the Great American Booboisie, wrote a parody in which he set forth the Declaration of Independence as it might have been written (or spoken) by Joe Sixpack in the mid-twentieth century. Here the target is not the original document but the twentieth-century American. The original document, you will remember, begins in this way:

> When in the Course of human events, it becomes necessary for one people to dissolve the political bands which have connected them with another, and to assume among the powers of the earth, the separate and equal station to which the Laws of Nature and of Nature's God entitle them, a decent respect to the opinions of mankind requires that they should declare the causes which impel them to the separation.

Now for Mencken's version:

> When things get so balled up that the people of a country got to cut loose from some other country, and go it on their own hook, without asking no permission from nobody, excepting maybe God Almighty, then they ought to let everybody know why they done it, so that everybody can see they are not trying to put nothing over on nobody.

WILLIAM CARLOS WILLIAMS

William Carlos Williams (1883–1963) was the son of an English traveling salesman and a Basque-Jewish woman. The couple met in Puerto Rico and settled in Rutherford, New Jersey, where Williams was born. He spent his life there, practicing as a pediatrician and writing poems in the moments between seeing patients.

This Is Just to Say

I have eaten
the plums
that were in
the icebox   4

and which
you were probably
saving
for breakfast   8

Forgive me
they were delicious
so sweet
and so cold   12

[1934]

Here are three parodies of Williams's poem, written by our students. The first is by Edward Rothko, the second by Julia Alfaro, and the third by Holly Chung.

I let out
the air
that was stored
in the tires

and which
your car
so badly
needed

I'm sorry
I like them
flat

    *   *   *

In your e-mail you said
that during spring break
we should meet
on the beach at Daytona

and we would have
fun, but I misread it
and here I am in Dayton

and I can't
forgive myself

    *   *   *

I always forget
to return
your phone calls

which you probably think
are so
important

Forgive me
but you are
such a pain
in the
neck

Topics for Critical Thinking and Writing

1. Do these poems sound like a poem by Williams? Why or why not? (We print other poems by Williams on pages 521 and 558.)
2. Write your own parody of "This Is Just to Say," apologizing for some action (real or imagined). Follow Williams's basic pattern: In the first stanza, state what you supposedly have done, in the second state what the person to whom you are apologizing probably was planning, and in the third stanza ask for forgiveness.

REVIEWING A DRAMATIC PRODUCTION

A review also is a response, since it normally includes an evaluation of the work, but at least at first glance it may seem to be an analytic essay. We'll talk about a review of a production of a play, but you can easily adapt what we say to a review of a book.

A review requires analytic skill, but it is not identical with an analysis. First of all, a reviewer normally assumes that the reader is unfamiliar with the production being reviewed, and unfamiliar with the play if the play is not a classic. Thus, the first paragraph usually provides a helpful introduction, along these lines:

> Marsha Norman's recent play, *'night, Mother*, a tragedy with only two actors and one set, shows us a woman's preparation for suicide. Jesse has concluded that she no longer wishes to live, and so she tries to put her affairs into order, which chiefly means preparing her rather uncomprehending mother to get along without her.

Inevitably some retelling of the plot is necessary if the play is new, and a summary of a sentence or two is acceptable even for a familiar play, but the review will chiefly be concerned with

1. describing,
2. analyzing, and, especially,
3. evaluating.

By the way, don't confuse description with analysis. Description tells what something—for instance, the set or the costumes—looks like; analysis tells us how it works, what it adds up to, what it contributes to the total effect.) If the play is new, much of the evaluation may center on the play itself, but if the play is a classic, the evaluation probably will be devoted chiefly to the acting, the set, and the direction.

Other points:

1. **Save the playbill.** It will give you the names of the actors, and perhaps a brief biography of the author, a synopsis of the plot, and a photograph of the set, all of which may be helpful.
2. **Draft your review as soon as possible,** while the performance is still fresh in your mind. If you can't draft it immediately after seeing the play, at least jot down some notes about the setting and the staging, the acting, and the audience's responses.
3. If possible, **read the play**—ideally, before the performance and again after it.
4. **In your first draft, don't worry about limitations of space.** Write as long a review as you can, putting down everything that comes to mind. Later you can cut it to the required length, retaining only the chief points and the necessary supporting details. But in your first draft try to produce a fairly full record of the performance and your response to it, so that a day or two later, when you revise, you won't have to trust a fading memory for details.

A Sample Review by a Student: "An Effective *Macbeth*"

If you read reviews of plays in *Time*, *Newsweek*, or a newspaper, you will soon develop a sense of what reviews do. The following example, an undergraduate's review of a college production of *Macbeth*, is typical except in one respect: Reviews of new plays, as we have already suggested, customarily include a few sentences summarizing the plot and classifying the play (a tragedy, a farce, a rock musical, or whatever), perhaps briefly putting it in the context of the author's other works. Because *Macbeth* is so widely known, however, the writer of this review chose not to risk offending her readers by telling them that *Macbeth* is a tragedy by Shakespeare.

PRELIMINARY JOTTINGS   During the two intermissions and immediately after the end of the performance, the reviewer made a few jottings, which the next day she rewrote:

Compare with last year's <u>Midsummer Night's Dream</u>
occasionally exciting production, strong visual effects
　　Useful?
witches: powerful, not funny
　　stage: battlefield? barren land?
　　costume: earth-colored rags
　　they seduce--even caress--Mac.
Macbeth
　　~~witches caress him~~
　　strong; also gentle (with Lady M)
Lady Macb.
　　sexy in speech about unsexing her
　　too attractive? Prob. ok
Banquo's ghost: naturalistic; covered with blood
Duncan: terrible; worst actor except for Lady Macduff's boy
costumes: leather, metal; only Duncan in robes
　　pipe framework used for D, and murder of Lady Macduff
　　forest; branches unrealistic; stylized? or cheesy?

THE FINISHED VERSION   The published review appears below, accompanied by some marginal notes in which we comment on its strengths.

Title implies thesis

An Effective *Macbeth*

Opening paragraph is informative, letting the reader know the reviewer's overall attitude

Macbeth at the University Theater is a thoughtful and occasionally exciting production, partly because the director, Mark Urice, has trusted Shakespeare and has not imposed a gimmick on the play. The characters do not wear cowboy costumes as they did in last year's production of *A Midsummer Night's Dream*.

Reviewer promptly turns to a major issue

Probably the chief problem confronting a director of *Macbeth* is how to present the witches so that they are powerful supernatural forces and not silly things that look as though they came from a Halloween party. Urice gives us ugly but not absurdly grotesque witches, and he introduces them most effectively. The stage seems to be a bombed-out battlefield littered with rocks and great chunks of earth, but some of these begin to stir—the earth seems to come alive—and the clods move, unfold, and become the witches, dressed in brown and dark gray rags. The suggestion is that the witches are a part of nature, elemental forces that can hardly be escaped. This effect is increased by the moans and creaking noises that they make, all of which could be comic but which in this production are impressive.

First sentence of this paragraph provides an effective transition

The witches' power over Macbeth is further emphasized by their actions. When the witches first meet Macbeth, they encircle him, touch him, caress him, even embrace him, and he seems helpless, almost their plaything. Moreover, in the scene in which he imagines that he sees a dagger, the director has arranged for one of the witches to appear, stand near Macbeth, and guide his hand toward the invisible dagger. This is, of course, not in the text, but the interpretation is reasonable rather than intrusive. Finally, near the end of the play, just before Macduff kills Macbeth, a witch appears and laughs at Macbeth as Macduff explains that he was not "born of woman." There is no doubt that throughout the tragedy Macbeth has been a puppet of the witches.

Paragraph begins with a broad assertion and then offers supporting details

Stephen Beers (Macbeth) and Tina Peters (Lady Macbeth) are excellent. Beers is sufficiently brawny to be convincing as a battlefield hero, but he also speaks the lines sensitively, so the audience feels that in addition to being a hero, he is a man of gentleness. One can believe Lady Macbeth when she says that she fears he is "too full o' the milk of human kindness" to murder Duncan. Lady Macbeth is especially effective in the scene in which she asks the spirits to "unsex her."

Reference to a particular scene

During this speech she is reclining on a bed and as she delivers the lines she becomes increasingly sexual in her bodily motions, deriving excitement from her own stimulating words. Her attachment to Macbeth is strongly sexual, and so is his attraction to her. The scene when she persuades him to kill Duncan ends with their passionately embracing. The strong attraction of each for the other, so evident in the early part of the play, disappears after the murder, when Macbeth keeps his distance from Lady Macbeth and does not allow her to touch him. The acting of the other performers is effective, except for John Berens (Duncan), who recites the lines mechanically and seems not to take much account of their meaning.

Description, but also analysis

The set consists of a barren plot, at the rear of which stands a spidery framework of piping of the sort used by construction companies, supporting a catwalk. This framework fits with the costumes (lots of armor, leather, heavy boots), suggesting a sort of elemental, primitive, and somewhat sadistic world. The catwalk, though effectively used when Macbeth goes off to murder Duncan (whose room is presumably upstairs and offstage), is not much used in later scenes. For the most part it is an interesting piece of scenery but not otherwise helpful. For instance, there is no reason why the scene with Macduff's wife and children is staged on it. The costumes are not in any way Scottish—no plaids—but in several scenes the sound of a bagpipe is heard, adding another weird or primitive tone to the production.

Concrete details to support evaluation

This *Macbeth* appeals to the eye, the ear, and the mind. The director has given us a unified production that makes sense and that is faithful to the spirit of Shakespeare's play.

Summary

Work Cited

Documentation

Macbeth. By William Shakespeare. Dir. Mark Urice. Perf. Stephen Beers, Tina Peters, and John Berens. University Theater, Medford, MA. 3 Mar. 1998.

The Review Reviewed

The marginal notes call attention to certain qualities in the review, but three additional points should be made:

1. The reviewer's feelings and evaluations are clearly expressed, not in such expressions as "furthermore I feel," and "it is also my opinion," but in such expressions as "a thoughtful and occasionally exciting production," "excellent," and "appeals to the eye, the ear, and the mind."
2. The evaluations are supported by details. For instance, the evaluation that the witches are effectively presented is supported by a brief description of their appearance.
3. The reviewer is courteous, even when (as in the discussion of the catwalk, in the next-to-last paragraph) she is talking about aspects of the production she doesn't care for.

Note: Another review by a student (of a film version of *Hamlet*) appears in Chapter 22, which includes a casebook on *Hamlet*.

6

Reading and Writing about Visual Culture

I am after the one unique picture whose composition possesses such vigor and richness, and whose content so radiates outwards from it, that this single picture is a whole story in itself.

HENRI CARTIER-BRESSON

THE LANGUAGE OF PICTURES

It may sound odd to talk about "reading" pictures and about the "language" of pictures, but pictures, like words, convey messages. Advertisers know this, and that's why their advertisements for soft drinks include images of attractive young couples frolicking at the beach. The not-so-hidden message is that consumers of these products are healthy, prosperous, relaxed, and sexually attractive.

Like compositions made of words—stories, poems, even vigorous sentences—many pictures are carefully constructed things, built up in a certain way in order to make a statement. To cite an obvious example, in medieval religious pictures Jesus or Mary may be shown larger than the surrounding figures to indicate their greater spiritual status. But even in realistic paintings the more important figures are likely to be given a greater share of the light or a more central position than the lesser figures. Such devices of composition are fairly evident in paintings, but we occasionally forget that photographs too are almost always constructed things. The photographer—even the amateur just taking a candid snapshot—adjusts a pillow under the baby's head, or suggests that the subject may want to step out of the shadow, and then the photographer backs up a little and bends his or her knees before clicking the shutter. Even when photographing something inanimate, the photographer searches for the best view, waits for a cloud to pass, and perhaps pushes out of the range of the camera some trash that would spoil the effect of a lovely fern growing beside a rock. Minor White was speaking for almost all photographers when he said, "I don't take pictures, I make them."

And we often make our photographs for a particular purpose—perhaps to have a souvenir of a trip, or to show what we look like in uniform, or to show grandparents what the new baby looks like. Even professional photographers have a variety of purposes—for instance, to provide wedding portraits, to report the news, to sell automobiles, or to record some visual phenomena that they think must be recorded. Sometimes these purposes can be mingled. During the depression of the early 1930s, for instance, the Resettlement Administration employed photographers such as Dorothea Lange to help convince the nation that migrant workers and dispossessed farmers needed help. These photographers were, so to speak, selling something, but they were also reporting the news and serving a noble social purpose. Later in this chapter we will reproduce Lange's most famous picture, *Migrant Mother*, along with some comments on it that students wrote in journals. We will follow these entries from journals with a finished essay, submitted by a student at the end of the term.

But before we get to Lange's photograph, we will give some questions that may help you to think about pictures.

What are some of the basic things to look for in understanding the language of pictures? It's possible to begin almost anywhere, but let's begin with the relationship among the parts:

- Do the figures share the space evenly, or does one figure overpower another, taking most of the space or the light?
- Are the figures harmoniously related, perhaps by a similar stance or shared action? Or are they opposed, perhaps by diagonals thrusting at each other? Generally speaking, diagonals may suggest instability, except when they form a triangle resting on its base. Horizontal lines suggest stability, as do vertical lines when connected by a horizontal line. Circular lines are often associated with motion, and sometimes—especially by men—with the female body and fertility. These simple formulas, however, must be applied cautiously, for they are not always appropriate.
- In a landscape, what is the relation between humans and nature? Are the figures at ease in nature, or are they dwarfed by it? Are they earthbound, beneath the horizon, or (because the viewpoint is low) do they stand out against the horizon and perhaps seem in touch with the heavens, or at least with open air? Do the natural objects in the landscape somehow reflect the emotions of the figures in it?
- If the picture is a portrait, how do the furnishings and the background and the angle of the head or the posture of the head and body (as well, of course, as the facial expression) contribute to our sense of the character of the person portrayed?
- What is the effect of light in the picture? Does it produce sharp contrasts, brightly illuminating some parts and throwing others into darkness? Or does it, by means of gentle gradations, unify most or all of the parts? Does the light seem theatrical or natural, disturbing or comforting? If the picture is in color, is the color realistic or is it expressive, or both?

You can stimulate responses to pictures by asking yourself two kinds of questions:

1. *What is this doing?* Why is this figure here and not there, why is this tree so brightly illuminated, why are shadows omitted, why is this seated figure leaning forward like that?
2. *Why do I have this response?* Why do I find this figure pathetic, this landscape oppressive, this child revoltingly sentimental but that child fascinating?

The first of these questions, "What is this doing?" requires you to identify yourself with the artist, wondering perhaps whether the fence or the side of the house is the better background for this figure, or whether both figures should sit or stand. The second question, "Why do I have this response?" requires you to trust your feelings. If you are amused, repelled, unnerved, or soothed, assume that these responses are appropriate and follow them up—at least until further study of the work elicits other responses.

ANALYZING A PICTURE: NAVAJO DANCERS ENTERTAINING A TOURIST TRAIN

Notes and a Sample Essay by a Student

If you take a course in art history, you will probably be asked to write a formal analysis. In such a context, the word *formal* is not the opposite of *informal*, as in a formal dance or a formal dinner, but simply means "related to the form or structure." In thinking about the form of an image—whether a painting, a photograph, or an advertisement—you can get some help by asking yourself the questions we listed earlier, such as "Do the figures share the space evenly?" But formal analyses of images are by no means limited to courses in art history. Almost any course that examines aspects of culture, for instance a course in religion or film or advertising or politics or journalism, is likely to consider images as well as words.

Consider a photograph taken in 1963, in Durango, Colorado. What does the picture tell us? Before beginning to draft an essay on this picture, one of our students made the following jottings:

George Hight. *Navajo Dancers Entertaining a Tourist Train, June 1963: Durango, Colorado.* (Courtesy of National Museum of the American Indian, Smithsonian Institution [N33190])

title: tourists, Navajo, in Colorado

the tourists (white) on the train are gawking at the Navajo, and the boy seems to be interested (at least he is smiling), BUT the man with the boy looks pretty grim, looks straight ahead, not at dancers. Superior? Uptight?

the Navajo are doing their stuff, at least the dancers are, BUT the girl (she's a Navajo too) is not part of the act (not dressed "Indian-style"). At side; not center-stage. Not being looked at-but she looks coolly at the photographer

the whole thing seems pretty grim-these Navajo (one at right even in a war bonnet) perform for a couple of minutes when the train pulls in, then probably wait an hour or maybe many hours, until the next train. They probably depend on coins or if they are lucky dollar bills that whites toss to them out of the train

the Navajo in the war bonnet seems to be drummer. Anyway, he is sort of offstage, with the girl.

Pretty strong separation of whites from Navajo. A white man and a boy are on the ground with Navajo, but whites' clothes clearly separate them from Navajo. These whites belong to the group on the train, that is, to the world on wheels that will soon pull out of this town.

lettering on train is like lettering on a "Wanted Poster"-to make the tourists think they are in the Wild West of the nineteenth century, even though reality is 1963!

These jottings served, with considerable amplification and reorganization, as the basis of an essay on the picture. Here is the student's finished essay.

Morales 1

Zoe Morales

English 10B

Mr. Shem

18 October 2004

Dancing at Durango: White Tourists and Navajo Performers

Today when people who are not Native Americans think about Native Americans, they probably think first of their terrible mistreatment by whites. The lands of the Native Americans were

Morales 2

stolen, and many of the tribes were nearly annihilated by diseases

introduced by whites. But this view seems to be fairly recent. A

common older view, forcefully presented in the Indian Wars of

the nineteenth century, can be summarized in the blunt words,

"The only good Indian is a dead Indian." These words are reported

to have been spoken by General Philip Henry Sheridan, who

achieved fame and acclaim as one of Lincoln's generals, and even

more fame and even more acclaim as an Indian fighter after the

Civil War.

By the beginning of the twentieth century the Native

Americans, their populations and their territories greatly

reduced by war and disease, were no longer a military threat to

the whites. In the popular white mind in the first half of the

twentieth century, Native Americans chiefly were of two sorts,

bad guys in cowboy films and quaint feather-wearing people in

tourist attractions. In films they were sometimes brave but more

often were cunning, and they were always defeated by whites; in

tourist sites they wore their feathers and beads and moccasins,

and they danced their dances, representing a colorful past that

the civilized world had outgrown.

George Hight's photograph, Navajo Dancers Entertaining a

Tourist Train, June 1963: Durango, Colorado, shows two

contrasting worlds, the white world with its railroad train, and

the Native American world with its costumes worn for the sake of

the tourists. But this railroad train is itself a bit of a fake, a

Morales 3

twentieth-century machine that, for the pleasure of white people,

uses a style of lettering that looks like a Wanted Poster to call to

mind the Wild West of a bygone day.

The train has stopped, some people have stepped off it, but

the strong diagonal line conveys a sense that this self-contained

world, this world which is decidedly separate from the Navajo,

will soon speed away, leaving the Navajo behind. Although a

white man and a boy are off the train and on the ground with the

Navajo--they are in Navajo territory for a minute, so to speak--

clearly there is no real intermingling. Their clothing separates

them, and so do their expressions: The man is grim-faced, the boy

is smiling and to that degree he is sympathetically entering into

the Navajo world, but there is no real contact between the two

dancers and the people safe in their train or the two whites who

have stepped off the train. This grim white man at the left faces

the same way that the Navajo in the bonnet at the right faces, but

this similarity only emphasizes the difference between them. The

chief connection between the two worlds, interestingly, is made

by the Navajo girl at the right, who is dressed like a white and

looks at the photographer and at us, that is, at the tourist world

in front of the picture. She lives in what we can call the real

Navajo world, the modern world, which whites dominate. And

this is the world to which the Navajo performers probably will

return. After the last performance the costumed men will put on

jeans and cotton shirts, and they will replace their beaded and feathered moccasins with sneakers. But the girl, standing at the side, dressed like a white, not performing, is a Native American who scarcely exists so far as the tourists are concerned.

I find the photograph very disturbing, and not simply because of the separation suggested between the worlds of the whites and the Navajo. The white man and the boy stride toward a dancer who leans, knees flexed, in their direction: Will the whites and this dancer collide? Certainly the white man does not look as though he is going to change his direction. Furthermore, the other dancer, in profile, bends forward and, as the scene is caught by the camera, blocks the movement of the white man. All of this troubling placement of the figures on the left-hand side is set in contrast to the firm vertical stances of the Indian wearing the headdress and the little girl on the right. A little to the right of the center of the picture, a man walks away (he seems to be wearing a cap, so he probably is a trainman of some sort), and further to the right two white women, also with their backs toward us, flank the bonneted Navajo and the girl. The man in the center and the two white women at the right take us in one direction, the white man and the boy at the left take us in the opposite direction. And as if all this contradictory motion were not enough, the train cars, which are stationary so that the tourists can take pictures, seem propelled forward to the left and also veering backward into the sharply receding right.

Morales 5

Most Native American dances had a social function: The Bear
Dance was danced to appease the soul of the animal which they
would kill; the Scalp Dance was a dance of victory; the Sun Dance
was danced in an effort to achieve divine guidance. Judging from
the hoops that hang on a post in the foreground, these Navajo
perform some sort of Hoop Dance. (According to Gladys A.
Reichard, Navaho Religions: A Study of Symbolism [1950], hoops
are used in many kinds of Navaho sacred dances.) But this dance
is performed not for any ritual that is an important part of the life
of the dancers; rather, it is performed for the entertainment of
outsiders. It has utterly lost its religious or healing function. But
not quite. It is still life-giving, since it gains some money, helping
the Native Americans to survive in the narrow world that the
whites have pushed them into--the space between the train and the
presumably white tourist who took the picture.

To my eye and mind, it is tragic that these Navajo are
performing their dances not as religious rites but just to
entertain outsiders and to make a few dollars. Imagine if some
Christians, Jews, Muslims, or Buddhists were so poor that today
they had to make money by performing their sacred ceremonies
to entertain people who do not have the faintest knowledge of or
interest in their religion, but who look at the ceremonies as the
strange doings of people who are not part of the modern world.
On the other hand, we don't know how these Indians felt when
they were dancing for tourists. Maybe they believed--and maybe

Morales 6

they were right--that they were communicating at least some of

their culture to strangers, were showing that although much of

their traditional way of life had been forcibly taken from them,

they nevertheless retained important parts of it, and were willing

to share these with the whites. The whites in a moment will be

speeding down the railroad tracks to the next tourist attraction,

but maybe some of them will be mysteriously touched by what

they saw. We can't know, but we can guess that the photographer

was touched enough to record the image.

The Analysis Analyzed

- The title of the essay is not simply "An analysis. . . "; rather, the title arouses interest.
- The essay includes some *description* ("The train has stopped, some people have stepped off," the train "uses a style of lettering that looks like a Wanted Poster"), but, more important, it includes *analysis*. That is, it sees how these elements work to make a meaningful whole. Thus, when Zoe Morales tells us that the photo shows a man and boy who have stepped off the train she is being descriptive, but when she goes on to say that they wear clothing that makes them clearly distinguishable from the other characters on the ground she is being analytic. Similarly, the statement that the train is labeled with lettering of the Wanted Poster sort is a descriptive statement, but the statement that this lettering is meant to suggest a romantic past is analytic.
- Formal analysis dominates the third and fourth paragraphs, but the essay also includes the writer's reflections on the image, especially in the final paragraph.

Topics for Critical Thinking and Writing

1. What do the first two paragraphs contribute to the essay? What would be the effect if these were omitted?
2. Does this essay present a thesis? Does a formal analysis require one?
3. Do you find the ending too indefinite, or just right?
4. What grade would you give this essay? Why?

THINKING ABOUT DOROTHEA LANGE'S *MIGRANT MOTHER, NIPOMO, CALIFORNIA*

Let's look now at a photograph by Dorothea Lange, an American photographer who made her reputation with photographs of migrant laborers in California during the depression that began in 1929. Lange's *Migrant Mother, Nipomo, California* (1936) is probably the best-known image of the period. One of our students made the following entry in his journal. (The student was given no information about the photograph other than the name of the photographer and the title of the picture.)

> This woman seems to be thinking. In a way, the picture reminds me of a statue called <u>The Thinker</u>, of a seated man who is bent over, with his chin resting on his fist. But I wouldn't say that this photograph is really so much about thinking as it is about other things. I'd say that it is about several other things. First (but not really in any particular order), fear. The children must be afraid, since they have turned to their mother. Second, the

Figure A. Dorothea Lange. *Migrant Mother, Nipomo, California,* 1936.

picture is about love. The children press against their mother, sure of her love. The mother does not actually show her love--for instance, by kissing them, or even hugging them--but you feel she loves them. Third, the picture is about hopelessness. The mother doesn't seem to be able to offer any comfort. Probably they have very little food; maybe they are homeless. I'd say the picture is also about courage. Although the picture seems to me to show hopelessness, I also think the mother, even though she does not know how she will be able to help her children shows great strength in her face. She also has a lot of dignity. She hasn't broken down in front of the children: she is going to do her best to get through the day and the next day and the next.

Another student wrote:

I remember from American Lit that good literature is not sentimental. (When we discussed the word, we concluded that "sentimental" meant "sickeningly sweet.") Some people might think that Lange's picture, showing a mother and two little children, is sentimental, but I don't think so. Although the children must be upset, and maybe they even are crying, the mother seems to be very strong. I feel that with a mother like this, the children are in very good hands. She is not "sickeningly sweet." She may be almost overcome with despair, but she doesn't seem to ask us to pity her.

A third student wrote:

It's like those pictures of the homeless in the newspapers and on TV. A photographer sees some man sleeping in a cardboard box, or a woman with shopping bags sitting in a doorway, and he takes their picture. I suppose the photographer could say that he is calling the public's attention to "the plight of the homeless," but I'm not convinced that he's doing anything more than making money by selling photographs. Homeless people have almost no privacy, and then some photographer comes along and invades even their doorways and cardboard houses. Sometimes the people are sleeping, or even if they are awake they may be in so much despair that they don't bother to tell the photographer to get lost. Or they may be mentally ill and don't know what's happening. In the case of this picture, the woman is not asleep, but she seems so preoccupied that she isn't aware of the photographer. Maybe she has just been told there is no work for her, or maybe she has been told she can't stay if she keeps the children. Should the photographer have intruded on this woman's sorrow? This picture may be art, but it bothers me.

All of these entries seem to us to be thoughtful, interesting, and helpful, though even taken together they do not provide the last word.

Here are a few additional points. First, it happens that Lange has written about the picture. She said that she had spent the winter of 1935–1936 taking photographs of migrants, and now, in March, she was preparing to drive five hundred miles to her home when she noticed a sign that said, "Pea-Pickers Camp." Having already taken hundreds of pictures, she drove on for twenty miles, but something preyed on her mind, and she made a U-turn and visited the camp. Here is part of what she wrote:

I saw and approached the hungry and desperate mother, as if drawn by a magnet. I do not remember how I explained my presence or my camera to her, but I do remember she asked me no questions. I made five exposures, working closer and closer from the same direction. I did not ask her name or her history. She told me her age, that she was thirty-two. She said that they had been living on frozen vegetables from the surrounding fields, and birds that the children killed. She had just sold the tires from her car to buy food. There she sat in that lean-to tent with her children huddled around her, and seemed to know that my pictures might help her, and so she helped me. There was a sort of equality about it. . . . What I am trying to tell other photographers is that had I not been deeply involved in my undertaking on that field trip, I would not have had to turn back. What I am trying to say is that I believe this inner compulsion to be the vital ingredient in our work.

Lange does not say anything about posing the woman and her child, and we can assume that she had too much decency to ask a woman and children in these circumstances to arrange themselves into an interesting pictorial composition. Furthermore, it seems obvious that unlike, say, a figure in a wedding portrait, the woman is not striking a pose. She has not deliberately prepared herself for a picture that will represent her to the public. Nevertheless, the composition—the way things are put together—certainly contributes to the significance of the picture. Of course the subject matter, a mother with children, may suggest the traditional Madonna and Child of the Middle Ages and the Renaissance, but the resemblance is not just in the subject matter. Lange's photograph may remind us of paintings in which the Madonna and the infant Jesus form a unified composition, their heads and limbs harmonizing and echoing each other.

The photograph, with its near-balance—a child on each side, the mother's bare right arm balanced by the child's bare arm, the mother's hand at one side of her neck echoed by the child's hand at the other side—achieves a stability, or harmony, that helps make the painfulness of the subject acceptable. That is, although the subject may be painful, it is possible to take some pleasure in the way in which it is presented. That the faces of the children are turned away probably helps make the subject acceptable. If we saw not only the woman's face but also the faces of two hungry children, we might feel that Lange was tugging too vigorously at our heartstrings. Finally, speaking of faces, it is worth mentioning that the woman does not look at us. We don't know why, but we can guess that she takes no notice of us because she is preoccupied with issues far beyond us.

A Sample Documented Essay by a Student

We have already given extracts from the journals of three students. A week after the journals were due, students were asked to write essays on the picture. Notice in the following essay that the student draws not only on his own experience as an amateur photographer but also on material that he found in the college library.

Dean 1

Bruce Dean

Professor Garcia

English 2B

20 March 2004

Did Dorothea Lange Pose Her Subject for Migrant Mother?

In doing research for this essay, I was surprised to find that

Dorothea Lange's Migrant Mother (figure A) is one of six pictures

of this woman and her children. Migrant Mother is so much an

image of the period, an icon of the Depression, that it is hard to

believe it exists in any other form than the one we all know.[1]

In addition to the famous picture, four other pictures of this

subject (figures B-E) are illustrated in a recent book, Vincent

Virga's Eyes of the Nation, and still another picture (figure F) is

illustrated in Karen Tsujimoto's Dorothea Lange. When you think

about it, it is not surprising that Lange would take several

pictures of this woman and her children, anyone who takes

[1]Curiously, Lange in her short essay on the picture, "The

Assignment I'll Never Forget: Migrant Mother," in Popular

Photography 46 (February 1960): 43, says that she made five

exposures. A slightly abridged version of the essay is reprinted in

Milton Meltzer, Dorothea Lange: A Photographer's Life (New

York: Farrar Straus Giroux, 1978): 132-33. Because Meltzer's

book is more available than the magazine, when I quote from the

article I quote from his book.

Dean 2

Figure B.

snapshots knows that if photographers have the opportunity they
will take several pictures of a subject. What is surprising is that
the picture we all know, the one that has become an icon for the
period, is so much more moving than the others.

Two of the pictures include an older child, apparently a
teenager, sitting in a chair, so in a sense they are "truer" to the
fact, because they give us more information about the family. The
trunk, for instance, tells us that the people are on the move, and
the setting--a messy field, with a shabby tent or lean-to--tells us
that they are homeless. But sometimes less is more; the pictures

Figure C.

showing the tent, trunk, and all of the children seem to sprawl.

Perhaps we find ourselves wondering why people who seem to

have only a trunk and some canvas would carry with them so

bulky an object as a rocker. In saying that the two more inclusive

pictures are less effective--less impressive, less moving--than the

others, then, I don't think that I am simply expressing a personal

preference. I think that most or maybe even all viewers would

agree.

    Putting aside the two pictures that show the setting, and also

putting aside for the moment the most famous picture, we

Dean 4

Figure D.

probably can agree that the three remaining pictures of the woman

are approximately equally effective, one viewer might prefer one

picture, another viewer another, but compared with the two that

show the larger setting, all three of these pictures have the

advantage of emphasizing the mother-and-child motif. But the

remaining picture, the famous one, surely is far more memorable

than even the other three close-up pictures. Why? Partly, perhaps,

because it is a <u>closer</u> view, eliminating the tent pole and most of

Dean 5

Figure E.

the hanging cloth. Partly it is more effective because the children

have turned their faces from the camera, thereby conveying their

isolation from everything in the world except their mother. And

partly it is more effective because the woman, touching the side

of her face, has a faraway look of anxiety.

Thinking about this picture in the context of the other five,

if one has a cynical mind one might wonder if Lange staged it.

And this is exactly what Charles J. Shindo says she did, in his

recent book:

> In the course of this encounter Lange took six exposures,
>
> starting with a long shot of the lean-to with the mother and
>
> four children inside. . . . For the final shot Lange called
>
> back another of the children and had the children lean

Dean 6

Figure F.

   upon their mother with their backs to the camera. The

   woman raised her hand to her chin and struck the now

   famous pose of the <u>Migrant Mother</u>. . . . (50)

What evidence does Shindo give for his claim that "Lange called

back another of the children" and that she "had the children lean

upon their mother"? Absolutely none. He does not cite Lange, or

an eyewitness, or anyone who suggests that Lange customarily

posed her subjects. He ignores the basic evidence, Lange's own

words about how she took the picture:

   I saw and approached the hungry and desperate mother, as

   if drawn by a magnet. I do not remember how I explained

   my presence or my camera to her, but I do remember she

asked me no questions. I made five exposures, working closer and closer from the same direction. I did not ask her name or her history. She told me her age, that she was 32. She said that they had been living on frozen vegetables from the surrounding fields, and birds that the children killed. She had just sold the tires from her car to buy food. There she sat in that lean-to tent with her children huddled around her, and seemed to know that my pictures might help her, and so she helped me. There was a sort of equality about it.

The pea crop at Nipomo had frozen and there was no work for anybody. But I did not approach the tents and shelters of other stranded pea-pickers. It was not necessary; I knew I had recorded the essence of my assignment. . . .

(qtd. in Meltzer 133)

This is the <u>only</u> eye-witness account of how Lange photographed the woman and her children. Of course she may not have been telling the truth, but none of her contemporaries ever challenged the truth of her statement. Furthermore, everything that we know about Lange suggests that she did not pose her subjects. For instance, Rondal Partridge, a longtime friend and sometimes a co-worker, gave this description of Lange's method: "She did not ask people to hold a pose or repeat an action, instead she might ask a question: 'How much does that bag of cotton weigh?' And the man, wanting to give her a precise answer, would lift it onto the scales and Lange would make her photograph" (qtd. in Ohrn 61).

Rondal Patridge's comment harmonizes with comments that Lange herself made about her method. Asked about her approach to photography, she said, "First--hands off! Whatever I photograph, I do not molest or tamper with or arrange" (qtd. in Dixon 68). Elsewhere she explained that since she worked with a large camera, "You have to wait until certain decisions are made by the subject--what he's going to give to the camera, which is a very important decision; and the photographer--what he's going to choose to take" (qtd. in Ohrn 233). If I may add a personal comment, I want to say that as an amateur portrait photographer I know from my experience and from talking to other photographers, that posed photographs just don't come out successfully. You can't say to children, "Turn your faces toward your mother," and then say to the mother, "Please put your hand on your cheek," and get a good picture. Every photographer quickly learns that when the photographer specifies the poses, the pictures will be lifeless. The way to get a picture that is convincing is, as Lange's friend said, for the photographer to engage in some talk with the subject, which allows the subject to respond in some significant way. I imagine that while Lange talked, the children may have become uneasy at the sight of the woman with the big camera, and they may have turned and sought the security of their mother. (This is only a guess, but it is very different from Shindo's assertion, made without evidence, that "Lange called back another of the children and had the children lean upon their mother with their backs to the camera"). And perhaps Lange asked the woman

something like, "What do you think you will do now?" or "Do you

think you can get a friend to give your family a hitch to another

work-site?" or some such thing, and the woman responded

naturally. Again my view is different from Shindo's, who says

that the woman "struck the pose of the Migrant Mother," where

"struck the pose," in the context of his preceding sentences about

Lange coldly setting up the image, suggests that the whole thing

is a performance, with Lange as stage-manager and the woman

as the chief actor.

Anyone who has read a book about Dorothea Lange, and has

studied Lange's numerous comments about her ways of working

in Dorothea Lange, ed. Howard M. Levin and Katherine

Northrup, knows that posing figures was utterly foreign to her.

In 1923 she posted on her darkroom door these words from

Francis Bacon, and they guided her for the remaining thirty-odd

years of her career:

> The contemplation of things as they are
>
> without substitution or imposture
>
> without error or confusion
>
> is in itself a nobler thing
>
> than a whole harvest of invention. (qtd. in Stein 59)

In her photography Lange sought to show the viewer "things as

they are." She believed it was nobler to show life as it is than it is to

invent compositions.

Dean 10

There are, of course, questions about this picture, such as "Exactly what is the mother thinking about?" Is she thinking that the situation is hopeless? Or that somehow she and the children will get through? Does her face show despair, or does it show determination? These are questions that we cannot answer definitively. But if we ask the question, "Did Lange tell the children and the woman how to position themselves?" we must answer that all of the evidence suggests that she did not set the scene. She spoke to the woman, and she moved about, looking for the best shot, but a picture as great as this one can only have come from (to repeat Lange's own belief) what the subject is "going to give to the camera" and what the photographer is "going to choose to take."

[New page]

Dean 11

Works Cited

Dixon, Daniel. "Dorothea Lange." <u>Modern Photography</u> 16 (Dec. 1952). 68-77, 138-41.

Levin, Howard M., and Katherine Northrup. <u>Dorothea Lange</u>. 2 vols. Glencoe: Text-Fiche Press, 1980.

Meltzer, Milton. <u>Dorothea Lange: A Photographer's Life</u>. New York: Farrar, 1978.

Dean 12

Ohrn, Karin Becker. <u>Dorothea Lange and the Documentary</u>

    <u>Tradition</u>. Baton Rouge: Louisiana State UP, 1980.

Shindo, Charles J. <u>Dust Bowl Migrants in the American Imagination</u>.

    Lawrence: UP of Kansas, 1997.

Stein, Sally. "Peculiar Grace: Dorothea Lange and the Testimony of the

    Body." <u>Dorothea Lange: A Visual Life</u>. Ed. Elizabeth Partridge.

    Washington, D.C.: Smithsonian Institution, 1994. 57-89.

PHOTOGRAPHERS ON PHOTOGRAPHY

If your instructor asks you to write about a picture—perhaps one in this book—and if even after thinking about the questions on page 151 you don't quite know where to begin, you may want to think about it partly in terms of one of the following remarks by distinguished photographers. (But remember: A remark need not be true just because it was made by someone who is highly regarded as a photographer.)

> A great photograph is a full expression of what one feels about what is being photographed in the deepest sense, and is, thereby, a true expression of what one feels about life in its entirety.
>
> Ansel Adams

> It's the subject-matter that counts. I'm interested in revealing the subject in a new way to intensify it.
>
> Harry Callahan

> Documentary photography records the social scene of our time. It mirrors the present and documents for the future. Its focus is man in his relations to mankind.
>
> Dorothea Lange

> Photography is the simultaneous recognition, in a fraction of a second, of the significance of an event as well as of the precise organization of forms which give that event its proper expression.
>
> Henri Cartier-Bresson

> I am a passionate lover of the snapshot because of all photographic images it comes closest to truth. The snapshot is a specific spiritual moment. . . . What the eye sees is different from what the camera records. Whereas the eye sees in three dimensions, images are projected on a surface of two dimensions,

which for every image-maker is a great problem. The snap-shooter disregards this problem, and the result is that his pictures have an apparent disorder and imperfection, which is exactly their appeal and their style. . . . Out of this im-balance, and out of this not knowing, and out of this real innocence toward the medium comes an enormous vitality and expression of life.

Lisette Model

Or you might begin by thinking about a statement by Janet Malcolm, who in *Diana and Nikon* (a book about photography) said:

If "the camera can't lie," neither is it inclined to tell the truth, since it can re-flect only the usually ambiguous, and sometimes outright deceitful surface of reality.

Exercise: Find a picture that interests you, and write two or three paragraphs about it. Say whatever you want to say, but you may want to take a picture that allows you to draw on your technical knowledge, so that you can educate your reader. If you read any specialized magazines, for instance about sports or com-puters or automobiles or fashion or beekeeping, you probably know more about this area than the average person. From a magazine on this topic, take a picture that interests you—a picture that (a) stimulates you to reflect and that (b) allows you to educate your reader by elucidating technical details.

LOU JACOBS JR.

Lou Jacobs Jr., photographer and the author of several books on photography, is a frequent contributor of essays on the topic to The New York Times, *where this piece originally appeared.*

What Qualities Does a Good Photograph Have?

When amateur and professional photographers get together they often dis-cuss equipment and techniques at some length, but it is not often that photogra-phers take time to consider what makes a good picture.

Many photographic organizations list criteria similar to those described below when judging pictures submitted in a competition. Judges may offer opinions like "The composition is off balance," or "The expressions on people's faces tell the story well." But photographic criticism is not an exact art. In the media, critics tend to use esoteric terms that even an "in" group doesn't always grasp.

Therefore it's important to the average photographer that he or she develop a basis for understanding and verbalizing how pictures succeed or fail in their visual way, or how they happen to be a near-miss. The latter term describes an image that has some, but not enough, of the visual virtues discussed below.

Of course "a good picture" is a relative description because it's subjective, as is the judgment of all the qualities mentioned in the list that follows. However, there is enough agreement in the tastes of a variety of people to make certain standards general and valid, though the characteristics of a good picture are sub-ject to flexible interpretation. A little honest controversy about the visual success of a print or slide can be a healthy thing.

Ansel Adams. *Moonrise, Hernandez, New Mexico, 1941.*

5   **Impact:** This descriptive word comprises a collection of the qualities that help make a photograph appealing, interesting, impressive, or memorable. For instance, Ansel Adams's "Moonrise, Hernandez, NM," is a famous image that has been selling for astronomical prices at auctions because it has enormous pictorial or visual impact—among other reasons. The picture's impact evolves from many qualities such as the drama of the light, the mood invoked, and the magic sense of realism.

It is possible to translate such qualities into your own photographs when you consider how the subjects were treated, whether landscapes or people. Too seldom do we meet dramatic opportunities in nature as grand as those in "Moonrise," but with a well developed artistic sensitivity, ideal conditions can be captured on film.

Human Interest: Here is another rather general term to encompass emotional qualities, action, and things that people do which appeal to a lot of viewers. A shot of your children laughing or a picture of vendors in a marketplace might both show outstanding human interest. The success of such a photograph depends on how you compose it, on lighting, on timing to catch vivid expressions, and perhaps on camera angle or choice of lens. All of these ingredients of a good picture are coming up on the list.

There is another aspect of human interest in your own or others' photographs. Sometimes the unusualness of a subject and the way it's presented overshadows adequate technique. For instance, a good sports picture showing peak action in a scrimmage or a definitive play in baseball has intrinsic appeal.

A photograph of a pretty girl, a baby, and a sunset are in the same category, because in each case the subject matter grabs the viewer's attention. As a result, a mediocre composition, inferior lighting, a messy background, or other technical or esthetic weaknesses are ignored or excused because the subject is striking.

10   It's a good feeling when you can distinguish between the subject in a photograph and the way it was treated.

Galleries and museums often hang photographs that are "different," but they're not necessarily worthy of distinction. Many offbeat photographs we see are likely not to have lasting visual value, while fine photographs like those of Ansel Adams or Cartier-Bresson will still be admired in future decades.

Effective Composition: Like other qualities that underlie a good picture, composition can be controversial. There are somewhat conventional principles of design that we follow because they seem "natural," like placing the horizon line or a figure off-center to avoid a static effect.

But really effective composition is usually derived from the subject, and generally the urge to keep composition as simple as possible pays off. That's why plain backgrounds are often best for portraits, and if you relate someone to his/her environment, simplicity is also a virtue. Composition may be dynamic, placid, or somewhere between.

Study the compositional tendencies of fine photographers and painters for guidance. Be daring and experimental at times too, because a "safe" composition may also be dull.

15   **Spontaneity:** This characteristic of a good picture is related to human interest, realism and involvement. When you are involved with the subject, as you might be in photographing an aged father or mother, you prize most the images that include spontaneous expressions and emotional reactions. Get people involved with each other, too, so they forget the camera and your pictures are likely to be more believable—and credibility is often a pictorial asset.

If your camera lens is not fast enough to shoot at let's say 1/60th of a second at f/2.8, then you need flash. But you get more spontaneity when people aren't posed, waiting for the flash to go off. Natural light also adds to the realistic impression you capture of people and places, since flash-on-camera has an unavoidably artificial look in most cases.

Lighting: Certainly we have to shoot sometimes when the light is not pictorial, so we do the best we can. A tripod is often the answer to long exposures and exciting photographs. In some situations the light improves if we have the time and patience to wait. Outdoors plan to shoot when the sun is low in the early morning, and at sunset time. Mountains, buildings and people are more dramatic in low-angle light. Details lost in shadows don't seem to matter when the light quality itself is beautiful.

Lighting also helps to create mood, another element of a good picture. Mood is understandably an ethereal quality which includes mystery, gaiety, somberness, and other emotional aspects. Effective photographs may capitalize on the mood of a place especially when it's dramatic.

Color: In a painting a pronounced feeling of light and shadow is called chiaroscuro, and in photographs such effects are augmented by color which may be in strong contrasts, or part of important forms. Outstanding pictures may also be softly colored in pastels that can be as appealing as bright hues.

20   We tend to take color in photographs for granted, but we don't have to settle for literal color when a colored filter or a switch in film may improve a situation. Next time it rains, shoot some pictures through a car window or windshield, or keep your camera dry and shoot on foot—using indoor color film. The cold blue effects, particularly in slides, are terrific. You may later use an 85B filter to correct the color for normal outdoor or flash use.

Keep in mind that "pretty" or striking color may influence us to take pictures where there really is no worthwhile image. And when you view prints and slides, realize that theatrical color can influence your judgment about the total quality of a picture. A beautiful girl in brightly colored clothes, or an exotic South Seas beach scene may be photographed with creative skill, or insensitively, no matter how appealing the color is.

Contrast: Outstanding pictures may be based on the fact that they contain various contrasting elements, such as large and small, near and far, old and new, bright and subtle color, etc. In taking pictures and evaluating them, keep the contrast range in mind, although these values are often integral with other aspects of the picture.

Camera Angle and Choice of Lens: If someone standing next to you shoots a mid-town Manhattan street with a 50mm lens on a 35mm camera, and you do the same scene with a 35mm or 105mm lens from a crouch rather than standing, you might get a better picture. You can dramatize a subject through your choice of camera angle and lens focal length to alter perspective as well as the relationship of things in the scene. Distortion created this way can be pictorially exciting—or awkward and distracting. You may get good pictures by taking risks in visual ways, and later deciding if what you tried seems to work.

Imagination and Creativity: These two attributes of people who take pictures might have been first on the list if they were not abused words. Look each one up in the dictionary. Ponder how you would apply the definitions to your own pictures and to photographs you see in books or exhibitions.

25   It takes imagination to see the commonplace in an artistic way, but a certain amount of imagination and creativity should be involved every time we press the shutter button. These human capabilities are basic to understanding the other qualities that make good pictures.

[1981]

Topics for Critical Thinking and Writing

1. Evaluate the title and the first paragraph.
2. In paragraph 4 Jacobs says, "Of course 'a good picture' is a relative description because it's subjective. . . ." Do you agree? Look, for instance, at Dorothea Lange's photographs of a migrant laborer and her children, on page 159 and 163–167. Would you be willing to argue that the famous picture (the one showing the children turned away from the camera) is clearly—objectively—a better picture than one of the other pictures? Explain.
3. In paragraph 5 Jacobs praises Ansel Adam's *Moonrise, Hernandez, NM*, but this picture, showing a cemetery with crosses illumined by a silvery moon, has been disparaged by some critics on the grounds that it is sentimental. How would you define sentimentality? And is it a bad thing in a photograph? Explain.

4. In paragraph 7 Jacobs speaks of "human interest," and he cites "a shot of your children laughing or a picture of vendors in a marketplace." Given these examples, what does "human interest" seem to mean? What might be some examples of photographs of people that do *not* have "human interest"?

5. In paragraph 23 Jacobs says that "you can dramatize a subject through your choice of camera angle. . . ." Find an example of such a photo in a newspaper or newsmagazine, or perhaps in this book, and explain how the camera angle "dramatizes" the subject.

6. Take a photo, perhaps one in this book, and in 500 words analyze and evaluate it in Jacobs's terms. Then consider whether Jacobs's essay has helped you to see and enjoy the photograph.

7. Write your own short essay (250–500 words) on "What Qualities Does a Good Photograph Have?" Illustrate it with photocopies of two or three photographs, from this book or from any other source that you wish to draw on. (You may want to choose two examples of good photographs, or one of a good photograph and one of a poor photograph.)

An American Picture Album:
Ten Images

Grant Wood. *American Gothic*, 1930.

Gordon Parks. *American Gothic.* Photograph of cleaning woman Ella Watson. Washington, 1942.

Lewis W. Hine. *Singer Power Machine Sewing Group*, Dec. 1936–July 1937.

Albert Bresnik. *Amelia Earhart.*

Lewis W. Hine. *Icarus, Empire State Building,* 1930.

Ernest C. Withers. *No White People Allowed in Zoo Today*, 1950s.

Alon Reininger. *Pledging Allegiance.*

Marilyn Monroe.

Charlotte Perkins Gilman at a Suffrage Rally.

Neil Armstrong. *Buzz Aldrin on the Moon*, 1969.

PART II

Up Close

Thinking Critically about Literary Works and Literary Forms

7

Critical Thinking: Asking Questions and Making Comparisons

WHAT IS CRITICAL THINKING?

The verb *to think* has several meanings, such as *to imagine* ("Think how he'll hit the ceiling when you tell him this"), *to expect or hope* ("I think I'll get the job"), and—the meaning we will chiefly be concerned with—*to consider closely, especially by exercising one's powers of reason* ("I've been thinking about why she did it, and I've come to some conclusions").

When we engage in this last sort of thinking, close consideration, we are keenly aware of what we are doing. We are, for instance, studying an effect and are searching for its causes. "This story bores me, but exactly *why* does it bore me?" Is the plot too familiar? Are the characters unrealistic? Is the language trite? Or so technical that I can't follow it? Does the author use too many words to say too little? Or: "I loved the book but hated the movie. Why?" And again we start to consider the problem closely, probably (again) by examining the parts that make up the whole. And here we are at the heart of *critical thinking*.

The words *critic*, *critical*, and *criticism* come from a Greek word *krinein*, meaning "to separate." In ordinary talk, *to criticize* is to find fault or to judge severely. But in the sense we are concerned with here, *to criticize* is to examine and to judge, not necessarily to find fault.

Having said that critical thinking does not necessarily involve fault-finding, we want to modify this statement. There is one writer whose work you should indeed judge severely. The writer is you. When you read a draft of your work, adopt a skeptical spirit. As you read the draft, ask yourself if assertions are supported with sufficient evidence, and ask if other interpretations of the evidence might reasonably be offered. If you engage in this process, you are engaged in critical thinking.

ASKING AND ANSWERING QUESTIONS

Critical thinking is a matter of separating the whole into parts, in order to see relationships. If you ask yourself questions about a work—whether the work is something reprinted in this book or is something that you have just drafted—you will almost surely set yourself thinking about how the parts relate to each other and to the whole, their context. Here are some typical questions:

- What expectations does the title arouse in a reader?
- Does the middle drag?
- Do certain characters or settings seem to be symbolic, suggesting more than themselves?
- Is the end satisfactory, and if so, why? Because it is surprising? Because, on the contrary, foreshadowing caused us to anticipate it, and it therefore fulfills our expectations?

When you ask yourself questions such as these, you will find that you are deepening your understanding of how a work (perhaps an essay, story, poem, or play in this book, perhaps an essay of your own) works. Because thinking about questions is an excellent way to deepen your understanding, we include questions along with most of the literature in this book. And we include numerous checklists—in effect, lists of questions for you to ask yourself when you are writing—in order to help you think about your own productions.

A process that in effect is synonymous with critical thinking is **analysis**; this word also comes from a Greek word, meaning *to separate into parts*. And because the point of analysis is to understand how things connect, how things work, and because the point of writing an analysis is to share your understanding with your readers, your essay normally will include a **synthesis**, "a putting together." It can almost be said that essays based on critical thinking will propose a **thesis**, and will support the thesis by giving **reasons**, that is, by giving evidence: "X is so, *because* . . . ."

Writing of this sort, in which evidence is offered, commonly is the result of conscious reasoning, but it must be admitted that sometimes insights come unsought. Two examples are famous. Legend says that the Greek mathematician Archimedes (287–212 B.C.), asked by the ruler of Syracuse to determine if a gold crown really was pure gold or was alloyed with silver, was baffled. To relax, he visited a public bath, and idly observed the overflow of water. "*Eureka!*" ("I have found it"), he shouted, leaping out of the water and (in his excitement) running home naked. What he had found was not the cake of soap but the solution to the problem: Since gold is denser than silver, a given weight of gold represents a smaller volume than an equal weight of silver. A one-pound crown of gold will therefore displace less water than a one-pound crown that is made of gold alloyed with silver. (The crown in question *was* alloyed.) A second (and better documented) example is the discovery by the great German chemist F. A. Kekulé, who, dozing in front of the fireplace, developed the ring theory of the molecular structure of benzene. Kekulé dreamed of a snake biting its own tail, and according to his report, he "awoke as though from a flash of lightning," and spent the rest of the night in working out the consequences of the hypothesis.

Confronted with the difficult but exciting and rewarding job of writing a thoughtful paper, you cannot count on inspiration, no matter how many baths you take or how many fires you contemplate sleepily. You probably will find, like almost everyone else, that your best thoughts come to you when you start to put them into writing, whether with pencil and paper or with a keyboard and a computer. Although our chief concern in this book is with writing about literature, and in a moment we will look at a short poem, let's start indirectly by thinking analytically, thinking critically, about a picture. (Our method will be in accord with Polonius's advice in *Hamlet*, "By indirections find directions out.")

COMPARING AND CONTRASTING

This photograph of Sitting Bull and Buffalo Bill was taken by a Canadian photographer, William Notman. Buffalo Bill—William F. Cody—got his name from his activities as a supplier of buffalo meat for workers on the Kansas Pacific Railway, but his fame came chiefly from his exploits as an army scout and a fighter against the Sioux Indians, and later from Buffalo Bill's Wild West. Buffalo Bill's Wild West was a show (though he never used this word because he insisted that the exhibition recreated recent Western history) consisting of mock battles with Indians, an attack on a stage coach, and feats of horsemanship and sharpshooting. Sitting Bull, a Sioux chief, had defeated Custer at the Battle of Little Bighorn ten years before this picture was taken, but he had fled to Canada soon after the battle. In 1879 he was granted amnesty and returned to the United States, and in 1885 he appeared in Buffalo Bill's Wild West. The photograph, entitled *Foes in '76, Friends in '85*, was used to publicize the show.

In Chapter 4 we talked about writing a comparison (pp. 67–69), but we now want to add a few things. The writer Howard Nemerov once said, "If you really want to see something, look at something else." He was talking about the

William Notman, *Foes in '76, Friends in '85*. The Sioux chief appeared for one season in William F. Cody's show, which was called *Buffalo Bill's Wild West*. Souvenir cards with this picture were sold. (Buffalo Bill Historical Center, Cody, WY [P.69.2125])

power of comparison to illuminate. We compare X and Y, not for the sake of making lists of similarities and differences, but for the sake of seeing X (or Y) more clearly. This book chiefly offers material for you to read with pleasure, and one source of pleasure is understanding. Your understanding of one work may be heightened by thinking about it in comparison with another work. We offer several *case studies* that present a writer *in depth*. For example, we give three stories by Raymond Carver—in fact, we give two versions of one of the stories so thinking about one story in comparison with another, or within this context, will enrich your understanding. Similarly, we offer several thematic chapters, for instance a chapter on "Love and Hate," where, again, works invite comparison.

Suppose we want to think about the picture of Sitting Bull and Buffalo Bill, in order to deepen our understanding of it and to share our understanding with others. To say that the photograph's dimensions are such-and-such or even to say that it shows two people is merely to *describe* it, not to do anything that can be called thinking. But if we look more closely, and compare the two figures, our mind is energized. (Strictly speaking, **to compare** is to take note of similarities, and **to contrast** is to take note of differences, but in ordinary usage *compare* covers both activities.) Comparing greatly stimulates the mind; by comparing X with Y, we notice things that we might otherwise pass over. Suppose we ask these questions:

- What resemblances and differences do we see in the clothes of the two figures?
- What about their facial expressions?
- How do their poses compare?
- Is the setting significant?

If we try to answer these and other questions that come to mind, we may find ourselves jotting down phrases and sentences along these lines:

> Buffalo Bill is in fancy clothing (shiny boots, a mammoth buckle, a decorated jacket)
>
> BB is striking a pose—very theatrical, his right hand on his heart, his head tilted slightly back, his eyes looking off as though he is gazing into the future. He seems to be working hard to present a grand image of himself.
>
> Sitting Bull simply stands there, apparently looking downward. One feels that he is going along with what is expected of him—after all, he had joined the show—but he refuses to make a fool of himself.
>
> Sitting Bull lets BB have upper hand (literally—on gun)
>
> BB in effect surrounds SB (Bill's right shoulder is behind Sitting Bull and Bill's left leg is in front of him).

ANALYZING AND EVALUATING EVIDENCE

If we continue to look closely, we probably notice that the landscape is fake—not the great outdoors but a set, a painted backdrop and probably a fake grass mat. If we see these things, we may formulate the thesis that Buffalo Bill here is all show biz, and that Sitting Bull retains his dignity. And if in our essay we support these assertions by pointing to **evidence**, we are demonstrating critical thinking.

Here, in fact, is the final paragraph from an essay that a student wrote on this picture:

> Buffalo Bill is obviously the dominant figure in this photograph, but he is not the outstanding one. His efforts to appear great only serve to make him appear small. His attempt to outshine Sitting Bull strikes us as faintly ridiculous. We do not need nor want to know any more about Buffalo Bill's personality; it is spread before us in the picture. Sitting Bull's inwardness and dignity make him more interesting than Buffalo Bill, and make us wish to prove our intuition and to ascertain that this proud Sioux was a great chief.

We think this analysis is excellent, but when we did some of our own research on Buffalo Bill we found that he was more complicated and more interesting than we at first thought. But this is to get ahead of the story.

THINKING CRITICALLY: ASKING QUESTIONS AND COMPARING— E. E. CUMMINGS'S "BUFFALO BILL 'S"

Let's look now at a short poem by E. E. Cummings, probably written in 1917, the year Buffalo Bill died, but not published until 1920. Cummings did not give it a title, but included it in a group of poems called "Portraits." (In line 6, *pigeons* are clay targets used in skeet shooting or in exhibitions of marksmanship.)

<pre>
Buffalo Bill 's
defunct
        who used to
        ride a watersmooth-silver
                              stallion   5
and break onetwothreefourfive pigeonsjustlikethat
                                        Jesus
he was a handsome man
                    and what i want to know is
how do you like your blueeyed boy   10
Mister Death
</pre>

Read the poem, preferably aloud, at least two or three times, and with as open a mind as possible. *Don't* assume that because the photograph shows us a man for whom we probably would not want to work, this poem necessarily conveys the same attitude.

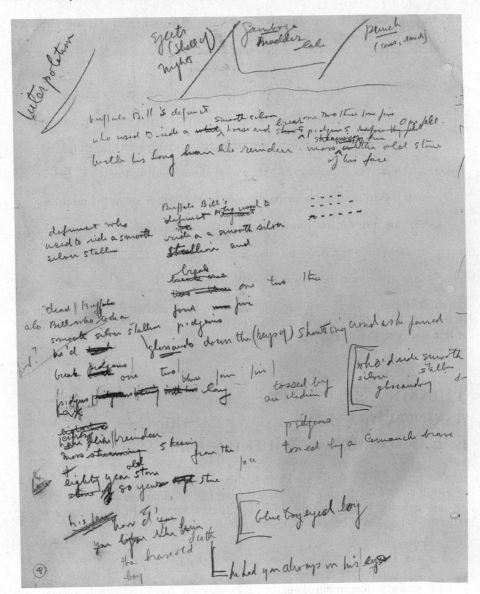

Manuscript of the draft of E. E. Cummings's poem (the final version is printed on page 193). (By permission of the Houghton Library, Harvard University. MS Am 1823.7 [21])

Ultimately you will want to ask your own questions about the poem and about your responses, but for a start you may find it useful to put down tentative answers to some or all of these questions:

1. What is the speaker's attitude toward Buffalo Bill? (How do you know? What *evidence* can you point to?)
2. In line 6, why do you suppose the poet ran the words together?
3. Why do you think Cummings spaced the poem as he does? One student suggested that the lines form an arrowhead pointing to the right. Do you

```
 1          buffalo Bill [in]'s defunct
 2                          smooth silver  break one two three four five  one fell.
 3          who used to ride a ~~white~~ horse and ~~shoot~~ pidgens ~~before they fell~~.
 4                          streaming from
 5                              ~~xxxx~~
 6          with his long hair like reindeer moss, ~~in~~ the old stone
 7                                        of his face
 8                              Buffalo Bill's
 9                                      who used to      - - - -
10    defunct who             defunct ~~defunct~~        - - - - -
11    used to ride a smooth        ~~who~~
12    silver stallion         ride a a smooth silver  r - - - - -
13                            [~~horse~~] stallion and
14                              break
15                            ~~break one~~
16    dead ‖Buffalo           ~~two three~~  one  two  three
17          'd
18  alo Bill who rode a       four ~~xxxx~~ five
19    smooth silver stallion  pidgens
20    he'd ~~break~~
21  how?        pidgens/        glissando down the (happy) shouting crowd as he passed
22    break ~~break~~
23              one      two
24                       three  four   five
25                                              |          who'd ride smooth
26    pidgens ~~pidgens being with his~~ long                silver ' stallion
27      ax                           tossed by          glissandoing  do
28    ~~eighty-two~~                 an indian
29    curls
30    hair like ‖ reindeer                    ~~pidgens~~
31              streaming
32    moss ~~streaming~~     from the      tossed by a Comanche brave
33                          face
34    x          old
35  ~~xxx~~ eighty year stone
36    stone ~~xx~~ 80 years ~~xxx~~ stone
37    his ~~long~~
38          how d'~~you~~
39    ~~you [like]~~ you like [it] him    blue ~~boy~~ eye[e]d boy
40                      death
41          the brave old
42          boy
43                              he had you always in his | ey[es]e |
```

Modern transcription of the draft reproduced on page 194. (By permission of the Houghton Library, Harvard University. MS Am 1823.7 [80].)

find merit in this suggestion? If not, what better explanation(s) can you offer?

4. What do you make out of the address to "Mister Death"? Why "Mister Death" rather than "Mr. Death" or "Death"? If Mister Death could speak, what answer do you think he might give to the speaker's question?
5. What do you make of the use of "defunct" (as opposed to "dead") in line 2?
6. What do you make of "Jesus" in line 7? What is the effect of placing the word on a line by itself? Is Cummings being blasphemous? Is he inviting us

The Farewell Shot, 1910. A poster from
what was billed as a farewell performance.
(Buffalo Bill Historical Center, Cody, WY
[1.69.137])

to compare Buffalo Bill with Jesus? Again, support your response with *evidence*.

7. Compare the published poem with the manuscript draft. In the manuscript (see page 194, and for a scholar's transcription of it, see page 195) you will notice that Cummings wrote, near the start, "with his long hair like reindeer moss streaming from the old stone of his face." These words do not appear in the final version. Do you think Cummings showed good judgment in deleting the line? Explain.

8. Some readers say that Cummings is satirizing Buffalo Bill, others that he is satirizing death. Do you agree with either of these views? Why? (In a sentence or two define *satire*—feel free to consult a dictionary—and perhaps give a clear example. By the way, it's possible to satirize the common human fear of death, but can death be satirized? How might that be done? And what would be the point?)

You may want to discuss some or all of these questions, and others that you generate for yourself, with classmates and with your instructor. It will be interesting to see whether at least some differences of opinion can be resolved by discussion, by pointing to evidence.

Finally, after you have thought about the preceding questions, and any questions that you may initiate, consider these two opinions, from published discussions of the poem:

1. Buffalo Bill, in the poem, functions as a destroyer, an agent of death.

Buffalo Bill on a favorite horse, around 1910.
(Buffalo Bill Historical Center, Cody, WY
[P.69.862])

2. The picture of Buffalo Bill on his "watersmooth-silver stallion," riding to the center of the tent to accept the adulation of the crowd before his demonstration of crack marksmanship is, I think, acidly ironic.

Do you agree with either, or with both? What evidence in the poem can you point to, in order to support or rebut these assertions?

EMILY DICKINSON: THREE VERSIONS OF A POEM, AND MORE

Here, for study and comparison, we present Emily Dickinson's "I felt a Funeral, in my Brain," in multiple versions: the poem as we know it today; the poem in manuscript; and the poem in its first published version. Then, two more poems, which are similar in phrasing to one another and show an affinity to "I felt a Funeral, in my Brain." Read each version carefully, asking questions about its style and structure and comparing it to the others. Look for details, and ask yourself why the detail—the use of a specific image, or a change in the organization of a line, for example—is significant.

This is the version of "I felt a Funeral, in my Brain" as we know it today. It is printed as #280 in *The Complete Poems of Emily Dickinson*, ed. Thomas H. Johnson (Boston: Little, Brown, and Company, 1957). This edition follows the text that Johnson presented in his three-volume scholarly edition, *The Poems of Emily*

Dickinson (Cambridge: Harvard University Press, 1955). Johnson proposes a date of sometime in 1861 for this poem. The editor of a new scholarly edition, *The Poems of Emily Dickinson: Variorum Edition*, 3 vols. (Cambridge: Harvard University Press, 1998), R. W. Franklin, while agreeing with Johnson's version of the poem, suggests a date of summer 1862.

I felt a Funeral, in my Brain

I felt a Funeral, in my Brain,
And Mourners to and fro
Kept treading—treading—till it seemed
That Sense was breaking through—   4

And when they all were seated,
A Service, like a Drum—
Kept beating—beating—till I thought
My Mind was going numb—   8

Dickinson's manuscript for "I felt a Funeral, in my Brain."

And then I heard them lift a Box
And creak across my Soul
With those same Boots of Lead, again,
Then Space—began to toll,   12

As all the Heavens were a Bell
And Being, but an Ear,
And I, and Silence, some strange Race
Wrecked, solitary, here—   16

And then a Plank in Reason, broke,
And I dropped down, and down—
And hit a World, at every plunge,
And Finished knowing—then—   20

[1861 or 1862]

On pages 198–199, we show the poem as it appears in Dickinson's own hand. Our copy is taken from *The Manuscript Books of Emily Dickinson*, 2 vols., ed. R. W. Franklin (Cambridge: Harvard University Press, 1981). Like nearly all of Dickinson's poems, this one was not published in her lifetime. She wrote her poems on sheets of letter paper, which she then bound together with string into packets. Perhaps these personal manuscript books or "fascicles" (that is, a small bundle, or the divisions of a book published in parts) represented for Dickinson a form of publication—though a very private one.

Notice that in line 10, Dickinson wrote "Brain," but then crossed it out and selected the word "Soul" instead. Notice also that in manuscript, the poem concludes with a line not in the poem, but that seems to give alternatives for words in lines 19 and 20. Refer to the poem as we know it to see how Thomas Johnson has worked from the manuscript to make his choices about how the poem should read. As you compare the published poem to the manuscript, ask yourself why Johnson made these choices and whether you agree with them.

In her will Dickinson stipulated that upon her death, her papers and letters should be burned. But her sister Lavinia, who discovered the poems, decided that her sister's request did not include them, and she soon became determined to see the poems published. This task was taken up by Mabel Loomis Todd (1856–1932), who was a friend of Dickinson's—and the lover of Austin Dickinson, Emily's older (and already married) brother. With help from the critic and man of letters Thomas Wentworth Higginson, Todd edited two series of Dickinson's poems (1890, 1891). She then edited a third series (1896) and the *Letters of Emily Dickinson* (2 vols., 1894) herself. Both Todd and Higginson removed many of the boldly original features of the poems' language, structure, and punctuation. They sought to make Dickinson more conventional, more like other poets of the age. This, in their view, was the best way to make her less difficult and hence more accessible to readers. But the result was that they eliminated the daring, brilliant innovations that make Dickinson extraordinary. The following poem is taken from *Poems by Emily Dickinson*, third series (Boston: Little, Brown, 1896). As you read Todd's version, consider its similarities to and differences from both the manuscript version and the poem as Johnson presents it.

> I felt a funeral in my brain,
> And mourners, to and fro,
> Kept treading, treading, till it seemed
> That sense was breaking through.   4
>
> And when they all were seated,
> A service like a drum
> Kept beating, beating, till I thought
> My mind was going numb.   8
>
> And then I heard them lift a box,
> And creak across my soul
> With those same boots of lead, again.
> Then space began to toll   12
>
> As all the heavens were a bell,
> And Being but an ear,
> And I and silence some strange race,
> Wrecked, solitary, here.   16

Here are two more poems, similar to one another and somewhat similar to "I felt a Funeral, in my Brain." Thomas Johnson dates the first one as having been written in 1864, and the second in the following year. The second, Johnson explains, is not so much a separate poem as a variant on the first. Dickinson probably sent this version to her sister-in-law Susan Gilbert Dickinson, who was married to Dickinson's brother Austin. In his more recent edition, R. W. Franklin says more firmly that the poem was written in early 1864 and that, without address or signature, Dickinson sent a version of its second stanza to Susan.

Here again, ask yourself questions about the style and structure of each poem in its own right, and then about how each compares to the other. Then, focus your attention on more general questions, as you review the analyses and comparisons you have performed: What has this question-asking exploration of multiple versions of "I felt a Funeral, in my Brain" taught you about Dickinson as a writer? What makes her a challenging, and unconventional, poet? What are the features of her style that make her poetry distinctive, different from other poets you have read and studied?

I felt a Cleaving in my Mind—

I felt a Cleaving in my Mind—
As if my Brain had split—
I tried to match it—Seam by Seam—
But could not make them fit.   4

The thought behind, I strove to join
Unto the thought before—
But Sequence ravelled out of Sound
Like Balls—upon a Floor.   8

[1864]

The Dust behind I strove to join

The Dust behind I strove to join
Unto the Disk before—
But Sequence ravelled out of Sound
Like Balls upon a Floor—

[1865]

IMAGINATIVE PLAY: THINKING ABOUT FOUR POEMS

Earlier in this book, in Chapter 5 (pp. 140–141), we included three versions of W. B. Yeats's "Leda and the Swan," dating from 1923 to 1933, along with a brief biographical note. Yeats used the swan in a number of poems, giving it various symbolic meanings: Sometimes, for example, the floating swan suggests the drifting imagination, or inspiration, and the mounting swan suggests the soul.

The following poem, "The Wild Swans at Coole," written in 1916, is Yeats's first important use of the swan. Coole Park was the name of the estate, in

Galway, Ireland, of Yeats's patron, Lady Gregory. (*Coole* is from an Irish word meaning "a niche" or "a retreat," hence its appropriateness for the name of a place of retirement or retreat.) Yeats was a frequent visitor there, beginning in 1897. Writing in 1916, in lines 7–8 he alludes to his first visit: "The nineteenth autumn has come upon me / Since I first made my count." At the time of this first visit, he was grieving because the woman he loved had rejected him. In a prose work he characterized his emotional state at the time of the first visit to Coole Park: "I was involved in a miserable love affair . . . My devotion might as well have been offered to an image in a milliner's window, or to a statue in a wax museum. . . ."

We follow Yeats's poem with an utterly unrelated work, Gwendolyn Brooks's "We Real Cool"—unrelated except for the accidental resemblance of "Coole" and "Cool." And we follow Brooks's poem with a witty piece by Andrew Hudgins, who brings the two preceding poems together by using Yeats's imagery and Brooks's lineation or versification. His work is a sort of parody of each author, but clearly—we think—he is motivated not by malice but by admiration and affection. And we end with an anonymous poem, set to music by Orlando Gibbons.

WILLIAM BUTLER YEATS

The Wild Swans at Coole

The trees are in their autumn beauty,
The woodland paths are dry,
Under the October twilight the water
Mirrors a still sky;
Upon the brimming water among the stones   5
Are nine-and-fifty swans.

The nineteenth autumn has come upon me
Since I first made my count;
I saw, before I had well finished,
All suddenly mount   10
And scatter wheeling in great broken rings
Upon their clamorous wings.

I have looked upon those brilliant creatures,
And now my heart is sore.
All's changed since I, hearing at twilight,   15
The first time on this shore,
The bell-beat of their wings above my head,
Trod with a lighter tread.

Unwearied still, lover by lover,
They paddle in the cold   20
Companionable streams or climb the air;
Their hearts have not grown old;
Passion or conquest, wander where they will,
Attend upon them still.

But now they drift on the still water,   25
Mysterious, beautiful;
Among what rushes will they build,
By what lake's edge or pool
Delight men's eyes when I awake some day
To find they have flown away?   30

[1916]

Topics for Critical Thinking and Writing

1. Do you find this a beautiful poem? Or would you be inclined to use a different term to characterize it? Is there a special element in this poem or in other poems you have read, or perhaps a special feeling that this poem or others give you, that leads you to say, "Now this is a beautiful poem"?
2. The key transition comes at line 15, in the exact middle: "All's changed since I. . . ." What is the scene that the speaker describes from lines 1–14? And what is the nature of the change that he describes in lines 15–30?
3. Yeats says in line 13 that the swans are "brilliant creatures." What does he mean by this phrase?
4. Can you explain the meaning of the question with which the speaker ends the poem? Do you think it is a good idea to end a poem with a question? What would be your argument in favor of such a choice? What would be your argument against it?
5. Have you ever had an experience similar to Yeats's—an experience, for example, of an eagle's flight, or of a group of horses in the wild, that has given you a feeling of connection? Or, maybe, a feeling of hope, or loss, or of something else that was powerful and profound? What was this experience? What was the response you had when it happened? Do you think about the experience differently now?

GWENDOLYN BROOKS

Gwendolyn Brooks (1917–2000) was born in Topeka, Kansas, but was raised on Chicago's South Side, where she spent most of her life. In 1950, when she won the Pulitzer Prize for Poetry, she became the first African American writer to win a Pulitzer Prize.

We Real Cool

The Pool Players.
Seven at the Golden Shovel.

We real cool. We
Left school. We

Lurk late. We
Strike straight. We   4

Sing sin. We
Thin gin. We

Jazz June. We
Die soon.

8

[1960]

Topics for Critical Thinking and Writing

1. What does it mean for the pool players to say that they are "cool," and not just "cool," but "real cool"?
2. Why does Brooks give seven speakers? Why not simply one, as in "I real cool" and so on? Would that have been more focused and thus more effective?
3. The stanzas could have been written:

> We real cool.
> We left school.
>
> We lurk late.
> We strike straight.

And so on. What does Brooks gain by organizing the lines as she does?
4. Brooks presents the poem in a first-person plural voice, "we." If someone claimed that Brooks would have made the poem more objective, and hence better, if she had presented it in third-personal plural, "they," what would be your argument in response?
5. One commentary we consulted says that this poem describes "pool-playing gang members at a bar called The Golden Shovel on the South Side of Chicago." Does this specific information add to or detract from your experience of the poem?

ANDREW HUDGINS

Andrew Hudgins was born in Killeen, Texas in 1951, and educated at Huntingdon College, the University of Alabama, and the University of Iowa. The author of a book of essays and of five volumes of poems, Hudgins has received numerous awards. He teaches at the University of Cincinnati.

The Wild Swans Skip School

We beat wings. We
fly rings. We

scorn Yeats. We
have mates. We

won't stay. We
fly 'way.

4

[2001]

Topics for Critical Thinking and Writing

1. In what way is Hudgins responding to Yeats? In what way is he responding to Brooks? Why do you think he would want to do something like this?
2. Does this poem make you laugh, or at least smile? Does it seem silly to you?
3. Is there anything serious about this poem, or is it a comic poem and no more than that?
4. If you were unfamiliar with the poems by Yeats and Brooks, what would your response be to Hudgins's poem?
5. Imagine that someone says to you, "This poem isn't any good: it's too short and too simple." What kind of argument could you present to convince this person that this is in fact a good poem?
6. Now imagine that someone says to you, "This poem is short and simple and I find it delightful." What kind of argument could you present that takes a more skeptical point of view?

ANONYMOUS

The ancient Greeks thought that the swan was silent throughout its life until the moment just before death, when it sang melodiously, hence the term "swan song" to denote a person's last action or last words. The following poem was first published in Orlando Gibbons's First Set of Madrigals and Motets *(1612).*

Cantus I (soprano I) vocal part from Orlando Gibbons's five-voice setting of 1612.

The Silver Swan

The silver swan, who living had no note,
When death approached, unlocked her silent throat;
Leaning her breast against the reedy shore,
Thus sung her first and last, and sung no more:
"Farewell, all joys; Oh death, come close mine eyes;   5
More geese than swans now live, more fools than wise."

[1612]

Topics for Critical Thinking and Writing

1. It is untrue that swans are silent until just before their death, at which point they sing. In fact, it is doubly untrue: (a) when angry, swans make hissing sounds, and (b) no kind of swan utters anything that can reasonably be called a song (though the whistling swan does a bit more than hiss). But does the truth or falsehood of the legend have any relevance to the value of the poem?

2. Suppose the final two lines were:

   > Farewell all joys; Oh death, come close mine eyes;
   > I leave the water now, for heavenly skies.

   Or:

   > Farewell all joys; Oh death, come close mine eyes;
   > A swan sings only once before it dies.

   Which version do you prefer? Why?

8

Reading and Writing about Essays

The word *essay* entered the English language in 1597, when Francis Bacon called a small book of ten short prose pieces *Essays*. Bacon borrowed the word from Michel de Montaigne, a French writer who in 1580 had published some short prose pieces under the title *Essais*—that is, "testings," or "attempts," from the French verb *essayer*, "to try." Montaigne's title indicated that his graceful and personal jottings—the fruit of pleasant study and meditation—were not fully thought-out treatises but rather sketches that could be amplified and amended.

If you keep a journal, you are working in Montaigne's tradition. You jot down your tentative thoughts, perhaps your responses to a work of literature, partly to find out what you think and how you feel. Montaigne said, in the preface to his book, "I am myself the subject of my book," and in all probability you are the real subject of your journal. Your entries—your responses to other writers and your reflections on those responses—require you to examine yourself.

TYPES OF ESSAYS

If you have already taken a course in composition (or even if you haven't), you are probably familiar with the chief kinds of essays. Essays are usually classified—roughly, of course—along the following lines: meditation (or speculation or reflection), argument (or persuasion), exposition (or information), narration, and description.

Of these, the **meditative** (or **speculative** or **reflective**) **essay** is the closest to Montaigne. In a meditative essay, the writer seems chiefly concerned with exploring an idea or a feeling. The organization usually seems casual, not a careful and evident structure but a free flow of thought—what the Japanese (who wrote with brush and ink) called "following the brush." The essayist is thinking, but he or she is not especially concerned with arguing a case, or even with being logical. We think along with the essayist, chiefly because we find the writer's tentative thoughts engaging. Of course the writer may in the long run be pressing a point, advancing an argument, but the emphasis is on the free play of mind, not on an orderly and logical analysis.

In the **argumentative** (or **persuasive**) **essay**, the organization probably is apparent, and it is reasonable: For instance, the essay may announce a problem, define some terms, present and refute solutions that the writer considers to be inadequate, and then, by way of a knockdown ending, offer what the writer considers to be the correct solution.

The **expository essay**, in which the writer is chiefly concerned with giving information (for instance on how to annotate a text, or how to read a poem, or how to use a word processor), ordinarily has an equally clear organization. A clear organization is necessary in such an essay because the reader is reading not in order to come into contact with an interesting mind that may keep doubling back on its thinking (as in a meditative essay), and not in order to come to a decision about some controversial issue (as in an argumentative essay), but in order to gain information.

Narrative and **descriptive essays** usually really are largely meditative essays. For instance, a narrative essay may recount some happening—often a bit of autobiography—partly to allow the writer and the reader to meditate on it. Similarly, a description, let's say of a spider spinning a web or of children playing in the street, usually turns out to be offered not so much as information—it thus is unlike the account of how to annotate a text—but rather as something for the writer and reader to enjoy in itself, and perhaps to think further about.

Of course most essays are not pure specimens. For instance, an informative essay, let's say on how to use a word processing program on a computer, may begin with a paragraph that seeks to persuade you to use this particular software. Or it might begin with a very brief narrative, an anecdote of a student who switched from program X to program Y, again in order to persuade the reader to use this software (Y, of course). Similarly, an argument—and probably most of the essays that you write in English courses will be arguments advancing a thesis concerning the meaning or structure of a literary work—may include some exposition, for instance a very brief summary to remind the reader of the gist of the work you will be arguing about.

THE ESSAYIST'S PERSONA

Many of the essays that give readers the most pleasure are, like entries in a journal, chiefly reflective. An essay of this kind sets forth the writer's attitudes or states of mind, and the reader's interest in the essay is almost entirely in the way the writer sees things. It's not so much *what* the writers see and say as *how* they say what they see. Even in essays that are narrative—that is, in essays that recount events, such as a bit of biography—our interest is more in the essayists' *responses* to the events than in the events themselves. When we read an essay, we almost say, "So that's how it feels to be you," and "Tell me more about the way you see things." The bit of history is less important than the memorable presence of the writer.

Voice

When you read an essay in this chapter or in a later chapter, try to imagine the kind of person who wrote it, the kind of person who seems to be speaking it. Then slowly reread the essay, noticing *how* the writer conveyed this personality or persona or "voice" (even while he or she was writing about a topic "out there"). The writer's persona may be revealed by common or uncommon words, for example, by short or long sentences, by literal or figurative language, or by familiar or erudite examples.

Let's take a simple, familiar example of words that establish a persona. Lincoln begins the Gettysburg Address with "Four score and seven years ago . . ." He might have said "Eighty-seven years ago"—but the language would have lacked the biblical echo, and the persona would thus have been that of an ordinary person rather than that of a man who has about him something of the tone of an Old Testament prophet. This religious tone of "four score and seven years" is entirely fitting, since

- President Lincoln was speaking at the dedication of a cemetery for "these hallowed dead" and
- he was urging the members of his audience to give all of their energies to ensure that the dead men had not died in vain.

By such devices as the choice of words, the length of sentences, and the sorts of evidence offered, an author sounds to the reader solemn or agitated or witty or genial or severe. If you are familiar with Martin Luther King's "I Have a Dream," you may recall that he begins the piece (originally it was a speech, delivered at the Lincoln Memorial on the one-hundredth anniversary of Lincoln's Emancipation Proclamation) with these words: "Five score years ago. . . ." King is deliberately echoing Lincoln's words, partly in tribute to Lincoln, but also to help establish himself as the spiritual descendant of Lincoln and, further back, of the founders of the Judeo-Christian tradition.

Tone

Only by reading closely can we hear in the mind's ear the writer's tone—friendly, or bitter, or indignant, or ironic (characterized by wry understatement or over-statement). Perhaps you have heard the line from Owen Wister's novel *The Virginian*: "When you call me that, smile!" Words spoken with a smile mean something different from the same words forced through clenched teeth. But while speakers can communicate—or, we might say, can guide the responses of their audience—by body language and by gestures, by facial expressions and by changes in tone of voice, writers have only words in ink on paper. As a writer, you are learning control of tone as you learn to take pains in your choice of words, in the way you arrange sentences, and even in the punctuation marks you may find yourself changing in your final draft. These skills will pay off doubly if you apply them to your reading, by putting yourself in the place of the writer whose work you are reading. As a reader, you must make some effort to "hear" the writer's tone as part of the meaning the words communicate. Skimming is not adequate to that task. Thinking carefully about the works in this book means, first of all, reading them carefully, listening for the sound of the speaking voice, so that you can respond to the persona—the personality or character the author presents in the essay.

Consider the following paragraph from the middle of "Black Men and Public Space," a short essay by Brent Staples. Staples is talking about growing up in a tough neighborhood. Of course the paragraph is only a small example; the tone depends, finally, on the entire essay, which we will print in a moment.

As a boy, I saw countless tough guys locked away; I have since buried several, too. They were babies, really—a teenage cousin, a brother of twenty-two, a childhood friend in his mid-twenties—all gone down in episodes of bravado played out in the streets. I came to doubt the virtues of intimidation early on. I chose, perhaps unconsciously, to remain a shadow—timid, but a survivor.

Judging only from these few lines, what sense of Staples do we get? Perhaps you will agree that we can probably say something along these lines:

- He is relatively quiet and gentle. We sense this not simply because he tells us that he was "timid" but because (at least in this passage) he does not raise his voice either in a denunciation of white society for creating a system that produces black violence or in a denunciation of those blacks of his youth who engaged in violence.
- He is perceptive; he sees that the "tough guys," despite the fact that some were in their twenties, were babies; their bravado was infantile and destructive.
- He speaks with authority; he is giving a firsthand report.
- He doesn't claim to be especially shrewd; he modestly says that he may have "unconsciously" adopted the behavior that enabled him to survive.
- In saying that he is a "survivor" he displays a bit of wry humor. The usual image of a survivor is a guy in a Banana Republic outfit, gripping a knife, someone who survived a dog-eat-dog world by being tougher than the others. But Staples almost comically says he is a "survivor" who is "timid."

If your responses to the paragraph are somewhat different, jot them down and in a few sentences try to explain them.

PRE-WRITING: IDENTIFYING THE TOPIC AND THESIS

Although we have emphasized the importance of the essayist's personality, essayists also make a point. They have a thesis or argument, and an argument implies taking a specific viewpoint toward a topic. In reading an essay, then, try to identify the topic. The topic of "Do-It-Yourself Brain Surgery" can't really be brain surgery; it must be do-it-yourself books, and the attitude probably will be amused contempt for such books. Even an essay that is largely narrative, like Brent Staples's, recounting a personal experience or a bit of history, probably will include an attitude toward the event that is being narrated. It is that attitude—the interpretation of the event rather than the event itself—that may be the real topic of the essay.

It's time to look at Staples's essay. (Following the essay you will find a student's outline of it and another student's version of its thesis.)

BRENT STAPLES

Brent Staples, born in 1951, received a bachelor's degree from Widener University in Chester, Pennsylvania, and a PhD from the University of Chicago. After working as a journalist in Chicago, he joined The New York Times *in 1985, and he is now on the newspaper's editorial board, where he writes on politics and culture. His essay was first published in* Ms. *magazine in 1986 and reprinted in a slightly revised form—the form we give here—in* Harper's *in 1987.*

Black Men and Public Space

My first victim was a woman—white, well dressed, probably in her late twenties. I came upon her late one evening on a deserted street in Hyde Park, a relatively affluent neighborhood in an otherwise mean, impoverished section of Chicago.

As I swung onto the avenue behind her, there seemed to be a discreet, unin-flammatory distance between us. Not so. She cast back a worried glance. To her, the youngish black man—a broad six feet two inches with a beard and billowing hair, both hands shoved into the pockets of a bulky military jacket—seemed menacingly close. After a few more quick glimpses, she picked up her pace and was soon running in earnest. Within seconds, she disappeared into a cross street.

That was more than a decade ago. I was twenty-two years old, a graduate student newly arrived at the University of Chicago. It was in the echo of that terri-fied woman's footfalls that I first began to know the unwieldy inheritance I'd come into—the ability to alter public space in ugly ways. It was clear that she thought herself the quarry of a mugger, a rapist, or worse. Suffering a bout of in-somnia, however, I was stalking sleep, not defenseless wayfarers. As a softy who is scarcely able to take a knife to a raw chicken—let alone hold one to a person's throat—I was surprised, embarrassed, and dismayed all at once. Her flight made me feel like an accomplice in tyranny. It also made it clear that I was indistin-guishable from the muggers who occasionally seeped into the area from the sur-rounding ghetto. That first encounter, and those that followed, signified that a vast, unnerving gulf lay between nighttime pedestrians—particularly women—and me. And I soon gathered that being perceived as dangerous is a hazard in itself. I only needed to turn a corner into a dicey situation, or crowd some frightened, armed person in a foyer somewhere, or make an errant move after being pulled over by a policeman. Where fear and weapons meet—and they often do in urban America—there is always the possibility of death.

In that first year, my first away from my hometown, I was to become thor-oughly familiar with the language of fear. At dark, shadowy intersections, I could cross in front of a car stopped at a traffic light and elicit the *thunk*, thunk, thunk, thunk of the driver—black, white, male, or female—hammering down the door locks. On less traveled streets after dark, I grew accustomed to but never comfort-able with people crossing to the other side of the street rather than pass me. Then there were the standard unpleasantries with policemen, doormen, bouncers, cab-drivers, and others whose business it is to screen out troublesome individuals *before* there is any nastiness.

I moved to New York nearly two years ago and I have remained an avid night walker. In central Manhattan, the near-constant crowd cover minimizes tense one-on-one street encounters. Elsewhere—in SoHo, for example, where sidewalks are narrow and tightly spaced buildings shut out the sky—things can get very taut indeed.

5   After dark, on the warrenlike streets of Brooklyn where I live, I often see women who fear the worst from me. They seem to have set their faces on neutral, and with their purse straps strung across their chests bandolier-style, they forge ahead as though bracing themselves against being tackled. I understand, of course, that the danger they perceive is not a hallucination. Women are particu-larly vulnerable to street violence, and young black males are drastically overrep-resented among the perpetrators of that violence. Yet these truths are no solace against the kind of alienation that comes of being ever the suspect, a fearsome en-tity with whom pedestrians avoid making eye contact.

It is not altogether clear to me how I reached the ripe old age of twenty-two without being conscious of the lethality nighttime pedestrians attributed to me. Perhaps it was because in Chester, Pennsylvania, the small, angry industrial town where I came of age in the 1960s, I was scarcely noticeable against a backdrop of gang warfare, street knifings, and murders. I grew up one of the good boys, had perhaps a half-dozen fistfights. In retrospect, my shyness of combat has clear sources.

As a boy, I saw countless tough guys locked away; I have since buried several, too. They were babies, really—a teenage cousin, a brother of twenty-two, a childhood friend in his mid-twenties—all gone down in episodes of bravado played out in the streets. I came to doubt the virtues of intimidation early on. I chose, perhaps unconsciously, to remain a shadow—timid, but a survivor.

The fearsomeness mistakenly attributed to me in public places often has a perilous flavor. The most frightening of these confusions occurred in the late 1970s and early 1980s, when I worked as a journalist in Chicago. One day, rushing into the office of a magazine I was writing for with a deadline story in hand, I was mistaken for a burglar. The office manager called security and, with an ad hoc posse, pursued me through the labyrinthine halls, nearly to my editor's door. I had no way of proving who I was. I could only move briskly toward the company of someone who knew me.

Another time I was on assignment for a local paper and killing time before an interview. I entered a jewelry store on the city's affluent Near North Side. The proprietor excused herself and returned with an enormous red Doberman pinscher straining at the end of a leash. She stood, the dog extended toward me, silent to my questions, her eyes bulging nearly out of her head. I took a cursory look around, nodded, and bade her good night.

10   Relatively speaking, however, I never fared as badly as another black male journalist. He went to nearby Waukegan, Illinois, a couple of summers ago to work on a story about a murderer who was born there. Mistaking the reporter for the killer, police officers hauled him from his car at gunpoint and but for his press credentials would probably have tried to book him. Such episodes are not uncommon. Black men trade tales like this all the time.

Over the years, I learned to smother the rage I felt at so often being taken for a criminal. Not to do so would surely have led to madness. I now take precautions to make myself less threatening. I move about with care, particularly late in the evening. I give a wide berth to nervous people on subway platforms during the wee hours, particularly when I have exchanged business clothes for jeans. If I happen to be entering a building behind some people who appear skittish, I may walk by, letting them clear the lobby before I return, so as not to seem to be following them. I have been calm and extremely congenial on those rare occasions when I've been pulled over by the police.

And on late-evening constitutionals I employ what has proved to be an excellent tension-reducing measure: I whistle melodies from Beethoven and Vivaldi and the more popular classical composers. Even steely New Yorkers hunching toward nighttime destinations seem to relax, and occasionally they even join in the tune. Virtually everybody seems to sense that a mugger wouldn't be warbling bright, sunny selections from Vivaldi's *Four Seasons*. It is my equivalent of the cowbell that hikers wear when they know they are in bear country.

[1986]

SUMMARIZING

Summary should be clearly distinguished from analysis. The word *summary* is related to *sum*, the total something adds up to. (We say "adds *up* to" because the Greeks and Romans counted upward and wrote the total at the top.)

A summary is a condensation or abridgement; it briefly gives the reader the gist of a longer work. It boils down the longer work, resembling the longer work as a bouillon cube resembles a bowl of soup. A summary of Staples's "Black Men and Public Space" will reduce the essay, perhaps to a paragraph or two or even to a sentence. It will not call attention to Staples's various strategies, and it will not evaluate his views or his skill as a writer; it will merely present the gist of what he says.

Summary and Analysis

If, then, you are asked to write an analysis of something you have read, you should not hand in a summary. On the other hand, a very brief summary may appropriately appear within an analytic essay. Usually, in fact, the reader needs some information, and the writer of the essay will briefly summarize this information. For example, a student who wrote about Staples's essay is *summarizing* when she writes

> Staples says that he is aware that his presence frightens many whites, especially women.

She is summarizing because she is reporting, without personal comment, what Staples said.

On the other hand, she is *analyzing* when she writes

> By saying at the outset, "My first victim was a woman--white, well dressed, probably in her late twenties," Staples immediately catches the reader's attention and sets up expectations that will be undermined in the next paragraph.

In this sentence the writer is not reporting *what* Staples said but is explaining *how* he achieved an effect.

In Chapter 5 we discussed a few principles that govern summaries (see the list on pages 130–131). Here is a summary of our comments on "summary":

> A summary is a condensation or abridgment. Its chief characteristics are that (1) it is rarely more than one-fourth as long as the original; (2) its brevity is usually achieved by leaving out most of the concrete details of the original; (3) it is accurate; (4) it may rearrange the organization of the original, especially if a rearrangement will make things clearer; (5) it normally is in the present tense; and (6) quoted words need not be enclosed in quotation marks.

Preparing a Summary

If you are summarizing an essay, you may find that the essay includes its own summary, perhaps at the start or more likely near the end. If it does, you're in luck.

If it doesn't, we suggest that on rereading you jot down, after reading each paragraph, a sentence summarizing the gist of the paragraph. (A very long or poorly unified paragraph may require two sentences, but make every effort to boil the paragraph down to a dozen or so words.) Of course if a paragraph consists merely of a transitional sentence or two ("We will now turn to another example") you will lump it with the next paragraph. Similarly, if for some reason you encounter a series of very short paragraphs—for instance, three examples, each briefly stated, and all illustrating the same point—you probably will find that you can cover them with a single sentence. But if a paragraph runs to half a page or more of print, it's probably worth its own sentence of summary. In fact, your author may summarize the paragraph in the paragraph's opening sentence or in its final sentence.

Here is a student's paragraph-by-paragraph summary of Staples's "Black Men and Public Space." The numbers refer to Staples's paragraphs.

1. "First victim" was a white woman in Chicago, who hurried away.
2. Age 22, he realized--to his surprise and embarrassment--that he (a "youngish black man") could be perceived by strangers as a mugger. And, since his presence created fear, he was in a dangerous situation.
3,4,5. At intersections he heard drivers of cars lock their doors, and elsewhere he sensed hostility of bouncers and others. In NY, lots of tension on narrow sidewalks. Women are esp. afraid of him; he knows why, but that's "no solace."
6. He's not sure why it took him 22 years to see that others fear him, but prob. because in his hometown of Chester, Pa., there was lots of adolescent violence, though he stayed clear of it.
7. As a boy, he saw young toughs killed, and he kept clear, "timid, but a survivor."
8,9,10. Though he is gentle, he looks fearsome. Once, working as a journalist, he was mistaken for a burglar. Another time, in a jewelry store, the clerk brought out a guard dog. Another black journalist was covering a crime, but the police thought the journalist was the killer. Many blacks have had such experiences.
11. He has learned to smother his rage--and he keeps away from nervous people.
12. Walking late at night, he whistles familiar classical music, trying to reassure others that he is not a mugger.

When you have written your sentence summarizing the last paragraph, you may have done enough if the summary was intended simply for your own private use, for example, to help you review material for an examination. But if you are going to use it as the basis of a summary within an essay you are writing, you probably won't want to include a summary longer than three or four sentences, so your job will be to reduce and combine the sentences you have jotted down. Indeed, you may even want to reduce the summary to a single sentence.

A Suggested Exercise: Assuming that you find the sentences summarizing "Black Men and Public Space" acceptable, reduce them to a summary no longer than four readable sentences. Then compare your version with the versions of two other students and, working as a group, produce a summary.

Stating the Thesis of an Essay

Summarizing each stage of the essay forces a reader to be attentive and can assist the reader to formulate a **thesis sentence**, a sentence that (in the reader's opinion) sets forth the writer's central point. If an essay is essentially an argument—for example, a defense of (or an argument against) capital punishment—it will probably include one or more sentences that directly assert the thesis. "Black Men and Public Space," chiefly a narrative essay, is much less evidently an argument, but it does have a point, and some of its sentences come pretty close to summarizing the point. Here are three of those sentences:

> And I soon gathered that being perceived as dangerous is a hazard in itself. (2)
> The fearsomeness mistakenly attributed to me in public places often has a perilous flavor. (8)
> I now take precautions to make myself less threatening. (11)

We asked our students to formulate their own thesis sentence for Staples's essay. One student came up with the following sentence after first drafting a couple of tentative versions and then rereading the essay in order to modify them:

> In "Black Men and Public Space" Staples recognizes that because many whites fear a young black man and therefore may do violence to him, he may do well to try to cool the situation by making himself unthreatening.

Notice, again, that a thesis sentence states the *point* of the work. Don't confuse a thesis sentence with a summary of a narrative, such as "Staples at the age of twenty-two came to realize that his presence was threatening to whites, and he has since taken measures to make himself less threatening." This sentence, though true, doesn't clearly get at the point of the essay, the generalization that can be drawn from Staples's example.

Look again at the student's formulation of a thesis sentence (*not* the narrative summary sentence that we have just given). If you don't think that it fairly represents Staples's point, you may (if you are writing an essay about Staples's essay) want to come up with a sentence that seems more precise to you. Whether you use the sentence we have quoted or a sentence that you formulate for yourself, you can in any case of course disagree very strongly with what you take to be Staples's point. Your version of Staples's thesis should accurately reflect your understanding of Staples's point, but you need not agree with the point. You may think, for instance, that Staples is hypersensitive or (to mention only one other possibility) that he is playing the Uncle Tom.

A thesis sentence, then, whether the words are your own or the author's, is a very brief summary of the argument (not of the narrative) of the work. If you are writing an essay about an essay, you'll probably want to offer a sentence that reminds your reader of the point of the work you are discussing or gives the reader the gist of an unfamiliar work:

> Black males, however harmless, are in a perilous situation because whites, especially white women, perceive them as threatening.

Or:

> In "Black Men and Public Space" Brent Staples recognizes that because many whites fear young black men and may therefore do violence to them, black men may do well to try to cool the situation by making themselves nonthreatening.

Drafting a Summary

Sometimes, however, a fuller statement may be useful. For instance, if you are writing about a complex essay that makes six points, you may help your reader if you briefly restate all six. The length of your summary will depend on your purpose and the needs of your audience.

The following principles may help you to write your summary:

1. First, after having written sentences that summarize each paragraph or group of paragraphs, formulate the essay's thesis sentence. Formulating the sentence in writing will help you to stay with what you take to be the writer's main point.

2. Next, write a first draft by turning your summaries of the paragraphs into fewer and better sentences. For example, the student who wrote the paragraph-by-paragraph summary (p. 214) of Staples's essay turned her first five sentences (on Staples's first paragraphs) into this:

> Staples's "first victim" was a white woman in Chicago. When she hurried away from him, he realized--to his surprise and embarrassment--that because he was large and black and young he seemed to her to be a mugger. And since his presence created fear, he was in a dangerous situation. Other experiences, such as hearing drivers lock their cars when they were waiting at an intersection, have made him aware of the hostility of others. Women are especially afraid of him, and although he knows why, this knowledge is "no solace."

The student turned the remaining sentences of the outline into the following summary:

> Oddly, it took him twenty-two years to see that others fear him. Perhaps it took this long because he grew up in a violent neighborhood, though he kept clear, "timid, but a survivor." Because he is black and large, whites regard him as fearsome and treat him accordingly (once a clerk in a jewelry store brought out a guard dog), but other blacks have been treated worse. He has learned to smother his rage, and in order to cool things he tries to reassure nervous people by keeping away from them and (when he is walking late at night) by whistling classical music.

3. Write a lead-in sentence, probably incorporating the gist of the thesis sentence. Here is an example:

> Brent Staples, in "Black Men and Public Space," tells how his awareness that many white people regarded him as dangerous caused him to realize that he was in danger. His implicitly recommended

solution is to try to cool the anxiety by adopting nonthreatening behavior.

After writing a lead-in, revise the draft of your summary, eliminating needless repetition, providing transitions, and adding whatever you think may be needed to clarify the work for someone who is unfamiliar with it. You may rearrange the points if you think the rearrangement will clarify matters.

4. Edit your draft for errors in grammar, punctuation, and spelling. Read it aloud to test it once more for readability. Sometimes only by reading aloud do writers detect needless repetition or confusing phrases.

Some Writing Assignments

1. In a paragraph or two, set forth what you take to be Staples's *purpose*. Do you think he was writing chiefly to clarify some ideas for himself—for instance, to explore how he came to discover the "alienation that comes of being ever the suspect"? Or writing to assist blacks? Or to assist whites? Or what? (You may of course conclude that none of these suggestions, or all, are relevant.)

2. If you think the essay is effective, in a paragraph or two addressed to your classmates try to account for its effectiveness. Do certain examples strike you as particularly forceful? If so, why? Do certain sentences seem especially memorable? Again, why? For example, if the opening and concluding paragraphs strike you as effective, explain why. On the other hand, if you are unimpressed by part or all of the essay, explain why.

3. The success of a narrative as a piece of writing often depends on the reader's willingness to identify with the narrator. From an examination of "Black Men and Public Space," what explanations can you give for your willingness (or unwillingness) to identify yourself with Staples? (Probably you will want to say something about his persona as you sense it from the essay.) In the course of a 500-word essay explaining your position, very briefly summarize Staples's essay and state his thesis.

4. Have *you* ever unintentionally altered public space? For instance, you might recall an experience in which, as a child, your mere presence caused adults to alter their behavior—for instance, to stop quarreling.

   After a session of brainstorming, in which you produce some possible topics, you'll want to try to settle on one. After you have chosen a topic and produced a first draft, if you are not satisfied with your first paragraph—for instance, if you feel that it is not likely to get and hold the reader's attention—you may want to imitate the strategy that Staples adopted for his first paragraph.

5. If you have ever been in the position of one of Staples's "victims," that is, if you have ever shown fear or suspicion of someone who, it turned out, meant you no harm (or if you can imagine being in that position), write an essay from the "victim's" point of view. Explain what happened, what you did and thought. Did you think at the time about the feelings of the person you avoided or fled from? Has reading Staples's essay prompted further reflections on your experience? (Suggested length: 750 words.)

✓ CHECKLIST: *Getting Ideas for Writing about Essays*

Persona and Tone

❏ What sort of *persona* does the writer create?

❏ How does the writer create this persona? (For example, does the writer use colloquial language or formal language or technical language? Short sentences or long ones? Personal anecdotes? Quotations from authorities?)

❏ What is the *tone* of the essay? Is it, for example, solemn, or playful? Is the tone consistent? If not, how do the shifts affect your understanding of the writer's point or your identification of the writer's persona? Who is the *audience*?

Kind of Essay

❏ What kind of essay is it? Is it chiefly a presentation of facts (for example, an exposition, a report, a history)? Or is it chiefly an argument? Or a meditation? (Probably the essay draws on several kinds of writing, but which kind is it primarily? How are the other kinds related to the main kind?) What is the overall *purpose* of the essay?

❏ What does it seem to add up to? If the essay is chiefly meditative or speculative, how much emphasis is placed on the persona? That is, if the essay is a sort of thinking-out-loud, is your interest chiefly in the announced or ostensible topic, or in the writer's mood and personality? If the essay is chiefly a presentation of facts, does it also have a larger implication? For instance, if it narrates a happening (history), does the reader draw an inference—find a meaning—in the happening? If the essay is chiefly an argument, what is the thesis? How is the thesis supported? (Is it supported, for example, by induction, deduction, analogy, or emotional appeal?) Do you accept the assumptions (explicit and implicit)?

Structure

❏ Is the title appropriate? Propose a better title, if possible.

❏ Did the opening paragraph interest you? Why, or why not? Did the essay continue more or less as expected, or did it turn out to be rather different from what you anticipated?

❏ Prepare an outline of the essay. What effect does the writer seem to be aiming at by using this structure?

Value

❏ What is especially good (or bad) about the essay? Is it logically persuasive? Or entertaining? Or does it introduce an engaging persona? Or (if it is a narrative) does it tell a story effectively, using (where appropriate) description, dialogue, and commentary, and somehow make you feel that this story is worth reporting?

❏ Does the writer seem to hold values that you share? Or cannot share? Explain.

❏ Do you think that most readers will share your response, or do you think that for some reason—for example, your age, or your cultural background—your responses are unusual? Explain.

Your Turn: Essays for Analysis

Langston Hughes

Langston Hughes (1902–1967) was born in Joplin, Missouri. He lived part of his youth in Mexico, spent a year at Columbia University, served as a merchant seaman, and worked in a Paris nightclub, where he showed some of his poems to Dr. Alain Locke, a strong advocate of African American literature. After returning to the United States, Hughes went on to publish poetry, fiction, plays, essays, and biographies.

Salvation

I was saved from sin when I was going on thirteen. But not really saved. It happened like this. There was a big revival at my Auntie Reed's church. Every night for weeks there had been much preaching, singing, praying, and shouting, and some very hardened sinners had been brought to Christ, and the membership of the church had grown by leaps and bounds. Then just before the revival ended, they held a special meeting for children, "to bring the young lambs to the fold." My aunt spoke of it for days ahead. That night I was escorted to the front row and placed on the mourners' bench with all the other young sinners, who had not yet been brought to Jesus.

My aunt told me that when you were saved you saw a light, and something happened to you inside! And Jesus came into your life! And God was with you from then on! She said you could see and hear and feel Jesus in your soul. I believed her. I had heard a great many old people say the same thing and it seemed to me they ought to know. So I sat there calmly in the hot, crowded church, waiting for Jesus to come to me.

The preacher preached a wonderful rhythmical sermon, all moans and shouts and lonely cries and dire pictures of hell, and then he sang a song about the ninety and nine safe in the fold, but one little lamb was left out in the cold. Then he said: "Won't you come? Won't you come to Jesus? Young lambs, won't you come?" And he held out his arms to all us young sinners there on the mourners' bench. And the little girls cried. And some of them jumped up and went to Jesus right away. But most of us just sat there.

A great many old people came and knelt around us and prayed, old women with jet-black faces and braided hair, old men with work-gnarled hands. And the church sang a song about the lower lights are burning, some poor sinners to be saved. And the whole building rocked with prayer and song.

5   Still I kept waiting to *see* Jesus.

Finally all the young people had gone to the altar and were saved, but one boy and me. He was a rounder's son named Westley. Westley and I were surrounded by sisters and deacons praying. It was very hot in the church, and getting late now. Finally Westley said to me in a whisper: "God damn! I'm tired o' sitting here. Let's get up and be saved." So he got up and was saved.

Then I was left all alone on the mourners' bench. My aunt came and knelt at my knees and cried, while prayers and songs swirled all around me in the little church. The whole congregation prayed for me alone, in a mighty wail of moans and voices. And I kept waiting serenely for Jesus, waiting, waiting—but he didn't come. I wanted to see him, but nothing happened to me. Nothing! I wanted something to happen to me, but nothing happened.

I heard the songs and the minister saying: "Why don't you come? My dear child, why don't you come to Jesus? Jesus is waiting for you. He wants you. Why don't you come? Sister Reed, what is this child's name?"

"Langston," my aunt sobbed.

10   "Langston, why don't you come? Why don't you come and be saved? Oh, Lamb of God! Why don't you come?"

Now it was really getting late. I began to be ashamed of myself, holding everything up so long. I began to wonder what God thought about Westley, who certainly hadn't seen Jesus either, but who was now sitting proudly on the platform, swinging his knickerbockered legs and grinning down at me, surrounded by deacons and old women on their knees praying. God had not struck Westley dead for taking his name in vain or for lying in the temple. So I decided that maybe to save further trouble, I'd better lie, too, and say that Jesus had come, and get up and be saved.

So I got up.

Suddenly the whole room broke into a sea of shouting, as they saw me rise. Waves of rejoicing swept the place. Women leaped in the air. My aunt threw her arms around me. The minister took me by the hand and led me to the platform.

When things quieted down, in a hushed silence, punctuated by a few ecstatic "Amens," all the new young lambs were blessed in the name of God. Then joyous singing filled the room.

15   That night, for the last time in my life but one—for I was a big boy twelve years old—I cried. I cried, in bed alone, and couldn't stop. I buried my head under the quilts, but my aunt heard me. She woke up and told my uncle I was crying because the Holy Ghost had come into my life, and because I had seen Jesus. But I was really crying because I couldn't bear to tell her that I had lied, that I had deceived everybody in the church, and I hadn't seen Jesus, and that now I didn't believe there was a Jesus any more, since he didn't come to help me.

[1940]

Topics for Critical Thinking and Writing

1. Do you find the piece amusing, or serious, or both? Explain.

2. How would you characterize the style or voice of the first three sentences? Childlike, or sophisticated, or what? How would you characterize the final sentence? How can you explain the change in style or tone?

3. Why does Hughes bother to tell us, in paragraph 11, that Westley was "swinging his knickerbockered legs and grinning"? Do you think that Westley too may have cried that night? Give your reasons.

4. Is the episode told from the point of view of someone "going on thirteen," or from the point of view of a mature man? Cite evidence to support your position.

5. One of the golden rules of narrative writing is "Show, don't tell." In about 500 words, report an experience—for instance, a death in the family, or a severe (perhaps unjust) punishment, or the first day in a new school—that produced strong feelings. Like Hughes, you may want to draw on an experience in

which you were subjected to group pressure. Do not explicitly state what the feelings were; rather, let the reader understand the feelings chiefly through concretely detailed actions. But, like Hughes, you might state your thesis or basic position in your first paragraph and then indicate when and where the experience took place.

LAURA VANDERKAM

Laura Vanderkam wrote this essay a few months after graduating from Princeton University. At the time that it was published she was working as a Collegiate Network intern with the editorial board of USA Today.

Hookups Starve the Soul

The scene: my college dorm's basement bathroom on a Sunday morning early in my freshman year. As hungover girls crowded around the sinks, I caught a friend's eye in the mirror. What happened when she left last night's party with a boy neither of us had ever seen before?

"Oh," she said with a knowing look, "we hooked up."

No, not planes refueling in midair. Hookups are when a guy and girl get together for a physical encounter and don't expect anything else. They've all but replaced dating at most colleges, according to a study being released today by the Institute on American Values, a non-partisan family issues think tank. Only half of the women interviewed had been on six or more dates during college; a third had been on no more than two.

As a new college graduate, I can attest to this. I've had as many dates in my first 2 months in the real world as I had during my whole college career.

5   Lest you think college students are all libertines, hooking up doesn't mean having sex, although it can. The term includes all of the bases, and the ambiguity is intentional. Modest types can imply that less happened than did, and braggarts can hint at hitting a home run. Hookups are defined by alcohol, physical attraction and a lack of expectations in the morning.

While the study found that only 40% of the women interviewed admitted to hooking up, the practice pervades college culture. Dates and, for the most part, love affairs, are passé. Why bother asking someone to dinner when you can meet at a party, down a few drinks and go home together?

I hear the traditionalists clucking. Sex without commitment. Sounds like a male plot, right? But women are going along.

Some blame the sexual revolution. Some blame co-ed dorms and alcohol abuse. I blame something else. Hookups are part of a larger cultural picture. Today's college kids are the first generation to have had their entire childhoods scheduled. To them, dating is simply not a productive use of time.

Author David Brooks used the phrase "Organization Kid" in April's *Atlantic Monthly* to describe what he discovered at my alma mater, Princeton. After a lifetime of shuffling from soccer practice to scout meetings and piano lessons, today's college kids no longer want to spend hours debating the nature of good and evil, he noted. Once obsessed with getting into increasingly selective colleges—and now obsessed with getting great grades and even greater jobs—they no longer have hours to spend wooing a lover.

10   "I was amazed to learn how little dating goes on," Brooks wrote in the maga-zine. "Students go out in groups, and there is certainly a fair bit of partying on campus, but as one told me, 'People don't have time or energy to put into real relationships.'"

But 20-year-olds still have hormones, so they hook up instead. They stumble home together late Saturday night, roll around in bed, then pass out. The next morning, it's as if nothing happened.

Hookups do satisfy biology, but the emotional detachment doesn't satisfy the soul. And that's the real problem—not the promiscuity, but the lack of meaning.

People who don't bother with love affairs cut themselves off from life's head-ier emotions. What about Scarlett O'Hara's passion, or Juliet's? What about the mad jealousy of Dostoevsky's Dmitry Karamazov or even the illicit pleasures of Lady Chatterley and her lover? No great art will be inspired by the muse of Milwaukee's Best or a tryst that both parties are trying to forget.

In the same way, the Organization Kid's lack of soul-searching doesn't bode well for future poets and philosophers. Dostoevsky's Ivan wouldn't have had time to dream up the Grand Inquisitor if he spent his youth being carted from one sport to another and his early 20s obsessed with the perfect lab report.

15   Parents want the best for their kids—but some also want the perfect kid. Somewhere along the way to achieving these perfect children through structured activities, overachieving parents stunt the growth of their children's souls. Too much supervision creates kids who'd rather hook up than fall in love, who'd rather get the right answers on tests than ask the larger questions.

It's too late to bring back the dormitory mothers, curfews and traditional morals that forced courtships in the past. But the Organization Kid culture can be changed. If parents stop rigidly scheduling their children's lives, and if they no longer teach that life is only a series of concrete goals to be met and then ex-ceeded, then there will be more real lovers and truth-seekers in the future—and fewer hookups.

[2001]

Topics for Critical Thinking and Writing

1. Vanderkam's opening words—"The scene"—is unusual, since it sounds like the opening of a play. What other rhetorical devices does Vanderkam use in order to make her essay interesting?

2. In a sentence or two, state Vanderkam's thesis. (Please do not confuse a state-ment of the thesis—the point, the argument—with a summary of the essay.) Do you agree with her thesis? In whole, in part, or not at all? Whether you agree or disagree, write your own 500-word essay on hookups, or, alterna-tively, on a related topic, such as college dating.

AMY TAN

Amy Tan was born in 1952 in Oakland, California, two and a half years after her parents had emigrated from China. She entered Linfield College in Oregon but then followed a boyfriend to California State University at San Jose, where she shifted her major from premedical studies to English. After earning a master's degree in linguistics from San Jose, Tan worked as a language consultant and then, under the name of May Brown, as a freelance business writer.

In 1985, having decided to try her hand at fiction, she joined the Squaw Valley Community of Writers, a fiction workshop. In 1987 she visited China with her mother; on her return to the United States she learned that her agent had sold her first book, The Joy Luck Club, *a collection of 16 interwoven stories (including "Two Kinds") about four Chinese mothers and their four American daughters. She is also author of* The Kitchen God's Wife *(1991),* The Hundred Secret Senses *(1995),* The Bonesetter's Daughter *(2001), and* The Opposite of Faith *(2003), a collection of essays in which "fish cheeks" appears.*

fish cheeks

I fell in love with the minister's son the winter I turned fourteen. He was not Chinese, but as white as Mary in the manger. For Christmas I prayed for this blond-haired boy, Robert, and a slim new American nose.

When I found out that my parents had invited the minister's family over for Christmas Eve dinner, I cried. What would Robert think of our shabby Chinese Christmas? What would he think of our noisy Chinese relatives who lacked proper American manners? What terrible disappointment would he feel upon seeing not a roasted turkey and sweet potatoes but Chinese food?

On Christmas Eve, I saw that my mother had outdone herself in creating a strange menu. She was pulling black veins out of the backs of fleshy prawns. The kitchen was littered with appalling mounds of raw food: A slimy rock cod with bulging fish eyes that pleaded not to be thrown into a pan of hot oil. Tofu, which looked like stacked wedges of rubbery white sponges. A bowl soaking dried fungus back to life. A plate of squid, crisscrossed with knife markings so they resembled bicycle tires.

And then they arrived—the minister's family and all my relatives in a clamor of doorbells and rumpled Christmas packages. Robert grunted hello, and I pretended he was not worthy of existence.

5   Dinner threw me deeper into despair. My relatives licked the ends of their chopsticks and reached across the table, dipping into the dozen or so plates of food. Robert and his family waited patiently for platters to be passed to them. My relatives murmured with pleasure when my mother brought out the whole steamed fish. Robert grimaced. Then my father poked his chopsticks just below the fish eye and plucked out the soft meat. "Amy, your favorite," he said, offering me the tender fish cheek. I wanted to disappear.

At the end of the meal my father leaned back and belched loudly, thanking my mother for her fine cooking. "It's a polite Chinese custom, to show you are satisfied," he explained to our astonished guests. Robert was looking down at his plate with a reddened face. The minister managed to muster a quiet burp. I was stunned into silence for the rest of the night.

After all the guests had gone, my mother said to me, "You want be same like American girls on the outside." She handed me an early gift. It was a miniskirt in beige tweed. "But inside, you must always be Chinese. You must be proud you different. You only shame is be ashame."

And even though I didn't agree with her then, I knew that she understood how much I had suffered during the evening's dinner. It wasn't until many years later—long after I had gotten over my crush on Robert—that I was able to appreciate fully her lesson and the true purpose behind our particular menu. For Christmas Eve that year, she had chosen all my favorite foods.

[2003]

Topics for Critical Thinking and Writing

1. In the first paragraph Tan prays for "a slim new American nose," and in the second paragraph she speaks of "our shabby Chinese Christmas" and of "our noisy Chinese relatives." Find some other examples in the essay where the author indicates her embarrassment with her ethnic origin. Next, thinking about the essay as a whole, explain why Tan devotes much of the essay to emphasizing her uneasiness with Chinese traditions.

2. Were you surprised that Tan's mother gave her a miniskirt for a Christmas gift? Gifts are often symbolic; why do you think the mother chose this gift? Write an essay (500 words) on a gift that you gave or received.

3. Let's assume that a classmate has told you that he or she does not understand the point of the final paragraph. What is your explanation?

4. If you were grading this essay, what grade would you give it? Why?

9

Reading and Writing about Fiction

STORIES TRUE AND FALSE

The word *story* comes from *history*; the stories that historians, biographers, and journalists narrate are supposed to be true accounts of what happened. The stories of novelists and short-story writers, however, are admittedly untrue; they are "fiction," things made up, imagined, manufactured. As readers, we come to a supposedly true story with expectations different from those we bring to fiction.

Consider the difference between reading a narrative in a newspaper and one in a book of short stories. If, while reading a newspaper, we come across a story of, say, a subway accident, we assume that the account is true, and we read it for the information about a relatively unusual event. Anyone hurt? What sort of people? In our neighborhood? Whose fault? When we read a book of fiction, however, we do not expect to encounter literal truths; we read novels and short stories not for facts but for pleasure and for some insight or for a sense of what an aspect of life means to the writer. Consider the following short story by Grace Paley.

GRACE PALEY

Born in New York City, Grace Paley attended Hunter College and New York University but left without a degree. (She now is an affiliate faculty member at Sarah Lawrence College.) While raising two children she wrote poetry and then, in the 1950s, turned to writing fiction.

Paley's chief subject is the life of little people struggling in the Big City. Of life she has said, "How daily life is lived is a mystery to me. You write about what's mysterious to you. What is it like? Why do people do this?" Of the short story she has said, "It can be just telling a little tale, or writing a complicated philosophical story. It can be a song, almost."

Samuel

Some boys are very tough. They're afraid of nothing. They are the ones who climb a wall and take a bow at the top. Not only are they brave on the roof, but they make a lot of noise in the darkest part of the cellar where even the super hates to go. They also jiggle and hop on the platform between the locked doors of the subway cars.

Four boys are jiggling on the swaying platform. Their names are Alfred, Calvin, Samuel, and Tom. The men and the women in the cars on either side watch them. They don't like them to jiggle or jump but don't want to interfere. Of course some of the men in the cars were once brave boys like these. One of them had ridden the tail of a speeding truck from New York to Rockaway Beach without getting off, without his sore fingers losing hold. Nothing happened to him then or later. He had made a compact with other boys who preferred to watch: Starting at Eighth Avenue and Fifteenth Street, he would get to some specified place, maybe Twenty-third and the river, by hopping the tops of the moving trucks. This was hard to do when one truck turned a corner in the wrong direction and the nearest truck was a couple of feet too high. He made three or four starts before succeeding. He had gotten his idea from a film at school called *The Romance of Logging*. He had finished high school, married a good friend, was in a responsible job and going to night school.

These two men and others looked at the four boys jumping and jiggling on the platform and thought, It must be fun to ride that way, especially now the weather is nice and we're out of the tunnel and way high over the Bronx. Then they thought, These kids do seem to be acting sort of stupid. They *are* little. Then they thought of some of the brave things they had done when they were boys and jiggling didn't seem so risky.

The ladies in the car became very angry when they looked at the four boys. Most of them brought their brows together and hoped the boys could see their extreme disapproval. One of the ladies wanted to get up and say, Be careful you dumb kids, get off that platform or I'll call a cop. But three of the boys were Negroes and the fourth was something else she couldn't tell for sure. She was afraid they'd be fresh and laugh at her and embarrass her. She wasn't afraid they'd hit her, but she was afraid of embarrassment. Another lady thought, Their mothers never know where they are. It wasn't true in this particular case. Their mothers all knew that they had gone to see the missile exhibit on Fourteenth Street.

5   Out on the platform, whenever the train accelerated, the boys would raise their hands and point them up to the sky to act like rockets going off, then they rat-tat-tatted the shatterproof glass pane like machine guns, although no machine guns had been exhibited.

For some reason known only to the motorman, the train began a sudden slowdown. The lady who was afraid of embarrassment saw the boys jerk forward and backward and grab the swinging guard chains. She had her own boy at home. She stood up with determination and went to the door. She slid it open and said, "You boys will be hurt. You'll be killed. I'm going to call the conductor if you don't just go into the next car and sit down and be quiet."

Two of the boys said, "Yes'm," and acted as though they were about to go. Two of them blinked their eyes a couple of times and pressed their lips together. The train resumed its speed. The door slid shut, parting the lady and the boys. She leaned against the side door because she had to get off at the next stop.

The boys opened their eyes wide at each other and laughed. The lady blushed. The boys looked at her and laughed harder. They began to pound each other's back. Samuel laughed the hardest and pounded Alfred's back until Alfred coughed and the tears came. Alfred held tight to the chain hook. Samuel pounded him even harder when he saw the tears. He said, "Why you bawling? You a baby, huh?" and laughed. One of the men whose boyhood had been more watchful than brave became angry. He stood up straight and looked at the boys for a couple of seconds. Then he walked in a citizenly way to the end of the car, where he pulled the emergency cord. Almost at once, with a terrible hiss, the pressure of air abandoned the brakes and the wheels were caught and held.

People standing in the most secure places fell forward, then backward. Samuel had let go of his hold on the chain so he could pound Tom as well as Alfred. All the passengers in the cars whipped back and forth, but he pitched only forward and fell head first to be crushed and killed between the cars.

10   The train had stopped hard, halfway into the station, and the conductor called at once for the trainmen who knew about this kind of death and how to take the body from the wheels and brakes. There was silence except for passengers from other cars who asked, What happened! What happened! The ladies waited around wondering if he might be an only child. The men recalled other afternoons with very bad endings. The little boys stayed close to each other, leaning and touching shoulders and arms and legs.

When the policeman knocked at the door and told her about it, Samuel's mother began to scream. She screamed all day and moaned all night, though the doctors tried to quiet her with pills.

Oh, oh, she hopelessly cried. She did not know how she could ever find another boy like that one. However, she was a young woman and she became pregnant. Then for a few months she was hopeful. The child born to her was a boy. They brought him to be seen and nursed. She smiled. But immediately she saw that this baby wasn't Samuel. She and her husband together have had other children, but never again will a boy exactly like Samuel be known.

[1968]

Topics for Critical Thinking and Writing

1. Paley wrote the story, but an unspecified person *tells* it. Describe the voice of this narrator in the first paragraph. Is the voice neutral and objective, or do you hear some sort of attitude, a point of view? If you do hear an attitude, what words or phrases in the story indicate it?

2. What do you know about the setting—the locale—of "Samuel"? What can you infer about the neighborhood?

3. In the fourth paragraph we are told that "three of the boys were Negroes and the fourth was something else." Is race important in this story? Is Samuel "Negro" or "something else"? Does it matter?

4. Exactly *why* did a man walk "in a citizenly way to the end of the car, where he pulled the emergency cord"? Do you think the author blames him? What evidence can you offer to support your view? Do *you* blame him? Or do you blame the boys? Or anyone? Explain.

5. The story is called "Samuel," and it is, surely, about him. But what happens after Samuel dies? (You might want to list the events.) What else is the story about? (You might want to comment on why you believe the items in your list are important.)

6. Can you generalize about what the men think of the jigglers and about what the women think? Is Paley saying something about the sexes? About the attitudes of onlookers in a big city?

ELEMENTS OF FICTION

You might think about the ways in which "Samuel" differs from a newspaper story of an accident in a subway. (You might even want to write a newspaper version of the happening.) In some ways, of course, Paley's story faintly resembles an account that might appear in a newspaper. Journalists are taught to give information about

- who,
- what,
- when,
- where, and
- why,

and Paley does provide this material. Thus, the **characters** (Samuel and others) are the journalist's Who; the **plot** (the boys were jiggling on the platform, and when a man pulled the emergency cord one of them was killed) is the What; the **setting** (the subway, presumably in modern times) is the When and the Where; the **motivation** (the irritation of the man who pulls the emergency cord) is the Why.

To write about fiction you would think about these elements of fiction, asking yourself questions about each, both separately and how they work together. Much of the rest of this chapter will be devoted to examining such words as *character* and *plot*, but before you read those pages notice the questions we've posed about "Samuel" and try responding to them. Your responses will teach you a good deal about what fiction is, and some of the ways in which it works.

Plot and Character

In some stories, such as adventure stories, the emphasis is on physical action—wanderings and strange encounters. In Paley's "Samuel," however, although there is a violent death in the subway, the emphasis is less on an unusual happening than on other things: for instance, the contrast between some of the adults, the contrast between uptight adults and energetic children, and the impact of the death on Samuel's mother.

The novelist E. M. Forster, in a short critical study entitled *Aspects of the Novel* (1927), introduced a distinction between **flat characters** and **round characters**. A *flat character* is relatively simple and usually has only one trait: loving wife (or jealous wife), tyrannical husband (or meek husband), braggart, pedant, hypocrite, or whatever. Thus, in "Samuel" we are told about a man "whose boyhood had been more watchful than brave." This man walks "in a citizenly way" to the end of the subway car, where he pulls the emergency cord. He is, so to speak, the conventional solid citizen. He is flat, or uncomplicated, but that is probably part of what the author is getting at. A *round character*, on the other hand, embodies several or even many traits that cohere to form a complex personality. Of course in a story as short as "Samuel" we can hardly expect to find fully rounded characters, but we can say that, at least by comparison with the "citizenly" man, the man who had once been a wild kid, had gone to night school, and now holds a "responsible job" is relatively round. Paley's story asserts rather than shows the development of the character, but much fiction does show such a development. Whereas a flat character is usually *static* (at the end of the story the character is pretty much what he or she was at the start), a round character is likely to be *dynamic*, changing considerably as the story progresses.

A frequent assignment in writing courses is to set forth a character sketch, describing some person in the story or novel. In preparing such a sketch, take these points into consideration:

- what the character says (but consider that what he or she says need not be taken at face value; the character may be hypocritical, or self-deceived, or biased—you will have to detect this from the context),
- what the character does,
- what other characters say about the character, and
- what others *do*. (A character who serves as a contrast to another character is called a **foil**.)

A character sketch can be complex and demanding, but usually you will want to do more than write a character sketch. You will probably discuss the character's function, or trace the development of his or her personality, or contrast the character with another. (One of the most difficult topics, the narrator's personality, is discussed later in this chapter under the heading "Narrative Point of View.") In writing on one of these topics you will probably still want to keep in mind the four suggestions for getting at a character, but you will also want to go further, relating your findings to additional matters that we discuss later.

Most discussions of fiction are concerned with happenings and with *why* they happen. Why does Samuel die? Because (to put it too simply) his youthful high spirits clash with the values of a "citizenly" adult. Paley never explicitly says anything like this, but a reader of the story tries to make sense out of the details, filling in the gaps.

Things happen, in most good fiction, at least partly because the people have certain personalities or character traits (moral, intellectual, and emotional qualities) and, given their natures, because they respond plausibly to other personalities. What their names are and what they look like may help you to understand them, but probably the best guide to characters is what they do and what they say. As we get to know more about their drives and goals—and especially about the choices they make—we enjoy seeing the writer complete the portraits, finally presenting us with a coherent and credible picture of people in action. In this view, plot and character are inseparable. Plot is not simply a series of happenings, but happenings that come out of character, that reveal character, and that influence character. Henry James puts it thus: "What is character but the determination of incident? What is incident but the illustration of character?" James goes on: "It is an incident for a woman to stand up with her hand resting on a table and look out at you in a certain way."

Foreshadowing

Although some stories depend heavily on a plot with a surprise ending, other stories prepare the reader for the outcome, at least to some degree. The **foreshadowing** that would eliminate surprise, or greatly reduce it, and thus destroy a story that has nothing else to offer, is a powerful tool in the hands of a writer of serious fiction. In "Samuel," the reader perhaps senses even in the first paragraph that these "tough" boys who "jiggle and hop on the platform" may be vulnerable, may come to an unfortunate end. When a woman says, "You'll be killed," the reader doesn't yet know if she is right, but a seed has been planted.

Even in such a story as Faulkner's "A Rose for Emily" (p. 702), where we are surprised to learn near the end that Miss Emily has slept beside the decaying corpse of her dead lover, from the outset we expect something strange; that is, we are not surprised by the surprise, only by its precise nature. The first sentence of the story tell us that after Miss Emily's funeral (the narrator begins at the end) the townspeople cross her threshold "out of curiosity to see the inside of her house, which no one save an old manservant . . . had seen in at least ten years." As the story progresses, we see Miss Emily prohibiting people from entering the house, we hear that after a certain point no one ever sees Homer Barron again, that "the front door remained closed," and (a few paragraphs before the end of the story) that the townspeople "knew that there was one room in that region above the stairs which no one had seen in forty years." The paragraph preceding the revelation that "the man himself lay in the bed" is devoted to a description of Homer's dust-covered clothing and toilet articles. In short, however much we are unprepared for the precise revelation, we are prepared for some strange thing in the house; and, given Miss Emily's purchase of poison and Homer's disappearance, we have some idea of what will be revealed.

The full meaning of a passage will not become apparent until you have read the entire story. In a sense, a story has at least three lives:

- when we read the story sentence by sentence, trying to turn the sequence of sentences into a consistent whole,
- when we have finished reading the story and we think back on it as a whole, even if we think no more than "That was a waste of time,"
- when we reread a story, knowing already even as we read the first line how it will turn out at the end.

Setting and Atmosphere

Foreshadowing normally makes use of **setting**. The setting or environment is not mere geography, not mere locale: It provides an **atmosphere**, an air that the characters breathe, a world in which they move. Narrowly speaking, the setting is the physical surroundings—the furniture, the architecture, the landscape, the climate—and these often are highly appropriate to the characters who are associated with them. Thus, in Emily Brontë's *Wuthering Heights* the passionate Earnshaw family is associated with Wuthering Heights, the storm-exposed moorland, whereas the mild Linton family is associated with Thrushcross Grange in the sheltered valley below.

Broadly speaking, setting includes not only the physical surroundings but also a point (or several points) in time. The background against which we see the characters and the happenings may be specified as morning or evening, spring or fall. In a good story, this temporal setting will probably be highly relevant; it will probably be part of the story's meaning, perhaps providing an ironic contrast to or exerting an influence on the characters.

Symbolism

When we read, we may feel that certain characters and certain things in the story stand for more than themselves, or hint at larger meanings. We feel, that is, that they are **symbolic**. But here we must be careful. How does a reader know that this or that figure or place is symbolic? In Hemingway's "Cat in the Rain" (p. 688), is the cat symbolic? Is the innkeeper? Is the rain? Reasonable people may differ in their answers. Again, in Chopin's "The Story of an Hour" (p. 13), is the railroad accident a symbol? Is Josephine a symbol? Is the season (springtime) a symbol? And again, reasonable people may differ in their responses.

Let's assume for the moment, however, that if writers use symbols, they want readers to perceive—at least faintly—that certain characters or places or seasons or happenings have rich implications, stand for something more than what they are on the surface. How do writers help us to perceive these things? By emphasizing them—for instance, by describing them at some length, or by introducing them at times when they might not seem strictly necessary, or by calling attention to them repeatedly.

Consider, for example, Chopin's treatment of the season in which "The Story of an Hour" takes place. The story has to take place at *some* time, but Chopin does not simply say, "On a spring day," or an autumn day, and let things go at that. Rather, she tells us about the sky, the trees, the rain, the twittering sparrows—and all of this in an extremely short story where we might think there is no time for talk about the setting. After all, none of this material is strictly necessary to a story about a woman who has heard that her husband was killed in an accident, who grieves, then recovers, and then dies when he suddenly reappears.

Why, then, does Chopin give such emphasis to the season? Because, we think, she is using the season symbolically. In this story, the spring is not just a bit of detail added for realism. It is rich with suggestions of renewal, of the new life that Louise achieves for a moment. But here, a caution. We think that the spring in this story is symbolic, but this is not to say that whenever spring appears in a story, it always stands for renewal, any more than whenever winter appears it always symbolizes death. Nor does it mean that since spring recurs, Louise will be reborn. In short, in *this* story Chopin uses the season to convey specific implications.

Is the railroad accident in "The Story of an Hour" also a symbol? Our answer is no—though we don't expect all readers to agree with us. We think that the railroad accident in "The Story of an Hour" is just a railroad accident. It's our sense that Chopin is *not* using this event to say something about (for instance) modern travel, or about industrialism. The steam-propelled railroad train could of course be used, symbolically, to say something about industrialism displacing an agrarian economy, but does Chopin give her train any such suggestion? We don't think so. Had she wished to do so, she would probably have talked about the enormous power of the train, the shriek of its whistle, the smoke pouring out of the smokestack, the intense fire burning in the engine, its indifference as it charged through the countryside, and so forth. Had she done so, the story would be a different story. Or she might have made the train a symbol of fate overriding human desires. But, again in our opinion, Chopin does not endow her train with such suggestions. She gives virtually no emphasis to the train, and so we believe it has virtually no significance for the reader.

What of Chopin's "Ripe Figs" (p. 3)? Maman-Nainaine tells Babette that when the figs are ripe Babette can visit her cousins. Of course Maman may merely be setting an arbitrary date, but as we read the story we probably feel—because of the emphasis on the *ripening* of the figs, which occurs in the spring or early summer—that the ripening of the figs in some way suggests the maturing of Babette. If we do get such ideas, we will in effect be saying that the story is not simply an anecdote about an old woman whose behavior is odd. True, the narrator of the story, after telling us of Maman-Nainaine's promise, adds, "Not that the ripening of figs had the least thing to do with it, but that is the way Maman-Nainaine was." The narrator sees nothing special—merely Maman-Nainaine's eccentricity—in the connection between the ripening of the figs and Babette's visit to her cousins. Readers, however, may see more than the narrator sees or says. They may see in Babette a young girl maturing; they may see in Maman-Nainaine an older woman who, almost collaborating with nature, helps Babette to mature.

And here, of course, as we talk about symbolism we are getting into the theme of the story. An apparently inconsequential and even puzzling action, such as is set forth in "Ripe Figs," may cast a long shadow. As Robert Frost once said,

> There is no story written that has any value at all, however straightforward it looks and free from doubleness, double entendre, that you'd value at all if it didn't have intimations of something more than itself.

The stranger, the more mysterious the story, the more likely we are to suspect some sort of significance, but even realistic stories such as Chopin's "The Storm" and "The Story of an Hour" may be rich in suggestions. This is not to say, however, that the suggestions (rather than the details of the surface) are what count. A reader does not discard the richly detailed, highly specific narrative (Mrs. Mallard learned that her husband was dead and reacted in such-and-such a way) in favor of some supposedly universal message or theme that it implies. We do not throw away the specific narrative—the memorable characters or the interesting things that happen in the story—and move on to some "higher truth." Robert Frost went on to say, "The anecdote, the parable, the surface meaning has got to be good and got to be sufficient in itself."

Narrative Point of View

An author must choose a **point of view** (or sometimes, several points of view) from which he or she will narrate the story. The choice will contribute to the total effect of the story.

Narrative points of view can be divided into two sorts: **participant** (or **first-person**) and **nonparticipant** (or **third-person**). That is, the narrator may or may not be a character who participates in the story. Each of these two divisions can be subdivided:

I. Participant (first-person narrative)
    A. Narrator as a major character
    B. Narrator as a minor character
II. Nonparticipant (third-person narrative)
    A. Omniscient
    B. Selective omniscient
    C. Objective

PARTICIPANT POINTS OF VIEW   Toni Bambara's "The Lesson" (p. 648) begins thus:

> Back in the days when everyone was old and stupid or young and foolish and me and Sugar were the only ones just right, this lady moved on our block with nappy hair and proper speech and no makeup.

In this story, the narrator is a major character. Bambara is the author, but the narrator—the person who tells us the story—is a young girl who speaks of "me and Sugar," and the story is chiefly about the narrator. We can say, then, that Bambara uses a first-person (or participant) point of view. She has invented a young girl who tells us about the impact a woman in the neighborhood had on her: "[Sugar] can run if she want to and even run faster. But ain't nobody gonna beat me at nuthin." The narrator is a major character. She, and not Bambara, tells the story.

But sometimes a first-person narrator tells a story that focuses on someone other than the narrator; he or she is a minor character, a peripheral witness, for example, to a story about Sally Jones, and we get the story of Sally filtered through, say, the eyes of her friend or brother or cat.

Whether a major or a minor character, a first-person narrator is a particular character, seeing things in a particular way. The reader should not assume that the speaker is necessarily a reliable source. Some, in fact, are notably **unreliable narrators**, for instance young children, mentally impaired adults, and psychopaths. A story told by an unreliable narrator, let's say by a man consumed with vengeful thoughts, depends largely on the reader's perception of the gap between what the narrator says and what the facts presumably are.

NONPARTICIPANT POINTS OF VIEW   In a nonparticipant (third-person) point of view, the teller of the tale does not introduce himself or herself as a character. If the point of view is **omniscient**, the narrator relates what he or she wants to relate about the thoughts as well as the deeds of all the characters. The omniscient teller can enter the mind of any character; the first-person narrator can only say, "I was angry" or "Jack seemed angry," but the omniscient teller can say, "Jack was inwardly angry but gave no sign; Jill continued chatting, but she sensed his anger." Thus, in Paley's "Samuel," the narrator tells us that Samuel's mother was "hopeful," but when the new baby was born "immediately she saw that this baby wasn't Samuel."

Furthermore, a distinction can be made between **neutral omniscience** (the narrator recounts deeds and thoughts but does not judge) and **editorial omniscience** (the narrator not only recounts but also judges). An editorially omniscient narrator knows what goes on in the minds of all the characters and might comment approvingly or disapprovingly: "He closed the book, having finished the story, but, poor fellow, he had missed the meaning."

Because a short story can scarcely hope to develop a picture of several minds effectively, authors may prefer to limit their omniscience to the minds of a few of their characters, or even to that of only one of the characters; that is, they may use **selective omniscience** as the point of view. Selective omniscience provides a focus, especially if it is limited to a single character. When thus limited, the author sees one character from both outside and inside, but sees the other characters only from the outside and from the impact they have on the mind of this selected receptor. When selective omniscience attempts to record mental activity ranging from consciousness to the unconscious, from clear perceptions to confused longings, it is sometimes labeled the **stream-of-consciousness** point of view.

Finally, sometimes a third-person narrator does not enter even a single mind but records only what crosses an apparently dispassionate eye and ear. Such a point of view is **objective** (sometimes called the **camera** or **fly-on-the-wall** point of view). The absence of editorializing and of dissection of the mind often produces the effect of a play; we see and hear the characters in action. Much of Chekhov's

"Misery" (p. 238) is objective, consisting of bits of dialogue that make the story look like a play:

> "My head aches," says one of the tall ones. "At the Dukmasovs' yesterday Vaska and I drank four bottles of brandy between us."
>
> "I can't make out why you talk such stuff," says the other tall one angrily. "You lie like a brute."
>
> "Strike me dead, it's the truth! . . . "
>
> "It's about as true as that a louse coughs."

Style and Point of View

Obviously a story told by a first-person narrator will have a distinctive style—let's say the voice of an adolescent boy, or an elderly widow, or a madman. The voice of a third-person narrator—especially the voice of a supposedly objective narrator—will be much less distinctive, but if, especially on rereading, you listen carefully, you will probably hear a distinctive tone. (Look, for instance, at the first paragraph of Grace Paley's "Samuel.") Put it this way: Even a supposedly objective point of view is not purely objective, since it represents the writer's choice of a style, a way of reporting material with an apparently dispassionate voice.

After reading a story, you may want to think at least briefly about what the story might be like if told from a different point of view. You may find it instructive, for instance, to rewrite "Samuel" from the "citizenly" man's point of view, or "Ripe Figs" from Babette's.

Theme

First, we can distinguish between story (or plot) and theme in fiction. *Story* is concerned with "How does it turn out? What happens?" But **theme** is concerned with "What is it about? What does it add up to? What motif holds the happenings together? What does it make of life, and, perhaps, what wisdom does it offer?" In a good work of fiction, the details add up, or, to use Flannery O'Connor's words, they are "controlled by some overall purpose." In F. Scott Fitzgerald's *The Great Gatsby*, for example, there are many references to popular music, especially to jazz. These references contribute to our sense of the reality of Fitzgerald's depiction of America in the 1920s, but they do more: They help to comment on the shallowness of the white middle-class characters, and they sometimes (very gently) remind us of an alternative culture. A reader might study Fitzgerald's references to music with an eye toward getting a deeper understanding of what the novel is about.

Suppose we think for a moment about the theme of Paley's "Samuel." Do we sense an "overall purpose" that holds the story together? Different readers inevitably will come up with different readings, that is, with different views of what the story is about. Here is one student's version:

> Whites cannot understand the feelings of blacks.

This statement gets at an important element in the story—the conflict between the sober-minded adults and the jiggling boys—but it apparently assumes that all of the adults are white, an inference that cannot be supported by pointing to evidence in the story. Further, we cannot be certain that Samuel is black. And, finally, even if Samuel and his mother are black, surely white readers *do understand his youthful enthusiasm and his mother's inconsolable grief.*

Here is a second statement:

One should not interfere with the actions of others.

Does the story really offer such specific advice? This version of the theme seems to us to reduce the story to a too-simple code of action, a heartless rule of behavior, a rule that seems at odds with the writer's awareness of the mother's enduring grief.

A third version:

Middle-class adults, acting from what seem to them to be the best of motives, may cause irreparable harm and grief.

This last statement seems to us to be one that can be fully supported by checking it against the story, but other equally valid statements can probably be made. How would you put it?

✔ CHECKLIST: *Getting Ideas for Writing about Fiction*

Here are some questions that may help to stimulate ideas about stories. Not every question is, of course, relevant to every story; but if after reading a story and thinking about it, you then run your eye over these questions, you will probably find some questions that will help you to think further about the story—in short, that will help you to get ideas.

As we have said in earlier chapters, it's best to do your thinking with a pen or pencil in hand. If some of the following questions seem to you to be especially relevant to the story you will be writing about, jot down—freely, without worrying about spelling—your initial responses, interrupting your writing only to glance again at the story when you feel the need to check the evidence.

Plot

❏ Does the plot grow out of the characters, or does it depend on chance or coincidence? Did something at first strike you as irrelevant that later you perceived as relevant? Do some parts continue to strike you as irrelevant?

❏ Does surprise play an important role, or does foreshadowing? If surprise is very important, can the story be read a second time with any interest? If so, what gives it this further interest?

❏ What conflicts does the story include? Conflicts of one character against another? Of one character against the setting, or against society? Conflicts within a single character?

❏ Are certain episodes narrated out of chronological order? If so, were you puzzled? Annoyed? On reflection, does the arrangement of episodes seem effective? Why, or why not? Are certain situations repeated? If so, what do you make out of the repetitions?

Character

❏ Which character chiefly engages your interest? Why?

❏ What purposes do minor characters serve? Do you find some who by their similarities and differences help to define each other or help to define the major character? How else is a particular character defined—by his or her words, actions (including thoughts and emotions), dress, setting, narrative point of view? Do certain characters act differently in the same, or in a similar, situation?

❑ How does the author reveal character? By explicit authorial (editorial) comment, for instance, or, on the other hand, by revelation through dialogue? Through depicted action? Through the actions of other characters? How are the author's methods especially suited to the whole of the story?

❑ Is the behavior plausible—that is, are the characters well motivated?

❑ If a character changes, why and how does he or she change? (You may want to jot down each event that influences a change.) Or did you change your attitude toward a character not because the character changes but because you came to know the character better?

❑ Are the characters round or flat? Are they complex, or, on the other hand, highly typical (for instance, one-dimensional representatives of a social class or age)? Are you chiefly interested in a character's psychology, or does the character strike you as standing for something, such as honesty or the arrogance of power?

❑ How has the author caused you to sympathize with certain characters? How does your response—your sympathy or lack of sympathy—contribute to your judgment of the conflict?

Point of View

❑ Who tells the story? How much does the narrator know? Does the narrator strike you as reliable? What effect is gained by using this narrator?

❑ How does the point of view help shape the theme? After all, the basic story of "Little Red Riding Hood"—what happens—remains unchanged whether told from the wolf's point of view or the girl's, but (to simplify grossly) if we hear the story from the wolf's point of view, we may feel that the story is about terrifying yet pathetic compulsive behavior; if from the girl's point of view, about terrified innocence.

❑ It is sometimes said that the best writers are subversive, forcing readers to see something they do not want to see—something that is true but that violates their comfortable conventional ideas. Does this story oppose comfortable conventional views?

❑ Does the narrator's language help you to construct a picture of the narrator's character, class, attitude, strengths, and limitations? (Jot down some evidence, such as colloquial or—on the other hand—formal expressions, ironic comments, figures of speech.) How far can you trust the narrator? Why?

Setting

❑ Do you have a strong sense of the time and place? Is the story very much about, say, New England Puritanism, or race relations in the South in the late nineteenth century, or midwestern urban versus small-town life? If time and place are important, how and at what points in the story has the author conveyed this sense? If you do not strongly feel the setting, do you think the author should have made it more evident?

❑ What is the relation of the setting to the plot and the characters? (For instance, do houses or rooms or their furnishings say something about their residents?) Would anything be lost if the descriptions of the setting were deleted from the story or the setting were changed?

Symbolism

❏ Do certain characters seem to you to stand for something in addition to themselves? Does the setting—whether a house, a farm, a landscape, a town, a period—have an extra dimension?)

❏ If you do believe that the story has symbolic elements, do you think they are adequately integrated within the story, or do they strike you as being too obviously stuck in?

Style

❏ How has the point of view shaped or determined the style?

❏ How would you characterize the style? Simple? Understated? Figurative? Or what, and why?

❏ Do you think that the style is consistent? If it isn't—for instance, if there are shifts from simple sentences to highly complex ones—what do you make of the shifts?

Theme

❏ Is the title informative? What does it mean or suggest? Did the meaning seem to change after you read the story? Does the title help you to formulate a theme? If you had written the story, what title would you use?

❏ Do certain passages—dialogue or description—seem to you to point especially toward the theme? Do you find certain repetitions of words or pairs of incidents highly suggestive and helpful in directing your thoughts toward stating a theme? Flannery O'Connor, in *Mystery and Manners,* says, "In good fiction, certain of the details will tend to accumulate meaning from the action of the story itself, and when that happens, they become symbolic in the way they work." Does this story work that way?

❏ Is the meaning of the story embodied in the whole story, or does it seem stuck in, for example in certain passages of editorializing?

❏ Suppose someone asked you to state the point—the theme—of the story. Could you? And if you could, would you say that the theme of a particular story reinforces values you hold, or does it to some degree challenge them? Or is the concept of a theme irrelevant to this story?

YOUR TURN: SHORT STORIES FOR ANALYSIS

ANTON CHEKHOV

Anton Chekhov (1860–1904) was born in Russia, the son of a shopkeeper. While a medical student at Moscow University, Chekhov wrote stories, sketches, and reviews to help support his family and to finance his education. In 1884 he received his medical degree, began to practice medicine, published his first book of stories, and suffered the first of a series of hemorrhages from tuberculosis. In his remaining twenty years, in addition to writing several hundred stories, he wrote plays, half a dozen of which have established themselves as classics. He died from tuberculosis at the age of 44.

Misery

Translated by Constance Garnett

"To Whom Shall I Tell My Grief?"

The twilight of evening. Big flakes of wet snow are whirling lazily about the street lamps, which have just been lighted, and lying in a thin soft layer on roofs, horses' backs, shoulders, caps. Iona Potapov, the sledgedriver, is all white like a ghost. He sits on the box without stirring, bent as double as the living body can be bent. If a regular snowdrift fell on him it seems as though even then he would not think it necessary to shake it off. . . . His little mare is white and motionless too. Her stillness, the angularity of her lines, and the stick-like straightness of her legs make her look like a halfpenny gingerbread horse. She is probably lost in thought. Anyone who has been torn away from the plough, from the familiar gray landscapes, and cast into this slough, full of monstrous lights, of unceasing uproar and hurrying people, is bound to think.

It is a long time since Iona and his nag have budged. They came out of the yard before dinner-time and not a single fare yet. But now the shades of evening are falling on the town. The pale light of the street lamps changes to a vivid color, and the bustle of the street grows noisier.

"Sledge to Vyborgskaya!" Iona hears. "Sledge!"

Iona starts, and through his snow-plastered eyelashes sees an officer in a military overcoat with a hood over his head.

5   "To Vyborgskaya," repeats the officer. "Are you asleep? To Vyborgskaya!"

In token of assent Iona gives a tug at the reins which sends cakes of snow flying from the horse's back and shoulders. The officer gets into the sledge. The sledge-driver clicks to the horse, cranes his neck like a swan, rises in his seat, and more from habit than necessity brandishes his whip. The mare cranes her neck, too, crooks her stick-like legs, and hesitatingly sets off. . . .

"Where are you shoving, you devil?" Iona immediately hears shouts from the dark mass shifting to and fro before him. "Where the devil are you going? Keep to the r-right!"

"You don't know how to drive! Keep to the right," says the officer angrily.

A coachman driving a carriage swears at him; a pedestrian crossing the road and brushing the horse's nose with his shoulder looks at him angrily and shakes the snow off his sleeve. Iona fidgets on the box as though he were sitting on thorns, jerks his elbows, and turns his eyes about like one possessed, as though he did not know where he was or why he was there.

10   "What rascals they all are!" says the officer jocosely. "They are simply doing their best to run up against you or fall under the horse's feet. They must be doing it on purpose."

Iona looks at his fare and moves his lips. . . . Apparently he means to say something, but nothing comes out but a sniff.

"What?" inquires the officer.

Iona gives a wry smile, and straining his throat, brings out huskily: "My son . . . , er . . . my son died this week, sir."

"H'm! What did he die of?"

15   Iona turns his whole body round to his fare, and says:

"Who can tell! It must have been from fever. . . . He lay three days in the hospital and then he died. . . . God's will."

"Turn round, you devil!" comes out of the darkness. "Have you gone cracked, you old dog? Look where you are going!"

"Drive on! drive on! . . . " says the officer. "We shan't get there till tomorrow going on like this. Hurry up!"

The sledge-driver cranes his neck again, rises in his seat, and with heavy grace swings his whip. Several times he looks round at the officer, but the latter keeps his eyes shut and is apparently disinclined to listen. Putting his fare down at Vyborgskaya, Iona stops by a restaurant, and again sits huddled up on the box. . . . Again the wet snow paints him and his horse white. One hour passes, and then another. . . .

20 Three young men, two tall and thin, one short and hunchbacked, come up, railing at each other and loudly stamping on the pavement with their galoshes.

"Cabby, to the Police Bridge!" the hunchback cries in a cracked voice. "The three of us, . . . twenty kopecks!"

Iona tugs at the reins and clicks to his horse. Twenty kopecks is not a fair price, but he has no thoughts for that. Whether it is a rouble or whether it is five kopecks does not matter to him now so long as he has a fare. . . . The three young men, shoving each other and using bad language, go up to the sledge, and all three try to sit down at once. The question remains to be settled: Which are to sit down and which one is to stand? After a long altercation, ill-temper, and abuse, they come to the conclusion that the hunchback must stand because he is the shortest.

"Well, drive on," says the hunchback in his cracked voice, settling himself and breathing down Iona's neck. "Cut along! What a cap you've got, my friend! You wouldn't find a worse one in all Petersburg. . . ."

"He-he! . . . he-he! . . . " laughs Iona. "It's nothing to boast of!"

25 "Well, then, nothing to boast of, drive on! Are you going to drive like this all the way? Eh? Shall I give you one in the neck?"

"My head aches," says one of the tall ones. "At the Dukmasovs' yesterday Vaska and I drank four bottles of brandy between us."

"I can't make out why you talk such stuff," says the other tall one angrily. "You lie like a brute."

"Strike me dead, it's the truth! . . . "

"It's about as true as that a louse coughs."

30 "He-he!" grins Iona. "Me-er-ry gentlemen!"

"Tfoo! the devil take you!" cries the hunchback indignantly. "Will you get on, you old plague, or won't you? Is that the way to drive? Give her one with the whip. Hang it all, give it her well."

Iona feels behind his back the jolting person and quivering voice of the hunchback. He hears abuse addressed to him, he sees people, and the feeling of loneliness begins little by little to be less heavy on his heart. The hunchback swears at him, till he chokes over some elaborately whimsical string of epithets and is overpowered by his cough. His tall companions begin talking of a certain Nadyezhda Petrovna. Iona looks round at them. Waiting till there is a brief pause, he looks round once more and says:

"This week . . . er . . . my . . . er . . . son died!"

"We shall all die, . . . " says the hunchback with a sigh, wiping his lips after coughing. "Come, drive on! drive on! My friends, I simply cannot stand crawling like this! When will he get us there?"

35 "Well, you give him a little encouragement . . . one in the neck!"

"Do you hear, you old plague? I'll make you smart. If one stands on ceremony with fellows like you one may as well walk. Do you hear, you old dragon?
Or don't you care a hang what we say?"

And Iona hears rather than feels a slap on the back of his neck.

"He-he! . . . " he laughs. "Merry gentlemen . . . God give you health!"

"Cabman, are you married?" asks one of the tall ones.

40   "I? He-he! Me-er-ry gentlemen. The only wife for me now is the damp earth.
. . . He-ho-ho! . . . The grave that is! . . . Here my son's dead and I am alive. . . . It's
a strange thing, death has come in at the wrong door. . . . Instead of coming for
me it went for my son. . . ."

And Iona turns round to tell them how his son died, but at that point the
hunchback gives a faint sigh and announces that, thank God! they have arrived at
last. After taking his twenty kopecks, Iona gazes for a long while after the revel-
ers, who disappear into a dark entry. Again he is alone and again there is silence
for him. . . . The misery which has been for a brief space eased comes back again
and tears his heart more cruelly than ever. With a look of anxiety and suffering
Iona's eyes stray restlessly among the crowds moving to and fro on both sides of
the street: can he not find among those thousands someone who will listen to
him? But the crowds flit by heedless of him and his misery. . . . His misery is immense, beyond all bounds. If Iona's heart were to burst and his misery to flow
out, it would flood the whole world, it seems, but yet it is not seen. It has found a
hiding-place in such an insignificant shell that one would not have found it with a
candle by daylight. . . .

Iona sees a house-porter with a parcel and makes up his mind to address
him.

"What time will it be, friend?" he asks.

"Going on for ten. . . . Why have you stopped here? Drive on!"

45   Iona drives a few paces away, bends himself double, and gives himself up to
his misery. He feels it is no good to appeal to people. But before five minutes
have passed he draws himself up, shakes his head as though he feels a sharp
pain, and tugs at the reins. . . . He can bear it no longer.

"Back to the yard!" he thinks. "To the yard!"

And his little mare, as though she knew his thoughts, falls to trotting. An hour
and a half later Iona is sitting by a big dirty stove. On the stove, on the floor, and
on the benches are people snoring. The air is full of smells and stuffiness. Iona
looks at the sleeping figures, scratches himself, and regrets that he has come
home so early. . . .

"I have not earned enough to pay for the oats, even," he thinks. "That's why I
am so miserable. A man who knows how to do his work, . . . who has had
enough to eat, and whose horse has had enough to eat, is always at ease. . . ."

In one of the corners a young cabman gets up, clears his throat sleepily, and
makes for the waterbucket.

50   "Want a drink?" Iona asks him.

"Seems so."

"May it do you good. . . . But my son is dead, mate. . . . Do you hear? This
week in the hospital. . . . It's queer business. . . ."

Iona looks to see the effect produced by his words, but he sees nothing. The
young man has covered his head over and is already asleep. The old man sighs
and scratches himself. . . . Just as the young man had been thirsty for water, he
thirsts for speech. His son will soon have been dead a week, and he has not really
talked to anybody yet. . . . He wants to talk of it properly, with deliberation. . . .

He wants to tell how his son was taken ill, how he suffered, what he said before he died, how he died. . . . He wants to describe the funeral, and how he went to the hospital to get his son's clothes. He still has his daughter Anisya in the country. . . . And he wants to talk about her too. . . . Yes, he has plenty to talk about now. His listener ought to sigh and exclaim and lament. . . . It would be even better to talk to women. Though they are silly creatures, they blubber at the first word.

"Let's go out and have a look at the mare," Iona thinks. "There is always time for sleep. . . . You'll have sleep enough, no fear. . . ."

55   He puts on his coat and goes into the stables where his mare is standing. He thinks about oats, about hay, about the weather. . . . He cannot think about his son when he is alone. . . . To talk about him with someone is possible, but to think of him and picture him is insufferable anguish. . . .

"Are you munching?" Iona asks his mare, seeing her shining eyes. "There, munch away, munch away. . . . Since we have not earned enough for oats, we will eat hay. . . . Yes, . . . I have grown too old to drive. . . . My son ought to be driving, not I. . . . He was a real coachman. . . . He ought to have lived. . . ."

Iona is silent for a while, and then he goes on:

"That's how it is, old girl. . . . Kuzma Ionitch is gone. . . . He said goodby to me. . . . He went and died for no reason. . . . Now, suppose you had a little colt, and you were mother to that little colt. . . . And all at once that same little colt went and died. . . . You'd be sorry, wouldn't you? . . ."

The little mare munches, listens, and breathes on her master's hands. Iona is carried away and tells her all about it.

[1886]

Topics for Critical Thinking and Writing

1. What do you admire or not admire about Chekhov's story? Why?
2. Try to examine in detail your response to the ending. Do you think the ending is, in a way, a happy ending? Would you prefer a different ending? For instance, should the story end when the young cabman falls asleep? Or when Iona sets out for the stable? Or can you imagine a better ending? If so, what?

EUDORA WELTY

Eudora Welty (1909–2001) was born in Jackson, Mississippi. Although she earned a bachelor's degree at the University of Wisconsin, and she spent a year studying advertising in New York City at the Columbia University Graduate School of Business, she lived almost all of her life in Jackson.

In the preface to her Collected Stories *she says:*

> *I have been told, both in approval and in accusation, that I seem to love all my characters. What I do in writing of any character is to try to enter into the mind, heart and skin of a human being who is not myself.*

> *Whether this happens to be a man or a woman, old or young, with skin black or white, the primary challenge lies in making the jump itself. It is the act of a writer's imagination that I set most high.*

In addition to writing stories and novels, Welty wrote a book about fiction, The Eye of the Story *(1977), and a memoir,* One Writer's Beginnings *(1984).*

A Worn Path

It was December—a bright frozen day in the early morning. Far out in the country there was an old Negro woman with her head tied in a red rag, coming along a path through the pinewoods. Her name was Phoenix Jackson. She was very old and small and she walked slowly in the dark pine shadows, moving a little from side to side in her steps, with the balanced heaviness and lightness of a pendulum in a grandfather clock. She carried a thin, small cane made from an umbrella, and with this she kept tapping the frozen earth in front of her. This made a grave and persistent noise in the still air, that seemed meditative like the chirping of a solitary little bird.

She wore a dark striped dress reaching down to her shoe tops, and an equally long apron of bleached sugar sacks, with a full pocket: all neat and tidy, but every time she took a step she might have fallen over her shoelaces, which dragged from her unlaced shoes. She looked straight ahead. Her eyes were blue with age. Her skin had a pattern all its own of numberless branching wrinkles and as though a whole little tree stood in the middle of her forehead, but a golden color ran underneath, and the two knobs of her cheeks were illuminated by a yellow burning under the dark. Under the red rag her hair came down on her neck in the frailest of ringlets, still black, and with an odor like copper.

Now and then there was a quivering in the thicket. Old Phoenix said, "Out of my way, all you foxes, owls, beetles, jack rabbits, coons, and wild animals! . . . Keep out from under these feet, little bob-whites. . . . Keep the big wild hogs out of my path. Don't let none of those come running my direction. I got a long way." Under her small black-freckled hand her cane, limber as a buggy whip, would switch at the brush as if to rouse up any hiding things.

On she went. The woods were deep and still. The sun made the pine needles almost too bright to look at, up where the wind rocked. The cones dropped as light as feathers. Down in the hollow was the mourning dove—it was not too late for him.

5   The path ran up a hill. "Seem like there is chains about my feet, time I get this far," she said, in the voice of argument old people keep to use with themselves. "Something always take a hold of me on this hill—pleads I should stay."

After she got to the top she turned and gave a full, severe look behind her where she had come. "Up through pines," she said at length. "Now down through oaks."

Her eyes opened their widest, and she started down gently. But before she got to the bottom of the hill a bush caught her dress.

Her fingers were busy and intent, but her skirts were full and long, so that before she could pull them free in one place they were caught in another. It was not possible to allow the dress to tear. "I in the thorny bush," she said. "Thorns, you doing your appointed work. Never want to let folks pass—no sir. Old eyes thought you was a pretty little *green* bush."

Finally, trembling all over, she stood free, and after a moment dared to stoop for her cane.

10   "Sun so high!" she cried, leaning back and looking, while the thick tears went over her eyes. "The time getting all gone here."

At the foot of this hill was a place where a log was laid across the creek.

"Now comes the trial," said Phoenix.

Putting her right foot out, she mounted the log and shut her eyes. Lifting her skirt, levelling her cane fiercely before her, like a festival figure in some parade, she began to march across. Then she opened her eyes and she was safe on the other side.

"I wasn't as old as I thought," she said.

15   But she sat down to rest. She spread her skirts on the bank around her and folded her hands over her knees. Up above her was a tree in a pearly cloud of mistletoe. She did not dare to close her eyes, and when a little boy brought her a lit- tle plate with a slice of marble-cake on it she spoke to him. "That would be accept- able," she said. But when she went to take it there was just her own hand in the air.

So she left that tree, and had to go through a barbed-wire fence. There she had to creep and crawl, spreading her knees and stretching her fingers like a baby trying to climb the steps. But she talked loudly to herself: she could not let her dress be torn now, so late in the day, and she could not pay for having her arm or leg sawed off if she got caught fast where she was.

At last she was safe through the fence and risen up out in the clearing. Big dead trees, like black men with one arm, were standing in the purple stalks of the withered cotton field. There sat a buzzard.

"Who you watching?"

In the furrow she made her way along.

20   "Glad this not the season for bulls," she said, looking sideways, "and the good Lord made his snakes to curl up and sleep in the winter. A pleasure I don't see no two-headed snake coming around that tree, where it come once. It took a while to get by him, back in the summer."

She passed through the old cotton and went into a field of dead corn. It whis- pered and shook and was taller than her head. "Through the maze now," she said, for there was no path.

Then there was something tall, black, and skinny there, moving before her.

At first she took it for a man. It could have been a man dancing in the field. But she stood still and listened, and it did not make a sound. It was as silent as a ghost.

"Ghost," she said sharply, "who be you the ghost of? For I have heard of nary death close by."

25   But there was no answer—only the ragged dancing in the wind.

She shut her eyes, reached out her hand, and touched a sleeve. She found a coat and inside that an emptiness, cold as ice.

"You scarecrow," she said. Her face lighted. "I ought to be shut up for good," she said with laughter. "My senses is gone, I too old. I the oldest people I ever know. Dance, old scarecrow," she said, "while I dancing with you."

She kicked her foot over the furrow, and with mouth drawn down, shook her head once or twice in a little strutting way. Some husks blew down and whirled in streamers about her skirts.

Then she went on, parting her way from side to side with the cane, through the whispering field. At last she came to the end, to a wagon track where the sil- ver grass blew between the red ruts. The quail were walking around like pullets, seeming all dainty and unseen.

30   "Walk pretty," she said. "This the easy place. This the easy going."

She followed the track, swaying through the quiet bare fields, through the little strings of trees silver in their dead leaves, past cabins silver from weather, with the doors and windows boarded shut, all like old women under a spell sitting there. "I walking in their sleep," she said, nodding her head vigorously.

In a ravine she went where a spring was silently flowing through a hollow log. Old Phoenix bent and drank. "Sweet-gum makes the water sweet," she said, and drank more. "Nobody know who made this well, for it was here when I was born."

The track crossed a swampy part where the moss hung as white as lace from every limb. "Sleep on, alligators, and blow your bubbles." Then the track went into the road.

Deep, deep the road went down between the high green-colored banks. Overhead the live-oaks met, and it was as dark as a cave.

35   A black dog with a lolling tongue came up out of the weeds by the ditch. She was meditating, and not ready, and when he came at her she only hit him a little with her cane. Over she went in the ditch, like a little puff of milk-weed.

Down there, her senses drifted away. A dream visited her, and she reached her hand up, but nothing reached down and gave her a pull. So she lay there and presently went to talking. "Old woman," she said to herself, "that black dog come up out of the weeds to stall you off, and now there he sitting on his fine tail, smiling at you."

A white man finally came along and found her—a hunter, a young man, with his dog on a chain.

"Well, Granny!" he laughed. "What are you doing there?"

"Lying on my back like a June-bug waiting to be turned over, mister," she said, reaching up her hand.

40   He lifted her up, gave her a swing in the air, and set her down. "Anything broken, Granny?"

"No sir, them old dead weeds is springy enough," said Phoenix, when she had got her breath. "I thank you for your trouble."

"Where do you live, Granny?" he asked, while the two dogs were growling at each other.

"Away back yonder, sir, behind the ridge. You can't even see it from here."

"On your way home?"

45   "No, sir, I going to town."

"Why, that's too far! That's as far as I walk when I come out myself, and I get something for my trouble." He patted the stuffed bag he carried, and there hung down a little closed claw. It was one of the bob-whites, with its beak hooked bitterly to show it was dead. "Now you go on home, Granny!"

"I bound to go to town, mister," said Phoenix. "The time come around."

He gave another laugh, filling the whole landscape. "I know you old colored people! Wouldn't miss going to town to see Santa Claus!"

But something held Old Phoenix very still. The deep lines in her face went into a fierce and different radiation. Without warning, she had seen with her own eyes a flashing nickel fall out of the man's pocket onto the ground.

50   "How old are you, Granny?" he was saying.

"There is no telling, mister," she said, "no telling."

Then she gave a little cry and clapped her hands and said, "Git on away from here, dog! Look! Look at that dog!" She laughed as if in admiration. "He ain't scared of nobody. He a big black dog." She whispered, "Sic him!"

"Watch me get rid of that cur," said the man. "Sic him, Pete! Sic him!"

Phoenix heard the dogs fighting, and heard the man running and throwing sticks. She even heard a gunshot. But she was slowly bending forward by that time, further and further forward, the lids stretched down over her eyes, as if she were doing this in her sleep. Her chin was lowered almost to her knees. The yellow palm of her hand came out from the fold of her apron. Her fingers slid down and along the ground under the piece of money with the grace and care they would have in lifting an egg from under a sitting hen. Then she slowly straightened up, she stood erect, and the nickel was in her apron pocket. A bird flew by. Her lips moved. "God watching me the whole time. I come to stealing."

55   The man came back, and his own dog panted about them. "Well, I scared him off that time," he said, and then he laughed and lifted his gun and pointed it at Phoenix.

She stood straight and faced him.

"Doesn't the gun scare you?" he said, still pointing it.

"No, sir, I seen plenty go off closer by, in my day, and for less than what I done," she said, holding utterly still.

He smiled, and shouldered the gun. "Well, Granny," he said, "you must be a hundred years old, and scared of nothing. I'd give you a dime if I had any money with me. But you take my advice and stay home, and nothing will happen to you."

60   "I bound to go on my way, mister," said Phoenix. She inclined her head in the red rag. Then they went in different directions, but she could hear the gun shooting again and again over the hill.

She walked on. The shadows hung from the oak trees to the road like curtains. Then she smelled wood-smoke, and smelled the river, and she saw a steeple and the cabins on their steep steps. Dozens of little black children whirled around her. There ahead was Natchez shining. Bells were ringing. She walked on.

In the paved city it was Christmas time. There were red and green electric lights strung and crisscrossed everywhere, and all turned on in the daytime. Old Phoenix would have been lost if she had not distrusted her eyesight and depended on her feet to know where to take her.

She paused quietly on the sidewalk where people were passing by. A lady came along in the crowd, carrying an armful of red-, green-, and silver-wrapped presents; she gave off perfume like the red roses in hot summer, and Phoenix stopped her.

"Please, missy, will you lace up my shoe?" She held up her foot.

65   "What do you want, Grandma?"

"See my shoe," said Phoenix. "Do all right for out in the country, but wouldn't look right to go in a big building."

"Stand still then, Grandma," said the lady. She put her packages down on the sidewalk beside her and laced and tied both shoes tightly.

"Can't lace 'em with a cane," said Phoenix. "Thank you, missy. I doesn't mind asking a nice lady to tie up my shoe, when I gets out on the street."

Moving slowly and from side to side, she went into the big building and into a tower of steps, where she walked up and around and around until her feet knew to stop.

70   She entered a door, and there she saw nailed up on the wall the document that had been stamped with the gold seal and framed in the gold frame, which matched the dream that was hung up in her head.

"Here I be," she said. There was a fixed and ceremonial stiffness over her body.

"A charity case, I suppose," said an attendant who sat at the desk before her.

But Phoenix only looked above her head. There was sweat on her face, the wrinkles in her skin shone like a bright net.

"Speak up, Grandma," the woman said. "What's your name? We must have your history, you know. Have you been here before? What seems to be the trouble with you?"

75   Old Phoenix only gave a twitch to her face as if a fly were bothering her.

"Are you deaf?" cried the attendant.

But then the nurse came in.

"Oh, that's just old Aunt Phoenix," she said. "She doesn't come for herself— she has a little grandson. She makes these trips just as regular as clockwork. She lives away back off the old Natchez Trace." She bent down. "Well, Aunt Phoenix, why don't you just take a seat? We won't keep you standing after your long trip." She pointed.

The old woman sat down, bolt upright in the chair.

80   "Now, how is the boy?" asked the nurse.

Old Phoenix did not speak.

"I said, how is the boy?"

But Phoenix only waited and stared straight ahead, her face very solemn and withdrawn into rigidity.

"Is his throat any better?" asked the nurse. "Aunt Phoenix, don't you hear me? Is your grandson's throat any better since the last time you came for the medicine?"

85   With her hands on her knees, the old woman waited, silent, erect and motionless, just as if she were in armor.

"You mustn't take up our time this way, Aunt Phoenix," the nurse said. "Tell us quickly about your grandson, and get it over. He isn't dead, is he?"

At last there came a flicker and then a flame of comprehension across her face, and she spoke.

"My grandson. It was my memory had left me. There I sat and forgot why I made my long trip."

"Forgot?" The nurse frowned. "After you came so far?"

90   Then Phoenix was like an old woman begging a dignified forgiveness for waking up frightened in the night. "I never did go to school, I was too old at the Surrender," she said in a soft voice. "I'm an old woman without an education. It was my memory fail me. My little grandson, he is just the same, and I forgot it in the coming."

"Throat never heals, does it?" said the nurse, speaking in a loud, sure voice to Old Phoenix. By now she had a card with something written on it, a little list. "Yes. Swallowed lye. When was it—January—two-three years ago—"

Phoenix spoke unasked now. "No, missy, he not dead, he just the same. Every little while his throat begin to close up again, and he not able to swallow. He not get his breath. He not able to help himself. So the time come around, and I go on another trip for the soothing medicine."

"All right. The doctor said as long as you came to get it, you could have it," said the nurse. "But it's an obstinate case."

"My little grandson, he sit up there in the house all wrapped up, waiting by himself," Phoenix went on. "We is the only two left in the world. He suffer and it don't seem to put him back at all. He got a sweet look. He going to last. He wear a little patch quilt and peep out holding his mouth open like a little bird. I remembers so plain now. I not going to forget him again, no, the whole enduring time. I could tell him from all the others in creation."

95 "All right." The nurse was trying to hush her now. She brought her a bottle of medicine. "Charity," she said, making a check mark in a book.

Old Phoenix held the bottle close to her eyes and then carefully put it into her pocket.

"I thank you," she said.

"It's Christmas time, Grandma," said the attendant. "Could I give you a few pennies out of my purse?"

"Five pennies is a nickel," said Phoenix stiffly.

100 "Here's a nickel," said the attendant.

Phoenix rose carefully and held out her hand. She received the nickel and then fished the other nickel out of her pocket and laid it beside the new one. She stared at her palm closely, with her head on one side.

Then she gave a tap with her cane on the floor.

"This is what come to me to do," she said. "I going to the store and buy my child a little windmill they sells, made out of paper. He going to find it hard to believe there such a thing in the world. I'll march myself back where he waiting, holding it straight up in his hand."

She lifted her free hand, gave a little nod, turned round, and walked out of the doctor's office. Then her slow step began on the stairs, going down.

[1941]

Topics for Critical Thinking and Writing

1. If you do not know the legend of the phoenix, look it up in a dictionary or, better, in an encyclopedia. Then carefully reread the story, to learn whether the story in any way connects with the legend.
2. What do you think of the hunter?
3. What would be lost if the episode (with all of its dialogue) of Phoenix falling into the ditch and being helped out of it by the hunter were omitted?
4. Is Christmas a particularly appropriate time in which to set the story? Why or why not?
5. What do you make of the title?

OSCAR CASARES

Oscar Casares, born and raised in Brownsville, Texas, and now a resident of San Antonio, is a graduate of the Iowa Writers' Workshop. He has published widely and received numerous prizes, including the James Michener Award. We reprint a story from his collection, Brownsville Stories *(2003).*

Yolanda

When I can't sleep at night I think of Yolanda Castro. She was a woman who lived next door to us one summer when I was growing up. I've never told Maggie about her because it's not something she'd appreciate knowing. Trust me.

Tonight, like most nights, she fell asleep before I was even done brushing my teeth. And now all I can hear are little snores. Sometimes she even talks to herself, shouts out other people's names, and then in the morning says she can't remember any of it. Either way, I let her go on sleeping. She's over on her side of the bed. It's right where she ought to be. This thing with Yolanda doesn't really concern her.

I was only twelve years old when Frank and Yolanda Castro moved into the beige house with green trim. Frank pulled up on our street in a U-Haul he'd driven all the way from California to Texas. I remember it being a different neighborhood back then. Everybody knew everybody, and people left their doors unlocked at night. You didn't worry about people stealing shit you didn't lock up. I'm talking about more than twenty years ago now. I'm talking about before some drunk spent all afternoon in one of the cantinas on Fourteenth Street, then drove his car straight into the Rivas front yard and ran over the Baby Jesus that was still lying in the manger because Lonny Rivas was too flojo[1] to put it away a month after Christmas, and they the guy tried to run, but fell down, asleep, in our yard, and when the cops were handcuffing him all he could say was *ma-ri-juan-a*, which even then, at the age of fifteen, I knew wasn't a good thing to say when you were being arrested. This was before Pete Zuniga was riding his brand-new ten-speed from Western Auto and, next to the Friendship Garden, saw a white dude who'd been knifed a couple of dozen times and was floating in the green water of the resaca.[2] Before some crazy woman hired a curandera[3] to put a spell on her daughter's ex-boyfriend, which really meant hiring a couple of hit men from Matamoros to do a drive-by. Before the cops ever had to show up at El Disco de Oro Tortillería. Like holding up a 7-Eleven was getting old, right? You know, when you could sit at the Brownsville Coffee Shop #1 and not worry about getting it in the back while you ate your menudo.[4] When you didn't have to put an alarm *and* the Club on your car so it wouldn't end up in Reynosa. Before my father had to put iron bars on the windows and doors because some future convict from the junior high was always breaking into the house. And before my father had to put a fence in the front because, in his words, I'm sick and tired of all those damn dogs making poo in my yard. I guess what I'm trying to say is, things were different back then.

Frank Castro was an older man, in his fifties by that point, and Yolanda couldn't have been more than thirty, if that. My mother got along with Yolanda okay and even helped her get a job at the HEB store where she had worked since before I was born. You could say that was where the problems started, because Frank Castro didn't want his wife working at HEB, or any other place for that matter. You have no business being in that grocery store, I heard him yell one night when I was trying to fall asleep. I could hear almost everything Frank yelled that summer. Our houses were only a few yards apart, and my window was the closest to the action. My father's bougainvilleas were the dividing line between the two properties. I heard Yolanda beg Frank to please let her take the job. I heard Frank yell something in Spanish about how no woman in his family had ever worked behind a cosmetics counter, selling lipstick. I heard her promise she'd only work part-time, and she'd quit if they ever scheduled her on nights or weekends. I heard her tell him how much she loved him and how she'd never take a job that would keep them apart. Francisco, tú eres mi vida,[5] she said to him. I

---

[1]**flojo** weak-willed. [2]**resaca** dry streambed. [3]**curandera** mid-wife. [4]**menudo** tripe soup.
[5]**tú . . . vida** you are my life.

heard him get real quiet. Then I heard Frank and Yolanda Castro making love. I didn't know what making love sounded like back then, but I can tell you now that's what it was.

If you saw what Yolanda looked like, you might not have blamed Frank for not wanting her to leave the house. It also wouldn't have been a big mystery to you how she went into the store applying for a job in the meat department and ended up getting one in cosmetics. The only girl I'd ever seen that even came close to being as beautiful as Yolanda was in a *Playboy* I found under my parents' bed the summer before. The girl in the magazine had the same long black hair, light brown skin, and green eyes that Yolanda did, only she was sitting bareback on an Appaloosa.

5   The thing I remember most about Frank was his huge forearms. They were like Popeye's, except with a lot more black and gray hair mixed in. But the hair on his arms was just the beginning. There wasn't a time I saw the guy that he didn't look like he could've use a good shave. And it didn't help that his thick eyebrows were connected into one long eyebrow that stretched across the bottom of his forehead like a piece of electrical tape. He was average size, but he looked short and squatty when he stood next to Yolanda. Frank was a mechanic at the airport and, according to my father, probably made good money. I was with my father the first time he met Frank. He always made it a point to meet any new neighbors and then come back to the house and give a full report to my mother, who would later meet the neighbors herself and say he was exaggerating about how shifty so-and-so's eyes were or how rich he thought another neighbor might be because he had one of those new foreign cars in the driveway, un carro extranjero,[6] a Toyota or a Honda. Frank was beginning to mow his front yard when we walked up. My father introduced me as his boy, and I shook our neighbor's sweaty hand. I've lived thirty-six years on this earth and never shaken hands with a bear, but I have a good idea that it wouldn't be much different from shaking Frank Castro's hand. Even his fingers needed a haircut. Frank stood there answering a couple of my father's questions about whether he liked the neighborhood (he liked it) and how long he had lived in California before moving back to Texas (ten years—he held up both hands to show us exactly how many). Suddenly, my father nodded and said we had to go. He turned around and walked off, then looked over his shoulder and yelled at me to hurry up. This whole time, Frank had not shut off his mower. My father was forced to stand there and shout over the sound of the engine. The report on Frank wasn't pretty when we got back to the house. From that point on, my father would only refer to him as El Burro.

It wasn't just my father. Nobody liked Frank. He had this thing about his yard where he didn't want anybody getting near it. We found this out one day when Lonny and I were throwing the football around in the street. Lonny was showing off and he threw the ball over my head, way over, and it landed in Frank's yard. When I was getting the ball, Frank opened the front door and yelled something about it being private property. Then he went over, turned on the hose, and started watering his yard and half the street in front of his yard. He did this every afternoon from that day on. The hose with a spray gun in his right hand, and a Schlitz tallboy in his left. Lonny thought we should steal the hose when Frank wasn't home, or maybe poke a few holes in it, just to teach the fucker a lesson. One Saturday morning we even saw him turn the hose on some Jehovahs who

[6]**carro extranjero** foreign car.

were walking up the street towards his house. A skinny man wearing a tie and short-sleeve shirt kept trying to give him a pamphlet, but Frank wasn't listening.

My mother gave Yolanda a ride to work every day. In the afternoons, Yolanda got off work early enough to be waiting for Frank to pull up in his car and drive her back to the house. My mother told us at home that Yolanda had asked Frank to teach her how to drive when they first got married but that Frank had said she was his princesa now and any place she needed to go, he'd take her. One morning, when both my mother and Yolanda had the day off, my mother asked her if she wanted to learn how to drive. They drove out by the port, and my mother pulled over so Yolanda could take the wheel. I was hanging out at the Jiffy-Mart, down the street, when I saw Yolanda driving my mother's car. Yolanda honked the horn, and they both waved at me as they turned the corner.

That night—like a lot of nights that summer—I listened to Frank and Yolanda Castro. What they said went something like this:

"I can show you."

"I don't wanna see."

10 "Why not?"

"Because you have *no* business driving a car around town."

"But this way you don't have to pick me up every day. You can come straight home, and I'll be here already, waiting."

"I don't care. I'm talking about you learning to drive."

15 "Frank, it's nothing."

"You don't even have a car. What do you want with a license?"

"I can buy one."

"With what?"

"I've been getting bonuses. The companies gives us a little extra if we sell more of their makeup."

20 "Is that right?"

"It isn't that much, Frank."

"And then?"

"Well, maybe I can buy a used one."

"It's because of that store."

25 "What's wrong with the store?"

"It's putting ideas in your head."

"Frank, what ideas?"

"Ideas! Is there some place I haven't taken you?"

"No."

30 "Well, then?"

"Francisco."

"Don't 'Francisco' me."

"Baby . . ."

"¡Qué no!"[7]

35 They were beginning to remind me of one of my mother's novellas, which she was probably watching in the living room at that very moment. Things like that usually made me want to laugh—and I did a little, into my pillow, but it was only because I couldn't believe I was actually hearing it, and I could see Frank Castro pounding me into the ground with his big forearms if he ever found out.

"No! I said."

"I'm not Trini."

---

[7]**¡Qué no!** Why not?

"I never said . . ."

"Then stop treating me like her. ¿No sabes qué tanto te quiero, Francisco?"[8]

40   It got quiet for a while after that. Then there was the sound of something hitting the floor, the sound of two bodies dropping on a bed with springs that had seen better days (and nights), the sound of Yolanda saying, *Ay, Diosito,*[9] over and over and over again—just like my tía[10] Hilda did the day her son, my cousin Rudy, almost drowned in the swimming pool at the Civic Center—then the sound of the bed springs making their own crazy music, and the sound of what I imagine a bear is like when he's trying to make little bears.

Yolanda kept getting a ride to work with my mother, and Frank kept bringing her home in the afternoons. My mother had offered to drive Yolanda to the DPS office and let her borrow our car for the driving part of the test, but Yolanda said she'd changed her mind and didn't want to talk about it. I heard my mother telling my father what she'd said, and they agreed it probably had something to do with Frank. El Burro, my father let out when they didn't have anything else to say.

It was the Fourth of July when I got sick that summer. I remember my mother wouldn't let me go outside with Lonny. He kept yelling at me from the street that night to stop being a baby and come out of the house so I could pop some firecrackers. We'd been talking all week about shooting some bottle rockets in the direction of Frank's house. It didn't feel like anything at first, just a fever, but the next morning we knew it was the chicken pox. My mother had to miss a few days of work, staying home with me until I got over the worst part. After that, Yolanda volunteered to come look in on me when she wasn't working. But I told my mother I didn't want her coming over when I still looked like those dead people in that *Night of the Living Dead* movie. My mother said Yolanda would understand I was sick, and if she didn't, that's what I'd get for watching those kinds of movies. So for about a week she came over in the mornings and we watched *The Price Is Right* together. Yolanda was great at guessing the prices of things, and she said it was from working in a grocery store and having a good memory. I told her I thought she should go on the show. She laughed and said she probably wouldn't win anything, since she'd be too nervous. What I meant to say was that she should go on the show and be one of the girls who stands next to the car, smiling. She was prettier than any of them, but I never told her that, because I got embarrassed whenever I thought about saying it.

If Yolanda came over in the afternoon, we'd watch *General Hospital* together. She said she'd been watching it for years. There wasn't anything else on at that hour, so I didn't really care. Once, she brought over some lime sherbert, and we played Chinese checkers in my room until she had to get home to Frank Castro. Each time she left she'd reach down and give me a little kiss on the cheek, and each time her hair smelled like a different fruit. Sometimes like a pear, sometimes like a strawberry, sometimes like an apple. The strawberry was my favorite.

This was about the time when Frank said that from now on, he would take Yolanda to work in the morning—no matter how out of the way it was for him, or the fact that he and my mother were always pulling out of the driveway at the same time. A week or two went by, and then my mother told my father that Frank had started showing up at the store in the middle of the day, usually during his lunch hour, but sometimes also at two or three in the afternoon. He wouldn't talk

---

[8]**¿No . . . Francisco?** Don't you know how much I love you, Francisco?   [9]**Ay, Diosito** Oh, God. [10]**tía** aunt.

to Yolanda, but instead just hung out by the magazine rack, pretending to read a wrestling magazine. Yolanda tried to ignore him. My mother said she had talked to her in the break room, but Yolanda kept saying it was nothing, that Frank's hours had changed at the airport.

45   There was one Saturday when he was off from work, and as usual, he spent it in his front yard, sitting in a green lawn chair, drinking tallboys. He had turned on the sprinkler and was watching his grass and half the street get a good watering. Lonny and I were throwing the football around. Frank sat in that stupid chair all afternoon. He only went in to grab another beer and, I guess, take a piss. Each time he got up and turned around, we shot him the finger.

That night, I heard Frank's voice loud and clear. He wanted answers. Something about a phone number. Something about a customer he'd seen Yolanda talking to a couple of days earlier. Did she think he was blind? What the hell was so funny when the two of them were talking? How many times? he wanted to know. ¡Desgraciado![11] Where? Goddammit! he wanted to know. What game show? ¡El sanavabiche! Something shattered against the wall and then a few seconds later Yolanda screamed. I sat up. I didn't know if I could form words if I had to. What the hell were you doing listening anyway? they would ask me. There was another scream and then the sound of the back door slamming. I looked out my window and saw Frank Castro chase Yolanda into their backyard. She was wearing a nightgown that came down to her knees. Frank had on the same khakis and muscle shirt he'd worn that afternoon. He only ran a few feet down from the back steps before his head hit the clothesline, and he fell to the ground, hard. Yolanda didn't turn to look back and ran around the right side of their house. I thought she'd gone back inside to call the police. Then I heard footsteps and a tapping on my window. It was Yolanda whispering, Open it, open it.

I didn't say anything for a long time. Yolanda had climbed in and let down the blinds. We were lying on the bed, facing the window. She was behind me, holding me tight. I finally asked her is she wanted a glass of water or some Kool-Aid. I made it myself, I told her. It's the orange kind, I said. I didn't know what else to talk about. She said no, and then she told me to be quiet. I kept thinking, This has to be a dream and any minute now my mother's going to walk in and tell me the barbacoa[12] is sitting on the table and to come eat because we're going to eleven o'clock mass and don't even think about putting on those blue jeans with the patches in the knees ¿me entiendes?[13] But that wasn't happening, and something told me then that no matter what happened after tonight, this was something I'd never forget. There would always be a time *before* Yolanda crawled into my bed and a time *after*. As she held me, I could feel her heart beating. Then I felt her chiches[14] pressed against my back. And even though I couldn't see them, I knew they were perfect like the rest of her. I knew that they'd fit right in the palms of my hands, if only I had enough guts to turn around. Just turn around, that's all I had to do. I thought back to when she was tapping on the window, and I was sure she wasn't wearing a bra. I was sure there was nothing but Yolanda underneath her nightgown. I could have sworn I'd seen even more. I'd been close to a woman's body before. But this wasn't like when my tía Gloria came into town and couldn't believe how much I'd grown, and then she squeezed me so hard my head got lost in her huge and heavily perfumed chiches. And it wasn't anything like the Sears catalog where the girls had a tiny rose at the top of their panties.

[11]**Desgraciado** disgraceful.   [12]**barbacoa** baked lamb or goat.   [13]**me entiendes** do you understand me?   [14]**chiches** breasts.

No, this was Yolanda and she was in my bed, pressed up against my back, like it was the only place in the world for us to be.

I could go on and tell you the rest of the details—how I never turned around and always regretted it, how we stayed there and listened to Frank crying in his backyard, how Lonny's dad finally called the cops on his ass, how Yolanda had a cousin pick her up the next morning, how she ended up leaving Frank for a man who worked for one of the shampoo companies, how it didn't matter because she'd also been seeing an assistant manager and would be having his baby soon enough, and how it really didn't matter because the assistant manager was already married and wasn't about to leave his wife and kids, and how, actually, none of it mattered because she'd been taking money out of the register and was about to be caught—but that's not the part of the story I like to remember.

In that bed of mine, the one with the Dallas Cowboy pillows and covers, Yolanda and I were safe. We were safe from Frank Castro and safe from anybody else that might try to hurt us. And it was safe for me to fall asleep in Yolanda's arms, with her warm, beautiful body pressed against mine, and dream that we were riding off to some faraway place on an Appaloosa.

[2003]

Topics for Critical Thinking and Writing

1. Characterize the narrator. Characterize Frank.
2. In the next-to-last paragraph we learn that Yolanda has been "taking money out of the register." Did this statement surprise you? Why do you think the author included it?
3. Do you think that the narrator is or was in love with Yolanda? Explain.

10

Thinking and Writing Critically about Short Stories: Two Case Studies

Case Study: Writing about Flannery O'Connor

In this case study we give two short stories and several comments of O'Connor's on literature:

1. "A Good Man Is Hard to Find"
2. "Revelation"
3. Passages from five essays about fiction and a letter on "A Good Man Is Hard to Find"

We also include a page from the manuscript of "A Good Man Is Hard to Find," showing O'Connor's revisions.

 *Flannery O'Connor (1925–1964)—her first name was Mary but she did not use it—was born in Savannah, Georgia, but spent most of her life in Milledgeville, Georgia, where her family moved when she was 12. She was educated in parochial schools and at the local college and then went to the School for Writers at the University of Iowa, where she earned an MFA in 1946. For a few months she lived at a writers' colony in Saratoga Springs, New York, and then for a few weeks she lived in New York City, but most of her life was spent back in Milledgeville, where she tended her peacocks and wrote stories, novels, essays* (posthumously published as Mystery and Manners [1970]), *and letters (posthumously published under the title* The Habit of Being [1979]).

In 1951, when she was 25, Flannery O'Connor discovered that she was a victim of lupus erythematosus, an incurable autoimmune disease that had crippled and then killed her father ten years before. She died at the age of 39. O'Connor faced her illness with stoic courage, Christian fortitude—and tough humor. Here is a glimpse, from one of her letters, of how she dealt with those who pitied her:

> *An old lady got on the elevator behind me and as soon as I turned around she fixed me with a moist gleaming eye and said in a loud voice, "Bless you, darling!" I felt exactly like the Misfit [in "A Good Man Is Hard to Find"] and I gave her a weakly lethal look, whereupon greatly encouraged she grabbed my arm and whispered (very loud) in my ear, "Remember what they said to John at the gate, darling!" It was not my*

floor but I got off and I suppose the old lady was astounded at how quick I could get away on crutches. I have a one-legged friend and I asked her what they said to John at the gate. She said she reckoned they said, "The lame shall enter first." This may be because the lame will be able to knock everybody else aside with their crutches.

A devout Catholic, O'Connor forthrightly summarized the relation between her belief and her writing:

I see from the standpoint of Christian orthodoxy. This means that for me the meaning of life is centered in our Redemption by Christ and what I see in the world I see in its relation to that.

A Good Man Is Hard to Find

The grandmother didn't want to go to Florida. She wanted to visit some of her connections in east Tennessee and she was seizing every chance to change Bailey's mind. Bailey was the son she lived with, her only boy. He was sitting on the edge of his chair at the table, bent over the orange sports section of the *Journal.* "Now look here, Bailey," she said, "see here, read this," and she stood with one hand on her thin hip and the other rattling the newspaper at his bald head. "Here this fellow that calls himself The Misfit is aloose from the Federal Pen and headed toward Florida and you read here what it says he did to these people. Just you read it. I wouldn't take my children in any direction with a criminal like that aloose in it. I couldn't answer to my conscience if I did."

Bailey didn't look up from his reading so she wheeled around then and faced the children's mother, a young woman in slacks, whose face was as broad and innocent as a cabbage and was tied around with a green headkerchief that had two points on the top like rabbit's ears. She was sitting on the sofa, feeding the baby his apricots out of a jar. "The children have been to Florida before," the old lady said. "You all ought to take them somewhere else for a change so they would see different parts of the world and be broad. They never have been to east Tennessee."

The children's mother didn't seem to hear her, but the eight-year-old boy, John Wesley, a stocky child with glasses, said. "If you don't want to go to Florida, why dontcha stay at home?" He and the little girl, June Star, were reading the funny papers on the floor.

"She wouldn't stay at home to be queen for a day," June Star said without raising her yellow head.

5 "Yes, and what would you do if this fellow, The Misfit, caught you?" the grandmother said.

"I'd smack his face," John Wesley said.

"She wouldn't stay at home for a million bucks," June Star said. "Afraid she'd miss something. She has to go everywhere we go."

"All right, Miss," the grandmother said. "Just remember that the next time you want me to curl your hair."

June Star said her hair was naturally curly.

10 The next morning the grandmother was the first one in the car, ready to go. She had her big black valise that looked like the head of a hippopotamus in one corner, and underneath it she was hiding a basket with Pitty Sing, the cat, in it. She didn't intend for the cat to be left alone in the house for three days because he would miss her too much and she was afraid he might brush against one of the

2.

~~Of course who~~ *the grandmother* was the first one ready to load up the next morning at six
o'clock. She had Baby Brother's bucking bronco ~~that~~ and ~~basxxxkiss~~ what she
called her "~~Flee~~" and Pitty Sing, the cat, ~~xxxxxxx~~ *got the* packed in the car before
Boatwrite had a chance to ~~gatxxxxthingxxjxxxxbx~~ ~~cq~~ ~~out of the door with the~~
rest of the luggage.out of the hall. They got off at seven-thirty, Boatwrite
and ~~xxx~~ the children's mother in the front and Granny, John Wesley, Baby Brother,
Little Sister Mayy Ann, Pitty Sing, and the bucking bronco in the back.

"Why the hell did you bring that goddam rocking horse?" Boatwrite asked
because as soon as ~~the car out of the door on the smooth highway~~ ~~the car began to move~~, Baby Brother began to squall to get
on the bucking bronco. "He can't get on that thing in this car and that's final,"
his father, who was a stern man said.

"Can we open the lunch now?" Little Sister ~~Maxyxxxx~~ asked. "It'll shut
Baby Brother up. Mamma, can we open up the lunch?"

"No," their grandmother said. *It's only eight-thirty*

Their mother was ~~xxxxx~~ *still* reading SCREEN MOTHERS AND THEIR CHILDREN. "Yeah,
sure," she said.without looking up. She was all dressed up today. She had on
a purple silk dress and a hat and ~~gxxxxxxxx~~ a choker of pink beads and a new
pocket book, and high heel *colored* pumps.

"Let's go through Georgia quick so we won't have to look at it much," John
Wesley said. "~~I can't see why it's here.~~"

"You should see Tennessee," his grandmother said. "Now there is a *beautiful* state."

"Like hell," John Wesley said. "That's just a hillbilly dumping ground."

"Yes," his mother said, and nudged Boatwrite. "Didjer hear that?" *She was*
from Tennessee They ate their lunch and got along fine ~~after that~~ for a while until Pitty
Sing who had been asleep jumped into the front of the car and caused Boatwrite
to swerve to the right into a ditch. Pitty Sing was a large grey-striped cat
with a yellow hind leg and a ~~x~~ *big* soiled white face. Granny thought that she
was the only person in the world that he really loved but he had never ~~really~~ *the truth was*
~~looked xxfxxxxxxxxkxxfxxx xxx~~ *yet* farther than her middle and he didn't even
like other cats. He jumped snarling into ~~the front seat and Boatwrite's~~ shoulders

Typescript page from "A Good Man Is Hard to Find" with O'Connor's handwritten
changes.

gas burners and accidentally asphyxiate himself. Her son, Bailey, didn't like to arrive at a motel with a cat.

She sat in the middle of the back seat with John Wesley and June Star on either side of her. Bailey and the children's mother and the baby sat in front and
they left Atlanta at eight forty-five with the mileage on the car at 55890. The
grandmother wrote this down because she thought it would be interesting to say
how many miles they had been when they got back. It took them twenty minutes
to reach the outskirts of the city.

The old lady settled herself comfortably, removing her white cotton gloves and putting them up with her purse on the shelf in front of the back window. The children's mother still had on slacks and still had her head tied up in a green kerchief, but the grandmother had on a navy blue straw sailor hat with a bunch of white violets on the brim and a navy blue dress with a small white dot in the print. Her collars and cuffs were white organdy trimmed with lace and at her neckline she had pinned a purple spray of cloth violets containing a sachet. In case of an accident, anyone seeing her dead on the highway would know at once that she was a lady.

She said she thought it was going to be a good day for driving, neither too hot nor too cold, and she cautioned Bailey that the speed limit was fifty-five miles an hour and that the patrolmen hid themselves behind bill-boards and small clumps of trees and sped out after you before you had a chance to slow down. She pointed out interesting details of the scenery: Stone Mountain; the blue granite that in some places came up to both sides of the highway; the brilliant red clay banks slightly streaked with purple; and the various crops that made rows of green lace-work on the ground. The trees were full of silver-white sunlight and the meanest of them sparkled. The children were reading comic magazines and their mother had gone back to sleep.

"Let's go through Georgia fast so we won't have to look at it much," John Wesley said.

15 "If I were a little boy," said the grandmother, "I wouldn't talk about my native state that way. Tennessee has the mountains and Georgia has the hills."

"Tennessee is just a hillbilly dumping ground," John Wesley said, "and Georgia is a lousy state too."

"You said it," June Star said.

"In my time," said the grandmother, folding her thin veined fingers, "children were more respectful of their native states and their parents and everything else. People did right then. Oh look at the cute little pickaninny!" she said and pointed to a Negro child standing in the door of a shack. "Wouldn't that make a picture, now?" she asked and they all turned and looked at the little Negro out of the back window. He waved.

"He didn't have any britches on," June Star said.

20 "He probably didn't have any," the grandmother explained. "Little niggers in the country don't have things like we do. If I could paint, I'd paint that picture," she said.

The children exchanged comic books.

The grandmother offered to hold the baby and the children's mother passed him over the front seat to her. She set him on her knee and bounced him and told him about the things they were passing. She rolled her eyes and screwed up her mouth and stuck her leathery thin face into his smooth bland one. Occasionally he gave her a faraway smile. They passed a large cotton field with five or six graves fenced in the middle of it, like a small island. "Look at the graveyard!" the grandmother said, pointing it out. "That was the old family burying ground. That belonged to the plantation."

"Where's the plantation?" John Wesley asked.

"Gone With the Wind," said the grandmother. "Ha. Ha."

25 When the children finished all the comic books they had brought, they opened the lunch and ate it. The grandmother ate a peanut butter sandwich and an olive and would not let the children throw the box and the paper napkins out the window. When there was nothing else to do they played a game by choosing

a cloud and making the other two guess what shape it suggested. John Wesley took one the shape of a cow and June Star guessed a cow and John Wesley said, no, an automobile, and June Star said he didn't play fair, and they began to slap each other over the grandmother.

The grandmother said she would tell them a story if they would keep quiet. When she told a story, she rolled her eyes and waved her head and was very dramatic. She said once when she was a maiden lady she had been courted by a Mr. Edgar Atkins Teagarden from Jasper, Georgia. She said he was a very good-looking man and a gentleman and that he brought her a watermelon every Saturday afternoon with his initials cut in it, E.A.T. Well, one Saturday, she said, Mr. Teagarden brought the watermelon and there was nobody at home and he left it on the front porch and returned in his buggy to Jasper, but she never got the watermelon, she said, because a nigger boy ate it when he saw the initials, E.A.T.! This story tickled John Wesley's funny bone and he giggled and giggled but June Star didn't think it was any good. She said she wouldn't marry a man that just brought her a watermelon on Saturday. The grandmother said she would have done well to marry Mr. Teagarden because he was a gentleman and had bought Coca-Cola stock when it first came out and that he had died only a few years ago, a very wealthy man.

They stopped at The Tower for barbecued sandwiches. The Tower was a part-stucco and part-wood filling station and dance hall set in a clearing outside of Timothy. A fat man named Red Sammy Butts ran it and there were signs stuck here and there on the building and for miles up and down the highway saying, TRY RED SAMMY'S FAMOUS BARBECUE. NONE LIKE FAMOUS RED SAMMY'S! RED SAM! THE FAT BOY WITH THE HAPPY LAUGH. A VETERAN! RED SAMMY'S YOUR MAN!

Red Sammy was lying on the bare ground outside The Tower with his head under a truck while a gray monkey about a foot high, chained to a small chinaberry tree, chattered nearby. The monkey sprang back into the tree and got on the highest limb as soon as he saw the children jump out of the car and run toward him.

Inside, The Tower was a long dark room with a counter at one end and tables at the other and dancing space in the middle. They all sat down at a broad table next to the nickelodeon and Red Sam's wife, a tall burnt-brown woman with hair and eyes lighter than her skin, came and took their order. The children's mother put a dime in the machine and played "The Tennessee Waltz," and the grandmother said that tune always made her want to dance. She asked Bailey if he would like to dance but he only glared at her. He didn't have a naturally sunny disposition like she did and trips made him nervous. The grandmother's brown eyes were very bright. She swayed her head from side to side and pretended she was dancing in her chair. June Star said play something she could tap to so the children's mother put in another dime and played a fast number and June Star stepped out onto the dance floor and did her tap routine.

30   "Ain't she cute?" Red Sam's wife said, leaning over the counter. "Would you like to come be my little girl?"

"No, I certainly wouldn't," June Star said. "I wouldn't live in a broken-down place like this for a million bucks!" and she ran back to the table.

"Ain't she cute?" the woman repeated, stretching her mouth politely.

"Aren't you ashamed?" hissed the grandmother.

Red Sam came in and told his wife to quit lounging on the counter and hurry with these people's order. His khaki trousers reached just to his hip bones and his stomach hung over them like a sack of meal swaying under his shirt. He came over and sat down at a table nearby and let out a combination sigh and yodel. "You can't win," he said. "You can't win," and he wiped his sweating red face off with a gray handkerchief. "These days you don't know who to trust," he said. "Ain't that the truth?"

35   "People are certainly not nice like they used to be," said the grandmother.

"Two fellers come in here last week," Red Sammy said, "driving a Chrysler. It was an old beat-up car but it was a good one and these boys looked all right to me. Said they worked at the mill and you know I let them fellers charge the gas they bought? Now why did I do that?"

"Because you're a good man!" the grandmother said at once.

"Yes'm, I suppose so," Red Sam said as if he were struck with this answer.

His wife brought the orders, carrying the five plates all at once without a tray, two in each hand and one balanced on her arm. "It isn't a soul in this green world of God's that you can trust," she said. "And I don't count nobody out of that, not nobody," she repeated, looking at Red Sammy.

40   "Did you read about that criminal, The Misfit, that's escaped?" asked the grandmother.

"I wouldn't be a bit surprised if he didn't attack this place right here," said the woman. "If he hears about it being here, I wouldn't be none surprised to see him. If he hears it's two cent in the cash register, I wouldn't be a tall surprised if he . . ."

"That'll do," Red Sam said. "Go bring these people their Co'Colas," and the woman went off to get the rest of the order.

"A good man is hard to find," Red Sammy said. "Everything is getting terrible. I remember the day you could go off and leave your screen door unlatched. Not no more."

He and the grandmother discussed better times. The old lady said that in her opinion Europe was entirely to blame for the way things were now. She said the way Europe acted you would think we were made of money and Red Sam said it was no use talking about it, she was exactly right. The children ran outside into the white sunlight and looked at the monkey in the lacy chinaberry tree. He was busy catching fleas on himself and biting each one carefully between his teeth as if it were a delicacy.

45   They drove off again into the hot afternoon. The grandmother took cat naps and woke up every five minutes with her own snoring. Outside of Toombsboro she woke up and recalled an old plantation that she had visited in this neighborhood once when she was a young lady. She said the house had six white columns across the front and that there was an avenue of oaks leading up to it and two little wooden trellis arbors on either side in front where you sat down with your suitor after a stroll in the garden. She recalled exactly which road to turn off to get to it. She knew that Bailey would not be willing to lose any time looking at an old house, but the more she talked about it, the more she wanted to see it once again and find out if the little twin arbors were still standing. "There was a secret panel in this house," she said craftily, not telling the truth but wishing that she were, "and the story went that all the family silver was hidden in it when Sherman came through but it was never found . . ."

"Hey!" John Wesley said. "Let's go see it! We'll find it! We'll poke all the woodwork and find it! Who lives there? Where do you turn off at? Hey, Pop, can't we turn off there?"

"We never have seen a house with a secret panel!" June Star shrieked. "Let's go to the house with the secret panel! Hey, Pop, can't we go see the house with the secret panel!"

"It's not far from here, I know," the grandmother said. "It wouldn't take over twenty minutes."

Bailey was looking straight ahead. His jaw was as rigid as a horseshoe. "No," he said.

50   The children began to yell and scream that they wanted to see the house with the secret panel. John Wesley kicked the back of the front seat and June Star hung over her mother's shoulder and whined desperately into her ear that they never had any fun even on their vacation, that they could never do what THEY wanted to do. The baby began to scream and John Wesley kicked the back of the seat so hard that his father could feel the blows in his kidney.

"All right!" he shouted and drew the car to a stop at the side of the road. "Will you all shut up? Will you all just shut up for one second? If you don't shut up, we won't go anywhere."

"It would be very educational for them," the grandmother murmured.

"All right," Bailey said, "but get this. This is the only time we're going to stop for anything like this. This is the one and only time."

"The dirt road that you have to turn down is about a mile back," the grandmother directed. "I marked it when we passed."

55   "A dirt road," Bailey groaned.

After they had turned around and were headed toward the dirt road, the grandmother recalled other points about the house, the beautiful glass over the front doorway and the candle lamp in the hall. John Wesley said that the secret panel was probably in the fireplace.

"You can't go inside this house," Bailey said. "You don't know who lives there."

"While you all talk to the people in front, I'll run around behind and get in a window," John Wesley suggested.

"We'll all stay in the car," his mother said.

60   They turned onto the dirt road and the car raced roughly along in a swirl of pink dust. The grandmother recalled the times when there were no paved roads and thirty miles was a day's journey. The dirt road was hilly and there were sudden washes in it and sharp curves on dangerous embankments. All at once they would be on a hill, looking down over the blue tops of trees for miles around, then the next minute, they would be in a red depression with the dust-coated trees looking down on them.

"This place had better turn up in a minute," Bailey said, "or I'm going to turn around."

The road looked as if no one had traveled on it in months.

"It's not much farther," the grandmother said and just as she said it, a horrible thought came to her. The thought was so embarrassing that she turned red in the face and her eyes dilated and her feet jumped up, upsetting her valise in the corner. The instant the valise moved, the newspaper top she had over the basket under it rose with a snarl and Pitty Sing, the cat, sprang onto Bailey's shoulder.

The children were thrown to the floor and their mother, clutching the baby, was thrown out the door onto the ground; the old lady was thrown into the front seat. The car turned over once and landed right-side-up in a gulch on the side of the road. Bailey remained in the driver's seat with the cat—gray-striped with a broad white face and an orange nose—clinging to his neck like a caterpillar.

65   As soon as the children saw they could move their arms and legs, they scrambled out of the car, shouting, "We've had an ACCIDENT!" The grandmother was curled up under the dashboard, hoping she was injured so that Bailey's wrath

would not come down on her all at once. The horrible thought she had had before the accident was that the house she had remembered so vividly was not in Georgia but in Tennessee.

Bailey removed the cat from his neck with both hands and flung it out the window against the side of a pine tree. Then he got out of the car and started looking for the children's mother. She was sitting against the side of the red gutted ditch, holding the screaming baby, but she only had a cut down her face and a broken shoulder. "We've had an ACCIDENT!" the children screamed in a frenzy of delight.

"But nobody's killed," June Star said with disappointment as the grandmother limped out of the car, her hat still pinned to her head but the broken front brim standing up at a jaunty angle and the violet spray hanging off the side. They all sat down in the ditch, except the children, to recover from the shock. They were all shaking.

"Maybe a car will come along," said the children's mother hoarsely.

"I believe I have injured an organ," said the grandmother, pressing her side, but no one answered her. Bailey's teeth were clattering. He had on a yellow sport shirt with bright blue parrots designed in it and his face was as yellow as the shirt. The grandmother decided that she would not mention that the house was in Tennessee.

70   The road was about ten feet above and they could see only the tops of the trees on the other side of it. Behind the ditch they were sitting in there were more woods, tall and dark and deep. In a few minutes they saw a car some distance away on top of a hill, coming slowly as if the occupants were watching them. The grandmother stood up and waved both arms dramatically to attract their attention. The car continued to come on slowly, disappeared around a bend and appeared again, moving even slower on top of the hill they had gone over. It was a big black battered hearselike automobile. There were three men in it.

It came to a stop just over them and for some minutes, the driver looked down with a steady expressionless gaze to where they were sitting, and didn't speak. Then he turned his head and muttered something to the other two and they got out. One was a fat boy in black trousers and a red sweat shirt with a silver stallion embossed on the front of it. He moved around on the right side of them and stood staring, his mouth partly open in a kind of loose grin. The other had on khaki pants and a blue striped coat and a gray hat pulled down very low, hiding most of his face. He came around slowly on the left side. Neither spoke.

The driver got out of the car and stood by the side of it, looking down at them. He was an older man than the other two. His hair was just beginning to gray and he wore silver-rimmed spectacles that gave him a scholarly look. He had a long creased face and didn't have on any shirt or undershirt. He had on blue jeans that were too tight for him and was holding a black hat and a gun. The two boys also had guns.

"We've had an ACCIDENT!" the children screamed.

The grandmother had the peculiar feeling that the bespectacled man was someone she knew. His face was as familiar to her as if she had known him all her life but she could not recall who he was. He moved away from the car and began to come down the embankment, placing his feet carefully so that he wouldn't slip. He had on tan and white shoes and no socks, and his ankles were red and thin. "Good afternoon," he said. "I see you all had you a little spill."

75   "We turned over twice!" said the grandmother.

"Oncet," he corrected. "We seen it happen. Try their car and see will it run, Hiram," he said quietly to the boy with the gray hat.

"What you got that gun for?" John Wesley asked. "Whatcha gonna do with that gun?"

"Lady," the man said to the children's mother, "would you mind calling them children to sit down by you? Children make me nervous. I want all you to sit down right together there where you're at."

"What are you telling us what to do for?" June Star asked.

80   Behind them the line of woods gaped like a dark open mouth. "Come here," said their mother.

"Look here now," Bailey began suddenly, "we're in a predicament! We're in . . . "

The grandmother shrieked. She scrambled to her feet and stood staring. "You're The Misfit!" she said. "I recognized you at once!"

"Yes'm," the man said, smiling slightly as if he were pleased in spite of himself to be known, "but it would have been better for all of you, lady, if you hadn't of reckernized me."

Bailey turned his head sharply and said something to his mother that shocked even the children. The old lady began to cry and The Misfit reddened.

85   "Lady," he said, "don't you get upset. Sometimes a man says things he don't mean. I don't reckon he meant to talk to you thataway."

"You wouldn't shoot a lady, would you?" the grandmother said and removed a clean handkerchief from her cuff and began to slap at her eyes with it.

The Misfit pointed the toe of his shoe into the ground and made a little hole and then covered it up again. "I would hate to have to," he said.

"Listen," the grandmother almost screamed, "I know you're a good man. You don't look a bit like you have common blood. I know you must come from nice people!"

"Yes ma'm," he said, "finest people in the world." When he smiled he showed a row of strong white teeth. "God never made a finer woman than my mother and my daddy's heart was pure gold," he said. The boy with the red sweat shirt had come around behind them and was standing with his gun at his hip. The Misfit squatted down on the ground. "Watch them children, Bobby Lee," he said. "You know they make me nervous." He looked at the six of them huddled together in front of him and he seemed to be embarrassed as if he couldn't think of anything to say. "Ain't a cloud in the sky," he remarked, looking up at it. "Don't see no sun but don't see no cloud neither."

90   "Yes, it's a beautiful day," said the grandmother. "Listen," she said, "you shouldn't call yourself The Misfit because I know you're a good man at heart. I can just look at you and tell."

"Hush!" Bailey yelled, "Hush! Everybody shut up and let me handle this!" He was squatting in the position of a runner about to sprint forward but he didn't move.

"I pre-chate that, lady," The Misfit said and drew a little circle in the ground with the butt of his gun.

"It'll take a half a hour to fix this here car," Hiram called, looking over the raised hood of it.

"Well, first you and Bobby Lee get him and that little boy to step over yonder with you," The Misfit said, pointing to Bailey and John Wesley. "The boys want to ask you something," he said to Bailey. "Would you mind stepping back in them woods there with them?"

95   "Listen," Bailey began, "we're in a terrible predicament! Nobody realizes what this is," and his voice cracked. His eyes were as blue and intense as the parrots in his shirt and he remained perfectly still.

The grandmother reached up to adjust her hat brim as if she were going to the woods with him but it came off in her hand. She stood staring at it and after a second she let it fall on the ground. Hiram pulled Bailey up by the arm as if he were assisting an old man. John Wesley caught hold of his father's hand and Bobby Lee followed. They went off toward the woods and just as they reached the dark edge, Bailey turned and supporting himself against a gray naked pine trunk, he shouted, "I'll be back in a minute, Mamma, wait on me!"

"Come back this instant!" his mother shrilled but they all disappeared into the woods.

"Bailey Boy!" the grandmother called in a tragic voice but she found she was looking at The Misfit squatting on the ground in front of her. "I just know you're a good man," she said desperately. "You're not a bit common!"

"Nome, I ain't a good man," The Misfit said after a second as if he had considered her statement carefully, "but I ain't the worst in the world neither. My daddy said I was a different breed of dog from my brothers and sisters. 'You know,' Daddy said, 'It's some that can live their whole life without asking about it and it's others has to know why it is, and this boy is one of the latters. He's going to be into everything!'" He put on his black hat and looked up suddenly and then away deep into the woods as if he were embarrassed again. "I'm sorry I don't have on a shirt before you ladies," he said, hunching his shoulders slightly. "We buried our clothes that we had on when we escaped and we're just making do until we can get better. We borrowed these from some folks we met," he explained.

100 "That's perfectly all right," the grandmother said. "Maybe Bailey has an extra shirt in his suitcase."

"I'll look and see terrectly," The Misfit said.

"Where are they taking him?" the children's mother screamed.

"Daddy was a card himself," The Misfit said. "You couldn't put anything over on him. He never got in trouble with the Authorities though. Just had the knack of handling them."

"You could be honest too if you'd only try," said the grandmother. "Think how wonderful it would be to settle down and live a comfortable life and not have to think about somebody chasing you all the time."

105 The Misfit kept scratching in the ground with the butt of his gun as if he were thinking about it. "Yes'm, somebody is always after you," he murmured.

The grandmother noticed how thin his shoulder blades were just behind his hat because she was standing up looking down on him. "Do you ever pray?" she asked.

He shook his head. All she saw was the black hat wiggle between his shoulder blades. "Nome," he said.

There was a pistol shot from the woods, followed closely by another. Then silence. The old lady's head jerked around. She could hear the wind move through the tree tops like a long satisfied insuck of breath. "Bailey Boy!" she called.

"I was a gospel singer for a while," The Misfit said. "I been most everything. Been in the arm service, both land and sea, at home and abroad, been twict married, been an undertaker, been with the railroads, plowed Mother Earth, been in a tornado, seen a man burnt alive oncet," and he looked up at the children's mother and the little girl who were sitting close together, their faces white and their eyes glassy; "I even seen a woman flogged," he said.

110 "Pray, pray," the grandmother began, "pray, pray. . . ."

"I never was a bad boy that I remember of," The Misfit said in an almost dreamy voice, "but somewheres along the line I done something wrong and got sent to the penitentiary. I was buried alive," and he looked up and held her attention to him by a steady stare.

"That's when you should have started to pray," she said. "What did you do to get sent up to the penitentiary that first time?"

"Turn to the right, it was a wall," The Misfit said, looking up again at the cloudless sky. "Turn to the left, it was a wall. Look up it was a ceiling, look down it was a floor. I forget what I done, lady. I set there and set there, trying to remember what it was I done and I ain't recalled it to this day. Oncet in a while, I would think it was coming to me, but it never come."

"Maybe they put you in by mistake," the old lady said vaguely.

115 "Nome," he said. "It wasn't no mistake. They had the papers on me."

"You must have stolen something," she said.

The Misfit sneered slightly. "Nobody had nothing I wanted," he said. "It was a head-doctor at the penitentiary said what I had done was kill my daddy but I known that for a lie. My daddy died in nineteen ought nineteen of the epidemic flu and I never had a thing to do with it. He was buried in the Mount Hopewell Baptist churchyard and you can go there and see for yourself."

"If you would pray," the old lady said, "Jesus would help you."

"That's right," The Misfit said.

120 "Well then, why don't you pray?" she asked trembling with delight suddenly.

"I don't want no hep," he said. "I'm doing all right by myself."

Bobby Lee and Hiram came ambling back from the woods. Bobby Lee was dragging a yellow shirt with bright blue parrots on it.

"Throw me that shirt, Bobby Lee," The Misfit said. The shirt came flying at him and landed on his shoulder and he put it on. The grandmother couldn't name what the shirt reminded her of. "No, lady," The Misfit said while he was buttoning it up, "I found out the crime don't matter. You can do one thing or you can do another, kill a man or take a tire off his car, because sooner or later you're going to forget what it was you done and just be punished for it."

The children's mother had begun to make heaving noises as if she couldn't get her breath. "Lady," he asked, "would you and that little girl like to step off yonder with Bobby Lee and Hiram and join your husband?"

125 "Yes, thank you," the mother said faintly. Her left arm dangled helplessly and she was holding the baby, who had gone to sleep, in the other. "Hep that lady up, Hiram," The Misfit said as she struggled to climb out of the ditch, "and Bobby Lee, you hold onto that little girl's hand."

"I don't want to hold hands with him," June Star said. "He reminds me of a pig."

The fat boy blushed and laughed and caught her by the arm and pulled her off into the woods after Hiram and her mother.

Alone with The Misfit, the grandmother found that she had lost her voice. There was not a cloud in the sky nor any sun. There was nothing around her but woods. She wanted to tell him that he must pray. She opened and closed her mouth several times before anything came out. Finally she found herself saying, "Jesus, Jesus," meaning, Jesus will help you, but the way she was saying it, it sounded as if she might be cursing.

"Yes'm," The Misfit said as if he agreed. "Jesus thown everything off balance. It was the same case with Him as with me except He hadn't committed any crime and they could prove I had committed one because they had the papers on me. Of course," he said, "they never shown me my papers. That's why I sign myself now. I said long ago, you get you a signature and sign everything you do and keep a copy of it. Then you'll know what you done and you can hold up the crime to the punishment and see do they match and in the end you'll have something to prove you ain't been treated right. I call myself The

Misfit," he said, "because I can't make what all I done wrong fit what all I gone through in punishment."

130   There was a piercing scream from the woods, followed closely by a pistol report. "Does it seem right to you, lady, that one is punished a heap and another ain't punished at all?"

"Jesus!" the old lady cried. "You've got good blood! I know you wouldn't shoot a lady! I know you come from nice people! Pray! Jesus, you ought not to shoot a lady. I'll give you all the money I've got!"

"Lady," The Misfit said, looking beyond her far into the woods, "there never was a body that give the undertaker a tip."

There were two more pistol reports and the grandmother raised her head like a parched old turkey hen crying for water and called, "Bailey Boy, Bailey Boy!" as if her heart would break.

"Jesus was the only One that ever raised the dead," The Misfit continued, "and He shouldn't have done it. He thown everything off balance. If He did what He said, then it's nothing for you to do but thow away everything and follow Him, and if He didn't, then it's nothing for you to do but enjoy the few minutes you got left the best way you can—by killing somebody or burning down his house or doing some other meanness to him. No pleasure but meanness," he said and his voice had become almost a snarl.

135   "Maybe He didn't raise the dead," the old lady mumbled, not knowing what she was saying and feeling so dizzy that she sank down in the ditch with her legs twisted under her.

"I wasn't there so I can't say He didn't," The Misfit said. "I wisht I had of been there," he said, hitting the ground with his fist. "It ain't right I wasn't there because if I had of been there I would of known. Listen lady," he said in a high voice, "if I had of been there I would of known and I wouldn't be like I am now." His voice seemed about to crack and the grandmother's head cleared for an instant. She saw the man's face twisted close to her own as if he were going to cry and she murmured, "Why you're one of my babies. You're one of my own children!" She reached out and touched him on the shoulder. The Misfit sprang back as if a snake had bitten him and shot her three times through the chest. Then he put his gun down on the ground and took off his glasses and began to clean them.

Hiram and Bobby Lee returned from the woods and stood over the ditch, looking down at the grandmother who half sat and half lay in a puddle of blood with her legs crossed under her like a child's and her face smiling up at the cloudless sky.

Without his glasses, The Misfit's eyes were red-rimmed and pale and defenseless-looking. "Take her off and thow her where you thown the others," he said, picking up the cat that was rubbing itself against his leg.

"She was a talker, wasn't she?" Bobby Lee said, sliding down the ditch with a yodel.

140   "She would of been a good woman," The Misfit said, "if it had been somebody there to shoot her every minute of her life."

"Some fun!" Bobby Lee said.

"Shut up, Bobby Lee," The Misfit said. "It's no real pleasure in life."

[1953]

Revelation

The doctor's waiting room, which was very small, was almost full when the Turpins entered and Mrs. Turpin, who was very large, made it look even smaller by her presence. She stood looming at the head of the magazine table set in the center of it, a living demonstration that the room was inadequate and ridiculous. Her little bright black eyes took in all the patients as she sized up the seating situation. There was one vacant chair and a place on a sofa occupied by a blond child in a dirty blue romper who should have been told to move over and make room for the lady. He was five or six, but Mrs. Turpin saw at once that no one was going to tell him to move over. He was slumped down in the seat, his arms idle at his sides and his eyes idle in his head; his nose ran unchecked.

Mrs. Turpin put a firm hand on Claud's shoulder and said in a voice that included anyone who wanted to listen, "Claud, you sit in that chair there," and gave him a push down into the vacant one. Claud was florid and bald and sturdy, somewhat shorter than Mrs. Turpin, but he sat down as if he were accustomed to doing what she told him to.

Mrs. Turpin remained standing. The only man in the room besides Claud was a lean stringy old fellow with a rusty hand spread out on each knee, whose eyes were closed as if he were asleep or dead or pretending to be so as not to get up and offer her his seat. Her gaze settled agreeably on a well-dressed grey-haired lady whose eyes met hers and whose expression said: If that child belonged to me, he would have some manners and move over—there's plenty of room there for you and him too.

Claud looked up with a sigh and made as if to rise.

5   "Sit down," Mrs. Turpin said. "You know you're not supposed to stand on that leg. He has an ulcer on his leg," she explained.

Claud lifted his foot onto the magazine table and rolled his trouser leg up to reveal a purple swelling on a plump marble-white calf.

"My!" the pleasant lady said. "How did you do that?"

"A cow kicked him," Mrs. Turpin said.

"Goodness!" said the lady.

10   Claud rolled his trouser leg down.

"Maybe the little boy would move over," the lady suggested, but the child did not stir.

"Somebody will be leaving in a minute," Mrs. Turpin said. She could not understand why a doctor—with as much money as they made charging five dollars a day to just stick their head in the hospital door and look at you—couldn't afford a decent-sized waiting room. This one was hardly bigger than a garage. The table was cluttered with limp-looking magazines and at one end of it there was a big green glass ash tray full of cigaret butts and cotton wads with little blood spots on them. If she had had anything to do with the running of the place, that would have been emptied every so often. There were no chairs against the wall at the head of the room. It had a rectangular-shaped panel in it that permitted a view of the office where the nurse came and went and the secretary listened to the radio. A plastic fern in a gold pot sat in the opening and trailed its fronds down almost to the floor. The radio was softly playing gospel music.

Just then the inner door opened and a nurse with the highest stack of yellow hair Mrs. Turpin had ever seen put her face in the crack and called for the next patient. The woman sitting beside Claud grasped the two arms of her chair and hoisted herself up; she pulled her dress free from her legs and lumbered through the door where the nurse had disappeared.

Mrs. Turpin eased into the vacant chair, which held her tight as a corset. "I wish I could reduce," she said, and rolled her eyes and gave a comic sigh.

15   "Oh, *you* aren't fat," the stylish lady said.

"Ooooo I am too," Mrs. Turpin said. "Claud he eats all he wants to and never weighs over one hundred and seventy-five pounds, but me I just look at something good to eat and I gain some weight," and her stomach and shoulders shook with laughter. "You can eat all you want to, can't you, Claud?" she asked, turning to him.

Claud only grinned.

"Well, as long as you have such a good disposition," the stylish lady said, "I don't think it makes a bit of difference what size you are. You just can't beat a good disposition."

Next to her was a fat girl of eighteen or nineteen, scowling into a thick blue book which Mrs. Turpin saw was entitled *Human Development*. The girl raised her head and directed her scowl at Mrs. Turpin as if she did not like her looks. She appeared annoyed that anyone should speak while she tried to read. The poor girl's face was blue with acne and Mrs. Turpin thought how pitiful it was to have a face like that at that age. She gave the girl a friendly smile but the girl only scowled the harder. Mrs. Turpin herself was fat but she had always had good skin, and, though she was forty-seven years old, there was not a wrinkle in her face except around her eyes from laughing too much.

20   Next to the ugly girl was the child, still in exactly the same position, and next to him was a thin leathery old woman in a cotton print dress. She and Claud had three sacks of chicken feed in their pump house that was in the same print. She had seen from the first that the child belonged with the old woman. She could tell by the way they sat—kind of vacant and white-trashy, as if they would sit there until Doomsday if nobody called and told them to get up. And at right angles but next to the well-dressed pleasant lady was a lank-faced woman who was certainly the child's mother. She had on a yellow sweat shirt and wine-colored slacks, both gritty-looking, and the rims of her lips were stained with snuff. Her dirty yellow hair was tied behind with a little piece of red paper ribbon. Worse than niggers any day, Mrs. Turpin thought.

The gospel hymn playing was, "When I looked up and He looked down," and Mrs. Turpin, who knew it, supplied the last line mentally, "And wona these days I know I'll we-era crown."

Without appearing to, Mrs. Turpin always noticed people's feet. The well-dressed lady had on red and grey suede shoes to match her dress. Mrs. Turpin had on her good black patent leather pumps. The ugly girl had on Girl Scout shoes and heavy socks. The old woman had on tennis shoes and the white-trashy mother had on what appeared to be bedroom slippers, black straw with gold braid threaded through them—exactly what you would have expected her to have on.

Sometimes at night when she couldn't go to sleep, Mrs. Turpin would occupy herself with the question of who she would have chosen to be if she couldn't have been herself. If Jesus had said to her before he made her, "There's only two places available for you. You can either be a nigger or white-trash," what would she have said? "Please, Jesus, please," she would have said, "just let me wait until there's another place available," and he would have said, "No, you have to go right now and I have only those two places so make up your mind." She would have wiggled and squirmed and begged and pleaded but it would have been no use and finally she would have said, "All right, make me a nigger then—but that don't mean a trashy one." And he would have made her a neat clean respectable Negro-woman, herself but black.

Next to the child's mother was a red-headed youngish woman, reading one of the magazines and working a piece of chewing gum, hell for leather, as Claud would say. Mrs. Turpin could not see the woman's feet. She was not white-trash, just common. Sometimes Mrs. Turpin occupied herself at night naming the classes of people. On the bottom of the heap were most colored people, not the kind she would have been if she had been one, but most of them; then next to them—not above, just away from—were the white-trash; then above them were the home-owners, and above them the home-and-land owners, to which she and Claud belonged. Above she and Claud were people with a lot of money and much bigger houses and much more land. But here the complexity of it would begin to bear in on her, for some of the people with a lot of money were common and ought to be below she and Claud and some of the people who had good blood had lost their money and had to rent and then there were colored people who owned their homes and land as well. There was a colored dentist in town who had two red Lincolns and a swimming pool and a farm with registered white-face cattle on it. Usually by the time she had fallen asleep all the classes of people were moiling and roiling around in her head, and she would dream they were all crammed in together in a box car, being ridden off to be put in a gas oven.

25   "That's a beautiful clock," she said and nodded to her right. It was a big wall clock, the face encased in a brass sunburst.

"Yes, it's very pretty," the stylish lady said agreeably. "And right on the dot too," she added, glancing at her watch.

The ugly girl beside her cast an eye upward at the clock, smirked, then looked directly at Mrs. Turpin and smirked again. Then she returned her eyes to her book. She was obviously the lady's daughter because, although they didn't look anything alike as to disposition, they both had the same shape of face and the same blue eyes. On the lady they sparkled pleasantly but in the girl's seared face they appeared alternately to smolder and to blaze.

What if Jesus had said, "All right, you can be white-trash or a nigger or ugly"!

Mrs. Turpin felt an awful pity for the girl, though she thought it was one thing to be ugly and another to act ugly.

30   The woman with the snuff-stained lips turned around in her chair and looked up at the clock. Then she turned back and appeared to look a little to the side of Mrs. Turpin. There was a cast in one of her eyes. "You want to know wher you can get one of themther clocks?" she asked in a loud voice.

"No, I already have a nice clock," Mrs. Turpin said. Once somebody like her got a leg in the conversation, she would be all over it.

"You can get you one with green stamps," the woman said. "That's most likely wher he got hisn. Save you up enough, you can get you most anything. I got me some joo'ry."

Ought to have got you a wash rag and some soap, Mrs. Turpin thought.

"I get contour sheets with mine," the pleasant lady said.

35   The daughter slammed her book shut. She looked straight in front of her, directly through Mrs. Turpin and on through the yellow curtain and the plate glass window which made the wall behind her. The girl's eyes seemed lit all of a sudden with a peculiar light, an unnatural light like night road signs give. Mrs. Turpin turned her head to see if there was anything going on outside that she should see, but she could not see anything. Figures passing cast only a pale shadow through the curtain. There was no reason the girl should single her out for her ugly looks.

"Miss Finley," the nurse said, cracking the door. The gum chewing woman got up and passed in front of her and Claud and went into the office. She had on red high-heeled shoes.

Directly across the table, the ugly girl's eyes were fixed on Mrs. Turpin as if she had some very special reason for disliking her.

"This is wonderful weather, isn't it?" the girl's mother said.

"It's good weather for cotton if you can get the niggers to pick it," Mrs. Turpin said, "but niggers don't want to pick cotton any more. You can't get the white folks to pick it and now you can't get the niggers—because they got to be right up there with the white folks."

40   "They gonna *try* anyways," the white-trash woman said, leaning forward.

"Do you have one of those cotton-picking machines?" the pleasant lady asked.

"No," Mrs. Turpin said, "they leave half the cotton in the field. We don't have much cotton anyway. If you want to make it farming now, you have to have a little of everything. We got a couple of acres of cotton and a few hogs and chickens and just enough white-face that Claud can look after them himself."

"One thang I don't want," the white-trash woman said, wiping her mouth with the back of her hand. "Hogs. Nasty stinking things, a-gruntin and a-rootin all over the place."

Mrs. Turpin gave her the merest edge of her attention. "Our hogs are not dirty and they don't stink," she said. "They're cleaner than some children I've seen. Their feet never touch the ground. We have a pig-parlor—that's where you raise them on concrete," she explained to the pleasant lady, "and Claud scoots them down with the hose every afternoon and washes off the floor." Cleaner by far than that child right there, she thought. Poor nasty little thing. He had not moved except to put the thumb of his dirty hand into his mouth.

45   The woman turned her face away from Mrs. Turpin. "I know I wouldn't scoot down no hog with no hose," she said to the wall.

You wouldn't have no hog to scoot down, Mrs. Turpin said to herself.

"A-gruntin and a-rootin and a-groanin," the woman muttered.

"We got a little of everything," Mrs. Turpin said to the pleasant lady. "It's no use in having more than you can handle yourself with help like it is. We found enough niggers to pick our cotton this year but Claud he has to go after them and take them home again in the evening. They can't walk that half a mile. No they can't. I tell you," she said and laughed merrily, "I sure am tired of buttering up niggers, but you got to love em if you want em to work for you. When they come in the morning, I run out and I say, 'Hi yawl this morning?' and when Claud drives them off to the field I just wave to beat the band and they just wave back." And she waved her hand rapidly to illustrate.

"Like you read out of the same book," the lady said, showing she understood perfectly.

50   "Child, yes," Mrs. Turpin said. "And when they come in from the field, I run out with a bucket of icewater. That's the way it's going to be from now on," she said. "You may as well face it."

"One thang I know," the white-trash woman said. "Two thangs I ain't going to do: love no niggers or scoot down no hog with no hose." And she let out a bark of contempt.

The look that Mrs. Turpin and the pleasant lady exchanged indicated they both understood that you had to *have* certain things before you could *know* certain things. But every time Mrs. Turpin exchanged a look with the lady, she was aware that the ugly girl's peculiar eyes were still on her, and she had trouble bringing her attention back to the conversation.

"When you got something," she said, "you got to look after it." And when you ain't got a thing but breath and britches, she added to herself, you can afford to come to town every morning and just sit on the Court House coping and spit.

A grotesque revolving shadow passed across the curtain behind her and was thrown palely on the opposite wall. Then a bicycle clattered down against the outside of the building. The door opened and a colored boy glided in with a tray from the drug store. It had two large red and white paper cups on it with tops on them. He was a tall, very black boy in discolored white pants and a green nylon shirt. He was chewing gum slowly as if to music. He set the tray down in the office opening next to the fern and stuck his head through to look for the secretary. She was not in there. He rested his arms on the ledge and waited, his narrow bottom stuck out, swaying slowly to the left and right. He raised a hand over his head and scratched the base of his skull.

55   "You see that button there, boy?" Mrs. Turpin said. "You can punch that and she'll come. She's probably in the back somewhere."

"Is that right?" the boy said agreeably, as if he had never seen the button before. He leaned to the right and put his finger on it. "She sometime out," he said and twisted around to face his audience, his elbows behind him on the counter. The nurse appeared and he twisted back again. She handed him a dollar and he rooted in his pocket and made the change and counted it out to her. She gave him fifteen cents for a tip and he went out with the empty tray. The heavy door swung to slowly and closed at length with the sound of suction. For a moment no one spoke.

"They ought to send all them niggers back to Africa," the white-trash woman said. "That's wher they come from in the first place."

"Oh, I couldn't do without my good colored friends," the pleasant lady said.

"There's a heap of things worse than a nigger," Mrs. Turpin agreed. "It's all kinds of them just like it's all kinds of us."

60   "Yes, and it takes all kinds to make the world go round," the lady said in her musical voice.

As she said it, the raw-complexioned girl snapped her teeth together. Her lower lip turned downwards and inside out, revealing the pale pink inside of her mouth. After a second it rolled back up. It was the ugliest face Mrs. Turpin had ever seen anyone make and for a moment she was certain that the girl had made it at her. She was looking at her as if she had known and disliked her all her life— all of Mrs. Turpin's life, it seemed too, not just all the girl's life. Why, girl, I don't even know you, Mrs. Turpin said silently.

She forced her attention back to the discussion. "It wouldn't be practical to send them back to Africa," she said. "They wouldn't want to go. They got it too good here."

"Wouldn't be what they wanted—if I had anythang to do with it," the woman said.

"It wouldn't be a way in the world you could get all the niggers back over there," Mrs. Turpin said. "They'd be hiding out and lying down and turning sick on you and wailing and hollering and raring and pitching. It wouldn't be a way in the world to get them over there."

65   "They got over here," the trashy woman said. "Get back like they got over."

"It wasn't so many of them then," Mrs. Turpin explained.

The woman looked at Mrs. Turpin as if here was an idiot indeed but Mrs. Turpin was not bothered by the look, considering where it came from.

"Nooo," she said, "they're going to stay here where they can go to New York and marry white folks and improve their color. That's what they all want to do, every one of them, improve their color."

"You know what comes of that, don't you?" Claud asked.

70   "No, Claud, what?" Mrs. Turpin said.

Claud's eyes twinkled. "White-faced niggers," he said with never a smile.

Everybody in the office laughed except the white-trash and the ugly girl. The girl gripped the book in her lap with white fingers. The trashy woman looked around her from face to face as if she thought they were all idiots. The old woman in the feed sack dress continued to gaze expressionless across the floor at the high-top shoes of the man opposite her, the one who had been pretending to be asleep when the Turpins came in. He was laughing heartily, his hands still spread out on his knees. The child had fallen to the side and was lying now almost face down in the old woman's lap.

While they recovered from their laughter, the nasal chorus on the radio kept the room from silence.

> You go to blank blank
> And I'll go to mine
> But we'll all blank along
> To-geth-ther,
> And all along the blank
> We'll hep each other out
> Smile-ling in any kind of
> Weath-ther!

Mrs. Turpin didn't catch every word but she caught enough to agree with the spirit of the song and it turned her thoughts sober. To help anybody out that needed it was her philosophy of life. She never spared herself when she found somebody in need, whether they were white or black, trash or decent. And of all she had to be thankful for, she was most thankful that this was so. If Jesus had said, "You can be high society and have all the money you want and be thin and svelte-like, but you can't be a good woman with it," she would have had to say, "Well don't make me that then. Make me a good woman and it don't matter what else, how fat or how ugly or how poor!" Her heart rose. He had not made her a nigger or white-trash or ugly! He had made her herself and given her a little of everything. Jesus, thank you! she said. Thank you thank you thank you! Whenever she counted her blessings she felt as buoyant as if she weighed one hundred and twenty-five pounds instead of one hundred and eighty.

75   "What's wrong with your little boy?" the pleasant lady asked the white-trashy woman.

"He has a ulcer," the woman said proudly. "He ain't give me a minute's peace since he was born. Him and her are just alike," she said, nodding at the old woman, who was running her leathery fingers through the child's pale hair. "Look like I can't get nothing down them two but Co'Cola and candy."

That's all you try to get down em, Mrs. Turpin said to herself. Too lazy to light the fire. There was nothing you could tell her about people like them that she didn't know already. And it was not just that they didn't have anything. Because if you gave them everything, in two weeks it would all be broken or filthy or they would have chopped it up for lightwood. She knew all this from her own experience. Help them you must, but help them you couldn't.

All at once the ugly girl turned her lips inside out again. Her eyes were fixed like two drills on Mrs. Turpin. This time there was no mistaking that there was something urgent behind them.

Girl, Mrs. Turpin exclaimed silently, I haven't done a thing to you! The girl might be confusing her with somebody else. There was no need to sit by and let herself be intimidated. "You must be in college," she said boldly, looking directly at the girl. "I see you reading a book there."

80   The girl continued to stare and pointedly did not answer.

Her mother blushed at this rudeness. "The lady asked you a question, Mary Grace," she said under her breath.

"I have ears," Mary Grace said.

The poor mother blushed again. "Mary Grace goes to Wellesley College," she explained. She twisted one of the buttons on her dress. "In Massachusetts," she added with a grimace. "And in the summer she just keeps right on studying. Just reads all the time, a real book worm. She's done real well at Wellesley; she's taking English and Math and History and Psychology and Social Studies," she rattled on, "and I think it's too much. I think she ought to get out and have fun."

The girl looked as if she would like to hurl them all through the plate glass window.

85   "Way up north," Mrs. Turpin murmured and thought, well, it hasn't done much for her manners.

"I'd almost rather to have him sick," the white-trash woman said, wrenching the attention back to herself. "He's so mean when he ain't. Look like some children just take natural to meanness. It's some gets bad when they get sick but he was the opposite. Took sick and turned good. He don't give me no trouble now. It's me waitin to see the doctor," she said.

If I was going to send anybody back to Africa, Mrs. Turpin thought, it would be your kind, woman. "Yes, indeed," she said aloud, but looking up at the ceiling, "it's a heap of things worse than a nigger." And dirtier than a hog, she added to herself.

"I think people with bad dispositions are more to be pitied than anyone on earth," the pleasant lady said in a voice that was decidedly thin.

"I thank the Lord he has blessed me with a good one," Mrs. Turpin said. "The day has never dawned that I couldn't find something to laugh at."

90   "Not since she married me anyways," Claud said with a comical straight face.

Everybody laughed except the girl and the white-trash.

Mrs. Turpin's stomach shook. "He's such a caution," she said, "that I can't help but laugh at him."

The girl made a loud ugly noise through her teeth.

Her mother's mouth grew thin and tight. "I think the worst thing in the world," she said, "is an ungrateful person. To have everything and not appreciate it. I know a girl," she said, "who has parents who would give her anything, a little brother who loves her dearly, who is getting a good education, who wears the best clothes, but who can never say a kind word to anyone, who never smiles, who just criticizes and complains all day long."

95   "Is she too old to paddle?" Claud asked.

The girl's face was almost purple.

"Yes," the lady said. "I'm afraid there's nothing to do but leave her to her folly. Some day she'll wake up and it'll be too late."

"It never hurt anyone to smile," Mrs. Turpin said. "It just makes you feel better all over."

"Of course," the lady said sadly, "but there are just some people you can't tell anything to. They can't take criticism."

100   "If it's one thing I am," Mrs. Turpin said with feeling, "it's grateful. When I think who all I could have been besides myself and what all I got, a little of everything, and a good disposition besides, I just feel like shouting, 'Thank you, Jesus, for making everything the way it is!' It could have been different!" For one thing, somebody else could have got Claud. At the thought of this, she was flooded with gratitude and a terrible pang of joy ran through her. "Oh thank you, Jesus, Jesus, thank you!" she cried aloud.

The book struck her directly over her left eye. It struck almost at the same instant that she realized the girl was about to hurl it. Before she could utter a sound, the raw face came crashing across the table toward her, howling. The girl's fingers sank like clamps into the soft flesh of her neck. She heard the mother cry out and Claud shout, "Whoa!" There was an instant when she was certain that she was about to be in an earthquake.

All at once her vision narrowed and she saw everything as if it were happening in a small room far away, or as if she were looking at it through the wrong end of a telescope. Claud's face crumpled and fell out of sight. The nurse ran in, then out, then in again. Then the gangling figure of the doctor rushed out of the inner door. Magazines flew this way and that as the table turned over. The girl fell with a thud and Mrs. Turpin's vision suddenly reversed itself and she saw everything large instead of small. The eyes of the white-trashy woman were staring hugely at the floor. There the girl, held down on one side by the nurse and on the other by her mother, was wrenching and turning in their grasp. The doctor was kneeling astride her, trying to hold her arm down. He managed after a second to sink a long needle into it.

Mrs. Turpin felt entirely hollow except for her heart which swung from side to side as if it were agitated in a great empty drum of flesh.

"Somebody that's not busy call for the ambulance," the doctor said in the offhand voice young doctors adopt for terrible occasions.

105   Mrs. Turpin could not have moved a finger. The old man who had been sitting next to her skipped nimbly into the office and made the call, for the secretary still seemed to be gone.

"Claud!" Mrs. Turpin called.

He was not in his chair. She knew she must jump up and find him but she felt like someone trying to catch a train in a dream, when everything moves in slow motion and the faster you try to run the slower you go.

"Here I am," a suffocated voice, very unlike Claud's, said.

He was doubled up in the corner on the floor, pale as paper, holding his leg. She wanted to get up and go to him but she could not move. Instead, her gaze was drawn slowly downward to the churning face on the floor, which she could see over the doctor's shoulder.

110   The girl's eyes stopped rolling and focused on her. They seemed a much lighter blue than before, as if a door that had been tightly closed behind them was now open to admit light and air.

Mrs. Turpin's head cleared and her power of motion returned. She leaned forward until she was looking directly into the fierce brilliant eyes. There was no doubt in her mind that the girl did know her, knew her in some intense and personal way, beyond time and place and condition. "What you got to say to me?" she asked hoarsely and held her breath, waiting, as for a revelation.

The girl raised her head. Her gaze locked with Mrs. Turpin's. "Go back to hell where you came from, you old wart hog," she whispered. Her voice was low but clear. Her eyes burned for a moment as if she saw with pleasure that her message had struck its target.

Mrs. Turpin sank back in her chair.

After a moment the girl's eyes closed and she turned her head wearily to the side.

115   The doctor rose and handed the nurse the empty syringe. He leaned over and put both hands for a moment on the mother's shoulders, which were shaking. She was sitting on the floor, her lips pressed together, holding Mary Grace's hand in her lap. The girl's fingers were gripped like a baby's around her thumb. "Go on to the hospital," he said. "I'll call and make the arrangements."

"Now let's see that neck," he said in a jovial voice to Mrs. Turpin. He began to inspect her neck with his first two fingers. Two little moonshaped lines like pink fish bones were indented over her windpipe. There was the beginning of an angry red swelling above her eye. His fingers passed over this also.

"Lea' me be," she said thickly and shook him off. "See about Claud. She kicked him."

"I'll see about him in a minute," he said and felt her pulse. He was a thin gray-haired man, given to pleasantries. "Go home and have yourself a vacation the rest of the day," he said and patted her on the shoulder.

Quit your pattin me, Mrs. Turpin growled to herself.

120   "And put an ice pack over that eye," he said. Then he went and squatted down beside Claud and looked at his leg. After a moment he pulled him up and Claud limped after him into the office.

Until the ambulance came, the only sounds in the room were the tremulous moans of the girl's mother, who continued to sit on the floor. The white-trash woman did not take her eyes off the girl. Mrs. Turpin looked straight ahead at nothing. Presently the ambulance drew up, a long dark shadow, behind the curtain. The attendants came in and set the stretcher down beside the girl and lifted her expertly onto it and carried her out. The nurse helped the mother gather up her things. The shadow of the ambulance moved silently away and the nurse came back in the office.

"That ther girl is going to be a lunatic, ain't she?" the white-trash woman asked the nurse, but the nurse kept on to the back and never answered her.

"Yes, she's going to be a lunatic," the white-trash woman said to the rest of them.

"Po' critter," the old woman murmured. The child's face was still in her lap. His eyes looked idly out over her knees. He had not moved during the disturbance except to draw one leg up under him.

125   "I thank Gawd," the white-trash woman said fervently, "I ain't a lunatic."

Claud came limping out and the Turpins went home.

As their pick-up truck turned into their own dirt road and made the crest of the hill, Mrs. Turpin gripped the window ledge and looked out suspiciously. The land sloped gracefully down through a field dotted with lavender weeds and at the start of the rise their small yellow frame house, with its little flower beds spread out around it like a fancy apron, sat primly in its accustomed place between two giant hickory trees. She would not have been startled to see a burnt wound between two blackened chimneys.

Neither of them felt like eating so they put on their house clothes and lowered the shade in the bedroom and lay down, Claud with his leg on a pillow and herself with a damp washcloth over her eye. The instant she was flat on her back, the image of a razor-backed hog with warts on its face and horns coming out behind its ears snorted into her head. She moaned, a low quiet moan.

"I am not," she said tearfully, "a wart hog. From hell." But the denial had no force. The girl's eyes and her words, even the tone of her voice, low but clear, directed only to her, brooked no repudiation. She had been singled out for the message, though there was trash in the room to whom it might justly have been applied. The full force of this fact struck her only now. There was a woman there who was neglecting her own child but she had been overlooked. The message had been given to Ruby Turpin, a respectable, hard-working, church-going woman. The tears dried. Her eyes began to burn instead with wrath.

130   She rose on her elbow and the washcloth fell into her hand. Claud was lying on his back, snoring. She wanted to tell him what the girl had said. At the same time she did not wish to put the image of herself as a wart hog from hell into his mind.

"Hey, Claud," she muttered and pushed his shoulder.

Claud opened one pale baby blue eye.

She looked into it warily. He did not think about anything. He just went his way.

"Wha, whasit?" he said and closed the eye again.

"Nothing," she said. "Does your leg pain you?"

135   "Hurts like hell," Claud said.

"It'll quit terreckly," she said and lay back down. In a moment Claud was snoring again. For the rest of the afternoon they lay there. Claud slept. She scowled at the ceiling. Occasionally she raised her fist and made a small stabbing motion over her chest as if she was defending her innocence to invisible guests who were like the comforters of Job, reasonable-seeming but wrong.

About five-thirty Claud stirred. "Got to go after those niggers," he sighed, not moving.

She was looking straight up as if there were unintelligible handwriting on the ceiling. The protuberance over her eye had turned a greenish-blue. "Listen here," she said.

"What"?

140   "Kiss me."

Claud leaned over and kissed her loudly on the mouth. He pinched her side and their hands interlocked. Her expression of ferocious concentration did not change. Claud got up, groaning and growling, and limped off. She continued to study the ceiling.

She did not get up until she heard the pick-up truck coming back with the Negroes. Then she rose and thrust her feet in her brown oxfords, which she did not bother to lace, and stumped out onto the back porch and got her red plastic bucket. She emptied a tray of ice cubes into it and filled it half full of water and went out into the back yard. Every afternoon after Claud brought the hands in, one of the boys helped him put out hay and the rest waited in the back of the truck until he was ready to take them home. The truck was parked in the shade under one one of the hickory trees.

"Hi yawl this evening?" Mrs. Turpin asked grimly, appearing with the bucket and the dipper. There were three women and a boy in the truck.

"Us doin nicely," the oldest woman said. "Hi you doin?" and her gaze stuck

145   immediately on the dark lump on Mrs. Turpin's forehead. "You done fell down, ain't you?" she asked in a solicitous voice. The old woman was dark and almost toothless. She had on an old felt hat of Claud's set back on her head. The other two women were younger and lighter and they both had new bright green sun

hats. One of them had hers on her head; the other had taken hers off and the boy was grinning beneath it.

Mrs. Turpin set the bucket down on the floor of the truck. "Yawl hep yourselves," she said. She looked around to make sure Claud had gone. "No. I didn't fall down," she said, folding her arms. "It was something worse than that."

"Ain't nothing bad happen to you!" the old woman said. She said it as if they all knew Mrs. Turpin was protected in some special way by Divine Providence. "You just had you a little fall."

"We were in town at the doctor's office for where the cow kicked Mr. Turpin," Mrs. Turpin said in a flat tone that indicated they could leave off their foolishness. "And there was this girl there. A big fat girl with her face all broke out. I could look at that girl and tell she was peculiar but I couldn't tell how. And me and her mama were just talking and going along and all of a sudden WHAM! She throws this big book she was reading at me and . . . "

"Naw!" the old woman cried out.

150   "And then she jumps over the table and commences to choke me."

"Naw!" they all exclaimed, "naw!"

"Hi come she do that?" the old woman asked. "What ail her?"

Mrs. Turpin only glared in front of her.

"Somethin ail her," the old woman said.

155   "They carried her off in an ambulance," Mrs. Turpin continued, "but before she went she was rolling on the floor and they were trying to hold her down to give her a shot and she said something to me." She paused. "You know what she said to me?"

"What she say?" they asked.

"She said," Mrs. Turpin began, and stopped, her face very dark and heavy. The sun was getting whiter and whiter, blanching the sky overhead so that the leaves of the hickory tree were black in the face of it. She could not bring forth the words. "Something real ugly," she muttered.

"She sho shouldn't said nothin ugly to you," the old woman said. "You so sweet. You the sweetest lady I know."

"She pretty too," the one with the hat on said.

160   "And stout," the other one said. "I never knowed no sweeter white lady."

"That's the truth befo' Jesus," the old woman said. "Amen! You des as sweet and pretty as you can be."

Mrs. Turpin knew just exactly how much Negro flattery was worth and it added to her rage. "She said," she began again and finished this time with a fierce rush of breath, "that I was an old wart hog from hell."

There was an astounded silence.

"Where she at?" the youngest woman cried in a piercing voice.

165   "Lemme see her. I'll kill her!"

"I'll kill her with you!" the other one cried.

"She b'long in the sylum," the old woman said emphatically. "You the sweetest white lady I know."

"She pretty too," the other two said. "Stout as she can be and sweet. Jesus satisfied with her!"

"Deed he is," the old woman declared.

170   Idiots! Mrs. Turpin growled to herself. You could never say anything intelligent to a nigger. You could talk at them but not with them. "Yawl ain't drunk your water," she said shortly. "Leave the bucket in the truck when you're finished with it. I got more to do than just stand around and pass the time of day," and she moved off and into the house.

She stood for a moment in the middle of the kitchen. The dark protuberance over her eye looked like a miniature tornado cloud which might any moment sweep across the horizon of her brow. Her lower lip protruded dangerously. She squared her massive shoulders. Then she marched into the front of the house and out the side door and started down the road to the pig parlor. She had the look of a woman going single-handed, weaponless, into battle.

The sun was a deep yellow now like a harvest moon and was riding westward very fast over the far tree line as if it meant to reach the hogs before she did. The road was rutted and she kicked several good-sized stones out of her path as she strode along. The pig parlor was on a little knoll at the end of a lane that ran off from the side of the barn. It was a square of concrete as large as a small room, with a board fence about four feet high around it. The concrete floor sloped slightly so that the hog wash could drain off into a trench where it was carried to the field for fertilizer. Claud was standing on the outside, on the edge of the concrete, hanging onto the top board, hosing down the floor inside. The hose was connected to the faucet of a water trough nearby.

Mrs. Turpin climbed up beside him and glowered down at the hogs inside. There were seven long-snouted bristly shoats in it—tan with liver-colored spots— and an old sow a few weeks off from farrowing. She was lying on her side grunting. The shoats were running about shaking themselves like idiot children, their little slit pig eyes searching the floor for anything left. She had read that pigs were the most intelligent animal. She doubted it. They were supposed to be smarter than dogs. There had even been a pig astronaut. He had performed his assignment perfectly but died of a heart attack afterwards because they left him in his electric suit, sitting upright throughout his examination when naturally a hog should be on all fours.

A-gruntin and a-rootin and a-groanin.

175 "Gimme that hose," she said, yanking it away from Claud. "Go on and carry them niggers home and then get off that leg."

"You look like you might have swallowed a mad dog," Claud observed, but he got down and limped off. He paid no attention to her humors.

Until he was out of earshot, Mrs. Turpin stood on the side of the pen, holding the hose and pointing the stream of water at the hind quarter of any shoat that looked as if it might try to lie down. When he had had time to get over the hill, she turned her head slightly and her wrathful eyes scanned the path. He was nowhere in sight. She turned back again and seemed to gather herself up. Her shoulders rose and she drew in her breath.

"What do you send me a message like that for?" she said in a low fierce voice, barely above a whisper but with the force of a shout in its concentrated fury. "How am I a hog and me both? How am I saved and from hell too?" Her free fist was knotted and with the other she gripped the hose, blindly pointing the stream of water in and out of the eye of the old sow whose outraged squeal she did not hear.

The pig parlor commanded a view of the back pasture where their twenty beef cows were gathered around the hay-bales Claud and the boy had put out. The freshly cut pasture sloped down to the highway. Across it was their cotton field and beyond that a dark green dusty wood which they owned as well. The sun was behind the wood, very red, looking over the paling of trees like a farmer inspecting his own hogs.

180 "Why me?" she rumbled. "It's no trash around here, black or white, that I haven't given to. And break my back to the bone every day working. And do for the church."

She appeared to be the right size woman to command the arena before her. "How am I a hog?" she demanded. "Exactly how am I like them?" and she jabbed the stream of water at the shoats. "There was plenty of trash there. It didn't have to be me."

"If you like trash better, go get yourself some trash then," she railed. "You could have made me trash. Or a nigger. If trash is what you wanted why didn't you make me trash?" She shook her fist with the hose in it and a watery snake appeared momentarily in the air. "I could quit working and take it easy and be filthy," she growled. "Lounge about the sidewalks all day drinking root beer. Dip snuff and spit in every puddle and have it all over my face. I could be nasty."

"Or you could have made me a nigger. It's too late for me to be a nigger," she said with deep sarcasm, "but I could act like one. Lay down in the middle of the road and stop traffic. Roll on the ground."

In the deepening light everything was taking on a mysterious hue. The pasture was growing a peculiar glassy green and the streak of highway had turned lavender. She braced herself for a final assault and this time her voice rolled out over the pasture. "Go on," she yelled, "call me a hog! Call me a hog again. From hell. Call me a wart hog from hell. Put that bottom rail on top. There'll still be a top and bottom!"

185   A garbled echo returned to her.

A final surge of fury shook her and she roared, "Who do you think you are?"

The color of everything, field and crimson sky, burned for a moment with a transparent intensity. The question carried over the pasture and across the highway and the cotton field and returned to her clearly like an answer from beyond the wood.

She opened her mouth but no sound came out of it.

A tiny truck, Claud's, appeared on the highway, heading rapidly out of sight. Its gears scraped thinly. It looked like a child's toy. At any moment a bigger truck might smash into it and scatter Claud's and the niggers' brains all over the road.

190   Mrs. Turpin stood there, her gaze fixed on the highway, all her muscles rigid, until in five or six minutes the truck reappeared, returning. She waited until it had had time to turn into their own road. Then like a monumental statue coming to life, she bent her head slowly and gazed, as if through the very heart of the mystery, down into the pig parlor at the hogs. They had settled all in one corner around the old sow who was grunting softly. A red glow suffused them. They appeared to pant with a secret life.

Until the sun slipped finally behind the tree line, Mrs. Turpin remained there with her gaze bent to them as if she were absorbing some abysmal life-giving knowledge. At last she lifted her head. There was only a purple streak in the sky, cutting through a field of crimson and leading, like an extension of the highway, into the descending dusk. She raised her hands from the side of the pen in a gesture hieratic and profound. A visionary light settled in her eyes. She saw the streak as a vast swinging bridge extending upward from the earth through a field of living fire. Upon it a vast horde of souls were rumbling toward heaven. There were whole companies of white-trash, clean for the first time in their lives, and bands of black niggers in white robes, and battalions of freaks and lunatics shouting and clapping and leaping like frogs. And bringing up the end of the procession was a tribe of people whom she recognized at once as those who, like herself and Claud, had always had a little of everything and the God-given wit to use it right. She leaned forward to observe them closer. They were marching behind the others with great dignity, accountable as they had always been for good order and common sense and respectable behavior. They alone were on key. Yet she could see by their shocked and altered faces that even their virtues were being burned away. She lowered her hands and gripped the rail of the hog pen, her eyes small but fixed unblinkingly on what lay ahead. In a moment the vision faded but she remained where she was, immobile.

At length she got down and turned off the faucet and made her slow way on the darkening path to the house. In the woods around her the invisible cricket choruses had struck up, but what she heard were the voices of the souls climbing upward into the starry field and shouting hallelujah.

[1964]

REMARKS FROM ESSAYS AND LETTERS
From "The Fiction Writer and His Country"

In the greatest fiction, the writer's moral sense coincides with his dramatic sense, and I see no way for it to do this unless his moral judgment is part of the very act of seeing, and he is free to use it. I have heard it said that belief in Christian dogma is a hindrance to the writer, but I myself have found nothing further from the truth. Actually, it frees the storyteller to observe. It is not a set of rules which fixes what he sees in the world. It affects his writing primarily by guaranteeing his respect for mystery. . . .

When I look at stories I have written I find that they are, for the most part, about people who are poor, who are afflicted in both mind and body, who have little—or at best a distorted—sense of spiritual purpose, and whose actions do not apparently give the reader a great assurance of the joy of life.

Yet how is this? For I am no disbeliever in spiritual purpose and no vague believer. I see from the standpoint of Christian orthodoxy. This means that for me the meaning of life is centered in our Redemption by Christ and what I see in the world I see in its relation to that. . . .

The novelist with Christian concerns will find in modern life distortions which are repugnant to him, and his problem will be to make these appear as distortions to an audience which is used to seeing them as natural; and he may well be forced to take ever more violent means to get his vision across to this hostile audience. When you can assume that your audience holds the same beliefs you do, you can relax a little and use more normal means of talking to it; when you have to assume that it does not, then you have to make your vision apparent by shock—to the hard of hearing you shout, and for the almost-blind you draw large and startling figures.

From "Some Aspects of the Grotesque
in Southern Fiction"

If the writer believes that our life is and will remain essentially mysterious, if he looks upon us as beings existing in a created order to whose laws we freely respond, then what he sees on the surface will be of interest to him only as he can go through it into an experience of mystery itself. His kind of fiction will always be pushing its own limits outward toward the limits of mystery, because for this kind of writer, the meaning of a story does not begin except at a depth where adequate motivation and adequate psychology and the various determinations have been exhausted. Such a writer will be interested in what we don't understand rather than in what we do. He will be interested in possibility rather than in probability. He will be interested in characters who are forced out to meet evil and grace and who act on a trust beyond themselves—whether they know very clearly what it is they act upon or not. To the modern mind, this kind of character, and his creator, are typical Don Quixotes, tilting at what is not there.

From "The Nature and Aim of Fiction"

The novel works by a slower accumulation of detail than the short story does. The short story requires more drastic procedures than the novel because more has to be accomplished in less space. The details have to carry more immediate weight. In good fiction, certain of the details will tend to accumulate meaning from the story itself, and when this happens, they become symbolic in their action.

Now the word *symbol* scares a good many people off, just as the word *art* does. They seem to feel that a symbol is some mysterious thing put in arbitrarily by the writer to frighten the common reader—sort of a literary Masonic grip that is only for the initiated. They seem to think that it is a way of saying something that you aren't actually saying, and so if they can be got to read a reputedly symbolic work at all, they approach it as if it were a problem in algebra. Find x. And when they do find or think they find this abstraction, x, then they go off with an elaborate sense of satisfaction and the notion that they have "understood" the story. Many students confuse the *process* of understanding a thing with understanding it.

I think that for the fiction writer himself, symbols are something he uses simply as a matter of course. You might say that these are details that, while having their essential place in the literal level of the story, operate in depth as well as on the surface, increasing the story in every direction. . . .

People have a habit of saying, "What is the theme of your story?" and they expect you to give them a statement: "The theme of my story is the economic pressure of the machine on the middle class"—or some such absurdity. And when they've got a statement like that, they go off happy and feel it is no longer necessary to read the story.

Some people have the notion that you read the story and then climb out of it into the meaning, but for the fiction writer himself the whole story is the meaning, because it is an experience, not an abstraction.

From "Writing Short Stories"

Being short does not mean being slight. A short story should be long in depth and should give us an experience of meaning. . . .

Meaning is what keeps the short story from being short. I prefer to talk about the meaning in a story rather than the theme of a story. People talk about the theme of a story as if the theme were like the string that a sack of chicken feed is tied with. They think that if you can pick out the theme, the way you pick the right thread in the chicken-feed sack, you can rip the story open and feed the chickens. But this is not the way meaning works in fiction.

When you can state the theme of a story, when you can separate it from the story itself, then you can be sure the story is not a very good one. The meaning of a story has to be embodied in it, has to be made concrete in it. A story is a way to say something that can't be said any other way, and it takes every word in the story to say what the meaning is. You tell a story because a statement would be inadequate. When anybody asks what a story is about, the only proper thing is to tell him to read the story. The meaning of fiction is not abstract meaning but experienced meaning, and the purpose of making statements about the meaning of a story is only to help you to experience that meaning more fully.

On Interpreting "A Good Man Is Hard to Find"

A professor of English had sent Flannery the following letter: "I am writing as spokesman for three members of our department and some ninety university students in three classes who for a week now have been discussing your story 'A Good Man Is Hard to Find.' We have debated at length several possible interpretations, none of which fully satisfies us. In general we believe that the appearance of the Misfit is not 'real' in the same sense that the incidents of the first half of the story are real. Bailey, we believe, imagines the appearance of the Misfit, whose activities have been called to his attention on the night before the trip and again during the stopover at the roadside restaurant. Bailey, we further believe, identifies himself with the Misfit and so plays two roles in the imaginary last half of the story. But we cannot, after great effort, determine the point at which reality fades into illusion or reverie. Does the accident literally occur, or is it a part of Bailey's dream? Please believe me when I say we are not seeking an easy way out of our difficulty. We admire your story and have examined it with great care, but we are convinced that we are missing something important which you intended for us to grasp. We will all be very grateful if you comment on the interpretation which I have outlined above and if you will give us further comments about your intention in writing 'A Good Man Is Hard to Find.'"

She replied:

To a Professor of English

28 March 61

The interpretation of your ninety students and three teachers is fantastic and about as far from my intentions as it could get to be. If it were a legitimate interpretation, the story would be little more than a trick and its interest would be simply for abnormal psychology. I am not interested in abnormal psychology.

There is a change of tension from the first part of the story to the second where the Misfit enters, but this is no lessening of reality. This story is, of course, not meant to be realistic in the sense that it portrays the everyday doings of people in Georgia. It is stylized and its conventions are comic even though its meaning is serious.

Bailey's only importance is as the Grandmother's boy and the driver of the car. It is the Grandmother who first recognizes the Misfit and who is most concerned with him throughout. The story is a duel of sorts between the Grandmother and her superficial beliefs and the Misfit's more profoundly felt involvement with Christ's action which set the world off balance for him.

The meaning of a story should go on expanding for the reader the more he thinks about it, but meaning cannot be captured in an interpretation. If teachers are in the habit of approaching a story as if it were a research problem for which any answer is believable so long as it is not obvious, then I think students will never learn to enjoy fiction. Too much interpretation is certainly worse than too little and where feeling for a story is absent, theory will not supply it.

My tone is not meant to be obnoxious. I am in a state of shock.

"A Reasonable Use of the Unreasonable"

Last fall I received a letter from a student who said she would be "graciously appreciative" if I would tell her "just what enlightenment" I expected her to get from each of my stories. I suspect she had a paper to write. I wrote her back to forget about the enlightenment and just try to enjoy them. I knew that was the most unsatisfactory answer I could have given because, of course, she didn't want to enjoy them, she just wanted to figure them out.

In most English classes the short story has become a kind of literary specimen to be dissected. Every time a story of mine appears in a Freshman anthology, I have a vision of it, with its little organs laid open, like a frog in a bottle.

I realize that a certain amount of this what-is-the-significance has to go on, but I think something has gone wrong in the process when, for so many students, the story becomes simply a problem to be solved, something which you evaporate to get Instant Enlightenment.

A story really isn't any good unless it successfully resists paraphrase, unless it hangs on and expands in the mind. Properly, you analyze to enjoy, but it's equally true that to analyze with any discrimination, you have to have enjoyed already, and I think that the best reason to hear a story read is that it should stimulate that primary enjoyment.

I don't have any pretensions to being an Aeschylus or Sophocles and providing you in this story with a cathartic experience out of your mythic background, though this story I'm going to read certainly calls up a good deal of the South's mythic background, and it should elicit from you a degree of pity and terror, even though its way of being serious is a comic one. I do think, though, that like the Greeks you should know what is going to happen in this story so that any element of suspense in it will be transferred from its surface to its interior.

I would be most happy if you have already read it, happier still if you knew it well, but since experience has taught me to keep my expectations along these lines modest, I'll tell you that this is the story of a family of six which, on its way driving to Florida, gets wiped out by an escaped convict who calls himself the Misfit. The family is made up of the Grandmother and her son, Bailey, and his children, John Wesley and June Star and the baby, and there is also the cat and the children's mother. The cat is named Pitty Sing, and the Grandmother is taking him with them, hidden in a basket.

Now I think it behooves me to try to establish with you the basis on which reason operates in this story. Much of my fiction takes its character from a reasonable use of the unreasonable, though the reasonableness of my use of it may not always be apparent. The assumptions that underlie this use of it, however, are those of the central Christian mysteries. These are assumptions to which a large part of the modern audience takes exception. About this I can only say that there are perhaps other ways than my own in which this story could be read, but none other by which it could have been written. Belief, in my own case anyway, is the engine that makes perception operate.

The heroine of this story, the Grandmother, is in the most significant position life offers the Christian. She is facing death. And to all appearances she, like the rest of us, is not too well prepared for it. She would like to see the event postponed. Indefinitely.

I've talked to a number of teachers who use this story in class and who tell their students that the Grandmother is evil, that in fact, she's a witch, even down to the cat. One of these teachers told me that his students, and particularly his Southern students, resisted this interpretation with a certain bemused vigor, and he didn't understand why. I had to tell him that they resisted it because they all had grandmothers or great-aunts just like her at home, and they knew, from personal experience, that the old lady lacked comprehension, but that she had a good heart. The Southerner is usually tolerant of those weaknesses that proceed from innocence, and he knows that a taste for self-preservation can be readily combined with the missionary spirit.

This same teacher was telling his students that morally the Misfit was several cuts above the Grandmother. He had a really sentimental attachment to the Misfit. But then a prophet gone wrong is almost always more interesting than your grandmother, and you have to let people take their pleasures where they find them.

It is true that the old lady is a hypocritical old soul; her wits are no match for the Misfit's, nor is her capacity for grace equal to his; yet I think the unprejudiced reader will feel that the Grandmother has a special kind of triumph in this story which instinctively we do not allow to someone altogether bad.

I often ask myself what makes a story work, and what makes it hold up as a story, and I have decided that it is probably some action, some gesture of a character that is unlike any other in the story, one which indicates where the real heart of the story lies. This would have to be an action or a gesture which was both totally right and totally unexpected; it would have to be one that was both in character and beyond character; it would have to suggest both the world and eternity. The action or gesture I'm talking about would have to be on the anagogical level, that is, the level which has to do with the Divine life and our participation in it. It would be a gesture that transcended any neat allegory that might have been intended or any pat moral categories a reader could make. It would be a gesture which somehow made contact with mystery.

There is a point in this story where such a gesture occurs. The Grandmother is at last alone, facing the Misfit. Her head clears for an instant and she realizes, even in her limited way, that she is responsible for the man before her and joined to him by ties of kinship which have their roots deep in the mystery she has been merely prattling about so far. And at this point, she does the right thing, she makes the right gesture.

I find that students are often puzzled by what she says and does here, but I think myself that if I took out this gesture and what she says with it, I would have no story. What was left would not be worth your attention. Our age not only does not have a very sharp eye for the almost imperceptible intrusions of grace, it no longer has much feeling for the nature of the violences which precede and follow them. The devil's greatest wile, Baudelaire has said, is to convince us that he does not exist.

I suppose the reasons for the use of so much violence in modern fiction will differ with each writer who uses it, but in my own stories I have found that violence is strangely capable of returning my characters to reality and preparing them to accept their moment of grace. Their heads are so hard that almost nothing else will do the work. This idea, that reality is something to which we must be returned at considerable cost, is one which is seldom understood by the casual reader, but it is one which is implicit in the Christian view of the world.

I don't want to equate the Misfit with the devil. I prefer to think that, however unlikely this may seem, the old lady's gesture, like the mustard-seed, will grow to be a great crow-filled tree in the Misfit's heart, and will be enough of a pain to him there to turn him into the prophet he was meant to become. But that's another story.

This story has been called grotesque, but I prefer to call it literal. A good story is literal in the same sense that a child's drawing is literal. When a child draws, he doesn't intend to distort but to set down exactly what he sees, and as his gaze is direct, he sees the lines that create motion. Now the lines of motion that interest the writer are usually invisible. They are lines of spiritual motion. And in this story you should be on the lookout for such things as the action of grace in the Grandmother's soul, and not for the dead bodies.

We hear many complaints about the prevalence of violence in modern fiction, and it is always assumed that this violence is a bad thing and meant to be an end in itself. With the serious writer, violence is never an end in itself. It is the extreme situation that best reveals what we are essentially, and I believe these are times when writers are more interested in what we are essentially than in the tenor of our daily lives. Violence is a force which can be used for good or evil, and among other things taken by it is the kingdom of heaven. But regardless of what can be taken by it, the man in the violent situation reveals those qualities least dispensable in his personality, those qualities which are all he will have to take into eternity with him; and since the characters in this story are all on the verge of eternity, it is appropriate to think of what they take with them. In any case, I hope that if you consider these points in connection with the story, you will come to see it as something more than an account of a family murdered on the way to Florida.

[1957]

Case Study: Writing about John Updike

We give four short stories (as well as two previously unpublished manuscript pages from "A&P" and manuscript pages of "Pygmalion") and selections from Updike's comments about writing and reading short stories.

In this case study we give four stories and extracts from several of Updike's Critical Writings:

1. "A&P"
2. "Pygmalion"
3. "The Rumor"
4. Passages about the art of short fiction, from five essays and an interview.

John Updike (b. 1932) grew up in Shillington, Pennsylvania, where his father was a teacher and his mother a writer. After receiving a BA degree in 1954 from Harvard, where he edited the Harvard Lampoon *(for which he both wrote and drew), he studied drawing at Oxford for a year, but an offer from* The New Yorker *brought him back to the United States. He was hired as a reporter for the magazine but soon began contributing poetry, essays, and fiction. In 1957 he left* The New

Yorker *in order to write independently full-time, though his stories and book reviews appear regularly in it.*

*In 1959 Updike published his first book of stories (*The Same Door*) and also his first novel (*The Poorhouse Fair*); the next year he published* Rabbit, Run, *a highly successful novel whose protagonist, "Rabbit" Angstrom, has reappeared in three later novels:* Rabbit Redux *(1971),* Rabbit Is Rich *(1981), and* Rabbit at Rest *(1990). The first and the last Rabbit books each won a Pulitzer Prize.*

A & P

In walks these three girls in nothing but bathing suits. I'm in the third checkout slot, with my back to the door, so I don't see them until they're over by the bread. The one that caught my eye first was the one in the plaid green two-piece. She was a chunky kid, with a good tan and a sweet broad soft-looking can with those two crescents of white just under it, where the sun never seems to hit, at the top of the backs of her legs. I stood there with my hand on a box of HiHo crackers trying to remember if I rang it up or not. I ring it up again and the customer starts giving me hell. She's one of these cash-register-watchers, a witch about fifty with rouge on her cheekbones and no eyebrows, and I know it made her day to trip me up. She'd been watching cash registers for fifty years and probably never seen a mistake before.

By the time I got her feathers smoothed and her goodies into a bag—she gives me a little snort in passing, if she'd been born at the right time they would have burned her over in Salem—by the time I get her on her way the girls had circled around the bread and were coming back, without a pushcart, back my way along the counters, in the aisle between the checkouts and the Special bins. They didn't even have shoes on. There was this chunky one, with the two-piece—it was bright green and the seams of the bra were still sharp and her belly was still pretty pale so I guessed she just got it (the suit)—there was this one, with one of those chubby berry-faces, the lips all bunched together under her nose, this one, and a tall one, with black hair that hadn't quite frizzed right, and one of these sunburns right across under the eyes, and a chin that was way too long—you know, the kind of girl other girls think is very "striking" and "attractive" but never quite makes it, as they very well know, which is why they like her so much—and then the third one, that wasn't quite so tall. She was the queen. She kind of led them, the other two peeking around and making their shoulders round. She didn't look around, not this queen, she just walked straight on slowly, on these long white prima-donna legs. She came down a little hard on her heels, as if she didn't walk in her bare feet that much, putting down her heels and then letting the weight move along to her toes as if she was testing the floor with every step, putting a little deliberate extra action into it. You never know for sure how girls' minds work (do they really think it's a mind in there or just a little buzz like a bee in a glass jar?) but you got the idea she had talked the other two into coming in here with her, and now she was showing them how to do it, walk slow and hold yourself straight.

She had on a kind of dirty pink—beige maybe, I don't know—bathing suit with a little nubble all over it and, what got me, the straps were down. They were off her shoulders looped loose around the cool tops of her arms, and I guess as a result the suit had slipped on her, so all around the top of the cloth there was this shining rim. If it hadn't been there you wouldn't have known there could have been anything whiter than those shoulders. With the straps pushed off, there was

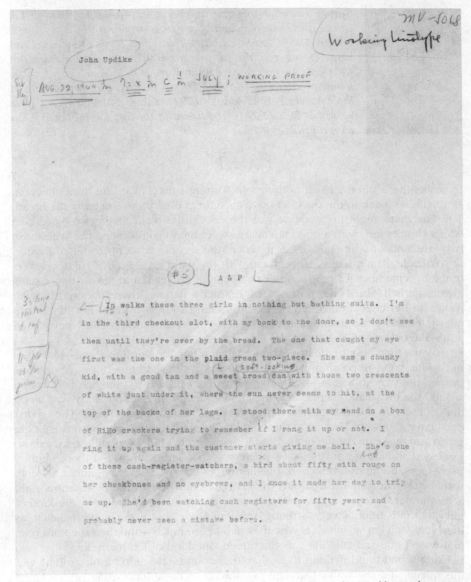

If you compare this paragraph with the printed text, you will see that Updike made small but significant changes.

nothing between the top of the suit and the top of her head except just *her*, this clean bare plane of the top of her chest down from the shoulder bones like a dented sheet of metal tilted in the light. I mean, it was more than pretty.

She had sort of oaky hair that the sun and salt had bleached, done up in a bun that was unravelling, and a kind of prim face. Walking into the A & P with your straps down, I suppose it's the only kind of face you *can* have. She held her head so high her neck, coming up out of those white shoulders, looked kind of stretched, but I didn't mind. The longer her neck was, the more of her there was.

5   She must have felt in the corner of her eye me and over my shoulder Stokesie in the second slot watching, but she didn't tip. Not this queen. She kept her eyes

moving across the racks, and stopped, and turned so slow it made my stomach rub the inside of my apron, and buzzed to the other two, who kind of huddled against her for relief, and then they all three of them went up the cat and dog food–breakfast cereal–macaroni–rice–raisins–seasonings–spreads–spaghetti–soft drinks–crackers–and–cookies aisle. From the third slot I look straight up this aisle to the meat counter, and I watched them all the way. The fat one with the tan sort of fumbled with the cookies, but on second thought she put the package back. The sheep pushing their carts down the aisle—the girls were walking against the usual traffic (not that we have one-way signs or anything)—were pretty hilarious. You could see them, when Queenie's white shoulders dawned on them, kind of jerk, or hop, or hiccup, but their eyes snapped back to their own baskets and on they pushed. I bet you could set off dynamite in the A & P and the people would by and large keep reaching and checking oatmeal off their lists and muttering "Let me see, there was a third thing, began with A, asparagus, no, ah, yes, apple-sauce!" or whatever it is they do mutter. But there was no doubt, this jiggled them. A few house slaves in pin curlers even look around after pushing their carts past to make sure what they had seen was correct.

You know, it's one thing to have a girl in a bathing suit down on the beach, where what with the glare nobody can look at each other much anyway, and an-other thing in the cool of the A & P, under the fluorescent lights, against all those stacked packages, with her feet paddling along naked over our checker-board green-and-cream, rubber-tile floor.

"Oh, Daddy," Stokesie said beside me. "I feel so faint."

"Darling," I said. "Hold me tight." Stokesie's married, with two babies chalked up on his fuselage already, but as far as I can tell that's the only difference. He's twenty-two, and I was nineteen this April.

"Is it done?" he asks, the responsible married man finding his voice. I forgot to say he thinks he's going to be a manager some sunny day, maybe in 1990 when it's called the Great Alexandrov and Petrooshki Tea Company or something.

10   What he meant was, our town is five miles from a beach, with a big summer colony out on the Point, but we're right in the middle of town, and the women generally put on a shirt or shorts or something before they get out of the car into the street. And anyway these are usually women with six children and varicose veins mapping their legs and nobody, including them, could care less. As I say, we're right in the middle of town, and if you stand at our front doors you can see two banks and the Congregational church and the newspaper store and three real estate offices and about twenty-seven old freeloaders tearing up Central Street be-cause the sewer broke again. It's not as if we're on the Cape; we're north of Boston and there's people in this town haven't seen the ocean for twenty years.

The girls had reached the meat counter and were asking McMahon some-thing. He pointed, they pointed, and they shuffled out of sight behind a pyramid of Diet Delight peaches. All that was left for us to see was old McMahon patting his mouth and looking after them sizing up their joints. Poor kids, I began to feel sorry for them, they couldn't help it.

Now here comes the sad part of the story, at least my family says it's sad, but I don't think it's so sad myself. The store's pretty empty, it being Thursday after-noon, so there was nothing much to do except lean on the register and wait for the girls to show up again. The whole store was like a pinball machine and I didn't know which tunnel they'd come out of. After a while they come around out of the far aisle, around the light bulbs, records at discount of the Caribbean Six or Tony Martin Sings or some such gunk you wonder they waste the wax on, six-packs of candy bars, and plastic toys done up in cellophane that fall apart when a kid looks at them anyway. Around they come, Queenie still leading the way, and holding a little gray jar in her hand. Slots Three through Seven are unmanned and I could see her wondering between Stokes and me, but Stokesie with his usual luck draws an old party in baggy gray pants who stumbles up with four giant cans of pineapple juice (what do these bums *do* with all that pineapple juice? I've often asked myself) so the girls come to me. Queenie puts down the jar and I take it into my fingers icy cold. Kingfish Fancy Herring Snacks in Pure Sour Cream: 49¢. Now her hands are empty, not a ring or a bracelet, bare as God made them, and I wonder where the money's coming from. Still with the prim look she lifts a folded dollar bill out of the hollow at the center of her nubbled pink top. The jar went heavy in my hand. Really, I thought that was so cute.

Then everybody's luck begins to run out. Lengel comes in from haggling with a truck full of cabbages on the lot and is about to scuttle into the door marked MANAGER behind which he hides all day when the girls touch his eye. Lengel's pretty dreary, teaches Sunday school and the rest, but he doesn't miss that much. He comes over and says, "Girls, this isn't the beach."

Queenie blushes, though maybe it's just a brush of sunburn I was noticing for the first time, now that she was so close. "My mother asked me to pick up a jar of herring snacks." Her voice kind of startled me, the way voices do when you see the people first, coming out so flat and dumb yet kind of tony, too, the way it ticked over "pick up" and "snacks." All of a sudden I slid right down her voice into her living room. Her father and the other men were standing around in ice-cream coats and bow ties and the women were in sandals picking up herring snacks on toothpicks off a big glass plate and they were all holding drinks the color of water with olives and sprigs of mint in them. When my parents have somebody over they get lemonade and if it's a real racy affair Schlitz in tall glasses with "They'll Do It Every Time" cartoons stencilled on.

15   "That's all right," Lengel said. "But this isn't the beach." His repeating this struck me as funny, as if it had just occurred to him, and he had been thinking all these years the A & P was a great big dune and he was the head lifeguard. He didn't like my smiling—as I say he doesn't miss much—but he concentrates on giving the girls that sad Sunday-school-superintendent stare.

Queenie's blush was no sunburn now, and the plump one in plaid, that I liked better from the back—a really sweet can—pipes up, "We weren't doing any shopping. We just came in for the one thing."

"That makes no difference," Lengel tells her, and I could see from the way his eyes went that he hadn't noticed she was wearing a two-piece before. "We want you decently dressed when you come in here."

"We *are* decent," Queenie says suddenly, her lower lip pushing, getting sore now that she remembers her place, a place from which the crowd that runs the A & P must look pretty crummy. Fancy Herring Snacks flashed in her very blue eyes.

"Girls, I don't want to argue with you. After this come in here with your shoulders covered. It's our policy." He turns his back. That's policy for you. Policy is what the kingpins want. What the others want is juvenile delinquency.

20   All this while, the customers had been showing up with their carts but, you know, sheep, seeing a scene, they had all bunched up on Stokesie, who shook open a paper bag as gently as peeling a peach, not wanting to miss a word. I could feel in the silence everybody getting nervous, most of all Lengel, who asks me, "Sammy, have you rung up this purchase?"

I thought and said "No" but it wasn't about that I was thinking. I go through the punches, 4, 9, GROC, TOT—it's more complicated than you think and after you do it often enough, it begins to make a little song, that you hear words to, in

10

your life," Lengel says, and I know that's true too, but remembering
how he made that pretty girl blush makes me so scrunchy inside I
punch the No Sale tab and the machine whirs "pee-pul" and the
drawer splats out. One advantage to this scene taking place in
summer, I can follow this up with a clean exit, there's no fumbling
around getting your coat and earmuffs, I just saunter into the
electric eye in my white shirt that my mother ironed the night
before, and the door heaves itself open, and outside the sunshine
is skating around on the asphalt.

I look around for my girls, but they're gone, of course.
There's nobody *(wasn't anybody)* but some young married screaming with her children
about some candy they didn't get by the door *(of)* a blue Falcon station
wagon. Looking back in the big windows, over the bags of peat moss
and aluminum furniture stacked on the pavement, I can *(could)* see Lengel in
my place in the slot, checking the sheep through. His face is *(was)* dark
gray and his back stiff, as if he'd just had an injection of iron,
and my stomach kind of falls *(fell)* as I realize *(felt)* how hard the world is *(was)* going
to be to me hereafter.

m   JOHN UPDIKE

LET me tell you about the beach. The old people are usually there by
the time I get down. They come down early because they have nothing
to do but have/forgotten how to sleep. Dressed in funny old suits,
with oval tops and frilly skirts, the ladies walk back and forth in
straw hats, back and forth, picking up shells and smiling at the
seagulls. There's an old gent, with *(a bald head and)* a brown barrel chest with white
hair all over it, who wears a very skimpy tight kind of French-style

---

As this typescript indicates, originally "A & P" continued after the point where the published version ends.

my case "Hello (*bing*) there, you (*gung*) hap-py *peepul* (*splat*)!"—the *splat* being the drawer flying out. I uncrease the bill, tenderly as you may imagine, it just having come from between the two smoothest scoops of vanilla I had ever known were there, and pass a half and a penny into her narrow pink palm and nestle the herrings in a bag and twist its neck and hand it over, all the time thinking.

The girls, and who'd blame them, are in a hurry to get out, so I say "I quit" to Lengel quick enough for them to hear, hoping they'll stop and watch me, their unsuspected hero. They keep right on going, into the electric eye; the door flies open and they flicker across the lot to their car, Queenie and Plaid and Big Tall Goony-Goony (not that as raw material she was so bad), leaving me with Lengel and a kink in his eyebrow.

"Did you say something, Sammy?"

"I said I quit."

25   "I thought you did."

"You didn't have to embarrass them."

"It was they who were embarrassing us."

I started to say something that came out "Fiddle-de-doo." It's a saying of my grandmother's, and I know she would have been pleased.

"I don't think you know what you're saying," Lengel said.

30   "I know you don't," I said. "But I do." I pull the bow at the back of my apron and start shrugging it off my shoulders. A couple customers that had been heading for my slot begin to knock against each other, like scared pigs in a chute.

Lengel sighs and begins to look very patient and old and gray. He's been a friend of my parents for years. "Sammy, you don't want to do this to your Mom and Dad," he tells me. It's true, I don't. But it seems to me that once you begin a gesture it's fatal not to go through with it. I fold the apron, "Sammy" stitched in red on the pocket, and put it on the counter, and drop the bow tie on top of it. The bow tie is theirs, if you've ever wondered. "You'll feel this for the rest of your life," Lengel says, and I know that's true, too, but remembering how he made that pretty girl blush makes me so scrunchy inside I punch the No Sale tab and the machine whirs "pee-pul" and the drawer splats out. One advantage to this scene taking place in summer, I can follow this up with a clean exit, there's no fumbling around getting your coat and galoshes, I just saunter into the electric eye in my white shirt that my mother ironed the night before, and the door heaves itself open, and outside the sunshine is skating round on the asphalt.

I look around for my girls, but they're gone, of course. There wasn't anybody but some young married screaming with her children about some candy they didn't get by the door of a powder-blue Falcon station wagon. Looking back in the big windows, over the bags of peat moss and aluminum lawn furniture stacked on the pavement, I could see Lengel in my place in the slot, checking the sheep through. His face was dark gray and his back stiff, as if he'd just had an injection of iron, and my stomach kind of fell as I felt how hard the world was going to be to me hereafter.

[1962]

Topics for Critical Thinking and Writing

1. In what sort of community is this A & P located? To what extent does this community resemble yours?

2. Do you think Sammy is a male chauvinist pig? Why, or why not? And if you think he is, do you find the story offensive? Again, why or why not?

3. In the last line of the story Sammy says, "I felt how hard the world was going to be to me hereafter." Do you think the world is going to be hard to Sammy? Why, or why not? And if it is hard to him, is this because of a virtue or a weakness in Sammy?

4. Write Lengel's version of the story (500–1000 words) as he might narrate it to his wife during dinner. Or write the story from Queenie's point of view.

5. In speaking of contemporary fiction, Updike said:

I want stories to startle and engage me within the first few sentences, and in their middle to widen or deepen or sharpen my knowledge of human activity, and to end by giving me a sensation of completed statement.

Let's assume that you share Updike's view of what a story should do. To what extent do you think "A & P" fulfills these demands? (You may want to put your response in the form of a letter to Updike.)

Pygmalion

What he liked about his first wife was her gift of mimicry; after a party, theirs or another couple's, she would vivify for him what they had seen, the faces, the voices, twisting her pretty mouth into small contortions that brought back, for a dazzling instant, the presence of an absent acquaintance. "Well, if I reawwy—how does Gwen talk?—if I *re*-awwy cared about conservation—" And he, the husband, would laugh and laugh, even though Gwen was secretly his mistress and would become his second wife. What he liked about *her* was her liveliness in bed, and what he disliked about his first wife was the way she would ask to have her backed rubbed and then, under his laboring hands, night after night, fall asleep.

For the first years of the new marriage, after he and Gwen had returned from a party, he would wait, unconsciously, for the imitations, the recapitulation, to begin. He would even prompt: "What did you make of our hostess's brother?"

"Oh," Gwen would simply say, "he seemed very pleasant." Sensing with feminine intuition that he expected more, she might add, "Harmless. Maybe a little stuffy." Her eyes flashed as she heard in his expectant silence an unvoiced demand, and with that touching, childlike impediment of hers she blurted out, "What are you reawy after?"

"Oh, nothing. Nothing. It's just—Marguerite met him once a few years ago and she was struck by what a pompous nitwit he was. That way he has of sucking his pipestem and ending every statement with 'Do you follow me?'"

5   "I thought he was perfectly pleasant," Gwen said frostily, and turned her back to remove her silvery, snug party dress. As she wriggled it down over her hips she turned her head and defiantly added, "He had a *lot* to say about tax shelters."

"I bet he did," Pygmalion scoffed feebly, numbed by the sight of his wife frontally advancing, nude, toward him as he lay on their marital bed. "It's awfully late," he warned her.

"Oh, come on," she said, the lights out.

The first imitation Gwen did was of Marguerite's second husband, Marvin; they had all unexpectedly met at a Save the Whales benefit ball, to which invitations had been sent out indiscriminately. "Oh-ho-*ho*," she boomed in the privacy of their bedroom afterwards, "so you're my noble predecessor!" In an aside she added, "Noble, my ass. He hates you so much you turned him on."

"I did?" he said. "I thought he was perfectly pleasant, in what could have been an awkward encounter."

10   "Yes, in*dee*dy," she agreed, imitating hearty Marvin, and for a dazzling second she allowed the man's slightly glassy and slack expression of forced benignity to invade her own usually petite and rounded features. "Nothing awkward about *us*, ho-ho," she went on, encouraged by her husband's laughter. "And tell me, old chap, why *is* it your child-support check is never on time anymore?"

```
                              PYGMALION

    What he liked about his first wife was her gift of mimickry; after a party,

    theirs or another couples, she would vivify for him what they had seen,

    the faces, the voices, ~~xxxxxxxxxxxxxxxx~~ twisting her mouth into small

    contortions that brought back, for a ~~startling~~ (dazzling) instant, the presence of an

    absent friend. "Well, if I reawy -- how does Fritzi talk? -- if I ~~xxxxxxxxx~~
                                                             the husband,
    re-awwy cared about conservation --" And he,would laugh uproariously, even

    though Fritzi was his ~~p~~ mistress and would become his second wife. What he

    liked about her was her liveliness in ~~x~~ bed, and what he disliked about his

    first wife was the way she would ask to have her back rubbed and then ~~f~~ under
                   night after night,
    his laboring hands,fall fast asleep.
                                      after            had
        Their first years of marriage, ~~when~~ he and Fritzi ~~xx~~ returned from a

    party, he would wait,~~for~~ unconsciously, for the ~~xxxxxxxxxxxxxxx~~ imitations,

    the recapitulation, to begin, and would even prompt: "What did you make of

    ~~thxxdixxxxxx xxxxxxxxxxxxxxxxxxxx~~ our hostess's brother?"

        "Oh," Fritzi would say, "he seemed pleasant." Seeing he expected more,

    she might add, "Harmless.~~\ xxxxxxxxxxxxxxxx xxxxxxxxx~~ A little stuffy."
                               expectant
    Her eyes flashed, sensing in his silence ~~xixxxxxxxxxxxxxxxxx~~ an unvoicable
                              with that touching impediment of ~~xxxx~~ hers, "What are you ~~xxxxxx~~
    demand, and she would blurt out, ~~Xthxxxxxxxxxxxxxxxxxxxxxxxxxxx~~ reawy after?"

        ~~Thxxxxxxx~~ "Oh, nothing. Nothing. It's just -- Marguerite met him once

    and she was ~~struck~~ struck by what an incredibly pompous nitwit he was. That
                                                              ending
    way ~~of~~ he has of sucking the ~~xxxxxxxxx~~ pipestem, and ~~finishing~~ every ~~xxxxxxxxx~~
    dogmatic statement with, 'Are you with me?'"
    ~~xxxxxxx paragraph with 'Do you follow me?'~~

        "I thought he had a good heart," Fritzi said stonily, and turned her back

    to remove her silvery, ~~xxxxsnug~~ party dress. ~~Xxxxxxxxx~~ As she wriggled it

    down over her hips, she turned her head and ~~xxxxxx defiantxxx~~ defiantly added,

    "He had to lot to say about tax shelters."

        "I bet he did,"~~xxxxxxxxxxxxxxxxxxxxxxx~~ he ~~xxxfinxxx~~ scoffed ~~xxxxxxx~~ feebly,
```

He laughed and laughed, entranced to see his bride arrive at what he conceived to be a proper womanliness—a plastic, alert sensitivity to the human environment, a susceptible responsiveness tugged this way and that by the currents of Nature herself. He could not know the world, was his fear, unless a woman translated it for him. Now, when they returned from a gathering, and he asked what she had made of so-and-so, Gwen would stand in her underwear and consider, as if onstage. "We-hell, my dear," she would announce in sudden, fluting parody, "if it weren't for Portugal there *rally* wouldn't be a *bear*able country left in Europe!"

"Oh, come on," he would protest, delighted at the way her pretty features distorted themselves into an uncanny, snobbish horsiness.

"How did she do it?" Gwen would ask, as if professionally intent. "Something with the chin, sort of rolling it from side to side without unclenching the teeth."

2

advancing,
numbed by the sight of her front~~ally~~ ~~xxxxxxxxxxx~~ nude, ~~xxxxx~~ toward him and
                              tiny "It's awfully late," he wanred her.
their marital bed. ~~Hex forgave her her deficiencies, once again.~~
  "Oh, come on," she said, the light out.
~~Xxxxxxxxxx~~ The first imitation she did was of Marguerite's second
                              Ed;
husband∧ they all unexpectedly met at a ~~kxxixxxxxxxxxxxxx~~ Save the Whales
~~where the~~ invitations had been sent out indiscriminately.
benefit ball, "Oh-ho-ho," Fritzie said in the~~ix~~ privacy of their bedroom

afterward, "so you're my noble predecessor! Noble, my ass. He hates you so

much you ~~t~~ really turned him on."

  "I ~~didx'xxx~~ ~~didx~~ did?" he said, dazzled. "I thought he was perfectly

pleasant, ~~xxxxxxxxxxxxx~~ in what could~~x~~ have been an awkward encounter."
                              hearty Ed,   magical
  "Yes, indeed," she ~~xx~~ agreed, imitating ~~thexxxxxxxxxxxxxx~~ and for a second
                         the man's   (heavy ponderous)
allowing ~~xxxxxxxxxxxxxxxxxxxxxxxxxx~~ his exact ~~xxxxxxx~~ slightly ~~pleesy~~ and
                              usually crisp
slack expression of forced benignity to invade her own ~~xxxxxxxxxxxxx~~ features.
                         ho ho,"   ~~hxxhxx~~ tell me
"Nothing ~~xxxxxxx~~ awkward about us," she went on, encouraged. "And ~~xxxxxxx~~
       old chap why your support check ~~kxx~~
~~xxxxxxxxxxxxxxxxxxxxxxxxxxxxxxxxxxxxxx~~ ~~xxxxxxxxxxxxx~~ is never on time
                   child   any more?"

  He laughed and laughed, her husband, ~~xxxxxxxxxx~~ entranced to see ~~hxx~~ his wife

arrive at what he took to be ~~xxxxxxxxxxxxxxxxx~~ proper womanliness -- a plastic,

alert sensitivity to the human environment, a responsive wit ~~hhkxxxxx~~ tugged
~~birdlike~~   ~~fxxxxx~~
this way and that by the currents ~~xxxx~~ of Nature herself. He ~~xxxxxxxxxx~~ could
                         he feared,
not know the world, ~~hxxfxxx was his feeling,~~ unless a woman translated it to

him. Now, when they returned from a gathering, and he asked what she made of
                              consider, as if on stage.
so-and-so, she would stand in her underwear and ~~xxxxxxxxxxxxxxxxxxxxxxxxxxx~~

~~consider for a second, like a nightclub performer~~ ~~xxxxxxxxxxxxxxxxxxx~~

~~tensing to knxxxxxxxx address the microphone.~~ "Well my dear," she would say

in fluting parody, "if it wasn't for ~~xxx~~ Portugal there ~~xxxxxxx~~ rally wouldn't

be any countries in Europe left!"

  "Oh, come ~~xxxxxxx~~ on" he would protest, laughing, to see her pretty little
                         brown
features ~~xxxxxxx~~ extend themselves ~~in knxxxxxxxxxxxxx~~ an uncanny horsiness.

  "How did she do ~~ixxxxxxxxxxxx~~ it? Something with the chin, sort of rolling

it from side to side without unclenching the teeth."

"You've got it!" he applauded.

15   "Of course you *knoaow*," she went on in the assumed voice, "there *used* to
be Greece, but now all these dreadful *Arabs* . . ."

    "Oh, yes, yes," he said, his face smarting from laughing so hard, so proudly.
She had become perfect for him.

    In bed she pointed out, "It's awfully late."

    "Want a back rub?"

    "Mmmm. That would be reawy nice." As his left hand labored on the smooth,
warm, pliable surface, his wife—that small something in her that was all her
own—sank out of reach; night after night, she fell asleep

[1981]

3

"You've got it!" he applauded. ~~xxxxxxxxxxxxxxxxxxxxxx~~

"Of course you know," ~~xxxxxx~~ she went on, "there used to be Greece, but now all these <u>Arabs</u> ..."

"Oh, yes," he ~~xx~~ said, his face ~~xxxxxxxxxxxxxxx~~ smarting from laughing so hard, so proudly.

In bed she said, "It's awfully late."

"Want a back rub?"

"Mmm." As ~~xxxxxxxxx~~ his hands labored on the smooth, pliable surface, his wife, ~~xxxxx~~ that in her which was all her ~~xxx~~ sank ~~xxxxx~~ out of reach; ex hausted by serving him, she fell asleep.

Topics for Critical Thinking and Writing

1. Although the man is once called Pygmalion, that probably is not his real name. If you are unfamiliar with the myth of Pygmalion, check an encyclopedia, or even a good dictionary. What is the relevance of the name to the story?
2. What is your attitude toward the man? How sympathetic (or unsympathetic) are you—at the start, and at the end?
3. Do you think the story is sexist? Is it your guess that males and females will, as groups, differ markedly in their response to the characters?

The Rumor

Frank and Sharon Whittier had come from the Cincinnati area and, with an inheritance of hers and a sum borrowed from his father, had opened a small art gallery on the fourth floor of a narrow building on West Fifty-seventh Street. They had known each other as children; their families had been in the same country-club set. They had married in 1971, when Frank was freshly graduated from Oberlin and Vietnam-vulnerable and Sharon was only nineteen, a sophomore at Antioch majoring in dance. By the time, six years later, they arrived in New York, they had two small children; the birth of a third led them to give up their apartment and the city struggle and move to a house in Hastings, a low stucco house with a wide-eaved Wright-style roof and a view, through massive beeches at the bottom of the yard, of the leaden, ongliding Hudson. They were happy, surely. They had dry Midwestern taste, and by sticking to representational painters and abstract sculptors they managed to survive the uglier Eighties styles—faux graffiti, neo-German expressionism, cathode-ray prole play, ecological-protest trash art—and bring their quiet, chaste string of fourth-floor rooms into the calm lagoon of Nineties eclectic revivalism and subdued recession chic. They prospered; their youngest child turned twelve, their oldest was filling out college applications.

When Sharon first heard the rumor that Frank had left her for a young homosexual with whom he was having an affair, she had to laugh, for, far from having left her, there he was, right in the lamplit study with her, ripping pages out of *ARTnews*.

"I don't think so, Avis," she said to the graphic artist on the other end of the line. "He's right here with me. Would you like to say hello?" The easy refutation was make additionally sweet by the fact that, some years before there had been a brief (Sharon thought) romantic flare-up between her husband and this caller, an overanimated redhead with protuberant cheeks and chin. Avis was a second-wave appropriationist who made color Xeroxes of masterpieces out of art books and then signed them in an ink mixed of her own blood and urine. How could she, who had actually slept with Frank, be imagining this grotesque thing?

The voice on the phone gushed as if relieved and pleased. "I know, it's wildly absurd, but I heard it from two sources, with absolutely solemn assurance."

5   "Who were these sources?"

"I'm not sure they'd like you to know. But it was Ed Jaffrey and then that boy who's been living with Walton Forney, what does he call himself, one of those names like Madonna—Jojo!"

"Well, then," Sharon began.

"But I've heard it from still others," Avis insisted. "All over town—it's in the air. Couldn't you and Frank *do* something about it, if it's not true?"

"If," Sharon protested, and her thrust of impatience carried, when she put down the receiver, into her conversation with Frank. "Avis says you're supposed to have run off with your homosexual lover."

10   "I don't have a homosexual lover," Frank said, too calmly, ripping an auction ad out of the magazine.

"She says all New York says you do."

"Well, what are you going to believe, all New York or your own experience? Here I sit, faithful to a fault, straight as a die, whatever that means. We made love just two nights ago."

It seemed possibly revealing to her that he so distinctly remembered, as if heterosexual performance were a duty he checked off. He was—had always been, for over twenty years—a slim blond man several inches under six feet tall, with a narrow head he liked to keep trim, even during those years when long hair was in fashion, milky-blue eyes set at a slight tilt, such as you see on certain taut Slavic or Norwegian faces, and a small, precise mouth he kept pursed over teeth a shade too prominent and yellow. He was reluctant to smile, as if giving something away, and was vain of his flat belly and lithe collegiate condition. He weighed himself every morning on the bathroom scale, and if he weighed a pound more than yesterday, he skipped lunch. In this, and in his general attention to his own person, he was as quietly fanatic as—it for the first time occurred to her—a woman.

"You know I've never liked the queer side of this business," he went on. "I've just gotten used to it. I don't even think anymore, who's gay and who isn't."

15   "Avis was *ju*bilant." Sharon said. "How could she think it?"

It took him a moment to focus on the question and realize that his answer was important to her. He became nettled. "Ask *her* how," he said. "Our brief and regrettable relationship, if that's what interests you, seemed satisfactory to me at least. What troubles and amazes me, if I may say so, is how *you* can be taking this ridiculous rumor so seriously."

"I'm *not*, Frank," she insisted, then backtracked. "But why would such a rumor come out of thin air? Doesn't there have to be *something*? Since we moved up here, we're not together so much, naturally, some days when I can't come into town you're gone sixteen hours . . . ."

"But *Shar*on," he said, like a teacher restoring discipline, removing his reading glasses from his almond-shaped eyes, with their stubby fair lashes. "Don't you *know* me? Ever since after that dance when you were sixteen, that time by the lake? . . ."

She didn't want to reminisce. Their early sex had been difficult for her; she had submitted to his advances out of a larger, more social, rather idealistic attraction. She knew that together they would have the strength to get out of Cincinnati and, singly or married to others, they would stay. "Well," she said, enjoying this sensation, despite the chill the rumor had awakened in her, of descending to a deeper level of intimacy than usual, "how well do you know even your own spouse? People are fooled all the time. Peggy Jacobson, for instance, when Henry ran off with that physical therapist, couldn't believe, even when the evidence was right there in front of her—"

20   "I'm *deeply* insulted," Frank interrupted, his mouth tense in that way he had when making a joke but not wanting to show his teeth. "My masculinity is insulted." But he couldn't deny himself a downward glance into his magazine; his tidy white hand jerked, as if wanting to tear out yet another item that might be useful to their business. Intimacy had always made him nervous. She kept at it, rather hopelessly. "Avis said two separate people had solemnly assured her."

"Who, exactly?"

When she told him, he said, exactly as she had done. "Well, then." He added. "You know how gays are. Malicious. Mischievous. They have all that time and money on their hands."

"You sound jealous." Something about the way he was arguing with her strengthened Sharon's suspicion that, outrageous as the rumor was—indeed, *because* it was outrageous—it was true.

In the days that followed, now that she was alert to the rumor's vaporous presence, she imagined it everywhere—on the poised young faces of their staff, in the delicate negotiatory accents of their artists' agents, in the heartier tones of their repeat customers, even in the gruff, self-occupied ramblings of the artists themselves. People seemed startled when she and Frank entered a room together: The desk receptionist and the security guard in their gallery halted their daily morning banter, and the waiters in their pet restaurant, over on Fifty-ninth, appeared especially effusive and attentive. Handshakes lasted a second too long, women embraced her with an extra squeeze, she felt herself ensnared in a soft net of unspoken pity.

25   Frank sensed her discomfort and took a certain malicious pleasure in it, enacting all the while his perfect innocence. He composed himself to appear, from her angle, aloof above the rumor. Dealing professionally in so much absurdity— the art world's frantic attention-getting, studied grotesqueries—he merely intensified the fastidious dryness that had sustained their gallery through wave after wave of changing fashion, and that had, like a rocket's heat-resistant skin, insulated their launch, their escape from the comfortable riverine smugness of this metropolis of dreadful freedom. The rumor amused him, and it amused him, too, to notice how she helplessly watched to see if in the metropolitan throngs his eyes now followed young men as once they had noticed and followed young women.

She observed his gestures—always a bit excessively graceful and precise—distrustfully, and listened for the buttery, reedy tone of voice that might signal an invisible sex change.

That even in some small fraction of her she was willing to believe the rumor justified a certain maliciousness on his part. He couldn't help teasing her—glancing over at her, say, when an especially magnetic young waiter served them, or at home, in their bedroom, pushing more brusquely than was his style at her increasing sexual unwillingness. More than once, at last away from the countless knowing eyes of their New York milieu, in the privacy of their Hastings upstairs, beneath the wide midwestern eaves, she burst into tears and struck out at him, his infuriating, impervious apparent blamelessness. He was like one of those photorealist nudes, merciless in every detail and yet subtly, defiantly not there, not human. "You're distant," she accused him. "You've always been."

"I don't mean to be. You didn't used to mind my manner. You thought it was quietly masterful."

"I was a teenage girl. I deferred to you."

"It worked out," he pointed out, lifting his hands in an effete, disclaiming way from his sides, to take in their room, their expansive house, their joint career. "What is it that bothers you, Sharon? The idea of losing me? Or the insult to your female pride? The people who started this ridiculous rumor don't even *see* women. Women to them are just background noise."

30   "It's *not* ridiculous—if it were, why does it keep on and on, even though we're seen together all the time?"

For, ostensibly to quiet her and to quench the rumor, he had all but ceased to go to the city alone, and took her with him even though it meant some neglect of the house and their sons.

Frank asked. "Who *says* it keeps on all the time? I've *never* heard it, never once, except from you. Who's mentioned it lately?"

"Nobody."

"Well, then." He smiled, his lips not quite parting on his curved teeth, tawny like a beaver's.

35   "You bastard!" Sharon burst out. "You have some stinking little secret!"

"I don't," he serenely half-lied.

The rumor had no factual basis. But was there, Frank asked himself, some truth to it after all? Not circumstantial truth, but some higher, inner truth? As a young man, slight of build, with artistic interests, had he not been fearful of being mistaken for a homosexual? Had he not responded to homosexual overtures as they arose, in bars and locker rooms, with a disproportionate terror and repugnance? Had not his early marriage, and then, ten years later, his flurry of adulterous womanizing, been an escape of sorts, into safe, socially approved terrain? When he fantasized, or saw a pornographic movie, was not the male organ the hero of the occasion for him, at the center of every scene? Were not those slavish, lapping starlets his robotlike delegates, with glazed eyes and undisturbed coiffures venturing where he did not dare? Did he not, perhaps, envy women their privilege of worshipping the phallus? But, Frank asked himself, in fairness, arguing both sides of the case, can homosexual strands be entirely disentangled from heterosexual in that pink muck of carnal excitement, of dream made flesh, of return to the presexual womb?

More broadly, had he not felt more comfortable with his father than with his mother? Was not this in itself a sinister reversal of the usual biology? His father had been a genteel Fourth Street lawyer, of no particular effectuality save that most of his clients were from the same social class, with the same accents and comfortably narrowed aspirations, here on this plateau by the swelling Ohio. Darker and taller than Frank, with the same long teeth and primly set mouth, his father had had the lawyer's gift of silence, of judicious withholding, and in his son's scattered memories of times together—a trip downtown on the trolley to buy Frank his first suit, each summer's one or two excursions to see the Reds play at old Crosley Field—the man said little. This prim reserve, letting so much go unstated and unacknowledged, was a relief after the daily shower of words and affection and advice Frank received from his mother. As an adult he was attracted, he noticed, to stoical men, taller than he and nursing an unexpressed sadness; his favorite college roommate had been of this saturnine type, and his pet tennis partner in Hastings, and artists he especially favored and encouraged—dour, weathered landscapists and virtually illiterate sculptors, welded solid into their crafts and stubborn obsessions. With these men he became a catering, wifely, subtly agitated presence that Sharon would scarcely recognize.

Frank's mother, once a fluffy belle from Louisville, had been gaudy, strident, sardonic, volatile, needy, demanding, loving; from her he had inherited his "artistic" side, as well as his pretty blondness, but he was not especially grateful. Less—as was proposed by a famous formula he didn't know as a boy—would have been more. His mother had given him an impression of women as complex, brightly-colored traps, attractive but treacherous, their petals apt to harden in an instant into knives. A certain wistful pallor, indeed, a limp helplessness, had drawn him to Sharon and, after the initial dazzlement of the Avises of the world faded and fizzled, always drew him back. Other women asked more than he could provide; he was aware of other, bigger, warmer men they had had. But with Sharon he had been a rescuing knight, slaying the dragon of the winding Ohio. Yet what more devastatingly, and less forgivably, confirmed the rumor's essential truth than her willingness, she who knew him best and owed him most, to entertain it? Her instinct had been to believe Avis even though, far from run off, he was sitting there right in front of her eyes.

40   He was unreal to her, he could not help but conclude: all those years of uxorious cohabitation, those nights of lovemaking and days of homemaking ungratefully absorbed and now suddenly dismissed because of an apparition, a shadow of gossip. On the other hand, now that the rumor existed, Frank had become more real in the eyes of José, the younger, daintier of the two security guards, whose daily greetings had edged beyond the perfunctory; a certain mischievous dance in the boy's sable eyes animated their employer-employee courtesies. And Jennifer, too, the severely beautiful receptionist, with her rather Sixties-reminiscent bangs and shawls and serapes, not treated him more relaxedly, even offhandedly, as if he had somehow dropped out of her calculations. She assumed with him a comradely slanginess—"The boss was in earlier but she went out to exchange something at Bergdorf's"—as if both he and she were in roughly parallel ironic bondage to "the boss." Frank's heart felt a reflex loyalty to Sharon, a single sharp beat, but then he too relaxed, as if his phantom male lover and the weightless, scandal-veiled life that lived with him in some glowing apartment had bestowed at last what the city had withheld from the overworked, child-burdened married couple who had arrived fourteen years ago—a halo of glamour, of debonair uncaring.

In Hastings, when he and his wife attended a suburban party, the effect was less flattering. The other couples, he imagined, were slightly unsettled by the Whittiers' stubbornly appearing together and became disjointed in their presence, the men drifting off in distaste, the women turning supernormal and laying up a chinkless wall of conversation about children's college applications, local zoning, and Wall Street layoffs. The women, it seemed to Frank, edged, with an instinctive animal movement, a few inches closer to Sharon and touched her with a deft, protective flicking on the shoulder or forearm, to express solidarity and sympathy.

Wes Robertson, Frank's favorite tennis partner, came over to him and grunted. "How's it going?"

"*Fine*," Frank said, staring up at Wes with what he hoped weren't unduly starry eyes. Wes, who had recently turned fifty, had an old motorcycle-accident scar on one side of his chin, a small pale rose of discoloration that seemed to concentrate the man's self-careless manliness. Frank gave him more of an answer than he might have wanted: "In the art game we're feeling the slowdown like everybody else, but the Japanese are keeping the roof from caving in. The trouble with the Japanese, though, is, from the standpoint of a marginal gallery like ours, they aren't adventurous—they want blue chips, they want guaranteed value, they can't grasp that in art, value has to be subjective to an extent. Look at their own stuff—it's all standardized. Who the hell can tell a Hiroshige from a Hokusai?[1] When you think about it, their whole society, their whole success, really, is based on everybody being alike, everybody agreeing. The notion of art as a struggle, a gamble, as the dynamic embodiment of an existential problem, they just don't get it." He was talking too much, he knew, but he couldn't help it; Wes's scowling presence, his melancholy scarred face, and his stringy alcoholic body, which nevertheless could still whip a backhand right across the forecourt, perversely excited Frank, made him want to flirt.

Wes grimaced and contemplated Frank glumly. "Be around for a game Sunday?" Meaning, had he really run off?

"Of course, Why wouldn't I be?" This was teasing the issue, and Frank tried to sober up, to rein in. He felt a flush on his face and a stammer coming on. He asked. "The usual time? Ten forty-five, more or less?"

Wes nodded. "Sure."

Frank chattered on: "Let's try to get court 5 this time. Those brats having their lessons on court 2 drove me crazy last time. We spent all our time retrieving their damn balls. And listening to their moronic chatter."

Wes didn't grant this attempt at evocation of past liaisons even a word, just continued his melancholy, stoical nodding. This was one of the things, it occurred to Frank, that he like about men: their relational minimalism, their gender-based realization that the cupboard of life, emotionally speaking, was pretty near bare. There wasn't that tireless, irksome, bright-eyed *hope* women kept fluttering at you.

Once, years ago, on a stag golfing trip to Bermuda, he and Wes had shared a room with two single beds, and Wes had fallen asleep within a minute and started snoring, keeping Frank awake for much of the night. Contemplating the unconscious male body on its moonlit bed, Frank had been struck by the tragic dignity of this supine form, like a stone knight eroding on a tomb—the snoring profile in motionless gray silhouette, the massive, sacred warrior weight helpless as Wes's breathing struggled from phase to phase of the sleep cycle, from deep to REM to a near-wakefulness that brought a few merciful minutes of silence. The next morning, Wes said Frank should have reached over and poked him in the side; that's what his wife did. But he wasn't his wife, Frank thought, though in the course of that night's ordeal, he had felt his heart make many curious motions, among them the heaving, all-but-impossible, effort women's hearts make in

---

[1]**Hiroshige . . . Hokusai** Ando Hiroshige (1797–1858) and Katsushika Hokusai (1760–1849) are chiefly know as designers of landscape prints.

overcoming men's heavy grayness and achieving—a rainbow born of drizzle—love.

50   At the opening of Ned Forschheimer's show—Forschheimer, a shy, rude, stubborn, and now elderly painter of tea-colored, wintry Connecticut landscapes, was one of Frank's pets, unfashionable yet sneakily salable—none other than Walton Forney came up to Frank, his round face lit by white wine and odd, unquenchable self-delight, and said, "Say, Frank, old boy. Methinks I owe you an apology. It was Charlie Whit*field*, who used to run that framing shop down on Eighth Street, who left his wife suddenly, with some little Guatemalan boy he was putting through CCNY on the side. They took off for Mexico and left the missus sitting with the shop mortgage up to its attic and about a hundred prints of wild ducks left unframed. The thing that must have confused me, Charlie came from Ohio, too—Columbus or Cleveland, one of those. It was—what do they call it—a Freudian slip, an understandable confusion. Avis Wasserman told me Sharon wasn't all that thrilled to get the word a while ago, and you must have wondered yourself what the hell was up."

"We ignored it." Frank said, in a voice firmer and less catering than his usual one. "We rose above it." Walton was a number of inches shorter than Frank, with yet a bigger head; his gleaming, thin-skinned face, bearing smooth jowls that had climbed into his sideburns, was shadowed blue here and there, like the moon. His bruised and powdered look somehow went with his small, spaced teeth and the horizontal red tracks his glasses had left in the fat in front of his ears.

The man gazed at Frank with a gleaming, sagging lower lip, his nearsighted little eyes trying to assess the damage, the depth of the grudge. "Well, mea culpa, mea culpa, I guess, though I *didn't* tell Jojo and that *poisonous* Ed Jaffrey to go blabbing it all over town."

"Well, thanks for telling me, Wally, I guess." Depending on which man he was standing with, Frank felt large and straight and sonorous or, as with Wes, gracile and flighty. Sharon, scenting blood amid the vacuous burble of the party, pushed herself through the crowd and joined the two men. To deny Walton the pleasure, Frank quickly told her, "Wally just confessed to me he started the rumor because Charlie Whitfield downtown, who did run off with somebody, came from Ohio, too. Toledo, as I remember."

"Oh, that rumor," Sharon said, blinking once, as if her party mascara were
55   sticking. "I'd forgotten it. Who could believe it, of Frank?"

"Everybody, evidently," Frank said. It was possible, given the strange, willful ways of women, that she had forgotten it, even while Frank had been brooding over its possible justice. If the rumor were truly dispersed—and Walton would undoubtedly tell the story of his Freudian slip around town as a self-promoting joke on himself—Frank would feel diminished. He would lose that small sadistic power to make her watch him watching waiters in restaurants, and to bring her into town as his chaperon. He would feel emasculated if she no longer thought he had a secret. Yet that night, at the party, Walton Forney's Jojo had come up to him. He had seemed, despite an earring the size of a faucet washer and a stripe of bleach in the center of his hair, unexpectedly intelligent and low-key, offering, not in so many words, a kind of apology, and praising the tea-colored landscapes being offered for sale. "I've been thinking, in my own work, of going, you know, more traditional. You get this feeling of, like, a dead end with abstraction." The boy had a bony, rueful face, with a silvery line of a scar under one eye, and seemed uncertain in manner, hesitantly murmurous, as if at a point in life where he needed direction. The fat fool Forney could certainly not provide that, and it pleased Frank to imagine that Jojo was beginning to realize it.

The car as he and Sharon drove home together along the Hudson felt close; the heater fan blew oppressively, parchingly. "*You* were willing to believe it at first," he reminded her.

"Well, Avis seemed so definite. But you convinced me."

"How?"

She placed her hand high on his thigh and dug her fingers in, annoyingly, infuriatingly. "You know," she said, in a lower register, meant to be sexy, but almost inaudible with the noise of the heater fan.

60   "That could be mere performance," he warned her. "Women are fooled that way all the time."

"Who says?"

"Everybody. Books. Proust.[2] People aren't that simple."

"They're simple enough." Sharon said, in a neutral, defensive tone, removing her presumptuous hand.

"If you say so," he said, somewhat stoically, his mind drifting. That silvery line of a scar under Jojo's left eye . . . lean long muscles snugly wrapped in white skin . . . lofts . . . Hellenic fellowship,[3] exercise machines . . . direct negotiations, a simple transaction among equals. The rumor might be dead in the world, but in him it had come alive.

[1990]

---

[2]**Proust** Marcel Proust (1871–1922), French homosexual novelist.   [3]**Hellenic fellowship** Greek friendship, with the implication of erotic love between a mature man and a youth.

Topics for Critical Thinking and Writing

1. What point of view is used in the first paragraph of the story?
2. Consider the following line from the story:

   "I don't have a homosexual lover," Frank said, too calmly, ripping an auction ad out of the catalog.

   What is the point of view?
3. How would you characterize the point of view in the following passage, from near the end of the story?

   She placed her hand high on his thigh and dug her fingers in, annoyingly, infuriatingly. "You know," she said in a lower register, meant to be sexy, but almost inaudible with the noise of the heater fan.

4. Suppose the story had been told entirely from Sharon's point of view. What might have been gained? What might have been lost?
5. In an essay on fiction (see page 291), Updike wrote:

   I want stories to startle and engage me within the first few sentences, and in their middle to widen or deepen or sharpen my knowledge of human activity, and to end by giving me a sensation of completed statement.

Is this what you want from stories? If not, in what ways do your desires differ from Updike's? A second question: Do you think "The Rumor" meets Updike's criteria? Explain.

Oliver's Evolution

His parents had not meant to abuse him; they had meant to love him, and did love him. But Oliver had come late in their little pack of offspring, at a time when the challenge of child-rearing was wearing thin, and he proved susceptible to mishaps. A big fetus, cramped in his mother's womb, he was born with in-turned feet, and learned to crawl with corrective casts up to his ankles. When they were at last removed, he cried in terror, because he thought those heavy plaster boots scraping and bumping along the floor had been part of himself.

One day in his infancy they found him on their dressing-room floor with a box of mothballs, some of which were wet with saliva; in retrospect they wondered if there had really been a need to rush him to the hospital and have his poor little stomach pumped. His face was gray-green afterwards. The following summer, when he had learned to walk, his parents had unthinkingly swum away off the beach together, striving for romantic harmony the morning after a late party and an alcoholic quarrel, and were quite unaware, until they saw the lifeguard racing along the beach, that Oliver had toddled after them and had been floating on his face for what might have been, given a less alert lifeguard, a fatal couple of minutes. This time, his face was blue, and he coughed for hours.

He was the least complaining of their children. He did not blame his parents when neither they nor the school authorities detected his "sleepy" right eye in time for therapy, with the result that when he closed that eye everything looked intractably fuzzy. Just the sight of the boy holding a schoolbook at a curious angle to the light made his father want to weep, impotently.

And it happened that he was just the wrong, vulnerable age when his parents went through their separation and divorce. His older brothers were off in boarding school and college, embarked on manhood, free of family. His younger sister was small enough to find the new arrangements—the meals in restaurants with her father, the friendly men who appeared to take her mother out—exciting. But Oliver, at thirteen, felt the weight of the household descend on him; he made his mother's sense of abandonment his own. Again, his father impotently grieved. It was he, and not the boy, who was at fault, really, when the bad grades began to come in from day school, and then from college, and Oliver broke his arm falling down the frat stairs, or leaping, by another account of the confused incident, from a girl's dormitory window. Not one but several family automobiles met a ruinous end with him at the wheel, though with no more injury, as it happened, than contused knees and loosened front teeth. The teeth grew firm again, thank God, for his innocent smile, slowly spreading across his face as the full humor of his newest misadventure dawned, was one of his best features. His teeth were small and round and widely spaced—baby teeth.

5   Then he married, which seemed yet another mishap, to go with the late nights, abandoned jobs, and fallen-through opportunities of his life as a young adult. The girl, Alicia, was as accident-prone as he, given to substance abuse and unwanted pregnancies. Her emotional disturbances left herself and others bruised. By comparison Oliver was solid and surefooted, and she looked up to

him. This was the key. What we expect of others, they endeavor to provide. He held on to a job, and she held on to her pregnancies. You should see him now, with their two children, a fair little girl and a dark-haired boy. Oliver has grown broad, and holds the two of them at once. They are birds in a nest. He is a tree, a sheltering boulder. He is a protector of the weak.

[2000]

Topics for Critical Thinking and Writing

1. At the end of the fourth paragraph Updike tells us that the mature Oliver's "teeth were small and round and widely spaced—baby teeth." Why do you suppose he gives us this detail?
2. How plausible does Oliver's life seem to you? Explain.
3. The story consists primarily of description and narration, but in the final paragraph Updike—or the narrator—offers a meditative comment: "What we expect of others, they endeavor to provide." Two questions here: Do you think this comment is useful in the story? Second, do you believe this comment by and large is true? Explain.
4. Here is a comment by Garrison Keillor, in his book entitled *Leaving Home* (1987), on parenting:

> Selective ignorance, a cornerstone of child rearing. You don't put kids under surveillance: it might frighten you. Parents should sit tall in the saddle and look upon their troops with a noble and benevolent and extremely nearsighted gaze.

Your view? Oliver's parents' view? Oliver's view?

JOHN UPDIKE ON THE ART OF FICTION
Thinking about an Author's Manuscripts

Some writers like the late Vladimir Nabokov have made a point of destroying all manuscripts and intermediate stages of their works of art, thus presenting to posterity an implacably clean face. Others, like Theodore Dreiser, have been so solicitous of their remnants as to keep carbons of even their love letters.

• • •

I myself find other writers' drafts and worksheets fascinating; one draws closer, bending over (say) Keats' first version of "Ode to a Nightingale" in the British Museum, to the sacred flame, the furnace of mental concentration wherein a masterpiece was still ductile and yielding to blows of the pen. But inspecting such material is (like most science) a form of prying—we should not forget that what we glimpse here is the long and winding middle of a human process whose end is a *published thing*—shiny, fragrant, infinitely distributable—and whose beginning is the belief on the author's part that he or she has something to say, *something to deliver*. Both this vague initial impetus and solid end-product partake of ecstasy: however tainted and flawed the vehicles of their essence, the essence is clean and good. The creative process is lit from two directions—by the remembered flash of the first innocent and thrilling vision, and by the anticipated steady glow of the perfected, delivered result, in its crisp trimmings of manufacture. It takes strong light and high hope to bring the writer through the dreary maze of writing. Most of writing is reading—reading again, to regrasp what is there. As writers go, I am not much of a reviser, but, seeing these numerous papers spread out, I quailed at how multiple and fallible are the procedures that work toward even a straightforward text, which then when published is not safe, as long as the author lives, from further revision.

> [from "Preface to a Partial Catalog of My Own Leavings," in Elizabeth
> A. Falsey, *The Art of Adding and the Art of Taking Away* (Cambridge,
> MA: Harvard College Library, 1987), 3]

What a Short Story Is

A short story, like a Japanese print, is a glimpse; but a glimpse which implies in itself the world or life of which is is a moment.

Designed with an eye (or ear) for relevant detail, its requirements are tension, economy and precision. In a sense it often gives the lie to the old dictum that a story must have a beginning, a middle, and an end, for it is possible for a short story to be nothing but a middle, if the beginning is inferred by implication and the end foreseeable.

It can be nothing but an ending if in itself the end determines what has gone before, or nothing but a beginning if by valid characterization the outcome is made to seem inevitable.

> [Updike in *Esprit* Winter 1959, p. 11 (publication of the University of
> Scranton), answering the question: "What Is a Short Story?"]

What Updike as a Reader Wants from a Short Story

I want—perhaps we all want—facts, words I can picture. I want stories to startle and engage me within the first few sentences, and in their middle to widen or deepen or sharpen my knowledge of human activity, and to end by giving me a sensation of completed statement. The ending is where the reader discovers whether he has been reading the same story the writer thought he was writing. Two chains of impression have been running in rough parallel: the ending . . . confirms or dissolves the imagined partnership. . . . To explain . . . one's sensation of rightness slightly suffocates it: the *echt* ending is finer than analysis, an inner release, as Aristotle said, of tensions aroused. A narrative is like a room on whose walls a number of false doors have been painted; while within the narrative, we have many apparent choices of exit, but when the author leads us to one particular door, we know it is the right one *because it opens.* [xvi–xvii]

· · ·

I tried to enter each microcosm as it rotated into view and to single out those that somehow, in addition to beginning energetically and ending intelligibly, gave me a sense of deep entry, of entry into life somewhat below the surface of dialogue and description: this nebulous sense of deep entry corresponds to the sensation we get in looking at some representational paintings that render not merely the color and contours but the heft and internal cohesion of actual objects, which therefore exist on the canvas not as tinted flat shapes but as palpables posed in atmosphere. Skill alone cannot produce this extra fidelity to the real: it needs passion. [xix]

. . .

The inner spaces that a good short story lets us enter are the old apartments of religion. People in fiction are not only as E. M. Forster pointed out in his *Aspects of the Novel*, more sensitive than people one meets: they are more religious. Religion and fiction both aver, with Kierkegaard, that "subjectivity is truth"; each claims importance for the ephemeral sensations of consciousness that material science must regard as accidents, as epiphenomena. [xix–xx]

. . .

Our information about each other remains, in the midst of a sophistication glut, wonderfully faulty, and for this reason we read short stories. Each is a glimpse into another country, an occasion for surprise, an excuse for wisdom, and an argument for charity. [xxii]

[from *Best American Short Stories 1984*]

Fiction is, in some ways, simpler than it seems. You're first of all trying to create a *thereness*—a place, a state of weather possibly, the look of people. . . . I've tended to err (if error is there) on the generous side, since I've enjoyed those writers who give me plenty of tactile, visual sensations. One hopes, of course, that the description of, say, the weather also in some way creates an emotion—and that it even carries a certain thematic–symbolic weight. But I think you begin with just trying to get the images planted in the reader's mind—and then move on. Fiction is difficult to boil down to prescriptive terms. It's in reading other writers that you begin to find out what you want to do.

["The Art of Fiction: A Conversation with John Updike," *Sewanee Review* Summer 1996, p. 423]

On His Own Early Stories

My generation, one called Silent, was, in considerable fraction of its white majority, a fortunate one—"too young to be warriors, too old to be rebels," as it is put in the story "I Will Not Let Thee Go, Except Thou Bless Me."

. . .

We were simple and hopeful enough to launch into idealistic careers and early marriages, and pragmatic enough to adjust, with an American shrug, to the ebb of old certainties. Yes, though spared many of the material deprivations and religious terrors that had dogged our parents, and awash in a disproportionate share of the world's resources, we continued prey to what Freud called "normal human unhappiness."

But when has happiness ever been the subject of fiction? The pursuit of it is just that—a pursuit. Death and its adjutants tax each transaction. What is possessed is devalued by what is coveted. Discontent, conflict, waste, sorrow, fear—these are the worthy, inevitable subjects. Yet our hearts expect happiness, as an underlying norm, "the fountain-light of all our day" in Wordsworth's words. Rereading, I found no lack of joy in these stories, though it arrives by the moment and not by the month, and no lack of affection and goodwill among characters caught in the human plight, the plight of limitation and mortality. Art hopes to sidestep mortality with feats of attention, of harmony, of illuminating connection, while enjoying, it might be said, at best a slower kind of mortality: paper yellows, language becomes old-fashioned, revelatory human news passes into general social wisdom. [xiv]

[Preface to *The Early Stories 1953–1975* (2003), p. xiv]

On a Writer's Early Years

I really don't think I'm alone among writers in caring about what they experienced in the first eighteen years of their life. . . . Nothing that happens to us after twenty is as free from self-consciousness because by then we have the vocation to write. Writers' lives break into two halves. At the point where you get your writerly vocation you diminish your receptivity to experience. Being able to write becomes a kind of shield, a way of hiding, a way of too instantly transforming pain into honey—whereas when you're young, you're so impotent you cannot help but strive and observe and feel.

[In James Plath, ed., *Conversations with John Updike*, pp. 28–29, reprinted from *Paris Review*, 1968; interview with Charles Samuels]

On the Importance of Fiction

Fiction is nothing less than the subtlest instrument for self-examination and self-display that Mankind has invented yet. Psychology and X-rays bring up some portentous shadows, and demographics and stroboscopic photography do some fine breakdowns, but for the full *parfum* and effluvia of being human, for feathery ambiguity and rank facticity, for the air and iron, fire and spit of our daily mortal adventure three is nothing like fiction: it makes sociology look priggish, history problematical, the cinema two-dimensional, and the *National Enquirer* as silly as last week's cereal box.

In fiction, everything that searchers for the important tend to leave out is left in, and what they would have in is left out. [86]

• • •

The fiction writer is the ombudsman who argues our humble, dubious case in the halls of eternal record. Are defecation, tipsy bar babble, days of accumulating small defeats, and tired, compromised, smelly connubial love part of our existence? Then put them into literature alongside of Homer, says *Ulysses*. Has a life been ill-spent in snobbery, inaction, neurasthenia, and heartache? Then make that life into a verbal cathedral, says *Remembrance of Things Past*. Do pathetic and senseless-seeming murders appear daily in the newspapers? Then show the humble aspiration and good intentions and small missteps that inexorably lead to such ruin, say *Tess of the D'Urbervilles* and *An American Tragedy*. Feeling nervous, and as though things don't quite add up? Then write like Virginia Woolf and give us actuality in its sliding, luminous increments. [86]

• • •

No soul or locale is too humble to be the site of entertaining and instructive fiction. Indeed, all other things being equal, the rich and glamorous are *less* fertile ground than the poor and plain, and the dusty corners of the world of more real interest than its glittering, already sufficiently publicized centers. [87]

. . .

What is important, if not the human individual? And where can individuality be better confronted, appraised, and enjoyed than in fiction's shapely lies? [87]

["The Importance of Fiction," first published in *Esquire* Aug 1984; reprinted here from *Odd Jobs* (1991)]

11

Fiction into Film

ASKING QUESTIONS, THINKING CRITICALLY, AND MAKING COMPARISONS

In this chapter we offer some comments about the nature of film, some definitions of indispensable technical terms, a few suggestions about topics, and a list of questions to consider as you begin to think about writing on a film derived from a story.

FILM AS A MEDIUM

Your first thought may be that a film (excluding cartoons, documentaries, newsreels, and so on) is rather like a play: A story is presented by means of actors. There are, however, crucial distinctions between film and drama. First, though drama uses such visual matters as gestures, tableaux effects, and scenery, the plays that we value most highly are *literature:* The word dominates, the visual component is subordinate. You need not be a film fanatic who believes that the invention of the sound track was an impediment to film in order to realize that a film is more a matter of pictures than of words. The camera usually roves, giving us crowded streets, empty skies, rainy nights, or close-ups of filled ashtrays and chipped coffee cups. A critic has aptly said that in Ingmar Bergman's *Smiles of a Summer Night* (1955) "the almost unbearably ornate crystal goblets, by their aspect and their positioning in the image, convey the oppressive luxuriousness of the diners' lives in purely and uniquely filmic terms."

In short, the speaker in a film does not usually dominate. In a play the speaker normally holds the spectator's attention, but in a film when a character speaks, the camera often gives us a **reaction shot**, focusing not on the speaker but on the face or gestures of a character who is affected by the speech, thus giving the spectator a visual interpretation of the words. In François Truffaut's *400 Blows* (1959), for example, we hear a reform school official verbally assault a boy, but we see the uncomfortable boy, not the official. Even when the camera does focus on the speaker, it is likely to offer an interpretation. An extreme example is a scene from David Lean's *Brief Encounter* (1945): A gossip is talking, and the camera gives us a close-up of her jabbering mouth, which monstrously fills the screen.

The distance between film and drama can be put another way: A film is more like a short story or a novel than it is like a play, the action being presented not directly by actors but by a narrator, in this case the camera. The camera, like a narrator telling a story from a particular point of view, *comments* on the story while telling it. Thus, a filmmaker may use out-of-focus shots or slow-motion shots to communicate the strangeness of an experience. At the end of Arthur

Penn's *Bonnie and Clyde* (1968), when Clyde is riddled with bullets, because his collapse is shot in slow motion he seems endowed not only with unusual grace but also with almost superhuman powers of endurance.

Even the choice of film stock is part of the comment. A highly sensitive or "fast" film needs less light to catch an image than a "slow" film does, but it is usually grainier. Perhaps because black-and-white newsreels often used fast film, a grainy quality may suggest authenticity or realism. Robert Enrico's film (1962) of Ambrose Bierce's short story "An Occurrence at Owl Creek Bridge" a story about the hanging of a civilian farmer who is a Southern sympathizer during the Civil War) begins with low-contrast stock that gives a rich gradation of tones from white to black, reminiscent of Civil War photographs. The director John Huston similarly chose to use black and white for his film version (1951) of Stephen Crane's *The Red Badge of Courage,* a novel about cowardice and courage in the Civil War. Different film stocks may be used within a single motion picture. In Bergman's *Wild Strawberries* (1957), for instance, Bergman uses high-contrast stock for the nightmare sequence, though elsewhere in the film the contrasts are subtle. Color film has its own methods of tone and texture control.

The medium, as everyone knows, is part of the message; Laurence Olivier made Shakespeare's *Henry V* (1944) in color but *Hamlet* (1948) in black and white because these media say different things. Similarly, although by 1971 most fiction films were being made in color, Peter Bogdanovich made *The Last Picture Show* (1971) in black and white, partly to convey a sense of the unexciting life of a small town in America in the 1950s and partly to evoke the films of the fifties. When a film is made in color, however, the colors may be symbolic (or at least suggestive) as well as realistic. In Stanley Kubrick's *A Clockwork Orange* (1971), for example, which is based on a novel of the same title by Anthony Burgess (1962), hot colors (oranges and reds) conveying vitality and aggressiveness in the first half of the film are displaced in the second half by cool colors (blues and greens) when the emphasis turns to "clockwork"—to mechanization.

The kind of lens used also helps determine what the viewer sees. In Mike Nichols's *The Graduate* (1967), Benjamin runs toward the camera (he is trying to reach a church before his girl marries another man), but he seems to make no progress because a **telephoto lens** was used and thus his size does not increase as it normally would. The lens, that is, helps communicate Benjamin's desperate sense of frustration. Similarly, in *An Occurrence at Owl Creek Bridge,* Peyton Farquhar runs toward his wife in the foreground, but the telephoto lens makes it seem that he is making no progress. Conversely, a **wide-angle lens** makes a character approach the camera with menacing rapidity; she or he quickly looms into the foreground. But of course filmmakers, though resembling fiction writers in offering a pervasive indirect comment, are not fiction writers any more than they are playwrights or directors of plays. The medium has its own techniques, and a filmmaker works with these techniques, not with those of a playwright or of a short-story writer.

Perhaps the most obvious way that a film may comment (as a story-writer may) on the events and characters is through the use of **voice-over**: The voice of the narrator or of an off-camera person speaks, while the visuals and other sounds (music, birds twittering, whatever) continue. Discussing the film version (1993) of a novel by Edith Wharton, *The Age of Innocence* (1920), Martin Scorsese said that he found the narrator's voice enjoyable for its satiric observations about New York society and important for an understanding of the characters, and thus he chose to present some phases of the film with a voice-over that sets the background for and interprets the action. Some reviewers criticized this decision, saying that the voice-over was imposed and artificial, as though Scorcese did not think he could trust the characters on screen to communicate their thoughts and feelings. The implication of their criticism was that Scorcese had not found visual equivalents for a fiction-writer's verbal techniques.

For the film version (1987) of James Joyce's story "The Dead" (1914), John Huston made a related, though somewhat different and perhaps more successful, choice. At the close of the story, Gabriel Conroy discovers that his wife Gretta has for many years harbored a deep affection for a young man who died a tragic early death. The narrator concludes by describing Gabriel's mournful feelings as he reflects on his wife, his family and friends, the past, and the approach of death (e.g., "The time had come for him to set out on his journey westward."). Huston adapted the narrator's words and gave them to Gabriel, who speaks them in a voice-over as the camera moves from one shot to the next, from inside to outside the hotel room where he and Gretta are staying. Perhaps in this way Huston avoids the distancing effect that reviewers complained about in Scorcese's film; in the case of *The Dead,* the voice speaking is that of a central character.

FILM TECHNIQUES

At this point it may be well to suspend generalizations temporarily and to look more methodically at some techniques of filmmaking. What follows is a brief grammar and dictionary of film, naming and explaining the cinematic devices that help filmmakers embody their vision in a work of art. An essay on film will discuss some of these devices, but there is no merit in mechanically trotting them all out.

Shots

A **shot** is what is recorded between the time a camera starts and the time it stops, that is, between the director's call for "action" and the call to "cut." Perhaps the average shot is about 10 seconds (very rarely a fraction of a second, and usually not more than 15 or so seconds). The average film is about an hour and a half, with about 600 shots, but Alfred Hitchcock's *The Birds* (1963) uses 1,360 shots. Three common shots are (1) a **long shot** or **establishing shot**, showing the main object at a considerable distance from the camera and thus presenting it in relation to its general surroundings (for example, captured soldiers, seen across a prison yard, entering the yard); (2) a **medium shot**, showing the object in relation to its immediate surroundings (a couple of soldiers, from the knees up, with the yard's wall behind them); and (3) a **close-up**, showing only the main object, or, more often, only a part of it (a soldier's face or his bleeding feet).

In the outside world we can narrow our vision to the detail that interests us by moving our head and by focusing our eyes, ignoring what is not of immediate interest. The close-up is the movie director's chief way of directing our vision and of emphasizing a detail. (Another way is to focus sharply on the significant image, leaving the rest of the image in soft focus.) The close-up, a way of getting emphasis, has been heavily used in recent years, not always successfully. As Dwight

Macdonald said of John Schlesinger's *Midnight Cowboy* (1969) and *Getting Straight* (1970):

> [A] movie told in close-ups is like a comic book, or like a novel composed in punchy one-sentence paragraphs and set throughout in large caps. How refreshing is a long or middle shot, a glimpse of the real world, so lovely and so *far away*, in the midst of those interminable processions of [a] hairy ogre face.

Two excellent film versions of Shakespeare's *Henry V* nicely show the different effects that long shots and close-ups can produce. Laurence Olivier's version (1944) uses abundant long shots and, on the whole, conveys a highly pictorial sweeping epic version of the war in which Henry was engaged. The film was made during World War II as a patriotic effort to inspire the English by showing the heroism of combat. On the other hand, Kenneth Branagh's version, made in 1989, uses lots of close-ups of soldiers with mud-splattered faces, emphasizing the grittiness of war. Olivier brought out the splendor and romance, Branagh the labor and pain, of war.

While taking a shot, the camera can move: It can swing to the right or left while its base remains fixed (a **pan shot**), up or down while fixed on its axis (a **tilt shot**), forward or backward (a **traveling shot**), or in and out and up and down fastened to a crane (a **crane shot**). The **zoom lens**, introduced in the 1950s and widespread by the middle 1960s, enables the camera to change its focus fluidly so that it can approach a detail—as a traveling shot does—while remaining fixed in place. Much will depend on the angle (high or low) from which the shots are made. If the camera is high (a **high-angle shot**), looking down on figures, it usually will dwarf them, perhaps even reduce them to crawling insects, making them vulnerable, pitiful, or contemptible. The higher the angle, the more likely it is to suggest a God's-eye view of entrapped people. If the camera is low (a **low-angle shot**), close to the ground and looking up, thereby showing figures against the sky, it probably will give them added dignity. In F. W. Murnau's *Last Laugh* (1924), we first get low-angle shots of the self-confident doorman, communicating his grand view of himself; later, when he loses his strength and is reduced to working as a lavatory attendant, we see him from above, and he seems dwarfed. But these are not inevitable principles. A shot in Enrico's film version of Bierce's "An Occurrence at Owl Creek Bridge" shows the hangman from below, making him seem threatening. And a shot in Orson Welles's *Citizen Kane* (1941) shows Kane from above, but it does not dwarf him; rather, it shows him dominating his wife and then in effect obliterating her by casting a shadow over her. Similarly, a low-angle shot does not always add dignity: Films in which children play important parts often have lots of low-angle shots showing adults as menacing giants.

In short, by its distance from the subject, its height from the ground, and its angle of elevation, the camera comments on or interprets what happens. It seems to record reality, but it offers its own version. It is only a slight exaggeration to say that the camera always lies, that is, gives a personal vision of reality.

Slow motion and **fast motion** also offer comments. In Kenneth Branagh's *Henry V* (1989), as in Orson Welles's *Falstaff* (1966; also titled *Chimes at Midnight*), part of the battle is filmed in slow motion; thus, the weariness of the soldiers is emphasized. In Enrico's *An Occurrence at Owl Creek Bridge*, Peyton Farquhar, imagining that he has escaped from his executioners, sees them in slow motion.

Sequences

A group of related scenes—such as the three scenes of soldiers mentioned earlier—is a **sequence**, though a sequence is more likely to have thirty scenes than three. A sequence corresponds roughly to a chapter in a novel, the shots being sentences and the scenes being paragraphs. Within a sequence may be an **intercut**, a switch to another action that, for example, provides an ironic comment on the main action of the sequence. If intercuts are so abundant in a sequence that, in effect, two or more sequences are going at once (for example, shots of the villain about to ravish the heroine, alternating with shots of the hero riding to her rescue), we have **parallel editing** (also called a **crosscut**). In the example just given, probably the tempo would increase, the shots being progressively shorter as we get to the rescue.

Within a sequence, the **transitions** normally are made by **straight cuts**—a strip of film is spliced to another, and the result is an instantaneous transfer from one shot to the next. Usually, an audience is scarcely (if at all) conscious of transitions from, say, a long shot of a character to a medium shot of her or him, or from a close-up of a speaker to a close-up of her or his auditor. But sometimes the director wants the audience to be fully aware of the change, as an author may emphasize a change by beginning a new paragraph or, even more sharply, by beginning a new chapter. Two older, and now rather unfashionable, relatively conspicuous transitions are sometimes still used, usually between sequences rather than within a sequence. These are the **dissolve** (the shot dissolves while a new shot appears to emerge from beneath it, there being a moment when we get a superimposition of both scenes), and the **fade** (in the **fade-out** the screen grows darker until black; in the **fade-in** the screen grows lighter until the new scene is fully visible).

In effect the camera is saying "Let us now leave X and turn to Y," or "Two weeks later." Two older methods, even less in favor today than the dissolve and the fade but used in many excellent old films and in some modern films that seek an archaic effect, are the **wipe** (a sort of windshield wiper crosses the screen, wiping off the first scene and revealing the next), and the **iris** (in an **iris-in**, the new scene first appears in the center of the previous scene and then this circle expands until it fills the screen; an **iris-out** shows the new scene first appearing around the perimeter and then the circle closes in on the previous scene). Charles Chaplin more than once ended a scene with an iris-out of the tramp walking jauntily toward the horizon. François Truffaut used iris shots in *The Wild Child* (1970), suggesting by the encircling darkness the boy's isolation from most of the world surrounding him as he concentrated on a single object before him.

Editing

All of the transitions just discussed are examples of editing techniques. A film, no less than a poem or a play or a picture or a palace, is something made, and it is not made by simply exposing some film footage. Shots—often taken at widely separated times and places—must be appropriately joined. For example, we see a man look off to the right, and then we get a shot of what he is looking at and then a shot of his reaction. Until the shots are assembled, we don't have a film—we merely have the footage. The Russian director V. I. Pudovkin put it this way: "The film is not *shot,* but built, built up from the separate strips of celluloid that are its raw material." This building-up is the process of **editing**.

More than a story can be told, of course; something of the appropriate emotion can be communicated by juxtaposing, say, a medium-long shot of a group of impassively advancing soldiers against a close-up of a single terrified victim. Similarly, emotion can be communicated by the duration of the shots (quick shots suggest haste; prolonged shots suggest slowness) and by the lighting (progressively darker shots can suggest melancholy; progressively lighter shots can suggest hope or joy). An extremely obvious but effective example occurs in Charlie Chaplin's *Modern Times* (1936), a satire on industrialism. We see a mass of workers hurrying to their jobs, and a moment later we see a herd of sheep on the move, this shot providing a bitter comic comment on the previous shot.

The Russian theorists of film called this process of building by quick cuts **montage**. The theory held that shots, when placed together, add up to more than the sum of the parts. Montage, for them, was what made a film a work of art and not a mere replica of reality. American writers commonly use the term merely to denote quick cutting, and French writers use it merely in the sense of cutting.

All this talk about ingenious shots and their arrangement, then, assumes that the camera is a sort of pen, carefully setting forth images and thus at every point guiding the perceiver. The director (through the actors, camera technicians, cutters, and a host of others) makes an artifact, rather as a novelist makes a book or a sculptor makes a statue, and this artifact is an elaborate contraption that manipulates the spectators by telling them at every second exactly how they ought to feel. But since the 1950s, a reaction has occurred against such artistry, a feeling that although the elaborate editing of Sergei Eisenstein and the other Russians is an aesthetic triumph, it is also a moral failure because by its insistent tricky commentary it seems to deny the inherent worth of the event in itself as it happens. Moreover, just as the nineteenth-century narrator in the novel, who continually guided the reader ("Do not fear, gentle reader, for even at this moment plans were being laid . . . ") was in the twentieth-century novel sloughed off, forcing the readers in large measure to deduce the story for themselves, so, too, some contemporary filmmakers emphasize improvisation, fully aware that the film thus made will not at every point guide or dominate the viewer.

Film affects us through sound as well as sight, and a good film usually succeeds in integrating the action with well-handled and carefully paced dialogue and keen choices of music. The long opening sequence of Francis Ford Coppola's *Apocalypse Now* (1979)—a film loosely based on Joseph Conrad's *Heart of Darkness*—unfolds to the music of the late 1960s/early 1970s rock group The Doors, as lead singer Jim Morrison sings the haunting song "The End." Later, an astonishingly vivid, breathtaking helicopter assault on a Vietnamese village takes place to the accompaniment of the German composer Richard Wagner's stirring "Ride of the Valkyries," which blasts from a speaker mounted on one of the attacking helicopters.

THEME

It is time now to point out that mastery of technique, though necessary to good filmmaking, will not in itself make a good film. A good film is not a bag of cinematic devices but the embodiment, through cinematic devices, of a vision, an underlying theme. What is this theme or vision? It is a filmmaker's perception of some aspect of existence that he or she thinks is worthy of our interest. Normally, this perception involves characters and a plot. Recent American films, relying heavily on color, rock music in surround sound, quick cutting, and the wide screen, have tended to emphasize the emotional experience and deemphasize narrative. Still, most of the best cinema—and virtually every film based on a short story—is concerned with what people do, that is, with character and plot. Character is what people are, plot is what happens, but the line between character and plot fades, for what people are is in large measure what they do, and what is done is in large measure the result of what people are.

COMPARING FILMED AND PRINTED STORIES

After seeing a film based on a novel or short story that we know, most of us are drawn to compare the two and make judgments about which one is better. If the film is not conspicuously faithful to the story, we may complain about the loss of this character or that episode; but if it is highly faithful we may find ourselves complaining, "What a disappointment! It was just like the book but it seemed so dead!" This second response is not surprising; as indicated earlier, good films use the camera creatively, and a film that is content merely to record a narrative is likely to be a dull film.

Most of the time we will conclude that the printed fiction is superior to what is shown on the screen. But we might do well on occasion not to emphasize which is better, but, rather, to observe how entertainingly, interestingly, each works on its own. It's true that the use of voice-over may feel a bit wrong or jarring in *The Age of Innocence* (see pages 309–310), but the film is so stunning visually that the voice-over seems only a minor element in it—a distraction perhaps, but hardly a serious flaw. A similar argument could be raised about the choices made in the film versions of E. M. Forster's novel *Maurice* (published posthumously in 1971; film version 1987) and Henry James's *The Wings of the Dove* (1902; film version 1997). The frontal nudity and explicit lovemaking depicted in these films seems very far removed from the restraint and indirection of the novels themselves, in which sexual desire and activity are implied rather than shown, frequently touched on but never in graphic detail. But we could claim nonetheless that the films are in a sense true to the meanings of the novels—dramatizing encounters and themes that Forster and James, writing many decades ago, simply could not render with the fully detailed candor that is now possible. These films, then, are not literally faithful to the novel—on the subject of sexuality, they show more, much more, than the novels do. But the changes in the films may be for the better, or at least may strike us as understandable and defensible on the ground that they are in keeping with the expectations of a contemporary audience. The novels become revitalized—made to feel contemporary—because of the films' greater openness about daring illicit behavior.

GETTING READY TO WRITE

Mastery of terminology does not make anyone a perceptive film critic, but it helps writers communicate their perceptions to their readers. Probably an essay on a film will not be primarily about the use of establishing shots or of wipes or of any such matters; rather, it will be about the reasons why a particular film pleases or displeases, succeeds or fails, seems significant or insignificant, and in discussing these large matters it is sometimes necessary (or at least economical) to use the commonest technical terms. Large matters are often determined in part by such seemingly small matters as the distance of the camera from its subject or how transitions are made, and the writer may as well use the conventional terms. But it is also true that a filmmaker's technique and technology alone cannot make a first-rate film. An idea, a personal vision, a theme must be embodied in all that is flashed on the screen.

Writing an essay about a new film—one not yet available for study on VHS or DVD—presents difficulties not encountered in writing about printed stories. Because we experience film in a darkened room, we cannot easily take notes, and because the film may be shown only once, we cannot always take another look at passages that puzzle us. But

- You can take some brief notes even in the dark; it is best to amplify them as soon as light is available, while you still know what the scrawls mean.
- If you can see the film more than once, do so, and of course if the script has been published, study it.
- Draft your paper as soon as possible after your first viewing, and then see the film again, if possible.
- If you can, check hazy memories of certain scenes and techniques with fellow viewers.

DRAFTING AN ESSAY

First—but you may not discover this until you have written a draft or two—you need to have a *point*, a *thesis*. Your essay must do more than say that the film of a story is faithful to the original in points A, B, C, and D, and departs from the original in points E, F, G, and H. Your readers doubtless can see these things for themselves. Probably in your preliminary notes you will indeed want to list such things, but you will then want to go on to think about the significance of the resemblances and the differences. What do you make of them? Given the fact that film is a visual medium, is it possible that too much fidelity to a story—for instance, failure to give us interesting pictures—has turned a memorable short story into a boring movie? You will want to think about the resemblances and the differences between the story and the film, and you will want to account for them, first to yourself (probably you will have to write and revise at least one draft before you can do this). Then in your essay, you will explain to your reader why you respond the way you do.

Early in the essay it is desirable to sketch enough of the plot to give readers an idea of what happens. Do not try to recount everything that happens; it can't be done, and the attempt will frustrate you and bore your readers. Once you introduce the main characters and devote a few sentences to the plot, thus giving the readers a comfortable seat, get down to the job of convincing them that you have something interesting to say about the film—that the plot is trivial, or that the hero is not really cool but cruel, or that the plot and the characters are fine achievements but the camera work is sometimes needlessly tricky, or that all is well.

Incidentally, a convenient way to give an actor's name in your essay is to put it in parentheses after the character's name or role, thus: "The detective (Humphrey Bogart) finds a clue . . . " Then, as you go on to talk about the film, use the names of the characters or the roles, not the names of the actors, except of course when you are talking about the actors themselves, as in "Bogart is exactly right for the part."

✔ CHECKLIST: *Getting Ideas for Writing about Film*

These questions may help to bring impressions out into the open and may with
some reworking provide topics for essays.

Preliminaries

❏ Is the title significant? If the film's title differs from that of the published story, account for and evaluate the change.

Literary Adaptations

❏ Does the film slavishly follow its original and neglect the potentialities of the camera? Or does it so revel in cinematic devices that it distorts the original work? (Of course, an adaptation need not go to either extreme. Enrico's *An Occurrence at Owl Creek Bridge* is a close adaptation of Ambrose Bierce's story, and yet it is visually interesting.)

❏ Does the film do violence to the theme of the original? Is the film better than its source? Are the additions or omissions due to the medium or to a crude or faulty interpretation of the original?

Plot and Character

❏ How faithful is the film to the story in plot and in character? Evaluate the changes, if any.

❏ In the film version (1984) of Henry James's novel *The Bostonians* (1886), one of the protagonists, an impassioned feminist reformer, delivers a speech to an unruly crowd in a theater, which significantly changes the effect of the novel itself, where the speech is not given. What is the impact of a decision like this one (which is so at odds with the plot as the author shaped it), and what is your assessment of it? Is the film to be faulted for such a change, or does the change make good sense for the film's development of character and theme, however unfaithful it might be to the author's story?

❏ Can film deal as effectively with inner action—mental processes—as with external, physical action? In a given film, how is the inner action conveyed? By voice-over? Or by visual equivalents?

Setting

❏ How effectively does the film convey the setting or settings that the author chose for his or her story? Do the film's settings somehow fall short of the expressive power that they possess in the story itself?

Editing

❏ Does the editing—for instance frequent sharp juxtapositions, or slow panoramic shots—convey qualities that the story writer conveyed by means of sentence length or sentence structure?

❏ Are shots and sequences adequately developed, or do they seem jerky? (A shot may be jerky by being extremely brief or at an odd angle; a sequence may be jerky by using discontinuous images or fast cuts. Sometimes, of course, jerkiness may be desirable.) If such cinematic techniques as wipes, dissolves, and slow motion are used, are they meaningful and effective?

❑ Are the actors appropriately cast? Was it a mistake to cast Robert Redford as Gatsby in Jack Clayton's film version (1974) of *The Great Gatsby* (1925)? John Huston, in his film (1951) of Stephen Crane's *The Red Badge of Courage* (1894) used Audie Murphy, one of the most highly decorated and best-known heroes of World War II, as Henry Fleming, the young soldier who flees from battle but later gets a second chance to fight bravely. What is the effect of this casting?

Symbolism

❑ If in the story certain objects acquire symbolic meanings, are these same objects similarly used in the film? Or does the film introduce new symbols?

❑ Is the lighting in the film realistic, symbolic, or both?

Soundtrack

❑ Does the soundtrack offer more than realistic dialogue? (In *An Occurrence at Owl Creek Bridge,* for instance, we hear—much louder than normal—the sound of soldiers' boots on railroad ties, and we even hear the sound of the hangman's rope rubbing on a crossbeam.) Is the music appropriate and functional? (Music may, among other things, imitate natural sounds, give a sense of locale or of ethnic group, suggest states of mind, provide ironic commentary, or—by repeated melodies—help establish connections.) Are volume, tempo, and pitch—whether of music or of such sounds as the wind blowing or cars moving—used to stimulate emotions?

SUGGESTIONS FOR FURTHER READING

For quick reference, see Ephraim Katz, *The Film Encyclopedia,* 3rd ed. (1998); Leslie Halliwell, *The Filmgoer's Companion,* 12th ed. (1997); and *Halliwell's Film and Video Guide 2000,* ed. Leslie Halliwell and John Walker (2000). For somewhat fuller discussions of directors, ranging from two or three pages to eight or ten pages, see Richard Roud, ed., *Cinema: A Critical Dictionary: The Major Film-Makers,* 2 vols. (1980).

Good introductory books include Gerald Mast, *A Short History of the Movies,* 7th ed., rev. Bruce F. Kawin (1999); Leo Braudy, *The World in a Frame* (1984); Bruce F. Kawin, *How Movies Work* (1992); Thomas Sobchack and Vivian C. Sobchack, *An Introduction to Film,* 2nd ed. (1987); David Bordwell, *Making Meaning: Inference and Rhetoric in the Interpretation of Cinema* (1989); Edward R. Branigan, *Point of View in Cinema* (1984); and Timothy Corrigan, *A Short Guide to Writing about Film,* 3rd ed. (1997).

For theory, see Tim Bywater, *An Introduction to Film Criticism: Major Critical Approaches to Narrative Film* (1989), and *Film Theory and Criticism: Introductory Readings,* ed. Leo Braudy and Marshall Cohen, 5th ed. (1998). Another helpful book is James Monaco, *How to Read a Film: The World of Movies, Media, and Multimedia: Art, Technology, Language, History, Theory,* 3rd ed. (2000).

For an influential feminist study, consult Laura Mulvey, *Visual and Other Pleasures* (1989). See also *Issues in Feminist Film Criticism,* ed. Patricia Erens (1991); Maggie Humm, *Feminism and Film* (1997); Anneke Smelik, *And the Mirror Cracked: Feminist Cinema and Film Theory* (1998); and *Feminist Film Theory: A Reader,* ed. Sue Thornham (1999).

On the depiction of African Americans in films, see two books by Thomas Cripps: *Slow Fade to Black: The Negro in American Film, 1900–1942* (1993), and *Making Movies Black: The Hollywood Message Movie from World War II to the Civil Rights Era* (1993). Also recommended is Donald Bogle, *Toms, Coons, Mulattoes, Mammies, and Bucks: An Interpretive History of Blacks in American Films* (1994).

JOYCE CAROL OATES

Joyce Carol Oates was born in 1938 in Millerport, New York. She won a scholarship to Syracuse University, from which she graduated (Phi Beta Kappa and valedictorian) in 1960. She then did graduate work in English, first at the University of Wisconsin and then at Rice University, but she withdrew from Rice in order to be able to devote more time to writing. Her first collection of stories, By the North Gate, *was published in 1963; since then she has published at least forty books—stories, poems, essays, and (in twenty-five years) twenty-two novels. She has received many awards, has been elected to the American Academy and Institute of Arts and Letters, and now teaches creative writing at Princeton University.*

Where Are You Going, Where Have You Been?

To Bob Dylan

Her name was Connie. She was fifteen and she had a quick nervous giggling habit of craning her neck to glance into mirrors or checking other people's faces to make sure her own was all right. Her mother, who noticed everything and knew everything and who hadn't much reason any longer to look at her own face, always scolded Connie about it. "Stop gawking at yourself, who are you? You think you're so pretty?" she would say. Connie would raise her eyebrows at these familiar complaints and look right through her mother, into a shadowy vision of herself as she was right at that moment: she knew she was pretty and that was everything. Her mother had been pretty once too, if you could believe those old snapshots in the album, but now her looks were gone and that was why she was always after Connie.

"Why don't you keep your room clean like your sister? How've you got your hair fixed—what the hell stinks? Hair spray? You don't see your sister using that junk."

Her sister June was twenty-four and still lived at home. She was a secretary in the high school Connie attended, and if that wasn't bad enough—with her in the same building—she was so plain and chunky and steady that Connie had to hear her praised all the time by her mother and her mother's sisters. June did this, June did that, she saved money and helped clean the house and cooked and Connie couldn't do a thing, her mind was all filled with trashy daydreams. Their father was away at work most of the time and when he came home he wanted supper and he read the newspaper at supper and after supper he went to bed. He didn't bother talking much to them, but around his bent head Connie's mother kept picking at her until Connie wished her mother was dead and she herself was dead and it was all over. "She makes me want to throw up sometimes," she complained to her friends. She had a high, breathless, amused voice which made everything she said sound a little forced, whether it was sincere or not.

There was one good thing: June went places with girlfriends of hers, girls who were just as plain and steady as she, and so when Connie wanted to do that her mother had no objections. The father of Connie's best girlfriend drove the girls the three miles to town and left them off at a shopping plaza, so that they could walk through the stores or go to a movie, and when he came to pick them up again at eleven he never bothered to ask what they had done.

5   They must have been familiar sights, walking around that shopping plaza in their shorts and flat ballerina slippers that always scuffed the sidewalk, with charm bracelets jingling on their thin wrists; they would lean together to whisper and laugh secretly if someone passed by who amused or interested them. Connie had long dark blond hair that drew anyone's eye to it, and she wore part of it pulled up on her head and puffed out and the rest of it she let fall down her back. She wore a pull-over jersey blouse that looked one way when she was at home and another way when she was away from home. Everything about her had two sides to it, one for home and one for anywhere that was not home: her walk that could be childlike and bobbing, or languid enough to make anyone think she was hearing music in her head, her mouth which was pale and smirking most of the time, but bright and pink on these evenings out, her laugh which was cynical and drawling at home—"Ha, ha, very funny"—but high-pitched and nervous anywhere else, like the jingling of the charms on her bracelet.

Sometimes they did go shopping or to a movie, but sometimes they went across the highway, ducking fast across the busy road, to a drive-in restaurant where older kids hung out. The restaurant was shaped like a big bottle, though squatter than a real bottle, and on its cap was a revolving figure of a grinning boy who held a hamburger aloft. One night in midsummer they ran across, breathless with daring, and right away someone leaned out a car window and invited them over, but it was just a boy from high school they didn't like. It made them feel good to be able to ignore him. They went up through the maze of parked and cruising cars to the bright-lit, fly-infested restaurant, their faces pleased and expectant as if they were entering a sacred building that loomed out of the night to give them what haven and what blessing they yearned for. They sat at the counter and crossed their legs at the ankles, their thin shoulders rigid with excitement, and listened to the music that made everything so good: the music was always in the background like music at a church service, it was something to depend upon.

A boy named Eddie came in to talk with them. He sat backward on his stool, turning himself jerkily around in semicircles and then stopping and turning again, and after a while he asked Connie if she would like something to eat. She said she did and so she tapped her friend's arm on her way out—her friend pulled her face up into a brave droll look—and Connie said she would meet her at eleven, across the way. "I just hate to leave her like that," Connie said earnestly, but the boy said that she wouldn't be alone for long. So they went out to his car and on the way Connie couldn't help but let her eyes wander over the windshields and faces all around her, her face gleaming with a joy that had nothing to do with Eddie or even this place; it might have been the music. She drew her shoulders up and sucked in her breath with the pure pleasure of being alive, and just at that moment she happened to glance at a face just a few feet from hers. It was a boy with shaggy black hair, in a convertible jalopy painted gold. He stared at her and then his lips widened into a grin. Connie slit her eyes at him and turned away, but she couldn't help glancing back and there he was still watching her. He wagged a finger and laughed and said, "Gonna get you, baby," and Connie turned away again without Eddie noticing anything.

She spent three hours with him, at the restaurant where they ate hamburgers and drank Cokes in wax cups that were always sweating, and then down an alley a mile or so away, and when he left her off at five to eleven only the movie house was still open at the plaza. Her girlfriend was there, talking with a boy. When Connie came up the two girls smiled at each other and Connie said, "How was the movie?" and the girl said, "*You* should know." They rode off with the girl's father, sleepy and pleased, and Connie couldn't help but look at the darkened shopping plaza with its big empty parking lot and its signs that were faded and ghostly now, and over at the drive-in restaurant where cars were still circling tirelessly. She couldn't hear the music at this distance.

Next morning June asked her how the movie was and Connie said, "So-so."

10   She and that girl and occasionally another girl went out several times a week that way, and the rest of the time Connie spent around the house—it was summer vacation—getting in her mother's way and thinking, dreaming, about the boys she met. But all the boys fell back and dissolved into a single face that was not even a face, but an idea, a feeling, mixed up with the urgent insistent pounding of the music and the humid night air of July. Connie's mother kept dragging her back to the daylight by finding things for her to do or saying, suddenly, "What's this about the Pettinger girl?"

And Connie would say nervously, "Oh, her. That dope." She always drew thick clear lines between herself and such girls, and her mother was simple and kindly enough to believe her. Her mother was so simple, Connie thought, that it was maybe cruel to fool her so much. Her mother went scuffling around the house in old bedroom slippers and complained over the telephone to one sister about the other, then the other called up and the two of them complained about the third one. If June's name was mentioned her mother's tone was approving, and if Connie's name was mentioned it was disapproving. This did not really mean she disliked Connie and actually Connie thought that her mother preferred her to June because she was prettier, but the two of them kept up a pretense of exasperation, a sense that they were tugging and struggling over something of little value to either of them. Sometimes, over coffee, they were almost friends, but something would come up—some vexation that was like a fly buzzing suddenly around their heads—and their faces went hard with contempt.

One Sunday Connie got up at eleven—none of them bothered with church— and washed her hair so that it could dry all day long, in the sun. Her parents and sister were going to a barbecue at an aunt's house and Connie said no, she wasn't interested, rolling her eyes to let her mother know just what she thought of it. "Stay home alone then," her mother said sharply. Connie sat out back in a lawn chair and watched them drive away, her father quiet and bald, hunched around so that he could back the car out, her mother with a look that was still angry and not at all softened through the windshield, and in the back seat poor old June all dressed up as if she didn't know what a barbecue was, with all the running yelling kids and the flies. Connie sat with her eyes closed in the sun, dreaming and dazed with the warmth about her as if this were a kind of love, the caresses of love, and her mind slipped over onto thoughts of the boy she had been with the night before and how nice he had been, how sweet it always was, not the way someone like June would suppose but sweet, gentle, the way it was in movies and promised in songs; and when she opened her eyes she hardly knew where she was, the back yard ran off into weeds and a fence line of trees and be- hind it the sky was perfectly blue and still. The asbestos "ranch house" that was now three years old startled her—it looked small. She shook her head as if to get awake.

It was too hot. She went inside the house and turned on the radio to drown out the quiet. She sat on the edge of her bed, barefoot, and listened for an hour and a half to a program called XYZ Sunday Jamboree, record after record of hard, fast, shrieking songs she sang along with, interspersed by exclamations from "Bobby King": "An' look here you girls at Napoleon's—Son and Charley want you to pay real close attention to this song coming up!"

And Connie paid close attention herself, bathed in a glow of slow-pulsed joy that seemed to rise mysteriously out of the music itself and lay languidly about the airless little room, breathed in and breathed out with each gentle rise and fall of her chest.

15   After a while she heard a car coming up the drive. She sat up at once, star- tled, because it couldn't be her father so soon. The gravel kept crunching all the way in from the road—the driveway was long—and Connie ran to the window. It was a car she didn't know. It was an open jalopy, painted a bright gold that caught the sunlight opaquely. Her heart began to pound and her fingers snatched at her hair, checking it, and she whispered "Christ, Christ," wondering how bad she looked. The car came to a stop at the side door and the horn sounded four short taps as if this were a signal Connie knew.

She went into the kitchen and approached the door slowly, then hung out the screen door, her bare toes curling down off the step. There were two boys in the car and now she recognized the driver: he had shaggy, shabby black hair that looked crazy as a wig and he was grinning at her.

"I ain't late, am I?" he said.

"Who the hell do you think you are?" Connie said.

"Toldja I'd be out, didn't I?"

20   "I don't even know who you are."

She spoke sullenly, careful to show no interest or pleasure, and he spoke in a fast bright monotone. Connie looked past him to the other boy, taking her time. He had fair brown hair, with a lock that fell onto his forehead. His sideburns gave him a fierce, embarrassed look, but so far he hadn't even bothered to glance at her. Both boys wore sunglasses. The driver's glasses were metallic and mirrored everything in miniature.

"You wanta come for a ride?" he said.

Connie smirked and let her hair fall loose over one shoulder.

"Don'tcha like my car? New paint job," he said. "Hey."

25   "What?"

"You're cute."

She pretended to fidget, chasing flies away from the door.

"Don'tcha believe me, or what?" he said.

"Look, I don't even know who you are," Connie said in disgust.

30   "Hey, Ellie's got a radio, see. Mine's broke down." He lifted his friend's arm and showed her the little transistor the boy was holding, and now Connie began to hear the music. It was the same program that was playing inside the house.

"Bobby King?" she said.

"I listen to him all the time. I think he's great."

"He's kind of great." Connie said reluctantly.

"Listen, that guy's *great*. He knows where the action is."

35   Connie blushed a little, because the glasses made it impossible for her to see just what this boy was looking at. She couldn't decide if she liked him or if he was just a jerk, and so she dawdled in the doorway and wouldn't come down or go back inside. She said, "What's all that stuff painted on your car?"

"Can'tcha read it?" He opened the door very carefully, as if he was afraid it might fall off. He slid out just as carefully, planting his feet firmly on the ground, the tiny metallic world in his glasses slowing down like gelatine hardening and in the midst of it Connie's bright green blouse. "This here is my name, to begin with," he said. ARNOLD FRIEND was written in tarlike black letters on the side, with a drawing of a round grinning face that reminded Connie of a pumpkin, except it wore sunglasses. "I wanta introduce myself, I'm Arnold Friend and that's my real name and I'm gonna be your friend, honey, and inside the car's Ellie Oscar, he's kinda shy." Ellie brought his transistor radio up to his shoulder and balanced it there. "Now these numbers are a secret code, honey," Arnold Friend explained. He read off the numbers 33, 19, 17 and raised his eyebrows at her to see what she thought of that, but she didn't think much of it. The left rear fender had been smashed and around it was written, on the gleaming gold background: DONE BY CRAZY WOMAN DRIVER. Connie had to laugh at that. Arnold Friend was pleased at her laughter and looked up at her. "Around the other side's a lot more—you wanta come and see them?"

"No."

"Why not?"

"Why should I?"

40   "Don'tcha wanta see what's on the car? Don'tcha wanta go for a ride?"

"I don't know."

"Why not?"

"I got things to do."

"Like what?"

45   "Things."

He laughed as if she had said something funny. He slapped his thighs. He was standing in a strange way, leaning back against the car as if he were balancing himself. He wasn't tall, only an inch or so taller than she would be if she came down to him. Connie liked the way he was dressed, which was the way all of them dressed: tight faded jeans stuffed into black, scuffed boots, a belt that pulled his waist in and showed how lean he was, and a white pullover shirt that was a little soiled and showed the hard small muscles of his arms and shoulders. He looked as if he probably did hard work, lifting and carrying things. Even his neck looked muscular. And his face was a familiar face, somehow: the jaw and chin and cheeks slightly darkened, because he hadn't shaved for a day or two, and the nose long and hawklike, sniffing as if she were a treat he was going to gobble up and it was all a joke.

"Connie, you ain't telling the truth. This is your day set aside for a ride with me and you know it," he said, still laughing. The way he straightened and recovered from his fit of laughing showed that it had been all fake.

"How do you know what my name is?" she said suspiciously.

"It's Connie."

50   "Maybe and maybe not."

"I know my Connie," he said, wagging his finger. Now she remembered him even better, back at the restaurant, and her cheeks warmed at the thought of how she sucked in her breath just at the moment she passed him—how she must have looked to him. And he had remembered her. "Ellie and I come out here especially for you," he said. "Ellie can sit in back. How about it?"

"Where?"

"Where what?"

"Where're we going?"

55   He looked at her. He took off the sunglasses and she saw how pale the skin around his eyes was, like holes that were not in shadow but instead in light. His eyes were like chips of broken glass that catch the light in an amiable way. He smiled. It was as if the idea of going for a ride somewhere, to some place, was a new idea to him.

"Just for a ride, Connie sweetheart."

"I never said my name was Connie," she said.

"But I know what it is. I know your name and all about you, lots of things," Arnold Friend said. He had not moved yet but stood still leaning back against the side of his jalopy. "I took a special interest in you, such a pretty girl, and found out all about you like I know your parents and sister are gone somewheres and I know where and how long they're going to be gone, and I know who you were with last night, and your best girlfriend's name is Betty. Right?"

He spoke in a simple lilting voice, exactly as if he were reciting the words to a song. His smile assured her that everything was fine. In the car Ellie turned up the volume on his radio and did not bother to look around at them.

60   "Ellie can sit in the back seat," Arnold Friend said. He indicated his friend with a casual jerk of his chin, as if Ellie did not count and she should not bother with him.

"How'd you find out all that stuff?" Connie said.

"Listen: Betty Schultz and Tony Fitch and Jimmy Pettinger and Nancy Pettinger," he said, in a chant. "Raymond Stanley and Bob Hutter—"

"Do you know all those kids?"

"I know everybody."

65   "Look, you're kidding. You're not from around here."

"Sure."

"But—how come we never saw you before?"

"Sure you saw me before," he said. He looked down at his boots, as if he were a little offended. "You just don't remember."

"I guess I'd remember you," Connie said.

70   "Yeah?" He looked up at this, beaming. He was pleased. He began to mark time with the music from Ellie's radio, tapping his fists lightly together. Connie looked away from his smile to the car, which was painted so bright it almost hurt her eyes to look at it. She looked at that name, ARNOLD FRIEND. And up at the front fender was an expression that was familiar—MAN THE FLYING SAUCERS. It was an expression kids had used the year before, but didn't use this year. She looked at it for a while as if the words meant something to her that she did not yet know.

"What're you thinking about? Huh?" Arnold Friend demanded. "Not worried about your hair blowing around in the car, are you?"

"No."

"Think I maybe can't drive good?"

"How do I know?"

75   "You're a hard girl to handle. How come?" he said. "Don't you know I'm your friend? Didn't you see me put my sign in the air when you walked by?"

"What sign?"

"My sign." And he drew an X in the air, leaning out toward her. They were maybe ten feet apart. After his hand fell back to his side the X was still in the air, almost visible. Connie let the screen door close and stood perfectly still inside it, listening to the music from her radio and the boy's blend together. She stared at Arnold Friend. He stood there so stiffly relaxed, pretending to be relaxed, with one hand idly on the door handle as if he were keeping himself up that way and had no intention of ever moving again. She recognized most things about him, the tight jeans that showed his thighs and buttocks and the greasy leather boots and the tight shirt, and even that slippery friendly smile of his, that sleepy dreamy smile that all the boys used to get across ideas they didn't want to put into words. She recognized all this and also the singsong way he talked, slightly mocking, kidding, but serious and a little melancholy, and she recognized the way he tapped one fist against the other in homage to the perpetual music behind him. But all these things did not come together.

She said suddenly, "Hey, how old are you?"

His smile faded. She could see then that he wasn't a kid, he was much older—thirty, maybe more. At this knowledge her heart began to pound faster.

80 "That's a crazy thing to ask. Can'tcha see I'm your own age?"

"Like hell you are."

"Or maybe a coupla years older, I'm eighteen."

"Eighteen?" she said doubtfully.

He grinned to reassure her and lines appeared at the corners of his mouth. His teeth were big and white. He grinned so broadly his eyes became slits and she saw how thick the lashes were, thick and black as if painted with a black tar-like material. Then he seemed to become embarrassed, abruptly, and looked over his shoulder at Ellie. "*Him,* he's crazy," he said. "Ain't he a riot, he's a nut, a real character." Ellie was still listening to the music. His sunglasses told nothing about what he was thinking. He wore a bright orange shirt unbuttoned halfway to show his chest, which was a pale, bluish chest and not muscular like Arnold Friend's. His shirt collar was turned up all around and the very tips of the collar pointed out past his chin as if they were protecting him. He was pressing the transistor radio up against his ear and sat there in a kind of daze, right in the sun.

85 "He's kinda strange," Connie said.

"Hey, she says you're kinda strange! Kinda strange!" Arnold Friend cried. He pounded on the car to get Ellie's attention. Ellie turned for the first time and Connie saw with shock that he wasn't a kid either—he had a fair, hairless face, cheeks reddened slightly as if the veins grew too close to the surface of his skin, the face of a forty-year-old baby. Connie felt a wave of dizziness rise in her at this sight and she stared at him as if waiting for something to change the shock of the moment, make it all right again. Ellie's lips kept shaping words, mumbling along, with the words blasting in his ear.

"Maybe you two better go away," Connie said faintly.

"What? How come?" Arnold Friend cried. "We come out here to take you for a ride. It's Sunday." He had the voice of the man on the radio now. It was the same voice, Connie thought. "Don'tcha know it's Sunday all day and honey, no matter who you were with last night today you're with Arnold Friend and don't you forget it!—Maybe you better step out here," he said, and this last was in a different voice. It was a little flatter, as if the heat was finally getting to him.

"No. I got things to do."

90 "Hey."

"You two better leave."

"We ain't leaving until you come with us."

"Like hell I am—"

"Connie, don't fool around with me. I mean, I mean, don't fool *around,*" he said, shaking his head. He laughed incredulously. He placed his sunglasses on top of his head, carefully, as if he were indeed wearing a wig, and brought the stems down behind his ears. Connie stared at him, another wave of dizziness and fear rising in her so that for a moment he wasn't even in focus but was just a blur, standing there against his gold car, and she had the idea that he had driven up the driveway all right but had come from nowhere before that and belonged nowhere and that everything about him and even about the music that was so familiar to her was only half real.

95   "If my father comes and sees you—"

"He ain't coming. He's at barbecue."

"How do you know that?"

"Aunt Tillie's. Right now they're—uh—they're drinking. Sitting around," he said vaguely, squinting as if he were staring all the way to town and over to Aunt Tillie's back yard. Then the vision seemed to get clear and he nodded energetically. "Yeah. Sitting around. There's your sister in a blue dress, huh? And high heels, the poor sad bitch—nothing like you, sweetheart! And your mother's helping some fat woman with the corn, they're cleaning the corn—husking the corn—"

"What fat woman?" Connie cried.

100   "How do I know what fat woman. I don't know every goddam fat woman in the world!" Arnold Friend laughed.

"Oh, that's Mrs. Hornby. . . . Who invited her?" Connie said. She felt a little light-headed. Her breath was coming quickly.

"She's too fat. I don't like them fat. I like them the way you are, honey," he said, smiling sleepily at her. They stared at each other for a while, through the screen door. He said softly, "Now what you're going to do is this: you're going to come out that door. You're going to sit up front with me and Ellie's going to sit in the back, the hell with Ellie, right? This isn't Ellie's date. You're my date. I'm your lover, honey."

"What? You're crazy—"

"Yes, I'm your lover. You don't know what that is but you will," he said. "I know that too. I know all about you. But look: it's real nice and you couldn't ask for nobody better than me, or more polite. I always keep my word. I'll tell you how it is, I'm always nice at first, the first time. I'll hold you so tight you won't think you have to try to get away or pretend anything because you'll know you can't. And I'll come inside you where it's all secret and you'll give in to me and you'll love me—"

105   "Shut up! You're crazy!" Connie said. She backed away from the door. She put her hands against her ears as if she'd heard something terrible, something not meant for her. "People don't talk like that, you're crazy," she muttered. Her heart was almost too big now for her chest and its pumping made sweat break out all over her. She looked out to see Arnold Friend pause and then take a step toward the porch lurching. He almost fell. But, like a clever drunken man, he managed to catch his balance. He wobbled in his high boots and grabbed hold of one of the porch posts.

"Honey?" he said. "You still listening?"

"Get the hell out of here!"

"Be nice, honey. Listen."

"I'm going to call the police—"

110   He wobbled again and out of the side of his mouth came a fast spat curse, an aside not meant for her to hear. But even this "Christ!" sounded forced. Then he began to smile again. She watched this smile come, awkward as if he were smiling from inside a mask. His whole face was a mask, she thought wildly, tanned down onto his throat but then running out as if he had plastered makeup on his face but had forgotten about his throat.

"Honey—? Listen, here's how it is. I always tell the truth and I promise you this: I ain't coming in that house after you."

"You better not! I'm going to call the police if you—if you don't—"

"Honey," he said, talking right through her voice, "honey, I'm not coming in there but you are coming out here. You know why?"

She was panting. The kitchen looked like a place she had never seen before, some room she had run inside but which wasn't good enough, wasn't going to help her. The kitchen window had never had a curtain, after three years, and there were dishes in the sink for her to do—probably—and if you ran your hand across the table you'd probably feel something sticky there.

115   "You listening, honey? Hey?"

"—going to call the police—"

"Soon as you touch the phone I don't need to keep my promise and can come inside. You won't want that."

She rushed forward and tried to lock the door. Her fingers were shaking. "But why lock it," Arnold Friend said gently, talking right into her face. "It's just a screen door. It's just nothing." One of his boots was at a strange angle, as if his foot wasn't in it. It pointed out to the left, bent at the ankle. "I mean, anybody can break through a screen door and glass and wood and iron or anything else if he needs to, anybody at all and specially Arnold Friend. If the place got lit up with a fire honey you'd come runnin' out into my arms, right into my arms an' safe at home—like you knew I was your lover and'd stopped fooling around. I don't mind a nice shy girl but I don't like no fooling around." Part of those words were spoken with a slight rhythmic lilt, and Connie somehow recognized them—the echo of a song from last year, about a girl rushing into her boyfriend's arms and coming home again—

Connie stood barefoot on the linoleum floor, staring at him. "What do you want?" she whispered.

120   "I want you," he said.

"What?"

"Seen you that night and thought, that's the one, yes sir. I never needed to look any more."

"But my father's coming back. He's coming to get me. I had to wash my hair first—" She spoke in a dry, rapid voice, hardly raising it for him to hear.

"No, your Daddy is not coming and yes, you had to wash your hair and you washed it for me. It's nice and shining and all for me, I thank you, sweetheart," he said, with a mock bow, but again he almost lost his balance. He had to bend and adjust his boots. Evidently his feet did not go all the way down; the boots must have been stuffed with something so that he would seem taller. Connie stared out at him and behind him Ellie in the car, who seemed to be looking off toward Connie's right into nothing. This Ellie said, pulling the words out of the air one after another as if he were just discovering them, "You want me to pull out the phone?"

125 "Shut your mouth and keep it shut," Arnold Friend said, his face red from bending over or maybe from embarrassment because Connie had seen his boots. "This ain't none of your business."

"What—what are you doing? What do you want?" Connie said. "If I call the police they'll get you, they'll arrest you—"

"Promise was not to come in unless you touch that phone, and I'll keep that promise," he said. He resumed his erect position and tried to force his shoulders back. He sounded like a hero in a movie, declaring something important. He spoke too loudly and it was as if he were speaking to someone behind Connie. "I ain't made plans for coming in that house where I don't belong but just for you to come out to me, the way you should. Don't you know who I am?"

"You're crazy," she whispered. She backed away from the door but did not want to go into another part of the house, as if this would give him permission to come through the door. "What do you . . . You're crazy, you . . ."

"Huh? What're you saying, honey?"

130 Her eyes darted everywhere in the kitchen. She could not remember what it was, this room.

"This is how it is, honey: you come out and we'll drive away, have a nice ride. But if you don't come out we're gonna wait till your people come home and then they're all going to get it."

"You want that telephone pulled out?" Ellie said. He held the radio away from his ear and grimaced, as if without the radio the air was too much for him.

"I toldja shut up, Ellie," Arnold Friend said, "you're deaf, get a hearing aid, right? Fix yourself up. This little girl's no trouble and's gonna be nice to me, so Ellie keep to yourself, this ain't your date—right? Don't hem in on me. Don't hog. Don't crush. Don't bird dog. Don't trail me," he said in a rapid meaningless voice, as if he were running through all the expressions he'd learned but was no longer sure which one of them was in style, then rushing on to new ones, making them up with his eyes closed, "Don't crawl under my fence, don't squeeze in my chipmunk hole, don't sniff my glue, suck my popsicle, keep your own greasy fingers on yourself!" He shaded his eyes and peered in at Connie, who was backed against the kitchen table. "Don't mind him honey he's just a creep. He's a dope. Right? I'm the boy for you and like I said you come out here nice like a lady and give me your hand, and nobody else gets hurt, I mean, your nice old bald-headed daddy and your mummy and your sister in her high heels. Because listen: why bring them in this?"

"Leave me alone," Connie whispered.

135 "Hey, you know that old woman down the road, the one with the chickens and stuff—you know her?"

"She's dead!"

"Dead? What? You know her?" Arnold Friend said.

"She's dead—"

"Don't you like her?"

140 "She's dead—she's—she isn't here any more—"

"But don't you like her, I mean, you got something against her? Some grudge or something?" Then his voice dipped as if he were conscious of a rudeness. He touched the sunglasses perched on top of his head as if to make sure they were still there. "Now you be a good girl."

"What are you going to do?"

"Just two things, or maybe three," Arnold Friend said. "But I promise it won't last long and you'll like me the way you get to like people you're close to. You

will. It's all over for you here, so come on out. You don't want your people in any
trouble, do you?"

She turned and bumped against a chair or something, hurting her leg, but she
ran into the back room and picked up the telephone. Something roared in her ear,
a tiny roaring, and she was so sick with fear that she could do nothing but listen
to it—the telephone was clammy and very heavy and her fingers groped down to
the dial but were too weak to touch it. She began to scream into the phone, into
the roaring. She cried out, she cried for her mother, she felt her breath start jerking back and forth in her lungs as if it were something Arnold Friend were stabbing her with again and again with no tenderness. A noisy sorrowful wailing rose
all about her and she was locked inside it the way she was locked inside the
house.

145   After a while she could hear again. She was sitting on the floor with her wet
back against the wall.

Arnold Friend was saying from the door, "That's a good girl. Put the phone
back."

She kicked the phone away from her.

"No, honey. Pick it up. Put it back right."

She picked it up and put it back. The dial tone stopped.

150   "That's a good girl. Now come outside."

She was hollow with what had been fear, but what was now just an emptiness. All that screaming had blasted it out of her. She sat, one leg cramped under
her, and deep inside her brain was something like a pinpoint of light that kept going and would not let her relax. She thought, I'm not going to see my mother
again. She thought, I'm not going to sleep in my bed again. Her bright green
blouse was all wet.

Arnold Friend said, in a gentle-loud voice that was like a stage voice, "The
place where you came from ain't there any more, and where you had in mind to
go is canceled out. This place you are now—inside your daddy's house—is nothing but a cardboard box I can knock down any time. You know that and always
did know it. You hear me?"

She thought, I have got to think. I have to know what to do.

"We'll go out to a nice field, out in the country here where it smells so nice
and it's sunny," Arnold Friend said. "I'll have my arms tight around you so you
won't need to try to get away and I'll show you what love is like, what it does.
The hell with this house! It looks solid all right," he said. He ran a fingernail down
the screen and the noise did not make Connie shiver, as it would have the day before. "Now put your hand on your heart, honey. Feel that? That feels solid too but
we know better, be nice to me, be sweet like you can because what else is there
for a girl like you but to be sweet and pretty and give in?—and get away before
her people come back?"

155   She felt her pounding heart. Her hand seemed to enclose it. She thought for
the first time in her life that it was nothing that was hers, that belonged to her, but
just a pounding, living thing inside this body that wasn't really hers either.

"You don't want them to get hurt," Arnold Friend went on. "Now get up,
honey. Get up all by yourself."

She stood up.

"Now turn this way. That's right. Come over here to me—Ellie, put that away,
didn't I tell you? You dope. You miserable creepy dope," Arnold Friend said. His
words were not angry but only part of an incantation. The incantation was kindly.
"Now come out through the kitchen to me honey, and let's see a smile, try it,

you're a brave sweet little girl and now they're eating corn and hot dogs cooked to bursting over an outdoor fire, and they don't know one thing about you and never did and honey you're better than them because not a one of them would have done this for you."

Connie felt the linoleum under her feet; it was cool. She brushed her hair back out of her eyes. Arnold Friend let go of the post tentatively and opened his arms for her, his elbows pointing in toward each other and his wrists limp, to show that this was an embarrassed embrace and a little mocking, he didn't want to make her self-conscious.

160   She put out her hand against the screen. She watched herself push the door slowly open as if she were safe back somewhere in the other doorway, watching this body and this head of long hair moving out into the sunlight where Arnold Friend waited.

"My sweet little blue-eyed girl," he said, in a half-sung sigh that had nothing to do with her brown eyes but was taken up just the same by the vast sunlit reaches of the land behind him and on all sides of him, so much land that Connie had never seen before and did not recognize except to know that she was going to it.

[1966]

Topics for Critical Thinking and Writing

1. Characterize Connie. Do you think the early characterization of Connie prepares us for her later behavior?
2. Is Arnold Friend clairvoyant—definitely, definitely not, maybe? Explain.
3. Evaluate the view that Arnold's friend is both Satan and the incarnation of Connie's erotic desires.
4. What do you make of the fact that Oates dedicated the story to Bob Dylan? Is she perhaps contrasting Dylan's music with the escapist (or in some other way unwholesome) music of other popular singers?
5. If you have read Flannery O'Connor's "A Good Man Is Hard to Find" (p. 255), compare and contrast Arnold Friend and the Misfit.

"Where Are You Going, Where Have You Been?" and Smooth Talk: *Short Story into Film*

Some years ago in the American Southwest there surfaced a tabloid psychopath known as "The Pied Piper of Tucson." I have forgotten his name, but his speciality was the seduction and occasional murder of teen-aged girls. He may or may not have had actual accomplices, but his bizarre activities were known among a circle of teenagers in the Tucson area; for some reason they kept his secret, deliberately did not inform parents or police. It was this fact, not the fact of the mass murderer himself, that struck me at the time. And this was a pre-Manson time, early or mid-1960s.

The Pied Piper mimicked teenagers in their talk, dress, and behavior, but he was not a teenager—he was a man in his early thirties. Rather short, he stuffed rags in his leather boots to give himself height. (And sometimes walked unsteadily as a consequence: did none among his admiring constituency notice?) He charmed his victims as charismatic psychopaths have always charmed their victims, to the bewilderment of others who fancy themselves free of all lunatic attractions. The Pied Piper of Tucson: a trashy dream, a tabloid archetype, sheer artifice, comedy, cartoon—surrounded, however improbably, and finally tragically, by real people. You think that, if you look twice, he won't be there. But there he is.

I don't remember any longer where I first read about this Pied Piper—very likely in *Life* Magazine. I do recall deliberately not reading the full article because I didn't want to be distracted by too much detail. It was not after all the mass murderer himself who intrigued me, but the disturbing fact that a number of teenagers—from "good" families—aided and abetted his crimes. This is the sort of thing authorities and responsible citizens invariably call "inexplicable" because they can't find explanations for it. *They* would not have fallen under this maniac's spell, after all.

An early draft of my short story, "Where Are you Going, Where Have You Been?"—from which the film *Smooth Talk* was adapted by Joyce Chopra and Tom Cole—had the rather too explicit title "Death and the Maiden." It was cast in a mode of fiction to which I am still partial—indeed, every third or fourth story of mine is probably in this mode—"realistic allegory," it might be called. It is Hawthornean, romantic, shading into parable. Like the medieval German engraving from which my title was taken, the story was minutely detailed yet clearly an allegory of the fatal attractions of death (or the devil). An innocent young girl is seduced by way of her own vanity; she mistakes death for erotic romance of a particularly American/trashy sort.

5   In subsequent drafts the story changed its tone, its focus, its language, its title. It became "Where Are You Going, Where Have You Been?" Written at a time when the author was intrigued by the music of Bob Dylan, particularly the hauntingly elegiac song "It's All Over Now, Baby Blue," it was dedicated to Bob Dylan. The charismatic mass murderer drops into the background and his innocent victim, a fifteen-year-old moves into the foreground. She becomes the true protagonist of the tale, courting and being courted by her fate, a self-styled 1950s pop figure, alternately absurd and winning. There is no suggestion in the published story that, "Arnold Friend" has seduced and murdered other young girls, or even that he necessarily intends to murder Connie. Is his interest "merely" sexual? (Nor is there anything about the complicity of other teenagers. I saved that yet more provocative note for a current story, "Testimony.") Connie is shallow, vain, silly, hopeful, doomed—but capable nonetheless of an unexpected gesture of heroism at the story's end. Her smooth-talking seducer, who cannot lie, promises her that her family will be unharmed if she gives herself to him; and so she does. The story ends abruptly at the point of her "crossing over." We don't know the nature of her sacrifice, only that she is generous enough to make it.

In adapting a narrative so spare and thematically foreshortened as "Where Are You Going, Where Have You Been?" film director Joyce Chopra and screenwriter Tom Cole were required to do a good deal of filling in, expanding, inventing. Connie's story becomes lavishly, and lovingly, textured; she is not an allegorical figure so much as a "typical" teenaged girl (if Laura Dern, spectacularly good-looking, can be so defined). Joyce Chopra, who has done documentary films on contemporary teenage culture and, yet more authoritatively, has an adolescent daughter of her own, creates in *Smooth Talk* a vivid and absolutely believable world for Connie to inhabit. Or worlds: as in the original story there is

Connie-at-home, and there is Connie-with-her-friends. Two fifteen-year-old girls, two finely honed styles, two voices, sometimes but not often overlapping. It is one of the marvelous visual features of the film that we *see* Connie and her friends transform themselves, once they are safely free of parental observation. The girls claim their true identities in the neighborhood shopping mall. What freedom, what joy!

Smooth Talk is, in a way, as much Connie's mother's story as it is Connie's; its center of gravity, its emotional nexus, is frequently with the mother—warmly and convincingly played by Mary Kay Place. (Though the mother's sexual jealousy of her daughter is slighted in the film.) Connie's ambiguous relationship with her affable, somewhat mysterious father (well played by Levon Helm) is an excellent touch: I had thought, subsequent to the story's publication, that I should have built up the father, suggesting, as subtly as I could, an attraction there paralleling the attraction Connie feels for her seducer, Arnold Friend. And Arnold Friend himself—"A. Friend" as he says —is played with appropriately overdone sexual swagger by Treat Williams, who is perfect for the part; and just the right age. We see that Arnold Friend isn't a teenager even as Connie, mesmerized by his presumed charm, does not seem to *see* him at all. What is so difficult to accomplish in prose—nudging the reader to look over the protagonist's shoulder, so to speak—is accomplished with enviable ease in film.

Treat Williams as Arnold Friend is supreme in his very awfulness, as, surely, the original Pied Piper of Tucson must have been. (Though no one involved in the film knew about the original source.) Mr. Williams flawlessly impersonates Arnold Friend as Arnold Friend impersonates—is it James Dean? James Dean regarding himself in mirrors, doing James Dean impersonations? That Connie's fate is so trashy is in fact her fate.

What is outstanding in Joyce Chopra's *Smooth Talk* is its visual freshness, its sense of motion and life; the attentive intelligence the director has brought to the semi-secret world of the American adolescent—shopping mall flirtations, drive-in restaurant romances, highway hitchhiking, the fascination of rock music played very, very loud. (James Taylor's music for the film is wonderfully appropriate. We hear it as Connie hears it; it is the music of her spiritual being.) Also outstanding, as I have indicated, and numerous critics have noted, are the acting performances. Laura Dern is so dazzlingly right as "my" Connie that I may come to think I modeled the fictitious girl on her, in the way that writers frequently delude themselves about motions of causality.

10 My difficulties with *Smooth Talk* have primarily to do with my chronic hesitation—about seeing/hearing work of mine abstracted from its contexture of language. All writers know that language is their subject; quirky word choices, patterns of rhythm, enigmatic pauses, punctuation marks. Where the quick scanner sees "quick" writing, the writer conceals nine tenths of the iceberg. Of course we all have "real" subjects, and we will fight to the death to defend those subjects, but beneath the tale-telling it is the tale-telling that grips us so very fiercely. The writer works in a single dimension, the director works in three. I assume they are professionals to their fingertips; authorities in their medium as I am an authority (if I am) in mine. I would fiercely defend the placement of a semicolon in one of my novels but I would probably have deferred in the end to Joyce Chopra's decision to reverse the story's conclusion, turn it upside down, in a sense, so that the film ends not with death, not with a sleepwalker's crossing over to her fate, but upon a scene of reconciliation, rejuvenation.

A girl's loss of virginity, bittersweet but not necessarily tragic. Not today. A girl's coming-of-age that involves her succumbing to, but then rejecting, the "trashy dreams" of her pop teenage culture. "Where Are You Going, Where Have You Been?" defines itself as allegorical in its conclusion: Death and Death's chariot (a funky souped-up convertible) have come for the Maiden. Awakening is, in the story's final lines, moving out into the sunlight where Arnold Friend waits:

> "My sweet little blue-eyed girl," he said in a half-sung sigh that had nothing to do with [Connie's] brown eyes but was taken up just the same by the vast sunlit reaches of the land behind him and on all sides of him—so much land that Connie had never seen before and did not recognize except to know that she was going to it.

—a conclusion impossible to transfigure into film.

[1986]

Your Turn: Thinking about Filming Fiction

When you read a story and consider its possibilities as a film, you may want to begin thinking along these lines:

- Which story included in this book is your favorite? Do you think that this story could be made into a good film? Are there features of the story—its setting, for example—that, in your view, would work very well in a film version? Are there also features of this story that would be hard to convey in a film?

- There have been film versions (in some instances, more than one) of a number of well-known novels by English and American authors, including Jane Austen, Emily and Charlotte Brontë, Charles Dickens, Thomas Hardy, Edith Wharton, E. M. Forster, and Ernest Hemingway, to name just a few. Have you seen a film version of a novel by one of these authors, or by another author whom you admire? What was your response to the film? (*Note:* If you'd like to check on whether a novel or story has been made into a film, you can search for the title on the Web site "The Internet Movie Database" at <http://www.us.imdb.com>.)

- What does it feel like to read a really absorbing story or novel? Do you have the same feeling, or a different one, when you watch an absorbing film? Which experience appeals to you more, reading literature or seeing films?

12

Reading and Writing about Drama

TYPES OF PLAYS

Most of the world's great plays written before the twentieth century may be regarded as one of two kinds: **tragedy** or **comedy**. Roughly speaking, tragedy dramatizes the conflict between the vitality of the individual life and the laws or limits of life. The tragic hero reaches a height, going beyond the experience of others but at the cost of his or her life. Comedy, on the other hand, dramatizes the vitality of the laws of social life. In comedy, the good life is seen to reside in the shedding of an individualism that isolates, in favor of a union with a genial and enlightened society. These points must be amplified a bit before we go on to the further point that, of course, any important play does much more than can be put into such crude formulas.

Tragedy

Tragic heroes usually go beyond the standards to which reasonable people adhere; they do some fearful deed which ultimately destroys them. This deed is often said to be an act of **hubris**, a Greek word meaning something like "overweening pride." It may involve, for instance, violating a taboo, such as that against taking life. But if the hubristic act ultimately destroys the man or woman who performs it, it also shows that person (paradoxically) to be in some way more fully a living being—a person who has experienced life more fully, whether by heroic action or by capacity for enduring suffering—than the other characters in the play. (If the tragic hero does not die, he or she is usually left in some deathlike state, as is the blind Oedipus in *Oedipus Rex*.) In tragedy we see humanity pushed to an extreme; the hero enters a world unknown to most and reveals magnificence. After the hero's departure from the stage, we are left in a world of littler people.

What has just been said may (or may not) be true of most tragedies, but it certainly is not true of all. If you are writing about a tragedy, you might consider whether the points just made are illustrated in your play. Is the hero guilty of hubris? Does the hero seem a greater person than the others in the play? An essay examining such questions probably requires not only a character sketch but also some comparison with other characters.

Tragedy commonly involves **irony** of two sorts: unconsciously ironic deeds and unconsciously ironic speeches. Ironic deeds have some consequence more or less the reverse of what the doer intends. Macbeth thinks that by killing Duncan he will gain happiness, but he finds that his deed brings him sleepless nights. Brutus thinks that by killing Caesar he will bring liberty to Rome, but he brings tyranny. In an unconsciously ironic speech, the words mean one thing to the speaker but something more significant to the audience, as when King Duncan, baffled by Cawdor's treason, says:

> There's no art
> To find the mind's construction in the face:
> He was a gentleman on whom I built
> An absolute trust.

At this moment Macbeth, whom we have already heard meditating the murder of Duncan, enters. Duncan's words are true, but he does not apply them to Macbeth, as the audience does. A few moments later Duncan praises Macbeth as "a peerless kinsman." Soon Macbeth will indeed become peerless, when he kills Duncan and ascends to the throne.[1] Sophocles' use of ironic deeds and speeches is so pervasive, especially in *Oedipus Rex,* that **Sophoclean irony** has become a critical term.

When the deed backfires or has a reverse effect, such as Macbeth's effort to gain happiness has, we have what Aristotle (the first—and still the greatest—drama critic) called a **peripeteia**, or a **reversal**. A character who comes to perceive what has happened (Macbeth's "I have lived long enough: my way of life / Is fall'n into the sere, the yellow leaf") experiences (in Aristotle's language) an **anagnorisis**, or **recognition**. Strictly speaking, for Aristotle the recognition was a matter of literal identification—for example, the recognition that Oedipus was the son of a man he killed. In *Macbeth,* the recognition in this sense is that Macduff, "from his mother's womb / Untimely ripped," is the man who fits the prophecy that Macbeth can be conquered only by someone not "of woman born."

In his analysis of drama, Aristotle says that the tragic hero comes to grief through his **hamartia**, a term sometimes translated as **tragic flaw** but perhaps better translated as **tragic error**, since *flaw* implies a moral fault. Thus it is a great error for Hamlet not to inspect the foils at the start of the deadly fencing match with Laertes; had he done so, he would have seen that one of the foils was blunt and one pointed. If we hold to the translation *flaw,* we begin to hunt for a fault in the tragic hero's character; and we say, for instance, that Hamlet is gullible, or some such thing. In doing this, we may diminish or even overlook the hero's grandeur.

Comedy

Although in tragedy the hero usually seems to embody certain values that are superior to those of the surrounding society, in comedy the fullest life is seen to reside *within* enlightened social norms: At the beginning of a comedy we find banished dukes, unhappy lovers, crabby parents, jealous husbands, and harsh laws; but at the end we usually have a unified and genial society, often symbolized by a marriage feast to which everyone, or almost everyone, is invited. Early in *A Midsummer Night's Dream,* for instance, we meet quarreling young lovers and a father who demands that his daughter either marry a man she does not love or enter a convent. Such is the Athenian law. At the end of the play the lovers are properly matched, to everyone's satisfaction.

---

[1]**Dramatic irony** (ironic deeds, or happenings, and unconsciously ironic speeches) must be distinguished from **verbal irony**, which is produced when the speaker is *conscious* that his words mean something different from what they say. In *Macbeth* Lennox says, "The gracious Duncan / Was pitied of Macbeth. Marry, he was dead! / And the right valiant Banquo walked too late./. . ./ Men must not walk too late." He *says* nothing about Macbeth having killed Duncan and Banquo, but he *means* that Macbeth has killed them.

Speaking broadly, most comedies fall into one of two classes: **satiric comedy** or **romantic comedy**. In satiric comedy, the emphasis is on the obstructionists— the irate fathers, hardheaded businessmen, and other members of the establishment who at the beginning of the play seem to hold all the cards, preventing joy from reigning. They are held up to ridicule because they are repressive monomaniacs enslaved to themselves, acting mechanistically (always irate, always hardheaded) instead of responding genially to the ups and downs of life. The outwitting of these obstructionists, usually by the younger generation, often provides the resolution of the plot. Ben Jonson, Molière, and George Bernard Shaw are in this tradition; their comedy, according to an ancient Roman formula, "chastens morals with ridicule"—that is, it reforms folly or vice by laughing at it. On the other hand, in romantic comedy (think of Shakespeare's *A Midsummer Night's Dream, As You Like It,* and *Twelfth Night*) the emphasis is on a pair or pairs of delightful people who engage our sympathies as they run their obstacle race to the altar. There are obstructionists here too, but the emphasis is on festivity.

In writing about comedy you may, of course, be concerned with the function of one scene or character. But whatever your topic, you may find it helpful to begin by trying to decide whether the play is primarily romantic or primarily satiric (or something else). One way of getting at this is to ask yourself to what degree you sympathize with the characters. Do you laugh *with* them, sympathetically, or on the other hand do you laugh *at* them, regarding them as at least somewhat contemptible?

ELEMENTS OF DRAMA
Theme

If we have read or seen a drama thoughtfully, we ought to be able to formulate its **theme**, its underlying idea—and perhaps we can even go so far as to say its moral attitudes, its view of life, its wisdom. Some critics, it is true, have argued that the concept of theme is meaningless. They hold that *Macbeth,* for example, gives us only an extremely detailed history of one imaginary man. In this view, *Macbeth* says nothing to you or me; it only says what happened to some imaginary man. Even *Julius Caesar* says nothing about the historical Julius Caesar or about the nature of Roman politics. Here we can agree; no one would offer Shakespeare's play as evidence of what the historical Caesar said or did. But surely the view that the concept of theme is meaningless, and that a work tells us only about imaginary creatures, is a desperate one. We *can* say that we see in *Julius Caesar* the fall of power, or (if we are thinking of Brutus) the vulnerability of idealism, or some such thing.

To the reply that these are mere truisms, we can counter: Yes, but the truisms are presented in such a way that they take on life and become a part of us rather than remain things of which we say, "I've heard it said, and I guess it's so." The play offers instruction, in a pleasant and persuasive way. And surely we are in no danger of equating the play with the theme that we sense underlies it. We recognize that the play presents the theme with such detail that our statement is only a wedge to help us enter into the play, so we can appropriate it more fully.

Some critics (influenced by Aristotle's statement that a drama is an imitation of an action) use **action** in a sense equivalent to theme. In this sense, the action is the underlying happening—the inner happening—for example, "the enlightenment of a character," or "the coming of unhappiness to a character," or "the finding of the self by self-surrender." It might be said that the theme of *Macbeth,* for example, is embodied in some words that Macbeth himself utters: "Blood will have blood." Of course this is not to say that these words and no other words embody the theme or the action; it is only to say that these words seem to the writer (and, if the essay is effective, to the reader) to bring us close to the center of the play.

Plot

Plot is variously defined, sometimes as equivalent to *story* (in this sense a synopsis of *Julius Caesar* has the same plot as *Julius Caesar*), but more often, and more usefully, as the dramatist's particular *arrangement of the story.* Thus, because Shakespeare's *Julius Caesar* begins with a scene dramatizing an encounter between plebeians and tribunes, its plot is different from that of a play on Julius Caesar in which such a scene (not necessary to the story) is omitted.

Handbooks on drama often suggest that a plot (arrangement of happenings) should have a **rising action**, a **climax**, and a **falling action**. This sort of plot can be diagramed as a pyramid: The tension rises through complications or **crises** to a climax, at which point the climax is the apex, and the tension allegedly slackens as we witness the **dénouement** (literally, *unknotting*). Shakespeare sometimes used a pyramidal structure, placing his climax neatly in the middle of what seems to us to be the third of five acts. In *Hamlet,* the protagonist proves to his own satisfaction Claudius's guilt in 3.2, with the play within the play; but almost immediately he begins to worsen his position, by failing to kill Claudius when he is an easy target (3.3) and by contaminating himself with the murder of Polonius (3.4). In *Romeo and Juliet,* the first half shows Romeo winning Juliet; but when in 3.1 he kills her cousin Tybalt, Romeo sets in motion the second half of the play, the losing of Juliet and of his own life.

Of course, no law demands such a structure, and a hunt for the pyramid usually causes the hunter to overlook all the crises but the middle one. William Butler Yeats once suggestively diagramed a good plot not as a pyramid but as a line moving diagonally upward, punctuated by several crises. Perhaps it is sufficient to say that a good plot has its moments of tension, but the location of these will vary with the play. They are the product of **conflict**, but it should be noted that not all conflict produces tension; there is conflict but little tension in a ball game when the home team is ahead 10–0 and the visiting pitcher comes to bat in the ninth inning with two out and none on base.

Regardless of how a plot is diagramed, the **exposition** is that part that tells the audience what it has to know about the past, the **antecedent action**. Two gossiping servants who tell each other that after a year away in Paris the young master is coming home tomorrow with a new wife are giving the audience the exposition. But the exposition may also extend far into the play, being given in small, explosive revelations.

Exposition has been discussed as though it consists simply of informing the audience about events, but exposition can do much more. It can give us an understanding of the characters who themselves are talking about other characters, it can evoke a mood, and it can generate tension. When we summarize the opening act, and treat it as "mere exposition," we are probably losing what is dramatic in it.

In fact, exposition usually includes **foreshadowing**. Details given in the exposition, which we may at first take as mere background, often turn out to be highly relevant to later developments. For instance, in the very short first scene of *Macbeth* the witches introduce the name of Macbeth, but in such words as "Fair is foul" and "when the battle's lost and won" they also give glimpses of what will happen: Macbeth will become foul, and though he will seem to win (he becomes king) he will lose the most important battle. Similarly, during the exposition in the second scene we learn that Macbeth has loyally defeated Cawdor, who betrayed King Duncan, and Macbeth has been given Cawdor's title. Later we will find that, like Cawdor, Macbeth betrays Duncan. That is, in giving us the background about Cawdor, the exposition is also telling us (though we don't know it, when we first see or read the play) something about what will happen to Macbeth.

In writing about an aspect of plot, you may want to consider one of the following topics:

- Is the plot improbable? If so, is the play therefore weak?
- Does a scene that might at first glance seem unimportant or even irrelevant serve an important function?
- If certain actions that could be shown onstage take place offstage, is there a reason? In *Macbeth,* for instance, why do you suppose the murder of Duncan takes place offstage, whereas Banquo and Macduff's family are murdered onstage? Why, then, might Shakespeare have preferred not to show us the murder of Duncan? What has he gained? (A good way to approach this sort of question is to think of what your own reaction would be if the action were shown on the stage.)
- If there are several conflicts—for example, between pairs of lovers or between parents and their children and also between the parents themselves—how are these conflicts related? Are they parallel? Or contrasting?
- Does the arrangement of scenes have a structure? For instance, do the scenes depict a rise and then a fall?
- Does the plot seem satisfactorily concluded? Are there loose threads? If so, is the apparent lack of a complete resolution a weakness in the play? Or does it serve a function?

Gestures

The language of a play, broadly conceived, includes the **gestures** that the characters make and the settings in which they make them. As Ezra Pound says, "The medium of drama is not words, but persons moving about on a stage using words." Because plays are meant to be seen, make every effort to visualize the action when you read a play. Ibsen is getting at something important when he tells us in a stage direction that Nora "walks cautiously over to the door to the study and listens." Her silent actions tell us as much about her as many of her speeches do.

Gesture can be interpreted even more broadly: The mere fact that a character enters, leaves, or does not enter may be highly significant. John Russell Brown comments on the actions and the absence of certain words that in *Hamlet* convey the growing separation between King Claudius and his wife, Gertrude:

Their first appearance together with a public celebration of marriage is a large and simple visual effect, and Gertrude's close concern for her son suggests a simple, and perhaps unremarkable modification. . . . But Claudius enters without Gertrude for his "Prayer Scene" (3.2) and, for the first time, Gertrude enters without him for the Closet Scene (3.4) and is left alone, again for the first time, when Polonius hides behind the arras. Thereafter earlier accord is revalued by an increasing separation, often poignantly silent and unexpected. When Claudius calls Gertrude to leave with him after Hamlet has dragged off

Polonius' body, she makes no reply; twice more he urges her and she is still silent. But he does not remonstrate or question; rather he speaks of his own immediate concerns and, far from supporting her with assurances, becomes more aware of his own fears:

> O, come away!
> My soul is full of discord and dismay. (4.1.44–45)

Emotion has been so heightened that it is remarkable that they leave together without further words. The audience has been aware of a new distance between Gertrude and Claudius, of her immobility and silence, and of his self-concern, haste, and insistence.[2]

Setting

Drama of the nineteenth and early twentieth centuries (for example, the plays of Henrik Ibsen, Anton Chekhov, and George Bernard Shaw) is often thought to be "realistic," but even a realistic playwright or stage designer selects from among many available materials. A **realistic setting** (indication of the **locale**), then, can say a great deal, and can even serve as a symbol. Over and over again in Ibsen we find the realistic setting of a nineteenth-century drawing room, with its heavy draperies and its bulky furniture, helping to convey his vision of a bourgeois world that oppresses the individual who struggles to affirm other values.

Twentieth-century dramatists are often explicit about the symbolic qualities of the setting. Here is an example from Eugene O'Neill's *Desire Under the Elms;* only a part of the initial stage direction is given:

> The house is in good condition but in need of paint. Its walls are a sickly grayish, the green of the shutters faded. Two enormous elms are on each side of the house. They bend their trailing branches down over the roof. They appear to protect and at the same time subdue. There is a sinister maternity in their aspect, a crushing, jealous absorption. . . . They are like exhausted women resting their sagging breasts and hands and hair on its roof.

Not surprisingly, the action in the play includes deeds of "sinister maternity" (a mother kills her infant) and "jealous absorption."

In *The Glass Menagerie* Tennessee Williams tells us that

> the apartment faces an alley and is entered by a fire-escape, a structure whose name is a touch of accidental poetic truth, for all of these huge buildings are always burning with the slow and implacable fires of human desperation.

Characterization and Motivation

Characterization, or personality, is defined, as in fiction (see pages 28–29), by what the characters do (a stage direction tells us that "Nora dances more and more wildly"), by what they say (she asks her husband to play the piano), by what others say about them, and by the setting in which they move. The characters are also defined in part by other characters whom they in some degree resemble or from whom they in some degree differ. Hamlet, Laertes, and Fortinbras have each lost their fathers, but Hamlet spares the praying King Claudius, whereas Laertes, seeking

---

[2]*Shakespeare's Plays in Performance* (New York: St. Martin's, 1967), p. 139.

vengeance on Hamlet for murdering Laertes's father, says he would cut Hamlet's throat in church; Hamlet meditates about the nature of action, but Fortinbras leads the Norwegians in a military campaign and ultimately acquires Denmark.

Other plays, of course, also provide examples of such **foils**, or characters who set one another off. Macbeth and Banquo both hear prophecies, but they act and react differently; Brutus is one kind of assassin, Cassius another, and Casca still another. Any analysis of a character, then, will probably have to take into account, in some degree, the other characters who help to show what he or she is, and who thus help to set forth his or her **motivation** (grounds for action, inner drives, goals).

ORGANIZING AN ANALYSIS OF A CHARACTER

As you read and reread, you'll annotate the text and will jot down (in whatever order they come to you) your thoughts about the character you are studying. Reading, with a view toward writing, you'll want to

1. jot down traits as they come to mind ("kind," "forgetful," "enthusiastic");
2. look back at the text, searching for supporting evidence (characteristic actions, brief supporting quotations); and of course you will also look for counterevidence so that you may modify your earlier impressions.

Brainstorming leads to an evaluation of your ideas and to a shaping of them. Evaluating and shaping lead to a tentative outline, and a tentative outline leads to the search for supporting evidence—the material that will constitute the body of your essay.

When you set out to write a first draft, review your annotations and notes and see if you can summarize your view of the character in one or two sentences:

> X is . . . ,

or

> Although X is . . . , she is also. . . .

That is, try to formulate a thesis sentence or a thesis paragraph, a proposition that you will go on to support.

You want to let your reader know early, probably in your first sentence—and almost certainly by the end of your first paragraph—which character you are writing about and what your overall thesis is.

First Draft

Here is the first draft of an **opening paragraph** that identifies the character and sets forth a thesis:

> Romeo is a very interesting character, I think. In the
>
> beginning of the play Romeo is very adolescent. Romeo is smitten
>
> with puppy love for a woman named Rosaline. He desires to show
>
> all of his friends that he knows how a lover is supposed to act.

When he sees Juliet he experiences true love. From the point when

he sees Juliet he experiences true love, and from this point he

steadily matures in <u>Romeo and Juliet</u>. He moves from a self-

centered man to a man who lives not for himself but only for Juliet.

Revised Draft

Later the student edited the draft. We reprint the original, with the additional editing in handwriting:

Romeo ~~is a very interesting character, I think. In the beginning~~
begins as an
~~of the play Romeo is very~~ adolescent. ~~Romeo is~~ smitten with puppy
                              and a desire
love for ~~a woman named~~ Rosaline. ~~He desires~~ to show all of his friends
                                                                however,
that he knows how a lover is supposed to act. When he sees Juliet, he
           and   this
experiences true love. ~~From the point when he sees Juliet he~~

~~experiences true love, and from this point~~ he steadily matures, in
       moving   *adolescent*
~~Romeo and Juliet. He moves~~ from a self-centered man to a man who

lives ~~not for himself but~~ only for Juliet.

Here is a revised version of another effective opening paragraph, effective partly because it identifies the character and offers a thesis:

In the last speech of <u>Macbeth</u>, Malcolm characterizes Lady

Macbeth as "fiend-like," and indeed she invokes evil spirits and

prompts her husband to commit murder. But despite her bold pose,

her role in the murder, and her belief that she will be untroubled by

guilt, she has a conscience that torments her and that finally drives

her to suicide. She is not a mere heartless villain; she is a human

being who is less strong—and more moral—than she thinks she is.

Notice that

- the paragraph quotes a word ("fiend-like") from the text. It happens that the writer goes on to argue that this word is *not* a totally accurate description, but the quotation nevertheless helps to bring the reader into close contact with the subject of the essay.
- in writing about literature we do not ordinarily introduce the thesis formally. We do not, that is, say "In this paper it is my intention to prove that . . ."

Such a sentence may be perfectly appropriate in a paper in political science, but in a paper on literature it sounds too stiff.

The body of your essay will be devoted, of course, to supporting your thesis. If you have asserted that although Lady Macbeth is cruel and domineering she nevertheless is endowed with a conscience, you will go on in your essay to support those assertions with references to passages that demonstrate them. This does *not* mean that you tell the plot of the whole work; an essay on a character is by no means the same as a summary of the plot. But since you must support your generalizations, you will have to make brief references to specific episodes that reveal her personality, and almost surely you will quote an occasional word or passage.

There are many possible **ways to organize** an essay on a character. Much will depend, of course, on your purpose and thesis. For instance,

- you may want to show how the character develops—gains knowledge, or matures, or disintegrates. Or, again,
- you may want to show what the character contributes to the story or play as a whole. Or, to give yet another example,
- you may want to show that the character is unbelievable.

Still, although no single organization is always right, two methods are common and effective. One is to let the organization of your essay follow closely the sequence of the literary work; that is, you might devote a paragraph to Lady Macbeth as we perceive her in the first act, and then in subsequent paragraphs go on to show that her character is later seen to be more complex than it at first appears. Such an essay may trace your changing responses. This does not mean that you need to write five paragraphs, one on her character in each of the five acts. But it does mean that you might begin with Lady Macbeth as you perceive her in, say, the first act, and then go on to the additional revelations of the rest of the play.

A second effective way of organizing an essay on a character is to set forth, early in the essay, the character's chief traits—let's say the chief strengths and two or three weaknesses—and then go on to study each trait you have listed. Here the organization would (to maintain the reader's interest) probably begin with the most obvious points and then move on to the less obvious, subtler points. The body of your essay, in any case, is devoted to offering evidence that supports your generalizations about the character.

What about a **concluding paragraph**? The concluding paragraph ought *not* to begin with the obviousness of "Thus we see," or "In conclusion," or "I recommend this play because . . . ." In fact, after you have given what you consider a sound sketch of the character, it may be appropriate simply to quit. Especially if your essay has moved from the obvious traits to the more subtle and more important traits, and if your essay is fairly short (say, fewer than 500 words), a reader may not need a conclusion. Further, there probably is no reason to blunt what you have just said by adding an unnecessary and merely repetitive summary. But if you do feel that a conclusion is necessary, you may find it effective to write a summary of the character, somewhat as you did in your opening. For the conclusion, relate the character's character to the entire drama—that is, try to give the reader a sense of the role that the character plays.

✔ CHECKLIST: *Getting Ideas for Writing about Drama*

The following questions may help you to formulate ideas for an essay on a play.

Plot and Conflict

❑ Does the exposition introduce elements that will be ironically fulfilled? During the exposition do you perceive things differently from the way the characters perceive them?

❑ Are certain happenings or situations recurrent? If so, what significance do you attach to them?

❑ If there is more than one plot, do the plots seem to you to be related? Is one plot clearly the main plot and another plot a sort of subplot, a minor variation on the theme?

❑ Do any scenes strike you as irrelevant?

❑ Are certain scenes so strongly foreshadowed that you anticipated them? If so, did the happenings in these scenes merely fulfill your expectations, or did they also surprise you?

❑ What kinds of conflict are there? One character against another, one group against another, one part of a personality against another part in the same person?

❑ How is the conflict resolved? By an unambiguous triumph of one side or by a triumph that is also in some degree a loss for the triumphant side? Do you find the resolution satisfying, or unsettling, or what? Why?

Character

❑ A dramatic character is not likely to be thoroughly realistic, a copy of someone we might know. Still, we can ask if the character is consistent and coherent. We can also ask if the character is complex or is, on the other hand, a rather simple representative of some human type.

❑ How is the character defined? Consider what the character says and does and what others say about him or her and do to him or her. Also consider other characters who more or less resemble the character in question, because the similarities—and the differences—may be significant.

❑ How trustworthy are the characters when they characterize themselves? When they characterize others?

❑ Do characters change as the play goes on, or do we simply know them better at the end?

❑ What do you make of the minor characters? Are they merely necessary to the plot, or are they foils to other characters? Or do they serve some other functions?

❑ If a character is tragic, does the tragedy seem to you to proceed from a moral flaw, from an intellectual error, from the malice of others, from sheer chance, or from some combination of these?

❑ What are the character's goals? To what degree do you sympathize with them? If a character is comic, do you laugh *with* or *at* the character?

❑ Do you think the characters are adequately motivated?

❑ Is a given character so meditative that you feel he or she is engaged less in a dialogue with others than in a dialogue with the self? If so, do you feel that this character is in large degree a spokesperson for the author, commenting not only on the world of the play but also on the outside world?

Nonverbal Language

❑ If the playwright does not provide full stage directions, try to imagine for at least one scene what gestures and tones might accompany each speech. (The first scene is usually a good one to try your hand at.)

❑ What do you make of the setting? Does it help to reveal character? Do changes of scene strike you as symbolic? If so, symbolic of what?

THINKING ABOUT A FILMED VERSION OF A PLAY

In Chapter 11, "Fiction into Film," we talked at some length about what can be called the language of film, discussing such things as "shots" (for instance, long shots, medium shots, close-ups, pan shots), "sequences" (shots connected by, for instance, crosscutting, dissolves, and fade-outs), and "editing" (the assembling of shots and sequences into a whole film). Although one might at first think that a film-version of a play is pretty much the play caught on film, as soon as one realizes that movies use such techniques as close-ups and high and low angle shots (the action is seen from above or below), one realizes that the filmed version of a play can be very different from the version on the stage, even though in both forms a story is told by means of actors. In Laurence Olivier's *Hamlet* (1944), dreamlike dissolves (the shot dissolves while a new shot appears to emerge from beneath it) suggest the prince's irresoluteness. Or consider the use of black-and-white versus color film; Olivier made Shakespeare's *Henry V* (1944) in color but *Hamlet* in black-and-white because, in Olivier's view, color conveyed a splendor appropriate to England's heroic history, whereas black-and-white seemed more suited to somber tragedy.

Filmmakers customarily "open out" plays, giving us scenes of skies, beaches, city streets, and so forth. In Olivier's *Hamlet* we get shots of the sea and the sky. The camera descends from a great height just before Hamlet delivers his first soliloquy, and when the Ghost leaves at 1.5.96 the camera soars into the air, as though with the Ghost, and then, from above the camera shows Hamlet fainting at the battlements. Even when the camera shows us scenes within the palace it in effect opens the play by panning and traveling through long empty corridors and over staircases, suggesting Hamlet's irresolute mind. (Kenneth Branagh's film version of *Hamlet* [1996] is very different; for a student's discussion of this film, see the essay by Will Saretta that we reprint in our casebook on *Hamlet*, page 1051.)

The 1987 film version of *The Glass Menagerie*, directed by Paul Newman, may suffer in part because the camera is not adventurous enough. Much of the play is shot close-up, with the result that this film of Williams's "Memory Play" has a realism, an in-your-face quality that is at odds with the dreaminess and fragility of the play. A stage production—usually set within a proscenium and making use of evidently theatrical lighting—has an illusionary or unrealistic quality appropriate to Williams's play, in which a narrator (Tom) conjures up scenes. Newman gives us almost all of Williams's dialogue, but he loses almost all of the magic of the play.

Getting Ready to Write

Mastery of terminology does not make anyone a perceptive film critic, but it helps writers communicate their perceptions to their readers. Probably an essay on a film will not be primarily about the use of establishing shots or of wipes or of any such matters; rather, it will be about the reasons why a particular film pleases or displeases, succeeds or fails, seems significant or insignificant, and in discussing these large matters it is sometimes necessary (or at least economical) to use common technical terms. Large matters are often determined in part by such seemingly small matters as the distance of the camera from its subject or the way in which transitions are made, and one may as well use the conventional terms. But it is also true that a filmmaker's technique and technology alone cannot make a first-rate film. An idea, a personal vision, a theme must be embodied in all that is flashed on the screen.

Writing an essay about a new film—one not yet available for study on DVD—presents difficulties not encountered in writing about stories, plays, or poems. Because we experience film in a darkened room, we cannot easily take notes, and because the film may be shown only once, we cannot always take another look at passages that puzzle us. But some brief notes can be taken even in the dark; it is best to amplify them as soon as light is available, while you still know what the scrawls mean. If you can see the film more than once, do so, and, of course, if the script has been published, study it. Draft your paper as soon as possible after your first viewing, and then see the film again. You can sometimes check hazy memories of certain scenes and techniques with fellow viewers. But even with multiple viewings and the aid of friends, it is almost impossible to get all of the details right; it is best for the writer to be humble and for the reader to be tolerant.

Reminder: For a sample essay by a student, see the essay on Kenneth Branagh's *Hamlet,* printed on page 1051.

✔ CHECKLIST: *Writing about a Filmed Play*

Preliminaries

❑ Is the title of the film the same as the title of the play? If not, what is implied?

Dramatic Adaptations

❑ Does the film closely follow its original and neglect the potentialities of the camera? Or does it so revel in cinematic devices that it distorts the original?

❑ Does the film do violence to the theme of the original? Is the film better than its source? Are the additions or omissions due to the medium or to a crude or faulty interpretation of the original?

Plot and Character

❑ Can film deal as effectively with inner action—mental processes—as with external, physical action? In a given film, how is the inner action conveyed? Olivier

used voice-over for parts of Hamlet's soliloquies—that is, we hear Hamlet's voice but his lips do not move.
❏ Are shots and sequences adequately developed, or do they seem jerky? (A shot may be jerky by being extremely brief or at an odd angle; a sequence may be jerky by using discontinuous images or fast cuts. Sometimes, of course, jerkiness may be desirable.) If such cinematic techniques as wipes, dissolves, and slow motion are used, are they meaningful and effective?
❏ Are the characters believable?
❏ Are the actors appropriately cast?

Sound Track

❏ Does the sound track offer more than realistic dialogue? Is the music appropriate and functional? (Music may, among other things, imitate natural sounds, give a sense of locale or of ethnic group, suggest states of mind, provide ironic commentary, or—by repeated melodies—help establish connections.) Are volume, tempo, and pitch—whether of music or of such sounds as the wind blowing or cars moving—used to stimulate emotions?

YOUR TURN: PLAYS FOR ANALYSIS
A Note on Greek Tragedy

Little or nothing is known for certain about the origin of Greek tragedy. The most common hypothesis holds that it developed from improvised speeches during choral dances honoring Dionysus, a Greek nature god associated with spring, fertility, and wine. Thespis (who perhaps never existed) is said to have introduced an actor into these choral performances in the sixth century B.C. Aeschylus (525–456 B.C.), Greece's first great writer of tragedies, added the second actor, and Sophocles (496?–406 B.C.) added the third actor and fixed the size of the chorus at fifteen. (Because the chorus leader often functioned as an additional actor, and because the actors sometimes doubled in their parts, a Greek tragedy could have more characters than might at first be thought.)

All of the extant great Greek tragedy is of the fifth century B.C. It was performed at religious festivals in the winter and early spring, in large outdoor amphitheaters built on hillsides. Some of these theaters were enormous; the one at Epidaurus held about fifteen thousand people. The audience sat in tiers, looking down on the *orchestra* (a dancing place), with the acting area behind it and the *skene* (the scene building) yet farther back. The scene building served as dressing room, background (suggesting a palace or temple), and place for occasional entrances and exits. Furthermore, this building helped to provide good acoustics, for speech travels well if there is a solid barrier behind the speaker and a hard, smooth surface in front of him, and if the audience sits in tiers. The wall of the scene building provided the barrier; the orchestra provided the surface in front of the actors; and the seats on the hillside fulfilled the third requirement. Moreover, the acoustics were somewhat improved by slightly elevating the actors above the orchestra, but it is not known exactly when this platform was first constructed in front of the scene building.

Greek theater at Epidaurus. (©Frederick Ayers/Photo Researchers)

A tragedy commonly begins with a *prologos* (prologue), during which the exposition is given. Next comes the *párodos,* the chorus's ode of entrance, sung while the chorus marches into the theater, through the side aisles, and onto the orchestra. The *epeisodion* (episode) is the ensuing scene; it is followed by a *stasimon* (choral song, ode). Usually there are four or five *epeisodia,* alternating with *stasima.* Each of these choral odes has a *strophe* (lines presumably sung while the chorus dances in one direction) and an *antistrophe* (lines presumably sung while the chorus retraces its steps). Sometimes a third part, an *epode,* concludes an ode. (In addition to odes that are *stasima,* there can be odes within episodes; the fourth episode of *Antigonê* contains an ode complete with *epode.*) After the last part of the last ode comes the *exodos,* the epilogue or final scene.

The actors (all male) wore masks, and they seem to have chanted much of the play. Perhaps the total result of combining speech with music and dancing was a sort of music-drama roughly akin to opera with some spoken dialogue, like Mozart's *Magic Flute.*

Thinking Critically about a Tragedy: Sophocles's *Antigonê*

SOPHOCLES

One of the three great writers of tragedies in ancient Greece, Sophocles (496?–406 B.C.) was born in Colonus, near Athens, into a well-to-do family. Well educated, he first won public acclaim as a tragic poet at the age of 27, in 468 B.C., when he defeated Aeschylus in a competition for writing a tragic play. He is said to have written some 120 plays, but only 7 tragedies are extant; among them are Oedipus the King, Antigonê, *and* Oedipus at Colonus. *He died, much honored, in his ninetieth year, in Athens, where he had lived his entire life.*

Antigonê

*An English Version by Dudley Fitts and Robert Fitzgerald**

LIST OF CHARACTERS

ANTIGONÊ
ISMENÊ
EURYDICÊ
CREON
HAIMON
TEIRESIAS
A SENTRY
A MESSENGER
CHORUS

SCENE: *Before the palace of* CREON, *king of Thebes. A central double door, and two lateral doors. A platform extends the length of the façade, and from this platform three steps lead down into the "orchestra," or chorus-ground.*
Time: *Dawn of the day after the repulse of the Argive army from the assault on Thebes.*

Prologue

ANTIGONÊ *and* ISMENÊ *enter from the central door of the palace.*

ANTIGONÊ.   Ismenê, dear sister,
    You would think that we had already suffered enough
    For the curse on Oedipus.°
    I cannot imagine any grief
    That you and I have not gone through. And now—   5

---

* Explanatory notes are indicated by a degree symbol (°) in the text and are keyed to the text by line number.

3 Oedipus, once King of Thebes, was the father of Antigonê and Ismenê, and of their brothers Polyneicês and Eteoclês. Oedipus unwittingly killed his father, Laïos, and married his own mother, Iocastê. When he learned what he had done, he blinded himself and left Thebes. Eteoclês and Polyneicês quarreled; Polyneicês was driven out but returned to assault Thebes. In the battle each brother killed the other; Creon became king and ordered that Polyneicês be left to rot unburied on the battlefield as a traitor.

Jane Lapotaire in *Antigonê*. National Theater, London, 1984. (Donald Cooper/Photostage)

	Have they told you of the new decree of our King Creon?	
ISMENÊ.	I have heard nothing: I know	
	That two sisters lost two brothers, a double death	
	In a single hour; and I know that the Argive army	
	Fled in the night; but beyond this, nothing.	10
ANTIGONÊ.	I thought so. And this is why I wanted you	
	To come out here with me. There is something we must do.	
ISMENÊ.	Why do you speak so strangely?	
ANTIGONÊ.	Listen, Ismenê:	
	Creon buried our brother Eteoclês	14
	With military honors, gave him a soldier's funeral,	
	And it was right that he should; but Polyneicês,	
	Who fought as bravely and died as miserably,—	
	They say that Creon has sworn	
	No one shall bury him, no one mourn for him,	20
	But his body must lie in the fields, a sweet treasure	
	For carrion birds to find as they search for food.	
	That is what they say, and our good Creon is coming here	
	To announce it publicly; and the penalty—	
	Stoning to death in the public square!	
	There it is,	25
	And now you can prove what you are:	
	A true sister, or a traitor to your family.	
ISMENÊ.	Antigonê, you are mad! What could I possibly do?	
ANTIGONÊ.	You must decide whether you will help me or not.	
ISMENÊ.	I do not understand you. Help you in what?	30
ANTIGONÊ.	Ismenê. I am going to bury him. Will you come?	

ISMENÊ.   Bury him! You have just said the new law forbids it.

ANTIGONÊ.   He is my brother. And he is your brother, too.

ISMENÊ.   But think of the danger! Think what Creon will do!

ANTIGONÊ.   Creon is not strong enough to stand in my way.   35

ISMENÊ.   Ah sister!
Oedipus died, everyone hating him
For what his own search brought to light, his eyes
Ripped out by his own hand; and Iocastê died,
His mother and wife at once: she twisted the cords   40
That strangled her life; and our two brothers died,
Each killed by the other's sword. And we are left:
But oh, Antigonê,
Think how much more terrible than these
Our own death would be if we should go against Creon   45
And do what he has forbidden! We are only women,
We cannot fight with men, Antigonê!
The law is strong, we must give in to the law
In this thing, and in worse. I beg the Dead
To forgive me, but I am helpless: I must yield   50
To those in authority. And I think it is dangerous business
To be always meddling.

ANTIGONÊ.   If that is what you think,
I should not want you, even if you asked to come.
You have made your choice, you can be what you want to be.
But I will bury him; and if I must die,   55
I say that this crime is holy: I shall lie down
With him in death, and I shall be as dear
To him as he to me.
                    It is the dead,
Not the living, who make the longest demands:
We die for ever. . . .
                    You may do as you like.   60
Since apparently the laws of the gods mean nothing to you.

ISMENÊ.   They mean a great deal to me; but I have no strength
To break laws that were made for the public good.

ANTIGONÊ.   That must be your excuse, I suppose. But as for me,
I will bury the brother I love.

ISMENÊ.   Antigonê,   65
I am so afraid for you!

ANTIGONÊ.   You need not be:
You have yourself to consider, after all.

ISMENÊ.   But no one must hear of this, you must tell no one!
I will keep it a secret, I promise!

ANTIGONÊ.   O tell it! Tell everyone!
Think how they'll hate you when it all comes out   70
If they learn that you knew about it all the time!

ISMENÊ.   So fiery! You should be cold with fear.

ANTIGONÊ.   Perhaps. But I am doing only what I must.

ISMENÊ.   But can you do it? I say that you cannot.

ANTIGONÊ.   Very well: when my strength gives out,
I shall do no more.   75

ISMENÊ.   Impossible things should not be tried at all.   75
ANTIGONÊ.   Go away, Ismenê:
    I shall be hating you soon, and the dead will too,
    For your words are hateful. Leave me my foolish plan:
    I am not afraid of the danger; if it means death,   80
    It will not be the worst of deaths—death without honor.
ISMENÊ.   Go then, if you feel that you must.
    You are unwise,
    But a loyal friend indeed to those who love you.

          Exit into the palace. ANTIGONÊ *goes off, left. Enter the* CHORUS.

                    Párodos

CHORUS.   Now the long blade of the sun, lying   *Strophe 1*
    Level east to west, touches with glory
    Thebes of the Seven Gates. Open, unlidded
    Eye of golden day! O marching light
    Across the eddy and rush of Dircê's stream,°   5
    Striking the white shields of the enemy
    Thrown headlong backward from the blaze of morning!
CHORAGOS.°   Polyneicês their commander
    Roused them with windy phrases,
    He the wild eagle screaming   10
    Insults above our land,
    His wings their shields of snow,
    His crest their marshalled helms.
CHORUS.   Against our seven gates in a yawning ring   *Antistrophe 1*
    The famished spears came onward in the night: 15
    But before his jaws were sated with our blood,
    Or pinefire took the garland of our towers,
    He was thrown back; and as he turned, great Thebes—
    No tender victim for his noisy power—
    Rose like a dragon behind him, shouting war.   20
CHORAGOS.   For God hates utterly
    The bray of bragging tongues;
    And when he beheld their smiling,
    Their swagger of golden helms,
    The frown of his thunder blasted   25
    Their first man from our walls.
CHORUS.   We heard his shout of triumph high in the air   *Strophe 2*
    Turn to a scream; far out in a flaming arc
    He fell with his windy torch, and the earth struck him.
    And others storming in fury no less than his   30
    Found shock of death in the dusty joy of battle.
CHORAGOS.   Seven captains at seven gates
    Yielded their clanging arms to the god
    That bends the battle-line and breaks it.
    These two only, brothers in blood,   35
    Face to face in matchless rage.
    Mirroring each the other's death,

Párodos 5 Dircê's stream a stream west of Thebes.   **8 Choragos** leader of the Chorus.

Clashed in long combat.

CHORUS.   But now in the beautiful morning of victory   *Antistrophe 2*
Let Thebes of the many chariots sing for joy!   40
With hearts for dancing we'll take leave of war:
Our temples shall be sweet with hymns of praise,
And the long nights shall echo with our chorus.

Scene I

CHORAGOS.   But now at last our new King is coming:
Creon of Thebes, Menoikeus' son.
In this auspicious dawn of his reign
What are the new complexities
That shifting Fate has woven for him?   5
What is his counsel? Why has he summoned
The old men to hear him?

Enter CREON *from the palace, center. He addresses the* CHORUS *from the top step.*

CREON.   Gentlemen: I have the honor to inform you that our Ship of State, which
recent storms have threatened to destroy, has come safely to harbor at last,
guided by the merciful wisdom of Heaven. I have summoned you here this   10
morning because I know that I can depend upon you: your devotion to King
Laïos was absolute; you never hesitated in your duty to our late ruler
Oedipus; and when Oedipus died, your loyalty was transferred to his children. Unfortunately, as you know, his two sons, the princes Eteoclês and
Polyneicês, have killed each other in battle; and I, as the next in blood, have   15
succeeded to the full power of the throne.

I am aware, of course, that no Ruler can expect complete loyalty from his
subjects until he has been tested in office. Nevertheless, I say to you at the very
outset that I have nothing but contempt for the kind of Governor who is afraid,
for whatever reason, to follow the course that he knows is best for the State;   20
and as for the man who sets private friendship above the public welfare,—I
have no use for him, either. I call God to witness that if I saw my country
headed for ruin, I should not be afraid to speak out plainly; and I need hardly
remind you that I would never have any dealings with an enemy of the people.
No one values friendship more highly than I: but we must remember that   25
friends made at the risk of wrecking our Ship are not real friends at all.

These are my principles, at any rate, and that is why I have made the following decision concerning the sons of Oedipus: Eteoclês, who died as a
man should die, fighting for his country, is to be buried with full military honors, with all the ceremony that is usual when the greatest heroes die; but his   30
brother Polyneicês, who broke his exile to come back with fire and sword
against his native city and the shrines of his fathers' gods, whose one idea
was to spill the blood of his blood and sell his own people into slavery—
Polyneicês, I say, is to have no burial: no man is to touch him or say the least
prayer for him; he shall lie on the plain, unburied; and the birds and the scav-   35
enging dogs can do with him whatever they like.

This is my command, and you can see the wisdom behind it. As long as I
am King, no traitor is going to be honored with the loyal man. But whoever
shows by word and deed that he is on the side of the State—he shall have my
respect while he is living and my reverence when he is dead.   40

CHORAGOS.   If that is your will, Creon son of Menoikeus,

You have the right to enforce it: we are yours.

CREON.   That is my will. Take care that you do your part.

CHORAGOS.   We are old men: let the younger ones carry it out.

CREON.   I do not mean that: the sentries have been appointed.   45

CHORAGOS.   Then what is it that you would have us do?

CREON.   You will give no support to whoever breaks this law.

CHORAGOS.   Only a crazy man is in love with death!

CREON.   And death it is; yet money talks, and the wisest
            Have sometimes been known to count a few coins too many.   50

   Enter SENTRY *from left.*

SENTRY.   I'll not say that I'm out of breath from running, King, because every time
   I stopped to think about what I have to tell you, I felt like going back. And all
   the time a voice kept saying, "You fool, don't you know you're walking
   straight into trouble?"; and then another voice: "Yes, but if you let somebody
   else get the news to Creon first, it will be even worse than that for you!" But   55
   good sense won out, at least I hope it was good sense, and here I am with a
   story that makes no sense at all; but I'll tell it anyhow, because, as they say,
   what's going to happen's going to happen and—

CREON.   Come to the point. What have you to say?

SENTRY.   I did not do it. I did not see who did it. You must not punish me for what   60
   someone else has done.

CREON.   A comprehensive defense! More effective, perhaps, if I knew its purpose.
   Come: what is it?

SENTRY.   A dreadful thing . . . I don't know how to put it—

CREON.   Out with it!

SENTRY.   Well, then;   65
            The dead man—
                  Polyneicês—

Pause. The SENTRY *is overcome, fumbles for words.* CREON *waits impassively.*

                              out there—
                        someone,—
            New dust on the slimy flesh!

Pause. No sign from CREON.

            Someone has given it burial that way, and
            Gone. . . .

Long pause. CREON *finally speaks with deadly control.*

CREON.   And the man who dared do this?

SENTRY.   I swear I   70
            Do not know! You must believe me!
                              Listen:
            The ground was dry, not a sign of digging, no,
            Not a wheeltrack in the dust, no trace of anyone.
            It was when they relieved us this morning: and one of them,
            The corporal, pointed to it.
                              There it was,   75
            The strangest—
                  Look:
            The body, just mounded over with light dust: you see?
            Not buried really, but as if they'd covered it

Just enough for the ghost's peace. And no sign
Of dogs or any wild animal that had been there.   80

And then what a scene there was! Every man of us
Accusing the other: we all proved the other man did it,
We all had proof that we could not have done it.
We were ready to take hot iron in our hands,
Walk through fire, swear by all the gods,   85
It was not I!
I do not know who it was, but it was not I!

CREON*'s rage has been mounting steadily, but the* SENTRY *is too intent upon
his story to notice it.*

And then, when this came to nothing, someone said
A thing that silenced us and made us stare
Down at the ground: you had to be told the news,   90
And one of us had to do it! We threw the dice,
And the bad luck fell to me. So here I am,
No happier to be here than you are to have me:
Nobody likes the man who brings bad news.
CHORAGOS.   I have been wondering, King: can it be that the gods have done this?   95
CREON [*furiously*].   Stop!
        Must you doddering wrecks
Go out of your heads entirely? "The gods"!
Intolerable!
The gods favor this corpse? Why? How had he served them?   100
Tried to loot their temples, burn their images,
Yes, and the whole State, and its laws with it!
Is it your senile opinion that the gods love to honor bad men?
A pious thought!—
                    No, from the very beginning
There have been those who have whispered together,   105
Stiff-necked anarchists, putting their heads together,
Scheming against me in alleys. These are the men,
And they have bribed my own guard to do this thing.
[*Sententiously.*] Money!
There's nothing in the world so demoralizing as money.   110
Down go your cities,
Homes gone, men gone, honest hearts corrupted.
Crookedness of all kinds, and all for money!
[*To* SENTRY.]   But you—!
I swear by God and by the throne of God,
The man who has done this thing shall pay for it!   115
Find that man, bring him here to me, or your death
Will be the least of your problems: I'll string you up
Alive, and there will be certain ways to make you
Discover your employer before you die;
And the process may teach you a lesson you seem to have missed: 120
The dearest profit is sometimes all too dear:
That depends on the source. Do you understand me?
A fortune won is often misfortune.

SENTRY.   King, may I speak?
CREON.   Your very voice distresses me.
SENTRY.   Are you sure that it is my voice, and not your conscience?   125
CREON.   By God, he wants to analyze me now!
SENTRY.   It is not what I say, but what has been done, that hurts you.
CREON.   You talk too much.
SENTRY.   Maybe; but I've done nothing.
CREON.   Sold your soul for some silver: that's all you've done.
SENTRY.   How dreadful it is when the right judge judges wrong!   130
CREON.   Your figures of speech
          May entertain you now; but unless you bring me the man,
          You will get little profit from them in the end.

                                                 Exit CREON *into the palace.*

SENTRY.   "Bring me the man"—!
          I'd like nothing better than bringing him the man!   135
          But bring him or not, you have seen the last of me here.
          At any rate, I am safe!   [*Exit* SENTRY.]

                              Ode I

CHORUS.   Numberless are the world's wonders, but not   *Strophe 1*
          More wonderful than man; the stormgray sea
          Yields to his prows, the huge crests bear him high;
          Earth, holy and inexhaustible, is graven
          With shining furrows where his plows have gone   5
          Year after year, the timeless labor of stallions.

          The lightboned birds and beasts that cling to cover,   *Antistrophe 1*
          The lithe fish lighting their reaches of dim water,
          All are taken, tamed in the net of his mind;
          The lion on the hill, the wild horse windy-maned,   10
          Resign to him; and his blunt yoke has broken
          The sultry shoulders of the mountain bull.

          Words also, and thought as rapid as air,   *Strophe 2*
          He fashions to his good use; statecraft is his,
          And his the skill that deflects the arrows of snow,   15
          The spears of winter rain: from every wind
          He has made himself secure—from all but one:
          In the late wind of death he cannot stand.

          O clear intelligence, force beyond all measure!   *Antistrophe 2*
          O fate of man, working both good and evil!   20
          When the laws are kept, how proudly his city stands!
          When the laws are broken, what of his city then?
          Never may the anarchic man find rest at my hearth,
          Never be it said that my thoughts are his thoughts.

                              Scene II

Reenter SENTRY *leading* ANTIGONÊ.

CHORAGOS.   What does this mean? Surely this captive woman
            Is the Princess, Antigonê. Why should she be taken?

SENTRY.   Here is the one who did it! We caught her
   In the very act of burying him.—Where is Creon?
CHORAGOS.   Just coming from the house.

   Enter CREON, *center.*

CREON.   What has happened?   5
   Why have you come back so soon?
SENTRY [*expansively*].   O King,
   A man should never be too sure of anything:
   I would have sworn
   That you'd not see me here again: your anger
   Frightened me so, and the things you threatened me with;   10
   But how could I tell then
   That I'd be able to solve the case so soon?
   No dice-throwing this time: I was only too glad to come!
   Here is this woman. She is the guilty one:
   We found her trying to bury him.   15
   Take her, then; question her; judge her as you will.
   I am through with the whole thing now, and glad of it.
CREON.   But this is Antigonê! Why have you brought her here?
SENTRY.   She was burying him, I tell you!
CREON [*severely*].   Is this the truth?
SENTRY.   I saw her with my own eyes. Can I say more?   20
CREON.   The details: come, tell me quickly!
SENTRY.   It was like this:
   After those terrible threats of yours, King,
   We went back and brushed the dust away from the body.
   The flesh was soft by now, and stinking,
   So we sat on a hill to windward and kept guard.   25
   No napping this time! We kept each other awake.
   But nothing happened until the white round sun
   Whirled in the center of the round sky over us:
   Then, suddenly,
   A storm of dust roared up from the earth, and the sky   30
   Went out, the plain vanished with all its trees
   In the stinging dark. We closed our eyes and endured it.
   The whirlwind lasted a long time, but it passed;
   And then we looked, and there was Antigonê!
   I have seen   35
   A mother bird come back to a stripped nest, heard
   Her crying bitterly a broken note or two
   For the young ones stolen. Just so, when this girl
   Found the bare corpse, and all her love's work wasted,
   She wept, and cried on heaven to damn the hands   40
   That had done this thing.
        And then she brought more dust
   And sprinkled wine three times for her brother's ghost.

   We ran and took her at once. She was not afraid,
   Not even when we charged her with what she had done.
   She denied nothing.
       And this was a comfort to me,   45

And some uneasiness: for it is a good thing
To escape from death, but it is no great pleasure
To bring death to a friend.
                                        Yet I always say
There is nothing so comfortable as your own safe skin!
CREON [*slowly, dangerously*].   And you, Antigonê,   50
     You with your head hanging,—do you confess this thing?
ANTIGONÊ.   I do. I deny nothing.
CREON [*to* SENTRY].   You may go.   [*Exit* SENTRY.]
     [*To* ANTIGONÊ.] Tell me, tell me briefly:
     Had you heard my proclamation touching this matter?
ANTIGONÊ.   It was public. Could I help hearing it?   55
CREON.   And yet you dared defy the law.
ANTIGONÊ.   I dared.
     It was not God's proclamation. That final Justice
     That rules the world below makes no such laws.

     Your edict, King, was strong.
     But all your strength is weakness itself against   60
     The immortal unrecorded laws of God.
     They are not merely now: they were, and shall be,
     Operative for ever, beyond man utterly.
     I knew I must die, even without your decree:
     I am only mortal. And if I must die   65
     Now, before it is my time to die,
     Surely this is no hardship: can anyone
     Living, as I live, with evil all about me,
     Think Death less than a friend? This death of mine
     Is of no importance; but if I had left my brother   70
     Lying in death unburied, I should have suffered.
     Now I do not.
                         You smile at me. Ah Creon,
     Think me a fool, if you like; but it may well be
     That a fool convicts me of folly.
CHORAGOS.   Like father, like daughter: both headstrong, deaf to reason!   75
     She has never learned to yield.
CREON.   She has much to learn.
     The inflexible heart breaks first, the toughest iron
     Cracks first, and the wildest horses bend their necks
     At the pull of the smallest curb.
                                        Pride? In a slave?
     This girl is guilty of a double insolence,   80
     Breaking the given laws and boasting of it.
     Who is the man here,
     She or I, if this crime goes unpunished?
     Sister's child, or more than sister's child,
     Or closer yet in blood—she and her sister   85
     Win bitter death for this!
     [*To* SERVANTS.]   Go, some of you,
     Arrest Ismenê. I accuse her equally.
     Bring her: you will find her sniffling in the house there.

Her mind's a traitor: crimes kept in the dark
Cry for light, and the guardian brain shudders;   85
But how much worse than this
Is brazen boasting of barefaced anarchy!

ANTIGONÊ.   Creon, what more do you want than my death?

CREON.   Nothing.
That gives me everything.

ANTIGONÊ.   Then I beg you: kill me.
This talking is a great weariness: your words   90
Are distasteful to me, and I am sure that mine
Seem so to you. And yet they should not seem so:
I should have praise and honor for what I have done.
All these men here would praise me
Were their lips not frozen shut with fear of you.   95
[*Bitterly.*] Ah the good fortune of kings,
Licensed to say and do whatever they please!

CREON.   You are alone here in that opinion.

ANTIGONÊ.   No, they are with me. But they keep their tongues in leash.

CREON.   Maybe. But you are guilty, and they are not.   100

ANTIGONÊ.   There is no guilt in reverence for the dead.

CREON.   But Eteoclês—was he not your brother too?

ANTIGONÊ.   My brother too.

CREON.   And you insult his memory?

ANTIGONÊ [*softly*].   The dead man would not say that I insult it.

CREON.   He would: for you honor a traitor as much as him.   105

ANTIGONÊ.   His own brother, traitor or not, and equal in blood.

CREON.   He made war on his country. Eteoclês defended it.

ANTIGONÊ.   Nevertheless, there are honors due all the dead.

CREON.   But not the same for the wicked as for the just.

ANTIGONÊ.   Ah Creon, Creon,   110
Which of us can say what the gods hold wicked?

CREON.   An enemy is an enemy, even dead.

ANTIGONÊ.   It is my nature to join in love, not hate.

CREON [*finally losing patience*].   Go join them then; if you must have your love,
Find it in hell!   115

CHORAGOS.   But see, Ismenê comes:

Enter ISMENÊ, *guarded.*

Those tears are sisterly, the cloud
That shadows her eyes rains down gentle sorrow.

CREON.   You too, Ismenê,
Snake in my ordered house, sucking my blood   120
Stealthily—and all the time I never knew
That these two sisters were aiming at my throne!
                                  Ismenê,
Do you confess your share in this crime, or deny it?
Answer me.

ISMENÊ.   Yes, if she will let me say so. I am guilty.   125

ANTIGONÊ [*coldly*].   No, Ismenê. You have no right to say so.
You would not help me, and I will not have you help me.

ISMENÊ.   But now I know what you meant: and I am here
To join you, to take my share of punishment.

ANTIGONÊ.   The dead man and the gods who rule the dead   135
   Know whose act this was. Words are not friends.

ISMENÊ.   Do you refuse me, Antigonê? I want to die with you:
   I too have a duty that I must discharge to the dead.

ANTIGONÊ.   You shall not lessen my death by sharing it.

ISMENÊ.   What do I care for life when you are dead?   140

ANTIGONÊ.   Ask Creon. You're always hanging on his opinions.

ISMENÊ.   You are laughing at me. Why, Antigonê?

ANTIGONÊ.   It's a joyless laughter, Ismenê.

ISMENÊ.   But can I do nothing?

ANTIGONÊ.   Yes. Save yourself. I shall not envy you.
   There are those who will praise you; I shall have honor, too.   145

ISMENÊ.   But we are equally guilty!

ANTIGONÊ.   No more, Ismenê.
   You are alive, but I belong to Death.

CREON [*to the* CHORUS].   Gentlemen, I beg you to observe these girls:
   One has just now lost her mind; the other,
   It seems, has never had a mind at all.   150

ISMENÊ.   Grief teaches the steadiest minds to waver, King.

CREON.   Yours certainly did, when you assumed guilt with the guilty!

ISMENÊ.   But how could I go on living without her?

CREON.   You are.
   She is already dead.

ISMENÊ.   But your own son's bride!

CREON.   There are places enough for him to push his plow.   155
   I want no wicked women for my sons!

ISMENÊ.   O dearest Haimon, how your father wrongs you!

CREON.   I've had enough of your childish talk of marriage!

CHORAGOS.   Do you really intend to steal this girl from your son?

CREON.   No; Death will do that for me.

CHORAGOS.   Then she must die?   160

CREON [*ironically*].   You dazzle me.
      —But enough of this talk!
  [*To* GUARDS.] You, there, take them away and guard them well:
  For they are but women, and even brave men run
  When they see Death coming.   *Exeunt* ISMENÊ, ANTIGONÊ, *and* GUARDS.

Ode II

CHORUS.   Fortunate is the man who has never tasted   *Strophe 1*
   God's vengeance!
   Where once the anger of heaven has struck, that house is shaken
   For ever: damnation rises behind each child
   Like a wave cresting out of the black northeast,
   When the long darkness under sea roars up   5
   And bursts drumming death upon the windwhipped sand.

   I have seen this gathering sorrow from time long past   *Antistrophe 1*
   Loom upon Oedipus' children: generation from generation
   Takes the compulsive rage of the enemy god.
   So lately this last flower of Oedipus' line   10

Drank the sunlight! but now a passionate word
And a handful of dust have closed up all its beauty.

What mortal arrogance   *Strophe 2*
Transcends the wrath of Zeus?
Sleep cannot lull him nor the effortless long months   15
Of the timeless gods: but he is young for ever,
And his house is the shining day of high Olympos.
All that is and shall be,
And all the past, is his.
No pride on earth is free of the curse of heaven.   20

The straying dreams of men   *Antistrophe 2*
May bring them ghosts of joy:
But as they drowse, the waking embers burn them;
Or they walk with fixed eyes, as blind men walk.
But the ancient wisdom speaks for our own time: 25

*Fate works most for woe
With Folly's fairest show.*

Man's little pleasure is the spring of sorrow.

Scene III

CHORAGOS.   But here is Haimon, King, the last of all your sons.
Is it grief for Antigonê that brings him here,
And bitterness at being robbed of his bride?

     Enter HAIMON.

CREON.   We shall soon see, and no need of diviners.
                              —Son,
You have heard my final judgment on that girl: 5
Have you come here hating me, or have you come
With deference and with love, whatever I do?
HAIMON.   I am your son, father. You are my guide.
You make things clear for me, and I obey you.
No marriage means more to me than your continuing wisdom.   10
CREON.   Good. That is the way to behave: subordinate
Everything else, my son, to your father's will.
This is what a man prays for, that he may get
Sons attentive and dutiful in his house,
Each one hating his father's enemies,   15
Honoring his father's friends. But if his sons
Fail him, if they turn out unprofitably,
What has he fathered but trouble for himself
And amusement for the malicious?
                           So you are right
Not to lose your head over this woman.   20
Your pleasure with her would soon grow cold, Haimon,
And then you'd have a hellcat in bed and elsewhere.
Let her find her husband in Hell!
Of all the people in this city, only she
Has had contempt for my law and broken it.   25

Do you want me to show myself weak before the people?
Or to break my sworn word? No, and I will not.
The woman dies.
I suppose she'll plead "family ties." Well, let her.
If I permit my own family to rebel,   30
How shall I earn the world's obedience?
Show me the man who keeps his house in hand,
He's fit for public authority.
                          I'll have no dealings
With lawbreakers, critics of the government:
Whoever is chosen to govern should be obeyed—   35
Must be obeyed, in all things, great and small,
Just and unjust! O Haimon,
The man who knows how to obey, and that man only,
Knows how to give commands when the time comes.
You can depend on him, no matter how fast   40
The spears come: he's a good soldier, he'll stick it out.

Anarchy, anarchy! Show me a greater evil!
This is why cities tumble and the great houses rain down,
This is what scatters armies!
No, no: good lives are made so by discipline.   45
We keep the laws then, and the lawmakers,
And no woman shall seduce us. If we must lose,
Let's lose to a man, at least! Is a woman stronger than we?

CHORAGOS.   Unless time has rusted my wits,
What you say, King, is said with point and dignity.   50

HAIMON   [*boyishly earnest*].   Father:
Reason is God's crowning gift to man, and you are right
To warn me against losing mine. I cannot say—
I hope that I shall never want to say!—that you
Have reasoned badly. Yet there are other men   55
Who can reason, too; and their opinions might be helpful.
You are not in a position to know everything
That people say or do, or what they feel:
Your temper terrifies—everyone
Will tell you only what you like to hear.   60
But I, at any rate, can listen; and I have heard them
Muttering and whispering in the dark about this girl.
They say no woman has ever, so unreasonably,
Died so shameful a death for a generous act:
"She covered her brother's body. Is this indecent?   65
She kept him from dogs and vultures. Is this a crime?
Death?—She should have all the honor that we can give her!"

This is the way they talk out there in the city.

You must believe me:
Nothing is closer to me than your happiness.   70
What could be closer? Must not any son
Value his father's fortune as his father does his?
I beg you, do not be unchangeable:
Do not believe that you alone can be right.

The man who thinks that, 75
The man who maintains that only he has the power
To reason correctly, the gift to speak, the soul—
A man like that, when you know him, turns out empty.

It is not reason never to yield to reason!
In flood time you can see how some trees bend, 80
And because they bend, even their twigs are safe,
While stubborn trees are torn up, roots and all.
And the same thing happens in sailing:
Make your sheet fast, never slacken,—and over you go,
Head over heels and under: and there's your voyage. 85
Forget you are angry! Let yourself be moved!
I know I am young; but please let me say this:
The ideal condition
Would be, I admit, that men should be right by instinct;
But since we are all too likely to go astray, 90
The reasonable thing is to learn from those who can teach.

CHORAGOS.   You will do well to listen to him, King,
If what he says is sensible. And you, Haimon,
Must listen to your father.—Both speak well.

CREON.   You consider it right for a man of my years and experience 95
To go to school to a boy?

HAIMON.   It is not right
If I am wrong. But if I am young, and right,
What does my age matter?

CREON.   You think it right to stand up for an anarchist?

HAIMON.   Not at all. I pay no respect to criminals. 100

CREON.   Then she is not a criminal?

HAIMON.   The City would deny it, to a man.

CREON.   And the City proposes to teach me how to rule?

HAIMON.   Ah. Who is it that's talking like a boy now?

CREON.   My voice is the one voice giving orders in this City! 105

HAIMON.   It is no City if it takes orders from one voice.

CREON.   The State is the King!

HAIMON.   Yes, if the State is a desert.

Pause.

CREON.   This boy, it seems, has sold out to a woman.

HAIMON.   If you are a woman: my concern is only for you.

CREON.   So? Your "concern"! In a public brawl with your father! 110

HAIMON.   How about you, in a public brawl with justice?

CREON.   With justice, when all that I do is within my rights?

HAIMON.   You have no right to trample on God's right.

CREON [*completely out of control*].   Fool, adolescent fool! Taken in by a woman!

HAIMON.   You'll never see me taken in by anything vile. 115

CREON.   Every word you say is for her!

HAIMON [*quietly, darkly*].   And for you.
And for me. And for the gods under the earth.

CREON.   You'll never marry her while she lives.

HAIMON.   Then she must die.—But her death will cause another.

CREON.   Another? 120
Have you lost your senses? Is this an open threat?

HAIMON.   There is no threat in speaking to emptiness.
CREON.   I swear you'll regret this superior tone of yours!
    You are the empty one!
HAIMON.   If you were not my father,
    I'd say you were perverse.   125
CREON.   You girlstruck fool, don't play at words with me!
HAIMON.   I am sorry. You prefer silence.
CREON.   Now, by God—
    I swear, by all the gods in heaven above us,
    You'll watch it, I swear you shall!
    [*To the* SERVANTS.] Bring her out!
    Bring the woman out! Let her die before his eyes!   130
    Here, this instant, with her bridegroom beside her!
HAIMON.   Not here, no; she will not die here, King.
    And you will never see my face again.
    Go on raving as long as you've a friend to endure you.   *Exit* HAIMON.

CHORAGOS.   Gone, gone.   135
    Creon, a young man in a rage is dangerous!
CREON.   Let him do, or dream to do, more than a man can.
    He shall not save these girls from death.
CHORAGOS.   These girls?
    You have sentenced them both?
CREON.   No, you are right.
    I will not kill the one whose hands are clean.   140
CHORAGOS.   But Antigonê?
CREON. [*somberly*].   I will carry her far away
    Out there in the wilderness, and lock her
    Living in a vault of stone. She shall have food,
    As the custom is, to absolve the State of her death.
    And there let her pray to the gods of hell: 145
    They are her only gods:
    Perhaps they will show her an escape from death,
    Or she may learn,
                  though late,
    That piety shown the dead is piety in vain.   [*Exit* CREON.]

Ode III

CHORUS.   Love, unconquerable   *Strophe*
    Waster of rich men, keeper
    Of warm lights and all-night vigil
    In the soft face of a girl:
    Sea-wanderer, forest-visitor!   5
    Even the pure Immortals cannot escape you,
    And the mortal man, in his one day's dusk,
    Trembles before your glory.

    Surely you swerve upon ruin   *Antistrophe*
    The just man's consenting heart,
    As here you have made bright anger   10

Strike between father and son—
And none has conquered by Love!
A girl's glance working the will of heaven:
Pleasure to her alone who mocks us,
Merciless Aphroditê.°   15

Scene IV

CHORAGOS [*as* ANTIGONÊ *enters guarded*].   But I can no longer stand in awe of this,
　　　Nor, seeing what I see, keep back my tears.
　　　Here is Antigonê, passing to that chamber
　　　Where all find sleep at last.

ANTIGONÊ.   Look upon me, friends, and pity me   *Strophe 1*   5
　　　Turning back at the night's edge to say
　　　Good-by to the sun that shines for me no longer;
　　　Now sleepy Death
　　　Summons me down to Acheron,° that cold shore:
　　　There is no bridesong there, nor any music.   10

CHORUS.   Yet not unpraised, not without a kind of honor,
　　　You walk at last into the underworld;
　　　Untouched by sickness, broken by no sword.
　　　What woman has ever found your way to death?

ANTIGONÊ.   How often I have heard the story of Niobê,°   *Antistrophe 1*   15
　　　Tantalos' wretched daughter, how the stone
　　　Clung fast about her, ivy-close: and they say
　　　The rain falls endlessly
　　　And sifting soft snow; her tears are never done.
　　　I feel the loneliness of her death in mine.   20

CHORUS.   But she was born of heaven, and you
　　　Are woman, woman-born. If her death is yours,
　　　A mortal woman's, is this not for you
　　　Glory in our world and in the world beyond?

ANTIGONÊ.   You laugh at me. Ah, friends, friends   *Strophe 2*   25
　　　Can you not wait until I am dead? O Thebes,
　　　O men many-charioted, in love with Fortune,
　　　Dear springs of Dircê, sacred Theban grove,
　　　Be witnesses for me, denied all pity,
　　　Unjustly judged! and think a word of love   30
　　　For her whose path turns
　　　Under dark earth, where there are no more tears.

CHORUS.   You have passed beyond human daring and come at last
　　　Into a place of stone where Justice sits.
　　　I cannot tell   35
　　　What shape of your father's guilt appears in this.

ANTIGONÊ.   You have touched it at last: *Antistrophe 2*
　　　That bridal bed
　　　Unspeakable, horror of son and mother mingling:

Ode III 16 Aphroditê goddess of love.   **9 Acheron** a river of the underworld, which was ruled
by Hades.   **15 Niobê** Niobê boasted of her numerous children, provoking Leto, the mother of
Apollo, to destroy them. Niobê wept profusely, and finally was turned to stone on Mount
Sipylus, whose streams are her tears.

Their crime, infection of all our family!
O Oedipus, father and brother!   40
Your marriage strikes from the grave to murder mine.
I have been a stranger here in my own land:
All my life
The blasphemy of my birth has followed me.

CHORUS.   Reverence is a virtue, but strength   45
Lives in established law: that must prevail.
You have made your choice,
Your death is the doing of your conscious hand.

ANTIGONÊ.   Then let me go, since all your words are bitter,   *Epode*
And the very light of the sun is cold to me.   50
Lead me to my vigil, where I must have
Neither love nor lamentation; no song, but silence.

    CREON *interrupts impatiently.*

CREON.   If dirges and planned lamentations could put off death,
Men would be singing for ever.
[*To the* SERVANTS.]   Take her, go!
You know your orders: take her to the vault   55
And leave her alone there. And if she lives or dies,
That's her affair, not ours: our hands are clean.

ANTIGONÊ.   O tomb, vaulted bride-bed in eternal rock,
Soon I shall be with my own again
Where Persephonê° welcomes the thin ghosts underground: 60
And I shall see my father again, and you, mother,
And dearest Polyneicês—
                dearest indeed
To me, since it was my hand
That washed him clean and poured the ritual wine:
And my reward is death before my time!   65
And yet, as men's hearts know, I have done no wrong,
I have not sinned before God. Or if I have,
I shall know the truth in death. But if the guilt
Lies upon Creon who judged me, then, I pray,
May his punishment equal my own.

CHORAGOS.   O passionate heart,   70
Unyielding, tormented still by the same winds!

CREON.   Her guards shall have good cause to regret their delaying.

ANTIGONÊ.   Ah! That voice is like the voice of death!

CREON.   I can give you no reason to think you are mistaken.

ANTIGONÊ.   Thebes, and you my fathers' gods,   75
And rulers of Thebes, you see me now, the last
Unhappy daughter of a line of kings,
Your kings, led away to death. You will remember
What things I suffer, and at what men's hands,
Because I would not transgress the laws of heaven.   80
[*To the* GUARDS, *simply.*] Come: let us wait no longer.

                    [*Exit* ANTIGONÊ, *left, guarded.*]

60 Persephonê queen of the underworld.

Ode IV

CHORUS.   All Danaê's° beauty was locked away   *Strophe 1*
              In a brazen cell where the sunlight could not come:
              A small room, still as any grave, enclosed her.
              Yet she was a princess too,
              And Zeus in a rain of gold poured love upon her.   5
              O child, child,
              No power in wealth or war
              Or tough sea-blackened ships
              Can prevail against untiring Destiny!

              And Dryas' son° also, that furious king,   *Antistrophe 1*
              Bore the god's prisoning anger for his pride: 10
              Sealed up by Dionysos in deaf stone,
              His madness died among echoes.
              So at the last he learned what dreadful power
              His tongue had mocked:
              For he had profaned the revels,   15
              And fired the wrath of the nine
              Implacable Sisters° that love the sound of the flute.

              And old men tell a half-remembered tale   *Strophe 2*
              Of horror where a dark ledge splits the sea
              And a double surf beats on the gray shores: 20
              How a king's new woman,° sick
              With hatred for the queen he had imprisoned,
              Ripped out his two sons' eyes with her bloody hands
              While grinning Arês° watched the shuttle plunge
              Four times: four blind wounds crying for revenge,   25

              Crying, tears and blood mingled.—Piteously born,   *Antistrophe 2*
              Those sons whose mother was of heavenly birth!
              Her father was the god of the North Wind
              And she was cradled by gales,
              She raced with young colts on the glittering hills
              And walked untrammeled in the open light: 30
              But in her marriage deathless Fate found means
              To build a tomb like yours for all her joy.

Scene V

Enter blind TEIRESIAS, *led by a boy. The opening speeches of* TEIRESIAS *should be in singsong contrast to the realistic lines of* CREON.

TEIRESIAS.   This is the way the blind man comes, Princes, Princes,
                Lock-step, two heads lit by the eyes of one.

---

1 Danaê A princess shut into a tower by her father because of a prophecy that the king would be killed by his grandson. Zeus nevertheless entered Danaê's chamber in the form of a shower of gold and impregnated her. She gave birth to Perseus, who accidentally killed the king with a discus.   **10 Dryas' son** Lycurgus, King of Thrace.   **18 Sisters** the Muses.   **22 king's new woman** Eidothea, second wife of King Phineus, blinded her stepsons. Their mother, Cleopatra, had been imprisoned in a cave. Phineus was the son of a king, and Cleopatra, his first wife, was the daughter of Boreas, the North Wind, but this illustrious ancestry could not protect his sons from violence and darkness.   **25 Arês** god of war.

CREON.   What new thing have you to tell us, old Teiresias?

TEIRESIAS.   I have much to tell you: listen to the prophet, Creon.

CREON.   I am not aware that I have ever failed to listen.   5

TEIRESIAS.   Then you have done wisely, King, and ruled well.

CREON.   I admit my debt to you. But what have you to say?

TEIRESIAS.   This, Creon: you stand once more on the edge of fate.

CREON.   What do you mean? Your words are a kind of dread.

TEIRESIAS.   Listen, Creon: 10
> I was sitting in my chair of augury, at the place
> Where the birds gather about me. They were all a-chatter,
> As is their habit, when suddenly I heard
> A strange note in their jangling, a scream, a
> Whirring fury; I knew that they were fighting,   15
> Tearing each other, dying
> In a whirlwind of wings clashing. And I was afraid.
> I began the rites of burnt-offering at the altar,
> But Hephaistos° failed me: instead of bright flame,
> There was only the sputtering slime of the fat thigh-flesh   20
> Melting: the entrails dissolved in gray smoke,
> The bare bone burst from the welter. And no blaze!
>
> This was a sign from heaven. My boy described it,
> Seeing for me as I see for others.
>
> I tell you, Creon, you yourself have brought   25
> This new calamity upon us. Our hearths and altars
> Are stained with the corruption of dogs and carrion birds
> That glut themselves on the corpse of Oedipus' son.
> The gods are deaf when we pray to them, their fire
> Recoils from our offering, their birds of omen   30
> Have no cry of comfort, for they are gorged
> With the thick blood of the dead.
>   O my son,
> These are no trifles! Think: all men make mistakes,
> But a good man yields when he knows his course is wrong,
> And repairs the evil. The only crime is pride.   35
>
> Give in to the dead man, then: do not fight with a corpse—
> What glory is it to kill a man who is dead?
> Think, I beg you:
> It is for your own good that I speak as I do.
> You should be able to yield for your own good.   40

CREON.   It seems that prophets have made me their especial province.
> All my life long
> I have been a kind of butt for the dull arrows
> Of doddering fortune-tellers!
>   No, Teiresias:
> If your birds—if the great eagles of God himself   45
> Should carry him stinking bit by bit to heaven,

---

19 Hephaistos god of fire.

I would not yield. I am not afraid of pollution:
No man can defile the gods.

                       Do what you will,
Go into business, make money, speculate
In India gold or that synthetic gold from Sardis,
Get rich otherwise than by my consent to bury him.   50
Teiresias, it is a sorry thing when a wise man
Sells his wisdom, lets out his words for hire!

TEIRESIAS.   Ah Creon! Is there no man left in the world—
CREON.   To do what?—Come, let's have the aphorism!   55
TEIRESIAS.   No man who knows that wisdom outweighs any wealth?
CREON.   As surely as bribes are baser than any baseness.
TEIRESIAS.   You are sick, Creon! You are deathly sick!
CREON.   As you say: it is not my place to challenge a prophet.
TEIRESIAS.   Yet you have said my prophecy is for sale.   60
CREON.   The generation of prophets has always loved gold.
TEIRESIAS.   The generation of kings has always loved brass.
CREON.   You forget yourself! You are speaking to your King.
TEIRESIAS.   I know it. You are a king because of me.
CREON.   You have a certain skill; but you have sold out.   65
TEIRESIAS.   King, you will drive me to words that—
CREON.   Say them, say them!
Only remember: I will not pay you for them.
TEIRESIAS.   No, you will find them too costly.
CREON.   No doubt. Speak:
Whatever you say, you will not change my will.
TEIRESIAS.   Then take this, and take it to heart!   70
The time is not far off when you shall pay back
Corpse for corpse, flesh of your own flesh.
You have thrust the child of this world into living night,
You have kept from the gods below the child that is theirs:
The one in a grave before her death, the other,   75
Dead, denied the grave. This is your crime:
And the Furies and the dark gods of Hell
Are swift with terrible punishment for you.

Do you want to buy me now, Creon?

                       Not many days,
And your house will be full of men and women weeping,   80
And curses will be hurled at you from far
Cities grieving for sons unburied, left to rot
Before the walls of Thebes.

These are my arrows, Creon: they are all for you.
[*To* BOY.] But come, child: lead me home.   85
Let him waste his fine anger upon younger men.
Maybe he will learn at last
To control a wiser tongue in a better head.   [*Exit* TEIRESIAS.]

CHORAGOS.   The old man has gone, King, but his words
Remain to plague us. I am old, too,   90
But I cannot remember that he was ever false.

CREON.   That is true. . . . It troubles me.
        Oh it is hard to give in! but it is worse
        To risk everything for stubborn pride.
CHORAGOS.   Creon: take my advice.
CREON.   What shall I do?   95
CHORAGOS.   Go quickly: free Antigonê from her vault
        And build a tomb for the body of Polyneicês.
CREON.   You would have me do this!
CHORAGOS.   Creon, yes!
        And it must be done at once: God moves
        Swiftly to cancel the folly of stubborn men.   100
CREON.   It is hard to deny the heart! But I
        Will do it: I will not fight with destiny.
CHORAGOS.   You must go yourself, you cannot leave it to others.
CREON.   I will go.
                    —Bring axes, servants:
        Come with me to the tomb. I buried her, I   105
        Will set her free.
                    Oh quickly!
        My mind misgives—
        The laws of the gods are mighty, and a man must serve them
        To the last day of his life!   [*Exit* CREON.]

                        Paean°

CHORAGOS.   God of many names   *Strophe 1*
CHORUS.   O Iacchos
                                son
        of Kadmeian Sémelê
                        O born of the Thunder!
        Guardian of the West
                          Regent
        of Eleusis' plain
                    O Prince of Maenad Thebes
        and the Dragon Field by rippling Ismenós:°   5
CHORAGOS.   God of many names   *Antistrophe 1*
CHORUS.   the flame of torches
        flares on our hills
                    the nymphs of Iacchos
        dance at the spring of Castalia:°
        from the vine-close mountain
                        come ah come in ivy:
        Evohé evohé! sings through the streets of Thebes   10
CHORAGOS.   God of many names   *Strophe 2*
CHORUS.   Iacchos of Thebes
        heavenly Child

Paean a hymn (here dedicated to Iacchos, also called Dionysos. His father was Zeus, his mother was Sémelê, daughter of Kadmos. Iacchos's worshipers were the Maenads, whose cry was "*Evohé evohé*")   **5 Ismenós** a river east of Thebes (from a dragon's teeth, sown near the river, there sprang men who became the ancestors of the Theban nobility).   **8 Castalia** a spring on Mount Parnassos.

of Sémelê bride of the Thunderer!
The shadow of plague is upon us:
          come
   with clement feet
      oh come from Parnassos
   down the long slopes
         across the lamenting water   15

CHORAGOS.   Iô Fire! Chorister of the throbbing stars!   *Antistrophe 2*
   O purest among the voices of the night!
   Thou son of God, blaze for us!
CHORUS.   Come with choric rapture of circling Maenads
   Who cry *Iô Iacche*!
           God of many names!   20

Exodos

Enter MESSENGER *from left.*

MESSENGER.   Men of the line of Kadmos,° you who live
   Near Amphion's citadel,°
                   I cannot say
Of any condition of human life "This is fixed,
This is clearly good, or bad." Fate raises up,
And Fate casts down the happy and unhappy alike: 5
No man can foretell his Fate.
           Take the case of Creon:
Creon was happy once, as I count happiness:
Victorious in battle, sole governor of the land,
Fortunate father of children nobly born.
And now it has all gone from him! Who can say   10
That a man is still alive when his life's joy fails?
He is a walking dead man. Grant him rich,
Let him live like a king in his great house:
If his pleasure is gone, I would not give
So much as the shadow of smoke for all he owns.   15
CHORAGOS.   Your words hint at sorrow: what is your news for us?
MESSENGER.   They are dead. The living are guilty of their death.
CHORAGOS.   Who is guilty? Who is dead? Speak!
MESSENGER.   Haimon.
Haimon is dead; and the hand that killed him
Is his own hand.
CHORAGOS.   His father's? or his own?   20
MESSENGER.   His own, driven mad by the murder his father had done.
CHORAGOS.   Teiresias, Teiresias, how clearly you saw it all!
MESSENGER.   This is my news: you must draw what conclusions you can from it.
CHORAGOS.   But look: Eurydicê, our Queen:
   Has she overheard us?   25

Enter EURYDICÊ *from the palace, center.*

EURYDICE.   I have heard something, friends:

---

1 Kadmos, who sowed the dragon's teeth, was founder of Thebes. **2 Amphion's citadel**
Amphion played so sweetly on his lyre that he charmed stones to form a wall around Thebes.

As I was unlocking the gate of Pallas'° shrine,
For I needed her help today, I heard a voice
Telling of some new sorrow. And I fainted
There at the temple with all my maidens about me.   30
But speak again: whatever it is, I can bear it:
Grief and I are no strangers.

MESSENGER.   Dearest Lady,
I will tell you plainly all that I have seen.
I shall not try to comfort you: what is the use,
Since comfort could lie only in what is not true?   35
The truth is always best.

                                   I went with Creon
To the outer plain where Polyneicês was lying,
No friend to pity him, his body shredded by dogs.
We made our prayers in the place to Hecatê
And Pluto,° that they would be merciful. And we bathed   40
The corpse with holy water, and we brought
Fresh-broken branches to burn what was left of it,
And upon the urn we heaped up a towering barrow
Of the earth of his own land.

                                   When we were done, we ran
To the vault where Antigonê lay on her couch of stone.   45
One of the servants had gone ahead,
And while he was yet far off he heard a voice
Grieving within the chamber, and he came back
And told Creon. And as the King went closer,
The air was full of wailing, the words lost,   50
And he begged us to make all haste. "Am I a prophet?"
He said, weeping, "And must I walk this road,
The saddest of all that I have gone before?
My son's voice calls me on. Oh quickly, quickly!
Look through the crevice there, and tell me   55
If it is Haimon, or some deception of the gods!"
We obeyed; and in the cavern's farthest corner
We saw her lying:
She had made a noose of her fine linen veil
And hanged herself. Haimon lay beside her,   60
His arms about her waist, lamenting her,
His love lost under ground, crying out
That his father had stolen her away from him.

When Creon saw him the tears rushed to his eyes
And he called to him: "What have you done, child?
Speak to me.   65
What are you thinking that makes your eyes so strange?
O my son, my son, I come to you on my knees!"
But Haimon spat in his face. He said not a word,
Staring—

27 **Pallas** Pallas Athene, goddess of wisdom.   40 **Hecatê / And Pluto** Hecatê and Pluto (also
known as Hades) were deities of the underworld.

And suddenly drew his sword
And lunged. Creon shrank back, the blade missed; and the boy,　　70
Desperate against himself, drove it half its length
Into his own side, and fell. And as he died
He gathered Antigonê close in his arms again,
Choking, his blood bright red on her white cheek.
And now he lies dead with the dead, and she is his　　75
At last, his bride in the house of the dead.

　　　　　　　　　　　　Exit EURYDICÊ *into the palace.*

CHORAGOS.　She has left us without a word. What can this mean?
MESSENGER.　It troubles me, too; yet she knows what is best,
　　Her grief is too great for public lamentation,
　　And doubtless she has gone to her chamber to weep　　80
　　For her dead son, leading her maidens in his dirge.

　　Pause.

CHORAGOS.　It may be so: but I fear this deep silence.
MESSENGER.　I will see what she is doing. I will go in.

　　　　　　　　　　　　Exit MESSENGER *into the palace.*

　　Enter CREON *with attendants, bearing* HAIMON's *body.*

CHORAGOS.　But here is the king himself: on look at him,
　　Bearing his own damnation in his arms.　　85
CREON.　Nothing you say can touch me any more.
　　My own blind heart has brought me
　　From darkness to final darkness. Here you see
　　The father murdering, the murdered son—
　　And all my civic wisdom!　　90

　　Haimon my son, so young, so young to die,
　　I was the fool, not you; and you died for me.
CHORAGOS.　That is the truth; but you were late in learning it.
CREON.　This truth is hard to bear. Surely a god
　　Has crushed me beneath the hugest weight of heaven,　　95
　　And driven me headlong a barbaric way
　　To trample out the thing I held most dear.

　　The pains that men will take to come to pain!

　　Enter MESSENGER *from the palace.*

MESSENGER.　The burden you carry in your hands is heavy,
　　But it is not all: you will find more in your house.　　100
CREON.　What burden worse than this shall I find there?
MESSENGER.　The Queen is dead.
CREON.　O port of death, deaf world,
　　Is there no pity for me? And you, Angel of evil,
　　I was dead, and your words are death again.　　105
　　Is it true, boy? Can it be true?
　　Is my wife dead? Has death bred death?
MESSENGER.　You can see for yourself.

　　The doors are opened and the body of EURYDICÊ *is disclosed within.*

　　CREON.　Oh pity!

All true, all true, and more than I can bear!   110
O my wife, my son!

MESSENGER.   She stood before the altar, and her heart
Welcomed the knife her own hand guided,
And a great cry burst from her lips for Megareus° dead,
And for Haimon dead, her sons; and her last breath   115
Was a curse for their father, the murderer of her sons.
And she fell, and the dark flowed in through her closing eyes.

CREON.   O God, I am sick with fear.
Are there no swords here? Has no one a blow for me?

MESSENGER.   Her curse is upon you for the deaths of both.   120

CREON.   It is right that it should be. I alone am guilty.
I know it, and I say it. Lead me in,
Quickly, friends.
I have neither life nor substance. Lead me in.

CHORAGOS.   You are right, if there can be right in so much wrong. 125
The briefest way is best in a world of sorrow.

CREON.   Let it come,
Let death come quickly, and be kind to me.
I would not ever see the sun again.

CHORAGOS.   All that will come when it will; but we, meanwhile,   130
Have much to do. Leave the future to itself.

CREON.   All my heart was in that prayer!

CHORAGOS.   Then do not pray any more: the sky is deaf.

CREON.   Lead me away. I have been rash and foolish.
I have killed my son and my wife.   135
I look for comfort; my comfort lies here dead.
Whatever my hands have touched has come to nothing.
Fate has brought all my pride to a thought of dust.

As CREON *is being led into the house, the* CHORAGOS *advances and speaks
directly to the audience.*

CHORAGOS.   There is no happiness where there is no wisdom;
No wisdom but in submission to the gods.   140
Big words are always punished,
And proud men in old age learn to be wise.

                                                          [c. 441 B.C.]

114 Megareus Megareus, brother of Haimon, had died in the assault on Thebes.

Topics for Critical Thinking and Writing

1. Would you use masks for some (or all) of the characters? If so, would they be masks that fully cover the face, Greek style, or some sort of half-masks? (A full mask enlarges the face, and conceivably the mouthpiece can amplify the voice, but only an exceptionally large theater might require such help. Perhaps half-

masks are enough if the aim is chiefly to distance the actors from the audience and from daily reality, and to force the actors to develop resources other than facial gestures. One director, arguing in favor of half-masks, has said that an actor who wears even a half-mask learns to act not with his eyes but with his neck.)

2. How would you costume the players? Would you dress them as the Greeks might have? Why? One argument sometimes used by those who hold the modern productions of Greek drama should use classical costumes is that Greek drama *ought* to be remote and ritualistic. Evaluate this view. What sort of modern dress might be effective?

3. If you were directing a college production of *Antigonê,* how large a chorus would you use? (Sophocles is said to have used a chorus of fifteen.) Would you have the chorus recite (or chant) the odes in unison, or would you assign lines to single speakers?

4. Although Sophocles called his play *Antigonê,* many critics say that Creon is the real tragic hero, pointing out that Antigonê is absent from the last third of the play. Evaluate this view.

5. In some Greek tragedies, fate plays a great role in bringing about the downfall of the tragic hero. Though there are references to the curse on the House of Oedipus in *Antigonê,* do we feel that Antigonê goes to her death as a result of the workings of fate? Do we feel that fate is responsible for Creon's fall? Are both Antigonê and Creon the creators of their own tragedy?

6. Are the words *hubris* (p. 333) and *hamartia* (p. 334) relevant to Antigonê? To Creon?

7. Why does Creon, contrary to the Chorus's advice, bury the body of Polyneices before he releases Antigonê? Does his action show a zeal for piety as short-sighted as his earlier zeal for law? Is his action plausible, in view of the facts that Teiresias has dwelt on the wrong done to Polyneices and that Antigonê has ritual food to sustain her? Or are we not to worry about Creon's motive?

8. A *foil* is a character who, by contrast, sets off or helps define another character. To what extent is Ismenê a foil to Antigonê? Is she entirely without courage?

9. What function does Eurydicê serve? How deeply do we feel about her fate?

AUGUST WILSON

August Wilson was born in Pittsburgh in 1945, the son of a black woman and a white man. After dropping out of school at the age of 15, Wilson took various odd jobs, such as stock clerk and short-order cook, in his spare time educating himself in the public library, chiefly by reading works by such black writers as Richard Wright, Ralph Ellison, Langston Hughes, and Amiri Baraka (LeRoi Jones). In 1978 the director of a black theater in St. Paul, Minnesota, who had known Wilson in Pittsburgh, invited him to write a play for the theater. Six months later Wilson moved permanently to St. Paul.

The winner of the Pulitzer Prize for drama in 1987, Wilson's Fences *was first presented as a staged reading in 1983 and was later performed in Chicago, Seattle, Rochester (New York), and New Haven (Connecticut) before reaching New York City in 1987. An earlier play,* Ma Rainey's Black Bottom, *was voted Best Play of the Year 1984–1985 by the New York Drama Critics' Circle. In 1981 when* Ma Rainey *was first read at the O'Neill Center in Waterford, Connecticut, Wilson met Lloyd Richards, a black director with whom he has continued to work closely.* The Piano Lesson, *directed by Richards, won Wilson a second Pulitzer Prize in 1990.*

Fences

for Lloyd Richards,
who adds to whatever he touches

When the sins of our fathers visit us
We do not have to play host.
We can banish them with forgiveness
As God, in His Largeness and Laws.

—August Wilson

LIST OF CHARACTERS

TROY MAXSON
JIM BONO, Troy's friend
ROSE, Troy's wife
LYONS, Troy's oldest son by previous marriage
GABRIEL, Troy's brother
CORY, Troy and Rose's son
RAYNELL, Troy's daughter

SETTING: *The setting is the yard which fronts the only entrance to the Maxson household, an ancient two-story brick house set back off a small alley in a big-city neighborhood. The entrance to the house is gained by two or three steps leading to a wooden porch badly in need of paint.*

A relatively recent addition to the house and running its full width, the porch lacks congruence. It is a sturdy porch with a flat roof. One or two chairs of dubious value sit at one end where the kitchen window opens onto the porch. An old-fashioned icebox stands silent guard at the opposite end.

The yard is a small dirt yard, partially fenced, except for the last scene, with a wooden saw horse, a pile of lumber, and other fence-building equipment set off to the side. Opposite is a tree from which hangs a ball made of rags. A baseball bat leans against the tree. Two oil drums serve as garbage receptacles and sit near the house at right to complete the setting.

THE PLAY: *Near the turn of the century, the destitute of Europe sprang on the city with tenacious claws and an honest and solid dream. The city devoured them. They swelled its belly until it burst into a thousand furnaces and sewing machines, a thousand butcher shops and bakers' ovens, a thousand churches and hospitals and funeral parlors and money-lenders. The city grew. It nourished itself and offered each man a partnership limited only by his talent, his guile, and his willingness and capacity for hard work. For the immigrants of Europe, a dream dared and won true.*

The descendants of African slaves were offered no such welcome or participation. They came from places called the Carolinas and the Virginias,

Fences in the Seattle Repertory Theater production with (left to right) Frances Foster as Rose, Keith Amos as Cory, William Jay as Gabriel, and Gilbert Lewis as Troy. (Photo © Chris Bennion/Photostage)

Georgia, Alabama, Mississippi, and Tennessee. They came strong, eager, searching. The city rejected them and they fled and settled along the riverbanks and under bridges in shallow, ramshackle houses made of sticks and tarpaper. They collected rags and wood. They sold the use of their muscles and their bodies. They cleaned houses and washed clothes, they shined shoes, and in quiet desperation and vengeful pride, they stole, and lived in pursuit of their own dream. That they could breathe free, finally, and stand to meet life with the force of dignity and whatever eloquence the heart could call upon.

By 1957, the hard-won victories of the European immigrants had solidified the industrial might of America. War had been confronted and won with new energies that used loyalty and patriotism as its fuel. Life was rich, full, and flourishing. The Milwaukee Braves won the World Series, and the hot winds of change that would make the sixties a turbulent, racing, dangerous, and provocative decade had not yet begun to blow full.

Act 1

Scene 1

It is 1957. TROY *and* BONO *enter the yard, engaged in conversation.* TROY *is fifty-three years old, a large man with thick, heavy hands; it is this largeness that he strives to fill out and make an accommodation with. Together with his blackness, his largeness informs his sensibilities and the choices he has made in his life.*

Of the two men, BONO *is obviously the follower. His commitment to their friendship of thirty-odd years is rooted in his admiration of* TROY'S *honesty, capacity for hard work, and his strength, which* BONO *seeks to emulate.*

It is Friday night, payday, and the one night of the week the two men engage in a ritual of talk and drink. TROY *is usually the most talkative and at times he can be crude and almost vulgar, though he is capable of rising to profound heights of expression. The men carry lunch buckets and wear or carry burlap aprons and are dressed in clothes suitable to their jobs as garbage collectors.*

BONO.   Troy, you ought to stop that lying!

TROY.   I ain't lying! The nigger had a watermelon this big. [*He indicates with his hands.*] Talking about . . . "What watermelon, Mr. Rand?" I liked to fell out! "What watermelon, Mr. Rand?" . . . And it sitting there big as life.

BONO.   What did Mr. Rand say?

TROY.   Ain't said nothing. Figure if the nigger too dumb to know he carrying a watermelon, he wasn't gonna get much sense out of him. Trying to hide that great big old watermelon under his coat. Afraid to let the white man see him carry it home.

BONO.   I'm like you . . . I ain't got no time for them kind of people.

TROY.   Now what he look like getting mad cause he see the man from the union talking to Mr. Rand?

BONO.   He come to me talking about . . . "Maxson gonna get us fired." I told him to get away from me with that. He walked away from me calling you a troublemaker. What Mr. Rand say?

TROY.   Ain't said nothing. He told me to go down the Commissioner's office next Friday. They called me down there to see them.

BONO.   Well, as long as you got your complaint filed, they can't fire you. That's what one of them white fellows tell me.

TROY.   I ain't worried about them firing me. They gonna fire me cause I asked a question? That's all I did. I went to Mr. Rand and asked him, "Why? Why you got the white mens driving and the colored lifting?" Told him, "What's the matter, don't I count? You think only white fellows got sense enough to drive a truck. That ain't no paper job! Hell, anybody can drive a truck. How come you got all whites driving and the colored lifting?" He told me "take it to the union." Well, hell, that's what I done! Now they wanna come up with this pack of lies.

BONO.   I told Brownie if the man come and ask him any questions . . . just tell the truth! It ain't nothing but something they done trumped up on you cause you filed a complaint on them.

TROY.   Brownie don't understand nothing. All I want them to do is change the job description. Give everybody a chance to drive the truck. Brownie can't see that. He ain't got that much sense.

BONO.   How you figure he be making out with that gal be up at Taylor's all the time . . . that Alberta gal?

TROY.   Same as you and me. Getting just as much as we is. Which is to say nothing.

BONO.   It is, huh? I figure you doing a little better than me . . . and I ain't saying what I'm doing.

TROY.   Aw, nigger, look here . . . I know you. If you had got anywhere near that gal, twenty minutes later you be looking to tell somebody. And the first one you gonna tell . . . that you gonna want to brag to . . . is me.

BONO.   I ain't saying that. I see where you be eyeing her.

TROY.   I eye all the women. I don't miss nothing. Don't never let nobody tell you Troy Maxson don't eye the women.

BONO.   You been doing more than eyeing her. You done bought her a drink or two.

TROY.   Hell yeah, I bought her a drink! What that mean? I bought you one, too. What that mean cause I buy her a drink? I'm just being polite.

BONO.   It's all right to buy her one drink. That's what you call being polite. But when you wanna be buying two or three . . . that's what you call eyeing her.

TROY.   Look here, as long as you known me . . . you ever known me to chase after women?

BONO.   Hell yeah! Long as I done known you. You forgetting I knew you when.

TROY.   Naw, I'm talking about since I been married to Rose?

BONO.   Oh, not since you been married to Rose. Now, that's the truth, there. I can say that.

TROY.   All right then! Case closed.

BONO.   I see you be walking up around Alberta's house. You supposed to be at Taylors' and you be walking up around there.

TROY.   What you watching where I'm walking for? I ain't watching after you.

BONO.   I seen you walking around there more than once.

TROY.   Hell, you liable to see me walking anywhere! That don't mean nothing cause you see me walking around there.

BONO.   Where she come from anyway? She just kinda showed up one day.

TROY.   Tallahassee. You can look at her and tell she one of them Florida gals. They got some big healthy women down there. Grow them right up out the ground. Got a little bit of Indian in her. Most of them niggers down in Florida got some Indian in them.

BONO.   I don't know about that Indian part. But she damn sure big and healthy. Woman wear some big stockings. Got them great big old legs and hips as wide as the Mississippi River.

TROY.   Legs don't mean nothing. You don't do nothing but push them out of the way. But them hips cushion the ride!

BONO.   Troy, you ain't got no sense.

TROY.   It's the truth! Like you riding on Goodyears!

ROSE *enters from the house. She is ten years younger than* TROY, *her devotion to him stems from her recognition of the possibilities of her life without him: a succession of abusive men and their babies, a life of partying and running the streets, the Church, or aloneness with its attendant pain and frustration. She recognizes* TROY*'s spirit as a fine and illuminating one and she either ignores or forgives his faults, only some of which she recognizes. Though she doesn't drink, her presence is an integral part of the Friday night rituals. She alternates between the porch and the kitchen, where supper preparations are under way.*

ROSE.   What you all out here getting into?

TROY.   What you worried about what we getting into for? This is men talk, woman.

ROSE.   What I care what you all talking about? Bono, you gonna stay for supper?

BONO.   No, I thank you, Rose. But Lucille say she cooking up a pot of pigfeet.

TROY.   Pigfeet! Hell, I'm going home with you! Might even stay the night if you got some pigfeet. You got something in there to top them pigfeet, Rose?

ROSE.   I'm cooking up some chicken. I got some chicken and collard greens.

TROY.   Well, go on back in the house and let me and Bono finish what we was talking about. This is men talk. I got some talk for you later. You know what kind of talk I mean. You go on and powder it up.

ROSE.   Troy Maxson, don't you start that now!

TROY [*puts his arm around her*].   Aw, woman . . . come here. Look here, Bono . . . when I met this woman . . . I got out that place, say, "Hitch up my pony, saddle up my mare . . . there's a woman out there for me somewhere. I looked here. Looked there. Saw Rose and latched on to her." I latched on to her and told her—I'm gonna tell you the truth—I told her, "Baby, I don't wanna marry, I just wanna be your man." Rose told me . . . tell him what you told me, Rose.

ROSE.   I told him if he wasn't the marrying kind, then move out the way so the marrying kind could find me.

TROY.   That's what she told me. "Nigger, you in my way. You blocking the view! Move out the way so I can find me a husband." I thought it over two or three days. Come back—

ROSE.   Ain't no two or three days nothing. You was back the same night.

TROY.   Come back, told her . . . "Okay, baby . . . but I'm gonna buy me a banty rooster and put him out there in the backyard . . . and when he see a stranger come, he'll flap his wings and crow . . . ." Look here, Bono, I could watch the front door by myself . . . it was that back door I was worried about.

ROSE.   Troy, you ought not talk like that. Troy ain't doing nothing but telling a lie.

TROY.   Only thing is . . . when we first got married . . . forget the rooster . . . we ain't had no yard!

BONO.   I hear you tell it. Me and Lucille was staying down there on Logan Street. Had two rooms with the outhouse in the back. I ain't mind the outhouse none. But when that goddamn wind blow through there in the winter . . . that's what I'm talking about! To this day I wonder why in the hell I ever stayed down there for six long years. But see, I didn't know I could do no better. I thought only white folks had inside toilets and things.

ROSE.   There's a lot of people don't know they can do no better than they doing now. That's just something you got to learn. A lot of folks still shop at Bella's.

TROY.   Ain't nothing wrong with shopping at Bella's. She got fresh food.

ROSE.   I ain't said nothing about if she got fresh food. I'm talking about what she charge. She charge ten cents more than the A&P.

TROY.   The A&P ain't never done nothing for me. I spends my money where I'm treated right. I go down to Bella, say, "I need a loaf of bread, I'll pay you Friday." She give it to me. What sense that make when I got money to go and spend it somewhere else and ignore the person who done right by me? That ain't in the Bible.

ROSE.   We ain't talking about what's in the Bible. What sense it make to shop there when she overcharge?

TROY.   You shop where you want to. I'll do my shopping where the people been good to me.

ROSE.   Well, I don't think it's right for her to overcharge. That's all I was saying.

BONO.   Look here . . . I got to get on. Lucille going be raising all kind of hell.

TROY.   Where you going, nigger? We ain't finished this pint. Come here, finish this pint.

BONO.   Well, hell, I am . . . if you ever turn the bottle loose.

TROY [*hands him the bottle*].   The only thing I say about the A&P is I'm glad Cory got that job down there. Help him take care of his school clothes and things. Gabe done moved out and things getting tight around here. He got that job. . . . He can start to look out for himself.

ROSE.   Cory done went and got recruited by a college football team.

TROY.   I told that boy about that football stuff. The white man ain't gonna let him get nowhere with that football. I told him when he first come to me with it. Now you come telling me he done went and got more tied up in it. He ought to go and get recruited in how to fix cars or something where he can make a living.

ROSE.   He ain't talking about making no living playing football. It's just something the boys in school do. They gonna send a recruiter by to talk to you. He'll tell you he ain't talking about making no living playing football. It's a honor to be recruited.

TROY.   It ain't gonna get him nowhere. Bono'll tell you that.

BONO.   If he be like you in the sports . . . he's gonna be all right. Ain't but two men ever played baseball as good as you. That's Babe Ruth and Josh Gibson.[1] Them's the only two men ever hit more home runs than you.

TROY.   What it ever get me? Ain't got a pot to piss in or a window to throw it out of.

ROSE.   Times have changed since you was playing baseball, Troy. That was before the war. Times have changed a lot since then.

TROY.   How in hell they done changed?

ROSE.   They got lots of colored boys playing ball now. Baseball and football.

BONO.   You right about that, Rose. Times have changed, Troy. You just come along too early.

TROY.   There ought not never have been no time called too early! Now you take that fellow . . . what's that fellow they had playing right field for the Yankees back then? You know who I'm talking about, Bono. Used to play right field for the Yankees.

ROSE.   Selkirk?

TROY.   Selkirk! That's it! Man batting .269, understand? .269. What kind of sense that make? I was hitting .432 with thirty-seven home runs! Man batting .269 and playing right field for the Yankees! I saw Josh Gibson's daughter yesterday. She walking around with raggedy shoes on her feet. Now I bet you Selkirk's daughter ain't walking around with raggedy shoes on the feet! I bet you that!

ROSE.   They got a lot of colored baseball players now. Jackie Robinson[2] was the first. Folks had to wait for Jackie Robinson.

TROY.   I done seen a hundred niggers play baseball better than Jackie Robinson. Hell, I know some teams Jackie Robinson couldn't even make! What you talking about Jackie Robinson. Jackie Robinson wasn't nobody. I'm talking about if you could play ball then they ought to have let you play. Don't care what color you were. Come telling me I come along too early. If you could play . . . then they ought to have let you play.

TROY *takes a long drink from the bottle.*

[1]**Josh Gibson** African American ballplayer (1911–1947), known as the Babe Ruth of the Negro leagues.   [2]**Jackie Robinson** In 1947 Robinson (1919–1972) became the first African American to play baseball in the major leagues.

ROSE.   You gonna drink yourself to death. You don't need to be drinking like that.

TROY.   Death ain't nothing. I done seen him. Done wrassled with him. You can't tell me nothing about death. Death ain't nothing but a fastball on the outside corner. And you know what I'll do to that! Lookee here, Bono . . . am I lying? You get one of them fastballs, about waist high, over the outside corner of the plate where you can get the meat of the bat on it . . . and good god! You can kiss it goodbye. Now, am I lying?

BONO.   Naw, you telling the truth there. I seen you do it.

TROY.   If I'm lying . . . that 450 feet worth of lying! [*Pause.*] That's all death is to me. A fastball on the outside corner.

ROSE.   I don't know why you want to get on talking about death.

TROY.   Ain't nothing wrong with talking about death. That's part of life. Everybody gonna die. You gonna die, I'm gonna die. Bono's gonna die. Hell, we all gonna die.

ROSE.   But you ain't got to talk about it. I don't like to talk about it.

TROY.   You the one brought it up. Me and Bono was talking about baseball . . . you tell me I'm gonna drink myself to death. Ain't that right, Bono? You know I don't drink this but one night out of the week. That's Friday night. I'm gonna drink just enough to where I can handle it. Then I cuts it loose. I leave it alone. So don't you worry about me drinking myself to death. 'Cause I ain't worried about Death. I done seen him. I done wrestled with him.

Look here, Bono . . . I looked up one day and Death was marching straight at me. Like Soldiers on Parade! The Army of Death was marching straight at me. The middle of July, 1941. It got real cold just like it be winter. It seem like Death himself reached out and touched me on the shoulder. He touched me just like I touch you. I got cold as ice and Death standing there grinning at me.

ROSE.   Troy, why don't you hush that talk.

TROY.   I say . . . what you want, Mr. Death? You be wanting me? You done brought your army to be getting me? I looked him dead in the eye. I wasn't fearing nothing. I was ready to tangle. Just like I'm ready to tangle now. The Bible say be ever vigilant. That's why I don't get but so drunk. I got to keep watch.

ROSE.   Troy was right down there in Mercy Hospital. You remember he had pneumonia? Laying there with a fever talking plumb out of his head.

TROY.   Death standing there staring at me . . . carrying that sickle in his hand. Finally he say, "You want bound over for another year?" See, just like that . . . "You want bound over for another year?" I told him, "Bound over hell! Let's settle this now!"

It seem like he kinda fell back when I said that, and all the cold went out of me. I reached down and grabbed that sickle and threw it just as far as I could throw it . . . and me and him commenced to wrestling.

We wrestled for three days and three nights. I can't say where I found the strength from. Everytime it seemed like he was gonna get the best of me, I'd reach way down deep inside myself and find the strength to do him one better.

ROSE.   Everytime Troy tell that story he find different ways to tell it. Different things to make up about it.

TROY.   I ain't making up nothing. I'm telling you the facts of what happened. I wrestled with Death for three days and three nights and I'm standing here to tell you about it. [*Pause.*] All right. At the end of the third night we done weakened each other to where we can't hardly move. Death stood up, throwed on his robe . . . had him a white robe with a hood on it. He throwed on that robe and went off to look for his sickle. Say, "I'll be back." Just like that. "I'll be back." I told him, say, "Yeah, but . . . you gonna have to find me!" I wasn't no fool. I wasn't going looking for him. Death ain't nothing to play with. And I know he's gonna get me. I know I got to join his army . . . his camp followers. But as long as I keep my strength and see him coming . . . as long as I keep up my vigilance . . . he's gonna have to fight to get me. I ain't going easy.

BONO.   Well, look here, since you got to keep up your vigilance . . . let me have the bottle.

TROY.   Aw hell, I shouldn't have told you that part. I should have left out that part.

ROSE.   Troy be talking that stuff and half the time don't even know what he be talking about.

TROY.   Bono know me better than that.

BONO.   That's right. I know you. I know you got some Uncle Remus[3] in your blood. You got more stories than the devil got sinners.

TROY.   Aw hell, I done seen him too! Done talked with the devil.

ROSE.   Troy, don't nobody wanna be hearing all that stuff.

LYONS *enters the yard from the street. Thirty-four years old,* TROY*'s son by a previous marriage, he sports a neatly trimmed goatee, sport coat, white shirt, tieless and buttoned at the collar. Though he fancies himself a musician, he is more caught up in the rituals and "idea" of being a musician than in the actual practice of the music. He has come to borrow money from* TROY, *and while he knows he will be successful, he is uncertain as to what extent his lifestyle will be held up to scrutiny and ridicule.*

LYONS.   Hey, Pop.

TROY.   What you come "Hey, Popping" me for?

LYONS.   How you doing, Rose? [*He kisses her.*] Mr. Bono. How you doing?

BONO.   Hey, Lyons . . . how you been?

TROY.   He must have been doing all right. I ain't seen him around here last week.

ROSE.   Troy, leave your boy alone. He come by to see you and you wanna start all that nonsense.

TROY.   I ain't bothering Lyons. [*Offers him the bottle.*] Here . . . get you a drink. We got an understanding. I know why he come by to see me and he know I know.

LYONS.   Come on, Pop . . . I just stopped by to say hi . . . see how you was doing.

TROY.   You ain't stopped by yesterday.

ROSE.   You gonna stay for supper, Lyons? I got some chicken cooking in the oven.

LYONS.   No, Rose . . . thanks. I was just in the neighborhood and thought I'd stop by for a minute.

TROY.   You was in the neighborhood all right, nigger. You telling the truth there. You was in the neighborhood cause it's my payday.

LYONS.   Well, hell, since you mentioned it . . . let me have ten dollars.

TROY.   I'll be damned! I'll die and go to hell and play blackjack with the devil before I give you ten dollars.

BONO.   That's what I wanna know about . . . that devil you done seen.

LYONS.   What . . . Pop done seen the devil? You too much, Pops.

---

[3]**Uncle Remus** narrator of traditional black tales in a book by Joel Chandler Harris.

TROY.   Yeah, I done seen him. Talked to him too!

ROSE.   You ain't seen no devil. I done told you that man ain't had nothing to do with the devil. Anything you can't understand, you want to call it the devil.

TROY.   Look here, Bono . . . I went down to see Hertzberger about some furniture. Got three rooms for two-ninety-eight. That what it say on the radio. "Three rooms . . . two-ninety-eight." Even made up a little song about it. Go down there . . . man tell me I can't get no credit. I'm working every day and can't get no credit. What to do? I got an empty house with some raggedy furniture in it. Cory ain't got no bed. He's sleeping on a pile of rags on the floor. Working every day and can't get no credit. Come back here—Rose'll tell you—madder than hell. Sit down . . . try to figure what I'm gonna do. Come a knock on the door. Ain't been living here but three days. Who know I'm here? Open the door . . . devil standing there bigger than life. White fellow . . . white fellow . . . got on good clothes and everything. Standing there with a clipboard in his hand. I ain't had to say nothing. First words come out of his mouth was . . . "I understand you need some furniture and can't get no credit." I liked to fell over. He say, "I'll give you all the credit you want, but you got to pay the interest on it." I told him, "Give me three rooms worth and charge whatever you want." Next day a truck pulled up here and two men unloaded them three rooms. Man what drove the truck give me a book. Say send ten dollars, first of every month to the address in the book and every thing will be all right. Say if I miss a payment the devil was coming back and it'll be hell to pay. That was fifteen years ago. To this day . . . the first of the month I send my ten dollars, Rose'll tell you.

ROSE.   Troy lying.

TROY.   I ain't never seen that man since. Now you tell me who else that could have been but the devil? I ain't sold my soul or nothing like that, you understand. Naw, I wouldn't have truck with the devil about nothing like that. I got my furniture and pays my ten dollars the first of the month just like clockwork.

BONO.   How long you say you been paying this ten dollars a month?

TROY.   Fifteen years!

BONO.   Hell, ain't you finished paying for it yet? How much the man done charged you?

TROY.   Ah hell, I done paid for it. I done paid for it ten times over! The fact is I'm scared to stop paying it.

ROSE.   Troy lying. We got that furniture from Mr. Glickman. He ain't paying no ten dollars a month to nobody.

TROY.   Aw hell, woman. Bono know I ain't that big a fool.

LYONS.   I was just getting ready to say . . . I know where there's a bridge for sale.

TROY.   Look here, I'll tell you this . . . it don't matter to me if he was the devil. It don't matter if the devil give credit. Somebody has got to give it.

ROSE.   It ought to matter. You going around talking about having truck with the devil . . . God's the one you gonna have to answer to. He's the one gonna be at the Judgment.

LYONS.   Yeah, well, look here, Pop . . . Let me have that ten dollars. I'll give it back to you. Bonnie got a job working at the hospital.

TROY.   What I tell you, Bono? The only time I see this nigger is when he wants something. That's the only time I see him.

LYONS.   Come on, Pop, Mr. Bono don't want to hear all that. Let me have the ten dollars. I told you Bonnie working.

TROY.   What that mean to me? "Bonnie working." I don't care if she working. Go ask her for the ten dollars if she working. Talking about "Bonnie working." Why ain't you working?

LYONS.   Aw, Pop, you know I can't find no decent job. Where am I gonna get a job at? You know I can't get no job.

TROY.   I told you I know some people down there. I can get you on the rubbish if you want to work. I told you that the last time you came by here asking me for something.

LYONS.   Naw, Pop . . . thanks. That ain't for me. I don't wanna be carrying nobody's rubbish. I don't wanna be punching nobody's time clock.

TROY.   What's the matter, you too good to carry people's rubbish? Where you think that ten dollars you talking about come from? I'm just supposed to haul people's rubbish and give my money to you cause you too lazy to work. You too lazy to work and wanna know why you ain't got what I got.

ROSE.   What hospital Bonnie working at? Mercy?

LYONS.   She's down at Passavant working in the laundry.

TROY.   I ain't got nothing as it is. I give you that ten dollars and I got to eat beans the rest of the week. Naw . . . you ain't getting no ten dollars here.

LYONS.   You ain't got to be eating no beans. I don't know why you wanna say that.

TROY.   I ain't got no extra money. Gabe done moved over to Miss Pearl's paying her the rent and things done got tight around here. I can't afford to be giving you every payday.

LYONS.   I ain't asked you to give me nothing. I asked you to loan me ten dollars. I know you got ten dollars.

TROY.   Yeah, I got it. You know why I got it? Cause I don't throw my money away out there in the streets. You living the fast life . . . wanna be a musician . . . running around in them clubs and things . . . . then, you learn to take care of yourself. You ain't gonna find me going and asking nobody for nothing. I done spent too many years without.

LYONS.   You and me is two different people, Pop.

TROY.   I done learned my mistake and learned to do what's right by it. You still trying to get something for nothing. Life don't owe you nothing. You owe it to yourself. Ask Bono. He'll tell you I'm right.

LYONS.   You got your way of dealing with the world . . . I got mine. The only thing that matters to me is the music.

TROY.   Yeah, I can see that! It don't matter how you gonna eat . . . where your next dollar is coming from. You telling the truth there.

LYONS.   I know I got to eat. But I got to live too. I need something that gonna help me to get out of the bed in the morning. Make me feel like I belong in the world. I don't bother nobody. I just stay with the music cause that's the only way I can find to live in the world. Otherwise there ain't no telling what I might do. Now I don't come criticizing you and how you live. I just come by to ask you for ten dollars. I don't wanna hear all that about how I live.

TROY.   Boy, your mamma did a hell of a job raising you.

LYONS.   You can't change me, Pop. I'm thirty-four years old. If you wanted to change me, you should have been there when I was growing up. I come by to see you . . . ask for ten dollars and you want to talk about how I was raised. You don't know nothing about how I was raised.

ROSE.   Let the boy have ten dollars, Troy.

TROY [*to* LYONS].   What the hell you looking at me for? I ain't got no ten dollars. You know what I do with my money. [*To* ROSE] Give him ten dollars if you want him to have it.

ROSE.   I will. Just as soon as you turn it loose.

TROY [*handing* ROSE *the money*].   There it is. Seventy-six dollars and forty-two cents. You see this, Bono? Now, I ain't gonna get but six of that back.

ROSE.   You ought to stop telling that lie. Here, Lyons. [*She hands him the money.*]

LYONS.   Thanks, Rose. Look . . . I got to run . . . I'll see you later.

TROY.   Wait a minute. You gonna say, "Thanks, Rose" and ain't gonna look to see where she got that ten dollars from? See how they do me, Bono?

LYONS.   I know she got it from you, Pop. Thanks. I'll give it back to you.

TROY.   There he go telling another lie. Time I see that ten dollars . . . he'll be owing me thirty more.

LYONS.   See you, Mr. Bono.

BONO.   Take care, Lyons!

LYONS.   Thanks, Pop. I'll see you again.

> LYONS *exits the yard.*

TROY.   I don't know why he don't go and get him a decent job and take care of that woman he got.

BONO.   He'll be all right, Troy. The boy is still young.

TROY.   The *boy* is thirty-four years old.

ROSE.   Let's not get off into all that.

BONO.   Look here . . . I got to be going. I got to be getting on. Lucille gonna be waiting.

TROY [*puts his arm around* ROSE].   See this woman, Bono? I love this woman. I love this woman so much it hurts. I love her so much . . . I done run out of ways of loving her. So I got to go back to basics. Don't you come by my house Monday morning talking about time to go to work . . . 'cause I'm still gonna be stroking!

ROSE.   Troy! Stop it now!

BONO.   I ain't paying him no mind, Rose. That ain't nothing but gin-talk. Go on, Troy. I'll see you Monday.

TROY.   Don't you come by my house, nigger! I done told you what I'm gonna be doing.

> *The lights go down to black.*

Scene 2

The lights come up on ROSE *hanging up clothes. She hums and sings softly to herself. It is the following morning.*

ROSE [*sings*].   Jesus, be a fence all around me every day
> Jesus, I want you to protect me as I travel on my way.
> Jesus, be a fence all around me every day.

> TROY *enters from the house.*

> Jesus, I want you to protect me
> As I travel on my way.

[*To* TROY.] Morning. You ready for breakfast? I can fix it soon as I finish hanging up these clothes.

TROY. I got the coffee on. That'll be all right. I'll just drink some of that this morning.

ROSE. That 651 hit yesterday. That's the second time this month. Miss Pearl hit for a dollar . . . seem like those that need the least always get lucky. Poor folks can't get nothing.

TROY. Them numbers don't know nobody. I don't know why you fool with them. You and Lyons both.

ROSE. It's something to do.

TROY. You ain't doing nothing but throwing your money away.

ROSE. Troy, you know I don't play foolishly. I just play a nickel here and a nickel there.

TROY. That's two nickels you done thrown away.

ROSE. Now I hit sometimes . . . that makes up for it. It always comes in handy when I do hit. I don't hear you complaining then.

TROY. I ain't complaining now. I just say it's foolish. Trying to guess out of six hundred ways which way the number gonna come. If I had all the money niggers, these Negroes, throw away on numbers for one week—just one week—I'd be a rich man.

ROSE. Well, you wishing and calling it foolish ain't gonna stop folks from playing numbers. That's one thing for sure. Besides . . . some good things come from playing numbers. Look where Pope done bought him that restaurant off of numbers.

TROY. I can't stand niggers like that. Man ain't had two dimes to rub together. He walking around with his shoes all run over bumming money for cigarettes. All right. Got lucky there and hit the numbers . . .

ROSE. Troy, I know all about it.

TROY. Had good sense, I'll say that for him. He ain't throwed his money away. I seen niggers hit the numbers and go through two thousand dollars in four days. Man bought him that restaurant down there . . . fixed it up real nice . . . and then didn't want nobody to come in it! A Negro go in there and can't get no kind of service. I seen a white fellow come in there and order a bowl of stew. Pope picked all the meat out of the pot for him. Man ain't had nothing but a bowl of meat! Negro come behind him and ain't got nothing but the potatoes and carrots. Talking about what numbers do for people, you picked a wrong example. Ain't done nothing but make a worser fool out of him than he was before.

ROSE. Troy, you ought to stop worrying about what happened at work yesterday.

TROY. I ain't worried. Just told me to be down there at the Commissioner's office on Friday. Everybody think they gonna fire me. I ain't worried about them firing me. You ain't got to worry about that. [*Pause.*] Where's Cory? Cory in the house? [*Calls.*] Cory?

ROSE. He gone out.

TROY. Out, huh? He gone out 'cause he know I want him to help me with this fence. I know how he is. That boy scared of work.

GABRIEL *enters. He comes halfway down the alley and, hearing* TROY*'s voice, stops.*

TROY [*continues*]. He ain't done a lick of work in his life.

ROSE. He had to go to football practice. Coach wanted them to get in a little extra practice before the season start.

TROY.   I got his practice . . . running out of here before he get his chores done.

ROSE.   Troy, what is wrong with you this morning? Don't nothing set right with you. Go on back in there and go to bed . . . get up on the other side.

TROY.   Why something got to be wrong with me? I ain't said nothing wrong with me.

ROSE.   You got something to say about everything. First it's the numbers . . . then it's the way the man runs his restaurant . . . then you done got on Cory. What's it gonna be next? Take a look up there and see if the weather suits you . . . or is it gonna be how you gonna put up the fence with the clothes hanging in the yard.

TROY.   You hit the nail on the head then.

ROSE.   I know you like I know the back of my hand. Go on in there and get you some coffee . . . see if that straighten you up. 'Cause you ain't right this morning.

TROY *starts into the house and sees* GABRIEL. GABRIEL *starts singing.* TROY's *brother, he is seven years younger than* TROY. *Injured in World War II, he has a metal plate in his head. He carries an old trumpet tied around his waist and believes with every fiber of his being that he is the Archangel Gabriel. He carries a chipped basket with an assortment of discarded fruits and vegetables he has picked up in the strip district and which he attempts to sell.*

GABRIEL [*singing*]   Yes, ma'am I got plums
             You ask me how I sell them
             Oh ten cents apiece
             Three for a quarter
             Come and buy now
             'Cause I'm here today
             And tomorrow I'll be gone

   GABRIEL *enters.*

Hey, Rose!

ROSE.   How you doing Gabe?

GABRIEL.   There's Troy . . . Hey, Troy!

TROY.   Hey, Gabe.

   Exit into kitchen.

ROSE [*to* GABRIEL].   What you got there?

GABRIEL.   You know what I got, Rose. I got fruits and vegetables.

ROSE [*looking in basket*].   Where's all these plums you talking about?

GABRIEL.   I ain't got no plums today, Rose. I was just singing that. Have some tomorrow. Put me in a big order for plums. Have enough plums tomorrow for St. Peter and everybody.

   TROY *reenters from kitchen, crosses to steps.*

[*To* ROSE.] Troy's mad at me.

TROY.   I ain't mad at you. What I got to be mad at you about? You ain't done nothing to me.

GABRIEL.   I just moved over to Miss Pearl's to keep out from in your way. I ain't mean no harm by it.

TROY.   Who said anything about that? I ain't said anything about that.

GABRIEL.   You ain't mad at me, is you?

TROY.   Naw . . . I ain't mad at you, Gabe. If I was mad at you I'd tell you about it.

GABRIEL.   Got me two rooms. In the basement. Got my own door too. Wanna see my key? [*He holds up a key.*] That's my own key! My two rooms!

TROY.   Well, that's good, Gabe. You got your own key . . . that's good.

ROSE.   You hungry, Gabe? I was just fixing to cook Troy his breakfast.

GABRIEL.   I'll take some biscuits. You got some biscuits? Did you know when I was in heaven . . . every morning me and St. Peter would sit down by the gate and eat some big fat biscuits? Oh, yeah! We had us a good time. We'd sit there and eat us them biscuits and then St. Peter would go off to sleep and tell me to wake him up when it's time to open the gates for the judgment.

ROSE.   Well, come on . . . I'll make up a batch of biscuits.

> ROSE *exits into the house.*

GABRIEL.   Troy . . . St. Peter got your name in the book. I seen it. It say . . . Troy Maxson. I say . . . I know him! He got the same name like what I got. That's my brother!

TROY.   How many times you gonna tell me that, Gabe?

GABRIEL.   Ain't got my name in the book. Don't have to have my name. I done died and went to heaven. He got your name though. One morning St. Peter was looking at his book . . . marking it up for the judgment . . . and he let me see your name. Got it in there under M. Got Rose's name . . . I ain't seen it like I seen yours . . . but I know it's in there. He got a great big book. Got everybody's name what was ever been born. That's what he told me. But I seen your name. Seen it with my own eyes.

TROY.   Go on in the house there. Rose going to fix you something to eat.

GABRIEL.   Oh, I ain't hungry. I done had breakfast with Aunt Jemimah. She come by and cooked me up a whole mess of flapjacks. Remember how we used to eat them flapjacks?

TROY.   Go on in the house and get you something to eat now.

GABRIEL.   I got to sell my plums. I done sold some tomatoes. Got me two quarters. Wanna see? [*He shows* TROY *his quarters.*] I'm gonna save them and buy me a new horn so St. Peter can hear me when it's time to open the gates. [GABRIEL *stops suddenly. Listens.*] Hear that? That's the hellhounds. I got to chase them out of here. Go on get out of here! Get out!

> GABRIEL *exits singing.*

> Better get ready for the judgment
> Better get ready for the judgment
> My Lord is coming down

> ROSE *enters from the house.*

TROY.   He's gone off somewhere.

GABRIEL. [*offstage*].   Better get ready for the judgment
> Better get ready for the judgment morning
> Better get ready for the judgment
> My God is coming down

ROSE.   He ain't eating right. Miss Pearl say she can't get him to eat nothing.

TROY.   What you want me to do about it, Rose? I done did everything I can for the man. I can't make him get well. Man got half his head blown away . . . what you expect?

ROSE.   Seem like something ought to be done to help him.

TROY.   Man don't bother nobody. He just mixed up from that metal plate he got in his head. Ain't no sense for him to go back into the hospital.

ROSE.   Least he be eating right. They can help him take care of himself.

TROY.   Don't nobody wanna be locked up, Rose. What you wanna lock him up for? Man go over there and fight the war . . . messin' around with them Japs, get half his head blow off . . . and they give him a lousy three thousand dollars. And I had to swoop down on that.

ROSE.   Is you fixing to go into that again?

TROY.   That's the only way I got a roof over my head . . . cause of that metal plate.

ROSE.   Ain't no sense you blaming yourself for nothing. Gabe wasn't in no condition to manage that money. You done what was right by him. Can't nobody say you ain't done what was right by him. Look how long you took care of him . . . till he wanted to have his own place and moved over there with Miss Pearl.

TROY.   That ain't what I'm saying, woman! I'm just stating the facts. If my brother didn't have that metal plate in his head . . . I wouldn't have a pot to piss in or a window to throw it out of. And I'm fifty-three years old. Now see if you can understand that!

TROY gets up from the porch and starts to exit the yard.

ROSE.   Where you going off to? You been running out of here every Saturday for weeks. I thought you was gonna work on this fence?

TROY.   I'm gonna walk down to Taylor's. Listen to the ball game. I'll be back in a bit. I'll work on it when I get back.

He exits the yard. The lights go to black.

Scene 3

The lights come up on the yard. It is four hours later. ROSE *is taking down the clothes from the line.* CORY *enters carrying his football equipment.*

ROSE.   Your daddy like to had a fit with you running out of here this morning without doing your chores.

CORY.   I told you I had to go to practice.

ROSE.   He say you were supposed to help him with this fence.

CORY.   He been saying that the last four or five Saturdays, and then he don't never do nothing, but go down to Taylors'. Did you tell him about the recruiter?

ROSE.   Yeah, I told him.

CORY.   What he say?

ROSE.   He ain't said nothing too much. You get in there and get started on your chores before he gets back. Go on and scrub down them steps before he gets back here hollering and carrying on.

CORY.   I'm hungry. What you got to eat, Mama?

ROSE.   Go on and get started on your chores. I got some meat loaf in there. Go on and make you a sandwich . . . and don't leave no mess in there.

CORY exits into the house. ROSE *continues to take down the clothes.* TROY *enters the yard and sneaks up and grabs her from behind.*

Troy! Go on, now. You liked to scared me to death. What was the score of the game? Lucille had me on the phone and I couldn't keep up with it.

TROY.   What I care about the game? Come here, woman.

[He tries to kiss her.]

ROSE.   I thought you went down Taylors' to listen to the game. Go on, Troy! You supposed to be putting up this fence.

TROY [*attempting to kiss her again*].   I'll put it up when I finish with what is at hand.

ROSE.   Go on, Troy. I ain't studying you.

TROY [*chasing after her*].   I'm studying you . . . fixing to do my homework!

ROSE.   Troy, you better leave me alone.

TROY.   Where's Cory? That boy brought his butt home yet?

ROSE.   He's in the house doing his chores.

TROY [*calling*].   Cory! Get your butt out here, boy!

ROSE *exits into the house with the laundry.* TROY *goes over to the pile of wood, picks up a board, and starts sawing.* CORY *enters from the house.*

TROY.   You just now coming in here from leaving this morning?

CORY.   Yeah, I had to go to football practice.

TROY.   Yeah, what?

CORY.   Yessir.

TROY.   I ain't but two seconds off you noway. The garbage sitting in there overflowing . . . you ain't done none of your chores . . . and you come in here talking about "Yeah."

CORY.   I was just getting ready to do my chores now, Pop . . .

TROY.   Your first chore is to help me with this fence on Saturday. Everything else come after that. Now get that saw and cut them boards.

CORY *takes the saw and begins cutting the boards.* TROY *continues working. There is a long pause.*

CORY.   Hey, Pop . . . why don't you buy a TV?

TROY.   What I want with a TV? What I want one of them for?

CORY.   Everybody got one. Earl, Ba Bra . . . Jesse!

TROY.   I ain't asked you who had one. I say what I want with one?

CORY.   So you can watch it. They got lots of things on TV. Baseball games and everything. We could watch the World Series.

TROY.   Yeah . . . and how much this TV cost?

CORY.   I don't know. They got them on sale for around two hundred dollars.

TROY.   Two hundred dollars, huh?

CORY.   That ain't that much, Pop.

TROY.   Naw, it's just two hundred dollars. See that roof you got over your head at night? Let me tell you something about that roof. It's been over ten years since that roof was last tarred. See now . . . the snow come this winter and sit up there on that roof like it is . . . and it's gonna seep inside. It's just gonna be a little bit . . . ain't gonna hardly notice it. Then the next thing you know, it's gonna be leaking all over the house. Then the wood rot from all that water and you gonna need a whole new roof. Now, how much you think it cost to get that roof tarred?

CORY.   I don't know.

TROY.   Two hundred and sixty-four dollars . . . cash money. While you thinking about a TV, I got to be thinking about the roof . . . and whatever else go wrong here. Now if you had two hundred dollars, what would you do . . . fix the roof or buy a TV?

CORY.   I'd buy a TV. Then when the roof started to leak . . . when it needed fixing . . . I'd fix it.

TROY.   Where you gonna get the money from? You done spent it for a TV. You gonna sit up and watch the water run all over your brand new TV.

CORY.   Aw, Pop. You got money. I know you do.

TROY.   Where I got it at, huh?

CORY.   You got it in the bank.

TROY.   You wanna see my bankbook? You wanna see that seventy-three dollars and twenty-two cents I got sitting up in there?

CORY.   You ain't got to pay for it all at one time. You can put a down payment on it and carry it on home with you.

TROY.   Not me. I ain't gonna owe nobody nothing if I can help it. Miss a payment and they come and snatch it right out of your house. Then what you got? Now, soon as I get two hundred dollars clear, then I'll buy a TV. Right now, as soon as I get two hundred and sixty-four dollars, I'm gonna have this roof tarred.

CORY.   Aw . . . Pop!

TROY.   You go on and get you two hundred dollars and buy one if ya want it. I got better things to do with my money.

CORY.   I can't get no two hundred dollars. I ain't never seen two hundred dollars.

TROY.   I'll tell you what . . . you get you a hundred dollars and I'll put the other hundred with it.

CORY.   All right, I'm gonna show you.

TROY.   You gonna show me how you can cut them boards right now.

> CORY *begins to cut the boards. There is a long pause.*

CORY.   The Pirates won today. That makes five in a row.

TROY.   I ain't thinking about the Pirates. Got an all-white team. Got that boy . . . that Puerto Rican boy . . . Clemente. Don't even half-play him. That boy could be something if they give him a chance. Play him one day and sit him on the bench the next.

CORY.   He gets a lot of chances to play.

TROY.   I'm talking about playing regular. Playing every day so you can get your timing. That's what I'm talking about.

CORY.   They got some white guys on the team that don't play every day. You can't play everybody at the same time.

TROY.   If they got a white fellow sitting on the bench . . . you can bet your last dollar he can't play! The colored guy got to be twice as good before he get on the team. That's why I don't want you to get all tied up in them sports. Man on the team and what it get him? They got colored on the team and don't use them. Same as not having them. All them teams the same.

CORY.   The Braves got Hank Aaron and Wes Covington. Hank Aaron hit two home runs today. That makes forty-three.

TROY.   Hank Aaron ain't nobody. That what you supposed to do. That's how you supposed to play the game. Ain't nothing to it. It's just a matter of timing . . . getting the right follow-through. Hell, I can hit forty-three home runs right now!

CORY.   Not off no major-league pitching, you couldn't.

TROY.   We had better pitching in the Negro leagues. I hit seven home runs off of Satchel Paige.[4] You can't get no better than that!

CORY.   Sandy Koufax. He's leading the league in strikeouts.

TROY.   I ain't thinking of no Sandy Koufax.

CORY.   You got Warren Spahn and Lew Burdette. I bet you couldn't hit no home runs off of Warren Spahn.

---

[4]**Satchel Paige** (1906–1982) was a pitcher in the Negro leagues.

TROY.   I'm through with it now. You go on and cut them boards. [*Pause.*] Your mama tell me you done got recruited by a college football team? Is that right?

CORY.   Yeah. Coach Zellman say the recruiter gonna be coming by to talk to you. Get you to sign the permission papers.

TROY.   I thought you supposed to be working down there at the A&P. Ain't you suppose to be working down there after school?

CORY.   Mr. Stawicki say he gonna hold my job for me until after the football season. Say starting next week I can work weekends.

TROY.   I thought we had an understanding about this football stuff? You suppose to keep up with your chores and hold that job down at the A&P. Ain't been around here all day on a Saturday. Ain't none of your chores done . . . and now you telling me you done quit your job.

CORY.   I'm going to be working weekends.

TROY.   You damn right you are! And ain't no need for nobody coming around here to talk to me about signing nothing.

CORY.   Hey, Pop . . . you can't do that. He's coming all the way from North Carolina.

TROY.   I don't care where he coming from. The white man ain't gonna let you get nowhere with that football noway. You go on and get your book-learning so you can work yourself up in that A&P or learn how to fix cars or build houses or something, get you a trade. That way you have something can't nobody take away from you. You go on and learn how to put your hands to some good use. Besides hauling people's garbage.

CORY.   I get good grades, Pop. That's why the recruiter wants to talk with you. You got to keep up your grades to get recruited. This way I'll be going to college. I'll get a chance . . .

TROY.   First you gonna get your butt down there to the A&P and get your job back.

CORY.   Mr. Stawicki done already hired somebody else 'cause I told him I was playing football.

TROY.   You a bigger fool than I thought . . . to let somebody take away your job so you can play some football. Where you gonna get your money to take out your girlfriend and whatnot? What kind of foolishness is that to let somebody take away your job?

CORY.   I'm still gonna be working weekends.

TROY.   Naw . . . naw. You getting your butt out of here and finding you another job.

CORY.   Come on, Pop! I got to practice. I can't work after school and play football too. The team needs me. That's what Coach Zellman say . . .

TROY.   I don't care what nobody else say. I'm the boss . . . you understand? I'm the boss around here. I do the only saying what counts.

CORY.   Come on, Pop!

TROY.   I asked you . . . did you understand?

CORY.   Yeah . . .

TROY.   What?!

CORY.   Yessir.

TROY.   You go on down there to that A&P and see if you can get your job back. If you can't do both . . . then you quit the football team. You've got to take the crookeds with the straights.

CORY.   Yessir. [*Pause.*] Can I ask you a question?

TROY.   What the hell you wanna ask me? Mr. Stawicki the one you got the questions for.

CORY.   How come you ain't never liked me?

TROY.   Liked you? Who the hell say I got to like you? What law is there say I got to like you? Wanna stand up in my face and ask a damn foolass question like that. Talking about liking somebody. Come here, boy, when I talk to you.

CORY *comes over to where* TROY *is working. He stands slouched over and* TROY *shoves him on his shoulder.*

Straighten up, goddammit! I asked you a question . . . what law is there say I got to like you?

CORY.   None.

TROY.   Well, all right then! Don't you eat every day? [*Pause.*] Answer me when I talk to you! Don't you eat every day?

CORY.   Yeah.

TROY.   Nigger, as long as you in my house, you put that sir on the end of it when you talk to me.

CORY.   Yes . . . sir.

TROY.   You eat every day.

CORY.   Yessir!

TROY.   Got a roof over your head.

CORY.   Yessir!

TROY.   Got clothes on your back.

CORY.   Yessir.

TROY.   Why you think that is?

CORY.   Cause of you.

TROY.   Ah, hell I know it's cause of me . . . but why do you think that is?

CORY [*hesitant*].   Cause you like me.

TROY.   Like you? I go out of here every morning . . . bust my butt . . . putting up with them crackers every day . . . cause I like you? You are the biggest fool I ever saw. [*Pause.*] It's my job. It's my responsibility! You understand that? A man got to take care of his family. You live in my house . . . sleep you behind on my bedclothes . . . fill you belly up with my food . . . cause you my son. You my flesh and blood. Not cause I like you! Cause it's my duty to take care of you. I owe a responsibility to you! Let's get this straight right here . . . before it go along any further . . . I ain't got to like you. Mr. Rand don't give me my money come payday cause he likes me. He gives me cause he owe me. I done give you everything I had to give you. I gave you your life! Me and your mama worked that out between us. And liking your black ass wasn't part of the bargain. Don't you try and go through life worrying about if somebody like you or not. You best be making sure they doing right by you. You understand what I'm saying boy?

CORY.   Yessir.

TROY.   Then get the hell out of my face, and get on down to that A&P.

ROSE *has been standing behind the screen door for much of the scene. She enters as* CORY *exits.*

ROSE.   Why don't you let the boy go ahead and play football, Troy? Ain't no harm in that. He's just trying to be like you with the sports.

TROY.   I don't want him to be like me! I want him to move as far away from my life as he can get. You the only decent thing that ever happened to me. I wish him that. But I don't wish him a thing else from my life. I decided seventeen years ago that boy wasn't getting involved in no sports. Not after what they did to me in the sports.

ROSE. Troy, why don't you admit you was too old to play in the major leagues? For once . . . why don't you admit that?

TROY. What do you mean too old? Don't come telling me I was too old. I just wasn't the right color. Hell, I'm fifty-three years old and can do better than Selkirk's .269 right now!

ROSE. How's was you gonna play ball when you were over forty? Sometimes I can't get no sense out of you.

TROY. I got good sense, woman. I got sense enough not to let my boy get hurt over playing no sports. You been mothering that boy too much. Worried about if people like him.

ROSE. Everything that boy do . . . he do for you. He wants you to say "Good job, son." That's all.

TROY. Rose, I ain't got time for that. He's alive. He's healthy. He's got to make his own way. I made mine. Ain't nobody gonna hold his hand when he get out there in that world.

ROSE. Times have changed from when you was young, Troy. People change. The world's changing around you and you can't even see it.

TROY [*slow, methodical*]. Woman . . . I do the best I can do. I come in here every Friday. I carry a sack of potatoes and a bucket of lard. You all line up at the door with your hands out. I give you the lint from my pockets. I give you my sweat and my blood. I ain't got no tears. I done spent them. We go upstairs in that room at night . . . and I fall down on you and try to blast a hole into forever. I get up Monday morning . . . find my lunch on the table. I go out. Make my way. Find my strength to carry me through to the next Friday. [*Pause.*] That's all I got, Rose. That's all I got to give. I can't give nothing else.

TROY *exits into the house. The lights go down to black.*

Scene 4

It is Friday. Two weeks later. CORY *starts out of the house with his football equipment. The phone rings.*

CORY [*calling*]. I got it! [*He answers the phone and stands in the screen door talking.*] Hello? Hey, Jesse. Naw . . . I was just getting ready to leave now.

ROSE [*calling*]. Cory!

CORY. I told you, man, them spikes is all tore up. You can use them if you want, but they ain't no good. Earl got some spikes.

ROSE [*calling*]. Cory!

CORY [*calling to* ROSE]. Mam? I'm talking to Jesse. [*Into phone.*] When she say that? [*Pause.*] Aw, you lying, man. I'm gonna tell her you said that.

ROSE [*calling*]. Cory, don't you go nowhere!

CORY. I got to go to the game, Ma! [*Into the phone.*] Yeah, hey, look, I'll talk to you later. Yeah, I'll meet you over Earl's house. Later. Bye, Ma.

CORY *exits the house and starts out the yard.*

ROSE. Cory, where you going off to? You got that stuff all pulled out and thrown all over your room.

CORY [*in the yard*]. I was looking for my spikes. Jesse wanted to borrow my spikes.

ROSE. Get up there and get that cleaned up before your daddy get back in here.

CORY. I got to go to the game! I'll clean it up *when I get back.*

CORY *exits.*

ROSE. That's all he need to do is see that room all messed up.

ROSE *exits into the house.* TROY *and* BONO *enter the yard.* TROY *is dressed in clothes other than his work clothes.*

BONO.   He told him the same thing he told you. Take it to the union.

TROY.   Brownie ain't got that much sense. Man wasn't thinking about nothing. He wait until I confront them on it . . . then he wanna come crying seniority. [*Calls.*] Hey, Rose!

BONO.   I wish I could have seen Mr. Rand's face when he told you.

TROY.   He couldn't get it out of his mouth! Liked to bit his tongue! When they called me down there to the Commissioner's office . . . he thought they was gonna fire me. Like everybody else.

BONO.   I didn't think they was gonna fire you. I thought they was gonna put you on the warning paper.

TROY.   Hey, Rose! [*To* BONO.] Yeah, Mr. Rand like to bit his tongue.

TROY *breaks the seal on the bottle, takes a drink, and hands it to* BONO.

BONO.   I see you run right down to Taylors' and told that Alberta gal.

TROY [*calling*].   Hey Rose! [*To* BONO.] I told everybody. Hey, Rose! I went down there to cash my check.

ROSE [*entering from the house*].   Hush all that hollering, man! I know you out here. What they say down there at the Commissioner's office?

TROY.   You supposed to come when I call you, woman. Bono'll tell you that. [*To* BONO.] Don't Lucille come when you call her?

ROSE.   Man, hush your mouth. I ain't no dog . . . talk about "come when you call me."

TROY [*puts his arm around* ROSE].   You hear this, Bono? I had me an old dog used to get uppity like that. You say, "C'mere, Blue!" . . . and he just lay there and look at you. End up getting a stick and chasing him away trying to make him come.

ROSE.   I ain't studying you and your dog. I remember you used to sing that old song.

TROY [*he sings*].   Hear it ring! Hear it ring! I had a dog his name was Blue.

ROSE.   Don't nobody wanna hear you sing that old song.

TROY [*sings*].   You know Blue was mighty true.

ROSE.   Used to have Cory running around here singing that song.

BONO.   Hell, I remember that song myself.

TROY [*sings*].   You know Blue was a good old dog.
    Blue treed a possum in a hollow log.

    That was my daddy's song. My daddy made up that song.

ROSE.   I don't care who made it up. Don't nobody wanna hear you sing it.

TROY [*makes a song like calling a dog*].   Come here, woman.

ROSE.   You come in here carrying on, I reckon they ain't fired you. What they say down there at the Commissioner's office?

TROY.   Look here, Rose . . . Mr. Rand called me into his office today when I got back from talking to them people down there . . . it come from up top . . . he called me in and told me they was making me a driver.

ROSE.   Troy, you kidding!

TROY.   No I ain't. Ask Bono.

ROSE.   Well, that's great, Troy. Now you don't have to hassle them people no more.

LYONS *enters from the street.*

TROY.   Aw hell, I wasn't looking to see you today. I thought you was in jail. Got it all over the front page of the *Courier* about them raiding Sefus's place . . . where you be hanging out with all them thugs.

LYONS.   Hey, Pop . . . that ain't got nothing to do with me. I don't go down there gambling. I go down there to sit in with the band. I ain't got nothing to do with the gambling part. They got some good music down there.

TROY.   They got some rogues . . . is what they got.

LYONS.   How you been, Mr. Bono? Hi, Rose.

BONO.   I see where you playing down at the Crawford Grill tonight.

ROSE.   How come you ain't brought Bonnie like I told you? You should have brought Bonnie with you, she ain't been over in a month of Sundays.

LYONS.   I was just in the neighborhood . . . thought I'd stop by.

TROY.   Here he come . . .

BONO.   Your daddy got a promotion on the rubbish. He's gonna be the first colored driver. Ain't got to do nothing but sit up there and read the paper like them white fellows.

LYONS.   Hey, Pop . . . if you knew how to read you'd be all right.

BONO.   Naw . . . naw . . . you mean if the nigger knew how to drive he'd be all right. Been fighting with them people about driving and ain't even got a license. Mr. Rand know you ain't got no driver's license?

TROY.   Driving ain't nothing. All you do is point the truck where you want it to go. Driving ain't nothing.

BONO.   Do Mr. Rand know you ain't got no driver's license? That's what I'm talking about. I ain't asked if driving was easy. I asked if Mr. Rand know you ain't got no driver's license.

TROY.   He ain't got to know. The man ain't got to know my business. Time he find out, I have two or three driver's licenses.

LYONS [*going into his pocket*].   Say, look here, Pop . . .

TROY.   I knew it was coming. Didn't I tell you, Bono? I know what kind of "Look here, Pop" that was. The nigger fixing to ask me for some money. It's Friday night. It's my payday. All them rogues down there on the avenue . . . the ones that ain't in jail . . . and Lyons is hopping in his shoes to get down there with them.

LYONS.   See, Pop . . . if you give somebody else a chance to talk sometimes, you'd see that I was fixing to pay you back your ten dollars like I told you. Here
. . . I told you I'd pay you when Bonnie got paid.

TROY.   Naw . . . you go ahead and keep that ten dollars. Put it in the bank. The next time you feel like you wanna come by here and ask me for something . . . you go on down there and get that.

LYONS.   Here's your ten dollars, Pop. I told you I don't want you to give me nothing. I just wanted to borrow ten dollars.

TROY.   Naw . . . you go on and keep that for the next time you want to ask me.

LYONS.   Come on, Pop . . . here go your ten dollars.

ROSE.   Why don't you go on and let the boy pay you back, Troy?

LYONS.   Here you go, Rose. If you don't take it I'm gonna have to hear about it for the next six months. [*He hands her the money.*]

ROSE.   You can hand yours over here too, Troy.

TROY.   You see this, Bono. You see how they do me.

BONO.   Yeah, Lucille do me the same way.

GABRIEL *is heard singing off stage. He enters.*

GABRIEL.   Better get ready for the Judgment! Better get ready for . . . Hey! . . . Hey! . . . There's Troy's boy!

LYONS.   How are you doing, Uncle Gabe?

GABRIEL.   Lyons . . . The King of the Jungle! Rose . . . hey, Rose. Got a flower for
  you. [*He takes a rose from his pocket.*] Picked it myself. That's the same rose
  like you is!

ROSE.   That's right nice of you, Gabe.

LYONS.   What you been doing, Uncle Gabe?

GABRIEL.   Oh, I been chasing hellhounds and waiting on the time to tell St. Peter
  to open the gates.

LYONS.   You been chasing hellhounds, huh? Well . . . you doing the right thing,
  Uncle Gabe. Somebody got to chase them.

GABRIEL.   Oh, yeah . . . I know it. The devil's strong. The devil ain't no pushover.
  Hellhounds snipping at everybody's heels. But I got my trumpet waiting on
  the judgment time.

LYONS.   Waiting on the Battle of Armageddon, huh?

GABRIEL.   Ain't gonna be too much of a battle when God get to waving that
  Judgment sword. But the people's gonna have a hell of a time trying to get
  into heaven if them gates ain't open.

LYONS [*putting his arm around* GABRIEL].   You hear this, Pop. Uncle Gabe, you all
  right!

GABRIEL [*laughing with* LYONS].   Lyons! King of the Jungle.

ROSE.   You gonna stay for supper, Gabe? Want me to fix you a plate?

GABRIEL.   I'll take a sandwich, Rose. Don't want no plate. Just wanna eat with my
  hands. I'll take a sandwich.

ROSE.   How about you, Lyons? You staying? Got some short ribs cooking.

LYONS.   Naw, I won't eat nothing till after we finished playing. [*Pause.*] You ought
  to come down and listen to me play, Pop.

TROY.   I don't like that Chinese music. All that noise.

ROSE.   Go on in the house and wash up, Gabe . . . I'll fix you a sandwich.

GABRIEL [*to* LYONS, *as he exits*].   Troy's mad at me.

LYONS.   What you mad at Uncle Gabe for, Pop?

ROSE.   He thinks Troy's mad at him cause he moved over to Miss Pearl's.

TROY.   I ain't mad at the man. He can live where he want to live at.

LYONS.   What he move over there for? Miss Pearl don't like nobody.

ROSE.   She don't mind him none. She treats him real nice. She just don't allow all
  that singing.

TROY.   She don't mind that rent he be paying . . . that's what she don't mind.

ROSE.   Troy, I ain't going through that with you no more. He's over there cause he
  want to have his own place. He can come and go as he please.

TROY.   Hell, he could come and go as he please here. I wasn't stopping him. I
  ain't put no rules on him.

ROSE.   It ain't the same thing, Troy. And you know it.

     GABRIEL *comes to the door.*

Now, that's the last I wanna hear about that. I don't wanna hear nothing else
  about Gabe and Miss Pearl. And next week . . .

GABRIEL.   I'm ready for my sandwich, Rose.

ROSE.   And next week . . . when that recruiter come from that school . . . I want
  you to sign that paper and go on and let Cory play football. Then that'll be
  the last I have to hear about that.

TROY [*to* ROSE *as she exits into the house*].   I ain't thinking about Cory nothing.

LYONS.   What . . . Cory got recruited? What school he going to?

TROY.   That boy walking around here smelling his piss . . . thinking he's grown.
  Thinking he's gonna do what he want, irrespective of what I say. Look here,

Bono . . . I left the Commissioner's office and went down to the A&P . . . that boy ain't working down there. He lying to me. Telling me he got his job back . . . telling me he working weekends . . . telling me he working after school . . . Mr. Stawicki tell me he ain't working down there at all!

LYONS.   Cory just growing up. He's just busting at the seams trying to fill out your shoes.

TROY.   I don't care what he's doing. When he get to the point where he wanna disobey me . . . then it's time for him to move on. Bono'll tell you that. I bet he ain't never disobeyed his daddy without paying the consequences.

BONO.   I ain't never had a chance. My daddy came on through .... but I ain't never knew him to see him . . . or what he had on his mind or where he went. Just moving on through. Searching out the New Land. That's what the old folks used to call it. See a fellow moving around from place to place . . .woman to woman . . . called it searching out the New Land. I can't say if he ever found it. I come along, didn't want no kids. Didn't know if I was gonna be in one place long enough to fix on them right as their daddy. I figured I was going searching too. As it turned out I been hooked up with Lucille near about as long as your daddy been with Rose. Going on sixteen years.

TROY.   Sometimes I wish I hadn't known my daddy. He ain't cared nothing about no kids. A kid to him wasn't nothing. All he wanted was for you to learn how to walk so he could start you to working. When it come time for eating . . . he ate first. If there was anything left over, that's what you got. Man would sit down and eat two chickens and give you the wing.

LYONS.   You ought to stop that, Pop. Everybody feed their kids. No matter how hard times is . . . everybody care about their kids. Make sure they have something to eat.

TROY.   The only thing my daddy cared about was getting them bales of cotton in to Mr. Lubin. That's the only thing that mattered to him. Sometimes I used to wonder why he was living. Wonder why the devil hadn't come and got him. "Get them bales of cotton in to Mr. Lubin" and find out he owe him money . . .

LYONS.   He should have just went on and left when he saw he couldn't get nowhere. That's what I would have done.

TROY.   How he gonna leave with eleven kids? And where he gonna go? He ain't knew how to do nothing but farm. No, he was trapped and I think he knew it. But I'll say this for him . . . he felt a responsibility toward us. Maybe he ain't treated us the way I felt he should have . . . but without that responsibility he could have walked off and left us . . . made his own way.

BONO.   A lot of them did. Back in those days what you talking about . . . they walk out their front door and just take on down one road or another and keep on walking.

LYONS.   There you go! That's what I'm talking about.

BONO.   Just keep on walking till you come to something else. Ain't you never heard of nobody having the walking blues? Well, that's what you call it when you just take off like that.

TROY.   My daddy ain't had them walking blues! What you talking about? He stayed right there with his family. But he was just as evil as he could be. My mama couldn't stand him. Couldn't stand that evilness. She run off when I was about eight. She sneaked off one night after he had gone to sleep. Told me she was coming back for me. I ain't never seen her no more. All his women run off and left him. He wasn't good for nobody.

When my turn come to head out, I was fourteen and got to sniffing around Joe Canewell's daughter. Had us an old mule we called Greyboy. My daddy sent me out to do some plowing and I tied up Greyboy and went to fooling around with Joe Canewell's daughter. We done found us a nice little spot, got real cozy with each other. She about thirteen and we done figured we was grown anyway . . . so we down there enjoying ourselves . . . ain't thinking about nothing. We didn't know Greyboy had got loose and wandered back to the house and my daddy was looking for me. We down there by the creek enjoying ourselves when my daddy come up on us. Surprised us. He had them leather straps off the mule and commenced to whupping me like there was no tomorrow. I jumped up, mad and embarrassed. I was scared of my daddy. When he commenced to whupping on me . . . quite naturally I run to get out of the way. [*Pause.*] Now I thought he was mad cause I ain't done my work. But I see where he was chasing me off so he could have the gal for himself. When I see what the matter of it was, I lost all fear of my daddy. Right there is where I become a man . . . at fourteen years of age. [*Pause.*] Now it was my turn to run him off. I picked up them same reins that he had used on me. I picked up them reins and commenced to whupping on him. The gal jumped up and run off . . . and when my daddy turned to face me, I could see why the devil had never come to get him . . . cause he was the devil himself. I don't know what happened. When I woke up, I was laying right there by the creek, and Blue . . . this old dog we had . . . was licking my face. I thought I was blind. I couldn't see nothing. Both my eyes were swollen shut. I laid there and cried. I didn't know what I was gonna do. The only thing I knew was the time had come for me to leave my daddy's house. And right there the world suddenly got big. And it was a long time before I could cut it down to where I could handle it.

Part of that cutting down was when I got to the place where I could feel him kicking in my blood and knew that the only thing that separated us was the matter of a few years.

GABRIEL *enters from the house with a sandwich.*

LYONS.   What you got there, Uncle Gabe?

GABRIEL.   Got me a ham sandwich. Rose gave me a ham sandwich.

TROY.   I don't know what happened to him. I done lost touch with everybody except Gabriel. But I hope he's dead. I hope he found some peace.

LYONS.   That's a heavy story, Pop. I didn't know you left home when you was fourteen.

TROY.   And didn't know nothing. The only part of the world I knew was the forty-two acres of Mr. Lubin's land. That's all I knew about life.

LYONS.   Fourteen's kinda young to be out on your own. [*Phone rings.*] I don't even think I was ready to be out on my own at fourteen. I don't know what I would have done.

TROY.   I got up from the creek and walked on down to Mobile. I was through with farming. Figured I could do better in the city. So I walked the two hundred miles to Mobile.

LYONS.   Wait a minute . . . you ain't walked no two hundred miles, Pop. Ain't nobody gonna walk no two hundred miles. You talking about some walking there.

BONO.   That's the only way you got anywhere back in them days.

LYONS.   Shhh. Damn if I wouldn't have hitched a ride with somebody!

TROY.   Who you gonna hitch it with? They ain't had no cars and things like they got now. We talking about 1918.

ROSE [*entering*].   What you all out here getting into?

TROY [*to* ROSE]. I'm telling Lyons how good he got it. He don't know nothing about this I'm talking.

ROSE. Lyons, that was Bonnie on the phone. She say you supposed to pick her up.

LYONS. Yeah, okay, Rose.

TROY. I walked on down to Mobile and hitched up with some of them fellows that was heading this way. Got up here and found out . . . not only couldn't you get a job . . . you couldn't find no place to live. I thought I was in freedom. Shhh. Colored folks living down there on the river banks in whatever kind of shelter they could find for themselves. Right down there under the Brady Street Bridge. Living in shacks made of sticks and tarpaper. Messed around there and went from bad to worse. Started stealing. First it was food. Then I figured, hell, if I steal money I can buy me some food. Buy me some shoes too! One thing led to another. Met your mama. I was young and anxious to be a man. Met your mama and had you. What I do that for? Now I got to worry about feeding you and her. Got to steal three times as much. Went out one day looking for somebody to rob . . . that's what I was, a robber. I'll tell you the truth. I'm ashamed of it today. But it's the truth. Went to rob this fellow . . . pulled out my knife . . . and he pulled out a gun. Shot me in the chest. I felt just like somebody had taken a hot branding iron and laid it on me. When he shot me I jumped at him with my knife. They told me I killed him and they put me in the penitentiary and locked me up for fifteen years. That's where I met Bono. That's where I learned how to play baseball. Got out that place and your mama had taken you and went on to make life without me. Fifteen years was a long time for her to wait. But that fifteen years cured me of that robbing stuff. Rose'll tell you. She asked me when I met her if I had gotten all that foolishness out of my system. And I told her, "Baby, it's you and baseball all what count with me." You hear me, Bono? I meant it too. She say, "Which one comes first?" I told her, "Baby, ain't no doubt it's baseball . . . but you stick and get old with me and we'll both outlive this baseball." Am I right, Rose? And it's true.

ROSE. Man, hush your mouth. You ain't said no such thing. Talking about, "Baby you know you'll always be number one with me." That's what you was talking.

TROY. You hear that, Bono. That's why I love her.

BONO. Rose'll keep you straight. You get off the track, she'll straighten you up.

ROSE. Lyons, you better get on up and get Bonnie. She waiting on you.

LYONS [*gets up to go*]. Hey, Pop, why don't you come on down to the Grill and hear me play?

TROY. I ain't going down there. I'm too old to be sitting around in them clubs.

BONO. You got to be good to play down at the Grill.

LYONS. Come on, Pop . . .

TROY. I got to get up in the morning.

LYONS. You ain't got to stay long.

TROY. Naw, I'm gonna get my supper and go on to bed.

LYONS. Well, I got to go. I'll see you again.

TROY. Don't you come around my house on my payday.

ROSE. Pick up the phone and let somebody know you coming. And bring Bonnie with you. You know I'm always glad to see her.

LYONS. Yeah, I'll do that, Rose. You take care now. See you, Pop. See you, Mr. Bono. See you, Uncle Gabe.

GABRIEL. Lyons! King of the Jungle!

LYONS *exits*.

TROY.   Is supper ready, woman? Me and you got some business to take care of. I'm gonna tear it up too.

ROSE.   Troy, I done told you now!

TROY [*puts his arm around* BONO].   Aw hell, woman . . . this is Bono. Bono like family. I done known this nigger since . . . how long I done know you?

BONO.   It's been a long time.

TROY.   I done know this nigger since Skippy was a pup. Me and him done been through some times.

BONO.   You sure right about that.

TROY.   Hell, I done know him longer than I known you. And we still standing shoulder to shoulder. Hey, look here, Bono . . . a man can't ask for no more than that. [*Drinks to him.*] I love you, nigger.

BONO.   Hell, I love you too . . . I got to get home see my woman. You got yours in hand. I got to get mine.

BONO *starts to exit as* CORY *enters the yard, dressed in his football uniform. He gives* TROY *a hard, uncompromising look.*

CORY.   What you do that for, Pop?

He throws his helmet down in the direction of TROY.

ROSE.   What's the matter? Cory . . . what's the matter?

CORY.   Papa done went up to the school and told Coach Zellman I can't play football no more. Wouldn't even let me play the game. Told him to tell the recruiter not to come.

ROSE.   Troy . . .

TROY.   What you Troying me for. Yeah, I did it. And the boy know why I did it.

CORY.   Why you wanna do that to me? That was the one chance I had.

ROSE.   Ain't nothing wrong with Cory playing football, Troy.

TROY.   The boy lied to me. I told the nigger if he wanna play football . . . to keep up his chores and hold down that job at the A&P. That was the conditions. Stopped down there to see Mr. Stawicki . . .

CORY.   I can't work after school during the football season, Pop! I tried to tell you that Mr. Stawicki's holding my job for me. You don't never want to listen to nobody. And then you wanna go and do this to me!

TROY.   I ain't done nothing to you. You done it to yourself.

CORY.   Just cause you didn't have a chance! You just scared I'm gonna be better than you, that's all.

TROY.   Come here.

ROSE.   Troy . . .

CORY *reluctantly crosses over to* TROY.

TROY.   All right! See. You done made a mistake.

CORY.   I didn't even do nothing!

TROY.   I'm gonna tell you what your mistake was. See . . . you swung at the ball and didn't hit it. That's strike one. See, you in the batter's box now. You swung and you missed. That's strike one. Don't you strike out!

Lights fade to black.

Act 2

Scene 1

The following morning. CORY *is at the tree hitting the ball with the bat. He tries to mimic* TROY, *but his swing is awkward, less sure.* ROSE *enters from the house.*

ROSE.   Cory, I want you to help me with this cupboard.

CORY.   I ain't quitting the team. I don't care what Poppa say.

ROSE.   I'll talk to him when he gets back. He had to go see about your Uncle Gabe. The police done arrested him. Say he was disturbing the peace. He'll be back directly. Come on in here and help me clean out the top of this cupboard.

> CORY *exits into the house.* ROSE *sees* TROY *and* BONO *coming down the alley.*

Troy . . . what they say down there?

TROY.   Ain't said nothing. I give them fifty dollars and they let him go. I'll talk to you about it. Where's Cory?

ROSE.   He's in there helping me clean out these cupboards.

TROY.   Tell him to get his butt out here.

> TROY *and* BONO *go over to the pile of wood.* BONO *picks up the saw and begins sawing.*

TROY [*to* BONO].   All they want is the money. That makes six or seven times I done went down there and got him. See me coming they stick out their hands.

BONO.   Yeah. I know what you mean. That's all they care about . . . that money. They don't care about what's right. [*Pause.*] Nigger, why you got to go and get some hard wood? You ain't doing nothing but building a little old fence. Get you some soft pine wood. That's all you need.

TROY.   I know what I'm doing. This is outside wood. You put pine wood inside the house. Pine wood is inside wood. This here is outside wood. Now you tell me where the fence is gonna be?

BONO.   You don't need this wood. You can put it up with pine wood and it'll stand as long as you gonna be here looking at it.

TROY.   How you know how long I'm gonna be here, nigger? Hell, I might just live forever. Live longer than old man Horsely.

BONO.   That's what Magee used to say.

TROY.   Magee's damn fool. Now you tell me who you ever heard of gonna pull their own teeth with a pair of rusty pliers.

BONO.   The old folks . . . my granddaddy used to pull his teeth with pliers. They ain't had no dentists for the colored folks back then.

TROY.   Get clean pliers! You understand? Clean pliers! Sterilize them! Besides we ain't living back then. All Magee had to do was walk over to Doc Goldblum's.

BONO.   I see where you and that Tallahassee gal . . . that Alberta . . . I see where you all done got tight.

TROY.   What you mean "got tight"?

BONO.   I see where you be laughing and joking with her all the time.

TROY.   I laughs and jokes with all of them, Bono. You know me.

BONO.   That ain't the kind of laughing and joking I'm talking about.

> CORY *enters from the house.*

CORY.   How you doing, Mr. Bono?

TROY.   Cory? Get that saw from Bono and cut some wood. He talking about the wood's too hard to cut. Stand back there, Jim, and let that young boy show you how it's done.

BONO.   He's sure welcome to it.

> CORY *takes the saw and begins to cut the wood.*

Whew-e-e! Look at that. Big old strong boy. Look like Joe Louis. Hell, must be getting old the way I'm watching that boy whip through that wood.

CORY.   I don't see why Mama want a fence around the yard noways.

TROY.   Damn if I know either. What the hell she keeping out with it? She ain't got nothing nobody want.

BONO.   Some people build fences to keep people out . . . and other people build fences to keep people in. Rose wants to hold on to you all. She loves you.

TROY.   Hell, nigger, I don't need nobody to tell me my wife loves me. Cory . . . go on in the house and see if you can find that other saw.

CORY.   Where's it at?

TROY.   I said find it! Look for it till you find it!

> CORY *exits into the house.*

What's that supposed to mean? Wanna keep us in?

BONO.   Troy . . . I done known you seem like damn near my whole life. You and Rose both. I done know both of you all for a long time. I remember when you met Rose. When you was hitting them baseball out the park. A lot of them old gals was after you then. You had the pick of the litter. When you picked Rose, I was happy for you. That was the first time I knew you had any sense. I said . . . My man Troy knows what he's doing . . . I'm gonna follow this nigger . . . he might take me somewhere. I been following you too. I done learned a whole heap of things about life watching you. I done learned how to tell where the shit lies. How to tell it from the alfalfa. You done learned me a lot of things. You showed me how to not make the same mistakes . . . to take life as it comes along and keep putting one foot in front of the other. [*Pause.*] Rose a good woman, Troy.

TROY.   Hell, nigger, I know she a good woman. I been married to her for eighteen years. What you got on your mind, Bono?

BONO.   I just say she a good woman. Just like I say anything. I ain't got to have nothing on my mind.

TROY.   You just gonna say she a good woman and leave it hanging out there like that? Why you telling me she a good woman?

BONO.   She loves you, Troy. Rose loves you.

TROY.   You saying I don't measure up. That's what you trying to say. I don't measure up cause I'm seeing this other gal. I know what you trying to say.

BONO.   I know what Rose means to you, Troy. I'm just trying to say I don't want to see you mess up.

TROY.   Yeah, I appreciate that, Bono. If you was messing around on Lucille I'd be telling you the same thing.

BONO.   Well, that's all I got to say. I just say that because I love you both.

TROY.   Hell, you know me . . . I wasn't out there looking for nothing. You can't find a better woman than Rose. I know that. But seems like this woman just stuck onto me where I can't shake her loose. I done wrestled with it, tried to throw her off me . . . but she just stuck on tighter. Now she's stuck on for good.

BONO.   You's in control . . . that's what you tell me all the time. You responsible for what you do.

TROY.   I ain't ducking the responsibility of it. As long as it sets right in my heart . . . then I'm okay. Cause that's all I listen to. It'll tell me right from wrong every time. And I ain't talking about doing Rose no bad turn. I love Rose. She done carried me a long ways and I love and respect her for that.

BONO.   I know you do. That's why I don't want to see you hurt her. But what you gonna do when she find out? What you got then? If you try and juggle both of them . . . sooner or later you gonna drop one of them. That's common sense.

TROY.   Yeah, I hear what you saying, Bono. I been trying to figure a way to work it out.

BONO.   Work it out right, Troy. I don't want to be getting all up between you and Rose's business . . . but work it so it come out right.

TROY.   Ah hell, I get all up between you and Lucille's business. When you gonna get that woman that refrigerator she been wanting? Don't tell me you ain't got no money now. I know who your banker is. Mellon don't need that money bad as Lucille want that refrigerator. I'll tell you that.

BONO.   Tell you what I'll do . . . when you finish building this fence for Rose . . . I'll buy Lucille that refrigerator.

TROY.   You done stuck your foot in your mouth now!

TROY *grabs up a board and begins to saw.* BONO *starts to walk out the yard.*

Hey, nigger . . . where you going?

BONO.   I'm going home. I know you don't expect me to help you now. I'm protecting my money. I wanna see you put that fence up by yourself. That's what I want to see. You'll be here another six months without me.

TROY.   Nigger, you ain't right.

BONO.   When it comes to my money . . . I'm right as fireworks on the Fourth of July.

TROY.   All right, we gonna see now. You better get out your bankbook.

BONO *exits, and* TROY *continues to work.* ROSE *enters from the house.*

ROSE.   What they say down there? What's happening with Gabe?

TROY.   I went down there and got him out. Cost me fifty dollars. Say he was disturbing the peace. Judge set up a hearing for him in three weeks. Say to show cause why he shouldn't be recommitted.

ROSE.   What was he doing that cause them to arrest him?

TROY.   Some kids was teasing him and he run them off home. Say he was howling and carrying on. Some folks seen him and called the police. That's all it was.

ROSE.   Well, what's you say? What'd you tell the judge?

TROY.   Told him I'd look after him. It didn't make no sense to recommit the man. He stuck out his big greasy palm and told me to give him fifty dollars and take him on home.

ROSE.   Where's he at now? Where'd he go off to?

TROY.   He's gone about his business. He don't need nobody to hold his hand.

ROSE.   Well, I don't know. Seem like that would be the best place for him if they did put him into the hospital. I know what you're gonna say. But that's what I think would be best.

TROY.   The man done had his life ruined fighting for what? And they wanna take and lock him up. Let him be free. He don't bother nobody.

ROSE.   Well, everybody got their own way of looking at it I guess. Come on and get your lunch. I got a bowl of lima beans and some cornbread in the oven. Come and get something to eat. Ain't no sense you fretting over Gabe.

ROSE *turns to go into the house.*

TROY.   Rose . . . got something to tell you.

ROSE.   Well, come on . . . wait till I get this food on the table.

TROY.   Rose!

She stops and turns around.

I don't know how to say this. [*Pause.*] I can't explain it none. It just sort of grows on you till it gets out of hand. It starts out like a little bush . . . and the next thing you know it's a whole forest.

ROSE.   Troy . . . what is you talking about?

TROY.   I'm talking, woman, let me talk. I'm trying to find a way to tell you . . . I'm
gonna be a daddy. I'm gonna be somebody's daddy.

ROSE.   Troy . . . you're not telling me this? You're gonna be . . . what?

TROY.   Rose . . . now . . . see . . .

ROSE.   You telling me you gonna be somebody's daddy? You telling your *wife* this?

GABRIEL *enters from the street. He carries a rose in his hand.*

GABRIEL.   Hey, Troy! Hey, Rose!

ROSE.   I have to wait eighteen years to hear something like this.

GABRIEL.   Hey, Rose . . . I got a flower for you. [*He hands it to her.*] That's a rose.
Same rose like you is.

ROSE.   Thanks, Gabe.

GABRIEL.   Troy, you ain't mad at me is you? Them bad mens come and put me
away. You ain't mad at me is you?

TROY.   Naw, Gabe, I ain't mad at you.

ROSE.   Eighteen years and you wanna come with this.

GABRIEL [*takes a quarter out of his pocket*].   See what I got? Got a brand new quarter.

TROY.   Rose . . . it's just . . .

ROSE.   Ain't nothing you can say, Troy. Ain't no way of explaining that.

GABRIEL.   Fellow that give me this quarter had a whole mess of them. I'm gonna
keep this quarter till it stop shining.

ROSE.   Gabe, go on in the house there. I got some watermelon in the Frigidaire.
Go on and get you a piece.

GABRIEL.   Say, Rose . . . you know I was chasing hellhounds and them bad mens
come and get me and take me away. Troy helped me. He come down there
and told them they better let me go before he beat them up. Yeah, he did!

ROSE.   You go on and get you a piece of watermelon, Gabe. Them bad mens is
gone now.

GABRIEL.   Okay, Rose . . . gonna get me some watermelon. The kind with the
stripes on it.

GABRIEL *exits into the house.*

ROSE.   Why, Troy? Why? After all these years to come dragging this in to me now.
It don't make no sense at your age. I could have expected this ten or fifteen
years ago, but not now.

TROY.   Age ain't got nothing to do with it, Rose.

ROSE.   I done tried to be everything a wife should be. Everything a wife could be.
Been married eighteen years and I got to live to see the day you tell me you
been seeing another woman and done fathered a child by her. And you know
I ain't never wanted no half nothing in my family. My whole family is half.
Everybody got different fathers and mothers . . . my two sisters and my
brother. Can't hardly tell who's who. Can't never sit down and talk about Papa
and Mama. It's your papa and your mama and my papa and my mama . . .

TROY.   Rose . . . stop it now.

ROSE.   I ain't never wanted that for none of my children. And now you wanna
drag your behind in here and tell me something like this.

TROY.   You ought to know. It's time for you to know.

ROSE.   Well, I don't want to know, goddamn it!

TROY.   I can't just make it go away. It's done now. I can't wish the circumstance
of the thing away.

ROSE. And you don't want to either. Maybe you want to wish me and my boy away. Maybe that's what you want? Well, you can't wish us away. I've got eighteen years of my life invested in you. You ought to have stayed upstairs in my bed where you belong.

TROY. Rose . . . now listen to me . . . we can get a handle on this thing. We can talk this out . . . come to an understanding.

ROSE. All of a sudden it's "we." Where was "we" at when you was down there rolling around with some godforsaken woman? "We" should have come to an understanding before you started making a damn fool of yourself. You're a day late and a dollar short when it comes to an understanding with me.

TROY. It's just . . . She gives me a different idea . . . a different understanding about myself. I can step out of this house and get away from the pressures and problems . . . be a different man. I ain't got to wonder how I'm gonna pay the bills or get the roof fixed. I can just be a part of myself that I ain't never been.

ROSE. What I want to know . . . is do you plan to continue seeing her. That's all you can say to me.

TROY. I can sit up in her house and laugh. Do you understand what I'm saying. I can laugh out loud . . . and it feels good. It reaches all the way down to the bottom of my shoes. [*Pause.*] Rose, I can't give that up.

ROSE. Maybe you ought to go on and stay down there with her . . . if she's a better woman than me.

TROY. It ain't about nobody being a better woman or nothing. Rose, you ain't the blame. A man couldn't ask for no woman to be a better wife than you've been. I'm responsible for it. I done locked myself into a pattern trying to take care of you all that I forgot about myself.

ROSE. What the hell was I there for? That was my job, not somebody else's.

TROY. Rose, I done tried all my life to live decent . . . to live a clean . . . hard . . . useful life. I tried to be a good husband to you. In every way I knew how. Maybe I come into the world backwards, I don't know. But . . . you born with two strikes on you before you come to the plate. You got to guard it closely . . . always looking for the curve ball on the inside corner. You can't afford to let none get past you. You can't afford a call strike. If you going down . . . you going down swinging. Everything lined up against you. What you gonna do. I fooled them, Rose. I bunted. When I found you and Cory and a halfway decent job . . . I was safe. Couldn't nothing touch me. I wasn't gonna strike out no more. I wasn't going back to the penitentiary. I wasn't gonna lay in the streets with a bottle of wine. I was safe. I had me a family. A job. I wasn't gonna get that last strike. I was on first looking for one of them boys to knock me in. To get me home.

ROSE. You should have stayed in my bed, Troy.

TROY. Then when I saw that gal . . . she firmed up my backbone. And I got to thinking that if I tried . . . I just might be able to steal second. Do you understand after eighteen years I wanted to steal second.

ROSE. You should have held me tight. You should have grabbed me and held on.

TROY. I stood on first base for eighteen years and I thought . . . well, goddamn it . . . go on for it!

ROSE. We're not talking about baseball! We're talking about you going off to lay in bed with another woman . . . and then bring it home to me. That's what we're talking about. We ain't talking about no baseball.

TROY. Rose, you're not listening to me. I'm trying the best I can to explain it to you. It's not easy for me to admit that I been standing in the same place for eighteen years.

ROSE.   I been standing with you! I been right here with you, Troy. I got a life too. I gave eighteen years of my life to stand in the same spot with you. Don't you think I ever wanted other things? Don't you think I had dreams and hopes? What about my life? What about me? Don't you think it ever crossed my mind to want to know other men? That I wanted to lay up somewhere and forget about my responsibilities? That I wanted someone to make me laugh so I could feel good? You not the only one who's got wants and needs. But I held on to you, Troy. I took all my feelings, my wants and needs, my dreams . . . and I buried them inside you. I planted a seed and watched and prayed over it. I planted myself inside you and waited to bloom. And it didn't take me no eighteen years to find out the soil was hard and rocky and it wasn't never gonna bloom.

But I held on to you, Troy. I held you tighter. You was my husband. I owed you everything I had. Every part of me I could find to give you. And upstairs in that room . . . with the darkness falling in on me . . . I gave everything I had to try and erase the doubt that you wasn't the finest man in the world. And wherever you was going . . . I wanted to be there with you. Cause you was my husband. Cause that's the only way I was gonna survive as your wife. You always talking about what you give . . . and what you don't have to give. But you take too. You take . . . and don't even know nobody's giving!

ROSE *turns to exit into the house;* TROY *grabs her arm.*

TROY.   You say I take and don't give!
ROSE.   Troy! You're hurting me!
TROY.   You say I take and don't give!
ROSE.   Troy . . . you're hurting my arm! Let go!
TROY.   I done give you everything I got. Don't you tell that lie on me.
ROSE.   Troy!
TROY.   Don't you tell that lie on me!

CORY *enters from the house.*

CORY.   Mama!
ROSE.   Troy. You're hurting me.
TROY.   Don't you tell me about no taking and giving.

CORY *comes up behind* TROY *and grabs him.* TROY, *surprised, is thrown off balance just as* CORY *throws a glancing blow that catches him on the chest and knocks him down.* TROY *is stunned, as is* CORY.

ROSE.   Troy. Troy. No!

TROY *gets to his feet and starts at* CORY.

Troy . . . no. Please! Troy!

ROSE *pulls on* TROY *to hold him back.* TROY *stops himself.*

TROY [*to* CORY].   All right. That's strike two. You stay away from around me, boy. Don't you strike out. You living with a full count. Don't you strike out.

TROY *exits out the yard as the lights go down.*

Scene 2

It is six months later, early afternoon. TROY *enters from the house and starts to exit the yard.* ROSE *enters from the house.*

ROSE.   Troy, I want to talk to you.
TROY.   All of a sudden, after all this time, you want to talk to me, huh? You ain't wanted to talk to me for months. You ain't wanted to talk to me last night. You ain't wanted no part of me then. What you wanna talk to me about now?

ROSE. Tomorrow's Friday.

TROY. I know what day tomorrow is. You think I don't know tomorrow's Friday? My whole life I ain't done nothing but look to see Friday coming and you got to tell me it's Friday.

ROSE. I want to know if you're coming home.

TROY. I always come home, Rose. You know that. There ain't never been a night I ain't come home.

ROSE. That ain't what I mean . . . and you know it. I want to know if you're coming straight home after work.

TROY. I figure I'd cash my check . . . hang out at Taylors' with the boys . . . maybe play a game of checkers . . .

ROSE. Troy, I can't live like this. I won't live like this. You livin' on borrowed time with me. It's been going on six months now you ain't been coming home.

TROY. I be here every night. Every night of the year. That's 365 days.

ROSE. I want you to come home tomorrow after work.

TROY. Rose . . . I don't mess up my pay. You know that now. I take my pay and I give it to you. I don't have no money but what you give me back. I just want to have a little time to myself . . . a little time to enjoy life.

ROSE. What about me? When's my time to enjoy life?

TROY. I don't know what to tell you, Rose. I'm doing the best I can.

ROSE. You ain't been home from work but time enough to change your clothes and run out . . . and you wanna call that the best you can do?

TROY. I'm going over to the hospital to see Alberta. She went into the hospital this afternoon. Look like she might have the baby early. I won't be gone long.

ROSE. Well, you ought to know. They went over to Miss Pearl's and got Gabe today. She said you told them to go ahead and lock him up.

TROY. I ain't said no such thing. Whoever told you that is telling a lie. Pearl ain't doing nothing but telling a big fat lie.

ROSE. She ain't had to tell me. I read it on the papers.

TROY. I ain't told them nothing of the kind.

ROSE. I saw it right there on the papers.

TROY. What it say, huh?

ROSE. It said you told them to take him.

TROY. Then they screwed that up, just the way they screw up everything. I ain't worried about what they got on the paper.

ROSE. Say the government send part of his check to the hospital and the other part to you.

TROY. I ain't got nothing to do with that if that's the way it works. I ain't made up the rules about how it work.

ROSE. You did Gabe just like you did Cory. You wouldn't sign the paper for Cory . . . but you signed for Gabe. You signed that paper.

The telephone is heard ringing inside the house.

TROY. I told you I ain't signed nothing, woman! The only thing I signed was the release form. Hell, I can't read, I don't know what they had on that paper! I ain't signed nothing about sending Gabe away.

ROSE. I said send him to the hospital . . . you said let him be free . . . now you done went down there and signed him to the hospital for half his money. You went back on yourself, Troy. You gonna have to answer for that.

TROY. See now . . . you been over there talking to Miss Pearl. She done got mad cause she ain't getting Gabe's rent money. That's all it is. She's liable to say anything.

ROSE.   Troy, I seen where you signed the paper.

TROY.   You ain't seen nothing I signed. What she doing got papers on my brother anyway? Miss Pearl telling a big fat lie. And I'm gonna tell her about it too! You ain't seen nothing I signed. Say . . . you ain't seen nothing I signed.

   ROSE *exits into the house to answer the telephone. Presently she returns.*

ROSE.   Troy . . . that was the hospital. Alberta had the baby.

TROY.   What she have? What is it?

ROSE.   It's a girl.

TROY.   I better get on down to the hospital to see her.

ROSE.   Troy . . .

TROY.   Rose . . . I got to go see her now. That's only right . . . what's the matter . . . the baby's all right, ain't it?

ROSE.   Alberta died having the baby.

TROY.   Died . . . you say she's dead? Alberta's dead?

ROSE.   They said they done all they could. They couldn't do nothing for her.

TROY.   The baby? How's the baby?

ROSE.   They say it's healthy. I wonder who's gonna bury her.

TROY.   She had family, Rose. She wasn't living in the world by herself.

ROSE.   I know she wasn't living in the world by herself.

TROY.   Next thing you gonna want to know if she had any insurance.

ROSE.   Troy, you ain't got to talk like that.

TROY.   That's the first thing that jumped out your mouth. "Who's gonna bury her?" Like I'm fixing to take on that task for myself.

ROSE.   I am your wife. Don't push me away.

TROY.   I ain't pushing nobody away. Just give me some space. That's all. Just give me some room to breathe.

   ROSE *exits into the house.* TROY *walks about the yard.*

TROY [*with a quiet rage that threatens to consume him*].   All right . . . Mr. Death. See now . . . I'm gonna tell you what I'm gonna do. I'm gonna take and build me a fence around this yard. See? I'm gonna build me a fence around what belongs to me. And then I want you to stay on the other side. See? You stay over there until you're ready for me. Then you come on. Bring your army. Bring your sickle. Bring your wrestling clothes. I ain't gonna fall down on my vigilance this time. You ain't gonna sneak up on me no more. When you ready for me . . . when the top of your list say Troy Maxson . . . that's when you come around here. You come up and knock on the front door. Ain't nobody else got nothing to do with this. This is between you and me. Man to man. You stay on the other side of that fence until you ready for me. Then you come up and knock on the front door. Anytime you want. I'll be ready for you.

   The lights go down to black.

Scene 3

The lights come up on the porch. It is late evening three days later. ROSE *sits listening to the ball game waiting for* TROY. *The final out of the game is made and* ROSE *switches off the radio.* TROY *enters the yard carrying an infant wrapped in blankets. He stands back from the house and calls.*

   ROSE *enters and stands on the porch. There is a long, awkward silence, the weight of which grows heavier with each passing second.*

TROY.   Rose . . . I'm standing here with my daughter in my arms. She ain't but a wee bittie little old thing. She don't know nothing about grownups' business. She innocent . . . and she ain't got no mama.

ROSE.   What you telling me for, Troy?

She turns and exits into the house.

TROY.   Well . . . I guess we'll just sit out here on the porch.

He sits down on the porch. There is an awkward indelicateness about the way he handles the baby. His largeness engulfs and seems to swallow it. He speaks loud enough for ROSE *to hear.*

A man's got to do what's right for him. I ain't sorry for nothing I done. It felt right in my heart. [*To the baby.*] What you smiling at? Your daddy's a big man. Got these great big old hands. But sometimes he's scared. And right now your daddy's scared cause we sitting out here and ain't got no home. Oh, I been homeless before. I ain't had no little baby with me. But I been homeless. You just be out on the road by your lonesome and you see one of them trains coming and you just kinda go like this . . .

He sings as a lullaby.

> Please, Mr. Engineer let a man ride the line
> Please, Mr. Engineer let a man ride the line
> I ain't got no ticket please let me ride the blinds.

ROSE *enters from the house.* TROY, *hearing her steps behind him, stands and faces her.*

She's my daughter, Rose. My own flesh and blood. I can't deny her no more than I can deny them boys. [*Pause.*] You and them boys is my family. You and them and this child is all I got in the world. So I guess what I'm saying is . . . I'd appreciate it if you'd help me take care of her.

ROSE.   Okay, Troy . . . you're right. I'll take care of your baby for you . . . cause . . . like you say . . . she's innocent . . . and you can't visit the sins of the father upon the child. A motherless child has got a hard time. [*She takes the baby from him.*] From right now . . . this child got a mother. But you a womanless man.

ROSE *turns and exits into the house with the baby. Lights go down to black.*

Scene 4

It is two months later. LYONS *enters the street. He knocks on the door and calls.*

LYONS.   Hey, Rose! [*Pause.*] Rose!

ROSE [*from inside the house*].   Stop that yelling. You gonna wake up Raynell. I just got her to sleep.

LYONS.   I just stopped by to pay Papa this twenty dollars I owe him. Where's Papa at?

ROSE.   He should be here in a minute. I'm getting ready to go down to the church. Sit down and wait on him.

LYONS.   I got to go pick up Bonnie over her mother's house.

ROSE.   Well, sit it down there on the table. He'll get it.

LYONS [*enters the house and sets the money on the table*].   Tell Papa I said thanks. I'll see you again.

ROSE.   All right, Lyons. We'll see you.

LYONS *starts to exit as* CORY *enters.*

CORY.   Hey, Lyons.

LYONS.   What's happening, Cory? Say man, I'm sorry I missed your graduation. You know I had a gig and couldn't get away. Otherwise, I would have been there, man. So what you doing?

CORY.   I'm trying to find a job.

LYONS.   Yeah I know how that go, man. It's rough out here. Jobs are scarce.

CORY.   Yeah, I know.

LYONS.   Look here, I got to run. Talk to Papa . . . he know some people. He'll be able to help get you a job. Talk to him . . . see what he say.

CORY.   Yeah . . . all right, Lyons.

LYONS.   You take care. I'll talk to you soon. We'll find some time to talk.

LYONS *exits the yard.* CORY *wanders over to the tree, picks up the bat, and assumes a batting stance. He studies an imaginary pitcher and swings. Dissatisfied with the result, he tries again.* TROY *enters. They eye each other for a beat.* CORY *puts the bat down and exits the yard.* TROY *starts into the house as* ROSE *exits with* RAYNELL. *She is carrying a cake.*

TROY.   I'm coming in and everybody's going out.

ROSE.   I'm taking this cake down to the church for the bake sale. Lyons was by to see you. He stopped by to pay you your twenty dollars. It's laying in there on the table.

TROY [*going into his pocket*].   Well . . . here go this money.

ROSE.   Put it in there on the table, Troy. I'll get it.

TROY.   What time you coming back?

ROSE.   Ain't no use in you studying me. It don't matter what time I come back.

TROY.   I just asked you a question, woman. What's the matter . . . can't I ask you a question?

ROSE.   Troy, I don't want to go into it. Your dinner's in there on the stove. All you got to do is heat it up. And don't you be eating the rest of them cakes in there. I'm coming back for them. We having a bake sale at the church tomorrow.

ROSE *exits the yard.* TROY *sits down on the steps, takes a pint bottle from his pocket, opens it, and drinks. He begins to sing.*

TROY.   Hear it ring! Hear it ring!
    Had an old dog his name was Blue
    You know Blue was mighty true
    You know Blue as a good old dog
    Blue trees a possum in a hollow log
    You know from that he was a good old dog.

BONO *enters the yard.*

BONO.   Hey, Troy.

TROY.   Hey, what's happening, Bono?

BONO.   I just thought I'd stop by to see you.

TROY.   What you stop by and see me for? You ain't stopped by in a month of Sundays. Hell, I must owe you money or something.

BONO.   Since you got your promotion I can't keep up with you. Used to see you every day. Now I don't even know what route you working.

TROY.   They keep switching me around. Got me out in Greentree now . . . hauling white folks' garbage.

BONO.   Greentree, huh? You lucky, at least you ain't got to be lifting them barrels. Damn if they ain't getting heavier. I'm gonna put in my two years and call it quits.

TROY.   I'm thinking about retiring myself.

BONO.   You got it easy. You can drive for another five years.

TROY.   It ain't the same, Bono. It ain't like working the back of the truck. Ain't got nobody to talk to . . . feel like you working by yourself. Naw, I'm thinking about retiring. How's Lucille?

BONO.   She all right. Her arthritis get to acting up on her sometime. Saw Rose on my way in. She going down to the church, huh?

TROY.   Yeah, she took up going down there. All them preachers looking for somebody to fatten their pockets. [*Pause.*] Got some gin here.

BONO.   Naw, thanks. I just stopped by to say hello.

TROY.   Hell, nigger . . . you can take a drink. I ain't never known you to say no to a drink. You ain't got to work tomorrow.

BONO.   I just stopped by. I'm fixing to go over to Skinner's. We got us a domino game going over his house every Friday.

TROY.   Nigger, you can't play no dominoes. I used to whup you four games out of five.

BONO.   Well, that learned me. I'm getting better.

TROY.   Yeah? Well, that's all right.

BONO.   Look here . . . I got to be getting on. Stop by sometime, huh?

TROY.   Yeah, I'll do that, Bono. Lucille told Rose you bought her a new refrigerator.

BONO.   Yeah, Rose told Lucille you had finally built your fence . . . so I figured we'd call it even.

TROY.   I knew you would.

BONO.   Yeah . . . okay. I'll be talking to you.

TROY.   Yeah, take care, Bono. Good to see you. I'm gonna stop over.

BONO.   Yeah. Okay, Troy.

> BONO *exits.* TROY *drinks from the bottle.*

TROY.   Old Blue died and I dig his grave
      Let him down with a golden chain
      Every night when I hear old Blue bark
      I know Blue treed a possum in Noah's Ark
      Hear it ring! Hear it ring!

> CORY *enters the yard. They eye each other for a beat.* TROY *is sitting in the middle of the steps.* CORY *walks over.*

CORY.   I got to get by.

TROY.   Say what? What's you say?

CORY.   You in my way. I got to get by.

TROY.   You got to get by where? This is my house. Bought and paid for. In full. Took me fifteen years. And if you wanna go in my house and I'm sitting on the steps . . . you say excuse me. Like your mama taught you.

CORY.   Come on, Pop . . . I got to get by.

> CORY *starts to maneuver his way past* TROY. TROY *grabs his leg and shoves him back.*

TROY.   You just gonna walk over top of me?

CORY.   I live here too!

TROY [*advancing toward him*].   You just gonna walk over top of me in my own house?

CORY.   I ain't scared of you.

TROY.   I ain't asked if you was scared of me. I asked you if you was fixing to walk over top of me in my own house? That's the question. You ain't gonna say excuse me? You just gonna walk over top of me?

CORY.   If you wanna put it like that.

TROY.   How else am I gonna put it?

CORY.   I was walking by you to go into the house cause you sitting on the steps drunk, singing to yourself. You can put it like that.

TROY.   Without saying excuse me???

> CORY *doesn't respond.*

I asked you a question. Without saying excuse me???

CORY.   I ain't got to say excuse me to you. You don't count around here no more.

TROY.   Oh, I see . . . I don't count around here no more. You ain't got to say excuse me to your daddy. All of a sudden you done got so grown that your daddy don't count around here no more . . . Around here in his own house and yard that he done paid for with the sweat of his brow. You done got so grown to where you gonna take over. You gonna take over my house. Is that right? You gonna wear my pants. You gonna go in there and stretch out on my bed. You ain't got to say excuse me cause I don't count around here no more. Is that right?

CORY.   That's right. You always talking this dumb stuff. Now, why don't you just get out my way?

TROY.   I guess you got someplace to sleep and something to put in your belly. You got that, huh? You got that? That's what you need. You got that, huh?

CORY.   You don't know what I got. You ain't got to worry about what I got.

TROY.   You right! You one hundred percent right! I done spent the last seventeen years worrying about what you got. Now it's your turn, see? I'll tell you what to do. You grown . . . we done established that. You a man. Now, let's see you act like one. Turn your behind around and walk out this yard. And when you get out there in the alley . . . you can forget about this house. See? Cause this is my house. You go on and be a man and get your own house. You can forget about this. Cause this is mine. You go on and get yours cause I'm through with doing for you.

CORY.   You talking about what you did for me . . . what'd you ever give me?

TROY.   Them feet and bones! That pumping heart, nigger! I give you more than anybody else is ever gonna give you.

CORY.   You ain't never gave me nothing! You ain't never done nothing but hold me back. Afraid I was gonna be better than you. All you ever did was try and make me scared of you. I used to tremble every time you called my name. Every time I heard your footsteps in the house. Wondering all the time . . . what's Papa gonna say if I do this? . . . What's he gonna say if I do that? . . . What's Papa gonna say if I turn on the radio? And Mama, too . . . she tries . . . but she's scared of you.

TROY.   You leave your mama out of this. She ain't got nothing to do with this.

CORY.   I don't know how she stand you . . . after what you did to her.

TROY.   I told you to leave your mama out of this!

> *He advances toward* CORY.

CORY.   What you gonna do . . . give me a whupping? You can't whup me no more. You're too old. You just an old man.

TROY [*shoves him on his shoulder*].   Nigger! That's what you are. You just another nigger on the street to me!

CORY.   You crazy! You know that?

TROY.   Go on now! You got the devil in you. Get on away from me!

CORY.   You just a crazy old man . . . talking about I got the devil in me.

TROY.   Yeah, I'm crazy! If you don't get on the other side of that yard . . . I'm gonna show you how crazy I am! Go on . . . get the hell out of my yard.

CORY.   It ain't your yard. You took Uncle Gabe's money he got from the army to buy this house and then you put him out.

TROY [*advances on* CORY].   Get your black ass out of my yard!

> TROY*'s advance backs* CORY *up against the tree.* CORY *grabs up the bat.*

CORY.   I ain't going nowhere! Come on . . . put me out! I ain't scared of you.

TROY.   That's my bat!

CORY.   Come on!

TROY.   Put my bat down!

CORY.   Come on, put me out.

> CORY *swings at* TROY, *who backs across the yard.*

What's the matter? You so bad . . . put me out!

> TROY *advances toward* CORY.

CORY [*backing up*].   Come on! Come on!

TROY.   You're gonna have to use it! You wanna draw that bat back on me . . . you're gonna have to use it.

CORY.   Come on! . . . Come on!

> CORY *swings the bat at* TROY *a second time. He misses.* TROY *continues to advance toward him.*

TROY.   You're gonna have to kill me! You wanna draw that bat back on me. You're gonna have to kill me.

> CORY, *backed up against the tree, can go no farther.* TROY *taunts him. He sticks out his head and offers him a target.*

Come on! Come on!

> CORY *is unable to swing the bat.* TROY *grabs it.*

TROY.   Then I'll show you.

> CORY *and* TROY *struggle over the bat. The struggle is fierce and fully engaged.* TROY *ultimately is the stronger and takes the bat from* CORY *and stands over him ready to swing. He stops himself.*

Go on and get away from around my house.

> CORY, *stung by his defeat, picks himself up, walks slowly out of the yard and up the alley.*

CORY.   Tell Mama I'll be back for my things.

TROY.   They'll be on the other side of that fence.

> CORY *exits.*

TROY.   I can't taste nothing. Helluljah! I can't taste nothing no more. [TROY *assumes a batting posture and begins to taunt Death, the fastball on the outside corner.*] Come on! It's between you and me now! Come on! Anytime you want! Come on! I be ready for you . . . but I ain't gonna be easy.

> *The lights go down on the scene.*

Scene 5

The time is 1965. The lights come up in the yard. It is the morning of TROY'S
*funeral. A funeral plaque with a light hangs beside the door. There is a small
garden plot off to the side. There is noise and activity in the house as* ROSE, LYONS,
and BONO *have gathered. The door opens and* RAYNELL, *seven years old, enters
dressed in a flannel nightgown. She crosses to the garden and pokes around with
a stick.* ROSE *calls from the house.*

ROSE.   Raynell!
RAYNELL.   Mam?
ROSE.   What you doing out there?
RAYNELL.   Nothing.

>   ROSE *comes to the door.*

ROSE.   Girl, get in here and get dressed. What you doing?
RAYNELL.   Seeing if my garden growed.
ROSE.   I told you it ain't gonna grow overnight. You got to wait.
RAYNELL.   It don't look like it never gonna grow. Dag!
ROSE.   I told you a watched pot never boils. Get in here and get dressed.
RAYNELL.   This ain't even no pot, Mama.
ROSE.   You just have to give it a chance. It'll grow. Now you come on and do
    what I told you. We got to be getting ready. This ain't no morning to be play-
    ing around. You hear me?
RAYNELL.   Yes, mam.

>   ROSE *exits into the house.* RAYNELL *continues to poke at her garden with a
stick.* CORY *enters. He is dressed in a Marine corporal's uniform, and carries a
duffelbag. His posture is that of a military man, and his speech has a clipped
sternness.*

CORY [*to* RAYNELL].   Hi. [*Pause.*] I bet your name is Raynell.
RAYNELL.   Uh huh.
CORY.   Is your mama home?

>   RAYNELL *runs up on the porch and calls through the screen door.*

RAYNELL.   Mama . . . there's some man out here. Mama?

>   ROSE *comes to the door.*

ROSE.   Cory? Lord have mercy! Look here, you all!

>   ROSE *and* CORY *embrace in a tearful reunion as* BONO *and* LYONS *enter from
the house dressed in funeral clothes.*

BONO.   Aw, looka here . . .
ROSE.   Done got all grown up!
CORY.   Don't cry, Mama. What you crying about?
ROSE.   I'm just so glad you made it.
CORY.   Hey Lyons. How you doing, Mr. Bono.

>   LYONS *goes to embrace* CORY.

LYONS.   Look at you, man. Look at you. Don't he look good, Rose. Got them
    Corporal stripes.
ROSE.   What took you so long?
CORY.   You know how the Marines are, Mama. They got to get all their paperwork
    straight before they let you do anything.

ROSE. Well, I'm sure glad you made it. They let Lyons come. Your Uncle Gabe's still in the hospital. They don't know if they gonna let him out or not. I just talked to them a little while ago.

LYONS. A Corporal in the United States Marines.

BONO. Your daddy knew you had it in you. He used to tell me all the time.

LYONS. Don't he look good, Mr. Bono?

BONO. Yeah, he remind me of Troy when I first met him. [*Pause.*] Say, Rose, Lucille's down at the church with the choir. I'm gonna go down and get the pallbearers lined up. I'll be back to get you all.

ROSE. Thanks, Jim.

CORY. See you, Mr. Bono.

LYONS [*with his arm around* RAYNELL]. Cory . . . look at Raynell. Ain't she precious? She gonna break a whole lot of hearts.

ROSE. Raynell, come and say hello to your brother. This is your brother, Cory. You remember Cory.

RAYNELL. No, Mam.

CORY. She don't remember me, Mama.

ROSE. Well, we talk about you. She heard us talk about you. [*To* RAYNELL.] This is your brother, Cory. Come on and say hello.

RAYNELL. Hi.

CORY. Hi. So you're Raynell. Mama told me a lot about you.

ROSE. You all come on into the house and let me fix you some breakfast. Keep up your strength.

CORY. I ain't hungry, Mama.

LYONS. You can fix me something, Rose. I'll be in there in a minute.

ROSE. Cory, you sure you don't want nothing? I know they ain't feeding you right.

CORY. No, Mama . . . thanks. I don't feel like eating. I'll get something later.

ROSE. Raynell . . . get on upstairs and get that dress on like I told you.

ROSE *and* RAYNELL *exit into the house.*

LYONS. So . . . I hear you thinking about getting married.

CORY. Yeah, I done found the right one, Lyons. It's about time.

LYONS. Me and Bonnie been split up about four years now. About the time Papa retired. I guess she just got tired of all them changes I was putting her through. [*Pause.*] I always knew you was gonna make something out yourself. Your head was always in the right direction. So . . . you gonna stay in . . . make it a career . . . put in your twenty years?

CORY. I don't know. I got six already, I think that's enough.

LYONS. Stick with Uncle Sam and retire early. Ain't nothing out here. I guess Rose told you what happened with me. They got me down the workhouse. I thought I was being slick cashing other people's checks.

CORY. How much time you doing?

LYONS. They give me three years. I got that beat now. I ain't got but nine more months. It ain't so bad. You learn to deal with it like anything else. You got to take the crookeds with the straights. That's what Papa used to say. He used to say that when he struck out. I seen him strike out three times in a row . . . and the next time up he hit the ball over the grandstand. Right out there in Homestead Field. He wasn't satisfied hitting in the seats . . . he want to hit it over everything! After the game he had two hundred people standing around waiting to shake his hand. You got to take the crookeds with the straights. Yeah, Papa was something else.

CORY.   You still playing?

LYONS.   Cory . . . you know I'm gonna do that. There's some fellows down there
we got us a band . . . we gonna try and stay together when we get out . . .
but yeah, I'm still playing. It still helps me to get out of bed in the morning.
As long as it do that I'm gonna be right there playing and trying to make
some sense out of it.

ROSE [*calling*].   Lyons, I got these eggs in the pan.

LYONS.   Let me go on and get these eggs, man. Get ready to go bury Papa.
[*Pause.*] How you doing? You doing all right?

CORY *nods.* LYONS *touches him on the shoulder and they share a moment of
silent grief.* LYONS *exits into the house.* CORY *wanders about the yard.* RAYNELL *enters.*

RAYNEL.   Hi.

CORY.   Hi.

RAYNELL.   Did you used to sleep in my room?

CORY.   Yeah . . . that used to be my room.

RAYNELL.   That's what Papa call it. "Cory's room." It got your football in the closet.

ROSE *comes to the door.*

ROSE.   Raynell, get in there and get them good shoes on.

RAYNELL.   Mama, can't I wear these? Them other one hurt my feet.

ROSE.   Well, they just gonna have to hurt your feet for a while. You ain't said they
hurt your feet when you went down to the store and got them.

RAYNELL.   They didn't hurt then. My feet done got bigger.

ROSE.   Don't you give me no backtalk now. You get in there and get them
shoes on.

RAYNELL *exits into the house.*

Ain't too much changed. He still got that piece of rag tied to that tree. He was out
here swinging that bat. I was just ready to go back in the house. He swung
that bat and then he just fell over. Seem like he swung it and stood there with
this grin on his face . . . and then he just fell over. They carried him on down
to the hospital, but I knew there wasn't no need . . . why don't you come on
in the house?

CORY.   Mama . . . I got something to tell you. I don't know how to tell you this . . .
but I've got to tell you . . . I'm not going to Papa's funeral.

ROSE.   Boy, hush your mouth. That's your daddy you talking about. I don't want
hear that kind of talk this morning. I done raised you to come to this? You
standing there all healthy and grown talking about you ain't going to your
daddy's funeral?

CORY.   Mama . . . listen . . .

ROSE.   I don't want to hear it, Cory. You just get that thought out of your head.

CORY.   I can't drag Papa with me everywhere I go. I've got to say no to him. One
time in my life I've got to say no.

ROSE.   Don't nobody have to listen to nothing like that. I know you and your
daddy ain't seen eye to eye, but I ain't got to listen to that kind of talk this
morning. Whatever was between you and your daddy . . . the time has come
to put it aside. Just take it and set it over there on the shelf and forget about
it. Disrespecting your daddy ain't gonna make you a man, Cory. You got to
find a way to come to that on your own. Not going to your daddy's funeral
ain't gonna make you a man.

CORY.   The whole time I was growing up . . . living in his house . . . Papa was like a shadow that followed you everywhere. It weighed on you and sunk into your flesh. It would wrap around you and lay there until you couldn't tell which one was you anymore. That shadow digging in your flesh. Trying to crawl in. Trying to live through you. Everywhere I looked, Troy Maxson was staring back at me . . . hiding under the bed . . . in the closet. I'm just saying I've got to find a way to get rid of that shadow, Mama.

ROSE.   You just like him. You got him in you good.

CORY.   Don't tell me that, Mama.

ROSE.   You Troy Maxson all over again.

CORY.   I don't want to be Troy Maxson. I want to be me.

ROSE.   You can't be nobody but who you are, Cory. That shadow wasn't nothing but you growing into yourself. You either got to grow into it or cut it down to fit you. But that's all you got to make life with. That's all you got to measure yourself against that world out there. Your daddy wanted you to be everything he wasn't . . . and at the same time he tried to make you into everything he was. I don't know if he was right or wrong . . . but I do know he meant to do more good than he meant to do harm. He wasn't always right. Sometimes when he touched he bruised. And sometimes when he took me in his arms he cut.

When I first met your daddy I thought . . . Here is a man I can lay down with and make a baby. That's the first thing I thought when I seen him. I was thirty years old and had done seen my share of men. But when he walked up to me and said, "I can dance a waltz that'll make you dizzy," I thought, Rose Lee, here is a man that you can open yourself up to and be filled to bursting. Here is a man that can fill all them empty spaces you been tipping around the edges of. One of them empty spaces was being somebody's mother.

I married your daddy and settled down to cooking his supper and keeping clean sheets on the bed. When your daddy walked through the house he was so big he filled it up. That was my first mistake. Not to make him leave some room for me. For my part in the matter. But at that time I wanted that. I wanted a house that I could sing in. And that's what your daddy gave me. I didn't know to keep up his strength I had to give up little pieces of mine. I did that. I took on his life as mine and mixed up the pieces so that you couldn't hardly tell which was which anymore. It was my choice. It was my life and I didn't have to live it like that. But that's what life offered me in the way of being a woman and I took it. I grabbed hold of it with both hands.

By the time Raynell came into the house, me and your daddy had done lost touch with one another. I didn't want to make my blessing off of nobody's misfortune . . . but I took on to Raynell like she was all them babies I had wanted and never had.

The phone rings.

Like I'd been blessed to relive a part of my life. And if the Lord see fit to keep up my strength . . . I'm gonna do her just like your daddy did you . . . I'm gonna give her the best of what's in me.

RAYNELL [*entering, still with her old shoes*].   Mama . . . Reverend Tollivier on the phone.

ROSE *exits into the house.*

RAYNELL.   Hi.

CORY.   Hi.

RAYNELL.   You in the Army or the Marines?

CORY.   Marines.

RAYNELL.   Papa said it was the Army. Did you know Blue?

CORY.   Blue? Who's Blue?

RAYNELL.   Papa's dog what he sing about all the time.

CORY [*singing*].   Hear it ring! Hear it ring!
> I had a dog his name was Blue
> You know Blue was mighty true
> You know Blue was a good old dog
> Blue treed a possum in a hollow log
> You know from that he was a good old dog.
> Hear it ring! Hear it ring!

RAYNELL *joins in singing.*

CORY AND RAYNELL.   Blue treed a possum out on a limb
> Blue looked at me and I looked at him
> Grabbed that possum and put him in a sack
> Blue stayed there till I came back
> Old Blue's feets was big and round
> Never allowed a possum to touch the ground.
>
> Old Blue died and I dug his grave
> I dug his grave with a silver spade
> Let him down with a golden chain
> And every night I call his name
> Go on Blue, you good dog you
> Go on Blue, you good dog you.

RAYNELL.   Blue laid down and died like a man
> Blue laid down and died . . .

BOTH.   Blue laid down and died like a man
> Now he's treeing possums in the Promised Land
> I'm gonna tell you this to let you know
> Blue's gone where the good dogs go
> When I hear old Blue bark
> When I hear old Blue bark
> Blue treed a possum in Noah's Ark
> Blue treed a possum in Noah's Ark.

ROSE *comes to the screen door.*

ROSE.   Cory, we gonna be ready to go in a minute.

CORY [*to* RAYNELL].   You go on in the house and change them shoes like Mama told you so we can go to Papa's funeral.

RAYNELL.   Okay, I'll be back.

RAYNELL *exits into the house.* CORY *gets up and crosses over to the tree.* ROSE *stands in the screen door watching him.* GABRIEL *enters from the alley.*

GABRIEL [*calling*].   Hey, Rose!

ROSE.   Gabe?

GABRIEL.   I'm here, Rose. Hey Rose, I'm here!

ROSE *enters from the house.*

ROSE.   Lord . . . Look here, Lyons!

LYONS. See, I told you, Rose . . . I told you they'd let him come.

CORY. How you doing, Uncle Gabe?

LYONS. How you doing, Uncle Gabe?

GABRIEL. Hey, Rose. It's time. It's time to tell St. Peter to open the gates. Troy, you ready? You ready, Troy. I'm gonna tell St. Peter to open the gates. You get ready now.

GABRIEL, *with great fanfare, braces himself to blow. The trumpet is without a mouthpiece. He puts the end of it into his mouth and blows with great force, like a man who has been waiting some twenty-odd years for this single moment. No sound comes out of the trumpet. He braces himself and blows again with the same result. A third time he blows. There is a weight of impossible description that falls away and leaves him bare and exposed to a frightful realization. It is a trauma that a sane and normal mind would be unable to withstand. He begins to dance. A slow, strange dance, eerie and life-giving. A dance of atavistic signature and ritual.* LYONS *attempts to embrace him.* GABRIEL *pushes* LYONS *away. He begins to howl in what is an attempt at song, or perhaps a song turning back into itself in an attempt at speech. He finishes his dance and the gates of heaven stand open as wide as God's closet.*

That's the way that go!

(BLACKOUT)

[1987]

Topics for Critical Thinking and Writing

1. What do you think Bono means when he says, early in Act 2 (p. 402), "Some people build fences to keep people out . . . and other people build fences to keep people in"? Why is the play called *Fences?* What is Troy fencing in? (You'll want to take account of Troy's last speech in 2.2, but don't limit your response to this speech.)

2. Would you agree that Troy's refusal to encourage his younger son's aspirations is one of the "fences" of the play? What do you think Troy's reasons are— conscious and unconscious—for not wanting Cory to play football at college?

3. Compare and contrast Cory and Lyons. Consider, too, in what ways they resemble Troy, and in what ways they differ from him.

4. In what ways is Troy like his father, and in what ways unlike?

5. What do you make of the prominence given to the song about Blue?

6. There is a good deal of anger in the play, but there is also humor. Which passages do you find humorous, and why?

7. Characterize Rose Maxson.

8. Some scenes begin by specifying that "the lights come up." Others do not, presumably beginning with an illuminated stage. All scenes except the last one— which ends with a sudden blackout—end with the lights slowly going down to blackness. How would you explain Wilson's use of lighting?

13

Thinking Critically about Drama

"The play's the thing," Hamlet says, and he is right, or almost right. The play exists as something on the stage, or on the page, but the thing that finally matters for each of us is the play in our minds, or, better, the play that we experience with every part of our being. When the villainous Claudius sees the play-within-the-play in Hamlet, it so unnerves him that he cannot bear to have it continue. Few plays will have a comparable effect on most of us, but we should not be ashamed of being moved. Literature, after all, is meant to affect us powerfully, and drama is perhaps the most striking case in point. The film director Alfred Hitchcock put it this way: "Drama is life with the dull bits left out."

In this chapter we reprint a play, *The Glass Menagerie,* and we follow it with an essay in which a student who has studied and responded to the play tells us how, in his view, the work is constructed and how the scenes function as parts of a whole.

The original cast of the New York production of *The Glass Menagerie* (1945). (New York Public Library/Art Resource, NY)

TENNESSEE WILLIAMS

Tennessee Williams (1914–1983) was born Thomas Lanier Williams in Columbus, Mississippi. During his childhood his family moved to St. Louis, where his father had accepted a job as manager of a shoe company. Williams has written that neither he nor his sister Rose could adjust to the change from the South to the Midwest, but the children had already been deeply troubled. Nevertheless, at the age of 16 he achieved some distinction as a writer when his prize-winning essay in a nationwide contest was published. After high school he attended the University of Missouri but flunked ROTC and was therefore withdrawn from school by his father. He worked in a shoe factory for a while, then attended Washington University, where he wrote several plays. He finally graduated from the University of Iowa with a major in playwrighting. After graduation he continued to write, supporting himself with odd jobs such as waiting on tables and running elevators. His first commercial success was The Glass Menagerie *(produced in Chicago in 1944, and in New York in 1945); among his other plays are* A Streetcar Named Desire *(1947),* Cat on a Hot Tin Roof *(1955), and* Suddenly Last Summer *(1958).*

The Glass Menagerie

> *nobody, not even the rain, has such small hands.*
> *—e. e. cummings*

LIST OF CHARACTERS

AMANDA WINGFIELD, the mother. A little woman of great but confused vitality clinging frantically to another time and place. Her characterization must be carefully created, not copied from type. She is not paranoiac, but her life is paranoia. There is much to admire in Amanda, and as much to love and pity as there is to laugh at. Certainly she has endurance and a kind of heroism, and though her foolishness makes her unwittingly cruel at times, there is tenderness in her slight person.

LAURA WINGFIELD, her daughter. Amanda, having failed to establish contact with reality, continues to live vitally in her illusions, but Laura's situation is even graver. A childhood illness has left her crippled, one leg slightly shorter than the other, and held in a brace. This defect need not be more than suggested on the stage. Stemming from this, Laura's separation increases till she is like a piece of her own glass collection, too exquisitely fragile to move from the shelf.

TOM WINGFIELD, her son. And the narrator of the play. A poet with a job in a warehouse. His nature is not remorseless, but to escape from a trap he has to act without pity.

JIM O'CONNOR, the gentleman caller. A nice, ordinary, young man.

SCENE: *An alley in St. Louis.*
PART I: *Preparation for a Gentleman Caller.*
PART II: *The Gentleman Calls.*
TIME: *Now and the Past.*

Scene I

The Wingfield apartment is in the rear of the building, one of those vast hive-like conglomerations of cellular living-units that flower as warty growths in overcrowded urban centers of lower middle-class population and are symptomatic of the impulse of this largest and fundamentally enslaved section of American society to avoid fluidity and differentiation and to exist and function as one interfused mass of automatism.

The apartment faces an alley and is entered by a fire-escape, a structure whose name is a touch of accidental poetic truth, for all of these huge buildings are always burning with the slow and implacable fires of human desperation. The fire-escape is included in the set—that is, the landing of it and steps descending from it.

The scene is memory and is therefore nonrealistic. Memory takes a lot of poetic license. It omits some details; others are exaggerated, according to the emotional value of the articles it touches, for memory is seated predominantly in the heart. The interior is therefore rather dim and poetic.

At the rise of the curtain, the audience is faced with the dark, grim rear wall of the Wingfield tenement. This building, which runs parallel to the footlights, is flanked on both sides by dark, narrow alleys which run into murky canyons of tangled clotheslines, garbage cans and the sinister latticework of neighboring fire-escapes. It is up and down these side alleys that exterior entrances and exits are made, during the play. At the end of TOM's *opening commentary, the dark tenement wall slowly reveals (by means of a transparency) the interior of the ground floor Wingfield apartment.*

Downstage is the living room, which also serves as a sleeping room for LAURA, *the sofa unfolding to make her bed. Upstage, center, and divided by a wide arch or second proscenium with transparent faded portieres (or second curtain), is the dining room. In an old-fashioned what-not in the living room are seen scores of transparent glass animals. A blown-up photograph of the father hangs on the wall of the living room, facing the audience, to the left of the archway. It is the face of a very handsome young man in a doughboy's First World War cap. He is gallantly smiling, ineluctably smiling, as if to say, "I will be smiling forever."*

The audience hears and sees the opening scene in the dining room through both the transparent fourth wall of the building and the transparent gauze portieres of the dining-room arch. It is during this revealing scene that the fourth wall slowly ascends, out of sight.

This transparent exterior wall is not brought down again until the very end of the play, during TOM's *final speech.*

The narrator is an undisguised convention of the play. He takes whatever license with dramatic convention as is convenient to his purposes.

TOM *enters dressed as a merchant sailor from alley, stage left, and strolls across the front of the stage to the fire-escape. There he stops and lights a cigarette. He addresses the audience.*

TOM.   Yes, I have tricks in my pocket, I have things up my sleeve. But I am the opposite of a stage magician. He gives you illusion that has the appearance of truth. I give you truth in the pleasant disguise of illusion. To begin with, I turn back time. I reverse it to that quaint period, the thirties, when the huge mid-dle class of America was matriculating in a school for the blind. Their eyes had failed them, or they had failed their eyes, and so they were having their fingers pressed forcibly down on the fiery Braille alphabet of a dissolving economy. In Spain there was revolution. Here there was only shouting and confusion. In Spain there was Guernica. Here there were disturbances of labor, sometimes pretty violent, in otherwise peaceful cities such as Chicago, Cleveland, Saint Louis. . . . This is the social background of the play.

[*Music.*]

The play is memory. Being a memory play, it is dimly lighted, it is sentimental, it is not realistic. In memory everything seems to happen to music. That explains the fiddle in the wings. I am the narrator of the play, and also a character in it. The other characters are my mother, Amanda, my sister, Laura, and a gentleman caller who appears in the final scenes. He is the most realistic character in the play, being an emissary from a world of reality that we were somehow set apart from. But since I have a poet's weakness for symbols, I am using this character also as a symbol; he is the long delayed but always expected something that we live for. There is a fifth character in the play who doesn't appear except in this larger-than-life photograph over the mantel. This is our father who left us a long time ago. He was a telephone man who fell in love with long distances; he gave up his job with the telephone company and skipped the light fantastic out of town. . . . The last we heard of him was a picture post-card from Mazatlan, on the Pacific coast of Mexico, containing a message of two words—"Hello—Goodbye!" and no address. I think the rest of the play will explain itself. . . .

AMANDA*'s voice becomes audible through the portieres.*
[*Legend on Screen: "Où Sont les Neiges?"*]
He divides the portieres and enters the upstage area.
AMANDA *and* LAURA *are seated at a drop-leaf table. Eating is indicated by gestures without food or utensils.* AMANDA *faces the audience.* TOM *and* LAURA *are seated in profile.*
The interior has lit up softly and through the scrim we see AMANDA *and* LAURA *seated at the table in the upstage area.*

AMANDA [*calling*].   Tom?
TOM.   Yes, Mother.
AMANDA.   We can't say grace until you come to the table!
TOM.   Coming, Mother. [*He bows slightly and withdraws reappearing a few moments later in his place at the table.*]
AMANDA [*to her son*].   Honey, don't *push* with your *fingers.* If you have to push with something, the thing to push with is a crust of bread. And chew—chew! Animals have sections in their stomachs which enable them to digest food without mastication, but human beings are supposed to chew their food before they swallow it down. Eat food leisurely, son, and really enjoy it. A well-cooked meal has lots of delicate flavors that have to be held in the mouth for appreciation. So chew your food and give your salivary glands a chance to function!

TOM *deliberately lays his imaginary fork down and pushes his chair back from the table.*

TOM.   I haven't enjoyed one bite of this dinner because of your constant directions on how to eat it. It's you that makes me rush through meals with your hawk-like attention to every bite I take. Sickening—spoils my appetite—all this discussion of animals' secretion—salivary glands—mastication!
AMANDA [*lightly*].   Temperament like a Metropolitan star! [*He rises and crosses downstage.*] You're not excused from the table.
TOM.   I am getting a cigarette.
AMANDA.   You smoke too much.

LAURA rises.

LAURA.   I'll bring in the blanc mange.

He remains standing with his cigarette by the portieres during the following.

AMANDA [*rising*].   No, sister, no, sister—you be the lady this time and I'll be the darky.

LAURA.   I'm already up.

AMANDA.   Resume your seat, little sister—I want you to stay fresh and pretty—for gentlemen callers!

LAURA.   I'm not expecting any gentlemen callers.

AMANDA [*crossing out to kitchenette. Airily*].   Sometimes they come when they are least expected! Why, I remember one Sunday afternoon in Blue Mountain— [*Enters kitchenette.*]

TOM.   I know what's coming!

LAURA.   Yes. But let her tell it.

TOM.   Again?

LAURA.   She loves to tell it.

AMANDA *returns with bowl of dessert.*

AMANDA.   One Sunday afternoon in Blue Mountain—your mother received— *seventeen!*—gentlemen callers! Why, sometimes there weren't chairs enough to accommodate them all. We had to send the nigger over to bring in folding chairs from the parish house.

TOM [*remaining at portieres*].   How did you entertain those gentlemen callers?

AMANDA.   I understood the art of conversation!

TOM.   I bet you could talk.

AMANDA.   Girls in those days *knew* how to talk, I can tell you.

TOM.   Yes?

[*Image:* AMANDA *as a Girl on a Porch Greeting Callers.*]

AMANDA.   They knew how to entertain their gentlemen callers. It wasn't enough for a girl to be possessed of a pretty face and a graceful figure—although I wasn't slighted in either respect. She also needed to have a nimble wit and a tongue to meet all occasions.

TOM.   What did you talk about?

AMANDA.   Things of importance going on in the world! Never anything coarse or common or vulgar. [*She addresses* TOM *as though he were seated in the vacant chair at the table though he remains by portieres. He plays this scene as though he held the book.*] My callers were gentlemen—all! Among my callers were some of the most prominent young planters of the Mississippi Delta— planters and sons of planters!

TOM *motions for music and a spot of light on* AMANDA.

Her eyes lift, her face glows, her voice becomes rich and elegiac. [*Screen Legend: "Où Sont les Neiges?"*]

There was young Champ Laughlin who later became vice-president of the Delta Planters Bank. Hadley Stevenson who was drowned in Moon Lake and left his widow one hundred and fifty thousand in Government bonds. There were the Cutrere brothers, Wesley and Bates. Bates was one of my bright particular beaux! He got in a quarrel with that wild Wainright boy. They shot it out on the floor of Moon Lake Casino. Bates was shot through the stomach. Died in the ambulance on his way to Memphis. His widow was also well-provided for, came into eight or ten thousand acres, that's all. She married him on the rebound—never loved her—carried my picture on him the night he died! And there was that boy that every girl in Delta had set her cap for! That beautiful, brilliant young Fitzhugh boy from Green County!

TOM.   What did he leave his widow?

AMANDA.   He never married! Gracious, you talk as though all of my old admirers had turned up their toes to the daisies!

TOM.   Isn't this the first you mentioned that still survives?

AMANDA.   That Fitzhugh boy went North and made a fortune—came to be known as the Wolf of Wall Street! He had the Midas touch, whatever he touched turned to gold! And I could have been Mrs. Duncan J. Fitzhugh, mind you! But—I picked your *father!*

LAURA [*rising*].   Mother, let me clear the table.

AMANDA.   No dear, you go in front and study your typewriter chart. Or practice your shorthand a little. Stay fresh and pretty!—It's almost time for our gentlemen callers to start arriving. [*She flounces girlishly toward the kitchenette.*] How many do you suppose we're going to entertain this afternoon?

> TOM *throws down the paper and jumps up with a groan.*

LAURA [*alone in the dining room*].   I don't believe we're going to receive any, Mother.

AMANDA [*reappearing, airily*].   What? No one—not one? You must be joking! [LAURA *nervously echoes her laugh. She slips in a fugitive manner through the half-open portieres and draws them gently behind her. A shaft of very clear light is thrown on her face against the faded tapestry of the curtains.*] [*Music: "The Glass Menagerie" Under Faintly.*] [*Lightly.*] Not one gentleman caller? It can't be true! There must be a flood, there must have been a tornado!

LAURA.   It isn't a flood, it's not a tornado, Mother. I'm just not popular like you were in Blue Mountain. . . . [TOM *utters another groan.* LAURA *glances at him with a faint, apologetic smile. Her voice catching a little.*] Mother's afraid I'm going to be an old maid.

> [*The Scene Dims Out with "Glass Menagerie" Music.*]

Scene II
"Laura, Haven't You Ever Liked Some Boy?"

On the dark stage the screen is lighted with the image of blue roses. Gradually LAURA*'s figure becomes apparent and the screen goes out. The music subsides.*

> LAURA *is seated in the delicate ivory chair at the small clawfoot table.*
> *She wears a dress of soft violet material for a kimono—her hair tied back from her forehead with a ribbon.*
> *She is washing and polishing her collection of glass.*
> AMANDA *appears on the fire-escape steps. At the sound of her ascent,* LAURA *catches her breath, thrusts the bowl of ornaments away and seats herself stiffly before the diagram of the typewriter keyboard as though it held her spellbound. Something has happened to* AMANDA. *It is written in her face as she climbs to the landing: a look that is grim and hopeless and a little absurd.*
> *She has on one of those cheap or imitation velvety-looking cloth coats with imitation fur collar. Her hat is five or six years old, one of those dreadful cloche hats that were worn in the late twenties, and she is clasping an enormous black patent-leather pocketbook with nickel clasp and initials. This is her full-dress outfit, the one she usually wears to the D.A.R.*
> *Before entering she looks through the door.*
> *She purses her lips, opens her eyes wide, rolls them upward and shakes her head.*
> *Then she slowly lets herself in the door. Seeing her mother's expression* LAURA *touches her lips with a nervous gesture.*

LAURA.   Hello, Mother, I was—[*She makes a nervous gesture toward the chart on the wall.* AMANDA *leans against the shut door and stares at* LAURA *with a martyred look.*]

AMANDA.   Deception? Deception? [*She slowly removes her hat and gloves, continuing the swift suffering stare. She lets the hat and gloves fall on the floor—a bit of acting.*]

LAURA [*shakily*].   How was the D.A.R. meeting? [AMANDA *slowly opens her purse and removes a dainty white handkerchief which she shakes out delicately and delicately touches to her lips and nostrils.*] Didn't you go to the D.A.R. meeting, Mother?

AMANDA [*faintly, almost inaudibly*].   —No.—No. [*Then more forcibly.*] I did not have the strength—to go to the D.A.R. In fact, I did not have the courage! I wanted to find a hole in the ground and hide myself in it forever! [*She crosses slowly to the wall and removes the diagram of the typewriter keyboard. She holds it in front of her for a second, staring at it sweetly and sorrowfully—then bites her lips and tears it in two pieces.*]

LAURA [*faintly*].   Why did you do that, Mother? [AMANDA *repeats the same procedure with the chart of the Gregg Alphabet.*] Why are you—

AMANDA.   Why? Why? How old are you, Laura?

LAURA.   Mother, you know my age.

AMANDA.   I thought that you were an adult; it seems that I was mistaken. [*She crosses slowly to the sofa and sinks down and stares at* LAURA.]

LAURA.   Please don't stare at me, Mother.

AMANDA *closes her eyes and lowers her head. Count ten.*

AMANDA.   What are we going to do, what is going to become of us, what is the future?

Count ten.

LAURA.   Has something happened, Mother? [AMANDA *draws a long breath and takes out the handkerchief again. Dabbing process.*] Mother, has—something happened?

AMANDA.   I'll be all right in a minute. I'm just bewildered—[*count five*]—by life. . . .

LAURA.   Mother, I wish that you would tell me what's happened.

AMANDA.   As you know, I was supposed to be inducted into my office at the D.A.R. this afternoon. [*Image: A Swarm of Typewriters.*] But I stopped off at Rubicam's Business College to speak to your teachers about your having a cold and ask them what progress they thought you were making down there.

LAURA.   Oh. . . .

AMANDA.   I went to the typing instructor and introduced myself as your mother. She didn't know who you were. Wingfield, she said. We don't have any such student enrolled at the school! I assured her she did, that you had been going to classes since early in January. "I wonder," she said, "if you could be talking about that terribly shy little girl who dropped out of school after only a few days' attendance?" "No," I said, "Laura, my daughter, has been going to school every day for the past six weeks!" "Excuse me," she said. She took the attendance book out and there was your name, unmistakably printed, and all the dates you were absent until they decided that you had dropped out of school. I still said, "No, there must have been some mistake! There must have been some mix-up in the records!" And she said, "No—I remember her perfectly now. Her hand shook so that she couldn't hit the right keys! The first time we gave a speed-test, she broke down completely—was sick at the stomach and almost had to be carried into the wash-room! After that morning she never

showed up any more. We phoned the house but never got any answer"—
while I was working at Famous and Barr, I suppose, demonstrating those—
Oh! I felt so weak I could barely keep on my feet. I had to sit down while
they got me a glass of water! Fifty dollars' tuition, all of our plans—my hopes
and ambitions for you—just gone up the spout, just gone up the spout like
that. [LAURA *draws a long breath and gets awkwardly to her feet. She crosses to
the victrola and winds it up.*] What are you doing?

LAURA.   Oh! [*She releases the handle and returns to her seat.*]

AMANDA.   Laura, where have you been going when you've gone out pretending
that you were going to business college?

LAURA.   I've just been going out walking.

AMANDA.   That's not true.

LAURA.   It is. I just went walking.

AMANDA.   Walking? Walking? In winter? Deliberately courting pneumonia in that
light coat? Where did you walk to, Laura?

LAURA.   It was the lesser of two evils, Mother. [*Image: Winter Scene in Park.*] I
couldn't go back up. I—threw up—on the floor!

AMANDA.   From half past seven till after five every day you mean to tell me you
walked around in the park, because you wanted to make me think that you
were still going to Rubicam's Business College?

LAURA.   It wasn't as bad as it sounds. I went inside places to get warmed up.

AMANDA.   Inside where?

LAURA.   I went in the art museum and the bird-houses at the Zoo. I visited the
penguins every day! Sometimes I did without lunch and went to the movies.
Lately I've been spending most of my afternoons in the Jewel-box, that big
glass house where they raise the tropical flowers.

AMANDA.   You did all this to deceive me, just for the deception? [LAURA *looks
down.*] Why?

LAURA.   Mother, when you're disappointed, you get that awful suffering look on
your face, like the picture of Jesus' mother in the museum!

AMANDA.   Hush!

LAURA.   I couldn't face it.

> *Pause. A whisper of strings.*
> [*Legend: "The Crust of Humility."*]

AMANDA [*hopelessly fingering the huge pocketbook*].   So what are we going to do the
rest of our lives? Stay home and watch the parades go by? Amuse ourselves with
the glass menagerie, darling? Eternally play those worn-out phonograph
records your father left as a painful reminder of him? We won't have a business
career—we've given that up because it gave us nervous indigestion! [*Laughs
wearily.*] What is there left but dependency all our lives? I know so well what
becomes of unmarried women who aren't prepared to occupy a position. I've
seen such pitiful cases in the South—barely tolerated spinsters living upon the
grudging patronage of sister's husband or brother's wife!—stuck away in some
little mousetrap of a room—encouraged by one in-law to visit another—little
birdlike women without any nest—eating the crust of humility all their life! Is
that the future that we've mapped out for ourselves? I swear it's the only alternative I can think of! It isn't a very pleasant alternative, is it? Of course—some girls
do marry. [LAURA *twists her hands nervously.*] Haven't you ever liked some boy?

LAURA.   Yes. I liked one once. [*Rises.*] I came across his picture a while ago.

AMANDA [*with some interest*].   He gave you his picture?

LAURA.   No, it's in the year-book.

AMANDA [*disappointed*].   Oh—a high-school boy.

[*Screen Image:* JIM *as a High-School Hero Bearing a Silver Cup.*]

LAURA.   Yes. His name was Jim. [LAURA *lifts the heavy annual from the clawfoot table.*] Here he is in *The Pirates of Penzance.*

AMANDA [*absently*].   The what?

LAURA.   The operetta the senior class put on. He had a wonderful voice and we sat across the aisle from each other Mondays, Wednesdays and Fridays in the Aud. Here he is with the silver cup for debating! See his grin?

AMANDA [*absently*].   He must have had a jolly disposition.

LAURA.   He used to call me—Blue Roses.

[*Image: Blue Roses.*]

AMANDA.   Why did he call you such a name as that?

LAURA.   When I had that attack of pleurosis—he asked me what was the matter when I came back. I said pleurosis—he thought that I said Blue Roses! So that's what he always called me after that. Whenever he saw me, he'd holler, "Hello, Blue Roses!" I didn't care for the girl that he went out with. Emily Meisenbach. Emily was the best-dressed girl at Soldan. She never struck me, though, as being sincere. . . . It says in the Personal Section—they're engaged. That's—six years ago! They must be married by now.

AMANDA.   Girls that aren't cut out for business careers usually wind up married to some nice man. [*Gets up with a spark of revival.*] Sister, that's what you'll do!

LAURA *utters a startled, doubtful laugh. She reaches quickly for a piece of glass.*

LAURA.   But, Mother—

AMANDA.   Yes? [*Crossing to photograph.*]

LAURA [*in a tone of frightened apology*].   I'm—crippled!

[*Image: Screen.*]

AMANDA.   Nonsense! Laura, I've told you never, never to use that word. Why, you're not crippled, you just have a little defect—hardly noticeable, even! When people have some slight disadvantage like that, they cultivate other things to make up for it—develop charm—and vivacity—and—*charm!* That's all you have to do! [*She turns again to the photograph.*] One thing your father had *plenty of*—was *charm!*

TOM *motions to the fiddle in the wings.*

[*The Scene Fades out with Music.*]

Scene III

[*Legend on the Screen: "After the Fiasco—"*]

TOM *speaks from the fire-escape landing.*

TOM.   After the fiasco at Rubicam's Business College, the idea of getting a gentleman caller for Laura began to play a more important part in Mother's calculations. It became an obsession. Like some archetype of the universal unconscious, the image of the gentleman caller haunted our small apartment. . . . [*Image: Young Man at Door with Flowers.*] An evening at home rarely passed without some allusion to this image, this specter, this hope. . . . Even when he wasn't mentioned, his presence hung in Mother's preoccupied look and in my sister's frightened, apologetic manner—hung like a sentence passed upon the Wingfields! Mother was a woman of action as well as words. She began to take logical steps in the planned direction. Late that winter and in the early spring—realizing that extra money would be needed to properly feather the nest and plume the bird—she conducted a vigorous campaign on the telephone, roping in subscribers to one of those magazines for matrons called *The Home-maker's Companion,* the type of journal that features the serialized sublimations of ladies of letters who think in terms of delicate cuplike breasts, slim, tapering waists, rich, creamy thighs, eyes like wood-smoke in autumn, fingers that soothe and caress like strains of music, bodies as powerful as Etruscan sculpture.

[*Screen Image: Glamor Magazine Cover.*]

AMANDA *enters with phone on long extension cord. She is spotted in the dim stage.*

AMANDA.   Ida Scott? This is Amanda Wingfield! We *missed* you at the D.A.R. last Monday! I said to myself: She's probably suffering with that sinus condition! How is that sinus condition? Horrors! Heaven have mercy!—You're a Christian martyr, yes, that's what you are, a Christian martyr! Well, I just now happened to notice that your subscription to the *Companion's* about to expire! Yes, it expires with the next issue, honey!—just when that wonderful new serial by Bessie Mae Hopper is getting off to such an exciting start. Oh, honey, it's something that you can't miss! You remember how *Gone With the Wind* took everybody by storm? You simply couldn't go out if you hadn't read it. All everybody *talked* was Scarlett O'Hara. Well, this is a book that critics already compare to *Gone With the Wind*. It's the *Gone With the Wind* of the post-World War generation—What?—Burning?—Oh, honey, don't let them burn, go take a look in the oven and I'll hold the wire! Heavens—I think she's hung up!

[*Dim Out.*]

[*Legend on Screen: "You Think I'm in Love with Continental Shoemakers?"*]

Before the stage is lighted, the violent voices of TOM *and* AMANDA *are heard. They are quarreling behind the portieres. In front of them stands* LAURA *with clenched hands and panicky expression.*

A clear pool of light on her figure throughout this scene.

TOM.   What in Christ's name am I—

AMANDA [*shrilly*].   Don't you use that—

TOM.   Supposed to do!

AMANDA.   Expression! Not in my—

TOM.   Ohhh!

AMANDA.   Presence! Have you gone out of your senses?

TOM.   I have, that's true, *driven* out!

AMANDA.   What is the matter with you, you—big—big—IDIOT!

TOM.   Look—I've got *no thing,* no single thing—

AMANDA.   Lower your voice!

TOM.   In my life here that I can call my OWN! Everything is—

AMANDA.   Stop that shouting!

TOM.   Yesterday you confiscated my books! You had the nerve to—

AMANDA.   I took that horrible novel back to the library—yes! That hideous book by that insane Mr. Lawrence. [TOM *laughs wildly.*] I cannot control the output of diseased minds or people who cater to them—[TOM *laughs still more wildly.*] BUT I WON'T ALLOW SUCH FILTH BROUGHT INTO MY HOUSE! No, no, no, no, no!

TOM.   House, house! Who pays rent on it, who makes a slave of himself to—

AMANDA [*fairly screeching*].   Don't you DARE to—

TOM.   No, no, *I* musn't say things! *I've* got to just—

AMANDA.   Let me tell you—

TOM.   I don't want to hear any more! [*He tears the portieres open. The upstage area is lit with a turgid smoky red glow.*]

AMANDA's *hair is in metal curlers and she wears a very old bathrobe, much too large for her slight figure, a relic of the faithless Mr. Wingfield.*

An upright typewriter and a wild disarray of manuscripts are on the dropleaf table. The quarrel was probably precipitated by AMANDA's *interruption of his creative labor. A chair lying overthrown on the floor.*

Their gesticulating shadows are cast on the ceiling by the fiery glow.

AMANDA.   You *will* hear more, you—

TOM.   No, I won't hear more, I'm going out!

AMANDA.   You come right back in—

TOM.   Out, out, out! Because I'm—

AMANDA.   Come back here, Tom Wingfield! I'm not through talking to you!

TOM.   Oh, go—

LAURA [*desperately*].   Tom!

AMANDA.   You're going to listen, and no more insolence from you! I'm at the end of my patience! [*He comes back toward her.*]

TOM.   What do you think I'm at? Aren't I supposed to have any patience to reach the end of, Mother? I know, I know. It seems unimportant to you, what I'm *doing*—what I *want* to do—having a little *difference* between them! You don't think that—

AMANDA.   I think you've been doing things that you're ashamed of. That's why you act like this. I don't believe that you go every night to the movies. Nobody goes to the movies night after night. Nobody in their right minds goes to the movies as often as you pretend to. People don't go to the movies at nearly midnight, and movies don't let out at two A.M. Come in stumbling. Muttering to yourself like a maniac! You get three hours' sleep and then go to work. Oh, I can picture the way you're doing down there. Moping, doping, because you're in no condition.

TOM [*wildly*].   No, I'm in no condition!

AMANDA.   What right have you got to jeopardize your job? Jeopardize the security of us all? How do you think we'd manage if you were—

TOM.   Listen! You think I'm crazy *about* the *warehouse?* [*He bends fiercely toward her slight figure.*] You think I'm in love with the Continental Shoemakers? You think I want to spend fifty-five *years* down there in that—*celotex interior!* with—*fluorescent—tubes!* Look! I'd rather somebody picked up a crowbar and battered out my brains—than go back mornings! *I go!* Every time you come in yelling that God damn "*Rise and Shine!*" "*Rise and Shine!*" I say to myself "How *lucky dead* people are!" But I get up. I *go!* For sixty-five dollars a month I give up all that I dream of doing and being *ever!* And you say self—*self*'s all I ever think of. Why, listen, if self is what I thought of, Mother, I'd be where he is—GONE! [*Pointing to father's picture.*] As far as the system of transportation reaches! [*He starts past her. She grabs his arm.*] Don't grab at me, Mother!

AMANDA.   Where are you going?

TOM.   I'm going to the *movies!*

AMANDA.   I don't believe that lie!

TOM [*crouching toward her, overtowering her tiny figure. She backs away, gasping*].   I'm going to opium dens! Yes, opium dens, dens of vice and criminals' hang-outs, Mother. I've joined the Hogan gang, I'm a hired assassin, I carry a tommy-gun in a violin case! I run a string of cat-houses in the Valley! They call me Killer, Killer Wingfield, I'm leading a double-life, a simple, honest ware-house worker by day, by night a dynamic *czar* of the *underworld, Mother.* I go to gambling casinos, I spin away fortunes on the roulette table! I wear a patch over one eye and a false mustache, sometimes I put on green whiskers. On those occasions they call me—*El Diablo!* Oh, I could tell you things to make you sleepless! My enemies plan to dynamite this place. They're going to blow us all sky-high some night! I'll be glad, very happy, and so will you! You'll go up, up on a broomstick, over Blue Mountain with seventeen gentlemen callers! You ugly—babbling old—*witch.* . . . [*He goes through a series of violent, clumsy movements, seizing his overcoat, lunging to the door, pulling it fiercely open. The women watch him, aghast. His arm catches in the sleeve of the coat as he struggles to pull it on. For a moment he is pinioned by the bulky garment. With an outraged groan he tears the coat off again, splitting the shoulders of it and hurls it across the room. It strikes against the shelf of* LAURA's *glass collection, there is a tinkle of shattering glass.* LAURA *cries out as if wounded.*]

[*Music Legend: "The Glass Menagerie."*]

LAURA [*shrilly*].   My glass!—menagerie. . . . [*She covers her face and turns away.*]

But AMANDA *is still stunned and stupefied by the "ugly witch" so that she barely notices this occurrence. Now she recovers her speech.*

AMANDA [*in an awful voice*].   I won't speak to you—until you apologize!

[*She crosses through portieres and draws them together behind her.* TOM *is left with* LAURA. LAURA *clings weakly to the mantel with her face averted.* TOM *stares at her stupidly for a moment. Then he crosses to shelf. Drops, awkwardly to his knees to collect the fallen glass, glancing at* LAURA *as if he would speak but couldn't.*]

"The Glass Menagerie" steals in as
[*The Scene Dims Out.*]

Scene IV

The interior is dark. Faint light in the alley.

A deep-voiced bell in a church is tolling the hour of five as the scene commences.

TOM *appears at the top of the alley. After each solemn boom of the bell in the tower, he shakes a little noise-maker or rattle as if to express the tiny spasm of man in contrast to the sustained power and dignity of the Almighty. This and the unsteadiness of his advance make it evident that he has been drinking.*

As he climbs the few steps to the fire-escape landing light steals up inside. LAURA *appears in night-dress, observing* TOM's *empty bed in the front room.*

TOM *fishes in his pockets for the door-key, removing a motley assortment of articles in the search, including a perfect shower of movie-ticket stubs and an empty bottle. At last he finds the key, but just as he is about to insert it, it slips from his fingers. He strikes a match and crouches below the door.*

TOM [*bitterly*].   One crack—and it falls through!

LAURA *opens the door.*

LAURA.   Tom! Tom, what are you doing?

TOM.   Looking for a door-key.

LAURA.   Where have you been all this time?

TOM.   I have been to the movies.

LAURA.   All this time at the movies?

TOM.   There was a very long program. There was a Garbo picture and a Mickey
      Mouse and a travelogue and a newsreel and a preview of coming attractions.
      And there was an organ solo and a collection for the milk-fund—simultane-
      ously—which ended up in a terrible fight between a fat lady and an usher!
LAURA [*innocently*].   Did you have to stay through everything?
TOM.   Of course! And, oh, I forgot! There was a big stage show! The headliner on
      this stage show was Malvolio the Magician. He performed wonderful tricks,
      many of them, such as pouring water back and forth between pitchers. First it
      turned to wine and then it turned to beer and then it turned to whiskey. I know
      it was whiskey it finally turned into because he needed somebody to come up
      out of the audience to help him, and I came up—both shows! It was Kentucky
      Straight Bourbon. A very generous fellow, he gave souvenirs. [*He pulls from his
      back pocket a shimmering rainbow-colored scarf.*] He gave me this. This is his
      magic scarf. You can have it, Laura. You wave it over a canary cage and you get
      a bowl of gold-fish. You wave it over the gold-fish bowl and they fly away ca-
      naries. . . . But the wonderfullest trick of all was the coffin trick. We nailed him
      into a coffin and he got out of the coffin without removing one nail. [*He has
      come inside.*] There is a trick that would come in handy for me—get me out of
      this 2 by 4 situation! [*Flops onto bed and starts removing shoes.*]
LAURA.   Tom—Shhh!
TOM.   What you shushing me for?
LAURA.   You'll wake up Mother.
TOM.   Goody, goody! Pay 'er back for all those "Rise an' Shines." [*Lies down,
      groaning.*] You know it don't take much intelligence to get yourself into a
      nailed-up coffin, Laura. But who in hell ever got himself out of one without
      removing one nail?

    As if in answer, the father's grinning photograph lights up.
    [*Scene Dims Out*]
    *Immediately following: The church bell is heard striking six. At the sixth
stroke the alarm clock goes off in* AMANDA'*s room, and after a few moments we
hear her calling: "Rise and Shine! Rise and Shine!* LAURA, *go tell your brother to
rise and shine!"*

TOM.   [*sitting up slowly*]. I'll rise—but I won't shine.

    The light increases.

AMANDA.   Laura, tell your brother his coffee is ready.

    LAURA *slips into front room.*

LAURA.   Tom! it's nearly seven. Don't make Mother nervous. [*He stares at her stu-
      pidly. Beseechingly.*] Tom, speak to Mother this morning. Make up with her,
      apologize, speak to her!
TOM.   She won't to me. It's her that started not speaking.
LAURA.   If you just say you're sorry she'll start speaking.
TOM.   Her not speaking—is that such a tragedy?
LAURA.   Please—please!
AMANDA [*calling from kitchenette*].   Laura, are you going to do what I asked you
      to do, or do I have to get dressed and go out myself?
LAURA.   Going, going—soon as I get on my coat! [*She pulls on a shapeless felt hat
      with nervous, jerky movement, pleadingly glancing at* TOM. *Rushes awkwardly
      for coat. The coat is one of* AMANDA'*s, inaccurately made-over the sleeves too
      short for* LAURA.] Butter and what else?
AMANDA [*entering upstage*].   Just butter. Tell them to charge it.

LAURA.   Mother, they make such faces when I do that.

AMANDA.   Sticks and stones may break my bones, but the expression on Mr.
Garfinkel's face won't harm us! Tell your brother his coffee is getting cold.

LAURA [*at door*].   Do what I asked you, will you, will you, Tom?

> *He looks sullenly away.*

AMANDA.   Laura, go now or just don't go at all!

LAURA [*rushing out*].   Going—going! [*A second later she cries out.* TOM *springs up
and crosses to the door.* AMANDA *rushes anxiously in.* TOM *opens the door.*]

TOM.   Laura?

LAURA.   I'm all right. I slipped, but I'm all right.

AMANDA [*peering anxiously after her*].   If anyone breaks a leg on those fire-escape
steps, the landlord ought to be sued for every cent he possesses!

> [*She shuts door. Remembers she isn't speaking and returns to other room.*]
> As TOM *enters listlessly for his coffee, she turns her back to him and stands
> rigidly facing the window on the gloomy gray vault of the areaway. Its light on
> her face with its aged but childish features is cruelly sharp, satirical as a Daumier
> print.*

> [*Music Under: "Ave Maria."*]

> TOM *glances sheepishly but sullenly at her averted figure and slumps at the
> table. The coffee is scalding hot; he sips it and gasps and spits it back in the cup.
> At his gasp,* AMANDA *catches her breath and half turns. Then catches herself and
> turns back to window.*

> TOM *blows on his coffee, glancing sidewise at his mother. She clears her
> throat.* TOM *clears his. He starts to rise. Sinks back down again, scratches his head,
> clears his throat again.* AMANDA *coughs.* TOM *raises his cup in both hands to blow
> on it, his eyes staring over the rim of it at his mother for several moments. Then he
> slowly sets the cup down and awkwardly and hesitantly rises from the chair.*

TOM [*hoarsely*].   Mother. I—I apologize. Mother. [AMANDA *draws a quick, shuddering breath. Her face works grotesquely. She breaks into childlike tears.*] I'm
sorry for what I said, for everything that I said, I didn't mean it.

AMANDA [*sobbingly*].   My devotion has made me a witch and so I make myself
hateful to my children!

TOM.   No you *don't.*

AMANDA.   I worry so much, don't sleep, it makes me nervous!

TOM [*gently*].   I understand that.

AMANDA.   I've had to put up a solitary battle all these years. But you're my right-
hand bower! Don't fall down, don't fail!

TOM [*gently*].   I try, Mother.

AMANDA [*with great enthusiasm*].   Try and you will SUCCEED! [*The notion makes her
breathless.*] Why, you—you're just *full* of natural endowments! Both of my
children—they're *unusual* children! Don't you think I know it? I'm so—
proud! Happy and—feel I've—so much to be thankful for but—Promise me
one thing, son!

TOM.   What, Mother?

AMANDA.   Promise, son, you'll—never be a drunkard!

TOM [*turns to her grinning*].   I will never be a drunkard, Mother.

AMANDA.   That's what frightened me so, that you'd be drinking! Eat a bowl of
Purina!

TOM.   Just coffee, Mother.

AMANDA.   Shredded wheat biscuit?

TOM.   No. No, Mother, just coffee.

AMANDA.   You can't put in a day's work on an empty stomach. You've got ten minutes—don't gulp! Drinking too-hot liquids makes cancer of the stomach. . . .
Put cream in.

TOM.   No, thank you.

AMANDA.   To cool it.

TOM.   No! No, thank you, I want it black.

AMANDA.   I know, but it's not good for you. We have to do all that we can to build
ourselves up. In these trying times we live in, all that we have to cling to is—
each other. . . . That's why it's so important to—Tom, I—I sent out your sister
so I could discuss something with you. If you hadn't spoken I would have
spoken to you. [*Sits down.*]

TOM [*gently*].   What is it, Mother, that you want to discuss?

AMANDA.   Laura!

> TOM *puts his cup down slowly.*
> [*Legend on Screen: "Laura."*]
> [*Music: "The Glass Menagerie."*]

TOM.   —Oh.—Laura . . .

AMANDA [*touching his sleeve*].   You know how Laura is. So quiet but—still water
runs deep! She notices things and I think she—broods about them. [TOM *looks
up.*] A few days ago I came in and she was crying.

TOM.   What about?

AMANDA.   You.

TOM.   Me?

AMANDA.   She has an idea that you're not happy here.

TOM.   What gave her that idea?

AMANDA.   What gives her any idea? However, you do act strangely. I—I'm not criticizing, understand *that!* I know your ambitions do not lie in the warehouse,
that like everybody in the whole wide world—you've had to—make sacrifices, but—Tom—Tom—life's not easy, it calls for—Spartan endurance!
There's so many things in my heart that I cannot describe to you! I've never
told you but I—*loved* your father. . . .

TOM [*gently*].   I know that, Mother.

AMANDA.   And you—when I see you taking after his ways! Staying out late—
and—well, you *had* been drinking the night you were in that—terrifying condition! Laura says that you hate the apartment and that you go out nights to
get away from it! Is that true, Tom?

TOM.   No. You say there's so much in your heart that you can't describe to me.
That's true of me, too. There's so much in my heart that I can't describe to
you! So let's respect each other's—

AMANDA.   But, why—*why*, Tom—are you always so *restless?* Where do you go to,
nights?

TOM.   I—go to the movies.

AMANDA.   Why do you go to the movies so much, Tom?

TOM.   I go to the movies because—I like adventure. Adventure is something I
don't have much of at work, so I go to the movies.

AMANDA.   But, Tom, you go to the movies *entirely too much!*

TOM.   I like a lot of adventure.

> AMANDA *looks baffled, then hurt. As the familiar inquisition resumes he
> becomes hard and impatient again.* AMANDA *slips back into her querulous attitude
> toward him.*
> [*Image on Screen: Sailing Vessel with Jolly Roger.*]

AMANDA.   Most young men find adventure in their careers.

TOM.   Then most young men are not employed in a warehouse.

AMANDA.   The world is full of young men employed in warehouses and offices and factories.

TOM.   Do all of them find adventure in their careers?

AMANDA.   They do or they do without it! Not everybody has a craze for adventure.

TOM.   Man is by instinct a lover, a hunter, a fighter, and none of those instincts are given much play at the warehouse!

AMANDA.   Man is by instinct! Don't quote instinct to me! Instinct is something that people have got away from! It belongs to animals! Christian adults don't want it!

TOM.   What do Christian adults want, then, Mother?

AMANDA.   Superior things! Things of the mind and the spirit! Only animals have to satisfy instincts! Surely your aims are somewhat higher than theirs! Than monkeys—pigs—

TOM.   I reckon they're not.

AMANDA.   You're joking. However, that isn't what I wanted to discuss.

TOM [*rising*].   I haven't much time.

AMANDA [*pushing his shoulders*].   Sit down.

TOM.   You want me to punch in red at the warehouse, Mother?

AMANDA.   You have five minutes. I want to talk about Laura.

>   [*Legend: "Plans and Provisions."*]

TOM.   All right! What about Laura?

AMANDA.   We have to be making plans and provisions for her. She's older than you, two years, and nothing has happened. She just drifts along doing nothing. It frightens me terribly how she just drifts along.

TOM.   I guess she's the type that people call home girls.

AMANDA.   There's no such type, and if there is, it's a pity! That is unless the home is hers, with a husband!

TOM.   What?

AMANDA.   Oh, I can see the handwriting on the wall as plain as I see the nose in the front of my face! It's terrifying! More and more you remind me of your father! He was out all hours without explanation—Then *left! Goodbye!* And me with the bag to hold. I saw that letter you got from the Merchant Marine. I know what you're dreaming of. I'm not standing here blindfolded. Very well, then. Then *do* it! But not till there's somebody to take your place.

TOM.   What do you mean?

AMANDA.   I mean that as soon as Laura has got somebody to take care of her, married, a home of her own, independent—why, then you'll be free to go wherever you please, on land, on sea, whichever way the wind blows! But until that time you've got to look out for your sister. I don't say me because I'm old and don't matter! I say for your sister because she's young and dependent. I put her in business college—a dismal failure! Frightened her so it made her sick to her stomach. I took her over to the Young People's League at the church. Another fiasco. She spoke to nobody, nobody spoke to her. Now all she does is fool with those pieces of glass and play those worn-out records. What kind of a life is that for a girl to lead!

TOM.   What can I do about it?

AMANDA.   Overcome selfishness! Self, self, self is all that you ever think of! [TOM *springs up and crosses to get his coat. It is ugly and bulky. He pulls on a cap with earmuffs.*] Where is your muffler? Put your wool muffler on! [*He snatches it angrily from the closet and tosses it around his neck and pulls both ends tight.*] Tom! I haven't said what I had in mind to ask you.

TOM.   I'm too late to—

AMANDA [*catching his arms—very importunately. Then shyly*].   Down at the warehouse, aren't there some—nice young men?

TOM.   No!

AMANDA.   There *must* be—*some.*

TOM.   Mother—

> *Gesture.*

AMANDA.   Find out one that's clean-living—doesn't drink and—ask him out for sister!

TOM.   What?

AMANDA.   For *sister!* To *meet!* Get *acquainted!*

TOM [*stamping to door*].   Oh, my go-osh!

AMANDA.   Will you? [*He opens door. Imploringly.*] Will you? [*He starts down.*] Will you? *Will* you dear?

TOM [*calling back*].   YES!

> AMANDA *closes the door hesitantly and with a troubled but faintly hopeful expression.*

> [*Screen Image: Glamor Magazine Cover.*]
>
> *Spot* AMANDA *at phone.*

AMANDA.   Ella Cartwright? This is Amanda Wingfield! How are you honey? How is that kidney condition? [*Count five.*] Horrors! [*Count five.*] You're a Christian martyr, yes, honey, that's what you are, a Christian martyr! Well, I just happened to notice in my little red book that your subscription to the *Companion* has just run out! I knew that you wouldn't want to miss out on the wonderful serial starting in this new issue. It's by Bessie Mae Hopper, the first thing she's written since *Honeymoon for Three.* Wasn't that a strange and interesting story? Well, this one is even lovelier, I believe. It has a sophisticated society background. It's all about the horsey set on Long Island!

> [*Fade Out.*]

Scene V

> [*Legend on Screen: "Annunciation."*] *Fade with music.*
>
> *It is early dusk of a spring evening. Supper has just been finished at the Wingfield apartment.* AMANDA *and* LAURA *in light colored dresses are removing dishes from the table, in the upstage area, which is shadowy, their movements formalized almost as a dance or ritual, their moving forms as pale and silent as moths.*
>
> TOM, *in white shirt and trousers, rises from the table and crosses toward the fire-escape.*

AMANDA [*as he passes her*].   Son, will you do me a favor?

TOM.   What?

AMANDA.   Comb your hair! You look so pretty when your hair is combed! [TOM *slouches on sofa with evening paper. Enormous caption "Franco Triumphs."*]
There is only one respect in which I would like you to emulate your father.

TOM.   What respect is that?

AMANDA.   The care he always took of his appearance. He never allowed himself to look untidy. [*He throws down the paper and crosses to fire-escape.*] Where are you going?

TOM.   I'm going out to smoke.

AMANDA.   You smoke too much. A pack a day at fifteen cents a pack. How much would that amount to in a month? Thirty times fifteen is how much, Tom? Figure it out and you will be astounded at what you could save. Enough to give you a night-school course in accounting at Washington U! Just think what a wonderful thing that would be for you, son!

TOM *is unmoved by the thought.*

TOM.   I'd rather smoke. [*He steps out on landing, letting the screen door slam.*]

AMANDA [*sharply*].   I know! That's the tragedy of it. . . . [*Alone, she turns to look at her husband's picture.*]

[*Dance Music: "All the World Is Waiting for the Sunrise!"*]

TOM [*to the audience*].   Across the alley from us was the Paradise Dance Hall. On evenings in spring the windows and doors were open and the music came outdoors. Sometimes the lights were turned out except for a large glass sphere that hung from the ceiling. It would turn slowly about and filter the dusk with delicate rainbow colors. Then the orchestra played a waltz or a tango, something that had a slow and sensuous rhythm. Couples would come outside, to the relative privacy of the alley. You could see them kissing behind ashpits and telephone poles. This was the compensation for lives that passed like mine, without any change or adventure. Adventure and change were imminent in this year. They were waiting around the corner for all these kids. Suspended in the mist over Berchtesgaden, caught in the folds of Chamberlain's umbrella—In Spain there was Guernica! But here there was only hot swing music and liquor, dance halls, bars, and movies, and sex that hung in the gloom like a chandelier and flooded the world with brief, deceptive rainbows. . . . All the world was waiting for bombardments!

AMANDA *turns from the picture and comes outside.*

AMANDA [*sighing*].   A fire-escape landing's a poor excuse for a porch. [*She spreads a newspaper on a step and sits down, gracefully and demurely as if she were settling into a swing on a Mississippi veranda.*] What are you looking at?

TOM.   The moon.

AMANDA.   Is there a moon this evening?

TOM.   It's rising over Garfinkel's Delicatessen.

AMANDA.   So it is! A little silver slipper of a moon. Have you made a wish on it yet?

TOM.   Um-hum.

AMANDA.   What did you wish for?

TOM.   That's a secret.

AMANDA.   A secret, huh? Well, I won't tell mine either. I will be just as mysterious as you.

TOM.   I bet I can guess what yours is.

AMANDA.   Is my head so transparent?

TOM.   You're not a sphinx.

AMANDA.   No, I don't have secrets. I'll tell you what I wished for on the moon. Success and happiness for my precious children! I wish for that whenever there's a moon, and when there isn't a moon, I wish for it, too.

TOM.   I thought perhaps you wished for a gentleman caller.

AMANDA.   Why do you say that?

TOM.   Don't you remember asking me to fetch one?

AMANDA.   I remember suggesting that it would be nice for your sister if you brought some nice young man from the warehouse. I think I've made that suggestion more than once.

TOM.   Yes, you have made it repeatedly.

AMANDA.   Well?

TOM.   We are going to have one.

AMANDA.   *What?*

TOM.   A gentleman caller!

[*The Annunciation Is Celebrated with Music.*]

AMANDA *rises.*

[*Image on Screen: Caller with Bouquet.*]

AMANDA.   You mean you have asked some nice young man to come over?

TOM.   Yep. I've asked him to dinner.

AMANDA.   You really did?

TOM.   I did!

AMANDA.   You did, and did he—*accept?*

TOM.   He did!

AMANDA.   Well, well—well, well! That's—lovely!

TOM.   I thought that you would be pleased.

AMANDA.   It's definite, then?

TOM.   Very definite.

AMANDA.   Soon?

TOM.   Very soon.

AMANDA.   For heaven's sake, stop putting on and tell me some things, will you?

TOM.   What things do you want me to tell you?

AMANDA.   Naturally I would like to know when he's *coming!*

TOM.   He's coming tomorrow.

AMANDA.   *Tomorrow?*

TOM.   Yep. Tomorrow.

AMANDA.   But, Tom!

TOM.   Yes, Mother?

AMANDA.   Tomorrow gives me no time!

TOM.   Time for what?

AMANDA.   Preparations! Why didn't you phone me at once, as soon as you asked him, the minute that he accepted? Then, don't you see, I could have been getting ready!

TOM.   You don't have to make any fuss.

AMANDA.   Oh, Tom, Tom, Tom, of course I have to make a fuss! I want things nice, not sloppy! Not thrown together. I'll certainly have to do some fast thinking, won't I?

TOM.   I don't see why you have to think at all.

AMANDA.   You just don't know. We can't have a gentleman caller in a pigsty! All my wedding silver has to be polished, the monogrammed table linen ought to be laundered! The windows have to be washed and fresh curtains put up. And how about clothes? We have to *wear* something, don't we?

TOM.   Mother, this boy is no one to make a fuss over!

AMANDA.   Do you realize he's the first young man we've introduced to your sister? It's terrible, dreadful, disgraceful that poor little sister has never received a single gentleman caller! Tom, come inside! [*She opens the screen door.*]

TOM.   What for?

AMANDA.   I want to ask you some things.

TOM.   If you're going to make such a fuss, I'll call it off, I'll tell him not to come.

AMANDA.   You certainly won't do anything of the kind. Nothing offends people worse than broken engagements. It simply means I'll have to work like a

Turk! We won't be brilliant, but we'll pass inspection. Come on inside. [TOM *follows, groaning.*] Sit down.

TOM.   Any particular place you would like me to sit?

AMANDA.   Thank heavens I've got that new sofa! I'm also making payments on a floor lamp I'll have sent out! And put the chintz covers on, they'll brighten things up! Of course I'd hoped to have these walls repapered. . . . What is the young man's name?

TOM.   His name is O'Connor.

AMANDA.   That, of course, means fish—tomorrow is Friday! I'll have that salmon loaf—with Durkee's dressing! What does he do? He works at the warehouse?

TOM.   Of course! How else would I—

AMANDA.   Tom, he—doesn't drink?

TOM.   Why do you ask me that?

AMANDA.   Your father *did!*

TOM.   Don't get started on that!

AMANDA.   He *does* drink, then?

TOM.   Not that I know of!

AMANDA.   Make sure, be certain! The last thing I want for my daughter's a boy who drinks!

TOM.   Aren't you being a little premature? Mr. O'Connor has not yet appeared on the scene!

AMANDA.   But will tomorrow. To meet your sister, and what do I know about his character? Nothing! Old maids are better off than wives of drunkards!

TOM.   Oh, my God!

AMANDA.   Be still!

TOM [*leaning forward to whisper*].   Lots of fellows meet girls whom they don't marry!

AMANDA.   Oh, talk sensibly, Tom—and don't be sarcastic! [*She has gotten a hairbrush.*]

TOM.   What are you doing?

AMANDA.   I'm brushing that cow-lick down! What is this young man's position at the warehouse?

TOM [*submitting grimly to the brush and the interrogation*].   This young man's position is that of a shipping clerk, Mother.

AMANDA.   Sounds to me like a fairly responsible job, the sort of a job *you* would be in if you just had more *get-up.* What is his salary? Have you got any idea?

TOM.   I would judge it to be approximately eighty-five dollars a month.

AMANDA.   Well—not princely, but—

TOM.   Twenty more than I make.

AMANDA.   Yes, how well I know! But for a family man, eighty-five dollars a month is not much more than you can just get by on. . . .

TOM.   Yes, but Mr. O'Connor is not a family man.

AMANDA.   He might be, mightn't he? Some time in the future?

TOM.   I see. Plans and provisions.

AMANDA.   You are the only man that I know of who ignores the fact that the future becomes the present, the present the past, and the past turns into everlasting regret if you don't plan for it!

TOM.   I will think that over and see what I can make of it.

AMANDA.   Don't be supercilious with your mother! Tell me some more about this—what do you call him?

TOM.   James D. O'Connor. The D. is for Delaney.

AMANDA.   Irish on *both* sides! *Gracious!* And doesn't drink?

TOM.   Shall I call him up and ask him right this minute?

AMANDA.   The only way to find out about those things is to make discreet inquiries at the proper moment. When I was a girl in Blue Mountain and it was
suspected that a young man drank, the girl whose attentions he had been receiving, if any girl *was,* would sometimes speak to the minister of his church,
or rather her father would if her father was living, and sort of feel him out on
the young man's character. That is the way such things are discreetly handled
to keep a young woman from making a tragic mistake!

TOM.   Then how did you happen to make a tragic mistake?

AMANDA.   That innocent look of your father's had everyone fooled! He *smiled—*
the world was *enchanted!* No girl can do worse than put herself at the mercy
of a handsome appearance! I hope that Mr. O'Connor is not too good-looking.

TOM.   No, he's not too good-looking. He's covered with freckles and hasn't too
much of a nose.

AMANDA.   He's not right-down homely, though?

TOM.   Not right-down homely. Just medium homely, I'd say.

AMANDA.   Character's what to look for in a man.

TOM.   That's what I've always said, Mother.

AMANDA.   You've never said anything of the kind and I suspect you would never
give it a thought.

TOM.   Don't be suspicious of me.

AMANDA.   At least I hope he's the type that's up and coming.

TOM.   I think he really goes in for self-improvement.

AMANDA.   What reason have you to think so?

TOM.   He goes to night school.

AMANDA [*beaming*].   Splendid! What does he do, I mean study?

TOM.   Radio engineering and public speaking!

AMANDA.   Then he has visions of being advanced in the world! Any young man
who studies public speaking is aiming to have an executive job some day!
And radio engineering? A thing for the future! Both of these facts are very illuminating. Those are the sort of things that a mother should know concerning any young man who comes to call on her daughter. Seriously or—not.

TOM.   One little warning. He doesn't know about Laura. I didn't let on that we
had dark ulterior motives. I just said, why don't you come have dinner with
us? He said okay and that was the whole conversation.

AMANDA.   I bet it was! You're eloquent as an oyster. However, he'll know about
Laura when he gets here. When he sees how lovely and sweet and pretty she
is, he'll thank his lucky stars he was asked to dinner.

TOM.   Mother, you mustn't expect too much of Laura.

AMANDA.   What do you mean?

TOM.   Laura seems all those things to you and me because she's ours and we love
her. We don't even notice she's crippled any more.

AMANDA.   Don't say crippled! You know that I never allow that word to be used!

TOM.   But face facts, Mother. She is and—that's not all—

AMANDA.   What do you mean "not all"?

TOM.   Laura is very different from other girls.

AMANDA.   I think the difference is all to her advantage.

TOM.   Not quite all—in the eyes of others—strangers—she's terribly shy and lives
in a world of her own and those things make her seem a little peculiar to
people outside the house.

AMANDA.   Don't say peculiar.

TOM.   Face the facts. She is.

[*The Dance-Hall Music Changes to a Tango that Has a Minor and Somewhat Ominous Tone.*]

AMANDA.   In what way is she peculiar—may I ask?

TOM [*gently*].   She lives in a world of her own—a world of—little glass ornaments, Mother. . . . [*Gets up.* AMANDA *remains holding brush, looking at him, troubled.*] She plays old phonograph records and—that's about all—[*He glances at himself in the mirror and crosses to door.*]

AMANDA [*sharply*].   Where are you going?

TOM.   I'm going to the movies. [*Out screen door.*]

AMANDA.   Not to the movies, every night to the movies! [*Follows quickly to screen door.*] I don't believe you always go to the movies! [*He is gone.* AMANDA *looks worriedly after him for a moment. Then vitality and optimism return and she turns from the door. Crossing to portieres.*] Laura! Laura! [LAURA *answers from kitchenette.*]

LAURA.   Yes, Mother.

AMANDA.   Let those dishes go and come in front! [*Laura appears with dish towel. Gaily.*] Laura, come here and make a wish on the moon!

LAURA   [*entering*]. Moon—moon?

AMANDA.   A little silver slipper of a moon. Look over your left shoulder, Laura, and make a wish! [LAURA *looks faintly puzzled as if called out of sleep.* AMANDA *seizes her shoulders and turns her at angle by the door.*] Now! Now, darling, *wish!*

LAURA.   What shall I wish for, Mother?

AMANDA.   [*her voice trembling and her eyes suddenly filling with tears*]. Happiness! Good Fortune!

The violin rises and the stage dims out.

Scene VI

[*Image: High School Hero.*]

TOM.   And so the following evening I brought Jim home to dinner. I had known Jim slightly in high school. In high school Jim was a hero. He had tremendous Irish good nature and vitality with the scrubbed and polished look of white chinaware. He seemed to move in a continual spotlight. He was a star in basketball, captain of the debating club, president of the senior class and the glee club and he sang the male lead in the annual light operas. He was always running or bounding, never just walking. He seemed always at the point of defeating the law of gravity. He was shooting with such velocity through his adolescence that you would logically expect him to arrive at nothing short of the White House by the time he was thirty. But Jim apparently ran into more interference after his graduation from Soldan. His speed had definitely slowed. Six years after he left high school he was holding a job that wasn't much better than mine.

[*Image: Clerk.*]

He was the only one at the warehouse with whom I was on friendly terms. I was valuable to him as someone who could remember his former glory, who had seen him win basketball games and the silver cup in debating. He knew of my secret practice of retiring to a cabinet of the washroom to work on poems when business was slack in the warehouse. He called me Shakespeare. And while the other boys in the warehouse regarded me with suspicious hostility, Jim took a humorous attitude toward me. Gradually his attitude affected the others, their hostility wore off and they also began to smile at me as people smile at an oddly fashioned dog who trots across their path at some distance.

I knew that Jim and Laura had known each other at Soldan, and I had heard Laura speak admiringly of his voice. I didn't know if Jim remembered her or not. In high school Laura had been as unobtrusive as Jim had been astonishing. If he did remember Laura, it was not as my sister, for when I asked him to dinner, he grinned and said, "You know, Shakespeare, I never thought of you as having folks!"

He was about to discover that I did. . . .

[Light up Stage]

[Legend on Screen: "The Accent of a Coming Foot."]

Friday evening. It is about five o'clock of a late spring evening which comes "scattering poems in the sky."

A delicate lemony light is in the Wingfield apartment.

AMANDA *has worked like a Turk in preparation for the gentleman caller. The results are astonishing. The new floor lamp with its rose-silk shade is in place, a colored paper lantern conceals the broken light fixture in the ceiling, new billowing white curtains are at the windows, chintz covers are on chairs and sofa, a pair of new sofa pillows make their initial appearance.*

Open boxes and tissue paper are scattered on the floor.

LAURA *stands in the middle with lifted arms while* AMANDA *crouches before her, adjusting the hem of the new dress, devout and ritualistic. The dress is colored and designed by memory. The arrangement of* LAURA*'s hair is changed; it is softer and more becoming. A fragile, unearthly prettiness has come out in* LAURA: *she is like a piece of translucent glass touched by light, given a momentary radiance, not actual, not lasting.*

AMANDA *[impatiently]*.   Why are you trembling?

LAURA.   Mother, you've made me so nervous!

AMANDA.   How have I made you nervous?

LAURA.   By all this fuss! You make it seem so important!

AMANDA.   I don't understand you, Laura. You couldn't be satisfied with just sitting home, and yet whenever I try to arrange something for you, you seem to resist it. *[She gets up.]* Now take a look at yourself. No, wait! Wait just a moment—I have an idea!

LAURA.   What is it now?

AMANDA *produces two powder puffs which she wraps in handkerchiefs and stuffs in* LAURA*'s bosom.*

LAURA.   Mother, what are you doing?

AMANDA.   They call them "Gay Deceivers"!

LAURA.   I won't wear them!

AMANDA.   You will!

LAURA.   Why should I?

AMANDA.   Because, to be painfully honest, your chest is flat.

LAURA.   You make it seem like we were setting a trap.

AMANDA.   All pretty girls are a trap, a pretty trap, and men expect them to be. *[Legend: "A Pretty Trap."]* Now look at yourself, young lady. This is the prettiest you will ever be! I've got to fix myself now! You're going to be surprised by your mother's appearance! *[She crosses through portieres, humming gaily.]*

LAURA *moves slowly to the long mirror and stares solemnly at herself.*

A wind blows the white curtains inward in a slow, graceful motion and with a faint sorrowful sighing.

AMANDA [*off stage*].   It isn't dark enough yet. [*She turns slowly before the mirror with a troubled look.*]

   [*Legend on Screen: "This Is My Sister: Celebrate Her with Strings!" Music.*]

AMANDA [*laughing, off*].   I'm going to show you something. I'm going to make a spectacular appearance!

LAURA.   What is it, Mother?

AMANDA.   Possess your soul in patience—you will see! Something I've resurrected from that old trunk! Styles haven't changed so terribly much after all. . . . [*She parts the portieres.*] Now just look at your mother! [*She wears a girlish frock of yellowed voile with a blue silk sash. She carries a bunch of jonquils—the legend of her youth is nearly revived. Feverishly.*] This is the dress in which I led the cotillion. Won the cakewalk twice at Sunset Hill, wore one spring to the Governor's ball in Jackson! See how I sashayed around the ballroom, Laura? [*She raises her skirt and does a mincing step around the room.*] I wore it on Sundays for my gentlemen callers! I had it on the day I met your fa- ther—I had malaria fever all that spring. The change of climate from East Tennessee to the Delta—weakened resistance—I had a little temperature all the time—not enough to be serious—just enough to make me restless and giddy! Invitations poured in—parties all over the Delta!—"Stay in bed," said Mother, "you have fever!"—but I just wouldn't.—I took quinine but kept on going, going!—Evenings, dances!—Afternoons, long, long rides! Picnics— lovely!—So lovely, that country in May.—All lacy with dogwood, literally flooded with jonquils!—That was the spring I had the craze for jonquils. Jonquils became an absolute obsession. Mother said, "Honey, there's no more room for jonquils." And still I kept bringing in more jonquils. Whenever, wherever I saw them, I'd say, "Stop! Stop! I see jonquils!" I made the young men help me gather the jonquils! It was a joke, Amanda and her jonquils! Finally there were no more vases to hold them, every available space was filled with jonquils. No vases to hold them? All right, I'll hold them myself! And then I—[*She stops in front of the picture.*] [*Music.*] met your father! Malaria fever and jonquils and then—this—boy. . . . [*She switches on the rose-colored lamp.*] I hope they get here before it starts to rain. [*She crosses upstage and places the jonquils in bowl on table.*] I gave your brother a little extra change so he and Mr. O'Connor could take the service car home.

LAURA [*with altered look*].   What did you say his name was?

AMANDA.   O'Connor.

LAURA.   What is his first name?

AMANDA.   I don't remember. Oh, yes, I do. It was—Jim!

   LAURA *sways slightly and catches hold of a chair.*
   [*Legend on Screen: "Not Jim!"*]

LAURA [*faintly*].   Not—Jim!

AMANDA.   Yes, that was it, it was Jim! I've never known a Jim that wasn't nice!

   [*Music: Ominous.*]

LAURA.   Are you sure his name is Jim O'Connor?

AMANDA.   Yes. Why?

LAURA.   Is he the one that Tom used to know in high school?

AMANDA.   He didn't say so. I think he just got to know him at the warehouse.

LAURA.   There was a Jim O'Connor we both knew in high school—[*Then, with effort.*] If that is the one that Tom is bringing to dinner—you'll have to excuse me, I won't come to the table.

AMANDA.   What sort of nonsense is this?

LAURA.   You asked me once if I'd ever liked a boy. Don't you remember I showed you this boy's picture?

AMANDA.   You mean the boy you showed me in the year-book?

LAURA.   Yes, that boy.

AMANDA.   Laura, Laura, were you in love with that boy?

LAURA.   I don't know, Mother. All I know is I couldn't sit at the table if it was him!

AMANDA.   It won't be him! It isn't the least bit likely. But whether it is or not, you will come to the table. You will not be excused.

LAURA.   I'll have to be, Mother.

AMANDA.   I don't intend to humor your silliness, Laura. I've had too much from you and your brother, both! So just sit down and compose yourself till they come. Tom has forgotten his key so you'll have to let them in, when they arrive.

LAURA [*panicky*].   Oh, Mother—*you* answer the door!

AMANDA   [*lightly*].   I'll be in the kitchen—busy!

LAURA.   Oh, Mother, please answer the door, don't make me do it!

AMANDA [*crossing into kitchenette*].   I've got to fix the dressing for the salmon. Fuss, fuss—silliness!—over a gentleman caller!

Door swings shut. LAURA *is left alone.*

[*Legend: "Terror!"*]

She utters a low moan and turns off the lamp—sits stiffly on the edge of the sofa, knotting her fingers together.

[*Legend on Screen: "The Opening of a Door!"*]

TOM *and* JIM *appear on the fire-escape steps and climb to landing. Hearing their approach,* LAURA *rises with a panicky gesture. She retreats to the portieres.*

The doorbell. LAURA *catches her breath and touches her throat. Low drums.*

AMANDA [*calling*].   Laura, sweetheart! The door!

LAURA *stares at it without moving.*

JIM.   I think we just beat the rain.

TOM.   Uh-huh. [*He rings again, nervously.* JIM *whistles and fishes for a cigarette.*]

AMANDA [*very, very gaily*].   Laura, that is your brother and Mr. O'Connor! Will you let them in, darling?

LAURA *crosses toward kitchenette door.*

LAURA [*breathlessly*].   Mother—you go to the door!

AMANDA *steps out of kitchenette and stares furiously at* LAURA. *She points imperiously at the door.*

LAURA.   Please, please!

AMANDA [*in a fierce whisper*].   What is the matter with you, you silly thing?

LAURA [*desperately*].   Please, you answer it, *please!*

AMANDA.   I told you I wasn't going to humor you, Laura. Why have you chosen this moment to lose your mind?

LAURA.   Please, please, please, you go!

AMANDA.   You'll have to go to the door because I can't!

LAURA [*despairingly*].   I can't either!

AMANDA.   Why?

LAURA.   I'm *sick!*

AMANDA.   I'm sick, too—of your nonsense! Why can't you and your brother be normal people? Fantastic whims and behavior! [TOM *gives a long ring.*] Preposterous
goings on! Can you give me one reason—[*Calls out lyrically.*] COMING! JUST ONE
SECOND!—why should you be afraid to open a door? Now you answer it, Laura!

LAURA.   Oh, oh, oh . . . [*She returns through the portieres. Darts to the victrola
and winds it frantically and turns it on.*]

AMANDA.   Laura Wingfield, you march right to that door!

LAURA.   Yes—yes, Mother!

A *faraway, scratchy rendition of "Dardanella" softens the air and gives her
strength to move through it. She slips to the door and draws it cautiously open.*

TOM *enters with caller,* JIM O'CONNOR.

TOM.   Laura, this is Jim. Jim, this is my sister, Laura.

JIM [*stepping inside*].   I didn't know that Shakespeare had a sister!

LAURA [*retreating stiff and trembling from the door*].   How—how do you do?

JIM [*heartily extending his hand*].   Okay!

LAURA *touches it hesitantly with hers.*

JIM.   Your hand's *cold,* Laura!

LAURA.   Yes, well—I've been playing the victrola. . . .

JIM.   Must have been playing classical music on it! You ought to play a little hot
swing music to warm you up!

LAURA.   Excuse me—I haven't finished playing the victrola. . . .

She *turns awkwardly and hurries into the front room. She pauses a second
by the victrola. Then catches her breath and darts through the portieres like a
frightened deer.*

JIM [*grinning*].   What was the matter?

TOM.   Oh—with Laura? Laura is—terribly shy.

JIM.   Shy, huh? It's unusual to meet a shy girl nowadays. I don't believe you ever
mentioned you had a sister.

TOM.   Well, now you know. I have one. Here is the *Post Dispatch.* You want a
piece of it?

JIM.   Uh-huh.

TOM.   What piece? The comics?

JIM.   Sports! [*Glances at it*]. Ole Dizzy Dean is on his bad behavior.

TOM [*disinterest*].   Yeah? [*Lights cigarette and crosses back to fire-escape door.*]

JIM.   Where are *you* going?

TOM.   I'm going out on the terrace.

JIM [*goes after him*].   You know, Shakespeare—I'm going to sell you a bill of goods!

TOM.   What goods?

JIM.   A course I'm taking.

TOM.   Huh?

JIM.   In public speaking! You and me, we're not the warehouse type.

TOM.   Thanks—that's good news. But what has public speaking got to do with it?

JIM.   It fits you for—executive positions!

TOM.   Awww.

JIM.   I tell you it's done a helluva lot for me.

[*Image: Executive at Desk.*]

TOM.   In what respect?

JIM.   In every! Ask yourself what is the difference between you an' me and men
in the office down front? Brains?—No!—Ability?—No! Then what? Just one little thing—

TOM.   What is that one little thing?

JIM.   Primarily it amounts to—social poise! Being able to square up to people and hold your own on any social level!

AMANDA [*off stage*].   Tom?

TOM.   Yes, Mother?

AMANDA.   Is that you and Mr. O'Connor?

TOM.   Yes, Mother.

AMANDA.   Well, you just make yourselves comfortable in there.

TOM.   Yes, Mother.

AMANDA.   Ask Mr. O'Connor if he would like to wash his hands.

JIM.   Aw—no—no—thank you—I took care of that at the warehouse. Tom—

TOM.   Yes?

JIM.   Mr. Mendoza was speaking to me about you.

TOM.   Favorably?

JIM.   What do you think?

TOM.   Well—

JIM.   You're going to be out of a job if you don't wake up.

TOM.   I am waking up—

JIM.   You show no signs.

TOM.   The signs are interior.

[*Image on Screen: The Sailing Vessel with Jolly Roger Again.*]

TOM.   I'm planning to change. [*He leans over the rail speaking with quiet exhilaration. The incandescent marquees and signs of the first-run movie houses light his face from across the alley. He looks like a voyager.*] I'm right at the point of committing myself to a future that doesn't include the warehouse and Mr. Mendoza or even a night-school course in public speaking.

JIM.   What are you gassing about?

TOM.   I'm tired of the movies.

JIM.   Movies!

TOM.   Yes, movies! Look at them—[*a wave toward the marvels of Grand Avenue.*] All of those glamorous people—having adventures—hogging it all, gobbling the whole thing up! You know what happens? People go to the *movies* instead of *moving!* Hollywood characters are supposed to have all the adventures for everybody in America, while everybody in America sits in a dark room and watches them have them! Yes, until there's a war. That's when adventure becomes available to the masses! *Everyone's* dish, not only Gable's! Then the people in the dark room come out of the dark room to have some adventures themselves—Goody, goody—It's our turn now, to go to the South Sea Island—to make a safari—to be exotic, far-off—But I'm not patient. I don't want to wait till then. I'm tired of the *movies* and I am *about* to *move!*

JIM [*incredulously*].   Move?

TOM.   Yes.

JIM.   When?

TOM.   Soon!

JIM.   Where? Where?

[*Theme three music seems to answer the question, while* TOM *thinks it over. He searches among his pockets.*]

TOM.   I'm starting to boil inside. I know I seem dreamy, but inside—well, I'm boiling! Whenever I pick up a shoe, I shudder a little thinking how short life is and what I am doing!—Whatever that means. I know it doesn't mean shoes—except as something to wear on a traveler's feet [*Finds paper.*] Look—

JIM.   What?

TOM.   I'm a member.

JIM [*reading*].   The Union of Merchant Seamen.

TOM.   I paid my dues this month, instead of the light bill.

JIM.   You will regret it when they turn the lights off.

TOM.   I won't be here.

JIM.   How about your mother?

TOM.   I'm like my father. The bastard son of a bastard! See how he grins? And he's been absent going on sixteen years!

JIM.   You're just talking, you drip. How does your mother feel about it?

TOM.   Shhh—Here comes Mother! Mother is not acquainted with my plans!

AMANDA [*enters portieres*].   Where are you all?

TOM.   On the terrace, Mother.

They start inside. She advances to them. TOM *is distinctly shocked at her appearance. Even* JIM *blinks a little. He is making his first contact with girlish Southern vivacity and in spite of the night-school course in public speaking is somewhat thrown off the beam by the unexpected outlay of social charm.*

Certain responses are attempted by JIM *but are swept aside by* AMANDA's *gay laughter and chatter.* TOM *is embarrassed but after the first shock* JIM *reacts very warmly. Grins and chuckles, is altogether won over.*

[*Image:* AMANDA *as a Girl.*]

AMANDA [*coyly smiling, shaking her girlish ringlets*].   Well, well, well, so this is Mr. O'Connor. Introductions entirely unnecessary. I've heard so much about you from my boy. I finally said to him, Tom—good gracious!—why don't you bring this paragon to supper? I'd like to meet this nice young man at the warehouse!—Instead of just hearing him sing your praises so much! I don't know why my son is so standoffish—that's not Southern behavior! Let's sit down and—I think we could stand a little more air in here! Tom, leave the door open. I felt a nice fresh breeze a moment ago. Where has it gone? Mmm, so warm already! And not quite summer, even. We're going to burn up when summer really gets started. However, we're having—we're having a very light supper. I think light things are better fo' this time of year. The same as light clothes are. Light clothes an' light food are what warm weather calls fo'. You know our blood gets so thick during th' winter—it takes a while fo' us to *adjust* ou'selves!—when the season changes. . . . It's come so quick this year, I wasn't prepared. All of a sudden—heavens! Already summer!—I ran to the trunk an' pulled out this light dress—Terribly old! Historical almost! But feels so good—so good an' co-ol, y'know. . . .

TOM.   Mother—

AMANDA.   Yes, honey?

TOM.   How about—supper?

AMANDA.   Honey, you go ask Sister if supper is ready! You know that Sister is in full charge of supper! Tell her you hungry boys are waiting for it. [*To* JIM.] Have you met Laura?

JIM.   She—

AMANDA.   Let you in? Oh, good, you've met already! It's rare for a girl as sweet an' pretty as Laura to be domestic! But Laura is, thank heavens, not only pretty but also very domestic. I'm not at all. I never was a bit. I never could make a thing but angel-food cake. Well, in the South we had so many servants. Gone, gone, gone. All vestiges of gracious living! Gone completely! I wasn't prepared for what the future brought me. All of my gentlemen callers were sons of planters and so of course I assumed that I would be married to one and raise my family on a large piece of land with plenty of servants. But man proposes—and woman accepts the proposal!—To vary that old, old saying a little bit—I married no planter! I married a man who worked for the telephone company!—that gallantly smiling gentleman over there! [*Points to the picture.*] A telephone man who—fell in love with long distance!—Now he travels and I don't even know where!—But what am I going on for about my—tribulations! Tell me yours—I hope you don't have any! Tom?

TOM [*returning*].   Yes, Mother?

AMANDA.   Is supper nearly ready?

TOM.   It looks to me like supper is on the table.

AMANDA.   Let me look—[*She rises prettily and looks through portieres.*] Oh, lovely—But where is Sister?

TOM.   Laura is not feeling well and she says that she thinks she'd better not come to the table.

AMANDA.   What?—Nonsense!—Laura? Oh, Laura!

LAURA [*off stage, faintly*].   Yes, Mother.

AMANDA.   You really must come to the table. We won't be seated until you come to the table! Come in, Mr. O'Connor. You sit over there and I'll—Laura? Laura Wingfield! You're keeping us waiting, honey! We can't say grace until you come to the table!

The back door is pushed weakly open and LAURA *comes in. She is obviously quite faint, her lips trembling, her eyes wide and staring. She moves unsteadily toward the table.*

[*Legend: "Terror!"*]

Outside a summer storm is coming abruptly. The white curtains billow inward at the windows and there is a sorrowful murmur and deep blue dusk.

LAURA *suddenly stumbles—She catches a chair with a faint moan.*

TOM.   Laura!

AMANDA.   Laura! [*There is a clap of thunder.*] [*Legend: "Ah!"*] [*Despairingly.*] Why, Laura, you *are* sick, darling! Tom, help your sister into the living room, dear! Sit in the living room, Laura—rest on the sofa. Well! [*To the gentleman caller.*] Standing over the hot stove made her ill!—I told her that it was just too warm this evening, but—[TOM *comes back in.* LAURA *is on the sofa.*] Is Laura all right now?

TOM.   Yes.

AMANDA.   What is that? Rain? A nice cool rain has come up! [*She gives the gentleman caller a frightened look.*] I think we may—have grace—now . . . [TOM *looks at her stupidly.*] Tom, honey—you say grace!

TOM.   Oh . . . "For these and all thy mercies—" [*They bow their heads.* AMANDA *stealing a nervous glance at* JIM. *In the living room* LAURA, *stretched on the sofa, clenches her hand to her lips, to hold back a shuddering sob.*] God's Holy Name be praised—

[*The Scene Dims Out.*]

Scene VII

A Souvenir

Half an hour later. Dinner is just being finished in the upstage area which is concealed by the drawn portieres.

As the curtain rises LAURA *is still huddled upon the sofa, her feet drawn under her, her head resting on a pale blue pillow, her eyes wide and mysteriously watchful. The new floor lamp with its shade of rose-colored silk gives a soft, becoming light to her face, bringing out the fragile, unearthly prettiness which usually escapes attention. There is a steady murmur of rain, but it is slackening and stops soon after the scene begins; the air outside becomes pale and luminous as the moon breaks out.*

    A moment after the curtain rises, the lights in both rooms flicker and go out.

JIM.   Hey, there, Mr. Light Bulb!

    AMANDA *laughs nervously.*

    [Legend: "Suspension of a Public Service."]

AMANDA.   Where was Moses when the lights went out? Ha-ha. Do you know the answer to that one, Mr. O'Connor?

JIM.   No, ma'am, what's the answer?

AMANDA.   In the dark! [JIM *laughs appreciatively.*] Everybody sit still. I'll light the candles. Isn't it lucky we have them on the table? Where's a match? Which of you gentlemen can provide a match?

JIM.   Here.

AMANDA.   Thank you, sir.

JIM.   Not at all, Ma'am!

AMANDA.   I guess the fuse has burnt out. Mr. O'Connor, can you tell a burnt-out fuse? I know I can't and Tom is a total loss when it comes to mechanics. [*Sound: Getting Up: Voices Recede a Little to Kitchenette.*] Oh, be careful you don't bump into something. We don't want our gentleman caller to break his neck. Now wouldn't that be a fine howdy-do?

JIM.   Ha-ha! Where is the fuse-box?

AMANDA.   Right here next to the stove. Can you see anything?

JIM.   Just a minute.

AMANDA.   Isn't electricity a mysterious thing? Wasn't it Benjamin Franklin who tied a key to a kite? We live in such a mysterious universe, don't we? Some people say that science clears up all the mysteries for us. In my opinion it only creates more! Have you found it yet?

JIM.   No, Ma'am. All these fuses look okay to me.

AMANDA.   Tom!

TOM.   Yes, Mother?

AMANDA.   That light bill I gave you several days ago. The one I told you we got the notices about?

TOM.   Oh.—Yeah.

    [Legend: "Ha!"]

AMANDA.   You didn't neglect to pay it by any chance?

TOM.   Why, I—

AMANDA.   Didn't! I might have known it!

JIM.   Shakespeare probably wrote a poem on that light bill, Mrs. Wingfield.

AMANDA.   I might have known better than to trust him with it! There's such a high price for negligence in this world!

JIM.   Maybe the poem will win a ten-dollar prize.

AMANDA.   We'll just have to spend the remainder of the evening in the nineteenth century, before Mr. Edison made the Mazda lamp!

JIM.   Candlelight is my favorite kind of light.

AMANDA.   That shows you're romantic! But that's no excuse for Tom. Well, we got through dinner. Very considerate of them to let us get through dinner before they plunged us into everlasting darkness, wasn't it, Mr. O'Connor?

JIM.   Ha-ha!

AMANDA.   Tom, as a penalty for your carelessness you can help me with the dishes.

JIM.   Let me give you a hand.

AMANDA.   Indeed you will not!

JIM.   I ought to be good for something.

AMANDA.   Good for something? [*Her tone is rhapsodic.*] *You?* Why, Mr. O'Connor, nobody, *nobody's* given me this much entertainment in years—as you have!

JIM.   Aw, now, Mrs. Wingfield!

AMANDA.   I'm not exaggerating, not one bit! But Sister is all by her lonesome. You go keep her company in the parlor! I'll give you this lovely old candelabrum that used to be on the altar at the Church of the Heavenly Rest. It was melted a little out of shape when the church burnt down. Lightning struck it one spring. Gypsy Jones was holding a revival at the time and he intimated that the church was destroyed because the Episcopalians gave card parties.

JIM.   Ha-ha.

AMANDA.   And how about coaxing Sister to drink a little wine? I think it would be good for her! Can you carry both at once?

JIM.   Sure. I'm Superman!

AMANDA.   Now, Thomas, get into this apron!

> The door of kitchenette swings closed on AMANDA's gay laughter; the flickering light approaches the portieres.
>
> LAURA *sits up nervously as he enters. Her speech at first is low and breathless from the almost intolerable strain of being alone with a stranger.*
>
> [*Legend: "I Don't Suppose You Remember Me at All!"*]
>
> *In her first speeches in this scene, before* JIM's *warmth overcomes her paralyzing shyness,* LAURA's *voice is thin and breathless as though she has run up a steep flight of stairs.*
>
> JIM's *attitude is gently humorous. In playing this scene it should be stressed that while the incident is apparently unimportant, it is to* LAURA *the climax of her secret life.*

JIM.   Hello, there, Laura.

LAURA [*faintly*]. Hello.   [*She clears her throat.*]

JIM.   How are you feeling now? Better?

LAURA.   Yes. Yes, thank you.

JIM.   This is for you. A little dandelion wine. [*He extends it toward her with extravagant gallantry.*]

LAURA.   Thank you.

JIM.   Drink it—but don't get drunk! [*He laughs heartily.* LAURA *takes the glass uncertainly; laughs shyly.*] Where shall I set the candles?

LAURA.   Oh—oh, anywhere . . .

JIM.   How about here on the floor? Any objections?

LAURA.   No.

JIM.   I'll spread a newspaper under to catch the drippings. I like to sit on the floor. Mind if I do?

LAURA.   Oh, no.

JIM.   Give me a pillow?

LAURA.   What?

JIM.   A pillow!

LAURA.   Oh . . . [*Hands him one quickly.*]

JIM.   How about you? Don't you like to sit on the floor?

LAURA.   Oh—yes.

JIM.   Why don't you, then?

LAURA.   I—will.

JIM.   Take a pillow! [LAURA *does. Sits on the other side of the candelabrum.* JIM *crosses his legs and smiles engagingly at her.*] I can't hardly see you sitting way over there.

LAURA.   I can—see you.

JIM.   I know, but that's not fair, I'm in the limelight. [LAURA *moves her pillow closer.*] Good! Now I can see you! Comfortable?

LAURA.   Yes.

JIM.   So am I. Comfortable as a cow. Will you have some gum?

LAURA.   No, thank you.

JIM.   I think that I will indulge, with your permission [*Musingly unwraps it and holds it up.*] Think of the fortune made by the guy that invented the first piece of chewing gum. Amazing, huh? The Wrigley Building is one of the sights of Chicago.—I saw it summer before last when I went up to the Century of Progress. Did you take in the Century of Progress?

LAURA.   No, I didn't.

JIM.   Well, it was quite a wonderful exposition. What impressed me most was the Hall of Science. Gives you an idea of what the future will be in America, even more wonderful than the present time is! [*Pause. Smiling at her.*] Your brother tells me you're shy. Is that right, Laura?

LAURA.   I—don't know.

JIM.   I judge you to be an old-fashioned type of girl. Well, I think that's a pretty good type to be. Hope you don't think I'm being too personal—do you?

LAURA [*hastily, out of embarrassment*].   I believe I *will* take a piece of gum, if you—don't mind. [*Clearing her throat.*] Mr. O'Connor, have you—kept up with your singing?

JIM.   Singing? Me?

LAURA.   Yes. I remember what a beautiful voice you had.

JIM.   When did you hear me sing?

[*Voice Offstage in the Pause*]
Voice [*offstage*].

> O blow, ye winds, heigh-ho.
> A-roving I will go!
> I'm off to my love
> With a boxing glove—
> Ten thousand miles away!

JIM.   You say you've heard me sing?

LAURA.   Oh, yes! Yes, very often . . . I—don't suppose you remember me—at all?

JIM [*smiling doubtfully*].   You know I have an idea I've seen you before. I had that idea soon as you opened the door. It seemed almost like I was about to remember your name. But the name that I started to call you—wasn't a name! And so I stopped myself before I said it.

LAURA.   Wasn't it—Blue Roses?

JIM [*springs up, grinning*].   Blue Roses! My gosh, yes—Blue Roses! That's what I had on my tongue when you opened the door! Isn't it funny what tricks your memory plays? I didn't connect you with the high school somehow or other. But that's where it was; it was high school. I didn't even know you were Shakespeare's sister! Gosh, I'm sorry.

LAURA.   I didn't expect you to. You—barely knew me!

JIM.   But we did have a speaking acquaintance, huh?

LAURA.   Yes, we—spoke to each other.

JIM.   When did you recognize me?

LAURA.   Oh, right away!

JIM.   Soon as I came in the door?

LAURA.   When I heard your name I thought it was probably you. I knew that Tom used to know you a little in high school. So when you came in the door— Well, then I was—sure.

JIM.   Why didn't you *say* something, then?

LAURA [*breathlessly*].   I didn't know what to say, I was—too surprised!

JIM.   For goodness' sakes! You know, this sure is funny!

LAURA.   Yes! Yes, isn't it, though. . . .

JIM.   Didn't we have a class in something together?

LAURA.   Yes, we did.

JIM.   What class was that?

LAURA.   It was—singing—Chorus!

JIM.   Aw!

LAURA.   I sat across the aisle from you in the Aud.

JIM.   Aw.

LAURA.   Mondays, Wednesdays and Fridays.

JIM.   Now I remember—you always came in late.

LAURA.   Yes, it was so hard for me, getting upstairs. I had a brace on my leg—it clumped so loud!

JIM.   I never heard any clumping.

LAURA [*wincing at the recollection*].   To me it sounded like—thunder!

JIM.   Well, well, well. I never even noticed.

LAURA.   And everybody was seated before I came in. I had to walk in front of all those people. My seat was in the back row. I had to go clumping all the way up the aisle with everyone watching!

JIM.   You shouldn't have been self-conscious.

LAURA.   I know, but I was. It was always such a relief when the singing started.

JIM.   Aw, yes, I've placed you now! I used to call you Blue Roses. How was it that I got started calling you that?

LAURA.   I was out of school a little while with pleurosis. When I came back you asked me what was the matter. I said I had pleurosis—you thought I said Blue Roses. That's what you always called me after that!

JIM.   I hope you didn't mind.

LAURA.   Oh, no—I liked it. You see, I wasn't acquainted with many—people. . . .

JIM.   As I remember you sort of stuck by yourself.

LAURA.   I—I—never had much luck at—making friends.

JIM.   I don't see why you wouldn't.

LAURA.   Well, I—started out badly.

JIM.   You mean being—

LAURA.   Yes, it sort of—stood between me—

JIM.   You shouldn't have let it!

LAURA.   I know, but it did, and—

JIM.   You were shy with people!

LAURA.   I tried not to be but never could—

JIM.   Overcome it?

LAURA.   No, I—I never could!

JIM.   I guess being shy is something you have to work out of kind of gradually.

LAURA [*sorrowfully*].   Yes—I guess it—

JIM.   Takes time!

LAURA.   Yes—

JIM.   People are not so dreadful when you know them. That's what you have to remember! And everybody has problems, not just you, but practically everybody has got some problems. You think of yourself as having the only problems, as being the only one who is disappointed. But just look around you and you will see lots of people as disappointed as you are. For instance, I hoped when I was going to high school that I would be further along at this time, six years after, than I am now—You remember that wonderful write-up I had in *The Torch?*

LAURA.   Yes! [*She rises and crosses to table.*]

JIM.   It said I was bound to succeed in anything I went into! [LAURA *returns with the annual.*] Holy Jeez! *The Torch!* [*He accepts it reverently. They smile across it with mutual wonder.* LAURA *crouches beside him and they begin to turn through it.* LAURA*'s shyness is dissolving in his warmth.*]

LAURA.   Here you are in *Pirates of Penzance!*

JIM [*wistfully*].   I sang the baritone lead in that operetta.

LAURA [*rapidly*].   So—*beautifully!*

JIM [*protesting*].   Aw—

LAURA.   Yes, yes—beautifully—beautifully!

JIM.   You heard me?

LAURA.   All three times!

JIM.   No!

LAURA.   Yes!

JIM.   All three performances?

LAURA [*looking down*].   Yes.

JIM.   Why?

LAURA.   I—wanted to ask you to—autograph my program.

JIM.   Why didn't you ask me to?

LAURA.   You were always surrounded by your own friends so much that I never had a chance to.

JIM.   You should have just—

LAURA.   Well, I—thought you might think I was—

JIM.   Thought I might think you was—what?

LAURA.   Oh—

JIM [*with reflective relish*].   I was beleaguered by females in those days.

LAURA.   You were terribly popular!

JIM.   Yeah—

LAURA.   You had such a—friendly way—

JIM.   I was spoiled in high school.

LAURA.   Everybody—liked you!

JIM.   Including you?

LAURA.   I—yes, I—I did, too—[*She gently closes the book in her lap.*]

JIM.   Well, well, well!—Give me that program, Laura. [*She hands it to him. He signs it with a flourish.*] There you are—better late than never!

LAURA.   Oh, I—what a—surprise!

JIM.   My signature isn't worth very much right now. But some day—maybe—it will increase in value! Being disappointed is one thing and being discouraged is something else. I am disappointed but I'm not discouraged. I'm twenty-three years old. How old are you?

LAURA.   I'll be twenty-four in June.

JIM.   That's not old age!

LAURA.   No, but—

JIM.   You finished high school?

LAURA [*with difficulty*].   I didn't go back.

JIM.   You mean you dropped out?

LAURA.   I made bad grades in my final examinations. [*She rises and replaces the book and the program. Her voice strained.*] How is—Emily Meisenbach getting along?

JIM.   Oh, that kraut-head!

LAURA.   Why do you call her that?

JIM.   That's what she was.

LAURA.   You're not still—going with her?

JIM.   I never see her.

LAURA.   It said in the Personal Section that you were—engaged!

JIM.   I know, but I wasn't impressed by that—propaganda!

LAURA.   It wasn't—the truth?

JIM.   Only in Emily's optimistic opinion!

LAURA.   Oh—

[*Legend: "What Have You Done since High School?"*]

JIM *lights a cigarette and leans indolently back on his elbows smiling at* LAURA *with a warmth and charm which light her inwardly with altar candles. She remains by the table and turns in her hands a piece of glass to cover her tumult.*

JIM [*after several reflective puffs on a cigarette*].   What have you done since high school? [*She seems not to hear him.*] Huh? [LAURA *looks up.*] I said what have you done since high school, Laura?

LAURA.   Nothing much.

JIM.   You must have been doing something these six long years.

LAURA.   Yes.

JIM.   Well, then, such as what?

LAURA.   I took a business course at business college—

JIM.   How did that work out?

LAURA.   Well, not very—well—I had to drop out, it gave me—indigestion—

JIM *laughs gently.*

JIM.   What are you doing now?

LAURA.   I don't do anything—much. Oh, please don't think I sit around doing nothing! My glass collection takes up a good deal of my time. Glass is something you have to take good care of.

JIM.   What did you say—about glass?

LAURA.   Collection I said—I have one—[*She clears her throat and turns away again, acutely shy.*]

JIM [*abruptly*].   You know what I judge to be the trouble with you? Inferiority complex! Know what that is? That's what they call it when someone low-rates himself! I understand it because I had it, too. Although my case was not so aggravated as yours seems to be. I had it until I took up public speaking, developed my voice, and learned that I had an aptitude for science. Before that time I never thought of myself as being outstanding in any way whatsoever! Now I've never made a regular study of it, but I have a friend who says I can analyze people better than doctors that make a profession of it. I don't claim that to be necessarily true, but I can sure guess a person's psychology, Laura! [*Takes out his gum.*] Excuse me, Laura. I always take it out when the flavor is gone. I'll use this scrap of paper to wrap it in. I know how it is to get it stuck on a shoe. Yep—that's what I judge to be your principal trouble. A lack of confidence in yourself as a person. You don't have the proper amount of faith in yourself. I'm basing that fact on a number of your remarks and also on certain observations I've made. For instance that clumping you thought was so awful in high school. You say that you even dreaded to walk into class. You see what you did? You dropped out of school, you gave up an education because of a clump, which as far as I know was practically nonexistent! A little physical defect is what you have. Hardly noticeable even! Magnified thousands of times by imagination! You know what my strong advice to you is? Think of yourself as *superior* in some way!

LAURA.   In what way would I think?

JIM.   Why, man alive, Laura! Just look about you a little. What do you see? A world full of common people! All of 'em born and all of 'em going to die! Which of them has one-tenth of your good points! Or mine! Or anyone else's, as far as that goes—Gosh! Everybody excels in some one thing. Some in many! [*Unconsciously glances at himself in the mirror.*] All you've got to do is discover in *what!* Take me, for instance. [*He adjusts his tie at the mirror.*] My interest happens to be in electrodynamics. I'm taking a course in radio engineering at night school, Laura, on top of a fairly responsible job at the warehouse. I'm taking that course and studying public speaking.

LAURA.   Ohhhh.

JIM.   Because I believe in the future of television! [*Turning back to her.*] I wish to be ready to go up right along with it. Therefore I'm planning to get in on the ground floor. In fact, I've already made the right connections and all that remains is for the industry itself to get under way! Full steam—[*His eyes are starry.*] *Knowledge*—Zzzzzp! *Money*—Zzzzzzp!—*Power!* That's the cycle democracy is built on! [*His attitude is convincingly dynamic.* LAURA *stares at him, even her shyness eclipsed in her absolute wonder. He suddenly grins.*] I guess you think I think a lot of myself!

LAURA.   No—o-o-o, I—

JIM.   Now how about you? Isn't there something you take more interest in than anything else?

LAURA.   Well, I do—as I said—have my—glass collection—

A peal of girlish laughter from the kitchen.

JIM.   I'm not right sure I know what you're talking about. What kind of glass is it?

LAURA.   Little articles of it, they're ornaments mostly! Most of them are little animals made out of glass, the tiniest little animals in the world. Mother calls them a glass menagerie! Here's an example of one, if you'd like to see it! This one is one of the oldest. It's nearly thirteen. [*He stretches out his hand.*] [*Music: "The Glass Menagerie."*] Oh, be careful—if you breathe, it breaks!

JIM.   I'd better not take it. I'm pretty clumsy with things.

LAURA.   Go on, I trust you with him! [*Places it in his palm.*] There now—you're holding him gently! Hold him over the light, he loves the light! You see how the light shines through him?

JIM.   It sure does shine!

LAURA.   I shouldn't be partial, but he is my favorite one.

JIM.   What kind of a thing is this one supposed to be?

LAURA.   Haven't you noticed the single horn on his forehead?

JIM.   A unicorn, huh?

LAURA.   Mmm-hmmm!

JIM.   Unicorns, aren't they extinct in the modern world?

LAURA.   I know!

JIM.   Poor little fellow, he must feel sort of lonesome.

LAURA [*smiling*].   Well, if he does he doesn't complain about it. He stays on a shelf with some horses that don't have horns and all of them seem to get along nicely together.

JIM.   How do you know?

LAURA [*lightly*].   I haven't heard any arguments among them!

JIM [*grinning*].   No arguments, huh? Well, that's a pretty good sign! Where shall I set him?

LAURA.   Put him on the table. They all like a change of scenery once in a while!

JIM [*stretching*].   Well, well, well, well—Look how big my shadow is when I stretch!

LAURA.   Oh, oh, yes—it stretches across the ceiling!

JIM [*crossing to door*].   I think it's stopped raining. [*Opens fire-escape door.*] Where does the music come from?

LAURA.   From the Paradise Dance Hall across the alley.

JIM.   How about cutting the rug a little, Miss Wingfield?

LAURA.   Oh, I—

JIM.   Or is your program filled up? Let me have a look at it. [*Grasps imaginary card.*] Why, every dance is taken! I'll just have to scratch some out. [*Waltz Music: "La Golondrina."*] Ahhh, a waltz! [*He executes some sweeping turns by himself then holds his arms toward* LAURA.]

LAURA [*breathlessly*].   I—can't dance!

JIM.   There you go, that inferiority stuff!

LAURA.   I've never danced in my life!

JIM.   Come on, try!

LAURA.   Oh, but I'd step on you!

JIM.   I'm not made out of glass.

LAURA.   How—how—how do we start?

JIM.   Just leave it to me. You hold your arms out a little.

LAURA.   Like this?

JIM.   A little bit higher. Right. Now don't tighten up, that's the main thing about it—relax.

LAURA [*laughing breathlessly*].   It's hard not to.

JIM.   Okay.

LAURA.   I'm afraid you can't budge me.

JIM.   What do you bet I can't? [*He swings her into motion.*]

LAURA.   Goodness, yes, you can!

JIM.   Let yourself go, now, Laura, just let yourself go.

LAURA.   I'm—

JIM.   Come on!

LAURA.   Trying!

JIM.   Not so stiff—Easy does it!

LAURA.   I know but I'm—

JIM.   Loosen th' backbone! There now, that's a lot better.

LAURA.   Am I?

JIM.   Lots, lots better! [*He moves her about the room in a clumsy waltz.*]

LAURA.   Oh, my!

JIM.   Ha-ha!

LAURA.   Goodness, yes you can!

JIM.   Ha-ha-ha! [*They suddenly bump into the table.* JIM *stops.*] What did we hit on?

LAURA. Table.

JIM. Did something fall off it? I think—

LAURA. Yes.

JIM. I hope that it wasn't the little glass horse with the horn!

LAURA. Yes.

JIM. Aw, aw, aw. Is it broken?

LAURA. Now it is just like all the other horses.

JIM. It's lost its—

LAURA. Horn! It doesn't matter. Maybe it's a blessing in disguise.

JIM. You'll never forgive me. I bet that that was your favorite piece of glass.

LAURA. I don't have favorites much. It's no tragedy, Freckles. Glass breaks so easily. No matter how careful you are. The traffic jars the shelves and things fall
off them.

JIM. Still I'm awfully sorry that I was the cause.

LAURA [*smiling*]. I'll just imagine he had an operation. The horn was removed to
make him feel less—freakish! [*They both laugh.*] Now he will feel more at
home with the other horses, the ones that don't have horns . . . .

JIM. Ha-ha, that's very funny! [*Suddenly serious.*] I'm glad to see that you have a
sense of humor. You know—you're—well—very different! Surprisingly different from anyone else I know! [*His voice becomes soft and hesitant with a genuine feeling.*] Do you mind me telling you that? [LAURA *is abashed beyond
speech.*] You make me feel sort of—I don't know how to put it! I'm usually
pretty good at expressing things, but—This is something that I don't know
how to say! LAURA *touches her throat and clears it—turns the broken unicorn
in her hands.*] [*Even softer*] Has anyone ever told you that you were pretty?
[*Pause: Music.*] [LAURA *looks up slowly, with wonder, and shakes her head.*]
Well, you are! In a very different way from anyone else. And all the nicer because of the difference, too. [*His voice becomes low and husky.* LAURA *turns
away, nearly faint with the novelty of her emotions.*] I wish that you were my
sister. I'd teach you to have some confidence in yourself. The different people
are not like other people, but being different is nothing to be ashamed of.
Because other people are not such wonderful people. They're one hundred
times one thousand. You're one times one! They walk all over the earth. You
just stay here. They're common as—weeds, but—you—well, you're *Blue
Roses!*

[*Image on Screen: Blue Roses.*]
[*Music Changes.*]

LAURA. But blue is wrong for—roses . . .

JIM. It's right for you—You're—pretty!

LAURA. In what respect am I pretty?

JIM. In all respects—believe me! Your eyes—your hair—are pretty! Your hands
are pretty! [*He catches hold of her hand.*] You think I'm making this up because I'm invited to dinner and have to be nice. Oh, I could do that! I could
put on an act for you, Laura, and say lots of things without being very sincere. But this time I am. I'm talking to you sincerely. I happened to notice
you had this inferiority complex that keeps you from feeling comfortable with
people. Somebody needs to build your confidence up and make you proud
instead of shy and turning away and—blushing—Somebody ought to—ought
to—*kiss* you. Laura! [*His hand slips slowly up her arm to her shoulder.*] [*Music
Swells Tumultuously.*] [*He suddenly turns her about and kisses her on the lips.*

When he releases her LAURA *sinks on the sofa with a bright, dazed look.* JIM *backs away and fishes in his pocket for a cigarette.*] [*Legend on Screen: "Souvenir."*] Stumble-john! [*He lights the cigarette, avoiding her look. There is a peal of girlish laughter from* AMANDA *in the kitchen.* LAURA *slowly raises and opens her hand. It still contains the little broken glass animal. She looks at it with a tender, bewildered expression.*] Stumble-john! I shouldn't have done that—That was way off the beam. You don't smoke, do you? [*She looks up, smiling, not hearing the question. He sits beside her a little gingerly. She looks at him speechlessly—waiting. He coughs decorously and moves a little farther aside as he considers the situation and senses her feelings, dimly, with perturbation. Gently.*] Would you—care for a—mint? [*She doesn't seem to hear him but her look grows brighter even.*] Peppermint—Life Saver? My pocket's a regular drug store—wherever I go . . . [*He pops a mint in his mouth. Then gulps and decides to make a clean breast of it. He speaks slowly and gingerly.*] Laura, you know, if I had a sister like you, I'd do the same thing as Tom. I'd bring out fellows—introduce her to them. The right type of boys of a type to—appreciate her. Only—well—he made a mistake about me. Maybe I've got no call to be saying this. That may not have been the idea in having me over. But what if it was? There's nothing wrong about that. The only trouble is that in my case—I'm not in a situation to—do the right thing. I can't take down your number and say I'll phone. I can't call up next week and—ask for a date. I thought I had better explain the situation in case you misunderstood it and—hurt your feelings. . . . [*Pause. Slowly, very slowly,* LAURA*'s look changes, her eyes returning slowly from his to the ornament in her palm.*]

AMANDA *utters another gay laugh in the kitchen.*

LAURA [*faintly*].   You—won't—call again?

JIM.   No, Laura, I can't [*He rises from the sofa.*] As I was just explaining, I've—got strings on me, Laura, I've—been going steady! I go out all the time with a girl named Betty. She's a home-girl like you, and Catholic, and Irish, and in a great many ways we—get along fine. I met her last summer on a moonlight boat trip up the river to Alton, on the *Majestic.* Well—right away from the start it was—love! [*Legend: Love!*] [LAURA *sways slightly forward and grips the arm of the sofa. He fails to notice, now enrapt in his own comfortable being.*] Being in love has made a new man of me! [*Leaning stiffly forward, clutching the arm of the sofa,* LAURA *struggles visibly with her storm. But* JIM *is oblivious, she is a long way off.*] The power of love is really pretty tremendous! Love is something that—changes the whole world, Laura! [*The storm abates a little and* LAURA *leans back. He notices her again.*] It happened that Betty's aunt took sick, she got a wire and had to go to Centralia. So Tom—when he asked me to dinner—I naturally just accepted the invitation, not knowing that you—that he—that I—[*He stops awkwardly.*] Huh—I'm a stumble-john! [*He flops back on the sofa. The holy candles in the altar of* LAURA*'s face have been snuffed out! There is a look of almost infinite desolation.* JIM *glances at her uneasily.*] I wish that you would—say something. [*She bites her lip which was trembling and then bravely smiles. She opens her hand again on the broken glass ornament. Then she gently takes his hand and raises it level with her own. She carefully places the unicorn in the palm of his hand, then pushes his fingers closed upon it.*] What are you—doing that for? You want me to have him?—Laura? [*She nods.*] What for?

LAURA.   A—souvenir . . .

She rises unsteadily and crouches beside the victrola to wind it up.

[*Legend on Screen: "Things Have a Way of Turning Out So Badly."*]
[*Or Image: "Gentleman Caller Waving Good-Bye!—Gaily."*]
    At this moment AMANDA *rushes brightly back in the front room. She bears a pitcher of fruit punch in an old-fashioned cut-glass pitcher and a plate of macaroons. The plate has a gold border and poppies painted on it.*

AMANDA.   Well, well, well! Isn't the air delightful after the shower? I've made you children a little liquid refreshment. [*Turns gaily to the gentleman caller.*] Jim, do you know that song about lemonade?

"Lemonade, lemonade
Made in the shade and stirred with a spade—
Good enough for any old maid!"

JIM [*uneasily*].   Ha-ha! No—I never heard it.
AMANDA.   Why, Laura! You look so serious!
JIM.   We were having a serious conversation.
AMANDA.   Good! Now you're better acquainted!
JIM [*uncertainly*].   Ha-ha! Yes.
AMANDA.   You modern young people are much more serious-minded than my generation. I was so gay as a girl!
JIM.   You haven't changed, Mrs. Wingfield.
AMANDA.   Tonight I'm rejuvenated! The gaiety of the occasion, Mr. O'Connor! [*She tosses her head with a peal of laughter. Spills lemonade.*] Oooo! I'm baptizing myself!
JIM.   Here—let me—
AMANDA [*setting the pitcher down*].   There now. I discovered we had some maraschino cherries. I dumped them in, juice and all!
JIM.   You shouldn't have gone to that trouble, Mrs. Wingfield.
AMANDA.   Trouble, trouble? Why it was loads of fun! Didn't you hear me cutting up in the kitchen? I bet your ears were burning! I told Tom how outdone with him I was for keeping you to himself so long a time! He should have brought you over much, much sooner! Well, now that you've found your way, I want you to be a very frequent caller! Not just occasional but all the time. Oh, we're going to have a lot of gay times together! I see them coming! Mmm, just breathe that air! So fresh, and the moon's so pretty! I'll skip back out—I know where my place is when young folks are having a—serious conversation!
JIM.   Oh, don't go out, Mrs. Wingfield. The fact of the matter is I've got to be going.
AMANDA.   Going, now? You're joking! Why, it's only the shank of the evening, Mr. O'Connor!
JIM.   Well, you know how it is.
AMANDA.   You mean you're a young workingman and have to keep workingmen's hours. We'll let you off early tonight. But only on the condition that next time you stay later. What's the best night for you? Isn't Saturday night the best night for you workingmen?
JIM.   I have a couple of time-clocks to punch, Mrs. Wingfield. One at morning, another one at night!
AMANDA.   My, but you *are* ambitious! You work at night, too?
JIM.   No, Ma'am, not work but—Betty! [*He crosses deliberately to pick up his hat. The band at the Paradise Dance Hall goes into a tender waltz.*]
AMANDA.   Betty? Betty? Who's—Betty! [*There is an ominous cracking sound in the sky.*]

JIM.   Oh, just a girl. The girl I go steady with! [*He smiles charmingly. The sky falls*.]

[*Legend: "The Sky Falls."*]

AMANDA [*a long-drawn exhalation*].   Ohhh . . . Is it a serious romance, Mr. O'Connor?

JIM.   We're going to be married the second Sunday in June.

AMANDA.   Ohhhh—how nice! Tom didn't mention that you were engaged to be married.

JIM.   The cat's not out of the bag at the warehouse yet. You know how they are. They call you Romeo and stuff like that. [*He stops at the oval mirror to put on his hat. He carefully shapes the brim and the crown to give a discreetly dashing effect.*] It's been a wonderful evening, Mrs. Wingfield. I guess this is what they mean by Southern hospitality.

AMANDA.   It really wasn't anything at all.

JIM.   I hope it don't seem like I'm rushing off. But I promised Betty I'd pick her up at the Wabash depot, an' by the time I get my jalopy down there her train'll be in. Some women are pretty upset if you keep 'em waiting.

AMANDA.   Yes, I know—The tyranny of women! [*Extends her hand*.] Good-bye, Mr. O'Connor. I wish you luck—and happiness—and success! All three of them, and so does Laura!—Don't you, Laura?

LAURA.   Yes!

JIM [*taking her hand*].   Goodbye, Laura. I'm certainly going to treasure that souvenir. And don't you forget the good advice I gave you. [*Raises his voice to a cheery shout.*] So long, Shakespeare! Thanks again, ladies—good night!

He grins and ducks jauntily out.
  Still bravely grimacing, AMANDA *closes the door on the gentleman caller.*
Then she turns back to the room with a puzzled expression. She and LAURA *don't dare to face each other.* LAURA *crouches beside the victrola to wind it.*

AMANDA [*faintly*].   Things have a way of turning out so badly. I don't believe that I would play the victrola. Well, well—well—Our gentleman caller was engaged to be married! Tom!

TOM [*from back*].   Yes, Mother?

AMANDA.   Come in here a minute. I want to tell you something awfully funny.

TOM [*enters with macaroon and a glass of the lemonade*].   Has the gentleman caller gotten away already?

AMANDA.   The gentleman caller has made an early departure. What a wonderful joke you played on us!

TOM.   How do you mean?

AMANDA.   You didn't mention that he was engaged to be married.

TOM.   Jim? Engaged?

AMANDA.   That's what he just informed us.

TOM.   I'll be jiggered! I didn't know about that.

AMANDA.   That seems very peculiar.

TOM.   What's peculiar about it?

AMANDA.   Didn't you call him your best friend down at the warehouse?

TOM.   He is, but how did I know?

AMANDA.   It seems extremely peculiar that you wouldn't know your best friend was going to be married!

TOM.   The warehouse is where I work, not where I know things about people!

AMANDA.   You don't know things anywhere! You live in a dream; you manufacture illusions! [*He crosses to door.*] Where are you going?

TOM.   I'm going to the movies.

AMANDA.   That's right, now that you've had us make such fools of ourselves. The effort, the preparations, all the expense! The new floor lamp, the rug, the clothes for Laura! All for what? To entertain some other girl's fiancé! Go to the movies, go! Don't think about us, a mother deserted, an unmarried sister who's crippled and has no job! Don't let anything interfere with your selfish pleasure! Just go, go, go—to the movies!

TOM.   All right, I will! The more you shout about my selfishness to me the quicker I'll go, and I won't go to the movies!

AMANDA.   Go, then! Then go to the moon—you selfish dreamer!

TOM *smashes his glass on the floor. He plunges out on the fire-escape, slamming the door.* LAURA *screams—cut by door.*

Dance-hall music up. TOM *goes to the rail and grips it desperately, lifting his face in the chill white moonlight penetrating the narrow abyss of the alley.*

[*Legend on Screen: "And So Good-Bye . . ."*]

TOM's *closing speech is timed with the interior pantomime. The interior scene is played as though viewed through sound-proof glass.* AMANDA *appears to be making a comforting speech to* LAURA *who is huddled upon the sofa. Now that we cannot hear the mother's speech, her silliness is gone and she has dignity and tragic beauty.* LAURA's *dark hair hides her face until at the end of the speech she lifts it to smile at her mother.* AMANDA's *gestures are slow and graceful, almost dancelike, as she comforts the daughter. At the end of her speech she glances a moment at the father's picture—then withdraws through the portieres. At close of* TOM's *speech,* LAURA *blows out the candles, ending the play.*

TOM.   I didn't go to the moon, I went much further—for time is the longest distance between two places—Not long after that I was fired for writing a poem on the lid of a shoe-box. I left Saint Louis. I descended the steps of this fire-escape for a last time and followed, from then on, in my father's footsteps, attempting to find in motion what was lost in space—I traveled around a great deal. The cities swept about me like dead leaves, leaves that were brightly colored but torn away from the branches. I would have stopped, but I was pursued by something. It always came upon me unawares, taking me altogether by surprise. Perhaps it was a familiar bit of music. Perhaps it was only a piece of transparent glass—Perhaps I am walking along a street at night, in some strange city, before I have found companions. I pass the lighted window of a shop where perfume is sold. The window is filled with pieces of colored glass, tiny transparent bottles in delicate colors, like bits of a shattered rainbow. Then all at once my sister touches my shoulder. I turn around and look into her eyes . . . Oh, Laura, Laura, I tried to leave you behind me, but I am more faithful than I intended to be! I reach for a cigarette, I cross the street, I run into the movies or a bar, I buy a drink, I speak to the nearest stranger—anything that can blow your candles out! [LAURA *bends over the candles.*]—for nowadays the world is lit by lightning! Blow out your candles, Laura—and so good-bye . . .

She blows the candles out.
[*The Scene Dissolves.*]

[1944]

TENNESSEE WILLIAMS'S PRODUCTION NOTES

Being a "memory play," *The Glass Menagerie* can be presented with unusual freedom of convention. Because of its considerably delicate or tenuous material, atmospheric touches and subtleties of direction play a particularly important part. Expressionism and all other unconventional techniques in drama have only one valid aim, and that is a closer approach to truth. When a play employs unconventional techniques, it is not, or certainly shouldn't be, trying to escape its responsibility of dealing with reality, or interpreting experience, but is actually or should be attempting to find a closer approach, a more penetrating and vivid expression of things as they are. The straight realistic play with its genuine frigidaire and authentic ice cubes, its characters that speak exactly as its audience speaks, corresponds to the academic landscape and has the same virtue of a photographic likeness. Everyone should know nowadays the unimportance of the photographic in art: that truth, life, or reality is an organic thing which the poetic imagination can represent or suggest, in essence, only through transformation, through changing into other forms than those which were merely present in appearance.

These remarks are not meant as comments only on this particular play. They have to do with a conception of a new, plastic theater which must take the place of the exhausted theater of realistic conventions if the theater is to resume vitality as a part of our culture.

The Screen Device

There is *only one important difference between the original and acting version of the play* and that is the *omission* in the latter of the device which I tentatively included in my *original* script. This device was the use of a screen on which were projected magic-lantern slides bearing images or titles. I do not regret the omission of this device from the . . . Broadway production. The extraordinary power of Miss Taylor's performance made it suitable to have the utmost simplicity in the physical production. But I think it may be interesting to some readers to see how this device was conceived. So I am putting it into the published manuscript. These images and legends, projected from behind, were cast on a section of wall between the front-room and dining-room areas, which should be indistinguishable from the rest when not in use.

The purpose of this will probably be apparent. It is to give accent to certain values in each scene. Each scene contains a particular point (or several) which is structurally the most important. In an episodic play, such as this, the basic structure or narrative line may be obscured from the audience; the effect may seem fragmentary rather than architectural. This may not be the fault of the play so much as a lack of attention in the audience. The legend or image upon the screen will strengthen the effect of what is merely allusion in the writing and allow the primary point to be made more simply and lightly than if the entire responsibility were on the spoken lines. Aside from this structural value, I think the screen will have a definite emotional appeal, less definable but just as important. An imaginative producer or director may invent many other uses for this device than those indicated in the present script. In fact the possibilities of the device seem much larger to me than the instance of this play can possibly utilize.

The Music

Another extra-literary accent in this play is provided by the use of music. A single recurring tune, "The Glass Menagerie," is used to give emotional emphasis to suitable passages. This tune is like circus music, not when you are on the grounds or in the immediate vicinity of the parade, but when you are at some distance and very likely thinking of something else. It seems under those circumstances to continue almost interminably and it weaves in and out of your preoccupied consciousness; then it is the lightest, most delicate music in the world and perhaps the saddest. It expresses the surface vivacity of life with the underlying strain of immutable and inexpressible sorrow. When you look at a piece of delicately spun glass you think of two things: how beautiful it is and how easily it can be broken. Both of those ideas should be woven into the recurring tune, which dips in and out of the play as if it were carried on a wind that changes. It serves as a thread of connection and allusion between the narrator with his separate point in time and space and the subject of his story. Between each episode it returns as reference to the emotion, nostalgia, which is the first condition of the play. It is primarily Laura's music and therefore comes out most clearly when the play focuses upon her and the lovely fragility of glass which is her image.

The Lighting

The lighting in the play is not realistic. In keeping with the atmosphere of memory, the stage is dim. Shafts of light are focused on selected areas or actors, sometimes in contradistinction to what is the apparent center. For instance, in the quarrel scene between Tom and Amanda, in which Laura has no active part, the clearest pool of light is on her figure. This is also true of the supper scene. The light upon Laura should be distinct from the others, having a peculiar pristine clarity such as light used in early religious portraits of female saints or madonnas. A certain correspondence to light in religious paintings, such as El Greco's, where the figures are radiant in atmosphere that is relatively dusky, could be effectively used throughout the play. (It will also permit a more effective use of the screen.) A free, imaginative use of light can be of enormous value in giving a mobile, plastic quality to plays of a more or less static nature.

Topics for Critical Thinking and Writing

1. When the play was produced in New York, the magic-lantern slides were omitted. Is the device an extraneous gimmick? Might it even interfere with the play, by oversimplifying and thus in a way belittling the actions?
2. What does the Victrola offer to Laura? Why is the typewriter a better symbol (for the purposes of the play) than, say, a piano? After all, Laura could have been taking piano lessons. Explain the symbolism of the unicorn, and the loss of its horn. What is Laura saying to Jim in the gesture of giving him the unicorn?
3. Laura escapes to her glass menagerie. To what do Amanda and Tom escape? How complete is Tom's escape at the end of the play?

4. What is meant at the end when Laura blows out the candles? Is she blowing out illusions? Or life? Or both?

5. Did Williams make a slip in having Amanda say Laura is "crippled" on page 461?

6. There is an implication that had Jim not been going steady he might have rescued Laura, but Jim also seems to represent (for example, in his lines about money and power) the corrupt outside world that no longer values humanity. Is this a slip on Williams's part, or is it an interesting complexity?

7. On page 461 Williams says, in a stage direction, "Now that we cannot hear the mother's speech, her silliness is gone and she has dignity and tragic beauty." Is Williams simply dragging in the word "tragic" because of its prestige, or is it legitimate? "Tragedy" is often distinguished from "pathos": In the tragic, the suffering is experienced by persons who act and are in some measure responsible for their suffering; in the pathetic, the suffering is experienced by the passive and the innocent. For example, in discussing Aeschylus's *The Suppliants* (in *Greek Tragedy*), H. D. F. Kitto says, "The Suppliants are not only pathetic, as the victims of outrage, but also tragic, as the victims of their own misconceptions." Given this distinction, to what extent are Amanda and Laura tragic? pathetic?

A SAMPLE ESSAY BY A STUDENT

The college essays you write about plays will be similar in many respects to analytic essays about fiction. Unless you are writing a review of a performance, you probably won't try to write about all aspects of a play. Rather, you'll choose one significant aspect as your topic. For instance, if you are writing about Tennessee Williams's *The Glass Menagerie,* you might compare the aspirations of Jim O'Connor and Tom Wingfield, or you might compare Tom's illusions with those of his sister, Laura, and his mother, Amanda. Or you might examine the symbolism, perhaps limiting your essay topic to the glass animals but perhaps extending it to include other symbols, such as the fire escape, the lighting, and the Victrola. Similarly, if you are writing an analysis, you might decide to study the construction of one scene of a play or (if the play does not have a great many scenes) even the construction of the entire play.

The following essay discusses the structure of *The Glass Menagerie*. It mentions various characters, but since its concern is with the arrangement of scenes, it does not (for instance) examine any of the characters in detail. Of course an essay might well be devoted to examining (for example) Williams's assertion that "There is much to admire in Amanda, and as much to love and pity as there is to laugh at," but an essay on the structure of the play is probably not the place to talk about Williams's characterization of Amanda.

Preliminary Notes

After deciding to write on the structure of the play, with an eye toward seeing the overall pattern that the parts form, the student reread *The Glass Menagerie,* jotted down some notes briefly summarizing each of the seven scenes, with an occasional comment, and then typed them. On rereading the typed notes, he added a few observations in handwriting.

nagging

1. begins with Tom talking to audience;
   ~~says he is a magician~~
   America, in 1930s
      "shouting and confusion"
   Father deserted
   Amanda nagging; ~~is she a bit cracked?~~
   Tom: bored, angry
   Laura: embarrassed, depressed
2. Laura: quit business school; sad, but Jim's name is mentioned, so, lighter tone introduced

out-and-out battle —3. Tom and Amanda argue
   Tom almost destroys glass menagerie
   Rage: Can things get any worse?

reconciliation, and false hopes—then final collapse

4. T and A reconciled
   T to try to get a "gentleman caller"
5. T tells A that Jim will visit
   things are looking up
6. Jim arrives; L terrified still, A thinks things can work out
7. Lights go out (foreshadowing dark ending?) Jim a jerk, clumsy; breaks unicorn, but L doesn't seem to mind. Maybe he *is* the right guy to draw her into normal world. Jim reveals he is engaged:
   "Desolation."
   Tom escapes into merchant marine, but can't escape memories. Speaks to audience. L. blows out candles (does this mean he forgets her? No, because he is remembering her right now. I don't get it, if the candles are supposed to be symbolic.)

   These notes enabled the student to prepare a rough draft, which he then submitted to some classmates for peer review. (On peer review, see page 26.)

Final Version of the Student's Essay: "The Solid Structure of *The Glass Menagerie*"

Notice that the final version of the essay, printed here, is *not* merely a summary (a brief retelling of the plot). Although it does indeed include summary, it chiefly is devoted to showing *how* the scenes are related.

Shapiro 1

Joel Shapiro

Professor Washington

English 1102

10 April 2004

Title is focused; it announces topic and thesis

The Solid Structure of The Glass Menagerie

In the "Production Notes" Tennessee Williams calls The Glass Menagerie a "memory

Opening paragraph closes in on thesis

play," a term that the narrator in the play also uses. Memories often consist of fragments of episodes that are so loosely connected that they seem chaotic, and therefore we might think that The Glass Menagerie will consist of very loosely related episodes. However, the play covers only one episode, and though it gives the illusion of random talk, it really has a firm structure and moves steadily toward a foregone conclusion.

Reasonable organization; the paragraph touches on the beginning and the end

Tennessee Williams divides the play into seven scenes. The first scene begins with a sort of prologue, and the last scene concludes with a sort of epilogue that is related to the prologue. In the prologue Tom addresses the audience and comments on the 1930s as a time when America

Brief but effective quotations

was "blind" and was a place of "shouting and confusion." Tom also mentions that our lives consist of expectations, and though he does not

Shapiro 2

say that our expectations are unfulfilled, near

the end of the prologue he quotes a postcard

that his father wrote to the family he deserted:

"Hello--Goodbye!" In the epilogue Tom tells us

that he followed his "father's footsteps,"

deserting the family. And just before the

epilogue, near the end of Scene VII, we see what

can be considered another desertion: Jim

explains to Tom's sister Laura that he is

engaged and therefore cannot visit Laura again.

Useful generalization based on earlier details

Thus the end is closely related to the beginning,

and the play is the steady development of the

initial implications.

Chronological organization is reasonable. Opening topic sentence lets readers know where they are going

The first three scenes show things going

from bad to worse. Amanda is a nagging mother

who finds her only relief in talking about the

past to her crippled daughter Laura and her

frustrated son Tom. When she was young she

was beautiful and was eagerly courted by rich

young men, but now the family is poor and this

harping on the past can only bore or infuriate

Tom and embarrass or depress Laura, who have

no happy past to look back to, who see no happy

future, and who can only be upset by Amanda's

insistence that they should behave as she

Shapiro 3

Brief plot summary supports thesis

behaved long ago. The second scene deepens the despair: Amanda learns that the timorous Laura has not been attending a business school but has retreated in terror from this confrontation with the contemporary world. Laura's helplessness is made clear to the audience, and so is Amanda's lack of understanding. Near the end of the second scene, however, Jim's name is introduced; he is a boy Laura had a crush on in high school, and so the audience gets a glimpse of a happier Laura and a sense that possibly Laura's world is wider than the stifling tenement in which she and her mother and brother live. But in the third scene things get worse, when Tom and Amanda have so violent an argument that they are no longer on speaking terms. Tom is so angry with his mother that he almost by accident destroys his sister's treasured collection of glass animals, the fragile, lifeless world that is her refuge. The apartment is literally full of the "shouting and confusion" that Tom spoke of in his prologue.

Useful summary and transition

The first three scenes have revealed a progressive worsening of relations; the next three scenes reveal a progressive improvement

Shapiro 4

in relations. In Scene IV Tom and his mother are
reconciled, and Tom reluctantly--apparently in
an effort to make up with his mother--agrees to
try to get a friend to come to dinner so that
Laura will have "a gentleman caller." In Scene V
Tom tells his mother that Jim will come to
dinner on the next night, and Amanda
brightens, because she sees a possibility of
security for Laura at last. In Scene VI Jim
arrives, and despite Laura's initial terror, there
seems, at least in Amanda's mind, to be the
possibility that things will go well.

The seventh scene, by far the longest, at
first seems to be fulfilling Amanda's hopes.
Despite the ominous fact that the lights go out
because Tom has not paid the electric bill, Jim is
at ease. He is an insensitive oaf, but that doesn't
seem to bother Amanda, and almost
miraculously he manages to draw Laura
somewhat out of her sheltered world. Even
when Jim in his clumsiness breaks the horn off
Laura's treasured glass unicorn, she is not
upset. In fact, she is almost relieved because the
loss of the horn makes the animal less "freakish"
and he "will feel more at home with the other

Shapiro 5

horses." In a way, of course, the unicorn symbolizes the crippled Laura, who at least for the moment feels less freakish and isolated now that she is somewhat reunited with society through Jim. But this is a play about life in a blind and confused world, and though in a previous age the father escaped, there can be no escape now. Jim reveals that he is engaged, Laura relapses into "desolation," Amanda relapses into rage and bitterness, and Tom relapses into dreams of escape. In a limited sense Tom does escape. He leaves the family and joins the merchant marine, but his last speech or epilogue tells us that he cannot escape the memory of his sister: "Oh, Laura, Laura, I tried to leave you behind me, but I am more faithful than I intended to be!" And so the end of the last scene brings us back again to the beginning of the first scene: we are still in a world of "the blind" and of "confusion." But now at the end of the play the darkness is deeper, the characters are lost forever in their unhappiness as Laura "blows the candles out," the darkness being literal but also symbolic of their extinguished hopes.

The essayist is thinking and commenting, not merely summarizing the plot

Shapiro 6

Numerous devices, such as repeated
references to the absent father, to Amanda's
youth, to Laura's Victrola, and of course to
Laura's glass menagerie help to tie the scenes

Useful, thoughtful
summary of thesis

together into a unified play. But beneath these
threads of imagery and recurring motifs is a
fundamental pattern that involves the
movement from nagging (Scenes I and II) to
open hostilities (Scene III) to temporary
reconciliation (Scene IV) to false hopes (Scenes V
and VI) to an impossible heightening of false
hopes and then, in a swift descent, to an
inevitable collapse (Scene VII). Tennessee
Williams has constructed his play carefully.
G. B. Tennyson says that a "playwright must

Effective quotation
from an outside
source

'build' his speeches, as the theatrical expression
has it" (13). But a playwright must do more; the
playwright must also build the play out of
scenes. Like Ibsen, if Williams had been
introduced to an architect he might have said,
"Architecture is my business too."

Shapiro 7

Works Cited

Tennyson, G. B. <u>An Introduction to Drama.</u> New

York: Holt, 1967.

Williams, Tennessee. <u>The Glass Menagerie.</u>

<u>Literature for Composition.</u> Ed. Sylvan

Barnet et al. 7th ed. New York:

Longman, 2005. 421-61.

14

Reading and Writing about Poetry

ELEMENTS OF POETRY

The Speaker and the Poet

The **speaker**, or **voice**, or **mask**, or **persona** (Latin for *mask*) that speaks a poem is not usually identical with the poet who writes it. The author assumes a role, or counterfeits the speech of a person in a particular situation. The nineteenth-century English poet Robert Browning, for instance, in "My Last Duchess" invented a Renaissance Italian duke who, in his palace, talks about his first wife and his art collection with an emissary from a count who is negotiating to offer his daughter in marriage to the duke.

In reading a poem, then, the first and most important question to ask yourself is this: Who is speaking? If an audience and a setting are suggested, keep them in mind, too, although these are not always indicated in a poem. Consider, for example, the following poem.

EMILY DICKINSON (1830–1886)

I'm Nobody! Who are you?
Are you—Nobody—too?
Then there's a pair of us!
Don't tell! they'd banish us—you know!   4

How dreary—to be—Somebody!
How public—like a Frog—
To tell your name—the livelong June—
To an admiring Bog!   8

[1861?]

We can't quite say that the speaker is Emily Dickinson, though if we have read a fair number of her poems we can say that the voice in this poem is familiar, and perhaps here we *can* talk of Dickinson rather than of "the speaker of the poem," since this speaker (unlike Browning's Renaissance duke) clearly is not a figure utterly remote from the poet.

Let's consider the sort of person we hear in "I'm Nobody! Who are you?" (Read it aloud, to see if you agree with what we say. In fact, you should test each of our assertions by reading the poem aloud.)

- The voice in the first line is rather like that of a child playing a game with a friend.
- In the second and third lines the speaker sees the reader as a fellow spirit ("Are you—Nobody—too?") and invites the reader to join her ("Then there's a pair of us!"), to form a sort of conspiracy of silence against outsiders ("Don't tell!").

In "they'd banish us," however, we hear a word that a child would not be likely to use, and we probably feel that the speaker is a shy but (with the right companion) playful adult, who here is speaking to an intimate friend, the reader. By means of "banish," a word that brings to mind images of a king's court, the speaker almost comically inflates and thereby makes fun of the "they" who are opposed to "us."

In the second stanza, or we might better say in the space between the two stanzas, the speaker puts aside the childlike manner. In "How dreary," the first words of the second stanza, we hear a sophisticated voice, one might even say a world-weary voice or a voice perhaps with more than a touch of condescension. But since by now we are paired with the speaker in a conspiracy against outsiders, we enjoy the contrast that the speaker makes between the Nobodies and the Somebodies. Who are these Somebodies, these people who would imperiously "banish" the speaker and the friend? What are the Somebodies like?

How dreary—to be—Somebody!
How public—like a Frog—
To tell your name—the livelong June—
To an admiring Bog!

The last two lines do at least two things:

- They amusingly explain to the speaker's new friend (the reader) in what way a Somebody is public (it proclaims its presence all day), and
- they indicate the absurdity of the Somebody-Frog's behavior (the audience is "an admiring Bog").

By the end of the poem we are quite convinced that it is better to be a Nobody (like Dickinson and the reader?) than a Somebody (a loudmouth).

Dickinson did not always speak in this persona, however. In "Wild Nights," probably written in the same year as "I'm Nobody! Who are you?", Dickinson speaks as an impassioned lover, but we need not assume that the beloved is actually in the presence of the lover. In fact, since the second line says, "Were I with thee," the reader must assume that the person addressed is *not* present. The poem apparently represents a state of mind—a sort of talking to oneself—rather than an address to another person.

Wild Nights—Wild Nights,
Were I with Thee
Wild Nights should be
Our luxury   4

Futile—the Winds
To a Heart in port—
Done with the Compass—
Done with the Chart!   8

Rowing in Eden—
Ah, the Sea!
Might I but moor—Tonight—
In Thee.   12

[c. 1861]

Clearly the speaker is someone passionately in love. The following questions invite you to look more closely at how the speaker of "Wild Nights" is characterized.

Topics for Critical Thinking and Writing

1. How does this poem communicate the speaker's state of mind? For example, in the first stanza (lines 1–4), what—beyond the meaning of the words—is communicated by the repetition of "Wild Nights"? In the last stanza (lines 9–12), what is the tone of "Ah, the Sea!"? ("Tone" means something like emotional coloring, as for instance a "businesslike tone," a "bitter tone," or an "eager tone.")
2. Paraphrase (that is, put into your own words) the second stanza. What does this stanza communicate about the speaker's love for the beloved? Compare your paraphrase and the original. What does the form of the original sentences (the *omission,* for instance, of the verbs of lines 5 and 6 and of the subject in lines 7 and 8) communicate?
3. Paraphrase the last stanza. How does "Ah, the Sea!" fit into your paraphrase? If you had trouble fitting it in, do you think the poem would be better off without it? If not, why not?

The voice speaking a poem may, of course, have the ring of the author's own voice, and to make a distinction between speaker and author may at times seem perverse. In fact, some poetry (especially contemporary American poetry) is highly autobiographical. Still, even in autobiographical poems it may be convenient to distinguish between author and speaker. The speaker of a given poem is, let's say, Sylvia Plath in her role as parent, or Sylvia Plath in her role as daughter, not simply Sylvia Plath the poet.

The Language of Poetry: Diction and Tone

How is a voice or mask or persona created? From the whole of language, the author consciously or unconsciously selects certain words and grammatical constructions; this selection constitutes the persona's diction. It is, then, partly by the diction that we come to know the speaker of a poem. Just as in life there is a difference between people who speak of a "belly button," a "navel," or an "umbilicus," so in poetry there is a difference between speakers who use one word rather than another. Of course it is also possible that all three of these words are part of a given speaker's vocabulary, and the speaker's choice among the three would depend on the situation. That is, in addressing a child, the speaker would probably use the word "belly button"; in addressing an adult other than a family member or close friend, the speaker might be more likely to use "navel"; and if the speaker is a physician addressing an audience of physicians, he or she might be most likely to use "umbilicus." But this is only to say, again, that the dramatic situation in which you find yourself helps to define yourself, helps to establish the particular role that you are playing.

Of course some words are used in virtually all poems: *I, see, and,* and the like. Still, the grammatical constructions in which they appear may help to define the speaker. In Dickinson's "Wild Nights," for instance, expressions such as "Were I with Thee" and "Might I" indicate a speaker of an earlier century than ours, and probably an educated speaker.

Speakers have attitudes toward

- themselves,
- their subjects, and
- their audiences,

and, consciously or unconsciously, they choose their words, pitch, and modulation accordingly; all these add up to their tone. In written literature, tone must be detected without the aid of the ear, although it's a good idea to read poetry aloud, trying to find the appropriate tone of voice. That is, the reader must understand by the selection and sequence of words the way the words are meant to sound— playful, angry, confidential, or ironic, for example. The reader must catch what Frost calls "the speaking tone of voice somehow entangled in the words and fastened to the page for the ear of the imagination."

WILLIAM SHAKESPEARE

William Shakespeare (1564–1616), born in Stratford-upon-Avon in England, is chiefly known as a dramatic poet, but he also wrote nondramatic poetry. In 1609 a volume of 154 of his sonnets was published, apparently without his permission. Probably he chose to keep his sonnets unpublished not because he thought that they were of little value, but because it was more prestigious to be an amateur poet (unpublished) than a professional (published). Although the sonnets were published in 1609, they were probably written in the mid-1590s, when there was a vogue for sonneteering. A contemporary writer in 1598 said that Shakespeare's "sugred Sonnets [circulate] among his private friends."

We print other sonnets on pages 56 and 482.

Sonnet 146

Poor soul, the center of my sinful earth,
[My sinful earth] these rebel pow'rs that thee array,
Why dost thou pine within and suffer dearth,
Painting thy outward walls so costly gay?   4
Why so large cost,° having so short a lease,
Dost thou upon thy fading mansion spend?
Shall worms, inheritors of this excess,
Eat up thy charge? Is this thy body's end?   8
Then, soul, live thou upon thy servant's loss,
And let that pine to aggravate thy store;
Buy terms divine° in selling hours of dross;
Within be fed, without be rich no more.   12
    So shalt thou feed on Death, that feeds on men,
    And death once dead, there's no more dying then.

[1609]

---

5 **cost** expense   11 **buy terms divine** buy ages of immortality

Topics for Critical Thinking and Writing

1. "My sinful earth," in line 2, is doubtless an error made by the printer of the first edition (1609), who mistakenly repeated the end of the first line. Among suggested replacements are "Thrall to," "Fooled by," "Rebuke," "Leagued with," and "Feeding." If you wish, suggest your own corrections. Which do you prefer?
2. In what tone of voice would you speak the first line? The last line? Trace the speaker's shifts in emotion throughout the poem.

Writing about the Speaker

Robert Frost once said:

> Everything written is as good as it is dramatic. . . . [A poem is] heard as sung or spoken by a person in a scene—in a character, in a setting. By whom, where and when is the question. By the dreamer of a better world out in a storm in autumn; by a lover under a window at night.

Suppose, in reading a poem Frost published in 1916, we try to establish "by whom, where and when" it is spoken. We may not be able to answer all three questions in great detail, but let's see what the poem suggests. As you read it, you'll notice—alerted by the quotation marks—that there are *two* speakers; the poem is a tiny drama. Thus, the closing quotation marks at the end of line 9 signal to us that the first speech is finished.

ROBERT FROST (1874–1963)

The Telephone

"When I was just as far as I could walk
From here today
There was an hour
All still
When leaning with my head against a flower   5
I heard you talk.
Don't say I didn't, for I heard you say—
You spoke from that flower on the window sill—
Do you remember what it was you said?"

"First tell me what it was you thought you heard."   10

"Having found the flower and driven a bee away,
I leaned my head,
And holding by the stalk,
I listened and I thought I caught the word—
What was it? Did you call me by my name?   15
Or did you say—
Someone said 'Come'—I heard it as I bowed."

"I may have thought as much, but not aloud."

"Well, so I came."

[1916]

Suppose we ask: Who are these two speakers? What is their relationship? What's going on between them? Where are they? We don't think that these questions can be answered with absolute certainty, but we do think some answers are more probable than others. For instance, line 8 ("You spoke from that flower on the window sill") tells us that the speakers are in a room, probably of a home—rather than, say, in a railroad station—but we can't say whether the home is a farmhouse, or a house in a village, town, or city, or an apartment.

Let's put the questions (even if they may turn out to be unanswerable) into a more specific form.

Topics for Critical Thinking and Writing

1. One speaker speaks lines 1–9, 11–17, and 19. The other speaks lines 10 and 18. Do you think you can tell the gender of each speaker? For sure, probably, or not at all? On what do you base your answer?
2. Try to visualize this miniature drama. In line 7 the first speaker says, "Don't say I didn't, . . . " What happens—what do you see in your mind's eye—after line 6 that causes the speaker to say this?
3. Why do you suppose the speaker of lines 10 and 18 says so little? How would you characterize the tone of these two lines? What sort of relationship do you think exists between the two speakers?
4. How would you characterize the tone of lines 11–17? Of the last line of the poem?

If you haven't jotted down your responses, we suggest that you do so before reading what follows.

Journal Entries

Given questions somewhat like the preceding ones, students were asked to try to identify the speakers by sex, to speculate on their relationship, and then to add whatever they wished to say. One student recorded the following thoughts:

> These two people care about each other--maybe husband and wife, or lovers--and a man is doing most of the talking, though I can't prove it. He has walked as far as possible--that is, as far as possible and still get back on the same day--and he seemed to hear the other person call him. He claims that she spoke to him "from that flower on the window sill," and that's why I think the second person is a woman. She's at home, near the window. Somehow I even imagine she was at the window near the kitchen sink, maybe working while he was out on this long walk.
>
> Then she speaks one line; she won't say if she did or didn't speak. She is very cautious, or suspicious: "First tell me what it was you thought you heard." Maybe she doesn't want to say something and then have her husband embarrass her by saying, "No, that's not what I thought." Or maybe she just doesn't feel like talking. Then he claims that he heard her speaking through a flower, as though the flower was a telephone, just as though it was hooked up to the flower on the window sill. But at first he won't say what he supposedly heard, or "thought" he heard. Instead, he

says that maybe it was someone else: "Someone said 'Come.'" Is he teasing her? Pretending that she may have a rival?

Then she speaks--again just one line, saying, "I may have thought as much, but not aloud." She won't admit that she did think this thought. And then the man says, "Well, so I came." Just like that; short and sweet. No more fancy talk about flowers as telephones. He somehow (through telepathy?) got the message, and so here he is. He seems like a sensitive guy, playful (the stuff about the flowers as telephones), but also he knows when to stop kidding around.

Another student also identified the couple as a man and woman and thought that this dialogue occurs after a quarrel:

As the poem goes on, we learn that the man wants to be with the woman, but it starts by telling us that he walked as far away from her as he could. He doesn't say why, but I think from the way the woman speaks later in the poem, they had a fight and he walked out. Then, when he stopped to rest, he thought he heard her voice. He really means that he was thinking of her and he was hoping she was thinking of him. So he returns, and he tells her he heard her calling him, but he pretends he heard her call him through a flower on their window sill. He can't admit that he was thinking about her. This seems very realistic to me; when someone feels a bit ashamed, it's sometimes hard to admit that you were wrong, and you want the other person to tell you that things are OK anyhow. And judging from line 7, when he says "Don't say I didn't," it seems that she is going to interrupt him by denying it. She is still angry, or maybe she doesn't want to make up too quickly. But he wants to pretend that she called him back. So when he says, "Do you remember what it was you said?" she won't admit that she was thinking of him, and she says, "First tell me what it was you thought you heard." She's testing him a little. So he goes on, with the business about flowers as telephones, and he says "someone" called him. He understands that she doesn't want to be pushed into forgiving him, so he backs off. Then she is willing to admit that she did think about him, but still she doesn't quite admit it. She is too proud to say openly that she wants him back but she does say, "I may have thought as much, . . . " And then, since they both have preserved their dignity, and also both have admitted that they care about the other, he can say, "Well, so I came."

Topics for Writing

1. In a paragraph or two or three, *evaluate* one of these two entries recorded by students. Do you think the comments are weak, plausible, or convincing, and *why* do you think so? Can you offer additional supporting evidence or, on the other hand, counterevidence? You may want to set forth your own scenario.

2. Two small questions: In a sentence or two, offer a suggestion as to why in line 11 Frost wrote, "and driven a bee away." After all, the bee plays no role in the poem. Second, in line 17 Frost has the speaker say, "I heard it as I bowed." Of

course "bowed" rhymes with "aloud," but let's assume that the need for a rhyme did not dictate the choice of this word. Do you think "I heard it as I bowed" is better than, say, "I heard it as I waited," or "I heard it as I listened"? Why?

3. Write an essay of 500 words either about an uncanny experience of your own or about a quarrel or disagreement that was resolved in a way you had not expected.

Figurative Language

Robert Frost has said, "Poetry provides the one permissible way of saying one thing and meaning another." This, of course, is an exaggeration, but it shrewdly suggests the importance of figurative language—saying one thing in terms of something else. Words have their literal meanings, but they can also be used so that something other than the literal meaning is implied. "My love is a rose" is, literally, nonsense, for a person is not a five-petaled, many-stamened plant with a spiny stem. But the suggestions of *rose* (at least for Robert Burns, who compared his beloved to a rose in the line "My love is like a red, red rose"), include "delicate beauty," "soft," and "perfumed," and thus the word *rose* can be meaningfully applied—figuratively rather than literally—to "my love." The girl is fragrant; her skin is perhaps like a rose in texture and (in some measure) color; she will not keep her beauty long. The poet, that is, has communicated his perception very precisely.

People who write about poetry have found it convenient to name the various kinds of figurative language. Just as the student of geology employs such special terms as *kames* and *eskers,* the student of literature employs special terms to name things as accurately as possible. The following paragraphs discuss the most common terms.

In a **simile**, items from different classes are explicitly compared by a connective such as *like, as,* or *than,* or by a verb such as *appears* or *seems.* (If the objects compared are from the same class, for example, "Tokyo is like Los Angeles," no simile is present.)

Float like a butterfly, sting like a bee.

—Muhammad Ali

It is a beauteous evening, calm and free.
The holy time is quiet as a Nun,
Breathless with adoration.

—William Wordsworth

All of our thoughts will be fairer than doves.

—Elizabeth Bishop

Seems he a dove? His feathers are but borrowed.

—Shakespeare

A **metaphor** asserts the identity, without a connective such as *like* or a verb such as *appears,* of terms that are literally incompatible.

Umbrellas clothe the beach in every hue.

—Elizabeth Bishop

whirlwind fife-and-drum of the storm bends the salt
marsh grass

—Marianne Moore

Two common types of metaphor have Greek names. In **synecdoche** the whole is replaced by the part, or the part by the whole. For example, *bread* in "Give us this day our daily bread" replaces all sorts of food. In **metonymy** something is named that replaces something closely related to it. For example, James Shirley names certain objects, using them to replace social classes (royalty and the peasantry) to which they are related:

> Scepter and crown must tumble down
> And in the dust be equal made
> With the poor crooked scythe and spade.

The attribution of human feelings or characteristics or abstractions to inanimate objects is called **personification**.

> Memory,
> that exquisite blunderer.
>
> —Amy Clampitt

> There's Wrath who has learnt every trick of guerilla warfare,
> The shamming dead, the night-raid, the feinted retreat.
>
> —W. H. Auden

> Hope, thou bold taster of delight.
>
> —Richard Crashaw

Crashaw's personification, "Hope, thou bold taster of delight," is also an example of the figure called **apostrophe**, an address to a person or thing not literally listening. Wordsworth begins a sonnet by apostrophizing Milton:

> Milton, thou shouldst be living at this hour.

What conclusions can we draw about figurative language? First, figurative language, with its literally incompatible terms, forces the reader to attend to the **connotations** (suggestions, associations) rather than to the **denotations** (dictionary definitions) of one of the terms. Second, although figurative language is said to differ from ordinary speech, it is found in ordinary speech as well as in poetry and other literary forms. "It rained cats and dogs," "War is hell," "Don't be a pig," "Mr. Know-it-all," and other tired figures are part of our daily utterances. But through repeated use, these, and most of the figures we use, have lost whatever impact they once had and are only a shade removed from expressions which, though once figurative, have become literal: the *eye* of a needle, a *branch* office, the *face* of a clock. Third, good figurative language is usually concrete, condensed, and interesting.

We should mention, too, that figurative language is not limited to literary writers; it is used by scientists and social scientists—by almost everyone who is concerned with effective expression. Take, for instance, R. H. Tawney's *Religion and the Rise of Capitalism* (1926), a classic of economics. Among the titles of Tawney's chapters are "The Economic Revolution," "The Puritan Movement," and "The New Medicine for Poverty," all of which include metaphors. (To take only the last: Poverty is seen as a sick person or a disease.) Or take this sentence from Tawney (almost any sentence will serve equally well to reveal his bent for metaphor): "By the end of the sixteenth century the divorce between religious theory and economic realities had long been evident." Figures are not a fancy way of speaking. Quite the opposite: Writers use figures because they are forceful and exact. Literal language would not only be less interesting, it would also be less precise.

We have already printed two sonnets by Shakespeare; here is a third, but before you read it we might mention that if you have read the other sonnets you may recall that they abound with figurative language. For instance, in Sonnet 73 (page 56), the speaker says that he is aging not by telling us how old he is but by saying

> he is like a tree with "yellow leaves" (we might say, again using a figure of speech, that he is in the autumn of his life),
> he is in his "twilight," and
> he is like a fire that now is merely embers lying on a bed of ashes.

In Sonnet 146 (p. 476) he compares his body to "earth" and to a "fading mansion," and he says that the body is the "servant" of the soul—expressions that are figurative, not literal. But in the following poem we see that Shakespeare can also laugh at figurative comparisons. His contemporaries wrote countless sonnets in which they compared their beloved's eyes to the sun, the redness of her lips to coral, her blonde hair to fine gold wire, her red and white complexion to damask roses (or perhaps to a silk called damask—mixed red and white), her breath to perfume, her speech to music, and her gait to that of a goddess (goddesses were said to walk on air, not on earth). Now see how Shakespeare describes his mistress. (But first, two cautions: In line 8, "reeks," in "the breath that from my mistress reeks," in Shakespeare's day did not have the strong negative suggestion that it has today; rather, it meant something like "emanates." Second, in the final line, "Any she belied with false compare" means "Any woman misrepresented by false comparisons.")

Sonnet 130

My mistress' eyes are nothing like the sun;
Coral is far more red than her lips' red;
If snow be white, why then her breasts are dun;
If hairs be wires, black wires grow on her head.   4
I have seen roses damasked, red and white,
But no such roses see I in her cheeks;
And in some perfumes is there more delight
Than in the breath that from my mistress reeks.   8
I love to hear her speak, yet well I know
That music hath a far more pleasing sound;
I grant I never saw a goddess go;
My mistress, when she walks, treads on the ground.   12
And yet, by heaven, I think my love as rare
As any she belied with false compare.

[1609]

Topic for Critical Thinking and Writing

As we said a moment ago, Shakespeare here seems to ridicule figurative language, yet he uses figurative language in his sonnets and his plays. How can this be explained?

Dana Gioia

Dana Gioia (pronounced "JOY uh"), born in 1950, is chair of the National Endowment for the Arts. He is a poet and the co-author of a textbook on literature, and he has also had a successful career as a businessman.

Money

Money is a kind of poetry.

—Walace Stevens

Money, the long green,
cash, stash, rhino, jack
or just plain dough.

Chock it up, fork it over,
shell it out. Watch it   5
burn holes through pockets.

To be made of it! To have it
to burn! Greenbacks, double eagles,
megabucks and Ginnie Maes.

It greases the palm, feathers a nest,   10
holds heads above water,
makes both ends meet.

Money breeds money.
Gathering interest, compounding daily.
Always in circulation   15

Money. You don't know where it's been,
but you put it where your mouth is.
And it talks.

[1991]

Topics for Critical Thinking and Writing

1. Are any of the terms in the poem unfamiliar to you? If so, check a dictionary, and if you don't find an explanation in a dictionary, turn to other resources— the Internet, and friends and classmates. Do some of the terms come from particular worlds of discourse, for instance banking, or gambling, or drug-dealing?
2. Suppose the last stanza had been placed first. Would the poem be better? Or worse? Why?
3. Write a somewhat comparable poem on a topic of your choice, for instance students, teachers, athletes, or work.

Although one is almost tempted to say that figurative language is essential to literature, in fact some literature, even some poetry, is not figurative. Consider this short piece.

ROBERT FROST (1874-1963)

The Hardship of Accounting

Never ask of money spent
Where the spender thinks it went.
Nobody was ever meant
To remember or invent
What he did with every cent.

[1936]

Topic for Critical Thinking and Writing

Do you consider Frost's lines to be a poem? Why, or why not? The lines rhyme, yes, but most people agree that not everything that rhymes is a poem. Consider:

> Thirty days hath September,
> April, June, and November;
> February has twenty-eight alone,
> All the rest have thirty-one,
> Excepting leap year, that's the time
> When February's days are twenty-nine.

Most teachers of literature would agree that although "Thirty days" is verse, it is not poetry. Why? And if "Thirty days" is not poetry, is Frost's "The Hardship of Accounting" poetry? Why or why not?

Imagery and Symbolism

When we read *rose* we may more or less call to mind a picture of a rose, or perhaps we are reminded of the odor or texture of a rose. Whatever in a poem appeals to any of our senses (including sensations of heat as well as of sight, smell, taste, touch, sound) is an image. In short, images are the sensory content of a work, whether literal or figurative. When a poet says "My rose" and is speaking about a rose, we have no figure of speech—though we still have an image. If, however, "My rose" is a shortened form of "My love is a rose," some would say that the poet is using a metaphor; but others would say that because the first term is omitted ("My love is"), the rose is a symbol. A poem about the transience of a rose might compel the reader to feel that the transience of female beauty is the larger theme even though it is never explicitly stated.

Some symbols are **conventional symbols**—people have agreed to accept them as standing for something other than their literal meanings: A poem about the cross would probably be about Christianity; similarly, the rose has long been a symbol for love. In Virginia Woolf's novel *Mrs. Dalloway,* the husband communicates his love by proffering this conventional symbol: "He was holding out flowers—roses, red and white roses. (But he could not bring himself to say he loved her; not in so many words.)" Here is a poem that uses the conventional symbol of the rose.

EDMUND WALLER

Edmund Waller (1606-1687), born into a country family of wealth in Bucking-hamshire in England, attended Eton and Cambridge before spending most of his life as a member of parliament. When the Puritans came to power, he was imprisoned and eventually banished to France, although he was soon allowed to return to England. When the monarchy was restored to the throne, he returned to parliament.

Song

Go, lovely rose,
Tell her that wastes her time and me,
That now she knows,
When I resemble her to thee,
How sweet and fair she seems to be.   5

Tell her that's young,
And shuns to have her graces spied,
That hadst thou sprung
In deserts where no men abide,
Thou must have uncommended died.   10

Small is the worth
Of beauty from the light retired:
Bid her come forth,
Suffer her self to be desired,
And not blush so to be admired.   15

Then die, that she
The common fate of all things rare
May read in thee,
How small a part of time they share,
That are so wondrous sweet and fair.   20.

[1645]

Topics for Critical Thinking and Writing

1. In the first stanza the poet says that the resemblance between the rose and the woman is that both are "sweet and fair," words that reappear at the end of the poem. In between these two passages, what additional resemblances does the poet say they are?

2. The poem contains a sort of narrative of the brief life and the imminent death of a rose. In the third stanza, however, the rose is momentarily forgotten while the poet meditates and speaks directly about the woman. If you agree that this third stanza could conceivably stand as an independent poem, explain why it becomes a better poem when placed within the context of the address to the rose.

Let's now look at yet another poem that speaks of a rose, but in a much less traditional way.

WILLIAM BLAKE (1757–1827)

The Sick Rose

O rose, thou art sick!
The invisible worm
That flies in the night,
In the howling storm,   4

Has found out thy bed
Of crimson joy,
And his dark secret love

Does thy life destroy.   8

[1794]

A reader might perhaps argue that the worm is invisible (line 2) merely because it is hidden within the rose, but an "invisible worm / That flies in the night"
is more than a long, slender, soft-bodied, creeping animal; and a rose that has, or
is, a "bed / Of crimson joy" is more than a gardener's rose. Blake's worm and rose
suggest things beyond themselves—a stranger, more vibrant world than the world
we are usually aware of. They are, in short, symbolic, though readers will doubtless differ in their interpretations. Perhaps we find ourselves half thinking, for example, that the worm is male, the rose female, and that the poem is about the violation of virginity. Or that the poem is about the destruction of beauty: Woman's
beauty, rooted in joy, is destroyed by a power that feeds on her.

But these interpretations are not fully satisfying: The poem presents a worm
and a rose, and yet it is not merely about a worm and a rose. These objects res-
onate, stimulating our thoughts toward something else, but the something else is
elusive. This is not to say, however, that symbols mean whatever any reader says
they mean. A reader could scarcely support, we imagine, an interpretation arguing
that the poem is about the need to love all aspects of nature. All interpretations are
not equally valid; it's the writer's job to offer a reasonably persuasive interpretation.

A symbol, then, is an image so loaded with significance that it is not simply literal, and it does not simply stand for something else; it is both itself *and* something
else that it richly suggests, a kind of manifestation of something too complex or too
elusive to be otherwise revealed. Blake's poem is about a blighted rose and at the
same time about much more. In a symbol, as Thomas Carlyle wrote, "the Infinite is
made to blend with the Finite, to stand visible, and as it were, attainable there."

LINDA PASTAN

*Linda Pastan was born in New York City in 1932. The author of ten books of po-
ems, she has won numerous prizes and has received grants from the National
Endowment for the Arts. In the following poem she wittily plays with repetitions
and with pauses.*

Jump Cabling

When our cars   touched
When you lifted the hood   of mine

To see the intimate workings   underneath,
When we were bound   together
By a pulse of pure   energy,   5
When my car like the   princess
In the tale woke with a   start,
I thought why not ride the rest of the way together?

[1984]

Topics for Critical Thinking and Writing

1. Suppose someone argued that this is merely prose broken up into arbitrary units. Would you agree? Explain.
2. As you read the poem aloud, think about the spacing that Pastan designed for it. What is the effect of the space between the first and second parts of the first seven lines? Why does she do something different for the final line?

Verbal Irony and Paradox

Among the most common devices in poems is **verbal irony**. The speaker's words mean more or less the opposite of what they seem to say. Sometimes verbal irony takes the form of **overstatement**, or **hyperbole**, as when Lady Macbeth says, while sleepwalking, "All the perfumes of Arabia will not sweeten this little hand." Sometimes it takes the form of **understatement**, as when Andrew Marvell's speaker in "To His Coy Mistress" remarks with cautious wryness, "The grave's a fine and private place, / But none, I think, do there embrace," or when Sylvia Plath sees an intended suicide as "the big strip tease." Speaking broadly, intensely emotional contemporary poems like those of Plath often use irony to undercut—and thus make acceptable—the emotion presented.

Another common device in poems is **paradox**: the assertion of an apparent contradiction, as in Marvell's "am'rous birds of prey" in "To His Coy Mistress." Normally we think of amorous birds as gentle—doves, for example—and not as birds of prey, such as hawks. Another example of an apparent contradiction: In "Auld Lang Syne" there is the paradox that the remembrance of joy evokes a kind of sadness.

Structure

The arrangement of the parts, the organization of the entire poem, is its **structure**. Sometimes the poem is divided into blocks of, say, four lines each, but even if the poem is printed as a solid block it probably has some principle of organization. It may move, for example, from sorrow in the first two lines to joy in the next two or from a question in the first three lines to an answer in the last line.

Consider this short poem by an English poet of the seventeenth century.

ROBERT HERRICK (1591–1674)

Upon Julia's Clothes

Whenas in silks my Julia goes,
Then, then (methinks) how sweetly flows
That liquefaction of her clothes.

Next, when I cast mine eyes, and see
That brave° vibration, each way free   5
O, how that glittering taketh me.

[1648]

5 **brave** splendid.

A Sample Essay by a Student: "Herrick's Julia, Julia's Herrick"

One student, Stan Wylie, began thinking about this poem by copying it, double-spaced, and by making the following notes on his copy:

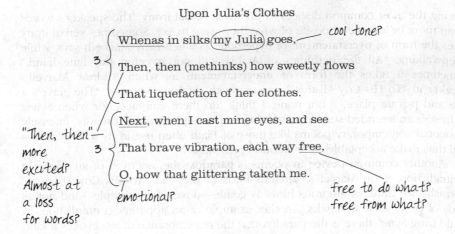

Stan got some further ideas by thinking about several of the questions that, in the checklist on pages 503–505, we suggest you ask yourself while rereading a poem. Among the questions are these:

- Does the poem proceed in a straightforward way, or at some point or points does the speaker reverse course, altering his or her tone or perception?
- What is the effect on you of the form?

With such questions in mind, Stan was stimulated to see if there is some sort of reversal or change in Herrick's poem, and if there is, how it is related to the structure. After rereading the poem several times, thinking about it in the light of these questions and perhaps others that came to mind, he produced the following notes:

> Two stanzas, each of three lines, with the same structure
> Basic structure of first stanza: When X (one line), then Y (two lines)
> Basic structure of second stanza: Next (one line), then Z (two lines)

When he marked the text, after reading the poem a few times, Stan noticed that the last line—an exclamation of delight ("O, how that glittering taketh me")—is much more personal than the rest of the poem. A little further thought enabled him to refine this last perception:

> Although the pattern of stanzas is repeated, the somewhat analytic, detached tone of the beginning ("Whenas," "Then," "Next") changes to an open, enthusiastic confession of delight in what the poet sees.

Further thinking led to this:

> Although the title is "Upon Julia's Clothes," and the first five lines describe Julia's silken dress, the poem finally is not only about Julia's clothing but about the effect of Julia (moving in silk that liquefies or seems to become a liquid) on the poet.

This is a nice observation, but when Stan looked again at the poem the next day, and started to write about it, he found that he was able to refine his observation.

> Even at the beginning, the speaker is not entirely detached, for he speaks of "<u>my</u> Julia."

In writing about Herrick's "Upon Julia's Clothes," Stan tells us, the thoughts did not come quickly or neatly. After two or three thoughts, he started to write. Only after drafting a paragraph, and rereading the poem, did he notice that the personal element appears not only in the last line ("taketh *me*") but even in the first line ("*my* Julia"). In short, for almost all of us, the only way to get to a good final essay is to read, to think, to jot down ideas, to write a draft, and to revise and revise again. Having gone through such processes, Stan came up with the following excellent essay.

By the way, Stan did not hit on the final version of his title ("Herrick's Julia, Julia's Herrick") until shortly before he typed his final version. His preliminary title was

Structure and Personality in
Herrick's "Upon Julia's Clothing"

That's a bit heavy-handed but at least it is focused, as opposed to such an uninformative title as "On a Poem." He soon revised his tentative title to

Julia, Julia's Clothing, and Julia's Poet

That's quite a good title: It is neat, and it is appropriate, since it moves (as the poem and the essay do) from Julia and her clothing to the poet. Of course it doesn't tell the reader exactly what the essay will be about, but it does stimulate the reader's interest. The essayist's final title, however, is even better:

Herrick's Julia, Julia's Herrick

Again, it is neat (the balanced structure, and structure is part of the student's topic), and it moves (as the poem itself moves) from Julia to the poet.

Stan Wiley

Professor Lloyd

English 112

19 April 2004

Herrick's Julia, Julia's Herrick

Robert Herrick's "Upon Julia's Clothes" begins as a

description of Julia's clothing and ends as an expression of the

poet's response not just to Julia's clothing but to Julia herself.

Despite the apparently objective or detached tone of the first

stanza and the first two lines of the second stanza, the poem

finally conveys a strong sense of the speaker's excitement.

The first stanza seems to say, "Whenas" X (one line), "Then" Y

(two lines). The second stanza repeats this basic structure of one

line of assertion and two lines describing the consequence: "Next"

(one line), "then" (two lines). But the logic or coolness of

"Whenas," "Then," and "Next," and of such rather scientific

language as "liquefaction" (a more technical-sounding word than

"melting") and "vibration," is undercut by the breathlessness or

excitement of "Then, then" (that is very different from a simple

"Then"). It is also worth mentioning that although there is a

personal rather than a fully detached note even in the first line,

in "my Julia," this expression scarcely reveals much feeling. In

fact, it reveals a touch of male chauvinism, a suggestion that the

woman is a possession of the speaker's. Not until the last line

does the speaker reveal that, far from Julia being his possession,

he is possessed by Julia: "O, how that glittering taketh me." If he

> Wiley 2
>
> begins coolly, objectively, and somewhat complacently, and uses a
>
> structure that suggests a somewhat detached mind, in the
>
> exclamatory "O" he nevertheless at last confesses (to our delight)
>
> that he is enraptured by Julia.

The Analysis Analyzed

Other things, of course, might be said about this poem. For instance, the writer says nothing about the changes in the basic iambic meter and their contributions to the poem. We have in mind not so much the trochees (a trochee is a metrical foot with a stressed syllable followed by an unstressed one) at the beginning of some lines, which is a fairly routine variation, but the spondees (two consecutive stresses) in "Then, then" and "O, how" and the almost-spondees in "Next, when," "each way free," and "that glittering." Also of interest are the two run-on lines (line 2 runs into 3, and 4 runs into 5) introducing related expressions, "That lique-faction" and "that brave vibration."

He also doesn't comment on the *s* and *z* sounds (*Whenas, silk, goes, thinks, sweetly flows*), which presumably imitate the sound of a silk gown in motion, a sound that can be said to resemble the sound of liquid, hence *liquefaction—* though the dress in motion also visually resembles flowing liquid. But the present essay seems excellent to us, and the neglected topics—sound effects in the poem—might be material for another essay.

CHRISTINA ROSSETTI (1830–1894)

In an Artist's Studio

One face looks out from all his canvases,
    One selfsame figure sits or walks or leans:
    We found her hidden just behind those screens,
That mirror gave back all her loveliness.   4
A queen in opal or in ruby dress,
    A nameless girl in freshest summer-greens
    A saint, an angel—every canvas means
The same one meaning, neither more nor less.   8
He feeds upon her face by day and night,
    And she with true kind eyes looks back on him,
Fair as the moon and joyful as the light:
    Not wan with waiting, not with sorrow dim;   12
Not as she is, but was when hope shone bright;
    Not as she is, but as she fills his dream.

[1856]

This poem is a sonnet. We discuss the form later, on page 502, but if you study the rhymes here you will notice that the first eight lines are united by rhymes, and the next six by different rhymes. A reader might, for a start at least, think about whether what is said has any relation to these units. The first eight lines are about the model, but are the next six equally about her or about someone else?

Topics for Critical Thinking

1. What do we know about the model in the first eight lines? What do we know about her in the last two lines?
2. How are the contrasts (between then and now, between model and painter) communicated by the repetition of "Not as she is," in lines 13 and 14?

EXPLICATION

As we said in Chapter 3, a line-by-line commentary on what is going on in a text is an explication (literally, unfolding, or spreading out). Although your explication will for the most part move steadily from the beginning to the end of the selection, try to avoid writing along these lines (or, we might say, along this one line): "In the first line. . . . In the second line. . . . In the third line. . . ." That is, don't hesitate to write such things as

> The poem begins. . . . In the next line. . . . The speaker immediately adds. . . .
> He then introduces. . . . The next stanza begins by complicating the tone. . . .

And of course you can discuss the second line before the first if that seems the best way of handling the passage.

An explication is not a paraphrase (a rewording, a sort of translation)—though it may include paraphrase if a passage in the original seems unclear, perhaps because of an unusual word or an unfamiliar expression. On the whole, however, an explication goes beyond paraphrase, seeking to make explicit what the reader perceives as implicit in the work. It is chiefly concerned with

- Connotations of words—for instance, "look" versus "behold"
- Implications of syntax—for instance, whether it is notably complex (thereby implying one sort of speaker) or notably simple (implying a very different sort of speaker)
- Implications of rhyme—for instance, the implied connection in meaning between "throne" and "alone"
- Patterns of imagery—for instance, commercial imagery in a love poem

As we said in Chapters 3 and 4, explication and analysis are not clearly distinct from each other; it is reasonable to think of explication as a kind of analysis operating on the level of verbal details.

An Example

Take this short poem (published in 1917) by the Irish poet William Butler Yeats. The "balloon" in the poem is a dirigible, a blimp.

WILLIAM BUTLER YEATS (1865–1939)

The Balloon of the Mind

Hands, do what you're bid:
Bring the balloon of the mind
That bellies and drags in the wind
Into its narrow shed.

[1917]

Annotations and Journal Entries

A student, Tina Washington, began thinking about the poem by copying it, double-spaced. Then she jotted down her first thoughts:

sounds abrupt

Hands, do what you're bid: *--balloon imagined by the mind? Or a mind like a balloon?*

Bring the balloon of the mind

That bellies and drags in the wind   *no real rhymes?*

Into its narrow shed.   *line seems to drag-- it's so long!*

Later she wrote some notes in a journal:

> I'm still puzzled about the meaning of the words "The balloon of the mind." Does "balloon of the mind" mean a balloon that belongs to the mind, sort of like "a disease of the heart"? If so, it means a balloon that the mind <u>has</u>, a balloon that the mind possesses, I guess by imagining it. Or does it mean that the mind is <u>like</u> a balloon, as when you say "he's a pig of a man," meaning he is like a pig, he is a pig? Can it mean both? What's a balloon that the mind imagines? Something like dreams of fame, wealth? Castles in Spain.
>
> Is Yeats saying that the "hands" have to work hard to make dreams a reality? Maybe. But maybe the idea really is that the mind is <u>like</u> a balloon-- hard to keep under control, floating around. Very hard to keep the mind on the job. If the mind is like a balloon, it's hard to get it into the hangar (shed).
>
> "Bellies." Is there such a verb? In this poem it seems to mean something like "puffs out" or "flops around in the wind." Just checked <u>The American Heritage Dictionary</u>, and it says "belly" can be a verb, "to swell out," "to bulge." Well, you learn something every day.

A later entry:

> OK; I think the poem is about a writer trying to keep his balloon-like mind from floating around, trying to keep the mind under control, trying to keep it working at the job of writing something, maybe writing something with the "clarity, unity, and coherence" I keep hearing about in this course.

A Sample Essay by a Student: Explication of W. B. Yeats's "The Balloon of the Mind"

Here is Tina Washington's final version of the explication:

Tina Washington

Professor Chase

English 102

2 November 2004

Explication of W. B. Yeats's "The Balloon of the Mind"

Yeats's "Balloon of the Mind" is about writing poetry,

specifically about the difficulty of getting one's floating thoughts

down in lines on the page. The first line, a short, stern, heavily

stressed command to the speaker's hands, perhaps implies by its

severe or impatient tone that these hands will be disobedient or

inept or careless if not watched closely: the poor bumbling body

so often fails to achieve the goals of the mind. The bluntness of

the command in the first line is emphasized by the fact that all

the subsequent lines have more syllables. Furthermore, the first

line is a grammatically complete sentence, whereas the thought

of line 2 spills over into the next lines, implying the difficulty of

fitting ideas into confining spaces, that is, of getting one's

thoughts into order, especially into a coherent poem.

Lines 2 and 3 amplify the metaphor already stated in the title

(the product of the mind is an airy but unwieldy balloon), and

they also contain a second command, "Bring." Alliteration ties this command, "Bring," to the earlier "bid"; it also ties both of

these verbs to their object, "balloon," and to the verb that most

effectively describes the balloon, "bellies." In comparison with the

abrupt first line of the poem, lines 2 and 3 themselves seem

almost swollen, bellying and dragging, an effect aided by using

adjacent unstressed syllables ("of the," "[bell]ies and," "in the") and

by using an eye rhyme ("mind" and "wind") rather than an exact

rhyme. And then comes the short last line: almost before we

could expect it, the cumbersome balloon--here, the idea that is to

be packed into the stanza--is successfully lodged in its "narrow

shed." Aside from the relatively colorless "into," the only words of

more than one syllable in the poem are "balloon," "bellies," and

"narrow," and all three emphasize the difficulty of the task. But

after "narrow"--the word itself almost looks long and narrow, in

this context like a hangar--we get the simplicity of the

monosyllable "shed." The difficult job is done, the thought is

safely packed away, the poem is completed--but again with an off-

rhyme ("bid" and "shed"), for neatness can go only so far when

hands and mind and a balloon are involved.

Note: The reader of an explication needs to see the text, and because the explicated text is usually short, it is advisable to quote it all. (Remember, your imagined audience probably consists of your classmates; even if they have already read the work you are explicating, they have not memorized it, and so you helpfully remind them of the work by quoting it.) You can quote the entire text at the outset, or you can quote the first unit (for example, a stanza), then explicate that unit, and then quote the next unit, and so on. And if the poem or passage of prose is longer than, say, six lines, it is advisable to number each line at the right for easy reference.

✔ CHECKLIST: *Explication*

On page 54 we provided an Explication Checklist. We include it again here, for convenience.

Overall Considerations

❏ Does the poem imply a story of some sort, for instance the speaker's report of a love affair, or of a response to nature? If so, what is its beginning, middle, and end?
❏ If you detect a story in the speaker's mind, a change of mood—for instance, a shift from bitterness that a love affair has ended to hope for its renewal—is this change communicated in part by the connotations of certain words? By syntax? By metrical shifts?

Detailed Considerations

❏ If the poem has a title other than the first line, what are the implications of the title?
❏ Are there clusters or patterns of imagery, for instance religious images, economic images, or images drawn from nature? If so, how do they contribute to the meaning of the poem?
❏ Is irony (understatement or overstatement) used? To what effect?
❏ How do the connotations of certain words (for instance, "dad" rather than "father") help to establish the meaning?
❏ What are the implications of the syntax—for instance, of notably simple or notably complex sentences? What do such sentences tell us about the speaker?
❏ Do metrical variations occur, and if so, what is their significance?
❏ Do rhyming words have some meaningful connection, as in the clichés "moon" and "June," "dove" and "love"?
❏ What are the implications of the appearance of the poem on the page—for example, of an indented line, or of the stanzaic pattern? (For instance, if the poem consists of two stanzas of four lines each, does the second stanza offer a reversal of the first?)

RHYTHM AND VERSIFICATION: A GLOSSARY FOR REFERENCE

Rhythm (most simply, in English poetry, stresses at regular intervals) has a power of its own. A highly pronounced rhythm is common in such forms of poetry as charms, college yells, and lullabies; all of them are aimed at inducing a special effect magically. It is not surprising that *carmen*, the Latin word for poem or song, is also the Latin word for *charm* and the word from which our word *charm* is derived.

In much poetry, rhythm is only half heard, but its presence is suggested by the way poetry is printed. Prose (from Latin *prorsus*, "forward," "straight on") keeps running across the paper until the right-hand margin is reached; then, merely because the paper has given out, the writer or printer starts again at the left, with a small letter. But verse (Latin *versus*, "a turning") often ends well short of the right-hand margin. The next line begins at the left—usually with a capital—

not because paper has run out but because the rhythmic pattern begins again. Lines of poetry are continually reminding us that they have a pattern.

Note that a mechanical, unvarying rhythm may be good to put the baby to sleep, but it can be deadly to readers who want to stay awake. Poets vary their rhythm according to their purposes; they ought not to be so regular that they are (in W. H. Auden's words) "accentual pests." In competent hands, rhythm contributes to meaning; it says something. Ezra Pound had a relevant comment: "Rhythm *must* have meaning. It can't be merely a careless dash off, with no grip and no real hold to the words and sense, a tumty tum tumty tum tum ta."

Consider this description of Hell from John Milton's *Paradise Lost* (stressed syllables are marked by ´, unstressed syllables by ˘:

Rócks, cáves, lákes, féns, bógs, déns, ańd shádes ŏf déath.

The normal line in *Paradise Lost* is written in iambic feet—alternate unstressed and stressed syllables—but in this line Milton immediately follows one heavy stress with another, helping to communicate the "meaning"—the oppressive monotony of Hell. As a second example, consider the function of the rhythm in two lines by Alexander Pope:

Wĥen Ájăx stríves some róck's vást wéight ĭo thrów,
Tĥe líne tóo lábŏrs, ańd tĥe wórds móve slów.

The stressed syllables do not merely alternate with the unstressed ones; rather the great weight of the rock is suggested by three consecutive stressed words, "rock's vast weight," and the great effort involved in moving it is suggested by another three consecutive stresses, "line too labors," and by yet another three, "words move slow." Note also the abundant pauses within the lines. In the first line, for example, unless one's speech is slovenly, one must pause at least slightly after "Ajax," "strives," "rock's," "vast," "weight," and "throw." The grating sounds in "Ajax" and "rock's" do their work, too, and so do the explosive *t*'s.

When Pope wishes to suggest lightness, he reverses his procedure, and he groups *un*stressed syllables:

Not so, when swift Camilla scours the plain,
Fliés o'ĕr th' ŭnbéndĭng córn, ańd skíms ălŏng tĥe máin.

This last line has twelve syllables and is thus longer than the line about Ajax, but the addition of *along* helps to communicate lightness and swiftness because in this line (it can be argued) neither syllable of *along* is strongly stressed. If *along* is omitted, the line still makes grammatical sense and becomes more "regular," but it also becomes less imitative of lightness.

The very regularity of a line may be meaningful too. Shakespeare begins a sonnet thus:

Wĥen Í đo cóunt tĥe clóck tĥat télls tĥe tíme.

This line about a mechanism runs with appropriate regularity. (It is worth noting, too, that "*c*ount the *c*lock" and "*t*ells the *t*ime" emphasize the regularity by the repetition of sounds and syntax.) But notice what Shakespeare does in the middle of the next line:

Ańd sée tĥe bráve dáy súnk ĭn hídeŏus níght.

The technical vocabulary of **prosody** (the study of the principles of verse structure, including meter, rhyme and other sound effects, and stanzaic patterns) is large. An understanding of these terms will not turn anyone into a poet, but it will enable you to write about some aspects of poetry more efficiently. The following are the chief terms of prosody.

Meter

Most poetry written in English has a pattern of stressed (accented) sounds. This pattern is the **meter** (from the Greek word for "measure"). Strictly speaking, we really should not talk of "unstressed" or "unaccented" syllables, since to utter a syllable—however lightly—is to give it some stress. It is really a matter of *relative* stress, but the fact is that "unstressed" or "unaccented" are parts of the established terminology of versification.

In a line of poetry, the **foot** is the basic unit of measurement. It is on rare occasions a single stressed syllable; but generally a foot consists of two or three syllables, one of which is stressed. The repetition of feet, then, produces a pattern of stresses throughout the poem.

Two cautions:

- A poem will seldom contain only one kind of foot throughout; significant variations usually occur, but one kind of foot is dominant.
- In reading a poem, one chiefly pays attention to the sense, not to presupposed metrical pattern. By paying attention to the sense, one often finds (reading aloud is a great help) that the stress falls on a word that according to the metrical pattern would be unstressed. Or a word that according to the pattern would be stressed may be seen to be unstressed. Furthermore, by reading for sense one finds that not all stresses are equally heavy; some are almost as light as unstressed syllables, and sometimes there is a **hovering stress**—that is, the stress is equally distributed over two adjacent syllables. To repeat: One reads for sense, allowing the syntax to help indicate the stresses.

METRICAL FEET   The most common feet in English poetry are the six listed here. **Iamb** (adjective: **iambic**): one unstressed syllable followed by one stressed syllable. The iamb, said to be the most common pattern in English speech, is surely the most common in English poetry. The following example has four iambic feet:

My héart ĭs líke ă síngĭng bírd.

—Christina Rossetti

Trochee (trochaic): one stressed syllable followed by one unstressed.

Wé wĕre vérȳ tírĕd, wé wĕre vérȳ mérrȳ

—Edna St. Vincent Millay

Anapest (anapestic): two unstressed syllables followed by one stressed.

Thĕre ăre mánȳ whŏ sáy thăt ă dóg hăs hĭs dáy.

—Dylan Thomas

Dactyl (dactylic): one stressed syllable followed by two unstressed. This trisyllabic foot, like the anapest, is common in light verse or verse suggesting joy, but its use is not limited to such material, as Longfellow's *Evangeline* shows. Thomas Hood's sentimental "The Bridge of Sighs" begins

Tăke hĕr ŭp ténderl̆y.

Spondee (spondaic): two stressed syllables; most often used as a substitute for an iamb or trochee.

Smárt lád, t̆o sl̆ip bĕtímes ăwáy.

—A. E. Housman

Pyrrhic: two unstressed syllables; it is often not considered a legitimate foot in English.

METRICAL LINES   A metrical line consists of one or more feet and is named for the number of feet in it. The following names are used:

monometer: one foot	**pentameter**: five feet
dimeter: two feet	**hexameter**: six feet
trimeter: three feet	**heptameter**: seven feet
tetrameter: four feet	

A line is scanned for the kind and number of feet in it, and the **scansion** tells you if it is, say, anapestic trimeter (three anapests):

Ăs Ĭ cáme t̆o th̆e édge ŏf th̆e wóods.

—Robert Frost

Or, in another example, iambic pentameter:

Th̆e súmm̆er thúnd̆er, l̆íke ă wóod̆en bĕll

—Louise Bogan

A line ending with a stress has a **masculine ending**; a line ending with an extra un-stressed syllable has a **feminine ending**. The **caesura** (usually indicated by the symbol / /) is a slight pause within the line. It need not be indicated by punctuation (notice the fourth and fifth lines in the following quotation), and it does not affect the metrical count:

Awake, my St. John! / / leave all meaner things
To low ambition, / / and the pride of kings.
Let us / / (since Life can little more supply
Than just to look about us / / and to die)
Expatiate free / / o'er all this scene of Man;
A mighty maze! / / but not without a plan;
A wild, / / where weeds and flowers promiscuous shoot;
Or garden, / / tempting with forbidden fruit.

—Alexander Pope

The varying position of the caesura helps to give Pope's lines an informality that plays against the formality of the pairs of rhyming lines.

    An **end-stopped line** concludes with a distinct syntactical pause, but a **run-on line** has its sense carried over into the next line without syntactical pause. (The running-on of a line is called **enjambment**.) In the following passage, only the first is a run-on line:

> Yet if we look more closely we shall find
> Most have the seeds of judgment in their mind:
> Nature affords at least a glimmering light;
> The lines, though touched but faintly, are drawn right.
>
> —Alexander Pope

Meter produces **rhythm**, recurrences at equal intervals, but rhythm (from a Greek word meaning "flow") is usually applied to larger units than feet. Often it depends most obviously on pauses. Thus, a poem with run-on lines will have a different rhythm from a poem with end-stopped lines, even though both are in the same meter. And prose, though it is unmetrical, can have rhythm, too.

In addition to being affected by syntactical pause, rhythm is affected by pauses attributable to consonant clusters and to the length of words. Polysyllabic words establish a different rhythm from monosyllabic words, even in metrically identical lines. We can say, then, that rhythm is altered by shifts in meter, syntax, and the length and ease of pronunciation. But even with no such shift, even if a line is repeated verbatim, a reader may sense a change in rhythm. The rhythm of the final line of a poem, for example, may well differ from that of the line before, even though in all other respects the lines are identical, as in Frost's "Stopping by Woods on a Snowy Evening" (p. 588), which concludes by repeating "And miles to go before I sleep." The reader may simply sense that this final line ought to be spoken, say, more slowly and with more stress on "miles."

Patterns of Sound

Though rhythm is basic to poetry, **rhyme**—the repetition of identical or similar stressed sound or sounds—is not. Rhyme is, presumably, pleasant in itself; it suggests order; and it also may be related to meaning, for it brings two words sharply together, often implying a relationship, as in the now trite *dove* and *love*, or in the more imaginative *throne* and *alone*.

Perfect rhyme (or **exact rhyme**): Differing consonant sounds are followed by identical stressed vowel sounds, and the following sounds, if any, are identical (*foe—toe; meet—fleet; buffer—rougher*). Notice that perfect rhyme involves identity of sound, not of spelling. *Fix* and *sticks,* like *buffer* and *rougher,* are perfect rhymes.

Half-rhyme (or **off-rhyme**): Only the final consonant sounds of the words are identical; the stressed vowel sounds as well as the initial consonant sounds, if any, differ (*soul—oil; mirth—forth; trolley—bully*).

Eye rhyme: The sounds do not in fact rhyme, but the words look as though they would rhyme (*cough—bough*).

Masculine rhyme: The final syllables are stressed and, after their differing initial consonant sounds, are identical in sound (*stark—mark; support—retort*).

Feminine rhyme (or **double rhyme**): Stressed rhyming syllables are followed by identical unstressed syllables (*revival—arrival; flatter—batter*). **Triple rhyme** is a kind of feminine rhyme in which identical stressed vowel sounds are followed by two identical unstressed syllables (*machinery—scenery; tenderly—slenderly*).

End rhyme (or **terminal rhyme**): The rhyming words occur at the ends of the lines.

Internal rhyme: At least one of the rhyming words occurs within the line (Oscar Wilde's "Each narrow *cell* in which we *dwell*").

Alliteration: sometimes defined as the repetition of initial sounds ("*A*ll the *a*wful *a*uguries," or "*B*ring me my *b*ow of *b*urning gold"), and sometimes as the prominent repetition of a consonant ("a*f*ter li*f*e's *f*it*f*ul *f*ever").

Assonance: the repetition, in words of proximity, of identical vowel sounds preceded and followed by differing consonant sounds. Whereas *tide* and *hide* are rhymes, *tide* and *mine* are assonantal.

Consonance: the repetition of identical consonant sounds and differing vowel sounds in words in proximity (*fail—feel; rough—roof; pitter—patter*). Sometimes consonance is more loosely defined merely as the repetition of a consonant (*fail—peel*).

Onomatopoeia: the use of words that imitate sounds, such as *hiss* and *buzz*. There is a mistaken tendency to see onomatopoeia everywhere—for example, in *thunder* and *horror*. Many words sometimes thought to be onomatopoeic are not clearly imitative of the thing they refer to; they merely contain some sounds that, when we know what the word means, seem to have some resemblance to the thing they denote. Tennyson's lines from "Come down, O maid" are usually cited as an example of onomatopoeia:

> The moan of doves in immemorial elms
> And murmuring of innumerable bees.

Stanzaic Patterns

Lines of poetry are commonly arranged in a rhythmical unit called a stanza (from an Italian word meaning "room" or "stopping-place"). Usually all the stanzas in a poem have the same rhyme pattern. A stanza is sometimes called a **verse**, though *verse* may also mean a single line of poetry. (In discussing stanzas, rhymes are indicated by identical letters. Thus, *abab* indicates that the first and third lines rhyme with each other, while the second and fourth lines are linked by a different rhyme. An unrhymed line is denoted by *x*.) Common stanzaic forms in English poetry are the following:

Couplet: a stanza of two lines, usually, but not necessarily, with end-rhymes. *Couplet* is also used for a pair of rhyming lines. The **octosyllabic couplet** is iambic or trochaic tetrameter:

> Had we but world enough, and time,
> This coyness, lady, were no crime.
>
> —Andrew Marvell

Heroic couplet: a rhyming couplet of iambic pentameter, often "closed," that is, containing a complete thought, with a fairly heavy pause at the end of the first line and a still heavier one at the end of the second. Commonly, there is a parallel or an *antithesis* (contrast) within a line or between the two lines. It is called heroic because in England, especially in the eighteenth century, it was much used for heroic (epic) poems.

> Some foreign writers, some our own despise;
> The ancients only, or the moderns, prize.
>
> —Alexander Pope

Triplet (or **tercet**): a three-line stanza, usually with one rhyme:

> Whenas in silks my Julia goes
> Then, then (methinks) how sweetly flows
> That liquefaction of her clothes.

> —Robert Herrick

Quatrain: a four-line stanza, rhymed or unrhymed. The **heroic** (or **elegiac**) **quatrain** is iambic pentameter, rhyming *abab*. That is, the first and third lines rhyme (so they are designated *a*), and the second and fourth lines rhyme (so they are designated *b*).

Sonnet: a fourteen-line poem, predominantly in iambic pentameter. The rhyme is usually according to one of two schemes. The **Italian** (or **Petrarchan**[1] **sonnet** has two divisions: The first eight lines (rhyming *abba abba*) are the **octave**, and the last six (rhyming *cd cd cd*, or a variant) are the **sestet** (p. 597). The second kind of sonnet, the **English** (or **Shakespearean**) **sonnet**, is usually arranged into three quatrains and a couplet, rhyming *abab cdcd efef gg*. (For examples see pages 56, 476, and 482.) In many sonnets there is a marked correspondence between the rhyme scheme and the development of the thought. Thus an Italian sonnet may state a generalization in the octave and a specific example in the sestet. Or an English sonnet may give three examples—one in each quatrain—and draw a conclusion in the couplet.

BILLY COLLINS

Born in New York City in 1941, Collins is a professor of English at Lehman College of the City University of New York. He is the author of six books of poetry and the recipient of numerous awards, including one from the National Endowment for the Arts. Collins's Sailing Alone Around the Room: New and Selected Poems *was published in 2001; in the same year, he was appointed poet laureate of the United States.*

The following sonnet uses the Petrarchan form, of an octave and a sestet. Petrarch is additionally present in the poem by the allusion in line 3 to "a little ship on love's storm-tossed seas," because Petrarch compared the hapless lover, denied the favor of his mistress, to a ship in a storm: The lover cannot guide his ship because the North Star is hidden (Petrarch's beloved Laura averts her eyes), and the sails of the ship are agitated by the lover's pitiful sighs. As you will see, Petrarch and Laura explicitly enter the poem in the last three lines.

In line 8 Collins refers to the stations of the cross. In Roman Catholicism, one of the devotions consists of prayers and meditations before each of fourteen crosses or images set up along a path that commemorates the fourteen places at which Jesus halted when, just before the Crucifixion, he was making his way in Jerusalem to Golgotha.

Sonnet

All we need is fourteen lines, well, thirteen now,
and after this next one just a dozen
to launch a little ship on love's storm-tossed seas,

---

[1]So called after Francesco Petrarch (1304–1374), the Italian poet who perfected and popularized the form.

then only ten more left like rows of beans.   4
How easily it goes unless you get Elizabethan
and insist the iambic bongos must be played
and rhymes positioned at the ends of lines,
one for every station of the cross.   8
But hang on here while we make the turn
into the final six where all will be resolved,
where longing and heartache will find an end,
where Laura will tell Petrarch to put down his pen,   12
take off those crazy medieval tights,
blow out the lights, and come at last to bed.

[1999]

Topics for Critical Thinking and Writing

1. The headnote explains the stations of the cross (line 8), but what is the point of introducing this image into a sonnet?
2. Normally the "turn" (*volta*) in an Italian sonnet occurs at the beginning of the ninth line; the first eight lines (the octave) establish some sort of problem, and the final six lines (the sestet) respond, for instance by answering a question, or by introducing a contrasting emotion. In your view, how satisfactorily does Collins handle this form?

Blank Verse and Free Verse

A good deal of English poetry is unrhymed, much of it in **blank verse**, that is, unrhymed iambic pentameter. Introduced into English poetry by Henry Howard, Earl of Surrey, in the middle of the sixteenth century, late in the century it became the standard medium (especially in the hands of Christopher Marlowe and Shakespeare) of English drama. In the seventeenth century, Milton used blank verse for *Paradise Lost,* and it has continued to be used in both dramatic and non-dramatic literature. For an example, see the first scene of *Hamlet* (p. 932), until the Ghost appears.

The second kind of unrhymed poetry fairly common in English, especially in the twentieth century, is **free verse** (or **vers libre**): rhythmical lines varying in length, adhering to no fixed metrical pattern and usually unrhymed. The pattern is often largely based on repetition and parallel grammatical structure. For an example, see T. S. Eliot's "The Love Song of J. Alfred Prufrock" (p. 601).

✔ CHECKLIST: *Getting Ideas for Writing about Poetry*

If you are going to write about a fairly short poem (say, under thirty lines), it's not a bad idea to copy out the poem, writing or typing it double-spaced. By writing it out you will be forced to notice details, down to the punctuation. After you have copied the poem, proofread it carefully against the original. Catching an error—even the addition or omission of a comma—may help you to notice a detail in the original that you might otherwise have overlooked. And of course, now that you have the poem with ample space between the lines, you have a worksheet with room for jottings.

A good essay is based on a genuine response to a poem; a response may be stimulated in part by first reading the poem aloud and then considering the following questions.

First Response

❑ What was your response to the poem on first reading? Did some parts especially please or displease you, or puzzle you? After some study—perhaps checking the meanings of some of the words in a dictionary and reading the poem several times—did you modify your initial response to the parts and to the whole?

Speaker and Tone

❑ Who is the speaker? (Consider age, sex, personality, frame of mind, and tone of voice.) Is the speaker defined fairly precisely (for instance, an older woman speaking to a child), or is the speaker simply a voice meditating? (Jot down your first impressions, then reread the poem and make further jottings, if necessary.)
❑ Do you think the speaker is fully aware of what he or she is saying, or does the speaker unconsciously reveal his or her personality and values? What is your attitude toward this speaker?
❑ Is the speaker narrating or reflecting on an earlier experience or attitude? If so, does he or she convey a sense of new awareness, such as of regret for innocence lost?

Audience

❑ To whom is the speaker speaking? What is the situation (including time and place)? (In some poems, a listener is strongly implied, but in others, especially those in which the speaker is meditating, there may be no audience other than the reader, who "overhears" the speaker.)

Structure and Form

❑ Does the poem proceed in a straightforward way, or at some point or points does the speaker reverse course, altering his or her tone or perception? If there is a shift, what do you make of it?
❑ Is the poem organized into sections? If so, what are these sections—stanzas, for instance—and how does each section (characterized, perhaps, by a certain tone of voice, or a group of rhymes) grow out of what precedes it?
❑ What is the effect on you of the form—say, quatrains (stanzas of four lines) or blank verse (unrhymed lines of ten syllables)? If the sense overflows the form, running without pause from (for example) one quatrain into the next, what effect is created?

Center of Interest and Theme

❑ What is the poem about? Is the interest chiefly in a distinctive character, or in meditation? That is, is the poem chiefly psychological or chiefly philosophical?
❑ Is the theme stated explicitly (directly) or implicitly? How might you state the theme in a sentence?

Diction

❑ Do certain words have rich and relevant associations that relate to other words and help to define the speaker or the theme or both?
❑ What is the role of figurative language, if any? Does it help to define the speaker or the theme?
❑ What do you think is to be taken figuratively or symbolically, and what literally?

Sound Effects

❑ What is the role of sound effects, including repetitions of sound (for instance, alliteration) and of entire words, and shifts in versification?
❑ If there are off-rhymes (for instance "dizzy" and "easy," or "home" and "come"), what effect do they have on you? Do they, for instance, add a note of tentativeness or uncertainty?
❑ If there are unexpected stresses or pauses, what do they communicate about the speaker's experience? How do they affect you?

YOUR TURN: POEMS ABOUT PEOPLE, PLACES, AND THINGS
People

ROBERT BROWNING

Born in a suburb of London into a middle-class family, Browning (1812–1889) was educated primarily at home, where he read widely. For a while he wrote for the stage, and in 1846 he married Elizabeth Barrett—herself a poet—and lived with her in Italy until her death in 1861. He then returned to England and settled in London with their son. Regarded as one of the most distinguished poets of the Victorian period, he is buried in Westminster Abbey.

My Last Duchess

Ferrara*

That's my last Duchess painted on the wall,
Looking as if she were alive. I call
That piece a wonder, now; Frà Pandolf's° hands
Worked busily a day, and there she stands.
Will't please you sit and look at her? I said   5
"Frà Pandolf" by design, for never read
Strangers like you that pictured countenance,
The depth and passion of its earnest glance,
But to myself they turned (since none puts by
The curtain I have drawn for you, but I)   10

---

* **Ferrara** town in Italy.   **3 Frà Pandolf** a fictitious painter.

And seemed as they would ask me, if they durst,
How such a glance came there; so, not the first
Are you to turn and ask thus. Sir, 'twas not
Her husband's presence only, called that spot
Of joy into the Duchess' cheek; perhaps   15
Frà Pandolf chanced to say "Her mantle laps
Over my lady's wrist too much," or, "Paint
Must never hope to reproduce the faint
Half-flush that dies along her throat." Such stuff
Was courtesy, she thought, and cause enough   20
For calling up that spot of joy. She had
A heart—how shall I say?—too soon made glad,
Too easily impressed; she liked whate'er
She looked on, and her looks went everywhere.
Sir, 'twas all one! My favor at her breast,   25
The dropping of the daylight in the west,
The bough of cherries some officious fool
Broke in the orchard for her, the white mule
She rode with round the terrace—all and each
Would draw from her alike the approving speech,   30
Or blush, at least. She thanked men—good! but thanked
Somehow—I know not how—as if she ranked
My gift of a nine-hundred-years-old name
With anybody's gift. Who'd stoop to blame
This sort of trifling? Even had you skill   35
In speech—(which I have not)—to make your will
Quite clear to such an one, and say, "Just this
Or that in you disgusts me; here you miss,
Or there exceed the mark"—and if she let
Herself be lessoned so, nor plainly set   40
Her wits to yours, forsooth, and made excuse,
—E'en then would be some stooping; and I choose
Never to stoop. Oh, Sir, she smiled, no doubt,
Whene'er I passed her; but who passed without
Much the same smile? This grew; I gave commands;   45
Then all smiles stopped together. There she stands
As if alive. Will't please you rise? We'll meet
The company below, then. I repeat,
The Count your master's known munificence
Is ample warrant that no just pretense   50
Of mine for dowry will be disallowed;
Though his fair daughter's self, as I avowed
At starting, is my object. Nay, we'll go
Together down, Sir. Notice Neptune, though,
Taming a sea-horse, thought a rarity,   55
Which Claus of Innsbruck° cast in bronze for me!

[1842]

56 **Claus of Innsbruck** a fictitious sculptor.

Topics for Critical Thinking and Writing

1. Who is speaking to whom? On what occasion?
2. What words or lines especially convey the speaker's arrogance? What is our attitude toward the speaker? Loathing? Fascination? Respect? Explain.
3. The time and place are Renaissance Italy; how do they affect our attitude toward the duke? What would be the effect if the poem were set in the twentieth century?
4. Years after writing this poem, Browning explained that the duke's "commands" (line 45) were "that she should be put to death, or he might have had her shut up in a convent." Should the poem have been more explicit? Does Browning's later uncertainty indicate that the poem is badly thought out? Suppose we did not have Browning's comment on line 45; could the line then mean only that he commanded her to stop smiling and that she obeyed? Explain.
5. Elizabeth Barrett (not yet Mrs. Browning) wrote to Robert Browning that it was not "by the dramatic medium that poets teach most impressively. . . . It is too difficult for the common reader to analyze, and to discern between the vivid and the earnest." She went on, urging him to teach "in the directest and most impressive way, the mask thrown off." What teaching, if any, is in this poem? If there is any teaching here, would it be more impressive if Browning had not used the mask of a Renaissance duke? Explain.
6. You are the envoy, writing to the count, your master, a 500-word report of your interview with the duke. What do you write?
7. You are the envoy, writing to the count, advising—as diplomatically as possible—for or against this marriage. Notice that this exercise, unlike #6, which calls for a *report,* calls for an *argument.*

E. E. CUMMINGS

E. E. Cummings was the pen name of Edwin Estlin Cummings (1894–1962), who grew up in Cambridge, Massachusetts, and was graduated from Harvard, where he became interested in modern literature and art, especially in the movements called Cubism and Futurism. His father, a conservative clergyman and a professor at Harvard, seems to have been baffled by the youth's interests, but Cummings's mother encouraged his artistic activities, including his use of unconventional punctuation and capitalization.

Politically liberal in his youth, Cummings became more conservative after a visit to Russia in 1931, but early and late his work emphasizes individuality and freedom of expression.

anyone lived in a pretty how town

anyone lived in a pretty how town
(with up so floating many bells down)

spring summer autumn winter
he sang his didn't he danced his did.   4

Women and men (both little and small)
cared for anyone not at all
they sowed their isn't they reaped their same
sun moon stars rain   8

children guessed (but only a few
and down they forgot as up they grew
autumn winter spring summer)
that noone loved him more by more   12

when by now and tree by leaf
she laughed his joy she cried his grief
bird by snow and stir by still
anyone's any was all to her   16

someones married their everyones
laughed their cryings and did their dance
(sleep wake hope and then) they
said their nevers they slept their dream   20

stars rain sun moon
(and only the snow can begin to explain
how children are apt to forget to remember
with up so floating many bells down)   24

one day anyone died i guess
(and noone stopped to kiss his face)
busy folk buried them side by side
little by little and was by was   28

all by all and deep by deep
and more by more they dream their sleep
noone and anyone earth by april
wish by spirit and if by yes.   32

Women and men (both dong and ding)
summer autumn winter spring
reaped their sowing and went their came
sun moon stars rain   36

[1940]

Topics for Critical Thinking and Writing

1. Put into normal order (as far as possible) the words of the first two stanzas and then compare your version with Cummings's. What does Cummings gain—or lose?

2. Characterize the "anyone" who "sang his didn't" and "danced his did." In your opinion, how does he differ from the people who "sowed their isn't they reaped their same"?

3. Some readers interpret "anyone died" (line 25) to mean that the child matured and became as dead as the other adults. How might you support or refute this interpretation?

SYLVIA PLATH

Sylvia Plath (1932–1963) was born in Boston, the daughter of German immigrants. While still an undergraduate at Smith College, she published in Seventeen *and* Mademoiselle, *but her years at college, like her later years, were marked by manic-depressive periods. After graduating from college she went to England to study at Cambridge University, where she met the English poet Ted Hughes, whom she married in 1956. The marriage was unsuccessful, and they separated. One day she committed suicide by turning on the kitchen gas.*

Daddy

You do not do, you do not do
Any more, black shoe
In which I have lived like a foot
For thirty years, poor and white,
Barely daring to breathe or Achoo.   5

Daddy, I have had to kill you.
You died before I had time—
Marble-heavy, a bag full of God,
Ghastly statue with one gray toe
Big as a Frisco seal   10

And a head in the freakish Atlantic
Where it pours bean green over blue
In the waters off beautiful Nauset.
I used to pray to recover you.
Ach, du.°   15

In the German tongue, in the Polish town
Scraped flat by the roller
Of wars, wars, wars.
But the name of the town is common.
My Polack friend   20

Says there are a dozen or two.
So I never could tell where you
Put your foot, your root,
I never could talk to you.
The tongue stuck in my jaw.   25

15 Ach, du O, you (German).

It stuck in a barb wire snare.
Ich, ich, ich, ich,°
I could hardly speak.
I thought every German was you.
And the language obscene   30

An engine, an engine
Chuffing me off like a Jew.
A Jew to Dachau, Auschwitz, Belsen.°
I began to talk like a Jew.
I think I may well be a Jew.   35

The snows of the Tyrol, the clear beer of Vienna
Are not very pure or true.
With my gypsy ancestress and my weird luck
And my Taroc pack and my Taroc pack
I may be a bit of a Jew.   40

I have always been scared of you,
With your Luftwaffe,° your gobbledygoo.
And your neat moustache
And your Aryan eye, bright blue,
Panzer-man,° panzer-man, O You—   45

Not God but a swastika
So black no sky could squeak through.
Every woman adores a Fascist,
The boot in the face, the brute
Brute heart of a brute like you.   50

You stand at the blackboard, daddy,
In the picture I have of you,
A cleft in your chin instead of your foot
But no less a devil for that, no not
Any less the black man who   55

Bit my pretty red heart in two.
I was ten when they buried you.
At twenty I tried to die
And get back, back, back to you.
I thought even the bones would do.   60

But they pulled me out of the sack,
And they stuck me together with glue,
And then I knew what to do.
I made a model of you,
A man in black with a Meinkampf° look   65

27 **Ich, ich, ich, ich** I, I, I, I.   33 **Dachau, Auschwitz, Belson** concentration camps.
42 **Luftwaffe** German air force.   45 **Panzer-man** member of a tank crew.   65 **Mein Kampf** *My Struggle* (title of Hitler's autobiography).

And a love of the rack and the screw.
And I said I do, I do.
So daddy, I'm finally through.
The black telephone's off at the root,
The voices just can't worm through.   70

If I've killed one man, I've killed two—
The vampire who said he was you
And drank my blood for a year,
Seven years, if you want to know.
Daddy, you can lie back now.   75

There's a stake in your fat black heart
And the villagers never liked you.
They are dancing and stamping on you.
They always *knew* it was you.
Daddy, daddy, you bastard, I'm through.   80

[1965]

Topics for Critical Thinking and Writing

1. Many readers find in this poem something that reminds them of nursery rhymes. If you are among these readers, specify the resemblance(s).
2. Some critics have called parts of the poem "surrealistic." Check a college dictionary, and then argue in a paragraph or two why the word is or is not appropriate.
3. Is this a poem whose experience a reader can share? Explain.

LOUISE ERDRICH

Louise Erdrich was born in Little Falls, Minnesota, in 1954 and raised in North Dakota; her father (born in Germany) and her mother (French Ojibwe) both worked for the Bureau of Indian Affairs. After graduating from Dartmouth College in 1976, she returned to North Dakota to teach in the Poetry in the Schools Program. In 1979 she received a master's degree in creative writing from Johns Hopkins University. She was married to late author and anthropologist Michael Dorris, a professor of Native American Studies at Dartmouth, and they successfully collaborated on multicultural literature. She now lives in Minneapolis, Minnesota, with her youngest three children. Although Erdrich is most widely known as a novelist, she has also won a reputation as a poet.

Indian Boarding School: The Runaways

Home's the place we head for in our sleep.
Boxcars stumbling north in dreams
don't wait for us. We catch them on the run.
The rails, old lacerations that we love,

shoot parallel across the face and break   5
just under Turtle Mountains.° Riding scars
you can't get lost. Home is the place they cross.
The lame guard strikes a match and makes the dark

less tolerant. We watch through cracks in boards
as the land starts rolling, rolling till it hurts   10
to be here, cold in regulation clothes.
We know the sheriff's waiting at midrun
to take us back. His car is dumb and warm.
The highway doesn't rock, it only hums
like a wing of long insults. The worn-down welts   15
of ancient punishment lead back and forth.

All runaways wear dresses, long green ones,
the color you would think shame was. We scrub
the sidewalks down because it's shameful work.
Our brushes cut the stone in watered arcs   20
and in the soak frail outlines shiver clear
a moment, things us kids pressed on the dark
face before it hardened, pale, remembering
delicate old injuries, the spines of names and leaves.

                                                                        [1984]

6 **Turtle Mountains** mountains in North Dakota and Manitoba.

Topics for Critical Thinking and Writing

1. In line 4 the railroad tracks are called "old lacerations." What is the connection
   between the two?
2. What other imagery of injury do you find in the poem? In lines 20–24, what—
   literally—is "the dark / face" that "hardened, pale"?

ETHERIDGE KNIGHT

*Etheridge Knight, born in Corinth, Mississippi, in 1931, dropped out of school in
the eighth grade. He served in the U.S. Army from 1947 to 1951, but after his discharge became addicted to drugs and soon was involved in a life of crime.
Arrested for robbery in 1960, Knight began to write poetry while in prison, encouraged by the African American poets Dudley Randall, Sonia Sanchez, and
Gwendolyn Brooks. His first book,* Poems from Prison, *was published in 1968 by
Randall's Broadside Press. Knight was a leading figure in the Black Arts movement of the 1960s and 1970s, a form of radical cultural activity (related to the
broader Black Power movement) that promoted "social engagement" as a crucial
feature of literary practice. His* Belly Song and Other Poems *(1973) was one of the
most influential books of the period for African American writers and critics.
Knight died in 1985.*

Malcolm X, June 29, 1963.

The following poem was written a year after the assassination of the charismatic African American militant, writer, and orator Malcolm X (nicknamed "Red"). Born in Omaha, Nebraska, in 1925, Malcolm Little moved to Boston in the early 1940s, and there and in New York City, he was a drug dealer and a thief. He was arrested in 1946 for armed robbery and spent the next six years in prisons in Massachusetts. While still in prison, he became acquainted with the teachings of Elijah Muhammed, the leader of the Nation of Islam, and he embarked upon an intensive program of self-education, especially in history. Upon his release from prison, Malcolm Little changed his name to Malcolm X, the "X" signifying the name, unknown to him, of his African ancestors who had been sold into slavery. He broke with Elijah Muhammed in 1963 and formed a rival organization, the Muslim Mosque, Inc. He then made a pilgrimage to Mecca, converted to orthodox Islam, and, while remaining a militant black nationalist, stated that he was no longer a racial separatist. In the Audubon Ballroom in Harlem, on February 21, 1965, Malcolm X was murdered by members of the Nation of Islam, though controversy still surrounds the conspiracy that led to his death. Malcolm X's writings and speeches are included in his Autobiography *(as told to Alex Haley, 1964) and* Malcolm X Speaks *(1965).*

For Malcolm, a Year After

Compose for Red a proper verse;
Adhere to foot and strict iamb;
Control the burst of angry words
Or they might boil and break the dam.

Or they might boil and overflow   5
And drench me, drown me, drive me mad.
So swear no oath, so shed no tear,
And sing no song blue Baptist sad.
Evoke no image, stir no flame,
And spin no yarn across the air.   10
Make empty anglo tea lace words—
Make them dead and white and dry bone bare.

Compose a verse for Malcolm man,
And make it rime and make it prim.
The verse will die—as all men do—   15
But not the memory of him!
Death might come singing sweet like C,
Or knocking like the old folk say,
The moon and stars may pass away,
But not the anger of that day.   20

[1966]

Topics for Critical Thinking and Writing

1. Knight's poem is both about Malcolm X and about the writing of a poem about him. Why might Knight have wanted to connect the subject of this poem to the act of writing the poem in the first place? Do you think that Knight should have presented a more straightforward tribute?
2. Explain the meaning of line 8. And of line 11. Which line is more effective? Are these lines more or less effective than other lines in the poem?
3. Are the first two lines of the second stanza puzzling? Why the word "prim"?
4. What is the relationship of the fourth line of the second stanza to the final line of the poem?
5. Do you think that Knight's poem remains powerful today? How does a poem keyed to a specific historical event or person retain its power decades after the event or after the person's death? Or is it the case, in your view, that the passing of time always diminishes the impact of a poem like this one?

Places

BASHO

If the name of any Japanese poet is known in the United States, it is probably Matsuo Basho (1644–1694). He lived most of his life in Edo (now called Tokyo), but he enjoyed traveling on foot in Japan and writing about his experiences. His most famous work, The Narrow Road to the Deep North *(1694), is a poetic diary recording one of his extended journeys. (It is available in several English translations.)*

We give here, however, a short poem in the form known as **haiku**. *A haiku has 17 syllables, arranged in 3 lines of 5, 7, and 5 syllables. Japanese poetry is unrhymed, but English versions—which may or may not follow the Japanese syllabic* *pattern—sometimes rhyme the first and third lines, as in the following translation of one of Basho's haiku:*

> On the withered bough
> A crow alone is perching;
> Autumn evening now.

The American poet Richard Wright wrote a number of poems grouped under the title "Hokku" (a variant of haiku), one of which goes thus:

> Keep straight down this block
> Then turn right where you will find
> A peach tree blooming.

The subject matter of a haiku can be high or low—the Milky Way or the screech of automobile brakes—but usually it is connected with the seasons, and it is described objectively and sharply. Here is Basho's most famous haiku. (The translation does not preserve the syllabic count of the original.)

An Old Pond

An old pond;
A frog jumps in—
The sound of the water.

Topic for Writing

Write at least one haiku. You need not use the 5-7-5 system if you don't want to; on the other hand, you may use rhyme if you wish. Some tips:

1. For a start, take some ordinary experience—tying your shoelaces, or seeing a cat at the foot of the stairs, or glancing out a window and seeing unexpected snowflakes, or hearing the alarm clock—and present it interestingly.
2. One way to make the experience interesting is to construct the poem in two parts—the first line balanced against the next two lines, or the first two lines balanced against the last line. If you construct a poem on this principle, the two sections should be related to each other, but they should also in some degree make a contrast with each other. Here is an example: "This handsome rooster / Struts before the clucking hens; / Inside, the pot is boiling." A second example, this one offering a contrast between pleasant sociability (the first two lines) and loneliness: "'Look, O look, there go / Fireflies,' I would like to say— / But I am alone."

THOMAS HARDY

Thomas Hardy (1840–1928) was born in Dorset, England, the son of a stonemason. Despite great obstacles he studied the classics and architecture, and in 1862 he moved to London to study and practice as an architect. Ill health forced him to return to Dorset, where he continued to work as an architect and to write. Best known for his novels, Hardy ceased writing fiction after the hostile reception of Jude the Obscure *in 1896 and turned to writing lyric poetry.*

Neutral Tones

We stood by a pond that winter day,
And the sun was white, as though chidden of God,
And a few leaves lay on the starving sod;
   —They had fallen from an ash, and were gray.   4

Your eyes on me were as eyes that rove
Over tedious riddles of years ago;
And some words played between us to and fro
   On which lost the more by our love.   8

The smile on your mouth was the deadest thing
Alive enough to have strength to die;
And a grin of bitterness swept thereby
   Like an ominous bird a-wing. . . .   12

Since then, keen lessons that love deceives,
And wrings with wrong, have shaped to me
Your face, and the God-cursed sun, and a tree,
   And a pond edged with grayish leaves.   16

[1898]

Topics for Critical Thinking and Writing

1. In a sentence or two, summarize the story implicit in the poem. What has happened between the time of the episode narrated and the time of this utterance?
2. Do you think that the speaker is actually addressing the woman, or is he recollecting her and addressing her image? Or does is matter?
3. Why do you think that "keen lessons that love deceives" always remind the speaker of this scene?
4. Characterize, in a sentence or two, the speaker's state of mind in the first stanza. Is he composed, or agitated? Bitter, or meditative? Or what? Next, characterize his mind as it seems to be revealed in the final stanza.

WILLIAM BUTLER YEATS

William Butler Yeats (1865–1939) was born in Dublin, Ireland. The early Yeats was much interested in highly lyrical, romantic poetry, often drawing on Irish mythology. The later poems, from about 1910 (and especially after Yeats met Ezra Pound in 1911), are often more colloquial. Although these later poems often employ mythological references too—"Leda and the Swan" on page 141 is an example—many believe that the poems are more down-to-earth. Yeats was awarded the Nobel Prize in Literature in 1923.

In the seventh century B.C. *the ancient Greeks founded the city of Byzantium in Thrace, where Istanbul, Turkey, now stands. (Constantine, the first Christian ruler of the Roman Empire, built a new city there in 330* A.D. *Named Constantinople, the city served as the capital of the Roman Empire until 1453, when the Turks captured it. In 1930 the name was officially changed to Istanbul.) The capital of the Roman Empire and the "holy city" of the Greek Orthodox Church, Byzantium had two golden ages. The first, in its early centuries, continued the traditions of the antique Greco-Roman world. The second, which is what Yeats had in mind, extended from the mid-ninth to the mid-thirteenth century and was a distinctive blend of classical, Christian, Slavic, and even Islamic culture. This period is noted for mysticism, for the preservation of ancient learning, and for exquisitely refined symbolic art. In short, Byzantium (as Yeats saw it) was wise and passionless. In* A Vision, *his prose treatment of his complex mystical system, Yeats says:*

> I think that in early Byzantium, maybe never before or since in recorded history, religious, aesthetic and practical life were one, that architect and artificers—though not, it may be, poets, for language has been the instrument of controversy and must have grown abstract— spoke to the multitude and the few alike. The painter, the mosaic worker, the worker in gold and silver, the illuminator of sacred books, were almost impersonal, almost perhaps without the consciousness of individual design, absorbed in their subject matter and that the vision of the whole people. They could copy out of old Gospel books those pictures that seemed as sacred as the text, and yet weave all into a vast design, the work of many that seemed the work of one, that made building, picture, pattern, metal-work of rail and lamp, seem but a single image.

Sailing to Byzantium

I

That is no country for old men. The young
In one another's arms, birds in the trees
—Those dying generations—at their song,
The salmon-falls, the mackerel-crowded seas,
Fish, flesh, or fowl, commend all summer long   5
Whatever is begotten, born, and dies.
Caught in that sensual music all neglect
Monuments of unaging intellect.

II

An aged man is but a paltry thing,
A tattered coat upon a stick, unless   10
Soul clap its hands and sing, and louder sing
For every tatter in its mortal dress.
Nor is there singing school but studying
Monuments of its own magnificence;
And therefore I have sailed the seas and come   15
To the holy city of Byzantium.

III

O sages standing in God's holy fire
As in the gold mosaic of a wall,
Come from the holy fire, perne° in a gyre,
And be the singing-masters of my soul.   20
Consume my heart away; sick with desire
And fastened to a dying animal
It knows not what it is; and gather me
Into the artifice of eternity.

IV

Once out of nature I shall never take   25
My bodily form from any natural thing,
But such a form as Grecian goldsmiths make
Of hammered gold and gold enameling
To keep a drowsy Emperor awake;
Or set upon a golden bough to sing   30
To lords and ladies of Byzantium
Of what is past, or passing, or to come.

[1926]

19 **perne** whirl down.

Topics for Critical Thinking and Writing

1. What is "that . . . country," mentioned in the first line?
2. By the end of the first stanza, the speaker seems to be dismissing the natural world. Do you agree that even in this stanza, however, he sounds attracted to it?
3. The poem is filled with oppositions, for instance "old men" versus "the young" (both in line 1), and "birds in the trees" (line 2) versus the mechanical bird in the final stanza. List as many opposites as you see in the poem, and then explain what Yeats is getting at.
4. The first stanza speaks of "monuments of unaging intellect." What might be some examples of these?
5. After reading and rereading this poem, do you think you will—even if only briefly—*act* differently, redirect any of your choices?
6. Have you ever visited any place—perhaps the place where you or your parents or grandparents were born, or perhaps a house of worship, or perhaps a college campus—that you have come to see symbolically, standing for a way of life or for some aspect of life? If so, describe the place and the significance that you give it.

JAMES WRIGHT

James Wright (1927–1980) was born in Martins Ferry, Ohio, which provided him with the locale for many of his poems. He is often thought of as a poet of the Midwest, but (as in the example that we give) his poems move beyond the scenery. Wright was educated at Kenyon College in Ohio and at the University of Washington. He wrote several books of poetry and published many translations of European and Latin American poetry.

Lying in a Hammock at William Duffy's Farm in Pine Island, Minnesota

Over my head, I see the bronze butterfly,
Asleep on the black trunk,
Blowing like a leaf in green shadow.
Down the ravine behind the empty house,
The cowbells follow one another   5
Into the distances of the afternoon.
To my right,
In a field of sunlight between two pines,
The droppings of last year's horses
Blaze up into golden stones.   10
I lean back, as the evening darkens and comes on.
A chicken hawk floats over, looking for home.
I have wasted my life.

[1963]

Topics for Critical Thinking and Writing

1. How important is it that the poet is "lying in a hammock"? That he is at some place other than his own home?
2. Do you take the last line as a severe self-criticism, or as a joking remark, or as something in between, or what?
3. Imagine yourself lying in a hammock—perhaps you can recall an actual moment in a hammock—or lying in bed, your eye taking in the surroundings. Write a description ending with some sort of judgment or concluding comment, as Wright does. You may want to parody Wright's poem, but you need not. (Keep in mind that the best parodies are written by people who regard the original with affection.)

ANONYMOUS

*Among the most memorable hymns produced in the United States are the spiritu-
als, or Sorrow Songs, created by black slaves in the United States, chiefly in the first
half of the nineteenth century. The origins of the spirituals are still a matter of
some dispute, but most specialists agree that the songs represent a distinctive
fusion of African rhythms with European hymns, and of course many of the texts
derive ultimately from biblical sources. A chief theme is the desire for release,
sometimes presented with imagery drawn from ancient Israel. Examples include
references to crossing the River Jordan (a river that runs from north of the Sea of
Galilee to the Dead Sea), the release of the Israelites from slavery in Egypt
(Exodus), Jonah's release from the whale (Book of Jonah), Daniel's deliverance
from the lions' den (Book of Daniel, chapter 6), and the deliverance of Shadrach,
Meshach, and Abednego from a fiery funace (Book of Daniel, chapter 3).*

*The texts were collected and published especially in the 1860s, for instance in
Slave Songs of the United States (1867). These books usually sought to reproduce
the singers' pronunciation, and we have followed the early texts in the example
that we give here, where we print "chillun" for "children."*

Deep River

Very slowly (with expression)

Deep———— riv - er, my home is ov - er

Jor- dan,———— Deep———— riv - er, Lord. I

want to cross o - ver in - to camp ground.

Deep river, my home is over Jordan, Deep river,
Lord, I want to cross over into campground,
Lord, I want to cross over into campground,
Lord, I want to cross over into campground.

Oh, chillun, Oh, don't you want to go to that gospel feast,   5
That promised land, that land, where all is peace?
Walk into heaven, and take my seat,
And cast my crown at Jesus' feet,
Lord, I want to cross over into campground,

Lord, I want to cross over into campground,   10
Lord, I want to cross over into campground.

Deep river, my home is over Jordan, Deep river
Lord, I want to cross over into campground,
Lord, I want to cross over into campground,
Lord, I want to cross over into campground, Lord!   15

Topic for Critical Thinking and Writing

Can a reader who does not believe in an afterlife enjoy this song?

Things

WILLIAM CARLOS WILLIAMS

*William Carlos Williams (1883–1963) was the son of an English traveling sales-
man and a Basque-Jewish woman. The couple met in Puerto Rico and settled in
Rutherford, New Jersey, where Williams was born. He spent his life there, practicing as a pediatrician and writing poems in the moments between seeing patients
who were visiting his office.*

The Red Wheelbarrow

so much depends
upon

a red wheel
barrow   4

glazed with rain
water

beside the white
chickens.   8

[1923]

Topics for Critical Thinking and Writing

1. Suppose lines 3 and 4 were printed as one line, and lines 5 and 6 were printed
   as one line. What difference, if any, would it make?
2. What, if anything, depends on a wet wheelbarrow next to white chickens?

WALT WHITMAN

Walt Whitman (1819–1892) was born on Long Island, the son of a farmer. The young Whitman taught school and worked as a carpenter, a printer, a newspaper editor, and, during the Civil War, as a volunteer nurse on the Union side. After the war he supported himself by doing secretarial jobs. In Whitman's own day his poetry was highly controversial because of its unusual form (formlessness, many people said) and (though not in the following poem) its abundant erotic implications.

A Noiseless Patient Spider

A noiseless patient spider,
I mark'd where on a little promontory it stood isolated,
Mark'd how to explore the vacant vast surrounding,
It launch'd forth filament, filament, filament, out of itself,
Ever unreeling them, ever tirelessly speeding them.   5

And you O my soul where you stand,
Surrounded, detached, in measureless oceans of space,
Ceaselessly musing, venturing, throwing, seeking the spheres to connect them,
Till the bridge you will need be form'd, till the ductile anchor hold,
Till the gossamer thread you fling catch somewhere, O my soul.   10

[1862–63]

Topics for Critical Thinking and Writing

1. How are the suggestions in "launch'd" (line 4) and "unreeling" (line 5) continued in the second stanza?
2. How are the varying lengths of lines 1, 4, and 8 relevant to their ideas?
3. The second stanza is not a complete sentence. Why? The poem is unrhymed. What effect does the near-rhyme (*hold—soul*) in the last two lines have on you?

THOMAS HARDY

For a biographical note, see page 515.

The Photograph

The flame crept up the portrait line by line
As it lay on the coals in the silence of night's profound,
    And over the arm's incline,
And along the marge of the silkworm superfine,
And gnawed at the delicate bosom's defenceless round.   5

Then I vented a cry of hurt, and averted my eyes;
The spectacle was one that I could not bear,
    To my deep and sad surprise;

But, compelled to heed, I again looked furtivewise
Till the flame had eaten her breasts, and mouth, and hair.   10

"Thank God, she is out of it now!" I said at last,
In a great relief of heart when the thing was done
    That had set my soul aghast,
And nothing was left of the picture unsheathed from the past
But the ashen ghost of the card it had figured on.   15

She was a woman long hid amid packs of years,
She might have been living or dead; she was lost to my sight,
    And the deed that had nigh drawn tears
Was done in a casual clearance of life's arrears;
But I felt as if I had put her to death that night! . . .   20

      •   •   •   •   •   •

—Well; she knew nothing thereof did she survive,
And suffered nothing if numbered among the dead;
    Yet—yet—if on earth alive
Did she feel a smart, and with vague strange anguish strive?
If in heaven, did she smile at me sadly and shake her head?

                          [1890]

Topics for Critical Thinking and Writing

1. What, if anything, does Hardy tell us about the speaker's motive for burning the photograph?
2. Trace the speaker's emotions, step by step, through the poem.
3. What does the speaker imply when he says that if the woman is in heaven she might "shake her head"?
4. Suppose you found a photograph of someone who once was part of your life but who now no longer is. Might you casually dispose of the picture, perhaps by tossing it into the fireplace, or do you think you probably could not bring yourself to do so? Whichever might be your reaction, explain it.

15

Thinking Critically about Poetry: Three Case Studies

Case Study: Writing about Emily Dickinson

In this case study, we give the texts of ten poems and an essay by a student that focuses on Emily Dickinson's religious poetry.

Dickinson is one of the most important and influential American poets, with an amazing gift for vivid, piercing language and an extraordinary ability to suggest and represent complex movements of thought and feeling. Dickinson is highly engaging and accessible in some poems, and difficult, and demanding, in many others. She is difficult in large measure because she is unique: No one wrote like this before her, and no one has written like this since. Spending time with Dickinson means rising to a special challenge, and at first this may strike you as a chore or a burden. But in truth it is an intellectual opportunity. Give this poet a chance, and you'll be amply rewarded.

For isn't this, after all, central to our interest in and love of literature? We want to be pushed, provoked, tested, and challenged. When we read Dickinson, it's true that we are often made uncomfortable: She gives immediate kinds of pleasure but also causes in us struggle and strain. She makes us reach and stretch. This is precisely what Dickinson—so innovative and complex and electrifying *alive*—sought to achieve in her verse and this is why we value her. She compels us to think and feel in ways we had not imagined possible.

Yet one of the ironies of Dickinson as a poet, and one of her sources of fascination for us, is that for all her impact, very few of her contemporaries were even aware that she wrote poetry, as the following brief biography indicates.

Except for brief trips in her youth to Boston, Worcester, and Cambridge, a longer visit to Washington and Philadelphia in 1855, and a few weeks in Cambridge in 1864 for treatment of an eye disorder, Emily Dickinson spent her entire life in Amherst, Massachusetts. She was capable of warmth, affection, and playful humor, but, especially as she became older, Dickinson made sure that she alone established (and secured) the terms for interacting with other people. She had no desire for any kind of public life or career; she had no interest in politics or reform movements; and, however fervent her feelings for both men and women may have been, she had no sexual relationship or sustained romance with anyone. She rigorously maintained her privacy in the family home; she dressed in white all the time and only allowed

a doctor to examine her as she walked by a door that was open a crack in an adjoining room.

Self-sentenced to confinement in her Amherst house, Dickinson baked bread, spent time in the garden, made brief appearances in this or that room or hallway and then vanished through a door or up a stairway. She sent many heightened, exuberant, often mirthful, and sometimes enigmatic notes and letters, above all to her sister-in-law Sue Gilbert, who lived next door.

Dickinson was complicatedly connected to the members of her family and to a few friends. There was, for example, her ambitious, aloof father, Edward Dickinson, who was an attorney, treasurer of Amherst College, and a one-term U.S. congressman, and her melancholy, detached, but wryly humorous mother, Emily Norcross. There was also the young lawyer B. F. Newton (who gave her a copy of Emerson's poems); the literary journalists and editors Josiah Holland and Samuel Bowles; Charles Wadsworth, a married Presbyterian minister and almost certainly the man, addressed as "Master," to whom Dickinson wrote passionate letters; the radical reformer and essayist Thomas Wentworth Higginson, with whom Dickinson corresponded about her poetry, and who visited her in 1870 (he told his wife, "I never was with anyone who drained my nerve power so much"); and Otis Phillips Lord, a crusty Whig politician and Massachusetts judge, two decades older than Dickinson, with whom she exchanged ardent letters late in her life.

Emotionally and intellectually (she felt special kinship with Shakespeare, Charlotte Brontë, Elizabeth Barrett Browning, and George Eliot), Dickinson was supercharged, as the nearly 1800 poems she composed—many of which she neatly sewed into booklets and hid away in the drawers of her bureau—demonstrate with a stunning, even shocking, thematic brilliance and technical daring. Extremely condensed in syntax and structure, idiosyncratic in punctuation, and breathtaking in imagery and phrasing, Dickinson's poems (and many of her letters, too) catch our attention immediately.

Only a handful of poems by Dickinson were published in her lifetime, all of them anonymously and probably without her consent. Through her father's friends and acquaintances, and familiar as she was with literary journals and papers, she could have published more, and in her own name, if publication had been a goal. But perhaps Dickinson understood poetry as writing to be done first and foremost for oneself and then in certain instances to be shared with friends and family members, as was the case with the poems she bestowed upon Sue Gilbert. Dickinson saved her poems and assembled many of them into bundles, but, her biographer Alfred Habegger acknowledges, there is not a single "explicit statement as to what the massive project meant to her."

Dickinson made her sister and brother promise that after her death they would burn all of her papers. As instructed, Lavinia proceeded to destroy all of the letters that Dickinson had saved. The poems, which were a revelation to her, she preserved, and many of them were published in the 1890s and in subsequent decades, though in editions that often revised and tampered with the wording and structure of the texts. Modern scholars, led by Thomas H. Johnson and R. W. Franklin, have restored the poems to the versions that Dickinson herself composed.

It is unnerving to realize that we know (and now can read in correct form) Dickinson's thrilling poems because of a broken promise. Possessed as she was with a fierce, ironic intelligence, Dickinson would have understood deeply both the love and betrayal that her sister's act displayed.

As you read the poems below, feel the excitement of, and take delight in, Dickinson's organizations of language as she explores her major themes and subjects, which include the meaning of death, the nature of identity, the beauty and mystery of nature, the anguish and ecstasy of love, and the majesty of God. But seek too, from poem to poem, to draw and develop for yourself a poetic portrait of Dickinson: What does she sound like? How does her mind work? What makes her so distinctive, so special?

I heard a Fly buzz—when I died—

I heard a Fly buzz—when I died—
The Stillness in the Room
Was like the Stillness in the Air—
Between the Heaves of Storm—   4

The Eyes around—had wrung them dry—
And Breaths were gathering firm
For the last Onset—when the King
Be witnessed—in the Room—   8

I willed my Keepsakes—Signed away
What portion of me be
Assignable—and then it was
There interposed a Fly—   12

With Blue—uncertain stumbling Buzz—
Between the light—and me—
And then the Windows failed—and then
I could not see to see—   16

[c. 1862]

The Soul selects her own Society

The Soul selects her own Society—
Then—shuts the Door—
To her divine Majority—
Present no more—   4

Unmoved—she notes the Chariots—pausing—
At her low Gate—
Unmoved—an Emperor be kneeling
Upon her Mat—   8

I've known her—from an ample nation—
Choose One—
Then—close the Valves° of her attention—
Like Stone—   12

[1862]

11 Valves the two halves of a hinged door, such as is now found on old telephone booths.
Possibly also an allusion to a bivalve, such as an oyster or a clam, having a shell consisting of
two hinged parts.

Manuscript of Emily Dickinson's "I heard a Fly buzz—when I died—"
(Reprinted from *The Manuscript Books of Emily Dickinson*, edited by Ralph W.
Franklin. Poetry text reprinted by permission of the publishers and the
Trustees of Akmherst College from *The Manuscript Books of Emily Dickinson:
A Facsimile Edition*, Ralph W. Franklin, ed. Cambridge, Mass.: The Belknap
Press of Harvard University Press, Copyright © 1981 by the President and
Fellows of Harvard College.)

These are the days when Birds come back

These are the days when Birds come back—
A very few—a Bird or two—
To take a backward look.

These are days when skies resume
The old—old sophistries° of June—   5
A blue and gold mistake.

O fraud that cannot cheat the Bee—
Almost thy plausibility
Induces my belief.

Till ranks of seeds their witness bear—   10
And softly thro' the altered air
Hurries a timid leaf.

Oh Sacrament of summer days,
Oh Last Communion in the Haze—
Permit a child to join.   15

Thy sacred emblems to partake—
Thy consecrated bread to take
And thine immortal wine!

[1859]

5 **sophistries** deceptively subtle arguments.

Papa above!

Papa above!
Regard a Mouse
O'erpowered by the Cat!
Reserve within thy kingdom
A "Mansion" for the Rat!   5

Snug in seraphic Cupboards
To nibble all the day,
While unsuspecting Cycles°
Wheel solemnly away!

[c. 1859]

8 **Cycles** long periods, eons.

There's a certain Slant of light

There's a certain Slant of light,
Winter Afternoons—
That oppresses, like the Heft°
Of Cathedral Tunes—   4

3 **Heft** weight.

Heavenly Hurt, it gives us—
We can find no scar,
But internal difference,
Where the Meanings, are—   8

None may teach it—Any—
'Tis the Seal Despair—
An imperial affliction .
Sent us of the Air—   12

When it comes, the Landscape listens—
Shadows—hold their breath—
When it goes, 'tis like the Distance
On the look of Death—   16

[c. 1861]

This World is not Conclusion

This World is not Conclusion.
A Species stands beyond—
Invisible, as Music—
But positive, as Sound—
It beckons, and it baffles—   5
Philosophy—dont know—
And through a Riddle, at the last—
Sagacity, must go—
To guess it, puzzles scholars—
To gain it, Men have borne   10
Contempt of Generations
And Crucifixion, shown—
Faith slips—and laughs, and rallies—
Blushes, if any see—
Plucks at a twig of Evidence—   15
And asks a Vane, the way—
Much Gesture, from the Pulpit—
Strong Hallelujahs roll—
Narcotics cannot still the Tooth
That nibbles at the soul—   20

[c. 1862]

I got so I could hear his name—

I got so I could hear his name—
Without—Tremendous gain—
That Stop-sensation—on my Soul—
And Thunder—in the Room—   4

I got so I could walk across
That Angle in the floor,
Where he turned so, and I turned—how—
And all our Sinew tore—   8

I got so I could stir the Box—
In which his letters grew
Without that forcing, in my breath—
As Staples—driven through—   12

Could dimly recollect a Grace—
I think, they call it "God"—
Renowned to ease Extremity—
When Formula, had failed—   16

And shape my Hands—
Petition's way,
Tho' ignorant of a word
That Ordination°—utters—   20

My Business, with the Cloud,
If any Power behind it, be,
Not subject to Despair—   24

It care, in some remoter way,
For so minute affair
As Misery—
Itself, too great, for interrupting—more—

[1861]

20 **Ordination** the ministry.

Those—dying, then

Those—dying, then
Knew where they went
They went to God's Right Hand—
The Hand is amputated now
And God cannot be found—   5

The abdication of Belief
Makes the Behavior small—
Better an ignis fatuus°
Than no illume at all—

[1882]

8 **ignis fatuus** a phosphorescent light that hovers over swampy ground, hence something deceptive.

Apparently with no surprise

Apparently with no surprise
To any happy Flower
The Frost beheads it at its play—
In accidental power—
The blonde Assassin passes on—   5
The Sun proceeds unmoved
To measure off another Day
For an Approving God.

[c. 1884]

Tell all the Truth but tell it slant

Tell all the Truth but tell it slant—
Success in Circuit lies
Too bright for our infirm Delight
The Truth's superb surprise

As Lightning to the Children eased
With explanation kind
The Truth must dazzle gradually
Or every man be blind—

4

8

[c. 1868]

A Sample Essay by a Student: "Religion and Religious Imagery in Emily Dickinson"

Gottsegen 1

Peter Gottsegen

Professor Diaz

English 150G

12 April 2004

Religion and Religious Imagery in Emily Dickinson

Emily Dickinson was not a preacher but a poet, so if we read

her poetry about God we should not be surprised if we do not find a

simple, consistent view, or even a clear development from one view--

for instance, belief--to another--for instance, loss of faith. Rather,

judging from some examples of her poetry, she explored various

views, and we should not try to convert this variety into unity.

We can begin by looking at extreme views, first two poems of

faith, and then a poem of doubt. One of the poems of faith, "Papa

above" (528), begins with a childlike or almost playful version of

Gottsegen 2

the Lord's Prayer. (In Matthew 6.9 Jesus begins a prayer by saying, "Our Father who art in heaven.") I think this poem says that God will see to it that even a mouse or rat will get into heaven, and will remain there for eternity. But Dickinson's God is not always concerned for all of the creatures of the world. In another poem that expresses belief in the existence of God, "Apparently with no surprise" (530), Dickinson describes the frost as beheading a flower--that is, beauty perishes--and she goes on to make the point that this occurs under the eyes of "an Approving God." Here she seems to be saying that evil takes place, and God approves of it. It is important to realize that in this poem Dickinson still says that God exists, even if he is indifferent to suffering.

In another poem, "Those--dying, then" (530), Dickinson expresses doubt that God exists. In olden days, she says, people mistakenly thought that God would protect them, but now, she says, "God cannot be found." She uses a particularly terrifying image to convey the loss of God. In the past, Dickinson says, the faithful went to "God's Right Hand," but, she goes on to say, "The Hand is amputated now. . . . " The faith in God that earlier people had was an illusion, but it was something, and it was "better" than the nothingness we now experience. This nothingness, or something not much more than nothingness, is the subject of "I heard a Fly buzz--when I died" (526). In this poem, the speaker expects "the King" (God) to appear to her as she dies, but all she sees is a fly, and then she hears its buzz. God ("the King") never

appears.

Even these few poems show that Dickinson held a variety of

views about God and religion, and it is difficult or perhaps

impossible for us to say exactly what her religious beliefs were.

But what is certain is that religious ideas were so important to

her, so much a part of her mind, that even when she was not

explicitly writing about the existence of a benevolent God or the

absence of God, she used religious imagery--for instance, to

describe impressive things in the natural world around her. In

"These are the days when Birds come back" (528), she talks about

what we call Indian summer, fall days that are like summer days.

But the poem is filled with religious words: "belief," "Sacrament,"

"Communion," "consecrated bread," "immortal wine." The fifth

stanza goes like this:

> Oh Sacrament of summer days,
>
> Oh Last Communion in the Haze--
>
> Permit a child to join.

I don't think Dickinson is really talking about traditional

religion here. Instead, she is using religious imagery to talk

about a particular precious moment in the seasons. As a second

example of her use of religious imagery in a poem that is about

nature and not about God, we might look at "There's a certain

Slant of light" (528-29). In this poem she says that on "Wintry

Afternoons" this particular light has "the Heft / Of Cathedral

Gottsegen 4

Tunes." That is, the wintry light has the solidity, the feel, the

"heft" of religious music. When we see this light, Dickinson says,

we are moved, in a way that we are moved by music in church.

She is not saying anything here about whether God is benevolent

or not, or whether he exists or not. Rather, she is drawing on

experiences in church--probably experiences shared by many

people even today--to help us to see nature more effectively.

    Speaking as someone who was brought up with traditional

religious beliefs but who does not go to church now, I can say

that Dickinson effectively represents the ideas of a believer and

also of a non-believer. But what I think is especially impressive is

that she sees that someone who no longer is a believer can't help

but still think in religious terms when he or she sees something

exceptionally beautiful, for instance on a winter day "a certain

Slant of light."

[New page]

Gottsegen 5

Work Cited

Barnet, Sylvan, et al. <u>Literature and Composition</u>. 7th ed. New York:

Longman, 2005.

Topics for Critical Thinking and Writing

1. In this essay Gottsegen comments on the following poems: "Papa above," "Apparently with no surprise," "Those—dying, then," "I heard a Fly buzz—when I died," "These are the days when Birds come back," and "There's a certain Slant of light." Read or reread each of these poems to see if you agree with Gottsegen's interpretations.

2. Are there other poems in the case study that you think Gottsegen could have used with better effect than some that he did use? Explain.

3. Reread the concluding paragraph. Do you think it is effective? Explain.

Case Study: America Sings the Blues: A Collection of Songs and Poems

Blues music, which emerged and developed during the late nineteenth and early twentieth centuries, embraces a range of styles and forms, including Delta blues (Mississippi and Louisiana), Texas blues, Piedmont blues (Georgia and the Carolinas), Chicago blues, and country blues, among others. It shaped and influenced rock and roll, rhythm and blues, and jazz, as well as religious and gospel music. Its roots are in the history and day-to-day experience of African Americans, reaching back to slavery (with its spirituals and work songs) and then emancipation in the 1860s and forward into the long, hard period of segregation. It is no accident that the blues came into prominence during the decades of the 1890s and the early 1900s—the period that one historian has termed "the nadir" of American race relations—when Jim Crow laws were introduced throughout the South and the horrific practice of lynching was widespread.

Focused on love, sex, grueling work, and death, the lyrics of blues songs are direct and vivid yet at the same time complex—simple-seeming things can indeed be complicated and subtle—and highly evocative. Often, a blues lyric expresses sorrow, anguish, or outright despair. But the blues are flexible and capacious; they can also be angry and defiant, and unabashedly paradoxical. In the blues one can locate humiliation and prideful boasting, beaten-down restraint and lusty exaggeration. One can even speak of some blues songs as happy/sad: The composer's (and the singer's) goal is to feel better, touched by joy and hope, by describing and working through wounded feelings and thereby gaining a measure of control over them.

American music's history includes many stellar composers and performers of the blues, who wrote and interpreted lyrics of stunning originality. Yet the blues are communal and collaborative. Key words, phrases, images, lines, and stanzas pass from one blues song to another, and from one generation to the next. It is perhaps misleading to refer to a "blues song" as such, since many of these songs, in their music and in their lyrics, exist in multiple versions. The words are rarely exactly the same, and even when they are, their expression in performance depends crucially on the style, approach, tone, and phrasing of the person who sings them or plays them on a guitar. Great performers of the blues maintained that they never sang a blues song the same way twice. For them, the same song was always different, a new turn, twist, or variation upon the original, and an original that itself was always a lot or a little in motion.

The blues were sung across the South before they were written down, transcribed, and recorded. W. C. Handy (see below), the author of the hit songs "Memphis Blues" (1912) and "St. Louis Blues" (1914), was the key figure in bringing the blues to the public's attention. His success led not only to an interest among white musicians and audiences in the blues, but also to an effort on the part of white musicians to learn and perform the blues themselves. These attempts were not always successful, and many white singers and bandleaders ended up doing little more than using the term "blues" in song titles or in parts of lyrics and in promotional materials.

Many white musicians, however, have deeply respected the blues and have honored such gifted African American pioneers and practitioners of the blues as W. C. Handy, Bessie Smith, Charley Patton, Son House, Robert Johnson, Blind Lemon Jefferson, Leadbelly, Muddy Waters, and Howlin' Wolf. This vast body of work, along with the blues-saturated achievements of the giants of jazz, including Louis Armstrong and Billie Holiday, inspired many of the best-known white performers in popular music and rock and roll, from Frank Sinatra and Elvis Presley to Mick Jagger and Keith Richards of The Rolling Stones. The impact of the blues has been so extensive, affecting painting and literature as well as music, that the blues may indeed be, as one scholar has said, "the most influential art form of the twentieth century."

Langston Hughes (see below) is often identified as the poet who introduced the blues into African American literature (his first book of poetry is titled *The Weary Blues*, 1926), but as a term, idea, inspiration, and feeling, the blues also appears in the poetry and prose of a number of other African American authors active in the first decades of the twentieth century—for instance, Paul Laurence Dunbar (see below), Sterling Brown, and Zora Neale Hurston. And for African American writers since World War II—for example, Ralph Ellison, James Baldwin, and Toni Morrison—the blues have proven a rich resource of formal and thematic elements.

What follows is a collection of blues songs, by W. C. Handy, Bessie Smith, Robert Johnson, Johnny Cash, and Merle Haggard, and blues poems, by Paul Laurence Dunbar, Langston Hughes, W. H. Auden, Linda Pastan, Allen Ginsberg, Charles Wright, and Sherman Alexie. As this range of selections bears witness, the blues have always been a treasure of African American culture but now have become central to multicultural American music and literature as a whole. It's all of America that's singing the blues.

SHORT VIEWS

Blue: (of a person or mood) melancholy, sad, or depressed.
    New Oxford American Dictionary

And every day I have the blues.
    Traditional

The blues are the roots; everything else is the fruits.
    Willie Dixon

The music of an unhappy people, of the children of disappointment: they tell of death and suffering and unvoiced longing toward a truer world, of misty wandering and hidden ways.
    W. E. B. DuBois, 1903

The blues is not the creation of a crushed-spirited people. It's the product of a forward-looking, upward-striving people.
    Albert Murray

The blues is where we came from and what we experience. The blues came from nothingness, from want, from desire.
    W. C. Handy

Staying in this dull place was enough to give anyone the blues.
    Joseph Conrad

White folks hear the blues come out, but they don't know how it got there.
    Ma Rainey

I got the blues thinking of the future, so I left off and made some marmalade. It's amazing how it cheers one up to shred oranges and scrub the floor.
    D. H. Lawrence

[The blues] contain sublimated bitterness and humility, pathos and bewilderment.
    Claude McKay

The blues can be real sad, else real mad, else real glad, and funny, too, all the same time. I ought to know. Me, I growed up with blues. I heard so many blues when I was a child until my shadow is blue.
    Langston Hughes

I've said that playing the blues is like having to be black twice. Stevie Ray Vaughan [a white blues-singer and guitarist] missed on both counts, but I never noticed.
    B. B. King

The blues sum up the universal challenge, the universal hope, the universal fear. . . . They contain the toughness that manages to make this experience articulate.
    James Baldwin

It's never hard to sing the blues. Everyone in the world has the blues.
    John Lee Hooker

Topics for Critical Thinking and Writing

1. What does it mean to say, "every day I have the blues?" Isn't that an exaggeration?
2. The African American composer W. C. Handy states, "the blues came from nothingness, from want, from desire." Explain each of these phrases and the relationship of the first to the second, and the second to the third.
3. The British novelist D. H. Lawrence tells of chasing away the blues by making marmalade and scrubbing the floor. Why did these activities manage to cheer him up? Can you name and describe activities that would work for you—that would rid you (for a while at least) of the blues? Explain the relationship, as clearly as you can, between what the blues are, and why your choice of activities is such a good antidote for them.
4. Both the essayist James Baldwin and the blues singer and guitarist John Lee Hooker claim that the blues are universal, that everyone feels them. Do you agree? Could you prove this claim? What would be your evidence?
5. Sometimes it is said of a performer, "he (or she) sings the blues but doesn't really feel them." What does this distinction mean? How can we tell when a singer "really feels" what he or she is singing? What is it that we perceive or sense?

W. C. HANDY

William Christopher Handy was born in 1873, in Florence, Alabama. The son and grandson of ministers, he attended Teachers' Agricultural and Mechanical College, in Huntsville, Alabama, and then worked as a schoolteacher and bandmaster. Handy secured a place in the history of American music by combining the blues idiom with the popular form of ragtime. As scholars have noted, his musical structures helped to spur improvisation, which proved central to the development of jazz. Among his best-known works are "Memphis Blue" (1912) and "St. Louis Blues" (1914), below, "the first great blues pop song" (as one critic has described it), which Handy published himself; it was one of the first ventures of a publishing firm he established and directed for decades. He also collected anthologies of blues, folk songs, and spirituals and encouraged the study of African American musicians. Honored as "the father of the blues," Handy died in 1958.

St. Louis Blues

I hate to see that evening sun go down
I hate to see that evening sun go down
'Cause, my baby, he's gone left this town

Feelin' tomorrow like I feel today
If I'm feelin' tomorrow like I feel today
I'll pack my truck and make my give-a-way

St. Louis woman with her diamond ring
Pulls that man around by her

If it wasn't for her and her
That man I love would have gone nowhere, nowhere

I got the St. Louis Blues
Blue as I can be
That man's got a heart like a rock cast in the sea
Or else he wouldn't have gone so far from me

I love my baby like a school boy loves his pie
Like a Kentucky colonel loves his mint'n rye
I love my man till the day I die

[1914]

Topics for Critical Thinking and Writing

1. W. C. Handy has been praised as a great pioneer and innovator, an "original," for his contributions to American music. Yet scholars of his work have noted that his songs adapt, derive from, borrow, and play variations upon countless blues pieces, songs, and tunes that Handy heard, studied, and transcribed. In your view, does this make him any less "original"?

2. Dictionaries define an "original" as "a person of fresh initiative or inventive capacity," someone who sets a level or standard of performance that others seek to emulate. From your knowledge of the arts, and the world of sports, please identify an "original." What makes this person so special, so original, in his or her field of expertise?

3. One commentator on "St. Louis Blues" has said "it is emphatically a woman's lyric all the way." What is the evidence in the song for this claim?

4. There are in fact many recordings of "St. Louis Blues" by male singers who have altered, shifted, and modified the lyrics to make them "fit" a male performer. How much of "St. Louis Blues" would have to be changed to make it work that way? Identify these places in the text, and suggest changes that you think would be effective.

5. What is the speaker's predicament in "St. Louis Blues"? What would you recommend to her as the step she should take next? How do you imagine she would reply to your advice?

BESSIE SMITH

Bessie Smith, the "Empress of the Blues," was born in 1895, in Chattanooga, Tennessee. She began her career as a singer while still a child, with the mentoring and support of Ma Rainey, a popular blues vocalist of the era. By her teens, Smith was touring with Ma Rainey's group, but it was not until the early 1920s that she gained national success. Her first hit-song was "Downhearted Blues," in 1923, and she quickly became one of the best-known African-American singers and entertainers in the United States Her career faltered, however, as a result of serious injuries she suffered in a car accident, and also from her alcoholism.

Smith died in 1937, a powerfully independent figure in the history of the blues and jazz, and one whose raw, aggressive approach to a song influenced Billie Holiday, Louis Armstrong, and countless other singers and musicians. As one literary scholar has noted, Smith also has been "identified by African-American feminist critics as an important foremother for black women writers, who celebrate her independence and forthright attitudes about race and sexuality." Somewhere between 150 and 160 of Smith's recordings survive.

Thinking Blues

Did you ever sit thinking with a thousand things on your mind?
Did you ever sit thinking with a thousand things on your mind?
Thinking about someone who has treated you so nice and kind

You'll get an old letter and you begin to read
You'll get an old letter and you begin to read
Got the blues so bad tell that man of mine I wanna be

Don't you hear me baby, knocking on your door?
Don't you hear me baby, knocking on your door?
Have you got the nerve to drive me from your door?

Have you got the nerve to say that you don't want me no more?
Have you got the nerve to say that you don't want me no more?
The good book said you got to reap what you sow

Take me back baby, try me one more time
Take me back baby, try me one more time
That's the only way I can get these thinking blues off my mind

[1928]

Topics for Critical Thinking and Writing

1. Is there a difference between "the blues" and the "thinking blues"? Please explain.
2. Like many blues songs, the second line of each stanza here repeats the first, and the third then responds to it. Can you recall an occasion when you sat "thinking with a thousand things on your mind?" What was this experience like? Where did all of this "thinking" lead you? What was the result?
3. In the third and fourth stanzas, the speaker asks how the other person "got the nerve" to do and say certain things. What does it mean to say to someone, "You've got a lot of nerve to say that to me"? How is this different from saying to someone in praise, "It took a lot of nerve for you to say that"?
4. The "good book" in the fourth stanza is the Bible, and the reference is to Galatians 6.7: "Be not deceived; God is not mocked: for whatsoever a man soweth, that shall he also reap." How is the speaker making use of this passage? Does it affect you as awkward, or just right?

5. From your reading of these lyrics, would you encourage the speaker to be hopeful about what she yearns for in the final stanza? Please compose a paragraph of "good advice" for her. Next, compose a paragraph of "bad advice."

ROBERT JOHNSON

The blues singer and guitarist Robert Johnson was born in 1911, the son of a Mississippi sharecropper. At a young age he learned to play the harmonica and the guitar, inspired by such Mississippi blues players as Son House and Charley Patton, whom Johnson knew personally and whose recordings he listened to. He traveled throughout the South and Midwest, and to New York, singing in venues of all kinds. He recorded twenty-nine songs in Texas, in 1936–1937. The best of these, including "Me and the Devil Blues," "Hellhound on My Trail," and "Love in Vain," he wrote himself, and he sings and plays the guitar with raw immediacy and haunting power. "Walkin' Blues," below, is another of Johnson's compositions, though some scholars have suggested that he may have based it on, or adapted it from, one of Son House's songs. Johnson died in 1938, in mysterious circumstances (he may have been poisoned), in a town in Mississippi.

Walkin' Blues

I woke up this mornin', feelin' 'round for my shoes.
Know 'bout 'at I got these old walkin' blues.
Woke up this mornin', feelin' 'round all for my shoes.
But you know 'bout 'at I got these old walkin' blues.
Lord, I feel like blowin' my, woh, old lonesome horn.   5
Got up this mornin', my little Bernice was gone,
Lord, I feel like blow-ooowin' my lonesome horn.
Well, I got up this mornin', woh, all I had was gone.
Well, ah leave this morn' if I have to, woh, ride the blind,° ah.
I feel mistreated and I don't mind dyin',   10
Leavin' this morn', ah, 'f I have to ride a blind.
Babe, I been mistreated, baby, and I don't mind dyin'.
Well, some people tell me that the worried blues ain't bad.
Worst old feelin' I most ever had,
Some people tell me that these old worried, old blues ain't bad.   15
It's the worst old feelin' I most ever had.
She got a Elgin movement° from her head down to her toes.
Break in on a dollar most any where she goes,
Ooooo-ooo, from her head down to her toes,
(spoken: 'Oh, honey')   20
Lord, she break in on a dollar most anywhere she goes.

[1936?]

9 Ride the blind Taking an illegal ride on a train; the "blind" is the walkway between two of the train's cars.   **17 Elgin movement** Elgin is the brand name of a watch or clock.

Topics for Critical Thinking and Writing

1. Why does Johnson include the name of the speaker's lover, Bernice? Does this make the song more or less effective?
2. Why is this speaker so afflicted by the blues? It's true that his lover left him, but he says he was mistreated. So why isn't he angry, rather than blue?
3. The story goes that Robert Johnson sold his soul to the devil in order to become a masterful singer and guitarist. Do you think this is farfetched? Or could it be literally true? What does it mean to say that a person "sold his (or her) soul to the devil?" Could you imagine ever being tempted to do this yourself?
4. The speaker at one point refers to "the worst old feelin'" he ever had. What does he mean by this? What is "the worst old feelin'" you have ever had?
5. "Walkin Blues" is included on a number of Robert Johnson CDs, including the 2-CD box set, *The Complete Recordings* (Sony). Before you listen to it, write a paragraph that describes what you think it will sound like. Then, after listening to it, write a paragraph that describes what it does sound like, and then explain, in another paragraph, how Johnson's performance did or did not fulfill your expectations.

PAUL LAURENCE DUNBAR

Born in Dayton, Ohio, in 1872, Paul Laurence Dunbar was the son of former slaves from Kentucky. He grew up poor, but his mother encouraged his enjoyment of literature—poetry and songs in particular—and urged him to excel in grammar and high school. The only African American in his high-school class, Dunbar compiled an excellent record. Soon he began to give readings of his verse (he had written his first poem when he was 6), and in 1892, his first book, Oak and Ivy, *appeared.*

Dunbar's second book, Majors and Minors *(1895), secured for him an even wider audience and national recognition. Many of the poems were written in dialect but many others were in standard English, drawing upon and extending Dunbar's wide reading in English Romantic poets and in popular nineteenth-century American poets, including Henry Wadsworth Longfellow and James Whitcomb Riley. Dunbar died of tuberculosis at age 33 in 1906.*

Blue

Standin' at de winder,
Feelin' kind o' glum,
Listenin' to de raindrops
Play de kettle drum,
Lookin' crost de medders
Swimmin' lak a sea;
Lawd 'a' mussy on us,
What's de good o' me?

Can't go out a-hoein',
Wouldn't ef I could;

Groun' too wet fu' huntin',
Fishin' ain't no good.
Too much noise fo' sleepin',
No 'one hyeah to chat;
Des mus' stan' an' listen
To dat pit-a-pat.

Hills is gittin' misty,
Valley's gittin' dahk;
Watch-dog's 'mence a-howlin',
Rathah have 'em ba'k
Dan a-moanin' solemn
Somewhaih out o' sight;
Rain-crow des a-chucklin'—
Dis is his delight.

Mandy, bring my banjo,
Bring de chillen in,
Come in f'om de kitchen,
I fell sick ez sin.
Call in Uncle Isaac,
Call Aunt Hannah, too,
Tain't no use in talkin',
Chile, I's sholy blue.

[1904]

Topics for Critical Thinking and Writing

1. "Blue," published in Dunbar's book *Li'l' Gal* in 1904, is in African American dialect. The dictionary defines "dialect" as "a local or regional variety of a language chiefly oral and orally transmitted and differing distinctively in vocabulary, grammar, and pronunciation from standard language." Why would Dunbar want to write this way? Dunbar's readers included both whites and African Americans. Do you think that this had an effect on the way someone in the early 1900s understood and responded to "Blue"?

2. When you encounter a literary work that uses dialect, what is your response? Do you feel less inclined to read it? Why is that?

3. Please read this poem aloud. What did it feel like to read it? Did you feel self-conscious as you did? How would you feel if you were asked to read "Blue" in a public setting, such as a college classroom?

4. In a paragraph of four to five sentences, summarize why this speaker is "blue." Did you find it hard or easy to write this summary?

5. Can you identify an experience when you felt "blue"? Can you identify an experience when you felt *really* "blue"? What was the difference between these two experiences? In each case, how did you manage to stop feeling blue?

W. H. AUDEN

One of the major poet-critics of the twentieth century, Wystan Hugh Auden was born in England in 1907 and educated at Oxford University. His first book, Poems, was published in 1930, and it established him as an important figure in both literary and left-wing political circles. After serving on the Republican side during the Spanish Civil War, Auden emigrated to the United States, where in 1946 he became an American citizen. He lectured and taught widely in U.S. colleges and universities, and in England as well, holding an appointment as professor of poetry at Oxford from 1956 to 1961. Auden died in 1973. His Collected Poems *was published three years later.*

Funeral Blues

Stop all the clocks, cut off the telephone,
Prevent the dog from barking with a juicy bone,
Silence the pianos and with muffled drum
Bring out the coffin, let the mourners come.   4

Let aeroplanes circle moaning overhead
Scribbling on the sky the message He Is Dead,
Put crêpe bows round the white necks of the public doves,
Let the traffic policemen wear black cotton gloves.   8

He was my North, my South, my East and West,
My working week and my Sunday rest,
My noon, my midnight, my talk, my song;
I thought that love would last for ever: I was wrong.   12

The stars are not wanted now; put out every one,
Pack up the moon and dismantle the sun,
Pour away the ocean and sweep up the wood;
For nothing now can ever come to any good.   16

[1940]

Topics for Critical Thinking and Writing

1. Auden's poem has been published both with and without the title "Funeral Blues." What does this title contribute to its structure and meaning? Is this title a good one? Could you imagine one that is better? Is there something in particular that the title of the poem should do, or not do?
2. Do you feel a "blues" tone and mood as you read and study this poem? Please explain.
3. How would you assess "Funeral Blues" as an expression of grief? Do you find touches of humor in it? Is that a mistake on Auden's part?

4. Teachers often say to us in essay-writing as well as poetry-writing courses, "Don't exaggerate." Doesn't Auden break this rule from beginning to end? How might he argue in defense of what he has done?
5. Write an essay of 1–2 pages in which you respond to the speaker. What would you say to him?

LANGSTON HUGHES

Langston Hughes was an accomplished short-story writer, playwright, essayist, autobiographer, editor, and author of children's books. But he is known above all for his poetry, and is now recognized as the premier African American poet of the twentieth century. He was born in Joplin, Missouri, but he was raised in Lawrence, Kansas, though with periods in Illinois, Ohio, and Mexico. He started as a student at Columbia University in 1921, but left in 1922 and worked at a number of low-paying jobs. He traveled to Africa and, later, to France, and he then returned in the mid-1920s to the United States to pursue a literary career.

The pace, structure, and tone of "the blues," mournful and yet resilient, shape many of the poems that Hughes included in his first two books: The Weary Blues *(1926) and* Fine Clothes to the Jew *(1927). He was a major figure in the Harlem or "New Negro" Renaissance of the 1920s and early 1930s, which led to a spirited array of race-conscious new production in literature and the arts. In an essay that became a manifesto for the movement, "The Negro and the Racial Mountain" (1926), Hughes maintained: "We younger Negro artists who create now intend to express our individual dark-skinned selves without fear or shame."*

Too Blue

I got those sad old weary blues.
I don't know where to turn.
I don't know where to go.
Nobody cares about you
When you sink so low.   5

What shall I do?
What shall I say?
Shall I take a gun
And put myself away?

I wonder if   10
One bullet would do?
As hard as my head is,
It would probably take two.

But I ain't got
Neither bullet nor gun—   15
And I'm too blue
To look for one.

[1943]

Topics for Critical Thinking and Writing

1. After reading and studying this poem, do you feel able to define the difference between feeling "blue" and feeling "too blue"? Is there evidence in the text that can help you to explain this difference?
2. Would you say that this speaker is depressed? Is being depressed the same as feeling blue?
3. What prevents the speaker from killing himself?
4. If your teacher assigned you to argue that this is (1) a comic poem, or (2) a serious poem, which position would you choose? Where in the poem is the support for your argument? Why do you prefer arguing for this position rather than for the other one? Is there no evidence for that one?
5. How would your response to "Too Blue" change if the poem ended with the third stanza? How would your response change if it ended with the second stanza? Do you conclude, then, that the fourth stanza is just right for the ending?
6. Please compose a new final (that is, a fifth) stanza for Hughes's poem. Next, give a good explanation for why the poem needs this stanza to end effectively.

JOHNNY CASH

One of the giants of country music, a singer and a songwriter who, in the words of one scholar, "always sought directness and simplicity" and composed "stark, austerely elegant music," Johnny Cash was born in Arkansas in 1932. After high school, he worked in an automobile factory in Detroit, Michigan, and later joined the U.S. Air Force. After completing military service, he settled in Memphis, Tennessee, and in 1955 made his debut as a singer with a recording for Sun Records. He was a popular performer during the late 1950s and 1960s, but he also suffered from drug addiction and other personal problems. In 1968, Cash married June Carter, a member of the Carter Family touring group, and he became a devout Christian. Cash received many honors, including eleven Grammy Awards. He was elected to the Rock and Roll Hall of Fame in 1992, and in 2001 he was awarded the National Medal of Arts. He died in 2003.

Folsom Prison Blues*

I hear the train a comin'; it's rollin' 'round the bend,
And I ain't seen the sunshine since I don't know when.
I'm stuck at Folsom Prison and time keeps draggin' on.
But that train keeps rollin' on down to San Antone.°   4

When I was just a baby, my mama told me, "Son,
Always be a good boy; don't ever play with guns."

---

* **Folsom Prison** Folsom State Prison, which opened in 1880, is one of the oldest prisons in California. **4 San Antone** San Antonio, Texas.

But I shot a man in Reno,° just to watch him die.
When I hear that whistle blowin' I hang my head and cry.　　8

I bet there's rich folk eatin' in a fancy dining car.
They're prob'ly drinkin' coffee and smokin' big cigars,
But I know I had it comin', I know I can't be free,
But those people keep a movin', and that's what tortures me.　　12

Well, if they freed me from this prison, if that railroad train was mine,
I bet I'd move on over a little farther down the line,
Far from Folsom Prison, that's where I want to stay,
And I'd let that lonesome whistle blow my blues away.　　16

[1968]

7 **Reno** Located in northwest Nevada, known for its gambling casinos.

Topics for Critical Thinking and Writing

1. Do you like country music? Do you know much about it—its history, its major singers and songwriters, its styles and traditions? Sometimes it is said that country music is "America's music." What does this mean? Do you agree?
2. Why did the speaker shoot "a man in Reno"? How does he respond to this incident, and what is our response to him?
3. Do you think that this speaker has a right to feel the blues? Is he the victim of bad fortune, or has he gotten what he deserves?
4. Have you ever been in a prison? What was the experience like? If you have not, do you think you would learn something from visiting a prison? What might you learn?
5. "Folsom Prison Blues" is available on a number of Johnny Cash's CDs. The best version is on *At Folsom Prison*, a live recording, in front of 2000 inmates, made in 1968 (reissued 1999). Listen to this, or to the version on another CD. How would you describe Cash's voice? What does his style as a vocalist bring out and develop in the lyrics?

MERLE HAGGARD

"He has written blues and folk songs," one music critic has said about Merle Haggard, "social commentaries and classic love songs, protest and anti-protest, gospel and ballads, prison and train songs, drinking songs, and updates of blues yodels." Another has compared him to the jazz and blues singer Billie Holiday, for his ability to communicate the depths of "heartache and depression."

　　Haggard was born in Bakersfield, California, in 1937; his parents had moved west from Oklahoma, making their home in an old railroad-car. He was a rebellious child and teenager, and even as he began in the 1950s to show talent as a singer, he was frequently in trouble with the law. Late in 1957, Haggard was arrested for robbery and sent to San Quentin prison; he was paroled in 1960 and turned his life around. During the early 1960s, reentering the country–music scene, he toured with his own band and gained renown as a singer, songwriter, and performer; one of his streaks, beginning in 1967, included thirty-seven consecutive top-ten hits, twenty-three of which reached number one. The recipient of many awards, Haggard was inducted into the Country Music Hall of Fame in 1994.

Working Man Blues

It's a big job just gettin' by with nine kids and a wife
I been a workin' man dang near all my life
I'll be working long as my two hands are fit to use
I'll drink my beer in a tavern,
Sing a little bit of these working man blues

I keep my nose on the grindstone, I work hard every day
Might get a little tired on the weekend, after I draw my pay
But I'll go back workin, come Monday morning I'm right back with the crew
I'll drink a little beer that evening,
Sing a little bit of these working man blues

Hey hey, the working man, the working man like me
I ain't never been on welfare, that's one place I won't be
Cause I'll be working long as my two hands are fit to use
I drink a little beer in a tavern,
Sing a little bit of these working man blues

Sometimes I think about leaving, do a little bummin around
I wanna throw my bills out the window catch a train to another town
But I go back working I gotta buy my kids a brand new pair of shoes
Yeah drink a little beer in a tavern,
Cry a little bit of these working man blues

Hey hey, the working man, the working man like me
I ain't never been on welfare, that's one place I won't be
Cause I'll be working long as my two hands are fit to use
I drink a little beer in a tavern,
Sing a little bit of these working man blues
Yeah drink a little beer in a tavern,
Cry a little bit of these working man blues

[1969]

Topics for Critical Thinking and Writing

1. What is your response to the fact that the speaker has "nine kids and a wife"? Do you sense that the speaker is a good husband and father? What kind of work does he do for a living?

2. Sometimes the word in the title is printed as "working," sometimes as "workin'." Does it make a difference?

3. The speaker insists he will never go "on welfare." Write him a letter of 1–2 pages, urging him to change his mind.
4. From your study of this song, can you give a summary of what the "working man blues" are? Is this an experience that you are familiar with? Have you ever felt "blue" about a job? How was your own experience similar to and different from the one that Merle Haggard depicts here?
5. "Working Man Blues" is included on a number of CDs, including Haggard's *For the Record: 43 Legendary Hits*, released in 1999, and *40 #1 Hits*, released in 2004. If you know the recording, describe Haggard's vocals, his interpretation of the words—the tone, mood, feeling. If you do not, describe how you imagine he would sound. What leads you to say this?

LINDA PASTAN

Born in 1932 and raised in New York City, Linda Pastan received her undergraduate degree from Radcliffe College and her master's degree from Brandeis University. A resident of Potomac, Maryland, outside Washington D.C., she served as poet laureate of her home state from 1991 to 1994. The best point of departure for surveying her achievement is Carnival Evening: New and Selected Poems, 1968–1998 *(1998).*

Mini Blues

Like a dinghy
I always lag
behind, awash
in somebody else's wake.
Or I answer
the low call
of the foghorn,
only to find
that what it meant
was keep away.

[1975]

Topics for Thinking and Writing

1. The first line introduces a simile. Lines 2–4 offer the first development of it, and lines 5–10 give the second. Examine the first ("I always lag . . ."): How is Pastan making use of the simile here? Now consider the second ("Or I answer . . ."): How is she making use of it in this section?
2. In what ways is this a "blues" poem? Why does Pastan say *"Mini Blues?"*
3. Is this poem too short? If someone asked you, "What is the best length for a poem?" what would be your reply?

ALLEN GINSBERG

Allen Ginsberg was born in Newark, New Jersey, in 1926, the son of Russian Jewish immigrants. He attended Columbia University and became friends in New York City with the writers Jack Kerouac and William S. Burroughs. After graduation and a few odd jobs, Ginsberg traveled to San Francisco, drawn to its atmosphere of radical politics, anarchist thought, and rebellious lifestyles.

Ginsberg made his big impact on the literary scene with the publication in 1956 of the fervent, fiery, bardic "Howl" and Other Poems—a book that led to the arrest of its publisher, Lawrence Ferlinghetti, because of the explicit sexuality and scandalous language it contained. Ginsberg first presented the poem in an oral performance in October 1955, an event that has assumed legendary proportions in the history of American literature and counter-culture.

Ginsberg wrote many books in later years, gave countless readings and speeches, traveled widely, and served as a counter-culture representative par excellence during the 1960s and beyond, the embodiment of the "Beat generation." He was active in the civil rights and anti-war movements, and, later, in the cause of gay liberation. He died in 1997.

Father Death Blues

Hey Father Death, I'm flying home
Hey poor man, you're all alone
Hey old daddy, I know where I'm going   3

Father Death, Don't cry any more
Mama's there, underneath the floor
Brother Death, please mind the store   6

Old Aunty Death   Don't hide your bones
Old Uncle Death   I hear your groans
O Sister Death   how sweet your moans   9

O Children Deaths go breathe your breaths
Sobbing breasts'll ease your Deaths
Pain is gone, tears take the rest   12

Genius Death   your art is done
Lover Death your body's gone
Father Death   I'm coming home   15

Guru Death your words are true
Teacher Death I do thank you
For inspiring me to sing this Blues   18

Buddha Death, I wake with you
Dharma Death, your mind is new
Sangha Death, we'll work it through   21

Suffering is what was born
Ignorance made me forlorn
Tearful truths I cannot scorn   24

Father Breath once more farewell
Birth you gave was no thing ill
My heart is still, as time will tell.   27

[1976]

Topics for Critical Thinking and Writing

1. What is the speaker's tone toward Father Death? When the speaker addresses Death by other names, does the tone change?
2. "Father Death Blues" was composed while Ginsberg was in a plane flying over Lake Michigan. Does this information add to your understanding of the poem? If you did not know this fact, would you miss something important?
3. Look up the words Buddha, Dharma, and Sangha, and explain how in lines 19–21 their meanings work together. Would you have advised Ginsberg to retain this stanza, or cut it?
4. What is the effect on the poem of the term "Blues" in the title? What are the differences between "Father Death Blues" and other possible titles, such as "Father Death" or "Forms of Death"?
5. One critic has said of "Father Death Blues": "Its mood is haunting but its unity is unclear." Do you agree, or do you perceive a beginning, middle, and end in the poem that this critic has overlooked?

CHARLES WRIGHT

The poet and translator Charles Wright was born in Pickwick Dam, Tennessee, in 1935, and educated at Davidson College and the University of Iowa. He began writing poetry in the late 1950s while he was serving in Verona, Italy, in the U.S. Army's Intelligence Unit. Wright has taught at the University of California in Irvine, and at the University of Virginia. His work as a poet has been collected in two volumes, Country Music: Selected Early Poems *(1982; 2nd ed., 1991) and* Negative Blue: Selected Later Poems *(2000).*

Laguna Blues

It's Saturday afternoon at the edge of the world.
White pages lift in the wind and fall.
Dust threads, cut loose from the heart, float up and fall.
Something's off-key in my mind.
Whatever it is, it bothers me all the time.   5

It's hot, and the wind blows on what I have had to say.
I'm dancing a little dance.
The crows pick up a thermal that angles away from the sea.
I'm singing a little song.
Whatever it is, it bothers me all the time.   10

It's Saturday afternoon and the crows glide down,
Black pages that lift and fall.
The castor beans and the pepper plant trundle their weary heads.
Something's off-key and unkind.
Whatever it is, it bothers me all the time.   15

[1981]

Topics for Critical Thinking and Writing

1. Laguna (Spanish for "lake" or "lagoon") Beach, located in Orange County, California, is a beautiful resort area. The rich and famous often vacation there, and it is well-known too for its theater, arts, and literary events and activities. Does this information add to your understanding of Wright's poem? Do you think that in order to appreciate the poem fully, you need to have spent some time in Laguna Beach yourself? If a poem needs or depends on personal experience of this kind, is there something wrong with it?
2. How does this poem draw upon and evoke the blues?
3. Why does Wright use the same line to end each stanza? Do you believe he gains something valuable from this device, or does it produce a monotonous effect?
4. What is the speaker's problem? How would you advise him to resolve it?
5. Have you ever lived in or traveled to a place that made you feel, "I want to write about this place"? What was it about your experience that gave you this feeling? Did you at some point write something? Why, or why not?
6. Have you ever lived in or traveled to a place that made you feel "blue," that gave you "the blues"? Describe this experience.

SHERMAN ALEXIE

A Spokane/Coeur d'Alene Indian, Sherman Alexie was born in 1966 on the Spokane Indian Reservation in Wellpinit, Washington. For his undergraduate work, he attended Gonzaga University in Spokane, Washington, but later he transferred to Washington State University in Pullman, graduating in 1991 with a degree in American Studies.

Alexie has written a number of fictional works, including The Lone Ranger and Tonto Fistfight in Heaven *(1993, stories),* Reservation Blues *(1994, novel),* Indian Killer *(1996, a murder mystery), and* The Toughest Indian in the World *(2000, stories). But he has noted: "My beginnings are as a poet. My first form of writing was poetry." His recent books of poetry include:* Water Flowing Home *(1995),* The Summer of Black Widows *(1996),* The Man Who Loves Salmon *(1998), and* One Stick Song *(2000). The recipient of many awards and honors, Alexie lives with his wife and son in Seattle, Washington.*

Reservation Blues

Dancing all alone, feeling nothing good
It's been so long since someone understood

All I've seen is, is why I weep
And all I had for dinner was some sleep

You know I'm lonely, I'm so lonely
My heart is empty and I've been so hungry
All I need is for my hunger to ease
Is anything that you can give me please

[chorus:]
I ain't got nothing, I heard no good news
I fill my pockets with those reservation blues
Those old, those old rez blues, those old reservation blues
And if you ain't got choices
What else do you choose?

[repeat chorus twice]

And if you ain't got choices
Ain't got much to lose

[1995]

Topics for Critical Thinking and Writing

1. After reading this poem, do you know what the "reservation blues" are? Please explain.
2. Is there too much self-pity in this poem? Do you think that Alexie would agree, or not?
3. The speaker says, "you ain't got choices." Can you recall an experience where you were conscious of "having no choice"? What was it? What did you do to resolve the situation?

Case Study: *Writing about Literary Visions (Word and Image)*

THINKING AND WRITING ABOUT POEMS AND PICTURES

Despite Mallarmé's witty remark that poems are not made with ideas but with words, and despite Archibald MacLeish's assertion that "A poem should not mean / But be," poems do include ideas, and they do have meanings. When you read the poems that we print along with pictures, you might think about some of the following questions:

- What is your own first response to the painting? In interpreting the painting, consider the subject matter, the composition (for instance, balanced masses, as opposed to an apparent lack of equilibrium), the technique (for instance, vigorous brush strokes of thick paint, as opposed to thinly applied strokes that leave no trace of the artist's hand), the color, and the title.
- After having read the poem, do you see the painting in a somewhat different way?
- To what extent does the poem illustrate the painting, and to what extent does it depart from the painting and make a very different statement?
- If the painting is based on a poem (see Demuth's painting on page 558), to what extent does the painting capture the poem?
- Beyond the subject matter, what (if anything) do the two works have in common?

A Sample Essay by a Student

On page 567 read (preferably aloud) Anne Sexton's "The Starry Night," which was inspired by van Gogh's painting of the same name. Then read the following essay.

Myers 1

Lisa Myers

Professor Peres

English 10G

12 November 2004

Two Ways of Looking at a Starry Night

About a hundred years ago Vincent van Gogh looked up into

the sky at night and painted what he saw, or what he felt. We

---

[continued on p. 579]

Word
and
Image

*Poetry is a
speaking picture,
painting is
silent poetry.*

— SIMONIDES

Vincent van Gogh. *Vincent's Bed in Arles.* (Oil on canvas, 72 × 90 cm. Vincent van Gogh Foundation/Van Gogh Museum, Amsterdam.)

JANE FLANDERS

Jane Flanders, born in Waynesboro, Pennsylvania, in 1940 and educated at Bryn Mawr College and Columbia University, is the author of three books of poems. Among her awards are poetry fellowships from the National Endowment for the Arts and the New York Foundation for the Arts.

Van Gogh's Bed

is orange,
like Cinderella's coach, like
the sun when he looked it
straight in the eye.   4

is narrow,
he slept alone, tossing
between two pillows, while it carried him
bumpily to the ball.   8

is clumsy,
but friendly. A peasant
built the frame; an old wife beat
the mattress till it rose like meringue.   12

is empty,
morning light pours in
like wine, melody, fragrance,
the memory of happiness

16

[1985]

Topics for Critical Thinking and Writing

Jane Flanders tells us that the poem is indebted not only to the painting but also
to two comments in letters that van Gogh wrote to his brother, Theo:

> I can tell you that for my part I will try to keep a straight course, and will
> paint the most simple, the most common things.
>
> [December 1884]

> My eyes are still tired, but then I had a new idea in my head and here is
> the sketch of it. . . . It's just simply my bedroom, only here color is to do
> everything, and giving by its simplification a grander style to things, is to
> be suggestive here of *rest* or of sleep in general. In a word, to look at the
> picture ought to rest the brain or rather the imagination.
>
> [September 1888]

1. Does the painting convey "rest" to you? If not, has van Gogh failed to paint a
   picture of interest? What *does* the picture convey to you?
2. In an earlier version, the last stanza of the poem went thus:

> empty,
> morning light pours in
> like wine; the sheets are what they are,
> casting no shadows.

Which version do you prefer? Why?

Charles Demuth. *I Saw the Figure 5 in Gold.* 1928. (Oil on composition board, 36 × 29¾ in. The Metropolitan Museum of Art, Alfred Stieglitz Collection, 1949. [49.59.1] Photograph © 1986 The Metropolitan Museum of Art.)

WILLIAM CARLOS WILLIAMS

William Carlos Williams (1883–1963) was the son of an English traveling sales-man and a Basque-Jewish woman. The couple met in Puerto Rico and settled in Rutherford, New Jersey, where Williams was born. He spent his life there, practicing as a pediatrician and writing poems in the moments between seeing patients who were visiting his office.

In his Autobiography *Williams gives an account of the origin of this poem. He was walking in New York City, on his way to visit a friend:*

> *As I approached his number I heard a great clatter of bells and the roar of a fire engine passing the end of the street down Ninth Avenue. I turned just in time to see a golden 5 on a red background flash by. The*

impression was so sudden and forceful that I took a piece of paper out of my pocket and wrote a short poem about it.

Several years later his friend Charles Demuth (1883–1939), an American painter who has been called a cubist-realist, painted this picture, inspired by the poem. The picture is one of a series of paintings about Demuth's friends.

The Great Figure

Among the rain
and lights
I saw the figure 5
in gold
on a red   5
fire truck
moving
tense
unheeded
to gong clangs   10
siren howls
and wheels rumbling
through the dark city

[1920]

Topic for Critical Thinking and Writing

Williams's draft for the poem runs thus:

Among the rain
and lights
I saw the figure 5
gold on red
moving
to gong clangs
siren howls
and wheels rumbling
tense
unheeded
through the dark city

Do you think the final version is better in all respects, some respects, or no respect? Explain.

John James Audubon. *Greater Flamingo, American Flamingo.* c. 1830. (Courtesy William S. Reese.)

GREG PAPE

Greg Pape was born in 1947 in Eureka, California, and educated at Fresno State College (now California State University, Fresno) and the University of Arizona. The author of several books of poems, he has served as writer-in-residence at several colleges and universities, and now teaches at Northern Arizona University, in Flagstaff.

American Flamingo

I know he shot them to know them.
I did not know the eyes of the flamingo
are blue, a deep live blue.   3

And the tongue is lined with many small
tongues, thirteen, in the sketch
by Audubon,° to function as a sieve.   6

I knew the long rose-pink neck,
the heavy tricolored down-sweeping bill,
the black primaries.   9

But I did not know the blue eye
drawn so passionately by Audubon
it seems to look out, wary, intense,   12

---

6 Audubon John James Audubon, American ornithologist and artist (1785–1851), author of the multivolume *Birds of America* (1827–1938).

from the paper it is printed on.
                    —*what*
Is man but his passion?   15

asked Robert Penn Warren.° In the background
of this sketch, tenderly subtitled *Old Male,*
beneath the over-draping feathered   18

monument of the body, between the long
flexible neck and the long bony legs
covered with pink plates of flesh,   21

Audubon has given us eight postures,
eight stunning movements in the ongoing
dance of the flamingos.   24

Once at Hialeah° in late afternoon
I watched the satin figures of the jockeys
perched like bright beetles on the backs   27

of horses pounding down the home
stretch, a few crops whipping
the lathering flanks, the loud flat   30

metallic voice of the announcer fading
as the flamingos, grazing the pond water
at the far end of the infield, rose   33

in a feathery blush, only a few feet
off the ground, and flew one long
clipped-winged ritual lap   36

in the heavy Miami light, a great
slow swirl of grace from the old world
that made tickets fall from hands,   39

stilled horses, and drew toasts from the stands
as they settled down again
like a rose-colored fog on the pond.   42
                                                          [1998]

16 Robert Penn Warren American poet, novelist, and literary critic (1905–1989).
25 Hialeah city in southeast Florida, site of Hialeah Park racetrack.

Topics for Critical Thinking and Writing

1. Why is the speaker preoccupied with the flamingo's eyes?
2. A transition occurs in lines 14–15, with the italicized quotation from Robert Penn Warren. What is the relationship of this to the description of the flamingo (and the speaker's reflections) that precede it?
3. From line 25 to the end, the speaker carefully describes a scene at Hialeah. Take note of the specific details and terms that the speaker presents, and explain how these make the poem both a vivid description and something more than that.

Edouard Manet. *Luncheon on the Grass (Déjeuner sur l'herbe)*. 1863. (Musée d'Orsay, Paris, France.)

CARL PHILLIPS

Carl Phillips was born in 1959 in Everett, Washington, and was educated at Harvard and at Boston University. African American, gay, a scholar of classical Greek and Latin, and the author of two books of poetry, he has taught creative writing at Harvard, and he now teaches English and African American Studies at Washington University in St. Louis.

Luncheon on the Grass

They're a curious lot. Manet's scandalous
lunch partners. The two men, lost
in cant and full dress, their legs sprawled
subway-style, as men's legs invariably are, seem
remarkably unruffled, all but oblivious to their nude   5
female companion. Her nudity is puzzling and
correct; clothes for her are surely only needed
to shrug a shoulder out of. She herself appears
baldly there-for-the-ride; her eyes, moving out
toward the viewer, are wide with the most banal,   10
detached surprise, as if to say, "where's
the *real* party?"

Now, in a comparable state of outdoor
undress, I'm beginning to have a fair idea
of what's going on in that scene. Watching   15
you, in clothes, remove one boot to work your
finger toward an itch in your athletic sock,
I look for any similarities between art
and our afternoon here on abandoned
property. The bather in the painting's   20
background, presumably there for a certain
balance of composition, is for us an ungainly,
rusted green dumpster, rising from overgrown
weeds that provide a contrast only remotely
pastoral. We are two to Manet's main group   25
of three, but the hum of the odd car or truck
on the highway below us offers a transient third.
Like the nude, I don't seem especially hungry,
partly because it's difficult eating naked when
everyone else is clothed, partly because   30
you didn't remember I hate chicken salad.
The beer you opened for me sits untouched,
going flat in the sun. I stroke the wet bottle
fitfully, to remind myself just how far
we've come or more probably have always been   35
from the shape of romance. My dear,
this is not art; we're not anywhere close
to Arcadia.°

[1993]

38 Arcadia an ancient region in Greece, traditionally associated in art and literature with
the simple, pastoral life, a Golden Age of unfailing romantic love.

Topics for Critical Thinking and Writing

1. The author is openly gay. Does knowledge of his sexual orientation affect the
   way in which you read the poem? Explain.
2. Do you agree that the speaker and the partner are "not anywhere close / to
   Arcadia"? Support your response with evidence.

Pablo Picasso. *Girl Before a Mirror.* 1932. (Museum of Modern
Art, New York. Gift of Mrs. Simon Guggenheim [2.1938].
© 2004 The Estate of Pablo Picasso/Artists Rights Society [ARS],
New York.)

JOHN UPDIKE

*John Updike, born in 1932, grew up in Shillington, Pennsylvania, where his father
was a teacher and his mother was a writer. After receiving a B.A. degree from
Harvard he studied drawing at Oxford for a year, but an offer from* The New
Yorker *magazine brought him back to the United States. He at first served as a re-
porter for the magazine, but soon began contributing poetry, essays, and fiction.
Today he is one of America's most prolific and well-known writers.*

Before the Mirror

How many of us still remember
when Picasso's *Girl Before a Mirror* hung
at the turning of the stairs in the pre-
expansion Museum of Modern Art?
Millions of us, maybe, but we form   5
a dwindling population. Garish
and brush-slashed and yet as balanced
as a cardboard queen in a deck of giant cards,

the painting proclaimed, *Enter here*
and abandon preconception. She bounced
the erotic balls of herself back and forth
between reflection and reality.

10

Now I discover, in the recent retro-
spective at the same establishment,
that the dazzling painting dates
from March of 1932,

15

the very month in which I first saw light,
squinting in quick nostalgia for the womb.
Inspecting, I bend closer. The blacks,
the stripy cyanide greens are still uncracked,

20

I note with satisfaction; the cherry reds
and lemon yellows full of childish juice.
No sag, no wrinkle. Fresh as paint. *Back then,*
I reflect, *they knew just how to lay it on.*

[1996]

Topics for Critical Thinking and Writing

1. The painting shows a young woman looking into a mirror. In viewing a picture with this subject, what associations might reasonably come to mind? Vanity? Mortality? Or what?

2. The woman (at the left) has two faces, one in profile. Do you think Picasso is showing us two views of the same face, or perhaps two stages in the woman's life? And what of the face in the mirror? Do you think it shows either or both of the faces at the left, or a third face or stage?

3. Why do you suppose the woman is reaching out toward the mirror? (There cannot be any way of proving whatever you or anyone else might offer as an answer, but *why* do you offer the explanation that you do offer?)

4. What do you think the poem is chiefly about? The distinctiveness of modern art (meaning the age of Picasso)? The excellent condition of the picture? The speaker's response to the picture? Explain.

5. The first twelve lines of this poem describe the speaker's thoughts "then," when he first saw *Girl Before a Mirror;* the last twelve lines describe his ideas and feelings "now." In two paragraphs, or in one extended paragraph, write a "Then and Now," describing a picture or a song or a scene—a lake, a house, a kitchen—or a person, then and now.

Pieter Brueghel the Elder. *Two Chained Monkeys*. c.1525–1592. (Oil on wood. Gemäldegalerie, Staaliche Museen zu Berlin, Berlin, Germany.)

WISLAWA SZYMBORSKA

Wislawa Szymborska (pronounced "Vislawa Zimborska"), born 1923, is one of Poland's leading poets. Her first book published in 1952, she has published seven later volumes. Some of her work is available in English, in Sounds, Feelings, Thoughts *(1981).*

Brueghel's Two Monkeys*

This is what I see in my dream about final exams:
two monkeys, chained to the floor, sit on the windowsill,
the sky behind them flutters,
the sea is taking its bath.

The exam is History of Mankind.   5
I stammer and hedge.

One monkey stares and listens with mocking disdain,
the other seems to be dreaming away—
but when it's clear I don't know what to say
he prompts me with a gentle   10
clinking of his chain.

[1983]

* Translated, from the Polish, by Stanislaw Baranczak and Clare Cavanagh.

Topics for Critical Thinking and Writing

1. What do we know, or guess, about the speaker from the poem's first line? Are we willing to listen to him (or her)?
2. We are not likely to be examined on "History of Mankind." Why do you suppose the speaker is being quizzed on it? What does the speaker do? (Paraphrase line 6.)
3. In the third stanza the speaker again does not know what to say. Do we know what the question is? Does the prompting (line 10) help?
4. Write a comment, in prose or verse, on Brueghel's painting.

Myers 2

know that he was a very religious man, but even if we had not heard this in an art course or read it in a book we would know it from his painting The Starry Night, which shows a glorious heaven, with stars so bright that they all have halos. Furthermore, almost in the lower center of the picture is a church, with its steeple rising above the hills and pointing to the heavens.

Anne Sexton's poem is about this painting, and also (we know from the line she quotes above the poem) about van Gogh's religious vision of the stars. But her poem is not about the heavenly comfort that the starry night offered van Gogh. It is a poem about her wish to die. As I understand the poem, she wants to die in a blaze of light, and to become extinct. She says, in the last line of the poem, that she wants to disappear with "no cry," but this seems to me to be very different from anything van Gogh is saying. His picture is about the glorious heavens, not about himself. Or if it is about himself, it is about how wonderful he feels when he sees God's marvelous creation. Van Gogh is concerned with praising God as God expresses himself in nature; Anne Sexton is concerned with expressing her anguish and with her hope that she can find extinction. Sexton's world is not ruled by a benevolent God but is ruled by an "old unseen serpent." The night is a "rushing beast," presided over by a "great dragon."

Sexton has responded to the painting in a highly unique way. She is not trying to put van Gogh's picture into words that he

Myers 3

might approve of. Rather, she has boldly used the picture as a

point of departure for her own word-picture.

Topics for Critical Thinking and Writing

1. Do you agree with Lisa Myers's analysis, especially her interpretation of Sexton's poem?
2. Has Washington cited and examined passages from the poem in a convincing way?
3. A general question: Do you think poets are obliged to be faithful to the paintings that they write about, or do poets enjoy the freedom—a kind of poetic license—to interpret a painting just as they choose, doing with it whatever the purpose of the poem requires?

PART III

Standing Back

Arguing Interpretations and Evaluations, and Understanding Critical Strategies

16

Arguing an Interpretation

In Chapter 2 we discussed arguing with yourself as a way of developing ideas; in Chapter 3 we discussed arguing about meanings or interpretations; and in Chapter 7 we discussed supporting arguments with evidence. Nevertheless, we have more to say about writing an argument, and we will say some of it in this chapter and in the next two chapters where we will consider assumptions and evidence.

INTERPRETATION AND MEANING

We can define **interpretation** as

- a setting forth of the meaning, or, better,
- a setting forth of one or more of the meanings of a work of literature.

This question of *meaning* versus *meanings* deserves a brief explanation. Although some critics believe that a work of literature has a single meaning, the meaning it had for the author, most critics hold that a work has several meanings, for instance the meaning it had for the author, the meaning(s) it had for its first readers (or viewers, if the work is a drama), the meaning(s) it had for later readers, and the meaning(s) it has for us today. Take *Hamlet* (1600–1601), for example. Perhaps this play about a man who has lost his father had a very special meaning for Shakespeare, who had recently lost his own father. Further, Shakespeare had earlier lost a son named Hamnet, a variant spelling of Hamlet. The play, then, may have had important psychological meanings for Shakespeare—but the audience could not have shared (or even known) these meanings.

What *did* the play mean to Shakespeare's audience? Perhaps the original audience of *Hamlet*—people living in a monarchy, presided over by Queen Elizabeth I—were especially concerned with the issue (specifically raised in *Hamlet*) of whether a monarch's subjects ever have the right to overthrow the monarch. But obviously for twenty-first-century Americans the interest in the play lies elsewhere, and the play must mean something else. If we are familiar with Freud, we may see in the play a young man who subconsciously lusts after his mother and seeks to kill his father (in the form of Claudius, Hamlet's uncle). Or we may see the play as largely about an alienated young man in a bourgeois society. Or—but the interpretations are countless.

Is the Author's Intention a Guide to Meaning?

Shouldn't we be concerned, you might ask, with the *intentions* of the author? The question is reasonable, but there are difficulties, as the members of the Supreme Court find when they try to base their decisions on the original intent of the writers of the Constitution. First, for older works we almost never know what the intention is. Authors did not leave comments about their intentions. We have *Hamlet,* but we do not have any statement of Shakespeare's intention concerning this or any other play. It might be argued that we can deduce Shakespeare's intention from the play itself, but to argue that we should study the play in the light of Shakespeare's intention, and that we can know his intention by studying the play, is to argue in a circle. We can say that Shakespeare must have intended to write a tragedy (if he intended to write a comedy he failed), but we can't go much further in talking about his intention.

Even if an author has gone on record expressing an intention, we may think twice before accepting the statement as decisive. The author may be speaking facetiously, deceptively, mistakenly, or (to be brief) unconvincingly. For instance, Thomas Mann said, probably sincerely and accurately, that he wrote one of his novels merely in order to entertain his family—but we may nevertheless take the book seriously and find it profound.

What Characterizes a Sound Interpretation?

Even the most vigorous advocates of the idea that meaning is indeterminate do not believe that all interpretations are equally significant. Rather, they believe that an interpretive essay is offered against a background of ideas, shared by essayist and reader, as to what constitutes a *persuasive argument.* Thus, an essay (even if it is characterized as "interpretive free play" or "creative engagement") will have to be

- coherent,
- plausible, and
- rhetorically effective.

The *presentation*—the rhetoric—as well as the interpretation is significant. This means (to repeat a point made in Chapter 2) that the essayist cannot merely set down random expressions of feeling or unsupported opinions. The essayist must, on the contrary, convincingly *argue* a thesis—must point to evidence so that the reader will not only know what the essayist believes but will also understand why he or she believes it.

There are lots of ways of making sense (and even more ways of making nonsense), but one important way of helping readers to see things from your point of view is to do your best to face all of the complexities of the work. Put it this way: Some interpretations strike a reader as better than others because they are *more inclusive,* that is, because they *account for more of the details of the work.* The less satisfactory interpretations leave a reader pointing to some aspects of the work—to some parts of the whole—and saying, "Yes, but your explanation doesn't take account of . . . ." This does not mean, of course, that a reader must feel that a persuasive interpretation says the last word about the work. We always realize that the work—if we value it highly—is richer than the discussion; but, again, for us to value an interpretation we must find the interpretation plausible and inclusive.

Interpretation often depends not only on making connections among various elements of the work (for instance, among the characters in a story or among the images in a poem), and among the work and other works by the author, but also on making connections between the particular work and a **cultural context**. The cultural context usually includes other writers and specific works of literature, since a given literary work participates in a tradition. That is, if a work looks toward life, it also looks toward other works. A sonnet, for example, is about human experience, but it is also part of a tradition of sonnet writing. The more works of literature you are familiar with, the better equipped you are to interpret any particular work. Here is the way Robert Frost put it, in the preface to *Aforesaid:*

> A poem is best read in the light of all the other poems ever written. We read A the better to read B (we have to start somewhere; we may get very little out of A). We read B the better to read C, C the better to read D, D the better to go back and get something more out of A. Progress is not the aim, but circulation. The thing is to get among the poems where they hold each other apart in their places as the stars do.

An Example: Interpreting Pat Mora's "Immigrants"

Let's think about interpreting a short poem by a contemporary poet, Pat Mora.

Immigrants

wrap their babies in the American flag,
feed them mashed hot dogs and apple pie,
name them Bill and Daisy,
buy them blonde dolls that blink   5
blue eyes or a football and tiny cleats
before the baby can even walk,
speak to them in thick English,
    hallo, babee, hallo.
whisper in Spanish or Polish   10
when the babies sleep, whisper
in a dark parent bed, that dark
parent fear, "Will they like
our boy, our girl, our fine american
boy, our fine american girl?"   15

[1986]

Perhaps most readers will agree that the poem expresses or dramatizes a desire, attributed to "immigrants," that their child grow up in an Anglo mode. (Mora is not saying that *all* immigrants have this desire; she has simply invented one speaker who says such-and-such. Of course *we* may say that Mora says all immigrants have this desire, but that is our interpretation.) For this reason the parents call their children Bill and Daisy (rather than, say, José and Juanita) and give them blonde dolls and a football (rather than dark-haired dolls and a soccer ball). Up to this point, the parents seem a bit silly in their mimicking of Anglo ways. But the second part of the poem gives the reader a more interior view of the parents, brings out the fear and hope and worried concern that lies behind the behavior: Some unspecified "they" may not "like / our boy, our girl." Who are "they"? Most readers probably will agree that "they" refers to native-born citizens, especially the blond, blue-eyed "all-American" Anglo types that until recently constituted the establishment in the United States.

We can raise further questions about the interpretation of the poem.

- Exactly what does the poet mean when she says that immigrants "wrap their babies in the American flag"? Are we to take this literally?
- If not, how are we to take it?

- And why in the last two lines is the word "american" not capitalized? Is Mora imitating the non-native speaker's uncertain grasp of English punctuation? (But if so, why does Mora capitalize "American" in the first line and "Spanish" and "Polish" later in the poem?) Or is she perhaps implying some mild reservation about becoming 100 percent American, some suggestion that in changing from Spanish or Polish to "american" there is some sort of loss?

A reader might seek Mora out and ask her why she didn't capitalize "american" in the last line, but Mora might not be willing to answer, or she might not give a straight answer, or she might say that she doesn't really know why—it just seemed right when she wrote the poem. Most authors do in fact take this last approach. When they are working as writers, they work by a kind of instinct, a kind of feel for the material. Later they can look critically at their writing, but that's another sort of experience.

To return to our basic question: What characterizes a good interpretation? The short answer is, *Evidence,* and especially evidence that seems to cover all relevant issues. In an essay it is not enough merely to assert an interpretation. Your readers don't expect you to make an airtight case, but because you are trying to help readers to understand a work—to see a work the way you do—you are obliged to

- offer reasonable supporting evidence, and
- take account of what might be set forth as counterevidence to your thesis.

Of course your essay may originate in an intuition or an emotional response, a sense that the work is about such-and-such, but this intuition or emotion must then be examined, and it must stand a test of reasonableness. (It's usually a good idea to jot down in a journal your first responses to a work, and in later entries to reflect on them.) It is not enough in an essay merely to set forth your response. Your readers will expect you to *demonstrate* that the response is something that they can to a large degree share. They may not be convinced that the interpretation is right or true, but they must at least feel that the interpretation is plausible and in accord with the details of the work, rather than, say, highly eccentric and irreconcilable with some details.

This book includes ten case studies, some of which include essays by critics advancing interpretations. When you read these interpretations, think about *why* you find some interpretations more convincing than others.

THINKING CRITICALLY ABOUT RESPONSES TO LITERATURE

Usually you will begin with a strong *response* to your reading—interest, boredom, bafflement, annoyance, shock, pleasure, or whatever. Fine. Then, if you are going to think critically about the work, you will go on to *examine* your response in order to understand it, or to deepen it, or to change it.

How can you change a response? Critical thinking involves seeing an issue from all sides, to as great a degree as possible. As you know, in ordinary language *to criticize* usually means to find fault, but in literary studies the term does not have a negative connotation. Rather, it means "to examine carefully." (The word *criticism* comes from a Greek verb meaning "to distinguish," "to decide," "to judge.") Nevertheless, in one sense the term *critical thinking* does approach the usual meaning, since critical thinking requires you to take a skeptical view of your response. You will, so to speak, argue with yourself, seeing if your response can stand up to doubts.

Let's say that you have found a story implausible. Question yourself:

- Exactly what is implausible in it?
- Is implausibility always a fault?
- If so, exactly why?

Your answers may deepen your response. Usually, in fact, you will find supporting evidence for your response, but in your effort to distinguish and to decide and to judge, try also (if only as an exercise) to find **counterevidence**. See what can be said against your position. (The best lawyers, it is said, prepare two cases—their own, and the other side's.) As you consider the counterevidence you will sometimes find that it requires you to adjust your thesis. Fine. You may even find yourself developing an entirely different response. That's also fine, though of course the paper that you ultimately hand in should clearly argue a thesis.

Critical thinking, in short, means examining or exploring one's own responses, by questioning and testing them. Critical thinking is not so much a skill (though it does involve the ability to understand a text) as it is a *habit of mind,* or, rather, several habits, including

- Open-mindedness
- Intellectual curiosity
- Willingness to work

It may involve, for instance, willingness to discuss the issues with others and to do research, a topic that will be treated separately in Appendix B, on writing a research paper.

TWO INTERPRETATIONS BY STUDENTS

Robert Frost, "Stopping by Woods on a Snowy Evening"

Read Frost's "Stopping by Woods on a Snowy Evening," and then read the first interpretation, written by a first-year student. This interpretation is followed by a discussion that is devoted chiefly to two questions:

- What is the essayist's thesis?
- Does the essayist offer convincing evidence to support the thesis?

A second essay by another first-year student, offering a different interpretation of the poem, provides further material for you to analyze critically.

ROBERT FROST

Robert Frost (1874–1963) was born in California. After his father's death in 1885 Frost's mother brought the family to New England, where she taught in high schools in Massachusetts and New Hampshire. Frost studied for part of one term at Dartmouth College in New Hampshire, then did odd jobs (including teaching), and from 1897 to 1899 was enrolled as a special student at Harvard. He then farmed in New Hampshire, published a few poems in local newspapers, left the farm and taught again, and in 1912 left for England, where he hoped to achieve more popular success as a writer. By 1915 he had won a

considerable reputation, and he returned to the United States, settling on a farm in New Hampshire and cultivating the image of the country-wise farmer-poet. In fact he was well read in the classics, the Bible, and English and American literature.

Stopping by Woods on a Snowy Evening

Whose woods these are I think I know.
His house is in the village though;
He will not see me stopping here
To watch his woods fill up with snow.　　　　4

My little horse must think it queer
To stop without a farmhouse near
Between the woods and frozen lake
The darkest evening of the year.　　　　8

He gives his harness bells a shake
To ask if there is some mistake.
The only other sound's the sweep
Of easy wind and downy flake.　　　　12

The woods are lovely, dark and deep.
But I have promises to keep,
And miles to go before I sleep,
And miles to go before I sleep.　　　　16

[1923]

Manuscript version of Frost's "Stopping by Woods on a Snowy Evening." The first part is lost. (Courtesy of the Jones Library, Inc., Amherst, Mass.)

Sample Essay by a Student:
"Stopping by Woods—and Going On"

MacDonald 1

Darrel MacDonald

Professor Conner

English 1102

4 October 2004

Stopping by Woods--and Going On

Robert Frost's "Stopping by Woods on a Snowy Evening" is

about what the title says it is. It is also about something more

than the title says.

When I say it is about what the title says, I mean that the

poem really does give us the thoughts of a person who pauses

(that is, a person who is "stopping") by woods on a snowy

evening. (This person probably is a man, since Robert Frost wrote

the poem and nothing in the poem clearly indicates that the

speaker is not a man. But, and this point will be important, the

speaker perhaps feels that he is not a very masculine man. As we

will see, the word "queer" appears in the poem, and, also, the

speaker uses the word "lovely," which sounds more like the word

a woman would use than a man.) In line 3 the speaker says he is

"stopping here," and it is clear that "here" is by woods, since

"woods" is mentioned not only in the title but also in the first line

of the poem, and again in the second stanza, and still again in the

last stanza. It is equally clear that, as the title says, there is snow,

and that the time is evening. The speaker mentions "snow" and "downy flake," and he says this is "The darkest evening of the year."

But in what sense is the poem about <u>more</u> than the title? The title does not tell us anything about the man who is "stopping by woods," but the poem--the man's meditation--tells us a lot about him. In the first stanza he reveals that he is uneasy at the thought that the owner of the woods may see him stopping by the woods. Maybe he is uneasy because he is trespassing, but the poem does not actually say that he has illegally entered someone else's property. More likely, he feels uneasy, almost ashamed, of watching the "woods fill up with snow." That is, he would not want anyone to see that he actually is enjoying a beautiful aspect of nature and is not hurrying about whatever his real business is in thrifty Yankee style.

The second stanza gives more evidence that he feels guilty about enjoying beauty. He feels so guilty that he even thinks the horse thinks there is something odd about him. In fact, he says that the horse thinks he is "queer," which of course may just mean odd, but also (as is shown by <u>The American Heritage Dictionary</u>) it can mean "gay," "homosexual." A real man, he sort of suggests, wouldn't spend time looking at snow in the woods.

So far, then, the speaker in two ways has indicated that he feels insecure, though perhaps he does not realize that he has given himself away. First, he expresses uneasiness that someone might see him watching the woods fill up with snow. Second, he expresses uneasiness when he suggests that even the horse

MacDonald 3

thinks he is strange, maybe even "queer" or unmanly, or at least

unbusinesslike. And so in the last stanza, even though he finds

the woods beautiful, he decides <u>not</u> to stop and to see the woods

fill up with snow. And his description of the woods as "lovely"--a

woman's word--sounds as though he may be something less than

a he-man. He seems to feel ashamed of himself for enjoying the

sight of the snowy woods and for seeing them as "lovely," and so

he tells himself that he has spent enough time looking at the

woods and that he must go on about his business. In fact, he tells

himself <u>twice</u> that he has business to attend to. Why? Perhaps he

is insisting too much. Just as we saw that he was excessively

nervous in the first stanza, afraid that someone might see him

trespassing and enjoying the beautiful spectacle, now at the end

he is again afraid that someone might see him loitering, and so

he very firmly, using repetition as a form of emphasis, tries to

reassure himself that he is not too much attracted by beauty and

is a man of business who keeps his promises.

Frost gives us, then, a man who indeed is seen "stopping by

woods on a snowy evening," but a man who, afraid of what

society will think of him, is also afraid to "stop" long enough to

fully enjoy the sight that attracts him, because he is driven by a

sense that he may be seen to be trespassing and also may be

thought to be unmanly. So after only a brief stop in the woods he

forces himself to go on, a victim (though he probably doesn't

know it) of the work ethic and of an over-simple idea of

manliness.

Let's examine this essay briefly.

The title is interesting. It gives the reader a good idea of which literary work will be discussed ("Stopping by Woods") and it arouses interest, in this case by a sort of wordplay ("Stopping . . . Going On"). A title of this sort is preferable to a title that merely announces the topic, such as "An Analysis of Frost's 'Stopping by Woods'" or "On a Poem by Robert Frost."

The opening paragraph helpfully names the exact topic (Robert Frost's poem) and arouses interest by asserting that the poem is about something more than its title. The writer's thesis presumably will be a fairly specific assertion concerning what else the poem is "about."

The body of the essay, beginning with the second paragraph, begins to develop the thesis. (The **thesis** perhaps can be summarized thus: "The speaker, insecure of his masculinity, feels ashamed that he responds with pleasure to the sight of the snowy woods.") The writer's evidence in the second paragraph is that the word "queer" (a word sometimes used of homosexuals) appears, and that the word "lovely" is "more like the word a woman would use than a man." Readers of MacDonald's essay may at this point be unconvinced by this evidence, but probably they suspend judgement. In any case, he has offered what he considers to be evidence in support of his thesis.

The next paragraph dwells on what is said to be the speaker's uneasiness, and the following paragraph returns to the word "queer," which, MacDonald correctly says, can mean "gay, homosexual." The question of course is whether *here,* in this poem, the word has this meaning. Do we agree with MacDonald's assertion, in the last sentence of this paragraph, that Frost is suggesting that "A real man . . . wouldn't spend time looking at snow in the woods"? Clearly this is the way MacDonald takes the poem—but is his response to these lines reasonable? After all, what Frost says is this: "My little horse must think it queer / To stop without a farmhouse near." Is it reasonable to see a reference to homosexuality (rather than merely to oddness) in *this* use of the word "queer"? Hasn't MacDonald offered a response that, so to speak, is private? It is *his* response—but are we likely to share it, to agree that we see it in Frost's poem?

The next paragraph, amplifying the point that the speaker is insecure, offers as evidence the argument that "lovely" is more often a woman's word than a man's. Probably most readers will agree on this point, though many or all might deny that only a gay man would use the word "lovely." And what do you think of MacDonald's assertions that the speaker of the poem "was excessively nervous in the first stanza" and is now "afraid that someone might see him loitering"? In your opinion, does the text lend much support to MacDonald's view?

The concluding paragraph effectively reasserts and clarifies MacDonald's thesis, saying that the speaker hesitates to stop and enjoy the woods because "he is driven by a sense that he may be seen to be trespassing and also may be thought to be unmanly."

The big questions, then, are these:

- Is the thesis *argued* rather than merely asserted, and
- Is it argued *convincingly?*

Or, to put it another way,

- Is the evidence adequate?

MacDonald certainly does argue (offer reasons) rather than merely assert, but does he offer enough evidence to make you think that his response is one that you can share? Has he helped you to enjoy the poem by seeing things that you may not have noticed—or has he said things that, however interesting, seem to you not to be in close contact with the poem as you see it?

Here is another interpretation of the same poem.

Sample Essay by a Student: "'Stopping by Woods on a Snowy Evening' as a Short Story"

Fong 1

Sara Fong

Professor Patel

English 102

3 December 2004

"Stopping by Woods on a Snowy Evening" as a Short Story

Robert Frost's "Stopping by Woods on a Snowy Evening" can

be read as a poem about a man who pauses to observe the beauty

of nature, and it can also be read as a poem about a man with a

death wish, a man who seems to long to give himself up

completely to nature and thus escape his responsibilities as a

citizen. Much depends, apparently, on what a reader wants to

emphasize. For instance, a reader can emphasize especially

appealing lines about the beauty of nature: "The only other

sound's the sweep / Of easy wind and downy flake," and "The

woods are lovely, dark and deep." On the other hand, a reader can

emphasize lines that show the speaker is fully aware of the

responsibilities that most of us agree we have. For instance, at

the very start of the poem he recognizes that the woods are not

his but are owned by someone else, and at the end of the poem he

recognizes that he has "promises to keep" and that before he

sleeps (dies?) he must accomplish many things (go for "miles").

Does a reader have to choose between these two interpretations? I don't think so; to the contrary, I think it makes sense to read the poem as a kind of very short story, with a character whose developing thoughts make up a plot with four stages. In the first stage, the central figure is an ordinary person with rather ordinary thoughts. His very first thought is of the owner of the woods. He knows who the owner is, and since the owner lives in the village, the poet feels safe in trespassing, or at least in watching the woods "fill up with snow." Then, very subtly, the poet begins to tell us that although this seems to be an ordinary person thinking ordinary thoughts, he is a somewhat special person in a special situation. First of all, the horse thinks something is strange. He shakes his bells, wondering why the driver doesn't keep moving, as presumably ordinary drivers would. Second, we are told that this is "The darkest evening of the year." Frost could simply have said that the evening is dark, but he goes out of his way to make the evening a special evening.

We are now through with the first ten lines, and only six lines remain, yet in these six lines the story goes through two additional phases. The first three of these lines ("The only other sound's the sweep / Of easy wind and downy flake" and "The woods are lovely, dark and deep") are probably the most beautiful lines, in the sense that they are the ones that make us say, "I wish I were there," or "I'd love to experience this." We feel that the poet has moved from the ordinary thoughts of the first stanza, about

Fong 3

such businesslike things as who owns the woods and where the

owner's house is, to less materialistic thoughts, thoughts about

the beauty of the nonhuman world of nature. And now, with the

three final lines, we get the fourth stage of the story, the return

to the ordinary world of people, the world of "promises." But this

world that we get at the end is not exactly the same as the world

we got at the beginning. The world at the beginning of the poem

is a world of property (who owns the woods, and where the house

is), but the world at the end of the poem is a world of unspecified

and rather mysterious responsibilities ("promises to keep," "miles

to go before I sleep"). It is almost as though the poet's experience

of the beauty of nature--a beauty that for a moment made him

forget the world of property--has in fact served to sharpen his

sense that human beings have responsibilities. He clearly sees

that "The woods are lovely, dark and deep," and then he says (I

add the italics), "<u>But</u> I have promises to keep." The "but" would be

logical if after saying that the woods are lovely, dark and deep, he

had said something like "But in the daylight they look different,"

or "But one can freeze to death in them." The logic of what Frost

says, however, is not at all clear: "The woods are lovely, dark and

deep, / But I have promises to keep." What is the logical

connection? We have to supply one, something like "but, <u>because</u>

<u>we are human beings we have responsibilities</u>; we can refresh

ourselves by perceiving the beauties of nature, and we can even

for a moment get so caught up that we seem to enter an

Fong 4

enchanted forest ('the woods are lovely, dark and deep'), but we

cannot forget our responsibilities."

My point is not that Frost ends with an important moral,

and it is also not that we have to choose between saying it is a

poem about nature or a poem about a man with a death wish.

Rather, my point is that the poem takes us through several

stages and that, although the poem begins and ends with the

speaker in the woods, the speaker has undergone mental

experiences--has, we might say, gone through a plot with a

conflict (the appeal of the snowy woods versus the call to return

to the human world). It's not a matter of good versus evil and of

one side winning. Frost in no way suggests that it is wrong to

feel the beauty of nature--even to the momentary exclusion of all

other thoughts. But the poem is certainly not simply a praise of

the beauty of nature. Frost shows us, in this mini-story or mini-

drama, one character who sees the woods as property, then sees

them as a place of almost overwhelming beauty, and then

(maybe refreshed by this experience) rejoins the world of chores

and responsibilities.

Topics for Critical Thinking and Writing

1. What is the thesis of the essay?
2. Does the essayist offer convincing evidence to support the thesis?
3. Do you consider the essay to be well written, poorly written, or something in between? On what evidence do you base your opinion?

YOUR TURN: POEMS FOR INTERPRETATION

JOHN MILTON

John Milton (1608–1674) was born into a well-to-do family in London, where from childhood he was a student of languages, mastering at an early age Latin, Greek, Hebrew, and a number of modern languages. Instead of becoming a minister in the Anglican Church, he resolved to become a poet and spent five years at his family's country home, reading. His attacks against the monarchy secured him a position in Oliver Cromwell's Puritan government as Latin secretary for foreign affairs. He became totally blind, but he continued his work through secretaries, one of whom was Andrew Marvell, author of "To His Coy Mistress" (page 755). With the restoration of the monarchy in 1660, Milton was for a time confined but was later pardoned in the general amnesty. Until his death he continued to work on many subjects, including his greatest poem, the epic Paradise Lost.

When I Consider How My Light Is Spent

When I consider how my light is spent
  Ere half my days, in this dark world and wide,
  And that one talent which is death to hide°
  Lodged with me useless,° though my soul more bent   4
To serve therewith my Maker, and present
  My true account, lest he returning chide;
  "Doth God exact day-labor, light denied?"
  I fondly° ask; but Patience to prevent°   8
That murmur, soon replies, "God doth not need
  Either man's work or his own gifts; who best
  Bear his mild yoke, they serve him best. His state
Is kingly. Thousands at his bidding speed   12
  And post o'er land and ocean without rest:
  They also serve who only stand and wait."

[1655]

3 There is a pun in *talent*, relating Milton's literary talent to Christ's Parable of the Talents (Matthew 25.14 ff.), in which a servant is rebuked for not putting his talent (a unit of money) to use. **4 useless** a pun on *use*, i.e., usury, interest. **8 fondly** foolishly. **prevent** forestall.

Topics for Critical Thinking and Writing

1. This Petrarchan sonnet (see page 502) is sometimes called "On His Blindness," though Milton never gave it a title. Do you think this title gets toward the heart of the poem? Explain. If you were to give it a title, what would the title be?
2. Read the parable in Matthew 25.14–30, and then consider how close the parable is to Milton's life as Milton describes it in this poem.

ROBERT FROST
Mending Wall

Something there is that doesn't love a wall,
That sends the frozen-ground-swell under it,
And spills the upper boulders in the sun;
And makes gaps even two can pass abreast.
The work of hunters is another thing: 5
I have come after them and made repair
Where they have left not one stone on a stone,
But they would have the rabbit out of hiding,
To please the yelping dogs. The gaps I mean,
No one has seen them made or heard them made,   10
But at spring mending-time we find them there.
I let my neighbor know beyond the hill;
And on a day we meet to walk the line
And set the wall between us once again.
We keep the wall between us as we go.   15
To each the boulders that have fallen to each.
And some are loaves and some so nearly balls
We have to use a spell to make them balance:
"Stay where you are until our backs are turned!"
We wear our fingers rough with handling them.   20
Oh, just another kind of outdoor game,
One on a side. It comes to little more:
There where it is we do not need the wall:
He is all pine and I am apple orchard.
My apple trees will never get across   25
And eat the cones under his pines, I tell him.
He only says, "Good fences make good neighbors."
Spring is the mischief in me, and I wonder
If I could put a notion in his head:
"*Why* do they make good neighbors? Isn't it   30
Where there are cows? But here there are no cows.
Before I built a wall I'd ask to know
What I was walling in or walling out,
And to whom I was like to give offense.
Something there is that doesn't love a wall,   35
That wants it down." I could say "Elves" to him,
But it's not elves exactly, and I'd rather
He said it for himself. I see him there
Bringing a stone grasped firmly by the top
In each hand, like an old-stone savage armed.   40
He moves in darkness as it seems to me,
Not of woods only and the shade of trees.
He will not go behind his father's saying,
And he likes having thought of it so well
He says again, "Good fences make good neighbors."   45

[1914]

Topics for Critical Thinking and Writing

1. The poem includes a scene, or action, in which the speaker and a neighbor are engaged. Briefly summarize the scene. What indicates that the scene has been enacted before and will be again?
2. Compare and contrast the speaker and the neighbor.
3. Notice that the speaker, not the neighbor, initiates the business of repairing the wall (line 12). Why do you think he does this?
4. Both the speaker and the neighbor repeat themselves; they each make one point twice in identical language. What do they say? And why does Frost allow the neighbor to have the last word?
5. "Something there is that doesn't love a wall" adds up to "Something doesn't love a wall." Or does it? Within the context of the poem, what is the difference between the two statements?
6. Write an essay of 500 words, telling of an experience in which you came to conclude that "good fences make good neighbors." Or tell of an experience that led you to conclude that fences (they can be figurative fences, of course) are "like to give offense" (see lines 32–34).

WILLIAM WORDSWORTH

William Wordsworth (1770–1850) grew up in the Lake District in England. After graduating from Cambridge University in 1791, he spent a year in France, where he fell in love with a French girl and fathered her child. His enthusiasm for the French Revolution waned, and he returned alone to England, where he devoted his life to poetry. We print a poem, written in 1799, that is one of five poems customarily called "Lucy poems," even though this particular poem, unlike the other four, does not mention the woman's name. It is not known if the poems refer to a real person.

A Slumber Did My Spirit Seal

A slumber did my spirit seal;
  I had no human fears;
She seemed a thing that could not feel
  The touch of earthly years.

4

No motion has she now, no force;
  She neither hears nor sees;
Rolled round in earth's diurnal course,
  With rocks, and stones, and trees.

8

[1799]

Topics for Critical Thinking and Writing

Each of the following assertions represents a brief interpretation. Evaluate each, citing evidence to support or rebut it.

1. The first stanza expresses the speaker's comforting but naive view (his *spirit,* i.e., his intelligence, was in a *slumber*) that his beloved was exempt from the pressures of this world; the second stanza expresses his horrified realization that, now dead, she is mere inanimate matter mechanistically hurled into violent motion.

2. The poem, by a pantheist—someone who identifies the Deity with everything in the universe—is about the poet's realization that the woman he loved, who seemed to be apart from everything else, is now (through her death) assimilated into the grandeur of all that is on the Earth; her death is a return to the life of nature.

3. The poem is ambiguous—just as, say, the following sentence is ambiguous: "Martha's mother died when she was twenty." (Who was twenty, Martha or her mother?) There is no way to decide between the first and second views expressed.

4. The word *diurnal* ("daily") adds a solemnity that makes it impossible to see the poem as a statement about the brutality of Lucy's death. Further, *diurnal* contains the word *urn,* thereby affirming that the entire Earth is her funeral urn.

5. Even if the second view correctly summarizes Wordsworth's pantheism, *for today's readers* the poem is about the brute fact of death.

6. The language is ambiguous, so the only intelligent way to decide between conflicting interpretations is to choose the interpretation that best fits in with what we know about the author.

7. Here, as in most poetry by males, the female is allowed no significant identity. She is a "thing" (line 3), she is the object of the poet's love, she seems to be above nature (thus she is the traditional woman on a pedestal), she is a nature spirit, she is the poet's inspiration—she is lots of things, but she is not a person.

   If none of the preceding statements seems to you to be just what you would say if you were asked to summarize your interpretation, set forth your own view, in 50–75 words, and then support it by pointing to details in the poem.

T. S. ELIOT

Thomas Stearns Eliot (1888–1965) was born into a New England family that had moved to St. Louis. He attended a preparatory school in Massachusetts, then graduated from Harvard and did further study in literature and philosophy in France, Germany, and England. In 1914 he began working for Lloyd's Bank in London, and three years later he published his first book of poems (it included "Prufrock"). In 1925 he joined a publishing firm, and in 1927 he became a British citizen and a member of the Church of England. Much of his later poetry, unlike "The Love Song of J. Alfred Prufrock," is highly religious. In 1948 Eliot received the Nobel Prize for Literature.

The Love Song of J. Alfred Prufrock

S'io credesse che mia risposta fosse
A persona che mai tornasse al mondo,
Questa fiamma staria senza piu scosse.
Ma perciocche giammai di questo fondo
Non torno vivo alcun. s'i' odo il vero,
*Senza tema d'infama ti rispondo.**

Let us go then, you and I,
When the evening is spread out against the sky
Like a patient etherized upon a table;
Let us go, through certain half-deserted streets,
The muttering retreats   5
Of restless nights in one-night cheap hotels
And sawdust restaurants with oyster-shells:
Streets that follow like a tedious argument
Of insidious intent
To lead you to an overwhelming question   10
Oh, do not ask, "What is it?"
Let us go and make our visit.

In the room the women come and go
Talking of Michelangelo.

The yellow fog that rubs its back upon the window-panes,   15
The yellow smoke that rubs its muzzle on the window-panes
Licked its tongue into the corners of the evening,
Lingered upon the pools that stand in drains,
Let fall upon its back the soot that falls from chimneys,
Slipped by the terrace, made a sudden leap,   20
And seeing that it was a soft October night,
Curled once about the house, and fell asleep.

And indeed there will be time
For the yellow smoke that slides along the street,
Rubbing its back upon the window-panes;   25
There will be time, there will be time
To prepare a face to meet the faces that you meet;
There will be time to murder and create,
And time for all the works and days° of hands
That lift and drop a question on your plate;   30
Time for you and time for me,
And time yet for a hundred indecisions,
And for a hundred visions and revisions,
Before the taking of a toast and tea.

*In Dante's *Inferno* XXVII:61–66, a damned soul who had sought absolution before committing a crime addresses Dante, thinking that his words will never reach the Earth: "If I believed that my answer were to a person who could ever return to the world, this flame would no longer quiver. But because no one ever returned from this depth, if what I hear is true without fear of infamy, I answer you."   **29 works and days** "Works and Days" is the title of a poem on farm life by Hesiod (eighth century B.C.).

In the room the women come and go   35
Talking of Michelangelo.

And indeed there will be time
To wonder, "Do I dare?" and, "Do I dare?"
Time to turn back and descend the stair,
With a bald spot in the middle of my hair—   40
[They will say: "How his hair is growing thin!"]
My morning coat, my collar mounting firmly to the chin,
My necktie rich and modest, but asserted by a simple pin—
[They will say: "But how his arms and legs are thin!"]
Do I dare   45
Disturb the universe?
In a minute there is time
For decisions and revisions which a minute will reverse.

For I have known them all already, known them all:—
Have known the evenings, mornings, afternoons,   50
I have measured out my life with coffee spoons;
I know the voices dying with a dying fall°
Beneath the music from a farther room.
        So how should I presume?

And I have known the eyes already, known them all—   55
The eyes that fix you in a formulated phrase,
And when I am formulated, sprawling on a pin,
When I am pinned and wriggling on the wall,
Then how should I begin
To spit out all the butt-ends of my days and ways?   60
        And how should I presume?

And I have known the arms already, known them all—
Arms that are braceleted and white and bare
[But in the lamplight, downed with light brown hair!]

Is it perfume from a dress   65
That makes me so digress?
Arms that lie along a table, or wrap about a shawl.
        And should I then presume?
        And how should I begin?

                                · · ·

Shall I say, I have gone at dusk through narrow streets   70
And watched the smoke that rises from the pipes
Of lonely men in shirt-sleeves, leaning out of windows? . . .

I should have been a pair of ragged claws
Scuttling across the floors of silent seas.

                                · · ·

And the afternoon, the evening, sleeps so peacefully!   75
Smoothed by long fingers,
Asleep . . . tired . . . or it malingers,

52 dying fall this line echoes Shakespeare's *Twelfth Night* 1.1.4.

Stretched on the floor, here beside you and me.
Should I, after tea and cakes and ices,
Have the strength to force the moment to its crisis?   80
But though I have wept and fasted, wept and prayed,
Though I have seen my head [grown slightly bald]
   brought in upon a platter,°
I am no prophet—and here's no great matter;
And I have seen the moment of my greatness flicker,
And I have seen the eternal Footman hold my coat, and snicker,   85
And in short, I was afraid.

And would it have been worth it, after all,
After the cups, the marmalade, the tea,
Among the porcelain, among some talk of you and me,
Would it have been worth while,   90
To have bitten off the matter with a smile,
To have squeezed the universe into a ball°
To roll it toward some overwhelming question,
To say: "I am Lazarus,° come from the dead,
Come back to tell you all, I shall tell you all"—   95
If one, settling a pillow by her head,
   Should say: "That is not what I meant at all.
   That is not it, at all."

And would it have been worth it, after all,
Would it have been worth while,   100
After the sunsets and the dooryards and the sprinkled streets.
After the novels, after the teacups, after the skirts that trail along the floor—
And this, and so much more?—
It is impossible to say just what I mean!
But as if a magic lantern threw the nerves in patterns on a screen: 105
Would it have been worth while
If one, settling a pillow or throwing off a shawl,
And turning toward the window, should say:
   "That is not it at all,
   That is not what I meant at all."   110

No! I am not Prince Hamlet, nor was meant to be;
Am an attendant lord, one that will do
To swell a progress, start a scene or two,
Advise the prince; no doubt, an easy tool,
Deferential, glad to be of use,   115
Politic, cautious, and meticulous;
Full of high sentence,° but a bit obtuse;°
At times, indeed, almost ridiculous—
Almost, at times, the Fool.

81–83 But . . . platter these lines allude to John the Baptist (see Matthew 14.1–11). **92 To have . . . ball** this line echoes lines 41–42 of Marvell's "To His Coy Mistress" (see page 755). **94 Lazarus** see Luke 16 and John 11.   **117 full of high sentence** see Chaucer's description of the Clerk of Oxford in the *Canterbury Tales*.   **112–117 Am . . . obtuse** these lines allude to Polonius and perhaps other figures in *Hamlet*.

I grow old . . . I grow old   120
I shall wear the bottoms of my trousers rolled.

Shall I part my hair behind? Do I dare to eat a peach?
I shall wear white flannel trousers, and walk upon the beach.
I have heard the mermaids singing, each to each.
I do not think that they will sing to me.   125

I have seen them riding seaward on the waves
Combing the white hair of the waves blown back
When the wind blows the water white and black.

We have lingered in the chambers of the sea
By sea-girls wreathed with seaweed red and brown   130
Till human voices wake us, and we drown.

[1910–11]

Topics for Critical Thinking and Writing

1. How does the speaker's name help to characterize him? What suggestions—of class, race, personality—do you find in it? Does the title of this poem strike you as ironic? If so, how or why?
2. What qualities of big-city life are suggested in the poem? How are these qualities linked to the speaker's mood? What other details of the setting—the weather, the time of day—express or reflect his mood? What images do you find especially striking?
3. The speaker's thoughts are represented in a stream-of-consciousness monologue, that is, in what appears to be an unedited flow of thought. Nevertheless, they reveal a story. What is the story?
4. In a paragraph, characterize Prufrock as he might be characterized by one of the women in the poem, and then, in a paragraph or two, offer your own characterization of him.
5. Consider the possibility that the "you" whom Prufrock is addressing is not a listener but is one aspect of Prufrock, and the "I" is another. Given this possibility, in a paragraph characterize the "you," and in another paragraph characterize the "I."
6. Prufrock has gone to a therapist, a psychiatrist, or a member of the clergy for help. Write a 500-word transcript of their session.

JOHN KEATS

John Keats (1795–1821), son of a London stablekeeper, was taken out of school when he was 15 and apprenticed to a surgeon and apothecary. In 1816 he was licensed to practice as an apothecary-surgeon, but he almost immediately abandoned medicine and decided to make a career as a poet. His progress was amazing: he published books of poems—to mixed reviews—in 1817, 1818, and 1820, before dying of tuberculosis at the age of 25. Today he is esteemed as one of England's greatest poets.

Ode on a Grecian Urn

I

Thou still unravished bride of quietness,
   Thou foster-child of silence and slow time,
Sylvan historian, who canst thus express
   A flowery tale more sweetly than our rhyme:
What leaf-fringed legend haunts about thy shape   5
   Of deities or mortals, or of both,
      In Tempe or the dales of Arcady?
   What men or gods are these? What maidens loth?
What mad pursuit? What struggle to escape?
      What pipes and timbrels? What wild ecstacy?   10

II

Heard melodies are sweet, but those unheard
   Are sweeter; therefore, ye soft pipes, play on;
Not to the sensual° ear, but, more endeared,
   Pipe to the spirit ditties of no tone:
Fair youth, beneath the trees, thou canst not leave   15
   Thy song, nor ever can those trees be bare;
      Bold Lover, never, never canst thou kiss,
Though winning near the goal—yet, do not grieve;
      She cannot fade, though thou hast not thy bliss,
   For ever wilt thou love, and she be fair!   20

III

Ah, happy, happy boughs! that cannot shed
   Your leaves, nor ever bid the Spring adieu;
And, happy melodist, unwearied,
   For ever piping songs for ever new;
More happy love! more happy, happy love!   25
   For ever warm and still to be enjoyed,
      For ever panting, and for ever young;
All breathing human passion far above,
   That leaves a heart high-sorrowful and cloyed,
      A burning forehead, and a parching tongue.   30

IV

Who are these coming to the sacrifice?
   To what green altar, O mysterious priest,
Lead'st thou that heifer lowing at the skies,
   And all her silken flanks with garlands drest?
What little town by river or sea shore,   35
   Or mountain-built with peaceful citadel,
      Is emptied of this folk, this pious morn?

13 sensual sensuous.

And, little town, thy streets for evermore
   Will silent be; and not a soul to tell
      Why thou art desolate can e'er return.   40

V

O Attic shape! Fair attitude! with brede°
   Of marble men and maidens overwrought,
With forest branches and the trodden weed;
   Thou, silent form, dost tease us out of thought
As doth eternity: Cold Pastoral!   45
When old age shall this generation waste,
     Thou shalt remain, in midst of other woe
     Than ours, a friend to man, to whom thou say'st,
"Beauty is truth, truth beauty,"—that is all
   Ye know on earth, and all ye need to know.   50

[1820]

41 **brede** design.

Topics for Critical Thinking and Writing

1. In the first stanza Keats calls the urn an "unravished bride of quietness," a "foster-child of silence and slow time," and a "Sylvan historian." Paraphrase each of these terms.
2. How much sense does it make to say (lines 11–12) that "Heard melodies are sweet, but those unheard / Are sweeter"?
3. In the second stanza Keats says that the youth will forever sing, the trees will forever have their foliage, and the woman will forever be beautiful. But what words in the stanza suggest that this scene is not entirely happy? Where else in the poem is it suggested that there are painful aspects to the images on the urn?
4. What arguments can you offer to support the view that "Beauty is truth, truth beauty"?
5. There is much uncertainty about whether everything in the last two lines should be enclosed within quotation marks, or only "Beauty is truth, truth beauty." If only these five words from line 49 should be enclosed within quotation marks, does the speaker address the rest of line 49 and the whole of line 50 to the urn, or to the reader of the poem?

17

Arguing an Evaluation

CRITICISM AND EVALUATION

Although, as previously noted, in ordinary usage *criticism* implies finding fault, and therefore implies evaluation—"This story is weak"—in fact most literary criticism is *not* concerned with evaluation. Rather, it is chiefly concerned with *interpretation* (the setting forth of meaning) and with *analysis* (examination of relationships among the parts, or of causes and effects). For instance, an interpretation may argue that in *Death of a Salesman* Willy Loman is the victim of a cruel capitalistic economy, and an analysis may show how the symbolic setting of the play (a stage direction tells us that "towering, angular shapes" surround the salesman's house) contributes to the meaning. In our discussion of "What Is Literature?" we saw that an analysis of Robert Frost's "The Span of Life" (p. 44) called attention to the contrast between the meter of the first line (relatively uneven or irregular, with an exceptional number of heavy stresses) and the meter of the second (relatively even and jingling). The analysis also called attention to the contrast between the content of the first line (the old dog) and the second (the speaker's memory of a young dog):

> The old dog barks backward without getting up.
> I can remember when he was a pup.

In our discussion we did not worry about whether this poem deserves an A, B, or C, nor did we consider whether it was better or worse than some other poem by Frost, or by some other writer. And, to repeat, if you read books and journals devoted to literary study, you find chiefly discussions of meaning. For the most part, critics assume that the works they are writing about have value and are good enough to merit attention, so critics largely concern themselves with other matters.

Still, some critical writing is indeed concerned with evaluation—with saying that works are good or bad, dated or classic, major or minor. (The language need not be as explicit as these words are: Evaluation can also be conveyed through words like *moving, successful, effective, important,* or, on the other hand, *tedious, unsuccessful, weak,* and *trivial.*) In reviews of plays, books, musical and dance performances, and films, professional critics usually devote much of their space to evaluating the work or the performance, or both. The reviewer seeks, finally, to tell readers whether to buy a book or a ticket—or to save their money and their time.

In short, although in our independent reading we read what we like, and we need not argue that one work is better than another, the issue of evaluation is evident all around us.

ARE THERE CRITICAL STANDARDS?

One approach to evaluating a work of literature, or, indeed, to evaluating any-thing at all, is to rely on personal taste. This approach is evident in a statement such as "I don't know anything about modern art, but I know what I like." The idea is old, at least as old as the Roman saying *De gustibus non est disputandum* ("There is no disputing tastes").

If we say "This is a good work" or "This book is greater than that book," are we saying anything beyond "I like this" and "I like this better than that"? Are all expressions of evaluation really nothing more than expressions of taste? Most peo-ple believe that if there are such things as works of art, or works of literature, there must be standards by which they can be evaluated, just as most other things are evaluated by standards. The standards for evaluating a scissors, for instance, are perfectly clear: It ought to cut cleanly, it ought not to need frequent sharpen-ing, and it ought to feel comfortable in the hand. We may also want it to look nice (perhaps to be painted—or on the contrary to reveal its stainless steel), and to be inexpensive, rustproof, and so on, but in any case we can easily state our stan-dards. Similarly, there are agreed-upon standards for evaluating figure skating, gymnastics, fluency in language, and so on.

But what are the standards for evaluating literature? In earlier pages we have implied one standard: In a good work of literature, all of the parts contribute to the whole, making a unified work. Some people would add that mere unity is not enough; a work of high quality needs not only to be unified but also to be com-plex. The writer offers a "performance in words" (Frost's words, again), and when we read, we can see if the writer has successfully kept all of the Indian clubs in the air. If, for instance, the stated content of the poem is mournful, yet the meter jingles, we can probably say that the performance is unsuccessful; at least one of the juggler's Indian clubs is clattering on the floor.

Here are some of the standards commonly set forth:

- Personal taste
- Truth, realism
- Moral content
- Esthetic qualities, for instance unity

Let's look at some of these in detail.

Morality and Truth as Standards

"It is always a writer's duty to make the world better." Thus wrote Samuel Johnson, in 1765, in his "Preface to Shakespeare." In this view, **morality** plays a large role: A story that sympathetically treats lesbian or gay love is, from a tradi-tional Judeo-Christian perspective, probably regarded as a bad story, or at least not as worthy as a story that celebrates heterosexual married love. On the other hand, a gay or lesbian critic, or anyone not committed to Judeo-Christian values, might regard the story highly because, in such a reader's view, it helps to educate readers and thereby does something "to make the world better."

But there are obvious problems. For one thing, a gay or lesbian story might strike even a reader with traditional values as a work that is effectively told, with believable and memorable characters, whereas a story of heterosexual married love might be unbelievable, awkwardly told, trite, sentimental. (More about sentimentality in a moment.) How much value should we give to the ostensible content of the story, the obvious moral or morality, and how much value should we give to the artistry exhibited in telling the story?

People differ greatly about moral (and religious) issues. Edward Fitzgerald's 1859 translation of *The Rubáiyát of Omar Khayyám* (a twelfth-century Persian poem) suggests that God doesn't exist, or—perhaps worse—if He does exist, He doesn't care about us. That God does not exist is a view held by many moral people; it is also a view opposed by many moral people. The issue then may become a matter of **truth.** Does the value of the poem depend on which view is right? In fact, does a reader have to subscribe to Fitzgerald's view to enjoy (and to evaluate highly) the following stanza from the poem, in which Fitzgerald suggests that the pleasures of this world are the only paradise that we can experience?

> A book of verses underneath the bough,
> A jug of wine, a loaf of bread—and thou
>   Beside me singing in the wilderness—
> Oh, wilderness were paradise enow!

Some critics can give high value to a literary work only if they share its beliefs, if they think that the work corresponds to reality. They measure the work against their vision of the truth.

Other readers can highly value a work of literature that expresses ideas they do not believe, arguing that literature does not require us to believe in its views. Rather, this theory claims, literature gives a reader a strong sense of *what it feels like* to hold certain views—even though the reader does not share those views. Take, for instance, a lyric poem in which Christina Rossetti (1830–1894), a devout Anglican, expresses both spiritual numbness and spiritual hope. Here is one stanza from "A Better Resurrection":

> My life is like a broken bowl,
>   A broken bowl that cannot hold
> One drop of water for my soul
>   Or cordial in the searching cold:
> Cast in the fire the perished thing:
>   Melt and remould it, till it be
> A royal cup for Him, my King:
>   O Jesus, drink of me.

One need not be an Anglican suffering a crisis to find this poem of considerable interest. It offers insight into a state of mind, and the truth or falsity of religious belief is not at issue. Similarly, we can argue that although *The Divine Comedy* by Dante Alighieri (1265–1321) is deeply a Roman Catholic work, the non-Catholic reader can read it with interest and pleasure because of (for example) its rich portrayal of a wide range of characters, the most famous of whom perhaps are the pathetic lovers Paolo and Francesca. In Dante's view, they are eternally damned because they were unrepentant adulterers, but a reader need not share this belief.

Other Ways of Thinking about Truth and Realism

Other solutions to the problem of whether a reader must share a writer's beliefs have been offered. One extreme view says that beliefs are irrelevant, since literature has nothing to do with truth. In this view, a work of art does not correspond to anything "outside" itself, that is, to anything in the real world. If a work of art has any "truth," it is only in the sense of being internally consistent. Thus Shakespeare's *Macbeth,* like, say, "Rock-a-bye Baby," isn't making assertions about reality. *Macbeth* has nothing to do with the history of Scotland, just as (in this view) Shakespeare's *Julius Caesar* has nothing to do with the history of Rome, although Shakespeare borrowed some of his material from history books. These tragedies, like lullabies, are worlds in themselves—not to be judged against historical accounts of Scotland or Rome—and we are interested in the characters in the plays only as they exist *in the plays.* We may require, for instance, that the characters be consistent, believable, and engaging, but we cannot require that they correspond to historical figures. Literary works are neither true nor false; they are only (when successful) coherent and interesting. The poet William Butler Yeats (1865–1939) perhaps had in mind something along these lines when he said that you can refute a philosopher, but you cannot refute the song of sixpence. And indeed "Sing a song of sixpence, / Pocket full of rye" has endured for a couple of centuries, perhaps partly because it has nothing to do with truth or falsity; it has created its own engaging world.

And yet it's possible to object, offering a commonsense response: Surely when we see a play, or read an engaging work of literature, whether it is old or new, we feel that somehow the work says something about the life around us, the real world. True, some of what we read—let's say, detective fiction—is chiefly fanciful: We read it to test our wits, or to escape, or to kill time. But most literature seems to be connected to life. This commonsense view, that literature is related to life, has an ancient history, and in fact almost everyone in the Western world believed it from the time of the ancient Greeks until the nineteenth century. And of course many people—including authors and highly skilled readers—still believe it today.

Certainly a good deal of literature, most notably the realistic short story and the novel, is devoted to giving a detailed picture that at least *looks like* the real world. One reason we read the fiction of Kate Chopin is to find out what "the real world" of Creole New Orleans in the late nineteenth century was like—as seen through Chopin's eyes, of course. (You need not be a Marxist to believe, with Karl Marx, that you can learn more about industrial England from the novels of Dickens and Mrs. Gaskell than from economic treatises.) Writers of stories, novels, and plays are concerned to give plausible, indeed precise and insightful, images of the relationships between people. Writers of lyric poems presumably are specialists in presenting human feelings—the experience of love, for instance, or of the loss of faith. And presumably we are invited to compare the writer's created world to the world that we live in, perhaps to be reminded that our own lives can be richer than they are.

Even when a writer describes an earlier time, the implication is that the description is accurate, and especially that people *did* behave the way the writer says they did—and the way our own daily experience shows us that people do behave. Here is George Eliot at the beginning of her novel *Adam Bede* (1859):

> With a single drop of ink for a mirror, the Egyptian sorcerer undertook to reveal to any chance comer far-reaching visions of the past. This is what I undertake to do for you, reader. With this drop of ink at the end of my pen, I will show you the roomy workshop of Jonathan Burge, carpenter and builder in the village of Hayslope, as it appeared on the 18th of June, in the year of Our Lord, 1799.

Why do novelists like George Eliot give us detailed pictures, and cause us to become deeply involved in the lives of their characters? Another novelist, D. H. Lawrence, offers a relevant comment in the ninth chapter of *Lady Chatterley's Lover* (1928):

> It is the way our sympathy flows and recoils that really determines our lives. And here lies the vast importance of the novel, properly handled. It can inform and lead into new places the flow of our sympathetic consciousness, and it can lead our sympathy away in recoil from things gone dead. Therefore, the novel, properly handled, can reveal the most secret places of life.

In Lawrence's view, we can evaluate a novel in terms of its moral effect on the reader: The good novel, Lawrence claims, leads us into worlds—human relationships —that deserve our attention, and leads us away from "things gone dead," presumably relationships and values—whether political, moral, or religious—that no longer deserve to survive. To be blunt, Lawrence claims that good books improve us. His comment is similar to a more violent comment, quoted earlier, by Franz Kafka: "A book must be an ice-axe to break the frozen sea inside us."

Realism, of course, is not the writer's only tool. In *Gulliver's Travels* Swift gives us a world of Lilliputians, people about six inches tall. Is his book pure fancy, unrelated to life? Not at all. We perceive that the Lilliputians are (except for their size) pretty much like ourselves, and we realize that their tiny stature is an image of human pettiness, an *un*realistic device that helps us to see the real world more clearly.

The view that we have been talking about—that writers do connect us to the world—does not require realism, but it does assume that writers see, understand, and, through the medium of their writings, give us knowledge, deepen our understanding, and even perhaps improve our character. If, the argument goes, a work distorts reality—let's say because the author sees women superficially—the work is inferior. Some such assumption is found, for instance, in a comment by Elaine Savory Fido, who says that the work of Derek Walcott, a Caribbean poet and dramatist, is successful when Walcott deals with racism and with colonialism but is unsuccessful when he deals with women. "His treatment of women," Fido says in an essay in *Journal of Commonwealth Literature* (1986),

> is full of clichés, stereotypes and negativity. I shall seek to show how some of his worst writing is associated with these portraits of women, which sometimes lead him to the brink of losing verbal control, or give rise to a retreat into abstract, conventional terms which prevent any real treatment of the subject. (109)

We need not here be concerned with whether Fido's evaluations of Walcott's works about women and about colonialism are convincing: What concerns us is her assumption that works can be—should be—evaluated in terms of the keenness of the writer's perception of reality.

Although we *need* not be concerned with an evaluation, we may wish to be concerned with it—and if so, we will probably find, perhaps to our surprise, that in the very process of arguing our evaluation (perhaps only to ourselves) we are also interpreting and reinterpreting. That is, we find ourselves observing passages closely, from a new point of view, and we may therefore find ourselves seeing them differently, finding new meanings in them.

Your Turn: Poems and A Story for Evaluation

Matthew Arnold

Matthew Arnold (1822–1888) was the son of a famous educator, Dr. Thomas Arnold, the headmaster of Rugby School. After graduating from Oxford, Matthew Arnold became an inspector of schools, a post he held until two years before his death. Besides writing poetry, Arnold wrote literary criticism and was appointed professor of poetry at Oxford from 1857 to 1867. He traveled widely on the Continent and lectured in the United States.

Dover Beach

The sea is calm to-night.
The tide is full, the moon lies fair
Upon the straits;—on the French coast the light
Gleams and is gone; the cliffs of England stand
Glimmering and vast, out in the tranquil bay.   5
Come to the window, sweet is the night-air!
Only, from the long line of spray
Where the sea meets the moon-blanch'd land,
Listen! you hear the grating roar
Of pebbles which the waves draw back, and fling,   10
At their return, up the high strand,
Begin, and cease, and then again begin,
With tremulous cadence slow, and bring
The eternal note of sadness in.

Sophocles long ago   15
Heard it on the Ægean, and it brought
Into his mind the turbid ebb and flow
Of human misery; we
Find also in the sound a thought,
Hearing it by this distant northern sea.   20

The Sea of Faith
Was once, too, at the full, and round earth's shore
Lay like the folds of a bright girdle furl'd.

But now I only hear
Its melancholy, long, withdrawing roar,   25
Retreating, to the breath
Of the night-wind, down the vast edges drear
And naked shingles° of the world.

Ah, love, let us be true
To one another! for the world, which seems   30
To lie before us like a land of dreams,
So various, so beautiful, so new,

28 shingles pebbled beaches.

Hath really neither joy, nor love, nor light,
Nor certitude, nor peace, nor help for pain;
And we are here as on a darkling plain   35
Swept with confused alarms of struggle and flight,
Where ignorant armies clash by night.

[c. 1851]

Topics for Critical Thinking and Writing

1. How would you characterize the speaker's tone of voice? Does the tone stay the same throughout?
2. What do we learn about the relationship between the speaker and the person whom he addresses? How is this relationship connected to the speaker's reflections on the general sorrow of life and the loss of faith?
3. What is your response to the simile that Arnold uses in line 23?
4. "Dover Beach" is included in many anthologies of literature and collections of verse. In your view, does this fact bear witness to the force of habit, or is there something about this poem that makes it especially important and memorable?

ANTHONY HECHT

Anthony Hecht was born in New York City in 1923, and educated at Bard College and Columbia University. He has taught at several institutions (since 1985 he has been at Georgetown University), and he has served as poetry consultant to the Library of Congress.

Like "The Dover Bitch," which assumes a reader's familiarity with Matthew Arnold's "Dover Beach," much of Hecht's work glances at earlier literature.

The Dover Bitch

A Criticism of Life
For Andrews Wanning

So there stood Matthew Arnold and this girl
With the cliffs of England crumbling away behind them,
And he said to her, "Try to be true to me,
And I'll do the same for you, for things are bad
All over, etc., etc."   5
Well now, I knew this girl. It's true she had read
Sophocles in a fairly good translation
And caught that bitter allusion to the sea.
But all the time he was talking she had in mind
The notion of what his whiskers would feel like   10
On the back of her neck. She told me later on
That after a while she got to looking out

At the lights across the channel, and really felt sad,
Thinking of all the wine and enormous beds
And blandishments in French and the perfumes.   15
And then she got really angry. To have been brought
All the way down from London, and then be addressed
As sort of a mournful cosmic last resort
Is really tough on a girl, and she was pretty.
Anyway, she watched him pace the room   20
And finger his watch-chain and seem to sweat a bit,
And then she said one or two unprintable things.
But you mustn't judge her by that. What I mean to say is,
She's really all right. I still see her once in a while
And she always treats me right.   25
We have a drink
And I give her a good time, and perhaps it's a year
Before I see her again, but there she is,
Running to fat, but dependable as they come,
And sometimes I bring her a bottle of *Nuit d'Amour.*   30

[1967]

Topics for Critical Thinking and Writing

1. Do you think that the first six lines of Hecht's poem are too chatty and informal? What might be the poet's purpose in writing in this style?
2. Line 8 seems somewhat puzzling. Is "that bitter allusion to the sea" the kind of
   phrase that the speaker of the first few lines would use? Take note as well of
   the word "blandishments" in line 15, and the phrase "mournful cosmic last resort," line 18. Are the tone and diction of these lines consistent with that of the
   rest of the poem?
3. What, finally, is the point of Hecht's poem? Is he simply making fun of the
   stuffy, solemn author of "Dover Beach," or, beyond that, does he seek to present and explore a point of view of his own—for example, on the nature of
   male/female relationships?
4. Does "The Dover Bitch," to be effective, require that we know "Dover Beach"?
   If you came across Hecht's poem by itself, and had never read Arnold's poem,
   what do you imagine your response to "The Dover Bitch" would be?

ROBERT FROST

*Robert Frost (1874–1963) was born in California. After his father's death in 1885
Frost's mother brought the family to New England, where she taught in high
schools in Massachusetts and New Hampshire. Frost studied for part of one term at
Dartmouth College in New Hampshire, then did odd jobs (including teaching),
and from 1897 to 1899 was enrolled as a special student at Harvard. He then
farmed in New Hampshire, published a few poems in local newspapers, left the
farm and taught again, and in 1912 left for England, where he hoped to achieve
more popular success as a writer. By 1915 he had won a considerable reputation,
and he returned to the United States, settling on a farm in New Hampshire and
cultivating the image of the country-wise farmer-poet. In fact he was well read in
the classics, the Bible, and English and American literature.*

Design

I found a dimpled spider, fat and white,
On a white heal-all, holding up a moth
Like a white piece of rigid satin cloth—
Assorted characters of death and blight   4
Mixed ready to begin the morning right,
Like the ingredients of a witches' broth—
A snow-drop spider, a flower like a froth,
And dead wings carried like a paper kite.   8

What had that flower to do with being white,
The wayside blue and innocent heal-all?
What brought the kindred spider to that height,
Then steered the white moth thither in the night?   12
What but design of darkness to appall?—
If design govern in a thing so small.

[1936]

Topics for Critical Thinking and Writing

1. Do you find the spider, as described in line 1, cute or disgusting? Why?
2. What is the effect of "If" in the last line?
3. The word *design* can mean "pattern" (as in "a pretty design"), or it can mean "intention," especially an evil intention (as in "He had designs on her"). Does Frost use the word in one sense or in both? Explain.

IRA GERSHWIN

Ira (originally Israel) Gershwin (1896–1983) was born in the Lower East Side of New York City, of Russian-Jewish immigrant parents. He attended City College of New York for two years (1914–16), but dropped out so that he could concentrate on his work for musical comedies. A writer of lyrics, he collaborated with his younger brother George on some twenty Broadway musicals, as well as with others—notably Moss Hart, Kurt Weill, Jerome Kern, and Harold Arlen. In 1932 he and his collabora-tors (Morrie Ryskind and George S. Kaufman) received a Pulitzer Prize for the musical satire, Of Thee I Sing *(1931).*

Among his best-known songs (in addition to "The Man That Got Away") are "The Man I Love," "I Got Rhythm," "Embraceable You," and (from Porgy and Bess *[1935]) "Summertime," "I Got Plenty o' Nuttin'," and "It Ain't Necessarily So." "The Man That Got Away" (music by Harold Arlen) was written for Judy Garland, in* A Star Is Born *(1954).*

Judy Garland (1922–1969) is best known for her roles in such film musicals as The Wizard of Oz *(1939),* Meet Me in St. Louis *(1944), and* Easter Parade *(1948). In* A Star Is Born, *the tragic story of an aging actor who helps a young, aspiring actress to fame, Garland excelled in both her musical and dramatic work.*

The Man That Got Away

The night is bitter,
The stars have lost their glitter,
The winds grow colder
And suddenly you're older—
And all because of the man that got away.   5

No more his eager call,
The writing's on the wall;
The dreams you've dreamed have all
        Gone astray.

The man that won you   10
Has run off and undone you.
That great beginning
Has seen the final inning.
Don't know what happened. It's all a crazy game.

No more that all-time thrill,   15
For you've been through the mill—
And never a new love will
        Be the same.

Good riddance, good bye!
        Ev'ry trick of his you're on to.   20
But, fools will be fools—
        And where's he gone to?

The road gets rougher,
It's lonelier and tougher.
With hope you burn up—   25
Tomorrow he may turn up.
There's just no let-up the live-long night and day.

Ever since this world began
        There is nothing sadder than
        A one man woman looking for   30
        The man that got away . . .
        The man that got away.

[1954]

Topics for Critical Thinking and Writing

1. Are these lyrics trash as poetry but great as lyrics for a song? Explain. While you are thinking about this issue, you may want to ponder some words by Edgar Allan Poe: "There are few cases in which mere popularity should be considered a proper test of merit; but the case of song-writing is, I think, one of the few."

2. Is the speaker making too much of a fuss? After all, it's only a man that she has lost.

3. Gershwin, in *Lyrics on Several Occasions* (1973), comments on the song. He mentions that some reviewers mistakenly called it "The Man Who Got Away," but, Gershwin says, this title is unacceptable because (1) it sounds like a whodunit title, and (2) it loses the echo of the fisherman's "You should have seen the one that got away." How valuable do you find these comments?

4. Gershwin also mentions that the word "man" in the title of a song usually limits it to female vocalists. Even if one makes some minimal switches (in "The Man I Love," changing to "the girl I love," and so forth) one is still left with something like "the girl I love; / And she'll be big and strong," which, Gershwin says, gives her "some undesirable attributes." But because Frank Sinatra wanted to do a recording of "The *Gal* That Got Away," Gershwin changed the ending thus:

> Ever since this world began
> There is nothing sadder than
> A lost, lost loser looking for
> The gal that got away.

What do you think of this revision? Try your hand at producing a better one.

KATHERINE MANSFIELD

Katherine Mansfield (1888–1923), née Kathleen Mansfield Beauchamp, was born in New Zealand. In 1902 she went to London for schooling; in 1906 she returned to New Zealand, but dissatisfied with its provincialism, in 1908 she returned to London to become a writer. After a disastrous marriage and a love affair, she went to Germany, where she wrote stories; in 1910 she returned to London, published a book of stories in 1911, and in 1912 met and began living with the writer John Middleton Murry. In 1918, after her first husband at last divorced her, she married Murry. She died of tuberculosis in 1923, a few months after her thirty-fourth birthday.

Mansfield published about seventy stories, and left some others unpublished. An early admirer of Chekhov, she read his works in German translations before they were translated into English.

Miss Brill

Although it was so brilliantly fine—the blue sky powdered with gold and great spots of light like white wine splashed over the Jardins Publiques[1]—Miss Brill was glad that she had decided on her fur. The air was motionless, but when you opened your mouth there was just a faint chill, like a chill from a glass of iced water before you sip, and now and again a leaf came drifting—from nowhere, from the sky. Miss Brill put up her hand and touched her fur. Dear little thing! It was nice to feel it again. She had taken it out of its box that afternoon, shaken out the moth-powder, given it a good brush, and rubbed the life back into the dim little eyes. "What has been happening to me?" said the sad little eyes. Oh, how sweet it was to see them snap at her again from the red eiderdown! . . . But the nose, which was of some black composition, wasn't at all firm. It must have had a

---

[1]**Jardins Publiques** Public Gardens (French).

knock, somehow. Never mind—a little dab of black sealing-wax when the time came—when it was absolutely necessary. . . . Little rogue! Yes, she really felt like that about it. Little rogue biting its tail just by her left ear. She could have taken it off and laid it on her lap and stroked it. She felt a tingling in her hands and arms, but that came from walking, she supposed. And when she breathed, something light and sad—no, not sad, exactly—something gentle seemed to move in her bosom.

There were a number of people out this afternoon, far more than last Sunday. And the band sounded louder and gayer. That was because the Season had begun. For although the band played all year round on Sundays, out of season it was never the same. It was like some one playing with only the family to listen; it didn't care how it played if there weren't any strangers present. Wasn't the conductor wearing a new coat, too? She was sure it was new. He scraped with his foot and flapped his arms like a rooster about to crow, and the bandsmen sitting in the green rotunda blew out their cheeks and glared at the music. Now there came a little "flutey" bit—very pretty!—a little chain of bright drops. She was sure it would be repeated. It was; she lifted her head and smiled.

Only two people shared her "special" seat: a fine old man in a velvet coat, his hands clasped over a huge carved walking-stick, and a big old woman, sitting upright, with a roll of knitting on her embroidered apron. They did not speak. This was disappointing, for Miss Brill always looked forward to the conversation. She had become really quite expert, she thought, at listening as though she didn't listen, at sitting in other people's lives just for a minute while they talked round her.

She glanced, sideways, at the old couple. Perhaps they would go soon. Last Sunday, too, hadn't been as interesting as usual. An Englishman and his wife, he wearing a dreadful Panama hat and she button boots. And she'd gone on the whole time about how she ought to wear spectacles; she knew she needed them; but that it was no good getting any; they'd be sure to break and they'd never keep on. And he'd been so patient. He'd suggested everything—gold rims, the kind that curved round your ears, little pads inside the bridge. No, nothing would please her. "They'll always be sliding down my nose!" Miss Brill had wanted to shake her.

5   The old people sat on the bench, still as statues. Never mind, there was always the crowd to watch. To and fro, in front of the flower-beds and the band rotunda, the couples and groups paraded, stopped to talk, to greet, to buy a handful of flowers from the old beggar who had his tray fixed to the railings. Little children ran among them, swooping and laughing; little boys with big white silk bows under their chins, little girls, little French dolls, dressed up in velvet and lace. And sometimes a tiny staggerer came suddenly rocking into the open from under the trees, stopped, stared, as suddenly sat down "flop," until its small high-stepping mother, like a young hen, rushed scolding to its rescue. Other people sat on the benches and green chairs, but they were nearly always the same, Sunday after Sunday, and—Miss Brill had often noticed—there was something funny about nearly all of them. They were odd, silent, nearly all old, and from the way they stared they looked as though they'd just come from dark little rooms or even—even cupboards!

Behind the rotunda the slender trees with yellow leaves down drooping, and through them just a line of sea, and beyond the blue sky with gold-veined clouds.

Tum-tum-tum tiddle-um! tiddle-um! tum tiddley-um tum ta! blew the band.

Two young girls in red came by and two young soldiers in blue met them, and they laughed and paired and went off arm-in-arm. Two peasant women with funny straw hats passed, gravely, leading beautiful smoke-colored donkeys. A cold, pale nun hurried by. A beautiful woman came along and dropped her bunch of violets, and a little boy ran after to hand them to her, and she took them and threw them away as if they'd been poisoned. Dear me! Miss Brill didn't know whether to admire that or not! And now an ermine toque[2] and a gentleman in grey met just in front of her. He was tall, stiff, dignified, and she was wearing the ermine toque she'd bought when her hair was yellow. Now everything, her hair, her face, even her eyes, was the same color as the shabby ermine, and her hand, in its cleaned glove, lifted to dab her lips, was a tiny yellowish paw. Oh, she was so pleased to see him—delighted! She rather thought they were going to meet that afternoon. She described where she'd been—everywhere, here, there, along by the sea. The day was so charming—didn't he agree? And wouldn't he, perhaps? . . . But he shook his head, lighted a cigarette, slowly breathed a great deep puff into her face, and, even while she was still talking and laughing, flicked the match away and walked on. The ermine toque was alone; she smiled more brightly than ever. But even the band seemed to know what she was feeling and played more softly, played tenderly, and the drum beat, "The Brute! The Brute!" over and over. What would she do? What was going to happen now? But as Miss Brill wondered, the ermine toque turned, raised her hand as though she'd seen some one else, much nicer, just over there, and pattered away. And the band changed again and played more quickly, more gaily than ever, and the old couple on Miss Brill's seat got up and marched away, and such a funny old man with long whiskers hobbled along in time to the music and was nearly knocked over by four girls walking abreast.

Oh, how fascinating it was! How she enjoyed it! How she loved sitting here, watching it all! It was like a play. It was exactly like a play. Who could believe the sky at the back wasn't painted? But it wasn't till a little brown dog trotted on solemn and then slowly trotted off, like a little "theatre" dog, a little dog that had been drugged, that Miss Brill discovered what it was that made it so exciting. They were all on the stage. They weren't only the audience, not only looking on; they were acting. Even she had a part and came every Sunday. No doubt somebody would have noticed if she hadn't been there; she was part of the performance after all. How strange she'd never thought of it like that before! And yet it explained why she made such a point of starting from home at just the same time each week—so as not to be late for the performance—and it also explained why she had quite a queer, shy feeling at telling her English pupils how she spent her Sunday afternoons. No wonder! Miss Brill nearly laughed out loud. She was on the stage. She thought of the old invalid gentleman to whom she read the newspaper four afternoons a week while he slept in the garden. She had got quite used to the frail head on the cotton pillow, the hollowed eyes, the open mouth and the high pinched nose. If he'd been dead she mightn't have noticed for weeks; she wouldn't have minded. But suddenly he knew he was having the paper read to him by an actress! "An actress!" The old head lifted; two points of light quivered in the old eyes. "An actress—are ye?" And Miss Brill smoothed the newspaper as though it were the manuscript of her part and said gently: "Yes, I have been an actress for a long time."

10   The band had been having a rest. Now they started again. And what they played was warm, sunny, yet there was just a faint chill—a something, what was it?—not sadness—no, not sadness—a something that made you want to sing. The

---

[2]**toque** a brimless, close-fitting woman's hat.

tune lifted, lifted, the light shone; and it seemed to Miss Brill that in another moment all of them, all the whole company, would begin singing. The young ones,
the laughing ones who were moving together, they would begin, and the men's
voices, very resolute and brave, would join them. And then she too, she too, and
the others on the benches—they would come in with a kind of accompaniment—
something low, that scarcely rose or fell, something so beautiful—moving. . . .
And Miss Brill's eyes filled with tears and she looked smiling at all the other members of the company. Yes, we understand, we understand, she thought—though
what they understood she didn't know.

Just at that moment a boy and a girl came and sat down where the old couple
had been. They were beautifully dressed; they were in love. The hero and heroine, of course, just arrived from his father's yacht. And still soundlessly singing,
still with that trembling smile, Miss Brill prepared to listen.

"No, not now," said the girl. "Not here, I can't."

"But why? Because of that stupid old thing at the end there?" asked the boy.
"Why does she come here at all—who wants her? Why doesn't she keep her silly
old mug at home?"

"It's her fu-fur which is so funny," giggled the girl. "It's exactly like a fried
whiting."[3]

15   "Ah, be off with you!" said the boy in an angry whisper. Then: "Tell me, my
petite chère[4]—"

"No, not here," said the girl. "Not *yet*."

On her way home she usually bought a slice of honey-cake at the baker's. It
was her Sunday treat. Sometimes there was an almond in her slice, sometimes
not. It made a great difference. If there was an almond it was like carrying home a
tiny present—a surprise—something that might very well not have been there.
She hurried on the almond Sundays and struck the match for the kettle in quite a
dashing way.

But today she passed the baker's by, climbed the stairs, went into the little
dark room—her room like a cupboard—and sat down on the red eiderdown. She
sat there for a long time. The box that the fur came out of was on the bed. She
unclasped the necklet quickly; quickly, without looking, laid it inside. But when
she put the lid on she thought she heard something crying.

[1920]

---

[3]**whiting** a kind of fish.   [4]*petite chère* darling.

Topics for Critical Thinking and Writing

1. Why do you think Mansfield did not give Miss Brill a first name?
2. What would be lost (or gained?) if the first paragraph were omitted?
3. Suppose someone said that the story is about a woman who is justly punished
   for her pride. What might be your response?

18

Writing about Literature: An Overview of Critical Strategies

THE NATURE OF CRITICAL WRITING

We have twice mentioned already that in everyday talk the commonest meaning of **criticism** is something like "finding fault." But a critic can see excellences as well as faults. Because we turn to criticism with the hope that the critic has seen something we have missed, the most valuable criticism is not that which shakes its finger at faults but that which calls our attention to interesting things going on in the work of art. Here is a statement by W. H. Auden (1907–1973), suggesting that criticism is most useful when it calls our attention to things worth attending to:

> What is the function of a critic? So far as I am concerned, he can do me one or more of the following services:
>
> 1. Introduce me to authors or works of which I was hitherto unaware.
> 2. Convince me that I have undervalued an author or a work because I had not read them carefully enough.
> 3. Show me relations between works of different ages and cultures which I could never have seen for myself because I do not know enough and never shall.
> 4. Give a "reading" of a work which increases my understanding of it.
> 5. Throw light upon the process of artistic "Making."
> 6. Throw light upon the relation of art to life, science, economics, ethics, religion, etc.
>
> *The Dyer's Hand* (New York, 1963), pp. 8–9

Auden does not neglect the delight we get from literature, but he extends (especially in his sixth point) the range of criticism to include topics beyond the literary work itself. Notice too the emphasis on observing, showing, and illuminating, which suggests that the function of critical writing is not very different from the commonest view of the function of imaginative writing.

Auden begins by saying that a critic can "introduce" him to an author. How would a critic introduce a reader to an author? It's not enough just to name the author; almost surely the advocate would give *reasons* why we should read the book. "It will really grip you"; "It's the funniest thing I've read in months"; "I was moved to tears." Auden lets the cat out of the bag in his next two assertions: the critic may "convince" him of something, or may "show" him something. Criticism

621

is largely a matter of convincing and showing—really, showing and thereby convincing. We can't just announce that we like or dislike something and expect people to agree; we have to point to evidence (that's the showing part) if we are going to convince.

In a moment we will return to the matter of evidence, but first let's hear another writer talk about criticism. The novelist D. H. Lawrence says,

> Literary criticism can be no more than a reasoned account of the feeling produced upon the critic by the book he is criticizing. Criticism can never be a science: it is, in the first place, much too personal, and in the second, it is concerned with values that science ignores.
>
> *Phoenix: The Posthumous Papers of D. H. Lawrence* (London, 1936), p. 539

We like Lawrence's assertion that criticism is *a reasoned account*—writing about literature is a rational activity, not a mere pouring out of emotion—but we equally like his assertion that it is rooted in *feeling*. As earlier chapters have suggested, when we read we respond (perhaps with an intense interest, perhaps with a yawn). Our responses are worth examining. *Why* do we find this character memorable, or that character unbelievable? As we examine our responses, and check the text to make sure that we have properly remembered it, we may of course find our responses changing, but finally we think we know what we think of the literary work, and we know *why* we think it. We are, in Lawrence's words, able to give "a reasoned account of the feeling produced . . . by the book."

CRITICISM AS ARGUMENT: ASSUMPTIONS AND EVIDENCE

In this process of showing and convincing (Auden's words) and of offering a reasoned account (Lawrence's words), even if we are talking about a so-so movie or television show, what we say depends in large measure on certain conscious or unconscious assumptions that we make:

- "I liked it because the characters were very believable" (here the assumption is that characters ought to be believable);
- "I didn't like it; there was too much violence" (here the assumption is that violence ought not to be shown, or if it is shown it should be condemned);
- "I didn't like it; it was awfully slow" (here the assumption probably is that there ought to be a fair amount of physical action, perhaps even changes of scene, rather than characters just talking in the kitchen);
- "I didn't like it; I don't think topics of this sort should be discussed publicly" (here the assumption is a moral one, that it is indecent to present certain topics);
- "I liked it partly because it was refreshing to hear such frankness" (here again the assumption is moral, and more or less the reverse of the previous one).

In short, whether we realize it or not, our responses are rooted in assumptions. These assumptions, we may believe, are so self-evident that they do not need to be stated. Our readers, however, may disagree.

If we are to hold our readers' interest, and perhaps convince them to see things the way we do, we must recognize our assumptions and must offer evidence—point to things in the work—that will convince the reader that our assumptions are reasonable. If we want to say that a short story ought to be realistic, we will call our reader's attention to unrealistic aspects in a particular story and will, with this evidence in front of the reader, argue that the story is not worth much. Or, conversely, we might say that in a satiric story realism of course is not a valid criterion; what readers want is (as in a political caricature in a newspaper) exaggeration and humor, and in our critical study we will call attention to the delight that this or that bit of exaggeration offers.

In brief, as we suggested in Chapters 16 and 17 ("Arguing an Interpretation" and "Arguing an Evaluation"), argument consists of offering statements that are *reasons* for other statements ("The work means X *because* . . . "), and the words that follow "because" normally point to the evidence that we believe supports the earlier assertion.

SOME CRITICAL STRATEGIES

Professional critics, like the ordinary moviegoer who recommends a movie to a friend, work from assumptions, but their assumptions are usually highly conscious, and the critics may define their assumptions at length. They regard themselves as, for instance, Freudians or Marxists or gay critics. They read all texts through the lens of a particular theory, and their focus enables them to see things that otherwise might go unnoticed. Most critics realize, however, that if a lens or critical perspective or interpretive strategy helps us to see certain things, it also limits our vision. They therefore regard their method not as an exclusive way of thinking but only as a useful tool.

What follows is a brief survey of the chief current approaches to literature. You may find, as you read these pages, that one or another approach sounds congenial, and you may want to make use of it in your reading and writing. On the other hand, it's important to remember that works of literature are highly varied, and we read them for various purposes—to kill time, to enjoy fanciful visions, to be amused, to learn about alien ways of feeling, and to learn about ourselves. It may be best, therefore, to try to respond to each text in the way that the text seems to require rather than to read all texts according to a single formula. You'll find, of course, that some works will lead you to want to think about them from several angles. A play by Shakespeare may stimulate you to read a book about the Elizabethan playhouse, and another that offers a Marxist interpretation of the English Renaissance, and still another that offers a feminist analysis of Shakespeare's plays. All of these approaches, and others, may help to deepen your understanding of the literary works that you read.

Formalist Criticism (New Criticism)

Formalist criticism emphasizes the work as an independent creation, a self-contained unity, something to be studied in itself, not as part of some larger context, such as the author's life or a historical period. This kind of study is called formalist criticism because the emphasis is on the *form* of the work, the relationships between the parts—the construction of the plot, the contrasts between characters, the functions of rhymes, the point of view, and so on. Formalist critics explain how and why literary works—*these* words, in *this* order—constitute unique, complex structures that embody or set forth meanings.

Cleanth Brooks, perhaps America's most distinguished formalist critic, in an essay in the *Kenyon Review* (Winter 1951), set forth what he called his "articles of faith":

> That literary criticism is a description and an evaluation of its object.
>
> That the primary concern of criticism is with the problem of unity—the kind of whole which the literary work forms or fails to form, and the relation of the various parts to each other in building up this whole.
>
> That the formal relations in a work of literature may include, but certainly exceed, those of logic.
>
> That in a successful work, form and content cannot be separated.
>
> That form is meaning.

Formalist criticism is, in essence, *intrinsic* criticism, rather than extrinsic, for it concentrates on the work itself, independent of its writer and the writer's background—that is, independent of biography, psychology, sociology, and history. The discussions of a proverb ("A rolling stone") and of a short poem by Frost ("The Span of Life") on page 44 are brief examples. The gist is that a work of literature is complex, unified, and freestanding. In practice, of course, we usually bring outside knowledge to the work. For instance, a reader who is familiar with, say, *Hamlet* can hardly study some other tragedy by Shakespeare, let's say *Romeo and Juliet*, without bringing to the second play some conception of what Shakespearean tragedy is or can be. A reader of Alice Walker's *The Color Purple* inevitably brings unforgettable outside material (perhaps the experience of being an African American, or some knowledge of the history of African Americans) to the literary work. It is hard to talk only about *Hamlet* or *The Color Purple* and not at the same time talk about, or at least have in mind, aspects of human experience.

Formalist criticism begins with a personal response to the literary work, but it goes on to try to account for the response by closely examining the work. It assumes that the author shaped the poem, play, or story so fully that the work guides the reader's responses. The assumption that "meaning" is fully and completely presented within the text is not much in favor today, when many literary critics argue that the active or subjective reader (or even what Judith Fetterley, a feminist critic, has called "the resisting reader"), and not the author of the text, makes the "meaning." Still, even if we grant that the reader is active, not passive or coolly objective, we can hold with the formalists that the author is active too, constructing a text that in some measure controls the reader's responses.

Formalist criticism usually takes one of two forms, **explication** (the unfolding of meaning, line by line or even word by word) and **analysis** (the examination of the relations of parts). The essay on Yeats's "The Balloon of the Mind" (p. 494) is an explication, a setting forth of the implicit meanings of the words. The essays on Kate Chopin's "The Story of an Hour" (p. 261) and on Tennessee Williams's *The Glass Menagerie* (p. 464) are analyses. The two essays on Frost's "Stopping by Woods on a Snowy Evening" (pp. 589 and 593) are chiefly analyses but with some passages of explication.

Formalist criticism, also called the **New Criticism** (to distinguish it from the historical and biographical writing that in earlier decades had dominated literary study), began to achieve prominence in the late 1920s and was dominant from the late 1930s until about 1970, and even today it is widely considered the best way for a student to begin to study a work of literature. Formalist criticism empowers the student; that is, the student confronts the work immediately and is not told first to spend days or weeks or months in preparation—for instance reading Freud and his followers in order to write a psychoanalytic essay or reading Marx and Marxists in order to write a Marxist essay, or doing research on "necessary historical background" in order to write a historical essay.

Deconstruction

Deconstruction or deconstructive or poststructuralist criticism, can almost be characterized as the opposite of everything that formalist criticism stands for. Deconstruction begins with the assumptions that language is unstable, elusive, unfaithful. (Language is all of these things because meaning is largely generated by opposition: *hot* means something in opposition to *cold,* but a hot day may be 90 degrees whereas a hot oven is at least 400 degrees, and a "hot item" may be of any temperature.) Deconstructionists seek to show that a literary work (usually called "a text" or "a discourse") inevitably is self-contradictory. Unlike formalist critics—who hold that an author constructs a coherent work with a stable meaning, and that competent readers can perceive this meaning—deconstructionists hold that a work has no coherent meaning at the center.

Despite the emphasis on indeterminacy, it is sometimes possible to detect in deconstructionist interpretations a view associated with Marxism. This is the idea that authors are "socially constructed" from the "discourses of power" or "signifying practices" that surround them. Thus, although authors may think they are individuals with independent minds, their works usually reveal—unknown to the authors—powerful social, cultural, or philosophic assumption. Deconstructionists "interrogate" a text, and they reveal what the authors were unaware of or had thought they had kept safely out of sight. That is, deconstructionists often find a rather specific meaning—though this meaning is one that might surprise the author.

Deconstruction is valuable insofar as—like the New Criticism—it encourages close, rigorous attention to the text. Furthermore, in its rejection of the claim that a work has a single stable meaning, deconstruction has had a positive influence on the study of literature. The problem with deconstruction, however, is that too often it is reductive, telling the same story about every text—that here, yet again, and again, we see how a text is incoherent and heterogeneous.

Reader-Response Criticism

Probably all reading includes some sort of response—"This is terrific," "This is a bore," "I don't know what's going on here"—and almost all writing about literature begins with some such response, but specialists in literature disagree greatly about the role that response plays, or should play, in experiencing literature and in writing about it.

At one extreme are those who say that our response to a work of literature should be a purely aesthetic response—a response to a work of art—and not the response we would have to something comparable in real life. To take an obvious point: If in real life we heard someone plotting a murder, we would intervene, perhaps by calling the police or by attempting to warn the victim. But when we hear Macbeth and Lady Macbeth plot to kill King Duncan, we watch with deep *interest;* we hear their words with *pleasure,* and maybe with horror and fascination we even look forward to seeing the murder and to what the characters then will say and what will happen to the murderers.

When you think about it, the vast majority of works of literature do not have a close, obvious resemblance to the reader's life. Most readers of *Macbeth* are not Scots, and no readers are Scottish kings or queens. (It's not just a matter of older literature; no readers of Toni Morrison's *Beloved* are nineteenth-century African Americans.) The connections that readers make between themselves and the lives in most of the books they read are not, on the whole, connections based on ethnic or professional identities. Rather, they are connections with states of consciousness, for instance a young person's sense of isolation from the family, or a young person's sense of guilt for initial sexual experiences. Before we reject a work either because it seems too close to us ("I'm a man and I don't like the depiction of this man"), or on the other hand too far from our experience ("I'm not a woman, so how can I enjoy reading about these women?"), we probably should try to follow the advice of Virginia Woolf, who said, "Do not dictate to your author; try to become him." Nevertheless, some literary works of the past may today seem intolerable, at least in part. There are passages in Mark Twain's *Huckleberry Finn,* where African Americans are stereotyped or called derogatory names, that deeply upset us today. We should, however, try to reconstruct the cultural assumptions of the age in which the work was written. If we do so, we may find that if in some ways it reflected its historical era, in other ways it challenged it.

Reader-response criticism, then, says that the "meaning" of a work is not merely something put into the work by the writer; rather, the "meaning" is an interpretation created or constructed or produced by the reader as well as the writer. Stanley Fish, an exponent of reader-response theory, in *Is There a Text in This Class?* (1980), puts it this way: "Interpretation is not the art of construing but of constructing. Interpreters do not decode poems; they make them" (327).

But does every reader see his or her individual image in each literary work? Even *Hamlet,* a play that has generated an enormous range of interpretation, is universally seen as a tragedy, a play that deals with painful realities. If someone were to tell us that *Hamlet* is a comedy, and that the end, with a pile of corpses, is especially funny, we would not say, "Oh, well, we all see things in our own way." Rather, we would conclude that we have just heard a misinterpretation.

Many people who subscribe to one version or another of a reader-response theory would agree that they are concerned not with all readers but with what they call *informed readers* or *competent readers*. Informed or competent readers are familiar with the conventions of literature. They understand misinterpretation, that in a play such as *Hamlet* the characters usually speak in verse. Such readers, then, do not express amazement that Hamlet often speaks metrically, and that he sometimes uses rhyme. These readers understand that verse is the normal language for most of the characters in the play, and therefore such readers do not characterize Hamlet as a poet. Informed, competent readers, in short, know the rules of the game. There will still be plenty of room for differences of interpretation. Some people will find Hamlet not at all blameworthy, others will find him somewhat blameworthy, and still others may find him highly blameworthy. In short, we can say that a writer works against a background that is *shared* by readers. As readers, we are familiar with various kinds of literature, and we read or see *Hamlet* as a particular kind of literary work, a tragedy, a play that evokes (in Shakespeare's words) "woe or wonder," sadness and astonishment. Knowing (in a large degree) how we ought to respond, our responses are not merely private.

Archetypal Criticism (Myth Criticism)

Carl G. Jung, the Swiss psychiatrist, in *Contributions to Analytical Psychology* (1928) postulates the existence of a "collective unconscious," an inheritance in our brains consisting of "countless typical experiences [such as birth, escape from danger, selection of a mate] of our ancestors." Few people today believe in an inherited "collective unconscious," but many people agree that certain repeated experiences, such as going to sleep and hours later awakening, or the perception of the setting and of the rising sun, or of the annual death and rebirth of vegetation, manifest themselves in dreams, myths, and literature—in these instances, as stories of apparent death and rebirth. This archetypal plot of death and rebirth is said to be evident in Coleridge's *The Rime of the Ancient Mariner* (1798), for example. The ship suffers a deathlike calm and then is miraculously restored to motion, and, in a sort of parallel rebirth, the mariner moves from spiritual death to renewed perception of the holiness of life. Another archetypal plot is the quest, which usually involves the testing and initiation of a hero, and thus essentially represents the movement from innocence to experience. In addition to archetypal plots there are archetypal characters, since an **archetype** is any recurring unit. Among archetypal characters are the scapegoat (as in Shirley Jackson's "The Lottery"), the hero (savior, deliverer), the terrible mother (witch, stepmother—even the wolf "grandmother" in the tale of Little Red Riding Hood), and the wise old man (father figure magician).

Because, the theory holds, both writer and reader share unconscious memories, the tale an author tells (derived from the collective unconscious) may strangely move the reader, speaking to his or her collective unconscious. As Maud Bodkin puts it, in *Archetypal Patterns in Poetry* (1934), something within us "leaps in response to the effective presentation in poetry of an ancient theme" (4). But this emphasis on ancient (or repeated) themes has made archetypal criticism vulnerable to the charge that it is reductive. The critic looks for certain characters or patterns of action and values the work if the motifs are there, meanwhile overlooking what is unique, subtle, distinctive, and truly interesting about the work. That is, a work is regarded as good if it closely resembles other works, with the usual motifs and characters. A second weakness in some archetypal criticism is that in its search for the deepest meaning of a work the critic may crudely impose a pattern, seeing (for instance) the quest in every walk down the street.

If archetypal criticism sometimes seems farfetched, it is nevertheless true that one of its strengths is that it invites us to use comparisons, and comparing is often an excellent way to see not only what a work shares with other works but what is distinctive in the work. The most successful practitioner of archetypal criticism was Northrop Frye (1912–1991), whose numerous books help readers to see fascinating connections between works. For Frye's explicit comments about archetypal criticism, as well as for examples of such criticism in action, see especially his *Anatomy of Criticism* (1957) and *The Educated Imagination* (1964). On archetypes see also Chapter 16, "Archetypal Patterns," in Norman Friedman, *Form and Meaning in Fiction* (1975).

Historical Criticism

Historical criticism studies a work within its historical context. Thus, a student of *Julius Caesar, Hamlet,* or *Macbeth*—plays in which ghosts appear—may try to find out about Elizabethan attitudes toward ghosts. We may find that the

Elizabethans took ghosts more seriously than we do, or, on the other hand, we may find that ghosts were explained in various ways, for instance sometimes as figments of the imagination and sometimes as shapes taken by the devil in order to mislead the virtuous. Similarly, a historical essay concerned with *Othello* may be devoted to Elizabethan attitudes toward Moors, or to Elizabethan ideas of love, or, for that matter, to Elizabethan ideas of a daughter's obligations toward her father's wishes concerning her suitor. The historical critic assumes (and the assumption can hardly be disputed) that writers, however individualistic, are shaped by the particular social contexts in which they live. Put another way, the goal of historical criticism is to understand how people in the past thought and felt. It assumes that such understanding can enrich our understanding of a particular work. The assumption is, however, disputable, since it may be argued that the artist may *not* have shared the age's view on this or that. All of the half-dozen or so Moors in Elizabethan plays other than *Othello* are villainous or foolish, but this evidence does not prove that *therefore* Othello is villainous or foolish.

BIOGRAPHICAL CRITICISM   One kind of historical research is the study of *biography*, which for our purposes includes not only biographies but also autobiographies, diaries, journals, letters, and so on. What experiences did (for example) Mark Twain undergo? Are some of the apparently sensational aspects of *Huckleberry Finn* in fact close to events that Twain experienced? If so, is he a "realist"? If not, is he writing in the tradition of the "tall tale"?

The really good biographies not only tell us about the life of the author—they enable us to return to the literary texts with a deeper understanding of how they came to be what they are. If, for example, you read Richard B. Sewall's biography of Emily Dickinson, you will find a wealth of material concerning her family and the world she moved in—for instance, the religious ideas that were part of her upbringing.

Biographical study may illuminate even the work of a living author. If you are writing about the poetry of Adrienne Rich, for example, you may want to consider what she has told us in many essays about her life, in *On Lies, Secrets, and Silence* (1979) and *Blood, Bread, and Poetry* (1986), especially about her relations with her father and her husband.

MARXIST CRITICISM   One form of historical criticism is **Marxist criticism**, named for Karl Marx (1818–1883). Actually, to say "one form" is misleading, since Marxist criticism today is varied, but essentially it sees history primarily as a struggle between socioeconomic classes, and it sees literature (and everything else, too) as the product of the economic forces of the period.

For Marxists, economics is the "base" or "infrastructure"; on this base rests a "superstructure" of ideology (law, politics, philosophy, religion, and the arts, including literature), reflecting the interests of the dominant class. Thus, literature is a material product, produced—like bread or battleships—in order to be consumed in a given society. Marxist critics are concerned, for instance, with Shakespeare's plays as part of a market economy—show *business,* the economics of the theater, including payments to authors and actors and revenue from audiences.

Few critics would disagree that works of art in some measure reflect the age that produced them, but most contemporary Marxist critics go further. First, they assert—in a repudiation of what has been called "vulgar Marxist theory"—that the deepest historical meaning of a literary work is to be found in what it does *not* say, what its ideology does not permit it to express. Second, Marxists take seriously Marx's famous comment that "the philosophers have only *interpreted* the world in various ways: the point is to *change* it." The critic's job is to change the world, by revealing the economic basis of the arts. Not surprisingly, most Marxists are skeptical of such concepts as "genius" and "masterpiece." These concepts, they say, are part of the bourgeois myth that idealizes the individual and detaches art from its economic context. For an introduction to Marxist criticism, see Terry Eagleton, *Marxism and Literary Criticism* (1976).

NEW HISTORICAL CRITICISM   A recent school of scholarship, called **New Historicism**, insists that there is no "history" in the sense of a narrative of indisputable past events. Rather, New Historicism holds that there is only our version—our narrative, our representation—of the past. In this view, each age projects its own preconceptions on the past: Historians may think they are revealing the past, but they are revealing only their own historical situation and their personal preferences. For example, in the nineteenth century and in the twentieth almost up to 1992, Columbus was represented as the heroic benefactor of humankind who discovered the New World. But even while plans were being made to celebrate the five-hundredth anniversary of his first voyage across the Atlantic, voices were raised in protest: Columbus did not "discover" a New World; after all, the indigenous people knew where they were, and it was Columbus who was lost, since he thought he was in India. In short, people who wrote history in, say, 1900 projected onto the past their current views (colonialism was a good thing), and people who wrote history in 1992 projected onto that same period a very different set of views (colonialism was a bad thing). Similarly, ancient Greece, once celebrated by historians as the source of democracy and rational thinking, is now more often regarded as a society that was built on slavery and on the oppression of women. And the Renaissance, once glorified as an age of enlightened thought, is now often seen as an age that tyrannized women, enslaved colonial people, and enslaved itself with its belief in witchcraft and astrology. Thinking about these changing views, we feel the truth of the witticism that the only thing more uncertain than the future is the past.

On the New Historicism, see H. Aram Veeser, ed., *The New Historicism* (1989), and Veeser, *The New Historicism Reader* (1994).

Psychological or Psychoanalytic Criticism

One form that biographical study may take is **psychological criticism** or *psychoanalytic criticism,* which usually examines the author and the author's writings in the framework of Freudian psychology. A central doctrine of Sigmund Freud (1856–1939) is the Oedipus complex, the view that all males (Freud seems not to have made his mind up about females) unconsciously wish to displace their fathers and to sleep with their mothers. According to Freud, hatred for the father and love of the mother, normally repressed, may appear disguised in dreams. Works of art, like dreams, are disguised versions of repressed wishes.

In *Hamlet and Oedipus* (1949) Ernest Jones, amplifying some comments by Freud, argued that Hamlet delays killing Claudius because Claudius (who has killed Hamlet's father and married Hamlet's mother) has done exactly what Hamlet himself wanted to do. For Hamlet to kill Claudius, then, would be to kill himself.

If this approach interests you, take a look at Norman N. Holland's *Psychoanalysis and Shakespeare* (1966) or Frederick Crews's study of Hawthorne, *The Sins of the Fathers* (1966). Crews finds in Hawthorne's work evidence of unresolved Oedipal conflicts, and he accounts for the appeal of the fictions thus: The stories "rest on fantasy, but on the shared fantasy of mankind, and this makes for a more penetrating fiction than would any illusionistic slice of life" (263). For applications to other authors, consider Simon O. Lesser's *Fiction and the Unconscious* (1957), or an anthology of criticism, *Literature and Psychoanalysis*, edited by Edith Kurzweil and William Phillips (1983).

Psychological criticism can also turn from the author and the work to the reader, seeking to explain why we, as readers, respond in certain ways. Why, for example, is *Hamlet* so widely popular? A Freudian answer is that it is universal because it deals with a universal (Oedipal) impulse. We can, however, ask whether it appeals as strongly to women as to men (again, Freud was unsure about the Oedipus complex in women) and, if so, why it appeals to them. Or, more generally, we can ask if males and females read in the same way.

Gender Criticism (Feminist, and Lesbian and Gay Criticism)

This last question brings us to **gender criticism**. As we have seen, writing about literature usually seeks to answer questions. Historical scholarship, for instance, tries to answer such questions as "What did Shakespeare and his contemporaries believe about ghosts?" or "How did Victorian novelists and poets respond to Darwin's theory of evolution?" Gender criticism, too, asks questions. It is especially concerned with two issues, one about reading and one about writing: "Do men and women read in different ways?" and "Do they write in different ways?"

Feminist criticism can be traced back to the work of Virginia Woolf (1882–1941), but chiefly it grew out of the women's movement of the 1960s. The women's movement at first tended to hold that women are pretty much the same as men and therefore should be treated equally, but much recent feminist criticism has emphasized and explored the differences between women and men. Because the experiences of the sexes are different, the argument goes, their values and sensibilities are different, and their responses to literature are different. Further, literature written by women is different from literature written by men. Works written by women are seen by some feminist critics as embodying the experiences of a minority culture—a group marginalized by the dominant male culture. (If you have read Susan Glaspell's *Trifles* [p. 1309] you'll recall that this literary work itself is largely concerned about the differing ways that males and females perceive the world.) Of course, not all women are feminist critics, and not all feminist critics are women. Further, there are varieties of feminist criticism, but for a good introduction see *The New Feminist Criticism: Essays on Women, Literature, and Theory* (1985), edited by Elaine Showalter, and *Feminism: An Anthology of Literary Theory and Criticism*, ed. Robyn R. Warhol and Diane Price Herndl, 2nd ed. (1997). For the role of men in feminist criticism, see *Engendering Men*, edited by Joseph A. Boone and Michael Cadden (1990).

Feminist critics rightly point out that men have established the conventions of literature and that men have established the canon—that is, the body of literature that is said to be worth reading. Speaking a bit broadly, in this patriarchal or male-dominated body of literature, men are valued for being strong and active, whereas women are expected to be weak and passive. Thus, in the world of fairy tales, the admirable male is the energetic hero (Jack, the Giant-Killer) but the admirable female is the passive Sleeping Beauty. Active women such as the wicked step-mother or—a disguised form of the same thing—the witch are generally villainous. (There are of course exceptions, such as Gretel in "Hansel and Gretel.") A woman hearing or reading the story of Sleeping Beauty or of Little Red Riding Hood (rescued by the powerful woodcutter), or any other work in which women seem to be trivialized, will respond differently than a man. For instance, a woman may be socially conditioned into admiring Sleeping Beauty, but only at great cost to her mental well-being. A more resistant female reader may recognize in herself no kinship with the beautiful, passive Sleeping Beauty and may respond to the story indignantly. Another way to put it is this: The male reader perceives a romantic story, but the resistant female reader perceives a story of oppression.

For discussions of the ways in which, it is argued, women *ought* to read, you may want to look at *Gender and Reading,* edited by Elizabeth A. Flynn and Patrocino Schweikart, and especially at Judith Fetterley's book *The Resisting Reader* (1978). In her discussion of Faulkner's "A Rose for Emily," Fetterley contends that the society made Emily a "lady"—society dehumanized her by elevating her. Emily's father, seeking to shape her life, stood in the doorway of their house and drove away her suitors. So far as he was concerned, Emily was a nonperson, a creature whose own wishes were not to be regarded; he alone would shape her future. Because society (beginning with her father) made her a "lady"—a creature so elevated that she is not taken seriously as a passionate human being—she is able to kill Homer Barron and not be suspected. Here is Fetterley speaking of the passage in which the townspeople crowd into her house when her death becomes known:

> When the would-be "suitors" finally get into her father's house, they discover the consequences of his oppression of her, for the violence contained in the rotted corpse of Homer Barron is the mirror image of the violence represented in the tableau, the back-flung front door flung back with a vengeance. (42)

"A Rose for Emily" is reprinted on pages 702–707.

Feminist criticism has been concerned not only with the depiction of women and men in a male-determined literary canon and with women's responses to these images but also with yet another topic: women's writing. Women have had fewer opportunities than men to become writers of fiction, poetry, and drama—for one thing, they have been less well educated in the things that the male patriarchy valued—but even when they *have* managed to write, men sometimes have neglected their work simply because it was written by a woman. Feminists have further argued that certain forms of writing have been especially the province of women—for instance journals, diaries, and letters; and predictably, these forms have not been given adequate space in the traditional, male-oriented canon.

In 1972, in an essay entitled "When We Dead Awaken: Writing as Re-Vision," the poet and essayist Adrienne Rich effectively summed up the matter:

> A radical critique of literature, feminist in its impulse, would take the work first of all as a clue to how we live, how we have been living, how we have been led to imagine ourselves, how our language has trapped as well as liberated us: and how we can begin to see—and therefore live—afresh. . . . We

need to know the writing of the past and know it differently than we have ever known it; not to pass on a tradition but to break its hold over us.

Much feminist criticism concerned with women writers has emphasized connections between the writer's biography and her work. Suzanne Juhasz, in her introduction to *Feminist Critics Read Emily Dickinson* (1983), puts it this way:

> The central assumption of feminist criticism is that gender informs the nature of art, the nature of biography, and the relation between them. Dickinson is a woman poet, and this fact is integral to her identity. Feminist criticism's sensitivity to the components of female experience in general and to Dickinson's identity as a woman generates essential insights about her. . . . Attention to the relationship between biography and art is a requisite of feminist criticism. To disregard it further strengthens those divisions continually created by traditional criticism, so that nothing about the woman writer can be seen whole. (1–5)

Feminist criticism has made many readers—men as well as women—increasingly aware of gender relationships within literary works.

Lesbian criticism and **gay criticism** have their roots in feminist criticism; that is, feminist criticism introduced many of the questions that these other, newer developments are now exploring.

Before turning to some of the questions that lesbian and gay critics address, it is necessary to say that lesbian criticism and gay criticism are not symmetrical, chiefly because lesbian and gay relationships themselves are not symmetrical. Straight society has traditionally been more tolerant of—or blinder to—lesbianism than male homosexuality. Further, lesbian literary theory has tended to see its affinities more with feminist theory than with gay theory: that is, the emphasis has been on gender (male/female) rather than on sexuality (homosexuality/bisexuality/heterosexuality). On the other hand, some gays and lesbians have been writing what is now being called queer theory.

Now for some of the questions that this criticism addresses: (1) Do lesbians and gays read in ways that differ from the ways straight people read? (2) Do they write in ways that differ from those of straight people? (3) How have straight writers portrayed lesbians and gays, and how have lesbian and gay writers portrayed straight women and men? (4) What strategies did lesbian and gay writers use to make their work acceptable to a general public in an age when lesbian and gay behavior was unmentionable?

Examination of gender by gay and lesbian critics obviously can help to illuminate literary works, but it should be added, too, that some—perhaps most—gay and lesbian critics write also as activists, reporting their findings not only to enable us to understand and to enjoy the works of (say) Whitman, but also to change society's view of sexuality. Thus, in *Disseminating Whitman* (1991), Michael Moon is impatient with earlier critical rhapsodies about Whitman's universalism. It used to be said that Whitman's celebration of the male body was a sexless celebration of brotherly love in a democracy, but the gist of Moon's view is that we must neither whitewash Whitman's poems with such high-minded talk nor reject them as indecent; rather, we must see exactly what Whitman is saying about a kind of experience to which society had shut its eyes, and we must take Whitman's view seriously.

One assumption in much lesbian and gay critical writing is that although gender greatly influences the ways in which we read, reading is a skill that can be learned, and therefore straight people—aided by lesbian and gay critics—can learn to read, with pleasure and profit, lesbian and gay writers. This assumption also underlies much feminist criticism, which often assumes that men must stop ignoring books by women and must learn (with the help of feminist critics) how to read them, and, in fact, how to read—with newly opened eyes—the sexist writings of men of the past and present.

In addition to the titles mentioned earlier concerning gay and lesbian criticism, consult Eve Kosofsky Sedgwick, *Between Men: English Literature and Male Homosocial Desire* (1985), and an essay by Sedgwick, "Gender Criticism," in *Redrawing the Boundaries,* ed. Stephen Greenblatt and Giles Gunn (1992).

In this book, works that concern gay or lesbian experience include those by A. E. Housman, Gloria Naylor, Adrienne Rich, and Walt Whitman.

This chapter began by making the obvious point that all readers, whether or not they consciously adopt a particular approach to literature, necessarily read through particular lenses. More precisely, a reader begins with a frame of interpretation and from within the frame selects one of the several competing methodologies. Critics often make great—even grandiose—claims for their approaches. For example, Frederic Jameson, a Marxist, begins *The Political Unconscious: Narrative as a Socially Symbolic Act* (1981) thus:

> This book will argue the priority of the political interpretation of literary texts. It conceives of the political perspective not as some supplemental method, not as an optional auxiliary to other interpretive methods current today—the psychoanalytic or the myth-critical, the stylistic, the ethical, the structural— but rather as the absolute horizon of all reading and all interpretation. (7)

Readers who are chiefly interested in politics may be willing to assume "the priority of the political interpretation . . . as the absolute horizon of all reading and all interpretation," but other readers may respectfully decline to accept this assumption.

In talking about a critical approach, sometimes the point is made by saying that readers decode a text by applying a grid to it: the grid enables them to see certain things clearly. Good; but what is sometimes forgotten is that a lens or a grid—an angle of vision or interpretive frame and a methodology—also prevents a reader from seeing certain other things. This is to be expected. What is important, then, is to remember this fact, and thus not to deceive ourselves by thinking that our keen tools enable us to see the whole. A psychoanalytic reading of, say, *Hamlet* may be helpful, but it does not reveal all that is in *Hamlet,* and it does not refute the perceptions of another approach, let's say a historical study. Each approach may illuminate aspects neglected by others.

It is too much to expect a reader to apply all useful methods (or even several) at once—that would be rather like looking through a telescope with one eye and through a microscope with the other—but it is not too much to expect readers to be aware of the limitations of their methods. If you read much criticism, you will find two kinds of critics. There are, on the one hand, critics who methodically and mechanically peer through a lens or grid, and they of course find what can be easily predicted they will find. On the other hand, there are critics who (despite what may be inevitable class and gender biases) are at least relatively open-minded in their approach—critics who, one might say, do not at the outset of their reading believe that their method assures them that they have got the text's number and that by means of this method they will expose the text for what it is. The philosopher Richard Rorty engagingly makes a distinction somewhat along these lines, in an essay he contributed to Umberto Eco's *Interpretation and Overinterpretation* (1992). There is a great difference, Rorty suggests,

> between knowing what you want to get out of a person or thing or text in advance and [on the other hand] hoping that the person or thing or text will help you want something different—that he or she or it will help you to change your purposes, and thus to change your life. This distinction, I think, helps us highlight the difference between methodical and inspired readings of texts. (106)

Rorty goes on to say he has seen an anthology of readings on Conrad's *Heart of Darkness,* containing a psychoanalytic reading, a reader-response reading, and so on. "None of the readers had, as far as I could see," Rorty says,

> been enraptured or destabilized by *Heart of Darkness.* I got no sense that the book had made a big difference to them, that they cared much about Kurtz or Marlow or the woman "with helmeted head and tawny cheeks" whom Marlow sees on the bank of the river. These people, and that book, had no more changed these readers' purposes than the specimen under the microscope changes the purpose of the histologist. (107)

The kind of criticism that Rorty prefers he calls "unmethodical" criticism and "inspired" criticism. It is, for Rorty, the result of an "encounter" with some aspect of a work of art "which has made a difference to the critic's conception of who she is, what she is good for, what she wants to do with herself . . . " (107). This is not a matter of "respect" for the text, Rorty insists. Rather, he says "love" and "hate" are better words, "for a great love or a great loathing is the sort of thing that changes us by changing our purposes, changing the uses to which we shall put people and things and texts we encounter later" (107).

YOUR TURN: PUTTING CRITICAL STRATEGIES TO WORK

1. Which of the critical strategies described in this chapter do you find the most interesting? Which interests you the least?
2. In Chapter 2, we present three stories by Kate Chopin: "The Story of an Hour," "The Storm," and "Désirée's Baby." Which critical strategy do you think is the most rewarding for the study of this author? Explain why, using your favorite story of the three as a "case study."
3. Select a poem in this book that you especially enjoy, and explain why you value it so highly. Next, reread and think about this poem in relation to each of the critical strategies outlined in this chapter. In what ways do these strategies, one by one, enable you to respond to and understand the poem more deeply? Does one of them seem to you especially helpful? Are any of them unhelpful?
4. Imagine that you have been assigned to prepare a mini-anthology of three or four poems and two or three stories that are particularly suited to one of these critical strategies. List your selections, and then explain how your critical strategy gives a special insight into each one, and into the group of works as a whole.
5. Do you think that any of these critical strategies could be usefully combined with one or more of the others? Could, for example, reader-response criticism

go hand-in-hand with gender criticism? Select a poem or a story to show how your combination of two or more strategies can be brought effectively together.

6. Do you find that some of these critical strategies are in conflict with one another? Can you, for instance, be a formalist critic and, say, a reader-response critic or a gender critic at the same time? Is it a problem if our interpretation of a literary work changes, depending on the critical strategy that we use?

7. As you review and think further about the critical strategies we have described, do you find anything missing? How would you respond to someone who says, "What really matters is our own interpretation of a literary work, not the interpretation that this or that critical strategy produces"?

SUGGESTIONS FOR FURTHER READING

Because a massive list of titles may prove discouraging rather than helpful, it seems advisable here to give a short list of basic titles. (Titles already mentioned in this chapter—which are good places to begin—are *not* repeated in the following list.)

Good selections of contemporary criticism can be found in *The Critical Tradition: Classic Texts and Contemporary Trends,* ed. David H. Richter, 2nd ed. (1998); and *The Norton Anthology of Literary Theory and Criticism,* ed. Vincent B. Leitch et al. (2001).

For a readable introduction to various approaches, written for students who are beginning the study of literary theory, see Steven Lynn, *Texts and Contexts,* 3rd ed. (2000). For a more advanced survey, that is, a work that assumes some familiarity with the material, see a short book by K. M. Newton, *Interpreting the Text: A Critical Introduction to the Theory and Practice of Literary Interpretation* (1990). A third survey, though considerably longer than the books by Lynn and Newton, is narrower because it confines itself to a study of critical writings about Shakespeare: Brian Vickers, *Appropriating Shakespeare: Contemporary Critical Quarrels* (1993), offers a stringent appraisal of deconstruction, New Historicism, psychoanalytic criticism, feminist criticism, and Marxist criticism. For collections of essays on Shakespeare written from some of the points of view that Vickers deplores, see Patricia Parker and Geoffrey Hartman, eds., *Shakespeare and the Question of Theory* (1985), and John Drakakis, ed., *Shakespearean Tragedy* (1992).

Sympathetic discussions (usually two or three pages long) of each approach, with fairly extensive bibliographic suggestions, are given in the appropriate articles in the following encyclopedic works: Wendell V. Harris, *Dictionary of Concepts in Literary Criticism* (1992); Irene Makaryk, ed., *Encyclopedia of Contemporary Literary Theory: Approaches, Scholars, Terms* (1993); and Alex Preminger and T. V. F. Brogan, *The New Princeton Encyclopedia of Poetry and Poetics* (1993). For essays discussing feminist, gender, Marxist, psychoanalytic, deconstructive, New Historicist, and cultural criticism—as well as other topics not covered in this chapter—see Stephen Greenblatt and Giles Gunn, eds., *Redrawing the Boundaries: The Transformation of English and American Literary Studies* (1992).

Formalist Criticism (The New Criticism)

Cleanth Brooks, *The Well Wrought Urn: Studies in the Structure of Poetry* (1947), especially Chapters 1 and 11 ("The Language of Paradox" and "The Heresy of

Paraphrase"); W. K. Wimsatt, *The Verbal Icon* (1954), especially "The Intentional Fallacy" and "The Affective Fallacy"; Murray Krieger, *The New Apologists for Poetry* (1956); *The New Criticism and Contemporary Literary Theory: Connections and Continuities,* ed. William J. Spurlin and Michael Fisher (1995); and, for an accurate overview of a kind of criticism often misrepresented today, Chapters 9–12 in Volume 6 of René Wellek, *A History of Modern Criticism: 1750–1950* (1986).

Deconstruction

Christopher Norris, *Deconstruction: Theory and Practice,* rev. ed. (1991); Vincent B. Leitch, *Deconstructive Criticism: An Advanced Introduction and Survey* (1983); Christopher Norris, ed., *What Is Deconstruction?* (1988); and Christopher Norris and Andrew Benjamin, *Deconstruction and the Interests of Theory* (1989); *Deconstruction: Critical Concepts in Literary and Cultural Studies,* ed. Jonathan Culler, 4 vols. (2003). For a negative assessment, consult John M. Ellis, *Against Deconstruction* (1989). More generally, see *Deconstruction: A Reader,* ed. Martin McQuillan (2001).

Reader-Response Criticism

Wolfgang Iser, *The Act of Reading: A Theory of Aesthetic Response* (1978); Iser, *Prospecting: From Reader Response to Literary Anthropology* (1993); Susan Suleiman and Inge Crossman, eds., *The Reader in the Text* (1980); Jane P. Tompkins, ed., *Reader-Response Criticism* (1980); Norman N. Holland, *The Dynamics of Literary Response* (1973, 1989); Steven Mailloux, *Interpretive Conventions: The Reader in the Study of American Fiction* (1982); Gerry Brenner, *Performative Criticism: Experiments in Reader Response* (2004).

Archetypal Criticism

G. Wilson Knight, *The Starlit Dome* (1941); Richard Chase, *Quest for Myth* (1949); Murray Krieger, ed., *Northrop Frye in Modern Criticism* (1966); Frank Lentricchia, *After the New Criticism* (1980); *Rereading Frye: The Published and Unpublished Works,* ed. David Boyd and Imre Salusinszky (1999). For a good survey of Frye's approach, see Robert D. Denham, *Northrop Frye and Critical Method* (1978).

Historical Criticism

For a brief survey of some historical criticism of the first half of this century, see René Wellek, *A History of Modern Criticism: 1750–1950,* Volume 6 (1986), Chapter 4 ("Academic Criticism"). E. M. W. Tillyard, *The Elizabethan World Picture* (1943), and Tillyard's *Shakespeare's History Plays* (1944), both of which relate Elizabethan literature to the beliefs of the age, are good examples of the historical approach. See also Roy Harvey Pearce, *Gesta Humanorum: Studies in the Historicist Mode* (1987); and David Levin, *Forms of Uncertainty: Essays in Historical Criticism* (1992).

Marxist Criticism

Raymond Williams, *Marxism and Literature* (1977); Tony Bennett, *Formalism and Marxism* (1979); Lydia Sargent, ed., *Women and Revolution: A Discussion of the Unhappy Marriage of Marxism and Feminism* (1981); and for a brief survey of American Marxist writers of the 1930s and 1940s, see Chapter 5 of Volume 6 of

René Wellek, *A History of Modern Criticism* (1986). Also helpful are Daniel Aaron, *Writers on the Left: Episodes in American Literary Communism* (1961; new ed., 1992), and Barbara Foley, *Radical Representations: Politics and Form in U.S. Proletarian Fiction, 1929–1941* (1993). Also stimulating is Terry Eagleton, *The Ideology of the Aesthetic* (1990). For a specialized study, see *Marxist Shakespeares*, ed. Jean E. Howard and Scott Cutler Shershow (2001).

New Historicism

Stephen Greenblatt, *Renaissance Self-Fashioning from More to Shakespeare* (1980), especially the first chapter; Brook Thomas, *The New Historicism and Other Old-Fashioned Topics* (1991). Greenblatt's other influential books include *Shakespearean Negotiations: The Circulation of Social Energy in Renaissance England* (1988), and, with Catherine Gallagher, *Practicing New Historicism* (2000). See also *Historicizing Theory*, ed. Peter C. Herman (2004).

Biographical Criticism

Leon Edel, *Literary Biography* (1957); Estelle C. Jellinek, ed., *Women's Autobiography: Essays in Criticism* (1980); James Olney, *Metaphors of Self: The Meaning of Autobiography* (1981); and *Women, Autobiography, Theory: A Reader,* ed. Sidonie Smith and Julia Watson. Important twentieth-century literary biographies are Richard Ellmann, *James Joyce* (1959, rev. ed., 1982); Juliet Barker, *The Brontës* (1994); Hermione Lee, *Virginia Woolf* (1997); Lyndall Gordon, *T. S. Eliot: An Imperfect Life* (1999); and Fred Kaplan, *The Singular Mark Twain: A Biography* (2003).

Psychological (or Psychoanalytical) Criticism

Edith Kurzweil and William Phillips, eds., *Literature and Psychoanalysis* (1983); Maurice Charney and Joseph Reppen, eds., *Psychoanalytic Approaches to Literature and Film* (1987); Madelon Sprengnether, *The Spectral Mother: Freud, Feminism, and Psychoanalysis* (1990); Frederick Crews, *Out of My System* (1975); and Graham Frankland, *Freud's Literary Culture* (2000).

Gender (Feminist, and Lesbian and Gay) Criticism

Gayle Greene and Coppèlia Kahn, eds., *Making a Difference: Feminist Literary Criticism* (1985), including an essay by Bonnie Zimmerman on lesbian criticism; Catherine Belsey and Jane Moore, eds., *The Feminist Reader: Essays in Gender and the Politics of Literary Criticism* (1989); Toril Moi, ed., *French Feminist Thought* (1987); Elizabeth A. Flynn and Patrocinio P. Schweikart, eds., *Gender and Reading: Essays on Readers, Texts, and Contexts* (1986); Barbara Christian, *Black Feminist Criticism: Perspectives on Black Women Writers* (1985); Shoshana Felman, *What Does a Woman Want? Reading and Sexual Difference* (1993); Robert Martin, *The Homosexual Tradition in American Poetry* (1979); Kathryn R. Kent, *Making Girls into Women: American Women's Writing and the Rise of Lesbian Identity;* and Rita Felski, *Literature After Feminism* (2003). Henry Abelove et al., eds., *The Lesbian and Gay Studies Reader* (1993), has only a few essays concerning literature, but it has an extensive bibliography on the topic.

Valuable reference works include *Encyclopedia of Feminist Literary Theory* (1997), ed. Beth Kowaleski-Wallace; *The Gay & Lesbian Literary Companion,* ed.

Sharon Malinowski and Christa Brelin (1995); and *The Gay and Lesbian Literary Heritage: A Reader's Companion to the Writers and Their Works, from Antiquity to the Present,* ed. Claude J. Summers (1995). See also Summers, *Gay Fictions: Wilde to Stonewall: Studies in a Male Homosexual Literary Tradition* (1990); *Novel Gazing: Queer Readings in Fiction,* ed. Eve Kosofsky Sedgwick (1997); and Gregory Woods, *A History of Gay Literature: The Male Tradition* (1998). For further discussion of queer theory, see Annamarie Jagose, *Queer Theory: An Introduction* (1996); Alan Sinfield, *Cultural Politics—Queer Reading* (1994); and *Feminism Meets Queer Theory* (1997), ed. Elizabeth Weed and Naomi Schor.

PART IV

A Thematic Anthology

19

Journeys

Short Views

Here are some brief comments about journeys—inner and outer. Read them carefully, and then write on one of the topics that appear after the last quotation.

If you don't know where you want to go, any road will take you there.
Traditional

They change their clime, not their disposition, who run across the sea.
Horace

Travel makes a wise man better, but a fool worse.
Thomas Fuller

Why do you wonder that globe-trotting does not help you, seeing that you always take yourself with you? The reason which set you wandering is ever at your heels.
Seneca, attributing the line to Socrates

Worth seeing, yes; but not worth going to see.
Samuel Johnson

We shall not cease from exploration
And the end of all our exploring
Will be to arrive where we started
And know the place for the first time.
T. S. Eliot

It is easier to sail many thousand miles through cold and storm and cannibals, in a government ship, with five hundred men and boys to assist one, than it is to explore the private sea, the Atlantic and Pacific Ocean of one's being alone...
Henry David Thoreau

I have traveled a good deal in Concord.
Henry David Thoreau

*I am not much an advocate for traveling. Who are you that have no task
to keep you at home?*
    Ralph Waldo Emerson

*The whole object of travel is not to set foot on foreign land; it is at last to
set foot on one's own country as a foreign land.*
    G. K. Chesterton

Before taking steps the wise man knows the object and end of his journey.
    W. E. B. Du Bois

*Without stirring abroad
One can know the whole world;
Without looking out of the window
One can see the way of heaven
The further one goes
The less one knows*
    Lao-Tzu, trans. D. C. Lau

*For my part, I travel not to go anywhere, but to go. I travel for travel's
sake. The great affair is to move; to feel the needs and hitches of our life
more nearly; to come down off this featherbed of civilization, and find
the globe granite underfoot and strewn with cutting flints.*
    Robert Louis Stevenson

*I always think that the most delightful thing about traveling is to always
be running into Americans and to always feel at home.*
    Anita Loos

*Travel spins us round in two ways at once: It shows us the sights and val-
ues and issues that we might ordinarily ignore; but it also, and more
deeply, shows us all the parts of ourselves that might otherwise grow rusty.
For in traveling to a truly foreign place, we inevitably travel to moods
and states of mind and hidden inward passages that we'd otherwise seldom have cause to visit. . . . Travel, then is a voyage into that famously
subjective zone, the imagination, and what the traveler brings back is—
and has to be—an ineffable compound of himself and the place, what's
really there and what's only in him.*
    Pico Iyer

Because it was there.
    George Mallory (answering the question why he wanted to climb Mt.
    Everest)

Like love, travel makes you innocent again.
    Diane Ackerman

Topics for Critical Thinking and Writing

1. Select a quotation that especially appeals to you, and make it the focus of an essay of about 500 words.

2. Take two of these passages—perhaps one that you especially like and one that you think is wrong-headed—and write a dialogue of about 500 words in which the two authors converse. They may each try to convince the other, or they may find that to some degree they share views and they may then work out a statement that both can accept. If you do take the first position—that one writer is on the correct track but the other is utterly mistaken—do try to be fair to the view that you think is mistaken. (As an experiment in critical thinking, imagine that you accept it, and make the best case for it that you possibly can.)

3. In a single paragraph, summarize the best, or the worst, consequence, of travel. Next, try to do the same in just a single sentence.

4. In one of the quotations above, Emerson says that he is "not much of an advocate for traveling." Imagine that you are an advocate *for* traveling, and that Emerson is your reader. List the key points of your argument. Then, working from this list, write an essay of two pages.

5. Review the essay, for Topic #3, that you wrote in defense of travel. What are the strengths and weaknesses of your argument? Do you see any weaknesses? How might you revise this essay to make it more effective? Do you think you should introduce counter-arguments into your essay—arguments "on the other side" that you could address and try to answer? Or would this prove confusing to your reader?

6. When someone says to you that he or she "hates to travel," what is your response? Do you think that such a position can really be defended? If you had to argue that traveling is a bad idea, what would be the main points you would make? Do you think you would cite any of the quotations given above? Which ones? What would you gain from such a citation? What, if anything, might you lose?

7. According to W. E. B. Du Bois, above, before a person travels, he or she should know "the object and end" of the journey. What is Du Bois saying? Do you agree? If Du Bois is right, then why is it said so often that a person should always travel "with an open mind"?

8. Once again, consider Du Bois's observation about travel. Have you ever traveled somewhere when you have known from the start "the object and end"? Please describe this experience. Have you ever traveled somewhere without knowing "the object and end"? Now, describe this experience.

9. If someone surprised you with the gift of a free trip, which destination would excite you the most? Which one would excite you the least?

10. Diane Ackerman suggests that travel restores a person's "innocence." What does this mean? Do you believe it? She also connects the experience of travel and love. What is her point? How would her point about travel change if the phrase "like love" were deleted?

11. Do you spend much time exploring your own thoughts and feelings? Do you set aside a specific time for this? Is there a specific place where it occurs? Is this an activity you undertake by yourself, or with someone else, or with some group? Describe an occasion when you explored your thoughts and feelings, and explain what happened next.

ESSAYS

JOAN DIDION

Joan Didion was born in Sacramento in 1934, and she was educated at the University of California, Berkeley. She has written essays, stories, screenplays, and novels.

On Going Home

I am home for my daughter's first birthday. By "home" I do not mean the house in Los Angeles where my husband and I and the baby live, but the place where my family is, in the Central Valley of California. It is a vital although troublesome distinction. My husband likes my family but is uneasy in their house, because once there I fall into their ways, which are difficult, oblique, deliberately inarticulate, not my husband's ways. We live in dusty houses ("D-U-S-T," he once wrote with his finger on surfaces all over the house, but no one noticed it) filled with mementos quite without value to him (what could the Canton dessert plates mean to him? How could he have known about the assay scales, why should he care if he did know?), and we appear to talk exclusively about people we know who have been committed to mental hospitals, about people we know who have been booked on drunk-driving charges, and about property, particularly about property, land, price per acre and C-2 zoning and assessments, and freeway access. My brother does not understand my husband's inability to perceive the advantage in the rather common real-estate transaction known as "sale-leaseback," and my husband in turn does not understand why so many of the people he hears about in my father's house have recently been committed to mental hospitals or booked on drunk-driving charges. Nor does he understand that when we talk about sale-leasebacks and right-of-way condemnations we are talking in code about the things we like best, the yellow fields and the cottonwoods and the rivers rising and falling and the mountain roads closing when they heavy snow comes in. We miss each other's points, have another drink and regard the fire. My brother refers to my husband, in his presence, as "Joan's husband." Marriage is the classic betrayal.

Or perhaps it is not any more. Sometimes I think that those of us who are now in our thirties were born into the last generation to carry the burden of "home," to find in family life the source of all tension and drama. I had by all objective accounts a "normal" and a "happy" family situation, and yet I was almost thirty years old before I could talk to my family on the telephone without crying after I had hung up. We did not fight. Nothing was wrong. And yet some nameless anxiety colored the emotional charges between me and the place that I came from. The question of whether or not you could go home again was a very real part of the sentimental and largely literary baggage with which we left home in the fifties; I suspect that it is irrelevant to the children born of the fragmentation after World War II. A few weeks ago in a San Francisco bar I saw a pretty young girl on crystal take off her clothes and dance for the cash prize in an "amateur-topless" contest. There was no particular sense of moment about this, none of the effect of romantic degradation, of "dark journey," for which my generation strived so assiduously. What sense could that girl possibly make of, say, *Long Day's Journey into Night?* Who is beside the point?

That I am trapped in this particular irrelevancy is never more apparent to me than when I am home. Paralyzed by the neurotic lassitude engendered by meeting one's past at every turn, around every corner, inside every cupboard, I go aimlessly from room to room. I decide to meet it head-on and clean out a drawer, and I spread the contents on the bed. A bathing suit I wore the summer I was seventeen. A letter of rejection from *The Nation*, an aerial photograph of the site for a shopping center my father did not build in 1954. Three teacups hand-painted with cabbage roses and signed "E.M.," my grandmother's initials. There is no final solution for letters of rejection from *The Nation* and teacups hand-painted in 1900. Nor is there any answer to snapshots of one's grandfather as a young man on skis, surveying around Donner Pass in the year 1910. I smooth out the snapshot and look into his face, and do and do not see my own. I close the drawer, and have another cup of coffee with my mother. We get along very well, veterans of a guerilla war we never understood.

Days pass. I see no one. I come to dread my husband's evening call, not only because he is full of news of what by now seems to me our remote life in Los Angeles, people he has seen, letters which require attention, but because he asks what I have been doing, suggests uneasily that I get out, drive to San Francisco or Berkeley. Instead I drive across the river to a family graveyard. It has been vandalized since my last visit and the monuments are broken, overturned in the dry grass. Because I once saw a rattlesnake in the grass I stay in the car and listen to a country-and-Western station. Later I drive with my father to a ranch he has in the foothills. The man who runs his cattle on it asks us to the roundup, a week from Sunday, and although I know I will be in Los Angeles I say, in the oblique way my family talks, that I will come. Once home I mention the broken monuments in the graveyard. My mother shrugs.

5   I go to visit my great-aunts. A few of them think now that I am my cousin, or their daughter who died young. We recall an anecdote about a relative last seen in 1948, and they ask if I still like living in New York City. I have lived in Los Angeles for three years, but I say that I do. The baby is offered a horehound drop, and I am slipped a dollar bill "to buy a treat." Questions trail off, answers are abandoned, the baby plays with the dust motes in a shaft of afternoon sun.

It is time for the baby's birthday party: a white cake, strawberry-marshmellow ice cream, a bottle of champagne saved from another party. In the evening, after she has gone to sleep, I kneel beside the crib and touch her face, where it is pressed against the slats, with mine. She is an open and trusting child, unprepared for and unaccustomed to the ambushes of family life, and perhaps it is just as well that I can offer her a little of that life. I would like to give her more. I would like to promise her that she will grow up with a sense of her cousins and of rivers and of her great-grandmother's teacups, would like to pledge her a picnic on a river with fried chicken and her hair uncombed, would like to give her *home* for her birthday, but we live differently now and I can promise her nothing like that. I give her a xylophone and a sundress from Madeira, and promise to tell her a funny story.

[1968]

Topics for Critical Thinking and Writing

1. Didion reveals that members of her family are difficult, inarticulate, poor housekeepers, and so forth. Do you find these revelations about her family distasteful? Would you mind seeing in print similarly unflattering things you had

written about your own family? How might such revelations be justified? Are they justified in this essay?

2. Summarize the point of the second paragraph. Do you find Didion's speculations about the difference between her generation and succeeding generations meaningful? Are they accurate for your generation?

3. Do you think that growing up necessarily involves estrangement from one's family?

CHARLES DE SECONDAT, BARON DE LA BRÈDE ET DE MONTESQUIEU

Montesquieu (1689–1755), French jurist, political philosopher, and writer, was born at La Brède, near Bordeaux. Today he is known chiefly for The Spirit of Laws *(1748), a study of three kinds of government (republic, monarchy, despotism), but he achieved fame in his own day with his* Persian Letters *(1721), letters supposedly written by two Persians (and their correspondents) traveling in Europe. Through the device of using narrators who are unsophisticated in European ways—innocent eyes, so to speak—he was able to satirize European social, political, religious, and literary customs. (If you are familiar with the fable of the emperor's clothes, in which a child sees that the emperor is naked, you are familiar with the device of using an innocent to tell the truth.)*

Persian Letters

Translated by J. Robert Loy

Letter 24: Rica to Ibben in Smyrna

We have been in Paris for a month and have been continually in motion. It takes much doing to find a place to live, to meet people to whom you are recommended, and to provide yourself with necessities all at the same time.

Paris is as large as Ispahan. The houses here are so high that you would swear they were all inhabited by astrologers. You can readily understand that a city built up in the air, with six or seven houses built one on top of the other, is an extremely populous city, and that when everyone is down in the streets, there is great confusion.

Perhaps you will not believe this, but for the month I have been here, I have seen nobody walking. There are no people in the world who get so much out of their carcasses as the French: they run; they fly. The slow carriages of Asia, the regular pace of our camels, would make them swoon. As for myself, I am not built that way, and when I go walking, as I do often, without changing my pace, I sometimes fume and rage like a Christian. For, passing over the fact that I am splashed from head to foot, still I cannot forgive the elbowings in my ribs that I collect regularly and periodically. A man walking behind me, passes me and turns me half-around; then another, coming toward me from the opposite direction, briskly puts me back into the position where the first fellow hit me. I have barely made a hundred paces before I am more bruised than if I had gone ten leagues.

Do not expect me to be able just now to talk to you seriously about European usages and customs. I have only a faint idea of them myself and have barely had time to be amazed by them.

5   The King of France is the most powerful prince of Europe. Unlike his neighbor the King of Spain, he has no gold mines. Yet he possesses greater riches, for he draws from the vanity of his subjects a wealth more inexhaustible than mines. He has been known to undertake and wage great wars with no other funds than honorary titles to sell, and by reason of this miracle of human pride, his troops are paid, his fortresses armed, and his navies fitted out.

Moreover, this king is a great magician. He exercises his empire over the very minds of his subjects and makes them think as he likes. If he has only one million crowns in his treasury and he needs two million, he has only to convince them that one crown equals two, and they believe him. If he is involved in a war that is difficult in the waging and finds himself short of money, he has only to put into their heads the notion that a slip of paper is money, and they are immediately convinced. He even goes so far as to make them believe that he can cure them of all manner of disease by touching them, so great is his strength and dominion over their minds. . . .

I shall continue to write to you, and I shall teach you things far removed from Persian character and spirit. It is certainly the same earth carrying both countries, but the men of this country where I am and those of the country where you are are quite different.

From Paris, the 4th of the Moon of Rebiab II, 1712

[1721]

Topics for Critical Thinking and Writing

1. In the third paragraph Montesquieu's narrator says of his stay in Paris, "I have seen nobody walking. . . . [T]hey run; they fly." He is writing in the eighteenth century, so "they fly" is a figure of speech. (A European friend of ours, visiting Los Angeles, wrote to us that he was the only person walking; everyone else was jogging or roller-blading.) Write your own Persian letter to a fellow-Persian, reporting on the strange behavior that surrounds you in the classroom, the streets, or (drawing on the newspapers and television) the nation. Or you may prefer to take on the persona of some other alleged innocent, for instance a creature from Mars, or an eighteenth-century person, who via a time machine, finds himself or herself in the twenty-first century.

2. Voltaire, Montesquieu's contemporary, said that *Persian Letters* was "a book which anybody might have written easily." Perhaps his thinking was along the lines of Samuel Johnson, who said of Jonathan Swift's *Gulliver's Travels* that once you thought of little people and big people, the rest was easy. If you have written your own Persian letter evaluate Voltaire's comment.

FICTION

TONI CADE BAMBARA

Toni Cade Bambara (1939–1995), an African American writer, was born in New York City and grew up in black districts of the city. After studying at the University of Florence in Italy and at City College in New York, where she received a master's degree, she worked for a while as a case investigator for the New York State Welfare Department. Later she directed a recreation program for hospital patients. After her literary reputation became established, she spent most of her time writing, though she also served as writer in residence at Spelman College in Atlanta.

The Lesson

Back in the days when everyone was old and stupid or young and foolish and me and Sugar were the only ones just right, this lady moved on our block with nappy hair and proper speech and no makeup. And quite naturally we laughed at her, laughed the way we did at the junk man who went about his business like he was some big-time president and his sorry-ass horse his secretary. And we kinda hated her too, hated the way we did the winos who cluttered up our parks and pissed on our handball walls and stank up our hallways and stairs so you couldn't halfway play hide-and-seek without a goddamn gas mask. Miss Moore was her name. The only woman on the block with no first name. And she was black as hell, cept for her feet, which were fish-white and spooky. And she was always planning these boring-ass things for us to do, us being my cousin, mostly, who lived on the block cause we all moved North the same time and to the same apartment then spread out gradual to breathe. And our parents would yank our heads into some kinda shape and crisp up our clothes so we'd be presentable for travel with Miss Moore, who always looked like she was going to church, though she never did. Which is just one of the things the grownups talked about when they talked behind her back like a dog. But when she came calling with some sachet she'd sewed up or some gingerbread she'd made or some book, why then they'd all be too embarrassed to turn her down and we'd get handed over all spruced up. She'd been to college and said it was only right that she should take responsibility for the young ones' education, and she not even related by marriage or blood. So they'd go for it. Specially Aunt Gretchen. She was the main gofer in the family. You got some ole dumb shit foolishness you want somebody to go for, you send for Aunt Gretchen. She been screwed into the go-along for so long, it's a blood-deep natural thing with her. Which is how she got saddled with me and Sugar and Junior in the first place while our mothers were in a la-de-da apartment up the block having a good ole time.

So this one day Miss Moore rounds us all up at the mailbox and it's puredee hot and she's knockin herself out about arithmetic. And school suppose to let up in summer I heard, but she don't never let up. And the starch in my pinafore scratching the shit outta me and I'm really hating this nappy-head bitch and her goddamn college degree. I'd much rather go to the pool or to the show where it's cool. So me and Sugar leaning on the mailbox being surly, which is a Miss Moore word. And Flyboy checking out what everybody brought for lunch. And Fat Butt already wasting his peanut-butter-and-jelly sandwich like the pig he is. And Junebug punchin on Q.T.'s arm for potato chips. And Rosie Giraffe shifting from one hip to the other waiting for somebody to step on her foot or ask her if she from Georgia so she can kick ass, preferably Mercedes'. And Miss Moore asking us do we know what money is, like we a bunch of retards. I mean real money, she say, like it's only poker chips or monopoly papers we lay on the grocer. So right away I'm tired of this and say so. And would much rather snatch Sugar and go to the Sunset and terrorize the West Indian kids and take their hair ribbons and their money too. And Miss Moore files that remark away for next week's lesson on brotherhood, I can tell. And finally I say we oughta get to the subway cause it's cooler and besides we might meet some cute boys. Sugar done swiped her mama's lipstick, so we ready.

So we heading down the street and she's boring us silly about what things cost and what our parents make and how much goes for rent and how money ain't divided up right in this country. And then she gets to the part about we all poor and live in the slums, which I don't feature. And I'm ready to speak on that, but she steps out in the street and hails two cabs just like that. Then she hustles half the crew in with her and hands me a five-dollar bill and tells me to calculate 10 percent tip for the driver. And we're off. Me and Sugar and Junebug and Flyboy hangin out the window and hollering to everybody, putting lipstick on each other cause Flyboy a faggot anyway, and making farts with our sweaty armpits. But I'm mostly trying to figure how to spend this money. But they all fascinated with the meter ticking and Junebug starts laying bets to how much it'll read when Flyboy can't hold his breath no more. Then Sugar lays bets as to how much it'll be when we get there. So I'm stuck. Don't nobody want to go for my plan, which is to jump out at the next light and run off to the first bar-b-que we can find. Then the driver tells us to get the hell out cause we there already. And the meter reads eighty-five cents. And I'm stalling to figure out the tip and Sugar say give him a dime. And I decide he don't need it as bad as I do, so later for him. But then he tries to take off with Junebug foot still in the door so we talk about his mama something ferocious. Then we check out that we on Fifth Avenue and everybody dressed up in stockings. One lady in a fur coat, hot as it is. White folks crazy.

"This is the place," Miss Moore say, presenting it to us in the voice she uses at the museum. "Let's look in the windows before we go in."

5   "Can we steal?" Sugar asks very serious like she's getting the ground rules squared away before she plays. "I beg your pardon," say Miss Moore, and we fall out. So she leads us around the windows of the toy store and me and Sugar screamin, "This is mine, that's mine, I gotta have that, that was made for me, I was born for that," till Big Butt drowns us out.

"Hey, I'm goin to buy that there."

"That there? You don't even know what it is, stupid."

"I do so," he say punchin on Rosie Giraffe. "It's a microscope."

"Whatcha gonna do with a microscope, fool?"

10   "Look at things."

"Like what, Ronald?" ask Miss Moore. And Big Butt ain't got the first notion. So here go Miss Moore gabbing about the thousands of bacteria in a drop of water and the somethinorother in a speck of blood and the million and one living things in the air around us is invisible to the naked eye. And what she say that for? Junebug go to town on that "naked" and we rolling. Then Miss Moore ask what it cost. So we all jam into the window smudgin it up and the price tag say $300. So

then she ask how long'd take for Big Butt and Junebug to save up their al-
lowances. "Too long," I say. "Yeh," adds Sugar, "outgrown it by that time." And
Miss Moore say no, you never outgrow learning instruments. "Why, even medical
students and interns and," blah, blah, blah. And we ready to choke Big Butt for
bringing it up in the first damn place.

"This here costs four hundred eighty dollars," say Rosie Giraffe. So we pile up
all over her to see what she pointin out. My eyes tell me it's a chunk of glass
cracked with something heavy, and different-color inks dripped into the splits, then
the whole thing put into a oven or something. But for $480 it don't make sense.

"That's a paperweight made of semi-precious stones fused together under
tremendous pressure," she explains slowly, and her hands doing the mining and
all the factory work.

"So what's a paperweight?" asks Rosie Giraffe.

15   "To weigh paper with, dumbbell," say Flyboy, the wise man from the East.

"Not exactly," say Miss Moore, which is what she say when you warm or way
off too. "It's to weigh paper down so it won't scatter and make your desk untidy."
So right away me and Sugar curtsy to each other and then to Mercedes who is
more the tidy type.

"We don't keep paper on top of the desk in my class," say Junebug, figuring
Miss Moore crazy or lyin one.

"At home, then," she say. "Don't you have a calendar and a pencil case and a
blotter and a letter-opener on your desk at home where you do your homework?"
And she know damn well what our homes look like cause she nosys around in
them every chance she gets.

"I don't even have a desk," say Junebug. "Do we?"

20   "No. And I don't get no homework neither," says Big Butt.

"And I don't even have a home," say Flyboy like he do at school to keep the
white folks off his back and sorry for him. Send this poor kid to camp posters, is
his specialty.

"I do," says Mercedes. "I have a box of stationery on my desk and a picture of
my cat. My godmother bought the stationery and the desk. There's a big rose on
each sheet and the envelopes smell like roses."

"Who wants to know about your smelly-ass stationery," say Rosie Giraffe fore
I can get my two cents in.

"It's important to have a work area all your own so that . . ."

25   "Will you look at this sailboat, please," say Flyboy, cuttin her off and pointin
to the thing like it was his. So once again we tumble all over each other to gaze at
this magnificent thing in the toy store which is just big enough to maybe sail two
kittens across the pond if you strap them to the posts tight. We all start reciting the
price tag like we in assembly. "Handcrafted sailboat of fiberglass at one thousand
one hundred ninety-five dollars."

"Unbelievable," I hear myself say and am really stunned. I read it again for
myself just in case the group recitation put me in a trance. Same thing. For some
reason this pisses me off. We look at Miss Moore and she lookin at us, waiting for
I dunno what.

"Who'd pay all that when you can buy a sailboat set for a quarter at Pop's, a
tube of glue for a dime, and a ball of string for eight cents? It must have a motor
and a whole lot else besides," I say. "My sailboat cost me about fifty cents."

"But will it take water?" say Mercedes with her smart ass.

"Took mine to Alley Pond Park once," say Flyboy. "String broke. Lost it. Pity."

30   "Sailed mine in Central Park and it keeled over and sank. Had to ask my father for another dollar."

"And you got the strap," laugh Big Butt. "The jerk didn't even have a string on it. My old man wailed on his behind."

Little Q.T. was staring hard at the sailboat and you could see he wanted it bad. But he too little and somebody'd just take it from him. So what the hell. "This boat for kids, Miss Moore?"

"Parents silly to buy something like that just to get all broke up," say Rosie Giraffe.

"That much money it should last forever," I figure.

35   "My father'd buy it for me if I wanted it."

"Your father, my ass," say Rosie Giraffe getting a chance to finally push Mercedes.

"Must be rich people shop here," say Q.T.

"You are a very bright boy," say Flyboy. "What was your first clue?" And he rap him on the head with the back of his knuckles, since Q.T. the only one he could get away with. Though Q.T. liable to come up behind you years later and get his licks in when you half expect it.

"What I want to know is," I says to Miss Moore though I never talk to her, I wouldn't give the bitch that satisfaction, "is how much a real boat costs? I figure a thousand'd get you a yacht any day."

40   "Why don't you check that out," she says, "and report back to the group?" Which really pains my ass. If you gonna mess up a perfectly good swim day least you could do is have some answers. "Let's go in," she say like she got something up her sleeve. Only she don't lead the way. So me and Sugar turn the corner to where the entrance is, but when we get there I kinda hang back. Not that I'm scared, what's there to be afraid of, just a toy store. But I feel funny, shame. But what I got to be shamed about? Got as much right to go in as anybody. But somehow I can't seem to get hold of the door, so I step away for Sugar to lead. But she hangs back too. And I look at her and she looks at me and this is ridiculous. I mean, damn, I have never ever been shy about doing nothing or going nowhere. But then Mercedes steps up and then Rosie Giraffe and Big Butt crowd in behind and shove, and next thing we all stuffed into the doorway with only Mercedes squeezing past us, smoothing out her jumper and walking right down the aisle. Then the rest of us tumble in like a glued-together jigsaw done all wrong. And people lookin at us. And it's like the time me and Sugar crashed into the Catholic church on a dare. But once we got in there and everything so hushed and holy and the candles and the bowin and the handkerchiefs on all the drooping heads, I just couldn't go through with the plan. Which was for me to run up to the altar and do a tap dance while Sugar played the nose flute and messed around in the holy water. And Sugar kept givin me the elbow. Then later teased me so bad I tied her up in the shower and turned it on and locked her in. And she'd be there till this day if Aunt Gretchen hadn't finally figured I was lyin about the boarder takin a shower.

Same thing in the store. We all walkin on tiptoe and hardly touchin the games and puzzles and things. And I watched Miss Moore who is steady watchin us like she waitin for a sign. Like Mama Drewery watches the sky and sniffs the air and takes note of just how much slant is in the bird formation. Then me and Sugar bump smack into each other, so busy gazing at the toys, 'specially the sailboat. But we don't laugh and go into our fat-lady bumpstomach routine. We just stare at that price tag. Then Sugar run a finger over the whole boat. And I'm jealous and want to hit her. Maybe not her, but I sure want to punch somebody in the mouth.

"Whatcha bring us here for, Miss Moore?"

"You sound angry, Sylvia. Are you mad about something?" Givin me one of them grins like she tellin a grown-up joke that never turns out to be funny. And she's lookin very closely at me like maybe she plannin to do my portrait from memory. I'm mad, but I won't give her that satisfaction. So I slouch around the store bein very bored and say, "Let's go."

Me and Sugar at the back of the train watchin the tracks whizzin by large then small then gettin gobbled up in the dark. I'm thinkin about this tricky toy I saw in the store. A clown that somersaults on a bar then does chin-ups just cause you yank lightly at his leg. Cost $35. I could see me askin my mother for a $35 birthday clown. "You wanna who that costs what?" she'd say, cocking her head to the side to get a better view of the hole in my head. Thirty-five dollars could buy new bunk beds for Junior and Gretchen's boy. Thirty-five dollars and the whole household could go visit Granddaddy Nelson in the country. Thirty-five dollars would pay for the rent and the piano bill too. Who are these people that spend that much for performing clowns and $1000 for toy sailboats? What kinda work they do and how they live and how come we ain't in on it? Where we are is who we are, Miss Moore always pointin out. But it don't necessarily have to be that way, she always adds then waits for somebody to say that poor people have to wake up and demand their share of the pie and don't none of us know what kind of pie she talkin about in the first damn place. But she ain't so smart cause I still got her four dollars from the taxi and she sure ain't gettin it. Messin up my day with this shit. Sugar nudges me in my pocket and winks.

45   Miss Moore lines us up in front of the mailbox where we started from, seem like years ago, and I got a headache for thinkin so hard. And we lean all over each other so we can hold up under the draggy-ass lecture she always finishes us off with at the end before we thank her for borin us to tears. But she just looks at us like she readin tea leaves. Finally she say, "Well, what do you think of F. A. O. Schwarz?"

Rosie Giraffe mumbles, "White folks crazy."

"I'd like to go there again when I get my birthday money," says Mercedes, and we shove her out the pack so she has to lean on the mailbox by herself.

"I'd like a shower. Tiring day," say Flyboy.

Then Sugar surprises me by sayin, "You know, Miss Moore, I don't think all of us here put together eat in a year what that sailboat costs." And Miss Moore lights up like somebody goosed her. "And?" she say, urging Sugar on. Only I'm standin on her foot so she don't continue.

50   "Imagine for a minute what kind of society it is in which some people can spend on a toy what it would cost to feed a family of six or seven. What do you think?"

"I think," say Sugar pushing me off her feet like she never done before, cause I whip her ass in a minute, "that this is not much of a democracy if you ask me. Equal chance to pursue happiness means an equal crack at the dough, don't it?" Miss Moore is besides herself and I am disgusted with Sugar's treachery. So I stand on her foot one more time to see if she'll shove me. She shuts up, and Miss Moore looks at me, sorrowfully I'm thinkin. And somethin weird is goin on, I can feel it in my chest.

"Anybody else learn anything today?" lookin dead at me. I walk away and Sugar has to run to catch up and don't even seem to notice when I shrug her arm off my shoulder.

"Well, we got four dollars anyway," she says.

"Uh hunh."

55 "We could go to Hascombs and get half a chocolate layer and then go to the Sunset and still have plenty money for potato chips and ice cream sodas."

"Uh hunh."

"Race you to Hascombs," she say.

We start down the block and she gets ahead which is O.K. by me cause I'm going to the West End and then over to the Drive to think this day through. She can run if she want to and even run faster. But ain't nobody gonna beat me at nuthin.

[1972]

Topics for Critical Thinking and Writing

1. What is the point of Miss Moore's lesson? Why does Sylvia resist it?
2. Describe the relationship between Sugar and Sylvia. What is Sugar's function in the story?
3. What does the last line of the story suggest?
4. In a paragraph or two, characterize the narrator. Do not summarize the story—assume that your reader is familiar with it—but support your characterization by some references to episodes in the story and perhaps by a few brief quotations.

BOBBIE ANN MASON

Bobbie Ann Mason, born in 1940 in rural western Kentucky and a graduate of the University of Kentucky, now lives in Pennsylvania. She took a master's degree at the State University of New York at Binghamton, and a PhD at the University of Connecticut, writing a dissertation on a novel by Vladimir Nabokov. Between graduate degrees she worked for various magazines, including T.V. Star Parade. *In 1974 she published her first book—the dissertation on Nabokov—and in 1975 she published her second,* The Girl Sleuth: A Guide to the Bobbsey Twins, Nancy Drew and Their Sisters. *She is, however, most widely known for her fiction, which usually deals with blue-collar people in rural Kentucky. "I write," she says, "about people trapped in circumstances. . . . I identify with people who are ambivalent about their situation. And I guess in my stories, I'm in a way imagining myself as I would have felt if I had not gotten away and gotten a different perspective on things—if, for example, I had gotten pregnant in high school and had to marry a truck driver as the woman did in my story 'Shiloh.'"*

Shiloh

Leroy Moffitt's wife, Norma Jean, is working on her pectorals. She lifts three-pound dumbbells to warm up, then progresses to a twenty-pound barbell. Standing with her legs apart, she reminds Leroy of Wonder Woman.

"I'd give anything if I could just get these muscles to where they're real hard," says Norma Jean. "Feel this arm. It's not as hard as the other one."

"That's cause you're right-handed," says Leroy, dodging as she swings the barbell in an arc.

"Do you think so?"

"Sure."

Leroy is a truckdriver. He injured his leg in a highway accident four months ago, and his physical therapy, which involves weights and a pulley, prompted Norma Jean to try building herself up. Now she is attending a body-building class. Leroy has been collecting temporary disability since his tractor-trailer jackknifed in Missouri, badly twisting his left leg in its socket. He has a steel pin in his hip. He will probably not be able to drive his rig again. It sits in the backyard, like a gigantic bird that has flown home to roost. Leroy has been home in Kentucky for three months, and his leg is almost healed, but the accident frightened him and he does not want to drive any more long hauls. He is not sure what to do next. In the meantime, he makes things from craft kits. He started by building a miniature log cabin from notched Popsicle sticks. He varnished it and placed it on the TV set, where it remains. It reminds him of a rustic Nativity scene. Then he tried string art (sailing ships on black velvet), a macramé owl kit, a snap-together B-17 Flying Fortress, and a lamp made out of a model truck, with a light fixture screwed in the top of the cab. At first the kits were diversions, something to kill time, but now he is thinking about building a full-scale log house from a kit. It would be considerably cheaper than building a regular house, and besides, Leroy has grown to appreciate how things are put together. He has begun to realize that in all the years he was on the road he never took time to examine anything. He was always flying past scenery.

"They won't let you build a log cabin in any of the new subdivisions," Norma Jean tells him.

"They will if I tell them it's for you," he says, teasing her. Ever since they were married, he has promised Norma Jean he would build her a new home one day. They have always rented, and the house they live in is small and nondescript. It does not even feel like a home, Leroy realizes now.

Norma Jean works at the Rexall drugstore, and she has acquired an amazing amount of information about cosmetics. When she explains to Leroy the three stages of complexion care, involving creams, toners, and moisturizers, he thinks happily of other petroleum products—axle grease, diesel fuel. This is a connection between him and Norma Jean. Since he has been home, he has felt unusually tender about his wife and guilty over his long absences. But he can't tell what she feels about him. Norma Jean has never complained about his traveling; she has never made hurt remarks, like calling his truck a "widow-maker." He is reasonably certain she has been faithful to him, but he wishes she would celebrate his permanent home-coming more happily. Norma Jean is often startled to find Leroy at home, and he thinks she seems a little disappointed about it. Perhaps he reminds her too much of the early days of their marriage, before he went on the road. They had a child who died as an infant, years ago. They never speak about their memories of Randy, which have almost faded, but now that Leroy is home all the time, they sometimes feel awkward around each other, and Leroy wonders if one of them should mention the child. He has the feeling that they are waking up out of a dream together—that they must create a new marriage, start afresh. They are lucky they are still married. Leroy has read that for most people losing a child destroys the marriage—or else he heard this on *Donahue*. He can't always remember where he learns things anymore.

At Christmas, Leroy bought an electric organ for Norma Jean. She used to play the piano when she was in high school. "It don't leave you," she told him once. "It's like riding a bicycle."

The new instrument had so many keys and buttons that she was bewildered by it at first. She touched the keys tentatively, pushed some buttons, then pecked out "Chopsticks." It came out in an amplified fox-trot rhythm, with marimba sounds.

"It's an orchestra!" she cried.

The organ had a pecan-look finish and eighteen preset chords, with optional flute, violin, trumpet, clarinet, and banjo accompaniments. Norma Jean mastered the organ almost immediately. At first she played Christmas songs. Then she bought *The Sixties Songbook* and learned every tune in it, adding variations to each with the rows of brightly colored buttons.

"I didn't like these old songs back then." she said. "But I have this crazy feeling I missed something."

15   "You didn't miss a thing," said Leroy.

Leroy likes to lie on the couch and smoke a joint and listen to Norma Jean play "Can't Take My Eyes Off You" and "I'll Be Back." He is back again. After fifteen years on the road, he is finally settling down with the woman he loves. She is still pretty. Her skin is flawless. Her frosted curls resemble pencil trimmings.

Now that Leroy has come home to stay, he notices how much the town has changed. Subdivisions are spreading across western Kentucky like an oil slick. The sign at the edge of town says "Pop: 11,500"—only seven hundred more than it said twenty years before. Leroy can't figure out who is living in all the new houses. The farmers who used to gather around the courthouse square on Saturday afternoons to play checkers and spit tobacco juice have gone. It has been years since Leroy has thought about the farmers, and they have disappeared without his noticing.

Leroy meets a kid named Stevie Hamilton in the parking lot at the new shopping center. While they pretend to be strangers meeting over a stalled car, Stevie tosses an ounce of marijuana under the front seat of Leroy's car. Stevie is wearing orange jogging shoes and a T-shirt that says CHATTAHOOCHEE SUPER-RAT. His father is a prominent doctor who lives in one of the expensive subdivisions in a new white-columned brick house that looks like a funeral parlor. In the phone book under his name there is a separate number, with the listing "Teenagers."

"Where do you get this stuff?" asks Leroy. "From your pappy?"

20   "That's for me to know and you to find out," Stevie says. He is slit-eyed and skinny.

"What else you got?"

"What you interested in?"

"Nothing special. Just wondered."

Leroy used to take speed on the road. Now he has to go slowly. He needs to be mellow. He leans back against the car and says, "I'm aiming to build me a log house, soon as I get time. My wife, though, I don't think she likes the idea."

25   "Well, let me know when you want me again," Stevie says. He has a cigarette in his cupped palm, as though sheltering it from the wind. He takes a long drag, then stomps it on the asphalt and slouches away.

Stevie's father was two years ahead of Leroy in high school. Leroy is thirty-four. He married Norma Jean when they were both eighteen, and their child Randy was born a few months later, but he died at the age of four months and three days. He would be about Stevie's age now. Norma Jean and Leroy were at the drive-in, watching a double feature (*Dr. Strangelove* and *Lover Come Back*), and the baby was sleeping in the back seat. When the first movie ended, the baby was dead. It was the sudden infant death syndrome. Leroy remembers handing Randy to a nurse at the emergency room, as though he were offering her a large doll as a present. A dead baby feels like a sack of flour. "It just happens sometimes," said the doctor, in what Leroy always recalls as a nonchalant tone. Leroy can hardly remember the child anymore, but he still sees vividly a scene from *Dr. Strangelove* in which the President of the United States was talking in a folksy voice on the hot line to the Soviet premier about the bomber accidentally headed toward Russia. He was in the War Room, and the world map was lit up. Leroy remembers Norma Jean standing catatonically beside him in the hospital and himself thinking: Who is this strange girl? He had forgotten who she was. Now scientists are saying that crib death is caused by a virus. Nobody knows anything, Leroy thinks. The answers are always changing.

When Leroy gets home from the shopping center, Norma Jean's mother, Mabel Beasley, is there. Until this year, Leroy has not realized how much time she spends with Norma Jean. When she visits, she inspects the closets and then the plants, informing Norma Jean when a plant is droopy or yellow. Mabel calls the plants "flowers," although there are never any blooms. She also notices if Norma Jean's laundry is piling up. Mabel is a short, overweight woman whose tight, brown-dyed curls look more like a wig than the actual wig she sometimes wears. Today she has brought Norma Jean an off-white dust ruffle she made for the bed; Mabel works in a custom-upholstery shop.

"This is the tenth one I made this year," Mabel says. "I got started and couldn't stop."

"It's real pretty," says Norma Jean.

30   "Now we can hide things under the bed," says Leroy, who gets along with his mother-in-law primarily by joking with her. Mabel has never really forgiven him for disgracing her by getting Norma Jean pregnant. When the baby died, she said that fate was mocking her.

"What's that thing?" Mabel says to Leroy in a loud voice, pointing to a tangle of yarn on a piece of canvas.

Leroy holds it up for Mabel to see. "It's my needlepoint," he explains. "This is a *Star Trek* pillow cover."

"That's what a woman would do," says Mabel. "Great day in the morning!"

"All the big football players on TV do it," he says.

35   "Why, Leroy, you're always trying to fool me. I don't believe you for one minute. You don't know what to do with yourself—that's the whole trouble. Sewing!"

"I'm aiming to build us a log house," says Leroy. "Soon as my plans come."

"Like *heck* you are," says Norma Jean. She takes Leroy's needlepoint and shoves it into a drawer. "You have to find a job first. Nobody can afford to build now anyway."

Mabel straightens her girdle and says, "I still think before you get tied down y'all ought to take a little run to Shiloh."

"One of these days, Mama," Norma Jean says impatiently.

40   Mabel is talking about Shiloh, Tennessee. For the past few years, she has been urging Leroy and Norma Jean to visit the Civil War battleground there. Mabel went there on her honeymoon—the only real trip she ever took. Her husband died of a perforated ulcer when Norma Jean was ten, but Mabel, who was accepted into the United Daughters of the Confederacy in 1975, is still preoccupied with going back to Shiloh.

"I've been to kingdom come and back in that truck out yonder," Leroy says to Mabel, "but we never yet set foot in that battleground. Ain't that something? How did I miss it?"

"It's not even that far," Mabel says.

After Mabel leaves, Norma Jean reads to Leroy from a list she has made. "Things you could do," she announces. "You could get a job as a guard at Union Carbide, where they'd let you set on a stool. You could get on at the lumberyard. You could do a little carpenter work, if you want to build so bad. You could—"

"I can't do something where I'd have to stand up all day."

45   "You ought to try standing up all day behind a cosmetics counter. It's amazing that I have strong feet, coming from two parents that never had strong feet at all." At the moment Norma Jean is holding on to the kitchen counter, raising her knees one at a time as she talks. She is wearing two-pound ankle weights.

"Don't worry," says Leroy. "I'll do something."

"You could truck calves to slaughter for somebody. You wouldn't have to drive any big old truck for that."

"I'm going to build you this house," says Leroy. "I want to make you a real home."

"I don't want to live in any log cabin."

50   "It's not a cabin. It's a house."

"I don't care. It looks like a cabin."

"You and me together could lift those logs. It's just like lifting weights."

Norma Jean doesn't answer. Under her breath, she is counting. Now she is marching through the kitchen. She is doing goose steps.

Before his accident, when Leroy came home he used to stay in the house with Norma Jean, watching TV in bed and playing cards. She would cook fried chicken, picnic ham, chocolate pie—all his favorites. Now he is home alone much of the time. In the mornings, Norma Jean disappears, leaving a cooling place in the bed. She eats a cereal called Body Buddies, and she leaves the bowl on the table, with the soggy tan balls floating in a milk puddle. He sees things about Norma Jean that he never realized before. When she chops onions, she stares off into a corner, as if she can't bear to look. She puts on her house slippers almost precisely at nine o'clock every evening and nudges her jogging shoes under the couch. She saves bread heels for the birds. Leroy watches the birds at the feeder. He notices the peculiar way goldfinches fly past the window. They close their wings, then fall, then spread their wings to catch and lift themselves. He wonders if they close their eyes when they fall. Norma Jean closes her eyes when they are in bed. She wants the lights turned out. Even then, he is sure she closes her eyes.

55   He goes for long drives around town. He tends to drive a car rather carelessly. Power steering and an automatic shift make a car feel so small and inconsequential that his body is hardly involved in the driving process. His injured leg stretches out comfortably. Once or twice he has almost hit something, but even the prospect of an accident seems minor in a car. He cruises the new subdivisions, feeling like a criminal rehearsing for a robbery. Norma Jean is probably right about a log house being inappropriate here in the new subdivision. All the houses look grand and complicated. They depress him.

One day when Leroy comes home from a drive he finds Norma Jean in tears. She is in the kitchen making a potato and mushroom-soup casserole, with grated cheese topping. She is crying because her mother caught her smoking.

"I didn't hear her coming. I was standing here puffing away pretty as you please," Norma Jean says, wiping her eyes.

"I knew it would happen sooner or later," says Leroy, putting his arm around her.

"She don't know the meaning of the word 'knock,'" says Norma Jean. "It's a wonder she hadn't caught me years ago."

60   "Think of it this way," Leroy says. "What if she caught me with a joint?"

"You better not let her!" Norma Jean shrieks. "I'm warning you, Leroy Moffitt!"

"I'm just kidding. Here, play me a tune. That'll help you relax."

Norma Jean puts the casserole in the oven and sets the timer. Then she plays a ragtime tune, with horns and banjo, as Leroy lights up a joint and lies on the couch, laughing to himself about Mabel's catching him at it. He thinks of Stevie Hamilton—a doctor's son pushing grass. Everything is funny. The whole town seems crazy and small. He is reminded of Virgil Mathis, a boastful policeman Leroy used to shoot pool with. Virgil recently led a drug bust in a back room at a bowling alley, where he seized ten thousand dollars' worth of marijuana. The newspaper had a picture of him holding up the bags of grass and grinning widely. Right now, Leroy can imagine Virgil breaking down the door and arresting him with a lungful of smoke. Virgil would probably have been alerted to the scene because of all the racket Norma Jean is making. Now she sounds like a hard-rock band. Norma Jean is terrific. When she switches to a Latin-rhythm version of "Sunshine Superman," Leroy hums along. Norma Jean's foot goes up and down, up and down.

"Well, what do you think?" Leroy says, when Norma Jean pauses to search through her music.

65   "What do I think about what?"

His mind has gone blank. Then he says, "I'll sell my rig and build us a house." That wasn't what he wanted to say. He wanted to know what she thought—what she *really* thought—about them.

"Don't start in on that again," says Norma Jean. She begins playing "Who'll Be the Next in Line?"

Leroy used to tell hitchhikers his whole life story—about his travels, his hometown, the baby. He would end with a question: "Well, what do you think?" It was just a rhetorical question. In time, he had the feeling that he'd been telling the same story over and over to the same hitchhikers. He quit talking to hitchhikers when he realized how his voice sounded—whining and self-pitying, like some teenage-tragedy song. Now Leroy has the sudden impulse to tell Norma Jean about himself, as if he had just met her. They have known each other so long they have forgotten a lot about each other. They could become reacquainted. But when the oven timer goes off and she runs to the kitchen, he forgets why he wants to do this.

The next day, Mabel drops by. It is Saturday and Norma Jean is cleaning. Leroy is studying the plans of his log house, which have finally come in the mail. He has them spread out on the table—big sheets of stiff blue paper, with diagrams and numbers printed in white. While Norma Jean runs the vacuum, Mabel drinks coffee. She sets her coffee cup on a blueprint.

70   "I'm just waiting for time to pass," she says to Leroy, drumming her fingers on the table.

As soon as Norma Jean switches off the vacuum, Mabel says in a loud voice, "Did you hear about the datsun dog that killed the baby?"

Norma Jean says, "The word is 'dachshund.'"

"They put the dog on trial. It chewed the baby's legs off. The mother was in the next room all the time." She raises her voice. "They thought it was neglect."

Norma Jean is holding her ears. Leroy manages to open the refrigerator and get some Diet Pepsi to offer Mabel. Mabel still has some coffee and she waves away the Pepsi.

75 "Datsuns are like that," Mabel says. "They're jealous dogs. They'll tear a place to pieces if you don't keep an eye on them."

"You better watch out what you're saying, Mabel," says Leroy.

"Well, facts is facts."

Leroy looks out the window at his rig. It is like a huge piece of furniture gathering dust in the backyard. Pretty soon it will be an antique. He hears the vacuum cleaner. Norma Jean seems to be cleaning the living room rug again.

Later, she says to Leroy, "She just said that about the baby because she caught me smoking. She's trying to pay me back."

80 "What are you talking about?" Leroy says, nervously shuffling blueprints.

"You know good and well," Norma Jean says. She is sitting in a kitchen chair with her feet up and her arms wrapped around her knees. She looks small and helpless. She says, "The very idea, her bringing up a subject like that! Saying it was neglect."

"She didn't mean that," Leroy says.

"She might not have *thought* she meant it. She always says things like that. You don't know how she goes on."

"But she didn't really mean it. She was just talking."

85 Leroy opens a king-sized bottle of beer and pours it into two glasses, dividing it carefully. He hands a glass to Norma Jean and she takes it from him mechanically. For a long time, they sit by the kitchen window watching the birds at the feeder.

Something is happening. Norma Jean is going to night school. She has graduated from her six-week body-building course and now she is taking an adult-education course in composition at Paducah Community College. She spends her evenings outlining paragraphs.

"First, you have a topic sentence," she explains to Leroy. "Then you divide it up. Your secondary topic has to be connected to your primary topic."

To Leroy, this sounds intimidating. "I never was any good in English," he says.

"It makes a lot of sense."

90 "What are you doing this for, anyhow?"

She shrugs. "It's something to do." She stands up and lifts her dumbbells a few times.

"Driving a rig, nobody cared about my English."

"I'm not criticizing your English."

Norma Jean used to say, "If I lose ten minutes' sleep, I just drag all day." Now she stays up late, writing compositions. She got a B on her first paper—a how-to theme on soup-based casseroles. Recently Norma Jean has been cooking unusual foods—tacos, lasagna, Bombay chicken. She doesn't play the organ anymore, though her second paper was called "Why Music Is Important to Me." She sits at the kitchen table, concentrating on her outlines, while Leroy plays with his log house plans, practicing with a set of Lincoln Logs. The thought of getting a truckload of notched, numbered logs scares him, and he wants to be prepared. As he and Norma Jean work together at the kitchen table, Leroy has the hopeful thought that they are sharing something, but he knows he is a fool to think this. Norma Jean is miles away. He knows he is going to lose her. Like Mabel, he is just waiting for time to pass.

95   One day, Mabel is there before Norma Jean gets home from work, and Leroy finds himself confiding in her. Mabel, he realizes, must know Norma Jean better than he does.

"I don't know what's got into that girl," Mabel says. "She used to go to bed with the chickens. Now you say she's up all hours. Plus her a-smoking. I like to died."

"I want to make her this beautiful home," Leroy says, indicating the Lincoln Logs. "I don't think she even wants it. Maybe she was happier with me gone."

"She don't know what to make of you, coming home like this."

"Is that it?"

100   Mabel takes the roof off his Lincoln Log cabin. "You couldn't get *me* in a log cabin," she says. "I was raised in one. It's no picnic, let me tell you."

"They're different now," says Leroy.

"I tell you what," Mabel says, smiling oddly at Leroy.

"What?"

"Take her on down to Shiloh. Y'all need to get out together, stir a little. Her brain's all balled up over them books."

105   Leroy can see traces of Norma Jean's features in her mother's face. Mabel's worn face has the texture of crinkled cotton, but suddenly she looks pretty. It occurs to Leroy that Mabel has been hinting all along that she wants them to take her with them to Shiloh.

"Let's all go to Shiloh," he says. "You and me and her. Come Sunday."

Mabel throws up her hand in protest. "Oh, no, not me. Young folks want to be by theirselves."

When Norma Jean comes in with groceries, Leroy says excitedly, "Your mama here's been dying to go to Shiloh for thirty-five years. It's about time we went, don't you think?"

"I'm not going to butt in on anybody's second honeymoon," Mabel says.

110   "Who's going on a honeymoon, for Christ's sake?" Norma Jean says loudly.

"I never raised no daughter of mine to talk that-a-way," Mabel says.

"You ain't seen nothing yet," says Norma Jean. She starts putting away boxes and cans, slamming cabinet doors.

"There's a log cabin at Shiloh," Mabel says. "It was there during the battle. There's bullet holes in it."

"When are you going to *shut up* about Shiloh, Mama?" asks Norma Jean.

115   "I always thought Shiloh was the prettiest place, so full of history," Mabel goes on. "I just hoped y'all could see it once before I die, so you could tell me about it." Later, she whispers to Leroy, "You do what I said. A little change is what she needs."

"Your name means 'the king,'" Norma Jean says to Leroy that evening. He is trying to get her to go to Shiloh, and she is reading a book about another century.

"Well, I reckon I ought to be right proud."

"I guess so."

"Am I still king around here?"

120   Norma Jean flexes her biceps and feels them for hardness. "I'm not fooling around with anybody, if that's what you mean," she says.

"Would you tell me if you were?"

"I don't know."

"What does *your* name mean?"

"It was Marilyn Monroe's real name."

125   "No kidding!"

"Norma comes from the Normans. They were invaders," she says. She closes her book and looks hard at Leroy. "I'll go to Shiloh with you if you'll stop staring at me."

On Sunday, Norma Jean packs a picnic and they go to Shiloh. To Leroy's relief Mabel says she does not want to come with them. Norma Jean drives, and Leroy, sitting beside her, feels like some boring hitchhiker she has picked up. He tries some conversation, but she answers him in monosyllables. At Shiloh, she drives aimlessly through the park, past bluffs and trails and steep ravines. Shiloh is an immense place, and Leroy cannot see it as a battleground. It is not what he expected. He thought it would look like a golf course. Monuments are everywhere, showing through the thick clusters of trees. Norma Jean passes the log cabin Mabel mentioned. It is surrounded by tourists looking for bullet holes.

"That's not the kind of log house I've got in mind," says Leroy apologetically.

"I know *that*."

130 "This is a pretty place. Your mama was right."

"It's O.K.," says Norma Jean. "Well, we've seen it. I hope she's satisfied."

They burst out laughing together.

At the park museum, a movie on Shiloh is shown every half hour, but they decide that they don't want to see it. They buy a souvenir Confederate flag for Mabel, and then they find a picnic spot near the cemetery. Norma Jean has brought a picnic cooler, with pimento sandwiches, soft drinks, and Yodels. Leroy eats a sandwich and then smokes a joint, hiding it behind the picnic cooler. Norma Jean has quit smoking altogether. She is picking cake crumbs from the cellophane wrapper, like a fussy bird.

Leroy says, "So the boys in gray ended up in Corinth. The Union soldiers zapped 'em finally. April 7, 1862."

135 They both know that he doesn't know any history. He is just talking about some of the historical plaques they have read. He feels awkward, like a boy on a date with an older girl. They are still just making conversation.

"Corinth is where Mama eloped to," says Norma Jean.

They sit in silence and stare at the cemetery for the Union dead and, beyond, at a tall cluster of trees. Campers are parked nearby, bumper to bumper, and small children in bright clothing are cavorting and squealing. Norma Jean wads up the cake wrapper and squeezes it tightly in her hand. Without looking at Leroy, she says, "I want to leave you."

Leroy takes a bottle of Coke out of the cooler and flips off the cap. He holds the bottle poised near his mouth but cannot remember to take a drink. Finally he says, "No, you don't."

"Yes, I do."

140 "I won't let you."

"You can't stop me."

"Don't do me that way."

Leroy knows Norma Jean will have her own way. "Didn't I promise to be home from now on?" he says.

"In some ways, a woman prefers a man who wanders," says Norma Jean. "That sounds crazy, I know."

145 "You're not crazy."

Leroy remembers to drink from his Coke. Then he says, "Yes, you *are* crazy. You and me could start all over again. Right back at the beginning."

"We *have* started all over again," says Norma Jean. "And this is how it turned out."

"What did I do wrong?"

"Nothing."

150   "Is this one of those women's lib things?" Leroy asks.

"Don't be funny."

The cemetery, a green slope dotted with white markers, looks like a subdivision site. Leroy is trying to comprehend that his marriage is breaking up, but for some reason he is wondering about white slabs in a graveyard.

"Everything was fine till Mama caught me smoking." says Norma Jean, standing up. "That set something off."

"What are you talking about?"

155   "She won't leave me alone—*you* won't leave me alone." Norma Jean seems to be crying, but she is looking away from him. "I feel eighteen again. I can't face that all over again." She starts walking away. "No, it *wasn't* fine. I don't know what I'm saying. Forget it."

Leroy takes a lungful of smoke and closes his eyes as Norma Jean's words sink in. He tries to focus on the fact that thirty-five hundred soldiers died on the grounds around him. He can only think of that war as a board game with plastic soldiers. Leroy almost smiles, as he compares the Confederates' daring attack on the Union camps and Virgil Mathis's raid on the bowling alley. General Grant, drunk and furious, shoved the Southerners back to Corinth, where Mabel and Jet Beasley were married years later, when Mabel was still thin and good-looking. The next day, Mabel and Jet visited the battleground, and then Norma Jean was born, and then she married Leroy and they had a baby, which they lost, and now Leroy and Norma Jean are here at the same battleground. Leroy knows he is leaving out a lot. He is leaving out the insides of history. History was always just names and dates to him. It occurs to him that building a house of logs is similarly empty—too simple. And the real inner workings of a marriage, like most of history, have escaped him. Now he sees that building a log house is the dumbest idea he could have had. It was clumsy of him to think Norma Jean would want a log house. It was a crazy idea. He'll have to think of something else, quickly. He will wad the blueprints into tight balls and fling them into the lake. Then he'll get moving again. He opens his eyes. Norma Jean has moved away and is walking through the cemetery, following a serpentine brick path.

Leroy gets up to follow his wife, but his good leg is asleep and his bad leg still hurts him. Norma Jean is far away, walking rapidly toward the bluff by the river, and he tries to hobble toward her. Some children run past him, screaming noisily. Norma Jean has reached the bluff, and she is looking out over the Tennessee River. Now she turns toward Leroy and waves her arms. Is she beckoning to him? She seems to be doing an exercise for her chest muscles. The sky is unusually pale—the color of the dust ruffle Mabel made for their bed.

[1982]

Topics for Critical Thinking and Writing

1. Whose feelings—Leroy's or Norma Jean's—are more fully presented in the story? Do we know exactly what Norma Jean wants? Do you think that she herself knows?

2. The story is written in the present tense, for instance, "Leroy Moffitt's wife, Norma Jean, is working on her pectorals," rather than (as would be more

common in fiction) ". . . was working on her pectorals." What is gained by using the present in this story?

3. Why is Leroy preoccupied with kits, and why is Norma Jean so eagerly attempting to improve her body and her mind?

4. When we first meet Mabel, Norma Jean's mother, we learn that she has made "an off-white dust ruffle for the bed." Leroy jokes about it, and Mason refers to it in the last line of the story, a place of great emphasis. Why this business about a dust ruffle for a bed?

5. Do you think "Shiloh" is a good title? Why?

ANONYMOUS JAPANESE FOLK TALE

The following text is adapted from the retelling by Lafcadio Hearn (1850–1904), a journalist and teacher. Hearn, born of a Greek mother and a British father on the Greek Island of Santa Maura, was raised in Dublin, settled in the United States in 1869 (chiefly in New Orleans), and moved to Japan in 1895, where he married a Japanese woman and became a Japanese citizen. Although he wrote novels he is chiefly known as an essayist and translator of Japanese material (e.g. In Ghostly Japan, where a version of the following story appears) and of West Indian material.

The following story tells of a young Buddhist priest who is climbing a mountain, aided by a bodhisattva. A bodhisattva is a being who has achieved the Enlightenment or Buddha-knowledge that Buddhists seek, but instead of entering nirvana—the state of liberation from the cycle of reincarnation—a bodhisattva chooses to remain in this world of birth, suffering, death, and rebirth in order to aid others to achieve the Enlightenment that will release them from the cycle of endless rebirth. If this is difficult to grasp, it may be useful to mention that the present Dalai Lama in The Good Heart: A Buddhist Perspective on the Teachings of Jesus has conjectured that Jesus may have been a bodhisattva.

The Mountain-Climber

At the hour of sunset they came to the foot of the mountain. There was no sign of life—not a token of water or a trace of a plant or even the shadow of a flying bird; there was nothing but desolation rising to desolation. And the summit was lost in heaven.

Under the stars they climbed—fast, fast—mounting by help of superhuman power. They passed high zones of mist and below them they saw, ever widening as they climbed, a silent flood of clouds, like a milky sea.

Hour after hour they climbed, and invisible forms yielded to their tread with dull soft crunching, and faint cold fires lighted and died at every crunch.

Then the Bodhisattva said to his young companion: "What you have asked to see will be shown to you. But the place of the Vision is far, and the way is difficult. Follow me, and do not fear: strength will be given you."

Twilight gloomed about them as they climbed. There was no beaten path, nor any mark of former human visitation, and the way took them over an endless heap of tumbled fragments that rolled or turned beneath the foot. Sometimes a dislodged mass would clatter down, echoing hollowly; sometimes the substance trodden would burst like an empty shell. . . . Stars disappeared, and the darkness deepened.

"Do not fear, my son," said the Bodhisattva, guiding: "There is no danger, though the way is grim."

And once the young pilgrim touched something smooth that was not stone, and he lifted it, and dimly saw a cheekless skull.

"Linger not thus, my son!" his teacher urged, "The summit that we must gain is far far away."

On through the dark they climbed, continually feeling beneath them the soft strange crunchings, and they saw the icy fires burn and die, until the rim of the night turned gray, and the stars began to fail and the east began to bloom.

Yet still they climbed—fast, fast—mounting by help of superhuman power. About them now was frigidness of death, and a tremendous silence. In the east they glimpsed a gold flame kindling. Then for the first time the pilgrim could see the bare steeps, and he was seized with fear and trembling. Beneath his feet there was no earth, only a monstrous, measureless heap of skulls and fragments of skulls and the dust of bones, with scattered teeth strewn through the drift, like the remnants of shells in the wrack of a tide.

"Do not fear, my son!" said the voice of the Bodhisattva, "Only the strong of heart can win to the place of the Vision!"

Behind them the world had vanished. Nothing remained but the clouds beneath and the sky above, and in between, slanting upward out of sight, the mountain of skulls.

The sun climbed with the climbers, but there was no warmth in its light, only sharp coldness. And the horror of stupendous height and the nightmare of stupendous depth, and the terror of stupendous silence grew and grew, weighing upon the pilgrim and holding his feet, so that suddenly all his strength left him and he moaned like a sleeper in dreams.

"Hasten, hasten, my son!" said the Bodhisattva: "the day is brief, and the summit is far away."

But the pilgrim shrieked, "I am afraid, I am afraid, my strength is gone."

"Your strength will return, my son," the Bodhisattva answered. "Look now below you and above you and about you, and tell me what you see."

"I cannot," the trembling pilgrim said, "I dare not look beneath! In front of me and all around me I see nothing but human skulls."

"And even now, my son," said the Bodhisattva, smiling compassionately, "and even now you still do not know of what this mountain is made."

The young monk, shuddering, repeated, "I am afraid, I am afraid! There is nothing but human skulls."

"Yes, it is a mountain of skulls," the Bodhisattva replied. "But know, my son, all of them *are you own*! Each skull has at some time been the nest of your dreams and your delusions and your desires. Not a single one is the skull of any other person. All, all, have been yours in your billions of former lives."

[1899]

Topic for Critical Thinking and Writing

If you do not believe in reincarnation, can this story have any significance for you? Consider this possibility: When the poet Tennyson says,

men may rise on stepping-stones
Of their dead selves to higher things,

he is not expressing a belief in reincarnation, but in the idea that we can learn from our mistakes. Our past actions may be like stones that enable us—for instance, by now acting more wisely or compassionately—to rise to "higher things," a better life. St. Augustine (354–430) has a memorable image: "We make a ladder of our vices, if we trample those same vices underfoot." Longfellow put it this way:

Saint Augustine! Well hast thou said,
That of our vices we can frame
A ladder, if we will but tread
Beneath our feet each deed of shame.

Your view?

POETRY

JOHN KEATS

John Keats (1795–1821), son of a London stable keeper, was taken out of school when he was 15 and was apprenticed to a surgeon and apothecary. In 1816 he was licensed to practice as an apothecary-surgeon, but he almost immediately abandoned medicine and decided to make a career as a poet. His progress was amazing; he quickly moved from routine verse to major accomplishments, publishing books of poems—to mixed reviews—in 1817, 1818, and 1820, before dying of tuberculosis at the age of 25.

On First Looking into Chapman's Homer*

Much have I traveled in the realms of gold,
And many goodly states and kingdoms seen;
Round many western islands have I been
Which bards in fealty to Apollo° hold.
Oft of one wide expanse have I been told   5
That deep-browed Homer ruled as his demesne;°
Yet did I never breathe its pure serene°
Till I heard Chapman speak out loud and bold;
Then felt I like some watcher of the skies
When a new planet swims into his ken;   10
Or like stout Cortez when with eagle eyes
He stared at the Pacific—and all his men
Looked at each other with a wild surmise—
Silent, upon a peak in Darien.

[1816]

* **Chapman's Homer** George Chapman (1559–1634?), Shakespeare's contemporary, is chiefly known for his translations (from the Greek) of Homer's *Odyssey* and *Iliad*. In lines 11–14 Keats mistakenly says that Cortés was the first European to see the Pacific, from the heights of darien, in panama. In fact, Balboa was the first. **4 Apollo** god of poetry. **6 demesne** domain. **7 serene** open space.

Topics for Critical Thinking and Writing

1. In line 1, what do you think "realms of gold" stands for? Chapman was an Elizabethan; how does this fact add relevance to the metaphor in the first line?.
2. Does line 9 introduce a totally new idea, or can you somehow connect it to the opening metaphor?

PERCY BYSSHE SHELLEY

Percy Bysshe Shelley (1792–1822) was born in Sussex in England, the son of a prosperous country squire. Educated at Eton, he went on to Oxford but was expelled for having written a pamphlet supporting a belief in atheism. Like John Keats he was a member of the second generation of English romantic poets. (The first generation included Wordsworth and Coleridge.) And like Keats, Shelley died young; he was drowned during a violent storm while sailing with a friend.

Ozymandias

I met a traveler from an antique land
Who said: Two vast and trunkless legs of stone
Stand in the desert . . . Near them, one the sand,
Half sunk, a shattered visage lies, whose frown,
And wrinkled lip, and sneer of cold command,   5
Tell that its sculptor well those passions read
Which yet survive, stamped on these lifeless things,
The hand that mocked them, and the heart that fed:
And on the pedestal these words appear:
"My name is Ozymandias, king of kings: 10
Look on my works, ye Mighty, and despair!"
Nothing beside remains. Round the decay
Of that colossal wreck, boundless and bare
The lone and level sands stretch far away.

[1817]

Lines 4–8 are somewhat obscure, but the gist is that the passions—still evident in the "shattered visage"—survive the sculptor's hand that "mocked"—that is, (1) imitated or copied, (2) derided—them, and the passions also survive the king's heart that had nourished them.

Topic for Critical Thinking and Writing

There is an irony of plot here: Ozymandias believed that he created enduring works, but his intentions came to nothing. However, another irony is also present: How are his words, in a way he did not intend, true?

ALFRED, LORD TENNYSON

Alfred, Lord Tennyson (1809–1892), the son of an English clergyman, was born in Lincolnshire, where he began writing verse at age 5. Educated at Cambridge, he had to leave without a degree when his father died and Alfred had to accept responsibility for bringing up his brothers and sisters. In fact, the family had inherited ample funds, but for some years the money was tied up by litigation. Following Wordsworth's death in 1850, Tennyson was made poet laureate. With his government pension he moved with his family to the Isle of Wight, where he lived in comfort until his death.

Ulysses*

It little profits that an idle king,
By this still hearth, among these barren crags,
Matched with an aged wife, I mete and dole
Unequal laws unto a savage race,
That hoard, and sleep, and feed, and know not me.   5
I cannot rest from travel; I will drink
Life to the lees. All times I have enjoyed
Greatly, have suffered greatly, both with those
That loved me, and alone; on shore, and when
Thro' scudding drifts the rainy Hyades   10
Vext the dim sea. I am become a name;
For always roaming with a hungry heart
Much have I seen and known,—cities of men
And manners, climates, councils, governments,
Myself not least, but honored of them all,—   15
And drunk delight of battle with my peers,
Far on the ringing plains of windy Troy.
I am a part of all that I have met
Yet all experience is an arch wherethro'
Gleams that untravelled world whose margin fades   20
For ever and for ever when I move.
How dull it is to pause, to make an end,
To rust unburnished, not to shine in use!
As tho' to breathe were life! Life piled on life
Were all too little, and of one to me   25
Little remains; but every hour is saved
From that eternal silence, something more,
A bringer of new things; and vile it were
For some three suns to store and hoard myself,
And this gray spirit yearning in desire   30
To follow knowledge like a sinking star
Beyond the utmost bound of human thought.

---

* **Ulysses** Odysseus, King of Ithaca, a leader of the Greeks in the Trojan War, famous for his ten years of journeying to remote places.

This is my son, mine own Telemachus,
To whom I leave the scepter and the isle,—
Well-loved of me, discerning to fulfill   35
This labor, by slow prudence to make mild
A rugged people, and thro' soft degrees
Subdue them to the useful and the good.
Most blameless is he, centered in the sphere
Of common duties, decent not to fail   40
In offices of tenderness, and pay
Meet adoration to my household gods,
When I am gone. He works his work, I mine.

There lies the port; the vessel puffs her sail;
There gloom the dark, broad seas. My mariners,   45
Souls that have toiled, and wrought, and thought with me,—
That ever with a frolic welcome took
The thunder and the sunshine, and opposed
Free hearts, free foreheads,—you and I are old;
Old age hath yet his honor and his toil.   50
Death closes all; but something ere the end,
Some work of noble note, may yet be done,
Not unbecoming men that strove with Gods.
The lights begin to twinkle from the rocks;
The long day wanes; the slow moon climbs; the deep   55
Moans round with many voices. Come, my friends.
'Tis not too late to seek a newer world.
Push off, and sitting well in order smite
The sounding furrows; for my purpose holds
To sail beyond the sunset, and the baths   60
Of all the western stars, until I die.
It may be that the gulfs will wash us down;
It may be we shall touch the Happy Isles,
And see the great Achilles, whom we knew.
Tho' much is taken, much abides; and tho'   65
We are not now that strength which in old days
Moved earth and heaven, that which we are, we are.
One equal temper of heroic hearts,
Made weak by time and fate, but strong in will
To strive, to seek, to find, and not to yield.   70

                                                     [1833]

Topics for Critical Thinking and Writing

1. Given the fact that Ulysses is a king and therefore a person with great responsibilities, does such a line as "I cannot rest from travel" (line 6) strike you as irresponsible? Explain.
2. It has been said that although at first glance the poem seems optimistic and
   highly positive—the final line is "To strive, to seek, to find, and not to yield"—
   the poem in fact is melancholy and filled with suggestions of death. Your view?

CARL SANDBURG

Carl Sandburg (1878–1967) was born in Galesburg, Illinois, the son of poor Swedish immigrants. As a boy he did odd jobs, and at the age of 17 he left home, traveling as a hobo on freight trains. In 1898 a friend urged him to enroll in Lombard College in Galesburg, where a teacher encouraged him to write. Sandburg later moved to Milwaukee, worked as a newspaper reporter and a writer of advertisements, and engaged in left-wing politics. He then moved to Chicago, where he became associated with Sherwood Anderson and other literary figures. He wrote several books of poems, all in somewhat Whitmanesque free verse, but today he is chiefly known for his six-volume biography of Abraham Lincoln, and for compilations of American folklore, notably The American Songbag *(1927).*

The following poem, from a book called Chicago Poems *(1919), gets its title from several express trains, for example The Twentieth Century Limited, that were renowned for their speed. "Limited" meant that they were limited to few or no stops between their start and their destination. Train service has greatly deteriorated in the past seventy-five years; in Sandburg's day the famous Twentieth Century Limited made the trip from New York to Chicago in twenty hours—less time than the same train trip takes today.*

Limited

I am riding on a limited express, one of the crack trains of the nation.
Hurtling across the prairie into blue haze and dark air go fifteen
All-steel coaches holding a thousand people.
(All coaches shall be scrap and rust, and all the men and women laughing
in the diners and sleepers shall pass to ashes)
I ask a man in the smoker where he is going and he answers: "Omaha".

[1916]

Topics for Critical Thinking and Writing

1. In the second line Sandburg says that the train hurtles "into blue haze and dark air." He could have written "into bright dawn and clear sky," or into "into clear day and high noon," or any number of other things. Which of the three versions—Sandburg's, and our two—do you prefer? Why?
2. Suppose the poem ended with "San Francisco" or "New York" or "Hollywood" instead of "Omaha." Would the meaning be different? Explain.
3. Imitate Sandburg's poem, setting the scene in an airplane.

COUNTEE CULLEN

Countee Cullen (1903–1946) was born Countee Porter in New York City, raised by his grandmother, and then adopted by the Reverend Frederick A Cullen, a Methodist minister in Harlem. Cullen received a bachelor's degree from New York University (Phi Beta Kappa) and a master's degree from Harvard. He earned his living as a high school teacher of French, but his literary gifts were recognized in his own day.

Incident

(For Eric Walrond)

Once riding in old Baltimore,
    Heart-filled, head-filled with glee,
I saw a Baltimorean
    Keep looking straight at me.   4

Now I was eight and very small,
    And he was no whit bigger,
And so I smiled, but he poked out
    His tongue, and called me, "Nigger."   8

I saw the whole of Baltimore
    From May until December;
Of all the things that happened there
    That's all that I remember.   12

[1925]

Topics for Critical Thinking and Writing

1. How would you define an "incident"? A serious occurrence? A minor occurrence, or what? Think about the word, and then think about Cullen's use of it
   as a title for the event recorded in this poem. Test out one or two other possible titles as a way of helping yourself to see the strengths or weaknesses of
   cullen's title.
2. The dedicatee, Eric Walrond (1989–1966), was an African American essayist and
   writer of fiction, who in an essay, "On Being Black," had described his experiences of racial prejudice. How does the presence of the dedication bear on our
   response to Cullen's account of the "incident"?
3. What is the tone of the poem? Indifferent? Angry? Or what? What do you think
   is the speaker's attitude toward the "incident"? What is your attitude?
4. Ezra Pound, poet and critic, once defined literature as "news that *stays* news."
   What do you think he meant by this? Do you think that the definition fits
   Cullen's poem?

WILLIAM STAFFORD

*William Stafford (1914–1993) was born in Hutchinson, Kansas, and was educated
at the University of Kansas and the State University of Iowa. A conscientious objector during World War II, he worked for the Brethren Service and the Church World
Service. After the war he taught at several universities and then settled at Lewis and
Clark College in Portland, Oregon. In addition to writing several books of poems,
Stafford wrote Down in My Heart (1947), an account of his experiences as a conscientious objector.*

Traveling Through the Dark

Traveling through the dark I found a deer
dead on the edge of the Wilson River road.
It is usually best to roll them into the canyon:
the road is narrow; to swerve might make more dead.   4

By glow of the tail-light I stumbled back of the car
and stood by the heap, a doe, a recent killing;
she had stiffened already, almost cold.
I dragged her off; she was large in the belly.   8

My fingers touching her side brought me the reason—
her side was warm; her fawn lay there waiting,
alive, still, never to be born.
Beside that mountain road I hesitated.   12

The car aimed ahead its lowered parking lights;
under the hood purred the steady engine.
I stood in the glare of the warm exhaust turning red;
around our group I could hear the wilderness listen.   16

I thought hard for us all—my only swerving—
Then pushed her over the edge into the river.

[1960]

Topics for Critical Thinking and Writing

1. Look at the first sentence (the first two lines) and try to recall what your impression of the speaker was, based only on these two lines, or pretend that you have not read the entire poem, and characterize him merely on these two lines. Then take the entire poem into consideration and characterize him.
2. What do you make of the title? Do you think it is a good title for this poem? Explain.

ROBERT FROST

For a biographical note, see page 587. After reading Frost's "The Pasture," please read the next poem, Berry's "Stay Home."

The Pasture

I'm going out to clean the pasture spring;
I'll only stop to rake the leaves away
(And wait to watch the water clear, I may):
I shan't be gone long.—You come too.   4

I'm going out to fetch the little calf
That's standing by the mother. It's so young,

It totters when she licks it with her tongue.
I shan't be gone long.—You come too.   8

[1913]

Topics for Critical Thinking and Writing

1. Would the poem be just as good—maybe better?—if it consisted of only one stanza, either the first or second? Explain.
2. Although Frost had already published books of poems, after he wrote "The Pasture" he always placed this poem first in any collected edition of his poems. Why do you suppose he did this?

WENDELL BERRY

Wendell Berry, born in rural Kentucky, received a bachelor's degree and a master's degree from the University of Kentucky, then studied at Stanford and lectured there on creative writing. Later he taught for several years at New York University, but then returned to Kentucky, where he has taught at the University of Kentucky and engaged in farming, while writing poetry, fiction, and essays.

Stay Home

I will wait here in the fields
to see how well the rain
brings on the grass.
In the labor of the fields
longer than a man's life   5
I am at home. Don't come with me.
You stay home too.

I will be standing in the woods
where the old trees
move only with the wind   10
and then with gravity.
In the stillness of the trees
I am home. Don't come with me.
You stay home too.

[1980]

Topic for Critical Thinking and Writing

Do you find the speaker offensive in his insistence on being alone? Explain.

ADRIENNE RICH

Adrienne Rich, born in 1929 in Baltimore, was educated at Radcliffe College. Her first book of poems, A Change of World, *published in 1951 when she was still an undergraduate, was selected by W. H. Auden for the Yale Series of Younger Poets. In 1953 she married an economist and had three sons, but as she indicates in several books, she felt confined by the full-time domestic role that she was expected to play, and the marriage did not last. Much of her poetry is concerned with issues of gender and power. When her ninth book,* Diving into the Wreck *(1973), won the National Book Award, Rich accepted the award not as an individual but on behalf of women everywhere.*

Diving into the Wreck

First having read the book of myths,
and loaded the camera,
and checked the edge of the knife-blade,
I put on
the body-armor of black rubber   5
the absurd flippers
the grave and awkward mask.
I am having to do this
not like Cousteau° with his
assiduous team   10
aboard the sun-flooded schooner
but here alone.

There is a ladder.
The ladder is always there
hanging innocently   15
close to the side of the schooner.
We know what it is for,
we who have used it.
Otherwise
it's a piece of maritime floss   20
some sundry equipment.

I go down.
Rung after rung and still
the oxygen immerses me
the blue light   25
the clear atoms

of our human air.
I go down.
My flippers cripple me,
I crawl like an insect down the ladder   30
and there is no one
to tell me when the ocean
will begin.

9 **Cousteau** Jacques Cousteau (1910–1997) French underwater explorer.

First the air is blue and then
it is bluer and then green and then   35
black I am blacking out and yet
my mask is powerful
it pumps my blood with power
the sea is another story
the sea is not a question of power   40
I have to learn alone
to turn my body without force
in the deep element.

And now: it is easy to forget
what I came for   45
among so many who have always
lived here
swaying their crenelated fans
between the reefs
and besides   50
you breathe differently down here.

I came to explore the wreck.
The words are purposes.
The words are maps.
I came to see the damage that was done   55
and the treasures that prevail.
I stroke the beam of my lamp
slowly along the flank
of something more permanent
than fish or weed   60

the thing I came for:
the wreck and not the story of the wreck
the thing itself and not the myth
the drowned face always staring
toward the sun   65
the evidence of damage

worn by salt and sway into this threadbare beauty
the ribs of the disaster
curving their assertion
among the tentative haunters.   70

This is the place.
And I am here, the mermaid whose dark hair
streams black, the mermaid in his armored body.
We circle silently
about the wreck   75
we dive into the hold.
I am she: I am he

whose drowned face sleeps with open eyes
whose breasts still bear the stress

whose silver, copper, vermillion cargo lies 80
obscurely inside barrels
half-wedged and left to rot
we are the half-destroyed instruments
that once held to a course
the water-eaten log 85
the fouled compass

We are, I am, you are
by cowardice or courage
the one who find our way
back to this scene
carrying a knife, a camera 90
a book of myths
in which
our names do not appear.

[1973]

DEREK WALCOTT

Derek Walcott, born in 1930 on the Caribbean island of St. Lucia, was awarded the Nobel Prize for Literature in 1992. Although in the United States he is known chiefly as a poet, Walcott is also an important playwright and director of plays. Much of his work is concerned with his mixed heritage—a black writer from the Caribbean, whose language is English and who lives part of the year in Massachusetts, where he teaches in the Creative Writing Program at Boston University. Walcott's books include Collected Poems *(1986) and* Omeros *(1989), a Caribbean epic that echoes Homer's* Iliad *and* Odyssey *as it explores the Caribbean's past and present.*

A Far Cry from Africa

A wind is ruffling the tawny pelt
Of Africa. Kikuyu,° quick as flies,
Batten upon the bloodstreams of the veldt.°
Corpses are scattered through a paradise.
Only the worm, colonel of carrion, cries: 5
'Waste no compassion on these separate dead!'
Statistics justify and scholars seize
The salients of colonial policy.
What is that to the white child hacked in bed?
To savages, expendable as Jews? 10

Threshed out by beaters, the long rushes break
In a white dust of ibises whose cries
Have wheeled since civilization's dawn

2 Kikuyu an African tribe that fought against British colonialists.   **3 veldt** grassland in southern Africa.

From the parched river or beast-teeming plain.
The violence of beast on beast is read   15
As natural law, but upright man
Seeks his divinity by inflicting pain.
Delirious as these worried beasts, his wars
Dance to the tightened carcass of a drum,
While he calls courage still that native dread   20
Of the white peace contracted by the dead.

Again brutish necessity wipes its hands
Upon the napkins of a dirty cause, again
A waste of our compassion, as with Spain,°
The gorilla wrestles with the superman.   25

I who am poisoned with the blood of both,
Where shall I turn, divided to the vein?
I who have cursed
The drunken officer of British rule, how choose
Between this Africa and the English tongue I love?   30
Betray them both, or give back what they give?
How can I face such slaughter and be cool?
How can I turn from Africa and live?

[1962]

24 **Spain** a reference to the triumph of fascism in Spain after the civil war of 1936–1939.

Topics for Critical Thinking and Writing

1. Now that you have read the poem, explain the meaning of the title.
2. Do you find the first stanza hard to understand? Why, or why not?
3. Focus on lines 15–17: What is Walcott saying here? Do you think that the poem might be even more effective if these lines were placed at the beginning? Or do they belong exactly where they are?
4. Imagine that Walcott sent this poem to you with a letter that asked for your response. In a letter ("Dear Mr. Walcott. . .") of one page in length, give your response to the poem.
5. What is the meaning of line 25?
6. Walcott uses the first-person "I" in the final stanza. How would you answer each of the questions he asks in it? Or do you think the point is that these questions cannot be answered?
7. What is your own experience of Africa? Have you lived or traveled there? Would you like to? Has Walcott given you a new perspective on Africa, its history and culture?

SHERMAN ALEXIE

Sherman Alexie, born in 1966 in Spokane, Washington, holds a BA from Washington State University. Author of novels, stories, and poems, and author and director of the highly praised film Smoke Signals *(1998), Alexie has been awarded a grant from the National Endowment for the Arts. Of his life and his work he says, "I am a Spokane Coeur d'Alene Indian.... I live on the Spokane Indian Reservation. Everything I do now, writing and otherwise, has its origin in that."*

On the Amtrak from Boston to New York City

The white woman across the aisle from me says, "Look,
look at all the history, that house
on the hill there is over two hundred years old,"
as she points out the window past me   4

into what she has been taught. I have learned
little more about American history during my few days
back East than what I expected and far less
of what we should all know of the tribal stories   8

whose architecture is 15,000 years older
than the corners of the house that sits
museumed on the hill. "Walden Pond,"°
the woman on the train asks, "Did you see Walden Pond?"   12

and I don't have a cruel enough heart to break
her own by telling her there are five Walden Ponds
on my little reservation out West
and at least a hundred more surrounding Spokane,   16

the city I pretend to call my home. "Listen,"
I could have told her. "I don't give a shit
about Walden. I know the Indians were living stories
around that pond before Walden's grandparents were born   20

and before his grandparents' grandparents were born.
I'm tired of hearing about Don-fucking-Henley° saving it, too,
because that's redundant. If Don Henley's brothers and sisters
and mothers and fathers hadn't come here in the first place   24

then nothing would need to be saved."
But I didn't say a word to the woman about Walden
Pond because she smiled so much and seemed delighted
that I thought to bring her an orange juice   28

back from the food car. I respect elders
of every color. All I really did was eat

11 Walden Pond site in Massachusetts where Henry David Thoreau (1817–1862) lived from 4 July 1845 to 6 September 1847, and about which he wrote in his most famous book, *Walden* (1854). **22 Don Henley** rock singer who was active in preserving Walden from building developers.

my tasteless sandwich, drink my Diet Pepsi
and nod my head whenever the woman pointed out   32

another little piece of her country's history
while I, as all Indians have done
since this war began, made plans
for what I would do and say the next time   36

somebody from the enemy thought I was one of their own.

[1993]

Topics for Critical Thinking and Writing

1. Characterize the speaker.
2. Take the common idea that "Columbus discovered America." What attitude toward the history of this land and toward Indians is implicit in these words?

CHRISTINA ROSSETTI

Christina Rossetti (1830–1894) was the daughter of an exiled Italian patriot who lived in London and the sister of the poet and painter Dante Gabriel Rossetti. After her father became an invalid, she led an extremely ascetic life, devoting most of her life to doing charitable work. Her first and best-known volume of poetry, Goblin Market and Other Poems, *was published in 1862.*

Uphill

Does the road wind uphill all the way?
   Yes, to the very end.
Will the day's journey take the whole long day?
   From morn to night, my friend.   4

But is there for the night a resting-place?
   A roof for when the slow dark hours begin.
May not the darkness hide it from my face?
   You cannot miss that inn.   8

Shall I meet other wayfarers at night?
   Those who have gone before.
Then must I knock, or call when just in sight?
   They will not keep you standing at that door.   12

Shall I find comfort, travel-sore and weak?
   Of labor you shall find the sum.
Will there be beds for me and all who seek?
   Yea, beds for all who come.   16

[1858]

Topics for Critical Thinking and Writing

1. Suppose that someone told you this poem is about a person preparing to go on a hike. The person is supposedly making inquiries about the road and the possible hotel arrangements. What would you reply?.
2. Who is the questioner? A woman? A man? All human beings collectively? "Uphill" does not use quotation marks to distinguish between two speakers. Can one say that in "Uphill" the questioner and the answerer are the same person?
3. Are the answers unambiguously comforting? Or can it, for instance, be argued that the "roof" is (perhaps among other things) the lid of a coffin—hence the questioner will certainly not be kept "standing at that door"? If the poem can be read along these lines, is it chilling rather than comforting?

EMILY DICKINSON

For a biographical note, see page 524.

Because I could not stop for Death

Because I could not stop for Death—
He kindly stopped for me—
The Carriage held but just Ourselves—
And Immortality.   4

We slowly drove—He knew no haste
And I had put away
My labor and my leisure too,
For His Civility—   8

We passed the School, where Children strove
At Recess—in the Ring—
We passed the Fields of Gazing Grain—
We passed the Setting Sun—   12

Or rather—He passed Us—
The Dews drew quivering and chill—
For only Gossamer, my Gown—
My Tippet°—only Tulle°—   16

We paused before a House that seemed
A Swelling of the Ground—
The Roof was scarcely visible—
The Cornice—in the Ground—   20

16 Tippet shawl; **Tulle** net of silk.

Since then—'tis Centuries—and yet
Feels shorter than the Day
I first surmised the Horses' Heads
Were toward Eternity—   24

[c. 1863]

Topics for Critical Thinking and Writing

1. Characterize death as it appears in lines 1–8.
2. What is the significance of the details and their arrangement in the third stanza? Why "strove" rather than "played" (line 9)? What meanings does "Ring" (line 10) have? Is "Gazing Grain" better than "Golden Grain"?
3. The "House" in the fifth stanza is a sort of riddle. What is the answer? Does this stanza introduce an aspect of death not present—or present only very faintly—in the rest of hte poem? Explain.
4. Evaluate this statement about the poem (from Yvor Winters's *In Defense of Reason*): "In so far as it concentrates on the life that is being left behind, it is wholly successful; in so far as it attempts to experience the death to come, it is fraudulent, however exquisitely."

20

Love and Hate

SHORT VIEWS

Love is a great beautifier.
    Louisa May Alcott

I do not think that what is called Love at first sight *is so great an absurdity a it is sometimes imagined to be. We generally make up our minds beforehand to the sort of person we should like, grave or gay, black, brown, or fair; with golden tresses or raven locks—and when we meet with a complete example of the qualities we admire, the bargain is soon struck.*
    William Hazlitt

For what is love itself, for the one we love best?—an enfolding of immeasurable cares which yet are better than any joys outside our love.
    George Eliot

We've got this gift of love, but love is like a precious plant. You can't just accept it and leave it in the cupboard or just think it's going to get on by itself. You've got to keep watering it. You've got to really look after it and nurture it.
    John Lennon

Lovers should also have their days off.
    Natalie Clifford Barney

In love, there is always one who kisses and one who offers the cheek.
    French proverb

Love is the word used to label the sexual excitement of the young, the habituation of the middle-aged, and the mutual dependence of the old.
    John Ciardi

A man falls in love through his eyes, a woman through her ears. What is said to [women] and what they believe about a man's status is usually more important than the superficiality of good looks.
    Woodrow Wyatt

Now hatred is by far the longest pleasure,
Men love in haste, but they detest at leisure.
    Lord Byron

Men hate more steadily than they love.
    Samuel Johnson

The price of hating other human beings is loving oneself less.
    Eldridge Cleaver

In hatred as in love, we grow like the thing we brood upon. What we
loathe, we graft into our very soul.
    Mary Renault

I tell you, there is such a thing as creative hate.
    Willa Cather

Never in this world can hatred be stilled by hatred; it will be stilled only
by non-hatred: This is the law Eternal.
    Buddha

Topics for Critical Thinking and Writing

1. Do you think it is possible to love lots of people? Or is love so special that it can only be felt for a few people? Would you go further and say that love—real love, love in the deepest sense—can in truth only be felt for one person in your life?
2. How do we know when we have moved from "liking" someone to "loving" him or her? What are the signs? What is the evidence?
3. What does it mean to say that we have "fallen out of love" with someone? Is this change in us the result of something specific? Or does it, somehow, simply happen? Once you fall out of love, can you ever fall back in, or is that feeling lost forever?
4. Have you ever hated someone? How did this come about? Do you still hate the person, or have your feelings changed?
5. "Love" is a term that is often used in literature courses—love poetry, for instance, or love in the modern novel. What do you imagine a course in literature could teach you about love? Have you read a literary work that made you think and feel differently about love?
6. Do you find it hard to say, "I love you"? Why is that?
7. Do you think that it is a good experience to write about personal feelings, such as love and hate? Would you prefer not to? Would you like to do more of this kind of personal writing in your courses, or less?
8. Are you a religious person? Do you love God? How is this love felt and expressed in your life from day to day?

ESSAYS

SEI SHŌNAGON

Sei Shōnagon was a Japanese woman who, in the tenth century, served for some ten years as a lady-in-waiting to the empress in Kyoto. Her Pillow Book—*a marvelous collection of lists, eyewitness reports, and brief essays—established the Japanese tradition of* zuihitsu, *"spontaneous writing" (literally, "to follow the brush").*

Not much is known about Sei Shōnagon. Her book tells us nothing of her early years, and the date and circumstances of her death are unknown. Scholars conjecture that she was born about 965 and that she became a lady-in-waiting during the early 990s. It is evident from her book that she was witty, snobbish, and well versed in the etiquette of love at court.

The passage that we here reprint appears in a list entitled "Hateful Things."

A Lover's Departure

A lover who is leaving at dawn announces that he has to find his fan and his paper. "I know I put them somewhere last night," he says. Since it is pitch dark, he gropes about the room, bumping into the furniture and muttering, "Strange! Where on earth can they be?" Finally he discovers the objects. He thrusts the paper into the breast of his robe with a great rustling sound; then he snaps open his fan and busily fans away with it. Only now is he ready to take his leave. What charmless behavior! "Hateful" is an understatement.

Equally disagreeable is the man who, when leaving in the middle of the night, takes care to fasten the cord of his headdress. This is quite unnecessary; he could perfectly well put it gently on his head without tying the cord. And why must he spend time adjusting his cloak or hunting costume? Does he really think someone may see him at this time of night and criticize him for not being impeccably dressed?

A good lover will behave as elegantly at dawn as at any other time. He drags himself out of bed with a look of dismay on his face. The lady urges him on: "Come, my friend, it's getting light. You don't want anyone to find you here." He gives a deep sigh, as if to say that the night has not been nearly long enough and that it is agony to leave. Once up, he does not instantly pull on his trousers. Instead he comes close to the lady and whispers whatever was left unsaid during the night. Even when he is dressed, he still lingers, vaguely pretending to be fastening his sash.

Presently he raises the lattice, and the two lovers stand together by the side door while he tells her how he dreads the coming day, which will keep them apart; then he slips away. The lady watches him go, and this moment of parting will remain among her most charming memories.

Indeed, one's attachment to a man depends largely on the elegance of his leave-taking. When he jumps out of bed, scurries about the room, tightly fastens his trouser-sash, rolls up the sleeves of his Court cloak, overrobe, or hunting costume, stuffs his belongings into the breast of his robe and then briskly secures the outer sash—one really begins to hate him.

Topics for Critical Thinking and Writing

1. What are your first responses to this passage? Later—even if only thirty minutes later—reread the passage and think about whether your responses have changed.
2. On the basis of this short extract, how would you characterize Sei Shōnagon? Can you imagine that you and she might become close friends or lovers?
3. Write a journal entry or two on the topic "Hateful Things."

JUDITH ORTIZ COFER

Born in Puerto Rico in 1952 of a Puerto Rican mother and a United States mainland father who served in the Navy, Judith Ortiz Cofer was educated both in Puerto Rico and on the mainland. After earning a bachelor's and a master's degree in English, she did further graduate work at Oxford and then taught English in Florida. She has published seven volumes of poetry.

The following selection comes from an autobiography, Silent Dancing *(1990).*

I Fell in Love, or My Hormones Awakened

I fell in love, or my hormones awakened from their long slumber in my body, and suddenly the goal of my days was focused on one thing: to catch a glimpse of my secret love. And it had to remain secret, because I had, of course, in the great tradition of tragic romance, chosen to love a boy who was totally out of my reach. He was not Puerto Rican; he was Italian and rich. He was also an older man. He was a senior at the high school when I came in as a freshman. I first saw him in the hall, leaning casually on a wall that was the border line between girlside and boyside for underclassmen. He looked extraordinarily like a young Marlon Brando—down to the ironic little smile. The total of what I knew about the boy who starred in every one of my awkward fantasies was this: that he was the nephew of the man who owned the supermarket on my block; that he often had parties at his parents' beautiful home in the suburbs which I would hear about; that his family had money (which came to our school in many ways)—and this fact made my knees weak: and that he worked at the store near my apartment building on weekends and in the summer.

My mother could not understand why I became so eager to be the one sent out on her endless errands. I pounced on every opportunity from Friday to late Saturday afternoon to go after eggs, cigarettes, milk (I tried to drink as much of it as possible, although I hated the stuff)—the staple items that she would order from the "American" store.

Week after week I wandered up and down the aisles, taking furtive glances at the stock room in the back, breathlessly hoping to see my prince. Not that I had a plan. I felt like a pilgrim waiting for a glimpse of Mecca. I did not expect him to notice me. It was sweet agony.

One day I did see him. Dressed in a white outfit like a surgeon: white pants and shirt, white cap, and (gross sight, but not to my love-glazed eyes) blood-smeared butcher's apron. He was helping to drag a side of beef into the freezer storage area of the store. I must have stood there like an idiot, because I remember that he did see me, he even spoke to me! I could have died. I think he said, "Excuse me," and smiled vaguely in my direction.

5   After that, I *willed* occasions to go to the supermarket. I watched my mother's pack of cigarettes empty ever so slowly. I wanted her to smoke them fast. I drank milk and forced it on my brother (although a second glass for him had to be bought with my share of Fig Newton cookies which we both liked, but we were restricted to one row each). I gave my cookies up for love, and watched my mother smoke her L&M's with so little enthusiasm that I thought (God, no!) that she might be cutting down on her smoking or maybe even giving up the habit. At this crucial time!

I thought I had kept my lonely romance a secret. Often I cried hot tears on my pillow for the things that kept us apart. In my mind there was no doubt that he would never notice me (and that is why I felt free to stare at him—I was invisible). He could not see me because I was a skinny Puerto Rican girl, a freshman who did not belong to any group he associated with.

At the end of the year I found out that I had not been invisible. I learned one little lesson about human nature—adulation leaves a scent, one that we are all equipped to recognize, and no matter how insignificant the source, we seek it.

In June the nuns at our school would always arrange for some cultural extravaganza. In my freshman year it was a Roman banquet. We had been studying Greek drama (as a prelude to church history—it was at a fast clip that we galloped through Sophocles and Euripedes toward the early Christian martyrs), and our young, energetic Sister Agnes was in the mood for spectacle. She ordered the entire student body (it was a small group of under 300 students) to have our mothers make us togas out of sheets. She handed out a pattern on mimeo pages fresh out of the machine. I remember the intense smell of the alcohol on the sheets of paper, and how almost everyone in the auditorium brought theirs to their noses and inhaled deeply—mimeographed handouts were the school-day buzz that the new Xerox generation of kids is missing out on. Then, as the last couple of weeks of school dragged on, the city of Paterson becoming a concrete oven, and us wilting in our uncomfortable uniforms, we labored like frantic Roman slaves to build a splendid banquet hall in our small auditorium. Sister Agnes wanted a raised dais where the host and hostess would be regally enthroned.

She had already chosen our Senator and Lady from among our ranks. The Lady was to be a beautiful new student named Sophia, a recent Polish immigrant, whose English was still practically unintelligible, but whose features, classically perfect without a trace of makeup, enthralled us. Everyone talked about her gold hair cascading past her waist, and her voice which could carry a note right up to heaven in choir. The nuns wanted her for God. They kept saying that she had vocation. We just looked at her in awe, and the boys seemed afraid of her. She just smiled and did as she was told. I don't know what she thought of it all. The main privilege of beauty is that others will do almost everything for you, including thinking.

10   Her partner was to be our best basketball player, a tall, red-haired senior whose family sent its many offspring to our school. Together, Sophia and her senator looked like the best combination of immigrant genes our community could

produce. It did not occur to me to ask then whether anything but their physical beauty qualified them for the starring roles in our production. I had the highest average in the church history class, but I was given the part of one of many "Roman Citizens." I was to sit in front of the plastic fruit and recite a greeting in Latin along with the rest of the school when our hosts came into the hall and took their places on their throne.

On the night of our banquet, my father escorted me in my toga to the door of our school. I felt foolish in my awkwardly draped sheet (blouse and skirt required underneath). My mother had no great skill as a seamstress. The best she could do was hem a skirt or a pair of pants. That night I would have traded her for a peasant woman with a golden needle. I saw other Roman ladies emerging from their parents' cars looking authentic in sheets of material that folded over their bodies like the garments on a statue by Michelangelo. How did they do it? How was it that I always got it just slightly wrong, and worse, I believed that other people were just too polite to mention it. "The poor little Puerto Rican girl," I could hear them thinking. But in reality, I must have been my worst critic, self-conscious as I was.

Soon, we were all sitting at our circle of tables joined together around the dais. Sophia glittered like a golden statue. Her smile was beatific: a perfect, silent Roman lady. Her "senator" looked uncomfortable, glancing around at his buddies, perhaps waiting for the ridicule that he would surely get in the locker room later. The nuns in their black habits stood in the background watching us. What were they supposed to be, the Fates? Nubian slaves? The dancing girls did their modest little dance to tinny music from their finger cymbals, then the speeches were made. Then the grape juice "wine" was raised in a toast to the Roman Empire we all knew would fall within the week—before finals anyway.

All during the program I had been in a state of controlled hysteria. My secret love sat across the room from me looking supremely bored. I watched his every move, taking him in gluttonously. I relished the shadow of his eyelashes on his ruddy cheeks, his pouty lips smirking sarcastically at the ridiculous sight of our little play. Once he slumped down on his chair, and our sergeant-at-arms nun came over and tapped him sharply on his shoulder. He drew himself up slowly, with disdain. I loved his rebellious spirit. I believed myself still invisible to him in my "nothing" status as I looked upon my beloved. But toward the end of the evening, as we stood chanting our farewells in Latin, he looked straight across the room and into my eyes! How did I survive the killing power of those dark pupils? I trembled in a new way. I was not cold—I was burning! Yet I shook from the inside out, feeling light-headed, dizzy.

The room began to empty and I headed for the girls' lavatory. I wanted to relish the miracle in silence. I did not think for a minute that anything more would follow. I was satisfied with the enormous favor of a look from my beloved. I took my time, knowing that my father would be waiting outside for me, impatient, perhaps glowing in the dark in his phosphorescent white Navy uniform. The others would ride home. I would walk home with my father, both of us in costume. I wanted as few witnesses as possible. When I could no longer hear the crowds in the hallway, I emerged from the bathroom, still under the spell of those mesmerizing eyes.

15   The lights had been turned off in the hallway and all I could see was the lighted stairwell, at the bottom of which a nun would be stationed. My father would be waiting just outside. I nearly screamed when I felt someone grab me by the waist. But my mouth was quickly covered by someone else's mouth. I was being kissed. My first kiss and I could not even tell who it was. I pulled away to see

that face not two inches away from mine. It was he. He smiled down at me. Did I have a silly expression on my face? My glasses felt crooked on my nose. I was unable to move or to speak. More gently, he lifted my chin and touched his lips to mine. This time I did not forget to enjoy it. Then, like the phantom lover that he was, he walked away into the darkened corridor and disappeared.

I don't know how long I stood there. My body was changing right there in the hallway of a Catholic school. My cells were tuning up like musicians in an orchestra, and my heart was a chorus. It was an opera I was composing, and I wanted to stand very still and just listen. But, of course, I heard my father's voice talking to the nun. I was in trouble if he had had to ask about me. I hurried down the stairs making up a story on the way about feeling sick. That would explain my flushed face and it would buy me a little privacy when I got home.

The next day Father announced at the breakfast table that he was leaving on a six month tour of Europe with the Navy in a few weeks and that at the end of the school year my mother, my brother, and I would be sent to Puerto Rico to stay for half a year at Mamá's (my mother's mother) house. I was devastated. This was the usual routine for us. We had always gone to Mamá's to stay when Father was away for long periods. But this year it was different for me. I was in love, and . . . my heart knocked against my bony chest at this thought . . . he loved me too? I broke into sobs and left the table.

In the next week I discovered the inexorable truth about parents. They can actually carry on with their plans right through tears, threats, and the awful spectacle of a teenager's broken heart. My father left me to my mother who impassively packed while I explained over and over that I was at a crucial time in my studies and that if I left my entire life would be ruined. All she would say was, "You are an intelligent girl, you'll catch up." Her head was filled with visions of *casa*[1] and family reunions, long gossip sessions with her mamá and sisters. What did she care that I was losing my one chance at true love?

In the meantime I tried desperately to see him. I thought he would look for me too. But the few times I saw him in the hallway, he was always rushing away. It would be long weeks of confusion and pain before I realized that the kiss was nothing but a little trophy for his ego. He had no interest in me other than as his adorer. He was flattered by my silent worship of him, and he had *bestowed* a kiss on me to please himself, and to fan the flames. I learned a lesson about the battle of the sexes then that I have never forgotten: the object is not always to win, but most times simply to keep your opponent (synonymous at times with "the loved one") guessing.

20   But this is too cynical a view to sustain in the face of that overwhelming rush of emotion that is first love. And in thinking back about my own experience with it, I can be objective only to the point where I recall how sweet the anguish was, how caught up in the moment I felt, and how every nerve in my body was involved in this salute to life. Later, much later, after what seemed like an eternity of dragging the weight of unrequited love around with me, I learned to make myself visible and to relish the little battles required to win the greatest prize of all. And much later, I read and understood Camus'[2] statement about the subject that concerns both adolescent and philosopher alike: if love were easy, life would be too simple.

[1990]

---

[1]*casa* home.   [2]**Albert Camus** (1913–1960), French novelist and philosopher.

Topics for Critical Thinking and Writing

1. If you agree with us that Cofer's essay is amusing, try to analyze the sources of its humor. *Why* are some passages funny?
2. In paragraph 9 Cofer says, "The main privilege of beauty is that others will do almost everything for you, including thinking." Do you agree that the beautiful are privileged? If so, draw on your experience (as one of the privileged or the unprivileged) to recount an example or two. By the way, Cofer seems to imply (paragraph 10) that the academically gifted should be privileged, or at least should be recognized as candidates for leading roles (e.g., that of "a perfect, silent Roman lady") in school productions. Is it any fairer to privilege brains than to privilege beauty? Explain.
3. In her final paragraph Cofer speaks of the experience as a "salute to life." What do you think she means by that?
4. Cofer is describing a state that is (or used to be) called "puppy love." If you have experienced anything like what Cofer experienced, write your own autobiographical essay. (You can of course amplify or censor as you wish.) If you have experienced a love that you think is more serious, more lasting, write about *that*.

FICTION

ERNEST HEMINGWAY

Ernest Hemingway (1899–1961) was born in Oak Park, Illinois. After graduating from high school in 1917 he worked on the Kansas City Star, *but left to serve as a volunteer ambulance driver in Italy, where he was wounded in action. He returned home, married, and then served as European correspondent for the* Toronto Star, *but he soon gave up journalism for fiction. In 1922 he settled in Paris, where he moved in a circle of American expatriates that included Ezra Pound, Gertrude Stein, and F. Scott Fitzgerald. It was in Paris that he wrote stories and novels about what Gertrude Stein called a "lost generation" of rootless Americans in Europe. (For Hemingway's reminiscences of the Paris years, see his posthumously published* A Moveable Feast.) *He served as a journalist during the Spanish civil war and during the Second World War, but he was also something of a private soldier.*

After the Second World War his reputation sank, though he was still active as a writer (for instance, he wrote The Old Man and the Sea *in 1952). In 1954 Hemingway was awarded the Nobel Prize in Literature, but in 1961, depressed by a sense of failing power, he took his own life.*

Cat in the Rain

There were only two Americans stopping at the hotel. They did not know any of the people they passed on the stairs on their way to and from their room. Their room was on the second floor facing the sea. It also faced the public garden and the war monument. There were big palms and green benches in the public garden. In the good weather there was always an artist with his easel. Artists liked the way the palms grew and the bright colors of the hotels facing the gardens and the sea. Italians came from a long way off to look up at the war monument. It was made of bronze and glistened in the rain. It was raining. The rain dripped from the palm trees. Water stood in pools on the gravel paths. The sea broke in a long line in the rain and slipped back down the beach to come up and break again in a long line in the rain. The motor cars were gone from the square by the war monument. Across the square in the doorway of the café a waiter stood looking out at the empty square.

The American wife stood at the window looking out. Outside right under their window a cat was crouched under one of the dripping green tables. The cat was trying to make herself so compact that she would not be dripped on.

"I'm going down and get that kitty," the American wife said.

"I'll do it," her husband offered from the bed.

5   "No, I'll get it. The poor kitty is out trying to keep dry under a table."

The husband went on reading, lying propped up with the two pillows at the foot of the bed.

"Don't get wet," he said.

The wife went downstairs and the hotel owner stood up and bowed to her as she passed the office. His desk was at the far end of the office. He was an old man and very tall.

"Il piove,"[1] the wife said. She liked the hotel-keeper.

10   "Si, si, Signora, brutto tempo. It is very bad weather."

He stood behind his desk in the far end of the dim room. The wife liked him. She liked the deadly serious way he received any complaints. She liked his dignity. She liked the way he wanted to serve her. She liked the way he felt about being a hotel-keeper. She liked his old, heavy face and big hands.

Liking him she opened the door and looked out. It was raining harder. A man in a rubber cape was crossing the empty square to the café. The cat would be around to the right. Perhaps she could go along under the eaves. As she stood in the doorway an umbrella opened behind her. It was the maid who looked after their room.

"You must not get wet," she smiled, speaking Italian. Of course, the hotel-keeper had sent her.

With the maid holding the umbrella over her, she walked along the gravel path until she was under their window. The table was there, washed bright green in the rain, but the cat was gone. She was suddenly disappointed. The maid looked up at her.

15   "Ha perduto qualque cosa, Signora?"[2]

"There was a cat," said the American girl.

"A cat?"

"Si, il gatto."

"A cat?" the maid laughed. "A cat in the rain?"

20   "Yes," she said, "under the table." Then. "Oh. I wanted it so much. I wanted a kitty."

When she talked English the maid's face tightened.

---

[1]**Il piove** It's raining (Italian).   [2]**Ha . . . Signora** Have you lost something, Madam?

"Come, Signora," she said. "We must get back inside. You will be wet."

"I suppose so," said the American girl.

They went back along the gravel path and passed in the door. The maid stayed outside to close the umbrella. As the American girl passed the office, the padrone bowed from his desk. Something felt very small and tight inside the girl. The padrone made her feel very small and at the same time really important. She had a momentary feeling of being of supreme importance. She went on up the stairs. She opened the door of the room. George was on the bed, reading.

25   "Did you get the cat?" he asked, putting the book down.

"It was gone."

"Wonder where it went to," he said, resting his eyes from reading.

She sat down on the bed.

"I wanted it so much," she said. "I don't know why I wanted it so much. I wanted that poor kitty. It isn't any fun to be a poor kitty out in the rain."

30   George was reading again.

She went over and sat in front of the mirror of the dressing table looking at herself with the hand glass. She studied her profile, first one side and then the other. Then she studied the back of her head and her neck.

"Don't you think it would be a good idea if I let my hair grow out?" she asked, looking at her profile again.

George looked up and saw the back of her neck, clipped close like a boy's.

"I like it the way it is."

35   "I get so tired of it," she said. "I get so tired of looking like a boy."

George shifted his position in the bed. He hadn't looked away from her since she started to speak.

"You look pretty darn nice," he said.

She laid the mirror down on the dresser and went over to the window and looked out. It was getting dark.

"I want to pull my hair back tight and smooth and make a big knot at the back that I can feel," she said. "I want to have a kitty to sit on my lap and purr when I stroke her."

40   "Yeah?" George said from the bed.

"And I want to eat at a table with my own silver and I want candles. And I want it to be spring and I want to brush my hair out in front of a mirror and I want a kitty and I want some new clothes."

"Oh, shut up and get something to read," George said. He was reading again.

His wife was looking out of the window. It was quite dark now and still raining in the palm trees.

"Anyway, I want a cat," she said, "I want a cat. I want a cat now. If I can't have long hair or any fun, I can have a cat."

45   George was not listening. He was reading his book. His wife looked out of the window where the light had come on in the square.

Someone knocked at the door.

"Avanti,"[3] George said. He looked up from his book.

In the doorway stood the maid. She held a big tortoise-shell cat pressed tight against her and swung down against her body.

"Excuse me," she said, "the padrone asked me to bring this for the Signora."

[1925]

---

[3] **Avanti** Come in.

A Student's Notes and Journal Entries on "Cat in the Rain"

When you read a story—or, perhaps more accurately, when you reread a story before discussing it or writing about it—you'll find it helpful to jot an occasional note (for instance, a brief response or a question) in the margins and to underline or highlight passages that strike you as especially interesting. Here is part of the story, with the annotations of a student, Bill Yanagi.

Is he making a joke? Or maybe he just isn't even thinking about what he is saying?

The cat was trying to make herself so compact that she would not be dripped on.

"I'm going down and get that kitty," the American wife said.

"I'll do it," her husband offered from the bed.

He doesn't make a move

"No, I'll get it. The poor kitty is out trying to keep dry under a table."

The husband <u>went on reading</u>, lying propped up with the two pillows at the foot of the bed.

still doesn't move

"Don't get wet," he said.

contrast with the husband

The wife went downstairs and the <u>hotel owner stood up and bowed to her</u> as she passed the office. His desk was at the far end of the office. He was an old man and very tall.

"Il piove," the wife said. She liked the hotel-keeper.

"Si, si, Signora, brutto tempo. It is very bad weather."

He stood behind his desk in the far end of the dim room. <u>The wife liked him.</u> She liked the deadly serious way he received any complaints. <u>She liked his dignity.</u> She liked the way he wanted to serve her. She liked the way he felt about being a hotel-keeper. She liked his old, heavy face and big hands.

She respects him and she is pleased by the attention he shows

to emphasize the bad weather??

Liking him she opened the door and looked out. It was raining harder. <u>A man in a rubber cape</u> was crossing the <u>empty square</u> to the café. The cat would be around to the right.

Asking Questions about a Story

Everything in a story presumably is important, but having read the story once, probably something has especially interested (or puzzled) you, such as the relationship between two people, or the way the end of the story is connected to the beginning. On rereading, then, pen in hand, you'll find yourself noticing things that you missed or didn't find especially significant on your first reading. Now that you know the end of the story, you will read the beginning in a different way.

And of course if your instructor asks you to think about certain questions, you'll keep these in mind while you reread, and you will find ideas coming to you. In "Cat in the Rain," suppose you are asked (or you ask yourself) if the story might just as well be about a dog in the rain. Would anything be lost?

Here are a few questions that you can ask of almost any story. (On pages 235–237, in Chapter 9, we give a fuller list.) After scanning the questions, you will want to reread the story, pen in hand, and then jot down your responses on a sheet of paper. As you write, doubtless you will go back and reread the story or at least parts of it.

1. *What happens?* In two or three sentences—say 25–50 words—summarize what happens in the story.
2. *What sorts of people are the chief characters?* In "Cat in the Rain" the chief characters are George, George's wife, and the innkeeper (the padrone). Jot down the traits that each seems to possess, and next to each trait briefly give some supporting evidence.
3. *What especially pleased or displeased you in the story?* Devote at least a sentence or two to the end of the story. Do you find the end satisfying? Why or why not?
4. *Have you any thoughts about the title?* If so, what are they? If the story did not have a title, what would you call it?

After you have made your own jottings, compare them with these responses by a student. No two readers will respond in exactly the same way, but all readers can examine their responses and try to account for them, at least in part. If your responses are substantially different, how do you account for the differences?

1. A summary. A young wife, stopping with her husband at an Italian hotel, from her room sees a cat in the rain. She goes to get it, but it is gone, and so she returns empty-handed. A moment later the maid knocks at the door, holding a tortoise-shell cat.
2. The characters: The woman.
   kind-hearted (pities cat in rain)
   appreciates innkeeper's courtesy ("liked the way he wanted to serve her")
       and admires him ("She liked his dignity")
   unhappy (wants a cat, wants to change her hair, wants to eat at a table
       with her own silver)
   The husband, George.
   not willing to put himself out (says he'll go to garden to get cat but
       doesn't move)
   doesn't seem very interested in wife (hardly talks to her--he's reading;
       tells her to "shut up")
   but he does say he finds her attractive ("You look pretty darn nice")
   The innkeeper.
   serious, dignified ("She liked the deadly serious way he received any
       complaints. She liked his dignity")
   courteous, helpful (sends maid with umbrella; at end sends maid
       with cat)
3. Dislikes and likes. "Dislikes" is too strong, but I was disappointed that more didn't happen at the end. What is the husband's reaction to the cat? Or his final reaction to his wife? I mean, what did he think about his wife when the maid brings the cat? And, for that matter, what is the wife's reaction? Is she satisfied? Or does she realize that the cat can't really make her happy? Now for the likes. (1) I guess I did like the way it turned out; it's sort of a happy ending, I think, since she wants the cat

and gets it. (2) I also especially like the innkeeper. Maybe I like him partly because the wife likes him, and if she likes him he must be nice. And he <u>is</u> nice--very helpful. And I also like the way Hemingway shows the husband. I don't mean that I like the man himself, but I like the way Hemingway shows he is such a bastard--not getting off the bed to get the cat, telling his wife to shut up and read.

Another thing about him is that the one time he says something nice about her, it's about her hair, and she isn't keen on the way her hair is. She says it makes her look "like a boy," and she is "tired" of looking like a boy. There's something wrong with this marriage. George hardly pays attention to his wife, but he wants her to look like a boy. Maybe the idea is that this macho guy wants to keep her looking like an inferior (immature) version of himself. Anyway, he certainly doesn't seem interested in letting her fulfill herself as a woman.

<u>I think my feelings add up to this</u>: I like the way Hemingway shows us the relation between the husband and wife (even though the relation is pretty bad), and I like the innkeeper. Even if the relation with the couple ends unhappily, the story has a sort of happy ending, so far as it goes, since the innkeeper does what he can to please his guest: he sends the maid, with the cat. There's really nothing more that he can do.

<u>More about the ending.</u> The more I think about it, the more I feel that the ending is as happy as it can be. George is awful. When his wife says "I want a cat and I want a cat now," Hemingway tells us "George was not listening." And then, a moment later, almost like a good fairy the maid appears and grants the wife's wish.

4. <u>The title.</u> I don't suppose that I would have called it "Cat in the Rain," but I don't know what I would have called it. Maybe "An American Couple in Italy." Or maybe "The Innkeeper." I really do think that the innkeeper is very important, even though he only has a few lines. He's very impressive--not only to the girl, but to me (and maybe to all readers), since at the end of the story we see how careful the innkeeper is.

But the more I think about Hemingway's title, the more I think that maybe it also refers to the girl. Like the "poor kitty" in the rain, the wife is in a pretty bad situation. "It isn't any fun to be a poor kitty out in the rain." Of course the woman is indoors, but her husband generates lots of unpleasant weather. She may as well be out in the rain. She says "I want to have a kitty to sit on my lap and purr when I stroke her." This shows that she wants to be affectionate and that she also wants to have someone respond to her affection. She <u>is</u> like a cat in the rain.

The responses of this student probably include statements that you want to take issue with. Or perhaps you feel that the student did not even mention some things that you think are important. You may want to jot down some notes and raise some questions in class.

A Sample Essay by a Student: "Hemingway's American Wife"

The responses that we have quoted were written by Bill Yanagi, who later wrote an essay developing one of them. Here is the essay.

Yanagi 1

Bill Yanagi

Professor Costello

English 10B

20 October 2004

Hemingway's American Wife

My title alludes not to any of the four women to whom

Hemingway was married, but to "the American wife" who is twice

called by this term in his short story, "Cat in the Rain." We first

meet her in the first sentence of the story ("There were only two

Americans stopping at the hotel"), and the next time she is

mentioned (apart from a reference to the wife and her husband as

"they") it is as "the American wife," at the beginning of the second

paragraph of the story. The term is used again at the end of the

third paragraph.

She is, then, at least in the early part of this story, just an

American or an American wife--someone identified only by her

nationality and her marital status, but not at all by her

personality, her individuality, her inner self. She first becomes

something of an individual when she separates herself from her

husband by leaving the hotel room and going to look for a cat

that she has seen in the garden, in the rain. This act of

separation, however, has not the slightest effect on her husband,

who "went on reading" (689).

When she returns, without the cat, he puts down his book

and speaks to her, but it is obvious that he has no interest in her, beyond as a physical object ("You look pretty darn nice"). This

comment is produced when she says she is thinking of letting

her hair grow out, because she is "so tired of looking like a boy"

(690). Why, a reader wonders, does her husband, who has paid

almost no attention to her up to now, assure her that she looks

"pretty darn nice"? I think it is reasonable to conclude that he

wants her to look like someone who is not truly a woman, in

particular someone who is immature. That she does not feel she

has much identity is evident when she continues to talk about

letting her hair grow, and she says "I want to pull my hair back

tight and smooth and make a big knot at the back that I can feel"

(690). Long hair is, or at least was, the traditional sign of a

woman; she wants long hair, and at the same time she wants to

keep it under her control by tying it in a "big knot," a knot that

she can feel, a knot whose presence reminds her, because she can

feel it, of her feminine nature.

She goes on to say that she wants to brush her hair "in front

of a mirror." That is, she wants to see and to feel her femininity,

since her husband apparently--so far as we can see in the story, at

least--scarcely recognizes it or her. Perhaps her desire for the cat

("I want a cat") is a veiled way of saying that she wants to express

her animal nature, and not be simply a neglected woman who is

made by her husband to look like a boy. Hemingway tells us,

however, that when she looked for the cat in the garden she could

not find it, a sign, I think, of her failure to break from the man.

Yanagi 3

At the end of the story the maid brings her the cat, but a woman

cannot just be handed a new nature and accept it, just like that.

She has to find it herself, and in herself, so I think the story ends

with "the American wife" still nothing more than an American

wife.

[New page]

Yanagi 4

Work Cited

Literature for Composition. Ed. Sylvan Barnet et al. 7th ed. New York:

Longman, 2005 688-90.

A few comments and questions may be useful.

- Do you find the essay interesting? Explain your response.
- Do you find the essay well written? Explain.
- Do you find the essay convincing? Can you suggest ways of strengthening it, or do you think its argument is mistaken? Carefully reread "Cat in the Rain," taking note of passages that give further support to this student's argument, or that seem to challenge or qualify it.
- We often say that a good critical essay sends us back to the literary work with a fresh point of view. Our rereading differs from our earlier reading. Does this essay change your reading of Hemingway's story?

Topics for Critical Thinking and Writing

1. Can we be certain that the cat at the end of the story is the cat that the woman saw in the rain? (When we first hear about the cat in the rain we are not told anything about its color, and at the end of the story we are not told that the tortoise-shell cat is wet.) Does it matter if there are two cats?
2. One student argued that the cat represents the child that the girl wants to have. Do you think there is something to this idea? How might you support or refute it?

3. Consider the following passage:

> As the American girl passed the office, the padrone bowed from his desk. Something felt very small and tight inside the girl. The padrone made her feel very small and at the same time really important. She had a momentary feeling of being of supreme importance.

Do you think there is anything sexual here? And if so, that the passage tells us something about her relations with her husband? Support your view.

4. What do you suppose Hemingway's attitude was toward each of the three chief characters? How might you support your hunch?

5. Hemingway wrote the story in Italy, when his wife Hadley was pregnant. In a letter to F. Scott Fitzgerald he said,

> Cat in the Rain wasn't about Hadley.... When I wrote that we were at Rapallo but Hadley was 4 months pregnant with Bumby. The Inn Keeper was the one at Cortina D'Ampezzo.... Hadley never made a speech in her life about wanting a baby because she had been told various things by her doctor and I'd—no use going into all that. (*Letters* 180)

According to some biographers, the story shows that Hemingway knew his marriage was going on the rocks (Hemingway and Hadley divorced). Does knowing that Hemingway's marriage turned out unhappily help you to understand the story? Does it make the story more interesting? And do you think that the story tells a biographer something about Hemingway's life?

6. It is sometimes said that a good short story does two things at once: It provides a believable picture of the surface of life, and it also illuminates some moral or psychological complexity that we feel is part of the essence of human life. This dual claim may not be true, but for the moment accept it. Do you think that Hemingway's story fulfills either or both of these specifications? Support your view.

A Second Example: An Essay Drawing on Related Material in the Chapter

Another student, Holly Klein, wrote about "Cat in the Rain," but she thought about it partly in terms of a familiar saying, "All the world loves a lover." She also draws on a less familiar quotation; it wouldn't have hurt to have cited the source of the unfamiliar quotation, but since the words are attributed to an author and are given within quotation marks, there is of course no problem of plagiarism. Here are her first notes, and the essay that she developed from them.

Journal Entries

"All the world loves a lover? Not necessarily. In real life, few emotions are less sociable than romantic passion." Certainly there's not much romantic passion in this story. But are these people in love?

Is it true that love stories are about people who are happy in love, or are they mostly about people who are unhappy? Many lovers may suffer and some even die (Leonardo DiCaprio in Titanic), but aren't they happy anyway? They are happy in their unhappiness. (And Rose—Kate Winslet—survives, happy and unhappy in her love.)

Is "Cat" really a love story anyway? Yes, in the sense it is about people who must at least at some time in the past have been lovers--happy lovers-- but who now seem stuck with each other. The wife still seems to be in love, or maybe she is trying to bring a dead love back to life.

Is there something to the idea (as Wilcox says), that "love is a mood" to men but is "life or death" to women? Does this add up to saying that for men, love is something of the moment, and is trivial, but for women it is enduring and important? And do men and women react differently to love stories? Someone in class-- and there was plenty of agreement and almost no disagreement-- said that <u>Titanic</u> is a "woman's picture." But Mark liked it as much as I did. Or at least he said so.

A Sample Essay by a Student: "Hemingway's Unhappy Lovers"

Here is the final version of Holly Klein's essay:

Klein 1

Holly Klein

Professor Chung

English 1102

30 April 2004

Hemingway's Unhappy Lovers

In class someone suggested that <u>Romeo and Juliet</u> is not so

much about how happy two people are but about how unhappy

they are. This statement, which at first I thought was ridiculous,

now strikes me as true, or for the most part true. The lovers in

<u>Romeo and Juliet</u>, <u>West Side Story</u>, and in the television drama

<u>All My Children</u> (Haley, Mateo, Lisa, and several other young

adults) would not give up being in love, but during most of the

time they are unhappy. I have heard a saying, "Love means not

ever having to say you are sorry," but some of these lovers, and

other lovers in daytime television programs, are always saying

they are sorry, and always feeling sorry for themselves. And we

---

feel sorry for them. Our interest in them is not in their

happiness, but in their unhappiness.

Certainly in Ernest Hemingway's "Cat in the Rain" the

woman is unhappy--and who wouldn't be unhappy, with a

husband like hers? She says she is going out into the rain to get

the cat, and he says "Don't get wet" (689), and he goes right on

reading, obviously uninterested in what his wife is doing, or in

her needs. The wife never explicitly says she is unhappy, but it is

obvious that she is. Her husband pays very little attention to her,

and then, when he does--he goes so far as to say "You look pretty

darn nice"--it's only after she tells him she wants to change her

appearance: "I get so tired of looking like a boy." When she adds

that she wants to change her hair, his response is, "Yeah?" And a

moment later he says, "Oh, shut up and get something to read"

(690). I felt like hitting him, and I suddenly realized that, at least

for this story, lovers are unhappy. If Hemingway's lovers were

happy and spent their time cooing at each other, the story

probably would have been boring. What's interesting here is,

paradoxically, the man's lack of interest in his wife--he is

probably affectionate only when he wants sex--and the woman's

basic unhappiness. Her unhappiness is revealed partly by her

almost desperate attempt to give affection to the cat, and to

receive some affection from it: "I want to have a kitty to sit on my

lap and purr when I stroke her" (690). Ella Wheeler Wilcox may

be overstating the matter, but, allowing for what is called poetic license, there is something sound in her view that "love is a mood--

no more--to man, / And love to a woman is life or death".

Many people probably do not make a distinction between the

attitudes of men and women toward love, and they therefore don't

distinguish between the responses of men and of women to love

stories. I think it is probably true that most love stories are

chiefly about unhappiness, but it is probably also true that

women in love are more likely than men to express in words their

unhappiness. (I think there are psychological or sociological

studies that support this view.) In any case, in support of the idea

that love stories are chiefly about unhappiness, I can say that

"Cat in the Rain" interested me not because the lovers keep

expressing their romantic passion but because the man does <u>not</u>

express his love, and the woman expresses her frustration. In

this story about lovers, the man is in bed—but he spends most of

his time <u>reading</u> in bed, and (as I said) about the best he can say

to the woman is that she looks "pretty darn nice"). The wife holds

our interest because she is unhappy, stuck with this guy, and she

is so grateful for a kind word from the hotel-keeper. She doesn't

explicitly say that she is desperately unhappy, but she does

express very vigorously a desire for a life different from the one

she is now living, and we do feel that (at least for her) love is not

just a "mood," as it probably is for the man, but is a matter of "life

or death." She is, so to speak, dying to be loved.

[New page]

Klein 4

Work Cited

<u>Literature for Composition</u>. Ed. Sylvan Barnet et al. 7th ed. New

York: Longman, 2005. 688-90.

We can ask of this essay the same questions that we asked of an earlier essay:

- Do you find the essay interesting? Explain your response.
- Do you find the essay well written? Explain.
- Do you find the essay convincing? Can you suggest ways of strengthening it, or do you think its argument is mistaken? Carefully reread "Cat in the Rain," taking note of passages that give further support to this student's argument, or that seem to challenge or qualify it.
- We often say that a good critical essay sends us back to the literary work with a fresh point of view. Our rereading differs from our earlier reading. Does this essay change your reading of Hemingway's story?

We can also ask one additional question:

- Sometimes writers make their essays far too impersonal, removing every trace of the writer as an individual human being, a distinct person. Do you think that this writer goes too far in the other direction, making the essay too personal? If you think that she does, what advice would you give her, to help her strike the right balance?

WILLIAM FAULKNER

 *William Faulkner (1897–1962) was brought up in Oxford, Mississippi. His great-grandfather had been a Civil War hero, and his father was treasurer of the University of Mississippi in Oxford; the family was no longer rich, but it was still respected. In 1918 he enrolled in the Royal Canadian Air Force, though he never saw overseas service. After the war he returned to Mississippi and went to the university for two years. He then moved to New Orleans, where he became friendly with Sherwood Anderson, who was already an established writer. In New Orleans Faulkner worked for the* Times-Picayune; *still later, even after he had established himself as a* major novelist with The Sound and the Fury *(1929), he had to do some work in Hollywood in order to make ends meet. In 1950 he was awarded the Nobel Prize in Literature.*

Almost all of Faulkner's writing is concerned with the people of Yoknapatawpha, an imaginary county in Mississippi. "I discovered," he said, "that my own little postage stamp of native soil was worth writing about and that I would never live long enough to exhaust it." Though he lived for brief periods in Canada, New Orleans, New York, Hollywood, and Virginia (where he died), he spent most of his life in his native Mississippi.

A Rose for Emily

I

When Miss Emily Grierson died, our whole town went to her funeral: the men through a sort of respectful affection for a fallen monument, the women mostly out of curiosity to see the inside of her house, which no one save an old manservant—a combined gardener and cook—had seen in at least ten years.

It was a big, squarish frame house that had once been white, decorated with cupolas and spires and scrolled balconies in the heavily lightsome style of the seventies, set on what had once been our most select street. But garages and cotton gins had encroached and obliterated even the august names of that neighborhood; only Miss Emily's house was left, lifting its stubborn and coquettish decay above the cotton wagons and the gasoline pumps—an eyesore among eyesores. And now Miss Emily had gone to join the representatives of those august names where they lay in the cedar-bemused cemetery among the ranked and anonymous graves of Union and Confederate soldiers who fell at the battle of Jefferson.

Alive, Miss Emily had been a tradition, a duty, and a care; a sort of hereditary obligation upon the town, dating from that day in 1894 when Colonel Sartoris, the mayor—he who fathered the edict that no Negro woman should appear on the streets without an apron—remitted her taxes, the dispensation dating from the death of her father on into perpetuity. Not that Miss Emily would have accepted charity. Colonel Sartoris invented an involved tale to the effect that Miss Emily's father had loaned money to the town, which the town, as a matter of business, preferred this way of repaying. Only a man of Colonel Sartoris' generation and thought could have invented it, and only a woman could have believed it.

When the next generation, with its more modern ideas, became mayors and aldermen, this arrangement created some little dissatisfaction. On the first of the year they mailed her a tax notice. February came, and there was no reply. They wrote her a formal letter, asking her to call at the sheriff's office at her convenience. A week later the mayor wrote her himself, offering to call or to send his car for her, and received in reply a note on paper of an archaic shape, in a thin, flowing calligraphy in faded ink, to the effect that she no longer went out at all. The tax notice was also enclosed, without comment.

5   They called a special meeting of the Board of Aldermen. A deputation waited upon her, knocked at the door through which no visitor had passed since she ceased giving china-painting lessons eight or ten years earlier. They were admitted by the old Negro into a dim hall from which a staircase mounted into still more shadow. It smelled of dust and disuse—a close, dank smell. The Negro led them into the parlor. It was furnished in heavy, leather-covered furniture. When the Negro opened the blinds of one window they could see that the leather was cracked; and when they sat down, a faint dust rose sluggishly about their thighs, spinning with slow motes in the single sunray. On a tarnished gilt easel before the fireplace stood a crayon portrait of Miss Emily's father.

They rose when she entered—a small, fat woman in black, with a thin gold chain descending to her waist and vanishing into her belt, leaning on an ebony cane with a tarnished gold head. Her skeleton was small and spare; perhaps that was why what would have been merely plumpness in another was obesity in her. She looked bloated, like a body long submerged in motionless water, and of that pallid hue. Her eyes, lost in the fatty ridges of her face, looked like two small pieces of coal pressed into a lump of dough as they moved from one face to another while the visitors stated their errand.

She did not ask them to sit. She just stood in the door and listened quietly until the spokesman came to a stumbling halt. Then they could hear the invisible watch ticking at the end of the gold chain.

Her voice was dry and cold. "I have no taxes in Jefferson. Colonel Sartoris explained it to me. Perhaps one of you can gain access to the city records and satisfy yourselves."

"But we have. We are the city authorities, Miss Emily. Didn't you get a notice from the sheriff, signed by him?"

10 "I received a paper, yes," Miss Emily said. "Perhaps he considers himself the sheriff. . . . I have no taxes in Jefferson."

"But there is nothing on the books to show that, you see. We must go by the—"

"See Colonel Sartoris. I have no taxes in Jefferson."

"But, Miss Emily—"

"See Colonel Sartoris." (Colonel Sartoris had been dead almost ten years.) "I have no taxes in Jefferson. Tobe!" The Negro appeared. "Show these gentlemen out."

II

15 So she vanquished them, horse and foot, just as she had vanquished their fathers thirty years before about the smell. That was two years after her father's death and a short time after her sweetheart—the one we believed would marry her—had deserted her. After her father's death she went out very little; after her sweetheart went away, people hardly saw her at all. A few of the ladies had the temerity to call, but were not received, and the only sign of life about the place was the Negro man—a young man then—going in and out with a market basket.

"Just as if a man—any man—could keep a kitchen properly," the ladies said; so they were not surprised when the smell developed. It was another link between the gross, teeming world and the high and mighty Griersons.

A neighbor, a woman, complained to the mayor, Judge Stevens, eighty years old.

"But what will you have me do about it, madam?" he said.

"Why, send her word to stop it," the woman said. "Isn't there a law?"

20 "I'm sure that won't be necessary," Judge Stevens said. "It's probably just a snake or a rat that nigger of hers killed in the yard. I'll speak to him about it."

The next day he received two more complaints, one from a man who came in diffident deprecation. "We really must do something about it, Judge. I'd be the last one in the world to bother Miss Emily, but we've got to do something." That night the Board of Aldermen met—three graybeards and one younger man, a member of the rising generation.

"It's simple enough," he said. "Send her word to have her place cleaned up. Give her a certain time to do it in, and if she don't . . . "

"Dammit, sir," Judge Stevens said, "will you accuse a lady to her face of smelling bad?"

So the next night, after midnight, four men crossed Miss Emily's lawn and slunk about the house like burglars, sniffing along the base of the brickwork and at the cellar openings while one of them performed a regular sowing motion with his hand out of a sack slung from his shoulder. They broke open the cellar door and sprinkled lime there, and in all the out-buildings. As they recrossed the lawn, a window that had been dark was lighted and Miss Emily sat in it, the light behind her, and her upright torso motionless as that of an idol. They crept quietly across the lawn and into the shadow of the locusts that lined the street. After a week or two the smell went away.

25   That was when people had begun to feel really sorry for her. People in our town remembering how old lady Wyatt, her great-aunt, had gone completely crazy at last, believed that the Griersons held themselves a little too high for what they really were. None of the young men were quite good enough for Miss Emily and such. We had long thought of them as a tableau; Miss Emily a slender figure in white in the background, her father a spraddled silhouette in the foreground, his back to her and clutching a horsewhip, the two of them framed by the back-flung front door. So when she got to be thirty and was still single, we were not pleased exactly, but vindicated; even with insanity in the family she wouldn't have turned down all of her chances if they had really materialized.

When her father died, it got about that the house was all that was left to her; and in a way, people were glad. At last they could pity Miss Emily. Being left alone, and a pauper, she had become humanized. Now she too would know the old thrill and the old despair of a penny more or less.

The day after his death all the ladies prepared to call at the house and offer condolence and aid, as is our custom. Miss Emily met them at the door, dressed as usual and with no trace of grief on her face. She told them that her father was not dead. She did that for three days, with the ministers calling on her, and the doctors, trying to persuade her to let them dispose of the body. Just as they were about to resort to law and force, she broke down, and they buried her father quickly.

We did not say she was crazy then. We believed she had to do that. We remembered all the young men her father had driven away, and we knew that with nothing left, she would have to cling to that which had robbed her, as people will.

III

She was sick for a long time. When we saw her again, her hair was cut short, making her look like a girl, with a vague resemblance to those angels in colored church windows—sort of tragic and serene.

30   The town had just let the contracts for paving the sidewalks, and in the summer after her father's death they began to work. The construction company came with niggers and mules and machinery, and a foreman named Homer Barron, a Yankee—a big, dark, ready man, with a big voice and eyes lighter than his face. The little boys would follow in groups to hear him cuss the niggers, and the niggers singing in time to the rise and fall of picks. Pretty soon he knew everybody in town. Whenever you heard a lot of laughing anywhere about the square, Homer Barron would be in the center of the group. Presently we began to see him and Miss Emily on Sunday afternoons driving in the yellow-wheeled buggy and the matched team of bays from the livery stable.

At first we were glad that Miss Emily would have an interest, because the ladies all said, "Of course a Grierson would not think seriously of a Northerner, a day laborer." But there were still others, older people, who said that even grief could not cause a real lady to forget *noblesse oblige*—without calling it *noblesse oblige*. They just said, "Poor Emily. Her kinsfolk should come to her." She had some kin in Alabama; but years ago her father had fallen out with them over the estate of old lady Wyatt, the crazy woman, and there was no communication between the two families. They had not even been represented at the funeral.

And as soon as the old people said, "Poor Emily," the whispering began. "Do you suppose it's really so?" they said to one another. "Of course it is. . . ." This behind their hands; rustling of craned silk and satin behind jalousies closed upon the sun of Sunday afternoon as the thin, swift clop-clop-clop of the matched team passed: "Poor Emily."

She carried her head high enough—even when we believed that she was fallen. It was as if she demanded more than ever the recognition of her dignity as the last Grierson; as if it had wanted that touch of earthiness to reaffirm her imperviousness. Like when she bought the rat poison, the arsenic. That was over a year after they had begun to say "Poor Emily," and while the two female cousins were visiting her.

"I want some poison," she said to the druggist. She was over thirty then, still a slight woman, though thinner than usual, with cold, haughty black eyes in a face the flesh of which was strained across the temples and about the eyesockets as you imagine a lighthouse-keeper's face ought to look. "I want some poison," she said.

35 "Yes, Miss Emily. What kind? For rats and such? I'd recom—"

"I want the best you have. I don't care what kind."

The druggist named several. "They'll kill anything up to an elephant. But what you want is—"

"Arsenic," Miss Emily said. "Is that a good one?"

"Is . . . arsenic? Yes ma'am. But what you want—"

40 "I want arsenic."

The druggist looked down at her. She looked back at him, erect, her face like a strained flag. "Why, of course," the druggist said. "If that's what you want. But the law requires you to tell what you are going to use it for."

Miss Emily just stared at him, her head tilted back in order to look him eye for eye, until he looked away and went and got the arsenic and wrapped it up. The Negro delivery boy brought her the package; the druggist didn't come back. When she opened the package at home there was written on the box, under the skull and bones: "For rats."

IV

So the next day we all said, "She will kill herself"; and we said it would be the best thing. When she had first begun to be seen with Homer Barron, we had said, "She will marry him." Then we said, "She will persuade him yet," because Homer himself had remarked—he liked men, and it was known that he drank with the younger men in the Elks' Club—that he was not a marrying man. Later we said, "Poor Emily," behind the jalousies as they passed on Sunday afternoon in the glittering buggy, Miss Emily with her head high and Homer Barron with his hat cocked and a cigar in his teeth, reins and whip in a yellow glove.

Then some of the ladies began to say that it was a disgrace to the town and a bad example to the young people. The men did not want to interfere, but at last the ladies forced the Baptist minister—Miss Emily's people were Episcopal—to call upon her. He would never divulge what happened during that interview, but he refused to go back again. The next Sunday they again drove about the streets, and the following day the minister's wife wrote to Miss Emily's relations in Alabama.

45   So she had blood-kin under her roof again and we sat back to watch developments. At first nothing happened. Then we were sure that they were to be married. We learned that Miss Emily had been to the jeweler's and ordered a man's toilet set in silver, with the letters H.B. on each piece. Two days later we learned that she had bought a complete outfit of men's clothing, including a nightshirt, and we said, "They are married." We were really glad. We were glad because the two female cousins were even more Grierson than Miss Emily had ever been.

So we were surprised when Homer Barron—the streets had been finished some time since—was gone. We were a little disappointed that there was not a public blowing-off but we believed that he had gone on to prepare for Miss Emily's coming, or to give a chance to get rid of the cousins. (By that time it was a cabal, and we were all Miss Emily's allies to help circumvent the cousins.) Sure enough, after another week they departed. And, as we had expected all along, within three days Homer Barron was back in town. A neighbor saw the Negro man admit him at the kitchen door at dusk one evening.

And that was the last we saw of Homer Barron. And of Miss Emily for some time. The Negro man went in and out with the market basket, but the front door remained closed. Now and then we would see her at a window for a moment, as the men did that night when they sprinkled the lime, but for almost six months she did not appear on the streets. Then we knew that this was to be expected too; as if that quality of her father which had thwarted her woman's life so many times had been too virulent and too furious to die.

When we next saw Miss Emily, she had grown fat and her hair was turning gray. During the next few years it grew grayer and grayer until it attained an even pepper-and-salt iron-gray, when it ceased turning. Up to the day of her death at seventy-four it was still that vigorous iron-gray, like the hair of an active man.

From that time on her front door remained closed, save for a period of six or seven years, when she was about forty, during which she gave lessons in china-painting. She fitted up a studio in one of the downstairs rooms, where the daughters and granddaughters of Colonel Sartoris' contemporaries were sent to her with the same regularity and in the same spirit that they were sent on Sundays with a twenty-five cent piece for the collection plate. Meanwhile her taxes had been remitted.

50   Then the newer generation became the backbone and the spirit of the town, and the painting pupils grew up and fell away and did not send their children to her with boxes of color and tedious brushes and pictures cut from the ladies' magazines. The front door closed upon the last one and remained closed for good. When the town got free postal delivery Miss Emily alone refused to let them fasten the metal numbers above her door and attach a mailbox to it. She would not listen to them.

Daily, monthly, yearly we watched the Negro grow grayer and more stooped, going in and out with the market basket. Each December we sent her a tax notice, which would be returned by the post office a week later, unclaimed. Now and then we could see her in one of the downstairs windows—she had evidently shut up the top floor of the house—like the carven torso of an idol in a niche, looking or not looking at us, we could never tell which. Thus she passed from generation to generation—dear, inescapable, impervious, tranquil, and perverse.

And so she died. Fell ill in the house filled with dust and shadows, with only a doddering Negro man to wait on her. We did not even know she was sick; we had long since given up trying to get any information from the Negro. He talked to no one, probably not even to her, for his voice had grown harsh and rusty, as if from disuse.

She died in one of the downstairs rooms, in a heavy walnut bed with a curtain, her gray head propped on a pillow yellow and moldy with age and lack of sunlight.

V

The Negro met the first of the ladies at the front door and let them in, with their hushed, sibilant voices and their quick, curious glances, and then he disappeared. He walked right through the house and out the back and was not seen again.

55   The two female cousins came at once. They held the funeral on the second day, with the town coming to look at Miss Emily beneath a mass of bought flowers, with the crayon face of her father musing profoundly above the bier and the ladies sibilant and macabre; and the very old men—some in their brushed Confederate uniforms—on the porch and the lawn, talking of Miss Emily as if she had been a contemporary of theirs, believing that they had danced with her and courted her perhaps, confusing time with its mathematical progression, as the old do, to whom all the past is not a diminishing road, but, instead, a huge meadow which no winter ever quite touches, divided from them now by the narrow bottleneck of the most recent decade of years.

Already we knew that there was one room in that region above stairs which no one had seen in forty years, and which would have to be forced. They waited until Miss Emily was decently in the ground before they opened it.

The violence of breaking down the door seemed to fill this room with pervading dust. A thin, acrid pall as of the tomb seemed to lie everywhere upon this room decked and furnished as for a bridal: upon the valance curtains of faded rose color, upon the rose-shaded lights, upon the dressing table, upon the delicate array of crystal and the man's toilet things backed with tarnished silver, silver so tarnished that the monogram was obscured. Among them lay a collar and tie, as if they had just been removed, which, lifted, left upon the surface a pale crescent in the dust. Upon a chair hung the suit, carefully folded; beneath it the two mute shoes and the discarded socks.

The man himself lay in the bed.

For a long while we just stood there, looking down at the profound and fleshless grin. The body had apparently once lain in the attitude of an embrace, but now the long sleep that outlasts love, that conquers even the grimace of love, had cuckolded him. What was left of him, rotted beneath what was left of the nightshirt, had become inextricable from the bed in which he lay; and upon him and upon the pillow beside him lay that even coating of the patient and biding dust.

60   Then we noticed that in the second pillow was the indentation of a head. One of us lifted something from it, and leaning forward, that faint and invisible dust dry and acrid in the nostrils, we saw a long strand of iron-gray hair.

[1930]

dust and shadows, with only a doddering negro man to wait on
her. We did not even know she was sick; we had long since given up
trying to get any information from the negro. He talked to no
one, probably not even to her, for his voice had grown ⱡⱥⱥⱡⱡ
harsh and ⱡⱥⱡ rusty, as though with disuse; the sparse words
which he did speak sounded as though he had learned them that
morning by rote---just enough of them to carry him through .
the day.

She died in one of the downstairs rooms, in a heavy
walnut bed with a curtain, her gray head propped on a pillow
yellow and moldy with age and lack of sunlight, her voice
cold and strong to the last.

"But not till I'm gone," she said. "Dont you let a
soul in until I'm gone, do you hear?" Standing beside the bed,
his head in the dim light nimbused by a faint halo of napped,
perfectly white hair, the negro made a brief gesture with his
hand. Miss Emily lay with her eyes open, gazing into the opposite shadows of the room. Upon the coverlet her hands lay on
her breast, gnarled, blue with age, motionless. "Hah," she said.
"Then they can. Let 'em go up there and see what's in that
room. ⱥ&ⱥ/ⱡⱥⱥ/ⱥⱥⱥⱡ/ⱡⱥ/ⱡⱥⱥ/ⱡⱥⱥⱡ/ⱥⱥⱥ/ⱥⱥⱥⱥ Fools. ⱥⱥⱥ Let
'em. ⱥⱥⱥ/ⱡⱥⱥ/ⱥⱥⱥⱡ/ⱡⱥ/ⱡⱥⱥ/ⱡⱥⱥⱡ/ⱥⱥⱥ Satisfy their minds that
I am crazy. Do you think I am?" The negro made no reply, no
movement. He stood above the bed, ⱥⱡⱥⱥⱥⱥⱥ/ⱥⱥⱡⱥⱥⱥ/ⱡⱡⱥⱥ/ⱥⱥ/ⱥⱥ/
ⱥⱥⱡ/ motionless, musing: a secret and unfathomable soul behind
the death-mask of an ape and haloed like an angel. "Let 'em
go up there and open that door. And you wont be the last one,

13.

The printed version of Faulkner's "A Rose for Emily" omitted several passages of dialogue
(shown here are pages 13 to 15 of the typed manuscript) between Miss Emily and her
longtime manservant.

either. Will you?"

"I wont have to," the negro said. "I know what's in that room. I dont have to see."

"Hah," Miss Emily said. "You do, do you. How long have you known?" Again he made that brief sign with his hand. Miss Emily had not turned her head. She stared into the shadows where the high ceiling was lost. "You should be glad. Now you can go to Chicago, like you've been talking about for thirty years. And with what you'll get for the house and furniture.... Colonel Sartoris has the will. He'll see they dont rob you."

"I dont want any house," the negro said.

"You cant help yourself. It's signed and sealed thirty-five years ago. Wasn't that our agreement when I found I couldn't pay you any wages? that you were to have everything that was left if you outlived me, and I was to bury you ~~with~~ in a coffin with your name on a gold plate if I outlived you?" He said nothing. "Wasn't it?" Miss Emily said.

"I was young then. Wanted to be rich. But now I dont want any house."

"Not when you have wanted to go to Chicago for thirty years?" Their breathing was alike: each that harsh, rasping breath of the old, the short inhalations that do not reach the bottom of the lungs: tireless, precarious, on the verge of cessation for all time, as if anything might suffice: a word, a look. "What are you going to do, then?"

"Going to the poorhouse."

"The poorhouse? When I'm trying to fix you so you'll

14.

have neither to worry nor lift your hand as long as you live?

"I dont want nothing," the negro said. "I'm going t.
the poorhouse. I already told them."

"Well," Miss Emily said. She had not moved her head,
not moved at all. "Do you mind telling me why you want to go
to the poorhouse?"

Again he mused. The room was still save for their brea
ing: it was as though they had both quitted all living and all
dying; all the travail of mortality and of breath. "So I can
set on that hill in the sun all day and watch them trains pass.
See them at night too, with the engine puffing and lights in
all the windows.

"Oh," Miss Emily said. Motionless, her knotted hands
lying on the yellowed coverlet beneath her chin and her chin
resting upon her breast, she appeared to muse intently, as
though she were listening to dissolution setting up within her.
"Hah," she said.

Then she died, and the negro met the first of the ladies at the front door and let them in, with their hushed sibilant voices and their quick curious glances, and he went on
to the back and disappeared. He walked right through the house
and out the back and was not seen again.

The two female cousins came at once. They held the
funeral on the second day, with the town coming to look at
Miss Emily beneath a mass of bought flowers, with the crayon
face of her father musing profoundly above the bier and the la-

15.

grin cemented into what had once been a pillow by a substance like
hardened sealing-wax. One side of the covers was flung back, as
though he were preparing to rise; we lifted the covers completely
away, liberating still another sluggish cloud of infinitesimal
dust, invisible and tainted. The body had apparently once lain
in the attitude of an embrace, but now the long sleep that outlasts love, that conquers even the grimace of love, had cuckolded
him: what was left of him lay beneath what was left of the
nightshirt, becoms inextricable with the bed in which he lay,
and upon him and upon the pillow beside him lay that even coating of the patient and biding dust. /p/ Then we noticed that in
the second pillow was the indentation of a head; one of us
lifted something from it, and leaning forward, that faint and
invisible dust lean and acrid in the nostrils, we saw a long
strand of iron-gray hair.

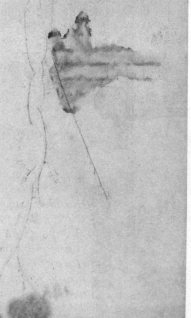

The final paragraph of the typed manuscript was reworded and made into two paragraphs
in the published version.

Topics for Critical Thinking and Writing

1. Why does the narrator begin with what is almost the end of the story—the death of Miss Emily—rather than save this information for later? What devices does Faulkner use to hold the reader's interest throughout?
2. In a paragraph, offer a conjecture about Miss Emily's attitudes toward Homer Barron after he was last seen alive.
3. In a paragraph or two, characterize Miss Emily, calling attention not only to her eccentricities or even craziness, but also to what you conjecture to be her moral values.
4. In paragraph 44 we are told that the Baptist minister "would never divulge what happened" during the interview with Miss Emily. Why do you suppose Faulkner does not narrate or describe the interview? Let's assume that in his first draft of the story he *did* give a paragraph of narration or a short dramatic scene. Write such an episode.
5. Suppose that Homer Barron's remains had been discovered before Miss Emily died, and that she was arrested and charged with murder. You are the prosecutor and you are running for a statewide political office. In 500 words, set forth your argument that—despite the fact that she is a public monument—she should be convicted. Or: You are the defense attorney, also running for office. In 500 words, set forth your defense.
6. Assume that Miss Emily kept a journal—perhaps even from her days as a young girl. Write some entries for the journal, giving her thoughts about some of the episodes reported in Faulkner's story.

ZORA NEALE HURSTON

Zora Neale Hurston (1891–1960) was brought up in Eatonville, Florida, a town said to be the first all-black self-governing town in the United States. Her mother died in 1904, and when Hurston's father remarried, Hurston felt out of place. In 1914, she joined a traveling theatrical group as a maid, hoping to save money for school. Later, by working at such jobs as manicurist and waitress, she put herself through college, entering Howard University in 1923. After receiving a scholarship, she transferred in 1926 to Barnard College in New York, where she was the first black student in the college. After graduating from Barnard in 1928 she taught drama, worked as an editor, and studied anthropology. But when grant money ran out in 1932 she returned to Eatonville to edit the folk material that she had collected during four years of fieldwork, and to do some further writing. She steadily published from 1932 to 1938—stories, folklore, and two novels—but she gained very little money. Further, although she played a large role in the Harlem Renaissance in the 1930s, she was criticized by Richard Wright and other influential black authors for portraying blacks as stereotypes and for being politically conservative. To many in the 1950s her writing seemed reactionary, almost embarrassing in an age of black protest, and she herself—working as a

domestic, a librarian, and a substitute teacher—was almost forgotten. She died in a county welfare home in Florida and is buried in an unmarked grave.

Sweat

It was eleven o'clock of a Spring night in Florida. It was Sunday. Any other night, Delia Jones would have been in bed for two hours by this time. But she was a washwoman, and Monday morning meant a great deal to her. So she collected the soiled clothes on Saturday when she returned the clean things. Sunday night after church, she sorted them and put the white things to soak. It saved her almost a half day's start. A great hamper in the bedroom held the clothes that she brought home. It was so much neater than a number of bundles lying around.

She squatted in the kitchen floor beside the great pile of clothes, sorting them into small heaps according to color, and humming a song in a mournful key, but wondering through it all where Sykes, her husband, had gone with her horse and buckboard.[1]

Just then something long, round, limp and black fell upon her shoulders and slithered to the floor beside her. A great terror took hold of her. It softened her knees and dried her mouth so that it was a full minute before she could cry out or move. Then she saw that it was the big bull whip her husband liked to carry when he drove.

She lifted her eyes to the door and saw him standing there bent over with laughter at her fright. She screamed at him.

5   "Sykes, what you throw dat whip on me like dat? You know it would skeer me—looks just like a snake, an' you knows how skeered Ah is of snakes."

"Course Ah knowed it! That's how come Ah done it." He slapped his leg with his hand and almost rolled on the ground in his mirth. "If you such a big fool dat you got to have a fit over a earth worm or a string, Ah don't keer how bad Ah skeer you."

"You aint got no business doing it. Gawd knows it's a sin. Some day Ah'm gointuh drop dead from some of yo' foolishness. 'Nother thing, where you been wid mah rig? Ah feeds dat pony. He aint fuh you to be drivin' wid no bull whip."

"Yo sho is one aggravatin' nigger woman!" he declared and stepped into the room. She resumed her work and did not answer him at once. "Ah done tole you time and again to keep them white folks' clothes outa dis house."

He picked up the whip and glared down at her. Delia went on with her work. She went out into the yard and returned with a galvanized tub and set it on the washbench. She saw that Sykes had kicked all of the clothes together again, and now stood in her way truculently, his whole manner hoping, *praying,* for an argument. But she walked calmly around him and commenced to re-sort the things.

10   "Next time, Ah'm gointer to kick 'em outdoors," he threatened as he struck a match along the leg of his corduroy breeches.

Delia never looked up from her work, and her thin, stooped shoulders sagged further.

"Ah aint for no fuss t'night Sykes. Ah just come from taking sacrament at the church house."

He snorted scornfully. "Yeah, you just come from de church house on a Sunday night, but heah you is gone to work on them clothes. You aint nothing

---

[1]**buckboard** an open wagon.

but a hypocrite. One of them amen-corner Christians—sing, whoop, shout, then come home and wash white folks clothes on the Sabbath."

He stepped roughly upon the whitest pile of things, kicking them helter-skelter as he crossed the room. His wife gave a little scream of dismay, and quickly gathered them together again.

15   "Sykes, you quit grindin' dirt into these clothes! How can Ah git through by Sat'day if Ah don't start on Sunday?"

"Ah don't keer if you never git through. Anyhow, Ah done promised Gawd and a couple of other men, Ah aint gointer have it in mah house. Don't gimme no lip neither, else Ah'll throw 'em out and put mah fist up side yo' head to boot."

Delia's habitual meekness seemed to slip from her shoulders like a blown scarf. She was on her feet; her poor little body, her bare knuckly hands bravely defying the strapping hulk before her.

"Looka heah, Sykes, you done gone too fur. Ah been married to you fur fifteen years, and Ah been takin' in washin' for fifteen years. Sweat, sweat, sweat! Work and sweat, cry and sweat, pray and sweat!"

"What's that got to do with me?" he asked brutally.

20   "What's it got to do with you, Sykes? Mah tub of suds is filled yo' belly with vittles more times than yo' hands is filled it. Mah sweat is done paid for this house and Ah reckon Ah kin keep on sweatin in it."

She seized the iron skillet from the stove and struck a defensive pose, which act surprised him greatly, coming from her. It cowed him and he did not strike her as he usually did.

"Naw you won't," she panted, "that ole snaggle-toothed black woman you runnin' with aint comin' heah to pile up on *mah* sweat and blood. You aint paid for nothin' on this place, and Ah'm gointer stay right heah till Ah'm toted out foot foremost."

"Well, you better quit gittin' me riled up, else they'll be totin' you out sooner than you expect. Ah'm so tired of you Ah don't know whut to do. Gawd! how Ah hates skinny wimmen!"

A little awed by this new Delia, he sidled out of the door and slammed the back gate after him. He did not say where he had gone, but she knew too well. She knew very well that he would not return until nearly daybreak also. Her work over, she went on to bed but not to sleep at once. Things had come to a pretty pass!

25   She lay awake, gazing upon the debris that cluttered their matrimonial trail. Not an image left standing along the way. Anything like flowers had long ago been drowned in the salty stream that had been pressed from her heart. Her tears, her sweat, her blood. She had brought love to the union and he had brought a longing for the flesh. Two months after the wedding, he had given her the first brutal beating. She had the memory of numerous trips to Orlando with all of his wages when he had returned to her penniless, even before the first year had passed. She was young and soft then, but now she thought of her knotty, muscled limbs, her harsh knuckly hands, and drew herself up into an unhappy little ball in the middle of the big feather bed. Too late now to hope for love, even if it were not Bertha it would be someone else. This case differed from the others only in that she was bolder than the others. Too late for everything except her little home. She had built it for her old days, and planted one by one the trees and flowers there. It was lovely to her, lovely.

Somehow before sleep came, she found herself saying aloud: "Oh well, whatever goes over the Devil's back, is got to come under his belly. Sometime or ruther, Sykes, like everybody else, is gointer reap his sowing." After that she was able to build a spiritual earthworks against her husband. His shells could no longer reach her. *Amen*. She went to sleep and slept until he announced his presence in bed by kicking her feet and rudely snatching the cover away.

"Gimme some kivah heah, an' git yo' damn foots over on yo' own side! Ah oughter mash you in yo' mouf fuh drawing dat skillet on me."

Delia went clear to the rail without answering him. A triumphant indifference to all that he was or did.

The week was as full of work for Delia as all other weeks, and Saturday found her behind her little pony, collecting and delivering clothes.

30   It was a hot, hot day near the end of July. The village men on Joe Clarke's porch even chewed cane listlessly. They did not hurl the cane-knots as usual. They let them dribble over the edge of the porch. Even conversation had collapsed under the heat.

"Heah comes Delia Jones," Jim Merchant said, as the shaggy pony came round the bend of the road toward them. The rusty buckboard was heaped with baskets of crisp, clean laundry.

"Yep," Joe Lindsay agreed, "Hot or col', rain or shine, jes ez reg'lar ez de weeks roll roun' Delia carries 'em an' fetches 'em on Sat'day."

"She better if she wanter eat," said Moss. "Syke Jones aint wuth de shot an' powder hit would tek tuh kill 'em. Not to *bub* he aint."

"He sho' aint," Walter Thomas chimed in. "It's too bad, too, cause she wuz a right pritty lil trick when he got huh. Ah'd uh mah'ied huh mahseft' it' he hadnter beat me to it."

35   Delia nodded briefly at the men as she drove past.

"Too much knockin will ruin *any* 'oman. He done beat huh nough tuh kill three women. let 'lone change they looks," said Elijah Mosely. "How Syke kin stommuck dat big black greasy Mogu[2] he's layin' roun' wid, gits me. Ah swear dat eight-rock couldn't kiss a sardine can Ah done thowed out de back do' 'way las' yeah."

"Aw, she's fat, thass how come. He's allus been crazy 'bout fat women," put in Merchant. "He'd a' been tied up wid one long time ago if he could a' found one tuh have him. Did Ah tell yuh 'bout him come sidlin' roun *mah* 'wife—bringin' her a basket uh pec-cans outa his yard fuh a present? Yes-sir, mah wife! She tol' him tuh take 'em right straight back home, cause Delia works so hard ovah dat washtub she reckon everything en de place taste lak sweat an' soap-suds. Ah jus' wisht Ah'd a' caught 'im 'roun' dere! Ah'd a' made his hips ketch on fiah down dat shell road."

"Ah know he done it, too. Ah sees 'im grinnin' at every 'oman dat passes," Walter Thomas said. "But even so, he useter eat some mighty big hunks uh humble pie tuh git dat lil' 'oman he got. She wuz ez pritty ez a speckled pup! Dat wuz fifteen yeahs ago. He useter be so skeered uh losin' huh, she could make him do some parts of a husband's duty. Dey never wuz de same in de mind."

"There oughter be a law about him," said Lindsay. "He aint fit tuh carry guts tuh a bear."

40   Clarke spoke for the first time. "Taint no law on earth dat kin make a man be decent if it aint in 'im. There's plenty men dat takes a wife lak dey do a joint uh sugar-cane. It's round, juicy an' sweet when dey gits it. But dey squeeze an' grind, squeeze an' grind an' wring tell dey wring every drop uh pleasure dat's in 'em out. When dey's satisfied dat dey is wring dry, dey treats 'em jes lak dey do a cane-chew. Dey thows 'em away. Dey knows whut dey is doin' while dey is at it,

---

[2]**Mogu** big person.

an' hates theirselves fuh it but they keeps on hangin' after huh tell she's empty. Den dey hates huh fuh bein' a cane-chew an' in de way."

"We oughter take Syke an' dat stray 'oman uh his'n down in Lake Howell swamp an' lay on de rawhide till they cain't say 'Lawd a' mussy.' He allus wuz uh ovahbearin' niggah, but since dat white 'oman from up north done teached 'im how to run a automobile, he done got too biggety to live—an' we oughter kill 'im," Old Man Anderson advised.

A grunt of approval went around the porch. But the heat was melting their civic virtue and Elijah Moseley began to bait Joe Clarke.

"Come on, Joe, git a melon outa dere an' slice it up for yo' customers. We'se all sufferin' wid de heat. De bear's done got *me!*"

"Thass right. Joe, a watermelon is jes' whut Ah needs tuh cure de eppizudicks."[3] Walter Thomas joined forces with Moseley. "Come on dere, Joe. We all is steady customers an' you aint set us up in a long time. Ah chooses dat long, bow-legged Floridy favorite."

45   "A god, an' be dough. You all gimme twenty cents and slice away," Clarke retorted. "Ah needs a col' slice m'self. Heah, everybody chip in. Ah'll lend y'll mah meat knife."

The money was quickly subscribed and the huge melon brought forth. At that moment, Sykes and Bertha arrived. A determined silence fell on the porch and the melon was put away again.

Merchant snapped down the blade of his jackknife and moved toward the store door.

"Come on in, Joe, an' gimme a slab uh sow belly an' uh pound uh coffee—almost fuhgot 'twas Sat'day. Got to git on home." Most of the men left also.

Just then Delia drove past on her way home, as Sykes was ordering magnificently for Bertha. It pleased him for Delia to see.

50   "Git whutsoever yo' heart desires, Honey. Wait a minute, Joe. Give huh two bottles uh strawberry soda-water, uh quart uh parched groundpeas, an' a block uh chewin' gum."

With all this they left the store, with Sykes reminding Bertha that this was his town and she could have it if she wanted it.

The men returned soon after they left, and held their watermelon feast. "Where did Syke Jones git dat 'oman from nohow?" Lindsay asked.

"Ovah Apopka. Guess dey musta been cleanin' out de town when she lef. She don't look lak a thing but a hunk uh liver wid hair on it."

"Well, she sho' kin squall," Dave Carter contributed. "When she gits ready tuh laff, she jes' opens huh mouf an' latches it back tuh de las' notch. No ole grandpa alligator down in Lake Bell aint got nothin' on huh."

55   Bertha had been in town three months now. Sykes was still paying her room rent at Della Lewis'—the only house in town that would have taken her in. Sykes took her frequently to Winter Park to "stomps."[4] He still assured her that he was the swellest man in the state.

"Sho' you kin have dat lil' ole house soon's Ah kin git dat 'oman outa dere. Everything b'longs tuh me an' you sho' kin have it. Ah sho' 'bominates uh skinny 'oman. Lawdy, you sho' is got one portly shape on you! You kin git *anything* you wants. Dis is *mah* town an' you sho' kin have it.

---

[3]**eppizudicks** i.e., epizootic, an epidemic among animals.   [4]**stomps** dances.

Delia's work-worn knees crawled over the earth in Gethsemane and on the rocks of Calvary[5] many, many times during these months. She avoided the villagers and meeting places in her effort to be blind and deaf. But Bertha nullified this to a degree, by coming to Delia's house to call Sykes out to her at the gate.

Delia and Sykes fought all the time now with no peaceful interludes. They slept and ate in silence. Two or three times Delia had attempted a timid friendliness, but she was repulsed each time. It was plain that the breaches must remain agape.

The sun had burned July to August. The heat streamed down like a million hot arrows, smiting all things living upon the earth. Grass withered, leaves browned, snakes went blind in shedding and men and dogs went mad. Dog days!

60   Delia came home one day and found Sykes there before her. She wondered, but started to go on into the house without speaking, even though he was standing in the kitchen door and she must either stoop under his arm or ask him to move. He made no room for her. She noticed a soap box beside the steps, but paid no particular attention to it, knowing that he must have brought it there. As she was stooping to pass under his outstretched arm, he suddenly pushed her backward, laughingly.

"Look in de box dere Delia. Ah done brung yuh somethin'!"

She nearly fell upon the box in her stumbling, and when she saw what it held, she all but fainted outright.

"Syke! Syke, mah Gawd! You take dat rattlesnake 'way from heah! You *gottuh*. Oh, Jesus, have mussy!"

"Ah aint gut tuh do nuthin' uh de kin'—fact is Ah aint got tuh do nothin' but die. Taint no use uh you puttin' on airs makin' out lak you sceered uh dat snake—he's gointer stay right heah tell he die. He wouldn't bite me cause Ah knows how tuh handle 'im. Nohow he wouldn't risk breakin' out his fangs 'gin *yo'* skinny laigs."

65   "Naw, now Syke, don't keep dat thing 'roun' heah tuh skeer me tuh death. You knows Ah'm even feared uh earth worms. Thass de biggest snake Ah evah did see. Kill 'im Syke, please."

"Doan ast me tuh do nothin 'fuh yuh. Goin' 'roun' tryin' to be so damn asterperious. Naw, Ah aint gonna kill it. Ah think uh damn sight mo' uh him dan you! Dat's a nice snake an' anybody doan lak 'im kin jes' hit de grit."

The village soon heard that Sykes had the snake, and came to see and ask questions.

"How de hen-fire did you ketch dat six-foot rattler, Syke?" Thomas asked.

"He's full uh frogs so he caint hardly move, thass how Ah eased up on 'm. But Ah'm a snake charmer an' knows how tuh handle 'em. Shux, dat aint nothin'. Ah could ketch one eve'y day if Ah so wanted tuh."

70   "Whut he needs is a heavy hick'ry club leaned real heavy on his head. Dat's de bes 'way tuh charm a rattlesnake."

"Naw, Walt, y'll jes' don't understand dese diamon' backs lak Ah do," said Sykes in a superior tone of voice.

The village agreed with Walter, but the snake stayed on. His box remained by the kitchen door with its screen wire covering. Two or three days later it had digested its meal of frogs and literally came to life. It rattled at every movement in

---

[5]**Gethsemane** was the garden where Jesus prayed just before he was betrayed (Matthew 26.36–47); **Calvary** was the hill where he was crucified.

the kitchen or the yard. One day as Delia came down the kitchen steps she saw his chalky-white fangs curved like scimitars hung in the wire meshes. This time she did not run away with averted eyes as usual. She stood for a long time in the doorway in a red fury that grew bloodier for every second that she regarded the creature that was her torment.

That night she broached the subject as soon as Sykes sat down to the table.

"Syke, Ah wants you tuh take dat snake 'way fum heah. You done starved me an' Ah put up widcher, you done beat me an Ah took dat, but you done kilt all mah insides bringin' dat varmint heah."

75   Sykes poured out a saucer full of coffee and drank it deliberately before he answered her.

"A whole lot Ah keer 'bout how you feels inside uh out. Dat snake aint goin' no damn wheah till Ah gits ready fuh 'im tuh go. So fur as beatin' is concerned, yuh aint took near all dat you gointer take ef yuh stay 'roun' me."

Delia pushed back her plate and got up from the table. "Ah hates you, Sykes," she said calmly. "Ah hates you tuh de same degree dat Ah useter love yuh. Ah done took an' took till mah belly is full up tuh mah neck. Dat's de reason Ah got mah letter fum de church an' moved mah membership tuh Woodbridge—so Ah don't haftuh take no sacrament wid yuh. Ah don't wantuh see yuh, 'roun' me atall. Lay 'roun' wid dat 'oman all yuh wants tuh, but gwan 'way fum me an' mah house. Ah hates yuh lak uh suck-egg dog."

Sykes almost let the huge wad of corn bread and collard greens he was chewing fall out of his mouth in amazement. He had a hard time whipping himself to the proper fury to try to answer Delia.

"Well, Ah'm glad you does hate me. Ah'm sho' tiahed uh you hangin' ontuh me. Ah don't want yuh. Look at yuh stringey ole neck! Yo' raw-bony laigs an' arms is enough tuh cut uh man tuh death. You looks jes' lak de devvul's doll-baby tuh *me*. You cain't hate me no worse dan Ah hates you. Ah been hatin' *you* fuh years."

80   "Yo' ole black hide don't look lak nothin' tuh me, but uh passle uh wrinkled up rubber, wid yo' big ole yeahs flappin' on each side lak uh paih uh buzzard wings. Don't think Ah'm gointuh be run 'way fum mah house neither. Ah'm goin' tuh de white folks about *you,* mah young man, de very nex' time you lay yo' han's on me. Mah cup is done run ovah." Delia said this with no signs of fear and Sykes departed from the house, threatening her, but made not the slightest move to carry out any of them.

That night he did not return at all, and the next day being Sunday, Delia was glad that she did not have to quarrel before she hitched up her pony and drove the four miles to Woodbridge.

She stayed to the night service—"love feast"—which was very warm and full of spirit. In the emotional winds her domestic trials were borne far and wide so that she sang as she drove homeward.

"Jurden water,[6] black an' col'
Chills de body, not de soul
An' Ah wantah cross Jurden in uh calm time."
She came from the barn to the kitchen door and stopped.

"Whut's de mattah, ol' satan, you aint kickin' up yo' racket?" She addressed the snake's box. Complete silence. She went on into the house with a new hope

---

[6]**Jurden** the River Jordan, which the Israelites had to cross in order to reach the Promised Land.

in its birth struggles. Perhaps her threat to go to the white folks had frightened Sykes! Perhaps he was sorry! Fifteen years of misery and suppression had brought Delia to the place where she would hope *anything* that looked towards a way over or through her wall of inhibitions.

85   She felt in the match safe behind the stove at once for a match. There was only one there.

"Dat niggah wouldn't fetch nothin heah tuh save his rotten neck, but he kin run thew whut Ah brings quick enough. Now he done toted off nigh on tuh haff uh box uh matches. He done had dat 'oman heah in mah house, too."

Nobody but a woman could tell how she knew this even before she struck the match. But she did and it put her into a new fury.

Presently she brought in the tubs to put the white things to soak. This time she decided she need not bring the hamper out of the bedroom; she would go in there and do the sorting. She picked up the pot-bellied lamp and went in. The room was small and the hamper stood hard by the foot of the white iron bed. She could sit and reach through the bedposts—resting as she worked.

"Ah wantah cross Jurden in uh calm time." She was singing again. The mood of the "love feast" had returned. She threw back the lid of the basket almost gaily. Then, moved by both horror and terror, she sprang back toward the door. *There lay the snake in the basket!* He moved sluggishly at first, but even as she turned round and round, jumped up and down in an insanity of fear, he began to stir vigorously. She saw him pouring his awful beauty from the basket upon the bed, then she seized the lamp and ran as fast as she could to the kitchen. The wind from the open door blew out the light and the darkness added to her terror. She sped to the darkness of the yard, slamming the door after her before she thought to set down the lamp. She did not feel safe even on the ground, so she climbed up in the hay barn.

90   There for an hour or more she lay sprawled upon the hay a gibbering wreck.

Finally she grew quiet, and after that, coherent thought. With this, stalked through her a cold, bloody rage. Hours of this. A period of introspection, a space of retrospection, then a mixture of both. Out of this an awful calm.

"Well, Ah done de bes' Ah could. If things aint right, Gawd knows taint mah fault."

She went to sleep—a twitchy sleep—and woke up to a faint gray sky. There was a loud hollow sound below. She peered out. Sykes was at the wood-pile, demolishing a wire-covered box.

He hurried to the kitchen door, but hung outside there some minutes before he entered, and stood some minutes more inside before he closed it after him.

95   The gray in the sky was spreading. Delia descended without fear now, and crouched beneath the low bedroom window. The drawn shade shut out the dawn, shut in the night. But the thin walls held back no sound.

"Dat ol' scratch is woke up now!" She mused at the tremendous whirr inside, which every woodsman knows, is one of the sound illusions. The rattler is a ventriloquist. His whirr sounds to the right, to the left, straight ahead, behind, close under foot—everywhere but where it is. Woe to him who guesses wrong unless he is prepared to hold up his end of the argument! Sometimes he strikes without rattling at all.

Inside, Sykes heard nothing until he knocked a pot lid off the stove while trying to reach the match safe in the dark. He had emptied his pockets at Bertha's.

The snake seemed to wake up under the stove and Sykes made a quick leap into the bedroom. In spite of the gin he had had, his head was clearing now.

"Mah Gawd!" he chattered. "Ef Ah could only strack uh light!"

100   The rattling ceased for a moment as he stood paralyzed. He waited. It seemed that the snake waited also.

"Oh, fuh de light! Ah thought he'd be too sick"—Sykes was muttering to himself when the whirr began again, closer, right underfoot this time. Long before this, Sykes' ability to think had been flattened down to primitive instinct and he leaped—onto the bed.

Outside Delia heard a cry that might have come from a maddened chimpanzee, a stricken gorilla. All the terror, all the horror, all the rage that man possibly could express, without a recognizable human sound.

A tremendous stir inside there, another series of animal screams, the intermittent whirr of the reptile. The shade torn violently down from the window, letting in the red dawn, a huge brown hand seizing the window stick, great dull blows upon the wooden floor punctuating the gibberish of sound long after the rattle of the snake had abruptly subsided. All this Delia could see and hear from her place beneath the window, and it made her ill. She crept over to the four-o'clocks[7] and stretched herself on the cool earth to recover.

She lay there. "Delia, Delia!" She could hear Sykes calling in a most despairing tone as one who expected no answer. The sun crept on up, and he called. Delia could not move—her legs were gone flabby. She never moved, he called, and the sun kept rising.

105   "Mah Gawd!" She heard him moan. "Mah Gawd fum Heben!" She heard him stumbling about and got up from her flower-bed. The sun was growing warm. As she approached the door she heard him call out hopefully. "Delia, is dat you Ah heah?"

She saw him on his hands and knees as soon as she reached the door. He crept an inch or two toward her—all that he was able, and she saw his horribly swollen neck and his one open eye shining with hope. A surge of pity too strong to support bore her away from that eye that must, could not, fail to see the tubs. He would see the lamp. Orlando with its doctors was too far. She could scarcely reach the Chinaberry tree, where she waited in the growing heat while inside she knew the cold river was creeping up and up to extinguish that eye which must know by now that she knew.

[1926]

---

[7]**four-o'clocks** flowers that open in the late afternoon.

Topics for Critical Thinking and Writing

1. Summarize the relationship of Delia and Sykes before the time of the story.
2. How do the men on Joe Clark's porch further your understanding of Delia and Sykes and of the relationship between the two?
3. To what extent is Delia responsible for Sykes's death? To what extent is Sykes responsible? Do you think that Delia's action (or inaction) at the end of the story is immoral? Why, or why not?
4. To what extent does the relationship between African Americans and whites play a role in the lives of the characters in "Sweat" and in the outcome of the story?

5. Are the African Americans in "Sweat" portrayed stereotypically, as some of Hurston's critics charged? (See the biographical note, page 712.) How, on the evidence available in this story, might Hurston's fiction be defended from that charge?

BEL KAUFMAN

Bel Kaufman, born in Berlin, Germany, came to the United States in her early years. She holds a bachelor's degree from Hunter College and a master's degree from Columbia University, and she has served as adjunct professor at the City University of New York.

In 1965 Kaufman won national fame with Up the Down Staircase, *a work of fiction that was later made into a popular film. She is also the author of another novel,* Love *(1979), and of essays and prize-winning short stories.*

Sunday in the Park

It was still warm in the late-afternoon sun, and the city noises came muffled through the trees in the park. She put her book down on the bench, removed her sunglasses, and sighed contentedly. Morton was reading the *Times Magazine* section, one arm flung around her shoulder; their three-year-old son, Larry, was playing in the sandbox: a faint breeze fanned her hair softly against her cheek. It was five-thirty of a Sunday afternoon, and the small playground, tucked away in a corner of the park, was all but deserted. The swings and seesaws stood motionless and abandoned, the slides were empty, and only in the sandbox two little boys squatted diligently side by side. *How good this is,* she thought, and almost smiled at her sense of well-being. They must go out in the sun more often; Morton was so city-pale, cooped up all week inside the gray factorylike university. She squeezed his arm affectionately and glanced at Larry, delighting in the pointed little face frowning in concentration over the tunnel he was digging. The other boy suddenly stood up and with a quick, deliberate swing of his chubby arm threw a spadeful of sand at Larry. It just missed his head. Larry continued digging; the boy remained standing, shovel raised, stolid and impassive.

"No, no, little boy." She shook her finger at him, her eyes searching for the child's mother or nurse. "We mustn't throw sand. It may get in someone's eyes and hurt. We must play nicely in the nice sandbox." The boy looked at her in unblinking expectancy. He was about Larry's age but perhaps ten pounds heavier, a husky little boy with none of Larry's quickness and sensitivity in his face. Where was his mother? The only other people left in the playground were two women and a little girl on roller skates leaving now through the gate, and a man on a bench a few feet away. He was a big man, and he seemed to be taking up the whole bench as he held the Sunday comics close to his face. She supposed he was the child's father. He did not look up from his comics, but spat once deftly out of the corner of his mouth. She turned her eyes away.

At that moment, as swiftly as before, the fat little boy threw another spadeful of sand at Larry. This time some of it landed on his hair and forehead. Larry looked up at his mother, his mouth tentative; her expression would tell him whether to cry or not.

Her first instinct was to rush to her son, brush the sand out of his hair, and punish the other child, but she controlled it. She always said that she wanted Larry to learn to fight his own battles.

5   "Don't *do* that, little boy," she said sharply, leaning forward on the bench. "You mustn't throw sand!"

The man on the bench moved his mouth as if to spit again, but instead he spoke. He did not look at her, but at the boy only.

"You go right ahead, Joe," he said loudly. "Throw all you want. This here is a *public* sandbox."

She felt a sudden weakness in her knees as she glanced at Morton. He had become aware of what was happening. He put his *Times* down carefully on his lap and turned his fine, lean face toward the man, smiling the shy, apologetic smile he might have offered a student in pointing out an error in his thinking. When he spoke to the man, it was with his usual reasonableness.

"You're quite right," he said pleasantly, "but just because this is a public place. . . ."

10   The man lowered his funnies and looked at Morton. He looked at him from head to foot, slowly and deliberately. "Yeah?" His insolent voice was edged with menace. "My kid's got just as good right here as yours, and if he feels like throwing sand, he'll throw it, and if you don't like it, you can take your kid the hell out of here."

The children were listening, their eyes and mouths wide open, their spades forgotten in small fists. She noticed the muscle in Morton's jaw tighten. He was rarely angry; he seldom lost his temper. She was suffused with a tenderness for her husband and an impotent rage against the man for involving him in a situation so alien and so distasteful to him.

"Now, just a minute," Morton said courteously, "you must realize. . . ."

"Aw, shut up," said the man.

Her heart began to pound. Morton half rose; the *Times* slid to the ground. Slowly the other man stood up. He took a couple of steps toward Morton, then stopped. He flexed his great arms, waiting. She pressed her trembling knees together. Would there be violence, fighting? How dreadful, how incredible. . . . She must do something, stop them, call for help. She wanted to put her hand on her husband's sleeve, to pull him down, but for some reason she didn't.

15   Morton adjusted his glasses. He was very pale. "This is ridiculous," he said unevenly. "I must ask you. . . ."

"Oh, yeah?" said the man. He stood with his legs spread apart, rocking a little, looking at Morton with utter scorn. "You and who else?"

For a moment the two men looked at each other nakedly. Then Morton turned his back on the man and said quietly, "Come on, let's get out of here." He walked awkwardly, almost limping with self-consciousness, to the sandbox. He stooped and lifted Larry and his shovel out.

At once Larry came to life; his face lost its rapt expression and he began to kick and cry. "I don't *want* to go home, I want to play better, I don't *want* any supper, I don't *like* supper. . . ." It became a chant as they walked, pulling their child between them, his feet dragging on the ground. In order to get to the exit gate they had to pass the bench where the man sat sprawling again. She was careful not to look at him. With all the dignity she could summon, she pulled Larry's sandy, perspiring little hand, while Morton pulled the other. Slowly and with head high she walked with her husband and child out of the playground.

Her first feeling was one of relief that a fight had been avoided, that no one was hurt. Yet beneath it there was a layer of something else, something heavy and inescapable. She sensed that it was more than just an unpleasant incident, more than defeat of reason by force. She felt dimly it had something to do with her and Morton, something acutely personal, familiar, and important.

20   Suddenly Morton spoke. "It wouldn't have proved anything."

"What?" she asked.

"A fight. It wouldn't have proved anything beyond the fact that he's bigger than I am."

"Of course," she said.

"The only possible outcome," he continued reasonably, "would have been—what? My glasses broken, perhaps a tooth or two replaced, a couple of days' work missed—and for what? For justice? For truth?"

25   "Of course," she repeated. She quickened her step. She wanted only to get home and to busy herself with her familiar tasks; perhaps then the feeling, glued like heavy plaster on her heart, would be gone. *Of all the stupid, despicable bullies,* she thought, pulling harder on Larry's hand. The child was still crying. Always before she had felt a tender pity for his defenseless little body, the frail arms, the narrow shoulders with sharp, winglike shoulder blades, the thin and unsure legs, but now her mouth tightened in resentment.

"Stop crying," she said sharply. "I'm ashamed of you!" She felt as if all three of them were tracking mud along the street. The child cried louder.

If there had been an issue involved, she thought, *if there had been something to fight for. . . . But what else could he possibly have done? Allow himself to be beaten? Attempt to educate the man? Call a policeman? "Officer, there's a man in the park who won't stop his child from throwing sand on mine. . . ."* The whole thing was as silly as that, and not worth thinking about.

"Can't you keep him quiet, for Pete's sake?" Morton asked irritably.

"What do you suppose I've been trying to do?" she said.

30   Larry pulled back, dragging his feet.

"If you can't discipline this child, I will," Morton snapped, making a move toward the boy.

But her voice stopped him. She was shocked to hear it, thin and cold and penetrating with contempt. "Indeed?" she heard herself say. "You and who else?"

[1985]

Topics for Critical Thinking and Writing

1. When you first saw the title of this story, did it arouse any particular expectations? If so, of what sort?

2. Reread the first paragraph, in order to remind yourself of the way in which Bel Kaufman introduces the characters to the reader. How (after reading the first paragraph) did you feel about the woman and Morton?

3. What is the woman's attitude toward her husband at the end of the story? Is it appropriate? At the end of the story, what is your attitude toward Morton? Toward the woman? How do you account for these attitudes? Do you judge either character morally?

Case Study: Writing about Raymond Carver

RAYMOND CARVER

Raymond Carver (1938–1988) was born in Clatskanie, a logging town in Oregon. In 1963 he graduated from Humboldt State College in northern California and then did further study at the University of Iowa.

His early years were not easy—he married while still in college, divorced a little later, and sometimes suffered from alcoholism. In his last years he found domestic happiness, but he died of cancer at the age of fifty.

As a young man he wrote poetry while working at odd jobs (janitor, deliveryman, etc.); later he turned to fiction, though he continued to write poetry. Most of Carver's fiction narrates, in a spare, understated style, stories about bewildered and sometimes exhausted men and women.

This case study consists of the following material:

1. Two versions of a very short story, originally called "Mine" (1977). In 1981 Carver published a revised version, with a new title, "Popular Mechanics" (1981), and in 1986 he published the same revised version but under yet another title, "Little Things"
2. Two longer stories, "What We Talk about When We Talk about Love" and "Cathedral"
3. Two pieces by Carver on the art of writing—the first an interview, the second an essay about revising
4. A parody of a Carver story

Mine

During the day the sun had come out and the snow melted into dirty water. Streaks of water ran down from the little, shoulder-high window that faced the back yard. Cars slushed by on the street outside. It was getting dark, outside and inside.

He was in the bedroom pushing clothes into a suitcase when she came to the door.

I'm glad you're leaving. I'm glad you're leaving! she said. Do you hear?

He kept on putting his things into the suitcase and didn't look up.

5   Sonofabitch! I'm so glad you're leaving! She began to cry. You can't even look me in the face, can you?

Little Things

Early that day the weather turned and the snow was melting into dirty water. Streaks of it ran down from the little shoulder-high window that faced the backyard. Cars slushed by on the street outside, where it was getting dark. But it was getting dark on the inside too.

He was in the bedroom pushing clothes into a suitcase when she came to the door.

I'm glad you're leaving! I'm glad you're leaving! she said. Do you hear?

He kept on putting his things into the suitcase.

5   Son of a bitch! I'm so glad you're leaving! She began to cry. You can't even look me in the face, can you?

Then she noticed the baby's picture on the bed and picked it up.

He looked at her and she wiped her eyes and stared at him before turning and going back to the living room.

Bring that back.

Just get your things and get out, she said.

He did not answer. He fastened the suitcase, put on his coat, and looked at the bedroom before turning off the light. Then he went out to the living room. She stood in the doorway of the little kitchen, holding the baby.

10   I want the baby, he said.

Are you crazy?

No, but I want the baby. I'll get someone to come by for his things.

You can go to hell! You're not touching this baby.

The baby had begun to cry and she uncovered the blanket from around its head.

15   Oh, oh, she said, looking at the baby.

He moved towards her.

For God's sake! she said. She took a step back into the kitchen.

I want the baby.

Get out of here!

20   She turned and tried to hold the baby over in a corner behind the stove as he came up.

He reached across the stove and tightened his hands on the baby.

Let go of him, he said.

Get away, get away! she cried.

The baby was red-faced and screaming. In the scuffle they knocked down a little flower pot that hung behind the stove.

25   He crowded her into the wall then, trying to break her grip, holding onto the baby and pushing his weight against her arm.

Let go of him, he said.

Don't, she said, you're hurting him!

He didn't talk again. The kitchen window gave no light. In the near dark he worked on her fisted fingers

Then she noticed the baby's picture on the bed and picked it up.

He looked at her and she wiped her eyes and stared at him before turning and going back to the living room.

Bring that back, he said.

Just get your things and get out, she said.

10   He did not answer. He fastened the suitcase, put on his coat, looked around the bedroom before turning off the light. Then he went out to the living room.

She stood in the doorway of the little kitchen, holding the baby.

I want the baby, he said.

Are you crazy?

No, but I want the baby. I'll get someone to come by for his things.

15   You're not touching this baby, she said.

The baby had begun to cry and she uncovered the blanket from around his head.

Oh, oh, she said, looking at the baby.

He moved toward her.

For God's sake! she said. She took a step back into the kitchen.

20   I want the baby.

Get out of here!

She turned and tried to hold the baby over in a corner behind the stove.

But he came up. He reached across the stove and tightened his hands on the baby.

Let go of him, he said.

25   Get away, get away! she cried.

The baby was red-faced and screaming. In the scuffle they knocked down a flowerpot that hung behind the stove.

He crowded her into the wall then, trying to break her grip. He held on to the baby and pushed with all his weight.

Let go of him, he said.

Don't, she said. You're hurting the baby, she said.

with one hand and with the other 30 hand he gripped the screaming baby up under an arm near the shoulder.

She felt her fingers being forced open and the baby going from her. No, she said, just as her hands came loose. She would have it, this baby whose chubby face gazed up at them from the picture on the table. She grabbed for the baby's other arm. She caught the baby around the wrist and leaned back.

30   He would not give. He felt the baby going out of his hands and he pulled back hard. He pulled back very hard.

In this manner they decided the issue.

[1977]

I'm not hurting the baby, he said.

The kitchen window gave no light. In the near-dark he worked on her fisted fingers with one hand and with the other hand he gripped the screaming baby up under an arm near the shoulder.

She felt her fingers being forced open. She felt the baby going from her.

No! she screamed just as her hands came loose.

She would have it, this baby. She grabbed for the baby's other arm. She caught the baby around the wrist and leaned back.

35   But he would not let go. He felt the baby slipping out of his hands and he pulled back very hard.

In this manner, the issue was decided.

[1981]

What We Talk about When We Talk about Love

My friend Mel McGinnis was talking. Mel McGinnis is a cardiologist, and sometimes that gives him the right.

The four of us were sitting around his kitchen table drinking gin. Sunlight filled the kitchen from the big window behind the sink. There were Mel and me and his second wife, Teresa—Terri, we called her—and my wife, Laura. We lived in Albuquerque then. But we were all from somewhere else.

There was an ice bucket on the table. The gin and the tonic water kept going around, and we somehow got on the subject of love. Mel thought real love was nothing less than spiritual love. He said he'd spent five years in a seminary before quitting to go to medical school. He said he still looked back on those years in the seminary as the most important years in his life.

Terri said the man she lived with before she lived with Mel loved her so much he tried to kill her. Then Terri said, "He beat me up one night. He dragged me around the living room by my ankles. He kept saying, 'I love you, I love you, you bitch.' He went on dragging me around the living room. My head kept knocking on things." Terri looked around the table. "What do you do with love like that?"

5   She was a bone-thin woman with a pretty face, dark eyes, and brown hair that hung down her back. She liked necklaces made of turquoise, and long pendant earrings.

"My God, don't be silly. That's not love, and you know it," Mel said. "I don't know what you'd call it, but I sure know you wouldn't call it love."

"Say what you want to, but I know it was," Terri said. "It may sound crazy to you, but it's true just the same. People are different, Mel. Sure, sometimes he may have acted crazy. Okay. But he loved me. In his own way maybe, but he loved me. There was love there, Mel. Don't say there wasn't."

Mel let out his breath. He held his glass and turned to Laura and me. "The man threatened to kill me," Mel said. He finished his drink and reached for the gin bottle. "Terri's a romantic. Terri's of the kick-me-so-I'll-know-you-love-me school. Terri, hon, don't look that way." Mel reached across the table and touched Terri's cheek with his fingers. He grinned at her.

"Now he wants to make up," Terri said.

10   "Make up what?" Mel said. "What is there to make up? I know what I know. That's all."

"How'd we get started on this subject, anyway?" Terri said. She raised her glass and drank from it. "Mel always has love on his mind," she said. "Don't you, honey?" She smiled, and I thought that was the last of it.

"I just wouldn't call Ed's behavior love. That's all I'm saying, honey," Mel said. "What about you guys?" Mel said to Laura and me. "Does that sound like love to you?"

"I'm the wrong person to ask," I said. "I didn't even know the man. I've only heard his name mentioned in passing. I wouldn't know. You'd have to know the particulars. But I think what you're saying is that love is an absolute."

Mel said, "The kind of love I'm talking about is. The kind of love I'm talking about, you don't try to kill people."

15   Laura said, "I don't know anything about Ed, or anything about the situation. But who can judge anyone else's situation?"

I touched the back of Laura's hand. She gave me a quick smile. I picked up Laura's hand. It was warm, the nails polished, perfectly manicured. I encircled the broad wrist with my fingers, and I held her.

"When I left, he drank rat poison," Terri said. She clasped her arms with her hands. "They took him to the hospital in Sante Fe. That's where we lived then, about ten miles out. They saved his life. But his gums went crazy from it. I mean they pulled away from his teeth. After that, his teeth stood out like fangs. My God," Terri said. She waited a minute, then let go of her arms and picked up her glass.

"What people won't do!" Laura said.

"He's out of the action now," Mel said. "He's dead."

20   Mel handed me the saucer of limes. I took a section, squeezed it over my drink, and stirred the ice cubes with my finger.

"It gets worse," Terri said. "He shot himself in the mouth. But he bungled that too. Poor Ed," she said. Terri shook her head.

"Poor Ed nothing," Mel said. "He was dangerous."

Mel was forty-five years old. He was tall and rangy with curly soft hair. His face and arms were brown from the tennis he played. When he was sober, his gestures, all his movements, were precise, very careful.

"He did love me though, Mel. Grant me that," Terri said. "That's all I'm asking. He didn't love me the way you love me. I'm not saying that. But he loved me. You can grant me that, can't you?"

25   "What do you mean, he bungled it?" I said.

Laura leaned forward with her glass. She put her elbows on the table and held her glass in both hands. She glanced from Mel to Terri and waited with a look of bewilderment on her open face, as if amazed that such things happened to people you were friendly with.

"How'd he bungle it when he killed himself?" I said.

"I'll tell you what happened," Mel said. "He took this twenty-two pistol he'd bought to threaten Terri and me with. Oh, I'm serious, the man was always threatening. You should have seen the way we lived in those days. Like fugitives. I even bought a gun myself. Can you believe it? A guy like me? But I did. I bought one for self-defense and carried it in the glove compartment. Sometimes I'd have to leave the apartment in the middle of the night. To go to the hospital, you know? Terri and I weren't married then, and my first wife had the house and kids, the dog, everything, and Terri and I were living in this apartment here. Sometimes, as I say, I'd get a call in the middle of the night and have to go in to the hospital at two or three in the morning. It'd be dark out there in the parking lot, and I'd break into a sweat before I could even get to my car. I never knew if he was going to come up out of the shrubbery or from behind a car and start shooting. I mean, the man was crazy. He was capable of wiring a bomb, anything. He used to call my service at all hours and say he needed to talk to the doctor, and when I'd return the call, he'd say, 'Son of a bitch, your days are numbered.' Little things like that. It was scary, I'm telling you."

"I still feel sorry for him," Terri said.

30 "It sounds like a nightmare," Laura said. "But what exactly happened after he shot himself?"

Laura is a legal secretary. We'd met in a professional capacity. Before we knew it, it was a courtship. She's thirty-five, three years younger than I am. In addition to being in love, we like each other and enjoy one another's company. She's easy to be with.

"What happened?" Laura said.

Mel said, "He shot himself in the mouth in his room. Someone heard the shot and told the manager. They came in with a passkey, saw what had happened, and called an ambulance. I happened to be there when they brought him in, alive but past recall. The man lived for three days. His head swelled up to twice the size of a normal head. I'd never seen anything like it, and I hope I never do again. Terri wanted to go in and sit with him when she found out about it. We had a fight over it. I didn't think she should see him like that. I didn't think she should see him, and I still don't."

"Who won the fight?" Laura said.

35 "I was in the room with him when he died," Terri said. "He never came up out of it. But I sat with him. He didn't have anyone else."

"He was dangerous," Mel said. "If you call that love, you can have it."

"It was love," Terri said. "Sure, it's abnormal in most people's eyes. But he was willing to die for it. He did die for it."

"I sure as hell wouldn't call it love," Mel said. "I mean, no one knows what he did it for. I've seen a lot of suicides, and I couldn't say anyone ever knew what they did it for."

Mel put his hands behind his neck and tilted his chair back. "I'm not interested in that kind of love," he said. "If that's love, you can have it."

40 Terri said, "We were afraid. Mel even made a will out and wrote to his brother in California who used to be a Green Beret. Mel told him who to look for if something happened to him."

Terri drank from her glass. She said, "But Mel's right—we lived like fugitives. We were afraid. Mel was, weren't you, honey? I even called the police at one point, but they were no help. They said they couldn't do anything until Ed actually did something. Isn't that a laugh?" Terry said.

She poured the last of the gin into her glass and waggled the bottle. Mel got up from the table and went to the cupboard. He took down another bottle.

"Well, Nick and I know what love is," Laura said. "For us, I mean," Laura said. She bumped my knee with her knee. "You're supposed to say something now," Laura said, and turned her smile on me.

For an answer, I took Laura's hand and raised it to my lips. I made a big production out of kissing her hand. Everyone was amused.

45   "We're lucky," I said.

"You guys," Terri said. "Stop that now. You're making me sick. You're still on the honeymoon, for God's sake. You're still gaga, for crying out loud. Just wait. How long have you been together now? How long has it been? A year? Longer than a year?"

"Going on a year and a half," Laura said, flushed and smiling.

"Oh, now," Terri said. "Wait a while."

She held her drink and gazed at Laura.

50   "I'm only kidding," Terri said.

Mel opened the gin and went around the table with the bottle.

"Here, you guys," he said. "Let's have a toast. I want to propose a toast. A toast to love. To true love," Mel said.

We touched glasses.

"To love," we said.

55   Outside in the backyard, one of the dogs began to bark. The leaves of the aspen that leaned past the window ticked against the glass. The afternoon sun was like a presence in this room, the spacious light of ease and generosity. We could have been anywhere, somewhere enchanted. We raised our glasses again and grinned at each other like children who had agreed on something forbidden.

"I'll tell you what real love is," Mel said. "I mean, I'll give you a good example. And then you can draw your own conclusions." He poured more gin into his glass. He added an ice cube and a sliver of lime. We waited and sipped our drinks. Laura and I touched knees again. I put a hand on her warm thigh and left it there.

"What do any of us really know about love?" Mel said. "It seems to me we're just beginners at love. We say we love each other and we do, I don't doubt it. I love Terri and Terri loves me, and you guys love each other too. You know the kind of love I'm talking about now. Physical love, that impulse that drives you to someone special, as well as love of the other person's being, his or her essence, as it were. Carnal love and, well, call it sentimental love, the day-to-day caring about the other person. But sometimes I have a hard time accounting for the fact that I must have loved my first wife too. But I did, I know I did. So I suppose I am like Terri in that regard. Terri and Ed." He thought about it and then he went on. "There was a time when I thought I loved my first wife more than life itself. But now I hate her guts. I do. How do you explain that? What happened to that love? What happened to it, is what I'd like to know. I wish someone could tell me. Then there's Ed. Okay, we're back to Ed. He loves Terri so much he tries to kill her and he winds up killing himself." Mel stopped talking and swallowed from his glass. "You guys have been together eighteen months and you love each other. It shows all over you. You glow with it. But you both loved other people before you met each other. You've both been married before, just like us. And you probably loved other people before that too, even. Terri and I have been together five years, been married for four. And the terrible thing, the terrible thing is, but the good thing too, the saving grace, you might say, is that if something happened to one of us—excuse me for saying this—but if something happened to one of us tomorrow I think the other one, the other person, would grieve for a while, you know, but then the surviving party would go out and love again, have someone else soon enough. All this, all of this love we're talking about, it would just be a memory. Maybe not even a memory. Am I wrong? Am I way off base? Because I want you to set me straight if you think I'm wrong. I want to know. I mean, I don't know anything, and I'm the first one to admit it."

"Mel, for God's sake," Terri said. She reached out and took hold of his wrist. "Are you getting drunk? Honey? Are you drunk?"

"Honey, I'm just talking," Mel said. "All right? I don't have to be drunk to say what I think. I mean, we're all just talking, right?" Mel said. He fixed his eyes on her.

60   "Sweetie, I'm not criticizing," Terri said.

She picked up her glass.

"I'm not on call today," Mel said. "Let me remind you of that. I am not on call," he said.

"Mel, we love you," Laura said.

Mel looked at Laura. He looked at her as if he could not place her, as if she was not the woman she was.

65   "Love you too, Laura," Mel said. "And you, Nick, love you too. You know something?" Mel said. "You guys are our pals," Mel said.

He picked up his glass.

Mel said, "I was going to tell you about something. I mean, I was going to prove a point. You see, this happened a few months ago, but it's still going on right now, and it ought to make us feel ashamed when we talk like we know what we're talking about when we talk above love."

"Come on now," Terri said. "Don't talk like you're drunk if you're not drunk."

"Just shut up for once in your life," Mel said very quietly. "Will you do me a favor and do that for a minute? So as I was saying, there's this old couple who had this car wreck out on the interstate. A kid hit them and they were all torn to shit and nobody was giving them much chance to pull through."

70   Terri looked at us and then back at Mel. She seemed anxious, or maybe that's too strong a word.

Mel was handing the bottle around the table.

"I was on call that night," Mel said. "It was May or maybe it was June. Terri and I had just sat down to dinner when the hospital called. There'd been this thing out on the interstate. Drunk kid, teenager, plowed his dad's pickup into this camper with this old couple in it. They were up in their mid-seventies, that couple. The kid—eighteen, nineteen, something—he was DOA. Taken the steering wheel through his sternum. The old couple, they were alive, you understand. I mean, just barely. But they had everything. Multiple fractures, internal injuries, hemorrhaging, contusions, lacerations, the works, and they each of them had themselves concussions. They were in a bad way, believe me. And, of course, their age was two strikes against them. I'd say she was worse off than he was. Ruptured spleen along with everything else. Both kneecaps broken. But they'd been wearing their seatbelts and, God knows, that's what saved them for the time being."

"Folks, this is an advertisement for the National Safety Council," Terri said. "This is your spokesman, Dr. Melvin R. McGinnis, talking." Terri laughed. "Mel," she said, "sometimes you're just too much. But I love you, hon," she said.

"Honey, I love you," Mel said.

75   He leaned across the table. Terri met him halfway. They kissed.

"Terri's right," Mel said as he settled himself again. "Get those seatbelts on. But seriously, they were in some shape, those oldsters. By the time I got down there, the kid was dead, as I said. He was off in a corner, laid out on a gurney. I took one look at the old couple and told the ER nurse to get me a neurologist and an orthopedic man and a couple of surgeons down there right away."

He drank from his glass. "I'll try to keep this short," he said. "So we took the two of them up to the OR and worked like fuck on them most of the night. They had these incredible reserves, those two. You see that once in a while. So we did everything that could be done, and toward morning we're giving them a fifty-fifty chance, maybe less than that for her. So here they are, still alive the next morning. So, okay, we move them into the ICU, which is where they both kept plugging away at it for two weeks, hitting it better and better on all the scopes. So we transfer them out to their own room."

Mel stopped talking. "Here," he said, "let's drink this cheapo gin the hell up. Then we're going to dinner, right? Terri and I know a new place. That's where we'll go, to this new place we know about. But we're not going until we finish up this cut-rate, lousy gin."

Terri said, "We haven't actually eaten there yet. But it looks good. From the outside, you know."

80   "I like food," Mel said. "If I had it to do all over again, I'd be a chef, you know? Right, Terri?" Mel said.

He laughed. He fingered the ice in his glass.

"Terri knows," he said. "Terri can tell you. But let me say this. If I could come back again in a different life, a different time and all, you know what? I'd like to come back as a knight. You were pretty safe wearing all that armor. It was all right being a knight until gunpowder and muskets and pistols came along."

"Mel would like to ride a horse and carry a lance," Terri said.

"Carry a woman's scarf with you everywhere," Laura said.

85   "Or just a woman," Mel said.

"Shame on you," Laura said.

Terri said, "Suppose you came back as a serf. The serfs didn't have it so good in those days," Terri said.

"The serfs never had it good," Mel said. "But I guess even the knights were vessels to someone. Isn't that the way it worked? But then everyone is always a vessel to someone. Isn't that right? Terri? But what I liked about knights, besides their ladies, was that they had that suit of armor, you know, and they couldn't get hurt very easy. No cars in those days, you know? No drunk teenagers to tear into your ass."

"Vassals," Terri said.

90   "What?" Mel said.

"Vassals," Terri said. "They were called vassals, not vessels."

"Vassals, vessels," Mel said, "what the fuck's the difference? You knew what I meant anyway. All right," Mel said. "So I'm not educated. I learned my stuff. I'm a heart surgeon, sure, but I'm just a mechanic. I go in and I fuck around and I fix things. Shit," Mel said.

"Modesty doesn't become you," Terri said.

"He's just a humble sawbones," I said. "But sometimes they suffocated in all that armor, Mel. They'd even have heart attacks if it got too hot and they were too tired and worn out. I read somewhere that they'd fall off their horses and not be able to get up because they were too tired to stand with all that armor on them. They got trampled by their own horses sometimes."

95   "That's terrible," Mel said. "That's a terrible thing, Nicky. I guess they'd just lay there and wait until somebody came along and made a shish kebab out of them."

"Some other vessel," Terri said.

"That's right," Mel said. "Some vassal would come along and spear the bastard in the name of love. Or whatever the fuck it was they fought over in those days."

"Same things we fight over these days," Terri said.

Laura said, "Nothing's changed."

100   The color was still high in Laura's cheeks. Her eyes were bright. She brought her glass to her lips.

Mel poured himself another drink. He looked at the label closely as if studying a long row of numbers. Then he slowly put the bottle down on the table and slowly reached for the tonic water.

"What about the old couple?" Laura said. "You didn't finish that story you started."

Laura was having a hard time lighting her cigarette. Her matches kept going out.

The sunshine inside the room was different now, changing, getting thinner. But the leaves outside the window were still shimmering, and I stared at the pattern they made on the panes and on the Formica counter. They weren't the same patterns, of course.

105   "What about the old couple?" I said.

"Older but wiser," Terri said.

Mel stared at her.

Terri said, "Go on with your story, hon. I was only kidding. Then what happened?"

"Terri, sometimes," Mel said.

110   "Please, Mel," Terri said. "Don't always be so serious, sweetie. Can't you take a joke?"

"Where's the joke?" Mel said.

He held his glass and gazed steadily at his wife.

"What happened?" Laura said.

Mel fastened his eyes on Laura. He said, "Laura, if I didn't have Terri and if I didn't love her so much, and if Nick wasn't my best friend, I'd fall in love with you, I'd carry you off, honey," he said.

115   "Tell your story," Terri said. "Then we'll go to that new place, okay?"

"Okay," Mel said. "Where was I?" he said. He stared at the table and then he began again.

"I dropped in to see each of them every day, sometimes twice a day if I was up doing other calls anyway. Casts and bandages, head to foot, the both of them. You know, you've seen it in the movies. That's just the way they looked, just like in the movies. Little eye-holes and nose-holes and mouth-holes. And she had to have her legs slung up on top of it. Well, the husband was very depressed for the longest while. Even after he found out that his wife was going to pull through, he was still very depressed. Not about the accident, though. I mean, the accident was one thing, but it wasn't everything. I'd get up to his mouth-hole, you know, and he'd say no, it wasn't the accident exactly but it was because he couldn't see her through his eye-holes. He said that was what was making him feel so bad. Can you imagine? I'm telling you, the man's heart was breaking because he couldn't turn his goddamn head and *see* his goddamn wife."

Mel looked around the table and shook his head at what he was going to say.

"I mean, it was killing the old fart just because he couldn't *look* at the fucking woman."

120   We all looked at Mel.

"Do you see what I'm saying?" he said.

Maybe we were a little drunk by then. I know it was hard keeping things in focus. The light was draining out of the room, going back through the window where it had come from. Yet nobody made a move to get up from the table to turn on the overhead light.

"Listen," Mel said. "Let's finish this fucking gin. There's about enough left here for one shooter all around. Then let's go eat. Let's go to the new place."

"He's depressed," Terri said. "Mel, why don't you take a pill?"

125   Mel shook his head. "I've taken everything there is."

"We all need a pill now and then," I said.

"Some people are born needing them," Terri said.

She was using her finger to rub at something on the table. Then she stopped rubbing.

"I think I want to call my kids," Mel said. "Is that all right with everybody? I'll call my kids," he said.

130   Terri said, "What if Marjorie answers the phone? You guys, you've heard us on the subject of Marjorie? Honey, you know you don't want to talk to Marjorie. It'll make you feel even worse."

"I don't want to talk to Marjorie," Mel said. "But I want to talk to my kids."

"There isn't a day goes by that Mel doesn't say he wishes she'd get married again. Or else die," Terri said. "For one thing," Terri said, "she's bankrupting us. Mel says it's just to spite him that she won't get married again. She has a boyfriend who lives with her and the kids, so Mel is supporting the boyfriend too."

"She's allergic to bees," Mel said. "If I'm not praying she'll get married again, I'm praying she'll get herself stung to death by a swarm of fucking bees."

"Shame on you," Laura said.

135   "Bzzzzzzz," Mel said, turning his fingers into bees and buzzing them at Terri's throat. Then he let his hands drop all the way to his sides.

"She's vicious," Mel said. "Sometimes I think I'll go up there dressed like a bee-keeper. You know, that hat that's like a helmet with the plate that comes down over your face, the big gloves, and the padded coat? I'll knock on the door and let loose a hive of bees in the house. But first I'd make sure the kids were out, of course."

He crossed one leg over the other. It seemed to take him a lot of time to do it. Then he put both feet on the floor and leaned forward, elbows on the table, his chin cupped in his hands.

"Maybe I won't call the kids, after all. Maybe it isn't such a hot idea. Maybe we'll just go eat. How does that sound?"

"Sounds fine to me," I said. "Eat or not eat. Or keep drinking. I could head right on out into the sunset."

140   "What does that mean, honey?" Laura said.

"It just means what I said," I said. "It means I could just keep going. That's all it means."

"I could eat something myself," Laura said. "I don't think I've ever been so hungry in my life. Is there something to nibble on?"

"I'll put out some cheese and crackers," Terri said.

But Terri just sat there. She did not get up to get anything.

145   Mel turned his glass over. He spilled it out on the table.

"Gin's gone," Mel said.

Terri said, "Now what?"

I could hear my heart beating. I could hear everyone's heart. I could hear the human noise we sat there making, not one of us moving, not even when the room went dark.

[1981]

Cathedral

This blind man, an old friend of my wife's, he was on his way to spend the night. His wife had died. So he was visiting the dead wife's relatives in Connecticut. He called my wife from his in-laws'. Arrangements were made. He would come by train, a five-hour trip, and my wife would meet him at the station. She hadn't seen him since she worked for him one summer in Seattle ten years ago. But she and the blind man had kept in touch. They made tapes and mailed them back and forth. I wasn't enthusiastic about his visit. He was no one I knew. And his being blind bothered me. My idea of blindness came from the movies. In the movies, the blind moved slowly and never laughed. Sometimes they were led by seeing-eye dogs. A blind man in my house was not something I looked forward to.

That summer in Seattle she had needed a job. She didn't have any money. The man she was going to marry at the end of the summer was in officers' training school. He didn't have any money, either. But she was in love with the guy, and he was in love with her, etc. She'd seen something in the paper: HELP WANTED— *Reading to Blind Man,* and a telephone number. She phoned and went over, was hired on the spot. She'd worked with this blind man all summer. She read stuff to him, case studies, reports, that sort of thing. She helped him organize his little office in the county social-service department. They'd become good friends, my wife and the blind man. How do I know these things? She told me. And she told me something else. On her last day in the office, the blind man asked if he could touch her face. She agreed to this. She told me he touched his fingers to every part of her face, her nose—even her neck! She never forgot it. She even tried to write a poem about it. She was always trying to write a poem. She wrote a poem or two every year, usually after something really important had happened to her.

When we first started going out together, she showed me the poem. In the poem, she recalled his fingers and the way they had moved around over her face. In the poem, she talked about what she had felt at the time, about what went through her mind when the blind man touched her nose and lips. I can remember I didn't think much of the poem. Of course, I didn't tell her that. Maybe I just don't understand poetry. I admit it's not the first thing I reach for when I pick up something to read.

Anyway, this man who'd first enjoyed her favors, the officer-to-be, he'd been her childhood sweetheart. So okay. I'm saying that at the end of the summer she let the blind man run his hands over her face, said goodbye to him, married her childhood etc., who was now a commissioned officer, and she moved away from Seattle. But they'd kept in touch, she and the blind man. She made the first contact after a year or so. She called him up one night from an Air Force base in Alabama. She wanted to talk. They talked. He asked her to send a tape and tell him about her life. She did this. She sent the tape. On the tape, she told the blind man about her husband and about their life together in the military. She told the blind man she loved her husband but she didn't like it where they lived and she didn't like it that he was part of the military-industrial thing. She told the blind man she'd written a poem and he was in it. She told him that she was writing a poem about what it was like to be an Air Force officer's wife. The poem wasn't finished yet. She was still writing it. The blind man made a tape. He sent her the tape. She made a tape. This went on for years. My wife's officer was posted to one base and then another. She sent tapes from Moody AFB, McGuire, McConnell, and finally Travis, near Sacramento, where one night she got to feeling lonely and cut off from people she kept losing in that moving-around life. She got to feeling she couldn't go it another step. She went in and swallowed all the pills and capsules in the medicine chest and washed them down with a bottle of gin. Then she got into a hot bath and passed out.

5   But instead of dying, she got sick. She threw up. Her officer—why should he have a name? he was the childhood sweetheart, and what more does he want?—came home from somewhere, found her, and called the ambulance. In time, she put it all on a tape and sent the tape to the blind man. Over the years, she put all kinds of stuff on tapes and sent the tapes off lickety-split. Next to writing a poem every year, I think it was her chief means of recreation. On one tape, she told the blind man she'd decided to live away from her officer for a time. On another tape, she told him about her divorce. She and I began going out, and of course she told her blind man about it. She told him everything, or so it seemed to me. Once she asked me if I'd like to hear the latest tape from the blind man. This was a year ago. I was on the tape, she said. So I said okay, I'd listen to it. I got us drinks and we settled down in the living room. We made ready to listen. First she inserted the tape into the player and adjusted a couple of dials. Then she pushed a lever. The tape squeaked and someone began to talk in this loud voice. She lowered the volume. After a few minutes of harmless chitchat, I heard my own name in the mouth of this stranger, this blind man I didn't even know! And then this: "From all you've said about him, I can only conclude—" But we were interrupted, a knock at the door, something, and we didn't ever get back to the tape. Maybe it was just as well. I'd heard all I wanted to.

Now this same blind man was coming to sleep in my house.

"Maybe I could take him bowling," I said to my wife. She was at the draining board doing scalloped potatoes. She put down the knife she was using and turned around.

"If you love me," she said, "you can do this for me. If you don't love me, okay. But if you had a friend, any friend, and the friend came to visit, I'd make him feel comfortable." She wiped her hands with the dish towel.

"I don't have any blind friends," I said.

10   "You don't have *any* friends," she said. "Period. Besides," she said, "goddamn it, his wife's just died! Don't you understand that? The man's lost his wife!"

I didn't answer. She'd told me a little about the blind man's wife. Her name was Beulah. Beulah! That's a name for a colored woman.

"Was his wife a Negro?" I asked.

"Are you crazy?" my wife said. "Have you just flipped or something?" She picked up a potato. I saw it hit the floor, then roll under the stove. "What's wrong with you?" she said. "Are you drunk?"

"I'm just asking," I said.

15   Right then my wife filled me in with more detail than I cared to know. I made a drink and sat at the kitchen table to listen. Pieces of the story began to fall into place.

Beulah had gone to work for the blind man the summer after my wife had stopped working for him. Pretty soon Beulah and the blind man had themselves a church wedding. It was a little wedding—who'd want to go to such a wedding in the first place?—just the two of them, plus the minister and the minister's wife. But it was a church wedding just the same. It was what Beulah had wanted, he'd said. But even then Beulah must have been carrying the cancer in her glands. After they had been inseparable for eight years—my wife's word, *inseparable*—Beulah's health went into a rapid decline. She died in a Seattle hospital room, the blind man sitting beside the bed and holding on to her hand. They'd married, lived and worked together, slept together—had sex, sure—and then the blind man had to bury her. All this without his having ever seen what the goddamned woman looked like. It was beyond my understanding. Hearing this, I felt sorry for the blind man for a little bit. And then I found myself thinking what a pitiful life this woman must have led. Imagine a woman who could never see herself as she was seen in the eyes of her loved one. A woman who could go on day after day and never receive the smallest compliment from her beloved. A woman whose husband could never read the expression on her face, be it misery or something better. Someone who could wear makeup or not—what difference to him? She could, if she wanted, wear green eye-shadow around one eye, a straight pin in her nostril, yellow slacks, and purple shoes, no matter. And then to slip off into death, the blind man's hand on her hand, his blind eyes streaming tears—I'm imagining now—her last thought maybe this: that he never even knew what she looked like, and she on an express to the grave. Robert was left with a small insurance policy and a half of a twenty-peso Mexican coin. The other half of the coin went into the box with her. Pathetic.

So when the time rolled around, my wife went to the depot to pick him up. With nothing to do but wait—sure, I blamed him for that—I was having a drink and watching the TV when I heard the car pull into the drive. I got up from the sofa with my drink and went to the window to have a look.

I saw my wife laughing as she parked the car. I saw her get out of the car and shut the door. She was still wearing a smile. Just amazing. She went around to the other side of the car to where the blind man was already starting to get out. This blind man, feature this, he was wearing a full beard! A beard on a blind man! Too much, I say. The blind man reached into the back seat and dragged out a suitcase. My wife took his arm, shut the car door, and, talking all the way, moved him down the drive and then up the steps to the front porch. I turned off the TV. I finished my drink, rinsed the glass, dried my hands. Then I went to the door.

My wife said, "I want you to meet Robert. Robert, this is my husband. I've told you all about him." She was beaming. She had this blind man by his coat sleeve.

20   The blind man let go of his suitcase and up came his hand. I took it. He squeezed hard, held my hand, and then he let it go.

"I feel like we've already met," he boomed.

"Likewise," I said. I didn't know what else to say. Then I said, "Welcome. I've heard a lot about you." We began to move then, a little group, from the porch into the living room, my wife guiding him by the arm. The blind man was carrying his suitcase in his other hand. My wife said things like, "To your left here, Robert. That's right. Now watch it, there's a chair. That's it. Sit down right here. This is the sofa. We just bought this sofa two weeks ago."

I started to say something about the old sofa. I'd liked that old sofa. But I didn't say anything. Then I wanted to say something else, small-talk, about the scenic ride along the Hudson. How going *to* New York, you should sit on the right-hand side of the train, and coming *from* New York, the left-hand side.

"Did you have a good train ride?" I said. "Which side of the train did you sit on, by the way?"

25   "What a question, which side!" my wife said. "What's it matter which side?" she said.

"I just asked," I said.

"Right side," the blind man said. "I hadn't been on a train in nearly forty years. Not since I was a kid. With my folks. That's been a long time. I'd nearly forgotten the sensation. I have winter in my beard now," he said. "So I've been told, anyway. Do I look distinguished, my dear?" the blind man said to my wife.

"You look distinguished, Robert," she said. "Robert," she said. "Robert, it's just so good to see you."

My wife finally took her eyes off the blind man and looked at me. I had the feeling she didn't like what she saw. I shrugged.

30   I've never met, or personally known, anyone who was blind. This blind man was late forties, a heavy-set, balding man with stooped shoulders, as if he carried a great weight there. He wore brown slacks, brown shoes, a light-brown shirt, a tie, a sports coat. Spiffy. He also had this full beard. But he didn't use a cane and he didn't wear dark glasses. I'd always thought dark glasses were a must for the blind. Fact was, I wished he had a pair. At first glance, his eyes looked like anyone else's eyes. But if you looked close, there was something different about them. Too much white in the iris, for one thing, and the pupils seemed to move around in the sockets without his knowing it or being able to stop it. Creepy. As I stared at his face, I saw the left pupil turn in toward his nose while the other made an effort to keep in one place. But it was only an effort, for that eye was on the roam without his knowing it or wanting it to be.

I said, "Let me get you a drink. What's your pleasure? We have a little of everything. It's one of our pastimes."

"Bub, I'm a Scotch man myself," he said fast enough in this big voice.

"Right," I said. Bub! "Sure you are. I knew it."

He let his fingers touch his suitcase, which was sitting alongside the sofa. He was taking his bearings. I didn't blame him for that.

35   "I'll move that up to your room," my wife said.

"No, that's fine," the blind man said loudly. "It can go up when I go up."

"A little water with the Scotch?" I said.

"Very little," he said.

"I knew it," I said.

40   He said, "Just a tad. The Irish actor, Barry Fitzgerald? I'm like that fellow. When I drink water, Fitzgerald said, I drink water. When I drink whiskey, I drink whiskey." My wife laughed. The blind man brought his hand up under his beard. He lifted his beard slowly and let it drop.

I did the drinks, three big glasses of Scotch with a splash of water in each. Then we made ourselves comfortable and talked about Robert's travels. First the long flight from the West Coast to Connecticut, we covered that. Then from Connecticut up here by train. We had another drink concerning that leg of the trip.

I remembered having read somewhere that the blind didn't smoke because, as speculation had it, they couldn't see the smoke they exhaled. I thought I knew that much and that much only about blind people. But this blind man smoked his cigarette down to the nubbin and then lit another one. This blind man filled his ashtray and my wife emptied it.

When we sat down at the table for dinner, we had another drink. My wife heaped Robert's plate with cube steak, scalloped potatoes, green beans. I buttered him up two slices of bread. I said, "Here's bread and butter for you." I swallowed some of my drink. "Now let us pray," I said, and the blind man lowered his head. My wife looked at me, her mouth agape. "Pray the phone won't ring and the food doesn't get cold," I said.

We dug in. We ate everything there was to eat on the table. We ate like there was no tomorrow. We didn't talk. We ate. We scarfed. We grazed that table. We were into serious eating. The blind man had right away located his foods, he knew just where everything was on his plate. I watched with admiration as he used his knife and fork on the meat. He'd cut two pieces of meat, fork the meat into his mouth, and then go all out for the scalloped potatoes, the beans next, and then he'd tear off a hunk of buttered bread and eat that. He'd follow this up with a big drink of milk. It didn't seem to bother him to use his fingers once in a while, either.

45   We finished everything, including half a strawberry pie. For a few moments, we sat as if stunned. Sweat beaded on our faces. Finally, we got up from the table and left the dirty places. We didn't look back. We took ourselves into the living room and sank into our places again. Robert and my wife sat on the sofa. I took the big chair. We had us two or three more drinks while they talked about the major things that had come to pass for them in the past ten years. For the most part, I just listened. Now and then I joined in. I didn't want him to think I'd left the room, and I didn't want her to think I was feeling left out. They talked of things that had happened to them—to them!—these past ten years. I waited in vain to hear my name on my wife's sweet lips: "And then my dear husband came into my life"—something like that. But I heard nothing of the sort. More talk of Robert. Robert had done a little of everything, it seemed, a regular blind jack-of-all-trades. But most recently he and his wife had had an Amway distributorship, from which, I gathered, they'd earned their living, such as it was. The blind man was also a ham radio operator. He talked in his loud voice about conversations he'd had with fellow operators in Guam, in the Philippines, in Alaska, and even in Tahiti. He said he'd have a lot of friends there if he ever wanted to go visit those places. From time to time, he'd turn his blind face toward me, put his hand under his beard, ask me something. How long had I been in my present position? (Three years.) Did I like my work? (I didn't.) Was I going to stay with it? (What were the options?) Finally, when I thought he was beginning to run down, I got up and turned on the TV.

My wife looked at me with irritation. She was heading toward a boil. Then she looked at the blind man and said, "Robert, do you have a TV?"

The blind man said, "My dear, I have two TVs. I have a color set and a black-and-white thing, an old relic. It's funny, but if I turn the TV on, and I'm always turning it on, I turn on the color set. It's funny, don't you think?"

I didn't know what to say to that. I had absolutely nothing to say to that. No opinion. So I watched the news program and tried to listen to what the announcer was saying.

"This is a color TV," the blind man said. "Don't ask me how, but I can tell."

50   "We traded up a while ago," I said.

The blind man had another taste of his drink. He lifted his beard, sniffed it, and let it fall. He leaned forward on the sofa. He positioned his ashtray on the coffee table, then put the lighter to his cigarette. He leaned back on the sofa and crossed his legs at the ankles.

My wife covered her mouth, and then she yawned. She stretched. She said, "I think I'll go upstairs and put on my robe. I think I'll change into something else. Robert, you make yourself comfortable," she said.

"I'm comfortable," the blind man said.

"I want you to feel comfortable in this house," she said.

55   "I am comfortable," the blind man said.

After she'd left the room, he and I listened to the weather report and then to the sports roundup. By that time, she'd been gone so long I didn't know if she was going to come back. I thought she might have gone to bed. I wished she'd come back downstairs. I didn't want to be left alone with a blind man. I asked him if he wanted another drink, and he said sure. Then I asked if he wanted to smoke some dope with me. I said I'd just rolled a number. I hadn't, but I planned to do so in about two shakes.

"I'll try some with you," he said.

"Damn right," I said. "That's the stuff."

I got our drinks and sat down on the sofa with him. Then I rolled us two fat numbers. I lit one and passed it. I brought it to his fingers. He took it and inhaled.

60   "Hold it as long as you can," I said. I could tell he didn't know the first thing.

My wife came back downstairs wearing her pink robe and her pink slippers.

"What do I smell?" she said.

"We thought we'd have us some cannabis," I said.

My wife gave me a savage look. Then she looked at the blind man and said, "Robert, I didn't know you smoked."

65   He said, "I do now, my dear. There's a first time for everything. But I don't feel anything yet."

"This stuff is pretty mellow," I said. "This stuff is mild. It's dope you can reason with," I said. "It doesn't mess you up."

"Not much it doesn't, bub," he said, and laughed.

My wife sat on the sofa between the blind man and me. I passed her the number. She took it and toked and then passed it back to me. "Which way is this going?" she said. Then she said, "I shouldn't be smoking this. I can hardly keep my eyes open as it is. That dinner did me in. I shouldn't have eaten so much."

"It was the strawberry pie," the blind man said. "That's what did it," he said, and he laughed his big laugh. Then he shook his head.

70   "There's more strawberry pie," I said.

"Do you want some more, Robert?" my wife said.

"Maybe in a little while," he said.

We gave our attention to the TV. My wife yawned again. She said, "Your bed is made up when you feel like going to bed, Robert. I know you must have had a long day. When you're ready to go to bed, say so." She pulled his arm. "Robert?"

He came to and said, "I've had a real nice time. This beats tapes, doesn't it?"

75   I said, "Coming at you," and I put the number between his fingers. He inhaled, held the smoke, and then let it go. It was like he'd been doing it since he was nine years old.

"Thanks, bub," he said. "But I think this is all for me. I think I'm beginning to feel it," he said. He held the burning roach out for my wife.

"Same here," she said. "Ditto. Me, too." She took the roach and passed it to me. "I may just sit here for a while between you two guys with my eyes closed.

But don't let me bother you, okay? Either one of you. If it bothers you, say so. Otherwise, I may just sit here with my eyes closed until you're ready to go to bed," she said. "Your bed's made up, Robert, when you're ready. It's right next to our room at the top of the stairs. We'll show you up when you're ready. You wake me up now, you guys, if I fall asleep." She said that and then she closed her eyes and went to sleep.

The news program ended. I got up and changed the channel. I sat back down on the sofa. I wished my wife hadn't pooped out. Her head lay across the back of the sofa, her mouth open. She'd turned so that her robe slipped away from her legs, exposing a juicy thigh. I reached to draw her robe back over her, and it was then that I glanced at the blind man. What the hell! I flipped the robe open again.

"You say when you want some strawberry pie," I said.

80   "I will," he said.

I said, "Are you tired? Do you want me to take you up to your bed? Are you ready to hit the hay?"

"Not yet," he said. "No, I'll stay up with you, bub. If that's all right. I'll stay up until you're ready to turn in. We haven't had a chance to talk. Know what I mean? I feel like me and her monopolized the evening." He lifted his beard and he let it fall. He picked up his cigarettes and his lighter.

"That's all right," I said. Then I said, "I'm glad for the company."

And I guess I was. Every night I smoked dope and stayed up as long as I could before I fell asleep. My wife and I hardly ever went to bed at the same time. When I did go to sleep, I had these dreams. Sometimes I'd wake up from one of them, my heart going crazy.

85   Something about the church and the Middle Ages was on the TV. Not your run-of-the-mill TV fare. I wanted to watch something else. I turned to the other channels. But there was nothing on them, either. So I turned back to the first channel and apologized.

"Bub, it's all right," the blind man said. "It's fine with me. Whatever you want to watch is okay. I'm always learning something. Learning never ends. It won't hurt me to learn something tonight. I got ears," he said.

We didn't say anything for a time. He was leaning forward with his head turned at me, his right ear aimed in the direction of the set. Very disconcerting. Now and then his eyelids drooped and then they snapped open again. Now and then he put his fingers into his beard and tugged, like he was thinking about something he was hearing on the television.

On the screen, a group of men wearing cowls was being set upon and tormented by men dressed in skeleton costumes and men dressed as devils. The men dressed as devils wore devil masks, horns, and long tails. This pageant was part of a procession. The Englishman who was narrating the thing said it took place in Spain once a year. I tried to explain to the blind man what was happening.

"Skeletons," he said. "I know about skeletons," he said, and he nodded.

90   The TV showed this one cathedral. Then there was a long, slow look at another one. Finally, the picture switched to the famous one in Paris, with its flying buttresses and its spires reaching up to the clouds. The camera pulled away to show the whole of the cathedral rising above the skyline.

There were times when the Englishman who was telling the thing would shut up, would simply let the camera move around the cathedrals. Or else the camera would tour the countryside, men in fields walking behind oxen. I waited as long as I could. Then I felt I had to say something. I said, "They're showing the outside of this cathedral now. Gargoyles. Little statues carved to look like monsters. Now I guess they're in Italy. Yeah, they're in Italy. There's paintings on the walls of this one church."

"Are those fresco paintings, bub?" he asked, and he sipped from his drink.

I reached for my glass. But it was empty. I tried to remember what I could remember. "You're asking me are those frescoes?" I said. "That's a good question. I don't know."

The camera moved to a cathedral outside Lisbon. The differences in the Portuguese cathedral compared with the French and Italian were not that great. But they were there. Mostly the interior stuff. Then something occurred to me, and I said, "Something has occurred to me. Do you have any idea what a cathedral is? What they look like, that is? Do you follow me? If somebody says cathedral to you, do you have any notion what they're talking about? Do you know the difference between that and a Baptist church, say?"

95   He let the smoke dribble from his mouth. "I know they took hundreds of workers fifty or a hundred years to build," he said. "I just heard the man say that, of course. I know generations of the same families worked on a cathedral. I heard him say that, too. The men who began their life's work on them, they never lived to see the completion of their work. In that wise, bub, they're no different from the rest of us, right?" He laughed. Then his eyelids drooped again. His head nodded. He seemed to be snoozing. Maybe he was imagining himself in Portugal. The TV was showing another cathedral now. This one was in Germany. The Englishman's voice droned on. "Cathedrals," the blind man said. He sat up and rolled his head back and forth. "If you want the truth, bub, that's about all I know. What I just said. What I heard him say. But maybe you could describe one to me? I wish you'd do it. I'd like that. If you want to know, I really don't have a good idea."

I stared hard at the shot of the cathedral on the TV. How could I even begin to describe it? But say my life depended on it. Say my life was being threatened by an insane guy who said I had to do it or else.

I stared some more at the cathedral before the picture flipped off into the countryside. There was no use. I turned to the blind man and said, "To begin with, they're very tall." I was looking around the room for clues. "They reach way up. Up and up. Toward the sky. They're so big, some of them, they have to have these supports. To help hold them up, so to speak. These supports are called buttresses. They remind me of viaducts, for some reason. But maybe you don't know viaducts, either? Sometimes the cathedrals have devils and such carved into the front. Sometimes lords and ladies. Don't ask me why this is," I said.

He was nodding. The whole upper part of his body seemed to be moving back and forth.

"I'm not doing so good, am I?" I said.

100   He stopped nodding and leaned forward on the edge of the sofa. As he listened to me, he was running his fingers through his beard. I wasn't getting through to him, I could see that. But he waited for me to go on just the same. He nodded, like he was trying to encourage me. I tried to think what else to say. "They're really big," I said. "They're massive. They're built of stone. Marble, too, sometimes. In those olden days, when they built cathedrals, men wanted to be close to God. In those olden days, God was an important part of everyone's life.

You could tell this from their cathedral-building. I'm sorry," I said, "but it looks like that's the best I can do for you. I'm just no good at it."

"That's all right, bub," the blind man said. "Hey, listen. I hope you don't mind my asking you. Can I ask you something? Let me ask you a simple question, yes or no. I'm just curious and there's no offense. You're my host. But let me ask if you are in any way religious? You don't mind my asking?"

I shook my head. He couldn't see that, though. A wink is the same as a nod to a blind man. "I guess I don't believe in it. In anything. Sometimes it's hard. You know what I'm saying?"

"Sure, I do," he said.

"Right," I said.

105 The Englishman was still holding forth. My wife sighed in her sleep. She drew a long breath and went on with her sleeping.

"You'll have to forgive me," I said. "But I can't tell you what a cathedral looks like. It just isn't in me to do it. I can't do any more than I've done."

The blind man sat very still, his head down, as he listened to me.

I said, "The truth is, cathedrals don't mean anything special to me. Nothing. Cathedrals. They're something to look at on late-night TV. That's all they are."

It was then that the blind man cleared his throat. He brought something up. He took a handkerchief from his back pocket. Then he said, "I get it, bub. It's okay. It happens. Don't worry about it," he said. "Hey, listen to me. Will you do me a favor? I got an idea. Why don't you find us some heavy paper? And a pen. We'll do something. We'll draw one together. Get us a pen and some heavy paper. Go on, bub, get the stuff," he said.

110 So I went upstairs. My legs felt like they didn't have any strength in them. They felt like they did after I'd done some running. In my wife's room, I looked around. I found some ballpoints in a little basket on her table. And then I tried to think where to look for the kind of paper he was talking about.

Downstairs, in the kitchen, I found a shopping bag with onion skins in the bottom of the bag. I emptied the bag and shook it. I brought it into the living room and sat down with it near his legs. I moved some things, smoothed the wrinkles from the bag, spread it out on the coffee table.

The blind man got down from the sofa and sat next to me on the carpet.

He ran his fingers over the paper. He went up and down the sides of the paper. The edges, even the edges. He fingered the corners.

"All right," he said. "All right, let's do her."

115 He found my hand, the hand with the pen. He closed his hand over my hand. "Go ahead, bub, draw," he said. "Draw. You'll see. I'll follow along with you. It'll be okay. Just begin now like I'm telling you. You'll see. Draw," the blind man said.

So I began. First I drew a box that looked like a house. It could have been the house I lived in. Then I put a roof on it. At either end of the roof, I drew spires. Crazy.

"Swell," he said. "Terrific. You're doing fine," he said. "Never thought anything like this could happen in your lifetime, did you, bub? Well, it's a strange life, we all know that. Go on now. Keep it up."

I put in windows with arches. I drew flying buttresses. I hung great doors. I couldn't stop. The TV station went off the air. I put down the pen and closed and opened my fingers. The blind man felt around over the paper. He moved the tips of his fingers over the paper, all over what I had drawn, and he nodded.

"Doing fine," the blind man said.

120   I took up the pen again, and he found my hand. I kept at it. I'm no artist. But I kept drawing just the same.

My wife opened up her eyes and gazed at us. She sat up on the sofa, her robe hanging open. She said, "What are you doing? Tell me, I want to know."

I didn't answer her.

The blind man said, "We're drawing a cathedral. Me and him are working on it. Press hard," he said to me. "That's right. That's good," he said. "Sure. You got it, bub, I can tell. You didn't think you could. But you can, can't you? You're cooking with gas now. You know what I'm saying? We're going to really have us something here in a minute. How's the old arm?" he said. "Put some people in there now. What's a cathedral without people?"

My wife said, "What's going on? Robert, what are you doing? What's going on?"

125   "It's all right," he said to her. "Close your eyes now," the blind man said to me. I did it. I closed them just like he said.

"Are they closed?" he said. "Don't fudge."

"They're closed," I said.

"Keep them that way," he said. He said, "Don't stop now. Draw."

130   So we kept on with it. His fingers rode my fingers as my hand went over the paper. It was like nothing else in my life up to now.

Then he said, "I think that's it. I think you got it," he said. "Take a look. What do you think?"

But I had my eyes closed. I thought I'd keep them that way for a little longer. I thought it was something I ought to do.

"Well?" he said. "Are you looking?"

My eyes were still closed. I was in my house. I knew that. But I didn't feel like I was inside anything.

135   "It's really something," I said.

[1983]

TALKING ABOUT STORIES

Larry McCaffery and Sinda Gregory have interviewed many contemporary authors and have published some of the interviews in a collection entitled Alive and Writing *(1987). In the following selections from a long interview, Carver talks about his life and work.*

SINDA GREGORY.   Many of your stories either open with the ordinary being slightly disturbed by this sense of menace you've just mentioned, or they develop in that direction. Is this tendency the result of your conviction that the world *is* menacing for most people? Or does it have more to do with an aesthetic choice—that menace contains more interesting possibilities for storytelling?

RAYMOND CARVER.   The world is a menacing place for many of the people in my stories, yes. The people I've chosen to write about *do* feel menace, and I think, many, if not most, people feel the world is a menacing place. Probably not so many people who will see this interview feel menace in the sense I'm talking about. Most of our friends and acquaintances, yours and mine, don't feel this way. But try living on the other side of the tracks for a while. Menace is there, and it's palpable. As to the second part of your question, that's true, too. Menace does contain, for me at least, more interesting possibilities to explore. . . .

SINDA GREGORY.   A reader is immediately struck with the "pared down" quality of your work, especially your work before *Cathedral*. Was this style something that evolved, or had it been with you from the beginning?

RAYMOND CARVER.   From the very beginning I loved the rewriting process as much as the initial execution. I've always loved taking sentences and playing with them, rewriting them, paring them down to where they seem solid somehow. This may have resulted from being John Gardner's student, because he told me something I immediately responded to: If you can say it in fifteen words rather than twenty or thirty words, then say it in fifteen words. That struck me with the force of revelation. There I was, groping to find my own way, and here someone was telling me something that somehow conjoined with what I already wanted to do. It was the most natural thing in the world for me to go back and refine what was happening on the page and eliminate the padding. The last few days I've been reading Flaubert's letters, and he says some things that seem relevant to my own aesthetic. At one point when Flaubert was writing *Madame Bovary,* he would knock off at midnight or one in the morning and write letters to his mistress, Louise Colet, about the construction of the book and his general notion of aesthetics. One passage he wrote her that really struck me was when he said, "The artist in his work must be like God in his creation—invisible and all powerful; he must be everywhere felt but nowhere seen." I like the last part of that especially. There's another interesting remark when Flaubert is writing to his editors at the magazine that published the book in installments. They were just getting ready to serialize *Madame Bovary* and were going to make a lot of cuts in the text because they were afraid they were going to be closed down by the government if they published it just as Flaubert wrote it, so Flaubert tells them that if they make the cuts they can't publish the book, but they'll still be friends. The last line of this letter is: "I know how to distinguish between literature and literary business"—another insight I respond to. Even in these letters his prose is astonishing: "Prose must stand upright from one end to the other, like a wall whose ornamentation continues down to its very base." "Prose is architecture." "Everything must be done coldly, with poise." "Last week I spent five days writing one page." One of the interesting things about the Flaubert book is the way it demonstrates how self-consciously he was setting out to do something very special and different with prose. He consciously tried to make prose an art form. If you look at what else was being published in Europe in 1855, when *Madame Bovary* was published, you realize what an achievement the book really is. . . .

LARRY MCCAFFERY.   Another distinctive feature of your work is that you usually present characters that most writers don't deal with—that is, people who are basically inarticulate, who can't verbalize their plights, who often don't seem to really grasp what is happening to them.

RAYMOND CARVER.   I don't think of this as being especially "distinctive" or nontraditional because I feel perfectly comfortable with these people while I'm working. I've known people like this all my life. Essentially, I *am* one of those confused, befuddled people, I come from people like that, those are the people I've worked with and earned my living beside for years. That's why I've never had any interest whatsoever in writing a story or a poem that has anything to do with the academic life, with teachers or students and so forth. I'm just not that interested. The things that have made an indelible impression on me are the things I saw in lives I witnessed being lived around me, and in the life I myself lived. These were lives where people really *were* scared when someone knocked on their door, day or night, or when the telephone rang; they didn't know how they were going to pay the rent or what they could do if their refrigerator went out. Anatole Broyard tries to criticize my story "Preservation" by saying, "So the refrigerator breaks—why don't they just call a repairman and get it fixed?" That kind of remark is dumb. You bring a repairman out to fix your refrigerator and it's sixty bucks to *fix* it; and who knows how much if the thing is completely broken? Well, Broyard may not be aware of it, but some people can't afford to bring in a repairman if it's going to cost them sixty bucks, just like they don't get a doctor if they don't have insurance, and their teeth go bad because they can't afford to go to a dentist when they need one. That kind of situation doesn't seem unrealistic or artificial to me. It also doesn't seem that, in focusing on this group of people, I have really been doing anything all that different from other writers. Chekhov was writing about a submerged population a hundred years ago. Short story writers have always been doing that. Not all of Chekhov's stories are about people who are down and out, but a significant number of them deal with that submerged population I'm talking about. He wrote about doctors and businessmen and teachers sometimes, but he also gave voice to people who were not so articulate. He found a means of letting those people have their say as well. So in writing about people who aren't so articulate and who are confused and scared, I'm not doing anything radically different.

LARRY MCCAFFERY.   Aren't there formal problems in writing about this group of people? I mean, you can't have them sit around in drawing rooms endlessly analyzing their situations, the way James does, or, in a different sense, the way Bellow does. I suppose setting the scene, composing it, must be especially important from a technical standpoint.

RAYMOND CARVER.   If you mean literally just setting the scene, that's the least of my worries. The scene is easy to set: I just open the door and see what's inside. I pay a lot of attention to trying to make the people talk the right way. By this I don't mean just *what* they say, but *how* they say it, and *why*. I guess *tone* is what I'm talking about, partly. There's never any chit-chat in my stories. Everything said is for a reason and adds, I want to think, to the overall impression of the story.

SINDA GREGORY.   People usually emphasize the realistic aspects of your work, but I feel there's a quality about your fiction that is *not* basically realistic. It's as if something is happening almost off the page, a dreamy sense of irrationality, almost like Kafka's fiction.

RAYMOND CARVER.   Presumably my fiction is in the realistic tradition (as opposed to the really far-out side), but just telling it like it is bores me. It really does. People couldn't possibly read pages of description about the way people *really* talk, about what *really* happens in their lives. They'd just snore away, of course. If you look carefully at my stories, I don't think you'll find people talking the way people do in real life. People always say that Hemingway had a great ear for dialogue, and he did. But no one ever talked in real life like they do in Hemingway's fiction. At least not until after they've *read* Hemingway.

On Rewriting

The following paragraph comes from Carver's afterword to Fires *(1983).*

I like to mess around with my stories. I'd rather tinker with a story after writing it, and then tinker some more, changing this, changing that, than have to write the story in the first place. That initial writing just seems to me the hard place I have to get to in order to go on and have fun with the story. Rewriting for me is not a chore—it's something I like to do. I think by nature I'm more deliberate and careful than I am spontaneous, and maybe that explains something. Maybe not. Maybe there's no connection except the one I'm making. But I do know that revising the work once it's done is something that comes naturally to me and is something I take pleasure in doing. Maybe I revise because it gradually takes me into the heart of what the story is *about.* I have to keep trying to see if I can find that out. It's a process more than a fixed position.

Michael Gerber and Jonathan Schwarz

Among the publications of Gerber and Schwarz is The Bull Street Journal *(1997).*
We print here a parody of Raymond Carver that Gerber and Schwarz published in The New Yorker *magazine. A parody (from the Greek "counter song" or "burlesque song") is a literary composition that imitates the style (for instance, the vocabulary and sentence structure) of another work, but that normally for comic purposes substitutes a very different subject matter. Parody is a very old device, reaching back at least as far as Aristophanes and Plato, both of whom made effective use of it. Aristotle mentions it in the* Poetics, *and among later authors, it figures in the writings of Chaucer, Shakespeare, Cervantes, and James Joyce.*
Parodists make fun of the original, and they may indeed be scathing. But they may also be genial, and if some parodies are motivated by contempt for the original author, other parodies are motivated by affection. It has been said that a parody is often a form of tribute, in that a parody succeeds only when the original is widely known and perhaps much admired. We might laugh while reading a parody, yet feel too that the parody is drawing our attention to something important in the style of the original. In this way it can function as an entertaining and enlightening form of literary criticism.

What We Talk about When We Talk about Doughnuts

My friend Jim Forrer was talking. Jim Forrer is a professional fish measurer, and sometimes that gives him the right.

We were sitting around the kitchen table drinking gin and smoking. There was Jim and me and his wife, Elizabeth—Lisa, we called her, or sometimes Frank—and my wife, Carol.

There was a bowl of peanuts sitting on the table, but nobody ate many of them, because we were drinking and smoking. We were talking to ourselves like this: "Some of us are drinking more than we are smoking, and some of us are smoking more than we are drinking. Some of us are drinking and smoking about the same amount."

We went on drinking and smoking for a while, and somehow we got on the subject of doughnuts. Jim thought that real doughnuts were nothing less than spiritual doughnuts. He said he had spent ten minutes at a seminary before he had gone to fish-measuring school. He said he still looked back on those ten minutes as the most important minutes of his life.

5   Lisa said that the man she lived with before Jim had really liked doughnuts. She said he liked them so much that sometimes he would shoot at them with his gun, or flush them down the toilet. Sometimes, she said, he would put them on the living-room rug, climb up on the coffee table, and then jump off directly on top of them.

"It was scary," she said.

Carol and I smiled at each other.

Just then I dropped a peanut on the floor. It rolled behind the refrigerator. It was hard to get it out. It was very hard. But not so hard as other things. Other things had been harder.

"I like doughnuts as much as anyone," said Jim. He took a sip of his drink. "I like them at breakfast, and sometimes lunch."

10   "Now, hon, you know that's not true," said Lisa.

"What do you mean?" said Jim. "I like doughnuts a lot."

"No, you don't," said Lisa. "And I've never seen you eat a doughnut at lunch."

"Has it ever occurred to you once in your goddam life that I might not always tell you when I eat a goddam doughnut? Has that ever occurred to you once?" said Jim. "*Christ.*"

He took a sip from his drink, and then stopped, so he could smoke.

15   Jim's dog was scratching at the door, but we couldn't let him out. We were drinking and smoking.

When I met Jim he was still married to Nancy, his forty-fifth wife. They had been very much in love, but one day she inhaled too much helium and just floated away. Then he met Lisa.

When I introduced Jim to Carol he said that she was "a real person." I was glad, because my college girlfriend, Hillary, was a facsimile person. She was warm and loving, and with the proper equipment could be sent across the country in seconds. But things didn't work out.

"Has anyone ever seen a really big doughnut?" said Carol. "I did once. At a pawnshop in Maine." She paused. But she didn't say anything afterward, so actually it was less like a pause and more like a full stop.

"No," said Jim, taking a sip of his drink, "but I ate some miniature doughnuts once." He took a sip of the gin he was drinking. "I ate ten or twelve of them." Jim leaned back, rubbed his temples, and took a sip from his glass. "I thought," he said, pausing to take a sip of his drink, "that they were pretty," he continued, sipping from his drink, "good." Jim took one last sip, this time of my drink.

20   We reminisced about the best doughnuts we had had in our lives. "The best doughnut I ever had," said Jim, "was when I was working for Harry Niven. Do you remember Harry, honey?"

"Of course," said Lisa.

"Compared to him I can't measure fish at all," said Jim. "I mean, there was a man who could measure a fish!"

We went on talking.

"The best doughnut I ever had," said Lisa, "was when I was dating Daniel." We all knew about Daniel. They had been deeply in love and on the brink of marriage when Lisa realized that he was a hologram.

25   "Hold on a second, hon," Carol said to Lisa. She turned to me. "Do you want to get divorced?"

"O.K.," I said.

Carol and I left and got divorced. Then we came back with our new spouses, Dave and Terri.

We all sat there talking, the six of us in the dark. We went on talking and talking, even after the gin ran out. Talking about doughnuts. Talking about doughnuts in the dark.

[1999]

POETRY

ANONYMOUS

Western Wind

Westron wind, when will thou blow?
The small rain down can rain.
Christ, that my love were in my arms,
And I in my bed again.

[c. 1500]

Topics for Critical Thinking and Writing

1. In "Western Wind," what do you think is the tone of the speaker's voice in the first two lines? Angry? Impatient? Supplicating? Be as precise as possible. What is the tone in the next two lines?
2. In England, the west wind, warmed by the Gulf Stream, rises in the spring. What associations link the wind and rain of lines 1 and 2 with lines 3 and 4?
3. Ought we to have been told why the lovers are separated? Explain.

CHRISTOPHER MARLOWE

Christopher Marlowe (1564–1593), English poet and playwright, was born in the same year as Shakespeare. An early death, in a tavern brawl, cut short what might have been a brilliant career.

Marlowe's "Come Live with Me" is a pastoral poem; it depicts shepherds and shepherdesses in an idyllic, timeless setting. This poem engendered many imitations and replies, two of which we reprint after Marlowe's.

Come Live with Me and Be My Love

Come live with me and be my love,
And we will all the pleasures prove,
That valleys, groves, hills, and fields,
Woods or steepy mountain yields.

4

There we will sit upon the rocks,
And see the shepherds feed their flocks,
By shallow rivers to whose falls
Melodious birds sing madrigals.   8

And I will make thee beds of roses
With a thousand fragrant posies,
A cap of flowers, and a kirtle
Embroidered all with leaves of myrtle;   12

A gown made of the finest wool
Which from our pretty lambs we pull;
Fair lined slippers for the cold,
With buckles of the purest gold;   16

A belt of straw and ivy buds,
With coral clasps and amber studs:
And if these pleasures may thee move,
Come live with me and be my love.   20

The shepherds' swains shall dance and sing
For thy delight each May morning:
If these delights thy mind may move,
Then live with me and be my love.   24

[1599–1600]

Topic for Critical Thinking and Writing

Read the poem two or three times, preferably aloud. Of course Marlowe's poem is
not to be taken seriously as a picture of the pastoral (shepherd) life, but if you
have enjoyed the poem, exactly what have you enjoyed?

SIR WALTER RALEIGH

*Walter Raleigh (1552–1618) is known chiefly as a soldier and a colonizer—he was
the founder of the settlement in Virginia, and he introduced tobacco into Europe—
but in his own day he was known also as a poet.*

The Nymph's Reply to the Shepherd

If all the world and love were young,
And truth in every shepherd's tongue,
These pretty pleasures might me move,
To live with thee, and be thy love.   4

Time drives the flocks from field to fold,
When rivers rage, and rocks grow cold,

And Philomel° becometh dumb,
The rest complains of cares to come.   8

The flowers do fade, and wanton fields,
To wayward winter reckoning yields,
A honey tongue, a heart of gall,
Is fancy's spring, but sorrow's fall.   12

Thy gowns, thy shoes, thy beds of roses,
Thy cap, thy kirtle, and thy posies,
Soon break, soon wither, soon forgotten:
In folly ripe, in reason rotten.   16

Thy belt of straw and ivy buds,
Thy coral clasps and amber studs,
All these in me no means can move,
To come to thee, and be thy love.   20

But could youth last, and love still breed,
Had joys no date, nor age no need,
Then these delights my mind might move,
To live with thee and be thy love.   24

[c. 1600]

7 Philomel in Greek mythology, Philomela was a beautiful woman who was raped and later transformed into a chattering sparrow, but in most Roman versions she is transformed into the nightingale, noted for its beautiful song.

Topics for Critical Thinking and Writing

1. What is the season in Marlowe's poem? What season(s) does Raleigh envision?
2. Some readers find puns in line 12, in "fancy's spring, but sorrow's fall." How do you paraphrase and interpret the line? .
3. How would you describe the tone of the final stanza?
4. Now that you have read Raleigh's poem, reread Marlowe's. Do you now, in the context of Raleigh's poem, enjoy Marlowe's more than before, or less? Why?

JOHN DONNE

John Donne (1572–1631) wrote religious poetry as well as love poetry. In the fol-
lowing lyric, he alters Marlowe's pastoral setting to a setting involving people en-
gaged in fishing. The poem thus belongs to a type called piscatory lyric (Latin
piscis, "fish"). For a fuller biographical note, and another poem, see page 753.

The Bait

Come live with me, and be my love,
And we will some new pleasures prove
Of golden sands, and crystal brooks,
With silken lines, and silver hooks.   4

There will the river whispering run
Warmed by thy eyes, more than the Sun.
And there th'enamored fish will stay,
Begging themselves they may betray.   8

When thou wilt swim in that live bath,
Each fish, which every channel hath,
Will amorously to thee swim,
Gladder to catch thee, than thou him.   12

If thou, to be so seen, beest loath,
By Sun, or Moon, thou darknest both,
And if my self have leave to see,
I need not their light, having thee.   16

Let others freeze with angling reeds,
And cut their legs, with shells and weeds,
Or treacherously poor fish beset,
With strangling snare, or windowy net: 20

Let coarse bold hands, from slimy nest
The bedded fish in banks out-wrest,
Or curious traitors, sleavesilk flies
Bewitch poor fishes' wandring eyes.   24

For thee, thou needst no such deceit,
For thou thy self art thine own bait;
That fish, that is not catched thereby,
Alas, is wiser far than I.   28

[1633]

Topics for Critical Thinking and Writing

1. In Donne's first stanza, which words especially indicate that we are (as in Marlowe's poem) in an idealized world?
2. Which words later in Donne's poem indicate what (for Donne) the real world of fishing is?
3. Paraphrase the last stanza, making it as clear as possible.

WILLIAM SHAKESPEARE

Shakespeare (1564–1616) was born into a middle-class family in Stratford-upon-Avon. Although we have a fair number of records about his life—documents concerning marriage, the birth of children, the purchase of property, and so forth—it is not known exactly why and when he turned to the theater. What we do know, however, is important. He was an actor and a shareholder in a play-house, and he did write the plays that are attributed to him. The dates of some of the plays can be set precisely, but the dates of some others can be only roughly set. Hamlet was probably written between 1600 and 1601. Most of Shakespeare's

154 sonnets were probably written in the late 1590s, but they were not published until 1609.

Sonnet 29

When, in disgrace with Fortune and men's eyes,
I all alone beweep my outcast state,
And trouble deaf heaven with my bootless° cries,
And look upon myself and curse my fate,   4
Wishing me like to one more rich in hope,
Featured like him, like him° with friends possessed,
Desiring this man's art and that man's scope,
With what I most enjoy contented least;   8
Yet in these thoughts myself almost despising,
Haply° I think on thee, and then my state,
Like to the lark at break of day arising
From sullen earth, sings hymns at heaven's gate;   12
    For thy sweet love rememb'red such wealth brings,
    That then I scorn to change my state with kings.

[c. 1600]

3 **bootless** useless.   6 **like him, like him** like a second man, like a third man.
10 **Haply** perchance.

Topics for Critical Thinking and Writing

1. Paraphrase the first eight lines. Then, in a sentence, summarize the speaker's state of mind to this point in the poem.
2. Summarize the speaker's state of mind in lines 9–12. What does "sullen earth" (line 12) suggest to you?
3. Notice that every line in the poem except line 11 ends with a comma or semi-colon, indicating a pause. How does the lack of punctuation at the end of line 11 affect your reading of this line and your understanding of the speaker's emotion?
4. In the last two lines of a sonnet Shakespeare often summarizes the preceding lines. In this sonnet, how does the *structure* (the organization) of the summary differ from that of the statement in the first twelve lines? Why? (Try reading the last lines as if they were reversed. Thus:

   > For then I scorn to change my state with kings.
   > Since thy sweet love rememb'red such wealth brings.)

   Which version do you like better? Why?
5. The "thee" of this poem is almost certainly a man, not a woman. Is the "love" of the poem erotic love, or can it be taken as something like brotherly love or even as loving-kindness?
6. Write a paragraph (or a sonnet) describing how thinking of someone you love—or hate—changes your mood.

Sonnet 116

Let me not to the marriage of true minds
Admit impediments; love is not love
Which alters when it alteration finds,
Or bends with the remover to remove.   4
O, no, it is an ever-fixèd mark°
That looks on tempests and is never shaken;
It is the star° to every wand'ring bark,
Whose worth's unknown, although his height be taken.   8
Love's not Time's fool,° though rosy lips and cheeks
Within his bending sickle's compass° come;
Love alters not with his° brief hours and weeks
But bears° it out even to the edge of doom.°   12
    If this be error and upon° me proved,
    I never writ, nor no man ever loved.

[c. 1600]

5 ever-fixèd mark seamark, guide to mariners.   **7 the star** the North Star.   **9 fool** plaything.
10 compass range, circle.   **11 his** Time's.   **12 bears** survives;   **doom** Judgment Day.
13 upon against.

Topics for Critical Thinking and Writing

1. Paraphrase (that is, put into your own words) "Let me not to the marriage of true minds / Admit impediments." Is there more than one appropriate meaning of "Admit"?
2. Notice that the poem celebrates "the marriage of true minds," not bodies. In a sentence or two, using only your own words, summarize Shakespeare's idea of the nature of such love, both what it is and what it is not.
3. Paraphrase lines 13–14. What is the speaker's tone here? Would you say that the tone is different from the tone in the rest of the poem?
4. Write a paragraph or a poem defining either love or hate. Or see if you can find such a definition in a popular song. Bring the lyrics to class.

JOHN DONNE

John Donne (1572–1631) was born into a Roman Catholic family in England, but in the 1590s he abandoned that faith. In 1615 he became an Anglican priest and soon was known as a great preacher. A hundred and sixty of his sermons survive, including one with the famous line "No man is an island, entire of itself; every man is a piece of the continent, a part of the main; if a clod be washed away by the sea, Europe is the less. . . ; and therefore never send to know for whom the bell tolls; it tolls for thee." From 1621 until his death Donne was dean of St. Paul's Cathedral in London. His love poems (often bawdy and cynical) are said to be his early work, and his "Holy Sonnets" (among the greatest religious poems written in English) his later work.

A Valediction: Forbidding Mourning

As virtuous men pass mildly away,
    And whisper to their souls, to go,
Whilst some of their sad friends do say,
    "The breath goes now," and some say, "No":   4

So let us melt, and make no noise.
    No tear-floods, nor sigh-tempests move.
'Twere profanation of our joys
    To tell the laity our love.   8

Moving of the earth° brings harms and fears,
    Men reckon what it did and meant;
But trepidation of the spheres,
    Though greater far, is innocent.°   12

Dull sublunary° lovers' love
    (Whose soul is sense) cannot admit
Absence, because it doth remove
    Those things which elemented it.   16

But we, by a love so much refined
    That our selves know not what it is,
Inter-assurèd of the mind,
    Care less, eyes, lips, and hands to miss.   20

Our two souls therefore, which are one,
    Though I must go, endure not yet
A breach, but an expansion,
    Like gold to airy thinness beat.   24

If they be two, they are two so
    As stiff twin compasses° are two:
Thy soul, the fixed foot, makes no show
    To move, but doth, if the other do.   28

And though it in the center sit,
    Yet when the other far doth roam,
It leans, and hearkens after it,
    And grows erect, as that comes home.   32

Such wilt thou be to me, who must
    Like the other foot, obliquely run:
Thy firmness makes my circle just,
    And makes me end where I begun.   36

[1611]

---

9 Moving of the earth an earthquake.   **11–12 But trepidation . . . innocent** But the movement of the heavenly spheres (in Ptolemaic astronomy), though far greater, is harmless.
13 sublunary under the moon, i.e., earthly.   **26 compasses** i.e., a carpenter's compass.

Topics for Critical Thinking and Writing

1. The first stanza describes the death of "virtuous men." To what is their death compared in the second stanza?

2. Who is the speaker of this poem? To whom does he speak, and what is the occasion? Explain the title.

3. What is the meaning of "laity" in line 8? What does it imply about the speaker and his beloved?

4. In the fourth stanza the speaker contrasts the love of "dull sublunary lovers" (i.e., ordinary mortals) with the love he and his beloved share. What is the difference?

5. In the figure of the carpenter's or draftsperson's compass (lines 25–36) the speaker offers reasons—some stated clearly, some not so clearly—why he will end where he began. In 250 words explain these reasons.

6. In line 35 Donne speaks of his voyage as a "circle." Explain in a paragraph why the circle is traditionally a symbol of perfection.

7. Write a farewell note—or poem—to someone you love (or hate).

ANDREW MARVELL

Born in 1621 near Hull in England, Marvell attended Trinity College, Cambridge, and graduated in 1638. During the Civil War he was tutor to the daughter of Sir Thomas Fairfax in Yorkshire at Nun Appleton House, where most of his best-known poems were written. In 1657 he was appointed assistant to John Milton, the Latin Secretary for the Commonwealth. After the Restoration of the monarchy in 1659 until his death, Marvell represented Hull as a member of Parliament. Most of his poems were not published until after his death in 1678.

To His Coy Mistress

Had we but world enough, and time,
This coyness, lady, were no crime.
We would sit down, and think which way
To walk, and pass our long love's day.
Thou by the Indian Ganges' side   5
Should'st rubies find: I by the tide
Of Humber° would complain.° I would
Love you ten years before the Flood,
And you should, if you please, refuse
Till the conversion of the Jews.   10
My vegetable° love should grow
Vaster than empires, and more slow.
An hundred years should go to praise

---

7 Humber river in England;   **complain** write love poems.   **11 vegetable** slowly growing.

Thine eyes, and on thy forehead gaze:
Two hundred to adore each breast: 15
But thirty thousand to the rest.
An age at least to every part,
And the last age should show your heart.
For, lady, you deserve this state,
Nor would I love at lower rate,   20
    But at my back I always hear
Time's winged chariot hurrying near;
And yonder all before us lie
Deserts of vast eternity.
Thy beauty shall no more be found,   25
Nor in thy marble vault shall sound
My echoing song; then worms shall try
That long preserved virginity,
And your quaint honor turn to dust,
And into ashes all my lust.   30
The grave's a fine and private place,
But none, I think, do there embrace.
    Now therefore, while the youthful hue
Sits on thy skin like morning dew,
And while thy willing soul transpires   35
At every pore with instant fires,
Now let us sport us while we may;
And now, like am'rous birds of prey,
Rather at once our time devour,
Than languish in his slow-chapt° power,   40
Let us roll all our strength, and all
Our sweetness, up into one ball;
And tear our pleasures with rough strife
Thorough° the iron gates of life.
Thus, though we cannot make our sun   45
Stand still, yet we will make him run.

[1641]

---

40 **slow-chapt** slowly devouring.   44 **thorough** through.

Topics for Critical Thinking and Writing

1. What does "coy" mean in the title, and "coyness" in line 2?
2. Do you think that the speaker's claims in lines 1–20 are so inflated that we detect behind them a playfully ironic tone? Explain. Why does the speaker say in line 8 that he would love "ten years before the Flood," rather than merely "since the Flood"?
3. What do you make of lines 21–24? Why is time behind the speaker, and eternity in front of him? Is this "eternity" the same as the period discussed in lines 1–20? Discuss the change in the speaker's tone after line 20.

WILLIAM BLAKE

William Blake (1757–1827) was born in London and at 14 was apprenticed for seven years to an engraver. A Christian visionary poet, he made his living by giving drawing lessons and by illustrating books, including his own Songs of Innocence *(1789) and* Songs of Experience *(1794). These two books represent, he said, "two contrary states of the human soul." In 1809 Blake exhibited his art, but the show was a failure. Not until he was in his sixties, when he stopped writing poetry, did he achieve any public recognition—and then it was as a painter.*

The Garden of Love

I went to the Garden of Love,
And saw what I never had seen:
A Chapel was built in the midst,
Where I used to play on the green.   4

And the gates of this Chapel were shut,
And "Thou shalt not" writ over the door;
So I turn'd to the Garden of Love,
That so many sweet flowers bore,   8

And I saw it was filled with graves,
And tomb-stones where flowers should be;
And Priests in black gowns were walking their rounds,
And binding with briars my joys & desires.   12

[1794]

Topics for Critical Thinking and Writing

1. What is the speaker's mood as he surveys "the Garden of Love"? What does he report?
2. Does the form of the poem contribute to the speaker's mood? Try taking out the *ands* wherever you can, consistent with the meaning of the sentences. There is a change in effect, but can you say what it is?
3. In a brief essay (500 words) compare Blake's "The Echoing Green" (p. 914) with "The Garden of Love."

A Poison Tree

I was angry with my friend:
I told my wrath, my wrath did end.
I was angry with my foe:
I told it not, my wrath did grow.   4

And I watered it in fears,
Night and morning with my tears:
And I sunnèd it with smiles,
And with soft deceitful wiles.   8

"The Garden of Love" by William Blake, from *Songs of Experience*. (By kind permission of the Provost and Scholars of King's College, Cambridge.)

And it grew both day and night,
Till it bore an apple bright.
And my foe beheld it shine,
And he knew that it was mine.   12

And into my garden stole
When the night had veiled the pole:
In the morning glad I see
My foe outstretched beneath the tree.   16

[1794]

Topics for Critical Thinking and Writing

1. In the first stanza, the speaker describes two actions. What is the difference between them? Does the poem indicate that we should choose one action over
   the other?
2. What reaction do you have to the speaker in stanza 2?
3. In stanzas 3 and 4, what does the "foe" do? Paraphrase line 14.
4. The poem ends, "In the morning glad I see / My foe outstretched beneath the
   tree." Does the reader share this gladness to any degree? Explain.
5. Like many of Blake's other poems, this one has a childlike tone. Does the tone
   enrich or does it impoverish the poem? Why?

WALT WHITMAN

*Walt Whitman (1819–1892) was born in a farmhouse in rural Long Island, New
York, but was brought up in Brooklyn, then an independent city in New York. He
attended public school for a few years (1825–1830), apprenticed as a printer in
the 1830s, and then worked as a typesetter, journalist, and newspaper editor. In
1855 he published the first edition of a collection of his poems,* Leaves of Grass, *a
book that he revised and republished throughout the remainder of his life. During
the Civil War, he served as a volunteer nurse for the Union army.*

In the third edition of Leaves of Grass *(1860) Whitman added two groups of
poems, one called "Children of Adam" and the other (named for an aromatic grass
that grows near ponds and swamps) called "Calamus." "Children of Adam" celebrates heterosexual relations, whereas "Calamus" celebrates what Whitman called
"manly love." Although the "Calamus" poems seem clearly homosexual, perhaps
the very fact that Whitman published them made them seem relatively innocent; in
any case, those nineteenth-century critics who condemned Whitman for the sexuality of his writing concentrated on the poems in "Children of Adam."*

*We give two poems from the "Calamus" section. Both were originally published
in the third edition of* Leaves of Grass *(1860), and both were revised into their final forms in the 1867 edition. We give them in the 1867 versions. We also include
the manuscript for one of the poems, showing it in its earliest extant versions.*

Calamus 20
p. 364

II

I saw in Louisiana a
    live-oak growing,
All alone stood it, and the
    moss hung down from the
    branches,
Without any companion it grew
    there, glistening out ~~with~~
    joyous leaves of dark green,
And its look, rude, unbending,
    lusty, made me think of
        myself;
But I wondered how it could
    utter joyous leaves, standing
    alone there without its friend,
    its lover — For I knew I could
    not;
And I plucked a twig with
    a certain number of leaves
    upon it, and twined around
    it a little moss, and brought
    it away — And I have placed
    it in sight in my room,

2

Walt Whitman, "I Saw in Louisiana a Live-Oak Growing," manuscript of 1860. On the first
leaf, in line 3 Whitman deleted "with." On the second leaf, in the third line (line 8 of the
printed text) he added, with a caret, "lately." In the sixth line on this leaf he deleted, "I
write these pieces, and name them after it," replacing the deletion with "it makes me think

It is not needed to remind
me as of my friends, (for I
believe lately think of little
else than of them,)
Yet it remains to me a
curious token - it makes
~~me think of manl love,~~
~~those pieces and name~~
~~them after it~~;
For all that, and though the
~~live oak~~
~~tree~~ glistens there in Louisiana, solitary in a wide
flat space, uttering joyous
leaves all its life, without
a friend, a lover, near - I
know very well I could
not.

3

of manly love." In the next line he deleted "tree" and inserted "live oak." When he reprinted
the poem in the 1867 version of *Leaves of Grass,* he made further changes, as you will see
if you compare the printed text with this manuscript version. (Walt Whitman Collection,
Clifton Waller Barrett Library of American Literature, The Albery Shirley Small Special
Collections Library, University of Virginia Library.)

When I Heard at the Close of the Day

When I heard at the close of the day how my name had been receiv'd with
    plaudits in the capitol, still it was not a happy night for me that follow'd,
And else when I carous'd, or when my plans were accomplish'd, still I was
    not happy,
But the day when I rose at dawn from the bed of perfect health, refresh'd,
    singing, inhaling the ripe breath of autumn,
When I saw the full moon in the west grow pale and disappear in the
    morning light,
When I wander'd alone over the beach, and undressing bathed, laughing
    with the cool waters, and saw the sun rise,   5
And when I thought how my dear friend my lover was on his way coming,
    O then I was happy,
O then each breath tasted sweeter, and all that day my food nourish'd me
    more, and the beautiful day pass'd well.
And the next came with equal joy, and with the next at evening came my
    friend,
And that night while all was still I heard the waters roll slowly continually up
    the shores,
I heard the hissing rustle of the liquid and sands as directed to me
    whispering to congratulate me,   10
For the one I love most lay sleeping by me under the same cover in the cool
    night,
In the stillness in the autumn moonbeams his face was inclined toward me,
And his arm lay lightly around my breast—and that night I was happy.

[1867]

Topics for Critical Thinking and Writing

1. Let's assume that the word *plot*—the gist of what happens—can be applied not
   only to prose fiction and to plays but also to lyric poems. How would you
   summarize the plot of this poem?
2. If someone were to ask you why "When I Heard at the Close of the Day" is regarded as a poem rather than as prose arranged to look like a poem, what
   would you reply?

I Saw in Louisiana a Live-Oak Growing

I saw in Louisiana a live-oak growing,
All alone stood it and the moss hung down from the branches,
Without any companion it grew there uttering joyous leaves of dark green,
And its look, rude, unbending, lusty, made me think of myself,
But I wonder'd how it could utter joyous leaves standing alone there without
    its friend near, for I knew I could not,   5
And I broke off a twig with a certain number of leaves upon it, and twined
    around it a little moss,

And brought it away, and I have placed it in sight in my room,
It is not needed to remind me as of my own dear friends,
(For I believe lately I think of little else than of them,)
Yet it remains to me a curious token, it makes me think of manly love;   10
For all that, and though the live-oak glistens there in Louisiana solitary in a
    wide flat space,
Uttering joyous leaves all its life without a friend a lover near,
I know very well I could not.

[1867]

Topic for Critical Thinking and Writing

Compare the final version (1867) of the poem with the manuscript version of 1860. Which version do you prefer? Why?

EDNA ST. VINCENT MILLAY

Edna St. Vincent Millay (1892–1950) was born in Rockland, Maine. Even as a child she wrote poetry, and by the time she graduated from Vassar College (1917) she had achieved some note as a poet. Millay settled for a while in Greenwich Village, a center of Bohemian activity in New York City, where she wrote, performed in plays, and engaged in feminist causes. In 1923, the year she married, she became the first woman to win the Pulitzer Prize for Poetry. Numerous other awards followed. Though she is best known as a lyric poet—especially as a writer of sonnets—she also wrote memorable political poetry and nature poetry as well as short stories, plays, and a libretto for an opera.

Love Is Not All: It Is Not Meat nor Drink

Love is not all: it is not meat nor drink
Nor slumber nor a roof against the rain;
Nor yet a floating spar to men that sink
And rise and sink and rise and sink again;   4
Love can not fill the thickened lung with breath,
Nor clean the blood, nor set the fractured bone;
Yet many a man is making friends with death
Even as I speak, for lack of love alone.   8

It well may be that in a difficult hour,
Pinned down by pain and moaning for release,
Or nagged by want past resolution's power,
I might be driven to sell your love for peace,   12
Or trade the memory of this night for food.
It well may be. I do not think I would.

[1931]

Topics for Critical Thinking and Writing

1. "Love Is Not All" is a sonnet. Using your own words, briefly summarize the argument of the octet (the first 8 lines). Next, paraphrase the sestet, line by line. On the whole, does the sestet repeat the idea of the octet, or does it add a new idea? Whom did you imagine to be speaking the octet? What does the sestet add to your knowledge of the speaker and the occasion? (And how did you paraphrase line 11?)
2. The first and last lines of the poem consist of words of one syllable, and both lines have a distinct pause in the middle. Do you imagine the lines to be spoken in the same tone of voice? If not, can you describe the difference and account for it?
3. Lines 7 and 8 appear to mean that the absence of love can be a cause of death. To what degree do you believe that to be true?
4. Would you call "Love Is Not All" a love poem? Why or why not? Describe the kind of person who might include the poem in a love letter or valentine, or who would be happy to receive it. (One of our friends recited it at her wedding. What do you think of that idea?)

ROBERT FROST

Robert Frost (1874–1963) was born in California. After his father's death in 1885, Frost's mother brought the family to New England, where she taught in high schools in Massachusetts and New Hampshire. Frost studied for part of one term at Dartmouth College in New Hampshire, then did odd jobs (including teaching), and from 1897 to 1899 was enrolled as a special student at Harvard. He later farmed in New Hampshire, published a few poems in local newspapers, left the farm and taught again, and in 1912 left for England, where he hoped to achieve more popular success as a writer. By 1915 he had won a considerable reputation, and he returned to the United States, settling on a farm in New Hampshire and cultivating the image of the country-wise farmer-poet. In fact he was well read in the classics, in the Bible, and in English and American literature.

Among Frost's many comments about literature, here are three: "Writing is unboring to the extent that it is dramatic"; "Every poem is . . . a figure of the will braving alien entanglements"; and, finally, a poem "begins in delight and ends in wisdom. . . . It runs a course of lucky events, and ends in a clarification of life—not necessarily a great clarification, such as sects and cults are founded on, but in a momentary stay against confusion."

The Silken Tent

She is as in a field a silken tent
At midday when a sunny summer breeze
Has dried the dew and all its ropes relent,
So that in guys it gently sways at ease,   4
And its supporting central cedar pole,
That is its pinnacle to heavenward
And signifies the sureness of the soul,
Seems to owe naught to any single cord,   8

The handwritten draft of "The Silken Tent" showing Frost's revisions:

The Silken Tent

She is as in a field a silken tent
At midday when a summer breeze
Has dried the dew and all its ropes relent,
So that in guys it gently sways at ease,
And its supporting central cedar pole,
That is its pinnacle to heavenward
And signifies the sureness of the soul,
Seems to owe naught to any single cord,
But strictly held by none, is loosely bound
By countless silken ties of love and thought
To everything on earth the compass round,
And only by one's going slightly taut
In the capriciousness of summer air,
Is of the slightest bondage made aware.

Page from Frost's notebooks, showing "The Silken Tent." (Printed with the permission of The Poetry/Rare Books Collection, University Libraries, State University of New York at Buffalo.)

But strictly held by none, is loosely bound
By countless silken ties of love and thought
To everything on earth the compass round,
And only by one's going slightly taut   12
In the capriciousness of summer air
Is of the slightest bondage made aware.

[1943]

Topics for Critical Thinking and Writing

1. The second line places the scene at "midday" in "summer." In addition to giving us the concreteness of a setting, do these words help to characterize the woman whom the speaker describes? If so, how?

2. The tent is supported by "guys" (not men, but the cords or "ties" of line 10) and by its "central cedar pole." What does Frost tell us about these ties? What does he tell us about the pole?

3. What do you make of lines 12–14?

4. In a sentence, a paragraph, or a poem, construct a simile that explains a relationship.

ADRIENNE RICH

Adrienne Rich was born in Baltimore in 1929. Since the selection of her first volume by W. H. Auden for the Yale Series of Younger Poets in 1951, her work has continually broken new ground, moving from closed forms to feminist poetics and radical politics. A selection of her poems is collected in The Fact of a Doorframe: Poems 1950–2001 *(2002). Her prose works include* On Lies, Secrets, and Silence *(1979),* Blood, Bread, and Poetry *(1986), and* What Is Found There *(1993). Her work has received many awards—most notably the Lenore Marshall/Nation Award, the Lambda Literary Award, the Frost Medal from the Poetry Society of America, the Wallace Stevens Award of the Academy of American Poets, the Lannan Foundation Lifetime Achievement Award, and the Bollingen Prize.*

Novella

Two people in a room, speaking harshly.
One gets up, goes out to walk.
(That is the man.)
The other goes out into the next room
and washes the dishes, cracking one.   5
(That is the woman.)
It gets dark outside.
The children quarrel in the attic.
She has no blood left in her heart.
The man comes back to a dark house.   10
The only light is in the attic.
He has forgotten his key.
He rings at his own door
and hears sobbing on the stairs.
The lights go on in the house.   15
The door closes behind him.
Outside, separate as minds.
the stars too come alight.

                                                        [1967]

*XI.**

Every peak is a crater. This is the law of volcanoes,
making them eternally and visibly female.
No height without depth, without a burning core,
though our straw soles shred on the hardened lava.
I want to travel with you to every sacred mountain   5
smoking within like the sibyl stooped over her tripod,
I want to reach for your hand as we scale the path,
to feel your arteries glowing in my clasp,
never failing to note the small, jewel-like flower
unfamiliar to us, nameless till we rename her,   10

---

* From *Twenty-One Love Poems.*

that clings to the slowly altering rock—
that detail outside ourselves that brings us to ourselves,
was here before us, knew we would come, and sees beyond us.

[1978]

ROBERT PACK

Robert Pack, born in New York City in 1929, was educated at Dartmouth College and at Columbia University. The author of several books of poems, he teaches at Middlebury College in Vermont.

The Frog Prince

(A Speculation on Grimm's Fairy Tale)

Imagine the princess' surprise!
Who would have thought a frog's cold frame
Could hold the sweet and gentle body
Of a prince? How can I name
The joy she must have felt to learn   5
His transformation was the wonder
Of her touch—that she too, in
Her way, had been transformed under
Those clean sheets? Such powers were
Like nothing she had ever read.   10
And in the morning when her mother
Came and saw them there in bed,
Heard how a frog became a prince;
What was it that her mother said?

[1980]

Topics for Critical Thinking and Writing

1. Fairy-tale characters seldom have characteristics that go beyond the legend they are in. What characteristics does Pack give to the princess? How do you understand "she too, in / Her way, had been transformed" (lines 7–8)?
2. And "What was it that her mother said?"
3. Transform a fairy tale that you know by giving one character or two some realistic traits. Retell the story, or one scene from it.

JOSEPH BRODSKY

The poet and critic Joseph Brodsky (1940–1996) was born in St. Petersburg (then Leningrad), Russia in 1940. Because of his resistance to Soviet authority, he was sentenced in the 1960s to a labor camp and later, in 1972, was expelled from the country. He emigrated to the United States, and taught and lectured at a number of colleges and universities. He received the Nobel Prize in Literature in 1987 and was named Poet Laureate by the Library of Congress in 1991. His books include a collection of poems, To Urania *(1988), and* Less Than One: Selected Essays *(1986).*

Love Song

If you were drowning, I'd come to the rescue,
    wrap you in my blanket and pour hot tea.
If I were a sheriff, I'd arrest you
    and keep you in the cell under lock and key.

If you were a bird, I'd cut a record   5
    and listen all night long to your high-pitched trill.
If I were a sergeant, you'd be my recruit,
    and boy I can assure you you'd love the drill.

If you were Chinese, I'd learn the language,
    burn a lot of incense, wear funny clothes.   10
If you were a mirror, I'd storm the Ladies,
    give you my red lipstick and puff your nose.

If you loved volcanoes, I'd be lava
    relentlessly erupting from my hidden source.
And if you were my wife, I'd be your lover   15
    because the church is firmly against divorce.

                                                         [1996]

Topics for Critical Thinking and Writing

1. This poem is structurally simple: four stanzas long, it is based on a series of if/then sentences (although the "then" is only implied). Start with the first of these in lines 1–2. How does this scene portray the speaker and the person being addressed? Now move to the next, in lines 3–4, and explain as clearly as you can how this if/then differs in tone and emphasis from the one before. And so on through the poem as a whole.

2. Lines 15–16 bring the poem to a close with a line that begins with "And" rather than "If." Put the speaker's witty point here into your own words. Are these final lines comic or serious or both?

NIKKI GIOVANNI

Nikki Giovanni was born in Knoxville, Tennessee, in 1943 and educated at Fisk University, the University of Pennsylvania School of Social Work, and Columbia University. She has taught at Queens College, Rutgers University, and The Ohio State University, and she now teaches creative writing at Mt. St. Joseph on the Ohio. Giovanni has published many books of po-ems, an autobiography (Gemini: An Extended Autobiographical Statement on My First Twenty-Five Years of Being a Black Poet), *a book of essays, and a book consisting of a conversation with James Baldwin (1972).*

Love in Place

I really don't remember falling in love all that much
I remember wanting to bake corn bread and boil a ham and I
certainly remember making lemon pie and when I used to smoke I
stopped in the middle of my day to contemplate

I know I must have fallen in love once because I quit biting   5
my cuticles and my hair is gray and that must indicate
something and I all of a sudden had a deeper appreciation
for Billie Holiday° and Billy Strayhorn° so if it wasn't love I don't
know what it was

I see the old photographs and I am smiling and I'm sure quite   10
happy but what I mostly see is me
through your eyes
and I am still young and slim and very much committed to the
love we still have

                                                                                    [1997]

8 **Billie Holiday** jazz singer (1915–1959); **Billy Strayhorn** jazz composer and musician (1915–1967).

Topics for Critical Thinking and Writing

1. What reasons does the speaker offer for supposing that she once fell in love? How seriously does she expect us to take those reasons?
2. Read the poem again, but begin with the third stanza and then read the first and second stanzas. Does it make a difference? If so, what is the difference?
3. In line 14 we learn of the "love we still have." Does "still" refer to the present, or to the time of the "old photographs" (10), as the "still" in line 13 does?
4. Why do you suppose Giovanni puts extra space between the words?
5. What do you make of the title?
6. In the first line Giovanni speaks of "falling in love," and she returns to the idea in the fifth line. Judging from your own experience (which includes your knowledge of the people around you), is the term "falling in love" apt, or do people come to love one another in a more gradual fashion than "falling in

love" implies? In responding to this question, in an essay of 500 words, you may want to take into consideration a remark by the English essayist William Hazlitt (1778–1830), in his *Table Talk* (1822):

> I do not think that what is called *Love at first sight* is so great an absurdity as it is sometimes imagined to be. We generally make up our minds beforehand to the sort of person we should like, grave or gay, black, brown, or fair; with golden tresses or raven locks;—and when we meet with a complete example of the qualities we admire, the bargain is soon struck.

CAROL MUSKE

Carol Muske was born in 1945 in St. Paul, Minnesota, and educated at Creighton University and San Francisco State College (now University). She has taught creative writing at several universities and was the founder and director of Free Space (a creative writing program) at the Women's House of Detention, Riker's Island, New York. She has written several books of poetry (and a novel, Dear Digby *[1989], published under her married name, Carol Muske-Dukes) and has been awarded distinguished fellowships, including a grant from the National Endowment for the Arts.*

Chivalry

In Benares°
the holiest city on earth
I saw an old man
toiling up the stone steps
to the ghat°   5
his dead wife in his arms
shrunken to the size
of a child—
lashed to a stretcher.

The sky filled with crows.   10
He held her up for a moment
then placed her
in the flames.

In my time on earth
I have seen few acts of true chivalry,   15
man's reverence
for woman.

---

1 Benares one of India's most ancient cities; located on the Ganges River, it is the holy city of the Hindus and the site of pilgrimages.   **5 ghat** a broad flight of steps on an Indian riverbank that provides access to the water.

But the memory of him
with her
in the cradle of his arms   20
placing her just so in the fire
so she would burn faster
so the kindling of the stretcher
would catch—
is enough for me now,   25
will suffice
for what remains on this earth
a gesture of bereavement
in the familiar carnage of love.

[1997]

Topics for Critical Thinking and Writing

1. Do you find the poem shocking? Even more to the point: do you find it shocking that the speaker refers to this scene as an example of chivalry?
2. What is the meaning of the final line? Why the word "carnage"? How does this word in particular fit (or, in your view, not fit) in the structure of the poem as a whole?

KITTY TSUI

Born in Hong Kong in 1953, Kitty Tsui lived there and in England until 1969, when she came to the United States. She is an actor, an artist, and a professional bodybuilder, as well as a writer. Her publications include Breathless: Erotica *(1996).*

A Chinese Banquet

for the one who was not invited

it was not a very formal affair but
all the women over twelve
wore long gowns and a corsage,
except for me.   4

it was not a very formal affair, just
the family getting together,
poa poa,° *kuw fu*° without *kuw mow*°
(her excuse this year is a headache).   8

aunts and uncles and cousins,
the grandson who is a dentist,

---

7 *poa poa* maternal grandmother; *kuw fu* uncle; *kuw mow* aunt.

the one who drives a mercedes benz,
sitting down for shark's fin soup.   12

they talk about buying a house and
taking a two week vacation in beijing.
i suck on shrimp and squab,
dreaming of the cloudscape in your eyes.   16

my mother, her voice beaded with sarcasm;
you're twenty six and not getting younger.
it's about time you got a decent job.
she no longer asks when i'm getting married.   20

you're twenty six and not getting younger.
what are you doing with your life?
you've got to make a living.
why don't you study computer programming?   24

she no longer asks when i'm getting married.
one day, wanting desperately to
bridge the boundaries that separate us,
wanting desperately to touch her,   28

tell her: mother, i'm gay,
mother i'm gay and so happy with her.
but she will not listen,
she shakes her head.   32

she sits across from me,
emotions invading her face.
her eyes are wet but
she will not let tears fall.   36

mother, i say,
you love a man.
i love a woman.
it is not what she wants to hear.   40

aunts and uncles and cousins,
very much a family affair.
but you are not invited,
being neither my husband nor my wife.   44

aunts and uncles and cousins
eating longevity noodles
fragrant with ham inquire:
sold that old car of yours yet?   48

i want to tell them: my back is healing,
i dream of dragons and water.
my home is in her arms,
our bedroom ceiling the wide open sky.   52

[1983]

Topic for Critical Thinking and Writing

An important element of the poem is the very conventional nature of the speaker's family, with its values and views so at odds with the speaker's. Do you think that the conflict between the speaker and her family might be too obvious, too predictable? If you do, how would you respond to the poet if she said, "But that's the way it really was"?

DRAMA

TERRENCE MCNALLY

Terrence McNally, born in 1939 in St. Petersburg, Florida, grew up in Corpus Christi, Texas, and did his undergraduate work at Columbia University. "I'm a gay man who writes plays," he has said, and most of his work concerns gay people—or the responses of straight people to gay people.

We give the original script of Andre's Mother *(1988); McNally later amplified it for a 1990 television broadcast (running time is 58 minutes) that was awarded an Emmy.*

Andre's Mother

CHARACTERS

Cal, a young man
Arthur, his father
Penny, his sister
Andre's Mother
Time: *Now*
Place: *New York City, Central Park*

   Four people—Cal, Arthur, Penny, and Andre's Mother—enter: They are nicely dressed and each carries a white helium-filled balloon on a string.

CAL: You know what's really terrible? I can't think of anything terrific to say. Good-bye. I love you. I'll miss you. And I'm supposed to be so great with words!
PENNY: What's that over there?
ARTHUR: Ask your brother.
CAL: It's a theatre. An outdoor theatre. They do plays there in the summer. Shakespeare's plays. *(To Andre's Mother.)* God, how much he wanted to play Hamlet again. he would have gone to Timbuktu to have another go at that part. The summer he did it in Boston, he was so happy!
PENNY: Cal, I don't think she . . . ! It's not the time. Later.
ARTHUR: Your son was a . . . the Jews have a word for it . . . .
PENNY *(quietly appalled):*   Oh my God!

ARTHUR: Mensch, I believe it is, and I think I'm using it right. It means warm, solid, the real thing. Correct me if I'm wrong.

PENNY: Fine, Dad, fine. Just quit while you're ahead.

ARTHUR: I won't say he was like a son to me. Even my son isn't always like a son to me. I mean . . . ! In my clumsy way, I'm trying to say how much I liked Andre. And how much he helped me to know my own boy. Cal was always two handsful but Andre and I could talk about anything under the sun. My wife was very fond of him, too.

PENNY: Cal, I don't understand about the balloons.

CAL: They represent the soul. When you let go, it means you're letting his soul ascend to Heaven. That you're willing to let go. Breaking the last earthly ties.

PENNY: Does the Pope know about this?

ARTHUR: Penny!

PENNY: Andre loved my sense of humor. Listen, you can hear him laughing. *(She lets go of her white balloon.)* So long, you glorious, wonderful, I-know-what-Cal-means-about-words . . . *man!* God forgive me for wishing you were straight every time I laid eyes on you. But if any man was going to have you, I'm glad it was my brother! Look how fast it went up. I bet that means something. Something terrific.

ARTHUR *(lets his balloon go):*   Good-bye. God speed.

PENNY: Cal?

CAL: I'm not ready yet.

PENNY: Okay. We'll be over there. Come on, Pop, you can buy your little girl a Good Humor.

ARTHUR: They still make Good Humor?

PENNY: Only now they're called Dove Bars and they cost twelve dollars.

(Penny takes Arthur off. Cal and Andre's Mother stand with their balloons.)

CAL: I wish I knew what you were thinking. I think it would help me. You know almost nothing about me and I only know what Andre told me about you. I'd always had it in my mind that one day we would be friends, you and me. But if you didn't know about Andre and me . . . If this hadn't happened, I wonder if he would have ever told you. When he was sick, if I asked him once I asked him a thousand times, tell her. She's your mother. She won't mind. But he was so afraid of hurting you and of your disapproval. I don't know which was worse. *(No response. He sighs.)* God, how many of us live in this city because we don't want to hurt our mothers and live in mortal terror of their disapproval. We lose ourselves here. Our lives aren't furtive, just our feelings toward people like you are! A city of fugitives from our parents' scorn or heartbreak. Sometimes he'd seem a little down and I'd say, "What's the matter, babe?" and this funny sweet, sad smile would cross his face and he'd say, "Just a little homesick, Cal, just a little bit." I always accused him of being a country boy just playing at being a hotshot, sophisticated New Yorker. *(He sighs.)*

It's bullshit. It's all bullshit. *(Still no response.)*

Do you remember the comic strip *Little Lulu?* Her mother had no name, she was so remote, so formidable to all the children. She was just Lulu's mother. "Hello, Lulu's Mother," Lulu's friends would say. She was almost anonymous in her remoteness. You remind me of her, Andre's Mother. Let me answer the questions you can't ask and then I'll leave you alone and you won't ever have to see me again. Andre died of AIDS. I don't know how he got it. I tested negative. He died bravely. You would have been proud of him. The only thing that frightened him was you. I'll have everything that was his sent to you. I'll pay for it. There isn't much. You should have come up the summer he played Hamlet. He was magnificent. Yes, I'm bitter. I'm bitter I've lost him. I'm bitter what's happening. I'm bitter even now, after all this, I can't reach you. I'm beginning to feel your disapproval and it's making me ill. *(He looks at his balloon.)* Sorry, old friend. I blew it. *(He lets go of the balloon.)*

Good night, sweet prince, and flights of angels sing thee to they rest![1] *(Beat.)*

Goodbye, Andre's Mother.

(He goes. Andre's Mother stands alone holding her white balloon. Her lips tremble. She looks on the verge of breaking down. She is about to let go of the balloon when she pulls it down to her. She looks at it awhile before she gently kisses it. She lets go of the balloon. She follows it with her eyes as it rises and rises. The lights are beginning to fade. Andre's Mother's eyes are still on the balloon. The lights fade.)

[1988]

Topics for Critical Thinking and Writing

1. Andre's Mother doesn't speak in the play, but we learn something about her through Cal's words, and something more through the description in the final stage direction. In a paragraph characterize Andre's Mother.

2. Let's assume that you drafted this play, and now, on rereading it you decide that you want to give Andre's Mother one speech, and one speech only. Write the speech—it can go anywhere in the play that you think best—and then in a brief essay explain why you think the speech is effective.

3. Cal tells Penny that the balloons "represent the soul. When you let go, it means you're letting his soul ascend to Heaven." Is that exactly the way you see the balloons, or would see them if you attended a funeral where white balloons were distributed? Explain.

---

[1]**Good night . . . rest!** Cal is quoting lines that Hamlet's friend Horatio speaks (5.2.336–37) at the moment of Hamlet's death.

21

Making Men and Women

SHORT VIEWS

The multitude will hardly believe the excessive force of education, and in the difference of modesty between men and women, ascribe that to nature which is altogether owing to early instruction. Miss is scarce three years old, but she's spoke to every day to hide her leg, and rebuked in good earnest if she shows it, whilst little Master *at the same age is bid to take up his coats and piss like a man.*
    Bernard Mandeville

We are all androgynous, not only because we are all born of a woman impregnated by the seed of a man but because each of us, helplessly and forever, contains the other—male in female, female in male, white in black and black in white. We are a part of each other. Many of my countrymen appear to find this fact exceedingly inconvenient and even unfair, and so, very often, do I. But none of us can do anything about it.
    James Baldwin

In the theory of gender I began from zero. There is no masculine power or privilege I did not covet. But slowly, step by step, decade by decade, I was forced to acknowledge that even a woman of abnormal will cannot escape her hormonal identity.
    Camille Paglia

A woman simply is, but a man must become. Masculinity is risky and elusive. It is achieved by a revolt from woman, and it is confirmed only by other men.
    Camille Paglia

One is not born, but rather becomes, a woman.
    Simone de Beauvoir

There is no female mind. The brain is not an organ of sex. As well speak of a female liver.
    Charlotte Perkins Gilman

Growing up female in America. What a liability! You grew up with your ears full of cosmetic ads, love songs, advice columns, whoreoscopes, Hollywood gossip, and moral dilemmas on the level of TV soap operas. What litanies the advertisers of the good life chanted at you! What curious catechisms.

Erica Jong

Men are not to be told anything they might find too painful; the secret depths of human nature, the sordid physicalities, might overwhelm or damage them. For instance, men often faint at the sight of their own blood, to which they are not accustomed. For this reason you should never stand behind one in the line at the Red Cross donor clinic.

Margaret Atwood

The true man wants two things: danger and play. For that reason he wants woman, as the most dangerous plaything.

Friedrich Nietzsche

Topics for Critical Thinking and Writing

1. Do you think it is beneficial for men and women to be together in the same college classroom? Can you recall a class discussion or debate when you were aware of sharp differences between how women and men were responding to an issue? Are there some subjects that you believe are best taught in a single-sex environment?

2. Plays, films, and TV shows often make use of the plot device of a man transformed into a woman, or of a woman who disguises herself as a man, and so on. Do you think you would gain from such an experience? How long would you like this experience to last?

3. What does it mean to be a feminist? Has feminism gone too far? Can a man be a feminist, or is that impossible?

4. Do you think that men and women should be free to enter into whatever kind of relationship, married or unmarried (that is, living together), gay or straight, they desire? Or is it your view that the government should play a leading role in defining proper and improper relationships?

5. Can you identify a literary work, or a film, that only a man, or a woman, can really understand and appreciate?

6. Who is better at keeping a secret, a man or a woman?

7. Many colleges and universities now offer courses in gay and lesbian literature. Have you taken such a course yourself? What did you learn from it? If you have not taken such a course, do you intend to?

8. If a straight student in a literature course is assigned to write a paper about a book by a gay author, but then tells the teacher that he or she disapproves of homosexuality on religious grounds, should this student be excused from having to do the paper?

ESSAYS

STEVEN DOLOFF

Steven Doloff, a professor of English and Humanities at Pratt Institute, has published essays on contemporary culture, education, and travel in numerous publications, including the New York Times, *the* Boston Globe, *and the* Philadelphia Inquirer.

The Opposite Sex

For just one day, imagine yourself a boy (wow!). A girl (ugh).

Having seen Dustin Hoffman's female impersonation in the movie, "Tootsie," I decided to give myself some reading over the Christmas recess by assigning in-class essays to my English composition students on how each would spend a day as a member of his or her respective opposite sex. From four classes I received approximately 100 essays. The sample, perhaps like the movie, proved both entertaining and annoying in its predictability.

The female students, as a group, took to the subject immediately and with obvious gusto, while the male students tended to wait a while (in several cases half the period), in something of a daze, before starting. The activities hypothetically engaged in by the women, whose ages averaged about 20, generally reflected two areas: envy of men's physical and social privileges, and curiosity regarding men's true feelings concerning women.

In their essays, women jauntily went places *alone*, and sometimes stayed out *all night*. They threw their clothes on the floor and left dishes in the sink. They hung out on the street and sweated happily in a variety of sports from football to weightlifting.

More than a third of them went out to cruise for dates. Appointing themselves in brand names of men's clothing and dousing themselves in men's cologne I have never heard of (I was instructed to read Gentleman's Quarterly magazine), they deliberately and aggressively accosted women, *many* women, on the street, in discos, in supermarkets. Others sought out the proverbial locker room for the kinds of bull sessions they hoped would reveal the real nitty-gritty masculine mind at work (on the subject of women).

5   At least two female students in each class spent chunks of their essays under the sheets with imaginary girlfriends, wives or strangers, finding out with a kind of scientific zeal what sex is like as a man.

Some, but not all of the women ended their essays with a formal, almost obligatory sounding statement of preference to be a female, and of gratitude in returning to their correct gender after a day as Mr. Hyde.

The male students, after their initial paralysis wore off, did not write as much as the females. They seemed envious of very little that was female, and curious about nothing. Three or four spent their day as women frantically seeking medical help to turn back into men more quickly. Those who accepted the assignment more seriously, if unenthusiastically, either stayed home and apathetically checked off a list of domestic chores or, more evasively, went off to work in an office and engaged in totally asexual business office routines.

A small percentage of the men ventured into the more feminine pursuits of putting on makeup and going to the beauty parlor. They agreed looking good was important.

If they stayed home as housewives, when their hypothetical husbands returned from work they ate dinner, watched some television and then went right to sleep. If they were businesswomen, they came directly home after work, ate some dinner, watched TV and went right to sleep. A handful actually went out on dates, had dinner in the most expensive restaurants they could cajole their escorts into taking them to, and then, after being taken home, very politely slammed the doors in their escorts' faces and went right to sleep. Not one male student let anybody lay a finger on him/her.

10   Finally, the sense of heartfelt relief at the end of the male students' essays, underscored by the much-repeated fervent anticipation of masculinity returning with the dawn, seemed equivalent to that of jumping up after having been forced to sit on a lit stove.

Granted, my flimsy statistical sample is nothing to go to the Ford Foundation with for research money. But on the other hand, do I really need to prove that young people even now are still burdened with sexist stereotypes and sexist self-images not nearly as vestigial as we would like to think? (One male student rhetorically crumpled up his paper after 10 minutes and growled, "You can't make me write this!") What does that imply about the rest of us? What would *you* do as a member of the opposite sex for a day? This last question is your essay assignment.

[1983]

Topics for Critical Thinking and Writing

1. In paragraphs 2–4 Doloff summarizes the essays that the women wrote, and in paragraphs 7–10 the essays that the men wrote. Do you think you would have written something fairly close to the essays he attributes to the persons of your sex? Explain.
2. Do you think Doloff's assignment is a good one? Why or why not?
3. Write an essay that fulfills Doloff's assignment and that honestly represents your thoughts, but that does *not* largely fit the pattern that Doloff finds.

GRETEL EHRLICH

Gretel Ehrlich, born in 1946, was educated at Bennington College, the UCLA Film School, and the New School for Social Research. She has written fiction and poetry, especially about open spaces (she has lived in Wyoming, Colorado, and Greenland), and has received numerous awards. The following selection comes from The Solace of Open Spaces *(1985).*

About Men

When I'm in New York but feeling lonely for Wyoming I look for the Marlboro ads in the subway. What I'm aching to see is horseflesh, the glint of a spur, a line of distant mountains, brimming creeks, and a reminder of the ranchers and cowboys I've ridden with for the last eight years. But the men I see in those posters with their stern, humorless looks remind me of no one I know here. In our hellbent earnestness to romanticize the cowboy we've ironically disesteemed his true character. If he's "strong and silent" it's because there's probably no one to talk to. If he "rides away into the sunset" it's because he's been on horseback since four in the morning moving cattle and he's trying, fifteen hours later, to get home to his family. If he's "a rugged individualist" he's also part of a team: ranch work is teamwork and even the glorified open-range cowboys of the 1880s rode up and down the Chisholm Trail in the company of twenty or thirty other riders. Instead of the macho, trigger-happy man our culture has perversely wanted him to be, the cowboy is more apt to be convivial, quirky, and softhearted. To be "tough" on a ranch has nothing to do with conquests and displays of power. More often than not, circumstances—like the colt he's riding or an unexpected blizzard—are overpowering him. It's not toughness but "toughing it out" that counts. In other words, this macho, cultural artifact the cowboy has become is simply a man who possesses resilience, patience, and an instinct for survival. "Cowboys are just like a pile of rocks—everything happens to them. They get climbed on, kicked, rained and snowed on, scuffed up by wind. Their job is 'just to take it,'" one old-timer told me.

A cowboy is someone who loves his work. Since the hours are long—ten to fifteen hours a day—and the pay is $30 he has to. What's required of him is an odd mixture of physical vigor and maternalism. His part of the beef-raising industry is to birth and nurture calves and take care of their mothers. For the most part his work is done on horseback and in a lifetime he sees and comes to know more animals than people. The iconic myth surrounding him is built on American notions of heroism: the index of a man's value as measured in physical courage. Such ideas have perverted manliness into a self-absorbed race for cheap thrills. In a rancher's world, courage has less to do with facing danger than with acting spontaneously—usually on behalf of an animal or another rider. If a cow is stuck in a boghole he throws a loop around her neck, takes his dally (a half hitch around the saddle horn), and pulls her out with horsepower. If a calf is born sick, he may take her home, warm her in front of the kitchen fire, and massage her legs until dawn. One friend, whose favorite horse was trying to swim a lake with hobbles on, dove under water and cut her legs loose with a knife, then swam her to shore, his arm around her neck lifeguard-style, and saved her from drowning. Because these incidents are usually linked to someone or something outside himself, the westerner's courage is selfless, a form of compassion.

The physical punishment that goes with cowboying is greatly underplayed. Once fear is dispensed with, the threshold of pain rises to meet the demands of the job. When Jane Fonda asked Robert Redford (in the film *Electric Horseman*) if he was sick as he struggled to his feet one morning, he replied, "No, just bent." For once the movies had it right. The cowboys I was sitting with laughed in agreement. Cowboys are rarely complainers; they show their stoicism laughing at themselves.

If a rancher or cowboy has been thought of as a "man's man"—laconic, harddrinking, inscrutable—there's almost no place in which the balancing act between male and female, manliness and femininity, can be more natural. If he's gruff, handsome, and physically fit on the outside, he's androgynous at the core. Ranchers are midwives, hunters, nurturers, providers, and conservationists all at once. What we've interpreted as toughness—weathered skin, calloused hands, a squint in the eye and a growl in the voice—only masks the tenderness inside. "Now don't go telling me these lambs are cute," one rancher warned me the first day I walked into the football-field-sized lambing sheds. The next thing I knew he was holding a black lamb. "Ain't this little rat good-lookin'?"

5   So many of the men who came to the West were Southerners—men looking for work and a new life after the Civil War—that chivalrousness and strict codes of honor were soon thought of as western traits. There were very few women in Wyoming during territorial days, so when they did arrive (some as mail-order brides from places like Philadelphia) there was a standoffishness between the sexes and a formality that persists now. Ranchers still tip their hats and say, "Howdy, ma'am" instead of shaking hands with me.

Even young cowboys are often evasive with women. It's not that they're Jekyll and Hyde creatures—gentle with animals and rough on women—but rather, that they don't know how to bring their tenderness into the house and lack the vocabulary to express the complexity of what they feel. Dancing wildly all night becomes a metaphor for the explosive emotions pent up inside, and when these are, on occasion, released, they're so battery-charged and potent that one caress of the face or one "I love you" will peal for a long while.

The geographical vastness and the social isolation here make emotional evolution seem impossible. Those contradictions of the heart between respectability, logic, and convention on the one hand, and impulse, passion, and intuition on the other, played out wordlessly against the paradisiacal beauty of the West, give cowboys a wide-eyed but drawn look. Their lips pucker up, not with kisses but with immutability. They may want to break out, staying up all night with a lover just to talk, but they don't know how and can't imagine what the consequences will be. Those rare occasions when they do bare themselves result in confusion. "I feel as if I'd sprained my heart," one friend told me a month after such a meeting.

My friend Ted Hoagland wrote, "No one is as fragile as a woman but no one is as fragile as a man." For all the women here who use "fragileness" to avoid work or as a sexual ploy, there are men who try to hide theirs, all the while clinging to an adolescent dependency on women to cook their meals, wash their clothes, and keep the ranch house warm in winter. But there is true vulnerability in evidence here. Because these men work with animals, not machines or numbers, because they live outside in landscapes of torrential beauty, because they are confined to a place and a routine embellished with awesome variables, because calves die in the arms that pulled others into life, because they go to the mountains as if on a pilgrimage to find out what makes a herd of elk tick, their strength is also a softness, their toughness, a rare delicacy.

[1985]

Topics for Critical Thinking and Writing

1. Early on, Ehrlich says: "In our hellbent earnestness to romanticize the cowboy we've ironically disesteemed his true character." What is she saying in this sentence? Do you find the sentence clear, or confusing? Please explain.
2. Later, Ehrlich says that cowboys are not like "Jekyll and Hyde." Identify and explain this reference. Where did you go to find this information?

3. In a paragraph of three or four sentences, summarize the main point that Ehrlich is making. Do you find it hard or easy to write this summary? What does your response suggest to you about Ehrlich's essay as a piece of writing?

4. Would you describe this essay as an "argument"? Or is it something different? After you read the essay, did your understanding of the topic change? In what way?

FICTION

CHARLOTTE PERKINS GILMAN

Charlotte Perkins Gilman (1860–1935), was born in Hartford, Connecticut. Her father deserted the family soon after Charlotte's birth; she was brought up by her mother, who found it difficult to make ends meet. For a while Charlotte worked as an artist and teacher of art, and in 1884, when she was 24, she married an artist. In 1885 she had a daughter, but soon after the birth of the girl Charlotte had a nervous breakdown. At her husband's urging she spent a month in the sanitarium of Dr. S. Weir Mitchell, a physician who specialized in treating women with nervous disorders. (Mitchell is specifically named in "The Yellow Wallpaper.") Because the treatment—isolation and total rest—nearly drove her to insanity, she fled Mitchell and her husband. In California she began a career as a lecturer and writer on feminist topics. (She also supported herself by teaching school and by keeping a boardinghouse.) Among her books are Women and Economics *(1899) and* The Man-Made World *(1911), which have been revived by the feminist movement. In 1900 she married a cousin, George Gilman. From all available evidence, the marriage was successful. Certainly it did not restrict her activities as a feminist. In 1935, suffering from inoperable cancer, she took her own life.*

"The Yellow Wallpaper," written in 1892—that is, written after she had been treated by S. Weir Mitchell for her nervous breakdown—was at first interpreted either as a ghost story or as a Poe-like study of insanity. Only in recent years has it been seen as a feminist story. (One might ask oneself if these interpretations are mutually exclusive.)

The Yellow Wallpaper

It is very seldom that mere ordinary people like John and myself secure ancestral halls for the summer.

A colonial mansion, a hereditary estate. I would say a haunted house, and reach the height of romantic felicity—but that would be asking too much of fate!

Still I will proudly declare that there is something queer about it.

Else, why should it be let so cheaply? And why have stood so long untenanted?

5   John laughs at me, of course, but one expects that in marriage.

John is practical in the extreme. He has no patience with faith, an intense horror of superstition, and he scoffs openly at any talk of things not to be felt and seen and put down in figures.

John is a physician, and *perhaps*—(I would not say it to a living soul, of course, but this is dead paper and a great relief to my mind)—*perhaps* that is one reason I do not get well faster.

You see he does not believe I am sick!

And what can one do?

10　If a physician of high standing, and one's own husband, assures friends and relatives that there is really nothing the matter with one but temporary nervous depression—a slight hysterical tendency—what is one to do?

My brother is also a physician, and also of high standing, and he says the same thing.

So I take phosphates or phosphites—whichever it is, and tonics, and journeys, and air, and exercise, and am absolutely forbidden to "work" until I am well again.

Personally, I disagree with their ideas.

Personally, I believe that congenial work, with excitement and change, would do me good.

15　But what is one to do?

I did write for a while in spite of them: but it *does* exhaust me a good deal—having to be so sly about it, or else meet with heavy opposition.

I sometimes fancy that in my condition if I had less opposition and more society and stimulus—but John says the very worst thing I can do is to think about my condition, and I confess it always makes me feel bad.

So I will let it alone and talk about the house.

The most beautiful place! It is quite alone, standing well back from the road, quite three miles from the village. It makes me think of English places that you read about, for there are hedges and walls and gates that lock, and lots of separate little houses for the gardeners and people.

20　There is a *delicious* garden! I never saw such a garden—large and shady, full of box-bordered paths, and lined with long grapecovered arbors with seats under them.

There were greenhouses, too, but they are all broken now. There was some legal trouble, I believe, something about the heirs and coheirs: anyhow, the place has been empty for years.

That spoils my ghostliness, I am afraid, but I don't care—there is something strange about the house—I can feel it.

I even said so to John one moonlight evening, but he said what I felt was a *draught,* and shut the window.

I get unreasonably angry with John sometimes. I'm sure I never used to be so sensitive. I think it is due to this nervous condition.

25　But John says if I feel so, I shall neglect proper self-control: so I take pains to control myself—before him, at least, and that makes me very tired.

I don't like our room a bit. I wanted one downstairs that opened on the piazza and had roses all over the window, and such pretty old-fashioned chintz hangings! but John would not hear of it.

He said there was only one window and not room for two beds, and no near room for him if he took another.

He is very careful and loving, and hardly lets me stir without special direction.

I have a schedule prescription for each hour in the day: he takes all care from me, and so I feel basely ungrateful not to value it more.

30　He said we came here solely on my account, that I was to have perfect rest and all the air I could get. "Your exercise depends on your strength, my dear," said he, "and your food somewhat on your appetite; but air you can absorb all the time." So we took the nursery at the top of the house.

It is a big, airy room, the whole floor nearly, with windows that look all ways, and air and sunshine galore. It was nursery first and then playroom and gymnasium, I should judge; for the windows are barred for little children, and there are rings and things in the walls.

The paint and paper look as if a boys' school had used it. It is stripped off—the paper—in great patches all around the head of my bed, about as far as I can reach, and in a great place on the other side of the room low down. I never saw a worse paper in my life.

One of those sprawling flamboyant patterns committing every artistic sin.

It is dull enough to confuse the eye in following, pronounced enough to constantly irritate and provoke study, and when you follow the lame uncertain curves for a little distance they suddenly commit suicide—plunge off at outrageous angles, destroy themselves in unheard of contradictions.

35   The color is repellent, almost revolting: a smouldering unclean yellow, strangely faded by the slow-turning sunlight.

It is a dull yet lurid orange in some places, a sickly sulphur tint in others.

No wonder the children hated it! I should hate it myself if I had to live in this room long.

There comes John, and I must put this away,—he hates to have me write a word.

We have been here two weeks, and I haven't felt like writing before, since that first day.

40   I am sitting by the window now, up in this atrocious nursery, and there is nothing to hinder my writing as much as I please, save lack of strength.

John is away all day, and even some nights when his cases are serious.

I am glad my case is not serious!

But these nervous troubles are dreadfully depressing.

John does not know how much I really suffer. He knows there is no *reason* to suffer, and that satisfies him.

45   Of course it is only nervousness. It does weigh on me so not to do my duty in any way!

I meant to be such a help to John, such a real rest and comfort, and here I am a comparative burden already!

Nobody would believe what an effort it is to do what little I am able,—to dress and entertain, and order things.

It is fortunate Mary is so good with the baby. Such a dear baby!

And yet I *cannot* be with him, it makes me so nervous.

50   I suppose John never was nervous in his life. He laughs at me so about this wallpaper!

At first he meant to repaper the room, but afterwards he said that I was letting it get the better of me, and that nothing was worse for a nervous patient than to give way to such fancies.

He said that after the wallpaper was changed it would be the heavy bed-stead, and then the barred windows, and then that gate at the head of the stairs, and so on.

"You know the place is doing you good," he said, "and really, dear, I don't care to renovate the house just for a three months' rental."

"Then do let us go downstairs," I said, "there are such pretty rooms there."

55   Then he took me in his arms and called me a blessed little goose, and said he would go down to the cellar, if I wished, and have it whitewashed into the bargain.

But he is right enough about the beds and windows and things.

It is an airy and comfortable room as any one need wish, and, of course, I would not be so silly as to make him uncomfortable just for a whim.

I'm really getting quite fond of the big room, all but that horrid paper.

Out of one window I can see the garden, those mysterious deep-shaded arbors, the riotous old-fashioned flowers, and bushes and gnarly trees.

60   Out of another I get a lovely view of the bay and a little private wharf belonging to the estate. There is a beautiful shaded lane that runs down there from the house. I always fancy I see people walking in these numerous paths and arbors, but John has cautioned me not to give way to fancy in the least. He says that with my imaginative power and habit of story-making, a nervous weakness like mine is sure to lead to all manner of excited fancies, and that I ought to use my will and good sense to check the tendency. So I try.

I think sometimes that if I were only well enough to write a little it would relieve the press of ideas and rest me.

But I find I get pretty tired when I try.

It is so discouraging not to have any advice and companionship about my work. When I get really well, John says we will ask Cousin Henry and Julia down for a long visit; but he says he would as soon put fireworks in my pillow-case as to let me have those stimulating people about now.

I wish I could get well faster.

65   But I must not think about that. This paper looks to me as if it *knew* what a vicious influence it had!

There is a recurrent spot where the pattern lolls like a broken neck and two bulbous eyes stare at you upside down.

I get positively angry with the impertinence of it and the everlastingness. Up and down and sideways they crawl, and those absurd, unblinking eyes are everywhere. There is one place where two breadths didn't match, and the eyes go all up and down the line, one a little higher than the other.

I never saw so much expression in an inanimate thing before, and we all know how much expression they have! I used to lie awake as a child and get more entertainment and terror out of blank walls and plain furniture than most children could find in a toystore.

I remember what a kindly wink the knobs of our big, old bureau used to have, and there was one chair that always seemed like a strong friend.

70   I used to feel that if any of the other things looked too fierce I could always hop into that chair and be safe.

The furniture in this room is no worse than inharmonious, however, for we had to bring it all from downstairs. I suppose when this was used as a playroom they had to take the nursery things out, and no wonder! I never saw such ravages as the children have made here.

The wallpaper, as I said before, is torn off in spots, and it sticketh closer than a brother—they must have had perseverance as well as hatred.

Then the floor is scratched and gouged and splintered, the plaster itself is dug out here and there, and this great heavy bed which is all we found in the room, looks as if it had been through the wars.

But I don't mind it a bit—only the paper.

75   There comes John's sister. Such a dear girl as she is, and so careful of me! I must not let her find me writing.

She is a perfect and enthusiastic housekeeper, and hopes for no better profession. I verily believe she thinks it is the writing which made me sick!

But I can write when she is out, and see her a long way off from these windows.

There is one that commands the road, a lovely shaded winding road, and one that just looks off over the country. A lovely country, too, full of great elms and velvet meadows.

This wallpaper has a kind of sub-pattern in a different shade, a particularly irritating one, for you can only see it in certain lights, and not clearly then.

80   But in the places where it isn't faded and where the sun is just so—I can see a strange, provoking, formless sort of figure, that seems to skulk about behind that silly and conspicuous front design.

There's sister on the stairs!

Well, the Fourth of July is over! The people are all gone and I am tired out. John thought it might do me good to see a little company, so we just had mother and Nellie and the children down for a week.

Of course I didn't do a thing. Jennie sees to everything now. But it tired me all the same.

John says if I don't pick up faster he shall send me to Weir Mitchell in the fall.

85   But I don't want to go there at all. I had a friend who was in his hands once, and she says he is just like John and my brother, only more so!

Besides, it is such an undertaking to go so far.

I don't feel as if it was worth while to turn my hand over for anything, and I'm getting dreadfully fretful and querulous.

I cry at nothing, and cry most of the time.

Of course I don't when John is here, or anybody else, but when I am alone.

90   And I am alone a good deal just now. John is kept in town very often by serious cases, and Jennie is good and lets me alone when I want her to.

So I walk a little in the garden or down that lovely lane, sit on the porch under the roses, and lie down up here a good deal.

I'm getting really fond of the room in spite of the wallpaper. Perhaps *because* of the wallpaper.

It dwells in my mind so!

I lie here on this great immovable bed—it is nailed down, I believe—and follow that pattern about by the hour. It is as good as gymnastics, I assure you. I start, we'll say, at the bottom, down in the corner over there where it has not been touched, and I determine for the thousandth time that I *will* follow that pointless pattern to some sort of a conclusion.

95   I know a little of the principle of design, and I know this thing was not arranged on any laws of radiation, or alternation, or repetition, or symmetry, or anything else that I ever heard of.

It is repeated, of course, by the breadths, but not otherwise.

Looked at in one way each breadth stands alone, the bloated curves and flourishes—a kind of "debased Romanesque" with *delirium tremens*—go waddling up and down in isolated columns of fatuity.

But, on the other hand, they connect diagonally, and the sprawling outlines run off in great slanting waves of optic horror, like a lot of wallowing seaweeds in full chase.

The whole thing goes horizontally, too, at least it seems so, and I exhaust myself in trying to distinguish the order of its going in that direction.

100   They have used a horizontal breadth for a frieze, and that adds wonderfully to the confusion.

There is one end of the room where it is almost intact, and there, when the crosslights fade and the low sun shines directly upon it, I can almost fancy radiation after all,—the interminable grotesques seem to form around a common center and rush off in headlong plunges of equal distraction.

It makes me tired to follow it. I will take a nap I guess.

I don't know why I should write this.

I don't want to.

105   I don't feel able.

And I know John would think it absurd. But I *must* say what I feel and think in some way—it is such a relief.

But the effort is getting to be greater than the relief!

Half the time now I am awfully lazy, and lie down ever so much.

John says I mustn't lose my strength, and has me take cod liver oil and lots of tonics and things, to say nothing of ale and wine and rare meat.

110   Dear John! He loves me very dearly, and hates to have me sick. I tried to have a real earnest reasonable talk with him the other day, and tell him how I wish he would let me go and make a visit to Cousin Henry and Julia.

But he said I wasn't able to go, nor able to stand it after I got there: and I did not make out a very good case for myself, for I was crying before I had finished.

It is getting to be a great effort for me to think straight. Just this nervous weakness I suppose.

And dear John gathered me up in his arms, and just carried me upstairs and laid me on the bed, and sat by me and read to me till it tired my head.

He said I was his darling and his comfort and all he had, and that I must take care of myself for his sake, and keep well.

115   He says no one but myself can help me out of it, that I must use my will and self-control and not let any silly fancies run away with me.

There's one comfort, the baby is well and happy, and does not have to occupy this nursery with the horrid wallpaper.

If we had not used it, that blessed child would have! What a fortunate escape! Why, I wouldn't have a child of mine, an impressionable little thing, live in such a room for worlds.

I never thought of it before, but it is lucky that John kept me here after all. I can stand it so much easier than a baby, you see.

Of course I never mention it to them any more—I am too wise,—but I keep watch of it all the same.

120   There are things in that paper that nobody knows but me, or ever will.

Behind that outside pattern the dim shapes get clearer every day.

It is always the same shape, only very numerous.

And it is like a woman stooping down and creeping about behind that pattern. I don't like it a bit. I wonder—I begin to think—I wish John would take me away from here!

It is so hard to talk with John about my case, because he is so wise, and because he loves me so.

125   But I tried last night.

It was moonlight. The moon shines in all around just as the sun does.

I hate to see it sometimes, it creeps so slowly, and always comes in by one window or another.

John was asleep and I hated to waken him, so I kept still and watched the moonlight on that undulating wallpaper till I felt creepy.

The faint figure behind seemed to shake the pattern, just as if she wanted to get out.

130   I got up softly and went to feel and see if the paper *did* move, and when I came back John was awake.

"What is it, little girl?" he said. "Don't go walking about like that—you'll get cold."

I thought it was a good time to talk, so I told him that I really was not gaining here, and that I wished he would take me away.

"Why darling!" said he, "our lease will be up in three weeks, and I can't see how to leave before."

"The repairs are not done at home, and I cannot possibly leave town just now. Of course if you were in any danger, I could and would, but you really are better, dear, whether you can see it or not. I am a doctor, dear, and I know. You are gaining flesh and color, your appetite is better, I feel really much easier about you."

135   "I don't weigh a bit more," said I, "nor as much: and my appetite may be better in the evening when you are here, but it is worse in the morning when you are away!"

"Bless her little heart!" said he with a big hug, "she shall be as sick as she pleases! But now let's improve the shining hours by going to sleep, and talk about it in the morning!"

"And you won't go away?" I asked gloomily.

"Why, how can I, dear? It is only three weeks more and then we will take a nice little trip of a few days while Jennie is getting the house ready. Really dear you are better!"

"Better in body perhaps—" I began, and stopped short, for he sat up straight and looked at me with such a stern, reproachful look that I could not say another word.

140   "My darling," said he, "I beg of you, for my sake and for our child's sake, as well as for your own, that you will never for one instant let that idea enter your mind! There is nothing so dangerous, so fascinating, to a temperament like yours. It is a false and foolish fancy. Can you not trust me as a physician when I tell you so?"

So of course I said no more on that score, and we went to sleep before long. He thought I was asleep first, but I wasn't and lay there for hours trying to decide whether that front pattern and the back pattern really did move together or separately.

On a pattern like this, by daylight, there is a lack of sequence, a defiance of law, that is a constant irritant to a normal mind.

The color is hideous enough, and unreliable enough, and infuriating enough, but the pattern is torturing.

You think you have mastered it, but just as you get well underway in following, it turns a back-somersault and there you are. It slaps you in the face, knocks you down, and tramples upon you. It is like a bad dream.

145   The outside pattern is a florid arabesque, reminding one of a fungus. If you can imagine a toadstool in joints, an interminable string of toadstools, budding and sprouting in endless convolutions—why, that is something like it.

That is, sometimes!

There is one marked peculiarity about this paper, a thing nobody seems to notice but myself, and that is that it changes as the light changes.

When the sun shoots in through the east window—I always watch for that first long, straight ray—it changes so quickly that I never can quite believe it.

That is why I watch it always.

150   By moonlight—the moon shines in all night when there is a moon—I wouldn't know it was the same paper.

At night in any kind of light, in twilight, candle light, lamplight, and worst of all by moonlight, it becomes bars! The outside pattern I mean, and the woman behind it is as plain as can be.

I didn't realize for a long time what the thing was that showed behind, that dim sub-pattern, but now I am quite sure it is a woman.

By daylight she is subdued, quiet. I fancy it is the pattern that keeps her so still. It is so puzzling. It keeps me quiet by the hour.

155 I lie down ever so much now. John says it is good for me, and to sleep all I can. Indeed he started the habit by making me lie down for an hour after each meal. It is a very bad habit I am convinced, for you see I don't sleep.

And that cultivates deceit, for I don't tell them I'm awake—O no!

The fact is I am getting a little afraid of John.

He seems very queer sometimes, and even Jennie has an inexplicable look.

160 It strikes me occasionally, just as a scientific hypothesis—that perhaps it is the paper!

I have watched John when he did not know I was looking, and come into the room suddenly on the most innocent excuses, and I've caught him several times *looking at the paper!* And Jennie too. I caught Jennie with her hand on it once.

She didn't know I was in the room, and when I asked her in a quiet, a very quiet voice, with the most restrained manner possible, what she was doing with the paper—she turned around as if she had been caught stealing, and looked quite angry—asked me why I should frighten her so!

Then she said that the paper stained everything it touched, that she had found yellow smooches on all my clothes and John's, and she wished we would be more careful!

Did not that sound innocent? But I know she was studying that pattern, and I am determined that nobody shall find it out but myself!

165 Life is very much more exciting now than it used to be. You see I have something more to expect, to look forward to, to watch. I really do eat better, and am more quiet than I was.

John is so pleased to see me improve! He laughed a little the other day, and said I seemed to be flourishing in spite of my wallpaper.

I turned it off with a laugh. I had no intention of telling him it was *because* of the wallpaper—he would make fun of me. He might even want to take me away.

I don't want to leave now until I have found it out. There is a week more, and I think that will be enough.

I'm feeling ever so much better! I don't sleep much at night, for it is so interesting to watch developments, but I sleep a good deal in the daytime.

170 In the daytime it is tiresome and perplexing.

There are always new shoots on the fungus, and new shades of yellow all over it. I cannot keep count of them, though I have tried conscientiously.

It is the strangest yellow, that wallpaper! It makes me think of all the yellow things I ever saw—not beautiful ones like buttercups, but old foul, bad yellow things.

But there is something else about that paper—the smell! I noticed it the moment we came into the room, but with so much air and sun it was not bad. Now we have had a week of fog and rain, and whether the windows are open or not, the smell is here.

It creeps all over the house.

175 I find it hovering in the dining-room, skulking in the parlor, hiding in the hall, lying in wait for me on the stairs.

It gets into my hair.

Even when I go to ride, if I turn my head suddenly and surprise it—there is that smell!

Such a peculiar odor, too! I have spent hours in trying to analyze it, to find what it smelled like.

It is not bad—at first, and very gentle, but quite the subtlest, most enduring odor I ever met.

In this damp weather it is awful, I wake up in the night and find it hanging over me.

It used to disturb me at first. I thought seriously of burning the house—to reach the smell.

But now I am used to it. The only thing I can think of that it is like is the *color* of the paper! A yellow smell.

There is a very funny mark on this wall, low down, near the mopboard. A streak that runs round the room. It goes behind every piece of furniture, except the bed, a long, straight, even *smooch,* as if it had been rubbed over and over.

I wonder how it was done and who did it, and what they did it for. Round and round and round—round and round and round—it makes me dizzy!

I really have discovered something at last.

Through watching so much at night, when it changes so, I have finally found out.

The front pattern *does* move—and no wonder! The woman behind shakes it!

Sometimes I think there are a great many women behind, and sometimes only one, and she crawls around fast, and her crawling shakes it all over.

Then in the very bright spots she keeps still, and in the very shady spots she just takes hold of the bars and shakes them hard.

And she is all the time trying to climb through. But nobody could climb through that pattern—it strangles so: I think that is why it has so many heads.

They get through, and then the pattern strangles them off and turns them upside down, and makes their eyes white!

If those heads were covered or taken off it would not be half so bad.

I think that woman gets out in the daytime!

And I'll tell you why—privately—I've seen her!

I can see her out of every one of my windows!

It is the same woman, I know, for she is always creeping, and most women do not creep by daylight.

I see her on that long road under the trees, creeping along, and when a carriage comes she hides under the blackberry vines.

I don't blame her a bit. It must be very humiliating to be caught creeping by daylight!

I always lock the door when I creep by daylight. I can't do it at night, for I know John would suspect something at once.

And John is so queer now, that I don't want to irritate him. I wish he would take another room! Besides, I don't want anybody to get that woman out at night but myself.

I often wonder if I could see her out of all the windows at once.

But, turn as fast as I can, I can only see out of one at one time. And though I always see her, she *may* be able to creep faster than I can turn!

I have watched her sometimes away off in the open country, creeping as fast as a cloud shadow in a high wind.

If only that top pattern could be gotten off from the under one! I mean to try it, little by little.

205   I have found out another funny thing, but I shan't tell at this time! It does not do to trust people too much.

There are only two more days to get this paper off, and I believe John is beginning to notice. I don't like the look in his eyes.

And I heard him ask Jennie a lot of professional questions about me. She had a very good report to give.

She said I slept a good deal in the daytime.

John knows I don't sleep very well at night, for all I'm so quiet!

210   He asked me all sorts of questions, too, and pretended to be very loving and kind.

As if I couldn't see through him!

Still, I don't wonder he acts so, sleeping under this paper for three months.

It only interests me, but I feel sure John and Jennie are secretly affected by it.

Hurrah! This is the last day, but it is enough. John is to stay in town over night, and won't be out until this evening.

215   Jennie wanted to sleep with me—the sly thing! But I told her I should undoubtedly rest better for a night all alone.

That was clever, for really I wasn't alone a bit! As soon as it was moonlight and that poor thing began to crawl and shake the pattern, I got up and ran to help her.

I pulled and she shook, I shook and she pulled, and before morning we had peeled off yards of that paper.

A strip about as high as my head and half round the room. And then when the sun came and that awful pattern began to laugh at me, I declared I would finish it to-day!

We go away to-morrow, and they are moving all the furniture down again to leave things as they were before.

220   Jennie looked at the wall in amazement, but I told her merrily that I did it out of pure spite at the vicious thing.

She laughed and said she wouldn't mind doing it herself, but I must not get tired.

How she betrayed herself that time!

But I am here, and no person touches this paper but me—not *alive!*

She tried to get me out of the room—it was too patent! But I said it was so quiet and empty and clean now that I believed I would lie down again and sleep all I could; and not to wake me even for dinner—I would call when I woke.

225   So now she is gone, and the servants are gone, and the things are gone, and there is nothing left but that great bedstead nailed down, with the canvas mattress we found on it.

We shall sleep downstairs to-night, and take the boat home to-morrow.

I quite enjoy the room, now it is bare again.

How those children did tear about here!

This bedstead is fairly gnawed!

230   But I must get to work.

I have locked the door and thrown the key down into the front path.

I don't want to go out, and I don't want to have anybody come in, till John comes.

I want to astonish him.

I've got a rope up here that even Jennie did not find. If that woman does get out, and tries to get away, I can tie her!

235 But I forgot I could not reach far without anything to stand on! This bed will *not* move!

I tried to lift and push it until I was lame, and then I got so angry I bit off a little piece at one corner—but it hurt my teeth.

Then I peeled off all the paper I could reach standing on the floor. It sticks horribly and the pattern just enjoys it! All those strangled heads and bulbous eyes and waddling fungus growths just shriek with derision!

I am getting angry enough to do something desperate. To jump out of the window would be admirable exercise, but the bars are too strong even to try.

Besides I wouldn't do it. Of course not, I know well enough that a step like that is improper and might be misconstrued.

240 I don't like to *look* out of the windows even—there are so many of those creeping women, and they creep so fast.

I wonder if they all come out of that wallpaper as I did?

But I am securely fastened now by my well-hidden rope—you don't get *me* out in the road there!

I suppose I shall have to get back behind the pattern when it comes night, and that is hard!

It is so pleasant to be out in this great room and creep around as I please!

245 I don't want to go outside. I won't, even if Jennie asks me to.

For outside you have to creep on the ground, and everything is green instead of yellow.

But here I can creep smoothly on the floor, and my shoulder just fits in that long smooch around the wall, so I cannot lose my way.

Why there's John at the door!

It is no use, young man, you can't open it!

250 How he does call and pound!

Now he's crying for an axe.

It would be a shame to break down that beautiful door!

"John dear!" said I in the gentlest voice, "the key is down by the front steps, under a plantain leaf!"

That silenced him for a few moments.

255 Then he said—very quietly indeed, "Open the door, my darling!"

"I can't," said I. "The key is down by the front door under a plantain leaf!"

And then I said it again, several times, very gently and slowly, and said it so often that he had to go and see, and he got it of course, and came in. He stopped short by the door.

"What is the matter?" he cried. "For God's sake, what are you doing!"

I kept on creeping just the same, but I looked at him over my shoulder.

260 "I've got out at last," said I, "in spite of you and Jane. And I've pulled off most of the paper, so you can't put me back!"

Now why should that man have fainted? But he did, and right across my path by the wall, so that I had to creep over him every time!

[1892]

Topics for Critical Thinking and Writing

1. Is the narrator insane at the start of the story, or does she become insane at some point during the narrative? Or can't we be sure? Support your view with evidence from the story.
2. How reliable do you think the narrator's characterization of her husband is? Support your answer with reasons.
3. The narrator says that she cannot get better because her husband is a physician. What do you take this to mean? Do you think the story is about a husband who deliberately drives his wife insane?

RICHARD WRIGHT

Richard Wright (1908–1960), the grandson of a slave and the son of an impoverished sharecropper couple, was born on a cotton plantation near Natchez, Mississippi. When Richard was 5 his father deserted the family; five years later his mother suffered the first of a series of strokes that left her partly paralyzed. Richard was then brought up by relatives in Jackson, Mississippi, and Memphis, Tennessee. He dropped out of school after completing the ninth grade, took a variety of odd jobs, and in 1927 moved to Chicago, where he worked as a porter, dishwasher, burial-insurance salesman, and postal clerk. He also worked for the WPA, first as a writer of guidebooks and then as a director of the Federal Negro Theater. In 1932 he joined the John Reed Club, a left-wing organization. In 1937 he moved to New York, where he became the Harlem editor of The Daily Worker, *a Communist newspaper. In the following year he published his first book,* Uncle Tom's Children: Four Novellas. *In 1947 Wright and his family moved to Paris, where they lived until he suffered a fatal heart attack in 1960.*

With Native Son *(1940), a novel about a black man who murders a white woman, Wright became the first black writer to reach a large white audience with a militant attack on racism. In the following year he wrote the text for* Twelve Million Black Voices, *a pictorial "folk history of the Negro in the United States." His next best-selling work was an autobiography,* Black Boy *(1945). Wright had already left the Communist Party in 1944, but material about his disillusionment with Communism was deleted from the manuscript of* Black Boy *and was first published in a posthumous book,* American Hunger *(1977). By the time he moved to France, then, Wright was strongly anti-Communist. He continued to write novels, though he also wrote nonfiction, including an account of a trip to Ghana.*

The Man Who Was Almost a Man

Dave struck out across the fields, looking homeward through paling light. Whut's the use talkin wid em niggers in the field? Anyhow, his mother was putting supper on the table. Them niggers can't understan nothing. One of these days he was going to get a gun and practice shooting, then they couldn't talk to him as though he were a little boy. He slowed, looking at the ground. Shucks, Ah ain scareda them even if they are biggern me! Aw, Ah know what Ahma do. Ahm going by ol Joe's sto n git that Sears Roebuck catlog n look at them guns. Mebbe Ma will lemme buy one when she gits mah pay from ol man Hawkins. Ahma beg her t gimme some money. Ahm ol ernough to hava gun. Ahm seventeen. Almost a man. He strode, feeling his long loose-jointed limbs. Shucks, a man oughta hava little gun aftah he done worked hard all day.

He came in sight of Joe's store. A yellow lantern glowed on the front porch. He mounted steps and went through the screen door, hearing it bang behind him. There was a strong smell of coal oil and mackerel fish. He felt very confident until he saw fat Joe walk in through the rear door, then his courage began to ooze.

"Howdy, Dave! Whutcha want?"

"How yuh, Mistah Joe? Aw, Ah don wanna buy nothing. Ah jus wanted t see ef yuhd lemme look at tha catlog erwhile."

5   "Sure! You wanna see it here?"

"Nawsuh. Ah wants t take it home wid me. Ah'll bring it back termorrow when Ah come in from the fiels."

"You plannin on buying something?"

"Yessuh."

"Your ma lettin you have your own money now?"

10   "Shucks. Mistah Joe, Ahm gittin t be a man like anybody else!"

Joe laughed and wiped his greasy white face with a red bandanna.

"Whut you plannin on buyin?"

Dave looked at the floor, scratched his head, scratched his thigh, and smiled. Then he looked up shyly.

"Ah'll tell yuh, Mistah Joe, ef yuh promise yuh won't tell."

15   "I promise."

"Waal, Ahma buy a gun."

"A gun? What you want with a gun?"

"Ah wanna keep it."

"You ain't nothing but a boy. You don't need a gun."

20   "Aw, lemme have the catlog, Mistah Joe. Ah'll bring it back."

Joe walked through the rear door. Dave was elated. He looked around at barrels of sugar and flour. He heard Joe coming back. He craned his neck to see if he were bringing the book. Yeah, he's got it. Gawddog, he's got it!

"Here, but be sure you bring it back. It's the only one I got."

"Sho, Mistah Joe."

"Say, if you wanna buy a gun, why don't you buy one from me? I gotta gun to sell."

25   "Will it shoot?"

"Sure it'll shoot."

"Whut kind is it?"

"Oh, it's kinda old . . . a left-hand Wheeler. A pistol. A big one."

"Is it got bullets in it?"

30   "It's loaded."

"Kin Ah see it?"

"Where's your money?"

"Whut yuh wan fer it?"

"I'll let you have it for two dollars."

35   "Just two dollahs? Shucks, Ah could buy tha when Ah git mah pay."

"I'll have it here when you want it."

"Awright, suh. Ah be in fer it."

He went through the door, hearing it slam again behind him. Ahma git some money from Ma n buy me a gun! Only two dollahs! He tucked the thick catalogue under his arm and hurried.

"Where yuh been, boy?" His mother held a steaming dish of blackeyed peas.

40 "Aw, Ma, Ah jus stopped down the road t talk wid the boys."

"Yuh know bettah t keep suppah waitin."

He sat down, resting the catalogue on the edge of the table.

"Yuh git up from there and git to the well n wash yosef! Ah ain feedin no hogs in mah house!"

She grabbed his shoulder and pushed him. He stumbled out of the room, then came back to get the catalogue.

45 "Whut this?"

"Aw, Ma, it's jusa catlog."

"Who yuh git it from?"

"From Joe, down at the sto."

"Waal, thas good. We kin use it in the outhouse."

50 "Naw, Ma." He grabbed for it. "Gimme ma catlog, Ma."

She held onto it and glared at him.

"Quit hollerin at me! Whut's wrong wid yuh? Yuh crazy?"

"But Ma, please. It ain mine! It's Joe's! He tol me t bring it back t im termorrow."

She gave up the book. He stumbled down the back steps, hugging the thick book under his arm. When he had splashed water on his face and hands, he groped back to the kitchen and fumbled in a corner for the towel. He bumped into a chair; it clattered to the floor. The catalogue sprawled at his feet. When he had dried his eyes he snatched up the book and held it again under his arm. His mother stood watching him.

55 "Now, ef yuh gonna act a fool over that ol book, Ah'll take it n burn it up."

"Naw, Ma, please."

"Waal, set down n be still!"

He sat down and drew the oil lamp close. He thumbed page after page, unaware of the food his mother set on the table. His father came in. Then his small brother.

"Whutcha got there, Dave?" his father asked.

60 "Jusa catlog," he answered, not looking up.

"Yeah, here they is!" His eyes glowed at blue-and-black revolvers. He glanced up, feeling sudden guilt. His father was watching him. He eased the book under the table and rested it on his knees. After the blessing was asked, he ate. He scooped up peas and swallowed fat meat without chewing. Buttermilk helped to wash it down. He did not want to mention money before his father. He would do much better by cornering his mother when she was alone. He looked at his father uneasily out of the edge of his eye.

"Boy, how come yuh don quit foolin wid tha book n eat yo suppah?"

"Yessuh."

"How you n ol man Hawkins gitten erlong?"

65 "Suh?"

"Can't yuh hear? Why don yuh lissen? Ah ast yu how wuz yuh n ol man Hawkins gittin erlong?"

"Oh, swell, Pa. Ah plows mo lan than anybody over there."

"Waal, yuh oughta keep you mind on what yuh doin."

"Yessuh."

70   He poured his plate full of molasses and sopped it up slowly with a chunk of cornbread. When his father and brother had left the kitchen, he still sat and looked again at the guns in the catalogue, longing to muster courage enough to present his case to his mother. Lawd, ef Ah only had tha pretty one! He could almost feel the slickness of the weapon with his fingers. If he had a gun like that he would polish it and keep it shining so it would never rust! N Ah'd keep it loaded, by Gawd!

"Ma?" His voice was hesitant.

"Hunh?"

"Ol man Hawkins give yuh mah money yit?"

"Yeah, but ain no usa yuh thinking bout throwin nona it erway. Ahm keeping tha money sos yuh kin have cloes t go to school this winter."

75   He rose and went to her side with the open catalogue in his palms. She was washing dishes, her head bent low over a pan. Shyly he raised the book. When he spoke, his voice was husky, faint.

"Ma, Gawd knows Ah wans one of these."

"One of whut?" she asked, not raising her eyes.

"One of these," he said again, not daring even to point. She glanced up at the page, then at him with wide eyes.

"Nigger, is yuh gone plumb crazy?"

80   "Aw, Ma—"

"Git outta here! Don yuh talk t me bout no gun! Yuh a fool!"

"Ma, Ah kin buy one fer two dollars."

"Not ef Ah knows it, yuh ain!"

"But yuh promised me one—"

85   "Ah don care what Ah promised! Yuh ain nothing but a boy yit!"

"Ma, ef yuh lemme buy one Ah'll *never* ast yuh fer nothing no mo."

"Ah tol yuh t git outta here! Yuh ain gonna toucha penny of tha money fer no gun! Thas how come Ah has Mistah Hawkins t pay yo wages t me, cause Ah knows yuh ain got no sense."

"But, Ma, we needa gun. Pa ain got no gun. We needa gun in the house. Yuh kin never tell whut might happen."

"Now don yuh try to maka fool outta me, boy! Ef we did hava gun, yuh wouldn't have it!"

90   He laid the catalogue down and slipped his arm around her waist.

"Aw, Ma, Ah done worked hard alla summer n ain ast yuh fer nothing, is Ah, now?"

"Thas what yuh spose t do!"

"But Ma, Ah wans a gun. Yuh kin lemme have two dollars outta mah money. Please, Ma. I kin give it to Pa. . . . Please, Ma! Ah loves yuh, Ma!"

When she spoke her voice came soft and low.

95   "What yu wan wida gun, Dave? Yuh don need no gun. Yuh'll git in trouble. N ef yo pa jus thought Ah let yuh have money t buy a gun he'd hava fit."

"Ah'll hide it, Ma. It ain but two dollars."

"Lawd, chil, whut's wrong wid yuh?"

"Ain nothin wrong, Ma. Ahm almos a man now. Ah wans a gun."

"Who gonna sell yuh a gun?"

100   "Ol Joe at the sto."

"N it don cos but two dollars?"

"Thas all, Ma. Jus two dollars. Please, Ma."

She was stacking the plates away; her hands moved slowly, reflectively. Dave kept an anxious silence. Finally, she turned to him.

"Ah'll let yuh git tha gun if yuh promise me one thing."

105   "What's tha, Ma?"

"Yuh bring it straight back t me, yuh hear? It be fer Pa."

"Yessum! Lemme go now, Ma."

She stooped, turned slightly to one side, raised the hem of her dress, rolled down the top of her stocking, and came up with a slender wad of bills.

"Here," she said. "Lawd knows yuh don need no gun. But yer pa does. Yuh bring it right back t me, yuh hear? Ahma put it up. Now ef yuh don, Ahma have yuh pa lick yuh so hard yuh won fergit it."

110   "Yessum."

He took the money, ran down the steps, and across the yard.

"Dave! Yuuuuuh Daaaaave!"

He heard, but he was not going to stop now. "Naw, Lawd!"

The first movement he made the following morning was to reach under the pillow for the gun. In the gray light of dawn he held it loosely, feeling a sense of power. Could kill a man with a gun like this. Kill anybody, black or white. And if he were holding his gun in his hand, nobody could run over him; they would have to respect him. It was a big gun, with a long barrel and a heavy handle. He raised and lowered it in his hand, marveling at its weight.

115   He had not come straight home with it as his mother had asked; instead he had stayed out in the fields, holding the weapon in his hand, aiming it now and then at some imaginary foe. But he had not fired it; he had been afraid that his father might hear. Also he was not sure he knew how to fire it.

To avoid surrendering the pistol he had not come into the house until he knew that they were all asleep. When his mother had tiptoed to his bedside late that night and demanded the gun, he had first played possum; then he had told her that the gun was hidden outdoors, that he would bring it to her in the morning. Now he lay turning it slowly in his hands. He broke it, took out the cartridges, felt them, and then put them back.

He slid out of bed, got a long strip of old flannel from a trunk, wrapped the gun in it, and tied it to his naked thigh while it was still loaded. He did not go in to breakfast. Even though it was not yet daylight he started for Jim Hawkins' plantation. Just as the sun was rising he reached the barns where the mules and plows were kept.

"Hey! That you, Dave?"

He turned. Jim Hawkins stood eyeing him suspiciously.

120   "What're yuh doing here so early?"

"Ah didn't know Ah wuz gittin up so early, Mistah Hawkins. Ah was fixin t hitch up ol Jenny n take her t the fiels."

"Good. Since you're so early, how about plowing that stretch down by the woods?"

"Suits me, Mistah Hawkins."

"O.K. Go to it!"

125   He hitched Jenny to a plow and started across the fields. Hot dog! This was just what he wanted. If he could get down by the woods, he could shoot his gun and nobody would hear. He walked behind the plow, hearing the traces creaking, feeling the gun tied tight to his thigh.

When he reached the woods, he plowed two whole rows before he decided to take out the gun. Finally, he stopped, looked in all directions, then untied the gun and held it in his hand. He turned to the mule and smiled.

"Know whut this is, Jenny? Naw, yuh wouldn know! Yuhs jusa ol mule! Anyhow, this is a gun, n it kin shoot, by Gawd!"

He held the gun at arm's length. Whut t hell, Ahma shoot this thing! He looked at Jenny again.

"Lissen here, Jenny! When Ah pull this ol trigger, Ah don wan yuh t run n acka fool now!"

130   Jenny stood with head down, her short ears pricked straight. Dave walked off about twenty feet, held the gun far out from him at arm's length, and turned his head. Hell, he told himself, Ah ain afraid. The gun felt loose in his fingers; he waved it wildly for a moment. Then he shut his eyes and tightened his forefinger. Bloom! A report half deafened him and he thought his right hand was torn from his arm. He heard Jenny whinnying and galloping over the field, and he found himself on his knees, squeezing his fingers hard between his legs. His hand was numb; he jammed it into his mouth, trying to warm it, trying to stop the pain. The gun lay at his feet. He did not quite know what had happened. He stood up and stared at the gun as though it were a living thing. He gritted his teeth and kicked the gun. Yuh almos broke mah arm! He turned to look for Jenny; she was far over the fields, tossing her head and kicking wildly.

"Hol on there, ol mule!"

When he caught up with her she stood trembling, walling her big white eyes at him. The plow was far away; the traces had broken. Then Dave stopped short, looking, not believing. Jenny was bleeding. Her left side was red and wet with blood. He went closer. Lawd, have mercy! Wondah did Ah shoot this mule? He grabbed for Jenny's mane. She flinched, snorted, whirled, tossing her head.

"Hol on now! Hol on."

Then he saw the hole in Jenny's side, right between the ribs. It was round, wet, red. A crimson stream streaked down the front leg, flowing fast. Good Gawd! Ah wuzn't shootin at tha mule. He felt panic. He knew he had to stop that blood, or Jenny would bleed to death. He had never seen so much blood in all his life. He chased the mule for half a mile, trying to catch her. Finally she stopped, breathing hard, stumpy tail half arched. He caught her mane and led her back to where the plow and gun lay. Then he stopped and grabbed handfuls of damp black earth and tried to plug the bullet hole. Jenny shuddered, whinnied, and broke from him.

135   "Hol on! Hol on now!"

He tried to plug it again, but blood came anyhow. His fingers were hot and sticky. He rubbed dirt into his palms, trying to dry them. Then again he attempted to plug the bullet hole, but Jenny shied away, kicking her heels high. He stood helpless. He had to do something. He ran at Jenny; she dodged him. He watched a red stream of blood flow down Jenny's leg and form a bright pool at her feet.

"Jenny . . . Jenny," he called weakly.

His lips trembled. She's bleeding t death! He looked in the direction of home, wanting to go back, wanting to get help. But he saw the pistol lying in the damp black clay. He had a queer feeling that if he only did something, this would not be; Jenny would not be there bleeding to death. When he went to her this time, she did not move. She stood with sleepy, dreamy eyes; and when he touched her she gave a low-pitched whinny and knelt to the ground, her front knees slopping in blood.

140   "Jenny . . . Jenny . . . " he whispered.

For a long time she held her neck erect; then her head sank, slowly. Her ribs swelled with a mighty heave and she went over.

Dave's stomach felt empty, very empty. He picked up the gun and held it gingerly between his thumb and forefinger. He buried it at the foot of a tree. He took a stick and tried to cover the pool of blood with dirt—but what was the use? There was Jenny lying with her mouth open and her eyes walled and glassy. He could not tell Jim Hawkins he had shot his mule. But he had to tell something. Yeah, Ah'll tel'em Jenny started gittin wil n fell on the joint of the plow. . . . But that would hardly happen to a mule. He walked across the field slowly, head down.

It was sunset. Two of Jim Hawkins' men were over near the edge of the woods digging a hole in which to bury Jenny. Dave was surrounded by a knot of people all of whom were looking down at the dead mule.

"I don't see how in the world it happened," said Jim Hawkins for the tenth time.

145 The crowd parted and Dave's mother, father, and small brother pushed into the center.

"Where Dave?" his mother called.

"There he is," said Jim Hawkins.

His mother grabbed him.

"Whut happened, Dave? Whut yuh done?"

150 "Nothin."

"C mon, boy, talk," his father said.

Dave took a deep breath and told the story he knew nobody believed.

"Waal," he drawled. "Ah brung ol Jenny down here sos Ah could do mah plowin. Ah plowed bout two rows, just like yuh see." He stopped and pointed at the long rows of upturned earth. "Then somethin musta been wrong wid ol Jenny. She wouldn ack right a-tall. She started snortin n kickin her heels. Ah tried t hol her, but she pulled erway, tearin n goin in. Then when the point of the plow was stickin up in the air, she swung erroun n twisted herself back on it. . . . She stuck herself n started t bleed. N fo Ah could do anything, she wuz dead."

"Did you ever hear anything like that in all your life?" asked Jim Hawkins.

155 There were white and black standing in the crowd. They murmured. Dave's mother came close to him and looked hard into his face. "Tell the truth, Dave," she said.

"Looks like a bullet hole to me," said one man.

"Dave, whut yuh do wid the gun?" his mother asked.

The crowd surged in, looking at him. He jammed his hands into his pockets, shook his head slowly from left to right, and backed away. His eyes were wide and painful.

"Did he hava gun?" asked Jim Hawkins.

160 "By Gawd, Ah tol yuh tha wuz a gun wound," said a man, slapping his thigh.

His father caught his shoulders and shook him till his teeth rattled.

"Tell whut happened, yuh rascal! Tell whut. . . ."

Dave looked at Jenny's stiff legs and began to cry.

"Whut yuh do wid tha gun?" his mother asked.

165 "What wuz he doin wida gun?" his father asked.

"Come on and tell the truth," said Hawkins. "Ain't nobody going to hurt you. . . ."

His mother crowded close to him.

"Did yuh shoot tha mule, Dave?"

Dave cried, seeing blurred white and black faces.

170 "Ahh ddinn gggo tt sshooot hher. . . . Ah ssswear ffo Gawd Ahh ddin. . . . Ah wuz a-tryin t sssee ef the old gggun would sshoot—"

"Where yuh git the gun from?" his father asked.

"Ah got it from Joe, at the sto."

"Where yuh git the money?"

"Ma give it t me."

175   "He kept worryin me, Bob. Ah had t. Ah tol im t bring the gun right back t me. . . . It was fer yuh, the gun."

"But how yuh happen to shoot that mule?" asked Jim Hawkins.

"Ah wuzn shootin at the mule, Mistah Hawkins. The gun jumped when Ah pulled the trigger. . . . N fo Ah knowed anythin Jenny was there a-bleedin."

Somebody in the crowd laughed. Jim Hawkins walked close to Dave and looked into his face.

"Well, looks like you have bought you a mule, Dave."

180   "Ah swear fo Gawd, Ah didn go t kill the mule, Mistah Hawkins!"

"But you killed her!"

All the crowd was laughing now. They stood on tiptoe and poked heads over one another's shoulders.

"Well, boy, looks like yuh done bought a dead mule! Hahaha!"

"Ain tha ershame."

185   "Hohohohoho."

Dave stood, head down, twisting his feet in the dirt.

"Well, you needn't worry about it, Bob," said Jim Hawkins to Dave's father. "Just let the boy keep on working and pay me two dollars a month."

"Whut yuh wan fer yo mule, Mistah Hawkins?"

Jim Hawkins screwed up his eyes.

190   "Fifty dollars."

"Whut yuh do wid tha gun?" Dave's father demanded.

Dave said nothing.

"Yuh wan me t take a tree n beat yuh till yuh talk!"

"Nawsuh!"

195   "Whut yuh do wid it?"

"Ah throwed it erway."

"Where?"

"Ah . . . . Ah throwed it in the creek."

"Waal, c mon home. N firs thing in the mawnin git to tha creek n fin tha gun."

200   "Yessuh."

"Whut yuh pay fer it?"

"Two dollahs."

"Take tha gun n git yo money back n carry it to Mistah Hawkins, yuh hear? N don fergit Ahma lam you black bottom good fer this! Now march yosef on home, suh!"

Dave turned and walked slowly. He heard people laughing. Dave glared, his eyes welling with tears. Hot anger bubbled in him. Then he swallowed and stumbled on.

205   That night Dave did not sleep. He was glad that he had gotten out of killing the mule so easily, but he was hurt. Something hot seemed to turn over inside him each time he remembered how they had laughed. He tossed on his bed, feeling his hard pillow. N Pa says he's gonna beat me. . . . He remembered other beatings, and his back quivered. Naw, naw, Ah sho don wan im t beat me tha way no mo. Dam em all! Nobody ever gave him anything. All he did was work. They treat me like a mule, n then they beat me. He gritted his teeth. N Ma had t tell on me.

Well, if he had to, he would take old man Hawkins that two dollars. But that meant selling the gun. And he wanted to keep that gun. Fifty dollars for a dead mule.

He turned over, thinking how he had fired the gun. He had an itch to fire it again. Ef other men kin shoota gun, by Gawd, Ah kin! He was still, listening. Mebbe they all sleepin now. The house was still. He heard the soft breathing of his brother. Yes, now! He would go down and get that gun and see if he could fire it. He eased out of bed and slipped into overalls.

The moon was bright. He ran almost all the way to the edge of the woods. He stumbled over the ground, looking for the spot where he had buried the gun. Yeah, here it is. Like a hungry dog scratching for a bone, he pawed it up. He puffed his black cheeks and blew dirt from the trigger and barrel. He broke it and found four cartridges unshot. He looked around; the fields were filled with silence and moonlight. He clutched the gun stiff and hard in his fingers. But, as soon as he wanted to pull the trigger, he shut his eyes and turned his head. Naw, Ah can't shoot wid mah eyes closed n mah head turned. With effort he held his eyes open: then he squeezed. *Blooooom!* He was stiff, not breathing. The gun was still in his hands. Dammit, he'd done it! He fired again. *Blooooom!* He smiled. *Blooooom! Blooooom! Click, click.* There! It was empty. If anybody could shoot a gun, he could. He put the gun into his hip pocket and started across the fields.

When he reached the top of a ridge he stood straight and proud in the moonlight, looking at Jim Hawkins' big white house, feeling the gun sagging in his pocket. Lawd, ef Ah had just one mo bullet Ah'd taka shot at tha house. Ah'd like t scare ol man Hawkins jusa little. . . . Jusa enough t let im know Dave Saunders is a man.

210   To his left the road curved, running to the tracks of the Illinois Central. He jerked his head, listening. From far off come a faint *boooof-boooof; boooof-boooof.* . . . He stood rigid. Two dollahs a mont. Les see now. . . . Tha means it'll take bout two years. Shucks! Ah'll be dam!

He started down the road, toward the tracks. Yeah, here she comes! He stood beside the track and held himself stiffly. Here she comes, erroun the ben. . . . C mon, yuh slow poke! C mon! He had his hand on his gun; something quivered in his stomach. Then the train thundered past, the gray and brown box cars tumbling and clinking. He gripped the gun tightly; then he jerked his hand out of his pocket. Ah betcha Bill wouldn't do it? Ah betcha. . . . The cars slid past, steel grinding upon steel. Ahm ridin yuh ternight, so hep me Gawd! He was hot all over. He hesitated just a moment; then he grabbed, pulled atop of a car, and lay flat. He felt his pocket; the gun was still there. Ahead the long rails were glinting in the moonlight, stretching away, away to somewhere, somewhere where he could be a man. . . .

[1940]

Topics for Critical Thinking and Writing

1. Why does Dave place such emphasis on owning a gun?
2. Do you assume that at the end of the story Dave is a man, or that he is only an immature boy who may come to a sad end? Explain.
3. Does the title strike you as odd? Would "The Boy Who Was Almost a Man" be more appropriate?

GLORIA NAYLOR

Gloria Naylor (b. 1950), a native of New York City, holds a bachelor's degree from Brooklyn College and a master's degree in Afro-American Studies from Yale University. "The Two" comes from The Women of Brewster Place *(1982), a book that won the American Book Award for First Fiction. Naylor has subsequently published two novels and* Centennial *(1986), a work of nonfiction.*

The Two

At first they seemed like such nice girls. No one could remember exactly when they had moved into Brewster. It was earlier in the year before Ben[1] was killed— of course, it had to be before Ben's death. But no one remembered if it was in the winter or spring of that year that the two had come. People often came and went on Brewster Place like a restless night's dream, moving in and out in the dark to avoid eviction notices or neighborhood bulletins about the dilapidated condition of their furnishings. So it wasn't until the two were clocked leaving in the mornings and returning in the evenings at regular intervals that it was quietly absorbed that they now claimed Brewster as home. And Brewster waited, cautiously prepared to claim them, because you never knew about young women, and obviously single at that. But when no wild music or drunken friends careened out of the corner building on weekends, and especially, when no slightly eager husbands were encouraged to linger around that first-floor apartment and run errands for them, a suspended sigh of relief floated around the two when they dumped their garbage, did their shopping, and headed for the morning bus.

The women of Brewster had readily accepted the lighter, skinny one. There wasn't much threat in her timid mincing walk and the slightly protruding teeth she seemed so eager to show everyone in her bell-like good mornings and evenings. Breaths were held a little longer in the direction of the short dark one—too pretty, and too much behind. And she insisted on wearing those thin Qiana dresses that the summer breeze molded against the maddening rhythm of the twenty pounds of rounded flesh that she swung steadily down the street. Through slitted eyes, the women watched their men watching her pass, knowing the bastards were praying for a wind. But since she seemed oblivious to whether these supplications went answered, their sighs settled around her shoulders too. Nice girls.

And so no one even cared to remember exactly when they had moved into Brewster Place, until the rumor started. It had first spread through the block like a sour odor that's only faintly perceptible and easily ignored until it starts growing in strength from the dozen mouths it had been lying in, among clammy gums and scum-coated teeth. And then it was everywhere—lining the mouths and whitening the lips of everyone as they wrinkled up their noses at its pervading smell, unable to pinpoint the source or time of its initial arrival. Sophie could—she had been there.

It wasn't that the rumor had actually begun with Sophie. A rumor needs no true parent. It only needs a willing carrier, and it found one in Sophie. She had been there—on one of those August evenings when the sun's absence is a mock-

---

[1]**Ben** the custodian of Brewster Place.

ery because the heat leaves the air so heavy it presses the naked skin down on your body, to the point that a sheet becomes unbearable and sleep impossible. So most of Brewster was outside that night when the two had come in together, probably from one of those air-conditioned movies downtown, and had greeted the ones who were loitering around their building. And they had started up the steps when the skinny one tripped over a child's ball and the darker one had grabbed her by the arm and around the waist to break her fall. "Careful, don't wanna lose you now." And the two of them had laughed into each other's eyes and went into the building.

5   The smell had begun there. It outlined the image of the stumbling woman and the one who had broken her fall. Sophie and a few other women sniffed at the spot and then, perplexed, silently looked at each other. Where had they seen that before? They had often laughed and touched each other—held each other in joy or its dark twin—but where had they seen *that* before? It came to them as the scent drifted down the steps and entered their nostrils on the way to their inner mouths. They had seen that—done that—with their men. That shared moment of invisible communion reserved for two and hidden from the rest of the world behind laughter or tears or a touch. In the days before babies, miscarriages, and other broken dreams, after stolen caresses in barn stalls and cotton houses, after intimate walks from church and secret kisses with boys who were now long forgotten or permanently fixed in their lives—that was where. They could almost feel the odor moving about in their mouths, and they slowly knitted themselves together and let it out into the air like a yellow mist that began to cling to the bricks on Brewster.

So it got around that the two in 312 were *that* way. And they had seemed like such nice girls. Their regular exits and entrances to the block were viewed with a jaundiced eye. The quiet that rested around their door on the weekends hinted of all sorts of secret rituals, and their friendly indifference to the men on the street was an insult to the women as a brazen flaunting of unnatural ways.

Since Sophie's apartment windows faced theirs from across the air shaft, she became the official watchman for the block, and her opinions were deferred to whenever the two came up in conversation. Sophie took her position seriously and was constantly alert for any telltale signs that might creep out around their drawn shades, across from which she kept a religious vigil. An entire week of drawn shades was evidence enough to send her flying around with reports that as soon as it got dark they pulled their shades down and put on the lights. Heads nodded in knowing unison—a definite sign. If doubt was voiced with a "But I pull my shades down at night too," a whispered "Yeah, but you're not *that* way" was argument enough to win them over.

Sophie watched the lighter one dumping their garbage, and she went outside and opened the lid. Her eyes darted over the crushed tin cans, vegetable peelings, and empty chocolate chip cookie boxes. What do they do with all them chocolate chip cookies? It was surely a sign, but it would take some time to figure that one out. She saw Ben go into their apartment, and she waited and blocked his path as he came out, carrying his toolbox.

"What ya see?" She grabbed his arm and whispered wetly in his face.

10   Ben stared at her squinted eyes and drooping lips and shook his head slowly. "Uh, uh, uh, it was terrible."

"Yeah?" She moved in a little closer.

"Worst busted faucet I seen in my whole life." He shook her hand off his arm and left her standing in the middle of the block.

"You old sop bucket," she muttered, as she went back up on her stoop. A broken faucet, huh? Why did they need to use so much water?

Sophie had plenty to report that day. Ben had said it was terrible in there. No, she didn't know exactly what he had seen, but you can imagine—and they did. Confronted with the difference that had been thrust into their predictable world, they reached into their imaginations and, using an ancient pattern, weaved themselves a reason for its existence. Out of necessity they stitched all of their secret fears and lingering childhood nightmares into this existence, because even though it was deceptive enough to try and look as they looked, talk as they talked, and do as they did, it had to have some hidden stain to invalidate it—it was impossible for them both to be right. So they leaned back, supported by the sheer weight of their numbers and comforted by the woven barrier that kept them protected from the yellow mist that enshrouded the two as they came and went on Brewster Place.

15   Lorraine was the first to notice the change in the people on Brewster Place. She was a shy but naturally friendly woman who got up early, and had read the morning paper and done fifty sit-ups before it was time to leave for work. She came out of her apartment eager to start her day by greeting any of her neighbors who were outside. But she noticed that some of the people who had spoken to her before made a point of having something else to do with their eyes when she passed, although she could almost feel them staring at her back as she moved on. The ones who still spoke only did so after an uncomfortable pause, in which they seemed to be peering through her before they begrudged her a good morning or evening. She wondered if it was all in her mind and she thought about mentioning it to Theresa, but she didn't want to be accused of being too sensitive again. And how would Tee even notice anything like that anyway? She had a lousy attitude and hardly ever spoke to people. She stayed in that bed until the last moment and rushed out of the house fogged-up and grumpy, and she was used to being stared at—by men at least—because of her body.

Lorraine thought about these things as she came up the block from work, carrying a large paper bag. The group of women on her stoop parted silently and let her pass.

"Good evening," she said, as she climbed the steps.

Sophie was standing on the top step and tried to peek into the bag. "You been shopping, huh? What ya buy?" It was almost an accusation.

"Groceries." Lorraine shielded the top of the bag from view and squeezed past her with a confused frown. She saw Sophie throw a knowing glance to the others at the bottom of the stoop. What was wrong with this old woman? Was she crazy or something?

20   Lorraine went into her apartment. Theresa was sitting by the window, reading a copy of *Mademoiselle*. She glanced up from her magazine. "Did you get my chocolate chip cookies?"

"Why good evening to you, too, Tee. And how was my day? Just wonderful." She sat the bag down on the couch. "The little Baxter boy brought in a puppy for show-and-tell, and the damn thing pissed all over the floor and then proceeded to chew the heel off my shoe, but, yes, I managed to hobble to the store and bring you your chocolate chip cookies."

Oh, Jesus, Theresa thought, she's got a bug up her ass tonight.

"Well, you should speak to Mrs. Baxter. She ought to train her kid better than that." She didn't wait for Lorraine to stop laughing before she tried to stretch her good mood. "Here, I'll put those things away. Want me to make dinner so you can rest? I only worked half a day, and the most tragic thing that went down was a broken fingernail and that got caught in my typewriter."

Lorraine followed Theresa into the kitchen. "No, I'm not really tired, and fair's fair, you cooked last night. I didn't mean to tick off like that; it's just that . . . well, Tee, have you noticed that people aren't as nice as they used to be?"

25   Theresa stiffened. Oh, God, here she goes again. "What people, Lorraine? Nice in what way?"

"Well, the people in this building and on the street. No one hardly speaks anymore. I mean, I'll come in and say good evening—and just silence. It wasn't like that when we first moved in. I don't know, it just makes you wonder; that's all. What are they thinking?"

"I personally don't give a shit what they're thinking. And their good evenings don't put any bread on my table."

"Yeah, but you didn't see the way that woman looked at me out there. They must feel something or know something. They probably—"

"They, they, they!" Theresa exploded. "You know, I'm not starting up with this again, Lorraine. Who in the hell are they? And where in the hell are we? Living in some dump of a building in this God-forsaken part of town around a bunch of ignorant niggers with the cotton still under their fingernails because of you and your theys. They knew something in Linden Hills, so I gave up an apartment for you that I'd been in for the last four years. And then they knew in Park Heights, and you made me so miserable there we had to leave. Now these mysterious theys are on Brewster Place. Well, look out that window, kid. There's a big wall down that block, and this is the end of the line for me. I'm not moving anymore, so if that's what you're working yourself up to—save it!"

30   When Theresa became angry she was like a lump of smoldering coal, and her fierce bursts of temper always unsettled Lorraine.

"You see, that's why I didn't want to mention it." Lorraine began to pull at her fingers nervously. "You're always flying up and jumping to conclusions—no one said anything about moving. And I didn't know your life has been so miserable since you met me. I'm sorry about that," she finished tearfully.

Theresa looked at Lorraine, standing in the kitchen door like a wilted leaf, and she wanted to throw something at her. Why didn't she ever fight back? The very softness that had first attracted her to Lorraine was now a frequent cause for irritation. Smoked honey. That's what Lorraine had reminded her of, sitting in her office clutching that application. Dry autumn days in Georgia woods, thick bloated smoke under a beehive, and the first glimpse of amber honey just faintly darkened about the edges by the burning twigs. She had flowed just that heavily into Theresa's mind and had stuck there with a persistent sweetness.

But Theresa hadn't known then that this softness filled Lorraine up to the very middle and that she would bend at the slightest pressure, would be constantly seeking to surround herself with the comfort of everyone's goodwill, and would shrivel up at the least touch of disapproval. It was becoming a drain to be continually called upon for this nurturing and support that she just didn't understand. She had supplied it at first out of love for Lorraine, hoping that she would harden eventually, even as honey does when exposed to the cold. Theresa was growing tired of being clung to—of being the one who was leaned on. She didn't want a child—she wanted someone who could stand toe to toe with her and be willing to slug it out at times. If they practiced that way with each other, then they could turn back to back and beat the hell out of the world for trying to invade their territory. But she had found no such sparring partner in Lorraine, and the strain of fighting alone was beginning to show on her.

"Well, if it was that miserable, I would have been gone a long time ago," she said, watching her words refresh Lorraine like a gentle shower.

35   "I guess you think I'm some sort of a sick paranoid, but I can't afford to have people calling my job or writing letters to my principal. You know I've already lost a position like that in Detroit. And teaching is my whole life, Tee."

"I know," she sighed, not really knowing at all. There was no danger of that ever happening on Brewster Place. Lorraine taught too far from this neighborhood for anyone here to recognize her in that school. No, it wasn't her job she feared losing this time, but their approval. She wanted to stand out there and chat and trade makeup secrets and cake recipes. She wanted to be secretary of their block association and be asked to mind their kids while they ran to the store. And none of that was going to happen if they couldn't even bring themselves to accept her good evenings.

Theresa silently finished unpacking the groceries. "Why did you buy cottage cheese? Who eats that stuff?"

"Well, I thought we should go on a diet."

"If *we* go on a diet, then you'll disappear. You've got nothing to lose but your hair."

40   "Oh, I don't know. I thought that we might want to try and reduce our hips or something." Lorraine shrugged playfully.

"No, thank you. We are very happy with our hips the way they are," Theresa said, as she shoved the cottage cheese to the back of the refrigerator. "And even when I lose weight, it never comes off there. My chest and arms just get smaller, and I start looking like a bottle of salad dressing."

The two women laughed, and Theresa sat down to watch Lorraine fix dinner. "You know, this behind has always been my downfall. When I was coming up in Georgia with my grandmother, the boys used to promise me penny candy if I would let them pat my behind. And I used to love those jawbreakers—you know, the kind that lasted all day and kept changing colors in your mouth. So I was glad to oblige them, because in one afternoon I could collect a whole week's worth of jawbreakers."

"Really. That's funny to you? Having some boy feeling all over you."

Theresa sucked her teeth. "We were only kids, Lorraine. You know, you remind me of my grandmother. That was one straight-laced old lady. She had a fit when my brother told her what I was doing. She called me into the smokehouse and told me in this real scary whisper that I could get pregnant from letting little boys pat my butt and that I'd end up like my cousin Willa. But Willa and I had been thick as fleas, and she had already given me a step-by-step summary of how she'd gotten into her predicament. But I sneaked around to her house that night just to double-check her story, since that old lady had seemed so earnest. 'Willa, are you sure?' I whispered through her bedroom window. 'I'm tellin' ya, Tee,' she said. 'Just keep both feet on the ground and you home free.' Much later I learned that advice wasn't too biologically sound, but it worked in Georgia because those country boys didn't have much imagination."

45   Theresa's laughter bounced off of Lorraine's silent, rigid back and died in her throat. She angrily tore open a pack of the chocolate chip cookies.

"Yeah," she said, staring at Lorraine's back and biting down hard into the cookie, "it wasn't until I came up north to college that I found out there's a whole lot of things that a dude with a little imagination can do to you even with both feet on the ground. You see, Willa forgot to tell me not to bend over or squat or—"

"Must you!" Lorraine turned around from the stove with her teeth clenched tightly together.

"Must I what, Lorraine? Must I talk about things that are as much a part of life as eating or breathing or growing old? Why are you always so uptight about sex or men?"

"I'm not uptight about anything. I just think its disgusting when you go on and on about—"

50   "There's nothing disgusting about it, Lorraine. You've never been with a man, but I've been with quite a few—some better than others. There were a couple who I still hope to this day will die a slow, painful death, but then there were some who were good to me—in and out of bed."

"If they were so great, then why are you with me?" Lorraine's lips were trembling.

"Because—" Theresa looked steadily into her eyes and then down at the cookie she was twirling on the table. "Because," she continued slowly, "you can take a chocolate chip cookie and put holes in it and attach it to your ears and call it an earring, or hang it around your neck on a silver chain and pretend it's a necklace—but it's still a cookie. See—you can toss it in the air and call it a Frisbee or even a flying saucer, if the mood hits you, and it's still just a cookie. Send it spinning on a table—like this—until it's a wonderful blur of amber and brown light that you can imagine to be a topaz or rusted gold or old crystal, but the law of gravity has got to come into play, sometime, and it's got to come to rest—sometime. Then all the spinning and pretending and hoopla is over with. And you know what you got?"

"A chocolate chip cookie," Lorraine said.

"Uh-huh." Theresa put the cookie in her mouth and winked. "A lesbian." She got up from the table. "Call me when dinner's ready. I'm going back to read." She stopped at the kitchen door. "Now, why are you putting gravy on that chicken, Lorraine? You know it's fattening."

[1982]

Topics for Critical Thinking and Writing

1. The first sentence says, "At first they seemed like such nice girls." What do we know about the person who says it? What does it tell us (and imply) about the "nice girls"?
2. What is Sophie's role in the story?
3. In the second part of the story, who is the narrator? Does she or he know Theresa's thoughts, or Lorraine's, or both?
4. How does the story end? What do you think will happen between Lorraine and Theresa?
5. Try writing a page or less that is the *end* of a story about two people (men, women, children—but *people*) whose relationship is going to end soon, or is going to survive, because of, or despite, its difficulties.

ALICE MUNRO

Alice Munro was born in 1931 in Wingham, Ontario, Canada, a relatively rural community and the sort of place in which she sets much of her fiction. She began publishing stories when she was an undergraduate at the University of Western Ontario. She left Western after two years, worked in a library and in a bookstore, then married, moved to Victoria, British Columbia, and founded a bookstore there. She continued to write while raising three children. She divorced and remarried; much of her fiction concerns marriage or divorce, which is to say it concerns shifting relationships in a baffling world.

Boys and Girls

My father was a fox farmer. That is, he raised silver foxes, in pens; and in the fall and early winter, when their fur was prime, he killed them and skinned them and sold their pelts to the Hudson's Bay Company or the Montreal Fur Traders. These companies supplied us with heroic calendars to hang, one on each side of the kitchen door. Against a background of cold blue sky and black pine forests and treacherous northern rivers, plumed adventurers planted the flags of England or of France: magnificent savages bent their backs to the portage.

For several weeks before Christmas, my father worked after supper in the cellar of our house. The cellar was whitewashed, and lit by a hundred-watt bulb over the worktable. My brother Laird and I sat on the top step and watched. My father removed the pelt inside-out from the body of the fox which looked surprisingly small, mean and rat-like, deprived of its arrogant weight of fur. The naked, slippery bodies were collected in a sack and buried at the dump. One time the hired man, Henry Bailey, had taken a swipe at me with this sack, saying, "Christmas present!" My mother thought that was not funny. In fact she disliked the whole pelting operation—that was what the killing, skinning, and preparation of the furs was called—and wished it did not have to take place in the house. There was the smell. After the pelt had been stretched inside-out on a long board my father scraped away delicately, removing the little clotted webs of blood vessels, the bubbles of fat; the smell of blood and animal fat, with the strong primitive odor of the fox itself, penetrated all parts of the house. I found it reassuringly seasonal, like the smell of oranges and pine needles.

Henry Bailey suffered from bronchial troubles. He would cough and cough until his narrow face turned scarlet, and his light blue, derisive eyes filled up with tears; then he took the lid off the stove, and, standing well back, shot out a great clot of phlegm—hsss—straight into the heart of the flames. We admired him for this performance and for his ability to make his stomach growl at will, and for his laughter, which was full of high whistlings and gurglings and involved the whole faulty machinery of his chest. It was sometimes hard to tell what he was laughing at, and always possible that it might be us.

After we had been sent to bed we could still smell fox and still hear Henry's laugh, but these things, reminders of the warm, safe, brightly lit downstairs world, seemed lost and diminished, floating on the stale cold air upstairs. We were afraid at night in the winter. We were not afraid of *outside* though this was the time of year when snowdrifts curled around our house like sleeping whales and the wind harassed us all night, coming up from the buried fields, the frozen swamp, with its old bugbear chorus of threats and misery. We were afraid of *inside,* the room where we slept. At this time the upstairs of our house was not finished. A brick chimney went up one wall. In the middle of the floor was a square hole, with a wooden railing around it; that was where the stairs came up. On the other side of the stairwell were the things that nobody had any use for any more—a soldiery roll of linoleum, standing on end, a wicker baby carriage, a fern basket, china jugs and basins with cracks in them, a picture of the Battle of Balaclava, very sad to look at. I had told Laird, as soon as he was old enough to understand such things, that bats and skeletons lived over there; whenever a man escaped from the county jail, twenty miles away, I imagined that he had somehow let himself in the window and was hiding behind the linoleum. But we had rules to keep us safe. When the light was on, we were safe as long as we did not step off the square of worn carpet which defined our bedroom-space; when the light was off no place was safe but the beds themselves. I had to turn out the light kneeling on the end of my bed, and stretching as far as I could to reach the cord.

5   In the dark we lay on our beds, our narrow life rafts, and fixed our eyes on the faint light coming up the stairwell, and sang songs. Laird sang "Jingle Bells," which he would sing any time, whether it was Christmas or not, and I sang "Danny Boy." I loved the sound of my own voice, frail and supplicating, rising in the dark. We could make out the tall frosted shapes of the windows now, gloomy and white. When I came to the part, *When I am dead, as dead I well may be*—a fit of shivering caused not by the cold sheets but by pleasurable emotion almost silenced me. *You'll kneel and say, an Ave there above me*—What was an Ave? Every day I forgot to find out.

Laird went straight from singing to sleep. I could hear his long, satisfied, bubbly breaths. Now for the time that remained to me, the most perfectly private and perhaps the best time of the whole day, I arranged myself tightly under the covers and went on with one of the stories I was telling myself from night to night. These stories were about myself, when I had grown a little older; they took place in a world that was recognizably mine, yet one that presented opportunities for courage, boldness and self-sacrifice, as mine never did. I rescued people from a bombed building (it discouraged me that the real war had gone on so far away from Jubilee). I shot two rabid wolves who were menacing the schoolyard (the teachers cowered terrified at my back). I rode a fine horse spiritedly down the main street of Jubilee, acknowledging the townspeople's gratitude for some yet-to-be-worked-out piece of heroism (nobody ever rode a horse there, except King Billy in the Orangemen's Day parade).[1] There was always riding and shooting in these stories, though I had only been on a horse twice—bareback because we did not own a saddle—and the second time I had slid right around and dropped under the horse's feet; it had stepped placidly over me. I really was learning to shoot, but I could not hit anything yet, not even tin cans on fence posts.

Alive, the foxes inhabited a world my father made for them. It was surrounded by a high guard fence, like a medieval town, with a gate that was padlocked at night. Along the streets of this town were ranged large, sturdy pens. Each of them had a real door that a man could go through, a wooden ramp along the wire, for the foxes to run up and down on, and a kennel—something like a clothes chest

---

[1]**Orangemen's Day parade** The Orange Society is named for William of Orange, who, as King William III of England, defeated James II of England at the Battle of the Boyne on 12 July 1609. It sponsors an annual procession on 12 July. (All notes to this reading are by the editors.)

with airholes—where they slept and stayed in winter and had their young. There were feeding and watering dishes attached to the wire in such a way that they could be emptied and cleaned from the outside. The dishes were made of old tin cans, and the ramps and kennels of odds and ends of old lumber. Everything was tidy and ingenious; my father was tirelessly inventive and his favorite book in the world was Robinson Crusoe. He had fitted a tin drum on a wheelbarrow, for bringing water to the pens. This was my job in summer, when the foxes had to have water twice a day. Between nine and ten o'clock in the morning, and again after supper, I filled the drum at the pump and trundled it down through the barnyard to the pens, where I parked it, and filled my watering can and went along the streets. Laird came too, with his little cream and green gardening can, filled too full and knocking against his legs and slopping water on his canvas shoes. I had the real watering can, my father's, though I could only carry it three-quarters full.

The foxes all had names, which were printed on a tin plate and hung beside their doors. They were not named when they were born, but when they survived the first year's pelting and were added to the breeding stock. Those my father had named were called names like Prince, Bob, Wally and Betty. Those I had named were called Star or Turk, or Maureen or Diana. Laird named one Maud after a hired girl we had when he was little, one Harold after a boy at school, and one Mexico, he did not say why.

Naming them did not make pets out of them, or anything like it. Nobody but my father ever went into the pens, and he had twice had blood-poisoning from bites. When I was bringing them their water they prowled up and down on the paths they had made inside their pens, barking seldom—they saved that for night-time, when they might get up a chorus of community frenzy—but always watching me, their eyes burning, clear gold, in their pointed, malevolent faces. They were beautiful for their delicate legs and heavy, aristocratic tails and the bright fur sprinkled on dark down their backs—which gave them their name—but especially for their faces, drawn exquisitely sharp in pure hostility, and their golden eyes.

10   Besides carrying water I helped my father when he cut the long grass, and the lamb's quarter and flowering money-musk, that grew between the pens. He cut with the scythe and I raked into piles. Then he took a pitchfork and threw fresh-cut grass all over the top of the pens to keep the foxes cooler and shade their coats, which were browned by too much sun. My father did not talk to me unless it was about the job we were doing. In this he was quite different from my mother, who, if she was feeling cheerful, would tell me all sorts of things—the name of a dog she had when she was a little girl, the names of boys she had gone out with later on when she was grown up, and what certain dresses of hers had looked like—she could not imagine now what had become of them. Whatever thoughts and stories my father had were private, and I was shy of him and would never ask him questions. Nevertheless I worked willingly under his eyes, and with a feeling of pride. One time a feed salesman came down into the pens to talk to him and my father said, "Like to have you meet my new hired man." I turned away and raked furiously, red in the face with pleasure.

"Could of fooled me," said the salesman. "I thought it was only a girl."

After the grass was cut, it seemed suddenly much later in the year. I walked on stubble in the earlier evening, aware of the reddening skies, the entering silences, of fall. When I wheeled the tank out of the gate and put the padlock on, it was almost dark. One night at this time I saw my mother and father standing on the little rise of ground we called the gangway, in front of the barn. My father had just come from the meathouse; he had his stiff bloody apron on, and a pail of cut-up meat in his hand.

It was an odd thing to see my mother down at the barn. She did not often come out of the house unless it was to do something—hang out the wash or dig potatoes in the garden. She looked out of place, with her bare lumpy legs, not touched by the sun, her apron still on and damp across the stomach from the supper dishes. Her hair was tied up in a kerchief, wisps of it falling out. She would tie her hair up like this in the morning, saying she did not have time to do it properly, and it would stay tied up all day. It was true, too; she really did not have time. These days our back porch was piled with baskets of peaches and grapes and pears, bought in town, and onions and tomatoes and cucumbers grown at home, all waiting to be made into jelly and jam and preserves, pickles and chili sauce. In the kitchen there was a fire in the stove all day, jars clinked in boiling water, sometimes a cheesecloth bag was strung on a pole between two chairs straining blue-black grape pulp for jelly. I was given jobs to do and I would sit at the table peeling peaches that had been soaked in the hot water, or cutting up onions, my eyes smarting and streaming. As soon as I was done I ran out of the house, trying to get out of earshot before my mother thought of what she wanted me to do next. I hated the hot dark kitchen in summer, the green blinds and the flypapers, the same old oilcloth table and wavy mirror and bumpy linoleum. My mother was too tired and preoccupied to talk to me, she had no heart to tell about the Normal School Graduation Dance; sweat trickled over her face and she was always counting under her breath, pointing at jars, dumping cups of sugar. It seemed to me that work in the house was endless, dreary and peculiarly depressing; work done out of doors, and in my father's service, was ritualistically important.

I wheeled the tank up to the barn, where it was kept, and I heard my mother saying, "Wait till Laird gets a little bigger, then you'll have a real help."

15   What my father said I did not hear. I was pleased by the way he stood listening, politely as he would to a salesman or a stranger, but with an air of wanting to get on with his real work. I felt my mother had no business down here and I wanted him to feel the same way. What did she mean about Laird? He was no help to anybody. Where was he now? Swinging himself sick on the swing, going around in circles, or trying to catch caterpillars. He never once stayed with me till I was finished.

"And then I can use her more in the house," I heard my mother say. She had a dead-quiet, regretful way of talking about me that always made me uneasy. "I just get my back turned and she runs off. It's not like I had a girl in the family at all."

I went and sat on a feed bag in the corner of the barn, not wanting to appear when this conversation was going on. My mother, I felt, was not to be trusted. She was kinder than my father and more easily fooled, but you could not depend on her, and the real reasons for the things she said and did were not to be known. She loved me, and she sat up late at night making a dress of the difficult style I wanted, for me to wear when school started, but she was also my enemy. She was always plotting. She was plotting now to get me to stay in the house more, although she knew I hated it (*because* she knew I hated it) and keep me from working for my father. It seemed to me she would do this simply out of perversity, and to try her power. It did not occur to me that she could be lonely, or jealous. No grown-up could be; they were too fortunate. I sat and kicked my heels monotonously against a feed bag, raising dust, and did not come out till she was gone.

At any rate, I did not expect my father to pay any attention to what she said. Who could imagine Laird doing my work—Laird remembering the padlock and cleaning out the watering dishes with a leaf on the end of a stick, or even wheeling the tank without it tumbling over? It showed how little my mother knew about the way things really were.

I have forgotten to say what the foxes were fed. My father's bloody apron reminded me. They were fed horsemeat. At this time most farmers still kept horses, and when a horse got too old to work, or broke a leg or got down and would not get up, as they sometimes did, the owner would call my father, and he and Henry went out to the farm in the truck. Usually they shot and butchered the horse there, paying the farmer from five to twelve dollars. If they had already too much meat on hand, they would bring the horse back alive, and keep it for a few days or weeks in our stable, until the meat was needed. After the war the farmers were buying tractors and gradually getting rid of horses altogether, so it sometimes happened that we got a good healthy horse, that there was just no use for any more. If this happened in the winter we might keep the horse in our stable till spring, for we had plenty of hay and if there was a lot of snow—and the plow did not always get our road cleared— it was convenient to be able to go to town with a horse and cutter.[2]

20   The winter I was eleven years old we had two horses in the stable. We did not know what names they had had before, so we called them Mack and Flora. Mack was an old black workhorse, sooty and indifferent. Flora was a sorrel mare, a driver. We took them both out in the cutter. Mack was slow and easy to handle. Flora was given to fits of violent alarm, veering at cars and even at other horses, but we loved her speed and high-stepping, her general air of gallantry and abandon. On Saturdays we went down to the stable and as soon as we opened the door on its cosy, animal-smelling darkness Flora threw up her head, rolled her eyes, whinnied despairingly and pulled herself through a crisis of nerves on the spot. It was not safe to go into her stall; she would kick.

This winter also I began to hear a great deal more on the theme my mother had sounded when she had been talking in front of the barn. I no longer felt safe. It seemed that in the minds of the people around me there was a steady undercurrent of thought, not to be deflected, on this one subject. The word *girl* had formerly seemed to me innocent and unburdened, like the word *child;* now it appeared that it was no such thing. A girl was not, as I had supposed, simply what I was; it was what I had to become. It was a definition, always touched with emphasis, with reproach and disappointment. Also it was a joke on me. Once Laird and I were fighting, and for the first time ever I had to use all my strength against him; even so, he caught and pinned my arm for a moment, really hurting me. Henry saw this, and laughed, saying, "Oh, that there Laird's gonna show you, one of these days!" Laird was getting a lot bigger. But I was getting bigger too.

My grandmother came to stay with us for a few weeks and I heard other things. "Girls don't slam doors like that." "Girls keep their knees together when they sit down." And worse still, when I asked some questions, "That's none of girls' business." I continued to slam the doors and sit as awkwardly as possible, thinking by such measures I kept myself free.

When spring came, the horses were let out in the barnyard. Mack stood against the barn wall trying to scratch his neck and haunches, but Flora trotted up and down and reared at the fences, clattering her hooves against the rails. Snow drifts dwindled quickly, revealing the hard gray and brown earth, the familiar rise and fall of the ground, plain and bare after the fantastic landscape of winter. There was

---

[2]**cutter** a small sleigh.

a great feeling of opening-out, of release. We just wore rubbers now, over our shoes; our feet felt ridiculously light. One Saturday we went to the stable and found all the doors open, letting in the unaccustomed sunlight and fresh air. Henry was there, just idling around looking at his collection of calendars which were tacked up behind the stalls in a part of the stable my mother had probably never seen.

"Come to say goodbye to your old friend Mack?" Henry said. "Here you give him a taste of oats." He poured some oats in Laird's cupped hands and Laird went to feed Mack. Mack's teeth were in bad shape. He ate very slowly, patiently shifting the oats around in his mouth, trying to find a stump of a molar to grind it on. "Poor old Mac," said Henry mournfully. "When a horse's teeth's gone, he's gone. That's about the way."

25   "Are you going to shoot him today?" I said. Mack and Flora had been in the stable so long I had almost forgotten they were going to be shot.

Henry didn't answer me. Instead he started to sing in a high, trembly, mocking-sorrowful voice. *Oh, there's no more work, for poor Uncle Ned, he's gone where the good darkies go.* Mack's thick, blackish tongue worked diligently at Laird's hand. I went out before the song was ended and sat down on the gangway.

I had never seen them shoot a horse, but I knew where it was done. Last summer Laird and I had come upon a horse's entrails before they were buried. We had thought it was a big black snake, coiled up in the sun. That was around in the field that ran up beside the barn. I thought that if we went inside the barn, and found a wide crack or a knothole to look through, we would be able to see them do it. It was not something I wanted to see; just the same, if a thing really happened, it was better to see, and know.

My father came down from the house, carrying the gun.

"What are you doing here?" he said.

30   "Nothing."

"Go on up and play around the house."

He sent Laird out of the stable. I said to Laird, "Do you want to see them shoot Mack?" and without waiting for an answer led him around to the front door of the barn, opened it carefully, and went in. "Be quiet or they'll hear us," I said. We could hear Henry and my father talking in the stable; then the heavy, shuffling steps of Mack being backed out of his stall.

In the loft it was cold and dark. Thin crisscrossed beams of sunlight fell through the cracks. The hay was low. It was a rolling country, hills and hollows, slipping under our feet. About four feet up was a beam going around the walls. We piled hay up in one corner and I boosted Laird up and hoisted myself. The beam was not very wide; we crept along it with our hands flat on the barn walls. There were plenty of knotholes, and I found one that gave me the view I wanted—a corner of the barnyard, the gate, part of the field. Laird did not have a knothole and began to complain.

I showed him a widened crack between two boards. "Be quiet and wait. If they hear you you'll get us in trouble."

35   My father came in sight carrying the gun. Henry was leading Mack by the halter. He dropped it and took out his cigarette papers and tobacco; he rolled cigarettes for my father and himself. While this was going on Mack nosed around in the old, dead grass along the fence. Then my father opened the gate and they took Mack through. Henry led Mack away from the path to a patch of ground and they talked together, not loud enough for us to hear. Mack again began searching for a mouthful of fresh grass, which was not to be found. My father walked away in a straight line, and stopped short a distance which seemed to suit him. Henry

was walking away from Mack too, but sideways, still negligently holding on to the halter. My father raised the gun and Mack looked up as if he had noticed something and my father shot him.

Mack did not collapse at once but swayed, lurched sideways and fell, first on his side; then he rolled over on his back and, amazingly, kicked his legs for a few seconds in the air. At this Henry laughed, as if Mack had done a trick for him. Laird, who had drawn a long, groaning breath of surprise when the shot was fired, said out loud, "He's not dead." And it seemed to me it might be true. But his legs stopped, he rolled on his side again, his muscles quivered and sank. The two men walked over and looked at him in a business-like way; they bent down and examined his forehead where the bullet had gone in, and now I saw his blood on the brown grass.

"Now they just skin him and cut him up," I said. "Let's go." My legs were a little shaky and I jumped gratefully down into the hay. "Now you've seen how they shoot a horse," I said in a congratulatory way, as if I had seen it many times before. "Let's see if any barn cat's had kittens in the hay." Laird jumped. He seemed young and obedient again. Suddenly I remembered how, when he was little, I had brought him into the barn and told him to climb the ladder to the top beam. That was in the spring, too, when the hay was low. I had done it out of a need for excitement, a desire for something to happen so that I could tell about it. He was wearing a little bulky brown and white checked coat, made down from one of mine. He went all the way up just as I told him, and sat down on the top beam with the hay far below him on one side, and the barn floor and some old machinery on the other. Then I ran screaming to my father. "Laird's up on the top beam!" My father came, my mother came, my father went up the ladder talking very quietly and brought Laird down under his arm, at which my mother leaned against the ladder and began to cry. They said to me, "Why weren't you watching him?" but nobody ever knew the truth. Laird did not know enough to tell. But whenever I saw the brown and white checked coat hanging in the closet, or at the bottom of the rag bag, which was where it ended up, I felt a weight in my stomach, the sadness of unexorcised guilt.

I looked at Laird, who did not even remember this, and I did not like the look on his thin, winter-pale face. His expression was not frightened or upset, but remote, concentrating. "Listen," I said, in an unusually bright and friendly voice, "you aren't going to tell, are you?"

"No," he said absently.

40   "Promise."

"Promise," he said. I grabbed the hand behind his back to make sure he was not crossing his fingers. Even so, he might have a nightmare; it might come out that way. I decided I had better work hard to get all thoughts of what he had seen out of his mind—which, it seemed to me, could not hold very many things at a time. I got some money I had saved and that afternoon we went into Jubilee and saw a show, with Judy Canova,[3] at which we both laughed a great deal. After that I thought it would be all right.

Two weeks later I knew they were going to shoot Flora. I knew from the night before, when I heard my mother ask if the hay was holding out all right, and my father said, "Well, after tomorrow there'll just be the cow, and we should be able to put her out to grass in another week." So I knew it was Flora's turn in the morning.

---

[3]**Judy Canova** American comedian, popular in films in the 1940s.

This time I didn't think of watching it. That was something to see just one time. I had not thought about it very often since, but sometimes when I was busy working at school, or standing in front of the mirror combing my hair and wondering if I would be pretty when I grew up, the whole scene would flash into my mind: I would see the easy, practiced way my father raised the gun, and hear Henry laughing when Mack kicked his legs in the air. I did not have any great feeling of horror and opposition, such as a city child might have had; I was too used to seeing the death of animals as a necessity by which we lived. Yet I felt a little ashamed, and there was a new wariness, a sense of holding-off, in my attitude to my father and his work.

It was a fine day, and we were going around the yard picking up tree branches that had been torn off in winter storms. This was something we had been told to do, and also we wanted to use them to make a teepee. We heard Flora whinny, and then my father's voice and Henry's shouting, and we ran down to the barnyard to see what was going on.

45   The stable door was open. Henry had just brought Flora out, and she had broken away from him. She was running free in the barnyard, from one end to the other. We climbed up on the fence. It was exciting to see her running, whinnying, going up on her hind legs, prancing and threatening like a horse in a Western movie, an unbroken ranch horse, though she was just an old driver, an old sorrel mare. My father and Henry ran after her and tried to grab the dangling halter. They tried to work her into a corner, and they had almost succeeded when she made a run between them, wild-eyed, and disappeared around the corner of the barn. We heard the rail clatter down as she got over the fence, and Henry yelled. "She's into the field now!"

That meant she was in the long L-shaped field that ran up by the house. If she got around the center, heading toward the lane, the gate was open; the truck had been driven into the field this morning. My father shouted to me, because I was on the other side of the fence, nearest the lane. "Go shut the gate!"

I could run very fast. I ran across the garden, past the tree where our swing was hung, and jumped across a ditch into the lane. There was the open gate. She had not got out, I could not see her up the road; she must have run to the other end of the field. The gate was heavy. I lifted it out of the gravel and carried it across the roadway. I had it halfway across when she came in sight, galloping straight toward me. There was just time to get the chain on. Laird came scrambling through the ditch to help me.

Instead of shutting the gate, I opened it as wide as I could. I did not make any decision to do this, it was just what I did. Flora never slowed down; she galloped straight past me, and Laird jumped up and down, yelling "Shut it, shut it!" even after it was too late. My father and Henry appeared in the field a moment too late to see what I had done. They only saw Flora heading for the township road. They would think I had not got there in time.

They did not waste any time asking about it. They went back to the barn and got the gun and the knives they used, and put these in the truck; then they turned the truck around and came bouncing up the field toward us. Laird called to them. "Let me go too, let me go too!" and Henry stopped the truck and they took him in. I shut the gate after they were all gone.

50   I supposed Laird would tell. I wondered what would happen to me. I had never disobeyed my father before, and I could not understand why I had done it. Flora would not really get away. They would catch up with her in the truck. Or if they did not catch her this morning somebody would see her and telephone us this afternoon or tomorrow. There was no wild country here for her to run to,

only farms. What was more, my father had paid for her, we needed the meat to feed the foxes, we needed the foxes to make our living. All I had done was make more work for my father who worked hard enough already. And when my father found out about it he was not going to trust me any more; he would know that I was not entirely on his side. I was on Flora's side, and that made me no use to anybody, not even to her. Just the same, I did not regret it; when she came running at me and I held the gate open, that was the only thing I could do.

I went back to the house, and my mother said, "What's all the commotion?" I told her that Flora had kicked down the fence and got away. "Your poor father," she said, "now he'll have to go chasing over the countryside. Well, there isn't any use planning dinner before one." She put up the ironing board. I wanted to tell her, but thought better of it and went upstairs, and sat on my bed.

Lately I had been trying to make my part of the room fancy, spreading the bed with old lace curtains, and fixing myself a dressing table with some leftovers of cretonne for a skirt. I planned to put up some kind of barricade between my bed and Laird's, to keep my section separate from his. In the sunlight, the lace curtains were just dusty rags. We did not sing at night any more. One night when I was singing Laird said, "You sound silly," and I went right on but the next night I did not start. There was not so much need to anyway, we were no longer afraid. We knew it was just old furniture over there, old jumble and confusion. We did not keep to the rules. I still stayed awake after Laird was asleep and told myself stories, but even in these stories something different was happening, mysterious alterations took place. A story might start off in the old way, with a spectacular danger, a fire or wild animals, and for a while I might rescue people; then things would change around, and instead, somebody would be rescuing me. It might be a boy from our class at school, or even Mr. Campbell, our teacher, who tickled girls under the arms. And at this point the story concerned itself at great length with what I looked like—how long my hair was, and what kind of dress I had on; by the time I had these details worked out the real excitement of the story was lost.

It was later than one o'clock when the truck came back. The tarpaulin was over the back, which meant there was meat in it. My mother had to heat dinner up all over again. Henry and my father had changed from their bloody overalls into ordinary working overalls in the barn, and they washed their arms and necks and faces at the sink, and splashed water on their hair and combed it. Laird lifted his arm to show off a streak of blood. "We shot old Flora," he said, "and cut her up in fifty pieces."

"Well I don't want to hear about it," my mother said. "And don't come to my table like that."

55   My father made him go and wash the blood off.

We sat down and my father said grace and Henry pasted his chewing gum on the end of his fork, the way he always did; when he took it off he would have us admire the pattern. We began to pass the bowls of steaming, overcooked vegetables. Laird looked across the table at me and said proudly, distinctly, "Anyway it was her fault Flora got away."

"What?" my father said.

"She could of shut the gate and she didn't. She just open' it up and Flora run out."

"Is that right?" my father said.

60   Everybody at the table was looking at me. I nodded, swallowing food with great difficulty. To my shame, tears flooded my eyes.

My father made a curt sound of disgust. "What did you do that for?"

I did not answer. I put down my fork and waited to be sent from the table, still not looking up.

But this did not happen. For some time nobody said anything, then Laird said matter-of-factly, "She's crying."

"Never mind," my father said. He spoke with resignation, even good humor, the words which absolved and dismissed me for good. "She's only a girl," he said.

65   I didn't protest that, even in my heart. Maybe it was true.

[1968]

Topics for Critical Thinking and Writing

1. Explain, in a paragraph, what the narrator means when she says (paragraph 21), "The word *girl* had formerly seemed to me innocent and unburdened, like the word *child;* now it appeared that it was no such thing. A girl was not, as I had supposed, simply what I was; it was what I had to become."
2. The narrator says that she "could not understand" why she disobeyed her father and allowed the horse to escape. Can you explain her action to her? If so, do so.
3. In a paragraph, characterize the mother.

POETRY

ANONYMOUS NURSERY RHYME

Nursery rhymes are of course found in books, but they survive because children find them memorable and pass them on to their playmates and, when they become adults, to their children. Nursery rhymes include lullabies ("Rock-a-by baby, on the tree tops"), counting-out rhymes ("eeny, meeny, miny, mo," "One potato, two potato"), charms ("rain, rain, go away"), short narratives ("Jack and Jill," "Mary had a little lamb"), and they are marked by emphatic rhymes. Scholars believe that perhaps half of the best-loved nursery rhymes of today go back to the eighteenth century, and many to the seventeenth. The earliest printed collections are *Tommy Thumb's Pretty Song Book* (1744) and *Mother Goose's Melody: or Sonnets for the Cradle* (1781).

The illustrations for "What are little boys made of" come from a book dated 1825.

Topic for Critical Thinking and Writing

When you read the following nursery rhyme (or call to mind others that you know), ask yourself this question: Do nursery rhymes indoctrinate children—that is, do they engender or reinforce attitudes about age, gender, and class? If so, how? And what should be done about it? Explain, using as examples these rhymes or others that you know.

Illustrations from a book published in 1825.

What Are Little Boys Made Of

What are little boys made of, made of?
What are little boys made of?
    Snips and snails
    And puppy-dogs' tails,
That's what little boys are made of.

What are little girls made of, made of?
What are little girls made of?
    Sugar and spice
    And all things nice,
That's what little girls are made of.

Topics for Critical Thinking and Writing

1. Do you imagine that boys like the description of what boys are made of? Do girls like the description of what girls are made of? Or is it only grown-ups who like these descriptions? Explain.
2. A version in 1846 gives two additional stanzas: "What are young men made of? / Sighs and leers and crocodile tears," and "What are young women made of? / Ribbons and laces, and sweet pretty faces." To the best of our knowledge, these two verses are not nearly so widely known as the first two. Why do you think this is so?

ANONYMOUS

The following lines have been attributed to various writers, including the American philosopher William James (1842–1910), but to the best of our knowledge the author is unknown.

Higamus, Hogamus,
Woman's monogamous;
Hogamus, Higamus,
Man is polygamous.

Topics for Critical Thinking and Writing

1. If you find these lines engaging, how do you account for their appeal? Does it make any difference—even a tiny difference—if the pairs are reversed; that is, if the first two lines are about men, and the second two about women?

2. The underlying idea largely coincides with the saying, "Men are from Mars, women are from Venus." But consider the four lines of verse: Do you agree that in the form we have just given them, they are more effective than "Men are from Mars, women are from Venus"? And how about "Women are from Venus, men are from Mars"? Admittedly the differences are small, but do you agree that one form is decidedly more effective than the others? If you do agree, how do you explain the greater effectiveness?

DOROTHY PARKER

Dorothy Parker (1893–1967) was born in West End, New Jersey, but brought up in New York City. From 1917 to 1920 she served as drama critic for the magazine Vanity Fair, *where her witty, satiric reviews gained her the reputation of being hard to please. She distinguished between wit and wisecracking: "Wit has truth in it; wisecracking is simply calisthenics with words."*

In addition to writing essays and stories, Parker also wrote light verse, especially about love.

General Review of the Sex Situation

Woman wants monogamy;
Man delights in novelty.
Love is woman's moon and sun;
Man has other forms of fun.   4

Woman lives but in her lord;
Count to ten, and man is bored.
With this the gist and sum of it,
What earthly good can come of it?   8

[1926]

Topics for Critical Thinking and Writing

1. How would you characterize Parker's message? (For instance, is it sad, happy, pitiful?) How would you characterize her tone—her attitude, as you perceive it?

2. How much truth do you think there is in Parker's lines? (Remember: No poem, or, for that matter, no novel—however long—can tell the whole truth about life.) As for truth, how would you compare it with the following passage, from Barbara Dafoe Whitehead's review (*The Times Literary Supplement,* June 9,

1995) of two sociological studies, *The Social Organization of Sexuality: Sexual Practice in the U.S.* and *Sex in America:*

> Men and women have different sexual interests, stakes and appetites, with men more oriented to the sex act and women more interested in sex as an expression of affiliative and romantic love.

RITA DOVE

Rita Dove was born in 1952 in Akron, Ohio. After graduating summa cum laude from Miami University (Ohio), she earned an M.F.A. at the Iowa Writers' Workshop. She has been awarded fellowships from the Guggenheim Foundation and the National Endowment for the Arts, and she now teaches at the University of Virginia. In 1993 she was appointed Poet Laureate of the United States for 1993–1994. In 2004 she was named Poet Laureate of the Commonwealth of Virginia. Dove is currently writing a book about the experiences of an African American volunteer regiment in France during World War I.

Daystar

She wanted a little room for thinking:
but she saw diapers steaming on the line,
a doll slumped behind the door.
So she lugged a chair behind the garage
to sit out the children's naps.   5

Sometimes there were things to watch—
the pinched armor of a vanished cricket,
a floating maple leaf. Other days
she stared until she was assured
when she closed her eyes   10
she'd see only her own vivid blood.

She had an hour, at best, before Liza appeared
pouting from the top of the stairs.
And just *what* was mother doing
out back with the field mice? Why,   15
building a palace. Later
that night when Thomas rolled over and
lurched into her, she would open her eyes
and think of the place that was hers
for an hour—where   20
she was nothing,
pure nothing, in the middle of the day.

[1986]

Topics for Critical Thinking and Writing

1. How would you characterize the woman who is the subject of the poem?
2. What do you make of the title?

ROBERT HAYDEN

Robert Hayden (1913–1980) was born in Detroit, Michigan. His parents divorced when he was a child, and he was brought up by a neighboring family, whose name he adopted. In 1942, at the age of 29, he graduated from Detroit City College (now Wayne State University); he received a master's degree from the University of Michigan. He taught at Fisk University from 1946 to 1969 and after that, for the remainder of his life, at the University of Michigan. In 1979 he was appointed Consultant in Poetry to the Library of Congress, the first African American to hold the post.

Those Winter Sundays

Sundays too my father got up early
and put his clothes on in the blueblack cold,
then with cracked hands that ached
from labor in the weekday weather made
banked fires blaze. No one ever thanked him.   5

I'd wake and hear the cold splintering, breaking.
When the rooms were warm, he'd call,
and slowly I would rise and dress,
fearing the chronic angers of that house.

Speaking indifferently to him,   10
who had driven out the cold
and polished my good shoes as well.
What did I know, what did I know
of love's austere and lonely offices?

[1962]

Topics for Critical Thinking and Writing

1. In line 1, what does the word *too* tell us about the father? What does it suggest about the speaker and the implied hearer of the poem?
2. How old do you believe the speaker was at the time he recalls in the second and third stanzas? What details suggest this age?
3. What is the meaning of *offices* in the last line? What does this word suggest that other words Hayden might have chosen do not?
4. What do you take to be the speaker's present attitude toward his father? What circumstances, do you imagine, prompted his memory of "Those Winter Sundays"?
5. In a page or two, try to get down the exact circumstances when you spoke "indifferently," or not at all, to someone who had deserved your gratitude.

THEODORE ROETHKE

Theodore Roethke (1908–1963) was born in Saginaw, Michigan, and educated at the University of Michigan and Harvard. From 1947 until his death he taught at the University of Washington in Seattle, where he exerted considerable influence on the next generation of poets. Many of Roethke's best poems are lyrical memories of his childhood.

My Papa's Waltz

The whiskey on your breath
Could make a small boy dizzy;
but I hung on like death:
Such waltzing was not easy.   4

We romped until the pans
Slid from the kitchen shelf;
My mother's countenance
Could not unfrown itself.   8

The hand that held my wrist
Was battered on one knuckle;
At every step you missed
My right ear scraped a buckle.   12

You beat time on my head
With a palm caked hard by dirt,
Then waltzed me off to bed
Still clinging to your shirt.   16

[1948]

Topics for Critical Thinking and Writing

1. Do the syntactical pauses vary much from stanza to stanza? Be specific. Would you say that the rhythm suggests lightness? Why?
2. Does the rhythm parallel or ironically contrast with the episode described? Was the dance a graceful waltz? Explain.
3. What would you say is the function of the stresses in lines 13–14?
4. How different would the poem be if the speaker were a female, and "girl" instead of "boy" appeared in line 2?

SHARON OLDS

Sharon Olds, born in San Francisco in 1942 and educated at Stanford University and Columbia University, has published several volumes of poetry and has received major awards.

Rites of Passage

As the guests arrive at my son's party
They gather in the living room—
short men, men in first grade
with smooth jaws and chins.
Hands in pockets, they stand around   5
jostling, jockeying for place, small fights
breaking out and calming. One says to another
How old are you? Six. I'm seven. So?
They eye each other, seeing themselves
tiny in the other's pupils. They clear their   10
throats a lot, a room of small bankers,
they fold their arms and frown. *I could beat you
up,* a seven says to a six,
the dark cake, round and heavy as a
turret, behind them on the table. My son,   15
freckles like specks of nutmeg on his cheeks,
chest narrow as the balsa keel of a
model boat, long hands
cool and thin as the day they guided him
out of me, speaks up as a host   20
for the sake of the group.
We could easily kill a two-year-old,
he says in his clear voice. The other
men agree, they clear their throats
like Generals, they relax and get down to   25
playing war, celebrating my son's life.

[1983]

Topics for Critical Thinking and Writing

1. Focus on the details that the speaker provides about the boys—how they look, how they speak. What do the details reveal about them?
2. Is the speaker's son the same as or different from the other boys?

3. Some readers find the ironies in this poem (e.g., "short men") to be somewhat comical, while others, noting such phrases as "kill a two-year-old" and
   "playing war," conclude that the poem as a whole is meant to be upsetting,
   even frightening. How would you describe the kinds of irony that Olds uses
   here?

4. An experiment in irony and point of view: Try writing a poem like this one,
   from the point of view of a father about the birthday party of his son, and
   then try writing another one, by either a father or mother about a daughter's
   party.

FRANK O'HARA

*Frank O'Hara (1926–1966), was born in Baltimore, and died
in a tragic accident—he was run over by a beach vehicle—on
Fire Island, New York. O'Hara was not only a prolific writer of
verse but also an astute critic of sculpture and painting who
worked as an assistant curator at the Museum of Modern Art, in
New York, and as an editor of* Art News. *O'Hara's first volume
of poetry was* A City Winter, and Other Poems *(1952);* Collected
Poems *was issued in 1971, but it was not complete. It has been
supplemented by two additional volumes,* Early Poems *(1977)
and* Poems Retrieved *(1977).*

Homosexuality

So we are taking off our masks, are we, and keeping
our mouths shut? as if we'd been pierced by a glance!

The song of an old cow is not more full of judgment
than the vapors which escape one's soul when one is sick;

so I pull the shadows around me like a puff   5
and crinkle my eyes as if at the most exquisite moment

of a very long opera, and then we are off!
without reproach and without hope that our delicate feet

will touch the earth again, let alone "very soon."
It is the law of my own voice I shall investigate.   10

I start like ice, my finger to my ear, my ear
to my heart, that proud cur at the garbage can

in the rain. It's wonderful to admire oneself
with complete candor, tallying up the merits of each

of the latrines. 14th Street is drunken and credulous,   15
53rd tries to tremble but is too at rest. The good

love a park and the inept a railway station,
and there are the divine ones who drag themselves up

and down the lengthening shadow of an Abyssinian head
in the dust, trailing their long elegant heels of hot air   20

crying to confuse the brave "It's a summer day,
and I want to be wanted more than anything else in the world."

[1971]

Topics for Critical Thinking and Writing

1. Describe your response to the word that O'Hara chooses for his title. In what ways does the poem define and explore the meanings of this word and our responses to it?
2. Characterize the point of view and tone of the speaker. Who is or are the "we" named in line 1?
3. In line 1 the speaker declares that "we are taking off our masks," but then immediately seems to confuse or contradict his point when he says "we" are "keeping / our mouths shut." Explain as clearly as you can what the speaker is suggesting in this first stanza.
4. Some of the language in this poem is ugly or unpleasant—for example, the "cur at the garbage can," "the latrines." What is the purpose of such language? What is its place in the structure of the poem as a whole?

TESS GALLAGHER

Tess Gallagher, born in 1943 in Port Angeles, Washington, was educated at the University of Washington and the University of Iowa. The author of books of poems and of short stories, she has been awarded a fellowship from the Guggenheim foundation and two National Endowment of the Arts Awards. Her collections of poetry include, Instructions to the Double *(1976), which won a Elliston Award;* Willingly *(1984), which consists of poems written to and about her third husband, Raymond carver;* My Black Horse: New and Selected Poems *(1995);* Owl-Spirit Dwelling *(1994); and* Moon Crossing Bridge *(1992). She has taught creative writing at several major universities.*

I Stop Writing the Poem

to fold the clothes. No matter who lives
or who dies, I'm still a woman.
I'll always have plenty to do.
I bring the arms of his shirt
together. Nothing can stop   5
our tenderness. I'll get back
to the poem. I'll get back to being
a woman. But for now
there's a shirt, a giant shirt
in my hands, and somewhere a small girl   10
standing next to her mother
watching to see how it's done.

[1992]

Topics for Critical Thinking and Writing

1. Why does the speaker say in line 2, "I'm still a woman"? How is this phrase connected to the phrase that precedes it?
2. Gallagher uses only two adjectives. Circle them and explain why they are there. How would the poem be different without them?
3. Is this a protest poem? If you think it is, explain what the nature of the speaker's protest is. If you do not think it is, then explain the point and purpose of the poem as you interpret it.

JULIA ALVAREZ

The Latina author Julia Alvarez has written fiction, poetry, and nonfictional prose. Her books include the novel How the Garcia Girls Lost Their Accents *(1991), which tells the story of four sisters and their parents who emigrate from the Dominican Republic to the United States;* Something to Declare: Essays *(1998); and* Homecoming: New and Collected Poems *(1996), which includes her first book,* Homecoming *(1984), as well as more recent work. The following poem is taken from that collection.*

Woman's Work

Who says a woman's work isn't high art?
She'd challenge as she scrubbed the bathroom tiles.
Keep house as if the address were your heart.   3

We'd clean the whole upstairs before we'd start
downstairs. I'd sigh, hearing my friends outside.
Doing her woman's work was a hard art   6

to practice when the summer sun would bar
the floor I swept till she was satisfied.
She kept me prisoner in her housebound heart.   9

She'd shine the tines of forks, the wheels of carts,
cut lacy lattices for all her pies.
Her woman's work was nothing less than art.   12

And, I, her masterpiece since I was smart,
was primed, praised, polished, scolded and advised
to keep a house much better than my heart.   15

I did not want to be her counterpart!
I struck out . . . but became my mother's child:
a woman working at home on her art,   18
housekeeping paper as if it were her heart.

[1996]

Topics for Critical Thinking and Writing

1. The poet explores the relationship between mother and daughter through the work that each performs. Describe this work, and in particular the lessons that the mother teaches through what she does and how she does it.
2. What is the meaning of line 3?
3. How do you interpret the phrase "I struck out"?

MARGE PIERCY

Marge Piercy, born in Detroit in 1936, was the first member of her family to attend college. After earning a bachelor's degree from the University of Michigan in 1957 and a master's degree from Northwestern University in 1958, she moved to Chicago. There she worked at odd jobs while writing novels (unpublished) and engaging in action on behalf of women and African Americans and against the war in Vietnam. In 1970— the year she moved to Wellfleet, Massachusetts, where she still lives—she published her first book, a novel. Since then she has published other novels, short stories, poems, and essays.

Barbie Doll

This girlchild was born as usual
and presented dolls that did pee-pee
and miniature GE stoves and irons
and wee lipsticks the color of cherry candy.
Then in the magic of puberty, a classmate said: 5
You have a great big nose and fat legs.

She was healthy, tested intelligent,
possessed strong arms and back,
abundant sexual drive and manual dexterity.
She went to and fro apologizing.   10
Everyone saw a fat nose on thick legs.

She was advised to play coy,
exhorted to come on hearty,
exercise, diet, smile and wheedle.
Her good nature wore out   15
like a fan belt.
So she cut off her nose and her legs
and offered them up.

In the casket displayed on satin she lay
with the undertaker's cosmetics painted on,   20
a turned-up putty nose,
dressed in a pink and white nightie.

Doesn't she look pretty? everyone said.
Consummation at last.
To every woman a happy ending.   25

[1969]

Topics for Critical Thinking and Writing

1. Why is the poem called "Barbie Doll"?
2. What voice do you hear in lines 1–4? Line 6 is, we are told, the voice of "a classmate." How do these voices differ? What voice do you hear in the first three lines of the second stanza?
3. Explain in your own words what Piercy is saying about women in this poem. Does her view seem to you fair, slightly exaggerated, or greatly exaggerated?

DRAMA

HENRIK IBSEN

Henrik Ibsen (1828–1906) was born in Skien, Norway, of wealthy parents who soon after his birth lost their money. Ibsen worked as a pharmacist's apprentice, but at the age of 22 he had written his first play, a promising melodrama entitled Cataline. *He engaged in theater work first in Norway and then in Denmark and Germany. By 1865 his plays had won him a state pension that enabled him to settle in Rome. After writing romantic, historic, and poetic plays, he turned to realistic drama with* The League of Youth *(1869). Among the major realistic "problem plays" are* A Doll's House *(1879),* Ghosts *(1881), and* An Enemy of the People *(1882). In* The Wild Duck *(1884) he moved toward a more symbolic tragic comedy, and his last plays, written in the nineties, are highly symbolic.* Hedda Gabler *(1890) looks backward to the plays of the eighties rather than forward to the plays of the nineties.*

A Doll's House

Translated by James McFarlane

CHARACTERS

TORVALD HELMER, a lawyer
NORA, his wife
DR. RANK
MRS. KRISTINE LINDE
NILS KROGSTAD
ANNE MARIE, the nursemaid
HELENE, the maid
THE HELMERS' THREE CHILDREN
A PORTER

The action takes place in the Helmers' flat.

A Doll's House (Harvard Theatre Collection, Houghton Library)

Act I

A pleasant room, tastefully but not expensively furnished. On the back wall, one door on the right leads to the entrance hall, a second door on the left leads to HELMER's *study. Between these two doors, a piano. In the middle of the left wall, a door; and downstage from it, a window. Near the window a round table with armchairs and a small sofa. In the right wall, upstage, a door; and on the same wall downstage, a porcelain stove with a couple of armchairs and a rocking chair. Between the stove and the door a small table. Etchings on the walls. A whatnot with china and other small objects d'art; a small bookcase with books in handsome bindings. Carpet on the floor; a fire burns in the stove. A winter's day.*

    The front door-bell rings in the hall; a moment later, there is the sound of the front door being opened. NORA *comes into the room, happily humming to herself. She is dressed in her outdoor things, and is carrying lots of parcels which she then puts down on the table, right. She leaves the door into the hall standing open; a* PORTER *can be seen outside holding a Christmas tree and a basket; he hands them to the* MAID *who has opened the door for them.*

NORA. Hide the Christmas tree away carefully, Helene. The children mustn't see it till this evening when it's decorated. [*To the* PORTER, *taking out her purse.*] How much?

PORTER. Fifty öre.

NORA. There's a crown. Keep the change.

    [*The* PORTER *thanks her and goes.* NORA *shuts the door. She continues to laugh quietly and happily to herself as she takes off her things. She takes a bag of macaroons out of her pocket and eats one or two; then she walks stealthily across and listens at her husband's door.*]

NORA.   Yes, he's in.

[*She begins humming again as she walks over to the table, right.*]

HELMER   [*in his study*].   Is that my little sky-lark chirruping out there?

NORA   [*busy opening some of the parcels*].   Yes, it is.

HELMER.   Is that my little squirrel frisking about?

NORA.   Yes!

HELMER.   When did my little squirrel get home?

NORA.   Just this minute. [*She stuffs the bag of macaroons in her pocket and wipes her mouth.*] Come on out, Torvald, and see what I've bought.

HELMER.   I don't want to be disturbed! [*A moment later, he opens the door and looks out, his pen in his hand.*] 'Bought', did you say? All that? Has my little spendthrift been out squandering money again?

NORA.   But, Torvald, surely this year we can spread ourselves just a little. This is the first Christmas we haven't had to go carefully.

HELMER.   Ah, but that doesn't mean we can afford to be extravagant, you know.

NORA.   Oh yes, Torvald, surely we can afford to be just a little bit extravagant now, can't we? Just a teeny-weeny bit. You are getting quite a good salary now, and you are going to earn lots and lots of money.

HELMER.   Yes, after the New Year. But it's going to be three whole months before the first pay cheque comes in.

NORA.   Pooh! We can always borrow in the meantime.

HELMER.   Nora! [*Crosses to her and takes her playfully by the ear.*] Here we go again, you and your frivolous ideas! Suppose I went and borrowed a thousand crowns today, and you went and spent it all over Christmas, then on New Year's Eve a slate fell and hit me on the head and there I was. . . .

NORA [*putting her hand over his mouth*].   Sh! Don't say such horrid things.

HELMER.   Yes, but supposing something like that did happen . . . what then?

NORA.   If anything as awful as that did happen, I wouldn't care if I owed anybody anything or not.

HELMER.   Yes, but what about the people I'd borrowed from?

NORA.   Them? Who cares about them! They are only strangers!

HELMER.   Nora, Nora! Just like a woman! Seriously though, Nora, you know what I think about these things. No debts! Never borrow! There's always something inhibited, something unpleasant, about a home built on credit and borrowed money. We two have managed to stick it out so far, and that's the way we'll go on for the little time that remains.

NORA [*walks over to the stove*].   Very well, just as you say, Torvald.

HELMER [*following her*].   There, there! My little singing bird mustn't go drooping her wings, eh? Has it got the sulks, that little squirrel of mine? [*Takes out his wallet.*] Nora, what do you think I've got here?

NORA [*quickly turning round*].   Money!

HELMER.   There! [*He hands her some notes.*] Good heavens, I know only too well how Christmas runs away with the housekeeping.

NORA [*counts*].   Ten, twenty, thirty, forty. Oh, thank you, thank you, Torvald! This will see me quite a long way.

HELMER.   Yes, it'll have to.

NORA.   Yes, yes, I'll see that it does. But come over here, I want to show you all the things I've bought. And so cheap! Look, some new clothes for Ivar . . . and a little sword. There's a horse and a trumpet for Bob. And a doll and a doll's cot for Emmy. They are not very grand but she'll have them all broken before long anyway. And I've got some dress material and some handkerchiefs for the maids. Though, really, dear old Anne Marie should have had something better.

HELMER.   And what's in this parcel here?

NORA [*shrieking*].   No, Torvald! You mustn't see that till tonight!

HELMER.   All right. But tell me now, what did my little spendthrift fancy for herself?

NORA.   For me? Puh, I don't really want anything.

HELMER.   Of course you do. Anything reasonable that you think you might like, just tell me.

NORA.   Well, I don't really know. As a matter of fact, though, Torvald . . .

HELMER.   Well?

NORA [*toying with his coat buttons, and without looking at him*].   If you did want to give me something, you could . . . you could always . . .

HELMER.   Well, well, out with it!

NORA [*quickly*].   You could always give me money, Torvald. Only what you think you could spare. And then I could buy myself something with it later on.

HELMER.   But Nora. . . .

NORA.   Oh, please, Torvald dear! Please! I beg you. Then I'd wrap the money up in some pretty gilt paper and hang it on the Christmas tree. Wouldn't that be fun?

HELMER.   What do we call my pretty little pet when it runs away with all the money?

NORA.   I know, I know, we call it a spendthrift. But please let's do what I said, Torvald. Then I'll have a bit of time to think about what I need most. Isn't that awfully sensible, now, eh?

HELMER [*smiling*].   Yes, it is indeed—that is, if only you really could hold on to the money I gave you, and really did buy something for yourself with it. But it just gets mixed up with the housekeeping and frittered away on all sorts of useless things, and then I have to dig into my pocket all over again.

NORA.   Oh but, Torvald. . . .

HELMER.   You can't deny it, Nora dear. [*Puts his arm round her waist.*] My pretty little pet is very sweet, but it runs away with an awful lot of money. It's incredible how expensive it is for a man to keep such a pet.

NORA.   For shame! How can you say such a thing? As a matter of fact I save everything I can.

HELMER [*laughs*].   Yes, you are right there. Everything you *can*. But you simply can't.

NORA [*hums and smiles quietly and happily*].   Ah, if you only knew how many expenses the likes of us sky-larks and squirrels have, Torvald!

HELMER.   What a funny little one you are! Just like your father. Always on the look-out for money, wherever you can lay your hands on it; but as soon as you've got it, it just seems to slip through your fingers. You never seem to know what you've done with it. Well, one must accept you as you are. It's in the blood. Oh yes, it is, Nora. That sort of thing is hereditary.

NORA.   Oh, I only wish I'd inherited a few more of Daddy's qualities.

HELMER.   And I wouldn't want my pretty little song-bird to be the least bit different from what she is now. But come to think of it, you look rather . . . rather . . . how shall I put it? . . . rather guilty today. . . .

NORA.   Do I?

HELMER.   Yes, you do indeed. Look me straight in the eye.

NORA [*looks at him*].   Well?

HELMER [*wagging his finger at her*].   My little sweet-tooth surely didn't forget herself in town today?

NORA.   No, whatever makes you think that?

HELMER.   She didn't just pop into the confectioner's for a moment?

NORA.   No, I assure you, Torvald . . . !

HELMER.   Didn't try sampling the preserves?

NORA.   No, really I didn't.

HELMER.   Didn't go nibbling a macaroon or two?

NORA.   No, Torvald, honestly, you must believe me . . . !

HELMER.   All right then! It's really just my little joke. . . .

NORA [*crosses to the table*].   I would never dream of doing anything you didn't want me to.

HELMER.   Of course not, I know that. And then you've given me your word. . . . [*Crosses to her.*] Well then, Nora dearest, you shall keep your little Christmas secrets. They'll all come out tonight, I dare say, when we light the tree.

NORA.   Did you remember to invite Dr. Rank?

HELMER.   No. But there's really no need. Of course he'll come and have dinner with us. Anyway, I can ask him when he looks in this morning. I've ordered some good wine. Nora, you can't imagine how I am looking forward to this evening.

NORA.   So am I. And won't the children enjoy it, Torvald!

HELMER.   Oh, what a glorious feeling it is, knowing you've got a nice, safe job, and a good fat income. Don't you agree? Isn't it wonderful, just thinking about it?

NORA.   Oh, it's marvellous!

HELMER.   Do you remember last Christmas? Three whole weeks beforehand you shut yourself up every evening till after midnight making flowers for the Christmas tree and all the other splendid things you wanted to surprise us with. Ugh, I never felt so bored in all my life.

NORA.   I wasn't the least bit bored.

HELMER [*smiling*].   But it turned out a bit of an anticlimax, Nora.

NORA.   Oh, you are not going to tease me about that again! How was I to know the cat would get in and pull everything to bits?

HELMER.   No, of course you weren't. Poor little Nora! All you wanted was for us to have a nice time—and it's the thought behind it that counts, after all. All the same, it's a good thing we've seen the back of those lean times.

NORA.   Yes, really it's marvellous.

HELMER.   Now there's no need for me to sit here all on my own, bored to tears. And you don't have to strain your dear little eyes, and work those dainty little fingers to the bone. . . .

NORA [*clapping her hands*].   No, Torvald, I don't, do I? Not any more. Oh, how marvellous it is to hear that! [*Takes his arm.*] Now I want to tell you how I've been thinking we might arrange things, Torvald. As soon as Christmas is over. . . . [*The door-bell rings in the hall.*] Oh, there's the bell. [*Tidies one or two things in the room.*] It's probably a visitor. What a nuisance!

HELMER.   Remember I'm not at home to callers.

MAID [*in the doorway*].   There's a lady to see you, ma'am.

NORA.   Show her in, please.

MAID [*to* HELMER].   And the doctor's just arrived, too, sir.

HELMER.   Did he go straight into my room?

MAID.   Yes, he did, sir.

[HELMER *goes into his study. The* MAID *shows in Mrs. Linde, who is in travelling clothes, and closes the door after her.*]

MRS. LINDE [*subdued and rather hesitantly*].   How do you do, Nora?

NORA [*uncertainly*].   How do you do?

MRS. LINDE.   I'm afraid you don't recognize me.

NORA.   No, I don't think I . . . And yet I seem to. . . . [*Bursts out suddenly*.] Why! Kristine! Is it really you?

MRS. LINDE.   Yes, it's me.

NORA.   Kristine! Fancy not recognizing you again! But how was I to, when . . . [*Gently*.] How you've changed, Kristine!

MRS. LINDE.   I dare say I have. In nine . . . ten years. . . .

NORA.   Is it so long since we last saw each other? Yes, it must be. Oh, believe me these last eight years have been such a happy time. And now you've come up to town, too? All that long journey in wintertime. That took courage.

MRS. LINDE.   I just arrived this morning on the steamer.

NORA.   To enjoy yourself over Christmas, of course. How lovely! Oh, we'll have such fun, you'll see. Do take off your things. You are not cold, are you? [*Helps her*.] There now! Now let's sit down here in comfort beside the stove. No, here, you take the armchair, I'll sit here on the rocking chair. [*Takes her hands*.] Ah, now you look a bit more like your old self again. It was just that when I first saw you. . . . But you are a little paler, Kristine . . . and perhaps even a bit thinner!

MRS. LINDE.   And much, much older, Nora.

NORA.   Yes, perhaps a little older . . . very, very little, not really very much. [*Stops suddenly and looks serious*.] Oh, what a thoughtless creature I am, sitting here chattering on like this! Dear, sweet Kristine, can you forgive me?

MRS. LINDE.   What do you mean, Nora?

NORA [*gently*].   Poor Kristine, of course you're a widow now.

MRS. LINDE.   Yes, my husband died three years ago.

NORA.   Oh, I remember now. I read about it in the papers. Oh, Kristine, believe me I often thought at the time of writing to you. But I kept putting it off, something always seemed to crop up.

MRS. LINDE.   My dear Nora, I understand so well.

NORA.   No, it wasn't very nice of me, Kristine. Oh, you poor thing, what you must have gone through. And didn't he leave you anything?

MRS. LINDE.   No.

NORA.   And no children?

MRS. LINDE.   No.

NORA.   Absolutely nothing?

MRS. LINDE.   Nothing at all . . . not even a broken heart to grieve over.

NORA [*looks at her incredulously*].   But, Kristine, is that possible?

MRS. LINDE [*smiles sadly and strokes* NORA*'s hair*].   Oh, it sometimes happens, Nora.

NORA.   So utterly alone. How terribly sad that must be for you. I have three lovely children. You can't see them for the moment, because they're out with their nanny. But now you must tell me all about yourself. . . .

MRS. LINDE.   No, no, I want to hear about you.

NORA.   No, you start. I won't be selfish today. I must think only about your affairs today. But there's just one thing I really must tell you. Have you heard about the great stroke of luck we've had in the last few days?

MRS. LINDE.   No. What is it?

NORA.   What do you think? My husband has just been made Bank Manager!

MRS. LINDE.   Your husband? How splendid!

NORA.   Isn't it tremendous! It's not a very steady way of making a living, you know, being a lawyer, especially if he refuses to take on anything that's the least bit shady—which of course is what Torvald does, and I think he's quite right. You can imagine how pleased we are! He starts at the Bank straight after New Year, and he's getting a big salary and lots of commission. From now on we'll be able to live quite differently . . . we'll do just what we want. Oh, Kristine, I'm so happy and relieved. I must say it's lovely to have plenty of money and not have to worry. Isn't it?

MRS. LINDE.   Yes. It must be nice to have enough, at any rate.

NORA.   No, not just enough, but pots and pots of money.

MRS. LINDE [*smiles*].   Nora, Nora, haven't you learned any sense yet? At school you used to be an awful spendthrift.

NORA.   Yes, Torvald still says I am. [*Wags her finger.*] But little Nora isn't as stupid as everybody thinks. Oh, we haven't really been in a position where I could afford to spend a lot of money. We've both had to work.

MRS. LINDE.   You too?

NORA.   Yes, odd jobs—sewing, crochet-work, embroidery and things like that. [*Casually.*] And one or two other things, besides. I suppose you know that Torvald left the Ministry when we got married. There weren't any prospects of promotion in his department, and of course he needed to earn more money than he had before. But the first year he wore himself out completely. He had to take on all kinds of extra jobs, you know, and he found himself working all hours of the day and night. But he couldn't go on like that; and he became seriously ill. The doctors said it was essential for him to go South.

MRS. LINDE.   Yes, I believe you spent a whole year in Italy, didn't you?

NORA.   That's right. It wasn't easy to get away, I can tell you. It was just after I'd had Ivar. But of course we had to go. Oh, it was an absolutely marvellous trip. And it saved Torvald's life. But it cost an awful lot of money, Kristine.

MRS. LINDE.   That I can well imagine.

NORA.   Twelve hundred dollars. Four thousand eight hundred crowns. That's a lot of money, Kristine.

MRS. LINDE.   Yes, but in such circumstances, one is very lucky if one has it.

NORA.   Well, we got it from Daddy, you see.

MRS. LINDE.   Ah, that was it. It was just about then your father died, I believe, wasn't it?

NORA.   Yes, Kristine, just about then. And do you know, I couldn't even go and look after him. Here was I expecting Ivar any day. And I also had poor Torvald, gravely ill, on my hands. Dear, kind Daddy! I never saw him again, Kristine. Oh, that's the saddest thing that has happened to me in all my married life.

MRS. LINDE.   I know you were very fond of him. But after that you left for Italy?

NORA.   Yes, we had the money then, and the doctors said it was urgent. We left a month later.

MRS. LINDE.   And your husband came back completely cured?

NORA.   Fit as a fiddle!

MRS. LINDE.   But . . . what about the doctor?

NORA.   How do you mean?

MRS. LINDE.   I thought the maid said something about the gentleman who came at the same time as me being a doctor.

NORA.   Yes, that was Dr. Rank. But this isn't a professional visit. He's our best friend and he always looks in at least once a day. No, Torvald has never had a day's illness since. And the children are fit and healthy, and so am I. [*Jumps up and claps her hands.*] Oh God, oh God, isn't it marvellous to be alive, and to be happy, Kristine! . . . Oh, but I ought to be ashamed of myself . . . Here I go on talking about nothing but myself. [*She sits on a low stool near* MRS. LINDE *and lays her arms on her lap.*] Oh, please, you mustn't be angry with me! Tell me, is it really true that you didn't love your husband? What made you marry him, then?

MRS. LINDE.   My mother was still alive; she was bedridden and helpless. And then I had my two young brothers to look after as well. I didn't think I would be justified in refusing him.

NORA.   No, I dare say you are right. I suppose he was fairly wealthy then?

MRS. LINDE.   He was quite well off, I believe. But the business was shaky. When he died, it went all to pieces, and there just wasn't anything left.

NORA.   What then?

MRS. LINDE.   Well, I had to fend for myself, opening a little shop, running a little school, anything I could turn my hand to. These last three years have been one long relentless drudge. But now it's finished, Nora. My poor dear mother doesn't need me any more, she's passed away. Nor the boys either; they're at work now, they can look after themselves.

NORA.   What a relief you must find it. . . .

MRS. LINDE.   No, Nora! Just unutterably empty. Nobody to live for any more. [*Stands up restless.*] That's why I couldn't stand it any longer being cut off up there. Surely it must be a bit easier here to find something to occupy your mind. If only I could manage to find a steady job of some kind, in an office perhaps. . . .

NORA.   But, Kristine, that's terribly exhausting; and you look so worn out even before you start. The best thing for you would be a little holiday at some quiet little resort.

MRS. LINDE [*crosses to the window*].   I haven't any father I can fall back on for the money, Nora.

NORA [*rises*].   Oh, please, you mustn't be angry with me!

MRS. LINDE [*goes to her*].   My dear Nora, you mustn't be angry with me either. That's the worst thing about people in my position, they become so bitter. One has nobody to work for, yet one has to be on the look-out all the time. Life has to go on, and one starts thinking only of oneself. Believe it or not, when you told me the good news about your step up, I was pleased not so much for your sake as for mine.

NORA.   How do you mean? Ah, I see. You think Torvald might be able to do something for you.

MRS. LINDE.   Yes, that's exactly what I thought.

NORA.   And so he shall, Kristine. Just leave things to me. I'll bring it up so cleverly . . . I'll think up something to put him in a good mood. Oh, I do so much want to help you.

MRS. LINDE.   It is awfully kind of you, Nora, offering to do all this for me, particularly in your case, where you haven't known much trouble or hardship in your own life.

NORA.   When I . . . ? I haven't known much . . . ?

MRS. LINDE [*smiling*].   Well, good heavens, a little bit of sewing to do and a few things like that. What a child you are, Nora!

NORA [*tosses her head and walks across the room*].   I wouldn't be too sure of that, if I were you.

MRS. LINDE.   Oh?

NORA.   You're just like the rest of them. You all think I'm useless when it comes to anything really serious. . . .

MRS. LINDE.   Come, come. . . .

NORA.   You think I've never had anything much to contend with in this hard world.

MRS. LINDE.   Nora dear, you've only just been telling me all the things you've had to put up with.

NORA.   Pooh! They were just trivialities! [*Softly.*] I haven't told you about the really big thing.

MRS. LINDE.   What big thing? What do you mean?

NORA.   I know you rather tend to look down on me, Kristine. But you shouldn't, you know. You are proud of having worked so hard and so long for your mother.

MRS. LINDE.   I'm sure I don't look down on anybody. But it's true what you say: I am both proud and happy when I think of how I was able to make Mother's life a little easier towards the end.

NORA.   And you are proud when you think of what you have done for your brothers, too.

MRS. LINDE.   I think I have every right to be.

NORA.   I think so too. But now I'm going to tell you something, Kristine. I too have something to be proud and happy about.

MRS. LINDE.   I don't doubt that. But what is it you mean?

NORA.   Not so loud. Imagine if Torvald were to hear! He must never on any account . . . nobody must know about it, Kristine, nobody but you.

MRS. LINDE.   But what is it?

NORA.   Come over here. [*She pulls her down on the sofa beside her.*] Yes, Kristine, I too have something to be proud and happy about. I was the one who saved Torvald's life.

MRS. LINDE.   Saved . . . ? How . . . ?

NORA.   I told you about our trip to Italy. Torvald would never have recovered but for that. . . .

MRS. LINDE.   Well? Your father gave you what money was necessary. . . .

NORA [*smiles*].   That's what Torvald thinks, and everybody else. But . . .

MRS. LINDE.   But . . . ?

NORA.   Daddy never gave us a penny. I was the one who raised the money.

MRS. LINDE.   You? All that money?

NORA.   Twelve hundred dollars. Four thousand eight hundred crowns. What do you say to that!

MRS. LINDE.   But, Nora, how was it possible? Had you won a sweepstake or something?

NORA [*contemptuously*].   A sweepstake? Pooh! There would have been nothing to it then.

MRS. LINDE.   Where did you get it from, then?

NORA [*hums and smiles secretively*].   H'm, tra-la-la!

MRS. LINDE.   Because what you couldn't do was borrow it.

NORA.   Oh? Why not?

MRS. LINDE.   Well, a wife can't borrow without her husband's consent.

NORA [*tossing her head*].   Ah, but when it happens to be a wife with a bit of a sense for business . . . a wife who knows her way about things, then. . . .

MRS. LINDE.   But, Nora, I just don't understand. . . .

NORA.   You don't have to. I haven't said I did borrow the money. I might have got it some other way. [*Throws herself back on the sofa.*] I might even have got it from some admirer. Anyone as reasonably attractive as I am. . . .

MRS. LINDE.   Don't be so silly!

NORA.   Now you must be dying of curiosity, Kristine.

MRS. LINDE.   Listen to me now, Nora dear—you haven't done anything rash, have you?

NORA [*sitting up again*].   Is it rash to save your husband's life?

MRS. LINDE.   I think it was rash to do anything without telling him. . . .

NORA.   But the whole point was that he mustn't know anything. Good heavens, can't you see! He wasn't even supposed to know how desperately ill he was. It was me the doctors came and told his life was in danger, that the only way to save him was to go South for a while. Do you think I didn't try talking him into it first? I began dropping hints about how nice it would be if I could be taken on a little trip abroad, like other young wives. I wept, I pleaded. I told him he ought to show some consideration for my condition, and let me have a bit of my own way. And then I suggested he might take out a loan. But at that he nearly lost his temper, Kristine. He said I was being frivolous, that it was his duty as a husband not to give in to all these whims and fancies of mine—as I do believe he called them. All right, I thought, somehow you've got to be saved. And it was then I found a way. . . .

MRS. LINDE.   Did your husband never find out from your father that the money hadn't come from him?

NORA.   No, never. It was just about the time Daddy died. I'd intended letting him into the secret and asking him not to give me away. But when he was so ill . . . I'm sorry to say it never became necessary.

MRS. LINDE.   And you never confided in your husband?

NORA.   Good heavens, how could you ever imagine such a thing! When he's so strict about such matters! Besides, Torvald is a man with a good deal of pride—it would be terribly embarrassing and humiliating for him if he thought he owed anything to me. It would spoil everything between us; this happy home of ours would never be the same again.

MRS. LINDE.   Are you never going to tell him?

NORA [*reflectively, half-smiling*].   Oh yes, some day perhaps . . . in many years time, when I'm no longer as pretty as I am now. You mustn't laugh! What I mean of course is when Torvald isn't quite so much in love with me as he is now, when he's lost interest in watching me dance, or get dressed up, or recite. Then it might be a good thing to have something in reserve. . . . [*Breaks off.*] What nonsense! That day will never come. Well, what have you got to say to my big secret, Kristine? Still think I'm not much good for anything? One thing, though, it's meant a lot of worry for me, I can tell you. It hasn't always been easy to meet my obligations when the time came. You know in business there is something called quarterly interest, and other things called instalments, and these are always terribly difficult things to cope with. So what I've had to do is save a little here and there, you see, wherever I could. I couldn't really save anything out of the housekeeping, because Torvald has to live in decent style. I couldn't let the children go about badly dressed either—I felt any money I got for them had to go on them alone. Such sweet little things!

MRS. LINDE.   Poor Nora! So it had to come out of your own allowance?

NORA.   Of course. After all, I was the one it concerned most. Whenever Torvald gave me money for new clothes and such-like, I never spent more than half. And always I bought the simplest and cheapest things. It's a blessing most things look well on me, so Torvald never noticed anything. But sometimes I did feel it was a bit hard, Kristine, because it is nice to be well dressed, isn't it?

MRS. LINDE.   Yes, I suppose it is.

NORA.   I have had some other sources of income, of course. Last winter I was lucky enough to get quite a bit of copying to do. So I shut myself up every night and sat and wrote through to the small hours of the morning. Oh, sometimes I was so tired, so tired. But it was tremendous fun all the same, sitting there working and earning money like that. It was almost like being a man.

MRS. LINDE.   And how much have you been able to pay off like this?

NORA.   Well, I can't tell exactly. It's not easy to know where you are with transactions of this kind, you understand. All I know is I've paid off just as much as I could scrape together. Many's the time I was at my wit's end. [*Smiles.*] Then I used to sit here and pretend that some rich old gentleman had fallen in love with me. . . .

MRS. LINDE.   What! What gentleman?

NORA.   Oh, rubbish! . . . and that now he had died, and when they opened his will, there in big letters were the words: 'My entire fortune is to be paid over, immediately and in cash, to charming Mrs. Nora Helmer.'

MRS. LINDE.   But my dear Nora—who is this man?

NORA.   Good heavens, don't you understand? There never was any old gentleman; it was just something I used to sit here pretending, time and time again, when I didn't know where to turn next for money. But it doesn't make very much difference; as far as I'm concerned, the old boy can do what he likes, I'm tired of him; I can't be bothered any more with him or his will. Because now all my worries are over. [*Jumping up.*] Oh God, what a glorious thought, Kristine! No more worries! Just think of being without a care in the world . . . being able to romp with the children, and making the house nice and attractive, and having things just as Torvald likes to have them! And then spring will soon be here, and blue skies. And maybe we can go away somewhere. I might even see something of the sea again. Oh yes! When you're happy, life is a wonderful thing!

[*The door-bell is heard in the hall.*]

MRS. LINDE [*gets up*].   There's the bell. Perhaps I'd better go.

NORA.   No, do stay, please. I don't suppose it's for me; it's probably somebody for Torvald . . .

MAID   [*in the doorway*].   Excuse me, ma'am, but there's a gentleman here wants to see Mr. Helmer, and I didn't quite know . . . because the Doctor is in there. . . .

NORA.   Who is the gentleman?

KROGSTAD [*in the doorway*].   It's me, Mrs. Helmer.

[MRS. LINDE *starts, then turns away to the window.*]

NORA [*tense, takes a step towards him and speaks in a low voice*].   You? What is it? What do you want to talk to my husband about?

KROGSTAD.   Bank matters . . . in a manner of speaking. I work at the bank, and I hear your husband is to be the new manager. . . .

NORA.   So it's . . .

KROGSTAD.   Just routine business matters, Mrs. Helmer. Absolutely nothing else.

NORA.   Well then, please go into his study.

[*She nods impassively and shuts the hall door behind him; then she walks across and sees to the stove.*]

MRS. LINDE.   Nora . . . who was that man?

NORA.   His name is Krogstad.

MRS. LINDE.   So it really was him.

NORA.   Do you know the man?

MRS. LINDE.   I used to know him . . . a good many years ago. He was a solicitor's clerk in our district for a while.

NORA.   Yes, so he was.

MRS. LINDE.   How he's changed!

NORA.   His marriage wasn't a very happy one, I believe.

MRS. LINDE.   He's a widower now, isn't he?

NORA.   With a lot of children. There, it'll burn better now.

[*She closes the stove door and moves the rocking chair a little to one side.*]

MRS. LINDE.   He does a certain amount of business on the side, they say?

NORA.   Oh? Yes, it's always possible. I just don't know. . . . But let's not think about business . . . it's all so dull.

[DR. RANK *comes in from* HELMER'*s study.*]

DR. RANK [*still in the doorway*].   No, no, Torvald, I won't intrude. I'll just look in on your wife for a moment. [*Shuts the door and notices* MRS. LINDE.] Oh, I beg your pardon. I'm afraid I'm intruding here as well.

NORA.   No, not at all! [*Introduces them.*] Dr. Rank . . . Mrs. Linde.

RANK.   Ah! A name I've often heard mentioned in this house. I believe I came past you on the stairs as I came in.

MRS. LINDE.   I have to take things slowly going upstairs. I find it rather a trial.

RANK.   Ah, some little disability somewhere, eh?

MRS. LINDE.   Just a bit run down, I think, actually.

RANK.   Is that all? Then I suppose you've come to town for a good rest—doing the rounds of the parties?

MRS. LINDE.   I have come to look for work.

RANK.   Is that supposed to be some kind of sovereign remedy for being run down?

MRS. LINDE.   One must live, Doctor.

RANK.   Yes, it's generally thought to be necessary.

NORA.   Come, come, Dr. Rank. You are quite as keen to live as anybody.

RANK.   Quite keen, yes. Miserable as I am, I'm quite ready to let things drag on as long as possible. All my patients are the same. Even those with a moral affliction are no different. As a matter of fact, there's a bad case of that kind in talking with Helmer at this very moment . . .

MRS. LINDE [*softly*].   Ah!

NORA.   Whom do you mean?

RANK.   A person called Krogstad—nobody you would know. He's rotten to the core. But even he began talking about having to *live,* as though it were something terribly important.

NORA.   Oh? And what did he want to talk to Torvald about?

RANK.   I honestly don't know. All I heard was something about the Bank.

NORA.   I didn't know that Krog . . . that this Mr. Krogstad had anything to do with the Bank.

RANK.   Oh yes, he's got some kind of job down there. [*To* MRS. LINDE.] I wonder if you've got people in your part of the country too who go rushing round sniffing out cases of moral corruption, and then installing the individuals concerned in nice, well-paid jobs where they can keep them under observation. Sound, decent people have to be content to stay out in the cold.

MRS. LINDE.   Yet surely it's the sick who most need to be brought in.

RANK [*shrugs his shoulders*].   Well, there we have it. It's that attitude that's turning society into a clinic.

[NORA, *lost in her own thoughts, breaks into smothered laughter and claps her hands.*]

RANK.   Why are you laughing at that? Do you know in fact what society is?

NORA.   What do I care about your silly old society? I was laughing about something quite different . . . something frightfully funny. Tell me, Dr. Rank, are all the people who work at the Bank dependent on Torvald now?

RANK.   Is that what you find so frightfully funny?

NORA [*smiles and hums*].   Never you mind! Never you mind! [*Walks about the room.*] Yes, it really is terribly amusing to think that we . . . that Torvald now has power over so many people. [*She takes the bag out of her pocket.*] Dr. Rank, what about a little macaroon?

RANK.   Look at this, eh? Macaroons. I thought they were forbidden here.

NORA.   Yes, but these are some Kristine gave me.

MRS. LINDE.   What? I . . . ?

NORA.   Now, now, you needn't be alarmed. You weren't to know that Torvald had forbidden them. He's worried in case they ruin my teeth, you know. Still . . . what's it matter once in a while! Don't you think so, Dr. Rank? Here! [*She pops a macaroon into his mouth.*] And you too, Kristine. And I shall have one as well; just a little one . . . or two at the most. [*She walks about the room again.*] Really I am so happy. There's just one little thing I'd love to do now.

RANK.   What's that?

NORA.   Something I'd love to say in front of Torvald.

RANK.   Then why can't you?

NORA.   No, I daren't. It's not very nice.

MRS. LINDE.   Not very nice?

RANK.   Well, in that case it might not be wise. But to us, I don't see why. . . . What is this you would love to say in front of Helmer?

NORA.   I would simply love to say: 'Damn.'

RANK.   Are you mad!

MRS. LINDE.   Good gracious, Nora . . . !

RANK.   Say it! Here he is!

NORA [*hiding the bag of macaroons*].   Sh! Sh!

[HELMER *comes out of his room, his overcoat over his arm and his hat in his hand.*]

NORA [*going over to him*].   Well, Torvald dear, did you get rid of him?

HELMER.   Yes, he's just gone.

NORA.   Let me introduce you. This is Kristine, who has just arrived in town. . . .

HELMER.   Kristine . . . ? You must forgive me, but I don't think I know . . .

NORA.   Mrs. Linde, Torvald dear. Kristine Linde.

HELMER.   Ah, indeed. A school-friend of my wife's, presumably.

MRS. LINDE.   Yes, we were girls together.

NORA.   Fancy, Torvald, she's come all this long way just to have a word with you.

HELMER.   How is that?

MRS. LINDE.   Well, it wasn't really . . .

NORA.   The thing is, Kristine is terribly clever at office work, and she's frightfully keen on finding a job with some efficient man, so that she can learn even more. . . .

HELMER.   Very sensible, Mrs. Linde.

NORA.   And then when she heard you'd been made Bank Manager—there was a bit in the paper about it—she set off at once. Torvald please! You *will* try and do something for Kristine, won't you? For my sake?

HELMER.   Well, that's not altogether impossible. You are a widow, I presume?

MRS. LINDE.   Yes.

HELMER.   And you've had some experience in business?

MRS. LINDE.   A fair amount.

HELMER.   Well, it's quite probable I can find you a job, I think. . . .

NORA   [*clapping her hands*].   There, you see!

HELMER.   You have come at a fortunate moment, Mrs. Linde. . . .

MRS. LINDE.   Oh, how can I ever thank you . . . ?

HELMER.   Not a bit. [*He puts on his overcoat.*] But for the present I must ask you to excuse me. . . .

RANK.   Wait. I'm coming with you.

[*He fetches his fur coat from the hall and warms it at the stove.*]

NORA.   Don't be long, Torvald dear.

HELMER.   Not more than an hour, that's all.

NORA.   Are you leaving too, Kristine?

MRS. LINDE   [*putting on her things*].   Yes, I must go and see if I can't find myself a room.

HELMER.   Perhaps we can all walk down the road together.

NORA [*helping her*].   What a nuisance we are so limited for space here. I'm afraid it just isn't possible. . . .

MRS. LINDE.   Oh, you mustn't dream of it! Goodbye, Nora dear, and thanks for everything.

NORA.   Goodbye for the present. But . . . you'll be coming back this evening, of course. And you too, Dr. Rank? What's that? If you are up to it? Of course you'll be up to it. Just wrap yourself up well.

[*They go out, talking, into the hall; children's voices can be heard on the stairs.*]

NORA.   Here they are! Here they are! [*She runs to the front door and opens it. Anne Marie, the* NURSEMAID, *enters with the children.*] Come in! Come in! [*She bends down and kisses them.*] Ah! my sweet little darlings. . . . You see them, Kristine? Aren't they lovely!

RANK.   Don't stand here chattering in this draught!

HELMER.   Come along, Mrs. Linde. The place now becomes unbearable for anybody except mothers.

[DR. RANK, HELMER *and* MRS. LINDE *go down the stairs: the* NURSEMAID *comes into the room with the children, then* NORA, *shutting the door behind her.*]

NORA.   How fresh and bright you look! My, what red cheeks you've got! Like apples and roses. [*During the following, the children keep chattering away to her.*] Have you had a nice time? That's splendid. And you gave Emmy and Bob a ride on your sledge? Did you now! Both together! Fancy that! There's a clever boy, Ivar. Oh, let me take her a little while, Anne Marie. There's my sweet little baby-doll! [*She takes the youngest of the children from the* NURSEMAID *and dances with her.*] All right, Mummy will dance with Bobby too. What? You've been throwing snowballs? Oh, I wish I'd been there. No, don't bother, Anne Marie, I'll help them off with their things. No, please, let me—I like doing it. You go on in, you look frozen. You'll find some hot coffee on the stove. [*The* NURSEMAID *goes into the room, left.* NORA *takes off the children's coats and hats and throws them down anywhere, while the children all talk at once.*] Really! A great big dog came running after you? But he didn't bite. No, the doggies wouldn't bite my pretty little dollies. You mustn't touch the parcels, Ivar! What are they? Wouldn't you like to know! No, no, that's nasty. Now? Shall we play something? What shall we play? Hide and seek? Yes, let's play hide and seek. Bob can hide first. Me first? All right, let me hide first.

[*She and the children play, laughing and shrieking, in this room and in the adjacent room on the right. Finally* NORA *hides under the table; the children come rushing in to look for her but cannot find her; they hear her stifled laughter, rush to the table, lift up the tablecloth and find her. Tremendous shouts of delight. She creeps out and pretends to frighten them. More shouts. Meanwhile there has been a knock at the front door, which nobody has heard. The door half opens, and* KROGSTAD *can be seen. He waits a little; the game continues.*]

KROGSTAD.   I beg your pardon, Mrs. Helmer. . . .

NORA [*turns with a stifled cry and half jumps up*].   Ah! What do you want?

KROGSTAD.   Excuse me. The front door was standing open. Somebody must have forgotten to shut it. . . .

NORA [*standing up*].   My husband isn't at home, Mr. Krogstad.

KROGSTAD.   I know.

NORA.   Well . . . what are you doing here?

KROGSTAD.   I want a word with you.

NORA.   With . . . ? [*Quietly, to the children.*] Go to Anne Marie. What? No, the strange man won't do anything to Mummy. When he's gone we'll have another game. [*She leads the children into the room, left, and shuts the door after them; tense and uneasy.*] You want to speak to me?

KROGSTAD.   Yes, I do.

NORA.   Today? But it isn't the first of the month yet. . . .

KROGSTAD.   No, it's Christmas Eve. It depends entirely on you what sort of Christmas you have.

NORA.   What do you want? Today I can't possibly . . .

KROGSTAD.   Let's not talk about that for the moment. It's something else. You've got a moment to spare?

NORA.   Yes, I suppose so, though . . .

KROGSTAD.   Good. I was sitting in Olsen's café, and I saw your husband go down the road . . .

NORA.   Did you?

KROGSTAD.   . . . with a lady.

NORA.   Well?

KROGSTAD.   May I be so bold as to ask whether that lady was a Mrs. Linde?

NORA.   Yes.

KROGSTAD.   Just arrived in town?

NORA.   Yes, today.

KROGSTAD.   And she's a good friend of yours?

NORA.   Yes, she is. But I can't see . . .

KROGSTAD.   I also knew her once.

NORA.   I know.

KROGSTAD.   Oh? So you know all about it. I thought as much. Well, I want to ask you straight: is Mrs. Linde getting a job in the Bank?

NORA.   How dare you cross-examine me like this, Mr. Krogstad? You, one of my husband's subordinates? But since you've asked me, I'll tell you. Yes, Mrs. Linde *has* got a job. And I'm the one who got it for her, Mr. Krogstad. Now you know.

KROGSTAD.   So my guess was right.

NORA [*walking up and down*].   Oh, I think I can say that some of us have a little influence now and again. Just because one happens to be a woman, that doesn't. . . . People in subordinate positions, ought to take care they don't offend anybody . . . who . . . hm . . .

KROGSTAD.   . . . has influence?

NORA.   Exactly.

KROGSTAD [*changing his tone*].   Mrs. Helmer, will you have the goodness to use your influence on my behalf?

NORA.   What? What do you mean?

KROGSTAD   Will you be so good as to see that I keep my modest little job at the Bank?

NORA.   What do you mean? Who wants to take it away from you?

KROGSTAD.   Oh, you needn't try and pretend to me you don't know. I can quite see that this friend of yours isn't particularly anxious to bump up against me. And I can also see now whom I can thank for being given the sack.

NORA.   But I assure you. . . .

KROGSTAD.   All right, all right. But to come to the point: there's still time. And I advise you to use your influence to stop it.

NORA.   But, Mr. Krogstad, I *have* no influence.

KROGSTAD.   Haven't you? I thought just now you said yourself . . .

NORA.   I didn't mean it that way, of course. Me? What makes you think I've got any influence of that kind over my husband?

KROGSTAD.   I know your husband from our student days. I don't suppose he is any more steadfast than other married men.

NORA.   You speak disrespectfully of my husband like that and I'll show you the door.

KROGSTAD.   So the lady's got courage.

NORA.   I'm not frightened of you any more. After New Year's I'll soon be finished with the whole business.

KROGSTAD [*controlling himself*].   Listen to me, Mrs. Helmer. If necessary I shall fight for my little job in the Bank as if I were fighting for my life.

NORA.   So it seems.

KROGSTAD.   It's not just for the money, that's the last thing I care about. There's something else . . . well, I might as well out with it. You see it's like this. You know as well as anybody that some years ago I got myself mixed up in a bit of trouble.

NORA.   I believe I've heard something of the sort.

KROGSTAD.   It never got as far as the courts; but immediately it was as if all paths were barred to me. So I started going in for the sort of business you know about. I had to do something, and I think I can say I haven't been one of the worst. But now I have to get out of it. My sons are growing up; for their sake I must try and win back what respectability I can. That job in the Bank was like the first step on the ladder for me. And now your husband wants to kick me off the ladder again, back into the mud.

NORA.   But in God's name, Mr. Krogstad, it's quite beyond my power to help you.

KROGSTAD.   That's because you haven't the will to help me. But I have ways of making you.

NORA.   You wouldn't go and tell my husband I owe you money?

KROGSTAD.   Suppose I did tell him?

NORA.   It would be a rotten shame. [*Half choking with tears.*] That secret is all my pride and joy—why should he have to hear about it in this nasty, horrid way . . . hear about it from *you*. You would make things horribly unpleasant for me. . . .

KROGSTAD.   Merely unpleasant?

NORA [*vehemently*].   Go on, do it then! It'll be all the worse for you. Because then my husband will see for himself what a bad man you are, and then you certainly won't be able to keep your job.

KROGSTAD.   I asked whether it was only a bit of domestic unpleasantness you were afraid of?

NORA.   If my husband gets to know about it, he'll pay off what's owing at once. And then we'd have nothing more to do with you.

KROGSTAD [*taking a pace towards her*].   Listen, Mrs. Helmer, either you haven't a very good memory, or else you don't understand much about business. I'd better make the position a little bit clearer for you.

NORA.   How do you mean?

KROGSTAD.   When your husband was ill, you came to me for the loan of twelve hundred dollars.

NORA.   I didn't know of anybody else.

KROGSTAD.   I promised to find you the money. . . .

NORA.   And you did find it.

KROGSTAD.   I promised to find you the money on certain conditions. At the time you were so concerned about your husband's illness, and so anxious to get the money for going away with, that I don't think you paid very much attention to all the incidentals. So there is perhaps some point in reminding you of them. Well, I promised to find you the money against an IOU which I drew up for you.

NORA.   Yes, and which I signed.

KROGSTAD.   Very good. But below that I added a few lines, by which your father was to stand security. This your father was to sign.

NORA.   Was to . . . ? He did sign it.

KROGSTAD.   I had left the date blank. The idea was that your father was to add the date himself when he signed it. Remember?

NORA.   Yes, I think. . . .

KROGSTAD.   I then gave you the IOU to post to your father. Wasn't that so?

NORA.   Yes.

KROGSTAD.   Which of course you did at once. Because only about five or six days later you brought it back to me with your father's signature. I then paid out the money.

NORA.   Well? Haven't I paid the instalments regularly?

KROGSTAD.   Yes, fairly. But . . . coming back to what we were talking about . . . that was a pretty bad period you were going through then, Mrs. Helmer.

NORA.   Yes, it was.

KROGSTAD.   Your father was seriously ill, I believe.

NORA.   He was very near the end.

KROGSTAD.   And died shortly afterwards?

NORA.   Yes.

KROGSTAD.   Tell me, Mrs. Helmer, do you happen to remember which day your father died? The exact date, I mean.

NORA.   Daddy died on 29 September.

KROGSTAD.   Quite correct. I made some inquiries. Which brings up a rather curious point [*takes out a paper*] which I simply cannot explain.

NORA.   Curious . . . ? I don't know . . .

KROGSTAD.   The curious thing is, Mrs. Helmer, that your father signed this document three days after his death.

NORA.   What? I don't understand. . . .

KROGSTAD.   Your father died on 29 September. But look here. Your father has dated his signature 2 October. Isn't that rather curious, Mrs. Helmer? [NORA *remains silent.*] It's also remarkable that the words '2 October' and the year are not in your father's handwriting, but in a handwriting I rather think I recognize. Well, perhaps that could be explained. Your father might have forgotten to date his signature, and then somebody else might have made a guess at the date later, before the fact of your father's death was known. There is nothing wrong in that. What really matters is the signature. And *that* is of course genuine, Mrs. Helmer? It really was your father who wrote his name here?

NORA   [*after a moment's silence, throws her head back and looks at him defiantly*]. No, it wasn't. It was me who signed father's name.

KROGSTAD.   Listen to me. I suppose you realize that that is a very dangerous confession?

NORA.   Why? You'll soon have all your money back.

KROGSTAD.   Let me ask you a question: why didn't you send that document to your father?

NORA.   It was impossible. Daddy was ill. If I'd asked him for his signature, I'd have to tell him what the money was for. Don't you see, when he was as ill as that I couldn't go and tell him that my husband's life was in danger. It was simply impossible.

KROGSTAD.   It would have been better for you if you had abandoned the whole trip.

NORA.   No, that was impossible. This was the thing that was to save my husband's life. I couldn't give it up.

KROGSTAD.   But did it never strike you that this was fraudulent . . . ?

NORA.   That wouldn't have meant anything to me. Why should I worry about you? I couldn't stand you, not when you insisted on going through with all those cold-blooded formalities, knowing all the time what a critical state my husband was in.

KROGSTAD.   Mrs. Helmer, it's quite clear you still haven't the faintest idea what it is you've committed. But let me tell you, my own offence was no more and no worse than that, and it ruined my entire reputation.

NORA.   You? Are you trying to tell me that you once risked everything to save your wife's life?

KROGSTAD.   The law takes no account of motives.

NORA.   Then they must be very bad laws.

KROGSTAD.   Bad or not, if I produce this document in court, you'll be condemned according to them.

NORA.   I don't believe it. Isn't a daughter entitled to try and save her father from worry and anxiety on his deathbed? Isn't a wife entitled to save her husband's life? I might not know very much about the law, but I feel sure of one thing: it must say somewhere that things like this are allowed. You mean to say you don't know that—you, when it's your job? You must be a rotten lawyer, Mr. Krogstad.

KROGSTAD.   That may be. But when it comes to business transactions—like the sort between us two—perhaps you'll admit I know something about *them?* Good. Now you must please yourself. But I tell you this: if I'm pitched out a second time, you are going to keep me company.

[*He bows and goes out through the hall.*]

NORA [*stands thoughtfully for a moment, then tosses her head*].   Rubbish! He's just trying to scare me. I'm not such a fool as all that. [*Begins gathering up the children's clothes; after a moment she stops.*] Yet . . . ? No, it's impossible! I did it for love, didn't I?

THE CHILDREN [*in the doorway, left*].   Mummy, the gentleman's just gone out of the gate.

NORA.   Yes, I know. But you mustn't say anything to anybody about that gentleman. You hear? Not even to Daddy!

THE CHILDREN.   All right, Mummy. Are you going to play again?

NORA.   No, not just now.

THE CHILDREN.   But Mummy, you promised!

NORA.   Yes, but I can't just now. Off you go now, I have a lot to do. Off you go, my darlings. [*She herds them carefully into the other room and shuts the door behind them. She sits down on the sofa, picks up her embroidery and works a few stitches, but soon stops.*] No! [*She flings her work down, stands up, goes to the hall door and calls out.*] Helene! Fetch the tree in for me, please. [*She walks across to the table, left, and opens the drawer; again pauses.*] No, really, it's quite impossible!

MAID [*with the Christmas tree*].   Where shall I put it, ma'am?

NORA.   On the floor there, in the middle.

MAID.   Anything else you want me to bring?

NORA.   No, thank you. I've got what I want.

   [*The* MAID *has put the tree down and goes out.*]

NORA [*busy decorating the tree*].   Candles here . . . and flowers here—Revolting man! It's all nonsense! There's nothing to worry about. We'll have a lovely Christmas tree. And I'll do anything you want me to, Torvald; I'll sing for you, dance for you. . . .

   [HELMER, *with a bundle of documents under his arm, comes in by the hall door.*]

NORA.   Ah, back again already?

HELMER.   Yes. Anybody been?

NORA.   Here? No.

HELMER.   That's funny. I just saw Krogstad leave the house.

NORA.   Oh? O yes, that's right. Krogstad was here a minute.

HELMER.   Nora, I can tell by your face he's been asking you to put a good word in for him.

NORA.   Yes.

HELMER.   And you were to pretend it was your own idea? You were to keep quiet about his having been here. He asked you to do that as well, didn't he?

NORA.   Yes, Torvald. But . . .

HELMER.   Nora, Nora, what possessed you to do a thing like that? Talking to a person like him, making him promises? And then on top of everything, to tell me a lie!

NORA.   A lie . . . ?

HELMER.   Didn't you say that nobody had been here? [*Wagging his finger at her.*] Never again must my little song-bird do a thing like that! Little song-birds must keep their pretty little beaks out of mischief; no chirruping out of tune! [*Puts his arm round her waist.*] Isn't that the way we want things to be? Yes, of course it is. [*Lets her go.*] So let's say no more about it. [*Sits down by the stove.*] Ah, nice and cosy here!

   [*He glances through his papers.*]

NORA [*busy with the Christmas tree, after a short pause*].   Torvald!

HELMER.   Yes.

NORA.   I'm so looking forward to the fancy dress ball at the Stenborgs on Boxing Day.

HELMER.   And I'm terribly curious to see what sort of surprise you've got for me.

NORA.   Oh, it's too silly.

HELMER.   Oh?

NORA.   I just can't think of anything suitable. Everything seems so absurd, so pointless.

HELMER.   Has my little Nora come to *that* conclusion?

NORA [*behind his chair, her arms on the chairback*].   Are you very busy, Torvald?

HELMER.   Oh. . . .

NORA.   What are all those papers?

HELMER.   Bank matters.

NORA.   Already?

HELMER.   I have persuaded the retiring manager to give me authority to make any changes in organisation or personnel I think necessary. I have to work on it over the Christmas week. I want everything straight by the New Year.

NORA.   So that was why that poor Krogstad. . . .

HELMER.   Hm!

NORA [*still leaning against the back of the chair, running her fingers through his hair*].   If you hadn't been so busy, Torvald, I'd have asked you to do me an awfully big favour.

HELMER.   Let me hear it. What's it to be?

NORA.   Nobody's got such good taste as you. And the thing is I do so want to look my best at the fancy dress ball. Torvald, couldn't you give me some advice and tell me what you think I ought to go as, and how I should arrange my costume?

HELMER.   Aha! So my impulsive little woman is asking for somebody to come to her rescue, eh?

NORA.   Please, Torvald, I never get anywhere without your help.

HELMER.   Very well, I'll think about it. We'll find something.

NORA.   That's sweet of you. [*She goes across to the tree again; pause.*] How pretty these red flowers look.—Tell me, was it really something terribly wrong this man Krogstad did?

HELMER.   Forgery. Have you any idea what that means?

NORA.   Perhaps circumstances left him no choice?

HELMER.   Maybe. Or perhaps, like so many others, he just didn't think. I am not so heartless that I would necessarily want to condemn a man for a single mistake like that.

NORA.   Oh no, Torvald, of course not!

HELMER.   Many a man might be able to redeem himself, if he honestly confessed his guilt and took his punishment.

NORA.   Punishment?

HELMER.   But that wasn't the way Krogstad chose. He dodged what was due to him by a cunning trick. And that's what has been the cause of his corruption.

NORA.   Do you think it would . . . ?

HELMER.   Just think how a man with a thing like that on his conscience will always be having to lie and cheat and dissemble; he can never drop the mask, not even with his own wife and children. And the children—*that's* the most terrible part of it, Nora.

NORA.   Why?

HELMER.   A fog of lies like that in a household, and it spreads disease and infection to every part of it. Every breath the children take in that kind of house is reeking with evil germs.

NORA [*closer behind him*].   Are you sure of that?

HELMER.   My dear Nora, as a lawyer I know what I'm talking about. Practically all juvenile delinquents come from homes where the mother is dishonest.

NORA.   Why mothers particularly?

HELMER.   It's generally traceable to the mothers, but of course fathers can have the same influence. Every lawyer knows that only too well. And yet there's

Krogstad been poisoning his own children for years with lies and deceit. That's the reason I call him morally depraved. [*Holds out his hands to her.*] That's why my sweet little Nora must promise me not to try putting in any more good words for him. Shake hands on it. Well? What's this? Give me your hand. There now! That's settled. I assure you I would have found it impossible to work with him. I quite literally feel physically sick in the presence of such people.

NORA [*draws her hand away and walks over to the other side of the Christmas tree*]. How hot it is in here! And I still have such a lot to do.

HELMER [*stands up and collects his papers together*].   Yes, I'd better think of getting some of this read before dinner. I must also think about your costume. And I might even be able to lay my hands on something to wrap in gold paper and hang on the Christmas tree. [*He lays his hand on her head.*] My precious little singing bird.

[*He goes into his study and shuts the door behind him.*]

NORA [*quietly, after a pause*].   Nonsense! It can't be. It's impossible. It *must* be impossible.

MAID [*in the doorway, left*].   The children keep asking so nicely if they can come in and see Mummy.

NORA.   No, no, don't let them in! You stay with them, Anne Marie.

MAID.   Very well, ma'am.

[*She shuts the door.*]

NORA [*pale with terror*].   Corrupt my children . . . ! Poison my home? [*Short pause; she throws back her head.*] It's not true! It could never, never be true!

Act II

The same room. In the corner beside the piano stands the Christmas tree, stripped, bedraggled and with its candles burnt out. NORA*'s outdoor things lie on the sofa.* NORA, *alone there, walks about restlessly; at last she stops by the sofa and picks up her coat.*

NORA [*putting her coat down again*].   Somebody's coming! [*Crosses to the door, listens.*] No, it's nobody. Nobody will come today, of course, Christmas Day— nor tomorrow, either. But perhaps. . . . [*She opens the door and looks out.*] No, nothing in the letter box; quite empty. [*Comes forward.*] Oh, nonsense! He didn't mean it seriously. Things like that *can't* happen. It's impossible. Why, I have three small children.

[*The* NURSEMAID *comes from the room, left, carrying a big cardboard box.*]

NURSEMAID.   I finally found it, the box with the fancy dress costumes.

NORA.   Thank you. Put it on the table, please.

NURSEMAID [*does this*].   But I'm afraid they are in an awful mess.

NORA.   Oh, if only I could rip them up into a thousand pieces!

NURSEMAID.   Good heavens, they can be mended all right, with a bit of patience.

NORA.   Yes, I'll go over and get Mrs. Linde to help me.

NURSEMAID.   Out again? In this terrible weather? You'll catch your death of cold, Ma'am.

NORA.   Oh, worse things might happen.—How are the children?

NURSEMAID.   Playing with their Christmas presents, poor little things, but . . .

NORA.   Do they keep asking for me?

NURSEMAID.   They are so used to being with their Mummy.

NORA.   Yes, Anne Marie, from now on I can't be with them as often as I was before.

NURSEMAID.   Ah well, children get used to anything in time.

NORA.   Do you think so? Do you think they would forget their Mummy if she went away for good?

NURSEMAID.   Good gracious—for good?

NORA.   Tell me, Anne Marie—I've often wondered—how on earth could you bear to hand your child over to strangers?

NURSEMAID.   Well, there was nothing else for it when I had to come and nurse my little Nora.

NORA.   Yes but . . . how could you *bring* yourself to do it?

NURSEMAID.   When I had the chance of such a good place? When a poor girl's been in trouble she must make the best of things. Because *he* didn't help, the rotter.

NORA.   But your daughter will have forgotten you.

NURSEMAID.   Oh no, she hasn't. She wrote to me when she got confirmed, and again when she got married.

NORA [*putting her arms round her neck*].   Dear old Anne Marie, you were a good mother to me when I was little.

NURSEMAID.   My poor little Nora never had any other mother but me.

NORA.   And if my little ones only had you, I know you would. . . . Oh, what am I talking about! [*She opens the box.*] Go in to them. I must . . . Tomorrow I'll let you see how pretty I am going to look.

NURSEMAID.   Ah, there'll be nobody at the ball as pretty as my Nora.

[*She goes into the room, left.*]

NORA [*begins unpacking the box, but soon throws it down*].   Oh, if only I dare go out. If only I could be sure nobody would come. And that nothing would happen in the meantime here at home. Rubbish—nobody's going to come. I mustn't think about it. Brush this muff. Pretty gloves, pretty gloves! I'll put it right out of my mind. One, two, three, four, five, six. . . . [*Screams.*] Ah, they are coming. . . . [*She starts towards the door, but stops irresolute.* MRS. LINDE *comes from the hall, where she has taken off her things*.] Oh, it's you, Kristine. There's nobody else out there, is there? I'm so glad you've come.

MRS. LINDE.   I heard you'd been over looking for me.

NORA.   Yes, I was just passing. There's something you must help me with. Come and sit beside me on the sofa here. You see, the Stenborgs are having a fancy dress party upstairs tomorrow evening, and now Torvald wants me to go as a Neapolitan fisher lass and dance the tarantella. I learned it in Capri, you know.

MRS. LINDE.   Well, well! So you are going to do a party piece?

NORA.   Torvald says I should. Look, here's the costume, Torvald had it made for me down there. But it's got all torn and I simply don't know. . . .

MRS. LINDE.   We'll soon have that put right. It's only the trimming come away here and there. Got a needle and thread? Ah, here's what we are after.

NORA.   It's awfully kind of you.

MRS. LINDE.   So you are going to be all dressed up tomorrow, Nora? Tell you what—I'll pop over for a minute to see you in all your finery. But I'm quite forgetting to thank you for the pleasant time we had last night.

NORA [*gets up and walks across the room*].   Somehow I didn't think yesterday was as nice as things generally are.—You should have come to town a little earlier, Kristine.—Yes, Torvald certainly knows how to make things pleasant about the place.

MRS. LINDE.   You too, I should say. You are not your father's daughter for nothing. But tell me, is Dr. Rank always as depressed as he was last night?

NORA.   No, last night it was rather obvious. He's got something seriously wrong with him, you know. Tuberculosis of the spine, poor fellow. His father was a horrible man, who used to have mistresses and things like that. That's why the son was always ailing, right from being a child.

MRS. LINDE [*lowering her sewing*].   But my dear Nora, how do you come to know about things like that?

NORA [*walking about the room*].   Huh! When you've got three children, you get these visits from . . . women who have had a certain amount of medical training. And you hear all sorts of things from them.

MRS. LINDE [*begins sewing again; short silence*].   Does Dr. Rank call in every day?

NORA.   Every single day. He was Torvald's best friend as a boy, and he's a good friend of *mine,* too. Dr. Rank is almost like one of the family.

MRS. LINDE.   But tell me—is he really genuine? What I mean is: doesn't he sometimes rather turn on the charm?

NORA.   No, on the contrary. What makes you think that?

MRS. LINDE.   When you introduced me yesterday, he claimed he'd often heard my name in this house. But afterwards I noticed your husband hadn't the faintest idea who I was. Then how is it that Dr. Rank should. . . .

NORA.   Oh yes, it was quite right what he said, Kristine. You see Torvald is so terribly in love with me that he says he wants me all to himself. When we were first married, it even used to make him sort of jealous if I only as much as mentioned any of my old friends from back home. So of course I stopped doing it. But I often talk to Dr. Rank about such things. He likes hearing about them.

MRS. LINDE.   Listen, Nora! In lots of ways you are still a child. Now, I'm a good deal older than you, and a bit more experienced. I'll tell you something: I think you ought to give up all this business with Dr. Rank.

NORA.   Give up what business?

MRS. LINDE.   The whole thing, I should say. Weren't you saying yesterday something about a rich admirer who was to provide you with money. . . .

NORA.   One who's never existed, I regret to say. But what of it?

MRS. LINDE.   Has Dr. Rank money?

NORA.   Yes, he has.

MRS. LINDE.   And no dependents?

NORA.   No, nobody. But . . . ?

MRS. LINDE.   And he comes to the house every day?

NORA.   Yes, I told you.

MRS. LINDE.   But how can a man of his position want to pester you like this?

NORA.   I simply don't understand.

MRS. LINDE.   Don't pretend, Nora. Do you think I don't see now who you borrowed the twelve hundred from?

NORA.   Are you out of your mind? Do you really think that? A friend of ours who comes here every day? The whole situation would have been absolutely intolerable.

MRS. LINDE.   It *really* isn't him?

NORA.   No, I give you my word. It would never have occurred to me for one moment. . . . Anyway, he didn't have the money to lend then. He didn't inherit it till later.

MRS. LINDE.   Just as well for you, I'd say, my dear Nora.

NORA.   No, it would never have occurred to me to ask Dr. Rank. . . . All the same I'm pretty certain if I were to ask him . . .

MRS. LINDE.   But of course you won't.

NORA.   No, of course not. I can't ever imagine it being necessary. But I'm quite certain if ever I were to mention it to Dr. Rank. . . .

MRS. LINDE.   Behind your husband's back?

NORA.   I have to get myself out of that other business. That's also behind his back. I *must* get myself out of that.

MRS. LINDE.   Yes, that's what I said yesterday. But . . .

NORA [*walking up and down*].   A man's better at coping with these things than a woman. . . .

MRS. LINDE.   Your own husband, yes.

NORA.   Nonsense! [*Stops.*] When you've paid everything you owe, you do get your IOU back again, don't you?

MRS. LINDE.   Of course.

NORA.   And you can tear it up into a thousand pieces and burn it—the nasty, filthy thing!

MRS. LINDE [*looking fixedly at her, puts down her sewing and slowly rises*].   Nora, you are hiding something from me.

NORA.   Is it so obvious?

MRS. LINDE.   Something has happened to you since yesterday morning. Nora, what is it?

NORA [*going towards her*].   Kristine! [*Listens.*] Hush! There's Torvald back. Look, you go and sit in there beside the children for the time being. Torvald can't stand the sight of mending lying about. Get Anne Marie to help you.

MRS. LINDE [*gathering a lot of the things together*].   All right, but I'm not leaving until we have thrashed this thing out.

[*She goes into the room, left; at the same time* HELMER *comes in from the hall.*]

NORA [*goes to meet him*].   I've been longing for you to be back, Torvald, dear.

HELMER.   Was that the dressmaker . . . ?

NORA.   No, it was Kristine; she's helping me with my costume. I think it's going to look very nice . . .

HELMER.   Wasn't that a good idea of mine, now?

NORA.   Wonderful! But wasn't it also nice of me to let you have your way?

HELMER [*taking her under the chin*].   Nice of you—because you let your husband have his way? All right, you little rogue, I know you didn't mean it that way. But I don't want to disturb you. You'll be wanting to try the costume on, I suppose.

NORA.   And I dare say you've got work to do?

HELMER.   Yes. [*Shows her a bundle of papers.*] Look at this. I've been down at the Bank. . . .

[*He turns to go into his study.*]

NORA.   Torvald!

HELMER [*stopping*].   Yes.

NORA.   If a little squirrel were to ask ever so nicely . . . ?

HELMER.   Well?

NORA.   Would you do something for it?

HELMER.   Naturally I would first have to know what it is.

NORA.   Please, if only you would let it have its way, and do what it wants, it'd scamper about and do all sorts of marvellous tricks.

HELMER.   What is it?

NORA.   And the pretty little sky-lark would sing all day long. . . .

HELMER.   Huh! It does that anyway.

NORA.   I'd pretend I was an elfin child and dance a moonlight dance for you, Torvald.

HELMER.   Nora—I hope it's not that business you started on this morning?

NORA [*coming closer*].   Yes, it is, Torvald. I implore you!

HELMER.   You have the nerve to bring that up again?

NORA.   Yes, yes, you *must* listen to me. You must let Krogstad keep his job at the Bank.

HELMER.   My dear Nora, I'm giving his job to Mrs. Linde.

NORA.   Yes, it's awfully sweet of you. But couldn't you get rid of somebody else in the office instead of Krogstad?

HELMER.   This really is the most incredible obstinacy! Just because you go and make some thoughtless promise to put in a good word for him, you expect me . . .

NORA.   It's not that, Torvald. It's for your own sake. That man writes in all the nastiest papers, you told me that yourself. He can do you no end of harm. He terrifies me to death. . . .

HELMER.   Aha, now I see. It's your memories of what happened before that are frightening you.

NORA.   What do you mean?

HELMER.   It's your father you are thinking of.

NORA.   Yes . . . yes, that's right. You remember all the nasty insinuations those wicked people put in the papers about Daddy? I honestly think they would have had him dismissed if the Ministry hadn't sent you down to investigate, and you hadn't been so kind and helpful.

HELMER.   My dear little Nora, there is a considerable difference between your father and me. Your father's professional conduct was not entirely above suspicion. Mine is. And I hope it's going to stay that way as long as I hold this position.

NORA.   But nobody knows what some of these evil people are capable of. Things could be so nice and pleasant for us here, in the peace and quiet of our home—you and me and the children, Torvald! That's why I implore you. . . .

HELMER.   The more you plead for him, the more impossible you make it for me to keep him on. It's already known down at the Bank that I am going to give Krogstad his notice. If it ever got around that the new manager had been talked over by his wife. . . .

NORA.   What of it?

HELMER.   Oh, nothing! As long as the little woman gets her own stubborn way . . . ! Do you want me to make myself a laughing stock in the office? . . . Give people the idea that I am susceptible to any kind of outside pressure? You can imagine how soon I'd feel the consequences of that! Anyway, there's one other consideration that makes it impossible to have Krogstad in the Bank as long as I am manager.

NORA.   What's that?

HELMER.   At a pinch I might have overlooked his past lapses. . . .

NORA.   Of course you could, Torvald!

HELMER.   And I'm told he's not bad at his job, either. But we knew each other rather well when we were younger. It was one of those rather rash friendships that prove embarrassing in later life. There's no reason why you shouldn't know we were once on terms of some familiarity. And he, in his tactless way, makes no attempt to hide the fact, particularly when other people are present. On the contrary, he thinks he has every right to treat me as an equal, with his 'Torvald this' and 'Torvald that' every time he opens his mouth. I find it extremely irritating, I can tell you. He would make my position at the Bank absolutely intolerable.

NORA.   Torvald, surely you aren't serious?

HELMER.   Oh? Why not?

NORA.   Well, it's all so petty.

HELMER.   What's that you say? Petty? Do you think I'm petty?

NORA.   No, not at all, Torvald dear! And that's why . . .

HELMER.   Doesn't make any difference! . . . You call my motives petty; so I must be petty too. Petty! Indeed! Well, we'll put a stop to that, once and for all. [*He opens the hall door and calls.*] Helene!

NORA.   What are you going to do?

HELMER [*searching among his papers*].   Settle things. [*The* MAID *comes in.*] See this letter? I want you to take it down at once. Get hold of a messenger and get him to deliver it. Quickly. The address is on the outside. There's the money.

MAID.   Very good, sir.

[*She goes with the letter.*]

HELMER [*putting his papers together*].   There now, my stubborn little miss.

NORA   [*breathless*].   Torvald . . . what was that letter?

HELMER.   Krogstad's notice.

NORA.   Get it back, Torvald! There's still time! Oh, Torvald, get it back! Please for my sake, for your sake, for the sake of the children! Listen, Torvald, please! You don't realize what it can do to us.

HELMER.   Too late.

NORA.   Yes, too late.

HELMER.   My dear Nora, I forgive you this anxiety of yours, although it is actually a bit of an insult. Oh, but it is, I tell you! It's hardly flattering to suppose that anything this miserable pen-pusher wrote could frighten *me!* But I forgive you all the same, because it is rather a sweet way of showing how much you love me. [*He takes her in his arms.*] This is how things must be, my own darling Nora. When it comes to the point, I've enough strength and enough courage, believe me, for whatever happens. You'll find I'm man enough to take everything on myself.

NORA [*terrified*].   What do you mean?

HELMER.   Everything, I said. . . .

NORA [*in command of herself*].   That is something you shall never, never do.

HELMER.   All right, then we'll share it, Nora—as man and wife. That's what we'll do. [*Caressing her.*] Does that make you happy now? There, there, don't look at me with those eyes, like a little frightened dove. The whole thing is sheer imagination.—Why don't you run through the tarantella and try out the tambourine? I'll go into my study and shut both the doors, then I won't hear anything. You can make all the noise you want. [*Turns in the doorway.*] And when Rank comes, tell him where he can find me.

[*He nods to her, goes with his papers into his room, and shuts the door behind him.*]

NORA [*wild-eyed with terror, stands as though transfixed*].   He's quite capable of doing it! He would do it! No matter what, he'd do it.—No, never in this world! Anything but that! Help? Some way out . . . ? [*The door-bell rings in the hall.*] Dr. Rank . . . ! Anything but that, *anything!* [*She brushes her hands over her face, pulls herself together and opens the door into the hall.* DR. RANK *is standing outside hanging up his fur coat. During what follows it begins to grow dark.*] Hello, Dr. Rank. I recognized your ring. Do you mind not going in to Torvald just yet, I think he's busy.

RANK.   And you?

[DR. RANK *comes into the room and she closes the door behind him.*]

NORA.   Oh, you know very well I've always got time for you.

RANK.   Thank you. A privilege I shall take advantage of as long as I am able.

NORA.   What do you mean—as long as you are able?

RANK.   Does that frighten you?

NORA.   Well, it's just that it sounds so strange. Is anything likely to happen?

RANK.   Only what I have long expected. But I didn't think it would come quite so soon.

NORA [*catching at his arm*].   What have you found out? Dr. Rank, you must tell me!

RANK.   I'm slowly sinking. There's nothing to be done about it.

NORA [*with a sigh of relief*].   Oh, it's *you* you're . . . ?

RANK.   Who else? No point in deceiving oneself. I am the most wretched of all my patients, Mrs. Helmer. These last few days I've made a careful analysis of my internal economy. Bankrupt! Within a month I shall probably be lying rotting up there in the churchyard.

NORA.   Come now, what a ghastly thing to say!

RANK.   The whole damned thing is ghastly. But the worst thing is all the ghastliness that has to be gone through first. I only have one more test to make; and when that's done I'll know pretty well when the final disintegration will start. There's something I want to ask you. Helmer is a sensitive soul; he loathes anything that's ugly. I don't want him visiting me. . . .

NORA.   But Dr. Rank. . . .

RANK.   On no account must he. I won't have it. I'll lock the door on him.—As soon as I'm absolutely certain of the worst, I'll send you my visiting card with a black cross on it. You'll know then the final horrible disintegration has begun.

NORA.   Really, you are being quite absurd today. And here was I hoping you would be in a thoroughly good mood.

RANK.   With death staring me in the face? Why should I suffer for another man's sins? What justice is there in that? Somewhere, somehow, every single family must be suffering some such cruel retribution. . . .

NORA [*stopping up her ears*].   Rubbish! Do cheer up!

RANK.   Yes, really the whole thing's nothing but a huge joke. My poor innocent spine must do penance for my father's gay subaltern life.

NORA [*by the table, left*].   Wasn't he rather partial to asparagus and *pâté de foie gras?*

RANK.   Yes, he was. And truffles.

NORA.   Truffles, yes. And oysters, too, I believe?

RANK.   Yes, oysters, oysters, of course.

NORA.   And all the port and champagne that goes with them. It does seem a pity all these delicious things should attack the spine.

RANK.   Especially when they attack a poor spine that never had any fun out of them.

NORA.   Yes, that is an awful pity.

RANK [*looks at her sharply*].   Hm. . . .

NORA [*after a pause*].   Why did you smile?

RANK.   No, it was you who laughed.

NORA.   No, it was you who smiled, Dr. Rank!

RANK [*getting up*].   You are a bigger rascal than I thought you were.

NORA.   I feel full of mischief today.

RANK. So it seems.

NORA [*putting her hands on his shoulders*]. Dear, dear Dr. Rank, you mustn't go and die on Torvald and me.

RANK. You wouldn't miss me for long. When you are gone, you are soon forgotten.

NORA [*looking at him anxiously*]. Do you think so?

RANK. People make new contacts, then . . .

NORA. Who make new contacts?

RANK. Both you and Helmer will, when I'm gone. You yourself are already well on the way, it seems to me. What was this Mrs. Linde doing here last night?

NORA. Surely you aren't jealous of poor Kristine?

RANK. Yes, I am. She'll be my successor in this house. When I'm done for, I can see this woman. . . .

NORA. Hush! Don't talk so loud, she's in there.

RANK. Today as well? There you are, you see!

NORA. Just to do some sewing on my dress. Good Lord, how absurd you are! [*She sits down on the sofa.*] Now Dr. Rank, cheer up. You'll see tomorrow how nicely I can dance. And you can pretend I'm doing it just for you—and for Torvald as well, of course. [*She takes various things out of the box.*] Come here, Dr. Rank. I want to show you something.

RANK [*sits*]. What is it?

NORA. Look!

RANK. Silk stockings.

NORA. Flesh-coloured! Aren't they lovely! Of course, it's dark here now, but to-morrow. . . . No, no, no, you can only look at the feet. Oh well, you might as well see a bit higher up, too.

RANK. Hm. . . .

NORA. Why are you looking so critical? Don't you think they'll fit?

RANK. I couldn't possibly offer any informed opinion about that.

NORA [*looks at him for a moment*]. Shame on you. [*Hits him lightly across the ear with the stockings.*] Take that! [*Folds them up again.*]

RANK. And what other delights am I to be allowed to see?

NORA. Not another thing. You are too naughty. [*She hums a little and searches among her things.*]

RANK [*after a short pause*]. Sitting here so intimately like this with you, I can't imagine . . . I simply cannot conceive what would have become of me if I had never come to this house.

NORA [*smiles*]. Yes, I rather think you do enjoy coming here.

RANK [*in a low voice, looking fixedly ahead*]. And the thought of having to leave it all . . .

NORA. Nonsense. You aren't leaving.

RANK [*in the same tone*]. . . . without being able to leave behind even the slightest token of gratitude, hardly a fleeting regret even . . . nothing but an empty place to be filled by the first person that comes along.

NORA. Supposing I were to ask you to . . . ? No . . .

RANK. What?

NORA. . . . to show me the extent of your friendship . . .

RANK. Yes?

NORA. I mean . . . to do me a tremendous favour. . . .

RANK. Would you really, for once, give me that pleasure?

NORA. You have no idea what it is.

RANK. All right, tell me.

NORA.   No, really I can't, Dr. Rank. It's altogether too much to ask . . . because I need your advice and help as well. . . .

RANK.   The more the better. I cannot imagine what you have in mind. But tell me anyway. You do trust me, don't you?

NORA.   Yes, I trust you more than anybody I know. You are my best and my most faithful friend. I know that. So I will tell you. Well then, Dr. Rank, there is something you must help me to prevent. You know how deeply, how passionately Torvald is in love with me. He would never hesitate for a moment to sacrifice his life for my sake.

RANK [*bending towards her*].   Nora . . . do you think he's the only one who . . . ?

NORA [*stiffening slightly*].   Who . . . ?

RANK.   Who wouldn't gladly give his life for your sake.

NORA [*sadly*].   Oh!

RANK.   I swore to myself you would know before I went. I'll never have a better opportunity. Well, Nora! Now you know. And now you know too that you can confide in me as in nobody else.

NORA [*rises and speaks evenly and calmly*].   Let me past.

RANK [*makes way for her, but remains seated*].   Nora. . . .

NORA [*in the hall doorway*].   Helene, bring the lamp in, please. [*Walks over to the stove.*] Oh, my dear Dr. Rank, that really was rather horrid of you.

RANK [*getting up*].   That I have loved you every bit as much as anybody? Is *that* horrid?

NORA.   No, but that you had to go and tell me. When it was all so unnecessary. . . .

RANK.   What do you mean? Did you know . . . ?

[*The* MAID *comes in with the lamp, puts it on the table, and goes out again.*]

RANK.   Nora . . . Mrs. Helmer . . . I'm asking you if you knew?

NORA.   How can I tell whether I did or didn't. I simply can't tell you. . . . Oh, how could you be so clumsy, Dr. Rank! When everything was so nice.

RANK.   Anyway, you know now that I'm at your service, body and soul. So you can speak out.

NORA [*looking at him*].   After this?

RANK.   I beg you to tell me what it is.

NORA.   I can tell you nothing now.

RANK.   You must. You can't torment me like this. Give me a chance—I'll do anything that's humanly possible.

NORA.   You can do nothing for me now. Actually, I don't really need any help. It's all just my imagination, really it is. Of course! [*She sits down in the rocking chair, looks at him and smiles.*] I must say, you are a nice one, Dr. Rank! Don't you feel ashamed of yourself, now the lamp's been brought in?

RANK.   No, not exactly. But perhaps I ought to go—for good?

NORA.   No, you mustn't do that. You must keep coming just as you've always done. You know very well Torvald would miss you terribly.

RANK.   And *you?*

NORA.   I always think it's tremendous fun having you.

RANK.   That's exactly what gave me wrong ideas. I just can't puzzle you out. I often used to feel you'd just as soon be with me as with Helmer.

NORA.   Well, you see, there are those people you love and those people you'd almost rather *be* with.

RANK.   Yes, there's something in that.

NORA. When I was a girl at home, I loved Daddy best, of course. But I also thought it great fun if I could slip into the maids' room. For one thing they never preached at me. And they always talked about such exciting things.

RANK. Aha! So it's their role I've taken over!

NORA [*jumps up and crosses to him*]. Oh, my dear, kind Dr. Rank, I didn't mean that at all. But you can see how it's a bit with Torvald as it was with Daddy. . . .

[*The* MAID *comes in from the hall.*]

MAID. Please, ma'am . . . !

[*She whispers and hands her a card.*]

NORA [*glances at the card*]. Ah!

[*She puts it in her pocket.*]

RANK. Anything wrong?

NORA. No, no, not at all. It's just . . . it's my new costume. . . .

RANK. How is that? There's your costume in there.

NORA. That one, yes. But this is another one. I've ordered it. Torvald mustn't hear about it. . . .

RANK. Ah, so that's the big secret, is it!

NORA. Yes, that's right. Just go in and see him, will you? He's in the study. Keep him occupied for the time being. . . .

RANK. Don't worry. He shan't escape me.

[*He goes into* HELMER'*s study.*]

NORA [*to the* MAID]. Is he waiting in the kitchen?

MAID. Yes, he came up the back stairs. . . .

NORA. But didn't you tell him somebody was here?

MAID. Yes, but it was no good.

NORA. Won't he go?

MAID. No, he won't till he's seen you.

NORA. Let him in, then. But quietly. Helene, you mustn't tell anybody about this. It's a surprise for my husband.

MAID. I understand, ma'am. . . .

[*She goes out.*]

NORA. Here it comes! What I've been dreading! No, no, it can't happen, it can't happen.

[*She walks over and bolts* HELMER'*s door. The* MAID *opens the hall door for* KROGSTAD *and shuts it again behind him. He is wearing a fur coat, over-shoes, and a fur cap.*]

NORA [*goes towards him*]. Keep your voice down, my husband is at home.

KROGSTAD. What if he is?

NORA. What do you want with me?

KROGSTAD. To find out something.

NORA. Hurry, then. What is it?

KROGSTAD. You know I've been given notice.

NORA. I couldn't prevent it, Mr. Krogstad, I did my utmost for you, but it was no use.

KROGSTAD. Has your husband so little affection for you? He knows what I can do to you, yet he dares. . . .

NORA. You don't imagine he knows about it!

KROGSTAD. No, I didn't imagine he did. It didn't seem a bit like my good friend Torvald Helmer to show that much courage. . . .

NORA.   Mr. Krogstad, I must ask you to show some respect for my husband.

KROGSTAD.   Oh, sure! All due respect! But since you are so anxious to keep this business quiet, Mrs. Helmer, I take it you now have a rather clearer idea of just what it is you've done, than you had yesterday.

NORA.   Clearer than *you* could ever have given me.

KROGSTAD.   Yes, being as I am such a rotten lawyer. . . .

NORA.   What do you want with me?

KROGSTAD.   I just wanted to see how things stood, Mrs. Helmer. I've been thinking about you all day. Even a mere money-lender, a hack journalist, a—well, even somebody like me has a bit of what you might call feeling.

NORA.   Show it then. Think of my little children.

KROGSTAD.   Did you or your husband think of mine? But what does it matter now? There was just one thing I wanted to say: you needn't take this business too seriously. I shan't start any proceedings, for the present.

NORA.   Ah, I knew you wouldn't.

KROGSTAD.   The whole thing can be arranged quite amicably. Nobody need know. Just the three of us.

NORA.   My husband must never know.

KROGSTAD.   How can you prevent it? Can you pay off the balance?

NORA.   No, not immediately.

KROGSTAD.   Perhaps you've some way of getting hold of the money in the next few days.

NORA.   None I want to make use of.

KROGSTAD.   Well, it wouldn't have been very much help to you if you had. Even if you stood there with the cash in your hand and to spare, you still wouldn't get your IOU back from me now.

NORA.   What are you going to do with it?

KROGSTAD.   Just keep it—have it in my possession. Nobody who isn't implicated need know about it. So if you are thinking of trying any desperate remedies . . .

NORA.   Which I am. . . .

KROGSTAD.   . . . if you happen to be thinking of running away . . .

NORA.   Which I am!

KROGSTAD.   . . . or anything worse . . .

NORA.   How did you know?

KROGSTAD.   . . . forget it!

NORA.   How did you know I was thinking of *that?*

KROGSTAD.   Most of us think of *that,* to begin with. I did, too; but I didn't have the courage. . . .

NORA [*tonelessly*].   I haven't either.

KROGSTAD [*relieved*].   So you haven't the courage either, eh?

NORA   No, I haven't! I haven't!

KROGSTAD.   It would also be very stupid. There'd only be the first domestic storm to get over. . . . I've got a letter to your husband in my pocket here. . . .

NORA.   And it's all in there?

KROGSTAD.   In as tactful a way as possible.

NORA [*quickly*].   He must never read that letter. Tear it up. I'll find the money somehow.

KROGSTAD.   Excuse me, Mrs. Helmer, but I've just told you. . . .

NORA.   I'm not talking about the money I owe you. I want to know how much you are demanding from my husband, and I'll get the money.

KROGSTAD.   I want no money from your husband.

NORA. What do you want?

KROGSTAD. I'll tell you. I want to get on my feet again, Mrs. Helmer; I want to get to the top. And your husband is going to help me. For the last eighteen months I've gone straight; all that time it's been hard going; I was content to work my way up, step by step. Now I'm being kicked out, and I won't stand for being taken back again as an act of charity. I'm going to get to the top, I tell you. I'm going back into that Bank—with a better job. Your husband is going to create a new vacancy, just for me. . . .

NORA. He'll never do that!

KROGSTAD. He will do it. I know him. He'll do it without so much as a whimper. And once I'm in there with him, you'll see what's what. In less than a year I'll be his right-hand man. It'll be Nils Krogstad, not Torvald Helmer, who'll be running that Bank.

NORA. You'll never live to see that day!

KROGSTAD. You mean you . . . ?

NORA. Now I have the courage.

KROGSTAD. You can't frighten me! A precious pampered little thing like you. . . .

NORA. I'll show you! I'll show you!

KROGSTAD. Under the ice, maybe? Down in the cold, black water? Then being washed up in the spring, bloated, hairless, unrecognizable. . . .

NORA. You can't frighten me.

KROGSTAD. You can't frighten me, either. People don't do that sort of thing, Mrs. Helmer. There wouldn't be any point to it, anyway, I'd still have him right in my pocket.

NORA. Afterwards? When I'm no longer . . .

KROGSTAD. Aren't you forgetting that your reputation would then be entirely in my hands? [NORA *stands looking at him, speechless.*] Well, I've warned you. Don't do anything silly. When Helmer gets my letter, I expect to hear from him. And don't forget: it's him who is forcing me off the straight and narrow again, your own husband! That's something I'll never forgive him for. Goodbye, Mrs. Helmer.

[*He goes out through the hall.* NORA *crosses to the door, opens it slightly, and listens.*]

NORA. He's going. He hasn't left the letter. No, no, that would be impossible! [*Opens the door further and further.*] What's he doing? He's stopped outside. He's not going down the stairs. Has he changed his mind? Is he . . . ? [*A letter falls into the letter-box. Then* KROGSTAD'*s footsteps are heard receding as he walks downstairs.* NORA *gives a stifled cry, runs across the room to the sofa table; pause.*] In the letter-box! [*She creeps stealthily across to the hall door.*] There it is! Torvald, Torvald! It's hopeless now!

MRS. LINDE [*comes into the room, left, carrying the costume*]. There, I think that's everything. Shall we try it on?

NORA [*in a low, hoarse voice*]. Kristine, come here.

MRS. LINDE [*throws the dress down on the sofa*]. What's wrong with you? You look upset.

NORA. Come here. Do you see that letter? *There,* look! Through the glass in the letter-box.

MRS. LINDE. Yes, yes, I can see it.

NORA. It's a letter from Krogstad.

MRS. LINDE. Nora! It was Krogstad who lent you the money!

NORA.   Yes. And now Torvald will get to know everything.

MRS. LINDE.   Believe me, Nora, it's best for you both.

NORA.   But there's more to it than that. I forged a signature. . . .

MRS. LINDE.   Heavens above!

NORA.   Listen, I want to tell you something, Kristine, so you can be my witness.

MRS. LINDE.   What do you mean 'witness'? What do you want me to . . . ?

NORA.   If I should go mad . . . which might easily happen . . .

MRS. LINDE.   Nora!

NORA.   Or if anything happened to me . . . which meant I couldn't be here. . . .

MRS. LINDE.   Nora, Nora! Are you out of your mind?

NORA.   And if somebody else wanted to take it all upon himself, the whole blame, you understand. . . .

MRS. LINDE.   Yes, yes. But what makes you think . . . ?

NORA.   Then you must testify that it isn't true, Kristine. I'm not out of my mind; I'm quite sane now. And I tell you this: nobody else knew anything, I alone was responsible for the whole thing. Remember that!

MRS. LINDE.   I will. But I don't understand a word of it.

NORA.   Why should you? You see something miraculous is going to happen.

MRS. LINDE.   Something miraculous?

NORA.   Yes, a miracle. But something so terrible as well, Kristine—oh, it must *never* happen, not for anything.

MRS. LINDE.   I'm going straight over to talk to Krogstad.

NORA.   Don't go. He'll only do you harm.

MRS. LINDE.   There was a time when he would have done anything for me.

NORA.   Him!

MRS. LINDE.   Where does he live?

NORA.   How do I know . . . ? Wait a minute. [*She feels in her pocket.*] Here's his card. But the letter, the letter . . . !

HELMER [*from his study, knocking on the door*].   Nora!

NORA [*cries out in terror*].   What's that? What do you want?

HELMER.   Don't be frightened. We're not coming in. You've locked the door. Are you trying on?

NORA.   Yes, yes, I'm trying on. It looks so nice on me, Torvald.

MRS. LINDE [*who has read the card*].   He lives just round the corner.

NORA.   It's no use. It's hopeless. The letter is there in the box.

MRS. LINDE.   Your husband keeps the key?

NORA.   Always.

MRS. LINDE.   Krogstad must ask for his letter back unread, he must find some sort of excuse. . . .

NORA.   But this is just the time that Torvald generally . . .

MRS. LINDE.   Put him off! Go in and keep him busy. I'll be back as soon as I can.

[*She goes out hastily by the hall door.* NORA *walks over to* HELMER'*s door, opens it and peeps in.*]

NORA.   Torvald!

HELMER [*in the study*].   Well, can a man get into his own living-room again now? Come along, Rank, now we'll see . . . [*In the doorway.*] But what's this?

NORA.   What, Torvald dear?

HELMER.   Rank led me to expect some kind of marvellous transformation.

RANK [*in the doorway*].   That's what I thought too, but I must have been mistaken.

NORA.   I'm not showing myself off to anybody before tomorrow.

HELMER.   Nora dear, you look tired. You haven't been practising too hard?

NORA.   No, I haven't practised at all yet.

HELMER.   You'll have to, though.

NORA.   Yes, I certainly must, Torvald. But I just can't get anywhere without your help: I've completely forgotten it.

HELMER.   We'll soon polish it up.

NORA.   Yes, do help me, Torvald. Promise? I'm so nervous. All those people. . . . You must devote yourself exclusively to me this evening. Pens away! Forget all about the office! Promise me, Torvald dear!

HELMER.   I promise. This evening I am wholly and entirely at your service . . . helpless little thing that you are. Oh, but while I remember, I'll just look first . . .

[*He goes towards the hall door.*]

NORA.   What do you want out there?

HELMER.   Just want to see if there are any letters.

NORA.   No, don't, Torvald!

HELMER.   Why not?

NORA.   Torvald, *please!* There aren't any.

HELMER.   Just let me see.

[*He starts to go.* NORA, *at the piano, plays the opening bars of the tarantella.*]

HELMER [*at the door, stops*].   Aha!

NORA.   I shan't be able to dance tomorrow if I don't rehearse it with you.

HELMER [*walks to her*].   Are you really so nervous, Nora dear?

NORA.   Terribly nervous. Let me run through it now. There's still time before supper. Come and sit here and play for me, Torvald dear. Tell me what to do, keep me right—as you always do.

HELMER.   Certainly, with pleasure, if that's what you want.

[*He sits at the piano.* NORA *snatches the tambourine out of the box, and also a long gaily-coloured shawl which she drapes round herself, then with a bound she leaps forward.*]

NORA. [*shouts*].   Now play for me! Now I'll dance!

[HELMER *plays and* NORA *dances;* DR. RANK *stands at the piano behind* HELMER *and looks on.*]

HELMER [*playing*].   Not so fast! Not so fast!

NORA.   I can't help it.

HELMER.   Not so wild, Nora!

NORA.   This is how it has to be.

HELMER [*stops*].   No, no, that won't do at all.

NORA [*laughs and swings the tambourine*].   Didn't I tell you?

RANK.   Let me play for her.

HELMER [*gets up*].   Yes, do. Then I'll be better able to tell her what to do.

[RANK *sits down at the piano and plays.* NORA *dances more and more wildly.* HELMER *stands by the stove giving her repeated directions as she dances; she does not seem to hear them. Her hair comes undone and falls about her shoulders; she pays no attention and goes on dancing.* MRS. LINDE *enters.*]

MRS. LINDE [*standing as though spellbound in the doorway*].   Ah . . . !

NORA [*dancing*].   See what fun we are having, Kristine.

HELMER.   But my dear darling Nora, you are dancing as though your life depended on it.

NORA.   It does.

HELMER.   Stop, Rank! This is sheer madness. Stop, I say.

[RANK *stops playing and* NORA *comes to a sudden halt.*]

HELMER [*crosses to her*].   I would never have believed it. You have forgotten every-thing I ever taught you.

NORA [*throwing away the tambourine*].   There you are, you see.

HELMER.   Well, some more instruction is certainly needed there.

NORA.   Yes, you see how necessary it is. You must go on coaching me right up to the last minute. Promise me, Torvald?

HELMER.   You can rely on me.

NORA.   You mustn't think about anything else but me until after tomorrow . . . mustn't open any letters . . . mustn't touch the letter-box.

HELMER.   Ah, you are still frightened of what that man might . . .

NORA.   Yes, yes, I am.

HELMER.   I can see from your face there's already a letter there from him.

NORA.   I don't know. I think so. But you mustn't read anything like that now. We don't want anything horrid coming between us until all this is over.

RANK [*softly to* HELMER].   I shouldn't cross her.

HELMER [*puts his arm round her*].   The child must have her way. But tomorrow night, when your dance is done. . . .

NORA.   Then you are free.

MAID [*in the doorway, right*].   Dinner is served, madam.

NORA.   We'll have champagne, Helene.

MAID.   Very good, madam.

[*She goes.*]

HELMER.   Aha! It's to be quite a banquet, eh?

NORA.   With champagne flowing until dawn. [*Shouts.*] And some macaroons, Helene . . . lots of them, for once in a while.

HELMER [*seizing her hands*].   Now, now, not so wild and excitable! Let me see you being my own little singing bird again.

NORA.   Oh yes, I will. And if you'll just go in . . . you, too, Dr. Rank. Kristine, you must help me to do my hair.

RANK [*softly, as they leave*].   There isn't anything . . . anything as it were, impend-ing, is there?

HELMER.   No, not at all, my dear fellow. It's nothing but these childish fears I was telling you about.

[*They go out to the right.*]

NORA.   Well?

MRS. LINDE.   He's left town.

NORA.   I saw it in your face.

MRS. LINDE.   He's coming back tomorrow evening. I left a note for him.

NORA.   You shouldn't have done that. You must let things take their course. Because really it's a case for rejoicing, waiting like this for the miracle.

MRS. LINDE.   What is it you are waiting for?

NORA.   Oh, you wouldn't understand. Go and join the other two. I'll be there in a minute.

[MRS. LINDE *goes into the dining-room.* NORA *stands for a moment as though to collect herself, then looks at her watch.*]

NORA.   Five. Seven hours to midnight. Then twenty-four hours till the next midnight. Then the tarantella will be over. Twenty-four and seven? Thirty-one
hours to live.

HELMER [*in the doorway, right*].   What's happened to our little sky-lark?

NORA [*running towards him with open arms*].   Here she is!

Act III

*The same room. The round table has been moved to the centre of the room, and
the chairs placed round it. A lamp is burning on the table. The door to the hall
stands open. Dance music can be heard coming from the floor above.* MRS. LINDE *is
sitting by the table, idly turning over the pages of a book; she tries to read, but
does not seem able to concentrate. Once or twice she listens, tensely, for a sound
at the front door.*

MRS. LINDE [*looking at her watch*].   Still not here. There isn't much time left. I only
hope he hasn't . . . [*She listens again.*] Ah, there he is. [*She goes out into the
hall, and cautiously opens the front door. Soft footsteps can be heard on the
stairs. She whispers.*] Come in. There's nobody here.

KROGSTAD [*in the doorway*].   I found a note from you at home. What does it all mean?

MRS. LINDE.   I *had* to talk to you.

KROGSTAD.   Oh? And did it have to be here, in this house?

MRS. LINDE.   It wasn't possible over at my place, it hasn't a separate entrance.
Come in. We are quite alone. The maid's asleep and the Helmers are at a
party upstairs.

KROGSTAD [*comes into the room*].   Well, well! So the Helmers are out dancing
tonight! Really?

MRS. LINDE.   Yes, why not?

KROGSTAD.   Why not indeed!

MRS. LINDE.   Well then, Nils. Let's talk.

KROGSTAD.   Have we two anything more to talk about?

MRS. LINDE.   We have a great deal to talk about.

KROGSTAD.   I shouldn't have thought so.

MRS. LINDE.   That's because you never really understood me.

KROGSTAD.   What else was there to understand, apart from the old, old story? A
heartless woman throws a man over the moment something more profitable
offers itself.

MRS. LINDE.   Do you really think I'm so heartless? Do you think I found it easy to
break it off?

KROGSTAD.   Didn't you?

MRS. LINDE.   You didn't really believe that?

KROGSTAD.   If that wasn't the case, why did you write to me as you did?

MRS. LINDE.   There was nothing else I could do. If I had to make the break, I felt in
duty bound to destroy any feeling that you had for me.

KROGSTAD [*clenching his hands*].   So that's how it was. And all that . . . was for
money!

MRS. LINDE.   You mustn't forget I had a helpless mother and two young brothers.
We couldn't wait for you, Nils. At that time you hadn't much immediate
prospect of anything.

KROGSTAD.   That may be. But you had no right to throw me over for somebody else.

MRS. LINDE.   Well, I don't know. Many's the time I've asked myself whether I was
justified.

KROGSTAD [*more quietly*].   When I lost you, it was just as if the ground had slipped away from under my feet. Look at me now: a broken man clinging to the wreck of his life.

MRS. LINDE.   Help might be near.

KROGSTAD.   It was near. Then you came along and got in the way.

MRS. LINDE.   Quite without knowing, Nils. I only heard today it's you I'm supposed to be replacing at the Bank.

KROGSTAD.   If you say so, I believe you. But now you do know, aren't you going to withdraw?

MRS. LINDE.   No, that wouldn't benefit you in the slightest.

KROGSTAD.   Benefit, benefit . . . ! I would do it just the same.

MRS. LINDE.   I have learned to go carefully. Life and hard, bitter necessity have taught me that.

KROGSTAD.   And life has taught me not to believe in pretty speeches.

MRS. LINDE.   Then life has taught you a very sensible thing. But deeds are something you surely must believe in?

KROGSTAD.   How do you mean?

MRS. LINDE.   You said you were like a broken man clinging to the wreck of his life.

KROGSTAD.   And I said it with good reason.

MRS. LINDE.   And I am like a broken woman clinging to the wreck of her life. Nobody to care about, and nobody to care for.

KROGSTAD.   It was your own choice.

MRS. LINDE.   At the time there was no other choice.

KROGSTAD.   Well, what of it?

MRS. LINDE.   Nils, what about us two castaways joining forces?

KROGSTAD.   What's that you say?

MRS. LINDE.   Two of us on one wreck surely stand a better chance than each on his own.

KROGSTAD.   Kristine!

MRS. LINDE.   Why do you suppose I came to town?

KROGSTAD.   You mean, you thought of me?

MRS. LINDE.   Without work I couldn't live. All my life I have worked, for as long as I can remember; that has always been my one great joy. But now I'm completely alone in the world, and feeling horribly empty and forlorn. There's no pleasure in working only for yourself. Nils, give me somebody and something to work for.

KROGSTAD.   I don't believe all this. It's only a woman's hysteria, wanting to be all magnanimous and self-sacrificing.

MRS. LINDE.   Have you ever known me hysterical before?

KROGSTAD.   Would you really do this? Tell me—do you know all about my past?

MRS. LINDE.   Yes.

KROGSTAD.   And you know what people think about me?

MRS. LINDE.   Just now you hinted you thought you might have been a different person with me.

KROGSTAD.   I'm convinced I would.

MRS. LINDE.   Couldn't it still happen?

KROGSTAD.   Kristine! You know what you are saying, don't you? Yes, you do. I can see you do. Have you really the courage . . . ?

MRS. LINDE.   I need someone to mother, and your children need a mother. We two need each other. Nils, I have faith in what, deep down, you are. With you I can face anything.

KROGSTAD [*seizing her hands*].   Thank you, thank you, Kristine. And I'll soon have everybody looking up to me, or I'll know the reason why. Ah, but I was forgetting. . . .

MRS. LINDE.   Hush! The tarantella! You must go!

KROGSTAD.   Why? What is it?

MRS. LINDE.   You hear that dance upstairs? When it's finished they'll be coming.

KROGSTAD.   Yes, I'll go. It's too late to do anything. Of course, you know nothing about what steps I've taken against the Helmers.

MRS. LINDE.   Yes, Nils, I do know.

KROGSTAD.   Yet you still want to go on. . . .

MRS. LINDE.   I know how far a man like you can be driven by despair.

KROGSTAD.   Oh, if only I could undo what I've done!

MRS. LINDE.   You still can. Your letter is still there in the box.

KROGSTAD.   Are you sure?

MRS. LINDE.   Quite sure. But . . .

KROGSTAD [*regards her searchingly*].   Is that how things are? You want to save your friend at any price? Tell me straight. Is that it?

MRS. LINDE.   When you've sold yourself *once* for other people's sake, you don't do it again.

KROGSTAD.   I shall demand my letter back.

MRS. LINDE.   No, no.

KROGSTAD.   Of course I will, I'll wait here till Helmer comes. I'll tell him he has to give me my letter back . . . that it's only about my notice . . . that he mustn't read it. . . .

MRS. LINDE.   No, Nils, don't ask for it back.

KROGSTAD.   But wasn't that the very reason you got me here?

MRS. LINDE.   Yes, that was my first terrified reaction. But that was yesterday, and it's quite incredible the things I've witnessed in this house in the last twenty-four hours. Helmer must know everything. This unhappy secret must come out. Those two must have the whole thing out between them. All this secrecy and deception, it just can't go on.

KROGSTAD.   Well, if you want to risk it. . . . But one thing I can do, and I'll do it at once. . . .

MRS. LINDE [*listening*].   Hurry! Go, go! The dance has stopped. We aren't safe a moment longer.

KROGSTAD.   I'll wait for you downstairs.

MRS. LINDE.   Yes, do. You must see me home.

KROGSTAD.   I've never been so incredibly happy before.

[*He goes out by the front door. The door out into the hall remains standing open.*]

MRS. LINDE [*tidies the room a little and gets her hat and coat ready*].   How things change! How things change! Somebody to work for . . . to live for. A home to bring happiness into. Just let me get down to it. . . . I wish they'd come. . . . [*Listens.*] Ah, there they are. . . . Get my things.

[*She takes her coat and hat. The voices of* HELMER *and* NORA *are heard outside. A key is turned and* HELMER *pushes* NORA *almost forcibly into the hall. She is dressed in the Italian costume, with a big black shawl over it. He is in evening dress, and over it a black cloak, open.*]

NORA [*still in the doorway, reluctantly*].   No, no, not in here! I want to go back up again. I don't want to leave so early.

HELMER.   But my dearest Nora . . .

NORA.   Oh, please, Torvald, I beg you. . . . *Please,* just for another hour.

HELMER.   Not another minute, Nora my sweet. You remember what we agreed. There now, come along in. You'll catch cold standing there.

[*He leads her, in spite of her resistance, gently but firmly into the room.*]

MRS. LINDE.   Good evening.

NORA.   Kristine!

HELMER.   Why, Mrs. Linde. You here so late?

MRS. LINDE.   Yes. You must forgive me but I did so want to see Nora all dressed up.

NORA.   Have you been sitting here waiting for me?

MRS. LINDE.   Yes, I'm afraid I wasn't in time to catch you before you went upstairs. And I felt I couldn't leave again without seeing you.

HELMER [*removing Nora's shawl*].   Well take a good look at her. I think I can say she's worth looking at. Isn't she lovely, Mrs. Linde?

MRS. LINDE.   Yes, I must say. . . .

HELMER.   Isn't she quite extraordinarily lovely? That's what everybody at the party thought, too. But she's dreadfully stubborn . . . the sweet little thing! And what shall we do about that? Would you believe it, I nearly had to use force to get her away.

NORA.   Oh Torvald, you'll be sorry you didn't let me stay, even for half an hour.

HELMER.   You hear that, Mrs. Linde? She dances her tarantella, there's wild applause—which was well deserved, although the performance was perhaps rather realistic . . . I mean, rather more so than was strictly necessary from the artistic point of view. But anyway! The main thing is she was a success, a tremendous success. Was I supposed to let her stay after that? Spoil the effect? No thank you! I took my lovely little Capri girl—my capricious little Capri girl, I might say—by the arm, whisked her once round the room, a curtsey all round, and then—as they say in novels—the beautiful vision vanished. An exit should always be effective, Mrs. Linde. But I just can't get Nora to see that. Phew! It's warm in here. [*He throws his cloak over a chair and opens the door to his study.*] What? It's dark. Oh yes, of course. Excuse me. . . .

[*He goes in and lights a few candles.*]

NORA [*quickly, in a breathless whisper*].   Well?

MRS. LINDE [*softly*].   I've spoken to him.

NORA.   And . . . ?

MRS. LINDE.   Nora . . . you must tell your husband everything.

NORA [*tonelessly*].   I knew it.

MRS. LINDE.   You've got nothing to fear from Krogstad. But you must speak.

NORA.   I won't.

MRS. LINDE.   Then the letter will.

NORA.   Thank you, Kristine. Now I know what's to be done. Hush . . . !

HELMER [*comes in again*].   Well, Mrs. Linde, have you finished admiring her?

MRS. LINDE.   Yes. And now I must say good night.

HELMER.   Oh, already? Is this yours, this knitting?

MRS. LINDE [*takes it*].   Yes, thank you. I nearly forgot it.

HELMER.   So you knit, eh?

MRS. LINDE.   Yes.

HELMER.   You should embroider instead, you know.

MRS. LINDE.   Oh? Why?

HELMER.   So much prettier. Watch! You hold the embroidery like this in the left hand, and then you take the needle in the right hand, like this, and you describe a long, graceful curve. Isn't that right?

MRS. LINDE.   Yes, I suppose so. . . .

HELMER.   Whereas knitting on the other hand just can't help being ugly. Look! Arms pressed into the sides, the knitting needles going up and down—there's something Chinese about it. . . . Ah, that was marvellous champagne they served tonight.

MRS. LINDE.   Well, good night, Nora! And stop being so stubborn.

HELMER.   Well said, Mrs. Linde!

MRS. LINDE.   Good night, Mr. Helmer.

HELMER [*accompanying her to the door*].   Good night, good night! You'll get home all right, I hope? I'd be only too pleased to. . . . But you haven't far to walk. Good night, good night! [*She goes; he shuts the door behind her and comes in again.*] There we are, got rid of her at last. She's a frightful bore, that woman.

NORA.   Aren't you very tired, Torvald?

HELMER.   Not in the least.

NORA.   Not sleepy?

HELMER.   Not at all. On the contrary, I feel extremely lively. What about you? Yes, you look quite tired and sleepy.

NORA.   Yes, I'm very tired. I just want to fall straight off to sleep.

HELMER.   There you are, you see! Wasn't I right in thinking we shouldn't stay any longer.

NORA.   Oh, everything you do is right.

HELMER [*kissing her forehead*].   There's my little sky-lark talking common sense. Did you notice how gay Rank was this evening?

NORA.   Oh, was he? I didn't get a chance to talk to him.

HELMER.   I hardly did either. But it's a long time since I saw him in such a good mood. [*Looks at Nora for a moment or two, then comes nearer her.*] Ah, it's wonderful to be back in our own home again, and quite alone with you. How irresistibly lovely you are, Nora!

NORA.   Don't look at me like that, Torvald!

HELMER.   Can't I look at my most treasured possession? At all this loveliness that's mine and mine alone, completely and utterly mine.

NORA [*walks round to the other side of the table*].   You mustn't talk to me like that tonight.

HELMER [*following her*].   You still have the tarantella in your blood, I see. And that makes you even more desirable. Listen! The guests are beginning to leave now. [*Softly.*] Nora . . . soon the whole house will be silent.

NORA.   I should hope so.

HELMER.   Of course you do, don't you, Nora my darling? You know, whenever I'm out at a party with you . . . do you know why I never talk to you very much, why I always stand away from you and only steal a quick glance at you now and then . . . do you know why I do that? It's because I'm pretending we are secretly in love, secretly engaged and nobody suspects there is anything between us.

NORA.   Yes, yes. I know your thoughts are always with me, of course.

HELMER.   And when it's time to go, and I lay your shawl round those shapely, young shoulders, round the exquisite curve of your neck . . . I pretend that you are my young bride, that we are just leaving our wedding, that I am taking you to our new home for the first time . . . to be alone with you for the first time . . . quite alone with your young and trembling loveliness! All evening

I've been longing for you, and nothing else. And as I watched you darting and swaying in the tarantella, my blood was on fire . . . I couldn't bear it any longer . . . and that's why I brought you down here with me so early. . . .

NORA.   Go away, Torvald! Please leave me alone. I won't have it.

HELMER.   What's this? It's just your little game isn't it, my little Nora. Won't! Won't! Am I not your husband. . . ?

[*There is a knock on the front door.*]

NORA [*startled*].   Listen . . . !

HELMER [*going towards the hall*].   Who's there?

RANK [*outside*].   It's me. Can I come in for a minute?

HELMER [*in a low voice, annoyed*].   Oh, what does he want now? [*Aloud.*] Wait a moment. [*He walks across and opens the door.*] How nice of you to look in on your way out.

RANK.   I fancied I heard your voice and I thought I would just look in. [*He takes a quick glance round.*] Ah yes, this dear, familiar old place! How cosy and comfortable you've got things here, you two.

HELMER.   You seemed to be having a pretty good time upstairs yourself.

RANK.   Capital! Why shouldn't I? Why not make the most of things in this world? At least as much as one can, and for as long as one can. The wine was excellent. . . .

HELMER.   Especially the champagne.

RANK.   You noticed that too, did you? It's incredible the amount I was able to put away.

NORA.   Torvald also drank a lot of champagne this evening.

RANK.   Oh?

NORA.   Yes, and that always makes him quite merry.

RANK.   Well, why shouldn't a man allow himself a jolly evening after a day well spent?

HELMER.   Well spent? I'm afraid I can't exactly claim that.

RANK [*clapping him on the shoulder*].   But I can, you see!

NORA.   Dr. Rank, am I right in thinking you carried out a certain laboratory test today?

RANK.   Exactly.

HELMER.   Look at our little Nora talking about laboratory tests!

NORA.   And may I congratulate you on the result?

RANK.   You may indeed.

NORA.   So it was good?

RANK.   The best possible, for both doctor and patient—certainty!

NORA [*quickly and searchingly*].   Certainty?

RANK.   Absolute certainty. So why shouldn't I allow myself a jolly evening after that?

NORA.   Quite right, Dr. Rank.

HELMER.   I quite agree. As long as you don't suffer for it in the morning.

RANK.   Well, you never get anything for nothing in this life.

NORA.   Dr. Rank . . . you are very fond of masquerades, aren't you?

RANK.   Yes, when there are plenty of amusing disguises. . . .

NORA.   Tell me, what shall we two go as next time?

HELMER.   There's frivolity for you . . . thinking about the next time already!

RANK.   We two? I'll tell you. You must go as Lady Luck. . . .

HELMER.   Yes, but how do you find a costume to suggest *that?*

RANK.   Your wife could simply go in her everyday clothes. . . .

HELMER.   That was nicely said. But don't you know what you would be?

RANK.   Yes, my dear friend, I know exactly what I shall be.

HELMER.   Well?

RANK.   At the next masquerade, I shall be invisible.

HELMER.   That's a funny idea!

RANK.   There's a big black cloak . . . haven't you heard of the cloak of invisibility? That comes right down over you, and then nobody can see you.

HELMER [*suppressing a smile*].   Of course, that's right.

RANK.   But I'm clean forgetting what I came for. Helmer, give me a cigar, one of the dark Havanas.

HELMER.   With the greatest of pleasure.

[*He offers his case.*]

RANK [*takes one and cuts the end off*].   Thanks.

NORA [*strikes a match*].   Let me give you a light.

RANK.   Thank you. [*She holds out the match and he lights his cigar.*] And now, goodbye!

HELMER.   Goodbye, goodbye, my dear fellow!

NORA.   Sleep well, Dr. Rank.

RANK.   Thank you for that wish.

NORA.   Wish me the same.

RANK.   You? All right, if you want me to. . . . Sleep well. And thanks for the light.

[*He nods to them both, and goes.*]

HELMER [*subdued*].   He's had a lot to drink.

NORA [*absently*].   Very likely.

[HELMER *takes a bunch of keys out of his pocket and goes out into the hall.*]

NORA.   Torvald . . . what do you want there?

HELMER.   I must empty the letter-box, it's quite full. There'll be no room for the papers in the morning. . . .

NORA.   Are you going to work tonight?

HELMER.   You know very well I'm not. Hello, what's this? Somebody's been at the lock.

NORA.   At the lock?

HELMER.   Yes, I'm sure of it. Why should that be? I'd hardly have thought the maids . . . ? Here's a broken hair-pin. Nora, it's one of yours. . . .

NORA [*quickly*].   It must have been the children. . . .

HELMER.   Then you'd better tell them not to. Ah . . . there . . . I've managed to get it open. [*He takes the things out and shouts into the kitchen.*] Helene! . . . Helene, put the light out in the hall. [*He comes into the room again with the letters in his hand and shuts the hall door.*] Look how it all mounts up. [*Runs through them.*] What's this?

NORA.   The letter! Oh no, Torvald, no!

HELMER.   Two visiting cards . . . from Dr. Rank.

NORA.   From Dr. Rank?

HELMER [*looking at them*].   Dr. Rank, Medical Practitioner. They were on top. He must have put them in as he left.

NORA.   Is there anything on them?

HELMER.   There's a black cross above his name. Look. What an uncanny idea. It's just as if he were announcing his own death.

NORA.   He is.

HELMER.   What? What do you know about it? Has he said anything to you?

NORA.   Yes. He said when these cards came, he would have taken his last leave of us. He was going to shut himself up and die.

HELMER.   Poor fellow! Of course I knew we couldn't keep him with us very long. But so soon. . . . And hiding himself away like a wounded animal.

NORA.   When it has to happen, it's best that it should happen without words. Don't you think so, Torvald?

HELMER [*walking up and down*].   He had grown so close to us. I don't think I can imagine him gone. His suffering and his loneliness seemed almost to provide a background of dark cloud to the sunshine of our lives. Well, perhaps it's all for the best. For him at any rate. [*Pauses.*] And maybe for us as well, Nora. Now there's just the two of us. [*Puts his arms round her.*] Oh, my darling wife, I can't hold you close enough. You know, Nora . . . many's the time I wish you were threatened by some terrible danger so I could risk everything, body and soul, for your sake.

NORA [*tears herself free and says firmly and decisively*].   Now you must read your letters, Torvald.

HELMER.   No, no, not tonight. I want to be with you, my darling wife.

NORA.   Knowing all the time your friend is dying . . . ?

HELMER.   You are right. It's been a shock to both of us. This ugly thing has come between us . . . thoughts of death and decay. We must try to free ourselves from it. Until then . . . we shall go our separate ways.

NORA [*her arms round his neck*].   Torvald . . . good night! Good night!

HELMER [*kisses her forehead*].   Goodnight, my little singing bird. Sleep well, Nora, I'll just read through my letters.

[*He takes the letters into his room and shuts the door behind him.*]

NORA [*gropes around her, wild-eyed, seizes* HELMER*'s cloak, wraps it round herself, and whispers quickly, hoarsely, spasmodically*].   Never see him again. Never, never, never. [*Throws her shawl over her head.*] And never see the children again either. Never, never. Oh, that black icy water. Oh, that bottomless . . . ! If only it were all over! He's got it now. Now he's reading it. Oh no, no! Not yet! Torvald, goodbye . . . and my children. . . .

[*She rushes out in the direction of the hall; at the same moment Helmer flings open his door and stands there with an open letter in his hand.*]

HELMER.   Nora!

NORA [*shrieks*].   Ah!

HELMER.   What is this? Do you know what is in this letter?

NORA.   Yes, I know. Let me go! Let me out!

HELMER [*holds her back*].   Where are you going?

NORA [*trying to tear herself free*].   You mustn't try to save me, Torvald!

HELMER [*reels back*].   True! Is it true what he writes? How dreadful! No, no, it can't possibly be true.

NORA.   It *is* true. I loved you more than anything else in the world.

HELMER.   Don't come to me with a lot of paltry excuses!

NORA [*taking a step towards him*].   Torvald . . . !

HELMER.   Miserable woman . . . what is this you have done?

NORA.   Let me go. I won't have you taking the blame for me. You mustn't take it on yourself.

HELMER.   Stop play-acting! [*Locks the front door.*] You are staying here to give an account of yourself. Do you understand what you have done? Answer me! Do you understand?

NORA [*looking fixedly at him, her face hardening*].   Yes, now I'm really beginning to understand.

HELMER [*walking up and down*].   Oh, what a terrible awakening this is. All these eight years . . . this woman who was my pride and joy . . . a hypocrite, a liar, worse than that, a criminal! Oh, how utterly squalid it all is! Ugh! Ugh! [*Nora remains silent and looks fixedly at him.*] I should have realized something like this would happen. I should have seen it coming. All your father's irresponsible ways. . . . Quiet! All your father's irresponsible ways are coming out in you. No religion, no morals, no sense of duty. . . . Oh, this is my punishment for turning a blind eye to him. It was for your sake I did it, and this is what I get for it.

NORA.   Yes, this.

HELMER.   Now you have ruined my entire happiness, jeopardized my whole future. It's terrible to think of. Here I am, at the mercy of a thoroughly unscrupulous person; he can do whatever he likes with me, demand anything he wants, order me about just as he chooses . . . and I daren't even whimper. I'm done for, a miserable failure, and it's all the fault of a feather-brained woman!

NORA.   When I've left this world behind, you will be free.

HELMER.   Oh, stop pretending! Your father was just the same, always ready with fine phrases. What good would it do me if you left this world behind, as you put it? Not the slightest bit of good. He can still let it all come out, if he likes; and if he does, people might even suspect me of being an accomplice in these criminal acts of yours. They might even think I was the one behind it all, that it was I who pushed you into it! And it's you I have to thank for this . . . and when I've taken such good care of you, all our married life. Now do you understand what you have done to me?

NORA [*coldly and calmly*].   Yes.

HELMER.   I just can't understand it, it's so incredible. But we must see about putting things right. Take that shawl off. Take it off, I tell you! I must see if I can't find some way or other of appeasing him. The thing must be hushed up at all costs. And as far as you and I are concerned, things must appear to go on exactly as before. But only in the eyes of the world, of course. In other words you'll go on living here; that's understood. But you will not be allowed to bring up the children, I can't trust you with them. . . . Oh, that I should have to say this to the woman I loved so dearly, the woman I still. . . . Well, that must be all over and done with. From now on, there can be no question of happiness. All we can do is save the bits and pieces from the wreck, preserve appearances. . . . [*The front door-bell rings.* HELMER *gives a start.*] What's that? So late? How terrible, supposing. . . . If he should . . . ? Hide, Nora! Say you are not well.

[NORA *stands motionless.* HELMER *walks across and opens the door into the hall.*]

MAID [*half dressed, in the hall*].   It's a note for Mrs. Helmer.

HELMER.   Give it to me. [*He snatches the note and shuts the door.*] Yes, it's from him. You can't have it. I want to read it myself.

NORA.   You read it then.

HELMER [*by the lamp*].   I hardly dare. Perhaps this is the end, for both of us. Well, I must know. [*He opens the note hurriedly, reads a few lines, looks at another enclosed sheet, and gives a cry of joy.*] Nora! [*Nora looks at him inquiringly.*] Nora! I must read it again. Yes, yes, it's true! I am saved! Nora, I am saved!

NORA.   And me?

HELMER.   You too, of course, we are both saved, you as well as me. Look, he's sent your IOU back. He sends his regrets and apologies for what he has done. . . .

His luck has changed. . . . Oh, what does it matter what he says. We are saved, Nora! Nobody can do anything to you now. Oh, Nora, Nora . . . but let's get rid of this disgusting thing first. Let me see. . . . [*He glances at the IOU.*] No, I don't want to see it. I don't want it to be anything but a dream. [*He tears up the IOU and both letters, throws all the pieces into the stove and watches them burn.*] Well, that's the end of that. He said in his note you'd known since Christmas Eve. . . . You must have had three terrible days of it, Nora.

NORA.   These three days haven't been easy.

HELMER.   The agonies you must have gone through! When the only way out seemed to be. . . . No, let's forget the whole ghastly thing. We can rejoice and say: It's all over! It's all over! Listen to me, Nora! You don't seem to understand: it's all over! Why this grim look on your face? Oh, poor little Nora, of course I understand. You can't bring yourself to believe I've forgiven you. But I have, Nora, I swear it. I forgive you everything. I know you did what you did because you loved me.

NORA.   That's true.

HELMER.   You loved me as a wife should love her husband. It was simply that you didn't have the experience to judge what was the best way of going about things. But do you think I love you any the less for that; just because you don't know how to act on your own responsibility? No, no, you just lean on me, I shall give you all the advice and guidance you need. I wouldn't be a proper man if I didn't find a woman doubly attractive for being so obviously helpless. You mustn't dwell on the harsh things I said in that first moment of horror, when I thought everything was going to come crashing down about my ears. I have forgiven you, Nora, I swear it! I have forgiven you!

NORA.   Thank you for your forgiveness.

[*She goes out through the door, right.*]

HELMER.   No, don't go! [*He looks through the doorway.*] What are you doing in the spare room?

NORA.   Taking off this fancy dress.

HELMER [*standing at the open door*].   Yes, do. You try and get some rest, and set your mind at peace again, my frightened little song-bird. Have a good long sleep; you know you are safe and sound under my wing. [*Walks up and down near the door.*] What a nice, cosy little home we have here, Nora! Here you can find refuge. Here I shall hold you like a hunted dove I have rescued unscathed from the cruel talons of the hawk, and calm your poor beating heart. And that will come, gradually, Nora, believe me. Tomorrow you'll see everything quite differently. Soon everything will be just as it was before. You won't need me to keep on telling you I've forgiven you; you'll feel convinced of it in your own heart. You don't really imagine me ever thinking of turning you out, or even of reproaching you? Oh, a real man isn't made that way, you know, Nora. For a man, there's something indescribably moving and very satisfying in knowing that he has forgiven his wife—forgiven her, completely and genuinely, from the depths of his heart. It's as though it made her his property in a double sense: he has, as it were, given her a new life, and she becomes in a way both his wife and at the same time his child. That is how you will seem to me after today, helpless, perplexed little thing that you are. Don't you worry your pretty little head about anything, Nora. Just you be frank with me, and I'll take all the decisions for you. . . . What's this? Not in bed? You've changed your things?

NORA [*in her everyday dress*].   Yes, Torvald, I've changed.

HELMER.   What for? It's late.

NORA.   I shan't sleep tonight.

HELMER.   But my dear Nora. . . .

NORA [*looks at her watch*].   It's not so terribly late. Sit down, Torvald. We two have a lot to talk about.

[*She sits down at one side of the table*]

HELMER.   Nora, what is all this? Why so grim?

NORA.   Sit down. It'll take some time. I have a lot to say to you.

HELMER [*sits down at the table opposite her*].   You frighten me, Nora. I don't understand you.

NORA.   Exactly. You don't understand me. And I have never understood you, either—until tonight. No, don't interrupt. I just want you to listen to what I have to say. We are going to have things out, Torvald.

HELMER.   What do you mean?

NORA.   Isn't there anything that strikes you about the way we two are sitting here?

HELMER.   What's that?

NORA.   We have now been married eight years. Hasn't it struck you this is the first time you and I, man and wife, have had a serious talk together?

HELMER.   Depends what you mean by 'serious.'

NORA.   Eight whole years—no, more, ever since we first knew each other—and never have we exchanged one serious word about serious things.

HELMER.   What did you want me to do? Get you involved in worries that you couldn't possibly help me to bear?

NORA.   I'm not talking about worries. I say we've never once sat down together and seriously tried to get to the bottom of anything.

HELMER.   But, my dear Nora, would that have been a thing for you?

NORA.   That's just it. You have never understood me . . . I've been greatly wronged, Torvald. First by my father, and then by you.

HELMER.   What! Us two! The two people who loved you more than anybody?

NORA [*shakes her head*].   You two never loved me. You only thought how nice it was to be in love with me.

HELMER.   But, Nora, what's this you are saying?

NORA.   It's right, you know, Torvald. At home, Daddy used to tell me what he thought, then I thought the same. And if I thought differently, I kept quiet about it, because he wouldn't have liked it. He used to call me his baby doll, and he played with me as I used to play with my dolls. Then I came to live in your house. . . .

HELMER.   What way is that to talk about our marriage?

NORA [*imperturbably*].   What I mean is: I passed out of Daddy's hands into yours. You arranged everything to your tastes, and I acquired the same tastes. Or I pretended to . . . I don't really know . . . I think it was a bit of both, sometimes one thing and sometimes the other. When I look back, it seems to me I have been living here like a beggar, from hand to mouth. I lived by doing tricks for you, Torvald. But that's the way you wanted it. You and Daddy did me a great wrong. It's your fault that I've never made anything of my life.

HELMER.   Nora, how unreasonable . . . how ungrateful you are! Haven't you been happy here?

NORA.   No, never. I thought I was, but I wasn't really.

HELMER.   Not . . . not happy!

NORA.   No, just gay. And you've always been so kind to me. But our house has never been anything but a play-room. I have been your doll wife, just as at home I was Daddy's doll child. And the children in turn have been my dolls. I thought it was fun when you came and played with me, just as they thought it was fun when I went and played with them. That's been our marriage, Torvald.

HELMER.   There is some truth in what you say, exaggerated and hysterical though it is. But from now on it will be different. Play-time is over; now comes the time for lessons.

NORA.   Whose lessons? Mine or the children's?

HELMER.   Both yours and the children's, my dear Nora.

NORA.   Ah, Torvald, you are not the man to teach me to be a good wife for you.

HELMER.   How can you say that?

NORA.   And what sort of qualifications have I to teach the children?

HELMER.   Nora!

NORA.   Didn't you say yourself, a minute or two ago, that you couldn't trust me with that job?

HELMER.   In the heat of the moment! You shouldn't pay any attention to that.

NORA.   On the contrary, you were quite right. I'm not up to it. There's another problem needs solving first. I must take steps to educate myself. You are not the man to help me there. That's something I must do on my own. That's why I'm leaving you.

HELMER [*jumps up*].   What did you say?

NORA.   If I'm ever to reach any understanding of myself and the things around me, I must learn to stand alone. That's why I can't stay here with you any longer.

HELMER.   Nora! Nora!

NORA.   I'm leaving here at once. I dare say Kristine will put me up for tonight. . . .

HELMER.   You are out of your mind! I won't let you! I forbid you!

NORA.   It's no use forbidding me anything now. I'm taking with me my own personal belongings. I don't want anything of yours, either now or later.

HELMER.   This is madness!

NORA.   Tomorrow I'm going home—to what used to be my home, I mean. It will be easier for me to find something to do there.

HELMER.   Oh, you blind, inexperienced . . .

NORA.   I must set about *getting* experience, Torvald.

HELMER.   And leave your home, your husband and your children? Don't you care what people will say?

NORA.   That's no concern of mine. All I know is that this is necessary for me.

HELMER.   This is outrageous! You are betraying your most sacred duty.

NORA.   And what do you consider to be my most sacred duty?

HELMER.   Does it take me to tell you that? Isn't it your duty to your husband and your children?

NORA.   I have another duty equally sacred.

HELMER.   You have not. What duty might *that* be?

NORA.   My duty to myself.

HELMER.   First and foremost, you are a wife and mother.

NORA.   That I don't believe any more. I believe that first and foremost I am an individual, just as much as you are—or at least I'm going to try to be. I know most people agree with you, Torvald, and that's also what it says in books. But I'm not content any more with what most people say, or with what it says in books. I have to think things out for myself, and get things clear.

HELMER.   Surely you are clear about your position in your own home? Haven't you an infallible guide in questions like these? Haven't you your religion?

NORA.   Oh, Torvald, I don't really know what religion is.

HELMER.   What do you say!

NORA.   All I know is what Pastor Hansen said when I was confirmed. He said religion was this, that and the other. When I'm away from all this and on my own, I'll go into that, too. I want to find out whether what Pastor Hansen told me was right—or at least whether it's right for *me*.

HELMER.   This is incredible talk from a young woman! But if religion cannot keep you on the right path, let me at least stir your conscience. I suppose you do have some moral sense? Or tell me—perhaps you don't?

NORA.   Well, Torvald, that's not easy to say. I simply don't know. I'm really very confused about such things. All I know is my ideas about such things are very different from yours. I've also learnt that the law is different from what I thought; but I simply can't get it into my head that that particular law is right. Apparently a woman has no right to spare her old father on his deathbed, or to save her husband's life, even. I just don't believe it.

HELMER.   You are talking like a child. You understand nothing about the society you live in.

NORA.   No, I don't. But I shall go into that too. I must try to discover who is right, society or me.

HELMER.   You are ill, Nora. You are delirious. I'm half inclined to think you are out of your mind.

NORA.   Never have I felt so calm and collected as I do tonight.

HELMER.   Calm and collected enough to leave your husband and children?

NORA.   Yes.

HELMER.   Then only one explanation is possible.

NORA.   And that is?

HELMER.   You don't love me any more.

NORA.   Exactly.

HELMER.   Nora! Can you say that?

NORA.   I'm desperately sorry, Torvald. Because you have always been so kind to me. But I can't help it. I don't love you any more.

HELMER [*struggling to keep his composure*].   Is that also a 'calm and collected' decision you've made?

NORA.   Yes, absolutely calm and collected. That's why I don't want to stay here.

HELMER.   And can you also account for how I forfeited your love?

NORA.   Yes, very easily. It was tonight, when the miracle didn't happen. It was then I realized you weren't the man I thought you were.

HELMER.   Explain yourself more clearly. I don't understand.

NORA.   For eight years I have been patiently waiting. Because, heavens, I knew miracles didn't happen every day. Then this devastating business started, and I became absolutely convinced the miracle *would* happen. All the time Krogstad's letter lay there, it never so much as crossed my mind that you would ever submit to that man's conditions. I was absolutely convinced you would say to him: Tell the whole wide world if you like. And when that was done . . .

HELMER.   Yes, then what? After I had exposed my own wife to dishonour and shame . . . !

NORA.   When that was done, I was absolutely convinced you would come forward and take everything on yourself, and say: I am the guilty one.

HELMER.   Nora!

NORA.   You mean I'd never let you make such a sacrifice for my sake? Of course not. But what would my story have counted for against yours?—That was the miracle I went in hope and dread of. It was to prevent it that I was ready to end my life.

HELMER.   I would gladly toil day and night for you, Nora, enduring all manner of sorrow and distress. But nobody sacrifices his *honour* for the one he loves.

NORA.   Hundreds and thousands of women have.

HELMER.   Oh, you think and talk like a stupid child.

NORA.   All right. But you neither think nor talk like the man I would want to share my life with. When you had got over your fright—and you weren't concerned about me but only about what might happen to you—and when all danger was past, you acted as though nothing had happened. I was your little sky-lark again, your little doll, exactly as before; except you would have to pro-tect it twice as carefully as before, now that it had shown itself to be so weak and fragile. [*Rises.*] Torvald, that was the moment I realised that for eight years I'd been living with a stranger, and had borne him three children. . . . Oh, I can't bear to think about it! I could tear myself to shreds.

HELMER [*sadly*].   I see. I see. There is a tremendous gulf dividing us. But, Nora, is there no way we might bridge it?

NORA.   As I am now, I am no wife for you.

HELMER.   I still have it in me to change.

NORA.   Perhaps . . . if you have your doll taken away.

HELMER.   And be separated from you! No, no, Nora, the very thought of it is in-conceivable.

NORA [*goes into the room, right*].   All the more reason why it must be done.

[*She comes back with her outdoor things and a small travelling bag which she puts on the chair beside the table.*]

HELMER.   Nora, Nora, not now! Wait till the morning.

NORA [*putting on her coat*].   I can't spend the night in a strange man's room.

HELMER.   Couldn't we go on living here like brother and sister . . . ?

NORA [*tying on her hat*].   You know very well that wouldn't last. [*She draws the shawl round her.*] Goodbye, Torvald. I don't want to see the children. I know they are in better hands than mine. As I am now, I can never be any-thing to them.

HELMER.   But some day, Nora, some day . . . ?

NORA.   How should I know? I've no idea what I might turn out to be.

HELMER.   But you are my wife, whatever you are.

NORA.   Listen, Torvald, from what I've heard, when a wife leaves her husband's house as I am doing now, he is absolved by law of all responsibility for her. I can at any rate free you from all responsibility. You must not feel in any way bound, any more than I shall. There must be full freedom on both sides. Look, here's your ring back. Give me mine.

HELMER.   That too?

NORA.   That too.

HELMER.   There it is.

NORA.   Well, that's the end of that. I'll put the keys down here. The maids know where everything is in the house—better than I do, in fact. Kristine will come in the morning after I've left to pack up the few things I brought with me from home. I want them sent on.

HELMER.   The end! Nora, will you never think of me?

NORA.   I dare say I'll often think about you and the children and this house.

HELMER.   May I write to you, Nora?

NORA.   No, never. I won't let you.

HELMER.   But surely I can send you . . .

NORA.   Nothing, nothing.

HELMER.   Can't I help you if ever you need it?

NORA.   I said 'no.' I don't accept things from strangers.

HELMER.   Nora, can I never be anything more to you than a stranger?

NORA [*takes her bag*].   Ah, Torvald, only by a miracle of miracles . . .

HELMER.   Name it, this miracle of miracles!

NORA.   Both you and I would have to change to the point where. . . . Oh, Torvald, I don't believe in miracles any more.

HELMER.   But I *will* believe. Name it! Change to the point where . . . ?

NORA.   Where we could make a real marriage of our lives together. Goodbye!

[*She goes out through the hall door.*]

HELMER [*sinks down on a chair near the door, and covers his face with his hands*]. Nora! Nora! [*He rises and looks round.*] Empty! She's gone! [*With sudden hope.*] The miracle of miracles . . . ?

[*The heavy sound of a door being slammed is heard from below.*]

[1879]

Topics for Critical Thinking and Writing

1. Near the beginning of the play, how does Mrs. Linde's presence help to define Nora's character? How does Nora's response to Krogstad's entrance tell us something about Nora?

2. What does Dr. Rank contribute to the play? If he were eliminated, what would be lost?

3. Can it be argued that although at the end Nora goes out to achieve self-realization, her abandonment of her children—especially to Torvald's loathsome conventional morality—is a crime? (By the way, exactly why does Nora leave the children? She seems to imply, in some passages, that because she forged a signature she is unfit to bring them up. But do you agree with her?)

4. Michael Meyer, in his splendid biography *Henrik Ibsen,* says that the play is not so much about women's rights as about "the need of every individual to find out the kind of person he or she really is, and to strive to become that person." What evidence can you offer to support or refute this interpretation?

5. In *The Quintessence of Ibsenism* Bernard Shaw says that Ibsen, reacting against a common theatrical preference for strange situations,

> saw that . . . the more familiar the situation, the more interesting the play. Shakespear had put ourselves on the stage but not our situations. Our uncles seldom murder our fathers and . . . marry our mothers. . . . Ibsen . . . gives us not only ourselves, but ourselves in our own situations. The things that happen to his stage figures are things that happen to us. One consequence is that his plays are much more important to us than Shakespear's. Another is that they are capable both of hurting us cruelly and of filling us with excited hopes of escape from idealistic tyrannies, and with visions of intenser life in the future.

How much of this do you believe?

22

Innocence and Experience

SHORT VIEWS

Children, I grant, should be innocent; but when the epithet is applied to men, or women, it is but a civil term for weakness.
    Mary Wollstonecraft

People who shut their eyes to reality simply invite their own destruction, and anyone who insists on remaining in a state of innocence long after that innocence is dead turns himself into a monster.
    James Baldwin

"Experience iz a good schoolmaster," but reason iz a better one.
    Josh Billings

Experience keeps a dear school, but Fools will learn in no other.
    Ben Franklin

A moment's insight is sometimes worth a life's experience.
    Oliver Wendell Holmes

What is the good of drawing conclusions from experience? I don't deny we sometimes draw the right conclusions, but don't we just as often draw the wrong ones?
    G. C. Lichtenberg

The power to guess the unseen from the seen, to trace the implications of things, to judge the whole piece by the pattern, the condition of feeling life in general so completely that you are well on your way to knowing any particular corner of it—this cluster of gifts may almost be said to constitute experience.
    Henry James

We should be careful to get out of an experience only the wisdom that is in it—and stop there; lest we be like the cat that sits down on a hot stove-lid. She will never sit down on a hot stove-lid again—and that is well; but also she will never sit down on a cold one anymore.
    Mark Twain

Topics for Critical Thinking and Writing

1. Sometimes we say a person is "so innocent." Is this a compliment, or a criticism?
2. Was there a moment in your own life when you moved in a significant way from "innocence" to "experience"? How did you feel when this event occurred? How do you feel about it now?
3. Do you think it is possible to know something well even without having direct experience of it? Can someone know what being a parent means, for example, if he or she does not have a child? Can someone comment expertly on baseball without having played on a major-league team?
4. Name and describe some things that you have experienced once, but never want to experience again.
5. Name and describe some things that you have not experienced, but that you hope to experience some day. If you do not experience them, will your life be affected a lot or a little?
6. Name and describe some things that you feel you must experience at some point in your life. Why are these so important to you?
7. If you could have been present at any historical event, however long ago, what would it be? Why would you want to be there? What would this experience give you that you do not now possess?

ESSAY

MAYA ANGELOU

Maya Angelou, born Marguerita Johnson in 1928 in St. Louis, spent her early years in California and Arkansas. She has worked as a cook, a streetcar conductor, a television screenwriter, and an actress, and she has written poems and five autobiographical books. The following selection comes from her first autobiography, I Know Why the Caged Bird Sings *(1970).*

Graduation

The children in Stamps trembled visibly with anticipation. Some adults were excited too, but to be certain the whole young population had come down with graduation epidemic. Large classes were graduating from both the grammar school and the high school. Even those who were years removed from their own day of glorious release were anxious to help with preparations as a kind of dry run. The junior students who were moving into the vacating classes' chairs were tradition-bound to show their talents for leadership and management. They strutted through the school and around the campus exerting pressure on the lower grades. Their authority was so new that occasionally if they pressed a little too hard it had to be overlooked. After all, next term was coming, and it never hurt a sixth grader to have a play sister in the eighth grade, or a tenth-year student to be able to call a twelfth grader Bubba. So all was endured in a spirit of shared understanding. But the graduating classes themselves were the nobility. Like travelers with exotic destinations on their minds, the graduates were remarkably forgetful. They came to school without their books, or tablets or even pencils. Volunteers fell over themselves to secure replacements for the missing equipment. When accepted, the willing workers might or might not be thanked, and it was of no importance to the pregraduation rites. Even teachers were respectful of the now quiet and aging seniors, and tended to speak to them, if not as equals, as beings only slightly lower than themselves. After tests were returned and grades given, the student body, which acted like an extended family, knew who did well, who excelled, and what piteous ones had failed.

Unlike the white high school, Lafayette County Training School distinguished itself by having neither lawn, nor hedges, nor tennis court, nor climbing ivy. Its two buildings (main classrooms, the grade school and home economics) were set on a dirt hill with no fence to limit either its boundaries or those of bordering farms. There was a large expanse to the left of the school which was used alternately as a baseball diamond or a basketball court. Rusty hoops on the swaying poles represented the permanent recreational equipment, although bats and balls could be borrowed from the P.E. teacher if the borrower was qualified and if the diamond wasn't occupied.

Over this rocky area relieved by a few shady tall persimmon trees the graduating class walked. The girls often held hands and no longer bothered to speak to the lower students. There was a sadness about them, as if this old world was not their home and they were bound for higher ground. The boys, on the other hand, had become more friendly, more outgoing. A decided change from the closed attitude they projected while studying for finals. Now they seemed not ready to give up the old school, the familiar paths and classrooms. Only a small percentage would be continuing on to college—one of the South's A & M (agricultural and mechanical) schools, which trained Negro youths to be carpenters, farmers, handymen, masons, maids, cooks and baby nurses. Their future rode heavily on their shoulders, and blinded them to the collective joy that had pervaded the lives of the boys and girls in the grammar school graduating class.

Parents who could afford it had ordered new shoes and ready-made clothes for themselves from Sears and Roebuck or Montgomery Ward. They also engaged the best seamstresses to make the floating graduating dresses and to cut down second-hand pants which would be pressed to a military slickness for the important event.

5   Oh, it was important, all right. Whitefolks would attend the ceremony, and two or three would speak of God and home, and the Southern way of life, and Mrs. Parsons, the principal's wife, would play the graduation march while the lower-grade graduates paraded down the aisles and took their seats below the platform. The high school seniors would wait in empty classrooms to make their dramatic entrance.

In the Store I was the person of the moment. The birthday girl. The center. Bailey had graduated the year before, although to do so he had had to forfeit all pleasures to make up for his time lost in Baton Rouge.

My class was wearing butter-yellow piqué dresses, and Momma launched out on mine. She smocked the yoke into tiny crisscrossing puckers, then shirred the rest of the bodice. Her dark fingers ducked in and out of the lemony cloth as she embroidered raised daisies around the hem. Before she considered herself finished she had added a crocheted cuff on the puff sleeves, and a pointy crocheted collar.

I was going to be lovely. A walking model of all the various styles of fine hand sewing and it didn't worry me that I was only twelve years old and merely graduating from the eighth grade. Besides, many teachers in Arkansas Negro schools had only that diploma and were licensed to impart wisdom.

The days had become longer and more noticeable. The faded beige of former times had been replaced with strong and sure colors. I began to see my classmates' clothes, their skin tones, and the dust that waved off pussy willows. Clouds that lazed across the sky were objects of great concern to me. Their shiftier shapes might have held a message that in my new happiness and with a little bit of time I'd soon decipher. During that period I looked at the arch of heaven so religiously my neck kept a steady ache. I had taken to smiling more often, and my jaws hurt from the unaccustomed activity. Between the two physical sore spots, I suppose I could have been uncomfortable, but that was not the case. As a member of the winning team (the graduating class of 1940) I had outdistanced unpleasant sensations by miles. I was headed for the freedom of open fields.

10   Youth and social approval allied themselves with me and we trammeled memories of slights and insults. The wind of our swift passage remodeled my features. Lost tears were pounded to mud and then to dust. Years of withdrawal were brushed aside and left behind, as hanging ropes of parasitic moss.

My work alone had awarded me a top place and I was going to be one of the first called in the graduating ceremonies. On the classroom blackboard, as well as on the bulletin board in the auditorium, there were blue stars and white stars and red stars. No absences, no tardinesses, and my academic work was among the best of the year. I could say the preamble to the Constitution even faster than Bailey. We timed ourselves often: "We the people of the United States in order to form a more perfect union . . ." I had memorized the Presidents of the United States from Washington to Roosevelt in chronological as well as alphabetical order.

My hair pleased me too. Gradually the black mass had lengthened and thickened, so that it kept at last to its braided pattern, and I didn't have to yank my scalp off when I tried to comb it.

Louise and I had rehearsed the exercises until we tired out ourselves. Henry Reed was class valedictorian. He was a small, very black boy with hooded eyes, a long, broad nose and an oddly shaped head. I had admired him for years because each term he and I vied for the best grades in our class. Most often he bested me, but instead of being disappointed I was pleased that we shared top places between us. Like many Southern Black children, he lived with his grandmother, who was as strict as Momma and as kind as she knew how to be. He was courteous, respectful and soft-spoken to elders, but on the playground he chose to play the roughest games. I admired him. Anyone, I reckoned, sufficiently afraid or sufficiently dull could be polite. But to be able to operate at a top level with both adults and children was admirable.

His valedictory speech was entitled "To Be or Not To Be." The rigid tenth-grade teacher had helped him to write it. He'd been working on the dramatic stresses for months.

15   The weeks until graduation were filled with heady activities. A group of small children were to be presented in a play about buttercups and daisies and bunny rabbits. They could be heard throughout the building practicing their hops and

their little songs that sounded like silver bells. The older girls (non-graduates, of course) were assigned the task of making refreshments for the night's festivities. A tangy scent of ginger, cinnamon, nutmeg and chocolate wafted around the home economics building as the budding cooks made samples for themselves and their teachers.

In every corner of the workshop, axes and saws split fresh timber as the woodshop boys made sets and stage scenery. Only the graduates were left out of the general bustle. We were free to sit in the library at the back of the building or look in quite detachedly, naturally, on the measures being taken for our event.

Even the minister preached on graduation the Sunday before. His subject was, "Let your light so shine that men will see your good works and praise your Father, Who is in Heaven." Although the sermon was purported to be addressed to us, he used the occasion to speak to backsliders, gamblers, and general ne'er-do-wells. But since he had called our names at the beginning of the service we were mollified.

Among Negroes the tradition was to give presents to children going only from one grade to another. How much more important this was when the person was graduating at the top of the class. Uncle Willie and Momma had sent away for a Mickey Mouse watch like Bailey's. Louise gave me four embroidered handkerchiefs. (I gave her three crocheted doilies.) Mrs. Sneed, the minister's wife, made me an underskirt to wear for graduation, and nearly every customer gave me a nickel or maybe even a dime with the instruction "Keep on moving to high ground," or some such encouragement.

Amazingly the great day finally dawned and I was out of bed before I knew it. I threw open the back door to see it more clearly, but Momma said, "Sister, come away from that door and put your robe on."

20   I hoped the memory of that morning would never leave me. Sunlight was it-self still young, and the day had none of the insistence maturity would bring it in a few hours. In my robe and barefoot in the backyard, under cover of going to see about my new beans; I gave myself up to the gentle warmth and thanked God that no matter what evil I had done in my life He had allowed me to live to see this day. Somewhere in my fatalism I had expected to die, accidentally, and never have the chance to walk up the stairs in the auditorium and gracefully receive my hard-earned diploma. Out of God's merciful bosom I had won reprieve.

Bailey came out in his robe and gave me a box wrapped in Christmas paper. He said he had saved his money for months to pay for it. It felt like a box of chocolates, but I knew Bailey wouldn't save money to buy candy when we had all we could want under our noses.

He was as proud of the gift as I. It was a soft-leather-bound copy of a collection of poems by Edgar Allan Poe, or, as Bailey and I called him, "Eap." I turned to "Annabel Lee" and we walked up and down the garden rows, the cool dirt between our toes, reciting the beautifully sad lines.

Momma made a Sunday breakfast although it was only Friday. After we finished the blessing, I opened my eyes to find the watch on my plate. It was a dream of a day. Everything went smoothly and to my credit, I didn't have to be reminded or scolded for anything. Near evening I was too jittery to attend to chores, so Bailey volunteered to do all before his bath.

Days before, we had made a sign for the Store and as we turned out the lights Momma hung the cardboard over the doorknob. It read clearly: CLOSED. GRADUATION.

25   My dress fitted perfectly and everyone said that I looked like a sunbeam in it. On the hill, going toward the school, Bailey walked behind with Uncle Willie, who muttered, "Go on, Ju." He wanted him to walk ahead with us because it embarrassed him to have to walk so slowly. Bailey said he'd let the ladies walk together, and the men would bring up the rear. We all laughed, nicely.

Little children dashed by out of the dark like fireflies. Their crepe-paper dresses and butterfly wings were not made for running and we heard more than one rip, dryly, and the regretful "uh uh" that followed.

The school blazed without gaiety. The windows seemed cold and unfriendly from the lower hill. A sense of ill-fated timing crept over me, and if Momma hadn't reached for my hand I would have drifted back to Bailey and Uncle Willie, and possibly beyond. She made a few slow jokes about my feet getting cold, and tugged me along to the now-strange building.

Around the front steps, assurance came back. There were my fellow "greats," the graduating class. Hair brushed back, legs oiled, new dresses and pressed pleats, fresh pocket handkerchiefs and little handbags, all homesewn. Oh, we were up to snuff, all right. I joined my comrades and didn't even see my family go in to find seats in the crowded auditorium.

The school band struck up a march and all classes filed in as had been rehearsed. We stood in front of our seats, as assigned, and on a signal from the choir director, we sat. No sooner had this been accomplished than the band started to play the national anthem. We rose again and sang the song, after which we recited the pledge of allegiance. We remained standing for a brief minute before the choir director and the principal signaled to us, rather desperately I thought, to take our seats. The command was so unusual that our carefully rehearsed and smooth-running machine was thrown off. For a full minute we fumbled for our chairs and bumped into each other awkwardly. Habits change or solidify under pressure, so in our state of nervous tension we had been ready to follow our usual assembly pattern: the American National Anthem, then the pledge of allegiance, then the song every Black person I knew called the Negro National Anthem. All done in the same key, with the same passion and most often standing on the same foot.

30   Finding my seat at last, I was overcome with a presentiment of worse things to come. Something unrehearsed, unplanned, was going to happen, and we were going to be made to look bad. I distinctly remember being explicit in the choice of pronoun. It was "we," the graduating class, the unit, that concerned me then.

The principal welcomed "parents and friends" and asked the Baptist minister to lead us in prayer. His invocation was brief and punchy, and for a second I thought we were getting back on the high road to right action. When the principal came back to the dais, however, his voice had changed. Sounds always affected me profoundly and the principal's voice was one of my favorites. During assembly it melted and lowed weakly into the audience. It had not been in my plan to listen to him, but my curiosity was piqued and I straightened up to give him my attention.

He was talking about Booker T. Washington, our "late great leader," who said we can be as close as the fingers on the hand, etc. . . . Then he said a few vague things about friendship and the friendship of kindly people to those less fortunate than themselves. With that his voice nearly faded, thin, away. Like a river diminishing to a stream and then to a trickle. But he cleared his throat and said, "Our speaker tonight, who is also our friend, came from Texarkana to deliver the commencement address, but due to the irregularity of the train schedule, he's going to, as they say, 'speak and run.'" He said that we understood and wanted the man to know that we were most grateful for the time he was able to give us and then something about how we were willing always to adjust to another's program, and without more ado—"I give you Mr. Edward Donleavy."

Not one but two white men came through the door offstage. The shorter one walked to the speaker's platform, and the tall one moved over to the center seat and sat down. But that was our principal's seat, and already occupied. The dislodged gentleman bounced around for a long breath or two before the Baptist minister gave him his chair, then with more dignity than the situation deserved, the minister walked off the stage.

Donleavy looked at the audience once (on reflection, I'm sure that he wanted only to reassure himself that we were really there), adjusted his glasses and began to read from a sheaf of papers.

35   He was glad "to be here and to see the work going on just as it was in the other schools."

At the first "Amen" from the audience I willed the offender to immediate death by choking on the word. But Amen's and Yes, sir's began to fall around the room like rain through a ragged umbrella.

He told us of the wonderful changes we children in Stamps had in store. The Central School (naturally, the white school was Central) had already been granted improvements that would be in use in the fall. A well-known artist was coming from Little Rock to teach art to them. They were going to have the newest microscopes and chemistry equipment for their laboratory. Mr. Donleavy didn't leave us long in the dark over who made these improvements available to Central High. Nor were we to be ignored in the general betterment scheme he had in mind.

He said that he had pointed out to people at a very high level that one of the first-line football tacklers at Arkansas Agricultural and Mechanical College had graduated from good old Lafayette County Training School. Here fewer Amen's were heard. Those few that did break through lay dully in the air with the heaviness of habit.

He went on to praise us. He went on to say how he had bragged that "one of the best basketball players at Fisk sank his first ball right here at Lafayette County Training School."

40   The white kids were going to have a chance to become Galileos and Madame Curies and Edisons and Gauguins, and our boys (the girls weren't even in on it) would try to be Jesse Owenses and Joe Louises.

Owens and the Brown Bomber were great heroes in our world, but what school official in the white-goddom of Little Rock had the right to decide that those two men must be our only heroes? Who decided that for Henry Reed to become a scientist he had to work like George Washington Carver, as a bootblack, to buy a lousy microscope? Bailey was obviously always going to be too small to be an athlete, so which concrete angel glued to what country seat had decided that if my brother wanted to become a lawyer he had to first pay penance for his skin by picking cotton and hoeing corn and studying correspondence books at night for twenty years?

The man's dead words fell like bricks around the auditorium and too many settled in my belly. Constrained by hard-learned manners I couldn't look behind me, but to my left and right the pro graduating class of 1940 had dropped their heads. Every girl in my row had found something new to do with her handkerchief. Some folded the tiny squares into love knots, some into triangles, but most were wadding them, then pressing them flat on their yellow laps.

On the dais, the ancient tragedy was being replayed. Professor Parsons sat, a sculptor's reject, rigid. His large, heavy body seemed devoid of will or willingness, and his eyes said he was no longer with us. The other teachers examined the flag (which was draped stage right) or their notes, or the windows which opened on our now-famous playing diamond.

Graduation, the hush-hush magic time of frills and gifts and congratulations and diplomas, was finished for me before my name was called. The accomplishment was nothing. The meticulous maps, drawn in three colors of ink, learning and spelling decasyllabic words, memorizing the whole of *The Rape of Lucrece*—it was nothing. Donleavy had exposed us.

45 We were maids and farmers, handymen and washerwomen, and anything higher that we aspired to was farcical and presumptuous. Then I wished that Gabriel Prosser and Nat Turner had killed all whitefolks in their beds and that Abraham Lincoln had been assassinated before the signing of the Emancipation Proclamation, and that Harriet Tubman had been killed by that blow on her head and Christopher Columbus had drowned in the *Santa Maria*.

It was awful to be Negro and have no control over my life. It was brutal to be young and already trained to sit quietly and listen to charges brought against my color and no chance of defense. We should all be dead. I thought I should like to see us all dead, one on top of the other. A pyramid of flesh with the whitefolks on the bottom, as the broad base, then the Indians with their silly tomahawks and teepees and wigwams and treaties, the Negroes with their mops and recipes and cotton sacks and spirituals sticking out of their mouths. The Dutch children should all stumble in their wooden shoes and break their necks. The French should choke to death on the Louisiana Purchase (1803) while silkworms ate all the Chinese with their stupid pigtails. As a species, we were an abomination. All of us.

Donleavy was running for election, and assured our parents that if he won we could count on having the only colored paved playing field in that part of Arkansas. Also—he never looked up to acknowledge the grunts of acceptance— also, we were bound to get some new equipment for the home economics building and the workshop.

He finished, and since there was no need to give any more than the most perfunctory thank-you's, he nodded to the men on the stage, and the tall white man who was never introduced joined him at the door. They left with the attitude that now they were off to something really important. (The graduation ceremonies at Lafayette County Training School had been a mere preliminary.)

The ugliness they left was palpable. An uninvited guest who wouldn't leave. The choir was summoned and sang a modern arrangement of "Onward, Christian Soldiers," with new words pertaining to graduates seeking their place in the world. But it didn't work. Elouise, the daughter of the Baptist minister, recited "Invictus," and I could have cried at the impertinence of "I am the master of my fate, I am the captain of my soul."

50 My name had lost its ring of familiarity and I had to be nudged to go and receive my diploma. All my preparations had fled. I neither marched up to the stage like a conquering Amazon, nor did I look in the audience for Bailey's nod of approval. Marguerite Johnson, I heard the name again, my honors were read, there were noises in the audience of appreciation, and I took my place on the stage as rehearsed.

I thought about colors I hated: ecru, puce, lavender, beige and black.

There was shuffling and rustling around me, then Henry Reed was giving his valedictory address, "To Be or Not to Be." Hadn't he heard the whitefolks? We couldn't *be*, so the question was a waste of time. Henry's voice came out clear and strong. I feared to look at him. Hadn't he got the message? There was no "nobler in the mind" for Negroes because the world didn't think we had minds, and they let us know it. "Outrageous fortune"? Now, that was a joke. When the ceremony was over I had to tell Henry Reed some things. That is, if I still cared. Not "rub," Henry, "erase." "Ah, there's the erase." Us.

Henry had been a good student in elocution. His voice rose on tides of promise and fell on waves of warnings. The English teacher had helped him to create a sermon winging through Hamlet's soliloquy. To be a man, a doer, a builder, a leader, or to be a tool, an unfunny joke, a crusher of funky toadstools. I marveled that Henry could go through with the speech as if we had a choice.

I had been listening and silently rebutting each sentence with my eyes closed; then there was a hush, which in an audience warns that something unplanned is happening. I looked up and saw Henry Reed, the conservative, the proper, the A student, turn his back to the audience and turn to us (the proud graduating class of 1940) and sing, nearly speaking,

> Lift ev'ry voice and sing
> Till earth and heaven ring
> Ring with the harmonies of Liberty . . .

55   It was the poem written by James Weldon Johnson. It was the music composed by J. Rosamond Johnson. It was the Negro National Anthem. Out of habit we were singing it.

Our mothers and fathers stood in the dark hall and joined the hymn of encouragement. A kindergarten teacher led the small children onto the stage and the buttercups and daisies and bunny rabbits marked time and tried to follow:

> Stony the road we trod
> Bitter the chastening rod
> Felt in the days when hope, unborn, had died.
> Yet with a steady beat
> Have not our weary feet
> Come to the place for which our fathers sighed?

Every child I knew had learned that song with his ABC's and along with "Jesus Loves Me This I Know." But I personally had never heard it before. Never heard the words, despite the thousands of times I had sung them. Never thought they had anything to do with me.

On the other hand, the words of Patrick Henry had made such an impression on me that I had been able to stretch myself tall and trembling and say, "I know not what course others may take, but as for me, give me liberty or give me death."

And now I heard, really for the first time:

> We have come over a way that with tears has been watered,
> We have come, treading our path through the blood of the slaughtered.

60   While echoes of the song shivered in the air, Henry Reed bowed his head, said "Thank you," and returned to his place in the line. The tears that slipped down many faces were not wiped away in shame.

We were on top again. As always, again. We survived. The depths had been icy and dark, but now a bright sun spoke to our souls. I was no longer simply a member of the proud graduating class of 1940; I was a proud member of the wonderful, beautiful Negro race.

Oh, Black known and unknown poets, how often have your auctioned pains sustained us? Who will compute the lonely nights made less lonely by your songs, or the empty pots made less tragic by your tales?

If we were a people much given to revealing secrets, we might raise monuments and sacrifice to the memories of our poets, but slavery cured us of that weakness. It may be enough, however, to have it said that we survive in exact relationship to the dedication of our poets (include preachers, musicians and blues singers).

[1969]

Topics for Critical Thinking and Writing

1. In the first paragraph, notice such overstatements as "glorious release," "the graduating classes themselves were the nobility," and "exotic destinations." Find further examples in the next few pages. What is the function of this diction?
2. How would you define "poets" as Angelou uses the word in the last sentence?
3. Characterize the writer as you perceive her up to the middle of paragraph 29. Support your characterizations with references to specific passages. Next, characterize her in the paragraph beginning "It was awful to be Negro" (paragraph 46). Next, characterize her on the basis of the entire essay. Finally, in a sentence, try to describe the change, telling the main attitudes or moods that she goes through.

FICTION

NATHANIEL HAWTHORNE

Nathaniel Hawthorne (1804–1864) was born in Salem, Massachusetts, the son of a sea captain. Two of his ancestors were judges; one had persecuted Quakers, and another had served at the Salem witch trials. After graduating from Bowdoin College in Maine, Hawthorne went back to Salem in order to write in relative seclusion. In 1835 he published "Young Goodman Brown."

From 1839 to 1841 Hawthorne worked in the Boston Customs House and then spent a few months as a member of a communal society, Brook Farm. In 1842 he married. From 1846 to 1849 he was a surveyor at the Salem Customs House; from 1849 to 1850 he wrote The Scarlet Letter, *the book that made him famous. From 1853 to 1857 he served as American consul in Liverpool, England, a plum awarded him in exchange for writing a campaign biography of a former college classmate, President Franklin Pierce. In 1860, after living in England and Italy, he returned to the United States, settling in Concord, Massachusetts.*

In his stories and novels Hawthorne keeps returning to the Puritan past, studying guilt, sin, and isolation.

Young Goodman Brown

Young Goodman Brown came forth at sunset into the street at Salem village; but put his head back, after crossing the threshold, to exchange a parting kiss with his young wife. And Faith, as the wife was aptly named, thrust her own pretty head into the street, letting the wind play with the pink ribbons of her cap while she called to Goodman Brown.

"Dearest heart," whispered she, softly and rather sadly, when her lips were close to his ear, "prithee put off your journey until sunrise and sleep in your own bed to-night. A lone woman is troubled with such dreams and such thoughts that she's afeared of herself sometimes. Pray tarry with me this night, dear husband, of all nights in the year."

"My love and my Faith," replied young Goodman Brown, "of all nights in the year, this one night must I tarry away from thee. My journey, as thou callest it, forth and back again, must needs be done 'twixt now and sunrise. What, my sweet, pretty wife, dost thou doubt me already, and we but three months married?"

"Then God bless you!" said Faith, with the pink ribbons; "and may you find all well when you come back."

5　　"Amen!" cried Goodman Brown. "Say thy prayers, dear Faith, and go to bed at dusk, and no harm will come to thee."

So they parted; and the young man pursued his way until, being about to turn the corner by the meeting-house, he looked back and saw the head of Faith still peeping after him with a melancholy air, in spite of her pink ribbons.

"Poor little Faith!" thought he, for his heart smote him. "What a wretch am I to leave her on such an errand! She talks of dreams, too. Methought as she spoke there was trouble in her face, as if a dream had warned her what work is to be done to-night. But no, no; 'twould kill her to think it. Well, she's a blessed angel on earth; and after this one night I'll cling to her skirts and follow her to heaven."

With this excellent resolve for the future, Goodman Brown felt himself justified in making more haste on his present evil purpose. He had taken a dreary road, darkened by all the gloomiest trees of the forest, which barely stood aside to let the narrow path creep through, and closed immediately behind. It was all as lonely as could be; and there is this peculiarity in such a solitude, that the traveler knows not who may be concealed by the innumerable trunks and the thick boughs overhead; so that with lonely footsteps he may yet be passing through an unseen multitude.

"There may be a devilish Indian behind every tree," said Goodman Brown to himself; and he glanced fearfully behind him as he added, "What if the devil himself should be at my very elbow!"

10　　His head being turned back, he passed a crook of the road, and, looking forward again, beheld the figure of a man, in grave and decent attire, seated at the foot of an old tree. He arose at Goodman Brown's approach and walked onward side by side with him.

"You are late, Goodman Brown," said he. "The clock of the Old South was striking as I came through Boston, and that is full fifteen minutes agone."

"Faith kept me back a while," replied the young man, with a tremor in his voice, caused by the sudden appearance of his companion, though not wholly unexpected.

It was now deep dusk in the forest, and deepest in that part of it where these two were journeying. As nearly as could be discerned, the second traveller was about fifty years old, apparently in the same rank of life as Goodman Brown, and bearing a considerable resemblance to him, though perhaps more in expression than features. Still they might have been taken for father and son. And yet, though the elder person was as simply clad as the younger, and as simple in manner too, he had an indescribable air of one who knew the world, and who would not have felt abashed at the governor's dinner table or in King William's court, were it possible that his affairs should call him thither. But the only thing about him that could be fixed upon as remarkable was his staff, which bore the likeness of a great black snake, so curiously wrought that it might almost be seen to twist and wriggle itself like a living serpent. This, of course, must have been an ocular deception, assisted by the uncertain light.

"Come, Goodman Brown," cried his fellow-traveller, "this is a dull pace for the beginning of a journey. Take my staff, if you are so soon weary."

15 "Friend," said the other, exchanging his slow pace for a full stop, "Having kept covenant by meeting thee here, it is my purpose now to return whence I came. I have scruples touching the matter thou wot'st of."

"Sayest thou so?" replied he of the serpent, smiling apart. "Let us walk on, nevertheless, reasoning as we go; and if I convince thee not thou shalt turn back. We are but a little way in the forest yet."

"Too far! too far!" exclaimed the goodman, unconsciously resuming his walk. "My father never went into the woods on such an errand, not his father before him. We have been a race of honest men and good Christians since the days of the martyrs; and shall I be the first of the name of Brown that ever took this path and kept—"

"Such company, thou wouldst say," observed the elder person, interpreting his pause. "Well said, Goodman Brown! I have been as well acquainted with your family as with ever a one among the Puritans; and that's no trifle to say. I helped your grandfather, the constable, when he lashed the Quaker woman so smartly through the streets of Salem; and it was I that brought your father a pitch-pine knot, kindled at my own hearth, to set fire to an Indian village, in King Philip's war. They were my good friends, both; and many a pleasant walk have we had along this path, and returned merrily after midnight. I would fain be friends with you for their sake."

"If it be as thou sayest," replied Goodman Brown, "I marvel they never spoke of these matters; or, verily, I marvel not, seeing that the least rumor of the sort would have driven them from New England. We are a people of prayer, and good works to boot, and abide no such wickedness."

20 "Wickedness or not," said the traveller with the twisted staff, "I have a very general acquaintance here in New England. The deacons of many a church have drunk the communion wine with me; the selectmen of divers towns make me their chairman; and a majority of the Great and General Court are firm supporters of my interest. The governor and I, too—But these are state secrets."

"Can this be so?" cried Goodman Brown, with a stare of amazement at his undisturbed companion. "Howbeit, I have nothing to do with the governor and council; they have their own ways, and are no rule for a simple husbandman like me. But, were I to go on with thee, how should I meet the eye of that good old man, our minister, at Salem village? Oh, his voice would make me tremble both Sabbath day and lecture day."

Thus far the elder traveller had listened with due gravity; but now burst into a fit of irrepressible mirth, shaking himself so violently that his snake-like staff actually seemed to wriggle in sympathy.

"Ha! ha! ha!" shouted he again and again; then composing himself, "Well, go on, Goodman Brown, go on; but, prithee, don't kill me with laughing."

"Well, then, to end the matter at once," said Goodman Brown, considerably nettled, "there is my wife, Faith. It would break her dear little heart; and I'd rather break my own."

"Nay, if that be the case," answered the other, "e'en go thy ways, Goodman Brown. I would not for twenty old women like the one hobbling before us that Faith should come to any harm."

As he spoke he pointed his staff at a female figure on the path, in whom Goodman Brown recognized a very pious and exemplary dame, who had taught him his catechism in youth, and was still his moral and spiritual adviser, jointly with the minister and Deacon Gookin.

"A marvel, truly, that Goody Cloyse should be so far in the wilderness at nightfall," said he. "But with your leave, friend, I shall take a cut through the woods until we have left this Christian woman behind. Being a stranger to you, she might ask whom I was consorting with and whither I was going."

"Be it so," said his fellow-traveller. "Betake you the woods, and let me keep the path."

Accordingly the young man turned aside, but took care to watch his companion, who advanced softly along the road until he had come within a staff's length of the old dame. She, meanwhile, was making the best of her way, with singular speed for so aged a woman, and mumbling some indistinct words—a prayer, doubtless—as she went. The traveller put forth his staff and touched her withered neck with what seemed the serpent's tail.

"The devil!" screamed the pious old lady.

"Then Goody Cloyse knows her old friend?" observed the traveller, confronting her and leaning on his writhing stick.

"Ah, forsooth, and is it your worship indeed?" cried the good dame. "Yea, truly is it, and in the very image of my old gossip, Goodman Brown, the grandfather of the silly fellow that now is. But—would your worship believe it?—my broomstick hath strangely disappeared, stolen, as I suspect, by that unhanged witch, Goody Cory, and that, too, when I was all anointed with the juice of small-age, and cinquefoil, and wolf's bane—"

"Mingled with fine wheat and the fat of a new-born babe," said the shape of old Goodman Brown.

"Ah, your worship knows the recipe," cried the old lady, cackling aloud. "So, as I was saying, being all ready for the meeting, and no horse to ride on, I made up my mind to foot it; for they tell me there is a nice young man to be taken into communion to-night. But now your good worship will lend me your arm, and we shall be there in a twinkling."

"That can hardly be," answered her friend. "I may not spare you my arm, Goody Cloyse; but here is my staff, if you will."

So saying, he threw it down at her feet, where, perhaps, it assumed life, being one of the rods which its owner had formerly lent to the Egyptian magi. Of this fact, however, Goodman Brown could not take cognizance. He had cast up his eyes in astonishment, and, looking down again, beheld neither Goody Cloyse nor the serpentine staff, but his fellow-traveller alone, who waited for him as calmly as if nothing had happened.

"That old woman taught me my catechism," said the young man; and there was a world of meaning in this simple comment.

They continued to walk onward, while the elder traveller exhorted his companion to make good speed and persevere in the path, discoursing so aptly that his arguments seemed rather to spring up in the bosom of his auditor than to be suggested by himself. As they went, he plucked a branch of maple to serve for a walking stick, and began to strip it of the twigs and the little boughs, which were wet with evening dew. The moment his fingers touched them they became strangely withered and dried up as with a week's sunshine. Thus the pair proceeded, at a good free pace, until suddenly, in a gloomy hollow of the road, Goodman Brown sat himself down on the stump of a tree and refused to go any farther.

"Friend," said he, stubbornly, "my mind is made up. Not another step will I budge on this errand. What if a wretched old woman do choose to go to the devil when I thought she was going to heaven: is that any reason why I should quit my dear Faith and go after her?"

40   "You will think better of this by and by," said his acquaintance, composedly. "Sit here and rest yourself a while; and when you feel like moving again, there is my staff to help you along."

Without more words, he threw his companion the maple stick, and was as speedily out of sight as if he had vanished into the deepening gloom. The young man sat a few moments by the roadside, applauding himself greatly, and thinking with how clear a conscience he should meet the minister in his morning walk, nor shrink from the eye of good old Deacon Gookin. And what calm sleep would be his that very night, which was to have been spent so wickedly, but so purely and sweetly now, in the arms of Faith! Amidst these pleasant and praiseworthy meditations, Goodman Brown heard the tramp of horses along the road, and deemed it advisable to conceal himself within the verge of the forest, conscious of the guilty purpose that had brought him thither, though now so happily turned from it.

On came the hoof tramps and the voices of the riders, two grave old voices, conversing soberly as they drew near. These mingled sounds appeared to pass along the road, within a few yards of the young man's hiding-place; but, owing doubtless to the depth of the gloom at that particular spot, neither the travellers nor their steeds were visible. Though their figures brushed the small boughs by the wayside, it could not be seen that they intercepted, even for a moment, the faint gleam from the strip of bright sky athwart which they must have passed. Goodman Brown alternately crouched and stood on tiptoe, pulling aside the branches and thrusting forth his head as far as he durst without discerning so much as a shadow. It vexed him the more, because he could have sworn, were such a thing possible, that he recognized the voices of the minister and Deacon Gookin, jogging along quietly, as they were wont to do, when bound to some ordination or ecclesiastical council. While yet within hearing, one of the riders stopped to pluck a switch.

"Of the two, reverend sir," said the voice like the deacon's, "I had rather miss an ordination dinner than to-night's meeting. They tell me that some of our community are to be here from Falmouth and beyond, and others from Connecticut and Rhode Island, besides several of the Indian powwows, who, after their fashion, know almost as much deviltry as the best of us. Moreover, there is a goodly young woman to be taken into communion."

"Mighty well, Deacon Gookin!" replied the solemn old tones of the minister. "Spur up, or we shall be late. Nothing can be done, you know, until I get on the ground."

45   The hoofs clattered again; and the voices, talking so strangely in the empty air, passed on through the forest, where no church had ever been gathered or solitary Christian prayed. Whither, then, could these holy men be journeying so deep into the heathen wilderness? Young Goodman Brown caught hold of a tree

for support, being ready to sink down on the ground, faint and overburdened with the heavy sickness of his heart. He looked up to the sky, doubting whether there really was a heaven above him. Yet there was the blue arch, and the stars brightening in it.

"With heaven above and Faith below, I will yet stand firm against the devil!" cried Goodman Brown.

While he still gazed upward into the deep arch of the firmament and had lifted his hands to pray, a cloud, though no wind was stirring, hurried across the zenith and hid the brightening stars. The blue sky was still visible, except directly overhead, where this black mass of cloud was sweeping swiftly northward. Aloft in the air, as if from the depths of the cloud, came a confused and doubtful sound of voices. Once the listener fancied that he could distinguish the accents of towns-people of his own, men and women, both pious and ungodly, many of whom he had met at the communion table, and had seen others rioting at the tavern. The next moment, so indistinct were the sounds, he doubted whether he had heard aught but the murmur of the old forest, whispering without a wind. Then came a stronger swell of those familiar tones, heard daily in the sunshine at Salem village, but never until now from a cloud of night. There was one voice, of a young woman, uttering lamentations, yet with an uncertain sorrow, and entreating for some favor, which, perhaps, it would grieve her to obtain; and all the unseen multitude, both saints and sinners, seemed to encourage her onward.

"Faith!" shouted Goodman Brown, in a voice of agony and desperation; and the echoes of the forest mocked him, crying, "Faith! Faith!" as if bewildered wretches were seeking her all through the wilderness.

The cry of grief, rage, and terror was yet piercing the night, when the unhappy husband held his breath for a response. There was a scream, drowned immediately in a louder murmur of voices, fading into far-off laughter, as the dark cloud swept away, leaving the clear and silent sky above Goodman Brown. But something fluttered lightly down through the air and caught on the branch of a tree. The young man seized it, and beheld a pink ribbon.

50   "My Faith is gone!" cried he, after one stupefied moment. "There is no good on earth; and sin is but a name. Come, devil; for to thee is this world given."

And, maddened with despair, so that he laughed loud and long, did Goodman Brown grasp his staff and set forth again, at such a rate that he seemed to fly along the forest path rather than to walk or run. The road grew wilder and drearier and more faintly traced, and vanished at length, leaving him in the heart of the dark wilderness, still rushing onward with the instinct that guides mortal man to evil. The whole forest was peopled with frightful sounds—the creaking of the trees, the howling of wild beasts, and the yell of Indians; while sometimes the wind tolled like a distant church bell, and sometimes gave a broad roar around the traveller, as if all Nature were laughing him to scorn. But he was himself the chief horror of the scene, and shrank not from its other horrors.

"Ha! ha! ha!" roared Goodman Brown when the wind laughed at him. "Let us hear which will laugh loudest. Think not to frighten me with your deviltry. Come witch, come wizard, come Indian powwow, come devil himself, and here comes Goodman Brown. You may as well fear him as he fear you."

In truth, all through the haunted forest there could be nothing more frightful than the figure of Goodman Brown. On he flew among the black pines, brandishing his staff with frenzied gestures, now giving vent to an inspiration of horrid blasphemy, and now shouting forth such laughter as set all the echoes of the forest laughing like demons around him. The fiend in his own shape is less hideous than when he rages in the breast of man. Thus sped the demoniac on his course, until, quivering among the trees, he saw a red light before him, as when the felled trunks and branches of a clearing have been set on fire, and throw up their lurid blaze against the sky, at the hour of midnight. He paused, in a lull of the tempest that had driven him onward, and heard the swell of what seemed a hymn, rolling solemnly from a distance with the weight of many voices. He knew the tune; it was a familiar one in the choir of the village meeting-house. The verse died heavily away, and was lengthened by a chorus, not of human voices, but of all the sounds of the benighted wilderness pealing in awful harmony together. Goodman Brown cried out, and his cry was lost to his own ear by its unison with the cry of the desert.

In the interval of silence he stole forward until the light glared full upon his eyes. At one extremity of an open space, hemmed in by the dark wall of the forest, arose a rock, bearing some rude, natural resemblance either to an altar or a pulpit, and surrounded by four blazing pines, their tops aflame, their stems untouched, like candles at an evening meeting. The mass of foliage that had overgrown the summit of the rock was all on fire, blazing high into the night and fitfully illuminating the whole field. Each pendent twig and leafy festoon was in a blaze. As the red light arose and fell, a numerous congregation alternately shone forth, then disappeared in shadow, and again grew, as it were, out of the darkness, peopling the heart of the solitary woods at once.

55   "A grave and dark-clad company," quoth Goodman Brown.

In truth they were such. Among them, quivering to and fro between gloom and splendor, appeared faces that would be seen next day at the council board of the province, and others which, Sabbath after Sabbath, looked devoutly heavenward, and benignantly over the crowded pews, from the holiest pulpits in the land. Some affirm that the lady of the governor was there. At least three were high dames well known to her, and wives of honored husbands, and widows, a great multitude, and ancient maidens, all of excellent repute, and fair young girls, who trembled lest their mothers should espy them. Either the sudden gleams of light flashing over the obscure field bedazzled Goodman Brown, or he recognized a score of the church members of Salem village famous for their especial sanctity. Good old Deacon Gookin had arrived, and waited at the skirts of that venerable saint, his revered pastor. But, irreverently consorting with these grave, reputable, and pious people, these elders of the church, these chaste dames and dewy virgins, there were men of dissolute lives and women of spotted fame, wretches given over to all mean and filthy vice, and suspected even of horrid crimes. It was strange to see that the good shrank not from the wicked, nor were the sinners abashed by the saints. Scattered also among their pale-faced enemies were the Indian priests, or powwows, who had often scared their native forest with more hideous incantations than any known to English witchcraft.

"But where is Faith?" thought Goodman Brown; and, as hope came into his heart, he trembled.

Another verse of the hymn arose, a slow and mournful strain, such as the pious love, but joined to words which expressed all that our nature can conceive of sin, and darkly hinted at far more. Unfathomable to mere mortals is the lore of fiends. Verse after verse was sung; and still the chorus of the desert swelled between like the deepest tone of a mighty organ; and with the final peal of that dreadful anthem there came a sound, as if the roaring wind, the rushing streams, the howling beasts, and every other voice of the unconcerted wilderness were mingling and according with the voice of guilty man in homage to the prince of all. The four blazing pines threw up a loftier flame, and obscurely discovered shapes and visages of horror on the smoke wreaths above the impious assembly. At the same moment the fire on the rock shot redly forth and formed a glowing arch above its base, where now appeared a figure. With reverence be it spoken, the figure bore no slight similitude, both in garb and manner, to some grave divine of the New England churches.

"Bring forth the converts!" cried a voice that echoed through the field and rolled into the forest.

60   At the word, Goodman Brown stepped forth from the shadow of the trees and approached the congregation, with whom he felt a loathful brotherhood by the sympathy of all that was wicked in his heart. He could have well-nigh sworn that the shape of his own dead father beckoned him to advance, looking downward from a smoke wreath, while a woman, with dim features of despair, threw out her hand to warn him back. Was it his mother? But he had no power to retreat one step, nor to resist, even in thought, when the minister and good old Deacon Gookin seized his arms and led him to the blazing rock. Thither came also the slender form of a veiled female, led between Goody Cloyse, that pious teacher of the catechism, and Martha Carrier, who had received the devil's promise to be queen of hell. A rampant hag was she. And there stood the proselytes beneath the canopy of fire.

"Welcome, my children," said the dark figure, "to the communion of your race. Ye have found thus young your nature and your destiny. My children, look behind you!"

They turned; and flashing forth, as it were, in a sheet of flame, the fiend worshippers were seen; the smile of welcome gleamed darkly on every visage.

"There," resumed the sable form, "are all whom ye have reverenced from youth. Ye deemed them holier than yourselves, and shrank from your own sin, contrasting it with their lives of righteousness and prayerful aspirations heavenward. Yet here are they all in my worshipping assembly. This night it shall be granted you to know their secret deeds: how hoary-bearded elders of the church have whispered wanton words to the young maids of their households; how many a woman, eager for widows' weeds, has given her husband a drink at bedtime and let him sleep his last sleep in her bosom; how beardless youths have made haste to inherit their fathers' wealth; and how fair damsels—blush not, sweet ones—have dug little graves in the garden, and bidden me, the sole guest, to an infant's funeral. By the sympathy of your human hearts for sin ye shall scent out all the places—whether in church, bedchamber, street, field, or forest—where crime has been committed, and shall exult to behold the whole earth one stain of guilt, one mighty blood spot. Far more than this. It shall be yours to penetrate, in every bosom, the deep mystery of sin, the fountain of all wicked arts, and which inexhaustibly supplies more evil impulses than human power—than my power at its utmost—can make manifest in deeds. And now, my children, look upon each other."

They did so; and, by the blaze of the hell-kindled torches, the wretched man beheld his Faith, and the wife her husband, trembling before that unhallowed altar.

65   "Lo, there ye stand, my children," said the figure, in a deep and solemn tone, almost sad with its despairing awfulness, as if his once angelic nature could yet mourn for our miserable race. "Depending upon one another's hearts, ye had still hoped that virtue were not all a dream. Now are ye undeceived. Evil is the nature of mankind. Evil must be your only happiness. Welcome again, my children, to the communion of your race."

"Welcome," repeated the fiend worshippers, in one cry of despair and triumph.

And there they stood, the only pair, as it seemed, who were yet hesitating on the verge of wickedness in this dark world. A basin was hollowed, naturally, in the rock. Did it contain water, reddened by the lurid light? or was it blood? or, perchance, a liquid flame? Herein did the shape of evil dip his hand and prepare to lay the mark of baptism upon their foreheads, that they might be partakers of the mystery of sin, more conscious of the secret guilt of others, both in deed and thought, than they could now be of their own. The husband cast one look at his pale wife, and Faith at him. What polluted wretches would the next glance show them to each other, shuddering alike at what they disclosed and what they saw!

"Faith! Faith!" cried the husband, "look up to heaven, and resist the wicked one."

Whether Faith obeyed he knew not. Hardly had he spoken when he found himself amid calm night and solitude, listening to a roar of the wind which died heavily away through the forest. He staggered against the rock, and felt it chill and damp; while a hanging twig, that had been all on fire, besprinkled his cheek with the coldest dew.

70   The next morning young Goodman Brown came slowly into the street of Salem village, staring around him like a bewildered man. The good old minister was taking a walk along the graveyard to get an appetite for breakfast and meditate his sermon, and bestowed a blessing, as he passed, on Goodman Brown. He shrank from the venerable saint as if to avoid an anathema. Old Deacon Gookin was at domestic worship, and the holy words of his prayer were heard through the open window. "What God doth the wizard pray to?" quoth Goodman Brown. Goody Cloyse, that excellent old Christian, stood in the early sunshine at her own lattice, catechizing a little girl who had brought her a pint of morning's milk. Goodman Brown snatched away the child as from the grasp of the fiend himself. Turning the corner by the meeting-house, he spied the head of Faith, with the pink ribbons, gazing anxiously forth, and bursting into such joy at sight of him that she skipped along the street and almost kissed her husband before the whole village. But Goodman Brown looked sternly and sadly into her face, and passed on without a greeting.

Had Goodman Brown fallen asleep in the forest and only dreamed a wild dream of a witch-meeting?

Be it so if you will; but alas! it was a dream of evil omen for young Goodman Brown. A stern, a sad, a darkly meditative, a distrustful, if not a desperate man did he become from the night of that fearful dream. On the Sabbath day, when the congregation were singing a holy psalm, he could not listen because an anthem of sin rushed loudly upon his ear and drowned all the blessed strain. When the minister spoke from the pulpit with power and fervid eloquence, and, with his hand on the open Bible, of the sacred truths of our religion, and of saint-like lives and triumphant deaths, and of future bliss or misery unutterable, then did Goodman Brown turn pale, dreading lest the roof should thunder down upon the gray blasphemer and his hearers. Often, awaking suddenly at midnight, he shrank from the bosom of Faith; and at morning or eventide, when the family knelt down at prayer, he scowled and muttered to himself, and gazed sternly at his wife, and turned away. And when he had lived long, and was borne to his grave a hoary corpse, followed by Faith, an aged woman, and children and grandchildren, a goodly procession, besides neighbors not a few, they carved no hopeful verse upon his tombstone, for his dying hour was gloom.

[1835]

Topics for Critical Thinking and Writing

1. What do you think Hawthorne gains (or loses) by the last sentence?
2. Evaluate the view that when young Goodman Brown enters the dark forest he is really entering his own evil mind. Why, by the way, does he go into the forest at night? (Hawthorne gives no explicit reason, but you may want to offer a conjecture.)
3. In a sentence or two summarize the plot, and then in another sentence or two state the theme of the story. (On theme, see pages 234–235.)
4. If you have undergone a religious experience, write an essay discussing your condition before, during, and after the experience.

JAMES JOYCE

James Joyce (1882–1941) was born into a middle-class family in Dublin, Ireland. His father drank, became increasingly irresponsible and unemployable, and the family sank in the social order. Still, Joyce received a strong classical education at excellent Jesuit schools and at University College, Dublin, where he studied modern languages. In 1902, at the age of 20, he left Ireland so that he might spend the rest of his life writing about life in Ireland. ("The shortest way to Tara," he said, "is via Holyhead," i.e., the shortest way to the heart of Ireland is to take ship away.) In Trieste, Zurich, and Paris he supported his family in a variety of ways, sometimes teaching English in a Berlitz language school. His fifteen stories, collected under the title of Dubliners, *were written between 1904 and 1907, but he could not get them published until 1914. Next came a highly autobiographical novel,* A Portrait of the Artist as a Young Man *(1916).* Ulysses *(1922), a large novel covering eighteen hours in Dublin, was for some years banned by the United States Post Office, though few if any readers today find it offensive. Joyce spent most of the rest of his life working on* Finnegans Wake *(1939).*

Nine years before he succeeded in getting Dubliners *published, Joyce described the manuscript in these terms:*

> *My intention was to write a chapter of the moral history of my country and I chose Dublin for the scene because that city seemed to me the centre of paralysis. . . . I have written it for the most part in a style of scrupulous meanness and with the conviction that he is a very bold man who dares to alter in the presentment, still more to deform, whatever he has seen and heard.*

Araby

North Richmond Street, being blind,[1] was a quiet street except at the hour when the Christian Brothers' School set the boys free. An uninhabited house of two stories stood at the blind end, detached from its neighbors in a square ground. The other houses of the street, conscious of decent lives within them, gazed at one another with brown imperturbable faces.

---

[1] **blind** a dead-end street. (All notes are by the editors.)

The former tenant of our house, a priest, had died in the back drawing-room. Air, musty from having long been enclosed, hung in all the rooms, and the waste room behind the kitchen was littered with old useless papers. Among these I found a few papercovered books, the pages of which were curled and damp: *The Abbot,* by Walter Scott, *The Devout Communicant* and *The Memoirs of Vidocq.*[2] I liked the last best because its leaves were yellow. The wild garden behind the house contained a central apple-tree and a few straggling bushes under one of which I found the late tenant's rusty bicycle-pump. He had been a very charitable priest; in his will he had left all his money to institutions and the furniture of his house to his sister.

When the short days of winter came dusk fell before we had well eaten our dinners. When we met in the street the houses had grown sombre. The space of sky above us was the colour of everchanging violet and towards it the lamps of the street lifted their feeble lanterns. The cold air stung us and we played till our bodies glowed. Our shouts echoed in the silent street. The career of our play brought us through the dark muddy lanes behind the houses where we ran the gauntlet of the rough tribes from the cottages, to the back doors of the dark dripping gardens where odours arose from the ashpits, to the dark odorous stables where a coachman smoothed and combed the horse or shook music from the buckled harness. When we returned to the street light from the kitchen windows had filled the areas. If my uncle was seen turning the corner we hid in the shadow until we had seen him safely housed. Or if Mangan's sister came out on the doorstep to call her brother in to his tea we watched her from our shadow peer up and down the street. We waited to see whether she would remain or go in and, if she remained, we left our shadow and walked up to Mangan's steps resignedly. She was waiting for us, her figure defined by the light from the half-opened door. Her brother always teased her before he obeyed and I stood by the railings looking at her. Her dress swung as she moved her body and the soft rope of her hair tossed from side to side.

Every morning I lay on the floor in the front parlour watching her door. The blind was pulled down to within an inch of the sash so that I could not be seen. When she came out on the doorstep my heart leaped. I ran to the hall, seized my books and followed her. I kept her brown figure always in my eye and, when we came near the point at which our ways diverged, I quickened my pace and passed her. This happened morning after morning. I had never spoken to her, except for a few casual words, and yet her name was like a summons to all my foolish blood.

5   Her image accompanied me even in places the most hostile to romance. On Saturday evenings when my aunt went marketing I had to go to carry some of the parcels. We walked through the flaring streets, jostled by drunken men and bargaining women, amid the curses of labourers, the shrill litanies of shop-boys who stood on guard by the barrels of pigs' cheeks, the nasal chanting of street-singers, who sang a *come-all-you* about O'Donovan Rossa,[3] or a ballad about the troubles in our native land. These noises converged in a single sensation of life for me: I imagined that I bore my chalice safely through a throng of foes. Her name sprang

---

[2]*The Abbot* one of Scott's popular historical romances; *The Devout Communicant* a Catholic religious manual; *The Memoirs of Vidocq* the memoirs of the chief of the French detective force.
[3]*O'Donovan Rossa* Jeremiah O'Donovan (1831–1915), a popular Irish leader who was jailed by the British for advocating violent rebellion; *come-all-you* a topical song that began "Come all you gallant Irishmen."

to my lips at moments in strange prayers and praises which I myself did not understand. My eyes were often full of tears (I could not tell why) and at times a flood from my heart seemed to pour itself out into my bosom. I thought little of the future. I did not know whether I would ever speak to her or not or, if I spoke to her, how I could tell her of my confused adoration. But my body was like a harp and her words and gestures were like fingers running upon the wires.

One evening I went into the back drawing-room in which the priest had died. It was a dark rainy evening and there was no sound in the house. Through one of the broken panes I heard the rain impinge upon the earth, the fine incessant needles of water playing in the sodden beds. Some distant lamp or lighted window gleamed below me. I was thankful that I could see so little. All my senses seemed to desire to veil themselves and, feeling that I was about to slip from them, I pressed the palms of my hands together until they trembled, murmuring: O *love!* O *love!* many times.

At last she spoke to me. When she addressed the first words to me I was so confused that I did not know what to answer. She asked me was I going to Araby.

I forget whether I answered yes or no. It would be a splendid bazaar, she said; she would love to go.

—And why can't you? I asked.

10   While she spoke she turned a silver bracelet round and round her wrist. She could not go, she said, because there would be a retreat that week in her convent. Her brother and two other boys were fighting for their caps and I was alone at the railings. She held one of the spikes, bowing her head towards me. The light from the lamp opposite our door caught the white curve of her neck, lit up her hair that rested there and, falling, lit up the hand upon the railing. It fell over one side of her dress and caught the white border of a petticoat, just visible as she stood at ease.

—It's well for you, she said.

—If I go, I said, I will bring you something.

What innumerable follies laid waste my waking and sleeping thoughts after that evening! I wished to annihilate the tedious intervening days. I chafed against the work of school. At night in my bedroom and by day in the classroom her image came between me and the page I strove to read. The syllables of the word *Araby* were called to me through the silence in which my soul luxuriated and cast an Eastern enchantment over me. I asked for leave to go to the bazaar on Saturday night. My aunt was surprised and hoped it was not some Freemason[4] affair. I answered few questions in class, I watched my master's face pass from amiability to sternness; he hoped I was not beginning to idle. I could not call my wandering thoughts together. I had hardly any patience with the serious work of life which, now that it stood between me and my desire, seemed to me child's play, ugly monotonous child's play.

On Saturday morning I reminded my uncle that I wished to go to the bazaar in the evening. He was fussing at the hallstand, looking for the hat-brush, and answered me curtly:

15   —Yes, boy, I know.

As he was in the hall I could not go into the front parlour and lie at the window. I left the house in bad humour and walked slowly towards the school. The air was pitilessly raw and already my heart misgave me.

When I came home to dinner my uncle had not yet been home. Still it was early. I sat staring at the clock for some time and, when its ticking began

---

[4]**Freemason** Irish Catholics viewed the Masons as their Protestant enemies.

to irritate me, I left the room. I mounted the staircase and gained the upper part of the house. The high cold empty gloomy rooms liberated me and I went from room to room singing. From the front window I saw my companions playing below in the street. Their cries reached me weakened and indistinct and, leaning my forehead against the cool glass, I looked over at the dark house where she lived. I may have stood there for an hour, seeing nothing but the brown-clad figure cast by my imagination, touched discreetly by the lamp-light at the curved neck, at the hand upon the railings and at the border below the dress.

When I came downstairs again I found Mrs Mercer sitting at the fire. She was an old garrulous woman, a pawnbroker's widow, who collected used stamps for some pious purpose. I had to endure the gossip of the tea-table. The meal was prolonged beyond an hour and still my uncle did not come. Mrs Mercer stood up to go: she was sorry she couldn't wait any longer, but it was after eight o'clock and she did not like to be out late, as the night air was bad for her. When she had gone I began to walk up and down the room, clenching my fists. My aunt said:

—I'm afraid you may put off your bazaar for this night of Our Lord.

20   At nine o'clock I heard my uncle's latchkey in the halldoor. I heard him talking to himself and heard the hallstand rocking when it had received the weight of his overcoat. I could interpret these signs. When he was midway through his dinner I asked him to give me the money to go to the bazaar. He had forgotten.

—The people are in bed and after their first sleep now, he said.

I did not smile. My aunt said to him energetically:

—Can't you give him the money and let him go? You've kept him late enough as it is.

My uncle said he was very sorry he had forgotten. He said he believed in the old saying: *All work and no play makes Jack a dull boy*. He asked me where I was going and, when I had told him a second time he asked me did I know *The Arab's Farewell to His Steed*.[5] When I left the kitchen he was about to recite the opening lines of the piece to my aunt.

25   I held a florin tightly in my hand as I strode down Buckingham Street towards the station. The sight of the streets thronged with buyers and glaring with gas recalled to me the purpose of my journey. I took my seat in a third-class carriage of a deserted train. After an intolerable delay the train moved out of the station slowly. It crept onward among ruinous houses and over the twinkling river. At Westland Row Station a crowd of people pressed to the carriage doors; but the porters moved them back, saying that it was a special train for the bazaar. I remained alone in the bare carriage. In a few minutes the train drew up beside an improvised wooden platform. I passed out on to the road and saw by the lighted dial of a clock that it was ten minutes to ten. In front of me was a large building which displayed the magical name.

I could not find any sixpenny entrance and, fearing that the bazaar would be closed, I passed in quickly through a turnstile, handing a shilling to a weary-looking man. I found myself in a big hall girdled at half its height by a gallery. Nearly all the stalls were closed and the greater part of the hall was in darkness. I recognised a silence like that which pervades a church after a service. I walked into the center of the bazaar timidly. A few people were gathered about the stalls

[5]*The Arab's Farewell to His Steed* "The Arab to His Favorite Steed" was a popular sentimental poem by Caroline Norton (1808–1877).

which were still open. Before a curtain, over which the words *Café Chantant* were written in coloured lamps, two men were counting money on a salver. I listened to the fall of the coins.

Remembering with difficulty why I had come I went over to one of the stalls and examined porcelain vases and flowered tea-sets. At the door of the stall a young lady was talking and laughing with two young gentlemen. I remarked their English accents and listened vaguely to their conversation.

—O, I never said such a thing!

—O, but you did!

30 —O, but I didn't!

—Didn't she say that?

—Yes! I heard her.

—O, there's a . . . fib!

Observing me the young lady came over and asked me did I wish to buy anything. The tone of her voice was not encouraging; she seemed to have spoken to me out of a sense of duty. I looked humbly at the great jars that stood like eastern guards at either side of the dark entrance to the stall and murmured:

35 —No, thank you.

The young lady changed the position of one of the vases and went back to the two young men. They began to talk of the same subject. Once or twice the young lady glanced at me over her shoulder.

I lingered before her stall, though I knew my stay was useless, to make my interest in her wares seem the more real. Then I turned away slowly and walked down the middle of the bazaar. I allowed the two pennies to fall against the sixpence in my pocket. I heard a voice call from one end of the gallery that the light was out. The upper part of the hall was now completely dark.

Gazing up into the darkness I saw myself as a creature driven and derided by vanity; and my eyes burned with anguish and anger.

[1905]

Topics for Critical Thinking and Writing

1. Joyce wrote a novel called *A Portrait of the Artist as a Young Man.* Write an essay of about 500 words on "Araby" as a portrait of the artist as a boy.

2. In an essay of about 500 words, consider the role of images of darkness and blindness and what they reveal to us about "Araby" as a story of the fall from innocence into painful awareness.

3. How old, approximately, is the narrator of "Araby" at the time of the experience he describes? How old is he at the time he tells his story? On what evidence do you base your estimates?

4. The boy, apparently an only child, lives with an uncle and aunt, rather than with parents. Why do you suppose Joyce put him in this family setting rather than some other?

5. The story is rich in images of religion. This in itself is not surprising, for the story is set in Roman Catholic Ireland, but the religious images are not simply references to religious persons or objects. In an essay of 500 to 750 words, discuss how these images reveal the narrator's state of mind.

LANGSTON HUGHES

Langston Hughes (1902–1967), an African American writer, was born in Joplin, Missouri. He lived part of his youth in Mexico, spent a year at Columbia University, served as a merchant seaman, and worked in a Paris nightclub. After returning to the United States, he showed some of his poems to Dr. Alain Locke, a strong advocate of African American literature. Encouraged by Locke, Hughes continued to write, publishing fiction, plays, essays, and biographies; he also founded theaters, gave public readings, and was, in short, a highly visible presence.

One Friday Morning

The thrilling news did not come directly to Nancy Lee, but it came in little indirections that finally added themselves up to one tremendous fact: she had won the prize! But being a calm and quiet young lady, she did not say anything, although the whole high school buzzed with rumors, guesses, reportedly authentic announcements on the part of students who had no right to be making announcements at all—since no student really knew yet who had won this year's art scholarship.

But Nancy Lee's drawing was so good, her lines so sure, her colors so bright and harmonious, that certainly no other student in the senior art class at George Washington High was thought to have very much of a chance. Yet you never could tell. Last year nobody had expected Joe Williams to win the Artist Club scholarship with that funny modernistic water color he had done of the high-level bridge. In fact, it was hard to make out there was a bridge until you had looked at the picture a long time. Still, Joe Williams got the prize, was feted by the community's leading painters, club women, and society folks at a big banquet at the Park-Rose Hotel, and was now an award student at the Art School—the city's only art school.

Nancy Lee Johnson was a colored girl, a few years out of the South. But seldom did her high-school classmates think of her as colored. She was smart, pretty, and brown, and fitted in well with the life of the school. She stood high in scholarship, played a swell game of basketball, had taken part in the senior musical in a soft, velvety voice, and had never seemed to intrude or stand out, except in pleasant ways, so it was seldom even mentioned—her color.

Nancy Lee sometimes forgot she was colored herself. She liked her classmates and her school. Particularly she liked her art teacher, Miss Dietrich, the tall red-haired woman who taught her law and order in doing things; and the beauty of working step by step until a job is done; a picture finished; a design created; or a block print carved out of nothing but an idea and a smooth square of linoleum, inked, proofs made, and finally put down on paper—clean, sharp, beautiful, individual, unlike any other in the world, thus making the paper have a meaning nobody else could give it except Nancy Lee. That was the wonderful thing about true creation. You made something nobody else on earth could make—but you.

5   Miss Dietrich was the kind of teacher who brought out the best in her students—but their own best, not anybody else's copied best. For anybody else's best, great though it might be, even Michelangelo's, wasn't enough to please Miss Dietrich, dealing with the creative impulses of young men and women living in an American city in the Middle West, and being American.

Nancy Lee was proud of being American, a Negro American with blood out of Africa a long time ago, too many generations back to count. But her parents had taught her the beauties of Africa, its strength, its song, its mighty rivers, its early smelting of iron, its building of the pyramids, and its ancient and important civilizations. And Miss Dietrich had discovered for her the sharp and humorous lines of African sculpture, Benin, Congo, Makonde. Nancy Lee's father was a mail carrier, her mother a social worker in a city settlement house. Both parents had been to Negro colleges in the South. And her mother had gotten a further degree in social work from a Northern university. Her parents were, like most Americans, simple, ordinary people who had worked hard and steadily for their education. Now they were trying to make it easier for Nancy Lee to achieve learning than it had been for them. They would be very happy when they heard of the award to their daughter—yet Nancy did not tell them. To surprise them would be better. Besides, there had been a promise.

Casually, one day, Miss Dietrich asked Nancy Lee what color frame she thought would be best on her picture. That had been the first inkling.

"Blue," Nancy Lee said. Although the picture had been entered in the Artist Club contest a month ago, Nancy Lee did not hesitate in her choice of a color for the possible frame, since she could still see her picture clearly in her mind's eye—for that picture waiting for the blue frame had come out of her soul, her own life, and had bloomed into miraculous being with Miss Dietrich's help. It was, she knew, the best water color she had painted in her four years as a high-school art student, and she was glad she had made something Miss Dietrich liked well enough to permit her to enter in the contest before she graduated.

It was not a modernistic picture in the sense that you had to look at it a long time to understand what it meant. It was just a simple scene in the city park on a spring day, with the trees still leaflessly lacy against the sky, the new grass fresh and green, a flag on a tall pole in the center, children playing, and an old Negro woman sitting on a bench with her head turned. A lot for one picture, to be sure, but it was not there in heavy and final detail like a calendar. Its charm was that everything was light and airy, happy like spring, with a lot of blue sky; paper-white clouds, and air showing through. You could tell that the old Negro woman was looking at the flag, and that the flag was proud in the spring breeze, and that the breeze helped to make the children's dresses billow as they played.

10   Miss Dietrich had taught Nancy Lee how to paint spring, people, and a breeze on what was only a plain white piece of paper from the supply closet. But Miss Dietrich had not said make it like any other spring-people-breeze ever seen before. She let it remain Nancy Lee's own. That is how the old Negro woman happened to be there looking at the flag—for in her mind the flag, the spring, and the woman formed a kind of triangle holding a dream Nancy Lee wanted to express. White stars on a blue field, spring, children, ever-growing life, and an old woman. Would the judges at the Artist Club like it?

One wet, rainy April afternoon Miss O'Shay, the girls' vice-principal, sent for Nancy Lee to stop by her office as school closed. Pupils without umbrellas or raincoats were clustered in doorways, hoping to make it home between showers. Outside the skies were gray. Nancy Lee's thoughts were suddenly gray, too.

She did not think she had done anything wrong, yet that tight little knot came in her throat just the same as she approached Miss O'Shay's door. Perhaps she had banged her locker too often and too hard. Perhaps the note in French she had written to Sallie halfway across the study hall just for fun had never gotten to Sallie but into Miss O'Shay's hands instead. Or maybe she was failing in some subject and wouldn't be allowed to graduate. Chemistry! A pang went through the pit of her stomach.

She knocked on Miss O'Shay's door. That familiarly solid and competent voice said, "Come in."

Miss O'Shay had a way of making you feel welcome, even if you came to be expelled.

15 "Sit down, Nancy Lee Johnson," said Miss O'Shay. "I have something to tell you." Nancy Lee sat down. "But I must ask you to promise not to tell anyone yet."

"I won't, Miss O'Shay," Nancy Lee said, wondering what on earth the principal had to say to her.

"You are about to graduate," Miss O'Shay said. "And we shall miss you. You have been an excellent student, Nancy, and you will not be without honors on the senior list, as I am sure you know."

At that point there was a light knock on the door. Miss O'Shay called out, "Come in," and Miss Dietrich entered. "May I be a part of this, too?" she asked, tall and smiling.

"Of course," Miss O'Shay said. "I was just telling Nancy Lee what we thought of her. But I hadn't gotten around to giving her the news. Perhaps, Miss Dietrich, you'd like to tell her yourself."

20 Miss Dietrich was always direct. "Nancy Lee," she said, "your picture has won the Artist Club scholarship."

The slender brown girl's eyes widened, her heart jumped, then her throat tightened again. She tried to smile, but instead tears came to her eyes.

"Dear Nancy Lee," Miss O'Shay said, "we are so happy for you." The elderly white woman took her hand and shook it warmly while Miss Dietrich beamed with pride.

Nancy Lee must have danced all the way home. She never remembered quite how she got there through the rain. She hoped she had been dignified. But certainly she hadn't stopped to tell anybody her secret on the way. Raindrops, smiles, and tears mingled on her brown cheeks. She hoped her mother hadn't yet gotten home and that the house was empty. She wanted to have time to calm down and look natural before she had to see anyone. She didn't want to be bursting with excitement—having a secret to contain.

Miss O'Shay's calling her to the office had been in the nature of a preparation and a warning. The kind, elderly vice-principal said she did not believe in catching young ladies unawares, even with honors, so she wished her to know about the coming award. In making acceptance speeches she wanted her to be calm, prepared, not nervous, overcome, and frightened. So Nancy Lee was asked to think what she would say when the scholarship was conferred upon her a few days hence, both at the Friday morning high-school assembly hour, when the announcement would be made, and at the evening banquet of the Artist Club. Nancy Lee promised the vice-principal to think calmly about what she would say.

25 Miss Dietrich had then asked for some facts about her parents, her background, and her life, since such material would probably be desired for the papers. Nancy Lee had told her how, six years before, they had come up from the Deep South, her father having been successful in achieving a transfer from the one post office to another, a thing he had long sought in order to give Nancy Lee a chance to go to school in the North. Now they lived in a modest Negro neighborhood, went to see the best plays when they came to town, and had been saving to send Nancy Lee to art school, in case she were permitted to enter. But the scholarship would help a great deal, for they were not rich people.

"Now Mother can have a new coat next winter," Nancy Lee thought, "because my tuition will all be covered for the first year. And once in art school, there are other scholarships I can win."

Dreams began to dance through her head, plans and ambitions, beauties she would create for herself, her parents, and the Negro people—for Nancy Lee possessed a deep and reverent race pride. She could see the old woman in her picture (really her grandmother in the South) lifting her head to the bright stars on the flag in the distance. A Negro in America! Often hurt, discriminated against, sometimes lynched—but always there were the stars on the blue body of the flag. Was there any other flag in the world that had so many stars? Nancy Lee thought deeply, but she could remember none in all the encyclopedias or geographies she had ever looked into.

"Hitch your wagon to a star," Nancy Lee thought, dancing home in the rain. "Who were our flag-makers?"

Friday morning came, the morning when the world would know—her high-school world, the newspaper world, her mother and dad. Dad could not be there at the assembly to hear the announcement, nor see her prize picture displayed on the stage, nor to listen to Nancy Lee's little speech of acceptance, but Mother would be able to come, although Mother was much puzzled as to why Nancy Lee was so insistent she be at school on that particular Friday morning.

30   When something is happening, something new and fine, something that will change your very life, it is hard to go to sleep at night for thinking about it, and hard to keep your heart from pounding, or a strange little knot of joy from gathering in your throat. Nancy Lee had taken her bath, brushed her hair until it glowed, and had gone to bed thinking about the next day, the big day, when before three thousand students, she would be the one student honored, her painting the one painting to be acclaimed as the best of the year from all the art classes of the city. Her short speech of gratitude was ready. She went over it in her mind, not word for word (because she didn't want it to sound as if she had learned it by heart), but she let the thoughts flow simply and sincerely through her consciousness many times.

When the president of the Artist Club presented her with the medal and scroll of the scholarship award, she would say:

"Judges and members of the Artist Club. I want to thank you for this award that means so much to me personally and through me to my people, the colored people of this city, who, sometimes, are discouraged and bewildered, thinking that color and poverty are against them. I accept this award with gratitude and pride, not for myself alone, but for my race that believes in American opportunity and American fairness—and the bright stars in our flag. I thank Miss Dietrich and the teachers who made it possible for me to have the knowledge and training that lie behind this honor you have conferred upon my painting. When I came here from the South a few years ago, I was not sure how you would receive me. You received me well. You have given me a chance and helped me along the road I wanted to follow. I suppose the judges know that every week here at assembly the students of this school pledge allegiance to the flag. I shall try to be worthy of that pledge, and of the help and friendship and understanding of my fellow citizens of whatever race or creed, and of our American dream of 'Liberty and justice for all'!"

That would be her response before the students in the morning. How proud and happy the Negro pupils would be, perhaps almost as proud as they were of the one colored star on the football team. Her mother would probably cry with happiness. Thus Nancy Lee went to sleep dreaming of a wonderful tomorrow.

The bright sunlight of an April morning woke her. There was breakfast with her parents—their half-amused and puzzled faces across the table, wondering what could be this secret that made her eyes so bright. The swift walk to school; the clock in the tower almost nine; hundreds of pupils streaming into the long, rambling old building that was the city's largest high school; the sudden quiet of the homeroom after the bell rang; then the teacher opening her record book to call the roll. But just before she began, she looked across the room until her eyes located Nancy Lee.

35   "Nancy," she said, "Miss O'Shay would like to see you in her office, please."

Nancy Lee rose and went out while the names were being called and the word *present* added its period to each name. Perhaps, Nancy Lee thought, the reporters from the papers had already come. Maybe they wanted to take her picture before assembly, which wasn't until ten o'clock. (Last year they had had the photograph of the winner of the award in the morning papers as soon as the announcement had been made.)

Nancy Lee knocked at Miss O'Shay's door.

"Come in."

The vice-principal stood at her desk. There was no one else in the room. It was very quiet.

40   "Sit down, Nancy Lee," she said. Miss O'Shay did not smile. There was a long pause. The seconds went by slowly. "I do not know how to tell you what I have to say," the elderly woman began, her eyes on the papers on her desk. "I am indignant and ashamed for myself and for this city." Then she lifted her eyes and looked at Nancy Lee in the neat blue dress, sitting there before her. "You are not to receive the scholarship this morning."

Outside in the hall the electric bells announcing the first period rang, loud and interminably long. Miss O'Shay remained silent. To the brown girl there in the chair, the room grew suddenly smaller, smaller, smaller, and there was no air. She could not speak.

Miss O'Shay said, "When the committee learned that you were colored, they changed their plans."

Still Nancy Lee said nothing, for there was no air to give breath to her lungs.

"Here is the letter from the committee, Nancy Lee." Miss O'Shay picked it up and read the final paragraph to her.

45   "'It seems to us wiser to arbitrarily rotate the award among the various high schools of the city from now on. And especially in this case since the student chosen happens to be colored, a circumstance which unfortunately, had we known, might have prevented this embarrassment. But there have never been any Negro students in the local art school, and the presence of one there might create difficulties for all concerned. We have high regard for the quality of Nancy Lee Johnson's talent, but we do not feel it would be fair to honor it with the Artist Club award.'" Miss O'Shay paused. She put the letter down.

"Nancy Lee, I am very sorry to have to give you this message."

"But my speech," Nancy Lee said, "was about. . . ." The words stuck in her throat. ". . . about America. . . ."

Miss O'Shay had risen; she turned her back and stood looking out the window at the spring tulips in the school yard.

"I thought, since the award would be made at assembly right after our oath of allegiance," the words tumbled almost hysterically from Nancy Lee's throat now, "I would put part of the flag salute in my speech. You know, Miss O'Shay, that part about 'liberty and justice for all.'"

50   "I know," said Miss O'Shay, slowly facing the room again. "But America is only what we who believe in it make it. I am Irish. You may not know, Nancy Lee, but years ago we were called the dirty Irish, and mobs rioted against us in the big cities, and we were invited to go back where we came from. But we didn't go. And we didn't give up, because we believed in the American dream, and in our power to make that dream come true. Difficulties, yes. Mountains to climb, yes. Discouragements to face, yes. Democracy to make, yes. That is it, Nancy Lee! We still have in this world of ours democracy to *make*. You and I, Nancy Lee. But the premise and the base are here, the lines of the Declaration of Independence and the words of Lincoln are here, and the stars in our flag. Those who deny you this scholarship do not know the meaning of those stars, but it's up to us to make them know. As a teacher in the public schools of this city, I myself will go before the school board and ask them to remove from our system the offer of any prizes or awards denied to any student because of race or color."

Suddenly Miss O'Shay stopped speaking. Her clear, clear blue eyes looked into those of the girl before her. The woman's eyes were full of strength and courage. "Lift up your head, Nancy Lee, and smile at me."

Miss O'Shay stood against the open window with the green lawn and the tulips beyond, the sunlight tangled in her gray hair, her voice an electric flow of strength to the hurt spirit of Nancy Lee. The Abolitionists who believed in freedom when there was slavery must have been like that. The first white teachers who went into the Deep South to teach the freed slaves must have been like that. All those who stand against ignorance, narrowness, hate, and mud on stars must be like that.

Nancy Lee lifted her head and smiled. The bell for assembly rang. She went through the long hall filled with students, toward the auditorium.

"There will be other awards," Nancy Lee thought. "There're schools in other cities. This won't keep me down. But when I'm a woman, I'll fight to see that these things don't happen to other girls as this has happened to me. And men and women like Miss O'Shay will help me."

55   She took her seat among the seniors. The doors of the auditorium closed. As the principal came onto the platform, the students rose and turned their eyes to the flag on the stage.

One hand went to the heart, the other outstretched toward the flag. Three thousand voices spoke. Among them was the voice of a dark girl whose cheeks were suddenly wet with tears, ". . . one nation indivisible, with liberty and justice for all."

"That is the land we must make," she thought.

[1941]

Topics for Critical Thinking and Writing

1. The third paragraph begins: "Nancy Lee Johnson was a colored girl. . . ." How would your response to the opening of the story change if this paragraph were placed at the very beginning?

2. Nancy Lee takes pride in her identity as both a "Negro" and an "American." How does she define and understand each of these terms? Does she perceive them to be at all at odds with one another? Is she admirable in her convictions, or is she simply naive?

3. This is a story about racism, but it is also a study (and an affirmation) of American ideals and principles. What is your response to Miss O'Shay's inspiring words to Nancy Lee at the end of the story? What is Nancy Lee's response to them, and your response to her? Does Hughes succeed in making us believe in, and accept, Nancy Lee's feelings at the conclusion?

ISAAC BASHEVIS SINGER

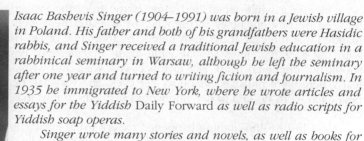

Isaac Bashevis Singer (1904–1991) was born in a Jewish village in Poland. His father and both of his grandfathers were Hasidic rabbis, and Singer received a traditional Jewish education in a rabbinical seminary in Warsaw, although he left the seminary after one year and turned to writing fiction and journalism. In 1935 he immigrated to New York, where he wrote articles and essays for the Yiddish Daily Forward *as well as radio scripts for Yiddish soap operas.*

Singer wrote many stories and novels, as well as books for juveniles and four autobiographies (including Lost in America, *1981). In 1978 his work received world attention when he was awarded the Nobel Prize in Literature.*

The Son from America

The village of Lentshin was tiny—a sandy marketplace where the peasants of the area met once a week. It was surrounded by little huts with thatched roofs or shingles green with moss. The chimneys looked like pots. Between the huts there were fields, where the owners planted vegetables or pastured their goats.

In the smallest of these huts lived old Berl, a man in his eighties, and his wife, who was called Berlcha (wife of Berl). Old Berl was one of the Jews who had been driven from their villages in Russia and had settled in Poland. In Lentshin, they mocked the mistakes he made while praying aloud. He spoke with a sharp "r." He was short, broad-shouldered, and had a small white beard, and summer and winter he wore a sheepskin hat, a padded cotton jacket, and stout boots. He walked slowly, shuffling his feet. He had a half acre of field, a cow, a goat, and chickens.

The couple had a son, Samuel, who had gone to America forty years ago. It was said in Lentshin that he became a millionaire there. Every month, the Lentshin letter carrier brought old Berl a money order and a letter that no one could read because many of the words were English. How much money Samuel sent his parents remained a secret. Three times a year, Berl and his wife went on foot to Zakroczym and cashed the money orders there. But they never seemed to use the money. What for? The garden, the cow, and the goat provided most of their needs. Besides, Berlcha sold chickens and eggs, and from these there was enough to buy flour for bread.

No one cared to know where Berl kept the money that his son sent him. There were no thieves in Lentshin. The hut consisted of one room, which contained all their belongings: the table, the shelf for meat, the shelf for milk foods, the two beds, and the clay oven. Sometimes the chickens roosted in the woodshed and sometimes, when it was cold, in a coop near the oven. The goat, too, found shelter inside when the weather was bad. The more prosperous villages had kerosene lamps, but Berl and his wife did not believe in newfangled gadgets. What was wrong with a wick in a dish of oil? Only for the Sabbath would Berlcha buy three tallow candles at the store. In summer, the couple got up at sunrise and retired with the chickens. In the long winter evenings, Berlcha spun flax at her spinning wheel and Berl sat beside her in the silence of those who enjoy their rest.

5   Once in a while when Berl came home from the synagogue after evening prayers, he brought news to his wife. In Warsaw there were strikers who demanded that the czar abdicate. A heretic by the name of Dr. Herzl[1] had come up with the idea that Jews should settle again in Palestine. Berlcha listened and shook her bonneted head. Her face was yellowish and wrinkled like a cabbage leaf. There were bluish sacks under her eyes. She was half deaf. Berl had to repeat each word he said to her. She would say, "The things that happen in the big cities!"

Here in Lentshin nothing happened except usual events: a cow gave birth to a calf, a young couple had a circumcision party, or a girl was born and there was no party. Occasionally, someone died. Lentshin had no cemetery, and the corpse had to be taken to Zakroczym. Actually, Lentshin had become a village with few young people. The young men left for Zakroczym, for Nowy Dwor, for Warsaw, and sometimes for the United States. Like Samuel's, their letters were illegible, the Yiddish mixed with the languages of the countries where they were now living. They sent photographs in which the men wore top hats and the women fancy dresses like squiresses.

Berl and Berlcha also received such photographs. But their eyes were failing and neither he nor she had glasses. They could barely make out the pictures. Samuel had sons and daughters with gentile names—and grandchildren who had married and had their own offspring. Their names were so strange that Berl and Berlcha could never remember them. But what difference do names make? America was far, far away on the other side of the ocean, at the edge of the world. A Talmud[2] teacher who came to Lentshin had said that Americans walked with their heads down and their feet up. Berl and Berlcha could not grasp this. How was it possible? But since the teacher said so it must be true. Berlcha pondered for some time and then she said, "One can get accustomed to everything."

And so it remained. From too much thinking—God forbid—one may lose one's wits.

One Friday morning, when Berlcha was kneading the dough for the Sabbath loaves, the door opened and a nobleman entered. He was so tall that he had to bend down to get through the door. He wore a beaver hat and a cloak bordered

---

[1]**Dr. Herzl** Theodore Herzl (1860–1904), the founder of Zionism.   [2]**Talmud** the collection of ancient rabbinic writings that constitute the basis of traditional Judaism.

with fur. He was followed by Chazkel, the coachman from Zakroczym, who carried two leather valises with brass locks. In astonishment Berlcha raised her eyes.

10   The nobleman looked around and said to the coachman in Yiddish, "Here it is." He took out a silver ruble and paid him. The coachman tried to hand him change but he said, "You can go now."

When the coachman closed the door, the nobleman said, "Mother, it's me, your son Samuel—Sam."

Berlcha heard the words and her legs grew numb. Her hands, to which pieces of dough were sticking, lost their power. The nobleman hugged her, kissed her forehead, both her cheeks. Berlcha began to cackle like a hen, "My son!" At that moment Berl came in from the woodshed, his arms piled with logs. The goat followed him. When he saw a nobleman kissing his wife, Berl dropped the wood and exclaimed, "What is this?"

The nobleman let go of Berlcha and embraced Berl. "Father!"

For a long time Berl was unable to utter a sound. He wanted to recite holy words that he had read in the Yiddish Bible, but he could remember nothing. Then he asked, "Are you Samuel?"

15   "Yes, Father, I am Samuel."

"Well, peace be with you." Berl grasped his son's hand. He was still not sure that he was not being fooled. Samuel wasn't as tall and heavy as this man, but then Berl reminded himself that Samuel was only fifteen years old when he had left home. He must have grown in that faraway country. Berl asked, "Why didn't you let us know that you were coming?"

"Didn't you receive my cable?" Samuel asked.

Berl did not know what a cable was.

Berlcha had scraped the dough from her hands and enfolded her son. He kissed her again and asked, "Mother, didn't you receive a cable?"

20   "What? If I lived to see this, I am happy to die," Berlcha said, amazed by her own words. Berl, too, was amazed. These were just the words he would have said earlier if he had been able to remember. After a while Berl came to himself and said, "Pescha, you will have to make a double Sabbath pudding in addition to the stew."

It was years since Berl had called Berlcha by her given name. When he wanted to address her, he would say, "Listen," or "Say." It is the young or those from the big cities who call a wife by her name. Only now did Berlcha begin to cry. Yellow tears ran from her eyes, and everything became dim. Then she called out, "It's Friday—I have to prepare for the Sabbath." Yes, she had to knead the dough and braid the loaves. With such a guest, she had to make a larger Sabbath stew. The winter day is short and she must hurry.

Her son understood what was worrying her, because he said, "Mother, I will help you."

Berlcha wanted to laugh, but a choked sob came out. "What are you saying? God forbid."

The nobleman took off his cloak and jacket and remained in his vest, on which hung a solid-gold watch chain. He rolled up his sleeves and came to the trough. "Mother, I was a baker for many years in New York," he said, and he began to knead the dough.

25   "What! You are my darling son who will say Kaddish[3] for me." She wept raspingly. Her strength left her, and she slumped onto the bed.

---

[3]**Kaddish** the prayer for the dead.

Berl said, "Women will always be women." And he went to the shed to get more wood. The goat sat down near the oven; she gazed with surprise at this strange man—his height and his bizarre clothes.

The neighbors had heard the good news that Berl's son had arrived from America and they came to greet him. The women began to help Berlcha prepare for the Sabbath. Some laughed, some cried. The room was full of people, as at a wedding. They asked Berl's son, "What is new in America?" And Berl's son answered, "America is all right."

"Do Jews make a living?"

"One eats white bread there on weekdays."[4]

30   "Do they remain Jews?"

"I am not a gentile."

After Berlcha blessed the candles, father and son went to the little synagogue across the street. A new snow had fallen. The son took large steps, but Berl warned him, "Slow down."

In the synagogue the Jews recited "Let Us Exult" and "Come, My Groom." All the time, the snow outside kept falling. After prayers, when Berl and Samuel left the Holy Place, the village was unrecognizable. Everything was covered in snow. One could see only the contours of the roofs and the candles in the windows. Samuel said, "Nothing has changed here."

Berlcha had prepared gefilte fish, chicken soup with rice, meat, carrot stew. Berl recited the benediction over a glass of ritual wine. The family ate and drank, and when it grew quiet for a while one could hear the chirping of the house cricket. The son talked a lot, but Berl and Berlcha understood little. His Yiddish was different and contained foreign words.

35   After the final blessing Samuel asked, "Father, what did you do with all the money I sent you?"

Berl raised his white brows. "It's here."

"Didn't you put it in a bank?"

"There is no bank in Lentshin."

"Where do you keep it?"

40   Berl hesitated. "One is not allowed to touch money on the Sabbath but I will show you." He crouched beside the bed and began to shove something heavy. A boot appeared. Its top was stuffed with straw. Berl removed the straw and the son saw that the boot was full of gold coins. He lifted it.

"Father, this is a treasure!" he called out.

"Well."

"Why didn't you spend it?"

"On what? Thank God, we have everything."

45   "Why didn't you travel somewhere?"

"Where to? This is our home."

The son asked one question after the other, but Berl's answer was always the same: they wanted for nothing. The garden, the cow, the goat, the chickens provided them with all they needed. The son said, "If thieves knew about this, your lives wouldn't be safe."

"There are no thieves here."

---

[4]**One eats white bread there on weekdays** In the poor communities of Europe, white bread was a luxury reserved for holidays such as the Sabbath.

"What will happen to the money?"

50   "You take it."

Slowly, Berl and Berlcha grew accustomed to their son and his American Yiddish. Berlcha could hear him better now. She even recognized his voice. He was saying, "Perhaps we should build a larger synagogue."

"The synagogue is big enough," Berl replied.

"Perhaps a home for old people."

"No one sleeps in the street."

55   The next day after the Sabbath meal was eaten, a gentile from Zakroczym brought a paper—it was the cable. Berl and Berlcha lay down for a nap. They soon began to snore. The goat, too, dozed off. The son put on his cloak and his hat and went for a walk. He strode with his long legs across the marketplace. He stretched out a hand and touched a roof. He wanted to smoke a cigar, but he remembered it was forbidden on the Sabbath. He had a desire to talk to someone, but it seemed that the whole of Lentshin was asleep. He entered the synagogue. An old man was sitting there, reciting psalms. Samuel asked, "Are you praying?"

"What else is there to do when one gets old?"

"Do you make a living?"

The old man did not understand the meaning of those words. He smiled, showing his empty gums, and then he said, "If God gives health, one keeps on living."

Samuel returned home. Dusk had fallen. Berl went to the synagogue for the evening prayers and the son remained with his mother. The room was filled with shadows.

60   Berlcha began to recite in a solemn singsong, "God of Abraham, Isaac, and Jacob, defend the poor people of Israel and Thy name. The Holy Sabbath is departing; the welcome week is coming to us. Let it be one of health, wealth, and good deeds."

"Mother, you don't need to pray for wealth," Samuel said. "You are wealthy already."

Berlcha did not hear—or pretended not to. Her face had turned into a cluster of shadows.

In the twilight Samuel put his hand into his jacket pocket and touched his passport, his checkbook, his letters of credit. He had come here with big plans. He had a valise filled with presents for his parents. He wanted to bestow gifts on the village. He brought not only his own money but funds from the Lentshin Society in New York, which had organized a ball for the benefit of the village. But this village in the hinterland needed nothing. From the synagogue one could hear hoarse chanting. The cricket, silent all day, started again its chirping. Berlcha began to sway and utter holy rhymes inherited from mothers and grandmothers:

> Thy holy sheep
> In mercy keep,
> In Torah[5] good deeds;
> Provide for all their needs,
> Shoes, clothes, and bread
> And the Messiah's tread.

[1973]

[5]**Torah** Jewish teachings, especially the first five books of the Hebrew Bible.

Topics for Critical Thinking and Writing

1. What is your attitude toward Berl and Berlcha? Admiration? Pity? Or what? (Of course you need not limit your answer to a single word. You may find that your response is complex.) What is your attitude toward Samuel?
2. Compare Samuel's values with those of his parents. What resemblances do you find? What differences?

POETRY

WILLIAM BLAKE

William Blake (1757–1827) was born in London and at 14 was apprenticed for seven years to an engraver. A Christian visionary poet, he made his living by giving drawing lessons and by illustrating books, including his own Songs of Innocence *(1789) and* Songs of Experience *(1794). These two books represent, he said, "two contrary states of the human soul." ("Infant Joy" comes from* Innocence, *"Infant Sorrow" and "The Echoing Green" come from* Experience.) *In 1809 Blake exhibited his art, but the show was a failure. Not until he was in his sixties, when he stopped writing poetry, did he achieve any public recognition—and then it was as a painter.*

Infant Joy

"I have no name,
I am but two days old."
What shall I call thee?
"I happy am,
Joy is my name."   5
Sweet joy befall thee!

Pretty joy!
Sweet joy but two days old,
Sweet joy I call thee;
Thou dost smile,   10
I sing the while—
Sweet joy befall thee.

[1789]

Infant Sorrow

My mother groand! my father wept.
Into the dangerous world I leapt,
Helpless, naked, piping loud;
Like a fiend hid in a cloud.   4

"Infant Joy" by William Blake, from *Songs of Innocence.* (By kind permission of the Provost and Scholars of King's College, Cambridge)

Struggling in my father's hands,
Striving against my swadling bands;
Bound and weary I thought best
To sulk upon my mother's breast.

8

[1794]

Topics for Critical Thinking and Writing

1. "Infant Joy" begins "I have no name," but by line 5 the infant says "Joy is my name." What does the mother reply? Does she know the infant's name?
2. In line 9 the mother says, "Sweet joy I call thee." Does the line suggest how the mother has learned the name? What is the child's response?

"Infant Sorrow" by William Blake, from *Songs of Innocence*. (By kind permission of the Provost and Scholars of King's College, Cambridge)

3. In "Infant Sorrow," why is the infant sorrowful? What does the baby struggle against? Does "Like a fiend" suggest that it is inherently wicked and therefore should be repressed? Or does the adult world wickedly repress energy?

4. Why does the mother groan? Why does the father weep? Is the world "dangerous" to the infant in other than an obviously physical sense? To what degree are its parents its enemies? To what degree does the infant yield to them? In the last line, one might expect a newborn baby to nurse. What does this infant do?

5. Compare "Infant Joy" with "Infant Sorrow." What differences in sound do you hear? In "Infant Sorrow," for instance, look at lines 3, 5, 6, and 7. What repeated sounds do you hear?

The Echoing Green

The Sun does arise,
And make happy the skies;
The merry bells ring

To welcome the Spring;
The skylark and thrush,
The birds of the bush,
Sing louder around
To the bells' cheerful sound,
While our sports shall be seen
On the Echoing Green.   10

Old John, with white hair,
Does laugh away care,
Sitting under the oak,
Among the old folk.
They laugh at our play,   15
And soon they all say:
"Such, such were the joys
When we all, girls and boys,
In our youth time were seen
On the Echoing Green."   20

Till the little ones, weary,
No more can be merry;
The sun does descend,
And our sports have an end.
Round the laps of their mothers   25
Many sisters and brothers,
Like birds in their nest,
Are ready for rest,
And sport no more seen
On the darkening Green.   30

[1789]

Topics for Critical Thinking and Writing

1. Who speaks the poem? (Go through the poem, picking up the clues that identify the speaker.)
2. When does the poem begin? And when does it end?
3. What is a "green," and why in this poem does it "echo"?
4. Try writing a piece entitled "Such, such were the joys . . ." You may need to pretend to be a bit older than you are, but try to get down what really were the joys of your childhood.

GERARD MANLEY HOPKINS

Gerard Manley Hopkins (1844–1889) was born near London and was educated at Oxford, where he studied the classics. A convert from Anglicanism to Roman Catholicism, he was ordained a Jesuit priest in 1877. After serving as a parish priest and teacher, he was appointed Professor of Greek at the Catholic University in Dublin.

Hopkins published only a few poems during his lifetime, partly because he be-lieved that the pursuit of literary fame was incompatible with his vocation as a priest, and partly because he was aware that his highly individual style might puzzle readers.

Spring and Fall

To a Young Child

Márgarét áre you grièving
Over Goldengrove unleaving?
Leáves, líke the thíngs of mán, you
With your fresh thoughts care for, can you?
Ah! ás the héart grows older   5
It will come to such sights colder
By and by, nor spare a sigh
Though worlds of wanwood leafmeal lie;
And yet you will weep and know why.
Now no matter, child, the name: 10
Sórrow's springs áre the same.
Nor mouth had, no nor mind, expressed
What héart heárd of, ghost° guéssed:
It iś the blíght mán was bórn for,
It is Margaret you mourn for.   15

[1880]

13 **ghost** spirit.

Topics for Critical Thinking and Writing

1. What is the speaker's age? His tone? What is the relevance of the title to Margaret? What meanings are in "Fall"? Is there more than one meaning to "Spring"? (Notice especially the title and line 11.)
2. What is meant by Margaret's "fresh thoughts" (line 4)? Paraphrase lines 3–4 and lines 12–13.
3. "Wanwood" and "leafmeal" are words coined by Hopkins. What are their suggestions?
4. What does "blight" mean in line 14?
5. Why is it not contradictory for the speaker to say that Margaret weeps for herself (line 15) after saying that she weeps for "Goldengrove unleaving" (line 2)?

A. E. HOUSMAN

Alfred Edward Housman (1859–1936) was born in rural Shropshire, England, and educated in the classics and philosophy at Oxford University. Although he was a brilliant student, his final examination was unexpectedly weak—in fact, he failed—and he did not receive the academic appointment that he had anticipated. He began working as a civil servant at the British Patent Office, but in his spare time he wrote scholarly articles on Latin literature, and these writings in 1892 won him an appointment as Professor of Latin at the University of London. In 1911 he was appointed to Cambridge. During his lifetime he published (in addition to his scholarly writings) only two thin books of poetry, A Shropshire Lad *(1898) and* Last Poems *(1922), and a highly readable lecture called* The Name and Nature of Poetry *(1933). After his death a third book of poems,* More Poems *(1936), was published.*

When I Was One-and-Twenty

When I was one-and-twenty
I heard a wise man say,
"Give crowns and pounds and guineas
But not your heart away;
Give pearls away and rubies   5
But keep your fancy free."
But I was one-and-twenty,
No use to talk to me.

When I was one-and-twenty
I heard him say again,   10
"The heart out of the bosom
Was never given in vain;
'Tis paid with sighs a plenty
And sold for endless rue."
And I am two-and-twenty,   15
And oh, 'tis true, 'tis true.

[1896]

Topics for Critical Thinking and Writing

1. In line 6, what does "fancy" mean?
2. In your own words, what is the advice of the "wise man"?
3. In a paragraph, indicate what you think the speaker's attitude is toward himself. In a second paragraph, indicate what *your* attitude toward him is.

E. E. CUMMINGS

Edwin Estlin Cummings (1894–1962), who used the pen name e. e. cummings, grew up in Cambridge, Massachusetts, and was graduated from Harvard, where he became interested in modern literature and art, especially in the movements called Cubism and Futurism. His father, a conservative clergyman and a professor at Harvard, seems to have been baffled by the youth's interests, but Cummings's mother encouraged his artistic activities, including unconventional punctuation.

Politically liberal in his youth, Cummings became more conservative after a visit to Russia in 1931, but early and late his work emphasizes individuality and freedom of expression.

in Just-

in Just-
spring   when the world is mud-
luscious the little
lame balloonman

whistles   far   and wee   5

and eddieandbill come
running from marbles and
piracies and it's
spring

when the world is puddle-wonderful   10

the queer
old balloonman whistles
far   and   wee
and bettyandisbel come dancing

from hop-scotch and jump-rope and   15

it's
spring
and
      the
            goat-footed   20

balloonMan   whistles
far
and
wee

[1920]

Topics for Critical Thinking and Writing

1. Why "eddieandbill" and "bettyandisbel" rather than "eddie and bill" and "betty and isabel"? And why not "eddie and betty," and "bill and isabel"?
2. What are some effects that Cummings may be getting at by his unusual arrangement of words on the page? Compare, for instance, the physical appearance of "Whistles far and wee" in line 5 with the appearance of the same words in lines 12–13 and 21–24.
3. Because the balloonman is "lame" (line 4) or "goat-footed" (line 20), many readers find an allusion to the Greek god Pan, the goat-footed god of woods, fields, and flocks, and the inventor of a primitive wind instrument consisting of a series of reeds, "Pan's pipes." (If you are unfamiliar with Pan, consult an encyclopedia or a guide to mythology.) Do you agree that Cummings is alluding to Pan? If so, what is the point of the allusion?

LOUISE GLÜCK

Louise Glück (b. 1943) was born in New York City and attended Sarah Lawrence College and Columbia University. She has taught at Goddard College in Vermont and at Warren Wilson College in North Carolina. Her volume of poems, The Triumph of Achilles *(1985), won the National Book Critics Circle Award for poetry.*

The School Children

The children go forward with their little satchels.
And all morning the mothers have labored
to gather the late apples, red and gold,
like words of another language.

And on the other shore   5
are those who wait behind great desks
to receive these offerings.

How orderly they are—the nails
on which the children hang
their overcoats of blue or yellow wool.   10

And the teachers shall instruct them in silence
and the mothers shall scour the orchards for a way out,
drawing to themselves the gray limbs of the fruit trees
bearing so little ammunition.

[1975]

Topics for Critical Thinking and Writing

1. Which words in the poem present a cute picture-postcard view of small children going to school?
2. Which words undercut this happy scene?
3. In the last stanza we read that "the teachers shall instruct" and "the mothers shall scour." What, if anything, is changed if we substitute "will" for "shall"?

Gretel in Darkness

This is the world we wanted. All who would have seen us dead
Are dead. I hear the witch's cry
Break in the moonlight through a sheet of sugar: God rewards.
Her tongue shrivels into gas. . . .

                    Now, far from women's arms   5
And memory of women, in our father's hut

We sleep, are never hungry.
Why do I not forget?
My father bars the door, bars harm
From this house, and it is years.   10

No one remembers. Even you, my brother,
Summer afternoons you look at me as though you meant
To leave, as though it never happened. But I killed for you.
I see armed firs, the spires of that gleaming kiln come back, come back—
Nights I turn to you to hold me but you are not there.   15
Am I alone? Spies
Hiss in the stillness, Hansel we are there still, and it is real, real,
That black forest, and the fire in earnest.

[1975]

Topics for Critical Thinking and Writing

1. How, as the poem develops, is the first sentence of the poem modified? Is this the world "we" wanted? What does Gretel believe that Hansel wants?
2. In stanza 3 Gretel says

    But I killed for you.
    I see . . . the spires of that gleaming kiln come back, come back—

    Whether or not you know the story from *Grimm's Fairy Tales,* how do you understand Gretel's plight?
3. Why is the poem called "Gretel in Darkness"? What does the poem seem to tell us about how men and women face danger?

DRAMA

Case Study: Writing about Shakespeare's Hamlet

This case study contains (in addition to illustrations of the original texts of *Hamlet,* the Elizabethan theater, and modern productions) the following material:

1. A note on the Elizabethan theater
2. A note on *Hamlet* on the stage
3. A note on the text of *Hamlet*
4. The text of *Hamlet*
5. A Freudian interpretation by Ernest Jones
6. Anne Barton's general comments on the play
7. Stanley Wells's analysis of the first soliloquy
8. Elaine Showalter's discussion of Ophelia
9. Claire Bloom's comments on her performance as Gertrude, in the BBC TV production
10. Bernice W. Kliman review of the BBC TV production of *Hamlet* (1980)
11. Stanley Kauffmann's review of Kenneth Branagh's film (1996)
12. A review by a student, Will Saretta, of Branagh's *Hamlet*

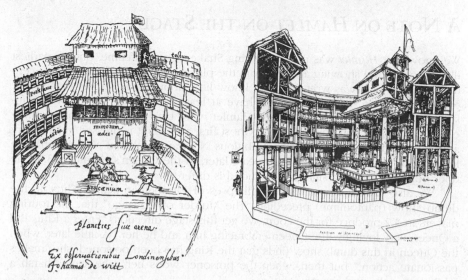

Left, Johannes de Witt, a Continental visitor to London, made a drawing of the Swan Theater in about the year 1596. The original drawing is lost; this is Arend van Buchel's copy of it. (Copyright the British Museum.) *Right,* C. Walter Hodges's drawing (1965) of an Elizabethan playhouse. (Courtesy C. Walter Hodges)

A NOTE ON THE ELIZABETHAN THEATER

Shakespeare's theater was wooden, round or polygonal (the Chorus in *Henry V* calls it a "wooden O"). About eight hundred spectators could stand in the yard in front of—and perhaps along the two sides of—the stage that jutted from the rear wall, and another fifteen hundred or so spectators could sit in the three roofed galleries that ringed the stage.

That portion of the galleries that was above the rear of the stage was sometimes used by actors. For instance, in *The Tempest,* 3.3, a stage direction following line 17 mentions "Prospero on the top, invisible," that is, he is imagined to be invisible to the characters in the play.

Entry to the stage was normally gained by doors at the rear, but apparently on rare occasions use was made of a curtained alcove—or perhaps a booth—between the doors, which allowed characters to be "discovered" (revealed) as in the modern proscenium theater, which normally employs a curtain. Such "discovery" scenes are rare.

Although the theater as a whole was unroofed, the stage was protected by a roof, supported by two pillars. These could serve (by an act of imagination) as trees behind which actors might pretend to conceal themselves.

A performance was probably uninterrupted by intermissions or by long pauses for the changing of scenery; a group of characters leaves the stage, another enters, and if the locale has changed the new characters somehow tell us. (Modern editors customarily add indications of locales to help a reader, but it should be remembered that the action on the Elizabethan stage was continuous.)

A NOTE ON *HAMLET* ON THE STAGE

We know that *Hamlet* was popular during Shakespeare's lifetime, but the earliest illustration (1709) showing a scene from the play was engraved more than a century after the play was written, so we know little about what *Hamlet* looked like on Shakespeare's stage. Still, we do have at least some idea. We know, for instance, that at least in the first scene Hamlet wore black (he speaks of his "inky cloak"), and we know that when the Ghost first appears it is dressed in "the very armor he had on / When he the ambitious Norway combated" (1.1.64–65). We know, too, that when the Ghost appears later, in the Queen's chamber (3.4), he does not wear armor, a sign that his mood is different.

We also have a few tantalizing glimpses of Elizabethan acting. Thus, in the dumb show (pantomime) preceding "The Murder of Gonzago" that the touring players in 3.2 produce for the court, we get this stage direction: "Enter a King and a Queen very lovingly: the Queen embracing him and he her." A little later, when the Queen in this dumb show finds that the King has been poisoned, she "makes passionate action," but then, when the poisoner woos her, "she seems harsh a while but in the end accepts love."

We know something, too, of the sound effects. Possibly the play begins with the bell tolling twelve (in 1.1 Bernardo says, "'Tis now struck twelve"), and certainly in the first scene we hear the crowing of a cock, which causes the Ghost to depart. Later we hear the sound of drums, trumpets, and cannon when Claudius drinks toasts, and the play ends with the sound of cannon, when Fortinbras orders the soldiers to pay tribute to the dead Hamlet.

What about costumes? In their own day, Elizabethan plays were staged chiefly in contemporary dress—doublet (close-fitting jacket) and hose (tights) for the men, gowns of various sorts for the women (whose roles were played by boy actors)—though for classical plays such as *Julius Caesar* some attempt was made in the direction of ancient costume, at least for the major characters. The seventeenth and eighteenth centuries, too, staged the plays in the costume of the day, which of course was not Elizabethan. But in much of the nineteenth century, and in the first third of the twentieth, a strong sense that the plays were "Elizabethan" caused producers to use Elizabethan costumes, although these costumes—contemporary when the plays were first performed—now had become historical costume, marking the plays as of an age remote from our own. In 1925 Barry Jackson staged a modern-dress production in London, in an effort to emphasize the play's contemporary relevance. Today, productions tend to be in modern dress in the sense that they avoid Elizabethan costume. Usually, in an effort to add some color to the stage as well as some (but not a great) sense of remoteness, they use costumes of the nineteenth century, which allow for splendid gowns and for military uniforms with sashes.

Figure 1

Figure 1. "The Murder of Gonzago" in 3.2. Because this episode is a play-within-the-play, Shakespeare uses a distinctive form of verse (pairs of rhyming line, eight syllables to a line) that sets it off from the language of the rest of the play (chiefly prose, or unrhymed lines of ten syllables). The language, too, is different, for it is conspicuously old-fashioned (the sun is called "Phoebus' cart," the ocean is called "Neptune's salt wash"). In this modern-dress production done at Stratford, England, in 1975, Claudius wore a blue business suit and Fortinbras wore combat gear, but the characters in the play-within-the-play were masked, to emphasize their theatricality.

Figure 2

Figure 2. The "closet" scene, in 3.4. A line in the preceding scene specifically tells us that Hamlet is "going to his mother's closet." (In Elizabethan language, a "closet" is a private room, rather than a public room—for instance a room in which a monarch might pray, or relax, as opposed to an audience chamber in which he or she would engage in official actions.) In the twentieth century, at least as early as John Gielgud's production in New York in 1935, and probably in response to Freudian interpretations of the play, the Queen's closet has been fitted with a bed on which Hamlet and Gertrude tussle, and indeed the scene is often wrongly called "the bedroom scene." In this 1989 Royal Shakespeare Company production, with Mark Rylance as Hamlet, a ranting Hamlet (at the left) confronts Gertrude. The Ghost, unknown to Gertrude, sits on the bed, presumably seeking to protect her from Hamlet's assault. The setting was not realistic but expressionistic; that is, the curtains stirred and the lighting changed not because a physical wind was blowing or the sources of illumination were changing, but to express the characters' passions.

Figure 3

Figures 3 and 4 (p. 926). Hamlet meditates on death in the grave yard, in 5.1.
Both of these productions used costumes that suggested the late nineteenth century. Kenneth Branagh portrayed Hamlet in 1993 for The Royal Shakespeare Theatre. In the photograph showing Kevin Kline as Hamlet (New York Shakespeare Festival), Horatio is played by an African American. Other than plays by black authors, and a very few plays by whites about blacks (such as Eugene O'Neill's *The Emperor Jones*), there are few roles in drama expressly written for blacks. Shakespeare offers only three: Othello, Aaron (a Moor in *Titus Andronicus*), and the Prince of Morocco (in *The Merchant of Venice*). The few black actors who played other Shakespearean roles, such as the great Ira Aldridge who in the nineteenth century was known for his King Lear, performed the roles in whiteface. Since the 1980s, however, directors have engaged in open casting, using blacks (and Asians) in any and all roles, and not requiring white makeup.

Figure 4

A NOTE ON THE TEXT OF *HAMLET*

Shakespeare's *Hamlet* comes to us in three versions. The first, known as the First Quarto (Q1), was published in 1603. It is an illegitimate garbled version, perhaps derived from the memory of the actor who played Marcellus (this part is conspicuously more accurate than the rest of the play) in a short version of the play.

The second printed version (Q2), which appeared in 1604–1605, is almost twice as long as Q1; all in all, it is the best text we have, doubtless published (as Q1 was not) with the permission of Shakespeare's theatrical company.

The third printed version, in the First Folio (the collected edition of Shakespeare's plays, published in 1623), is also legitimate, but it seems to be an acting version, for it lacks some two hundred lines of Q2.

On the other hand, the Folio text includes some ninety lines not found in Q2.

Because Q2 is the longest version, giving us more of the play as Shakespeare conceived it than either of the other texts, it serves as the basic version for this text. Unfortunately, the printers of it often worked carelessly: Words and phrases are omitted, there are plain misreadings of what must have been in Shakespeare's manuscript, and speeches are sometimes wrongly assigned. It was therefore necessary to turn to the First Folio for many readings. It has been found useful, also, to divide the play into acts and scenes; these divisions, not found in Q2 (and only a few are found in the Folio), are purely editorial additions, and they are therefore enclosed in square brackets.

We use the text edited by David Bevington.

The Tragedy of Hamlet

And so by continuance, and weakenesse of the braine
Into this frensie, which now possesseth him:
And if this be not true, take this from this.

  King Thinke you t'is so?

  Cor. How? so my Lord, I would very faine know
That thing that I haue saide t'is so, positiuely,
And it hath fallen out otherwise.
Nay, if circumstances leade me on,
Ile finde it out, if it were hid
As deepe as the centre of the earth.

  King. how should wee trie this same?

  Cor. Mary my good lord thus,
The Princes walke is here in the galery,
There let *Ofelia*, walke vntill hee comes:
Your selfe and I will stand close in the study,
There shall you heare the effect of all his hart,
And if it proue any otherwise then loue,
Then let my censure faile an other time.

  King. see where hee comes poring vppon a booke.

      Enter Hamlet.

  Cor. Madame, will it please your grace
To leaue vs here?

  Que. With all my hart.   *exit.*

  Cor. And here *Ofelia*, reade you on this booke,
And walke aloofe, the King shal be vnseene.

  Ham. To be, or not to be, I there's the point,
To Die, to sleepe, is that all? I all:
No, to sleepe, to dreame, I mary there it goes,
For in that dreame of death, when wee awake,
And borne before an euerlasting Iudge,
From whence no passenger euer retur'nd,
The vndiscouered countty, at whose sight
The happy smile, and the accursed damn'd.
But for this, the ioyfull hope of this,
Whol'd beare the scornes and flattery of the world,
Scorned by the right rich, the rich cursed of the poore?

                      The

On this page and on the next page, we give the text of "To be or not to be" from the First Quarto (Q1, 1603). On pages 929–930 we give the text from the Second Quarto (Q2, 1604–1605), and on page 931 we give a third version, from the First Folio (F1, 1623), beginning at the bottom of the left-hand column.

Prince of Denmarke

The widow being oppreſſed, the orphan wrong'd,
The taſte of hunger, or a tirants raigne,
And thouſand more calamities beſides,
To grunt and ſweate vnder this weary life,
When that he may his full *Quietus* make,
With a bare bodkin, who would this indure,
But for a hope of ſomething after death?
Which puſſes the braine, and deth confound the ſence,
Which makes vs rather beare thoſe euilles we haue,
Than flie to others that we know not of.
I that, O this conſcience makes cowardes of vs all,
Lady in thy orizons, be all my ſinnes remembred.

   Ofel. My Lord, I haue ſought opportunitie,which now
I haue,to redeliuer to your worthy handes, a ſmall remembrance,ſuch tokens which I haue receiued of you.

     Ham. Are you faire?

     Ofel. My Lord.

     Ham. Are you honeſt?

     Ofel. What meanes my Lord?

     Ham. That if you be faire and honeſt,
Your beauty ſhould admit no diſcourſe to your honeſty.

   Ofel. My Lord, can beauty haue better priviledge than
with honeſty?

   Ham. Yea mary may it; for Beauty may transforme
Honeſty, from what ſhe was into a bawd:
Then Honeſty can transforme Beauty:
This was ſometimes a Paradox,
But now the time giues it ſcope.
I neuer gaue you nothing.

   Ofel. My Lord, you know right well you did,
And with them ſuch earneſt vowes of loue,
As would haue moou'd the ſtonieſt breaſt aliue,
But now too true I finde,
Rich giftes waxe poore, when giuers grow vnkinde.

     Ham. I neuer loued you.

     Ofel. You made me beleeue you did.

         E   *Ham.*

That show of such an exercise may cullour
Yourlowlines; we are oft too blame in this,
Tis too much proou'd, that with deuotions visage
And pious action, we doe sugar ore
The deuill himselfe.

   King. O tis too true,
How smart a lash that speech doth giue my conscience,
The harlots cheeke beautied with plastring art,
Is not more ougly to the thing that helps it,
Then is my deede to my most painted word :
O heauy burthen.

Enter Hamlet.

   Pol. I heare him comming, with-draw my Lord.
   Ham. To be, or not to be, that is the question,
Whether tis nobler in the minde to suffer
The slings and arrowes of outragious fortune,
Or to take Armes against a sea of troubles,
And by opposing, end them; to die to sleepe
No more, and by a sleepe, to say we end
The hart-ake, and the thousand naturall shocks
That flesh is heire to; tis a consummation
Deuoutly to be wisht to die to sleepe,
To sleepe, perchance to dreame, I there's the rub,
For in that sleepe of death what dreames may come
When we haue shuffled off this mortall coyle
Must giue vs pause, there's the respect
That makes calamitie of so long life:
For who would beare the whips and scornes of time,
Th'oppressors wrong, the proude mans contumely,
The pangs of despiz'd loue, the lawes delay,
The insolence of office, and the spurnes
That patient merrit of th'vnworthy takes,
When he himselfe might his quietas make
With a bare bodkin; who would fardels beare,
To grunt and sweat vnder a wearie life,
But that the dread of something after death,
The vndiscouer'd country, from whose borne.

G 2

No

"To be or not to be," as given in the Second Quarto (Q2, 1604–1605).

The Tragedie of Hamlet

No trauiler returnes, puzzels the will,
And makes vs rather beare thofe ills we haue,
Then flie to others that we know not of.
Thus confcience dooes make cowards,
And thus the natiue hiew of refolution
Is fickled ore with the pale caft of thought,
And enterprifes of great pitch and moment,
With this regard theyr currents turne awry,
And loofe the name of action. Soft you now,
The faire *Ophelia*, Nimph in thy orizons
Be all my finnes remembred.

  Oph. Good my Lord,
How dooes your honour for this many a day?

  Ham. I humbly thanke you well.

  Oph. My Lord, I haue remembrances of yours
That I haue longed long to redeliuer.
I pray you now receiue them.

  Ham. No, not I, I neuer gaue you ought.

  Oph. My honor'd Lord, you know right well you did,
And with them words of fo fweet breath compofd
As made thefe things more rich, their perfume loft,
Take thefe againe, for to the noble mind
Rich gifts wax poore when giuers prooue vnkind,
There my Lord.

  Ham. Ha, ha, are you honeft.

  Oph. My Lord.

  Ham. Are you faire?

  Oph. What meanes your Lordfhip?

  Ham. That if you be honeft & faire, you fhould admit
no difcourfe to your beautie.

  Oph. Could beauty my Lord haue better comerfe
Then with honeftie?

  Ham. I truly, for the power of beautie will fooner transforme honeftie from what it is to a bawde, then the force of honeftie can tranf-
late beautie into his likenes, this was fometime a paradox, but now the
time giues it proofe, I did loue you once.

  Oph. Indeed my Lord you made me belieue fo.

  Ham. You fhould not haue beleeu'd me, for vertue cannot fo
enocutat our old ftock, but we fhall relifh of it, I loued you not.

The Tragedie of Hamlet.   265

With turbulent and dangerous Lunacy.
Rosin. He does confesse he feeles himselfe distracted,
But from what cause he will by no meanes speake.
Guil. Nor do we finde him forward to be sounded,
But with a crafty Madnesse keepes aloofe:
When we would bring him on to some Confession
Of his true state.
Qu. Did he receiue you well?
Rosin. Most like a Gentleman.
Guild. But with much forcing of his disposition.
Rosin. Niggard of question, but of our demands
Most free in his reply.
Qu. Did you assay him to any pastime?
Rosin. Madam, it so fell out, that certaine Players
We ore-wrought on the way: of these we told him,
And there did seeme in him a kinde of ioy
To heare of it: They are about the Court,
And (as I thinke) they haue already order
This night to play before him.
Pol. 'Tis most true:
And he beseech'd me to intreate your Maiesties
To heare, and see the matter.
King. With all my heart, and it doth much content me
To heare him so inclin'd. Good Gentlemen,
Giue him a further edge, and driue his purpose on
To these delights.
Rosin. We shall my Lord.   *Exeunt.*
King. Sweet *Gertrude* leaue vs too,
For we haue closely sent for *Hamlet* hither,
That he, as 'twere by accident, may there
Affront *Ophelia.* Her Father, and my selfe (lawful espials)
Will so bestow our selues, that seeing vnseene
We may of their encounter frankely iudge,
And gather by him, as he is behaued,
If't be th'affliction of his loue, or no.
That thus he suffers for.
Qu. I shall obey you,
And for your part *Ophelia*, I do wish
That your good Beauties be the happy cause
Of *Hamlets* wildenesse: so shall I hope your Vertues
Will bring him to his wonted way againe,
To both your Honors.
Ophe. Madam, I wish it may.
Pol. *Ophelia*, walke you heere. Gracious so please ye
We will bestow our selues: Reade on this booke,
That shew of such an exercise may colour
Your lonelinesse. We are oft too blame in this,
'Tis too much prou'd, that with Deuotions visage,
And pious Action, we do surge o're
The diuell himselfe.
King. Oh 'tis true:
How smart a lash that speech doth giue my Conscience?
The Harlots Cheeke beautied with plaist'ring Art
Is not more vgly to the thing that helpes it,
Then is my deede, to my most painted word.
Oh heauie burthen!
Pol. I heare him comming, let's withdraw my Lord.
                                    Exeunt.

Enter Hamlet.

Ham. To be, or not to be, that is the Question:
Whether 'tis Nobler in the minde to suffer
The Slings and Arrowes of outragious Fortune,
Or to take Armes against a Sea of troubles,
And by opposing end them: to dye, to sleepe
No more; and by a sleepe, to say we end
The Heart-ake, and the thousand Naturall shockes

That Flesh is heyre too? 'Tis a consummation
Deuoutly to be wish'd. To dye to sleepe,
To sleepe, perchance to Dreame; I, there's the rub,
For in that sleepe of death, what dreames may come,
When we haue shuffiel'd off this mortall coile,
Must giue vs pawse. There's the respect
That makes Calamity of so long life:
For who would beare the Whips and Scornes of time,
The Oppressors wrong, the poore mans Contumely,
The pangs of dispriz'd Loue, the Lawes delay,
The insolence of Office, and the Spurnes
That patient merit of the vnworthy takes,
When he himselfe might his *Quietus* make
With a bare Bodkin? Who would these Fardles beare
To grunt and sweat vnder a weary life,
But that the dread of something after death,
The vndiscouered Countrey, from whose Borne
No Traueller returnes, Puzels the will,
And makes vs rather beare those illes we haue,
Then flye to others that we know not of.
Thus Conscience does make Cowards of vs all,
And thus the Natiue hew of Resolution
Is sicklied o're, with the pale cast of Thought,
And enterprizes of great pith and moment,
With this regard their Currants turne away,
And loose the name of Action. Soft you now,
The faire *Ophelia?* Nimph, in thy Orizons
Be all my sinnes remembred.
Ophe. Good my Lord,
How does your Honor for this many a day?
Ham. I humbly thanke you: well, well, well.
Ophe. My Lord, I haue Remembrances of yours,
That I haue longed long to re-deliuer.
I pray you now, receiue them.
Ham. No, no, I neuer gaue you ought.
Ophe. My honor'd Lord, I know right well you did,
And with them words of so sweet breath compos'd,
As made the things more rich, then perfume left:
Take these againe, for to the Noble minde
Rich gifts wax poore, when giuers proue vnkinde.
There my Lord.
Ham. Ha, ha: Are you honest?
Ophe. My Lord.
Ham. Are you faire?
Ophe. What meanes your Lordship?
Ham. That if you be honest and faire, your Honesty
should admit no discourse to your Beautie.
Ophe. Could Beautie my Lord, haue better Comerce
then your Honestie?
Ham. I trulie: for the power of Beautie, will sooner
transforme Honestie from what it is, to a Bawd, then the
force of Honestie can translate Beautie into his likenesse.
This was sometime a Paradox, but now the time giues it
proofe. I did loue you once.
Ophe. Indeed my Lord, you made me beleeue so.
Ham. You should not haue beleeued me. For vertue
cannot so innocculate our old stocke, but we shall rellish
of it. I loued you not.
Ophe. I was the more deceiued.
Ham. Get thee to a Nunnerie. Why would'st thou
be a breeder of Sinners? I am my selfe indifferent honest,
but yet I could accuse me of such things, that it were better my Mother had not borne me. I am very prowd, re-
uengefull, Ambitious, with more offences at my becke,
then I haue thoughts to put them in imagination, to giue
them shape, or time to acte them in. What should such
                                         Fel-

"To be or not to be," as given in the First Folio (F1, 1623).

WILLIAM SHAKESPEARE

William Shakespeare (1564–1616) was born in Stratford–on–Avon, England, of middle-class parents. Nothing of interest is known about his early years, but by 1590 he was acting and writing plays in London. By the end of the following decade he had worked in all three Elizabethan dramatic genres—tragedy, comedy, and history. Romeo and Juliet, for example, was written about 1595, the year of Richard II. Hamlet was probably written in 1600–1601. Among the plays that followed were Othello (1603–1604), King Lear (1605–1606), Macbeth (1605–1606), and several "romances"—plays that have happy endings but that seem more meditative and closer to tragedy than such comedies as A Midsummer Night's Dream, As You Like It, and Twelfth Night.

The Tragedy of Hamlet, Prince of Denmark

DRAMATIS PERSONAE

GHOST *of Hamlet, the former King of Denmark*
CLAUDIUS, *King of Denmark, the former King's brother*
GERTRUDE, *Queen of Denmark, widow of the former King and now wife of*
           Claudius
HAMLET, *Prince of Denmark, son of the late King and of Gertrude*
POLONIUS, *councillor to the King*
LAERTES, *his son*
OPHELIA, *his daughter*
REYNALDO, *his servant*

HORATIO, *Hamlet's friend and fellow student*

VOLTIMAND,
CORNELIUS,
ROSENCRANTZ,
GUILDENSTERN,   } *members of the Danish court*
OSRIC,
A GENTLEMAN,
A LORD,

BERNARDO,
FRANCISCO,   } *officers and soldiers on watch*
MARCELLUS,

FORTINBRAS, *Prince of Norway*
CAPTAIN *in his army*
Three or Four PLAYERS, *taking the roles of* PROLOGUE, PLAYER KING, PLAYER QUEEN,
           and LUCIANUS
Two MESSENGERS
FIRST SAILOR
Two CLOWNS, *a gravedigger and his companion*
PRIEST
FIRST AMBASSADOR from England

Lords, Soldiers, Attendants, Guards, other Players, Followers of Laertes, other
     Sailors, another Ambassador or Ambassadors from England

SCENE: *Denmark*

1.1   *Enter* BERNARDO *and* FRANCISCO, *two sentinels* [*meeting*].

BERNARDO.   Who's there?
FRANCISCO.   Nay, answer me.° Stand and unfold yourself.°
BERNARDO.   Long live the King!
FRANCISCO.   Bernardo?
BERNARDO.   He.   5
FRANCISCO.   You come most carefully upon your hour.
BERNARDO.   'Tis now struck twelve. Get thee to bed, Francisco.
FRANCISCO.   For this relief much thanks. 'Tis bitter cold,
          And I am sick at heart.
BERNARDO.   Have you had quiet guard?   10
FRANCISCO.   Not a mouse stirring.
BERNARDO.   Well, good night.
          If you do meet Horatio and Marcellus,
          The rivals° of my watch, bid them make haste.

          Enter HORATIO *and* MARCELLUS.

FRANCISCO.   I think I hear them.—Stand, ho! Who is there?   15
HORATIO.   Friends to this ground.°
MARCELLUS.   And liegemen to the Dane.°
FRANCISCO.   Give° you good night.
MARCELLUS.   O, farewell, honest soldier. Who hath relieved you?
FRANCISCO.   Bernardo hath my place. Give you good night.   *Exit* FRANCISCO.   20
MARCELLUS.   Holla! Bernardo!
BERNARDO.   Say, what, is Horatio there?
HORATIO.   A piece of him.
BERNARDO.   Welcome, Horatio. Welcome, good Marcellus.
HORATIO.   What, has this thing appeared again tonight?   25
BERNARDO.   I have seen nothing.
MARCELLUS.   Horatio says 'tis but our fantasy,°
          And will not let belief take hold of him
          Touching this dreaded sight twice seen of us.
          Therefore I have entreated him along°   30
          With us to watch° the minutes of this night,
          That if again this apparition come
          He may approve° our eyes and speak to it.
HORATIO.   Tush, tush, 'twill not appear.
BERNARDO.   Sit down awhile,
          And let us once again assail your ears,   35
          That are so fortified against our story,
          What° we have two nights seen.

1.1 Location: Elsinore castle. A guard platform.   **2 me** (Francisco emphasizes that *he* is the
sentry currently on watch.);   **unfold yourself** reveal your identity.   **14 rivals** partners.
16 ground ground, land.   **17 liegemen to the Dane** men sworn to serve the Danish king.
18 Give i.e., may God give.   **27 fantasy** imagination.   **30 along** to come along.
31 watch keep watch during.   **33 approve** corroborate.   **37 What** with what.

HORATIO.   Well, sit we down,
     And let us hear Bernardo speak of this.
BERNARDO.   Last night of all,°
     When yond same star that's westward from the pole°   40
     Had made his° course t' illume° that part of heaven
     Where now it burns, Marcellus and myself,
     The bell then beating one—

     Enter GHOST.

MARCELLUS.   Peace, break thee off! Look where it comes again!
BERNARDO.   In the same figure like the King that's dead.   45
MARCELLUS.   Thou art a scholar.° Speak to it, Horatio.
BERNARDO.   Looks 'a° not like the King? Mark it, Horatio.
HORATIO.   Most like. It harrows me with fear and wonder.
BERNARDO.   It would be spoke to.°
MARCELLUS.   Speak to it, Horatio.
HORATIO.   What art thou that usurp'st° this time of night,   50
     Together with that fair and warlike form
     In which the majesty of buried Denmark°
     Did sometime° march? By heaven, I charge thee, speak!
MARCELLUS.   It is offended.
BERNARDO.   See, it stalks away.
HORATIO.   Stay! Speak, speak! I charge thee, speak!   *Exit* GHOST. 55
MARCELLUS.   'Tis gone and will not answer.
BERNARDO.   How now, Horatio? You tremble and look pale.
     Is not this something more than fantasy?
     What think you on 't?°
HORATIO.   Before my God, I might not this believe   60
     Without the sensible° and true avouch°
     Of mine own eyes.
MARCELLUS.   Is it not like the King?
HORATIO.   As thou art to thyself.
     Such was the very armor he had on
     When he the ambitious Norway° combated.   65
     So frowned he once when, in an angry parle,°
     He smote the sledded° Polacks° on the ice.
     'Tis strange.
MARCELLUS.   Thus twice before, and jump° at this dead hour,
     With martial stalk° hath he gone by our watch.   70
HORATIO.   In what particular thought to work° I know not,
     But in the gross and scope° of mine opinion
     This bodes some strange eruption to our state.

---

39 Last . . . all i.e., this *very* last night (emphatic).   **40 pole** Pole Star, North Star.   **41 his** its;
illume illuminate.   **46 scholar** one learned enough to know how to question a ghost properly.
47 'a he.   **49 It . . . to** (It was commonly believed that a ghost could not speak until spoken
to.)   **50 usurp'st** wrongfully takes over.   **52 buried Denmark** the buried King of Denmark.
53 sometime formerly.   **59 on 't** of it.   **61 sensible** confirmed by the sense;   **avouch** warrant
evidence.   **65 Norway** King of Norway.   **66 parle** parley.   **67 sledded** traveling on sleds;
Polacks Poles.   **69 jump** exactly.   **70 stalk** stride.   **71 to work** i.e., to collect my thoughts and
try to understand this.   **72 gross and scope** general drift.

MARCELLUS.   Good now,° sit down, and tell me, he that knows,
    Why this same strict and most observant watch   75
    So nightly toils° the subject° of the land,
    And why such daily cast° of brazen cannon
    And foreign mart° for implements of war,
    Why such impress° of shipwrights, whose sore task
    Does not divide the Sunday from the week.   80
    What might be toward,° that this sweaty haste
    Doth make the night joint-laborer with the day?
    Who is 't that can inform me?
HORATIO.   That can I;
    At least, the whisper goes so. Our last king,
    Whose image even but now appeared to us,   85
    Was, as you know, by Fortinbras of Norway,
    Thereto pricked on° by a most emulate° pride,°
    Dared to the combat; in which our valiant Hamlet—
    For so this side of our known world° esteemed him—
    Did slay this Fortinbras; who by a sealed° compact   90
    Well ratified by law and heraldry
    Did forfeit, with his life, all those his lands
    Which he stood seized° of, to the conqueror;
    Against the° which a moiety competent°
    Was gagèd° by our king, which had returned°   95
    To the inheritance° of Fortinbras
    Had he been vanquisher, as, by the same cov'nant°
    And carriage of the article designed,°
    His fell to Hamlet. Now, sir, young Fortinbras,
    Of unimprovèd mettle° hot and full,   100
    Hath in the skirts° of Norway here and there
    Sharked up° a list° of lawless resolutes°
    For food and diet° to some enterprise
    That hath a stomach° in 't, which is no other—
    As it doth well appear unto our state—   105
    But to recover of us, by strong hand
    And terms compulsatory, those foresaid lands
    So by his father lost. And this, I take it,
    Is the main motive of our preparations,

---

74 Good now (An expression denoting entreaty or expostulation.)   **76 toils** causes to toil;
subject subjects.   **77 cast** casting.   **78 mart** buying and selling.   **79 impress** impressment,
conscription.   **81 toward** in preparation.   **87 pricked on** incited;   **emulate** emulous, ambitious;
Thereto . . . pride (Refers to old Fortinbras, not the Danish King.)   **89 this . . . world** i.e., all
Europe, the Western world.   **90 sealed** certified, confirmed.   **93 seized** possessed.   **94 Against
the** in return for;   **moiety competent** corresponding portion.   **95 gagèd** engaged, pledged;   **had
returned** would have passed.   **96 inheritance** possession.   **97 cov'nant** i.e., the *sealed compact*
on line 90.   **98 carriage . . . designed** carrying out of the article or clause drawn up to cover the
point.   **100 unimprovèd mettle** untried, undisciplined spirits.   **101 skirts** outlying regions,
outskirts.   **102 Sharked up** gathered up, as a shark takes fish;   **list** i.e., troop;
resolutes desperadoes.   **103 For Food and diet** i.e., they are to serve as *food,* or "means," *to
some enterprises;* also they serve in return for the rations they get.   **104 stomach** (1) a spirit of
daring (2) an appetite that is fed by the *lawless resolutes.*

The source of this our watch, and the chief head°   110
Of this posthaste and rummage° in the land.
BERNARDO.   I think it be no other but e'en so.
Well may it sort° that this portentous figure
Comes armèd through our watch so like the King
That was and is the question° of these wars.   115
HORATIO.   A mote° it is to trouble the mind's eye.
In the most high and palmy° state of Rome,
A little ere the mightiest Julius fell,
The graves stood tenantless, and the sheeted° dead
Did squeak and gibber in the Roman streets;   120
As° stars with trains° of fire and dews of blood,
Disasters° in the sun; and the moist star°
Upon whose influence Neptune's° empire stands°
Was sick almost to doomsday° with eclipse.
And even the like precurse° of feared events,   125
As harbingers° preceding still° the fates
And prologue to the omen° coming on,
Have heaven and earth together demonstrated
Unto our climatures° and countrymen.

Enter GHOST.

But soft,° behold! Lo, where it comes again!   130
I'll cross° it, though it blast° me. [*It spreads his° arms.*]
    Stay, *illusion!*
If thou hast any sound or use of voice,
Speak to me!
If there be any good thing to be done
That may to thee do ease and grace to me,   135
Speak to me!
If thou art privy to° thy country's fate,
Which, happily,° foreknowing may avoid,
O, speak!
Or if thou hast uphoarded in thy life   140
Extorted treasure in the womb of earth,
For which, they say, you spirits oft walk in death,
Speak of it! [*The cock crows.*] Stay and speak!—Stop it, Marcellus.
MARCELLUS.   Shall I strike at it with my partisan?°
HORATIO.   Do, if it will not stand.   [*They strike at it.*]   145
BERNARDO.   'Tis here!

110 **head** source.   111 **rummage** bustle, commotion.   113 **sort** suit.   115 **question** focus of
contention.   116 **mote** speck of dust.   117 **palmy** flourishing.   119 **sheeted** shrouded.
121 **As** (This abrupt transition suggests that matter is possibly omitted between lines 120 and
121.);   **trains** trails.   122 **Disasters** unfavorable signs or aspects;   **moist star** i.e., moon,
governing tides.   123 **Neptune** god of the sea;   **stands** depends.   124 **sick . . . doomsday** (See
Matthew 24:29 and Revelation 6:12.)   125 **precurse** heralding, foreshadowing.
126 **harbingers** forerunners;   **still** continually.   127 **omen** calamitous event.
129 **climatures** regions.   130 **soft** i.e., enough, break off.   131 **cross** stand in its path,
confront;   **blast** wither, strike with a curse;   **s.d. his** its.   137 **privy to** in on the secret of.
138 **happily** haply, perchance.   144 **partisan** long-handled spear.

HORATIO.   'Tis here!   [*Exit* GHOST.]
MARCELLUS.   'Tis gone.
    We do it wrong, being so majestical,
    To offer it the show of violence,   150
    For it is as the air invulnerable,
    And our vain blows malicious mockery.
BERNARDO.   It was about to speak when the cock crew.
HORATIO.   And then it started like a guilty thing
    Upon a fearful summons. I have heard   155
    The cock, that is the trumpet° to the morn,
    Doth with his lofty and shrill-sounding throat
    Awake the god of day, and at his warning,
    Whether in sea or fire, in earth or air,
    Th' extravagant and erring° spirit hies°   160
    To his confine; and of the truth herein
    This present object made probation.°
MARCELLUS.   It faded on the crowing of the cock.
    Some say that ever 'gainst° that season comes
    Wherein our Savior's birth is celebrated,   165
    This bird of dawning singeth all night long,
    And then, they say, no spirit dare stir abroad;
    The nights are wholesome, then no planets strike,°
    No fairy takes,° nor witch hath power to charm,
    So hallowed and so gracious° is that time.   170
HORATIO.   So have I heard and do in part believe it.
    But, look, the morn in russet mantle clad
    Walks o'er the dew of yon high eastward hill.
    Break we our watch up, and by my advice
    Let us impart what we have seen tonight   175
    Unto young Hamlet; for upon my life,
    This spirit, dumb to us, will speak to him.
    Do you consent we shall acquaint him with it,
    As needful in our loves, fitting our duty?
MARCELLUS.   Let's do 't, I pray, and I this morning know   180
    Where we shall find him most conveniently.   *Exeunt.*

    1.2   *Flourish. Enter* CLAUDIUS, *King of Denmark,* GERTRUDE *the*
    Queen, [*the*] *Council, as*° POLONIUS *and his son* LAERTES, HAMLET,
    cum aliis° [*including* VOLTIMAND *and* CORNELIUS].

KING.   Though yet of Hamlet our° dear brother's death
    The memory be green, and that it us befitted
    To bear our hearts in grief and our whole kingdom
    To be contracted in one brow of woe,
    Yet so far hath discretion fought with nature   5
    That we with wisest sorrow think on him

---

156 trumpet trumpeter.   **160 extravagant and erring** wandering beyond bounds. (The words
have similar meaning.);   **hies** hastens.   **162 probation** proof.   **164 'gainst** just before.
168 strike destroy by evil influence.   **169 takes** bewitches.   **170 gracious** full of grace.
1.2. Location: The castle.   **s.d. as** i.e., such as, including;   **cum aliis** with others.   **1 our** my.
(The royal "we"; also in the following lines.)

Together with remembrance of ourselves.
Therefore our sometime° sister, now our queen,
Th' imperial jointress° to this warlike state,
Have we, as 'twere with a defeated joy—   10
With an auspicious and a dropping eye,°
With mirth in funeral and with dirge in marriage,
In equal scale weighing delight and dole°—
Taken to wife: Nor have we herein barred
Your better wisdoms, which have freely gone   15
With this affair along. For all, our thanks.
Now follows that you know° young Fortinbras,
Holding a weak supposal° of our worth,
Or thinking by our late dear brother's death
Our state to be disjoint and out of frame,   20
Co-leaguèd with° this dream of his advantage,°
He hath not failed to pester us with message
Importing° the surrender of those lands
Lost by his father, with all bonds° of law,
To our most valiant brother. So much for him.   25
Now for ourself and for this time of meeting.
Thus much the business is: we have here writ
To Norway, uncle of young Fortinbras—
Who, impotent° and bed-rid, scarcely hears
Of this his nephew's purpose—to suppress   30
His° further gait° herein, in that the levies,
The lists, and full proportions are all made
Out of his subject;° and we here dispatch
You, good Cornelius, and you, Voltimand,
For bearers of this greeting to old Norway,   35
Giving to you no further personal power
To business with the King more than the scope
Of these dilated° articles allow.   [*He gives a paper.*]
Farewell, and let your haste commend your duty.°
CORNELIUS, VOLTIMAND.   In that, and all things, will we show our duty.   40
KING.   We doubt it nothing.° Heartily farewell.
                                        [*Exeunt* VOLTIMAND *and* CORNELIUS.]
And now, Laertes, what's the news with you?
You told us of some suit; what is 't, Laertes?
You cannot speak of reason to the Dane°
And lose your voice.° What wouldst thou beg, Laertes,   45

8 sometime former.   **9 jointress** woman possessing property with her husband.   **11 With . . .
eye** with one eye smiling and the other weeping.   **13 dole** grief.   **17 that you know** what you
know already, that; or, that you be informed as follows.   **18 weak supposal** low estimate.
21 Co-leaguèd with joined to, allied with;   **dream . . . advantage** illusory hope of having the
advantage. (His only ally is this hope.)   **23 Importing** pertaining to.   **24 bonds** contracts.
29 impotent helpless.   **31 His** i.e., Fortinbras';   **gait** proceeding.   **31–33 in that . . .
subject** since the levying of troops and supplies is drawn entirely from the King of Norway's
own subjects.   **38 dilated** set out at length.   **39 let . . . duty** let your swift obeying of orders,
rather than mere words, express your dutifulness.   **41 nothing** not at all.   **44 the Dane** the
Danish king.   **45 lose your voice** waste your speech.

That shall not be my offer, not thy asking?
The head is not more native° to the heart,
The hand more instrumental° to the mouth,
Than is the throne of Denmark to thy father.
What wouldst thou have, Laertes?

LAERTES.   My dread lord,   50
Your leave and favor° to return to France,
From whence though willingly I came to Denmark
To show my duty in your coronation,
Yet now I must confess, that duty done,
My thoughts and wishes bend again toward France   55
And bow them to your gracious leave and pardon.°

KING.   Have you your father's leave? What says Polonius?

POLONIUS.   H'ath,° my lord, wrung from me my slow leave
By laborsome petition, and at last
Upon his will I sealed° my hard° consent.   60
I do beseech you, give him leave to go.

KING.   Take thy fair hour,° Laertes. Time be thine,
And thy best graces spend it at thy will!°
But now, my cousin° Hamlet, and my son—

HAMLET.   A little more than kin, and less than kind.°   65

KING.   How is it that the clouds still hang on you?

HAMLET.   Not so, my lord. I am too much in the sun.°

QUEEN.   Good Hamlet, cast thy nighted color° off,
And let thine eye look like a friend on Denmark.°
Do not forever with thy vailèd lids°   70
Seek for thy noble father in the dust.
Thou know'st 'tis common,° all that lives must die,
Passing through nature to eternity.

HAMLET.   Ay, madam, it is common.

QUEEN.   If it be,
Why seems it so particular° with thee?   75

HAMLET.   Seems, madam? Nay, it is. I know not "seems."
'Tis not alone my inky cloak, good Mother,
Nor customary° suits of solemn black,
Nor windy suspiration° of forced breath,

---

47 native closely connected, related.   **48 instrumental** serviceable.   **51 leave and favor** kind permission.   **56 bow . . . pardon** entreatingly make a deep bow, asking your permission to depart.   **58 H'ath** he has.   **60 sealed** (As if sealing a legal document.);   **hard** reluctant.
62 Take thy fair hour enjoy your time of youth.   **63 And . . . will** and may your finest qualities guide the way you choose to spend your time.   **64 cousin** any kin not of the immediate family.
65 A little . . . kind i.e., closer than an ordinary nephew (since I am stepson), and yet more separated in natural feeling (with pun on *kind* meaning "affectionate" and "natural," "lawful." This line is often read as an aside, but it need not be. The King chooses perhaps not to respond to Hamlet's cryptic and bitter remark.)   **67 the sun** i.e., the sunshine of the King's royal favor (with pun on *son*).   **68 nighted color** (1) mourning garments of black (2) dark melancholy.
69 Denmark the King of Denmark.   **70 vailèd lids** lowered eyes.   **72 common** of universal occurrence. (But Hamlet plays on the sense of "vulgar" in line 74.)   **75 particular** personal.
78 customary (1) socially conventional (2) habitual with me.   **79 suspiration** sighing.

No, nor the fruitful° river in the eye,
Nor the dejected havior° of the visage,
Together with all forms, moods,° shapes of grief,
That can denote me truly. These indeed seem,
For they are actions that a man might play.
But I have that within which passes show;   85
These but the trappings and the suits of woe.

KING.   'Tis sweet and commendable in your nature, Hamlet,
To give these mourning duties to your father.
But you must know your father lost a father,
That father lost, lost his, and the survivor bound   90
In filial obligation for some term
To do obsequious° sorrow. But to persever°
In obstinate condolement° is a course
Of impious stubbornness. 'Tis unmanly grief.
It shows a will most incorrect to heaven,   95
A heart unfortified,° a mind impatient,
An understanding simple° and unschooled.
For what we know must be and is as common
As any the most vulgar thing to sense,°
Why should we in our peevish opposition   100
Take it to heart? Fie, 'tis a fault to heaven,
A fault against the dead, a fault to nature,
To reason most absurd, whose common theme
Is death of fathers, and who still° hath cried,
From the first corpse° till he that died today,   105
"This must be so." We pray you, throw to earth
This unprevailing° woe and think of us
As of a father; for let the world take note,
You are the most immediate° to our throne,
And with no less nobility of love   110
Than that which dearest father bears his son
Do I impart toward° you. For° your intent
In going back to school° in Wittenberg,°
It is most retrograde° to our desire,
And we beseech you bend you° to remain   115
Here in the cheer and comfort of our eye,
Our chiefest courtier, cousin, and our son.

QUEEN.   Let not thy mother lose her prayers, Hamlet.
I pray thee, stay with us, go not to Wittenberg.

---

80 fruitful abundant.   **81 havior** expression.   **82 moods** outward expression of feeling.
92 obsequious suited to obsequies or funerals;   **persever** persevere.
93 condolement sorrowing.   **96 unfortified** i.e., against adversity.   **97 simple** ignorant.   **99 As
. . . sense** as the most ordinary experience.   **104 still** always.   **105 the first corpse** (Abel's.)
107 unprevailing unavailing, useless.   **109 most immediate** next in succession.   **112 impart
toward** i.e., bestow my affection on;   **For** as for.   **113 to school** i.e., to your studies;
Wittenberg famous German university founded in 1502.   **114 retrograde** contrary.   **115 bend
you** incline yourself.

HAMLET.   I shall in all my best° obey you, madam.   120

KING.   Why, 'tis a loving and a fair reply.
      Be as ourself in Denmark. Madam, come.
      This gentle and unforced accord of Hamlet
      Sits smiling to° my heart, in grace° whereof
      No jocund° health that Denmark drinks today   125
      But the great cannon to the clouds shall tell,
      And the King's rouse° the heaven shall bruit again,°
      Respeaking earthly thunder.° Come away.

Flourish. Exeunt all but HAMLET.

HAMLET.   O, that this too too sullied° flesh would melt,
      Thaw, and resolve itself into a dew!
      Or that the Everlasting had not fixed   130
      His canon° 'gainst self-slaughter! O God, God,
      How weary, stale, flat, and unprofitable
      Seem to me all the uses° of this world!
      Fie on 't, ah fie! 'Tis an unweeded garden   135
      That grows to seed. Things rank and gross in nature
      Possess it merely.° That it should come to this!
      But two months dead—nay, not so much, not two.
      So excellent a king, that was to° this
      Hyperion° to a satyr,° so loving to my mother   140
      That he might not beteem° the winds of heaven
      Visit her face too roughly. Heaven and earth,
      Must I remember? Why, she would hang on him
      As if increase of appetite had grown
      By what it fed on, and yet within a month—   145
      Let me not think on 't; frailty, thy name is woman!—
      A little month, or ere° those shoes were old
      With which she followed my poor father's body,
      Like Niobe;° all tears, why, she, even she—
      O God, a beast, that wants discourse of reason,°   150
      Would have mourned longer—married with my uncle,
      My father's brother, but no more like my father
      Than I to Hercules. Within a month,
      Ere yet the salt of most unrighteous tears
      Had left the flushing in her gallèd° eyes,   155
      She married. O, most wicked speed, to post°

---

120 in all my best to the best of my ability.   **124 to** i.e., at;   **grace** thanksgiving.
125 jocund merry.   **127 rouse** drinking of a draft of liquor;   **bruit again** loudly echo.
128 thunder i.e., of trumpet and kettledrum, sounded when the King drinks; see 1.4.8–12.
129 sullied defiled. (The early quartos read *sallied;* the Folio, *solid.*)   **132 canon** law.   **134 all
the uses** the whole routine.   **137 merely** completely.   **139 to** in comparison to.
140 Hyperion Titan sun-god, father of Helios;   **satyr** a lecherous creature of classical
mythology, half-human but with a goat's legs, tail, ears, and horns.   **141 beteem** allow.   **147 or
ere** even before.   **149 Niobe** Tantalus' daughter, Queen of Thebes, who boasted that she had
more sons and daughters than Leto; for this, Apollo and Artemis, children of Leto, slew her
fourteen children. She was turned by Zeus into a stone that continually dropped tears.
150 wants . . . reason lacks the faculty of reason.   **155 gallèd** irritated, inflamed.
156 post hasten.

With such dexterity to incestuous° sheets!
It is not, nor it cannot come to good.
But break, my heart, for I must hold my tongue.

Enter HORATIO, MARCELLUS *and* BERNARDO.

HORATIO.   Hail to your lordship!

HAMLET.   I am glad to see you well.   160
Horatio!—or I do forget myself.

HORATIO.   The same, my lord, and your poor servant ever.

HAMLET.   Sir, my good friend; I'll change that name° with you.
And what make you from° Wittenberg, Horatio?
Marcellus.   165

MARCELLUS.   My good lord.

HAMLET.   I am very glad to see you. [*To* BERNARDO.] Good even, sir.—
But what in faith make you from Wittenberg?

HORATIO.   A truant disposition, good my lord.

HAMLET.   I would not hear your enemy say so,   170
Nor shall you do my ear that violence
To make it truster of your own report
Against yourself. I know you are no truant.
But what is your affair in Elsinore?
We'll teach you to drink deep ere you depart.   175

HORATIO.   My lord, I came to see your father's funeral.

HAMLET.   I prithee, do not mock me, fellow student;
I think it was to see my mother's wedding.

HORATIO.   Indeed, my lord, it followed hard° upon.

HAMLET.   Thrift, thrift, Horatio! The funeral baked meats°   180
Did coldly° furnish forth the marriage tables.
Would I had met my dearest° foe in heaven
Or ever° I had seen that day, Horatio!
My father!—Methinks I see my father.

HORATIO.   Where, my lord?

HAMLET.   In my mind's eye, Horatio.   185

HORATIO.   I saw him once. 'A° was a goodly king.

HAMLET.   'A was a man. Take him for all in all,
I shall not look upon his like again.

HORATIO.   My lord, I think I saw him yesternight.

HAMLET.   Saw? Who?   190

HORATIO.   My lord, the King your father.

HAMLET.   The King my father?

HORATIO.   Season your admiration° for a while
With an attent° ear till I may deliver,
Upon the witness of these gentlemen,   195
This marvel to you.

HAMLET.   For God's love, let me hear!

---

157 incestuous (In Shakespeare's day, the marriage of a man like Claudius to his deceased brother's wife was considered incestuous.)   **163 change that name** i.e., give and receive reciprocally the name of "friend" (rather than talk of "servant").   **164 make you from** are you doing away from.   **179 hard** close.   **180 baked meats** meat pies.   **181 coldly** i.e., as cold leftovers.   **182 dearest** closest (and therefore deadliest).   **183 Or ever** before.   **186 'A** he.
193 Season your admiration restrain your astonishment.   **194 attent** attentive.

HORATIO. Two nights together had these gentlemen,
      Marcellus and Bernardo, on their watch,
      In the dead waste° and middle of the night,
      Been thus encountered. A figure like your father,   200
      Armèd at point° exactly, cap-à-pie,°
      Appears before them, and with solemn march
      Goes slow and stately by them. Thrice he walked
      By their oppressed and fear-surprisèd eyes
      Within his truncheon's° length, whilst they, distilled°   205
      Almost to jelly with the act° of fear,
      Stand dumb and speak not to him. This to me
      In dreadful° secrecy impart they did,
      And I with them the third night kept the watch,
      Where, as they had delivered, both in time,   210
      Form of the thing, each word made true and good,
      The apparition comes. I knew your father;
      These hands are not more like.

HAMLET.   But where was this?

MARCELLUS. My lord, upon the platform where we watch.

HAMLET. Did you not speak to it?

HORATIO.   My lord, I did,   215
      But answer made it none. Yet once methought
      It lifted up its head and did address
      Itself to motion, like as it would speak;°
      But even then° the morning cock crew loud,
      And at the sound it shrunk in haste away   220
      And vanished from our sight.

HAMLET.   'Tis very strange.

HORATIO. As I do live, my honored lord, 'tis true,
      And we did think it writ down in our duty
      To let you know of it.

HAMLET. Indeed, indeed, sirs. But this troubles me.   225
      Hold you the watch tonight?

ALL.   We do, my lord.

HAMLET. Armed, say you?

ALL. Armed, my lord.

HAMLET. From top to toe?

ALL. My lord, from head to foot.   230

HAMLET. Then saw you not his face?

HORATIO. O, yes, my lord, he wore his beaver° up.

HAMLET. What° looked he, frowningly?

HORATIO. A countenance more in sorrow than in anger.

HAMLET. Pale or red?   235

HORATIO. Nay, very pale.

HAMLET. And fixed his eyes upon you?

---

199 dead waste desolate stillness. **201 at point** correctly in every detail; **cap-à-pie** from head
to foot. **205 truncheon** officer's staff; **distilled** dissolved. **206 act** action, operation.
208 dreadful full of dread. **217–218 did . . . speak** began to move as though it were about to
speak. **219 even then** at that very instant. **232 beaver** visor on the helmet. **233 What** how.

HORATIO.   Most constantly.

HAMLET.   I would I had been there.

HORATIO.   It would have much amazed you.

HAMLET.   Very like, very like. Stayed it long?   240

HORATIO.   While one with moderate haste might tell° a hundred.

MARCELLUS, BERNARDO.   Longer, longer.

HORATIO.   Not when I saw 't.

HAMLET.   His beard was grizzled°—no?   245

HORATIO.   It was, as I have seen it in his life,
    A sable silvered.°

HAMLET.   I will watch tonight.
    Perchance 'twill walk again.

HORATIO.   I warrant° it will.

HAMLET.   If it assume my noble father's person,
    I'll speak to it though hell itself should gape   250
    And bid me hold my peace. I pray you all,
    If you have hitherto concealed this sight,
    Let it be tenable° in your silence still,
    And whatsoever else shall hap tonight,
    Give it an understanding but no tongue.   255
    I will requite your loves. So, fare you well.
    Upon the platform twixt eleven and twelve
    I'll visit you.

ALL.   Our duty to your honor.

HAMLET.   Your loves, as mine to you. Farewell.   *Exeunt* [*all but* HAMLET].
    My father's spirit in arms! All is not well.   260
    I doubt° some foul play. Would the night were come!
    Till then sit still, my soul. Foul deeds will rise,
    Though all the earth o'erwhelm them, to men's eyes.   *Exit.*

           1.3   *Enter* LAERTES *and* OPHELIA, *his sister.*

LAERTES.   My necessaries are embarked. Farewell.
    And, sister, as the winds give benefit
    And convoy is assistant,° do not sleep
    But let me hear from you.

OPHELIA.   Do you doubt that?

LAERTES.   For Hamlet, and the trifling of his favor,   5
    Hold it a fashion and a toy in blood,°
    A violet in the youth of primy° nature,
    Forward,° not permanent, sweet, not lasting,
    The perfume and suppliance° of a minute—
    No more.

OPHELIA.   No more but so?

LAERTES.   Think it no more.   10

---

242 tell count.   **245 grizzled** gray.   **247 sable silvered** black mixed with white.
248 warrant assure you.   **253 tenable** held.   **261 doubt** suspect.   **1.3. Location: Polonius'
chambers.   3 convoy is assistant** means of conveyance are available.   **6 toy in blood** passing
amorous fancy.   **7 primy** in its prime, springtime.   **8 Forward** precocious.
9 suppliance supply, filler.

For nature crescent° does not grow alone
In thews° and bulk, but as this temple° waxes
The inward service of the mind and soul
Grows wide withal.° Perhaps he loves you now,
And now no soil° nor cautel° doth besmirch   15
The virtue of his will,° but you must fear,
His greatness weighed,° his will is not his own.
For he himself is subject to his birth.
He may not, as unvalued persons do,
Carve° for himself, for on his choice depends   20
The safety and health of this whole state,
And therefore must his choice be circumscribed
Unto the voice and yielding° of that body
Whereof he is the head. Then if he says he loves you,
It fits your wisdom so far to believe it   25
As he in his particular act and place°
May give his saying deed, which is no further
Than the main voice° of Denmark goes withal.°
Then weigh what loss your honor may sustain
If with too credent° ear you list° his songs,   30
Or lose your heart, or your chaste treasure open
To his unmastered importunity.
Fear it, Ophelia, fear it, my dear sister,
And keep you in the rear of your affection,°
Out of the shot and danger of desire.   35
The chariest° maid is prodigal enough
If she unmask her beauty° to the moon.°
Virtue itself scapes not calumnious strokes.
The canker galls° the infants of the spring
Too oft before their buttons° be disclosed,°   40
And in the morn and liquid dew° of youth
Contagious blastments° are most imminent.
Be wary then; best safety lies in fear.
Youth to itself rebels,° though none else near.

OPHELIA.   I shall the effect of this good lesson keep   45
As watchman to my heart. But, good my brother,
Do not, as some ungracious° pastors do,
Show me the steep and thorny way to heaven,
Whiles like a puffed° and reckless libertine

---

11 **crescent** growing, waxing.   12 **thews** bodily strength;   **temple** i.e., body.   14 **Grows wide withal** grows along with it.   15 **soil** blemish;   **cautel** deceit.   16 **will** desire.   17 **His greatness weighed** if you take into account his high position.   20 **Carve** i.e., choose.   23 **voice and yielding** assent, approval.   26 **in . . . place** in his particular restricted circumstances.   28 **main voice** general assent;   **withal** along with.   30 **credent** credulous;   **list** listen to.   34 **keep . . . affection** don't advance as far as your affection might lead you (A military metaphor.)   36 **chariest** most scrupulously modest.   37 **If she unmask her beauty** if she does no more than show her beauty;   **moon** (Symbol of chastity.)   39 **canker galls** canker-worm destroys.   40 **buttons** buds;   **disclosed** opened.   41 **liquid dew** i.e., time when dew is fresh and bright.   42 **blastments** blights.   44 **Youth . . . rebels** youth is inherently rebellious.   47 **ungracious** ungodly.   49 **puffed** bloated, or swollen with pride.

  Himself the primrose path of dalliance treads,
  And recks° not his own rede.°

 Enter POLONIUS.

LAERTES.   O, fear me not.°
  I stay too long. But here my father comes.
  A double° blessing is a double grace;
  Occasion smiles upon a second leave.°
POLONIUS. Yet here, Laertes? Aboard, aboard, for shame!   55
  The wind sits in the shoulder of your sail,
  And you are stayed for. There—my blessing with thee!
  And these few precepts in thy memory
  Look° thou character.° Give thy thoughts no tongue,
  Nor any unproportioned° thought his° act.   60
  Be thou familiar,° but by no means vulgar.°
  Those friends thou hast, and their adoption tried,°
  Grapple them unto thy soul with hoops of steel,
  But do not dull thy palm° with entertainment
  Of each new-hatched, unfledged courage.° Beware   65
  Of entrance to a quarrel, but being in,
  Bear 't that° th' opposèd may beware of thee.
  Give every man thy ear, but few thy voice;
  Take each man's censure,° but reserve thy judgment.
  Costly thy habit° as thy purse can buy,   70
  But not expressed in fancy;° rich, not gaudy,
  For the apparel oft proclaims the man,
  And they in France of the best rank and station
  Are of a most select and generous chief in that.°
  Neither a borrower nor a lender be,   75
  For loan oft loses both itself and friend,
  And borrowing dulleth edge of husbandry.°
  This above all: to thine own self be true,
  And it must follow, as the night the day,
  Thou canst not then be false to any man.   80
  Farewell. My blessing season° this in thee!
LAERTES. Most humbly do I take my leave, my lord.
POLONIUS. The time invests° you. Go, your servants tend.°
LAERTES. Farewell, Ophelia, and remember well
  What I have said to you.   85

---

51 recks heeds; **rede** counsel; **fear me not** don't worry on my account. **53 double** (Laertes has already bid his father good-bye.) **54 Occasion . . . leave** happy is the circumstance that provides a second leave-taking. (The goddess Occasion, or Opportunity, smiles.) **59 Look** be sure that; **character** inscribe. **60 unproportioned** badly calculated, intemperate; **his** its. **61 familiar** sociable; **vulgar** common. **62 and their adoption tried** and also their suitability for adoption as friends having been tested. **64 dull thy palm** i.e., shake hands so often as to make the gesture meaningless. **65 courage** young man of spirit. **67 Bear 't that** manage it so that. **69 censure** opinion, judgment. **70 habit** clothing. **71 fancy** excessive ornament, decadent fashion. **74 Are . . . that** are of a most refined and well-bred preeminence in choosing what to wear. **77 husbandry** thrift. **81 season** mature. **83 invests** besieges, presses upon; **tend** attend, wait.

OPHELIA.   'Tis in my memory locked,
            And you yourself shall keep the key of it.
LAERTES.   Farewell.   *Exit* LAERTES.
POLONIUS.   What is 't, Ophelia, he hath said to you?
OPHELIA.   So please you, something touching the Lord Hamlet.   90
POLONIUS.   Marry,° well bethought.
            'Tis told me he hath very oft of late
            Given private time to you, and you yourself
            Have of your audience been most free and bounteous.
            If it be so—as so 'tis put on° me,   95
            And that in way of caution—I must tell you
            You do not understand yourself so clearly
            As it behooves° my daughter and your honor.
            What is between you? Give me up the truth.
OPHELIA.   He hath, my lord, of late made many tenders°   100
            Of his affection to me.
POLONIUS.   Affection? Pooh! You speak like a green girl,
            Unsifted° in such perilous circumstance.
            Do you believe his tenders, as you call them?
OPHELIA.   I do not know, my lord, what I should think.   105
POLONIUS.   Marry, I will teach you. Think yourself a baby
            That you have ta'en these tenders for true pay
            Which are not sterling.° Tender° yourself more dearly,
            Or—not to crack the wind° of the poor phrase,
            Running it thus—you'll tender me a fool.°   110
OPHELIA.   My lord, he hath importuned me with love
            In honorable fashion.
POLONIUS.   Ay, fashion° you may call it. Go to,° go to.
OPHELIA.   And hath given countenance° to his speech, my lord,
            With almost all the holy vows of heaven.   115
POLONIUS.   Ay, springes° to catch woodcocks.° I do know,
            When the blood burns, how prodigal° the soul
            Lends the tongue vows. These blazes, daughter,
            Giving more light than heat, extinct in both
            Even in their promise as it° is a-making,   120
            You must not take for fire. From this time
            Be something° scanter of your maiden presence.
            Set your entreatments° at a higher rate
            Than a command to parle.° For Lord Hamlet,

---

91 Marry i.e., by the Virgin Mary. (A mild oath.)   **95 put on** impressed on, told to.
98 behooves befits.   **100 tenders** offers.   **103 Unsifted** i.e., untried.   **108 sterling** legal
currency;   **Tender** hold, look after, offer.   **109 crack the wind** i.e., run it until it is broken-
winded.   **110 tender me a fool** (1) show yourself to me as a fool (2) show me up as a fool (3)
present me with a grandchild. (*Fool* was a term of endearment for a child.)   **113 fashion** mere
form, pretense;   **Go to** (An expression of impatience.)   **114 countenance** credit, confirmation.
116 springes snares;   **woodcocks** birds easily caught; here used to connote gullibility.
117 prodigal prodigally.   **120 it** i.e., the promise.   **122 something** somewhat.
123 entreatments negotiations for surrender. (A military term.)   **124 parle** discuss terms with
the enemy. (Polonius urges his daughter, in the metaphor of military language, not to meet with
Hamlet and consider giving in to him merely because he requests an interview.)

Believe so much in him° that he is young,
And with a larger tether may he walk
Than may be given you. In few,° Ophelia,
Do not believe his vows, for they are brokers,°
Not of that dye° which their investments° show,
But mere implorators° of unholy suits,   130
Breathing° like sanctified and pious bawds,
The better to beguile. This is for all:°
I would not, in plain terms, from this time forth
Have you so slander° any moment° leisure
As to give words or talk with the Lord Hamlet.   135
Look to 't, I charge you. Come your ways.°

OPHELIA.   I shall obey, my lord.   *Exeunt.*

1.4   *Enter* HAMLET, HORATIO, *and* MARCELLUS.

HAMLET.   The air bites shrewdly,° it is very cold.
HORATIO.   It is a nipping and an eager° air.
HAMLET.   What hour now?
HORATIO.   I think it lacks of° twelve.
MARCELLUS.   No, it is struck.
HORATIO.   Indeed? I heard it not.
It then draws near the season°   5
Wherein the spirit held his wont° to walk.
            A flourish of trumpets, and two pieces° go off [within].
What does this mean, my lord?
HAMLET.   The King doth wake° tonight and takes his rouse,°
Keeps wassail,° and the swaggering upspring° reels,°
And as he drains his drafts of Rhenish° down,   10
The kettledrum and trumpet thus bray out
The triumph of his pledge.°
HORATIO.   It is a custom?
HAMLET.   Ay, marry, is't,
But to my mind, though I am native here
And to the manner° born, it is a custom   15
More honored in the breach than the observance.°
This heavy-headed revel east and west°
Makes us traduced and taxed of° other nations.
They clepe° us drunkards, and with swinish phrase°

---

125 so . . . him this much concerning him.   **127 In few** briefly.   **128 brokers** go-betweens,
procurers.   **129 dye** color or sort;   **investments** clothes. (The vows are not what they seem.)
130 mere implorators out-and-out solicitors.   **131 Breathing** speaking.   **132 for all** once for
all, in sum.   **134 slander** abuse, misuse;   **moment** moment's.   **136 Come your ways** come
along.   **1.4. Location: The guard platform.**   **1 shrewdly** keenly, sharply.   **2 eager** biting.
3 lacks of is just short of.   **5 season** time.   **6 held his wont** was accustomed;   **s.d. pieces** i.e., of
ordnance, cannon.   **8 wake** stay awake and hold revel;   **takes his rouse** carouses.
9 wassail carousal;   **upspring** wild German dance;   **reels** dances.   **10 Rhenish** Rhine wine.
12 The triumph . . . pledge i.e., his feat in draining the wine in a single draft.
15 manner custom (of drinking).   **16 More . . . observance** better neglected than followed.
17 east and west i.e., everywhere.   **18 taxed of** censured by.   **19 clepe** call;   **with swinish
phrase** i.e., by calling us swine.

Soil our addition;° and indeed it takes   20
From our achievements, though performed at height,°
The pith and marrow of our attribute.°
So, oft it chances in particular men,
That for° some vicious mole of nature° in them,
As in their birth—wherein they are not guilty,   25
Since nature cannot choose his° origin—
By their o'ergrowth of some complexion,°
Oft breaking down the pales° and forts of reason,
Or by some habit that too much o'erleavens°
The form of plausive° manners, that these men,   30
Carrying, I say, the stamp of one defect,
Being nature's livery° or fortune's star,°
His virtues else,° be they as pure as grace,
As infinite as man may undergo,°
Shall in the general censure° take corruption   35
From that particular fault. The dram of evil
Doth all the noble substance often dout
To his own scandal.°

Enter GHOST.

HORATIO.   Look, my lord, it comes!
HAMLET.   Angels and ministers of grace° defend us!
Be thou° a spirit of health° or goblin damned,   40
Bring° with thee airs from heaven or blasts from hell,
Be thy intents° wicked or charitable,
Thou com'st in such a questionable° shape
That I will speak to thee. I'll call thee Hamlet,
King, father, royal Dane. O, answer me!   45
Let me not burst in ignorance, but tell
Why thy canonized° bones, hearsèd° in death,
Have burst their cerements;° why the sepulcher
Wherein we saw thee quietly inurned°
Hath oped his ponderous and marble jaws   50
To cast thee up again. What may this mean,
That thou, dead corpse, again in complete steel,°

20 **addition** reputation.   21 **at height** outstandingly.   22 **The pith . . . attribute** the essence of
the reputation that others attribute to us.   24 **for** on account of;   **mole of nature** natural
blemish in one's constitution.   26 **his** its.   27 **their o'ergrowth . . . complexion** the excessive
growth in individuals of some natural trait.   28 **pales** palings, fences (as of a fortification).
29 **o'erleavens** induces a change throughout (as yeast works in dough).   30 **plausive** pleasing.
32 **nature's livery** sign of one's servitude to nature;   **fortune's star** the destiny that chance
brings.   33 **His virtues else** i.e., the other qualities of *these men* (line 30).   34 **may undergo** can
sustain.   35 **general censure** general opinion that people have of him.   36–38 **The dram . . .
scandal** i.e., the small drop of evil blots out or works against the noble substance of the whole
and brings it into disrepute. To *dout* is to blot out. (A famous crux.)   39 **ministers of
grace** messengers of God.   40 **Be thou** whether you are;   **spirit of health** good angel.
41 **Bring** whether you bring.   42 **Be thy intents** whether your intentions are.
43 **questionable** inviting question.   47 **canonized** buried according to the canons of the church;
hearsèd coffined.   48 **cerements** grave clothes.   49 **inurned** entombed.   52 **complete steel** full
armor.

Revisits thus the glimpses of the moon,°
Making night hideous, and we fools of nature°
So horridly to shake our disposition°   55
With thoughts beyond the reaches of our souls?
Say, why is this? Wherefore? What should we do?

    [*The* GHOST] *beckons* [HAMLET].

HORATIO.   It beckons you to go away with it,
    As if it some impartment° did desire
    To you alone.
MARCELLUS.   Look with what courteous action   60
    It wafts you to a more removèd ground.
    But do not go with it.
HORATIO.   No, by no means.
HAMLET.   It will not speak. Then I will follow it.
HORATIO.   Do not, my lord!
HAMLET.   Why, what should be the fear?
    I do not set my life at a pin's fee,°   65
    And for my soul, what can it do to that,
    Being a thing immortal as itself?
    It waves me forth again. I'll follow it.
HORATIO.   What if it tempt you toward the flood,° my lord,
    Or to the dreadful summit of the cliff   70
    That beetles o'er° his° base into the sea,
    And there assume some other horrible form
    Which might deprive your sovereignty of reason°
    And draw you into madness? Think of it.
    The very place puts toys of desperation,°   75
    Without more motive, into every brain
    That looks so many fathoms to the sea
    And hears it roar beneath.
HAMLET.   It wafts me still.—Go on, I'll follow thee.
MARCELLUS.   You shall not go, my lord.   [*They try to stop him.*]
HAMLET.   Hold off your hands!   80
HORATIO.   Be ruled. You shall not go.
HAMLET.   My fate cries out,°
    And makes each petty° artery° in this body
    As hardy as the Nemean lion's° nerve.°
    Still am I called. Unhand me, gentlemen.
    By heaven, I'll make a ghost of him that lets° me!   85
    I say, away!—Go on, I'll follow thee.   *Exeunt* GHOST *and* HAMLET.
HORATIO.   He waxes desperate with imagination.

---

53 glimpses of the moon pale and uncertain moonlight.   **54 fools of nature** mere men, limited
to natural knowledge and subject to nature.   **55 So . . . disposition** to distress our mental
composure so violently.   **59 impartment** communication.   **65 fee** value.   **69 flood** sea.
71 beetles o'er overhangs threateningly (like bushy eyebrows); **his** its.   **73 deprive . . .
reason** take away the rule of reason over your mind.   **75 toys of desperation** fancies of
desperate acts, i.e., suicide.   **81 My fate cries out** my destiny summons me.   **82 petty** weak;
artery (through which the vital spirits were thought to have been conveyed).   **83 Nemean
lion** one of the monsters slain by Hercules in his twelve labors; **nerve** sinew.   **85 lets** hinders.

MARCELLUS.   Let's follow. 'Tis not fit thus to obey him.
HORATIO.   Have after.° To what issue° will this come?
MARCELLUS.   Something is rotten in the state of Denmark.   90
HORATIO.   Heaven will direct it.°
MARCELLUS.   Nay, let's follow him.   *Exeunt.*

1.5   *Enter* GHOST *and* HAMLET.

HAMLET.   Whither wilt thou lead me? Speak. I'll go no further.
GHOST.   Mark me.
HAMLET.   I will.
GHOST.   My hour is almost come,
When I to sulfurous and tormenting flames
Must render up myself.
HAMLET.   Alas, poor ghost!
GHOST.   Pity me not, but lend thy serious hearing   5
To what I shall unfold.
HAMLET.   Speak. I am bound° to hear.
GHOST.   So art thou to revenge, when thou shalt hear.
HAMLET.   What?
GHOST.   I am thy father's spirit,   10
Doomed for a certain term to walk the night,
And for the day confined to fast° in fires,
Till the foul crimes° done in my days of nature°
Are burnt and purged away. But that° I am forbid
To tell the secrets of my prison house,   15
I could a tale unfold whose lightest word
Would harrow up° thy soul, freeze thy young blood,
Make thy two eyes like stars start from their spheres,°
Thy knotted and combinèd locks° to part,
And each particular hair to stand on end   20
Like quills upon the fretful porcupine.
But this eternal blazon° must not be
To ears of flesh and blood. List, list, O, list!
If thou didst ever thy dear father love—
HAMLET.   O God!   25
GHOST.   Revenge his foul and most unnatural murder.
HAMLET.   Murder?
GHOST.   Murder most foul, as in the best ° it is,
But this most foul, strange, and unnatural.
HAMLET.   Haste me to know't, that I, with wings as swift   30
As meditation or the thoughts of love,
May sweep to my revenge.

---

89 Have after let's go after him;   **issue** outcome.   **91 it** i.e., the outcome.   **1.5. Location: The battlements of the castle.**   **7 bound** (1) ready (2) obligated by duty and fate. (The Ghost, in line 8, answers in the second sense.)   **12 fast** do penance by fasting.   **13 crimes** sins;   **of nature** as a mortal.   **14 But that** were it not that.   **17 harrow up** lacerate, tear.   **18 spheres** i.e., eye-sockets, here compared to the orbits or transparent revolving spheres in which, according to Ptolemaic astronomy, the heavenly bodies were fixed.   **19 knotted . . . locks** hair neatly arranged and confined.   **22 eternal blazon** revelation of the secrets of eternity.   **28 in the best** even at best.

GHOST.   I find thee apt;
          And duller shouldst thou be° than the fat° weed
          That roots itself in ease on Lethe° wharf,
          Wouldst thou not stir in this. Now, Hamlet, hear.   35
          'Tis given out that, sleeping in my orchard,°
          A serpent stung me. So the whole ear of Denmark
          Is by a forgèd process° of my death
          Rankly abused.° But know, thou noble youth,
          The serpent that did sting thy father's life   40
          Now wears his crown.
HAMLET.   O, my prophetic soul! My uncle!
GHOST.   Ay, that incestuous, that adulterate° beast,
          With witchcraft of his wit, with traitorous gifts°—
          O wicked wit and gifts, that have the power   45
          So to seduce!—won to his shameful lust
          The will of my most seeming-virtuous queen.
          O Hamlet, what a falling off was there!
          From me, whose love was of that dignity
          That it went hand in hand even with the vow°   50
          I made to her in marriage, and to decline
          Upon a wretch whose natural gifts were poor
          To° those of mine!
          But virtue, as it° never will be moved,
          Though lewdness court it in a shape of heaven,°   55
          So lust, though to a radiant angel linked,
          Will sate itself in a celestial bed°
          And prey on garbage.
          But soft, methinks I scent the morning air.
          Brief let me be. Sleeping within my orchard,   60
          My custom always of the afternoon,
          Upon my secure° hour thy uncle stole,
          With juice of cursèd hebona° in a vial,
          And in the porches of my ears° did pour
          The leprous distillment,° whose effect   65
          Holds such an enmity with blood of man
          That swift as quicksilver it courses through
          The natural gates and alleys of the body,
          And with a sudden vigor it doth posset°
          And curd, like eager° droppings into milk,   70
          The thin and wholesome blood. So did it mine,

---

33 shouldst thou be you would have to be;   **fat** torpid, lethargic.   **348 Lethe** the river of
forgetfulness in Hades.   **36 orchard** garden.   **38 forgèd process** falsified account.
39 abused deceived.   **43 adulterate** adulterous.   **44 gifts** (1) talents (2) presents.   **50 even
with the vow** with the very vow.   **53 To** compared to.   **54 virtue, as it** as virtue.   **55 shape of
heaven** heavenly form.   **57 sate . . . bed** cease to find sexual pleasure in a virtuously lawful
marriage.   **62 secure** confident, unsuspicious.   **63 hebona** a poison. (The word seems to be a
form of *ebony*, though it is thought perhaps to be related to *benbane*, a poison, or to *ebenus*,
"yew.")   **64 porches of my ears** ears as a porch or entrance of the body.   **65 leprous
distillment** distillation causing leprosylike disfigurement.   **69 posset** coagulate, curdle.
70 eager sour, acid.

And a most instant tetter° barked° about,
Most lazar-like,° with vile and loathsome crust,
All my smooth body.
Thus was I, sleeping, by a brother's hand   75
Of life, of crown, of queen at once dispatched,°
Cut off even in the blossoms of my sin,
Unhouseled,° disappointed,° unaneled,°
No reckoning° made, but sent to my account
With all my imperfections on my head.   80
O, horrible! O, horrible, most horrible!
If thou hast nature° in thee, bear it not.
Let not the royal bed of Denmark be
A couch for luxury° and damnèd incest.
But, howsoever thou pursues this act,   85
Taint not thy mind nor let thy soul contrive
Against thy mother aught. Leave her to heaven
And to those thorns that in her bosom lodge,
To prick and sting her. Fare thee well at once.
The glowworm shows the matin° to be near,   90
And 'gins to pale his° uneffectual fire.
Adieu, adieu, adieu! Remember me.   [*Exit.*]

HAMLET.   O all you host of heaven! O earth! What else?
And shall I couple° hell? O, fie! Hold,° hold, my heart,
And you, my sinews, grow not instant° old,   95
But bear me stiffly up. Remember thee?
Ay, thou poor ghost, whiles memory holds a seat
In this distracted globe.° Remember thee?
Yea, from the table° of my memory
I'll wipe away all trivial fond° records,   100
All saws° of books, all forms,° all pressures° past
That youth and observation copied there,
And thy commandment all alone shall live
Within the book and volume of my brain,
Unmixed with baser matter. Yes, by heaven!   105
O most pernicious woman!
O villain, villain, smiling, damnèd villain!
My tables°—meet it is° I set it down
That one may smile, and smile, and be a villain.
At least I am sure it may be so in Denmark.   [*Writing.*] 110
So uncle, there you are.° Now to my word:
It is "Adieu, adieu! Remember me."
I have sworn 't.

---

72 tetter eruption of scabs;   **barked** recovered with a rough covering, like bark on a tree.
73 lazar-like leperlike.   **76 dispatched** suddenly deprived.   **78 Unhouseled** without having
received the Sacrament;   **disappointed** unready (spiritually) for the last journey;
unaneled without having received extreme unction.   **79 reckoning** settling of accounts.
82 nature i.e., the promptings of a son.   **84 luxury** lechery.   **90 matin** morning.   **91 his** its.
94 couple add;   **Hold** hold together.   **95 instant** instantly.   **98 globe** (1) head (2) world.
99 table tablet, slate.   **100 fond** foolish.   **101 saws** wise sayings;   **forms** shapes or images
copied onto the slate; general ideas;   **pressures** impressions stamped.   **108 tables** writing
tablets;   **meet it is** it is fitting.   **111 there you are** i.e., there, I've written that down against you.

Enter HORATIO *and* MARCELLUS.

HORATIO.   My lord, my lord!

MARCELLUS.   Lord Hamlet!   115

HORATIO.   Heavens secure him!°

HAMLET.   So be it.

MARCELLUS.   Hilo, ho, ho, my lord!

HAMLET.   Hillo, ho, ho, boy! Come, bird, come.°

MARCELLUS.   How is 't, my noble lord?   120

HORATIO.   What news, my lord?

HAMLET.   O, wonderful!

HORATIO.   Good my lord, tell it.

HAMLET.   No, you will reveal it.

HORATIO.   Not I, my lord, by heaven.   125

MARCELLUS.   Nor I, my lord.

HAMLET.   How say you, then, would heart of man once° think it?
          But you'll be secret?

HORATIO, MARCELLUS.   Ay, by heaven, my lord.

HAMLET.   There's never a villain dwelling in all Denmark
          But he's an arrant° knave.   130

HORATIO.   There needs no ghost, my lord, come from the grave
          To tell us this.

HAMLET.   Why, right, you are in the right.
          And so, without more circumstance° at all,
          I hold it fit that we shake hands and part,
          You as your business and desire shall point you—   135
          For every man hath business and desire,
          Such as it is—and for my own poor part,
          Look you, I'll go pray.

HORATIO.   These are but wild and whirling words, my lord.

HAMLET.   I am sorry they offend you, heartily;   140
          Yes, faith, heartily.

HORATIO.   There's no offense, my lord.

HAMLET.   Yes, by Saint Patrick,° but there is, Horatio,
          And much offense° too. Touching this vision here,
          It is an honest ghost,° that let me tell you.
          For your desire to know what is between us,   145
          O'ermaster 't as you may. And now, good friends,
          As you are friends, scholars, and soldiers,
          Give me one poor request.

HORATIO.   What is 't, my lord? We will.

HAMLET.   Never make known what you have seen tonight.   150

HORATIO, MARCELLUS.   My lord, we will not.

HAMLET.   Nay, but swear 't.

---

116 secure him keep him safe.   **119 Hillo . . . come** (A falconer's call to a hawk in air. Hamlet mocks the halloing as though it were a part of hawking.)   **127 once** ever.
130 arrant thoroughgoing.   **133 circumstance** ceremony, elaboration.   **142 Saint Patrick** (The keeper of Purgatory and patron saint of all blunders and confusion.)   **143 offense** (Hamlet deliberately changes Horatio's "no offense against all decency.")   **144 an honest ghost** i.e., a real ghost and not an evil spirit.

HORATIO.   In faith, my lord, not I.°
MARCELLUS.   Nor I, my lord, in faith.
HAMLET.   Upon my sword.°   [*He holds out his sword.*]   155
MARCELLUS.   We have sworn, my lord, already.°
HAMLET.   Indeed, upon my sword, indeed.
GHOST [*cries under the stage*].   Swear.
HAMLET.   Ha, ha, boy, sayst thou so? Art thou there, truepenny?°
    Come on, you hear this fellow in the cellarage.   160
    Consent to swear.
HORATIO.   Propose the oath, my lord.
HAMLET.   Never to speak of this that you have seen,
    Swear by my sword.
GHOST [*beneath*].   Swear.   [*They swear.°*]
HAMLET.   *Hic et ubique?°* Then we'll shift our ground.   165
                         [*He moves to another spot.*]
    Come hither, gentlemen,
    And lay your hands again upon my sword.
    Swear by my sword
    Never to speak of this that you have heard.
GHOST [*beneath*].   Swear by his sword.   [*They swear.*]   170
HAMLET.   Well said, old mole. Canst work i' th' earth so fast?
    A worthy pioneer!°—Once more removed, good friends.
                            [*He moves again.*]
HORATIO.   O day and night, but this is wondrous strange!
HAMLET.   And therefore as a stranger° give it welcome.
    There are more things in heaven and earth, Horatio,   175
    Than are dreamt of in your philosophy.°
    But come;
    Here, as before, never, so help you mercy,°
    How strange or odd soe'er I bear myself—
    As I perchance hereafter shall think meet   180
    To put an antic° disposition on—
    That you, at such times seeing me, never shall,
    With arms encumbered° thus, or this headshake,
    Or by pronouncing of some doubtful phrase
    As "Well, we know," or "We could, an if° we would,"   185
    Or "If we list° to speak," or "There be, an if they might,"°
    Or such ambiguous giving out,° to note°

---

153 In faith . . . I i.e., I swear not to tell what I have seen. (Horatio is not refusing to swear.)
155 sword i.e., the hilt in the form of a cross.   **156 We . . . already** i.e., we swore in *faith*.
159 truepenny honest old fellow.   **164 s.d. They swear** (Seemingly they swear here, and at
lines 170 and 190, as they lay their hands on Hamlet's sword. Triple oaths would have particular
force; these three oaths deal with what they have seen, what they have heard, and what they
promise about Hamlet's *antic disposition*.)   **165 Hic et ubique** here and everywhere (Latin).
172 pioneer foot soldier assigned to dig tunnels and excavations.   **174 as a stranger** i.e.,
needing your hospitality.   **176 your philosophy** this subject called "natural philosophy" or
"science" that people talk about.   **178 so help you mercy** as you hope for God's mercy when
you are judged.   **181 antic** fantastic.   **1831 encumbered** folded.   **185 an if** if.
186 list wished;   **There . . . might** i.e., there are people here (we, in fact) who could tell news if
we were at liberty to do so.   **187 giving out** intimation;   **note** draw attention to the fact.

That you know aught° of me—this do swear,
So grace and mercy at your most need help you.
GHOST [*beneath*].   Swear.   [*They swear.*]   190
HAMLET.   Rest, rest, perturbèd spirit! So, gentlemen,
With all my love I do commend me to you;°
And what so poor a man as Hamlet is
May do t' express his love and friending° to you,
God willing, shall not lack.° Let us go in together,   195
And still° your fingers on your lips, I pray.
The time° is out of joint. O cursèd spite°
That ever I was born to set it right!   [*They wait for him to leave first.*]
Nay, come, let's go together.°   *Exeunt.*

2.1   *Enter old* POLONIUS *with his man* [REYNALDO].

POLONIUS.   Give him this money and these notes, Reynaldo.
                                       [*He gives money and papers.*]
REYNALDO.   I will, my lord.
POLONIUS.   You shall do marvelous° wisely, good Reynaldo,
Before you visit him, to make inquire°
Of his behavior.
REYNALDO.   My lord, I did intend it.   5
POLONIUS.   Marry, well said, very well said. Look you, sir,
Inquire me first what Danskers° are in Paris,
And how, and who, what means,° and where they keep,°
What company, at what expense; and finding
By this encompassment° and drift° of question   10
That they do know my son, come you more nearer
Than your particular demands will touch it.°
Take you,° as 'twere, some distant knowledge of him,
As thus, "I know his father and his friends,
And in part him." Do you mark this, Reynaldo?   15
REYNALDO.   Ay, very well, my lord.
POLONIUS.   "And in part him, but," you may say, "not well.
But if 't be he I mean, he's very wild,
Addicted so and so," and there put on° him
What forgeries° you please—marry, none so rank°   20
As may dishonor him, take heed of that,
But, sir, such wanton,° wild, and usual slips
As are companions noted and most known
To youth and liberty.

---

188 aught i.e., something secret.   **192 do . . . you** entrust myself to you.
194 friending friendliness.   **195 lack** be lacking.   **196 still** always.   **197 The time** the state of
affairs;   **spite** i.e., the spite of Fortune.   **199 let's go together** (Probably they wait for him to
leave first, but he refuses this ceremoniousness.)   **2.1 Location: Polonius' chambers.**
3 marvelous marvelously.   **4 inquire** inquiry.   **7 Danskers** Danes.   **8 what means** what wealth
(they have);   **keep** dwell.   **10 encompassment** roundabout talking;   **drift** gradual approach or
course.   **11–12 come . . . it** you will find out more this way than by asking pointed questions
(*particular demands*).   **13 Take you** assume, pretend.   **19 put on** impute to.
20 forgeries invented tales;   **rank** gross.   **22 wanton** sportive, unrestrained.

REYNALDO.   As gaming, my lord.   25
POLONIUS.   Ay, or drinking, fencing, swearing,
               Quarreling, drabbing°—you may go so far.
REYNALDO.   My lord, that would dishonor him.
POLONIUS.   Faith, no, as you may season° it in the charge.
               You must not put another scandal on him   30
               That he is open to incontinency;°
               That's not my meaning. But breathe his faults so quaintly°
               That they may seem the taints of liberty,°
               The flash and outbreak of a fiery mind,
               A savageness in unreclaimèd blood,   35
               Of general assault.°
REYNALDO.   But, my good lord—
POLONIUS.   Wherefore should you do this?
REYNALDO.   Ay, my lord, I would know that.
POLONIUS.   Marry, sir, here's my drift,   40
               And I believe it is a fetch of warrant.°
               You laying these slight sullies on my son,
               As 'twere a thing a little soiled wi' the working,°
               Mark you,
               Your party in converse,° him you would sound,°   45
               Having ever° seen in the prenominate crimes°
               The youth you breathe° of guilty, be assured
               He closes with you in this consequence:°
               "Good sir," or so, or "friend," or "gentleman,"
               According to the phrase or the addition°   50
               Of man and country.
REYNALDO.   Very good, my lord.
POLONIUS.   And then, sir, does 'a this—'a does—what was I about to say? By the
               Mass, I was about to say something. Where did I leave?
REYNALDO.   At "closes in the consequence."
POLONIUS.   At "closes in the consequence," ay, marry.   55
               He closes thus: "I know the gentleman,
               I saw him yesterday," or "th' other day,"
               Or then, or then, with such or such, "and as you say,
               There was 'a gaming," "there o'ertook in 's rouse,"°
               "There falling out° at tennis," or perchance   60
               "I saw him enter such a house of sale,"
               Videlicet° a brothel, or so forth. See you now,
               Your bait of falsehood takes this carp° of truth;
               And thus do we of wisdom and of reach,°

27 **drabbing** whoring.   29 **season** temper, soften.   31 **incontinency** habitual sexual excess.
32 **quaintly** artfully, subtly.   33 **taints of liberty** faults resulting from free living.   35–36 **A
savageness . . . assault** a wildness in untamed youth that assails all indiscriminately.   41 **fetch of
warrant** legitimate trick.   43 **soiled wi' the working** soiled by handling while it is being made,
i.e., by involvement in the ways of the world.   45 **converse** conversation;   **sound** i.e., sound
out.   46 **Having ever** if he has ever;   **prenominate crimes** before-mentioned offenses.
47 **breathe** speak.   48 **closes . . . consequence** takes you into his confidence in some fashion, as
follows.   50 **addition** title.   59 **o'ertook in 's rouse** overcome by drink.   60 **falling
out** quarreling.   62 **Videlicet** namely.   63 **carp** a fish.   64 **reach** capacity, ability.

With windlasses° and with assays of bias,°   65
By indirections find directions° out.
So by my former lecture and advice
Shall you my son. You have° me, have you not?
REYNALDO.   My lord, I have.
POLONIUS.   God b'wi'° ye; fare ye well.
REYNALDO.   Good my lord.   70
POLONIUS.   Observe his inclination in yourself.°
REYNALDO.   I shall, my lord.
POLONIUS.   And let him ply his music.
REYNALDO.   Well, my lord.
POLONIUS.   Farewell.   *Exit* REYNALDO.

    Enter OPHELIA.

                How now, Ophelia, what's the matter?   75
OPHELIA.   O my lord, my lord, I have been so affrighted!
POLONIUS.   With what, i' the name of God?
OPHELIA.   My lord, as I was sewing in my closet,°
  Lord Hamlet, with his doublet° all unbraced,°
  No hat upon his head, his stockings fouled,   80
  Ungartered, and down-gyvèd° to his ankle,
  Pale as his shirt, his knees knocking each other,
  And with a look so piteous in purport°
  As if he had been loosèd out of hell
  To speak of horrors—he comes before me.   85
POLONIUS.   Mad for thy love?
OPHELIA.   My lord, I do not know,
  But truly I do fear it.
POLONIUS.   What said he?
OPHELIA.   He took me by the wrist and held me hard.
  Then goes he to the length of all his arm,
  And, with his other hand thus o'er his brow   90
  He falls to such perusal of my face
  As° 'a would draw it. Long stayed he so.
  At last, a little shaking of mine arm
  And thrice his head thus waving up and down,
  He raised a sigh so piteous and profound   95
  As it did seem to shatter all his bulk°
  And end his being. That done, he lets me go,
  And with his head over his shoulder turned
  He seemed to find his way without his eyes,
  For out o' doors he went without their helps,   100
  And to the last bended their light on me.

---

65 windlasses i.e., circuitous paths. (Literally, circuits made to head off the game in hunting);
assays of bias attempts through indirection (like the curving path of the bowling ball, which is
biased or weighted to one side).   **66 directions** i.e., the way things really are.
68 have understand.   **69 b' wi'** be with.   **71 in yourself** in your own person (as well as by
asking questions).   **78 closet** private chamber.   **79 doublet** close-fitting jacket;
unbraced unfastened.   **81 down-gyvèd** fallen to the ankles (like gyves or fetters).   **83 in
purport** in what it expressed.   **92 As** as if (also in line 97).   **96 bulk** body.

POLONIUS.   Come, go with me. I will go seek the King.
          This is the very ecstasy° of love,
          Whose violent property° fordoes° itself
          And leads the will to desperate undertakings   105
          As oft as any passion under heaven
          That does afflict our natures. I am sorry.
          What, have you given him any hard words of late?
OPHELIA.   No, my good lord, but as you did command
          I did repel his letters and denied   110
          His access to me.
POLONIUS.   That hath made him mad.
          I am sorry that with better heed and judgment
          I had not quoted° him. I feared he did but trifle
          And meant to wrack° thee. But beshrew my jealousy!°
          By heaven, it is as proper to our age°   115
          To cast beyond° ourselves in our opinions
          As it is common for the younger sort
          To lack discretion. Come, go we to the King.
          This must be known,° which, being kept close,° might move
          More grief to hide than hate to utter love.°   120
          Come.   *Exeunt.*

          2.2 *Flourish. Enter* KING *and* QUEEN, ROSENCRANTZ, *and*
                  GUILDENSTERN [*with others*].

KING.   Welcome, dear Rosencrantz and Guildenstern.
          Moreover that° we much did long to see you,
          The need we have to use you did provoke
          Our hasty sending. Something have you heard
          Of Hamlet's transformation—so call it,   5
          Sith nor° th' exterior nor the inward man
          Resembles that° it was. What it should be,
          More than his father's death, that thus hath put him
          So much from th' understanding of himself,
          I cannot dream of. I entreat you both   10
          That, being of so young days° brought up with him,
          And sith so neighbored to° his youth and havior,°
          That you vouchsafe your rest° here in our court
          Some little time, so by your companies
          To draw him on to pleasures, and to gather   15

---

103 ecstasy madness.   **104 property** nature;   **fordoes** destroys.   **113 quoted** observed.
114 wrack ruin, seduce;   **beshrew my jealousy** a plague upon my suspicious nature.
115 proper . . . age characteristic of us (old) men.   **116 cast beyond** overshoot, miscalculate. (A
metaphor from hunting.)   **119 known** made known (to the King);   **close** secret.
119–120 might . . . love i.e., might cause more grief (because of what Hamlet might do) by
hiding the knowledge of Hamlet's strange behavior toward Ophelia than unpleasantness by
telling it.   **2.2. Location: The castle.**   **2 Moreover that** besides the fact that.   **6 Sith nor** since
neither.   **7 that** what.   **11 of . . . days** from such early youth.   **12 And sith so neighbored
to** and since you are (or, and since that time you are) intimately acquainted with;
havior demeanor.   **13 vouchsafe your rest** please to stay.

So much as from occasion° you may glean,
Whether aught to us unknown afflicts him thus
That, opened,° lies within our remedy.

QUEEN.   Good gentlemen, he hath much talked of you,
And sure I am two men there is not living   20
To whom he more adheres. If it will please you
To show us so much gentry° and good will
As to expend your time with us awhile
For the supply and profit of our hope,°
Your visitation shall receive such thanks   25
As fits a king's remembrance.°

ROSENCRANTZ.   Both Your Majesties
Might, by the sovereign power you have of° us,
Put your dread° pleasures more into command
Than to entreaty.

GUILDENSTERN.   But we both obey,
And here give up ourselves in the full bent°   30
To lay our service freely at your feet,
To be commanded.

KING.   Thanks, Rosencrantz and gentle Guildenstern.

QUEEN.   Thanks, Guildenstern and gentle Rosencrantz.
And I beseech you instantly to visit   35
My too much changèd son. Go, some of you,
And bring these gentlemen where Hamlet is.

GUILDENSTERN.   Heavens make our presence and our practices°
Pleasant and helpful to him!

QUEEN.   Ay, amen!

          Exeunt ROSENCRANTZ *and* GUILDENSTERN [*with some attendants*].

     Enter Polonius.

POLONIUS.   Th' ambassadors from Norway, my good lord,   40
Are joyfully returned.

KING.   Thou still° hast been the father of good news.

POLONIUS.   Have I, my lord? I assure my good liege
I hold° my duty, as° I hold my soul,
Both to my God and to my gracious king;   45
And I do think, or else this brain of mine
Hunts not the trail of policy° so sure
As it hath used to do, that I have found
The very cause of Hamlet's lunacy.

KING.   O, speak of that! That do I long to hear.   50

POLONIUS.   Give first admittance to th' ambassadors.
My news shall be the fruit° to that great feast.

KING.   Thyself do grace° to them and bring them in.   [*Exit* POLONIUS.]

---

16 occasion opportunity.   **18 opened** being revealed.   **22 gentry** courtesy.   **24 supply**...
hope aid and furtherance of what we hope for.   **26 As fits . . . remembrance** as would be a
fitting gift of a king who rewards true service.   **27 of** over.   **28 dread** inspiring awe.   **30 in**...
bent to the utmost degree of our capacity. (An archery metaphor.)   **38 practices** doings.
42 still always.   **44 hold** maintain;   **as** firmly as.   **47 policy** sagacity.   **52 fruit** dessert.
53 grace honor (punning on *grace* said before a *feast*, line 52.)

He tells me, my dear Gertrude, he hath found
The head and source of all your son's distemper.   55
QUEEN.   I doubt° it is no other but the main,°
His father's death and our o'erhasty marriage.

Enter Ambassadors VOLTIMAND *and* CORNELIUS, *with* POLONIUS.

KING.   Well, we shall sift him.°—Welcome, my good friends!
Say, Voltimand, what from our brother° Norway?
VOLTIMAND.   Most fair return of greetings and desires.°   60
Upon our first,° he sent out to suppress
His nephew's levies, which to him appeared
To be a preparation 'gainst the Polack,
But, better looked into, he truly found
It was against Your Highness. Whereat grieved   65
That so his sickness, age, and impotence°
Was falsely borne in hand,° sends out arrests°
On Fortinbras, which he, in brief, obeys,
Receives rebuke from Norway, and in fine°
Makes vow before his uncle never more   70
To give th' assay° of arms against Your Majesty.
Whereon old Norway, overcome with joy,
Gives him three thousand crowns in annual fee
And his commission to employ those soldiers,
So levied as before, against the Polack,   75
With an entreaty, herein further shown,   [*giving a paper*]
That it might please you to give quiet pass
Through your dominions for this enterprise
On such regards of safety and allowance°
As therein are set down.
KING.   It likes° us well,   80
And at our more considered° time we'll read,
Answer, and think upon this business.
Meantime we thank you for your well-took labor.
Go to your rest; at night we'll feast together.
Most welcome home!   *Exeunt Ambassadors.*
POLONIUS.   This business is well ended.   85
My liege, and madam, to expostulate°
What majesty should be, what duty is,
Why day is day, night night, and time is time,
Were nothing but to waste night, day, and time.
Therefore, since brevity is the soul of wit,°   90
And tediousness the limbs and outward flourishes,
I will be brief. Your noble son is mad.

---

56 doubt fear, suspect;   **main** chief point, principal concern.   **58 sift him** question Polonius closely.   **59 brother** fellow king.   **60 desires** good wishes.   **61 Upon our first** at our first words on the business.   **66 impotence** helplessness.   **67 borne in hand** deluded, taken advantage of;   **arrests** orders to desist.   **69 in fine** in conclusion.   **71 give th' assay** make trial of strength, challenge.   **78 On . . . allowance** i.e., with such considerations for the safety of Denmark and permission for Fortinbras.   **80 likes** pleases.   **81 considered** suitable for deliberation.   **86 expostulate** expound, inquire into.   **90 wit** sense or judgment.

Mad call I it, for, to define true madness,
What is't but to be nothing else but mad?
But let that go.

QUEEN.   More matter, with less art.   95

POLONIUS.   Madam, I swear I use no art at all.
That he's mad, 'tis true; 'tis true 'tis pity.
And pity 'tis 'tis true—a foolish figure,°
But farewell it, for I will use no art.
Mad let us grant him, then, and now remains   100
That we find out the cause of this effect,
Or rather say, the cause of this defect,
For this effect defective comes by cause.°
Thus it remains, and the remainder thus.
Perpend.°   105
I have a daughter—have while she is mine—
Who, in her duty and obedience, mark,
Hath given me this. Now gather and surmise.°
[*He reads the letter.*] "To the celestial and my soul's idol, the most beauti-
fied Ophelia"—   110
That's an ill phrase, a vile phrase; "beautified" is a vile phrase. But you
shall hear. Thus: [*He reads.*]
"In her excellent white bosom,° these,° etc."

QUEEN.   Came this from Hamlet to her?

POLONIUS.   Good madam, stay° awhile, I will be faithful.°   [*He reads.*]   115

"Doubt thou the stars are fire,
    Doubt that the sun doth move,
Doubt° truth to be a liar,
    But never doubt I love.

O dear Ophelia, I am ill at these numbers.° I have not art to reckon° my   120
groans. But that I love thee best, O most best, believe it. Adieu.
    Thine evermore, most dear lady, whilst this machine° is to him,
                                                                        Hamlet."

This in obedience hath my daughter shown me,
And, more above,° hath his solicitings,   125
As they fell out° by° time, by means, and place,
All given to mine ear.°

KING.   But how hath she
Received his love?

POLONIUS.   What do you think of me?

KING.   As of a man faithful and honorable.

POLONIUS.   I would fain° prove so. But what might you think,   130

---

98 figure figure of speech.   **103 For . . . cause** i.e., for this defective behavior, his madness, has
a cause.   **105 Perpend** consider.   **108 gather and surmise** draw your own conclusions.
113 In . . . bosom (The letter is poetically addressed to her heart.);   **these** i.e., the letter.
115 stay wait;   **faithful** i.e., in reading the letter accurately.   **118 Doubt** suspect.   **120 ill . . .
numbers** unskilled at writing verses.   **121 reckon** (1) count (2) number metrically, scan.
122 machine i.e., body.   **125 more above** moreover.   **126 fell out** occurred;   **by** according to.
127 given . . . ear i.e., told me about.   **130 fain** gladly.

When I had seen this hot love on the wing—
As I perceived it, I must tell you that,
Before my daughter told me—what might you,
Or my dear Majesty your queen here, think,
If I had played the desk or table book,°   135
Or given my heart a winking,° mute and dumb,
Or looked upon this love with idle sight?°
What might you think? No, I went round° to work,
And my young mistress thus I did bespeak:°
"Lord Hamlet is a prince out of thy star;°   140
This must not be." And then I prescripts° gave her,
That she should lock herself from his resort,°
Admit no messengers, receive no tokens.
Which done, she took the fruits of my advice;
And he, repellèd—a short tale to make—   145
Fell into a sadness, then into a fast,
Thence to a watch,° thence into a weakness,
Thence to a lightness,° and by this declension°
Into the madness wherein now he raves,
And all we° mourn for.

KING [*to the* QUEEN].   Do you think 'tis this?   150
QUEEN.   It may be, very like.
POLONIUS.   Hath there been such a time—I would fain know that—
    That I have positively said "'Tis so,"
    When it proved otherwise?
KING.   Not that I know.
POLONIUS.   Take this from this,° if this be otherwise.   155
    If circumstances lead me, I will find
    Where truth is hid, though it were hid indeed
    Within the center.°
KING.   How may we try° it further?
POLONIUS.   You know sometimes he walks four hours together
    Here in the lobby.
QUEEN.   So he does indeed.   160
POLONIUS.   At such a time I'll loose° my daughter to him.
    Be you and I behind an arras° then.
    Mark the encounter. If he love her not
    And be not from his reason fall'n thereon,°

---

135 played . . . table book i.e., remained shut up, concealing the information.   **136 given . . .
winking** closed the eyes of my heart to this.   **137 with idle sight** complacently or
incomprehendingly.   **138 round** roundly, plainly.   **139 bespeak** address.   **140 out of thy
star** above your sphere, position.   **141 prescripts** orders.   **142 his resort** his visits.
147 watch state of sleeplessness.   **148 lightness** lightheadedness;   **declension** decline,
deterioration (with a pun on the grammatical sense).   **150 all we** all of us, or, into everything
that we.   **155 Take this from this** (The actor probably gestures, indicating that he means his
head from his shoulders, or his staff of office or chain from his hands or neck, or something
similar.)   **158 center** middle point of the earth (which is also the center of the Ptolemaic
universe);   **try** test, judge.   **161 loose** (As one might release an animal that is being mated.)
162 arras hanging, tapestry.   **164 thereon** on that account.

Let me be no assistant for a state,   165
But keep a farm and carters.°

KING.   We will try it.

Enter HAMLET [*reading on a book*].

QUEEN.   But look where sadly° the poor wretch comes reading.

POLONIUS.   Away, I do beseech you both, away.
I'll board° him presently.° O, give me leave.°

Exeunt KING *and* QUEEN [*with attendants*].

How does my good Lord Hamlet?   170

HAMLET.   Well, God-a-mercy.°

POLONIUS.   Do you know me, my lord?

HAMLET.   Excellent well. You are a fishmonger.°

POLONIUS.   Not I, my lord.

HAMLET.   Then I would you were so honest a man.   175

POLONIUS.   Honest, my lord?

HAMLET.   Ay, sir. To be honest, as this world goes, is to be one man picked out of
ten thousand.

POLONIUS.   That's very true, my lord.

HAMLET.   For if the sun breed maggots in a dead dog, being a good kissing car-   180
rion°—Have you a daughter?

POLONIUS.   I have, my lord.

HAMLET.   Let her not walk i' the sun.° Conception° is a blessing, but as your
daughter may conceive, friend, look to 't.

POLONIUS [*aside*].   How say you by that? Still harping on my daughter. Yet he   185
knew me not at first; 'a° said I was a fishmonger. 'A is far gone. And truly
in my youth I suffered much extremity for love, very near this. I'll speak
to him again.—What do you read, my lord?

HAMLET.   Words, words, words.

POLONIUS.   What is the matter,° my lord?   190

HAMLET.   Between who?

POLONIUS.   I mean, the matter that you read, my lord.

HAMLET.   Slanders, sir; for the satirical rogue says here that old men have gray
beards, that their faces are wrinkled, their eyes purging° thick amber° and
plum-tree gum, and that they have a plentiful lack of wit,° together with   195
most weak hams. All which, sir, though I most powerfully and potently
believe, yet I hold it not honesty° to have it thus set down, for yourself,
sir, shall grow old° as I am, if like a crab you could go backward.

POLONIUS [*aside*].   Though this be madness, yet there is method in 't.—Will you
walk out of the air,° my lord?   200

---

166 carters wagon drivers.   **167 sadly** seriously.   **169 board** accost;   **presently** at once;   **give me leave** i.e., excuse me, leave me alone. (Said to those he hurries offstage, including the King and Queen.)   **171 God-a-mercy** God have mercy, i.e., thank you.   **173 fishmonger** fish merchant.   **180–181 a good kissing carrion** i.e., a good piece of flesh for kissing, or for the sun to kiss.   **183 i' the sun** in public (with additional implication of the sunshine of princely favors); **Conception** (1) understanding (2) pregnancy.   **186 'a** he.   **190 matter** substance. (But Hamlet plays on the sense of "basis for a dispute.")   **194 purging** discharging;   **amber** i.e., resin, like the resinous *plum-tree gum*.   **195 wit** understanding.   **197 honesty** decency, decorum. **198 old** as old.   **200 out of the air** (The open air was considered dangerous for sick people.)

HAMLET.   Into my grave.

POLONIUS.   Indeed, that's out of the air. [*Aside.*] How pregnant° sometimes his replies are! A happiness° that often madness hits on, which reason and sanity could not so prosperously° be delivered of. I will leave him and suddenly° contrive the means of meeting between him and my daugh-ter.—My honorable lord, I will most humbly take my leave of you.   205

HAMLET.   You cannot, sir, take from me anything that I will more willingly part withal°—except my life, except my life, except my life.

Enter GUILDENSTERN *and* ROSENCRANTZ.

POLONIUS.   Fare you well, my lord.

HAMLET.   These tedious old fools!°   210

POLONIUS.   You go to seek the Lord Hamlet. There he is.

ROSENCRANTZ [*to* POLONIUS].   God save you, sir!   [*Exit* POLONIUS.]

GUILDENSTERN.   My honored lord!

ROSENCRANTZ.   My most dear lord!

HAMLET.   My excellent good friends! How dost thou, Guildenstern? Ah,   215
Rosencrantz! Good lads, how do you both?

ROSENCRANTZ.   As the indifferent° children of the earth.

GUILDENSTERN.   Happy in that we are not overhappy.
On Fortune's cap we are not the very button.

HAMLET.   Nor the soles of her shoe?   220

ROSENCRANTZ.   Neither, my lord.

HAMLET.   Then you live about her waist, or in the middle of her favors?°

GUILDENSTERN.   Faith, her privates we.°

HAMLET.   In the secret parts of Fortune? O, most true, she is a strumpet.°
What news?   225

ROSENCRANTZ.   None, my lord, but the world's grown honest.

HAMLET.   Then is doomsday near. But your news is not true. Let me question more in particular. What have you, my good friends, deserved at the hands of Fortune that she sends you to prison hither?

GUILDENSTERN.   Prison, my lord?   230

HAMLET.   Denmark's a prison.

ROSENCRANTZ.   Then is the world one.

HAMLET.   A goodly one, in which there are many confines,° wards,° and dun-geons, Denmark being one o' the worst.

ROSENCRANTZ.   We think not so, my lord.   235

HAMLET.   Why then 'tis none to you, for there is nothing either good or bad but thinking makes it so. To me it is a prison.

ROSENCRANTZ.   Why then, your ambition makes it one. 'Tis too narrow for your mind.

HAMLET.   O God, I could be bounded in a nutshell and count myself a king of in-finite space, were it not that I have bad dreams.   240

---

202 pregnant quick-witted, full of meaning.   **203 happiness** felicity of expression.
204 prosperously successfully.   **205 suddenly** immediately.   **208 withal** with.   **210 old fools** i.e., old men like Polonius.   **217 indifferent** ordinary, at neither extreme of fortune or misfortune.   **222 favors** i.e., sexual favors.   **223 her privates we** i.e., (1) we are sexually intimate with Fortune, the fickle goddess who bestows her favors indiscriminately (2) we are her private citizens.   **224 strumpet** prostitute. (A common epithet for indiscriminate Fortune; see line 452.)   **233 confines** places of confinement;   **wards** cells.

GUILDENSTERN.   Which dreams indeed are ambition, for the very substance of the
ambitious° is merely the shadow of a dream.

HAMLET.   A dream itself is but a shadow.

ROSENCRANTZ.   Truly, and I hold ambition of so airy and light a quality that it is but
a shadow's shadow.   245

HAMLET.   Then are our beggars bodies,° and our monarchs and outstretched° heroes the beggars' shadows. Shall we to the court? For, by my fay,° I cannot reason.

ROSENCRANTZ, GUILDENSTERN.   We'll wait upon° you.

HAMLET.   No such matter. I will not sort° you with the rest of my servants, for, to   250
speak to you like an honest man, I am most dreadfully attended.° But, in
the beaten way° of friendship, what make° you at Elsinore?

ROSENCRANTZ.   To visit you, my lord, no other occasion.

HAMLET.   Beggar that I am, I am even poor in thanks; but I thank you, and sure,
dear friends, my thanks are too dear a halfpenny.° Were you not sent for?   255
Is it your own inclining? Is it a free° visitation? Come, come, deal justly
with me. Come, come. Nay, speak.

GUILDENSTERN.   What should we say, my lord?

HAMLET.   Anything but to the purpose.° You were sent for, and there is a kind of
confession in your looks which your modesties° have not craft enough to   260
color.° I know the good King and Queen have sent for you.

ROSENCRANTZ.   To what end, my lord?

HAMLET.   That you must teach me. But let me conjure° you, by the rights of our fellowship, by the consonancy of our youth,° by the obligation of our ever-
preserved love, and by what more dear a better° proposer could charge°   265
you withal, be even° and direct with me whether you were sent for or no.

ROSENCRANTZ [*aside to* GUILDENSTERN].   What say you?

HAMLET [*aside*].   Nay, then, I have an eye of° you.—If you love me, hold not off.°

GUILDENSTERN.   My lord, we were sent for.

HAMLET.   I will tell you why; so shall my anticipation prevent your discovery,° and   270
your secrecy to the King and Queen molt no feather,° I have of late—but
wherefore I know not—lost all my mirth, for-gone all custom of exercises; and indeed it goes so heavily with my disposition that this goodly
frame, the earth, seems to me a sterile promontory; this most excellent
canopy, the air, look you, this brave° o'erhanging firmament, this majesti-   275
cal roof fretted° with golden fire, why, it appeareth nothing to me but a

---

241–242 the very ... ambitious that seemingly very substantial thing that the ambitious pursue.
246 bodies i.e., solid substances rather than shadows (since beggars are not ambitious).
outstretched (1) far-reaching in their ambition (2) elongated as shadows.   **247 fay** faith.
249 wait upon accompany, attend. (But Hamlet uses the phrase in the sense of providing
menial service.)   **250 sort** class, categorize.   **251 dreadfully attended** waited upon in slovenly
fashion.   **252 beaten way** familiar path, tried-and-true course;   **make** do.   **255 too dear a**
halfpenny (1) too expensive at even a halfpenny, i.e., of little worth (2) too expensive *by* a
halfpenny in return for worthless kindness.   **256 free** voluntary.   **259 Anything but to the**
purpose anything except a straightforward answer. (Said ironically.)   **260 modesties** sense of
shame.   **261 color** disguise.   **263 conjure** adjure, entreat.   **264 the consonancy of our**
youth our closeness in our younger days.   **265 better** more skillful;   **charge** urge.
266 even straight, honest.   **268 of** on;   **hold not off** don't hold back.   **270 so ... discovery** in
that way my saying it first will spare you from revealing the truth.   **271 molt no feather** i.e., not
diminish in the least.   **275 brave** splendid.   **276 fretted** adorned (with fretwork, as in a vaulted
ceiling).

foul and pestilent congregation° of vapors. What a piece of work° is a man! How noble in reason, how infinite in faculties, in form and moving how express° and admirable, in action how like an angel, in apprehension° how like a god! The beauty of the world, the paragon of animals! And yet, to me, what is this quintessence° of dust? Man delights not me— no, nor woman neither, though by your smiling you seem to say so.   280

ROSENCRANTZ.   My lord, there was no such stuff in my thoughts.

HAMLET.   Why did you laugh, then, when I said man delights not me?

ROSENCRANTZ.   To think, my lord, if you delight not in man, what Lenten entertainment° the players shall receive from you. We coted° them on the way, and hither are they coming to offer you service.   285

HAMLET.   He that plays the king shall be welcome; His Majesty shall have tribute° of° me. The adventurous knight shall use his foil and target,° the lover shall not sigh gratis,° the humorous man° shall end his part in peace,° the clown shall make those laugh whose lungs are tickle o' the sear,° and the lady shall say her mind freely, or the blank verse shall halt° for 't. What players are they?   290

ROSENCRANTZ.   Even those you were wont to take such delight in, the tragedians° of the city.   295

HAMLET.   How chances it they travel? Their residence,° both in reputation and profit, was better both ways.

ROSENCRANTZ.   I think their inhibition° comes by the means of the late° innovation.°

HAMLET.   Do they hold the same estimation they did when I was in the city? Are they so followed?   300

ROSENCRANTZ.   No, indeed are they not.

HAMLET.   How comes it? Do they grow rusty?

ROSENCRANTZ.   Nay, their endeavor keeps° in the wonted° pace. But there is, sir, an aerie° of children, little eyases,° that cry out on the top of question° and are most tyrannically° clapped for 't. These are now the fashion, and so berattle° the common stages°—so they call them—that many wearing rapiers° are afraid of goose quills° and dare scarce come thither.   305

HAMLET.   What, are they children? Who maintains 'em? How are they escoted?° Will they pursue the quality° no longer than they can sing?° Will they not

277 **congregation** mass;   **piece of work** masterpiece.   279 **express** well-framed, exact, expressive.   279–280 **apprehension** power of comprehending.   281 **quintessence** the fifth essence of ancient philosophy, beyond earth, water, air, and fire, supposed to be the substance of the heavenly bodies and to be latent in all things.   285–286 **Lenten entertainment** meager reception (appropriate to Lent);   **coted** overtook and passed by.   288 **tribute** (1) applause (2) homage paid in money.   289 **of** from;   **foil and target** sword and shield.   290 **gratis** for nothing;   **humorous man** eccentric character, dominated by one trait or "humor";   **in peace** i.e., with full license.   291 **tickle o' the sear** easy on the trigger, ready to laugh easily. (A *sear* is part of a gunlock.)   292 **halt** limp.   294 **tragedians** actors.   296 **residence** remaining in their usual place, i.e., in the city.   298 **inhibition** formal prohibition (from acting plays in the city); **late** recent;   **innovation** i.e., the new fashion in satirical plays performed by boy actors in the "private" theaters; or possibly a political uprising; or the strict limitations set on theaters in London in 1600.   303 **keeps** continues;   **wonted** usual.   304 **aerie** nest;   **eyases** young hawks; **cry . . . question** speak shrilly, dominating the controversy (in decrying the public theaters). 305 **tyrannically** outrageously.   306 **berattle** berate, clamor against;   **common stages** public theaters.   306–307 **many wearing repiers** i.e., many men of fashion, afraid to patronize the common players for fear of being satirized by the poets writing for the boy actors;   **goose quills** i.e., pens of satirists.   308 **escoted** maintained.   309 **quality** (acting) profession;   **no longer . . . sing** i.e., only until their voices change.

say afterwards, if they should grow themselves to common° players—as   310
it is most like,° if their means are no better°—their writers do them
wrong to make them exclaim against their own succession?°

ROSENCRANTZ.   Faith, there has been much to-do° on both sides, and the nation holds
it no sin to tar° them to controversy. There was for a while no money bid for
argument unless the poet and the player went to cuffs in the question.°   315

HAMLET.   Is 't possible?

GUILDENSTERN.   O, there has been much throwing about of brains.

HAMLET.   Do the boys carry it away?°

ROSENCRANTZ.   Ay, that they do, my lord—Hercules and his load° too.°

HAMLET.   It is not very strange; for my uncle is King of Denmark, and those that   320
would make mouths° at him while my father lived give twenty, forty,
fifty, a hundred ducats° apiece for his picture in little.° 'Sblood,° there is
something in this more than natural, if philosophy° could find it out.

                                              A flourish [of trumpets within].

GUILDENSTERN.   There are the players.

HAMLET.   Gentlemen, you are welcome to Elsinore. Your hands, come then.   325
Th' appurtenance° of welcome is fashion and ceremony. Let me comply°
with you in this garb,° lest my extent° to the players, which, I tell you,
must show fairly outwards,° should more appear like entertainment° than
yours. You are welcome. But my uncle-father and aunt-mother are
deceived.   330

GUILDENSTERN.   In what, my dear lord?

HAMLET.   I am but mad north-north-west.° When the wind is southerly I know a
hawk from a handsaw.°

        Enter POLONIUS.

POLONIUS.   Well be with you, gentlemen!

HAMLET.   Hark you, Guildenstern, and you too; at each ear a hearer. That great   335
baby you see there is not yet out of his swaddling clouts.°

ROSENCRANTZ.   Haply° he is the second time come to them, for they say an old
man is twice a child.

HAMLET.   I will prophesy he comes to tell me of the players. Mark it.—You say
right, sir, o' Monday morning, 'twas then indeed.   340

---

310 **common** regular, adult.   311 **like** likely;   **if . . . better** if they find no better way to support
themselves.   312 **succession** i.e., future careers.   313 **to-do** ado.   314 **tar** set on (as dogs).
314–315 **There . . . question** i.e., for a while, no money was offered by the acting companies to
playwrights for the plot to a play unless the satirical poets who wrote for the boys and the adult
actors came to blows in the play itself.   318 **carry it away** i.e., win the day.   319 **Hercules . . .
load** (Thought to be an allusion to the sign of the Globe Theatre, which was Hercules bearing
the world on his shoulders.)   302–319 **How . . . load too** (The passage, omitted from the early
quartos, alludes to the so-called War of the Theaters, 1599–1602, the rivalry between the
children's companies and the adult actors.)   321 **mouths** faces.   322 **ducats** gold coins;   **in
little** in miniature;   **'Sblood** by God's (Christ's) blood.   323 **philosophy** i.e., scientific inquiry.
326 **appurtenance** proper accompaniment;   **comply** observe the formalities of courtesy.
327 **garb** i.e., manner;   **my extent** that which I extend, i.e., my polite behavior.   328 **show
fairly outwards** show every evidence of cordiality;   **entertainment** a (warm) reception.
332 **north-north-west** just off true north, only partly.   333 **hawk, handsaw** i.e., two very
different things, though also perhaps meaning a mattock (or *hack*) and carpenter's cutting tools,
respectively; also birds, with a play on *bernshaw*, or heron.   336 **swaddling clouts** cloths in
which to wrap a newborn baby.   337 **Haply** perhaps.

POLONIUS.   My lord, I have news to tell you.

HAMLET.   My lord, I have news to tell you. When Roscius° was an actor in Rome—

POLONIUS.   The actors are come hither, my lord.

HAMLET.   Buzz,° buzz!

POLONIUS.   Upon my honor—   345

HAMLET.   Then came each actor on his ass.

POLONIUS.   The best actors in the world, either for tragedy, comedy, history, pastoral, pastoral-comical, historical-pastoral, tragical-historical, tragical-comical-historical-pastoral, scene individable,° or poem unlimited.° Seneca° cannot be too heavy, nor Plautus° too light. For the law of writ   350 and the liberty,° these° are the only men.

HAMLET.   O Jephthah, judge of Israel,° what a treasure hadst thou!

POLONIUS.   What a treasure had he, my lord?

HAMLET.   Why,   355

   "One fair daughter, and no more,
   The which he lovèd passing° well."

POLONIUS [*aside*].   Still on my daughter.

HAMLET.   Am I not i' the right, old Jephthah?

POLONIUS.   If you call me Jephthah, my lord, I have a daughter that I love passing   360 well.

HAMLET.   Nay, that follows not.

POLONIUS.   What follows then, my lord?

HAMLET.   Why,

   "As by lot,° God wot,"°   365
and then, you know,
   "It came to pass, as most like° it was"—
the first row° of the pious chanson° will show you more, for look where my abridgement° comes.

Enter the PLAYERS.

You are welcome, masters; welcome, all. I am glad to see thee well.   370 Welcome, good friends. O, old friend! Why, thy face is valanced° since I saw thee last. Com'st thou to beard° me in Denmark? What, my young lady° and mistress! By 'r Lady,° your ladyship is nearer to heaven than when I saw you last, by the altitude of a chopine.° Pray God your voice, like a piece of uncurrent° gold, be not cracked within the ring.° Masters,   375

342 **Roscius** a famous Roman actor who died in 62 B.C.   344 **Buzz** (An interjection used to denote stale news.)   349 **scene individable** a play observing the unity of place; or perhaps one that is unclassifiable, or performed without intermission;   **poem unlimited** a play disregarding the unities of time and place; one that is all-inclusive.   350 **Seneca** writer of Latin tragedies; **Plautus** writer of Latin comedies.   350–351 **law . . . liberty** dramatic composition both according to the rules and disregarding the rules;   **these** i.e., the actors.   352 **Jephthah . . . Israel** (Jephthah had to sacrifice his daughter; see Judges 11. Hamlet goes on to quote from a ballad on the theme.)   357 **passing** surpassingly.   365 **lot** chance;   **wot** knows. 367 **like** likely, probable.   368 **row** stanza;   **chanson** ballad, song.   369 **my abridgement** something that cuts short my conversation; also, a diversion.   371 **valanced** fringed (with a beard).   372 **beard** confront, challenge (with obvious pun).   372–373 **young lady** i.e., boy playing women's parts;   **By 'r Lady** by Our Lady.   374 **chopine** thick-soled shoe of Italian fashion.   375 **uncurrent** not passable as lawful coinage;   **cracked . . . ring** i.e., changed from adolescent to male voice, no longer suitable for women's roles. (Coins featured rings enclosing the sovereign's head; if the coin was cracked within this ring, it was unfit for currency.)

you are all welcome. We'll e'en to 't° like French falconers, fly at anything
we see. We'll have a speech straight.° Come, give us a taste of your
quality.° Come, a passionate speech.

FIRST PLAYER.   What speech, my good lord?

HAMLET.   I heard thee speak me a speech once, but it was never acted, or if it   380
was, not above once, for the play, I remember, pleased not the million;
'twas caviar to the general.° But it was—as I received it, and others,
whose judgments in such matters cried in the top of° mine—an excellent
play, well digested° in the scenes, set down with as much modesty° as
cunning.° I remember one said there were no sallets° in the lines to   385
make the matter savory, nor no matter in the phrase that might indict°
the author of affection, but called it an honest method, as wholesome
as sweet, and by very much more handsome° than fine.° One speech in
't I chiefly loved: 'twas Aeneas' tale to Dido, and thereabout of it especially when he speaks of Priam's slaughter.° If it live in your memory, be-   390
gin at this line: let me see, let me see—

"The rugged Pyrrhus,° like th' Hyrcanian beast°"—

'Tis not so. It begins with Pyrrhus:

"The rugged° Pyrrhus, he whose sable° arms,
Black as his purpose, did the night resemble
When he lay couchèd° in the ominous horse,°   395
Hath now this dread and black complexion smeared
With heraldry more dismal.° Head to foot
Now is he total gules,° horridly tricked°
With blood of fathers, mothers, daughters, sons,
Baked and impasted° with the parching streets,°   400
That lend a tyrannous° and a damnèd light
To their lord's° murder. Roasted in wrath and fire,
And thus o'ersizèd° with coagulate gore,
With eyes like carbuncles,° the hellish Pyrrhus   405
Old grandsire Priam seeks."

So proceed you.

---

376 e'en to 't go at it.   **377 straight** at once.   **378 quality** professional skill.   **382 caviar to the
general** caviar to the multitude, i.e., a choice dish too elegant for coarse tastes.   **383 cried in the
top of** i.e., spoke with greater authority than.   **384 digested** arranged, ordered;
modesty moderation, restraint.   **385 cunning** skill;   **sallets** i.e., something savory, spicy
improprieties.   **386 indict** convict.   **388 handsome** well-proportioned;   **fine** elaborately
ornamented, showy.   **390 Priam's slaughter** the slaying of the ruler of Troy, when the Greeks
finally took the city.   **392 Pyrrhus** a Greek hero in the Trojan War, also known as
Neoptolemus, son of Achilles—another avenging son;   **Hyrcanian beast** i.e., tiger. (On the
death of Priam, see Virgil, *Aeneid*, 2.506 ff.; compare the whole speech with Marlowe's *Dido
Queen of Carthage*, 2.1.214. ff. On the *Hyrcanian* tiger, see *Aeneid*, 4.366–367. Hyrcania is on
the Caspian Sea.)   **394 rugged** shaggy, savage;   **sable** black (for reasons of camouflage during
the episode of the Trojan horse).   **396 couchèd** concealed;   **ominous horse** fateful Trojan
horse, by which the Greeks gained access to Troy.   **398 dismal** ill-omened.   **399 total
gules** entirely red. (A heraldic term);   **tricked** spotted and smeared. (Heraldic.)
401 impasted crusted, like a thick paste;   **with . . . streets** by the parching heat of the streets
(because of the fires everywhere).   **402 tyrannous** cruel.   **403 their lord's** i.e., Priam's.
404 o'ersizèd covered as with size or glue.   **405 carbuncles** large fiery-red precious stones
thought to emit their own light.

POLONIUS. 'Fore God, my lord, well spoken, with good accent and good discretion.
FIRST PLAYER.   "Anon he finds him
   Striking too short at Greeks. His antique° sword,   410
   Rebellious to his arm, lies where it falls,
   Repugnant° to command. Unequal matched,
   Pyrrhus at Priam drives, in rage strikes wide,
   But with the whiff and wind of his fell° sword
   Th' unnervèd° father falls. Then senseless Ilium,°   415
   Seeming to feel this blow, with flaming top
   Stoops to his° base, and with a hideous crash
   Takes prisoner Pyrrhus' ear. For, lo! His sword,
   Which was declining° on the milky° head
   Of reverend Priam, seemed i' th' air to stick.   420
   So as a painted° tyrant Pyrrhus stood,
   And, like a neutral to his will and matter,°
   Did nothing.
   But as we often see against° some storm
   A silence in the heavens, the rack° stand still,   425
   The bold winds speechless, and the orb° below
   As hush as death, anon the dreadful thunder
   Doth rend the region,° so, after Pyrrhus' pause,
   A rousèd vengeance sets him new a-work
   And never did the Cyclops'° hammers fall   430
   On Mars's armor forged for proof eterne°
   With less remorse° than Pyrrhus' bleeding sword
   Now falls on Priam.
   Out, out, thou strumpet Fortune! All you gods
   In general synod° take away her power!   435
   Break all the spokes and fellies° from her wheel,
   And bowl the round nave° down the hill of heaven°
   As low as to the fiends!"

POLONIUS.   This is too long.
HAMLET.   It shall to the barber's with your beard.—Prithee, say on. He's for a jig° 440
  or a tale of bawdry, or he sleeps. Say on; come to Hecuba.°
FIRST PLAYER.   "But who, ah woe! had° seen the moblèd° queen"—
HAMLET.   "The moblèd queen?"
POLONIUS.   That's good. "Moblèd queen" is good.
FIRST PLAYER.   "Run barefoot up and down, threat'ning the flames°   445

---

410 **antique** ancient, long-used.   412 **Repugnant** disobedient, resistant.   414 **fell** cruel.
415 **unnervèd** strengthless;   **senseless Ilium** inanimate citadel of Troy.   417 **his** its.
419 **declining** descending;   **milky** white-haired.   421 **painted** i.e., painted in a picture.
422 **like . . . matter** i.e., as though suspended between his intention and its fulfillment.
424 **against** just before.   425 **rack** mass of clouds.   426 **orb** globe, earth.   428 **region** sky.
430 **Cyclops** giant armor makers in the smithy of Vulcan.   431 **proof eterne** eternal resistance
to assault.   432 **remorse** pity.   435 **synod** assembly.   436 **fellies** pieces of wood forming the
rim of a wheel.   437 **nave** hub;   **hill of heaven** Mount Olympus.   440 **jig** comic song and
dance often given at the end of a play.   441 **Hecuba** wife of Priam.   442 **who . . . had** anyone
who had (also in line 469);   **moblèd** muffled.   445 **threat'ning the flames** i.e., weeping hard
enough to dampen the flames.

With bisson rheum,° a clout° upon that head
Where late° the diadem stood, and, for a robe,
About her lank and all o'erteemd° loins
A blanket, in the alarm of fear caught up—
Who this had seen, with tongue in venom steeped,   450
'Gainst Fortune's state° would treason have pronounced.°
But if the gods themselves did see her then
When she saw Pyrrhus make malicious sport
In mincing with his sword her husband's limbs,
The instant burst of clamor that she made,   455
Unless things mortal move them not at all,
Would have made milch° the burning eyes of heaven,°
And passion° in the gods."

POLONIUS.   Look whe'er° he has not turned his color and has tears in 's eyes.
Prithee, no more.   460

HAMLET.   'Tis well; I'll have thee speak out the rest of this soon.—Good my lord, will
you see the players well bestowed?° Do you hear, let them be well used,
for they are the abstract° and brief chronicles of the time. After your death
you were better have a bad epitaph than their ill report while you live.

POLONIUS.   My lord, I will use them according to their desert.   465

HAMLET.   God's bodikin,° man, much better. Use every man after his desert, and
who shall scape whipping? Use them after° your own honor and dignity.
The less they deserve, the more merit is in your bounty. Take them in.

POLONIUS.   Come, sirs.   [*Exit.*]

HAMLET.   Follow him, friends. We'll hear a play tomorrow. [*As they start to leave,*   470
HAMLET *detains the* FIRST PLAYER.] Dost thou hear me, old friend? Can you
play *The Murder of Gonzago?*

FIRST PLAYER.   Ay, my lord.

HAMLET.   We'll ha 't° tomorrow night. You could, for a need, study° a speech of
some dozen or sixteen lines which I would set down and insert in 't,   475
could you not?

FIRST PLAYER.   Ay, my lord.

HAMLET.   Very well. Follow that lord, and look you mock him not. [*Exeunt* PLAYERS.]
My good friends, I'll leave you till night. You are welcome to Elsinore.

ROSENCRANTZ.   Good my lord!   *Exeunt* [ROSENCRANTZ *and* GUILDENSTERN].   480

HAMLET.   Ay, so, goodbye to you.—Now I am alone.
O, what a rogue and peasant slave am I!
Is it not monstrous that this player here,
But° in a fiction, in a dream of passion,
Could force his soul so to his own conceit°   485
That from her working° all his visage wanned,°

---

446 bisson rheum blinding tears;   **clout** cloth.   **447 late** lately.   **448 all o'erteemèd** utterly
worn out with bearing children.   **451 state** rule, managing;   **pronounced** proclaimed.
457 milch milky, moist with tears;   **burning eyes of heaven** i.e., heavenly bodies.
458 passion overpowering emotion.   **459 whe'er** whether.   **462 bestowed** lodged.
463 abstract summary account.   **466 God's bodikin** by God's (Christ's) little body, *bodykin.*
(Not to be confused with *bodkin,* "dagger.")   **467 after** according to.   **474 ha 't** have it;
study memorize.   **484 But** merely.   **485 force . . . conceit** bring his innermost being so entirely
into accord with his conception (of the role).   **486 from her working** as a result of, or in
response to, his soul's activity;   **wanned** grew pale.

Tears in his eyes, distraction in his aspect,°
A broken voice, and his whole function suiting
With forms to his conceit?° And all for nothing!
For Hecuba!   490
What's Hecuba to him, or he to Hecuba,
That he should weep for her? What would he do
Had he the motive and the cue for passion
That I have? He would drown the stage with tears
And cleave the general ear° with horrid° speech,   495
Make mad the guilty and appall° the free,°
Confound the ignorant,° and amaze° indeed
The very faculties of eyes and ears. Yet I,
A dull and muddy-mettled° rascal, peak°
Like John-a-dreams,° unpregnant of° my cause,   500
And can say nothing—no, not for a king
Upon whose property° and most dear life
A damned defeat° was made. Am I a coward?
Who calls me villain? Breaks my pate° across?
Plucks off my beard and blows it in my face?   505
Tweaks me by the nose? Gives me the lie i' the throat°
As deep as to the lungs? Who does me this?
Ha, 'swounds,° I should take it; for it cannot be
But I am pigeon-livered° and lack gall
To make oppression bitter,° or ere this   510
I should ha' fatted all the region kites°
With this slave's offal.° Bloody, bawdy villain!
Remorseless,° treacherous, lecherous, kindless° villain!
O, vengeance!
Why, what an ass am I! This is most brave,°   515
That I, the son of a dear father murdered,
Prompted to my revenge by heaven and hell,
Must like a whore unpack my heart with words
And fall a-cursing, like a very drab,°
A scullion!° Fie upon 't, foh! About,° my brains!   520
Hum, I have heard
That guilty creatures sitting at a play
Have by the very cunning° of the scene°

487 aspect look, glance.   **488–489 his whole . . . conceit** all his bodily powers responding with
actions to suit his thought.   **495 the general ear** everyone's ear;   **horrid** horrible.
496 appall (Literally, make pale.);   **free** innocent.   **497 Confound the ignorant,** i.e.,
dumbfound those who know nothing of the crime that has been committed;   **amaze** stun.
499 muddy-mettled dull-spirited;   **peak** mope, pine.   **500 John-a-dreams** a sleepy, dreaming
idler;   **unpregnant of** not quickened by.   **502 property** i.e., the crown; also character, quality.
503 damned defeat damnable act of destruction.   **504 pate** head.   **506 Gives . . . throat** calls
me an out-and-out liar.   **508 'swounds** by his (Christ's) wounds.   **509 pigeon-livered** (The
pigeon or dove was popularly supposed to be mild because it secreted no gall.)   **510 bitter** i.e.,
bitter to me.   **511 region kites** kites (birds of prey) of the air.   **512 offal** entrails.
513 Remorseless pitiless;   **kindless** unnatural.   **515 brave** fine, admirable. (Said ironically.)
519 drab whore.   **520 scullion** menial kitchen servant (apt to be foul-mouthed);   **About** about
it, to work.   **523 cunning** art, skill;   **scene** dramatic presentation.

Been struck so to the soul that presently°
They have proclaimed their malefactions;   525
For murder, though it have no tongue, will speak
With most miraculous organ. I'll have these players
Play something like the murder of my father
Before mine uncle. I'll observe his looks;
I'll tent° him to the quick.° If 'a do blench,°   530
I know my course. The spirit that I have seen
May be the devil, and the devil hath power
T' assume a pleasing shape; yea, and perhaps,
Out of my weakness and my melancholy,
As he is very potent with such spirits,°   535
Abuses° me to damn me. I'll have grounds
More relative° than this. The play's the thing
Wherein I'll catch the conscience of the King.   *Exit.*

3.1   *Enter* KING, QUEEN, POLONIUS, OPHELIA, ROSENCRANTZ, GUILDERNSTERN, *lords.*

KING.   And can you by no drift of conference°
            Get from him why he puts on this confusion,
            Grating so harshly all his days of quiet
            With turbulent and dangerous lunacy?
ROSENCRANTZ.   He does confess he feels himself distracted,   5
            But from what cause 'a will by no means speak.
GUILDENSTERN.   Nor do we find him forward° to be sounded,°
            But with a crafty madness keeps aloof
            When we would bring him on to some confession
            Of his true state.
QUEEN.   Did he receive you well?   10
ROSENCRANTZ.   Most like a gentleman.
GUILDENSTERN.   But with much forcing of his disposition.°
ROSENCRANTZ.   Niggard° of question,° but of our demands
            Most free in his reply.
QUEEN.   Did you assay° him
            To any pastime?   15
ROSENCRANTZ.   Madam, it so fell out that certain players
            We o'erraught° on the way. Of these we told him,
            And there did seem in him a kind of joy
            To hear of it. They are here about the court,
            And, as I think, they have already order   20
            This night to play before him.
POLONIUS.   'Tis most true,
            And he beseeched me to entreat Your Majesties
            To hear and see the matter.
KING.   With all my heart, and it doth much content me

---

524 presently at once.   **530 tent** probe;   **the quick** the tender part of a wound, the core;
blench quail, flinch.   **535 spirits** humors (of melancholy).   **536 Abuses** deludes.
537 relative cogent, pertinent.   **3.1. Location:** The castle.   **1 drift of conference** directing of
conversation.   **7 forward** willing;   **sounded** questioned.   **12 dispositon** inclination.
13 Niggard stingy;   **question** conversation.   **14 assay** try to win.   **17 o'erraught** overtook.

To hear him so inclined. 25
Good gentlemen, give him a further edge°
And drive his purpose into these delights.
ROSENCRANTZ. We shall, my lord. *Exeunt* ROSENCRANTZ *and* GUILDENSTERN.
KING. Sweet Gertrude, leave us too
For we have closely° sent for Hamlet hither,
That he, as 'twere by accident, may here 30
Affront° Ophelia.
Her father and myself, lawful espials,°
Will so bestow ourselves that seeing, unseen,
We may of their encounter frankly judge,
And gather by him, as he is behaved, 35
If't be th' affliction of his love or no
That thus he suffers for.
QUEEN. I shall obey you.
And for your part, Ophelia, I do wish
That your good beauties be the happy cause
Of Hamlet's wildness. So shall I hope your virtues 40
Will bring him to his wonted° way again,
To both your honors.
OPHELIA. Madam, I wish it may. *[Exit* QUEEN.*]*
POLONIUS. Ophelia, walk you here.—Gracious,° so please you,
We will bestow° ourselves. *[To* OPHELIA.*]* Read on this book,

[giving her a book]

That show of such an exercise° may color° 45
Your loneliness.° We are oft to blame in this—
'Tis too much proved°—that with devotion's visage
And pious action we do sugar o'er
The devil himself.
KING *[aside].* O 'tis too true! 50
How smart a lash that speech doth give my conscience!
The harlot's cheek, beautied with plastering art,
Is not more ugly to° the thing° that helps it
Than is my deed to my most painted word.
O heavy burden! 55
POLONIUS. I hear him coming. Let's withdraw, my lord.

[The KING *and* POLONIUS *withdraw.°]*

Enter HAMLET. *[*OPHELIA *pretends to read a book.]*

HAMLET. To be, or not to be, that is the question:
Whether 'tis nobler in the mind to suffer
The slings° and arrows of outrageous fortune,
Or to take arms against a sea of troubles 60

---

26 edge incitement. **29 closely** privately. **31 Affront** confront, meet. **32 espials** spies.
41 wonted accustomed. **43 Gracious** Your Grace (i.e., the King). **44 bestow** conceal.
45 exercise religious exercise. (The book she reads is one of devotion.); **color** give a plausible
appearance to. **46 loneliness** being alone. **47 too much proved** too often shown to be true,
too often practiced. **53 to** compared to; **the thing** i.e., the cosmetic. **56 s.d. withdraw** (The
King and Polonius may retire behind an arras. The stage directions specify that they "enter"
again near the end of the scene.) **59 slings** missiles.

And by opposing end them. To die, to sleep—
No more—and by a sleep to say we end
The heartache and the thousand natural shocks
That flesh is heir to. 'Tis a consummation
Devoutly to be wished. To die, to sleep;   65
To sleep, perchance to dream. Ay, there's the rub,°
For in that sleep of death what dreams may come,
When we have shuffled° off this mortal coil,°
Must give us pause. There's the respect°
That makes calamity of so long life.°   70
For who would bear the whips and scorns of time,
Th' oppressor's wrong, the proud man's contumely,°
The pangs of disprized° love, the law's delay,
The insolence of office,° and the spurns°
That patient merit of th' unworthy takes,°   75
When he himself might his quietus° make
With a bare bodkin?° Who would fardels° bear,
To grunt and sweat under a weary life,
But that the dread of something after death,
The undiscovered country from whose bourn°   80
No traveler returns, puzzles the will,
And makes us rather bear those ills we have
Than fly to others that we know not of?
Thus conscience does make cowards of us all;
And thus the native hue° of resolution   85
Is sicklied o'er with the pale cast° of thought,
And enterprises of great pitch° and moment°
With this regard° their currents° turn awry
And lose the name of action.—Soft you° now,
The fair Ophelia. Nymph, in thy orisons°   90
Be all my sins remembered.

OPHELIA.   Good my lord,
How does your honor for this many a day?
HAMLET.   I humbly thank you; well, well, well.
OPHELIA.   My lord, I have remembrances of yours,
That I have longèd long to redeliver.   95
I pray you, now receive them.   *[She offers tokens.]*
HAMLET.   No, not I, I never gave you aught.
OPHELIA.   My honored lord, you know right well you did,
And with them words of so sweet breath composed
As made the things more rich. Their perfume lost,   100

---

66 rub (Literally, an obstacle in the game of bowls.)   **68 shuffled** sloughed, cast;   **coil** turmoil.
69 respect consideration.   **70 of . . . life** so long-lived, something we willingly endure for so
long (also suggesting that long life is itself a calamity).   **72 contumely** insolent abuse.
73 disprized unvalued.   **74 office** officialdom;   **spurns** insults.   **75 of . . . takes** receives from
unworthy persons.   **76 quietus** acquittance; here, death.   **77 a bare bodkin** a mere dagger,
unsheathed;   **fardels** burdens.   **80 bourn** frontier, boundary.   **85 native hue** natural color,
complexion.   **86 cast** tinge, shade of color.   **87 pitch** height (as of a falcon's flight.);
moment importance.   **88 regard** respect, consideration;   **currents** courses.   **89 Soft you** i.e.,
wait a minute, gently.   **90 orisons** prayers.

Take these again, for to the noble mind
Rich gifts wax poor when givers prove unkind.
There, my lord.   [*She gives tokens.*]

HAMLET.   Ha, ha! Are you honest?°

OPHELIA.   My lord?   105

HAMLET.   Are you fair?°

OPHELIA.   What means your lordship?

HAMLET.   That if you be honest and fair, your honesty° should admit no discourse
to° your beauty.

OPHELIA.   Could beauty, my lord, have better commerce° than with honesty?   110

HAMLET.   Ay, truly, for the power of beauty will sooner transform honesty from
what it is to a bawd than the force of honesty can translate beauty into
his° likeness. This was sometime° a paradox,° but now the time° gives it
proof. I did love you once.

OPHELIA.   Indeed, my lord, you made me believe so.   115

HAMLET.   You should not have believed me, for virtue cannot so inoculate° our
old stock but we shall relish of it.° I loved you not.

OPHELIA.   I was the more deceived.

HAMLET.   Get thee to a nunnery.° Why wouldst thou be a breeder of sinners? I am
myself indifferent honest,° but yet I could accuse me of such things that it   120
were better my mother had not borne me: I am very proud, revengeful, ambitious, with more offenses at my beck° than I have thoughts to put them in,
imagination to give them shape, or time to act them in. What should such
fellows as I do crawling between earth and heaven? We are arrant knaves
all; believe none of us. Go thy ways to a nunnery. Where's your father?   125

OPHELIA.   At home, my lord.

HAMLET.   Let the doors be shut upon him, that he may play the fool nowhere but
in's own house. Farewell.

OPHELIA.   O, help him, you sweet heavens!

HAMLET.   If thou dost marry, I'll give thee this plague for thy dowry: be thou as   130
chaste as ice, as pure as snow, thou shalt not escape calumny. Get thee
to a nunnery, farewell. Or, if thou wilt needs marry, marry a fool, for
wise men know well enough what monsters° you° make of them. To a
nunnery, go, and quickly too. Farewell.

OPHELIA.   Heavenly powers, restore him!   135

HAMLET.   I have heard of your paintings too, well enough. God hath given you
one face, and you make yourselves another. You jig,° you amble,° and
you lisp, you nickname God's creatures,° and make your wantonness
your ignorance.° Go to, I'll no more on 't;° it hath made me mad. I say

---

104 honest (1) truthful (2) chaste.   **106 fair** (1) beautiful (2) just, honorable.   **108 your
honesty** your chastity.   **108–109 discourse to** familiar dealings with.   **110 commerce** dealings,
intercourse.   **113 his** its;   **sometime** formerly;   **a paradox** a view opposite to commonly held
opinion;   **the time** the present age.   **116 inoculate** graft, be engrafted to.   **117 but . . . it** that
we do not still have about us a taste of the old stock, i.e., retain our sinfulness.
119 nunnery convent (with possibly an awareness that the word was also used derisively to
denote a brothel).   **120 indifferent honest** reasonably virtuous.   **122 beck** command.
133 monsters (An illusion to the horns of a cuckold.);   **you** i.e., you women.   **137 jig** dance;
amble move coyly.   **138 you nickname . . . creatures** i.e., you give trendy names to things in
place of their God-given names.   **139 make . . . ignorance** i.e., excuse your affectation on the
grounds of pretended ignorance;   **on 't** of it.

we will have no more marriage. Those that are married already—all but   140
one—shall live. The rest shall keep as they are. To a nunnery, go.

Exit.

OPHELIA.   O, what a noble mind is here o'erthrown!
    The courtier's, soldier's, scholar's, eye, tongue, sword,
    Th' expectancy° and rose° of the fair state,
    The glass of fashion and the mold of form,°   145
    Th' observed of all observers,° quite, quite down!
    And I, of ladies most deject and wretched,
    That sucked the honey of his music° vows,
    Now see that noble and most sovereign reason
    Like sweet bells jangled out of tune and harsh,   150
    That unmatched form and feature of blown° youth
    Blasted° with ecstasy.° O, woe is me,
    T' have seen what I have seen, see what I see!

    Enter KING *and* POLONIUS.

KING.   Love? His affections° do not that way tend;
    Nor what he spake, though it lacked form a little,   155
    Was not like madness. There's something in his soul
    O'er which his melancholy sits on brood,°
    And I do doubt° the hatch and the disclose°
    Will be some danger; which for to prevent,
    I have in quick determination   160
    Thus set it down:° he shall with speed to England
    For the demand of° our neglected tribute.
    Haply the seas and countries different
    With variable objects° shall expel
    This something-settled matter in his heart,°   165
    Whereon his brains still° beating puts him thus
    From fashion of himself.° What think you on 't?
POLONIUS.   It shall do well. But yet do I believe
    The origin and commencement of his grief
    Sprung from neglected love.—How now, Ophelia?   170
    You need not tell us what Lord Hamlet said;
    We heard it all.—My lord, do as you please,
    But, if you hold it fit, after the play
    Let his queen-mother° all alone entreat him
    To show his grief. Let her be round° with him;   175
    And I'll be placed, so please you, in the ear
    Of all their conference. If she find him not,°

144 **expectancy** hope;   **rose** ornament.   145 **The glass . . . form** the mirror of true fashioning
and the pattern of courtly behavior.   146 **Th' observed . . . observers** i.e., the center of attention
and honor in the court.   148 **music** musical, sweetly uttered.   151 **blown** blooming.
152 **Blasted** withered;   **ecstasy** madness.   154 **affections** emotions, feelings.   157 **sits on
brood** sits like a bird on a nest, about to *hatch* mischief (line 169).   158 **doubt** fear;
disclose disclosure, hatching.   161 **set it down** resolved.   162 **For . . . of** to demand.
164 **variable objects** various sights and surroundings to divert him.   165 **This something . . .
heart** the strange matter settled in his heart.   166 **still** continually.   167 **From . . . himself** out
of his natural manner.   174 **queen-mother** queen and mother.   175 **round** blunt.   177 **find
him not** fails to discover what is troubling him.

To England send him, or confine him where
Your wisdom best shall think.

KING.   It shall be so.
Madness in great ones must not unwatched go.   *Exeunt.*   180

3.2 *Enter* HAMLET *and three of the* PLAYERS.

HAMLET.   Speak the speech, I pray you, as I pronounced it to you, trippingly on
the tongue. But if you mouth it, as many of our players° do, I had as
lief° the town crier spoke my lines. Nor do not saw the air too much
with your hand, thus, but use all gently; for in the very torrent, tempest,
and, as I may say, whirlwind of your passion, you must acquire and   5
beget a temperance that may give it smoothness. O, it offends me to the
soul to hear a robustious° periwig-pated° fellow tear a passion to tatters,
to very rags, to split the ears of the groundlings,° who for the most part
are capable of° nothing but inexplicable dumb shows° and noise. I
would have such a fellow whipped for o'erdoing Termagant.° It out-   10
Herods Herod.° Pray you, avoid it.

FIRST PLAYER.   I warrant your honor.

HAMLET.   Be not too tame neither, but let your own discretion be your tutor. Suit
the action to the word, the word to the action, with this special observance, that you o'erstep not the modesty° of nature. For anything so o'er-   15
done is from° the purpose of playing, whose end, both at the first and
now, was and is to hold as 't were the mirror up to nature, to show virtue
her feature, scorn° her own image, and the very age and body of the
time° his° form and pressure.° Now this overdone or come tardy off,°
though it makes the unskillful° laugh, cannot but make the judicious   20
grieve, the censure of the which one° must in your allowance° o'erweigh
a whole theater of others. O, there be players that I have seen play, and
heard others praise, and that highly, not to speak it profanely,° that, neither having th' accent of Christians° nor the gait of Christian, pagan, nor
man,° have so strutted and bellowed that I have thought some of nature's   25
journeymen° had made men and not made them well, they imitated humanity so abominably.°

3.2. Location: The castle.   2 our players players nowadays.   **2–3 I had as lief** I would just as
soon.   **7 robustious** violent, boisterous;   **periwig-pated** wearing a wig.
8 groundlings spectators who paid least and stood in the yard of the theater.   **9 capable of** able
to understand;   **dumb shows** mimed performances, often used before Shakespeare's time to
precede a play or each act.   **10 Termagant** a supposed deity of the Mohammedans, not found
in any English medieval play but elsewhere portrayed as violent and blustering.
11 Herod Herod of Jewry. (A character in *The Slaughter of the Innocents* and other cycle plays.
The part was played with great noise and fury.)   **15 modesty** restraint, moderation.
16 from contrary to.   **18 scorn** i.e., something foolish and deserving of scorn.   **18–19 the very
. . . time** i.e., the present state of affairs;   **his** its;   **pressure** stamp, impressed character;   **come
tardy off** inadequately done.   **20 the unskillful** those lacking in judgment.   **21 the censure . . .
one** the judgment of even one of whom;   **your allowance** your scale of values.   **23 not . . .
profanely** (Hamlet anticipates his idea in lines 25–27 that some men were not made by God at
all.)   **24 Christians** i.e., ordinary decent folk.   **24–25 nor man** i.e., nor any human being at all.
26 journeymen laborers who are not yet masters in their trade.   **27 abominably** (Shakespeare's
usual spelling, *abbominably,* suggests a literal though etymologically incorrect meaning,
"removed from human nature.")

FIRST PLAYER.   I hope we have reformed that indifferently° with us, sir.

HAMLET.   O, reform it altogether. And let those that play your clowns speak no
more than is set down for them; for there be of them° that will them-   30
selves laugh, to set on some quantity of barren° spectators to laugh too,
though in the meantime some necessary question of the play be then to
be considered. That's villainous, and shows a most pitiful ambition in the
fool that uses it. Go make you ready.   [*Exeunt* PLAYERS.]

Enter POLONIUS, GUILDENSTERN *and* ROSENCRANTZ.

How now, my lord, will the King hear this piece of work?   35

POLONIUS.   And the Queen too, and that presently.°

HAMLET.   Bid the players make haste.   [*Exit* POLONIUS.]
Will you two help to hasten them?

ROSENCRANTZ.   Ay, my lord.   *Exeunt they two.*

HAMLET.   What ho, Horatio!

Enter HORATIO.

HORATIO.   Here, sweet lord, at your service.   40

HAMLET.   Horatio, thou art e'en as just a man
As e'er my conversation coped withal.°

HORATIO.   O, my dear lord—

HAMLET.   Nay, do not think I flatter,
For what advancement may I hope from thee
That no revenue hast but thy good spirits   45
To feed and clothe thee? Why should the poor be flattered?
No, let the candied° tongue lick absurd pomp,
And crook the pregnant° hinges of the knee
Where thrift° may follow fawning. Dost thou hear?
Since my dear soul was mistress of her choice   50
And could of men distinguish her election,°
Sh' hath sealed thee° for herself, for thou hast been
As one, in suffering all, that suffers nothing,
A man that Fortune's buffets and rewards
Hast ta'en with equal thanks; and blest are those   55
Whose blood° and judgment are so well commeddled°
That they are not a pipe for Fortune's finger
To sound what stop° she please. Give me that man
That is not passion's slave, and I will wear him
In my heart's core, ay, in my heart of heart,   60
As I do thee.—Something too much of this.—
There is a play tonight before the King.
One scene of it comes near the circumstance
Which I have told thee of my father's death.
I prithee, when thou seest that act afoot,   65

---

28 indifferently tolerably.   **30 of them** some among them.   **31 barren** i.e., of wit.
36 presently at once.   **42 my . . . withal** my dealings encountered.   **47 candied** sugared,
flattering.   **48 pregnant** compliant.   **49 thrift** profit.   **51 could . . . election** could make
distinguishing choices among persons.   **52 sealed thee** (Literally, as one would seal a legal
document to mark possession.)   **56 blood** passion;   **commeddled** commingled.   **58 stop** hole
in a wind instrument for controlling the sound.

Even with the very comment of thy soul°
Observe my uncle. If his occulted° guilt
Do not itself unkennel° in one speech,
It is a damnéd° ghost that we have seen,
And my imaginations are as foul   70
As Vulcan's stithy.° Give him heedful note,
For I mine eyes will rivet to his face,
And after we will both our judgments join
In censure of his seeming.°

HORATIO.   Well, my lord.
If 'a steal aught° the whilst this play is playing   75
And scape detecting, I will pay the theft.

[*Flourish.*] *Enter trumpets and kettledrums,* KING, QUEEN, POLONIUS, OPHELIA,
[ROSENCRANTZ, GUILDENSTERN, *and other lords, with guards carrying torches*].

HAMLET.   They are coming to the play. I must be idle.°
Get you a place.   [*The* KING, QUEEN, *and courtiers sit.*]

KING.   How fares our cousin° Hamlet?

HAMLET.   Excellent, i' faith, of the chameleon's dish:° I eat the air, promise-   80
crammed. You cannot feed capons° so.

KING.   I have nothing with° this answer, Hamlet. These words are not mine.°

HAMLET.   No, nor mine now.° [*To* POLONIUS.] My lord, you played once i' th' university, you say?

POLONIUS.   That did I, my lord, and was accounted a good actor.   85

HAMLET.   What did you enact?

POLONIUS.   I did enact Julius Caesar. I was killed i' the Capitol; Brutus killed me.

HAMLET.   It was a brute° part° of him to kill so capital a calf° there.—Be the players ready?

ROSENCRANTZ.   Ay, my lord. They stay upon° your patience.   90

QUEEN.   Come hither, my dear Hamlet, sit by me.

HAMLET.   No, good Mother, here's metal° more attractive.

POLONIUS [*to the* KING].   O, ho, do you mark that?

HAMLET.   Lady, shall I lie in your lap?   [*Lying down at* OPHELIA's *feet.*]

OPHELIA.   No, my lord.   95

HAMLET.   I mean, my head upon your lap?

OPHELIA.   Ay, my lord.

---

66 very . . . soul your most penetrating observation and consideration.   **67 occulted** hidden.
68 unkennel (As one would say of a fox driven from its lair.)   **69 damnéd** in league with Satan.
71 stithy smithy, place of stiths (anvils).   **74 censure of his seeming** judgment of his appearance
or behavior.   **75 If 'a steal aught** if he gets away with anything.   **77 idle** (1) unoccupied (2)
mad.   **79 cousin** i.e., close relative.   **80 chameleon's dish** (Chameleons were supposed to feed
on air. Hamlet deliberately misinterprets the King's *fares* as "feeds." By his phrase *eat the air* he
also plays on the idea of feeding himself with the promise of succession, of being the *heir*.)
81 capons roosters castrated and *crammed* with feed to make them succulent.   **82 have . . .
with** make nothing of, or gain nothing from;   **are not mine** do not respond to what I asked.
83 nor mine now (Once spoken, words are proverbially no longer the speaker's own—and
hence should be uttered warily.)   **88 brute** (The Latin meaning of *brutus*, "stupid," was often
used punningly with the name Brutus.);   **part** (1)deed (2) role;   **calf** fool.   **90 stay
upon** await.   **92 metal** substance that is *attractive*, i.e., magnetic, but with suggestion also of
mettle, "disposition."

HAMLET.   Do you think I meant country matters?°

OPHELIA.   I think nothing, my lord.

HAMLET.   That's a fair thought to lie between maids' legs.   100

OPHELIA.   What is, my lord?

HAMLET.   Nothing.°

OPHELIA.   You are merry, my lord.

HAMLET.   Who, I?

OPHELIA.   Ay, my lord.   105

HAMLET.   O God, your only jig maker.° What should a man do but be merry? For
look you how cheerfully my mother looks, and my father died within 's°
two hours.

OPHELIA.   Nay, 'tis twice two months, my lord.

HAMLET.   So long? Nay then, let the devil wear black, for I'll have a suit of sables.°   110
O heavens! Die two months ago, and not forgotten yet? Then there's
hope a great man's memory may outlive his life half a year. But, by 'r
Lady, 'a must build churches, then, or else shall 'a suffer not thinking
on,° with the hobbyhorse, whose epitaph is
"For O, for O, the hobbyhorse is forgot."°   115

The trumpets sound. Dumb show follows.

*Enter a King and a Queen [very lovingly]; the Queen embracing him, and
he her. [She kneels, and makes show of protestation unto him.] He takes her up,
and declines his head upon her neck. He lies him down upon a bank of flowers.
She, seeing him asleep, leaves him. Anon comes in another man, takes off his
crown, kisses it, pours poison in the sleeper's ears, and leaves him. The Queen
returns, finds the King dead, makes passionate action. The Poisoner with some
three or four come in again, seem to condole with her. The dead body is carried
away. The Poisoner woos the Queen with gifts; she seems harsh awhile, but in the
end accepts love.*

[Exeunt PLAYERS.*]*

OPHELIA.   What means this, my lord?

HAMLET.   Marry, this' miching mallico;° it means mischief.

OPHELIA.   Belike° this show imports the argument° of the play.

Enter PROLOGUE.

HAMLET.   We shall know by this fellow. The players cannot keep counsel;° they'll
tell all.   120

OPHELIA.   Will 'a tell us what this show meant?

98 country matters sexual intercourse (making a bawdy pun on the first syllable of *country*).
102 Nothing the figure zero or naught, suggesting the female sexual anatomy. (*Thing* not
infrequently has a bawdy connotation of male or female anatomy, and the reference here could
be male.)   **106 only jig maker** very best composer of jigs, i.e., pointless merriment. (Hamlet
replies sardonically to Ophelia's observation that he is merry by saying, "If you're looking for
someone who is really merry, you've come to the right person.")   **107 within 's** within this (i.e.,
these).   **110 suit of sables** garments trimmed with the fur of the sable and hence suited for a
wealthy person, not a mourner (but with a pun on *sable*, "black," ironically suggesting mourning
once again).   **113–114 suffer . . . on** undergo oblivion.   **115 For . . . forgot** (Verse of a song
occurring also in *Love's Labor's Lost*, 3.1.27–28. The hobbyhorse was a character made up to
resemble a horse and rider, appearing in the morris dance and such May-game sports. This song
laments the disappearance of such customs under pressure from the Puritans.)   **117 this'
miching mallico** this is sneaking mischief.   **118 Belike** probably;   **argument** plot.
119 counsel secret.

HAMLET.   Ay, or any show that you will show him. Be not you° ashamed to show,
   he'll not shame to tell you what it means.

OPHELIA.   You are naught,° you are naught. I'll mark the play.

PROLOGUE.   For us, and for our tragedy,   125
   Here stooping° to your clemency,
   We beg your hearing patiently.   [*Exit.*]

HAMLET.   Is this a prologue, or the posy of a ring?°

OPHELIA.   'Tis brief, my lord.

HAMLET.   As woman's love.   130

   Enter [two PLAYERS *as*] *King and Queen.*

PLAYER KING.   Full thirty times hath Phoebus' cart° gone round
   Neptune's salt wash° and Tellus'° orbèd ground,
   And thirty dozen moons with borrowed° sheen
   About the world have times twelve thirties been,
   Since love our hearts and Hymen° did our hands   135
   Unite commutual° in most sacred bands.°

PLAYER QUEEN.   So many journeys may the sun and moon
   Make us again count o'er ere love be done!
   But, woe is me, you are so sick of late,
   So far from cheer and from your former state,   140
   That I distrust° you. Yet, though I distrust,
   Discomfort° you, my lord, it nothing° must.
   For women's fear and love hold quantity;°
   In neither aught, or in extremity.°
   Now, what my love is, proof° hath made you know,   145
   And as my love is sized,° my fear is so.
   Where love is great, the littlest doubts are fear;
   Where little fears grow great, great love grows there.

PLAYER KING.   Faith, I must leave thee, love, and shortly too;
   My operant powers° their functions leave to do.°   150
   And thou shalt live in this fair world behind,°
   Honored, beloved; and haply one as kind
   For husband shalt thou—

PLAYER QUEEN.   O, confound the rest!
   Such love must needs be treason in my breast.
   In second husband let me be accurst!   155
   None° wed the second but who° killed the first.

HAMLET.   Wormwood,° wormwood.

---

122 Be not you provided you are not.   **124 naught** indecent. (Ophelia is reacting to Hamlet's
pointed remarks about not being ashamed to show all.)   **126 stooping** bowing.   **128 posy . . .
ring** brief motto in verse inscribed in a ring.   **131 Phoebus' cart** the sun-god's chariot, making
its yearly cycle.   **132 salt wash** the sea;   **Tellus** goddess of the earth, of the *orbèd ground*.
133 borrowed i.e., reflected.   **135 Hymen** god of matrimony.   **136 commutual** mutually;
bands bonds.   **141 distrust** am anxious about.   **142 Discomfort** distress;   **nothing** not at all.
143 hold quantity keep proportion with one another.   **144 In . . . extremity** i.e., women fear
and love either too little or too much, but the two, fear and love, are equal in either case.
145 proof experience.   **146 sized** in size.   **150 operant powers** vital functions;   **leave to
do** cease to perform.   **151 behind** after I have gone.   **156 None** i.e., let no woman;   **but
who** except the one who.   **157 Wormwood** i.e., how bitter. (Literally, a bitter-tasting plant.)

PLAYER QUEEN.   The instances° that second marriage move°
    Are base respects of thrift,° but none of love.
    A second time I kill my husband dead   160
    When second husband kisses me in bed.
PLAYER KING.   I do believe you think what now you speak,
    But what we do determine oft we break.
    Purpose is but the slave to memory,°
    Of violent birth, but poor validity,°   165
    Which° now, like fruit unripe, sticks on the tree,
    But fall unshaken when they mellow be.
    Most necessary 'tis that we forget
    To pay ourselves what to ourselves is debt.°
    What to ourselves in passion we propose,   170
    The passion ending, doth the purpose lose.
    The violence of either grief or joy
    Their own enactures° with themselves destroy.
    Where joy most revels, grief doth most lament;
    Grief joys, joy grieves, on slender accident.°   175
    This world is not for aye,° nor 'tis not strange
    That even our loves should with our fortunes change;
    For 'tis a question left us yet to prove,
    Whether love lead fortune, or else fortune love.
    The great man down,° you mark his favorite flies;   180
    The poor advanced makes friends of enemies.°
    And hitherto° doth love on fortune tend;°
    For who not needs° shall never lack a friend,
    And who in want° a hollow friend doth try°
    Directly seasons him° his enemy.   185
    But, orderly to end where I begun,
    Our wills and fates do so contrary run°
    That our devices still° are overthrown;
    Our thoughts are ours, their ends° none of our own.
    So think thou wilt no second husband wed,   190
    But die thy thoughts when thy first lord is dead.
PLAYER QUEEN.   Nor° earth to me give food, nor heaven light,
    Sport and repose lock from me day and night,°
    To desperation turn my trust and hope,

---

158 instances motives;   **move** motivate.   **159 base . . . thrift** ignoble considerations of material prosperity.   **164 Purpose . . . memory** our good intentions are subject to forgetfulness.
165 validity strength, durability.   **166 Which** i.e., purpose.   **168–169 Most . . . debt** it's inevitable that in time we forget the obligations we have imposed on ourselves.
173 enactures fulfillments.   **174–175 Where . . . accident** the capacity for extreme joy and grief go together, and often one extreme is instantly changed into its opposite on the slightest provocation.   **176 aye** ever.   **180 down** fallen in fortune.   **181 The poor . . . enemies** when one of humble station is promoted, you see his enemies suddenly becoming his friends.
182 hitherto up to this point in the argument, or, to this extent;   **tend** attend.   **183 who not needs** he who is not in need (of wealth).   **184 who in want** he who, being in need;   **try** test (his generosity).   **185 seasons him** ripens him into.   **187 Our . . . run** what we want and what we get go so contrarily.   **188 devices still** intentions continually.   **189 ends** results.
192 Nor let neither.   **193 Sport . . . night** may day deny me its pastimes and night its repose.

An anchor's cheer° in prison be my scope!°   195
Each opposite that blanks° the face of joy
Meet what I would have well and it destroy!°
Both here and hence° pursue me lasting strife
If, once a widow, ever I be wife!

HAMLET.   If she should break it now!   200

PLAYER KING.   'Tis deeply sworn. Sweet, leave me here awhile;
My spirits° grow dull, and fain I would beguile
The tedious day with sleep.

PLAYER QUEEN.   Sleep rock thy brain,
And never come mischance between us twain!

                              [*He sleeps.*] *Exit* [PLAYER QUEEN].

HAMLET.   Madam, how like you this play?   205

QUEEN.   The lady doth protest too much,° methinks.

HAMLET.   O, but she'll keep her word.

KING.   Have you heard the argument?° Is there no offense in 't?

HAMLET.   No, no, they do but jest,° poison in jest. No offense° i' the world.

KING.   What do you call the play?   210

HAMLET.   *The Mousetrap.* Marry, how? Tropically.° This play is the image of a murder done in Vienna. Gonzago is the Duke's° name, his wife, Baptista.
You shall see anon. 'Tis a knavish piece of work, but what of that? Your
Majesty, and we that have free° souls, it touches us not. Let the galled
jade° wince, our withers° are unwrung.°   215

          Enter LUCIANUS.

This is one Lucianus, nephew to the King.

OPHELIA.   You are as good as a chorus,° my lord.

HAMLET.   I could interpret° between you and your love, if I could see the puppets
dallying.°

OPHELIA.   You are keen,° my lord, you are keen.   220

HAMLET.   It would cost you a groaning to take off mine edge.

OPHELIA.   Still better, and worse.°

---

195 anchor's cheer anchorite's or hermit's fare;   **my scope** the extent of my happiness.
196 blanks causes to blanch or grow pale.   **196–197 Each . . . destroy** may every adverse thing
that causes the face of joy to turn pale meet and destroy everything that I desire to see prosper.
198 hence in the life hereafter.   **202 spirits** vital spirits.   **206 doth . . . much** makes too many
promises and protestations.   **208 argument** plot.   **209 jest** make believe.   **208–209 offense . . .
offense** cause for objection . . . actual injury, crime.   **211 Tropically** figuratively. (The First
Quarto reading, *trapically,* suggests a pun on *trap* in *Mousetrap.*)   **212 Duke's** i.e., King's (A
slip that may be due to Shakespeare's possible source, the alleged murder of the Duke of
Urbino by Luigi Gonzaga in 1538.)   **214 free** guiltless.   **214–215 galled jade** horse whose hide
is rubbed by saddle or harness.   **215 withers** the part between the horse's shoulder blades;
unwrung not rubbed sore.   **217 chorus** (In many Elizabethan plays, the forthcoming action was
explained by an actor known as the "chorus"; at a puppet show, the actor who spoke the
dialogue was known as an "interpreter," as indicated by the lines following.)   **218 interpret** (1)
ventriloquize the dialogue, as in a puppet show (2) act as pander.   **218–219 puppets
dallying** (With suggestion of sexual play, continued in *keen,* "sexually aroused," *groaning,*
"moaning in pregnancy," and *edge,* "sexual desire" or "impetuosity.")   **220 keen** sharp, bitter.
222 Still . . . worse more keen, always *bettering* what other people say with witty wordplay, but
at the same time more offensive.

HAMLET.   So° you mis-take° your husbands. Begin, murder; leave thy damnable faces and begin. Come, the croaking raven doth bellow for revenge.

LUCIANUS.   Thoughts black, hands apt, drugs fit, and time agreeing,   225
Confederate season,° else° no creature seeing,°
Thou mixture rank, of midnight weeds collected,
With Hecate's ban° thrice blasted, thrice infected,
Thy natural magic and dire property°
On wholesome life usurp immediately.   230

[He pours the poison into the sleeper's ear.]

HAMLET.   'A poisons him i' the garden for his estate.° His° name's Gonzago. The story is extant, and written in very choice Italian. You shall see anon how the murderer gets the love of Gonzago's wife.

[CLAUDIUS *rises.*]

OPHELIA.   The King rises.

HAMLET.   What, frighted with false fire?°   235

QUEEN.   How fares my lord?

POLONIUS.   Give o'er the play.

KING.   Give me some light. Away!

POLONIUS.   Lights, lights, lights!

Exeunt all but HAMLET *and* HORATIO.

HAMLET.

"Why,° let the strucken deer go weep,   240
    The hart ungallèd° play.
For some must watch,° while some must sleep;
    Thus runs the world away."°

Would not this,° sir, and a forest of feathers°—if the rest of my fortunes turn Turk with° me—with two Provincial roses° on my razed° shoes, get   245
me a fellowship in a cry° of players?°

HORATIO.   Half a share.

HAMLET.   A whole one, I.

"For thou dost know, O Damon° dear,
    This realm dismantled° was   250

---

223 So even thus (in marriage);   **mis-take** take falseheartedly and cheat on. (The marriage vows say "for better, for worse.")   **226 Confederate season** the time and occasion conspiring (to assist the murderer);   **else** otherwise;   **seeing** seeing me.   **228 Hecate's ban** the curse of Hecate, the goddess of witchcraft.   **229 dire property** baleful quality.   **231 estate** i.e., the kingship; **His** i.e., the King's.   **235 false fire** the blank discharge of a gun loaded with powder but no shot.   **240–243 Why . . . away** (Probably from an old ballad, with allusion to the popular belief that a wounded deer retires to weep and die; compare with *As You Like It,* 2.1.33–66.) **241 ungallèd** unafflicted.   **242 watch** remain awake.   **243 Thus . . . away** thus the world goes. **244 this** i.e., the play;   **feathers** (Allusion to the plumes that Elizabethan actors were fond of wearing.)   **245 turn Turk with** turn renegade against, go back on;   **Provincial roses** rosettes of ribbon, named for roses grown in a part of France;   **razed** with ornamental slashing. **246 cry** pack (of hounds);   **fellowship . . . players** partnership in a theatrical company. **249 Damon** the friend of Pythias, as Horatio is friend of Hamlet; or, a traditional pastoral name. **250 dismantled** stripped, divested.

> Of Jove himself, and now reigns here
>   A very, very—pajock."°

HORATIO.   You might have rhymed.

HAMLET.   O good Horatio, I'll take the ghost's word for a thousand pound.
Didst perceive?   255

HORATIO.   Very well, my lord.

HAMLET.   Upon the talk of the poisoning?

HORATIO.   I did very well note him.

> *Enter* ROSENCRANTZ *and* GUILDENSTERN.

HAMLET.   Aha! Come, some music! Come, the recorders.°

> "For if the King like not the comedy,   260
> Why then, belike, he likes it not, perdy."°

> Come, some music.

GUILDENSTERN.   Good my lord, vouchsafe me a word with you.

HAMLET.   Sir, a whole history.

GUILDENSTERN.   The King, sir—   265

HAMLET.   Ay, sir, what of him?

GUILDENSTERN.   Is in his retirement° marvelous distempered.°

HAMLET.   With drink, sir?

GUILDENSTERN.   No, my lord, with choler.°

HAMLET.   Your wisdom should show itself more richer to signify this to the doctor,   270
for for me to put him to his purgation° would perhaps plunge him into
more choler.

GUILDENSTERN.   Good my lord, put your discourse into some frame° and start° not
so wildly from my affair.

HAMLET.   I am tame, sir. Pronounce.   275

GUILDENSTERN.   The Queen, your mother, in most great affliction of spirit, hath
sent me to you.

HAMLET.   You are welcome.

GUILDENSTERN.   Nay, good my lord, this courtesy is not of the right breed.° If it
shall please you to make me a wholesome answer, I will do your   280
mother's commandment; if not, your pardon° and my return shall be the
end of my business.

HAMLET.   Sir, I cannot.

ROSENCRANTZ.   What, my lord?

250–252 This realm . . . pajock i.e., Jove, representing divine authority and justice, has
abandoned this realm to its own devices, leaving in his stead only a peacock or vain pretender
to virtue (though the rhyme-word expected in place of *pajock* or "peacock" suggests that the
realm is now ruled over by an "ass").   **259 recorders** wind instruments of the flute kind.
261 perdy (A corruption of the French *par dieu,* "by God.")   **267 retirement** withdrawal to his
chambers; **distempered** out of humor. (But Hamlet deliberately plays on the wider application
to any illness of mind or body, as in line 298, especially to drunkenness.)   **269 choler** anger.
(But Hamlet takes the word in its more basic humoral sense of "bilious disorder.")
271 purgation (Hamlet hints at something going beyond medical treatment to bloodletting and
the extraction of confession.)   **273 frame** order; **start** shy or jump away (like a horse; the
opposite of *tame* in line 275).   **279 breed** (1) kind (2) breeding, manners.
281 pardon permission to depart.

HAMLET. Make you a wholesome answer; my wit's diseased. But, sir, such answer   285
as I can make, you shall command, or rather, as you say, my mother.
Therefore no more, but to the matter. My mother, you say—

ROSENCRANTZ. Then thus she says: your behavior hath struck her into amazement
and admiration.°

HAMLET. O wonderful son, that can so stonish a mother! But is there no sequel at   290
the heels of this mother's admiration? Impart.

ROSENCRANTZ. She desires to speak with you in her closet° ere you go to bed.

HAMLET. We shall obey, were she ten times our mother. Have you any further
trade with us?

ROSENCRANTZ. My lord, you once did love me.   295

HAMLET. And do still, by these pickers and stealers.°

ROSENCRANTZ. Good my lord, what is your cause of distemper? You do surely bar
the door upon your own liberty° if you deny° your griefs to your friend.

HAMLET. Sir, I lack advancement.

ROSENCRANTZ. How can that be, when you have the voice of the King himself for   300
your succession in Denmark?

HAMLET. Ay, sir, but "While the grass grows"°—the proverb is something° musty.

Enter the PLAYERS° WITH RECORDERS.

O, the recorders. Let me see one. [*He takes a recorder.*]
To withdraw° with you: why do you go about to recover the wind° of
me, as if you would drive me into a toil?°   305

GUILDENSTERN. O, my lord, if my duty be too bold, my love is too unmannerly.°

HAMLET. I do not well understand that.° Will you play upon this pipe?

GUILDENSTERN. My lord, I cannot.

HAMLET. I pray you.

GUILDENSTERN. Believe me, I cannot.   310

HAMLET. I do beseech you.

GUILDENSTERN. I know no touch of it, my lord.

HAMLET. It is as easy as lying. Govern these ventages° with your fingers and
thumb, give it breath with your mouth, and it will discourse most eloquent music. Look you, these are the stops.   315

GUILDENSTERN. But these cannot I command to any utterance of harmony. I have
not the skill.

HAMLET. Why, look you now, how unworthy a thing you make of me! You would
play upon me, you would seem to know my stops, you would pluck out
the heart of my mystery, you would sound° me from my lowest note to   320
the top of my compass,° and there is much music, excellent voice, in this
little organ,° yet cannot you make it speak. 'Sblood, do you think I am

289 admiration bewilderment.   **292 closet** private chamber.   **296 pickers and stealers** i.e.,
hands. (So called from the catechism, "to keep my hands from picking and stealing.")
298 liberty i.e., being freed from *distemper,* line 297, but perhaps with a veiled threat as well;
deny refuse to share.   **302 While . . . grows** (The rest of the proverb is "the silly horse starves";
Hamlet may not live long enough to succeed to the kingdom.);   **something** somewhat;   **s.d.**
Players actors.   **304 withdraw** speak privately;   **recover the wind** get to the windward side
(thus driving the game into the *toil,* or "net").   **305 toil** snare.   **306 if . . . unmannerly** if I am
using an unmannerly boldness, it is my love that occasions it.   **307 I . . . that** i.e., I don't
understand how genuine love can be unmannerly.   **313 ventages** finger-holes or *stops* (line 319)
of the recorder.   **320 sound** (1) fathom (2) produce sound in.   **321 compass** range (of voice).
322 organ musical instrument.

easier to be played on than a pipe? Call me what instrument you will, though you can fret° me, you cannot play upon me.

Enter POLONIUS.

God bless you, sir!   325

POLONIUS.   My lord, the Queen would speak with you, and presently.°

HAMLET.   Do you see yonder cloud that's almost in shape of a camel?

POLONIUS.   By the Mass and 'tis, like a camel indeed.

HAMLET.   Methinks it is like a weasel.

POLONIUS.   It is backed like a weasel.   330

HAMLET.   Or like a whale.

POLONIUS.   Very like a whale.

HAMLET.   Then I will come to my mother by and by.° [*Aside.*] They fool me° to the top of my bent.°—I will come by and by.

POLONIUS.   I will say so.   [*Exit.*] 335

HAMLET.   "By and by" is easily said. Leave me, friends.

                                      [*Exeunt all but* HAMLET.]

'Tis now the very witching time° of night,
When churchyards yawn and hell itself breathes out
Contagion to this world. Now could I drink hot blood
And do such bitter business as the day   340
Would quake to look on. Soft, now to my mother.
O heart, lose not thy nature!° Let not ever
The soul of Nero° enter this firm bosom.
Let me be cruel, not unnatural;
I will speak daggers to her, but use none.   345
My tongue and soul in this be hypocrites:
How in my words soever° she be shent,°
To give them seals° never my soul consent!   *Exit.*

3.3   *Enter* KING, ROSENCRANTZ, *and* GUILDENSTERN.

KING.   I like him° not, nor stands it safe with us
To let his madness range. Therefore prepare you.
I your commission will forthwith dispatch,°
And he to England shall along with you.
The terms of our estate° may not endure
Hazard so near 's as doth hourly grow   5
Out of his brows.°

GUILDENSTERN.   We will ourselves provide.
Most holy and religious fear° it is

324 fret irritate (with a quibble on *fret,* meaning the piece of wood, gut, or metal that regulates the fingering on an instrument). **326 presently** at once. **333 by and by** quite soon. **fool me** trifle with me, humor my fooling. **334 top of my bent** limit of my ability or endurance. (Literally, the extent to which a bow may be bent.) **337 witching time** time when spells are cast and evil is abroad. **342 nature** natural feeling. **343 Nero** murderer of his mother, Agrippina. **347 How . . . soever** however much by my words; **shent** rebuked. **348 give them seals** i.e., confirm them with deeds. **3.3 Location: The castle.** **1 him** i.e., his behavior. **3 dispatch** prepare, cause to be drawn up. **5 terms of our estate** circumstances of my royal position. **7 Out of his brows** i.e., from his brain, in the form of plots and threats. **8 religious fear** sacred concern.

To keep those many many bodies safe
That live and feed upon Your Majesty.   10

ROSENCRANTZ.   The single and peculiar° life is bound
With all the strength and armor of the mind
To keep itself from noyance,° but much more
That spirit upon whose weal depends and rests
The lives of many. The cess° of majesty   15
Dies not alone, but like a gulf° doth draw
What's near it with it; or it is a massy° wheel
Fixed on the summit of the highest mount,
To whose huge spokes ten thousand lesser things
Are mortised° and adjoined, which, when it falls,°   20
Each small annexment, petty consequence,°
Attends° the boisterous ruin. Never alone
Did the King sigh, but with a general groan.

KING.   Arm° you, I pray you, to this speedy voyage,
For we will fetters put about this fear,   25
Which now goes too free-footed.

ROSENCRANTZ.   We will haste us.

         Exeunt gentlemen [ROSENCRANTZ *and* GUILDENSTERN].

    Enter POLONIUS.

POLONIUS.   My lord, he's going to his mother's closet.
Behind the arras° I'll convey myself
To hear the process.° I'll warrant she'll tax him home,°
And, as you said—and wisely was it said—   30
'Tis meet° that some more audience than a mother,
Since nature makes them partial, should o'erhear
The speech, of vantage.° Fare you well, my liege.
I'll call upon you ere you go to bed
And tell you what I know.

KING.   Thanks, dear my lord.   *Exit* [POLONIUS].   35
O, my offense is rank! It smells to heaven.
It hath the primal eldest curse° upon't,
A brother's murder. Pray can I not,
Though inclination be as sharp as will;°
My stronger guilt defeats my strong intent,   40
And like a man to double business bound°
I stand in pause where I shall first begin,

---

11 **single and peculiar** individual and private.   13 **noyance** harm.   15 **cess** decease, cessation.
16 **gulf** whirlpool.   17 **massy** massive.   20 **mortised** fastened (as with a fitted joint);   **when it
falls** i.e., when it descends, like the wheel of Fortune, bringing a king down with it.   21 **Each
. . . consequence** i.e., every hanger-on and unimportant person or thing connected with the King.
22 **Attends** participates in.   24 **Arm** prepare.   28 **arras** screen of tapestry placed around the
walls of household apartments. (On the Elizabethan stage, the arras was presumably over a door
or discovery space in the tiring-house facade.)   29 **process** proceedings;   **tax him
home** reprove him severely.   31 **meet** fitting.   33 **of vantage** from an advantageous place, or, in
addition.   37 **the primal eldest curse** the curse of Cain, the first murderer; he killed his brother
Abel.   39 **Though . . . will** though my desire is as strong as my determination.   41 **bound**
(1) destined (2) obliged. (The King wants to repent and still enjoy what he has gained.)

And both neglect. What if this cursèd hand
Were thicker than itself with brother's blood,
Is there not rain enough in the sweet heavens   45
To wash it white as snow? Whereto serves mercy
But to confront the visage of offense?°
And what's in prayer but this twofold force,
To be forestallèd° ere we come to fall,
Or pardoned being down? Then I'll look up.   50
My fault is past. But O, what form of prayer
Can serve my turn? "Forgive me my foul murder"?
That cannot be, since I am still possessed
Of those effects for which I did the murder:
My crown, mine own ambition, and my Queen.   55
May one be pardoned and retain th' offense?°
In the corrupted currents° of this world
Offense's gilded hand° may shove by° justice,
And oft 'tis seen the wicked prize° itself
Buys out the law. But 'tis not so above.   60
There° is no shuffling,° there the action lies°
In his° true nature, and we ourselves compelled,
Even to the teeth and forehead° of our faults,
To give in° evidence. What then? What rests?°
Try what repentance can. What can it not?   65
Yet what can it, when one cannot repent?
O wretched state, O bosom black as death,
limèd° soul that, struggling to be free,
Art more engaged!° Help, angels! Make assay.°
Bow, stubborn knees, and heart with strings of steel,   70
Be soft as sinews of the newborn babe!
All may be well.   [*He kneels.*]

    Enter HAMLET.

HAMLET.   Now might I do it pat,° now 'a is a-praying;
And now I'll do 't. [*He draws his sword.*] And so 'a goes to heaven,
And so am I revenged. That would be scanned:°   75
A villain kills my father, and for that,
I, his sole son, do this same villain send
To heaven.
Why, this is hire and salary, not revenge.
'A took my father grossly, full of bread,°   80

46–47 Whereto . . . offense what function does mercy serve other than to meet sin face to face?
49 forestallèd prevented (from sinning). **56 th' offense** the thing for which one offended.
57 currents courses. **58 gilded hand** hand offering gold as a bribe; **shove by** thrust aside.
59 wicked prize prize won by wickedness. **61 There** i.e., in heaven; **shuffling** escape by
trickery; **the action lies** the accusation is made manifest. (A legal metaphor.) **62 his** its.
63 to the teeth and forehead face to face, concealing nothing. **64 give in** provide;
rests remains. **68 limèd** caught as with birdlime, a sticky substance used to ensnare birds.
69 engaged entangled; **assay** trial. (Said to himself.) **73 pat** opportunely. **75 would be
scanned** needs to be looked into, or, would be interpreted as follows. **80 grossly, full of
bread** i.e., enjoying his worldly pleasures rather than fasting. (See Ezekiel 16:49.)

With all his crimes broad blown,° as flush° as May;
And how his audit° stands who knows save° heaven?
But in our circumstance and course of thought°
'Tis heavy with him. And am I then revenged,
To take him in the purging of his soul   85
When he is fit and seasoned° for his passage?
No!
Up, sword, and know thou a more horrid hent.°

                                      [*He puts up his sword.*]

When he is drunk asleep, or in his rage,°
Or in th' incestuous pleasure of his bed,   90
At game,° a-swearing, or about some act
That has no relish° of salvation in 't—
Then trip him, that his heels may kick at heaven,
And that his soul may be as damned and black
As hell, whereto it goes. My mother stays.°   95
This physic° but prolongs thy sickly days.   *Exit.*

KING.   My words fly up, my thoughts remain below.
        Words without thoughts never to heaven go.   *Exit.*

                3.4   *Enter* [QUEEN] GERTRUDE *and* POLONIUS.

POLONIUS.   'A will come straight. Look you lay home° to him.
            Tell him his pranks have been too broad° to bear with,
            And that Your Grace hath screened and stood between
            Much heat° and him. I'll shroud° me even here.
            Pray you, be round° with him.   5
HAMLET [*within*].   Mother, Mother, Mother!
QUEEN.   I'll warrant you, fear me not.
         Withdraw, I hear him coming.   [POLONIUS *hides behind the arras.*]

        Enter HAMLET.

HAMLET.   Now, Mother, what's the matter?
QUEEN.   Hamlet, thou hast thy father° much offended.   10
HAMLET.   Mother, you have my father much offended.
QUEEN.   Come, come, you answer with an idle° tongue.
HAMLET.   Go, go, you question with a wicked tongue.
QUEEN.   Why, how now, Hamlet?
HAMLET.   What's the matter now?

81 **crimes broad blown** sins in full bloom;   **flush** vigorous.   82 **audit** account;   **save** except for.
83 **in . . . thought** as we see it from our mortal perspective.   86 **seasoned** matured, readied.
88 **know . . . hent** await to be grasped by me on a more horrid occasion; **hent** act of seizing.
89 **drunk . . . rage** dead drunk, or in a fit of sexual passions.   91 **game** gambling.
92 **relish** trace, savor.   95 **stays** awaits (me).   96 **physic** purging (by prayer); or, Hamlet's
postponement of the killing.   3.4 **Location: The Queen's private chamber.**   1 **lay home** thrust
to the heart, reprove him soundly.   2 **broad** unrestrained.   4 **Much heat** i.e., the King's anger;
shroud conceal. (With ironic fitness to Polonius' imminent death. The word is only in the First
Quarto: the Second Quarto and the Folio read "silence.")   5 **round** blunt.   10 **thy father** i.e.,
your stepfather, Claudius.   12 **idle** foolish.

QUEEN.   Have you forgot me?°

HAMLET.   No, by the rood,° not so: 15
    You are the Queen your husband's brother's wife,
    And—would it were not so!—you are my mother.

QUEEN.   Nay, then, I'll set those to you that can speak.°

HAMLET.   Come, come, and sit you down; you shall not budge.
    You go not till I set you up a glass   20
    Where you may see the inmost part of you.

QUEEN.   What wilt thou do? Thou wilt not murder me?
    Help, ho!

POLONIUS [*behind the arras*].   What ho! Help!

HAMLET [*drawing*].   How now? A rat? Dead for a ducat,° dead!   25

                 [*He thrusts his rapier through the arras.*]

POLONIUS [*behind the arras*].   O, I am slain!   [*He falls and dies.*]

QUEEN.   O me, what hast thou done?

HAMLET.   Nay, I know not. Is it the King?

QUEEN.   O, what a rash and bloody deed is this!

HAMLET.   A bloody deed—almost as bad, good Mother,
    As kill a King, and marry with his brother.   30

QUEEN.   As kill a King!

HAMLET.   Ay, lady, it was my word.

          [*He parts the arras and discovers* POLONIUS.]

    Thou wretched, rash, intruding fool, farewell!
    I took thee for thy better. Take thy fortune.
    Thou find'st to be too busy° is some danger.—
    Leave wringing of your hands. Peace, sit you down,   35
    And let me wring your heart, for so I shall,
    If it be made of penetrable stuff,
    If damnèd custom° have not brazed° it so
    That it be proof° and bulwark against sense.°

QUEEN.   What have I done, that thou dar'st wag thy tongue
    In noise so rude against me?   40

HAMLET.   Such an act
    That blurs the grace and blush of modesty,
    Calls virtue hypocrite, takes off the rose
    From the fair forehead of an innocent love
    And sets a blister° there, makes marriage vows   45
    As false as dicers' oaths. O, such a deed
    As from the body of contraction° plucks
    The very soul, and sweet religion makes°
    A rhapsody° of words. Heaven's face does glow
    O'er this solidity and compound mass   50

---

15 forgot me i.e., forgotten that I am your mother;   **rood** cross of Christ.   **18 speak** i.e., to someone so rude.   **25 Dead for a ducat** i.e., I bet a ducat he's dead; or, a ducat is his life's fee.
34 busy nosey.   **38 damned custom** habitual wickedness;   **brazed** brazened, hardened.
39 proof armor;   **sense** feeling.   **45 sets a blister** i.e., brands as a harlot.   **47 contraction** the marriage contract.   **48 sweet religion makes** i.e., makes marriage vows.   **49 rhapsody** senseless string.

With tristful visage, as against the doom,
Is thought-sick at the act.°

QUEEN.   Ay me, what act,
That roars so loud and thunders in the index?°

HAMLET [*showing her two likenesses*].   Look here upon this picture, and on this,
The counterfeit presentment° of two brothers.   55
See what a grace was seated on this brow:
Hyperion's° curls, the front° of Jove himself,
An eye like Mars° to threaten and command,
A station° like the herald Mercury°
New-lighted° on a heaven-kissing hill—   60
A combination and a form indeed
Where every god did seem to set his seal°
To give the world assurance of a man.
This was your husband. Look you now what follows:
Here is your husband, like a mildewed ear,°   65
Blasting° his wholesome brother. Have you eyes?
Could you on this fair mountain leave° to feed
And batten° on this moor?° Ha, have you eyes?
You cannot call it love, for at your age
The heyday° in the blood° is tame, it's humble,   70
And waits upon the judgment, and what judgment
Would step from this to this? Sense,° sure, you have,
Else could you not have motion, but sure that sense
Is apoplexed,° for madness would not err,°
Nor sense to ecstasy was ne'er so thralled,   75
But° it reserved some quantity of choice
To serve in such a difference.° What devil was 't
That thus hath cozened° you at hoodman-blind?°
Eyes without feeling, feeling without sight,
Ears without hands or eyes, smelling sans° all   80
Or but a sickly part of one true sense
Could not so mope.° O shame, where is thy blush?
Rebellious hell,

49–52 Heaven's . . . act heaven's face blushes at this solid world compounded of the various elements, with sorrowful face as though the day of doom were near, and is sick with horror at the deed (i.e., Gertrude's marriage).   **54 index** table of contents, prelude or preface.
55 counterfeit presentment portrayed representation.   **57 Hyperion's** the sungod's;   **front** brow.
58 Mars god of war.   **59 station** manner of standing;   **Mercury** winged messenger of the gods.
60 New-lighted newly alighted.   **62 set his seal** i.e., affix his approval.   **65 ear** i.e., of grain.
66 Blasting blighting.   **67 leave** cease.   **68 batten** gorge;   **moor** barren or marshy ground (suggesting also "dark-skinned").   **70 heyday** state of excitement;   **blood** passion.
72 Sense perception through the five senses (the functions of the middle sensible soul).
74 apoplexed paralyzed (Hamlet goes on to explain that, without such a paralysis of will, mere madness would not so err, nor would the five senses so enthrall themselves to *ecstasy* or lunacy; even such deranged states of mind would be able to make the obvious choice between Hamlet Senior and Claudius.);   **err** so err.   **76 But** but that.   **77 To . . . difference** to help in making a choice between two such men.   **78 cozened** cheated;   **hoodman-blind** blindman's buff. (In this game, says Hamlet, the devil must have pushed Claudius toward Gertrude while she was blindfolded.)   **80 sans** without.   **82 mope** be dazed, act aimlessly.

If thou canst mutine° in a matron's bones,
To flaming youth let virtue be as wax   85
And melt in her own fire.° Proclaim no shame
When the compulsive ardor gives the charge,
Since frost itself as actively doth burn,
And reason panders will.°

QUEEN.   O Hamlet, speak no more!   90
Thou turn'st mine eyes into my very soul,
And there I see such black and grainèd° spots
As will not leave their tint.°

HAMLET.   Nay, but to live
In the rank sweat of an enseamèd° bed,
Stewed° in corruption, honeying and making love   95
Over the nasty sty!

QUEEN.   O, speak to me no more!
These words like daggers enter in my ears.
No more, sweet Hamlet!

HAMLET.   A murderer and a villain,
A slave that is not twentieth part the tithe°   100
Of your precedent lord,° a vice° of kings,
A cutpurse of the empire and the rule,
That from a shelf the precious diadem stole
And put it in his pocket!

QUEEN.   No more!   105

Enter GHOST [*in his nightgown*].

HAMLET.   A king of shreds and patches°—
Save me, and hover o'er me with your wings,
You heavenly guards! What would your gracious figure?

QUEEN.   Alas, he's mad!

HAMLET.   Do you not come your tardy son to chide,   110
That, lapsed° in time and passion, lets go by
Th' important° acting of your dread command?
O, say!

GHOST.   Do not forget. This visitation
Is but to whet thy almost blunted purpose.
But look, amazement° on thy mother sits.   115
O, step between her and her fighting soul!
Conceit° in weakest bodies strongest works.
Speak to her, Hamlet.

---

84 mutine incite mutiny.   **85–86 be as wax . . . fire** melt like a candle or stick of sealing wax held over the candle flame.   **86–89 Proclaim . . . will** call it no shameful business when the compelling ardor of youth delivers the attack, i.e., commits lechery, since the *frost* of advanced age burns with as active a fire of lust and reason perverts itself by fomenting lust rather than restraining it.   **92 grainèd** dyed in grain, indelible.   **93 leave their tint** surrender their color.
94 enseamèd saturated in the grease and filth of passionate lovemaking.   **95 Stewed** soaked, bathed (with a suggestion of "stew," brothel).   **100 tithe** tenth part.   **101 precedent lord** former husband;   **vice** buffoon. (A reference to the Vice of the morality plays.)   **106 shreds and patches** i.e., motley, the traditional costume of the clown or fool.   **111 lapsed** delaying.
112 important importunate, urgent.   **116 amazement** distraction.   **118 Conceit** imagination.

HAMLET.   How is it with you, lady?
QUEEN.   Alas, how is 't with you,   120
          That you do bend your eye on vacancy,
          And with th' incorporal° air do hold discourse?
          Forth at your eyes your spirits wildly peep,
          And, as the sleeping soldiers in th' alarm,°
          Your bedded° hair, like life in excrements,°   125
          Start up and stand on end. O gentle son,
          Upon the heat and flame of thy distemper°
          Sprinkle cool patience. Whereon do you look?
HAMLET.   On him, on him! Look you how pale he glares!
          His form and cause conjoined,° preaching to stones,   130
          Would make them capable.°—Do not look upon me,
          Lest with this piteous action you convert
          My stern effects.° Then what I have to do
          Will want true color—tears perchance for blood.°
QUEEN.   To whom do you speak this?   135
HAMLET.   Do you see nothing there?
QUEEN.   Nothing at all, yet all that is I see.
HAMLET.   Nor did you nothing hear?
QUEEN.   No, nothing but ourselves.
HAMLET.   Why, look you there, look how it steals away!   140
          My father, in his habit° as° he lived!
          Look where he goes even now out at the portal!   *Exit* GHOST.
QUEEN.   This is the very° coinage of your brain.
          This bodiless creation ecstasy
          Is very cunning in.°   145
HAMLET.   Ecstasy?
          My pulse as yours doth temperately keep time,
          And makes as healthful music. It is not madness
          That I have uttered. Bring me to the test,
          And I the matter will reword,° which madness   150
          Would gambol° from. Mother, for love of grace,
          Lay not that flattering unction° to your soul
          That not your trespass but my madness speaks.
          It will but skin° and film the ulcerous place,
          Whiles rank corruption, mining° all within,   155
          Infects unseen. Confess yourself to heaven,
          Repent what's past, avoid what is to come,

---

122 **incorporal** immaterial.   124 **as . . . alarm** like soldiers called out of sleep by an alarum.
125 **bedded** laid flat;   **like life in excrements** i.e., as though hair, an outgrowth of the body, had
a life of its own. (Hair was thought to be lifeless because it lacks sensation, and so its standing
on end would be unnatural and ominous.)   127 **distemper** disorder.   130 **His . . .
conjoined** his appearance joined to his cause for speaking.   131 **capable** receptive.
132–133 **convert . . . effects** divert me from my stern duty.   134 **want . . . blood** lack
plausibility so that (with a play on the normal sense of *color*) I shall shed colorless tears instead
of blood.   141 **habit** clothes;   **as** as when.   143 **very** mere.   144–145 **This . . . in** madness is
skillful in creating this kind of hallucination.   150 **reword** repeat word for word.
151 **gambol** skip away.   152 **unction** ointment.   154 **skin** grow a skin for.
155 **mining** working under the surface.

And do not spread the compost° on the weeds
To make them ranker. Forgive me this my virtue;°
For in the fatness° of these pursy° times   160
Virtue itself of vice must pardon beg,
Yea, curb° and woo for leave° to do him good.

QUEEN.   O Hamlet, thou hast cleft my heart in twain.

HAMLET.   O, throw away the worser part of it,
And live the purer with the other half.   165
Good night. But go not to my uncle's bed;
Assume a virtue, if you have it not.
That monster, custom, who all sense doth eat,°
Of habits devil,° is angel yet in this,
That to the use of actions fair and good   170
He likewise gives a frock or livery°
That aptly° is put on. Refrain tonight,
And that shall lend a kind of easiness
To the next abstinence; the next more easy;
For use° almost can change the stamp of nature,°   175
And either° . . . the devil, or throw him out
With wondrous potency. Once more, good night;
And when you are desirous to be blest,
I'll blessing beg of you.° For this same lord,   [*pointing to* POLONIUS.]
I do repent; but heaven hath pleased it so   180
To punish me with this, and this with me,
That I must be their scourge and minister.°
I will bestow° him, and will answer° well
The death I gave him. So, again, good night.
I must be cruel only to be kind.   185
This° bad begins, and worse remains behind.°
One word more, good lady.

QUEEN.   What shall I do?

HAMLET.   Not this by no means that I bid you do:
Let the bloat° King tempt you again to bed,
Pinch wanton° on your cheek, call you his mouse,   190
And let him, for a pair of reechy° kisses,
Or paddling° in your neck with his damned fingers,

---

158 compost manure.   **159 this my virtue** my virtuous talk in reproving you.
160 fatness grossness;   **pursy** flabby, out of shape.   **162 curb** bow, bend the knee;
leave permission.   **168 who . . . eat** which consumes all proper or natural feeling, all sensibility.
169 Of habits devil devil-like in prompting evil habits.   **171 livery** an outer appearance, a
customary garb (and hence a predisposition easily assumed in time of stress).
172 aptly readily.   **175 use** habit;   **the stamp of nature** our inborn traits.   **176 And either** (A
defective line, usually emended by inserting the word *master* after *either*, following the Fourth
Quarto and early editors.)   **178–179 when . . . you** i.e., when you are ready to be penitent and
seek God's blessing, I will ask your blessing as a dutiful son should.   **182 their scourge and
minister** i.e., agent of heavenly retribution. (By *scourge*, Hamlet also suggests that he himself will
eventually suffer punishment in the process of fulfilling heaven's will.)   **183 bestow** stow,
dispose of;   **answer** account or pay for.   **186 This** i.e., the killing of Polonius;   **behind** to
come.   **189 bloat** bloated.   **190 Pinch wanton** i.e., leave his love pinches on your cheeks,
branding you as wanton.   **191 reechy** dirty, filthy.   **192 paddling** fingering amorously.

Make you to ravel all this matter out°
That I essentially am not in madness,
But mad in craft.° 'Twere good° you let him know,   195
For who that's but a Queen, fair, sober, wise,
Would from a paddock,° from a bat, a gib,°
Such dear concernings° hide? Who would do so?
No, in despite of sense and secrecy,°
Unpeg the basket° on the house's top,   200
Let the birds fly, and like the famous ape,°
To try conclusions,° in the basket creep
And break your own neck down.°

QUEEN.   Be thou assured, if words be made of breath,
And breath of life, I have no life to breathe   205
What thou hast said to me.

HAMLET.   I must to England. You know that?

QUEEN.   Alack,
I had forgot. 'Tis so concluded on.

HAMLET.   There's letters sealed, and my two schoolfellows,
Whom I will trust as I will adders fanged,   210
They bear the mandate; they must sweep my way
And marshal me to knavery.° Let it work.°
For 'tis the sport to have the enginer°
Hoist with° his own petard,° and 't shall go hard
But I will° delve one yard below their mines°   215
And blow them at the moon. O, 'tis most sweet
When in one line° two crafts° directly meet.
This man shall set me packing.°
I'll lug the guts into the neighbor room.
Mother, good night indeed. This counselor   220
Is now most still, most secret, and most grave,
Who was in life a foolish prating knave.—
Come, sir, to draw toward an end° with you.—
Good night, Mother.

Exeunt [*separately,* HAMLET *dragging in* POLONIUS].

---

193 ravel . . . out unravel, disclose.   **195 in craft** by cunning;   **good** (Said sarcastically; also the
following eight lines.)   **197 paddock** toad;   **gib** tomcat.   **198 dear concernings** important
affairs.   **199 sense and secrecy** secrecy that common sense requires.   **200 Unpeg the
basket** open the cage, i.e., let out the secret.   **201 famous ape** (In a story now lost.)   **202 try
conclusions** test the outcome (in which the ape apparently enters a cage from which birds have
been released and then tries to fly out of the cage as they have done, falling to its death).
203 down in the fall; utterly.   **211–212 sweep . . . knavery** sweep a path before me and
conduct me to some *knavery* or treachery prepared for me;   **work** proceed.
213 enginer maker of military contrivances.   **214 Hoist with** blown up by;   **petard** an
explosive used to blow in a door or make a breach.   **214–215 't shall . . . will** unless luck is
against me, I will;   **mines** tunnels used in warfare to undermine the enemy's emplacements;
Hamlet will countermine by going under their mines.   **217 in one line** i.e., mines and
countermines on a collision course, or the countermines directly below the mines;   **crafts** acts
of guile, plots.   **218 set me packing** set me to making schemes, and set me to lugging (him),
and, also, send me off in a hurry.   **223 draw . . . end** finish up (with a pun on *draw*, "pull").

4.1   *Enter* KING *and* QUEEN,° *with* ROSENCRANTZ *and* GUILDENSTERN.

KING.   There's matter° in these sighs, these profound heaves.°
          You must translate; 'tis fit we understand them.
          Where is your son?
QUEEN.   Bestow this place on us a little while.

                              [*Exeunt* ROSENCRANTZ *and* GUILDENSTERN.]

          Ah, mine own lord, what have I seen tonight!   5
KING.   What, Gertrude? How does Hamlet?
QUEEN.   Mad as the sea and wind when both contend
          Which is the mightier. In his lawless fit,
          Behind the arras hearing something stir,
          Whips out his rapier, cries, "A rat, a rat!"   10
          And in this brainish apprehension° kills
          The unseen good old man.
KING.   O heavy° deed!
          It had been so with us,° had we been there.
          His liberty is full of threats to all—
          To you yourself, to us, to everyone.   15
          Alas, how shall this bloody deed be answered?°
          It will be laid to us, whose providence°
          Should have kept short,° restrained, and out of haunt°
          This mad young man. But so much was our love,
          We would not understand what was most fit,   20
          But, like the owner of a foul disease,
          To keep it from divulging,° let it feed
          Even on the pith of life. Where is he gone?
QUEEN.   To draw apart the body he hath killed,
          O'er whom his very madness, like some ore°   25
          Among a mineral° of metals base,
          Shows itself pure: 'a weeps for what is done.
KING.   O Gertrude, come away!
          The sun no sooner shall the mountains touch
          But we will ship him hence, and this vile deed   30
          We must with all our majesty and skill
          Both countenance° and excuse.—Ho, Guildenstern!

          Enter ROSENCRANTZ *and* GUILDENSTERN.

          Friends both, go join you with some further aid.
          Hamlet in madness hath Polonius slain,
          And from his mother's closet hath he dragged him.   35

4.1 Location: The castle.   s.d. Enter . . . Queen (Some editors argue that Gertrude never exits
in 3.4 and that the scene is continuous here, as suggested in the Folio, but the Second Quarto
marks an entrance for her and at line 35 Claudius speaks of Gertrude's *closet* as though it were
elsewhere. A short time has elapsed, during which the King has become aware of her highly
wrought emotional state.)   **1 matter** significance;   **heaves** heavy sighs.   **11 brainish
apprehension** headstrong conception.   **12 heavy** grievous.   **13 us** i.e., me. (The royal "we";
also in line 15.)   **16 answered** explained.   **17 providence** foresight.   **18 short** i.e., on a short
tether;   **out of haunt** secluded.   **22 divulging** becoming evident.   **25 ore** vein of gold.
26 mineral mine.   **32 countenance** put the best face on.

Go seek him out, speak fair, and bring the body
Into the chapel. I pray you, haste in this.

[*Exeunt* ROSENCRANTZ *and* GUILDENSTERN.]

Come, Gertrude, we'll call up our wisest friends
And let them know both what we mean to do
And what's untimely done°.......   40
Whose whisper o'er the world's diameter,°
As level° as the cannon to his blank,°
Transports his poisoned shot, may miss our name
And hit the woundless° air. O, come away!
My soul is full of discord and dismay.   *Exeunt.*   45

4.2   *Enter* HAMLET.

HAMLET.   Safely stowed.

ROSENCRANTZ, GUILDENSTERN [*within*].   Hamlet! Lord Hamlet!

HAMLET.   But soft, what noise? Who calls on Hamlet? O, here they come.

Enter ROSENCRANTZ *and* GUILDENSTERN.

ROSENCRANTZ.   What have you done, my lord, with the dead body?

HAMLET.   Compounded it with dust, whereto 'tis kin.   5

ROSENCRANTZ.   Tell us where 'tis, that we may take it thence
And bear it to the chapel.

HAMLET.   Do not believe it.

ROSENCRANTZ.   Believe what?

HAMLET.   That I can keep your counsel and not mine own.° Besides, to be demanded   10
of° a sponge, what replication° should be made by the son of a king?

ROSENCRANTZ.   Take you me for a sponge, my lord?

HAMLET.   Ay, sir, that soaks up the King's countenance,° his rewards, his authorities.° But such officers do the King best service in the end. He keeps
them, like an ape, an apple, in the corner of his jaw, first mouthed to be   15
last swallowed. When he needs what you have gleaned, it is but squeezing you, and, sponge, you shall be dry again.

ROSENCRANTZ.   I understand you not, my lord.

HAMLET.   I am glad of it. A knavish speech sleeps in° a foolish ear.

ROSENCRANTZ.   My lord, you must tell us where the body is and go with us to the   20
King.

HAMLET.   The body is with the King, but the King is not with the body.°
The King is a thing—

---

40 And . . . done (A defective line; conjectures as to the missing words include *So, haply,
slander* [Capell and others]; *For, haply, slander* [Theobald and others]; and *So envious slander*
[Jenkins].)   **41 diameter** extent from side to side.   **42 As level** with as direct aim;   **his blank** its
target at point-blank range.   **44 woundless** invulnerable.   **4.2. Location: The castle.**
10 That . . . own i.e., that I can follow your advice (by telling where the body is) and still keep
my own secret.   **10–11 demanded of** questioned by;   **replication** reply.
13 countenance favor.   **13–14 authorities** delegated power, influence.   **19 sleeps in** has no
meaning to.   **22 The . . . body** (Perhaps alludes to the legal commonplace of "the king's two
bodies," which drew a distinction between the sacred office of kingship and the particular
mortal who possessed it at any given time. Hence, although Claudius' body is necessarily a part
of him, true kingship is not contained in it. Similarly, Claudius will have Polonius' body when it
is found, but there is no kingship in this business either.)

GUILDENSTERN.   A thing, my lord?

HAMLET.   Of nothing.° Bring me to him. Hide fox, and all after!°   25

Exeunt [running].

4.3   *Enter* KING, *and two or three.*

KING.   I have sent to seek him, and to find the body.
How dangerous is it that this man goes loose!
Yet must not we put the strong law on him.
He's loved of° the distracted° multitude,
Who like not in their judgment, but their eyes,°   5
And where 'tis so, th' offender's scourge° is weighed,°
But never the offense. To bear all smooth and even,°
This sudden sending him away must seem
Deliberate pause.° Diseases desperate grown
By desperate appliance° are relieved,   10
Or not at all.

Enter ROSENCRANTZ, GUILDENSTERN, *and all the rest.*

How now, what hath befall'n?

ROSENCRANTZ.   Where the dead body is bestowed, my lord,
We cannot get from him.

KING.   But where is he?

ROSENCRANTZ.   Without, my lord; guarded, to know your pleasure.

KING.   Bring him before us.

ROSENCRANTZ.   Ho! Bring in the lord.   15

They enter [with HAMLET].

KING.   Now, Hamlet, where's Polonius?

HAMLET.   At supper.

KING.   At supper? Where?

HAMLET.   Not where he eats, but where 'a is eaten. A certain convocation of politic
worms° are e'en° at him. Your worm° is your only emperor for diet.° We   20
fat all creatures else to fat us, and we fat ourselves for maggots. Your fat
king and your lean beggar is but variable service°—two dishes, but to
one table. That's the end.

KING.   Alas, alas!

HAMLET.   A man may fish with the worm that hath eat° of a king, and eat of the   25
fish that hath fed of that worm.

KING.   What dost thou mean by this?

---

25 Of nothing (1) of no account (2) lacking the essence of kingship, as in lines 24–25 and note;
Hide . . . after (An old signal cry in the game of hide-and-seek, suggesting that Hamlet now runs
away from them.)   **4.3 Location: The castle.**   **4 of** by;   **distracted** fickle, unstable.   **5 Who
. . . eyes** who choose not by judgment but by appearance.   **6 scourge** punishment. (Literally,
blow with a whip.);   **weighed** sympathetically considered.   **7 To . . . even** to manage the
business in an unprovocative way.   **9 Deliberate pause** carefully considered action.
10 appliance remedies.   **19–20 politic worms** crafty worms (suited to a master spy like
Polonius);   **e'en** even now;   **Your worm** your average worm. (Compare *your fat king and your
lean beggar* in lines 21–22.);   **diet** food, eating (with a punning reference to the Diet of Worms,
a famous *convocation* held in 1521).   **22 variable service** different courses of a single meal.
25 eat eaten. (Pronounced *et.*)

HAMLET.   Nothing but to show you how a king may go a progress° through the
    guts of a beggar.

KING.   Where is Polonius?   30

HAMLET.   In heaven. Send thither to see. If your messenger find him not there,
    seek him i' th' other place yourself. But if indeed you find him not
    within this month, you shall nose him as you go up the stairs into the
    lobby.

KING [*to some attendants*].   Go seek him there.   35

HAMLET.   'A will stay till you come.   [*Exeunt attendants.*]

KING.   Hamlet, this deed, for thine especial safety—
    Which we do tender,° as we dearly° grieve
    For that which thou hast done—must send thee hence
    With fiery quickness. Therefore prepare thyself.   40
    The bark° is ready, and the wind at help,
    Th' associates tend,° and everything is bent°
    For England.

HAMLET.   For England!

KING.   Ay, Hamlet.   45

HAMLET.   Good.

KING.   So is it, if thou knew'st our purposes.

HAMLET.   I see a cherub° that sees them. But come, for England!
    Farewell, dear mother.

KING.   Thy loving father, Hamlet.   50

HAMLET.   My mother. Father and mother is man and wife, man and wife is one
    flesh, and so, my mother. Come, for England!   *Exit.*

KING.   Follow him at foot;° tempt him with speed aboard.
    Delay it not. I'll have him hence tonight.
    Away! For everything is sealed and done   55
    That else leans on° th' affair. Pray you, make haste.
                                  [*Exeunt all but the* KING.]
    And, England,° if my love thou hold'st at aught°—
    As my great power thereof may give thee sense,°
    Since yet thy cicatrice° looks raw and red
    After the Danish sword, and thy free awe°   60
    Pays homage to us—thou mayst not coldly set°
    Our sovereign process,° which imports at full,°
    By letters congruing° to that effect,
    The present° death of Hamlet. Do it, England,
    For like the hectic° in my blood he rages,   65
    And thou must cure me. Till I know 'tis done,
    Howe'er my haps,° my joys were ne'er begun.   *Exit.*

---

28 progress royal journey of state.   **38 tender** regard, hold dear;   **dearly** intensely.
41 bark sailing vessel.   **42 tend** wait;   **bent** in readiness.   **48 cherub** (Cherubim are angels of
knowledge. Hamlet hints that both he and heaven are onto Claudius' tricks.)   **53 at foot** close
behind, at heel.   **56 leans on** bears upon, is related to.   **57 England** i.e., King of England;   **at
aught** at any value.   **58 As . . . sense** for so my great power may give you a just appreciation of
the importance of valuing my love.   **59 cicatrice** scar.   **60 free awe** voluntary show of respect.
61 coldly set regard with indifference.   **62 process** command;   **imports at full** conveys specific
directions for.   **63 congruing** agreeing.   **64 present** immediate.   **65 hectic** persistent fever.
67 haps fortunes.

4.4 *Enter* FORTINBRAS *with his army over the stage.*

FORTINBRAS.   Go, Captain, from me greet the Danish king.
　　　　Tell him that by his license° Fortinbras
　　　　Craves the conveyance of° a promised march
　　　　Over his kingdom. You know the rendezvous.
　　　　If that His Majesty would aught with us,　　　　　　　　　5
　　　　We shall express our duty° in his eye;°
　　　　And let him know so.
CAPTAIN.   I will do 't, my lord.
FORTINBRAS.   Go softly° on.　　　　　　　　　*[Exeunt all but the* CAPTAIN.]

　　　Enter HAMLET, ROSENCRANTZ, [GUILDENSTERN,] *etc.*

HAMLET.   Good sir, whose powers° are these?　　　　　　　　10
CAPTAIN.   They are of Norway, sir.
HAMLET.   How purposed, sir, I pray you?
CAPTAIN.   Against some part of Poland.
HAMLET.   Who commands them, sir?
CAPTAIN.   The nephew to old Norway, Fortinbras.　　　　　　15
HAMLET.   Goes it against the main° of Poland, sir,
　　　　Or for some frontier?
CAPTAIN.   Truly to speak, and with no addition,°
　　　　We go to gain a little patch of ground
　　　　That hath in it no profit but the name.　　　　　　　　20
　　　　To pay° five ducats, five, I would not farm it;°
　　　　Nor will it yield to Norway or the Pole
　　　　A ranker° rate, should it be sold in fee.°
HAMLET.   Why, then the Polack never will defend it.
CAPTAIN.   Yes, it is already garrisoned.　　　　　　　　　　25
HAMLET.   Two thousand souls and twenty thousand ducats
　　　　Will not debate the question of this straw.°
　　　　This is th' impostume° of much wealth and peace,
　　　　That inward breaks, and shows no cause without
　　　　Why the man dies. I humbly thank you, sir.　　　　　　30
CAPTAIN.   God b' wi' you, sir.　　　　　　　　　　　　　*[Exit.]*
ROSENCRANTZ.　　Will 't please you go, my lord?
HAMLET.   I'll be with you straight. Go a little before.

　　　　　　　　　　　　　　　　[Exeunt all except HAMLET.]

　　　　How all occasions do inform against° me
　　　　And spur my dull revenge! What is a man,　　　　　　35
　　　　If his chief good and market of° his time
　　　　Be but to sleep and feed? A beast, no more.
　　　　Sure he that made us with such large discourse,°
　　　　Looking before and after,° gave us not

4.4 Location: The coast of Denmark. 2 license permission. **3 the conveyance of** escort during. **6 duty** respect; **eye** presence. **9 softly** slowly, circumspectly. **10 powers** forces. **16 main** main part. **18 addition** exaggeration. **21 To pay** i.e., for a yearly rental of; **farm it** take a lease on it. **23 ranker** higher; **in fee** fee simple, outright. **27 debate . . . straw** settle this trifling matter. **28 impostume** abscess. **33 inform against** denounce, betray; take shape against. **35 market of** profit of, compensation for. **37 discourse** power of reasoning. **38 Looking before and after** able to review past events and anticipate the future.

That capability and godlike reason   40
To fust° in us unused. Now, whether it be
Bestial oblivion,° or some craven° scruple
Of thinking too precisely° on th' event°—
A thought which, quartered, hath but one part wisdom
And ever three parts coward—I do not know   45
Why yet I live to say "This thing's to do,"
Sith° I have cause, and will, and strength, and means
To do 't. Examples gross° as earth exhort me:
Witness this army of such mass and charge,°
Led by a delicate and tender° prince,   50
Whose spirit with divine ambition puffed
Makes mouths° at the invisible event,°
Exposing what is mortal and unsure
To all that fortune, death, and danger dare,°
Even for an eggshell. Rightly to be great   55
Is not to stir without great argument,
But greatly to find quarrel in a straw
When honor's at the stake.° How stand I, then,
That have a father killed, a mother stained,
Excitements of° my reason and my blood,   60
And let all sleep, while to my shame I see
The imminent death of twenty thousand men
That for a fantasy° and trick° of fame
Go to their graves like beds, fight for a plot°
Whereon the numbers cannot try the cause,°   65
Which is not tomb enough and continent°
To hide the slain? O, from this time forth
My thoughts be bloody or be nothing worth!   *Exit.*

4.5   *Enter* HORATIO, [QUEEN] GERTRUDE, *and a* GENTLEMAN.

QUEEN.   I will not speak with her.
GENTLEMAN.   She is importunate,
        Indeed distract.° Her mood will needs be pitied.
QUEEN.   What would she have?
GENTLEMAN.   She speaks much of her father, says she hears
        There's tricks° i' the world, and hems,° and beats her heart,°   5
        Spurns enviously at straws,° speaks things in doubt°

---

41 fust grow moldy.   **42 oblivion** forgetfulness;   **craven** cowardly.   **43 precisely** scrupulously;
event outcome.   **47 Sith** since.   **48 gross** obvious.   **49 charge** expense.   **50 delicate and
tender** of fine and youthful qualities.   **52 Makes mouths** makes scornful faces;   **invisible event**
unforeseeable outcome.   **54 dare** could do (to him).   **55–58 Rightly . . . stake** true greatness
does not normally consist of rushing into action over some trivial provocation; however, when
one's honor is involved, even a trifling insult requires that one respond greatly (?); **at the
stake** (A metaphor from gambling or bear-baiting.)   **60 Excitements of** promptings by.
63 fantasy fanciful caprice, illusion;   **trick** trifle, deceit.   **64 plot** plot of ground.   **65 Whereon
. . . cause** on which there is insufficient room for the soldiers needed to engage in a military
contest.   **66 continent** receptacle; container.   **4.5. Location: The castle.**   **2 distract** distracted.
5 tricks deceptions;   **hems** makes "hmm" sounds;   **heart** i.e., breast.   **6 Spurns . . . straws** kicks
spitefully, takes offense at trifles;   **in doubt** obscurely.

That carry but half sense. Her speech is nothing,
Yet the unshapèd use° of it doth move
The hearers to collection;° they yawn° at it,
And botch° the words up fit to their own thoughts,   10
Which,° as her winks and nods and gestures yield° them,
Indeed would make one think there might be thought,°
Though nothing sure, yet much unhappily.°

HORATIO.   'Twere good she were spoken with, for she may strew
Dangerous conjectures in ill-breeding° minds.   15

QUEEN.   Let her come in.   [*Exit* GENTLEMAN.]
[*Aside.*] To my sick soul, as sin's true nature is,
Each toy° seems prologue to some great amiss.°
So full of artless jealousy is guilt,
It spills itself in fearing to be spilt.°   20

Enter OPHELIA° [*distracted*].

OPHELIA.   Where is the beauteous majesty of Denmark?
QUEEN.   How now, Ophelia?
OPHELIA   [*she sings*].

"How should I your true love know
    From another one?
By his cockle hat° and staff,   25
    And his sandal shoon."°

QUEEN.   Alas, sweet lady, what imports this song?
OPHELIA.   Say you? Nay, pray you, mark.

"He is dead and gone, lady,   [*Song.*]   30
    He is dead and gone;
At his head a grass-green turf,
    At his heels a stone."

O, ho!
QUEEN.   Nay, but Ophelia—   35
OPHELIA.   Pray you, mark.   [*Sings.*]

"White his shroud as the mountain snow"—

Enter KING.

QUEEN.   Alas, look here, my lord.
OPHELIA.

"Larded° with sweet flowers;   [*Song.*]   40
Which bewept to the ground did not go
    With true-love showers."°

---

9 unshapèd use incoherent manner.   **9 collection** inference, a guess at some sort of meaning;
yawn gape, wonder; grasp. (The Folio reading, *aim*, is possible.)   **10 botch** patch.
11 Which which words;   **yield** deliver, represent.   **12 thought** intended.
13 unhappily unpleasantly near the truth, shrewdly.   **15 ill-breeding** prone to suspect the worst
and to make mischief.   **18 toy** trifle;   **amiss** calamity.   **19–20 So . . . split** guilt is so full of
suspicion that it unskilfully betrays itself in fearing betrayal.   **s.d. Enter Ophelia** (In the First
Quarto, Ophelia enters, "playing on a lute, and her hair down, singing.")   **26 cockle hat** hat
with cockle-shell stuck in it as a sign that the wearer had been a pilgrim to the shrine of Saint
James of Compostela in Spain.   **27 shoon** shoes.   **40 Larded** decorated.   **42 showers** i.e.,
tears.

KING.   How do you, pretty lady?

OPHELIA.   Well, God 'ild° you! They say the owl° was a baker's daughter.
Lord, we know what we are, but know not what we may be. God be at   45
your table!

KING.   Conceit° upon her father.

OPHELIA.   Pray let's have no words of this; but when they ask you what it means,
say you this:

"Tomorrow is Saint Valentine's day,   *[Song.]*   50
    All in the morning betime,°
And I a maid at your window,
    To be your Valentine.
Then up he rose, and donned his clothes,
    And dupped° the chamber door,   55
Let in the maid, that out a maid
    Never departed more."

KING.   Pretty Ophelia—

OPHELIA.   Indeed, la, without an oath, I'll make an end on 't: *[Sings.]*

"By Gis° and by Saint Charity,   60
    Alack, and fie for shame!
Young men will do 't, if they come to 't;
    By Cock,° they are to blame.
Quoth she, 'Before you tumbled me,
    You promised me to wed.'"   65

He answers:

"'So would I ha' done, by yonder sun,
An° thou hadst not come to my bed.'"

KING.   How long hath she been thus?

OPHELIA.   I hope all will be well. We must be patient, but I cannot choose but   70
weep to think they would lay him i' the cold ground. My brother shall
know of it. And so I thank you for your good counsel. Come, my
coach! Good night, ladies, good night, sweet ladies, good night, good
night.   *[Exit.]*

KING [*to* HORATIO].   Follow her close. Give her good watch, I pray you.   75

[Exit HORATIO.]

O, this is the poison of deep grief; it springs
All from her father's death—and now behold!
O Gertrude, Gertrude,
When sorrows come, they come not single spies,°
But in battalions. First, her father slain;   80
Next, your son gone, and he most violent author

---

44 God 'ild God yield or reward;   **owl** (Refers to a legend about a baker's daughter who was
turned into an owl for being ungenerous when Jesus begged a loaf of bread.)
47 Conceit brooding.   **51 betime** early.   **55 dupped** did up, opened.   **60 Gis** Jesus.
63 Cock (A perversion of "God" in oaths; here also with a quibble on the slang word for penis.)
68 An if.   **79 spies** scouts sent in advance of the main force.

Of his own just remove;° the people muddied,°
Thick and unwholesome in their thoughts and whispers
For good Polonius' death—and we have done but greenly,°
In hugger-mugger° to inter him; poor Ophelia   85
Divided from herself and her fair judgment,
Without the which we are pictures or mere beasts;
Last, and as much containing° as all these,
Her brother is in secret come from France,
Feeds on this wonder, keeps himself in clouds,°   90
And wants° not buzzers° to infect his ear
With pestilent speeches of his father's death,
Wherein necessity,° of matter beggared,°
Will nothing stick our person to arraign
In ear and ear.° O my dear Gertrude, this,   95
Like to a murdering piece,° in many places
Gives me superfluous death.°   *A noise within.*

QUEEN.   Alack, what noise is this?
KING.   Attend!°
         Where is my Switzers?° Let them guard the door.   100

         Enter a MESSENGER.

         What is the matter?
MESSENGER.   Save yourself, my lord!
         The ocean, overpeering of his list,°
         Eats not the flats° with more impetuous° haste
         Than young Laertes, in a riotous head,°
         O'erbears your officers. The rabble call him lord,   105
         And, as° the world were now but to begin,
         Antiquity forgot, custom not known,
         The ratifiers and props of every word,°
         They cry, "Choose we! Laertes shall be king!"
         Caps,° hands, and tongues applaud it to the clouds, 110
         "Laertes shall be king, Laertes king!"
QUEEN.   How cheerfully on the false trail they cry! *A noise within.*
         O, this is counter,° you false Danish dogs!

         Enter LAERTES *with others.*

82 remove removal; **muddied** stirred up, confused.   **84 greenly** in an inexperienced way,
foolishly.   **85 hugger-mugger** secret haste.   **88 as much containing** as full of serious matter.
90 Feeds . . . clouds feeds his resentment or shocked grievance, holds himself inscrutable and
aloof amid all this rumor.   **91 wants** lacks;   **buzzers** gossipers, informers.   **93 necessity** i.e., the
need to invent some plausible explanation;   **of matter beggared** unprovided with facts.
94–95 Will . . . ear will not hesitate to accuse my (royal) person in everybody's ears.
96 murdering piece cannon loaded so as to scatter its shot.   **97 Gives . . . death** kills me over
and over.   **99 Attend** i.e., guard me.   **100 Switzers** Swiss guards, mercenaries.
102 overpeering of his list overflowing its shore, boundary.   **103 flats** i.e., flatlands near shore;
impetuous violent. (Perhaps also with the meaning of *impiteous* [*impitious,* Q2], "pitiless.")
104 head insurrection.   **106 as** as if.   **108 The ratifiers . . . word** i.e., *antiquity* (or tradition)
and *custom* ought to confirm (*ratify*) and underprop our every word or promise.
110 Caps (The caps are thrown in the air.)   **113 counter** (A hunting term, meaning to follow
the trail in a direction opposite to that which the game has taken.)

KING.   The doors are broke.

LAERTES.   Where is this King?—Sirs, stand you all without.   115

ALL.   No, let's come in.

LAERTES.   I pray you, give me leave.

ALL.   We will, we will.

LAERTES.   I thank you. Keep the door. [*Exeunt followers.*] O thou vile king,
    Give me my father!   120

QUEEN [*restraining him*].   Calmly, good Laertes.

LAERTES.   That drop of blood that's calm proclaims me bastard,
    Cries cuckold to my father, brands the harlot
    Even here, between° the chaste unsmirchèd brow
    Of my true mother.   125

KING.   What is the cause, Laertes,
    That thy rebellion looks so giantlike?
    Let him go, Gertrude. Do not fear our° person.
    There's such divinity doth hedge° a king
    That treason can but peep to what it would,°   130
    Acts little of his will.° Tell me, Laertes,
    Why thou art thus incensed. Let him go, Gertrude.
    Speak, man.

LAERTES.   Where is my father?

KING.   Dead.

QUEEN.   But not by him.

KING.   Let him demand his fill.   135

LAERTES.   How came he dead? I'll not be juggled with.°
    To hell, allegiance! Vows, to the blackest devil!
    Conscience and grace, to the profoundest pit!
    I dare damnation. To this point I stand,°
    That both the worlds I give to negligence,°   140
    Let come what comes, only I'll be revenged
    Most throughly° for my father.

KING.   Who shall stay you?

LAERTES.   My will, not all the world's.°
    And for° my means, I'll husband them so well   145
    They shall go far with little.

KING.   Good Laertes,
    If you desire to know the certainty
    Of your dear father, is 't writ in your revenge
    That, swoopstake,° you will draw both friend and foe,   150
    Winner and loser?

LAERTES.   None but his enemies.

KING.   Will you know them, then?

---

124 between in the middle of.   **128 fear our** fear for my.   **129 hedge** protect, as with a surrounding barrier.   **130 can . . . would** can only peep furtively, as through a barrier, at what it would intend.   **131 Acts . . . will** (but) performs little of what it intends.   **136 juggled with** cheated, deceived.   **139 To . . . stand** I am resolved in this.   **140 both . . . negligence** i.e. both this world and the next are of no consequence to me.   **142 throughly** thoroughly. **144 My will . . . world's** I'll stop (*stay*) when my will is accomplished, not for anyone else's. **145 for** as for.   **150 swoopstake** i.e., indiscriminately. (Literally, taking all stakes on the gambling table at once. *Draw* is also a gambling term, meaning "taken from.")

LAERTES.   To his good friends thus wide I'll ope my arms,
And like the kind life-rendering pelican°   155
Repast° them with my blood.
KING.   Why, now you speak
Like a good child and a true gentleman.
That I am guiltless of your father's death,
And am most sensibly° in grief for it,   160
It shall as level° to your judgment 'pear
As day does to your eye.   *A noise within.*
LAERTES.   How now, what noise is that?

    Enter OPHELIA.

KING.   Let her come in.
LAERTES.   O heat, dry up my brains! Tears seven times salt
Burn out the sense and virtue° of mine eye!   165
By heaven, thy madness shall be paid with weight°
Till our scale turn the beam.° O rose of May!
Dear maid, kind sister, sweet Ophelia!
O heavens, is 't possible a young maid's wits
Should be as mortal as an old man's life?   170
Nature is fine in° love, and where 'tis fine
It sends some precious instance° of itself
After the thing it loves.°
OPHELIA.   *[Song.]*

    "They bore him barefaced on the bier,   175
      Hey non nonny, nonny, hey nonny,
    And in his grave rained many a tear—"

    Fare you well, my dove!
LAERTES.   Hadst thou thy wits and didst persuade° revenge,
It could not move thus.   180
OPHELIA.   You must sing "A-down a-down," and you "call him a-down-a."°
O, how the wheel° becomes it! It is the false steward° that stole his master's daughter.
LAERTES.   This nothing's more than matter.°
OPHELIA.   There's rosemary,° that's for remembrance; pray you, love, remember.   185
And there is pansies;° that's for thoughts.
LAERTES.   A document° in madness, thoughts and remembrance fitted.

---

155 **pelican** (Refers to the belief that the female pelican fed its young with its own blood.)
156 **Repast** feed.   160 **sensibly** feelingly.   161 **level** plain.   165 **virtue** faculty, power.
166 **paid with weight** repaid, avenged equally or more.   167 **beam** crossbar of a balance.
171 **fine in** refined by.   172 **instance** token.   173 **After . . . loves** i.e., into the grave, along with Polonius.   179 **persuade** argue cogently for.   181 **You . . . a-down-a** (Ophelia assigns the singing of refrains, like her own "Hey non nonny," to others present.)   182 **wheel** spinning wheel as accompaniment to the song, or refrain; **false steward** (The story is unknown.)
184 **This . . . matter** this seeming nonsense is more eloquent than sane utterance.
185 **rosemary** (Used as a symbol of remembrance both at weddings and at funerals.)
186 **pansies** (Emblems of love and courtship; perhaps from French *pensées*, "thoughts.")
187 **document** instruction, lesson.

OPHELIA.   There's fennel° for you, and columbines.° There's rue° for you, and
here's some for me; we may call it herb of grace o' Sundays. You must
wear your rue with a difference.° There's a daisy.° I would give you   190
some violets,° but they withered all when my father died. They say 'a
made a good end—
[*Sings.*] "For bonny sweet Robin is all my joy."

LAERTES.   Thought° and affliction, passion,° hell itself,
She turns to favor° and to prettiness.   195

OPHELIA.   [*Song.*]

"And will 'a not come again?
And will 'a not come again?
    No, no, he is dead.
    Go to thy deathbed,   200
He never will come again.

"His beard was as white as snow,
All flaxen was his poll.°
    He is gone, he is gone,
    And we cast away moan.   205
God ha' mercy on his soul!"

And of all Christian souls, I pray God. God b' wi' you.
                                          [*Exit, followed by* GERTRUDE.]

LAERTES.   Do you see this, O God?

KING.   Laertes, I must commune with your grief,   210
Or you deny me right. Go but apart,
Make choice of whom° your wisest friends you will,
And they shall hear and judge twixt you and me.
If by direct or by collateral hand°
They find us touched,° we will our kingdom give,   215
Our crown, our life, and all that we call ours
To you in satisfaction; but if not,
Be you content to lend your patience to us,
And we shall jointly labor with your soul
To give it due content.

LAERTES.   Let this be so.   220
His means of death, his obscure funeral—
No trophy,° sword, nor hatchment° o'er his bones,
No noble rite, nor formal ostentation°—

---

188 **fennel** (Emblem of flattery.);   **columbines** (Emblems of unchastity or ingratitude.);
rue (Emblem of repentance—a signification that is evident in its popular name, *herb of grace*.)
190 **with a difference** (A device used in heraldry to distinguish one family from another on the
coat of arms, here suggesting that Ophelia and the others have different causes of sorrow and
repentance; perhaps with a play on *rue* in the sense of "ruth," "pity.");   **daisy** (Emblem of
dissembling, faithlessness.)   191 **violets** (Emblems of faithfulness.)   194 **Thought** melancholy;
passion suffering.   195 **favor** grace, beauty.   203 **poll** head.   212 **whom** whichever of.
214 **collateral hand** indirect agency.   215 **us touched** me implicated.   222 **trophy** memorial;
hatchment tablet displaying the armorial bearings of a deceased person.
223 **ostentation** ceremony.

Cry to be heard, as 'twere from heaven to earth,
That° I must call 't in question.°

KING.   So you shall,   225
And where th' offense is, let the great ax fall.
I pray you, go with me.   *Exeunt.*

4.6　*Enter* HORATIO *and others.*

HORATIO.　What are they that would speak with me?
GENTLEMAN.　Seafaring men, sir. They say they have letters for you.
HORATIO.　Let them come in.   [*Exit* GENTLEMAN.]
I do not know from what part of the world
I should be greeted, if not from Lord Hamlet.   5

Enter Sailors.

FIRST SAILOR.　God bless you, sir.
HORATIO.　Let him bless thee too.
FIRST SAILOR.　'A shall, sir, an 't° please him. There's a letter for you, sir—it came
from th' ambassador° that was bound for England—if your name be
Horatio, as I am let to know it is.   [*He gives a letter.*]   10
HORATIO [*reads*].　"Horatio, when thou shalt have overlooked° this, give these fel-
lows some means° to the King; they have letters for him. Ere we were
two days old at sea, a pirate of very warlike appointment° gave us chase.
Finding ourselves too slow of sail, we put on a compelled valor, and in
the grapple I boarded them. On the instant they got clear of our ship, so   15
I alone became their prisoner. They have dealt with me like thieves of
mercy,° but they knew what they did: I am to do a good turn for them.
Let the King have the letters I have sent, and repair° thou to me with as
much speed as thou wouldest fly death. I have words to speak in thine
ear will make thee dumb, yet are they much too light for the bore° of the   20
matter. These good fellows will bring thee where I am. Rosencrantz and
Guildenstern hold their course for England. Of them I have much to tell
thee. Farewell.
He that thou knowest thine, Hamlet."
Come, I will give you way° for these your letters,   25
And do 't the speedier that you may direct me
To him from whom you brought them.   *Exeunt.*

4.7　*Enter* KING *and* LAERTES.

KING.　Now must your conscience my acquittance seal,°
And you must put me in your heart for friend,
Sith° you have heard, and with a knowing ear,
That he which hath your noble father slain
Pursued my life.

---

225 That so that;　**call 't in question** demand an explanation.　**4.6. Location: The castle.**
8 an 't if it.　**9 th' ambassador** (Evidently Hamlet. The sailor is being circumspect.)
11 overlooked looked over.　**12 means** means of access.　**13 appointment** equipage.
16–17 thieves of mercy merciful thieves.　**18 repair** come.　**20 bore** caliber, i.e., importance.
25 way means of access.　**4.7 Location: The castle.**　**1 my acquittance seal** confirm or
acknowledge my innocence.　**3 Sith** since.

LAERTES.   It well appears. But tell me   5
            Why you proceeded not against these feats°
            So crimeful and so capital° in nature,
            As by your safety, greatness, wisdom, all things else,
            You mainly° were stirred up.

KING.   O, for two special reasons,   10
            Which may to you perhaps seem much unsinewed,°
            But yet to me they're strong. The Queen his mother
            Lives almost by his looks, and for myself—
            My virtue or my plague, be it either which—
            She is so conjunctive° to my life and soul   15
            That, as the star moves not but in his° sphere,°
            I could not but by her. The other motive
            Why to a public count° I might not go
            Is the great love the general gender° bear him,
            Who, dipping all his faults in their affection,   20
            Work° like the spring° that turneth wood to stone,
            Convert his gyves° to graces, so that my arrows,
            Too slightly timbered° for so loud° a wind,
            Would have reverted° to my bow again
            But not where I had aimed them.   25

LAERTES.   And so have I a noble father lost,
            A sister driven into desperate terms,°
            Whose worth, if praises may go back° again,
            Stood challenger on mount° of all the age
            For her perfections. But my revenge will come.   30

KING.   Break not your sleeps for that. You must not think
            That we are made of stuff so flat and dull
            That we can let our beard be shook with danger
            And think it pastime. You shortly shall hear more.
            I loved your father, and we love ourself;   35
            And that, I hope, will teach you to imagine—

            Enter a MESSENGER *with letters.*

            How now? What news?

MESSENGER.   Letters, my lord, from Hamlet:
            This to Your Majesty, this to the Queen.   [*He gives letters.*]

KING.   From Hamlet? Who brought them?   40

MESSENGER.   Sailors, my lord, they say. I saw them not.
            They were given me by Claudio. He received them
            Of him that brought them.

---

6 feats acts.   **7 capital** punishable by death.   **9 mainly** greatly.   **11 unsinewed** weak.
15 conjunctive closely united. (An astronomical metaphor.)   **16 his** its;   **sphere** one of the
hollow spheres in which, according to Ptolematic astronomy, the planets were supposed to
move.   **18 count** account, reckoning, indictment.   **19 general gender** common people.
21 Work operate, act;   **spring** i.e., a spring with such a concentration of lime that it coats a
piece of wood with limestone, in effect gilding and petrifying it.   **22 gyves** fetters (which, gilded
by the people's praise, would look like badges of honor).   **23 slightly timbered** light;
loud (suggesting public outcry on Hamlet's behalf).   **24 reverted** returned.   **27 terms** state,
condition.   **28 go back** i.e., recall what she was.   **29 on mount** set up on high.

KING.   Laertes, you shall hear them.—
        Leave us.   [*Exit* MESSENGER.]   45
        [*He reads.*] "High and mighty, you shall know I am set naked° on your
        kingdom. Tomorrow shall I beg leave to see your kingly eyes, when I
        shall, first asking your pardon,° thereunto recount the occasion of my
        sudden and more strange return.   Hamlet."
        What should this mean? Are all the rest come back?   50
        Or is it some abuse,° and no such thing?°

LAERTES.   Know you the hand?

KING.   'Tis Hamlet's character.° "Naked!"
        And in a postscript here he says "alone."
        Can you devise° me?   55

LAERTES.   I am lost in it, my lord. But let him come.
        It warms the very sickness in my heart
        That I shall live and tell him to his teeth,
        "Thus didst thou."°

KING.   If it be so, Laertes—
        As how should it be so? How otherwise?°—   60
        Will you be ruled by me?

LAERTES.   Ay, my lord,
        So° you will not o'errule me to a peace.

KING.   To thine own peace. If he be now returned,
        As checking at° his voyage, and that° he means
        No more to undertake it, I will work him   65
        To an exploit, now ripe in my device,°
        Under the which he shall not choose but fall;
        And for his death no wind of blame shall breathe,
        But even his mother shall uncharge the practice°
        And call it accident.

LAERTES.   My lord, I will be ruled,   70
        The rather if you could devise it so
        That I might be the organ.°

KING.   It falls right.
        You have been talked of since your travel much,
        And that in Hamlet's hearing, for a quality   75
        Wherein they say you shine. Your sum of parts°
        Did not together pluck such envy from him
        As did that one, and that, in my regard,
        Of the unworthiest siege.°

LAERTES.   What part is that, my lord?   80

KING.   A very ribbon in the cap of youth,

46 naked destitute, unarmed, without following.   **48 pardon** permission.   **51 abuse** deceit;   **no such thing** not what it appears.   **53 character** handwriting.   **55 devise** explain to.   **59 Thus didst thou** i.e., here's for what you did to my father.   **60 As . . . otherwise** how can this (Hamlet's return) be true? Yet how otherwise than true (since we have the evidence of his letter)?   **62 So** provided that.   **64 checking at** i.e., turning aside from (like a falcon leaving the quarry to fly at a chance bird);   **that** if.   **66 device** devising, invention.   **69 uncharge the practice** acquit the stratagem of being a plot.   **72 organ** agent, instrument.   **76 Your . . . parts** i.e., all your other virtues.   **79 unworthiest siege** least important rank.

Yet needful too, for youth no less becomes°
The light and careless livery that it wears
Than settled age his sables° and his weeds°
Importing health and graveness.° Two months since   85
Here was a gentleman of Normandy.
I have seen myself, and served against, the French,
And they can well° on horseback, but this gallant
Had witchcraft in 't; he grew unto his seat,
And to such wondrous doing brought his horse   90
As had he been incorpsed and demi-natured°
With the brave beast. So far he topped° my thought
That I in forgery° of shapes and tricks
Come short of what he did.

LAERTES.   A Norman was 't?

KING.   A Norman.   95

LAERTES.   Upon my life, Lamord.

KING.   The very same.

LAERTES.   I know him well. He is the brooch° indeed
And gem of all the nation.

KING.   He made confession° of you,   100
And gave you such a masterly report
For art and exercise in your defense,°
And for your rapier most especial,
That he cried out 'twould be a sight indeed
If one could match you. Th' escrimers° of their nation,   105
He swore, had neither motion, guard, nor eye
If you opposed them. Sir, this report of his
Did Hamlet so envenom with his envy
That he could nothing do but wish and beg
Your sudden° coming o'er, to play° with you.   110
Now, out of this—

LAERTES.   What out of this, my lord?

KING.   Laertes, was your father dear to you?
Or are you like the painting of a sorrow,
A face without a heart?

LAERTES.   Why ask you this?

KING.   Not that I think you did not love your father,   115
But that I know love is begun by time,°
And that I see, in passages of proof,°
Time qualifies° the spark and fire of it.
There lives within the very flame of love

---

82 **no less becomes** is no less suited by.   84 **his sables** its rich robes furred with sable;
weeds garments.   85 **Importing . . . graveness** signifying a concern for health and dignified
prosperity; also, giving an impression of comfortable prosperity.   88 **can well** are skilled.
91 **As . . . demi-natured** as if he had been of one body and nearly of one nature (like the
centaur).   92 **topped** surpassed.   93 **forgery** imagining.   98 **brooch** ornament.
100 **confession** testimonial, admission of superiority.   102 **For . . . defense** with respect to your
skill and practice with your weapon.   105 **escrimers** fencers.   110 **sudden** immediate;
play fence.   116 **begun by time** i.e., created by the right circumstance and hence subject to
change.   117 **passages of proof** actual instances that prove it.   118 **qualifies** weakens,
moderates.

A kind of wick or snuff° that will abate it,   120
And nothing is at a like goodness still,°
For goodness, growing to a pleurisy,°
Dies in his own too much.° That° we would do,
We should do when we would; for this "would" changes
And hath abatements° and delays as many   125
As there are tongues, are hands, are accidents,°
And then this "should" is like a spendthrift sigh,°
That hurts by easing.° But, to the quick o' th' ulcer:°
Hamlet comes back. What would you undertake
To show yourself in deed your father's son   130
More than in words?

LAERTES.   To cut his throat i' the church.

KING.   No place, indeed, should murder sanctuarize;°
Revenge should have no bounds. But good Laertes,
Will you do this,° keep close within your chamber.
Hamlet returned shall know you are come home.   135
We'll put on those shall° praise your excellence
And set a double varnish on the fame
The Frenchman gave you, bring you in fine° together,
And wager on your heads. He, being remiss,°
Most generous,° and free from all contriving,   140
Will not peruse the foils, so that with ease,
Or with a little shuffling, you may choose
A sword unbated,° and in a pass of practice°
Requite him for your father.

LAERTES.   I will do 't,
And for that purpose I'll anoint my sword.   145
I bought an unction° of a mountebank°
So mortal that, but dip a knife in it,
Where it draws blood no cataplasm° so rare,
Collected from all simples° that have virtue°
Under the moon,° can save the thing from death   150
That is but scratched withal. I'll touch my point
With this contagion, that if I gall° him slightly,
It may be death.

---

120 snuff the charred part of a candlewick.   **121 nothing . . . still** nothing remains at a constant level of perfection.   **122 pleurisy** excess, plethora. (Literally, a chest inflammation.)   **123 in . . . much** of its own excess;   **That** that which.   **125 abatements** diminutions.   **126 As . . . accidents** as there are tongues to dissuade, hands to prevent, and chance events to intervene.   **127 spendthrift sigh** (An allusion to the belief that sighs draw blood from the heart.)   **128 hurts by easing** i.e., costs the heart blood and wastes precious opportunity even while it affords emotional relief;   **quick o' th' ulcer** i.e., heart of the matter.   **132 sanctuarize** protect from punishment. (Alludes to the right of sanctuary with which certain religious places were invested.)   **134 Will you do this** if you wish to do this.   **136 put on those shall** arrange for some to.   **138 in fine** finally.   **139 remiss** negligently unsuspicious.   **140 generous** noble-minded.   **143 unbated** not blunted, having no button;   **pass of practice** treacherous thrust.   **146 unction** ointment;   **mountebank** quack doctor.   **148 cataplasm** plaster or poultice.   **149 simples** herbs;   **virtue** potency.   **150 Under the moon** i.e., anywhere (with reference perhaps to the belief that herbs gathered at night had a special power).   **152 gall** graze, wound.

KING.   Let's further think of this,
            Weigh what convenience both of time and means   155
            May fit us to our shape.° If this should fail,
            And that our drift look through our bad performance,°
            'Twere better not assayed. Therefore this project
            Should have a back or second, that might hold
            If this did blast in proof.° Soft, let me see.   160
            We'll make a solemn wager on your cunnings°—
            I ha 't!
            When in your motion you are hot and dry—
            As° make your bouts more violent to that end—
            And that he calls for drink, I'll have prepared him   165
            A chalice for the nonce,° whereon but sipping,
            If he by chance escape your venomed stuck,°
            Our purpose may hold there. [*A cry within.*] But stay, what noise?

            Enter QUEEN.

QUEEN.   One woe doth tread upon another's heel,
            So fast they follow. Your sister's drowned, Laertes.   170

LAERTES.   Drowned! O, where?

QUEEN.   There is a willow grows askant° the brook,
            That shows his hoar leaves° in the glassy stream;
            Therewith fantastic garlands did she make
            Of crowflowers, nettles, daisies, and long purples,°   175
            That liberal° shepherds give a grosser name,°
            But our cold° maids do dead men's fingers call them.
            There on the pendent° boughs her crownet° weeds
            Clamb'ring to hang, an envious sliver° broke,
            When down her weedy° trophies and herself   180
            Fell in the weeping brook. Her clothes spread wide,
            And mermaidlike awhile they bore her up,
            Which time she chanted snatches of old lauds,°
            As one incapable of° her own distress,
            Or like a creature native and endued°   185
            Unto that element. But long it could not be
            Till that her garments, heavy with their drink,
            Pulled the poor wretch from her melodious lay
            To muddy death.

LAERTES.   Alas, then she is drowned?

QUEEN.   Drowned, drowned.   190

---

156 shape part we propose to act.   **157 drift . . . performance** intention should be made visible by our bungling.   **160 blast in proof** burst in the test (like a cannon).   **161 cunnings** respective skills.   **164 As** i.e., and you should.   **166 nonce** occasion.   **167 stuck** thrust. (From *stoccado*, a fencing term.)   **172 askant** aslant.   **173 hoar leaves** white or gray undersides of the leaves. **175 long purples** early purple orchids.   **176 liberal** free-spoken;   **a grosser name** (The testicle-resembling tubers of the orchid, which also in some cases resemble *dead men's fingers*, have earned various slang names like "dogstones" and "cullions.")   **177 cold** chaste. **178 pendent** over-hanging;   **crownet** made into a chaplet or coronet.   **179 envious sliver** malicious branch.   **180 weedy** i.e., of plants.   **183 lauds** hymns.   **184 incapable of** lacking capacity to apprehend.   **185 endued** adapted by nature.

LAERTES.   Too much of water hast thou, poor Ophelia,
And therefore I forbid my tears. But yet
It is our trick;° nature her custom holds,
Let shame say what it will. [*He weeps.*] When these are gone,
The woman will be out.° Adieu, my lord.   195
I have a speech of fire that fain would blaze,
But that this folly douts° it.   *Exit.*

KING.   Let's follow, Gertrude.
How much I had to do to calm his rage!
Now fear I this will give it start again;   200
Therefore let's follow.   *Exeunt.*

5.1   *Enter two* CLOWNS° [*with spades and mattocks*].

FIRST CLOWN.   Is she to be buried in Christian burial, when she willfully seeks her
own salvation?°
SECOND CLOWN.   I tell thee she is; therefore make her grave straight.° The
crowner° hath sat on her,° and finds it° Christian burial.
FIRST CLOWN.   How can that be, unless she drowned herself in her own defense?   5
SECOND CLOWN.   Why, 'tis found so.°
FIRST CLOWN.   It must be *se offendendo*,° it cannot be else. For here lies the point:
if I drown myself wittingly, it argues an act, and an act hath three
branches—it is to act, to do, and to perform. Argal,° she drowned herself
wittingly.   10
SECOND CLOWN.   Nay, but hear you, goodman° delver—
FIRST CLOWN.   Give me leave. Here lies the water; good. Here stands the man;
good. If the man go to this water and drown himself, it is, will he, nill he,°
he goes, mark you that. But if the water come to him and drown him, he
drowns not himself. Argal, he that is not guilty of his own death shortens   15
not his own life.
SECOND CLOWN.   But is this law?
FIRST CLOWN.   Ay, marry, is 't—crowner's quest° law.
SECOND CLOWN.   Will you ha' the truth on 't? If this had not been a gentlewoman,
she should have been buried out o' Christian burial.   20
FIRST CLOWN.   Why, there thou sayst.° And the more pity that great folk should have
countenance° in this world to drown or hang themselves, more than their
even-Christian.° Come, my spade. There is no ancient° gentlemen but gardeners, ditchers, and grave makers. They hold up° Adam's profession.

---

193 It is our trick i.e., weeping is our natural way (when sad).   **194–195 When . . . out** when
my tears are all shed, the woman in me will be expended, satisfied.   **197 douts** extinguishes.
(The Second Quarto reads "drowns.")   **5.1 Location: A churchyard.   s.d. Clowns** rustics.
2 salvation (A blunder for "damnation," or perhaps a suggestion that Ophelia was taking her
own shortcut to heaven.)   **3 straight** straightway, immediately. (But with a pun on *strait,*
"narrow.")   **4 crowner** coroner;   **sat on her** conducted an inquest on her case;   **finds it** gives
his official verdict that her means of death was consistent with.   **6 found so** determined so in
the coroner's verdict.   **7 se offendendo** (A comic mistake for *se defendendo,* a term used in
verdicts of justifiable homicide.)   **9 Argal** (Corruption of *ergo,* "therefore.")   **11 goodman** (An
honorific title often used with the name of a profession or craft.)   **13 will he, nill he** whether he
will or no, willy-nilly.   **18 quest** inquest.   **21 there thou sayst** i.e., that's right.
22 countenance privilege.   **23 even-Christian** fellow Christians;   **ancient** going back to ancient
times.   **24 hold up** maintain.

SECOND CLOWN.   Was he a gentleman?   25

FIRST CLOWN.   'A was the first that ever bore arms.°

SECOND CLOWN.   Why, he had none.

FIRST CLOWN.   What, art a heathen? How dost thou understand the Scripture? The
Scripture says Adam digged. Could he dig without arms?° I'll put another
question to thee. If thou answerest me not to the purpose, confess thy-   30
self°—

SECOND CLOWN.   Go to.

FIRST CLOWN.   What is he that builds stronger than either the mason, the shipwright, or the carpenter?

SECOND CLOWN.   The gallows maker, for that frame° outlives a thousand tenants.   35

FIRST CLOWN.   I like thy wit well, in good faith. The gallows does well.° But how
does it well? It does well to those that do ill. Now thou dost ill to say the
gallows is built stronger than the church. Argal, the gallows may do well
to thee. To 't again, come.

SECOND CLOWN.   "Who builds stronger than a mason, a shipwright, or a carpenter?" 40

FIRST CLOWN.   Ay, tell me that, and unyoke.°

SECOND CLOWN.   Marry, now I can tell.

FIRST CLOWN.   To 't.

SECOND CLOWN.   Mass,° I cannot tell.

Enter HAMLET *and* HORATIO [*at a distance*].

FIRST CLOWN.   Cudgel thy brains no more about it, for your dull ass will not mend   45
his pace with beating; and when you are asked this question next, say "a
grave maker." The houses he makes lasts till doomsday. Go get thee in
and fetch me a stoup° of liquor.

[*Exit* SECOND CLOWN. FIRST CLOWN *digs.*]

Song.

"In youth, when I did love, did love,°
  Methought it was very sweet,   50
To contract—O—the time for—a—my behove,°
  O, methought there—a—was nothing—a—meet."°

HAMLET.   Has this fellow no feeling of his business, 'a° sings in gravemaking?

HORATIO.   Custom hath made it in him a property of easiness.°

HAMLET.   'Tis e'en so. The hand of little employment hath the daintier sense.°   55

FIRST CLOWN.   *Song.*

"But age with his stealing steps
  Hath clawed me in his clutch,

---

26 bore arms (To be entitled to bear a coat of arms would make Adam a gentleman, but as one
who bore a spade, our common ancestor was an ordinary delver in the earth.)   **29 arms** i.e.,
the arms of the body.   **30–31 confess thyself** (The saying continues, "and be hanged.")
35 frame (1) gallows (2) structure.   **36 does well** (1) is an apt answer (2) does a good turn.
41 unyoke i.e., after this great effort, you may unharness the team of your wits.   **44 Mass** by
the Mass.   **48 stoup** two-quart measure.   **49 In . . . love** (This and the two following stanzas,
with nonsensical variations, are from a poem attributed to Lord Vaux and printed in *Tottel's
Miscellany,* 1557. The *O* and *a* [for "ah"] seemingly are the grunts of the digger.)   **51 To
contract . . . behove** i.e., to shorten the time for my own advantage. (Perhaps he means to
prolong it.)   **52 meet** suitable, i.e., more suitable.   **53 'a** that he.   **54 property of
easiness** something he can do easily and indifferently.   **55 daintier sense** more delicate sense of
feeling.

And hath shipped me into the land,°
   As if I had never been such."   *[He throws up a skull.]*   60

HAMLET.   That skull had a tongue in it and could sing once. How the knave jowls°
it to the ground, as if 'twere Cain's jawbone, that did the first murder!
This might be the pate of a politician,° which this ass now o'erreaches,°
one that would circumvent God, might it not?

HORATIO.   It might, my lord.   65

HAMLET.   Or of a courtier, which could say, "Good morrow, sweet lord! How dost
thou, sweet lord?" This might be my Lord Such-a-one, that praised my
Lord Such-a-one's horse when 'a meant to beg it, might it not?

HORATIO.   Ay, my lord.

HAMLET.   Why, e'en so, and now my Lady Worm's, chapless,° and knocked about   70
the mazard° with a sexton's spade. Here's fine revolution,° an° we had
the trick to see° 't. Did these bones cost no more the breeding but to°
play at loggets° with them? Mine ache to think on 't.

FIRST CLOWN.   *Song.*

   "A pickax and a spade, a spade,   75
     For and° a shrouding sheet;
   O, a pit of clay for to be made
     For such a guest is meet."   *[He throws up another skull.]*

HAMLET.   There's another. Why may not that be the skull of a lawyer? Where be
his quiddities° now, his quillities,° his cases, his tenures,° and his tricks?   80
Why does he suffer this mad knave now to knock him about the sconce°
with a dirty shovel, and will not tell him of his action of battery?° Hum,
this fellow might be in 's time a great buyer of land, with his statutes, his
recognizances,° his fines, his double° vouchers,° his recoveries.° Is this
the fine of his fines and the recovery of his recoveries, to have his fine   85
pate full of fine dirt?° Will his vouchers vouch him no more of his pur-
chases, and double ones too, than the length and breadth of a pair of indentures?° The very conveyances° of his lands will scarcely lie in this
box,° and must th' inheritor° himself have no more, ha?

---

59 into the land i.e., toward my grave (?) (But note the lack of rhyme in *steps, land.*)
61 jowls dashes (with a pun on *jowl,* "jawbone").   **63 politician** schemer, plotter;
o'erreaches circumvents, gets the better of (with a quibble on the literal sense).
70 chapless having no lower jaw.   **71 mazard** i.e., head (Literally, a drinking vessel.);
revolution turn of Fortune's wheel, change;   **an** if.   **72 trick to see** knack of seeing;   **cost . . .
to** involve so little expense and care in upbringing that we may.   **73 loggets** a game in which
pieces of hard wood shaped like Indian clubs or bowling pins are thrown to lie as near as
possible to a stake.   **76 For and** and moreover.   **80 quiddities** subtleties, quibbles. (From Latin
quid, "a thing.");   **quillities** verbal niceties, subtle distinctions. (Variation of *quiddities.*);
tenures the holding of a piece of property or office, or the conditions or period of such holding.
81 sconce head.   **82 action of battery** lawsuit about physical assault.   **83–84 statutes,
recognizances** legal documents guaranteeing a debt by attaching land and property.   **84 fines,
recoveries** ways of converting entailed estates into "fee simple" or freehold;   **double** signed by
two signatories;   **vouchers** guarantees of the legality of a title to real estate.   **85–86 fine of his
fines . . . fine pate . . . fine dirt** end of his legal maneuvers . . . elegant head . . . minutely sifted
dirt.   **87–88 pair of indentures** legal document drawn up in duplicate on a single sheet and
then cut apart on a zigzag line so that each pair was uniquely matched. (Hamlet may refer to
two rows of teeth or dentures.)   **88 conveyances** deeds.   **89 box** (1) deed box (2) coffin.
("Skull" has been suggested.);   **inheritor** possessor, owner.

HORATIO.   Not a jot more, my lord.   90

HAMLET.   Is not parchment made of sheepskins?

HORATIO.   Ay, my lord, and of calves' skins too.

HAMLET.   They are sheep and calves which seek out assurance in that.° I will
speak to this fellow.—Whose grave's this, sirrah?°

FIRST CLOWN.   Mine, sir.   [*Sings.*]   95

> "O, pit of clay for to be made
> For such a guest is meet."

HAMLET.   I think it be thine, indeed, for thou liest in 't.

FIRST CLOWN.   You lie out on 't, sir, and therefore 'tis not yours. For my part, I do
not lie in 't, yet it is mine.   100

HAMLET.   Thou dost lie in 't, to be in 't and say it is thine. 'Tis for the dead, not for
the quick;° therefore thou liest.

FIRST CLOWN.   'Tis a quick lie, sir; 'twill away again from me to you.

HAMLET.   What man dost thou dig it for?

FIRST CLOWN.   For no man, sir.   105

HAMLET.   What woman, then?

FIRST CLOWN.   For none, neither.

HAMLET.   Who is to be buried in 't?

FIRST CLOWN.   One that was a woman, sir, but, rest her soul, she's dead.

HAMLET.   How absolute° the knave is! We must speak by the card,° or equivoca-   110
tion° will undo us. By the Lord, Horatio, this three years I have took°
note of it: the age is grown so picked° that the toe of the peasant comes
so near the heel of the courtier, he galls his kibe.°—How long hast thou
been grave maker?

FIRST CLOWN.   Of all the days i' the year, I came to 't that day that our last king   115
Hamlet overcame Fortinbras.

HAMLET.   How long is that since?

FIRST CLOWN.   Cannot you tell that? Every fool can tell that. It was that very day
that young Hamlet was born—he that is mad and sent into England.

HAMLET.   Ay, marry, why was he sent into England?   120

FIRST CLOWN.   Why, because 'a was mad. 'A shall recover his wits there, or if 'a do
not, 'tis no great matter there.

HAMLET.   Why?

FIRST CLOWN.   'Twill not be seen in him there. There the men are as mad as he.

HAMLET.   How came he mad?   125

FIRST CLOWN.   Very strangely, they say.

HAMLET.   How strangely?

FIRST CLOWN.   Faith, e'en with losing his wits.

HAMLET.   Upon what ground?°

FIRST CLOWN.   Why, here in Denmark. I have been sexton here, man and boy,   130
thirty years.

---

93 assurance in that safety in legal parchments.   **94 sirrah** (A term of address to inferiors.)
102 quick living.   **110 absolute** strict, precise;   **by the card** i.e., with precision. (Literally, by
the mariner's compass-card, on which the points of the compass were marked.)
111–112 equivocation ambiguity in the use of terms.   **111 took** taken;   **picked** refined,
fastidious.   **113 galls his kibe** chafes the courtier's chilblain.   **129 ground** cause. (But, in the
next line, the gravedigger takes the word in the sense of "land," "country.")

HAMLET.   How long will a man lie i' th' earth ere he rot?

FIRST CLOWN.   Faith, if 'a be not rotten before 'a die—as we have many pocky°
   corpses nowadays, that will scarce hold the laying in°—'a will last you°
   some eight year or nine year. A tanner will last you nine year.   135

HAMLET.   Why he more than another?

FIRST CLOWN.   Why, sir, his hide is so tanned with his trade that 'a will keep out
   water a great while, and your water is a sore° decayer of your whoreson°
   dead body. [*He picks up a skull.*] Here's a skull now hath lien you° i' th'
   earth three-and-twenty years.   140

HAMLET.   Whose was it?

FIRST CLOWN.   A whoreson mad fellow's it was. Whose do you think it was?

HAMLET.   Nay, I know not.

FIRST CLOWN.   A pestilence on him for a mad rogue! 'A poured a flagon of
   Rhenish° on my head once. This same skull, sir, was, sir, Yorick's skull,   145
   the King's jester.

HAMLET.   This?

FIRST CLOWN.   E'en that.

HAMLET.   Let me see. [*He takes the skull.*] Alas, poor Yorick! I knew him, Horatio, a
   fellow of infinite jest, of most excellent fancy. He hath bore° me on his   150
   back a thousand times, and now how abhorred in my imagination it is!
   My gorge rises° at it. Here hung those lips that I have kissed I know not
   how oft. Where be your gibes now? Your gambols, your songs, your
   flashes of merriment that were wont° to set the table on a roar? Not one
   now, to mock your own grinning?° Quite chopfallen?° Now get you to my   155
   lady's chamber and tell her, let her paint an inch thick, to this favor° she
   must come. Make her laugh at that. Prithee, Horatio, tell me one thing.

HORATIO.   What's that, my lord?

HAMLET.   Dost thou think Alexander looked o' this fashion i' th' earth?

HORATIO.   E'en so.   160

HAMLET.   And smelt so? Pah! [*He throws down the skull.*]

HORATIO.   E'en so, my lord.

HAMLET.   To what base uses we may return, Horatio! Why may not imagination
   trace the noble dust of Alexander till 'a find it stopping a bunghole?°

HORATIO.   'Twere to consider too curiously° to consider so.   165

HAMLET.   No, faith, not a jot, but to follow him thither with modesty° enough, and
   likelihood to lead it. As thus: Alexander died, Alexander was buried,
   Alexander returneth to dust, the dust is earth, of earth we make loam,°
   and why of that loam whereto he was converted might they not stop a
   beer barrel?   170
   Imperious° Caesar, dead and turned to clay,

---

133 pocky rotten, diseased. (Literally, with the pox, or syphilis.)   **134 hold the laying in** hold
together long enough to be interred;   **last you** last. (*You* is used colloquially here and in the
following lines.)   **138 sore** i.e., terrible, great;   **whoreson** i.e., vile, scurvy.   **139 lien you** lain.
(See the note at line 144.)   **145 Rhenish** Rhine wine.   **150 bore** borne.   **152 My gorge
rises** i.e., I feel nauseated.   **154 were wont** used.   **155 mock your own grinning** mock at the
way your skull seems to be grinning (just as you used to mock at yourself and those who
grinned at you);   **chopfallen** (1) lacking the lower jaw (2) dejected.   **156 favor** aspect,
appearance.   **164 bunghole** hole for filling or emptying a cask.   **165 curiously** minutely.
166 modesty plausible moderation.   **168 loam** mortar consisting chiefly of moistened clay and
straw.   **171 Imperious** imperial.

> Might stop a hole to keep the wind away.
> O, that that earth which kept the world in awe
> Should patch a wall t' expel the winter's flaw!°

Enter KING, QUEEN, LAERTES, *and the corpse* [*of* OPHELIA, *in procession, with*
PRIEST, *lords, etc.*].

> But soft,° but soft awhile! Here comes the King,   175
> The Queen, the courtiers. Who is this they follow?
> And with such maimèd° rites? This doth betoken
> The corpse they follow did with desperate hand
> Fordo° its own life. 'Twas of some estate.°
> Couch we° awhile and mark.   180

[*He and* HORATIO *conceal themselves.* OPHELIA'*s body is taken to the grave.*]

LAERTES.   What ceremony else?

HAMLET [*to* HORATIO].   That is Laertes, a very noble youth. Mark.

LAERTES.   What ceremony else?

PRIEST.   Her obsequies have been as far enlarged
> As we have warranty.° Her death was doubtful,   185
> And but that great command o'ersways the order°
> She should in ground unsanctified been lodged°
> Till the last trumpet. For° charitable prayers,
> Shards,° flints, and pebbles should be thrown on her.
> Yet here she is allowed her virgin crants,°   190
> Her maiden strewments,° and the bringing home
> Of bell and burial.°

LAERTES.   Must there no more be done?

PRIEST.   No more be done.
> We should profane the service of the dead   195
> To sing a requiem and such rest° to her
> As to peace-parted souls.°

LAERTES.   Lay her i' th' earth,
> And from her fair and unpolluted flesh
> May violets° spring! I tell thee, churlish priest,   200
> A ministering angel shall my sister be
> When thou liest howling.°

HAMLET [*to* HORATIO].   What, the fair Ophelia!

QUEEN [*scattering flowers*].   Sweets to the sweet! Farewell.
> I hoped thou shouldst have been my Hamlet's wife.   205
> I thought thy bride-bed to have decked, sweet maid,
> And not t' have strewed thy grave.

LAERTES.   O, treble woe
> Fall ten times treble on that cursèd head

174 flaw gust of wind.   **175 soft** i.e., wait, be careful.   **177 maimèd** mutilated, incomplete.
179 Fordo destroy; **estate** rank.   **180 Couch we** let's hide, lie low.   **185 warranty** i.e.,
ecclesiastical authority.   **186 great . . . order** orders from on high overrule the prescribed
procedures.   **187 She should . . . lodged** she should have been buried in unsanctified ground.
188 For in place of.   **189 Shards** broken bits of pottery.   **190 crants** garlands betokening
maidenhood.   **191 strewments** flowers strewn on a coffin.   **192 bringing . . . burial** laying the
body to rest, to the sound of the bell.   **196 such rest** i.e., to pray for such rest.   **197 peace-
parted souls** those who have died at peace with God.   **200 violets** (See 4.5.191 and note.)
202 howling i.e., in hell.

Whose wicked deed thy most ingenious sense°
Deprived thee of! Hold off the earth awhile,   210
Till I have caught her once more in mine arms.

[*He leaps into the grave and embraces* OPHELIA.]

Now pile your dust upon the quick and dead,
Till of this flat a mountain you have made
T' o'ertop old Pelion or the skyish head
Of blue Olympus.°   215

HAMLET [*coming forward*].   What is he whose grief
Bears such an emphasis,° whose phrase of sorrow
Conjures the wandering stars° and makes them stand
Like wonder-wounded° hearers? This is I,
Hamlet the Dane.°   220

LAERTES [*grappling with him*°].   The devil take thy soul!

HAMLET.   Thou pray'st not well.
I prithee, take thy fingers from my throat,
For though I am not splenitive° and rash,
Yet have I in me something dangerous,   225
Which let thy wisdom fear. Hold off thy hand.

KING.   Pluck them asunder.

QUEEN.   Hamlet, Hamlet!

ALL.   Gentlemen!

HORATIO.   Good my lord, be quiet.   230

[HAMLET *and* LAERTES *are parted*.]

HAMLET.   Why, I will fight with him upon this theme
Until my eyelids will no longer wag.°

QUEEN.   O my son, what theme?

HAMLET.   I loved Ophelia. Forty thousand brothers
Could not with all their quantity of love   235
Make up my sum. What wilt thou do for her?

KING.   O, he is mad, Laertes.

QUEEN.   For love of God, forbear him.°

HAMLET.   'Swounds,° show me what thou'lt do.
Woo't° weep? Woo't fight? Woo't fast? Woo't tear thyself? 240
Woo't drink up° eisel?° Eat a crocodile?°
I'll do 't. Dost come here to whine?

---

209 ingenious sense a mind that is quick, alert, of fine qualities.   **214–215 Pelion,
Olympus** sacred mountains in the north of Thessaly; see also *Ossa,* below, at line 248.
217 emphasis i.e., rhetorical and florid emphasis. (*Phrase* has a similar rhetorical connotation.)
218 wandering stars planets.   **219 wonder-wounded** struck with amazement.   **220 the
Dane** (This title normally signifies the King; see 1.1.17 and note.)   **221 s.d. grappling with
him** (The testimony of the First Quarto that "*Hamlet leaps in after Laertes*" and the "Elegy on
Burbage" ("Oft have I seen him leap into the grave") seem to indicate one way in which this
fight was staged; however, the difficulty of fitting two contenders and Ophelia's body into a
confined space (probably the trapdoor) suggests to many editors the alternative, that Laertes
jumps out of the grave to attack Hamlet.)   **224 splenitive** quick-tempered.   **232 wag** move. (A
fluttering eyelid is a conventional sign that life has not yet gone.)   **238 forbear him** leave him
alone.   **239 'Swounds** by His (Christ's) wounds.   **240 Woo't** wilt thou.   **241 drink up** drink
deeply;   **eisel** vinegar;   **crocodile** (Crocodiles were tough and dangerous, and were supposed
to shed hypocritical tears.)

To outface me with leaping in her grave?
Be buried quick° with her, and so will I.
And if thou prate of mountains, let them throw   245
Millions of acres on us, till our ground,
Singeing his pate° against the burning zone,°
Make Ossa° like a wart! Nay, an° thou'lt mouth,°
I'll rant as well as thou.

QUEEN.   This is mere° madness,
And thus awhile the fit will work on him;   250
Anon, as patient as the female dove
When that her golden couplets° are disclosed,°
His silence will sit drooping.

HAMLET.   Hear you, sir,
What is the reason that you use me thus?
I loved you ever. But it is no matter.   255
Let Hercules himself do what he may,
The cat will mew, and dog will have his day.°   *Exit* HAMLET.

KING.   I pray thee, good Horatio, wait upon him.   [*Exit*] HORATIO.
[*To* LAERTES.] Strengthen your patience in° our last night's speech;
We'll put the matter to the present push.°—   260
Good Gertrude, set some watch over your son.—
This grave shall have a living° monument.
An hour of quiet° shortly shall we see;
Till then, in patience our proceeding be.   *Exeunt.*

5.2 *Enter* HAMLET *and* HORATIO.

HAMLET.   So much for this, sir; now shall you see the other.°
You do remember all the circumstance?

HORATIO.   Remember it, my lord!

HAMLET.   Sir, in my heart there was a kind of fighting
That would not let me sleep. Methought I lay   5
Worse than the mutines° in the bilboes.° Rashly,°
And praised be rashness for it—let us know°
Our indiscretion° sometimes serves us well
When our deep plots do pall,° and that should learn° us
There's a divinity that shapes our ends,   10

---

244 quick alive.   **247 his pate** its head, i.e., top;   **burning zone** zone in the celestial sphere containing the sun's orbit, between the tropics of Cancer and Capricorn.   **248 Ossa** another mountain in Thessaly. (In their war against the Olympian gods, the giants attempted to heap Ossa on Pelion to scale Olympus.);   **an if;   mouth** i.e., rant.   **249 mere** utter.   **252 golden couplets** two baby pigeons, covered with yellow down;   **disclosed** hatched.   **256–257 Let . . . day** i.e., (1) even Hercules couldn't stop Laertes' theatrical rant (2) I, too, will have my turn; i.e., despite any blustering attempts at interference, every person will sooner or later do what he or she must do.   **259 in** i.e., by recalling.   **260 present push** immediate test.   **262 living** lasting. (For Laertes' private understanding, Claudius also hints that Hamlet's death will serve as such a monument.)   **263 hour of quiet** time free of conflict.   **5.2. Location: The castle.   1 see the other** hear the other news.   **6 mutines** mutineers;   **bilboes** shackles;   **Rashly** on impulse. (This adverb goes with lines 12 ff.)   **7 know** acknowledge   **8 indiscretion** lack of foresight and judgment (not an indiscreet act).   **9 pall** fail, falter, go stale;   **learn** teach.

Rough-hew° them how we will—

HORATIO.   That is most certain.

HAMLET.   Up from my cabin,
My sea-gown° scarfed° about me, in the dark
Groped I to find out them,° had my desire,
Fingered° their packet, and in fine° withdrew   15
To mine own room again, making so bold,
My fears forgetting manners, to unseal
Their grand commission; where I found, Horatio—
Ah, royal knavery!—an exact command,
Larded° with many several° sorts of reasons   20
Importing° Denmark's health and England's too,
With, ho! such bugs° and goblins in my life,°
That on the supervise,° no leisure bated,°
No, not to stay° the grinding of the ax,
My head should be struck off.

HORATIO.   Is't possible?   25

HAMLET [*giving a document*].
Here's the commission. Read it at more leisure.
But wilt thou hear now how I did proceed?

HORATIO.   I beseech you.

HAMLET.   Being thus benetted round with villainies—   30
Ere I could make a prologue to my brains,
They had begun the play°—I sat me down,
Devised a new commission, wrote it fair.°
I once did hold it, as our statists° do,
A baseness° to write fair, and labored much   35
How to forget that learning; but, sir, now
It did me yeoman's° service. Wilt thou know
Th' effect° of what I wrote?

HORATIO.   Ay, good my lord.

HAMLET.   An earnest conjuration° from the King,
As England was his faithful tributary,   40
As love between them like the palm° might flourish,
As peace should still° her wheaten garland° wear
And stand a comma° 'tween their amities,
And many suchlike "as"es° of great charge,°
That on the view and knowing of these contents,   45
Without debatement further more or less,
He should those bearers put to sudden death,

---

11 Rough-hew shape roughly.   **13 sea-gown** seaman's coat;   **scarfed** loosely wrapped.
14 them i.e., Rosencrantz and Guildenstern.   **15 Fingered** pilfered, pinched;   **in fine** finally, in
conclusion.   **20 Larded** garnished;   **several** different.   **21 Importing** relating to.
22 bugs bugbears, hobgoblins;   **in my life** i.e., to be feared if I were allowed to live.
23 supervise reading;   **leisure bated** delay allowed.   **24 stay** await.   **31–32 Ere . . . play** before
I could consciously turn my brain to the matter, it had started working on a plan.   **33 fair** in a
clear hand.   **34 statists** statesmen.   **35 baseness** i.e., lower-class trait.   **37 yeoman's** i.e.,
substantial, faithful, loyal.   **38 effect** purport.   **39 conjuration** entreaty.   **41 palm** (An image of
health; see Psalm 92:12.)   **42 still** always;   **wheaten garland** (Symbolic of fruitful agriculture, of
peace and plenty.)   **43 comma** (Indicating continuity, link.)   **44 "as"es** (1) the "whereases" of a
formal document (2) asses;   **charge** (1) import (2) burden (appropriate to asses).

Not shriving time° allowed.

HORATIO.   How was this sealed?

HAMLET.   Why, even in that was heaven ordinant.°
          I had my father's signet° in my purse,   50
          Which was the model° of that Danish seal;
          Folded the writ° up in the form of th' other,
          Subscribed° it, gave 't th' impression,° placed it safely,
          The changeling° never known. Now, the next day
          Was our sea fight, and what to this was sequent°   55
          Thou knowest already.

HORATIO.   So Guildenstern and Rosencrantz go to 't.

HAMLET.   Why, man, they did make love to this employment.
          They are not near my conscience. Their defeat°
          Does by their own insinuation° grow.   60
          'Tis dangerous when the baser° nature comes
          Between the pass° and fell° incensèd points
          Of mighty opposites.°

HORATIO.   Why, what a king is this!

HAMLET.   Does it not, think thee, stand me now upon°—
          He that hath killed my king and whored my mother,   65
          Popped in between th' election° and my hopes,
          Thrown out his angle° for my proper° life,
          And with such cozenage°—is 't not perfect conscience
          To quit° him with this arm? And is 't not to be damned
          To let this canker° of our nature come   70
          In° further evil?

HORATIO.   It must be shortly known to him from England
          What is the issue of the business there.

HAMLET.   It will be short. The interim is mine,
          And a man's life's no more than to say "one."°   75
          But I am very sorry, good Horatio,
          That to Laertes I forgot myself,
          For by the image of my cause I see
          The portraiture of his. I'll court his favors.
          But, sure, the bravery° of his grief did put me   80
          Into a tow'ring passion.

HORATIO.   Peace, who comes here?

Enter a Courtier [OSRIC].

OSRIC.   Your lordship is right welcome back to Denmark.

---

48 shriving time time for confession and absolution.   **49 ordinant** directing.   **50 signet** small
seal.   **51 model** replica.   **52 writ** writing.   **53 Subscribed** signed (with forged signature);
impression i.e., with a wax seal.   **54 changeling** i.e., substituted letter. (Literally, a fairy child
substituted for a human one.)   **55 was sequent** followed.   **59 defeat** destruction.
60 insinuation intrusive intervention, sticking their noses in my business.   **61 baser** of lower
social station.   **62 pass** thrust;   **fell** fierce.   **63 opposites** antagonists.   **64 stand me now
upon** become incumbent on me now.   **66 election** (The Danish monarch was "elected" by a
small number of high-ranking electors.)   **67 angle** fishhook;   **proper** very.
68 cozenage trickery.   **69 quit** requite, pay back.   **70 canker** ulcer.   **70–71 come In** grow into.
75 a man's . . . "one" one's whole life occupies such a short time, only as long as it takes to
count to 1.   **80 bravery** bravado.

HAMLET.   I humbly thank you, sir. [*To* HORATIO.] Dost know this water fly?

HORATIO.   No, my good lord.

HAMLET.   Thy state is the more gracious, for 'tis a vice to know him. He hath   85
much land, and fertile. Let a beast be lord of beasts, and his crib° shall
stand at the King's mess.° 'Tis a chuff,° but, as I say, spacious in the possession of dirt.

OSRIC.   Sweet lord, if your lordship were at leisure, I should impart a thing to you
from His Majesty.   90

HAMLET.   I will receive it, sir, with all diligence of spirit.
Put your bonnet° to his° right use; 'tis for the head.

OSRIC.   I thank your lordship, it is very hot.

HAMLET.   No, believe me, 'tis very cold. The wind is northerly.

OSRIC.   It is indifferent° cold, my lord, indeed.   95

HAMLET.   But yet methinks it is very sultry and hot for my complexion.°

OSRIC.   Exceedingly, my lord. It is very sultry, as 'twere—I cannot tell how.
My lord, His Majesty bade me signify to you that 'a has laid a great wager
on your head. Sir, this is the matter—

HAMLET.   I beseech you, remember.   100

[HAMLET *moves him to put on his hat.*]

OSRIC.   Nay, good my lord; for my ease,° in good faith. Sir, here is newly
come to court Laertes—believe me, an absolute° gentleman, full of
most excellent differences,° of very soft society° and great showing.°
Indeed, to speak feelingly° of him, he is the card° or calendar° of
gentry,° for you shall find in him the continent of what part a gentle-   105
man would see.°

HAMLET.   Sir, his definement° suffers no perdition° in you,° though I know to divide him inventorially° would dozy° th' arithmetic of memory, and yet
but yaw° neither° in respect of° his quick sail. But, in the verity of extolment,° I take him to be a soul of great article,° and his infusion° of such   110
dearth and rareness° as, to make true diction° of him, his semblable° is
his mirror and who else would trace° him his umbrage,° nothing more.

OSRIC.   Your lordship speaks most infallibly of him.

---

86 crib manger.   **86–87 Let . . . mess** i.e., if a man, no matter how beastlike, is as rich in
livestock and possessions as Osric, he may eat at the King's table.   **87 chuff** boor, churl. (The
Second Quarto spelling, *chough*, is a variant spelling that also suggests the meaning here of
"chattering jackdaw.")   **92 bonnet** any kind of cap or hat;   **his** its.   **95 indifferent** somewhat.
96 complexion temperament.   **101 for my ease** (A conventional reply declining the invitation to
put his hat back on.)   **102 absolute** perfect.   **103 differences** special qualities;   **soft
society** agreeable manners;   **great showing** distinguished appearance.   **104 feelingly** with just
perception;   **card** chart, map;   **calendar** guide.   **105 gentry** good breeding.   **105–106 the
continent . . . see** one who contains in him all the qualities a gentleman would like to see. (A
continent is that which contains.)   **107 definement** definition (Hamlet proceeds to mock Osric
by throwing his lofty diction back at him);   **perdition** loss, diminution;   **you** your description.
107–108 divide him inventorially enumerate his graces;   **dozy** dizzy.   **109 yaw** swing
unsteadily off course. (Said of a ship.);   **neither** for all that;   **in respect of** in comparison with.
109–110 in . . . extolment in true praise (of him).   **110 of great article** one with many articles
in his inventory;   **infusion** essence, character infused into him by nature.   **111 dearth and
rareness** rarity;   **make true diction** speak truly;   **semblable** only true likeness.   **112 who . . .
trace** any other person who would wish to follow;   **umbrage** shadow.

HAMLET.   The concernancy,° sir? Why do we wrap the gentleman in our more
rawer breath?°   115

OSRIC.   Sir?

HORATIO.   Is 't not possible to understand in another tongue?° You will do 't,° sir,
really.

HAMLET.   What imports the nomination° of this gentleman?

OSRIC.   Of Laertes?   120

HORATIO [*to* HAMLET].   His purse is empty already; all 's golden words are spent.

HAMLET.   Of him, sir.

OSRIC.   I know you are not ignorant—

HAMLET.   I would you did, sir. Yet in faith if you did, it would not much approve°
me. Well, sir?   125

OSRIC.   You are not ignorant of what excellence Laertes is—

HAMLET.   I dare not confess that, lest I should compare with him in excellence.
But to know a man well were to know himself.°

OSRIC.   I mean, sir, for° his weapon; but in the imputation laid on him by them,°
in his meed° he's unfellowed.°   130

HAMLET.   What's his weapon?

OSRIC.   Rapier and dagger.

HAMLET.   That's two of his weapons—but well.°

OSRIC.   The King, sir, hath wagered with him six Barbary horses, against the
which he° has impawned,° as I take it, six French rapiers and poniards,°   135
with their assigns,° as girdle, hangers,° and so.° Three of the carriages,°
in faith, are very dear to fancy,° very responsive° to the hilts, most deli-
cate° carriages, and of very liberal conceit.°

HAMLET.   What call you the carriages?

HORATIO [*to* HAMLET].   I knew you must be edified by the margent° ere you had   140
done.

OSRIC.   The carriages, sir, are the hangers.

HAMLET.   The phrase would be more germane to the matter if we could carry a
cannon by our sides; I would it might be hangers till then. But, on: six
Barbary horses against six French swords, their assigns, and three liberal-   145
conceited carriages; that's the French bet against the Danish. Why is this
impawned, as you call it?

---

114 concernancy import, relevance.   **115 rawer breath** unrefined speech that can only come
short in praising him.   **118 to understand . . . tongue** i.e., for you, Osric, to understand when
someone else speaks your language. (Horatio twits Osric for not being able to understand the
kind of flowery speech he himself uses, when Hamlet speaks in such a vein. Alternatively, all
this could be said to Hamlet.);   **You will do 't** i.e., you can if you try, or, you may well have to
try (to speak plainly).   **119 nomination** naming.   **124 approve** commend.   **127–128 I dare
. . . himself** I dare not boast of knowing Laertes' excellence lest I seem to imply a comparable
excellence in myself. Certainly, to know another person well, one must know oneself.
129 for i.e., with;   **imputation . . . them** reputation given him by others.   **130 meed** merit;
unfellowed unmatched.   **133 but well** but never mind.   **135 he** i.e., Laertes;
impawned staked, wagered;   **poniards** daggers.   **136 assigns** appurtenances;   **hangers** straps
on the sword belt (*girdle*), from which the sword hung;   **and so** and so on;   **carriages** (An
affected way of saying *hangers;* literally, gun carriages.)   **137 dear to fancy** delightful to the
fancy;   **responsive** corresponding closely, matching or well adjusted.   **137–138 delicate** (i.e., in
workmanship);   **liberal conceit** elaborate design.   **140 margent** margin of a book, place for
explanatory notes.

OSRIC. The King, sir, hath laid,° sir, that in a dozen passes° between yourself and
him, he shall not exceed you three hits. He hath laid on twelve for nine,
and it would come to immediate trial, if your lordship would vouchsafe   150
the answer.°

HAMLET. How if I answer no?

OSRIC. I mean, my lord, the opposition of your person in trial.

HAMLET. Sir, I will walk here in the hall. If it please His Majesty, it is the breathing
time° of day with me. Let° the foils be brought, the gentleman willing,   155
and the King hold his purpose. I will win for him an I can; if not, I will
gain nothing but my shame and the odd hits.

OSRIC. Shall I deliver you° so?

HAMLET. To this effect, sir—after what flourish your nature will.

OSRIC. I commend° my duty to your lordship.   160

HAMLET. Yours, yours. [*Exit* OSRIC.] 'A does well to commend it himself; there are
no tongues else for 's turn.°

HORATIO. This lapwing° runs away with the shell on his head.

HAMLET. 'A did comply with his dug° before 'a sucked it. Thus has he—and many
more of the same breed that I know the drossy° age dotes on—only got the   165
tune° of the time and, out of an habit of encounter,° a kind of yeasty° collection,° which carries them through and through the most fanned and win-
nowed opinions;° and do° but blow them to their trial, the bubbles are
out.°

    Enter a LORD.

LORD. My lord, His Majesty commended him to you by young Osric, who brings   170
back to him that you attend him in the hall. He sends to know if your
pleasure hold to play with Laertes, or that° you will take longer time.

HAMLET. I am constant to my purposes; they follow the King's pleasure. If his fitness
speaks, mine is ready;° now or whensoever, provided I be so able as now.

LORD. The King and Queen and all are coming down.   175

HAMLET. In happy time.°

---

148 laid wagered;   **passes** bouts. (The odds of the betting are hard to explain. Possibly the King
bets that Hamlet will win at least five out of twelve, at which point Laertes raises the odds
against himself by betting he will win nine.)   **150–151 vouchsafe the answer** be so good as to
accept the challenge. (Hamlet deliberately takes the phrase in its literal sense of replying.)
154–155 breathing time exercise period;   **Let** i.e., if.   **158 deliver you** report what you say.
160 commend commit to your favor. (A conventional salutation, but Hamlet wryly uses a more
literal meaning, "recommend," "praise," in line 161.)   **162 for 's turn** for his purposes, i.e., to do
it for him.   **163 lapwing** (A proverbial type of youthful forwardness. Also, a bird that draws
intruders away from its nest and was thought to run about with its head in the shell when newly
hatched; a seeming reference to Osric's hat.)   **164 comply . . . dug** observe ceremonious
formality toward his nurse's or mother's teat.   **165 drossy** laden with scum and impurities,
frivolous.   **166 tune** temper, mood, manner of speech;   **an habit of encounter** a demeanor in
conversing (with courtiers of his own kind);   **yeasty** frothy.   **166–167 collection** i.e., of current
phrases.   **167–168 carries . . . opinions** sustains them right through the scrutiny of persons
whose opinions are select and refined. (Literally, like grain separated from its chaff. Osric is both
the chaff and the bubbly froth on the surface of the liquor that is soon blown away.)   **168 and
do** yet do.   **168–169 blow . . . out** test them by merely blowing on them, and their bubbles
burst.   **172 that** if.   **173–174 If . . . ready** if he declares his readiness, my convenience waits
on his.   **176 In happy time** (A phrase of courtesy indicating that the time is convenient.)

LORD.   The Queen desires you to use some gentle entertainment° to Laertes be-
    fore you fall to play.

HAMLET.   She well instructs me.   [*Exit* LORD.]

HORATIO.   You will lose, my lord.   180

HAMLET.   I do not think so. Since he went into France, I have been in continual
    practice; I shall win at the odds. But thou wouldst not think how ill all's
    here about my heart; but it is no matter.

HORATIO.   Nay, good my lord—

HAMLET.   It is but foolery, but it is such a kind of gaingiving° as would perhaps   185
    trouble a woman.

HORATIO.   If your mind dislike anything, obey it. I will forestall their repair° hither
    and say you are not fit.

HAMLET.   Not a whit, we defy augury. There is special providence in the fall of a
    sparrow. If it be now, 'tis not to come; if it be not to come, it will be   190
    now; if it be not now, yet it will come. The readiness is all. Since no man
    of aught he leaves knows, what is 't to leave betimes? Let be.°

    A table prepared. [Enter] trumpets, drums, and officers with cushions; KING,
QUEEN, [OSRIC,] *and all the state; foils, daggers, [and wine borne in;] and* LAERTES.

KING.   Come, Hamlet, come and take this hand from me.

    [*The* KING *puts* LAERTES' *hand into* HAMLET'*s*.]

HAMLET [*to* LAERTES].   Give me your pardon, sir. I have done you wrong,
    But pardon 't as you are a gentleman.   195
    This presence° knows,
    And you must needs have heard, how I am punished°
    With a sore distraction. What I have done
    That might your nature, honor, and exception°
    Roughly awake, I here proclaim was madness.   200
    Was 't Hamlet wronged Laertes? Never Hamlet.
    If Hamlet from himself be ta'en away,
    And when he's not himself does wrong Laertes,
    Then Hamlet does it not, Hamlet denies it.
    Who does it, then? His madness. If 't be so,   205
    Hamlet is of the faction° that is wronged;
    His madness is poor Hamlet's enemy.
    Sir, in this audience
    Let my disclaiming from a purposed evil
    Free me so far in your most generous thoughts   210
    That I have° shot my arrow o'er the house
    And hurt my brother.

LAERTES.   I am satisfied in nature,°
    Whose motive° in this case should stir me most
    To my revenge. But in my terms of honor
    I stand aloof, and will no reconcilement   215

---

177 entertainment greeting.   **185 gaingiving** misgiving.   **187 repair** coming.   **191–192 Since
. . . Let be** since no one has knowledge of what he is leaving behind, what does an early death
matter after all? Enough; don't struggle against it.   **196 presence** royal assembly.
197 punished afflicted.   **199 exception** disapproval.   **206 faction** party.   **211 That I have** as if
I had.   **212 in nature** i.e., as to my personal feelings.   **213 motive** prompting.

Till by some elder masters of known honor
I have a voice° and precedent of peace°
To keep my name ungored.° But till that time
I do receive your offered love like love,
And will not wrong it.

HAMLET.   I embrace it freely,   220
And will this brothers' wager frankly° play.—
Give us the foils. Come on.

LAERTES.   Come, one for me.

HAMLET.   I'll be your foil,° Laertes. In mine ignorance
Your skill shall, like a star i' the darkest night,
Stick fiery off° indeed.

LAERTES.   You mock me, sir.   225

HAMLET.   No, by this hand.

KING.   Give them the foils, young Osric. Cousin Hamlet,
You know the wager?

HAMLET.   Very well, my lord.
Your Grace has laid the odds o'° the weaker side.

KING.   I do not fear it; I have seen you both.   230
But since he is bettered,° we have therefore odds.

LAERTES.   This is too heavy. Let me see another.

[He exchanges his foil for another.]

HAMLET.   This likes me° well. These foils have all a length?

[They prepare to play.]

OSRIC.   Ay, my good lord.

KING.   Set me the stoups of wine upon that table.   235
If Hamlet give the first or second hit,
Or quit in answer of the third exchange,°
Let all the battlements their ordnance fire.
The King shall drink to Hamlet's better breath,°
And in the cup an union° shall he throw   240
Richer than that which four successive kings
In Denmark's crown have worn. Give me the cups,
And let the kettle° to the trumpet speak,
The trumpet to the cannoneer without,
The cannons to the heavens, the heaven to earth,   245
"Now the King drinks to Hamlet." Come, begin.   *Trumpets the while.*
And you, the judges, bear a wary eye.

HAMLET.   Come on, sir.

LAERTES.   Come, my lord.   *[They play.* HAMLET *scores a hit.]*

HAMLET.   One.   250

---

217 voice authoritative pronouncement;   **of peace** for reconciliation.   **218 name
ungored** reputation unwounded.   **221 frankly** without ill feeling or the burden of rancor.
223 foil thin metal background which sets a jewel off (with pun on the blunted rapier for
fencing).   **225 Stick fiery off** stand out brilliantly.   **229 laid the odds o'** bet on, backed.
231 is bettered has improved; is the odds-on favorite. (Laertes' handicap is the "three hits"
specified in line 149.)   **233 likes me** pleases me.   **237 Or . . . exchange** i.e., or requites Laertes
in the third bout for having won the first two.   **239 better breath** improved vigor.
240 union pearl. (So called, according to Pliny's *Natural History,* 9, because pearls are *unique,*
never identical.)   **243 kettle** kettledrum.

LAERTES.   No.

HAMLET.   Judgment.

OSRIC.   A hit, a very palpable hit.

Drum, trumpets, and shot. Flourish. A piece goes off.

LAERTES.   Well, again.

KING.   Stay, give me drink. Hamlet, this pearl is thine.

[*He drinks, and throws a pearl in* HAMLET's *cup.*]

          Here's to thy health. Give him the cup.   255

HAMLET.   I'll play this bout first. Set it by awhile.

          Come. [*They play.*] Another hit; what say you?

LAERTES.   A touch, a touch, I do confess 't.

KING.   Our son shall win.

QUEEN.   He's fat° and scant of breath.

          Here, Hamlet, take my napkin,° rub thy brows.   260

          The Queen carouses° to thy fortune, Hamlet.

HAMLET.   Good madam!

KING.   Gertrude, do not drink.

QUEEN.   I will, my lord, I pray you pardon me.   [*She drinks.*]

KING [*aside*].   It is the poisoned cup. It is too late.   265

HAMLET.   I dare not drink yet, madam; by and by.

QUEEN.   Come, let me wipe thy face.

LAERTES [*to* KING].   My lord, I'll hit him now.

KING.   I do not think 't.

LAERTES [*aside*].   And yet it is almost against my conscience.   270

HAMLET.   Come, for the third, Laertes. You do but dally.

          I pray you, pass° with your best violence;

          I am afeard you make a wanton of me.°

LAERTES.   Say you so? Come on. [*They play.*]

OSRIC.   Nothing neither way.   275

LAERTES.   Have at you now!

[LAERTES *wounds* HAMLET; *then, in scuffling, they change rapiers,° and* HAMLET *wounds* LAERTES.]

KING.   Part them! They are incensed.

HAMLET.   Nay, come, again.   [*The* QUEEN *falls.*]

OSRIC.   Look to the Queen there, ho!

HORATIO.   They bleed on both sides. How is it, my lord?

OSRIC.   How is 't, Laertes?

LAERTES.   Why, as a woodcock° to mine own springe,° Osric;   280

          I am justly killed with mine own treachery.

HAMLET.   How does the Queen?

KING.   She swoons to see them bleed.

QUEEN.   No, no, the drink, the drink—O my dear Hamlet—

          The drink, the drink! I am poisoned.   [*She dies.*]

---

259 fat not physically fit, out of training.   **260 napkin** handkerchief.   **261 carouses** drinks a toast.
272 pass thrust.   **273 make . . . me** i.e., treat me like a spoiled child, trifle with me.   **276 s.d. in scuffling,
they change rapiers** (This stage direction occurs in the Folio. According to a widespread stage tradition,
Hamlet receives a scratch, realizes that Laertes' sword is unbated, and accordingly forces an exchange.)
280 woodcock a bird, a type of stupidity or as a decoy;   **springe** trap, snare.

HAMLET.   O villainy! Ho, let the door be locked!   285
                Treachery! Seek it out.   [LAERTES *falls. Exit* OSRIC.]
LAERTES.   It is here, Hamlet. Hamlet, thou art slain.
                No med'cine in the world can do thee good;
                In thee there is not half an hour's life.
                The treacherous instrument is in thy hand,   290
                Unbated° and envenomed. The foul practice°
                Hath turned itself on me. Lo, here I lie,
                Never to rise again. Thy mother's poisoned.
                I can no more. The King, the King's to blame.
HAMLET.   The point envenomed too? Then, venom, to thy work.   295

                                                        [*He stabs the* KING.]

ALL.   Treason! Treason!
KING.   O, yet defend me, friends! I am but hurt.
HAMLET [*forcing the* KING *to drink.*]
                Here, thou incestuous, murderous, damnèd Dane,
                Drink off this potion. Is thy union° here?   300
                Follow my mother.   [*The* KING *dies.*]
LAERTES.   He is justly served.
                It is a poison tempered° by himself.
                Exchange forgiveness with me, noble Hamlet.
                Mine and my father's death come not upon thee,
                Nor thine on me!   [*He dies.*]   305
HAMLET.   Heaven make thee free of it! I follow thee.
                I am dead, Horatio. Wretched Queen, adieu!
                You that look pale and tremble at this chance,°
                That are but mutes° or audience to this act,
                Had I but time—as this fell° sergeant,° Death,   310
                Is strict° in his arrest°—O, I could tell you—
                But let it be. Horatio, I am dead;
                Thou livest. Report me and my cause aright
                To the unsatisfied.
HORATIO.   Never believe it.
                I am more an antique Roman° than a Dane.   315
                Here's yet some liquor left.

        [*He attempts to drink from the poisoned cup.* HAMLET *prevents him.*]

HAMLET.   As thou't a man,
                Give me the cup! Let go! By heaven, I'll ha 't.
                O God, Horatio, what a wounded name,
                Things standing thus unknown, shall I leave behind me!
                If thou didst ever hold me in thy heart,
                Absent thee from felicity awhile,   320
                And in this harsh world draw thy breath in pain

---

291 Unbated not blunted with a button;   **practice** plot.   **300 union** pearl. (See line 240; with
grim puns on the word's other meanings: marriage, shared death.)   **302 tempered** mixed.
308 chance mischance.   **309 mutes** silent observers. (Literally, actors with nonspeaking parts.)
310 fell cruel;   **sergeant** sheriff's officer.   **311 strict** (1) severely just (2) unavoidable;
arrest (1) taking into custody (2) stopping my speech.   **315 Roman** (Suicide was an honorable
choice for many Romans as an alternative to a dishonorable life.)

To tell my story.   *A march afar off* [*and a volley within*].
What warlike noise is this?

Enter OSRIC.

OSRIC.   Young Fortinbras, with conquest come from Poland,   325
To th' ambassadors of England gives
This warlike volley.

HAMLET.   O, I die, Horatio!
The potent poison quite o'ercrows° my spirit.
I cannot live to hear the news from England,
But I do prophesy th' election lights   330
On Fortinbras. He has my dying voice.°
So tell him, with th' occurents° more and less
Which have solicited°—the rest is silence.   [*He dies.*]

HORATIO.   Now cracks a noble heart. Good night, sweet prince,
And flights of angels sing thee to thy rest!   [*March within.*] 335
Why does the drum come hither?

Enter FORTINBRAS, *with the* [*English*] *Ambassadors* [*with drum, colors, and*
attendants].

FORTINBRAS.   Where is this sight?

HORATIO.   What is it you would see?
If aught of woe or wonder, cease your search.

FORTINBRAS.   This quarry° cries on havoc.° O proud Death,
What feast° is toward° in thine eternal cell,   340
That thou so many princes at a shot
So bloodily hast struck?

FIRST AMBASSADOR.   The sight is dismal,
And our affairs from England come too late.
The ears are senseless that should give us hearing,
To tell him his commandment is fulfilled,   345
That Rosencrantz and Guildenstern are dead.
Where should we have our thanks?

HORATIO.   Not from his° mouth,
Had it th' ability of life to thank you.
He never gave commandment for their death.
But since, so jump° upon this bloody question,°   350
You from the Polack wars, and you from England,
And here arrived, give order that these bodies
High on a stage° be placèd to the view,
And let me speak to th' yet unknowing world
How these things came about. So shall you hear   355
Of carnal, bloody, and unnatural acts,
Of accidental judgments,° casual° slaughters,

---

328 o'ercrows triumphs over (like the winner in a cockfight).   **331 voice** vote.
332 occurrents events, incidents.   **333 solicited** moved, urged. (Hamlet doesn't finish saying
what the events have prompted—presumably, his acts of vengeance, or his reporting of those
events to Fortinbras.)   **339 quarry** heap of dead;   **cries on havoc** proclaims a general slaughter.
340 feast i.e., Death feasting on those who have fallen;   **toward** in preparation.   **347 his** i.e.,
Claudius'.   **350 jump** precisely, immediately;   **question** dispute, affair.   **353 stage** platform.
357 judgments retributions;   **casual** occurring by chance.

Of deaths put on° by cunning and forced cause,°
And, in this upshot, purposes mistook
Fall'n on th' inventors' heads. All this can I   360
Truly deliver.
FORTINBRAS.   Let us haste to hear it,
And call the noblest to the audience.
For me, with sorrow I embrace my fortune.
I have some rights of memory° in this kingdom,
Which now to claim my vantage° doth invite me.   365
HORATIO.   Of that I shall have also cause to speak,
And from his mouth whose voice will draw on more.°
But let this same be presently° performed,
Even while men's minds are wild, lest more mischance
On° plots and errors happen.
FORTINBRAS.   Let four captains   370
Bear Hamlet, like a soldier, to the stage,
For he was likely, had he been put on,°
To have proved most royal; and for his passage,°
The soldiers' music and the rite of war
Speak° loudly for him.   375
Take up the bodies. Such a sight as this
Becomes the field,° but here shows much amiss.
Go bid the soldiers shoot.
Exeunt [marching, bearing off the dead bodies; a peal of ordnance is shot off].

358 put on instigated;   **forced cause** contrivance.   **364 of memory** traditional, remembered,
unforgotten.   **365 vantage** favorable opportunity.   **367 voice . . . more** vote will influence still
others.   **368 presently** immediately.   **370 On** on the basis of; on top of.   **372 put on** i.e.,
invested in royal office and so put to the test.   **373 passage** i.e., from life to death.
375 Speak let them speak.   **377 Becomes the field** suits the field of battle.

Topics for Critical Thinking and Writing

Act 1

1. The first scene (like many other scenes in this play) is full of expressions of uncertainty. What are some are these uncertainties? The Ghost first appears at
   1.1.43. Does his appearance surprise us, or have we been prepared for it? Or is
   there both preparation and surprise? Do the last four speeches of 1.1 help to
   introduce a note of hope? If so, how?
2. Does the King's opening speech in 1.2 reveal him to be an accomplished public speaker—or are lines 10–14 offensive? In his second speech (lines 41–49),
   what is the effect of naming Laertes four times? Claudius sometimes uses the
   royal pronouns ("we," "our"), sometimes the more intimate "I" and "my." Study
   his use of these in lines 1–4 and in 106–117. What do you think he is getting at?
3. Hamlet's first soliloquy (1.2.129–159) reveals that more than just his father's
   death distresses him. Be as specific as possible about the causes of Hamlet's
   anguish here. What traits does Hamlet reveal in his conversation with Horatio
   (1.2.160–258)?

4. What do you make of Polonius's advice to Laertes (1.3.55–81)? Is it sound? Sound advice, but here uttered by a fool? Ignoble advice? How would one follow the advice of line 78: "to thine own self be true"? In his words to Ophelia in 1.3.102–136, what does he reveal about himself?

5. Can 1.4.17–38 reasonably be taken as a speech on the "tragic flaw"? (On this idea, see page 334.) Or is the passage a much more limited discussion, a comment simply on Danish drinking habits?

6. Hamlet is convinced in 1.5.93–105 that the Ghost has told the truth, indeed, the only important truth. But do we detect in 105–112 a hint of a tone suggesting that Hamlet delights in hating villainy? If so, can it be said that later this delight grows, and that in some scenes (e.g., 3.3) we feel that Hamlet has almost become a diabolic revenger? Explain.

Act 2

1. Characterize Polonius on the basis of 2.1.1–75.

2. In light of what we have seen of Hamlet, is Ophelia's report of his strange behavior when he visits her understandable?

3. Why does 2.2.33–34 seem almost comic? How do these lines help us to form a view about Rosencrantz and Guildenstern?

4. Is "the hellish Pyrrhus" (2.2.405) Hamlet's version of Claudius? Or is he Hamlet, who soon will be responsible for the deaths of Polonius, Rosencrantz and Guildenstern, Claudius, Gertrude, Ophelia, and Laertes? Explain.

5. Is the speech that Hamlet and the First Player recite, with some interruptions (2.2.392–453), an absurdly bombastic speech? If so, why? To distinguish it from the poetry of the play itself? To characterize the bloody deeds that Hamlet cannot descend to?

6. In 2.2.482–520 Hamlet rebukes himself for not acting. Why has he not acted? Because he is a coward (line 503)? Because he has a conscience? Because no action can restore his father and his mother's purity? Because he doubts the Ghost? What reason(s) can you offer?

Act 3

1. What do you make out of Hamlet's assertion to Ophelia: "I loved you not" (3.1.117)? Of his characterization of himself as full of "offenses" (3.1.121–25)? Why is Hamlet so harsh to Ophelia?

2. In 3.3.36–72 Claudius's conscience afflicts him. But is he repentant? What makes you say so?

3. Is Hamlet other than abhorrent in 3.3.73–96? Do we want him to kill Claudius at this moment, when Claudius (presumably with his back to Hamlet) is praying? Why?

4. The Ghost speaks of Hamlet's "almost blunted purpose" (3.4.115). Is the accusation fair? Explain.

5. How would you characterize the Hamlet who speaks in 3.4.209–24?

Act 4

1. Is Gertrude protecting Hamlet when she says he is mad (4.1.7), or does she believe that he is mad? If she believes he is mad, does it follow that she no longer feels ashamed and guilty? Explain.

2. Why should Hamlet hide Polonius's body (in 4.2)? Is he feigning madness? Is he on the edge of madness? Explain.
3. How can we explain Hamlet's willingness to go to England (4.3.52)?
4. Judging from 4.5, what has driven Ophelia mad? Is Laertes heroic, or somewhat foolish? Consider also the way Claudius treats him in 4.7.

Act 5

1. Would anything be lost if the gravediggers in 5.1 were omitted?
2. To what extent do we judge Hamlet severely for sending Rosencrantz and Guildenstern to their deaths, as he reports in 5.2? On the whole, do we think of Hamlet as an intriguer? What other intrigues has he engendered? How successful were they?
3. Does 5.2.189–192 show a paralysis of the will, or a wise recognition that more is needed than mere human scheming? Explain.
4. Does 5.2.276 suggest that Laertes takes advantage of a momentary pause and unfairly stabs Hamlet? Is the exchange of weapons accidental, or does Hamlet (as in Olivier's film version), realizing that he has been betrayed, deliberately get possession of Laertes's deadly weapon?
5. Fortinbras is often cut from the play. How much is lost by the cut? Explain.
6. Fortinbras gives Hamlet a soldier's funeral. Is this ridiculous? Can it fairly be said that, in a sense, Hamlet has been at war? Explain.

General Questions

1. Hamlet in 5.2.10–11 speaks of a "divinity that shapes our ends." To what extent does "divinity" (or Fate or mysterious Chance) play a role in the happenings?
2. How do Laertes, Fortinbras, and Horatio help to define Hamlet for us?
3. T. S. Eliot says (in "Shakespeare and the Stoicism of Seneca") that Hamlet, having made a mess, "dies fairly well pleased with himself." Evaluate.

ERNEST JONES
*Hamlet and the Oedipus Complex**

In short, the whole picture presented by Hamlet, his deep depression, the hopeless note in his attitude towards the world and towards the value of life, his dread of death, his repeated reference to bad dreams, his self-accusations, his desperate efforts to get away from the thoughts of his duty, and his vain attempts to find an excuse for his procrastination: all this unequivocally points to a *tortured conscience,* to some hidden ground for shirking his task, a ground which he dare not or cannot avow to himself.

. . .

Extensive studies of the past half century, inspired by Freud, have taught us that a psychoneurosis means a state of mind where the person is unduly, and often painfully, driven or thwarted by the "unconscious" part of his mind, that buried part that was once the infant's mind and still lives on side by side with the

---

* The title is the editors'. Footnotes are abridged.

adult mentality that has developed out of it and should have taken its place. It signifies *internal* mental conflict. We have here the reason why it is impossible to discuss intelligently the state of mind of anyone suffering from a psychoneurosis, whether the description is of a living person or an imagined one, without correlating the manifestations with what must have operated in his infancy and is *still operating*. That is what I propose to attempt here.

For some deep-seated reason, which is to him unacceptable, Hamlet is plunged into anguish at the thought of his father being replaced in his mother's affections by someone else. It is as if his devotion to his mother had made him so jealous for her affection that he had found it hard enough to share this even with his father and could not endure to share it with still another man. Against this thought, however, suggestive as it is, may be urged three objections. First, if it were in itself a full statement of the matter, Hamlet would have been aware of the jealousy, whereas we have concluded that the mental process we are seeking is hidden from him. Secondly, we see in it no evidence of the arousing of an old and forgotten memory. And, thirdly, Hamlet is being deprived by Claudius of no greater share in the Queen's affection than he had been by his own father, for the two brothers made exactly similar claims in this respect—namely, those of a loved husband. The last-named objection, however, leads us to the heart of the situation. How if, in fact, Hamlet had in years gone by, as a child, bitterly resented having had to share his mother's affection even with his own father, had regarded him as a rival, and had secretly wished him out of the way so that he might enjoy undisputed and undisturbed the monopoly of that affection? If such thoughts had been present in his mind in childhood days they evidently would have been "repressed," and all traces of them obliterated, by filial piety and other educative influences. The actual realization of his early wish in the death of his father at the hands of a jealous rival would then have stimulated into activity these "repressed" memories, which would have produced, in the form of depression and other suffering, an obscure aftermath of his childhood's conflict. This is at all events the mechanism that is actually found in the real Hamlets who are investigated psychologically.

The explanation, therefore, of the delay and self-frustration exhibited in the endeavour to fulfil his father's demand for vengeance is that to Hamlet the thought of incest and parricide combined is too intolerable to be borne. One part of him tries to carry out the task, the other flinches inexorably from the thought of it. How fain would he blot it out in that "bestial oblivion" which unfortunately for him his conscience contemns. He is torn and tortured in an insoluble inner conflict.

• • •

5   Now comes the father's death and the mother's second marriage. The association of the idea of sexuality with his mother, buried since infancy, can no longer be concealed from his consciousness. As Bradley well says: "Her son was forced to see in her action not only an astounding shallowness of feeling, but an eruption of coarse sensuality, 'rank and gross,' speeding post-haste to its horrible delight." Feelings which once, in the infancy of long ago, were pleasurable desires can now, because of his repressions, only fill him with repulsion. The long "repressed" desire to take his father's place in his mother's affection is stimulated to unconscious activity by the sight of someone usurping this place exactly as he himself had once longed to do. More, this someone was a member of the same family, so that the actual usurpation further resembled the imaginary one in being incestuous. Without his being in the least aware of it these ancient desires are ringing in his mind, are once more struggling to find conscious expression, and

need such an expenditure of energy again to "repress" them that he is reduced to the deplorable mental state he himself so vividly depicts.

There follows the Ghost's announcement that the father's death was a willed one, was due to murder. Hamlet, having at the moment his mind filled with natural indignation at the news, answers normally enough with the cry (Act I, Sc. 5):

> Haste me to know 't, that I with wings as swift
> As meditation or the thoughts of love,
> May sweep to my revenge.

The momentous words follow revealing who was the guilty person, namely a relative who had committed the deed at the bidding of lust.[1] Hamlet's second guilty wish had thus also been realized by his uncle, namely to procure the fulfilment of the first—the possession of the mother—by a personal deed, in fact by murder of the father. The two recent events, the father's death and the mother's second marriage, seemed to the world to have no inner causal relation to each other, but they represented ideas which in Hamlet's unconscious phantasy had always been closely associated. These ideas now in a moment forced their way to conscious recognition in spite of all "repressing forces," and found immediate expression in his almost reflex cry: "O my prophetic soul! My uncle?" The frightful truth his unconscious had already intuitively divined, his consciousness had now to assimilate as best it could. For the rest of the interview Hamlet is stunned by the effect of the internal conflict thus re-awakened, which from now on never ceases, and into the essential nature of which he never penetrates.

[1] It is not maintained that this was by any means Claudius's whole motive, but it was evidently a powerful one and the one that most impressed Hamlet.

ANNE BARTON

*The Promulgation of Confusion**

The length of the play suggests that it was never, not even in Shakespeare's time, performed uncut. Other plays by Shakespeare are long; no other violates so strikingly the limits of audience attention, or asks for so much from its leading actor. Like *Titus,* like *The Spanish Tragedy* and that lost source play, the so-called *Ur-Hamlet,* which was probably the work of Kyd, Shakespeare's *Hamlet* is a tragedy of revenge. It concentrates, like them, upon a single, essentially sympathetic hero and it confronts precisely the same structural problem: how to linger out his vengeance for the necessary five acts. Kyd's Hieronymo (and probably his Hamlet), Shakespeare's Titus and Hamlet all require proof of the villain's identity before they can act. They are temporarily deflected from their purpose, not only by difficulties of strategy, but by a madness partly assumed and partly real. All make use of some kind of dramatic show to further their intention and all accomplish, in the end, a vengeance which, whatever the original provocation, has by this time become more than a little suspect.

As a tragic predicament, revenge has several inherent advantages. Intrigue and spectacle, madness and violence, are not the only elements native to the genre. The isolation naturally imposed upon the revenger not only encourages introspection, it destroys normal human relationships in a fundamentally tragic way.

* The title is the editors'.

A detached, satirist's view of the society against which they war almost forces itself upon these characters. Their situation generates a corrosive doubt, reaching out to attack religious, moral and legal institutions. Kyd, Marlowe in *The Jew of Malta,* and the young Shakespeare of *Titus,* had all recognized and explored these inbuilt opportunities, at least to some extent. It was only with *Hamlet,* however, that a dramatist seized upon the form to trigger off an enquiry into the whole basis of human existence. Debate over man's right to encroach upon the prerogative of Heaven by undertaking himself what was properly God's act of retributive justice had been and, in the Jacobean period, would continue to be a feature of revenge tragedy.

· · ·

Only *Hamlet* side-steps the ethic of revenge entirely. It is one of several great silences at the heart of this play. Deliberately, Shakespeare has shifted attention away from an expected centre, from the problem of whether the prince *ought* to kill Claudius—or even whether in practical terms he *can*—to the far more complicated and subjective issue of whether or not he ultimately *will.* It is not the peculiar status of acts of private vengeance that is under review here, but the validity of all and any human action.

Although other dramatists (Marston, Webster and Tourneur especially) later used *Hamlet* as a spring-board for their own exploration of the revenge form, none of them dared to attempt a focus so wide. The range of the play and, above all, of the role of Hamlet himself, is so great that any performance must necessarily be a matter of selection, of emphases more or less arbitrarily imposed. The impossibility of presenting *Hamlet* whole and uncut is not entirely a feature of its great length. It is also bound up with its inclusiveness, with the fact that Shakespeare seems to have been determined to subject a bewildering number of people, ideas, values, kinds of relationship, emotions and social forms to the distorted but strangely clear scrutiny of a revenger so complicated himself that no attempt to describe, or act, him can be more than partial. Even more than most plays of Shakespeare, *Hamlet* is a warning against the fallacy that any critical interpretation or stage production can be definitive, or even complete.

5   When Hamlet cautioned Rosencrantz and Guildenstern, after the play scene, against the attempt to "pluck out the heart of my mystery . . . sound me from my lowest note to the top of my compass" (3.2.319–321), he also provided a useful counsel for literary critics. The play as a whole is built upon contradiction, upon the promulgation of confusion. Shakespeare gives every indication of having constructed an imaginary Denmark intended to baffle, to resist explanation as stubbornly as those mysterious facts of human existence which it illuminates without rationalizing. A distrust of what might be described as a "play-shaped" view of the world of the falseness of clearly defined moral, theological or formal patterns imposed upon reality in the interests of art is, I think, characteristic of him throughout his dramatic career. It was to become particularly strong in his Jacobean plays. This antipathy may account, in part, for Shakespeare's apparent suspicion of *tragedy* as a term, and also for the variety and restlessness of his own formal development.

Certainly, the eschatology of *Hamlet* defies explication. The ghost of a murdered king appears from an almost embarrassingly specific Catholic Purgatory, a place of "sulph'rous and tormenting flames" (1.5.3) to which it has been confined "till the foul crimes done in my days of nature / Are burnt and purged away" (1.5.13–14). This spirit urges upon its beloved only son a revenge for which, by immutable Christian law, that son must be damned perpetually—sent not to

Purgatory, but to the far greater torments of Hell. Neither Hamlet, the sensible Horatio nor the ghost itself ever remark upon this illogicality. Hamlet's worry is only about the truth of the ghost's accusation. If Claudius is guilty, and the Mouse-trap proves that he is, he must be killed. Not for an instant does Hamlet doubt the justice of such a course, let alone the propriety of a repentant soul spending its time in Purgatory meditating a murder. A similar inconsistency adds complications to what is already, on psychological grounds, a most ambiguous scene in Act 3. Hamlet declines to kill the king at prayers because he fears that Claudius' soul will ascend to Heaven. This, at least, is the reason he gives. He will wait to find his enemy

> drunk asleep, or in his rage,
> Or in th'incestuous pleasure of his bed,
> At game, a-swearing, or about some act
> That has no relish of salvation in't,
> Then trip him that his heels may kick at heaven,
> And that his soul may be as damned and black
> As hell whereto it goes.

(3.3.89–95)

Here, the odd fact that Hamlet never considers that his own soul would be damned irrecoverably by the requirements of such a theology, is cunningly mingled with doubts as to whether he really means what he is saying in this speech, or whether it is a feeble excuse for postponing an explicably distasteful task.

In *Hamlet,* Shakespeare affirms a Christian supernatural in one moment to deny it in the next. The hereafter involves Purgatory, hell fire, and flights of angels. It is also silence, an eternal sleep that has nothing to do with punishment or reward. The prince talks about death as "the undiscovered country, from whose bourn / No traveller returns" (3.1.80–81) out of an anguish of mind created by the return of just such a traveller. A special Providence guides the fall of the sparrow, or at least Hamlet asserts that it does just before the fatal game with the foils in Act 5. He seems to die, however, in the agnostic spirit which, a moment later, prompts Horatio's account of the catastrophe as "accidental judgements, casual slaughters" (5.2.357). These conflicting views follow one another so closely in the action, and they are treated by the dramatist with such a non-committal equality, that it becomes impossible to characterize the supernatural in the play. Although we stumble from time to time over the partially submerged rocks of old beliefs, their presence only makes the obscurity of the total picture more poignant. In effect, Shakespeare has created his own, infinitely more complex version of the divided worlds of [Pickering's] *Horestes* and [Kyd's] *The Spanish Tragedy*. Hamlet's questions, instead of being halted artificially as Hieronymo's were by a tidy, Senecan supernatural visible to us in the audience although not to the hero, grope their way into a darkness without form or limit. Like Pickering, Shakespeare placed his spirit of Revenge inside the play itself, as a character who addresses the protagonist directly. Having done so, he proceeded disconcertingly to associate the ghost with a Christian hereafter, and refused to judge its ethic of blood vengeance. *Hamlet* never explains the nature of that silence towards which the hero moves gradually, away from us, and into which he finally vanishes. This is one reason why the tragedy has a terror, and also a relevance to the world as we know it, lacking in Pickering and Kyd.

More perhaps than any other Shakespearean tragedy, *Hamlet* is a play obsessed with words themselves. It displaces the accustomed centre of earlier revenge drama by subordinating plot for its own sake to a new concern with the mysterious gap between thought and action, between the verbal formulation of intent and its concrete realization. The prince himself is the most articulate of Shakespeare's tragic heroes, but he combines verbal fluency with a curious paralysis of the will. When Claudius asks Laertes in Act 4 what he would do "to show yourself your father's son in deed / More than in words" (4.7.130–131), Laertes replies instantly that, to be avenged, he would be happy to cut Hamlet's throat "i' the church." A demonstration that "in deed more than words" he is his father's son is conspicuously what the Hamlet of "O, what a rogue and peasant slave am I" and "How all occasions do inform against me" has not managed. We may respect him for this failing. Certainly, the sharply contrasted readiness of Laertes to act without thinking is unlovely. The fact remains that Hamlet is a man suffering from a peculiar malaise. In his mind, speech and event, language and its realization have become separate and disjunct. He can initiate action only when he has no time to subject it, first, to words: when he stabs impulsively through the arras and kills Polonius, when he sends Rosencrantz and Guildenstern to death *before* "I could make a prologue to my brains" (5.2.31), boards the pirate ship in the heat of the moment or finally, without premeditation, kills the king. The Norwegian captain tells Hamlet in the fourth scene of Act 4 that Fortinbras is hazarding twenty thousand ducats and an army of two thousand men to gain "a little patch of ground / That hath in it no profit but the name" (4.4.19–20). Fortinbras here, as in other respects, is Hamlet's diametric opposite. He has converted a mere word, a name, into a pretext for action. Hamlet, on the other hand, allows a tangible situation, the fact of a father's murder, to dissolve into words alone.

STANLEY WELLS

On the First Soliloquy

More than most plays, *Hamlet* is a series of opportunities for virtuosity. This is true above all of the role of Hamlet himself. "Hamlet," wrote Max Beerbohm, is "a hoop through which every very eminent actor must, sooner or later, jump." There is no wonder that it has been such a favourite part with actors, and even with actresses. The performer has the opportunity to demonstrate a wide range of ability, to be melancholy and gay, charming and cynical, thoughtful and flippant, tender and cruel, calm and impassioned, noble and vindictive, downcast and witty, all within a few hours. He can wear a variety of costumes, he need not disguise good looks, he can demonstrate athletic ability, he has perhaps the longest role in drama—he could scarcely ask for more, except perhaps the opportunity to sing and dance.

And if the role of Hamlet is the greatest reason for the play's popularity with actors, the character of Hamlet is surely the greatest reason for its popularity with audiences. Hamlet is the most sympathetic of tragic heroes. We are drawn to him by his youth, his intelligence, and his vulnerability. As soon as he appears we are conscious of one of the sources of his appeal: his immense capacity for taking life seriously. It may sound like a slightly repellent quality, but I don't mean to imply that he is excessively gloomy or over-earnest. Often he is deeply dejected: but he has good cause. There is nothing exceptional about his emotional reactions except perhaps their intensity. He has a larger-than-life capacity for experience, a fullness of response, a depth of feeling, a vibrancy of living, which mark him out from the ordinary. He is a raw nerve in the court of Denmark, disconcertingly liable to make the instinctive rather than the conditioned response. This cuts him off from those around him, but it puts him into peculiar contact with the audience. And as Hamlet is to the other figures of the play, so his soliloquies are to the role, for in them Shakespeare shows us the raw nerves of Hamlet himself.

The use of soliloquy is one of the most brilliant features of the play, for in these speeches Shakespeare solves a major technical problem in the presentation of his central character. The young man who takes himself seriously, who persists in explaining himself and his problems, is someone we are apt—perhaps too apt— to regard as a bore. We have all had experience of him, and so probably have most of our friends. On the other hand, the desire to know someone to the depths is fundamental to human nature. Here was both a problem and a challenge: how to let Hamlet reveal himself without becoming an almighty bore? Shakespeare found a double solution. First, he caused Hamlet to conduct his deepest self-communings in solitude, so that there is none of the awkwardness associated with the presence of a confidant. And secondly, the soliloquies are written in a style which presents us not with conclusions but with the very processes of Hamlet's mind.

There had been nothing like this in drama before: nothing which, while retaining a verse form, at the same time so vividly revealed what Shakespeare elsewhere calls "the quick forge and working-house of thought" (*Henry the Fifth* [5.Pro.23]). Vocabulary, syntax, and rhythm all contribute to the effect. Consider the second half of Hamlet's first soliloquy, beginning with his contrast between his uncle and his dead father:

> That it should come to this—
> But two months dead—nay, not so much, not two—
> So excellent a king, that was to this
> Hyperion to a satyr, so loving to my mother
> That he might not beteem the winds of heaven
> Visit her face too roughly! Heaven and earth,
> Must I remember? Why, she would hang on him
> As if increase of appetite had grown
> By what it fed on, and yet within a month—
> Let me not think on't; frailty, thy name is woman—
> A little month, or ere those shoes were old
> With which she followed my poor father's body,
> Like Niobe, all tears, why she, even she—
> O God, a beast that wants discourse of reason
> Would have mourned longer!—married with mine uncle,
> My father's brother, but no more like my father
> Than I to Hercules; within a month,
> Ere yet the salt of most unrighteous tears
> Had left the flushing of her gallèd eyes,
> She married. O most wicked speed, to post
> With such dexterity to incestuous sheets!
> It is not, nor it cannot come to good.
> But break, my heart, for I must hold my tongue.

(1.2.137–159)

5   The anguish that it causes Hamlet to think of his mother's over-hasty marriage is conveyed as much by the tortured syntax as by direct statement; we share his

difficulty as he tries—and fails—to assimilate these unwelcome facts into his consciousness, seeking to bring under emotional control the discordant elements of his disrupted universe: his love of his dead father, his love of his mother combined with disgust at her marriage to the uncle whom he loathes, and the disillusion with womankind that this has provoked in him. The short exclamations interrupting the sentence structure point his horror: the rhythms of ordinary speech within the verse give immediacy to the contrasts in phrases such as "Hyperion to a satyr" and "Than I to Hercules"; and the concreteness of the imagery betrays the effort it costs him to master the unwelcome nature of the facts which it expresses: his mother's haste to marry "or ere those shoes were old/With which she followed my poor father's body"—it is as if only by concentrating on the matter-of-fact, physical aspects of the scene can he bear to contemplate it, or bring it within his belief. He ends on a note of utter helplessness: he alone sees the truth; he knows that his mother's actions, which both he and she see as evil, must bring forth evil; but he, the only emotionally honest person there, cannot express his emotion—except to us.

ELAINE SHOWALTER

Representing Ophelia

"Of all the characters in *Hamlet*," Bridget Lyons has pointed out, "Ophelia is most persistently presented in terms of symbolic meanings." Her behavior, her appearance, her gestures, her costume, her props, are freighted with emblematic significance, and for many generations of Shakespearean critics her part in the play has seemed to be primarily iconographic. Ophelia's symbolic meanings, moreover, are specifically feminine. Whereas for Hamlet madness is metaphysical, linked with culture, for Ophelia it is a product of the female body and female nature, perhaps that nature's purest form. On the Elizabethan stage, the conventions of female insanity were sharply defined. Ophelia dresses in white, decks herself with "fantastical garlands" of wild flowers, and enters, according to the stage directions of the "Bad" Quarto, "distracted" playing on a lute with her "hair down singing." Her speeches are marked by extravagant metaphors, lyrical free associations, and "explosive sexual imagery." She sings wistful and bawdy ballads, and ends her life by drowning.

All of these conventions carry specific messages about femininity and sexuality. Ophelia's virginal and vacant white is contrasted with Hamlet's scholar's garb, his "suits of solemn black." Her flowers suggest the discordant double images of female sexuality as both innocent blossoming and whorish contamination; she is the "green girl" of pastoral, the virginal "Rose of May" and the sexually explicit madwoman who, in giving away her wild flowers and herbs, is symbolically deflowering herself. The "weedy trophies" and phallic "long purples" which she wears to her death intimate an improper and discordant sexuality that Gertrude's lovely elegy cannot quite obscure. In Elizabethan and Jacobean drama, the stage direction that a woman enters with dishevelled hair indicates that she might either be mad or the victim of a rape; the disordered hair, her offense against decorum, suggests sensuality in each case. The mad Ophelia's bawdy songs and verbal license, while they give her access to "an entirely different range of experience" from what she is allowed as the dutiful daughter, seem to be her one sanctioned form of self-assertion as a woman, quickly followed, as if in retribution, by her death.

Drowning too was associated with the feminine, with female fluidity as opposed to masculine aridity. In his discussion of the "Ophelia complex," the phenomenologist Gaston Bachelard traces the symbolic connections between women, water, and death. Drowning, he suggests, becomes the truly feminine death in the dramas of literature and life, one which is a beautiful immersion and submersion in the female element. Water is the profound and organic symbol of the liquid woman whose eyes are so easily drowned in tears, as her body is the repository of blood, amniotic fluid, and milk. A man contemplating this feminine suicide understands it by reaching for what is feminine in himself, like Laertes, by a temporary surrender to his own fluidity—that is, his tears; and he becomes a man again in becoming once more dry—when his tears are stopped.

Clinically speaking, Ophelia's behavior and appearance are characteristic of the malady the Elizabethans would have diagnosed as female love-melancholy, or erotomania. From about 1580, melancholy had become a fashionable disease among young men, especially in London, and Hamlet himself is a prototype of the melancholy hero. Yet the epidemic of melancholy associated with intellectual and imaginative genius "curiously bypassed women." Women's melancholy was seen instead as biological, and emotional in origins.

CLAIRE BLOOM
Playing Gertrude on Television

Editors' note: Claire Bloom played Gertrude in the BBC TV production (1980), directed by Rodney Bennett, with Patrick Stewart as Claudius. In the following passage she discusses the role.

It's very hard to play because strangely enough Gertrude has very few lines; I've always known it was a wonderful part and it *is,* but when you come to play it you realise you have to find many ways around the fact that she in actual fact says little!

You come to rehearse a part like this with certain preconceived notions, which you usually leave! I can only describe them as a battering ram—you knock down the first wall then what is inside is something quite different from what you'd imagined. I was convinced that she was guilty, not of the murder, but certainly that she had found out from Claudius that he had killed her husband. But there's nothing in the text that bears that out and many things that contradict it. I had thought it would make her less of a victim, more of a performer in the world, but [she laughs at herself] it isn't so. Like anyone if you live with a man, she must know there was something more, but I now believe that when Hamlet confronts her with "as kill a king . . . ay, madam, it was my word," it's the first time she's realised. I think from then on she knows and she must accept the fact that Claudius did it, and there is a change in their relationship. But there isn't a break—you don't break with someone suddenly like that. It changes; perhaps if they'd lived another twenty years they would have drifted apart. But there isn't a complete withdrawal. The hold they have on each other is too strong for that to happen. That caused me great difficulty; the scene after the closet scene is with Claudius, when he repeats twice "Gertrude, come away," and she doesn't reply. It's very mysterious. It's a kind of underwritten scene until you realise, or I realised, that there is no real choice for her. For the moment she doesn't go with him, but the next day she does. Hamlet knows it when he says, "Go not to my uncle's bed."

She never replies and says "I won't"; she just says, "Thou hast cleft my heart in twain." She's a woman who goes with whatever is happening at the time. She's a weak-willed woman, but most of us are weak-willed if we're in the power of somebody who is very strong—and Claudius and Hamlet are both pretty strong fellows.

The "mysterious" scene with Claudius was one of the hardest to deal with in rehearsal. . . . We tried backwards, forwards, upside down and inside out and didn't really find it until a couple of days before we shot it. The minute we found it we knew it was the right one, but at other times we'd go away saying, "We've got it," then both Patrick and I would come in the next day depressed and say to Rodney, "Could we please do that scene again because it doesn't make sense when you think about it." There are questions that I'm sure have been asked by every cast of every *Hamlet* since Burbage[1] and for Gertrude they are: Was there a decision to go with Claudius or not to go with Claudius? How far was she lying about Hamlet's madness? I do think part of her believes he's mad, but when she says to the king "He's mad," I think that's protection, or overstating a fact she believes is possibly true. And of course she withholds information from Claudius; she says, "Behind the arras hearing something stir . . . [he] kills the unseen good old man," but she *doesn't* say he said "Is it the king?" That is a very important bit of information which she certainly doesn't pass on!

[1]**Burbage** Richard Burbage (c. 1567–1619), the first actor to play Shakepeare's Hamlet.

BERNICE W. KLIMAN

The BBC Hamlet: A Television Production

With *Hamlet,* the producers of the BBC Shakespeare Plays have finally met the demands of Shakespeare-on-television by choosing a relatively bare set, conceding only a few richly detailed movable panels and props to shape key locales. By avoiding both location and realistic settings, they point up the natural affinity between Shakespeare's stage and the undisguised sound set. This starkness of setting admits poetry, heightened intensity—and "what not that's sweet and happy."

The producers have thus made a valid choice from among television's three faces: one, broadcast films, whether made for television or not, which exploit location settings, long shots, and all the clichés we associate with movies, including sudden shifts of space and time and full use of distance, from the most extreme long shots to "eyes only" closeups; two, studio-shot television drama with naturalistic settings, such as the hospital corridors and middle-class living rooms of sitcoms and soap operas, mostly in mid- to close-shots, often interspersed, to be sure, with a bit of stock footage of highways and skylines to establish a realistic environment. This second style varies from a close representation of real action to frankly staged action, where canned laughter or even shadowy glimpses of the studio audience can heighten the staged effect. Three, there is bare space with little or no effort made to disguise that this is a televised activity with a television crew out of sight but nearby. News broadcasts, talk shows and some television drama fit into this third category. Because of its patently unrepresentational quality, this last type offers the most freedom in shooting style. To all three kinds of settings we bring particular expectations in response to their conventions.

Shakespeare's plays work best in the last kind of television space, I believe, because it avoids the clash between realism and poetry, between the unity often expected in realistic media and the disunity and ambiguity of many of the plays, especially *Hamlet*. Yet, while closest to the kind of stage Shakespeare wrote for, the bare television set can be stretched through creative camera work. For example, when Hamlet follows the ghost in the BBC play, the two repeatedly walk across the frame and out of it, first from one direction, then from another; framing fosters the illusion of extended space. Freeing this *Hamlet* from location (as in the BBC *As You Like It*) and from realistic sets (as in the BBC *Measure for Measure*—however well those sets worked for that play) allows the play to be as inconsistent as it is, with, as Bernard Beckerman has so brilliantly explained in *Shakespeare at the Globe, 1599–1609,* a rising and falling action in each individual scene rather than through the course of the drama as a whole. It also allows for acting, the bravura kind that Derek Jacobi is so capable of.

Although gradually coalescing like the pointillism of impressionistic paintings into a subtly textured portrait, at first his mannerisms suggesting madness seem excessive. It is to be expected, perhaps, that Hamlet is a bit unhinged after the ghost scene, but Jacobi's rapid, hard blows to his forehead with the flat of his hand as he says "My tables" recall the desperation of Lear's cry: "O, let me not be mad, not mad, sweet heaven." And soon after, following the last couplet of the scene, Hamlet, maniacally playful, widens his eyes and points, pretending to see the ghost again, then guffaws at Marcellus's fears. Even more unsettling is his laughter when he is alone, as while he is saying "The play's the thing / Wherein I'll catch the conscience of the King." More significantly, he breaks up his own "Mousetrap" by getting right into the play, destroying the distance between audience and stage (a very real raked proscenium-arch stage), spoiling it as a test, because Claudius has a right to be incensed at Hamlet's behavior. Of course, Hamlet does so because Claudius never gives himself away, an unusual and provocative but not impossible interpretation. Thus, Claudius can only have the court's sympathy as he calmly calls for light and uses it to examine Hamlet closely. Hamlet, in response, covers his face, then laughs.

5   Hamlet himself thinks he is mad. To Ophelia he says, as if the realization had suddenly struck him, "It *hath* made me mad [emphasis his]" (III.i.147). To his mother he stresses the word "essentially" in "I *essentially* am not in madness" (III.iv.187). That is, in all essential matters he can be considered sane, though mad around the edges. This indeed turns out to be the explanation.

However doubtful about Hamlet's sanity Jacobi's acting leaves us, in this production this question does not seem to make a difference because it does not have a bearing on the tragedy, and this is true at least partly because in each scene on this nonrealistic set we seem to start anew, ready to let Hamlet's behavior tell us if he is mad or not. Moreover, if Hamlet is mad, it is not so totally as to obscure reason or sensibility. Far from it. It is more as if exacerbated reason and sensibility sometimes tip him into madness. This madness is no excuse for action or delay; it is simply part of the suffering that Hamlet is heir to.

Hamlet, then, is left to struggle against himself—surely where Shakespeare intended the struggle to abide. One of the conflicts in this Hamlet results from his affinity, perhaps, more to the bureaucratic Claudius who handles war-scares with diplomacy and who sits at a desk while brooding over his sins than to the warlike King Hamlet who comes in full armor. Hamlet may admire Fortinbras but is himself more like the bookish Horatio. Through nuance of gesture, through body movement, through a face that is indeed a map of all emotions, Jacobi shapes a

Hamlet who loves his father too much to disregard his command, yet who cannot hate his step-father enough to attend to it. Because Jacobi conveys so fully Hamlet's aloneness and vulnerability, one could be struck, for the first time, by the ghost's silence about his son. There is no declaration of love, no concern about Hamlet's ascension to the throne. Hamlet is doomed, it seems, to care about those who consistently care more for others than for him.

All of this production's richness and suggestiveness was realized not only because Jacobi is a marvelous actor—as indeed he is—but also because within the set's spareness that acting could unfold, an acting style that subsumes and transcends the "real." This production's space tells us what is possible for television presentations of Shakespeare. The more bare the set, it seems, the more glowing the words, the more immediate our apprehension of the enacted emotion.

STANLEY KAUFFMANN

At Elsinore

Kenneth Branagh wins two victories in *Hamlet* (Castle Rock [1996]). He has made a vital, exciting film; and he has triumphed over the obstacles he put in his own way.

Let's first rejoice in the virtues. Branagh confirms what was known from the opening shot of *Henry V:* he has fine cinematic skills. His directing keeps *Hamlet* flowing, endows scenes that might become static with germane movement. Many of his touches illuminate. One of them: Hamlet comes into a huge mirrored room in the palace, sees himself full-length and, after a moment, begins "To be or not to be." Two selves speak that speech and give it an added edge.

Then there's the text itself. Branagh has used the complete First Folio text, has included a scene from the Second Quarto that is not in the Folio, to make a film that runs four hours plus intermission. I could find only a few alterations, trifles compared with the chopped, twisted, insulting text that Olivier used in his 155-minute version. Branagh's film looks splendid. He sets it in the mid-nineteenth century—with Blenheim Palace serving as the exterior of Elsinore—and Alex Byrne's costumes fully exploit the period. The cinematographer, Alex Thomson, using 70-mm wide-screen format, has nonetheless created lighting that seems naturally evolved from the hundreds of candles. And as for the music, Patrick Doyle again does wonders. He wrote the scores for Branagh's two previous Shakespeare films, and here again he provides music that rises unobtrusively to benefit scene after scene.

Every supporting role of significance has been superbly cast and is superbly played. I can't imagine a better Claudius than Derek Jacobi, who brings to it force and cunning and manipulative charm. The sequences in which he converts the furious Laertes from enemy to accomplice are masterpieces of guile manifested as honesty. (Jacobi, by the way, was the first Hamlet that Branagh ever saw; and years later Jacobi directed Branagh in a theater production.)

5   Jacobi is no surprise: Julie Christie is. This Golden Girl of the 1960s virtually disappeared for a while, then reappeared in a London production of Pinter's *Old Times*. She was so dull that I thought she was being used just for her name. But here, as Gertrude, she is emotionally rich. She brings to the role the apt quality of overblown sex object, and, presumably with Branagh's help, she completely fulfills the woman. In Gertrude's key moment, the closet scene, Christie bursts with

the frightened despair of a guilty woman who thinks that her behavior may have driven her son mad.

Kate Winslet, dear to us already through *Sense and Sensibility* and *Jude,* gives Ophelia the kind of vulnerability that almost invites the man she loves to wound her. Polonius gets the obtuse officiousness that he needs from Richard Briers. It's immediately clear why Horatio, done by Nicholas Farrell, is Hamlet's dearest friend: anybody would want him for a friend. Laertes, a role always in danger of being as much of a blowhard as his father, Polonius, is realized in his confusions by Michael Maloney. Branagh, as he did in *Much Ado About Nothing,* has sprinkled some American actors through his cast. The best of these is Charlton Heston as the Player King, sounding and (even) looking plummy, home at last.

Hamlet is unique in Shakespeare. I can think of no other role in the plays in which an actor is so compelled, commanded, to present *himself.* Macbeth, Othello, Iago, the Richards and the Henrys—run through the roster, and always the actor selects and nurtures what there is in his imagination and experience and technique that will make the man come alive. No such selections for Hamlet. The whole actor is the whole character. So, when we see a Hamlet, we are looking at an actor in a unique way.

Branagh's Hamlet—or, one might say, Hamlet's Branagh—is attractive, keen, nobly intended, tender with regret for Ophelia, torn with disgust for the chicaneries of the world, fiery, quite susceptible to cracking into frenzy. (In appearance, he is fair—not Olivier's platinum blond—with a somewhat darker moustache and goatee.)

This is a man we could meet and understand. What this Hamlet lacks is what possibly we could not understand: his sense of falling upward into the metaphysical. This is what is sometimes called the "poetic" nature of Hamlet, this linkage with a spirit walking the earth in quest of purgation; and this linkage, in mystery and awe and uncertainty, leads to what Granville Barker called "a tragedy of inaction." Branagh's Hamlet doesn't attain this quality: it doesn't quite seem to be in him. Not long ago Ralph Fiennes, burdened with an unworthy director and cast, nevertheless did a Hamlet on Broadway that took us out into the spheres. Not Branagh. Every word he speaks is true. But in Hamlet that is not quite enough.

10   Now the lesser aspects of the film. First, the obverse side of Branagh's directing skill. He is too eager for spectacle, even if it's pointless or harmful. When Gertrude and Claudius exit at the end of the first court scene, confetti rains down on them. For the moment, it's startling, pretty. Then we wonder who planned it and who threw it. Answer: the director. When the Ghost speaks to Hamlet, the earth splits and flames leap. Is this God overseeing unpurged souls? Or the special effects department? Rosencrantz and Guildenstern arrive on a toy locomotive. Who put that model train and tracks on the palace grounds? Old King Hamlet? Claudius? Or the director? When Hamlet and Laertes duel, the civilized sport explodes into Errol Flynn antics, with ropes and chandeliers—another directorial intrusion. Branagh sets the whole film in winter, which allows for some breathtaking vistas but makes us wonder why the old king was sleeping outdoors in his snow-covered orchard on the afternoon of his murder and how the brookside flowers could be present when Ophelia drowns.

Another obverse side, one that may sound odd: the use of the complete text. Admirable though it is in Branagh to aim at "classic" status, not every word is helpful today, especially in a film. To hear Marcellus discourse on "the bird of dawning" at Christmastime, just after the Ghost's second appearance, is a soft indulgence in Elizabethan folklore. To hear Gertrude include a small dirty joke, about "long purples," when she tells Laertes of his sister's death is to coddle the lad from Stratford who couldn't always keep rustic humor out of his plays. And the sad fact is that, when Shakespeare takes time out from drama for moral commentary, the result is sometimes mere homiletics. Hamlet's speech about "the dram of evil" is not only a brusque lapse in the action, it captures perfectly the quality in Shakespeare that Bernard Shaw called "the atmosphere of the rented pew."

Sex. Branagh has searched for chances to get it into the film. While Polonius is warning Ophelia to be careful in her behavior with Hamlet, to avoid the prince completely, Branagh includes flashback shots of her and Hamlet naked in bed together. Presumably Branagh takes his license from the bawdy song that Ophelia later sings when she is mad—"Young men will do't if they come to't," etc.—a song that is usually viewed as the raving of a sexually repressed virgin. Whether or not Hamlet and Ophelia actually had an affair is possibly arguable, but what seems clear is that, if they have made love, it detracts considerably from the fierce, Savonarola-like outburst of the "get thee to a nunnery" passages.

Then, too, Polonius is given a visiting whore in the scene with Reynaldo, who is apparently her pimp. (Ophelia bursts in without knocking—fortuitously, just after Reynaldo and the whore leave.) Branagh's purpose is to lend irony to the old man's instructions to Reynaldo, about checking on Laertes's behavior in Paris, but the episode smacks of opportunism.

Politics. Of course *Hamlet* is, among other elements, a political play. One cause for Hamlet's hatred of Claudius is that his uncle has "popp'd in between th'election and my hopes." Branagh's use of the mid-century period affords the ambiance of the "Age of Metternich," but it misplaces in time the Denmark-England-Norway-Poland relationships of the original. Further, Branagh distorts the political action of the closing scenes. Early in the play we learn that the young Fortinbras of Norway wants to reconquer some lands that his country lost to Denmark, but the Norwegian king dissuades him. Fortinbras swears never to attack Denmark, but he will ask for the right of passage through Denmark to attack Poland. Toward the end of the play Fortinbras leads an army into Denmark and sends a messenger to Claudius to ask for that right of passage.

15   Incomprehensibly, in Branagh's film, Fortinbras then attacks Elsinore. (Real reason: Branagh wants to heat up the film's closing moments.) Shots of this violence are intercut with the Hamlet-Laertes duel. Just as Hamlet dies, the Norwegian soldiers burst into the court, destroying as they come. Fortinbras ought to feel a bit foolish, not only having broken his word but to find out that, just before Hamlet expired, the prince named him as his successor. ("He has my dying voice.") Instead, Fortinbras is shown as a glowering conqueror moderately disturbed by the prince's death. The very last shot is of old King Hamlet's statue being toppled and smashed. Why did Branagh choose that shot as the moment toward which the entire film moved?

Some other points might be called matters of interpretation—Claudius's slapping of Hamlet in anger at the chaffing about Polonius's corpse, the straitjacketing of Ophelia in a padded cell—but one Branagh touch seems just plain misreading. Claudius (in Act III, Scene 1) says he has "closely sent for Hamlet" so that the prince can meet Ophelia while Claudius and Polonius are hidden and watching. They do hide. Hamlet enters, finds the chamber empty though he has been sent for, muses aloud while waiting ("To be or not to be"). Then Ophelia enters—the girl who, for days, has been forbidden to see him. And it was the king who summoned him here. Surely, in simple reason, Hamlet must be suspicious that this is

a set-up from the moment she appears. Instead, Branagh plays it merely petulantly until, after the nunnery speech, he hears a noise behind the door and the
deception dawns on him. Branagh's treatment not only makes Hamlet less acute
than we are, it takes the bite out of "Are you honest?"

Interpretations and innovations have different weights in a Shakespeare film
from such matters in a theater production. When I saw Ingmar Bergman's production of *Hamlet,* with his sluttish Ophelia wandering through scenes in which
Shakespeare forgot to include her, I was relieved that Bergman had not filmed it.
Branagh's film, warts and all, will be with us for some time to come.

On the whole, this is good news. Though his *Henry V* and *Much Ado
About Nothing* were closer to perfection, *Hamlet* is more difficult in every way.
Flaws, problems, bumps, yes; but the film surpasses them finally through
Branagh's talent and the talents of his colleagues. And, not to be slighted, there
is Branagh's infectious joy—the right word even for *Hamlet*—in doing
Shakespeare.

WILL SARETTA

*What follows is an undergraduate's review, published in a college newspaper, of
Kenneth Branagh's film version of Hamlet (1996).*

Branagh's Film of Hamlet

Kenneth Branagh's *Hamlet* opened last night at the Harmon Auditorium, and
will be shown again on Wednesday and Thursday at 7:30 p.m. According to the
clock the evening will be long—the film runs for four hours, and in addition
there is one ten-minute intermission—but you will enjoy every minute of it.

Well, almost every minute. Curiously, the film begins and ends relatively
weakly, but most of what occurs in between is good and much of it is wonderful.
The beginning is weak because it is too strong; Bernardo, the sentinel, offstage
says "Who's there?" but before he gets a reply he crashes onto the screen and
knocks Francisco down. The two soldiers grapple, swords flash in the darkness,
and Francisco finally says, "Nay, answer me. Stand and unfold yourself."
Presumably Branagh wanted to begin with a bang, but here, as often, more is less.
A quieter, less physical opening in which Bernardo, coming on duty, hears a
noise and demands that the maker of the noise identify himself and Francisco, the
sentinel on duty, rightly demands that the newcomer identify *himself,* would catch
the uneasiness and the mystery that pervades the play much better than does
Branagh's showy beginning.

Similarly, at the end of the film, we get too much. For one thing, shots of
Fortinbras's army invading Elsinore alternate with shots of the duel between
Hamlet and King Claudius's pawn, Laertes, and they merely distract us from what
really counts in this scene, the duel itself, which will result in Hamlet's death but
also in Hamlet's successful completion of his mission to avenge his father. Second,
at the very end we get shots of Fortinbras's men pulling down a massive statue of
Hamlet Senior, probably influenced by television and newspaper shots of statues
of Lenin being pulled down when the Soviet Union was dissolved a few years earlier. This is ridiculous; *Hamlet* is not a play about the fall of Communism, or about
one form of tyranny replacing another. Shakespeare's *Hamlet* is not about the triumph of Fortinbras. It is about Hamlet's brave and ultimately successful efforts to
do what is right, against overwhelming odds, and to offer us the consolation that

in a world where death always triumphs there nevertheless is something that can be called nobility.

What, then, is good about the film? First of all, the film gives us the whole play, whereas almost all productions, whether on the stage or in the movie house, give us drastically abbreviated versions. Although less is often more, when it comes to the text of *Hamlet,* more is better, and we should be grateful to Branagh for letting us hear all of the lines. Second, it is very well performed, with only a few exceptions. Jack Lemmon as Marcellus is pretty bad, but fortunately the part is small. Other big-name actors in small parts—Charlton Heston as the Player King, Robin Williams as Osric, and Billy Crystal as the First Grave-digger—are admirable. But of course the success or failure of any production of *Hamlet* will depend chiefly on the actor who plays Hamlet, and to a considerable degree on the actors who play Claudius, Gertrude, Polonius, Ophelia, Laertes, and Horatio. There isn't space here to comment on all of these roles, but let it be said that Branagh's Prince Hamlet is indeed princely, a man who strikes us as having the ability to become a king, not a wimpy whining figure. When at the end Fortinbras says that if Hamlet had lived to become the king, he would "have proved most royal," we believe him. And his adversary, King Claudius, though morally despicable, is a man of great charm and great ability. The two men are indeed "mighty opposites," to use Hamlet's own words.

5   Branagh's decision to set the play in the late nineteenth century rather than in the Elizabethan period of Shakespeare's day and rather than in our own day contributes to this sense of powerful forces at work. If the play were set in Shakespeare's day, the men would wear tights, and if it were set in our day they would wear suits or trousers and sports jackets and sweaters, but in the film all of the men wear military costumes (black for Hamlet, scarlet for Claudius, white for Laertes) and the women wear ball gowns of the Victorian period. Branagh gives us a world that is closer to our own than would Elizabethan costumes, but yet it is, visually at least, also distant enough to convey a sense of grandeur, which modern dress cannot suggest. Of course *Hamlet* can be done in modern dress, just as *Romeo and Juliet* was done, successfully, in the recent film starring Claire Danes and Leonardo DiCaprio, set in a world that seemed to be Miami Beach, but *Romeo and Juliet* is less concerned with heroism and grandeur than *Hamlet* is, so Branagh probably did well to avoid contemporary costumes.

Although Branagh is faithful to the text, in that he gives us the entire text, he knows that a good film cannot be made merely by recording on film a stage production, and so he gives us handsome shots of landscape, and of rich interiors—for instance, a great mirrored hall—that would be beyond the resources of any theatrical production. I have already said that at the end, when Fortinbras's army swarms over the countryside and then invades the castle we get material that is distracting, indeed irrelevant, but there are also a few other distractions. It is all very well to let us *see* the content of long narrative speeches (for instance, when the Player King talks of the fall of Troy and the death of King Priam and the lament of Queen Hecuba, Branagh shows us these things, with John Gielgud as Priam and Judi Dench as Hecuba, performing in pantomime), but there surely is no need for us to see a naked Hamlet and a naked Ophelia in bed, when Polonius is warning Ophelia that Hamlet's talk of love cannot be trusted. Polonius's warning is not so long or so undramatic that we need to be entertained visually with an invention that finds not a word of support in the text. On the contrary, all of Ophelia's lines suggest that she would not be other than a dutiful young woman, obedient to the morals of the times and to her father's authority.

Yet another of Branagh's unfortunate inventions is the prostitute who appears in Polonius's bedroom, during Polonius's interview with Reynaldo. A final example of unnecessary spectacle is Hamlet's killing of Claudius: He hurls his rapier the length of the hall, impaling Claudius, and then like some 1930's movie star he swings on the chandelier and drops down on Claudius to finish him off.

But it is wrong to end this review by pointing out faults in Branagh's film of *Hamlet*. There is so much in this film that is exciting, so much that is moving, so much that is . . . , well, so much that is *Hamlet* (which is to say that is a great experience), that the film must be recommended without reservation. Go to see it. The four hours will fly.

A postscript. It is good to see that Branagh uses color-blind casting. Voltemand, Fortinbras's Captain, and the messenger who announces Laertes's return are all blacks—the messenger is a black woman—although of course medieval Denmark and Elizabethan England, and, for that matter, Victorian England, would not have routinely included blacks. These performers are effective, and it is appropriate that actors of color take their place in the world's greatest play.

23

Studying America in Crisis: Responding to Literature of the Civil War, the Great Depression, the Vietnam War, and September 11, 2001

THE CIVIL WAR

SHORT VIEWS

It seems almost incredible that the advocates of liberty should conceive of the idea of selling a fellow creature to slavery.
> James Forten, "Letters from a Man of Colour on a Late Senate Bill Before the Senate of Pennsylvania," 1813

Go where you may, search where you will, roam through all the monarchies and despotisms of the Old World, travel through South America, search out every abuse and when you have found the last, lay your facts by the side of the every-day practices of this nation, and you will say with me, that, for revolting barbarity and shameless hypocrisy, America reigns without a rival.
> Frederick Douglas, "What to the Slave is the Fourth of July?", speech in Rochester, New York, July 5, 1852

What do you propose, gentlemen of the Free-Soil party? Do you propose to better the condition of slavery? Not at all. . . . You say that you are opposed to the expansion of slavery. . . . Is the slave to be benefited by it? Not at all. It is not humanity that influences you. . . . It is that you may have an opportunity of cheating us that you want to limit slave territory. . . . It is that you may have a majority in the Congress of the United States and convert the Government into an engine of Northern aggrandizement. . . . You want by an unjust system of legislation to promote the industry of the United States at the expense of the people of the South.
> Senator Jefferson Davis, Mississippi, to his Northern colleagues, 1852

*A house divided against itself cannot stand. I believe this government
cannot endure permanently half slave and half free. I do not expect the
Union to be dissolved. I do not expect the house to fall. But I do expect it
will cease to be divided. It will become all one thing, or all the other.*
> Abraham Lincoln, at the Republican State Convention, Springfield, 1858

*Let me tell you what is coming. . . . Your fathers and husbands, your sons
and brothers, will be herded at the point of the bayonet. . . . You may, after the sacrifice of countless millions of treasure and hundreds of thousands of lives, as a bare possibility, win Southern independence. . . . But
I doubt it. I tell you that, while I believe with you in the doctrine of States
Rights, the North is determined to preserve this Union. They are not a
fiery, impulsive people as you are, for they live in colder climates. But
when they begin to move in a given direction . . . they move with the
steady momentum and perseverance of a mighty avalanche.*
> Sam Houston, Governor of Texas, warning against secession

*I cannot raise my hand against my birthplace, my home, my children. I
should like, above all things, that our difficulties might be peaceably
arranged. . . . Whatever may be the result of the contest I foresee that the
country will have to pass through a terrible ordeal, a necessary expiation
for our national sins. May God direct all for our good, and shield and
preserve you and yours.*
> Robert E. Lee, accepting the command of the Army of Virginia, 1861

*[The Northerners] say our [i.e. Southerners'] crowning misdemeanor is to
hold in slavery still those Africans they brought over here from Africa, or
sold to us when they found to own them did not pay. They gradually slid
them off down here, giving themselves years to get rid of them in a remu-
nerative way. We want to spread them too, west and south, or northwest,
where the climate would free them or kill them; would improve them out
of the world as the Yankees do Indians. If they had been forced to keep
them in New England, I dare say they would have shared the Indians'
fate; for they are wise in their generation these Yankee children of light.*
> Mary Boykin Chesnut, daughter of a governor of South Carolina,
> diary, 1861

*My paramount object in this struggle is to save the Union and is not ei-
ther to save or destroy slavery. If I could save the Union without freeing
any slave, I would do it; and if I could save it by freeing all the slaves, I
would do it; and if I could save it by freeing some and leaving others
alone, I would also do that. . . . I have here stated my purpose according
to my official duty; and I intend no modification of my oft-expressed
personal wish that all men everywhere could be free.*
> Abraham Lincoln, letter to Horace Greeley, 1862

*My son went in the 54th regiment [of African-American soldiers, formed
in Massachusetts]. I am a colored woman and my son was strong and*

*able as any to fight for his country and the colored people have as much
to fight for as any.*
    Hannah Johnson, letter to Abraham Lincoln, July 31, 1863

*GENERAL ORDER, No. 14: AN ACT to increase the military force of the
Confederate States. The Congress of the Confederate States of America do
enact, That, in order to provide additional forces to repel invasion,
maintain the rightful possession of the Confederate States, secure their independence, and preserve their institutions, the President be, and he is
hereby, authorized to ask for and accept from the owners of slaves, the
services of such number of able-bodied negro men as he may deem expedient, for and during the war, to perform military service in whatever capacity he may direct.*
    Confederate Law authorizing the enlistment of Black soldiers,
    March, 13, 1865

*I have fought against the people of the North because I believed they were
seeking to wrest from the South its dearest rights. But I have never cher-
ished toward them bitter or vindictive feelings, and I have never seen the
day when I did not pray for them.*
    Robert E. Lee

*With malice toward none, with charity for all, with firmness in the right,
as God gives us to see the right, let us strive to finish the work we are in,
to bind up the nation's wounds, to care for him who shall have borne the
battle, and for his widow and orphans, to do all which may achieve and
cherish a just and lasting peace among ourselves, and with all nations.*
    Abraham Lincoln, Second Inaugural Address, 1865

In the South, the war is what A.D. is elsewhere: they date from it.
    Mark Twain, *Life on the Mississippi* (1883)

*I feel that we are on the eve of a new era, when there is to be a great har-
mony between the Federal and the Confederate. I cannot stay to be a living witness to this prophesy, but I feel it within me that it is so.*
    Ulysses S. Grant, in his *Personal Memoirs* (1886)

*We are constantly thinking of the great war . . . which saved the Union
. . . but it was a war that did a great deal more than that. It created in
this country what had never existed before—a national consciousness. It
was not the salvation of the Union, it was the rebirth of the Union.*
    Woodrow Wilson, Memorial Day Address, 1915

*There will never be anything in America more interesting than the Civil
War never.*
    Gertrude Stein, *Everybody's Autobiography* (1937)

Topics for Critical Thinking and Writing

1. The conflict we know as the American Civil War was often referred to during the nineteenth century, and into the twentieth century, by different names. Many in the North used the phrase "The War of the Rebellion," while in the South the common phrase was "The War Between the States." How does our understanding of the conflict change, depending on how we identify it?
2. How might Senator Jefferson Davis and Robert E. Lee respond to the anti-slavery statements by James Forten and Frederick Douglass? What would be Forten's and Douglass's replies to them?
3. Do you think that the Civil War was inevitable?
4. Both Mark Twain and Gertrude Stein make very big claims about the signifi-cance of the Civil War. Explain clearly what each of them is saying. Do you agree with them, or do you think that they exaggerate?
5. Which of these quotations surprised you the most? Surprised you the least? What is the most important lesson that the study of the Civil War teaches?

ESSAYS

JEFFERSON DAVIS

Born in 1808, Jefferson Davis began his career as a statesman and political leader in 1845 when he was elected to Congress, but soon he resigned in order to serve in the military during the Mexican War. In 1849, Davis returned to political life as U.S. senator from Mississippi, and he remained in the Senate during the 1850s, ex-cept for a term as secretary of war under President Franklin Pierce. A forceful, de-termined supporter of slavery and the extension of slavery into new territories and states, Davis resigned his senate seat when Mississippi seceded from the Union and in 1861 was elected president of the Confederate States of America. In the after-math of the Confederacy's defeat in 1865, Davis was captured and from 1865 to 1867 he was imprisoned. The author of The Rise and Fall of Confederate Govern-ment *(1881), he died in 1889.*

Inaugural Address of Jefferson Davis

Delivered at the Capitol, Monday, 18 February 1861

Gentlemen of the Congress of the Confederate States of America, Friends and Fellow-Citizens:

Called to the difficult and responsible station of Chief Executive of the Pro-visional Government which you have instituted, I approach the discharge of the du-ties assigned to me with an humble distrust of my abilities, but with a sustaining confidence in the wisdom of those who are to guide and aid me in the administra-tion of public affairs, and an abiding faith in the virtue and patriotism of the people.

Looking forward to the speedy establishment of a permanent government to take the place of this, and which, by its greater moral and physical power, will be better able to combat with the many difficulties which arise from the conflicting interests of separate nations, I enter upon the duties of the office, to which I have been chosen, with the hope that the beginning of our career, as a Confederacy, may not be obstructed by hostile opposition to our enjoyment of the separate existence and independence which we have asserted, and, with the blessing of Providence, intend to maintain. Our present condition, achieved in a manner unprecedented in the history of nations, illustrates the American idea that governments rest upon the consent of the governed, and that it is the right of the people to alter or abolish governments whenever they become destructive of the ends for which they were established.

The declared purpose of the compact of union from which we have withdrawn, was "to establish justice, insure domestic tranquility, provide for the common defense, promote the general welfare," and when in the judgment of the sovereign States now composing this Confederacy, it had been perverted from the purposes for which it was ordained, and had ceased to answer the ends for which it was established, a peaceful appeal to the ballot-box, declared that so far as they were concerned, the government created by that compact should cease to exist. In this they merely asserted a right which the Declaration of Independence of 1776 had defined to be inalienable. Of the time and occasion for its exercise, they as sovereigns, were the final judges, each for itself. The impartial and enlightened verdict of mankind will vindicate the rectitude of our conduct, and he, who knows the hearts of men, will judge of the sincerity with which we labored to preserve the government of our fathers in its spirit. The right solemnly proclaimed at the birth of the States and which has been affirmed and re-affirmed in the bills of right of States subsequently admitted into the Union of 1789, undeniably recognizes in the people the power to resume the authority delegated for the purposes of government. Thus the sovereign States, here represented, proceeded to form this Confederacy, and it is by abuse of language that their act has been denominated a revolution. They formed a new alliance, but within each State its government has remained, and the rights of person and property have not been disturbed. The agent, through whom they communicated with foreign nations, is changed; but this does not necessarily interrupt their international relations.

5   Sustained by the consciousness that the transition from the former Union to the present Confederacy has not proceeded from a disregard on our part of just obligations, or any failure to perform any constitutional duty; moved by no interest or passion to invade the rights of others; anxious to cultivate peace and commerce with all nations, if we may not hope to avoid war, we may at least expect that posterity will acquit us of having needlessly engaged in it. Doubly justified by the absence of wrong on our part, and by wanton aggression on the part of others, there can be no cause to doubt that the courage and patriotism of the people of the Confederate States will be found equal to any measures of defense which honor and security may require.

An agricultural people, whose chief interest is the export of a commodity required in every manufacturing country, our true policy is peace and the freest trade which our necessities will permit. It is alike our interest, and that of all those to whom we would sell and from whom we would buy, that there should be fewest practicable restrictions upon the interchange of commodities. There can be but little rivalry between ours and any manufacturing or navigating community, such as the northeastern States of the American Union. It must follow, therefore, that a mutual interest would invite good will and kind offices. If, however, passion or the lust of dominion should cloud the judgment or inflame the ambition of those States, we must prepare to meet the emergency, and to maintain, by the final arbitrament of the sword, the position which we have assumed among the nations of the earth. We have entered upon the career of independence, and it must be inflexibly pursued. Through many years of controversy with our late associates, the Northern States, we have vainly endeavored to secure tranquility, and to obtain respect for the rights to which we are entitled. As a necessity, not a choice, we have resorted to the remedy of separation; and henceforth our energies must be directed to the conduct of our own affairs, and the perpetuity of the Confederacy which we have formed. If a just perception of mutual interest shall permit us peaceably to pursue our separate political career, my most earnest desire will have been fulfilled; but if this be denied to us, and the integrity of our territory and jurisdiction be assailed, it will but remain for us, with firm resolve, to appeal to arms and invoke the blessings of Providence on a just cause.

As a consequence of our new condition, and with a view to meet anticipated wants, it will be necessary to provide for the speedy and efficient organization of branches of the Executive Department, having special charge of foreign intercourse, finance, military affairs, and the postal service.

For purposes of defense, the Confederate States may, under ordinary circumstances, rely mainly upon the militia; but it is deemed advisable, in the present condition of affairs, that there should be a well-instructed and disciplined army, more numerous than would usually be required on a peace establishment. I also suggest that, for the protection of our harbors and commerce on the high seas, a navy adapted to those objects will be required. These necessities have doubtless engaged the attention of Congress.

With a constitution differing only from that of our fathers, in so far as it is explanatory of their well-known intent, freed from the sectional conflicts which have interfered with the pursuit of the general welfare, it is not unreasonable to expect that States from which we have recently parted, may seek to unite their fortunes with ours under the government which we have instituted. For this your constitution makes adequate provision; but beyond this, if I mistake not, the judgment and will of the people, a re-union with the States from which we have separated is neither practicable nor desirable. To increase the power, develop the resources, and promote the happiness of the Confederacy, it is requisite that there should be so much homogeneity that the welfare of every portion shall be the aim of the whole. Where this does not exist, antagonisms are engendered which must and should result in separation.

10   Actuated solely by the desire to preserve our own rights and promote our own welfare, the separation of the Confederate States has been marked by no aggression upon others, and followed by no domestic convulsion. Our industrial pursuits have received no check; the cultivation of our fields has progressed as heretofore; and even should we be involved in war, there would be no considerable diminution in the production of the staples which have constituted our exports, and in which the commercial world has an interest scarcely less than our own. This common interest of the producer and consumer can only be interrupted by an exterior force, which should obstruct its transmission to foreign markets—a course of conduct which would be as unjust towards us as it would be detrimental to manufacturing and commercial interests abroad. Should reason guide the action of the government for which we have separated, a policy so detrimental to the civilized world, the Northern States included, could not be dictated by even the strongest desire to inflict injury upon us; but if otherwise, a terrible responsibility will rest upon it, and the suffering of millions will bear testimony to the folly and wickedness of our aggressors. In the meantime, there will remain to us, besides the ordinary means before suggested, the well-known resources for retaliation upon the commerce of the enemy.

Experience in public stations, of subordinate grades to this which your kindness has conferred, has taught me that care, and toil, and disappointment, are the price of official elevation. You will see many errors to forgive, many deficiencies to tolerate, but you shall not find in me either a want of zeal or fidelity to the cause that is to me highest in hope and of most enduring affection. Your generosity has bestowed upon me an undeserved distinction—one which I never sought nor desired. Upon the continuance of that sentiment, and upon your wisdom and patriotism, I rely to direct and support me in the performance of the duty required at my hands.

We have changed the constituent parts but not the system of our government. The constitution formed by our fathers is that of these Confederate States, in their exposition of it; and, in the judicial construction it has received, we have a light that reveals its true meaning.

Thus instructed as to the just interpretation of the instrument, and ever remembering that all offices are but trusts held for the people, and that delegated powers are to be strictly construed, I will hope by due diligence in the performance of my duties, though I may disappoint your expectations, yet to retain, when retiring, something of the good will and confidence which welcomed my entrance into the office.

It is joyous, in the midst of perilous times, to look around upon a people united in heart, where one purpose of high resolve animates and actuates the whole—where the sacrifices to be made are not weighed in the balance against honor, and right, and liberty, and equality. Obstacles may retard—they cannot long prevent—the progress of a movement sanctified by its justice, and sustained by a virtuous people. Reverently let us invoke the God of our fathers to guide and protect us in our efforts to perpetuate the principles which, by his blessing, they were able to vindicate, establish, and transmit to their posterity, and with a continuance of his favor, ever gratefully acknowledged, we may hopefully look forward to success, to peace, and to prosperity.

[1861]

Topics for Critical Thinking and Writing

1. Noting that in 1860–1861, there were nearly four million slaves in the South, an American historian has recently concluded: "On the eve of the Civil War, slavery remained a dynamic and expanding system, not an antiquated labor system on its way to extinction." How does Jefferson Davis refer to and deal with slavery in his Inaugural Address? What is your response to his approach? If you had been one of his advisors, would you have recommended the same approach, or a different one?

2. Setting slavery to the side, do you judge that Davis presents a good argument for Southern secession from the Union? What are the key elements of his argument? Do you find it convincing?

3. Do you think it is possible to "set slavery to the side" when we read Davis's Address?

4. Is Davis a good writer? What are the identifying features of a good writer, as opposed to a bad one?

5. In an essay of 1–2 pages, present a counterargument to Davis. What do you imagine his response to your argument would be? Do you think you could argue with him, or not? And what are the implications of your answer to this question?

MARY BOYKIN MILLER CHESNUT

Mary Boykin Miller Chesnut (1823–1886)—a rich white Southerner—was born in Statesboro, South Carolina. Her father was a U.S. Senator, and in 1826 he was elected governor of South Carolina. Mary in 1840 married James Chesnut, who later served in the South Carolina senate and still later in the U.S. Senate, though he resigned in 1869 when Lincoln was elected president. James Chesnut in fact helped to draft the Confederate ordinance of secession and the Confederate constitution, and he served as an aide to Jefferson Davis, president of the Confederacy.

During the Civil War Mary kept a diary, running to some 400,000 words, but it was not published until 1905, and then in an abridged form. For a modern edition, see A Diary from Dixie, *ed. Ben Ames Williams (1980).*

November 28, 1861

On one side Mrs. Stowe, Greeley, Thoreau, Emerson, Sumner.[1] They live in nice New England homes, clean, sweet-smelling, shut up in libraries, writing books which ease their hearts of their bitterness against us. What self-denial they do practice is to tell John Brown to come down here and cut our throats in Christ's name. Now consider what I have seen of my mother's life, my grandmother's, my mother-in-law's. These people were educated at Northern schools, they read the same books as their Northern contemporaries, the same daily papers, the same Bible. They have the same ideas of right and wrong, are high-bred, lovely, good, pious, doing their duty as they conceive right and wrong. They live in Negro villages. They do not preach and teach hate as a gospel, and the sacred duty of murder and insurrection; but they strive to ameliorate the condition of these Africans in every particular. They set them the example of a perfect life, a life of utter self-abnegation. Think of these holy New Englanders forced to have a Negro village walk through their houses whenever they see fit, dirty, slatternly, idle, ill-smelling by nature. These women I love have less chance to live their own lives in peace than if they were African missionaries. They have a swarm of blacks about them like children under their care, not as Mrs. Stowe's fancy painted them, and they hate slavery worse than Mrs. Stowe does. Book-making which leads you to a round of visits among crowned heads is an easier way to be a saint than martyrdom down here, doing unpleasant duty among the Negroes with no reward but the threat of John Brown hanging like a drawn sword over your head in this world, and threats of what is to come to you from blacker devils in the next.

The Mrs. Stowes have the plaudits of crowned heads; we take our chances, doing our duty as best we may among the woolly heads. My husband supported his plantation by his law practice. Now it is running him in debt. Our people have never earned their own bread. Take this estate, what does it do, actually? It all goes back in some shape to what are called slaves here, called operatives, or tenants, or peasantry elsewhere. I doubt if ten thousand in money ever comes to this old gentlemen's hands. When Mrs. Chesnut married South, her husband was as wealthy as her brothers-in-law. How is it now? Their money has accumulated for their children. This old man's goes to support a horde of idle dirty Africans, while he is abused as a cruel slave owner. I say we are no better than our judges in the North, and no worse. We are human beings of the nineteenth century and slavery has to go, of course. All that has been gained by it goes to the North and to

[1]**Mrs. Stowe . . . Sumner** New Englanders who opposed slavery.

Negroes. The slave owners, when they are good men and women, are the martyrs. I hate slavery. I even hate the harsh authority I see parents think it their duty to exercise toward their children.

[1861]

Topics for Critical Thinking and Writing

1. Clearly Mrs. Chesnut did not have a high view of blacks. She speaks of them as "dirty, slatternly, idle, ill-smelling by nature," "a swarm" (as though they are insects), "devils," "woolly heads," and "idle dirty Africans," yet she was a thoughtful person, and apparently someone who was made uneasy by the sight of power being exerted over another human being. How can you explain her descriptions of African Americans? Can you conceive that you might think of some ethnic group as "idle [and] dirty?" Or as having some other quality that you disapprove of—for instance, "fanatic," "mercenary," "raucous," "domineering"? If you can think of a group this way, are you drawing on your experience or on the reports of others?
2. Putting aside (if possible) the distressing view of African Americans, can you see any virtues in Mrs. Chesnut's writing? Are some sentences especially effective for one reason or another? If you find some or all of the writing effective, point to two or three sentences and explain why you think they are of special interest.

ABRAHAM LINCOLN

Abraham Lincoln (1809–1865), sixteenth president of the United States, is not usually thought of as a writer, but his published speeches and writings comprise about 1,078,000 words, the equivalent of about four thousand pages of double-spaced typing. They were all composed without the assistance of a speech writer.

The Gettysburg campaign—a series of battles fought near Gettysburg in southeastern Pennsylvania—took place in June and July of 1863. Each side lost something like twenty-three thousand men. The battle is regarded as a turning point in the war, but the Confederate army escaped and the war continued until April 1865.

On November 19, 1863, Lincoln delivered a short speech (printed below) at the dedication of a national cemetery on the battlefield of Gettysburg.

Address at the Dedication of the Gettysburg National Cemetery

Four score and seven years ago our fathers brought forth on this continent, a new nation, conceived in Liberty, and dedicated to the proposition that all men are created equal.

Now we are engaged in a great civil war; testing whether that nation, or any nation so conceived and so dedicated, can long endure. We are met on a great battlefield of that war. We have come to dedicate a portion of that field as a final resting-place for those who here gave their lives that that nation might live. It is altogether fitting and proper that we should do this.

But, in a larger sense, we cannot dedicate—we cannot consecrate—we cannot hallow—this ground. The brave men, living and dead, who struggled here have consecrated it, far above our poor power to add or detract. The world will little note, nor long remember, what we say here, but it can never forget what they did here. It is for us the living, rather, to be dedicated here to the unfinished work they who fought here have thus far so nobly advanced. It is rather for us to be here dedicated to the great task remaining before us—that from these honored dead we take increased devotion to that cause for which they gave the last full measure of devotion; that we here highly resolve that these dead shall not have died in vain; that this nation, under God, shall have a new birth of freedom; and that government of the people, by the people, for the people, shall not perish from the earth.

[1863]

Topics for Critical Thinking and Writing

1. Why do you suppose Lincoln began by saying "Four score and seven years ago" rather than "Eighty-seven years ago"?
2. What other words in the Gettysburg Address belong to what we can call the same world or the same discourse—the same community of speech—as "four score"?
3. Speaking a bit broadly we can say that the Address moves from the past to the present to the future. Trace this pattern in as much detail as possible.

MARTHA LIGGAN

Martha Liggan was a local woman in Virginia who in May 1864 cared for a dying Confederate soldier named O. H. Middleton. After his death, she wrote a letter to the soldier's mother.

Dear Madam

Long Meadow Hanover
County Va
Mrs Middleton

Dear Madam,

I now seat myself to reply to your letter for the purpose of giving you the particulars concerning the death of your noble son, who was mortaly wounded here on 30th of May.

The ball sruck the left arm between the shoulder and the elbow, entering the body little below the arm pit passing through the lungs, came out under the left shoulder blade bone. Our Cavelry was repulsed here, about seven O'clock P.M. Your son was brought to the house about sun down, by my father and one of the Yankeys. They found him a very little distance from the house. It is supposed he had been lying there some time, for he was very near speechless, when they got him here. I bathed his wound, washed his face and hands. That revived him very much. He would raise his head from the pillow and speak very distinctly. I asked him his name. He told me O. H. Middleton. I asked him his father's name and address. He told me the same name he was named after his father. The reason we asked him those questions, we could see that he would die, and we thought if he died we could let his relatives know where he died. I think he suspicioned why we asked him those questions, for he asked us please to write and let his father know that he was wounded.

He was conscious until two hours before he died. He died about three O'clock in the morning. Just a little while before he became delerious, he said, Oh! my dear mother if I only could see you once more before I die! While delerious, he would call some names I suppose of his companions, such as Tom, Charlie, and Jerry. The last I heard him say was Mr Blake please send for the surgeon. He suffered very much, But he bore it patiently, like the rest of our noble Sons.

Sometimes he was resless, because we couldn't move him on the bed to ease him, his wound was so painful. I do assure you your son resieved the very best attention we possible could give him, being in the enemy's lines. We hardly knew ourselves having the enemy all around us, and enoying us with there numerous questions.

Although your son was a stranger to me, I have shed many a tear over his corpse and now over his grave. He is buried in our family burying ground, But not coffined as we wish him to be. He was wraped in a blanket. My father is now in the reserve class militia, he says if he can come home, him and another one of our neighbors are going to take him up before he decays and put him in a coffin, so that his remains can be removed more conveniently.

He didn't receive any surgical attention at all. We tried to get him a surgeon and beged the yankeys to send him one, But it was impossible to get one. He would ask us please to try to get him a surgeon. He thought something could be done for him. Oh, he did crave a surgeon. We asked the Yankeys to let us send for our family physician, they told us no they could not do that. Oh, vile and unfeeling wretches. I hope they may receive their reward.

M. E. L.
[1864]

Topics for Critical Thinking and Writing

1. If Mrs. Liggan gave you a draft of this letter to read before she mailed it, would you keep it as it is, or would you be inclined to suggest changes?
2. Does your reading and study of this letter give you a new insight into the Civil War? What other kinds of letters would you want to examine to gain a fuller picture of the War? How would you go about finding these letters?
3. Is Mrs. Liggan's letter a "literary work," or is it something else?
4. Imagine that this soldier, even as he neared death, somehow found the strength to write his own letter to his mother. Compose this letter, a page or so in length. And then please explain what it felt like to write such a letter.
5. Now imagine you are Mrs. Middleton, and that you have just received and read Mrs. Liggan's letter. Please write Mrs. Middleton's letter of reply. What did it feel like to write this letter?

W. E. B. DU BOIS

W. E. B. Du Bois (1868–1963) led an extraordinary life that spanned ninety-five years, from the presidency of Andrew Johnson and the period of Reconstruction that followed the Civil War to the presidency of John F. Kennedy and the political tensions of the Cold War. He was born in 1868 in Great Barrington, western Massachusetts, a town of 5000 residents that included an African American community numbering about fifty. After graduating with honors from the local high school in 1885, he attended Fisk University, in Nashville, Tennessee, from 1885 to 1888, and then Harvard College, where he received a second bachelor's degree, cum laude, in 1890. He pursued graduate study at Harvard (M.A., 1891; Ph.D., 1895) and the University of Berlin (1892–1894).

Du Bois's first book, based on his dissertation and excerpted below, was The Suppression of the African Slave Trade to the United States of America, 1638–1870 *(1896). He wrote many other books and essays during his long and illustrious career. His best-known work is* The Souls of Black Folk, *published in 1903, in which he examines the history of slavery and segregation in the United States, emphasizing throughout that "the problem of the Twentieth Century is the problem of the color line."*

The Lesson for Americans

It may be doubted if ever before such political mistakes as the slavery compromises of the Constitutional Convention had such serious results, and yet, by a succession of unexpected accidents, still left a nation in position to work out its destiny. No American can study the connection of slavery with United States history, and not devoutly pray that his country may never have a similar social problem to solve, until it shows more capacity for such work than it has shown in the past. It is neither profitable nor in accordance with scientific truth to consider that whatever the constitutional fathers did was right, or that slavery was a plague sent from God and fated to be eliminated in due time. We must face the fact that this problem arose principally from the cupidity and carelessness of our ancestors. It was the plain duty of the colonies to crush the trade and the system in its infancy: they preferred to enrich themselves on its profits. It was the plain duty of a Revolution based upon "Liberty" to take steps toward the abolition of slavery: it preferred promises to straightforward action. It was the plain duty of the Constitutional Convention, in founding a new nation, to compromise with a threatening social evil only in case its settlement would thereby be postponed to a more favorable time: this was not the case in the slavery and the slave-trade compromises; there never was a time in the history of America when the system had a slighter economic, political, and moral justification than in 1787; and yet with this real, existent, growing evil before their eyes, a bargain largely of dollars and cents was allowed to open the highway that led straight to the Civil War. Moreover, it was due to no wisdom and foresight on the part of the fathers that fortuitous circumstances made the result of that war what it was, nor was it due to exceptional philanthropy on the part of their descendants that that result included the abolition of slavery.

With the faith of the nation broken at the very outset, the system of slavery untouched, and twenty years' respite given to the slave-trade to feed and foster it, there began, with 1787, that system of bargaining, truckling, and compromising with a moral, political, and economic monstrosity, which makes the history of our dealing with slavery in the first half of the nineteenth century so discreditable to a great people. Each generation sought to shift its load upon the next, and the burden rolled on, until a generation came which was both too weak and too strong to bear it longer. One cannot, to be sure, demand of whole nations exceptional moral foresight and heroism; but a certain hard common-sense in facing the complicated phenomena of political life must be expected in every progressive people. In some respects we as a nation seem to lack this; we have the somewhat inchoate idea that we are not destined to be harassed with great social questions, and that even if we are, and fail to answer them, the fault is with the question and not with us. Consequently we often congratulate ourselves more on getting rid of a problem than on solving it. Such an attitude is dangerous; we have and shall have, as other peoples have had, critical, momentous, and pressing questions to answer. The riddle of the Sphinx may be postponed, it may be evasively answered now; sometime it must be fully answered.

It behooves the United States, therefore, in the interest both of scientific truth and of future social reform, carefully to study such chapters of her history as that of the suppression of the slave-trade. The most obvious question which this study suggests is: How far in a State can a recognized moral wrong safely be compromised? And although this chapter of history can give us no definite answer suited to the ever-varying aspects of political life, yet it would seem to warn any nation from allowing, through carelessness and moral cowardice, any social evil to grow. No persons would have seen the Civil War with more surprise and horror than the Revolutionists of 1776; yet from the small and apparently dying institution of their day arose the walled and castled Slave-Power. From this we may conclude that it behooves nations as well as men to do things at the very moment when they ought to be done.

[1896]

Topics for Critical Thinking and Writing

1. One reviewer rebuked Du Bois for his "bitter" tone. Do you think that this is an accurate criticism? Can you locate passages to support it? What does it mean to say that a writer comes across in his or her tone as "bitter"? Is this always a bad thing?

2. How would you defend the Founding Fathers from the charges that Du Bois advances against them? What would be the key points of your counter-argument? And what, in turn, would be Du Bois's rebuttal?

3. Do you think that slavery is the biggest problem that America has ever faced? Is there any problem comparable to it? Do you agree with the claim made recently by one scholar that "the problem of slavery has never been solved"? Or does this strike you as an overstatement?

4. Du Bois says at one point that Americans do not like to deal with "great social questions." What does he mean by this? Is he exaggerating for effect? Or do you believe that he truly means what he says?

5. Is there a "great social question" facing Americans today? Is it more serious, or less serious, than the problem of slavery that Du Bois describes? Does the history of slavery in the United States teach us a "lesson" (Du Bois's term) that can help us to understand and respond to "great social questions" now?

6. This selection invites you to "think big," about major problems, issues, and crises across the span of American history. Do you like to "think big"? Why or why not? What is the value of this kind of thinking? What are the limitations of "thinking big"? How would you compensate for them?

FICTION

Ambrose Bierce

Ambrose Bierce (1842–1914?) was born in Horse Creek, Ohio, but his family soon moved to Indiana, where at the age of 19 he enlisted in the Union Army. In the next four years he fought in several of the bloodiest battles of the Civil War, was wounded twice, and rose to the rank of lieutenant. After the war he worked as a journalist in San Francisco, in England, and again in San Francisco. In 1912 he went to Mexico to cover the Mexican Revolution, but he disappeared there and it is assumed he died in 1914.

Bierce's literary reputation rests chiefly on one story, "An Occurrence at Owl Creek Bridge," but he wrote other stories of interest.

A Horseman in the Sky

I

One sunny afternoon in the autumn of the year 1861 a soldier lay in a clump of laurel by the side of a road in western Virginia. He lay at full length upon his stomach, his feet resting upon the toes, his head upon the left forearm. His extended right hand loosely grasped his rifle. But for the somewhat methodical disposition of his limbs and a slight rhythmic movement of the cartridge-box at the back of his belt he might have been thought to be dead. He was asleep at his post of duty. But if detected he would be dead shortly afterward, death being the just and legal penalty of his crime.

The clump of laurel in which the criminal lay was in the angle of a road which after ascending southward a steep acclivity to that point turned sharply to the west, running along the summit for perhaps one hundred yards. There it turned southward again and went zigzagging downward through the forest. At the salient of that second angle was a large flat rock, jutting out northward, overlooking the deep valley from which the road ascended. The rock capped a high cliff; a stone dropped from its outer edge would have fallen sheer downward one thousand feet to the tops of the pines. The angle where the soldier lay was on another spur of the same cliff. Had he been awake he would have commanded a view, not only of the short arm of the road and the jutting rock, but of the entire profile of the cliff below. If might well have made him giddy to look.

The country was wooded everywhere except at the bottom of the valley to the northward, where there was a small natural meadow, through which flowed a stream scarcely visible from the valley's rim. This open ground looked hardly any larger than an ordinary door-yard, but was really several acres in extent. Its green was more vivid than that of the inclosing forest. Away beyond it rose a line of giant cliffs similar to those upon which we are supposed to stand in our survey of the savage scene, and through which the road had somehow made its climb to the summit. The configuration of the valley, indeed, was such that from this point of observation it seemed entirely shut in, and one could but have wondered how the road which found a way out of it had found a way into it, and whence came and whither went the waters of the stream that parted the meadow more than a thousand feet below.

No country is so wild and difficult but men will make it a theatre of war; concealed in the forest at the bottom of the military rat-trap, in which half a hundred men in possession of the exits might have starved an army to submission, lay five regiments of Federal infantry. They had marched all the previous day and night and were resting. At nightfall they would take to the road again, climb to the place where their unfaithful sentinel now slept, and descending the other slope of the ridge fall upon a camp of the enemy at about midnight. Their hope was to surprise it, for the road led to the rear of it. In case of failure, their position would be perilous in the extreme; and fail they surely would should accident or vigilance apprise the enemy of the movement.

II

5   The sleeping sentinel in the clump of laurel was a young Virginian named Carter Druse. He was the son of wealthy parents, an only child, and had known such ease and cultivation and high living as wealth and taste were able to command in the mountain country of western Virginia. His home was but a few miles from where he now lay. One morning he had risen from the breakfast-table and said, quietly but gravely: "Father, a Union regiment has arrived at Grafton. I am going to join it."

The father lifted his leonine head, looked at the son a moment in silence, and replied, "Well, go, sir, and whatever may occur do what you conceive to be your duty. Virginia, to which you are a traitor, must get on without you. Should we both live to the end of the war, we will speak further of the matter. Your mother, as the physician has informed you, is in a most critical condition; at the best she cannot be with us longer than a few weeks, but that time is precious. It would be better not to disturb her."

So Carter Druse, bowing reverently to his father, who returned the salute with a stately courtesy that masked a breaking heart, left the home of his childhood to go soldiering. By conscience and courage, by deeds of devotion and daring, he soon commended himself to his fellows and his officers; and it was to these qualities and to some knowledge of the country that he owed his selection for his present perilous duty at the extreme outpost. Nevertheless, fatigue had been stronger than resolution and he had fallen asleep. What good or bad angel came in a dream to rouse him from his state of crime, who shall say? Without a movement, without a sound, in the profound silence and the languor of the late afternoon, some invisible messenger of fate touched with unsealing finger the eyes of his consciousness—whispered into the ear of his spirit the mysterious awakening word which no human lips ever have spoken, no human memory ever has recalled. He quietly raised his forehead from his arm and looked between the masking stems of the laurels, instinctively closing his right hand about the stock of his rifle.

His first feeling was a keen artistic delight. On a colossal pedestal, the cliff— motionless at the extreme edge of the capping rock and sharply outlined against the sky—was an equestrian statue of impressive dignity. The figure of the man sat the figure of the horse, straight and soldierly, but with the repose of a Grecian god carved in the marble which limits the suggestion of activity. The gray costume harmonized with its aërial background; the metal of accoutrement and caparison was softened and subdued by the shadow; the animal's skin had no points of high light. A carbine strikingly foreshortened lay across the pommel of the saddle, kept in place by the right hand grasping it at the "grip"; the left hand, holding the bridle rein, was invisible. In silhouette against the sky the profile of the horse was cut with the sharpness of a cameo; it looked across the heights of air to the confronting cliffs beyond. The face of the rider, turned slightly away, showed only an outline of temple and beard, he was looking downward to the bottom of the valley. Magnified by its lift against the sky and by the soldier's testifying sense of the formidableness of a near enemy the group appeared of heroic, almost colossal, size.

For an instant Druse had a strange, half-defined feeling that he had slept to the end of the war and was looking upon a noble work of art reared upon that eminence to commemorate the deeds of an heroic past of which he had been an inglorious part. The feeling was dispelled by a slight movement of the group: the horse, without moving its feet, had drawn its body slightly backward from the verge; the man remained immobile as before. Broad awake and keenly alive to the significance of the situation, Druse now brought the butt of his rifle against his cheek by cautiously pushing the barrel forward through the bushes, cocked the piece, and glancing through the sights covered a vital spot of the horseman's breast. A tough upon the trigger and all would have been well with Carter Druse. At that instant the horseman turned his head and looked in the direction of his concealed foeman seemed to look into his very face, into his eyes, into his brave, compassionate heart.

10   It is then so terrible to kill an enemy in war—an enemy who has surprised a secret vital to the safety of one's self and comrades—an enemy more formidable for his knowledge than all his army for its numbers? Carter Druse grew pale; he shook in every limb, turned faint, and saw the statuesque group before him as black figures, rising, falling, moving unsteadily in arcs of circles in a fiery sky. His hand fell away from his weapon, his head slowly dropped until his face rested on the leaves in which he lay. This courageous gentleman and hardy soldier was near swooning from intensity of emotion.

It was not for long; in another moment his face was raised from earth, his hands resumed their places on the rifle, his forefinger sought the trigger; mind, heart, and eyes were clear, conscience and reason sound. He could not hope to capture that enemy; to alarm him would but send him dashing to his camp with his fatal news. The duty of the soldier was plain: the man must be shot dead from ambush—without warning, without a moment's spiritual preparation, with never so much as an unspoken prayer, he must be sent to his account. But no—there is a hope; he may have discovered nothing—perhaps he is but admiring the sublimity of the landscape. If permitted, he may turn and ride carelessly away in the direction whence he came. Surely it will be possible to judge at the instant of his withdrawing whether he knows. It may well be that his fixity of attention—Druse turned his head and looked through the deeps of air downward, as from the surface to the bottom of a translucent sea. He saw creeping across the green meadow a sinuous line of figures of men and horses—some foolish commander was permitting the soldiers of his escort to water their beasts in the open, in plain view from a dozen summits!

Druse withdrew his eyes from the valley and fixed them again upon the group of man and horse in the sky, and again it was through the sights of his rifle. But this time his aim was at the horse. In his memory, as if they were a divine mandate, rang the words of his father at their parting: "Whatever may occur, do what you conceive to be your duty." He was calm now. His teeth were firmly but not rigidly closed; his nerves were as tranquil as a sleeping babe's—not a tremor affected any muscle of his body; his breathing, until suspended in the act of taking aim, was regular and slow. Duty had conquered; the spirit had said to the body; "Peace, be still." He fired.

III

An officer of the Federal force, who in a spirit of adventure or in quest of knowledge had left the hidden *bivouac* in the valley, and with aimless feet had made his way to the lower edge of a small open space near the foot of the cliff, was considering what he had to gain by pushing his exploration further. At a distance of a quarter-mile before him, but apparently at a stone's throw, rose from its fringe of pines the gigantic face of rock, towering to so great a height above him that it made him giddy to look up to where its edge cut a sharp, rugged line against the sky. It presented a clean, vertical profile against a background of blue sky to a point half the way down, and of distant hills, hardly less blue, thence to the tops of the trees at its base. Lifting his eyes to the dizzy altitude of its summit the officer saw an astonishing sight—a man on horseback riding down into the valley through the air!

Straight upright sat the rider, in military fashion, with a firm seat in the saddle, a strong clutch upon the rein to hold his charger from too impetuous a plunge. From his bare head his long hair streamed upward, waving like a plume. His hands were concealed in the cloud of the horse's lifted mane. The animal's body was as level as if every hoof encountered the resistant earth. Its motions were those of a wild gallop, but even as the officer looked they ceased, with all the legs thrown sharply forward as in the act of alighting from a leap. But this was a flight!

15   Filled with amazement and terror by this apparition of a horseman in the sky—half believing himself the chosen scribe of some new Apocalypse the officer was overcome by the intensity of his emotions; his legs failed him and he fell. Almost at the same instant he heard a crashing sound in the trees—a sound that died without an echo—and all was still.

The officer rose to his feet, trembling. The familiar sensation of an abraded shin recalled his dazed faculties. Pulling himself together he ran rapidly obliquely away from the cliff to a point distant from its foot; thereabout he expected to find his man; and thereabout he naturally failed. In the fleeting instant of his vision his imagination had been so wrought upon by the apparent grace and ease and intention of the marvelous performance that it did not occur to him that the line of march of aërial cavalry is directly downward, and that he could find the objects of his search at the very foot of the cliff. A half-hour later he returned to his camp.

This officer was a wise man; he knew better than to tell an incredible truth. He said nothing of what he had seen. But when the commander asked him if in his scout he had learned anything of advantage to the expedition he answered: "Yes, sir; there is no road leading down into this valley from the southward." The commander, knowing better, smiled.

IV

20   After firing his shot, Private Carter Druse reloaded his rifle and resumed his watch. Ten minutes had hardly passed when a Federal sergeant crept cautiously

to him on hands and knees. Druse neither turned his head nor looked at him, but lay without motion or sign of recognition.

"Did you fire?" the sergeant whispered.

"Yes."

"At what?"

"A horse. It was standing on yonder rock—pretty far out. You see it is no longer there. It went over the cliff."

25   The man's face was white, but he showed no other sign of emotion. Having answered, he turned away his eyes and said no more. The sergeant did not understand.

"See here, Druse," he said, after a moment's silence, "it's no use making a mystery. I order you to report. Was there anybody on the horse?"

"Yes."

"Well?"

"My father."

30   The sergeant rose to his feet and walked away. "Good God!" he said.

[1889]

Topics for Critical Thinking and Writing

1. The narrator ends the first paragraph by telling us that death is "the just and legal penalty" for a soldier who falls asleep at his post, and the second paragraph speaks of the sleeping sentinel as a "criminal." Is Bierce inventing a narrator who is supposed to make us uneasy, or is he speaking simply as a man who knows the rules of war, and whose ideals we are supposed to share?

2. Bierce shows us, at the beginning of Part 2, the rather formal exchange between the father and son. Does the exchange seem believable? Believable and admirable? Believable but less than admirable? Unbelievable? Explain.

3. In the middle of paragraph 7 Bierce speaks of "some invisible messenger of fate." Does the story as a whole suggest that our destinies are fated?

4. Beginning in paragraph 7 Bierce emphasizes Druse's "aesthetic delight" in his perception of "an equestrian statue of impressive dignity." In the next paragraph he speaks of a "noble work of art." Why the emphasis on the horseman as a work of art?

5. Is the story so improbable that it is of no interest, no value? Explain your position.

STEPHEN CRANE

Stephen Crane (1871–1900) was born in Newark, New Jersey, six years after the Civil War ended. His fame largely rests on his short novel about war, The Red Badge of Courage (1895), a novel so convincing that many readers who are vague about dates assume that Crane participated in the war.

By the time he was 20, Crane had dropped out of several institutions of higher learning. He turned to journalism to make a living, spending some of his time observing life in the slums, and in 1891, when he was 21, he finished a novel, Maggie, a Girl of the Streets, *about the slum life that he had seen.* Maggie *drew mixed reviews,* but The Red Badge of Courage *established him as a writer, and in the six months following its publication he wrote five more stories of the Civil War, including "An Episode of War." In his few remaining years—Crane died of tuberculosis before he was 30—he continued his careers as a journalist, a writer of fiction, and a poet.*

An Episode of War

The lieutenant's rubber blanket lay on the ground, and upon it he had poured the company's supply of coffee. Corporals and other representatives of the grimy and hot-throated men who lined the breast-work[1] had come for each squad's portion.

The lieutenant was frowning and serious at this task of division. His lips pursed as he drew with his sword various crevices in the heap, until brown squares of coffee, astoundingly equal in size, appeared on the blanket. He was on the verge of a great triumph in mathematics, and the corporals were thronging forward, each to reap a little square, when suddenly the lieutenant cried out and looked quickly at a man near him as if he suspected it was a case of personal assault. The others cried out also when they saw blood upon the lieutenant's sleeve.

He had winced like a man stung, swayed dangerously, and then straightened. The sound of his hoarse breathing was plainly audible. He looked sadly, mystically, over the breast-work at the green face of a wood, where now were many little puffs of white smoke. During this moment the men about him gazed statue-like and silent, astonished and awed by this catastrophe which happened when catastrophes were not expected—when they had leisure to observe it.

As the lieutenant stared at the wood, they too swung their heads, so that for another instant all hands, still silent, contemplated the distant forest as if their minds were fixed upon the mystery of a bullet's journey.

5   The officer had, of course, been compelled to take his sword into his left hand. He did not hold it by the hilt. He gripped it at the middle of the blade, awkwardly. Turning his eyes from the hostile wood, he looked at the sword as he held it there, and seemed puzzled as to what to do with it, where to put it. In short, this weapon had of a sudden become a strange thing to him. He looked at it in a kind of stupefaction, as if he had been endowed with a trident, a sceptre, or a spade.

Finally he tried to sheathe it. To sheathe a sword held by the left hand, at the middle of the blade, in a scabbard hung at the left hip, is a feat worthy of a sawdust ring.[2] This wounded officer engaged in a desperate struggle with the sword and the wobbling scabbard, and during the time of it he breathed like a wrestler.

But at this instant the men, the spectators, awoke from their stonelike poses and crowded forward sympathetically. The orderly-sergeant took the sword and tenderly placed it in the scabbard. At the time, he leaned nervously backward, and did not allow even his finger to brush the body of the lieutenant. A wound gives a strange dignity to him who bears it. Well men shy from this new and terrible majesty. It is as if the wounded man's hand is upon the curtain which hangs before the revelations of all existence—the meaning of ants, potentates, wars,

---

[1]**breast-work** a rough and temporary fortification, about chest-high, used as defense against an enemy; a parapet.   [2]**sawdust ring** a circus act; that which is performed in the ring of a circus.

cities, sunshine, snow, a feather dropped from a bird's wing; and the power of it sheds radiance upon a bloody form, and makes the other men understand sometimes that they are little. His comrades look at him with large eyes thoughtfully. Moreover, they fear vaguely that the weight of a finger upon him might send him headlong, precipitate the tragedy, hurl him at once into the dim, grey unknown. And so the orderly-sergeant, while sheathing the sword, leaned nervously backward.

There were others who proffered assistance. One timidly presented his shoulder and asked the lieutenant if he cared to lean upon it, but the latter waved him away mournfully. He wore the look of one who knows he is the victim of a terrible disease and understands his helplessness. He again stared over the breastwork at the forest, and then, turning, went slowly rearward. He held his right wrist tenderly in his left hand as if the wounded arm was made of very brittle glass.

And the men in silence stared at the wood, then at the departing lieutenant; then at the wood, then at the lieutenant.

10   As the wounded officer passed from the line of battle, he was enabled to see many things which as a participant in the fight were unknown to him. He saw a general on a black horse gazing over the lines of blue infantry at the green woods which veiled his problems. An aide galloped furiously, dragged his horse suddenly to a halt, saluted, and presented a paper. It was, for a wonder, precisely like a historical painting.

To the rear of the general and his staff a group, composed of a bugler, two or three orderlies, and the bearer of the corps standard, all upon maniacal horses, were working like slaves to hold their ground, preserve their respectful interval, while the shells boomed in the air about them, and caused their chargers to make furious quivering leaps.

A battery, a tumultuous and shining mass, was swirling toward the right. The wild thud of hoofs, the cries of the riders shouting blame and praise, menace and encouragement, and, last, the roar of the wheels, the slant of the glistening guns, brought the lieutenant to an intent pause. The battery swept in curves that stirred the heart; it made halts as dramatic as the crash of a wave on the rocks, and when it fled onward this aggregation of wheels, levers, motors had a beautiful unity, as if it were a missile. The sound of it was a war-chorus that reached into the depths of man's emotion.

The lieutenant, still holding his arm as it were of glass, stood watching this battery until all detail of it was lost, save the figures of the riders, which rose and fell and waved lashes over the black mass.

Later, he turned his eyes toward the battle, where the shooting sometimes crackled like bush-fires, sometimes sputtered with exasperating irregularity, and sometimes reverberated like the thunder. He saw the smoke rolling upward and saw crowds of men who ran and cheered, or stood and blazed away at the inscrutable distance.

15   He came upon some stragglers, and they told him how to find the field hospital. They described its exact location. In fact, these men, no longer having part in the battle, knew more of it than others. They told the performance of every corps, every division, the opinion of every general. The lieutenant, carrying his wounded arm rearward, looked upon them with wonder.

At the roadside a brigade was making coffee and buzzing with talk like a girls' boarding-school. Several officers came out to him and inquired concerning things of which he knew nothing. One, seeing his arm, began to scold, "Why, man, that's no way to do. You want to fix that thing." He appropriated the lieutenant and the lieutenant's wound. He cut the sleeve and laid bare the arm, every nerve of which softly fluttered under his touch. He bound his handkerchief over the wound, scolding away in the meantime. His tone allowed one to think that he was in the habit of being wounded every day. The lieutenant hung his head, feeling, in this presence, that he did not know how to be correctly wounded.

The low white tents of the hospital were grouped around an old schoolhouse. There was here a singular commotion. In the foreground two ambulances interlocked wheels in the deep mud. The drivers were tossing the blame of it back and forth, gesticulating and berating, while from the ambulances, both crammed with wounded, there came an occasional groan. An interminable crowd of bandaged men were coming and going. Great numbers sat under the trees nursing heads or arms or legs. There was a dispute of some kind raging on the steps of the schoolhouse. Sitting with his back against a tree a man with a face as grey as a new army blanket was serenely smoking a corncob pipe. The lieutenant wished to rush forward and inform him that he was dying.

A busy surgeon was passing near the lieutenant. "Good morning," he said, with a friendly smile. Then he caught sight of the lieutenant's arm, and his face at once changed. "Well, let's have a look at it." He seemed possessed suddenly of a great contempt for the lieutenant. This wound evidently placed the latter on a very low social plane. The doctor cried out impatiently: "What mutton-head had tied it up that way anyhow?" The lieutenant replied, "Oh, a man."

When the wound was disclosed the doctor fingered it disdainfully. "Humph," he said. "You come along with me and I'll tend to you." His voice contained the same scorn as if he were saying: "You will have to go to jail."

20   The lieutenant had been very meek, but now his face was flushed, and he looked into the doctor's eyes. "I guess I won't have it amputated," he said.

"Nonsense, man! Nonsense! Nonsense!" cried the doctor. "Come along, now. I won't amputate it. Come along. Don't be a baby."

"Let go of me," said the lieutenant, holding back wrathfully, his glance fixed upon the door of the old schoolhouse, as sinister to him as the portals of death.

And this is the story of how the lieutenant lost his arm. When his reached home, his sisters, his mother, his wife, sobbed for a long time at the sight of the flat sleeve. "Oh, well," he said, standing shamefaced amid these tears, "I don't suppose it matters so much as all that."

[1899]

Topics for Critical Writing and Thinking

1. Why do you suppose that Crane has the officer wounded while *not* engaged in combat? Would the story be a very different story if, say, shots had been exchanged and the lieutenant, in an effort to see where the enemy soldiers were, had bravely left a concealed position and in the process was wounded?
2. In paragraph 10 we are told that when the lieutenant leaves the line of battle he sees a general on a horse, an aide who is galloping and who suddenly halts his horse and salutes, very much "like a historical painting." And in paragraph

12 he sees a battery that "stirred the heart . . . [and that] reached into the depths of a man's emotion." What is Crane saying about war?

3. What do you make of the last line of the story, where the lieutenant, attended by his sobbing family, says of the loss of his arm, "I don't suppose it matters so much as all that"?

POETRY

DANIEL DECATUR EMMETT

Daniel Decatur Emmett (1815–1904) was born in Mount Vernon, Ohio. At the age of 16 he ran away, joined a traveling circus, and performed songs of his own composition while playing the banjo. In 1842 he and three friends formed the Virginia Minstrels, the first black-face minstrel company in the United States. The company was highly successful, and their makeup and costume—burnt cork, and white trousers, striped shirt, and blue swallowtail coat—became standard for all later minstrels. Tradition says that in December, 1859, when business was slow, he was urged to create a new song, "something the bands will play and the boys will whistle in the street." A few days later, still uninspired, he said to his wife, "What a morning! I wish I was in Dixie, in Dixie," a show-biz term used when things were not going well, meaning, in effect, "I wish I were south of the Mason-Dixon line, where the weather is good." According to Emmett, this remark provided the inspiration that he needed.

The first performance in the South seems to have been in Charleston, South Carolina, in December, 1860; by the spring of 1861 it had been adopted in the South as a militant, defiant song, a sort of counterpart to the North's use of "John Brown's Body." It was played in Montgomery, Alabama, when the Confederacy was provisionally established, and it was the first song played at the inauguration of Jefferson Davis.

Emmett is also reputed to be the author of "Old Dan Tucker" and "The Blue-Tail Fly" ("Jimmy Crack Corn").

The spelling in the song below is an attempt to capture the pronunciation of African Americans in the South. Such efforts to reproduce the speech of particular groups—Yankees, Irish Americans, the descendants of the French in Louisiana, and so forth—are part of the Local Color movement in American literature, a movement that sought to convey the distinctive qualities of the people of a particular region. Mark Twain and Joel Chandler Harris, writing about the South, were part of this movement, and Mary E. Wilkins Freeman and Sarah Orne Jewett, writing about New England, were as well. The tradition continued into the first third of the twentieth century in the work, for example, of Zora Neale Hurston, an African American writer and a professional student of folklore, whose story "Sweat" we include in this book. (The first line of dialogue in the story is, "Sykes, what you throw dat whip on me like dat?")

Dixie's Land

I wish I was in de land ob cotton,
Old times dar am not forgotten,
   Look away! Look away! Look away! Dixie Land.

In Dixie Land whar I was born in,
Early on one frosty mornin,   5
   Look away! Look away! Look away! Dixie Land.

    Den I wish I was in Dixie
     Hooray! Hooray!
   In Dixie Land, I'll took my stand,
    To lib an die in Dixie,   10
   Away, Away, Away down south in Dixie,
   Away, Away, Away down south in Dixie.

Old Missus marry "Will-de-weaber,"
Willium was a gay deceaber,"
   Look away! Look away! Look away! Dixie Land.   15
But when he put his arm around 'er,
He smiled as fierce as a forty pounder.
   Look away! Look away! Look away! Dixie Land.

   Chorus.

His face was sharp as butcher's cleaber,
But dat did not seem to greab 'er;   20
   Look away! Look away! Look away! Dixie Land.
Old Missus acted de foolish part,
And died for a man dat broke her heart.
   Look away! Look away! Look away! Dixie Land.

   Chorus.

Now here's a health to the next old Missus,   25
An all de gals dat want to kiss us;
   Look away! Look away! Look away! Dixie Land
But if you want to drive 'way sorrow,
Come and hear dis song to-morrow.
   Look away! Look away! Look away! Dixie Land.   30

   Chorus.

Dar's buck-wheat cakes an Ingen' batter,
Makes you fat or a little fatter;
   Look away! Look away! Look away! Dixie Land.
Den hoe it down an scratch your grabble,
To Dixie land I'm bound to trabble.
   Look away! Look away! Look away! Dixie Land.   35

   Chorus.

Topics for Critical Thinking and Writing

1. Do you find the representation of African American speech in this song to be offensive? When dialect or "local color" idioms are used in a song or literary work, does it make a difference who the author is? A member of the group? Someone who is not a member of the group?

2. Putting aside the dialect—imagine that the words are all spelled correctly—do you think the song is demeaning to African Americans? Explain.
3. Perhaps you have played or sung "Dixie," and even if you have not you know that it is popular. How do you account for its popularity?
4. Emmett's song originally included the following verse, but it was omitted because he was advised that religious people might object to it.

> Dis worl' was made in jiss six days,
> An' finished up in various ways;
> > Look away! Look away! Look away! Dixie Land!
> Dey den made Dixie trim and nice,
> But Adam called it "paradise,"
> > Look away! Look away! Look away! Dixie Land!

If you are a believer, do you find the lines offensive? Why, or why not? If you are not a believer, try to put yourself in the shoes of someone who is, and then give your response.

JULIA WARD HOWE

Julia Ward Howe (1819–1910) was born in New York City. A social reformer, her work for the emancipation of African Americans and the right of women to vote is notable. She was the first woman to be elected to the American Academy of Arts and Letters.

Battle Hymn of the Republic

> Mine eyes have seem the glory of the coming of the Lord;
> He is trampling out the vintage where the grapes of wrath are stored;
> He hath loosed the fateful lightning of his terrible swift sword;
> > His truth is marching on.   4

> *Chorus*
> > Glory! glory! Hallelujah!
> > Glory! glory! Hallelujah!
> > Glory! glory! Hallelujah!
> > > His truth is marching on!   8

> I have seen him in the watch-fires of a hundred circling camps;
> They have builded him an altar in the evening dews and damps;
> I can read his righteous sentence by the dim and flaring lamps;
> > His day is marching on.   12

> I have read a fiery gospel, writ in burnished rows of steel;
> "As ye deal with my contemners, so with you my grace shall deal;
> Let the Hero, born of woman, crush the serpent with his heel;
> > Since God is marching on."   16

> He has sounded forth the trumpet that shall never call retreat;
> He is sifting out the hearts of men before his judgment seat;
> Oh, be swift, my soul, to answer him! be jubilant, my feet!
> > Our God is marching on.   20

In the beauty of the lilies Christ was born across the sea,
With a glory is his bosom that transfigures you and me;
As he died to make men holy, let us die to make men free,
    While God is marching on.   24

[1861]

Topics for Critical Thinking and Writing

1. This poem of the Civil War, written to the tune of "John Brown's Body," draws some of its militant imagery from the Bible, especially from Isaiah 63.1–6 and Revelation 19.11–15. Do you think the lines about Christ are inappropriate here? Explain.
2. If you know the tune to which "Battle Hymn of the Republic" is sung, think about the interplay between the music and the words. Do you think people have a different response to Howe's words when they read her text as a poem, rather than experienced it as a song?

HERMAN MELVILLE

Herman Melville (1819–1891) was born into a prosperous family in New York City. The bankruptcy and death of his father when Melville was 12 forced the boy to leave school. During his early years he worked first as a bank clerk, then as a farm laborer, then as a store clerk and a bookkeeper, and then as a schoolmaster. In 1837 he sailed to England as a cabin boy and signed on for other voyages, notably on whalers in the South Pacific, where he spent time in the Marquesas Islands and Tahiti. Out of his marine adventures he produced commercially successful books, Typee *(1846),* Omoo *(1847),* Mardi *(1849), and* Redburn *(1849), but the book for which he is best known today,* Moby Dick *(1851), was a commercial failure. In 1866 a book of poems about the Civil War—we print three of the poems here—was published, but it, too, was a failure. Abandoning his attempt to live by his pen, Melville survived on some inherited money, and on a political appointment as a customs inspector in New York City.*

The March into Virginia,

*Ending in the First Manassas.**

(July, 1861)

Did all the lets° and bars appear
    To every just or larger end,
Whence should come the trust and cheer?
    Youth must its ignorant impulse lend—
Age finds place in the rear.   5

---

* **First Manassas** or the First Battle of Bull Run (July 1861), fought near Manassas, Virginia, was a Confederate victory. The final line of the poem alludes to the Second Battle of Manassas, fought in August 1862, when Union forces were again defeated.   **1 lets** impediments.

All wars are boyish, and are fought by boys,
The champions and enthusiasts of the state:
    Turbid ardors and vain joys
        Not barrenly abate—
    Stimulants to the power mature,   10
        Preparatives of fate.

Who here forecasteth the event?°
What heart but spurns at precedent
And warning of the wise,
Contemned foreclosures of surprise?   15
The banners play, the bugles call,
The air is blue and prodigal.
    No berrying party, pleasure-wooed,
No picnic party in the May,
Ever went less loth than they   20
    Into that leafy neighborhood.
In Bacchic glee° they file toward Fate,
Moloch's° uninitiate;
Expectancy; and glad surmise
Of battle's unknown mysteries.   25

All they feel is this: 'tis glory,
A rapture sharp, though transitory,
Yet lasting in belaureled story.
So they gayly go to fight,
Chatting left and laughing right.   30

But some who this blithe mood present,
    As on in lightsome files they fare,
Shall die experienced ere three days are spent—
    Perish, enlightened by the vollied glare;
Or shame survive, and, like to adamant,   35
    The throe of Second Manassas share.

[1866]

12 **event** outcome.   22 **Bacchic glee** with the glee inspired by Bacchus, Roman god of wine.
23 **Moloch** ancient Semite god to whom children were sacrificed.

Topics for Critical Thinking and Writing

1. Taking into account the entire first stanza, explicate Melville's assertion (line 6) that "All wars are boyish, and are fought by boys." Further, putting aside the issue of whether you agree that "all wars are boyish," write an essay of 250 words indicating why you do or do not think the first stanza offers a tiresome lecture.
2. In line 18 Melville speaks of a "berrying party." Some readers find a grim pun here on "burying-party." There is no way of knowing if Melville intended a pun or not, but do you think the pun enriches the line? Why, or why not? And, speaking of puns, do you agree that in line 34 Melville must have intended a pun in "enlightened"?

DuPont's Round Fight*

(November, 1861)

In time and measure perfect moves
    All Art whose aim is sure;
Evolving rhyme and stars divine
    Have rules, and they endure.   4

Nor less the Fleet that warred for Right,
    And, warring so, prevailed,
In geometric beauty curved,
    And in an orbit sailed.   8

The rebel at Port Royal felt
    The Unity overawe,
And rued the spell. A type was here,
    And victory of LAW.   12

[1866]

* At the Battle of Port Royal Sound (South Carolina), November 7, 1861, Commander Samuel Francis DuPont led a Union squadron of ships that sailed down the Broad River, assaulted Fort Beauregard on the north, reloaded on the elliptical return, bombarded Fort Walker, two and a half miles south, and continued the circuit to bombard Fort Beauregard again, and so on for four and a half hours, finally destroying and capturing both forts.

Topics for Critical Thinking and Writing

1. In the first stanza Melville says that all art is characterized by "measure." Take any art in which you have some interest—poetry, potting, dancing, music, whatever—and explain in an essay of 250 words how "measure" is essential.
2. In the third line Melville says that the stars no less than poems "have rules." What is he getting at?
3. Check a dictionary for the various meanings of "type," and see which meaning best fits line 11.

Shiloh*

A Requiem

(April, 1862)

Skimming lightly, wheeling still,
    The swallows fly low
Over the field in clouded days,
    The forest-field of Shiloh—

* **Shiloh,** Tennessee, was the scene of a Confederate victory on Sunday, April 10, 1862, but the losses on both sides were enormous.

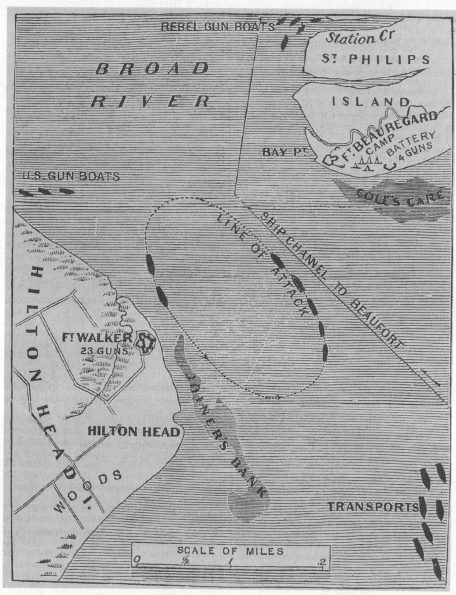

Plan of the Battle of Port Royal, South Carolina. Printed in the *New York Herald Tribune* showing the elliptical movement that DuPont's squadron took, destroying Fort Beauregard in the upper right, and Fort Walker on the left. Melville almost certainly used this map as the basis for his poem. (Map by G.C. Plicque from "The Rebellion Record" by GP Putnam, 1862.)

Over the field where April rain   5
Solaced the parched ones stretched in pain
Through the pause of night
That followed the Sunday fight
    Around the church of Shiloh—
The church so lone, the log-built one,   10

That echoed to many a parting grown
    And natural prayer
Of dying foemen mingled there—
Foemen at morn, but friends at eve—
    Fame or country least their care: 15
(What like a bullet can undeceive!)
    But now they lie low,
While over them the swallows skim,
    And all is hushed at Shiloh.

[1866]

Topic for Critical Thinking and Writing

Certainly the speaker feels deeply sympathetic toward the dead, but what does he feel besides sympathy? To what degree is it suggested that the battle was fought in vain? What paradoxes are here? Are the paradoxes in the language or in the situation?

SIDNEY LANIER

*Sidney Lanier (1842–1881), born in Macon, Georgia, served with the Confederate Army and was taken as prisoner of war. After the war, he wrote a novel based on his war experience (*Tiger-Lilies *[1867]), and he then turned to lecturing on English literature at Johns Hopkins. An accomplished musician, in* The Science of English Verse *(1880) Lanier set forth the theory that music and poetry are governed by the same principles, and that therefore time, not accent, is the chief element in poetry.*

    We reprint Lanier's poem on the death of General Thomas J. Jackson, known as Stonewall Jackson, the Confederate general who was accidentally killed by his own men at the Battle of Chancellorsville (1863). The Confederate Army won the battle, but it cost them one of their best officers, and it was their last important victory.

The Dying Words of Jackson

"Order A. P. Hill to prepare for battle."
"Tell Major Hawks to advance the Commissary train."
"Let us cross the river and rest in the shade."

The stars of Night contain the glittering Day,
And rain his glory down with sweeter grace
Upon the dark World's grand, enchanted face
    All loth to turn away.   4

And so the Day, about to yield his breath,
Utters the Stars unto the listening Night

Women at the grave of Stonewall Jackson. (Photograph by Bonde & Miley, 1866. Virginia Military Institute.)

To stand for burning fare-thee-wells of light
    Said on the verge of death.   8

O hero-life that lit us like the Sun!
O hero-words that glittered like the Stars
And stood and shone above the gloomy wars
    When the hero-life was done!   12

The Phantoms of a battle came to dwell
In the fitful vision of his dying eyes—
Yet even in battle-dreams, he sends supplies
    To those he loved so well.   16

His army stands in battle-line arrayed:
His couriers fly: all's done—now God decide!
And not till then saw he the Other Side
    Or would accept the Shade.   20

Thou Land whose Sun is gone, thy Stars remain!
Still shine the words that miniature his deeds—
O Thrice-Beloved, where'er they great heart bleeds,
    Solace has thou for pain!   24

[1865]

Topics for Critical Thinking and Writing

1. The first three lines, in italic type, are Jackson's dying words. What do they reveal of Jackson? (See especially lines 13–20.)
2. The first stanza is perhaps a bit obscure. How would you paraphrase it?
3. Jackson is compared to the sun and the stars. What are the points of comparison? Does it make sense to compare any human being to celestial bodies? What are some other poems that make such comparisons?
4. Speaking of comparisons, Jackson's nickname, "Stonewall," involves a comparison. (If you don't know how he acquired the name, check a biographical account.) If you can think of any other military figures who acquired nicknames that characterized them, jot them down and be prepared in class to discuss the persons and the figures of speech.
5. Summarize each stanza in a phrase or sentence, and then see if the poem has a shape, a pattern. Does it seem to progress meaningfully or could the stanzas just as well be rearranged? Please explain your response.

WALT WHITMAN

Walt Whitman (1819–1892) was born on Long Island, the son of a farmer. The young Whitman taught school, worked as a carpenter, a printer, a newspaper editor, and, during the Civil War, as a volunteer nurse on the Union side. In Whitman's own day, his poetry was highly controversial because of its expansive form (formlessness, many people said) and its eroticism. His major work, Leaves of Grass, *was first published in 1855, and he revised and expanded it a number of times. One admirer, Ralph Waldo Emerson, told Whitman in 1855 that he found* Leaves of Grass *"the most extraordinary piece of wit and wisdom that America has yet contributed." Another, Henry David Thoreau, wrote in a letter in 1856 to a friend that* Leaves of Grass *"exhilarated" and "encouraged" him: "we ought greatly to rejoice in Whitman."*

Reconciliation

Word over all, beautiful as the sky,
Beautiful that war and all its deeds of carnage must in time be utterly lost.
That the hands of the sisters Death and Night incessantly softly wash again,
    and ever again, this soil'd world;
For my enemy is dead, a man divine as myself is dead,
I look where he lies white-faced and still in the coffin—I draw near,   5
Bend down and touch lightly with my lips the white face in the coffin.

[1865–66]

Topics for Critical Thinking and Writing

1. "Reconcile" means to "restore to friendship, compatibility, or harmony." What is happening in the scene of reconciliation that Whitman describes?
2. Does this poem make you uncomfortable? How would Whitman reply to someone who had such as response?
3. Whitman wrote this poem in the same year that the Civil War ended, a war in which, in the words of one scholar, "at least 618,000 Americans died, 360,000 on the Union side and 258,000 on the Confederate." Wasn't Whitman mistaken to imagine that "reconciliation" could take place so soon?
4. Do you think we should always become "reconciled" with our enemies? Can you imagine a situation when this would be impossible?
5. In the second line of the poem, Whitman seems to be claiming that the passage of time will cause the horrors of war to become "lost," to disappear from memory. Does he really believe this? Do you believe it? If you do not, how does this affect your response to the poem?

Vigil Strange I Kept on the Field One Night

Vigil strange I kept on the field one night;
When you my son and my comrade dropt at my side that day,
One look I but gave which your dear eyes return'd with a look I shall never
    forget,
One touch of your hand to mine O boy, reach'd up as you lay on the
    ground,
Then onward I sped in the battle, the even-contested battle,   5
Till late in the night reliev'd to the place at last again I made my way,
Found you in death so cold dear comrade, found your body son of
    responding kisses, (never again on earth responding,)
Bared your face in the starlight, curious the scene, cool blew the moderate
    night-wind,
Long there and then in vigil I stood, dimly around me the battlefield
    spreading,
Vigil wondrous and vigil sweet there in the fragrant silent night,   10
But not a tear fell, not even a long-drawn sigh, long I gazed,
Then on the earth partially reclining sat by your side leaning my chin in my
    hands,
Passing sweet hours, immortal and mystic hours with you dearest comrade
    — not a tear, not a word,
Vigil of silence, love and death, vigil for you my son and my soldier,
As onward silently stars aloft, eastward new ones upward stole,   15
Vigil final for you brave boy, (I could not save you, swift was your death,
I faithfully loved you and cared for you living, I think we shall surely meet
    again,)
Till at latest lingering of the night, indeed just as the dawn appear'd,
My comrade I wrapt in his blanket, envelop'd well his form,

Folded the blanket well, tucking it carefully over head and
    carefully under feet,   20
And there and then and bathed by the rising sun, my son in his grave, in
    his rude-dug grave I deposited,
Ending my vigil strange with that, vigil of night and battle-field dim,
Vigil for boy of responding kisses, (never again on earth responding,)
Vigil for comrade swiftly slain, vigil I never forget, how as day brighten'd,
I rose from the chill ground and folded my soldier well in his blanket,   25
And buried him where he fell.

[1865–66]

Topics for Critical Thinking and Writing

1. "Vigil" has a number of related but different meanings: "a watch formerly kept on the night before a religious feast and customarily spent in prayer or other devotions; the day before a religious feast observed as a day of spiritual preparation; a religious service on the morning of the day before a holy day; evening or nocturnal devotions or prayers; the act or action of keeping awake especially at times when sleep is customary." What is the nature of the "vigil" that Whitman depicts?
2. Do you find this poem erotic? Do you think that Whitman did?
3. One scholar has praised this poem ass "hauntingly beautiful," while another has said that he finds it "creepy and disturbing." Which of these responses do you share? Where in the text do you find evidence for your response?
4. This poem is longer and more detailed than "Reconciliation." Which poem is better? How would you seek to prove your case? Can we really show that one poem is better than another, or is it finally just a matter of personal preference?

ANDREW HUDGINS

Andrew Hudgins was born in Killen, Texas in 1951, and educated at Huntington College, the University of Alabama, and the University of Iowa. The author of several books of poetry and a book of essays, The Glass Anvil *(1997), Hudgins has received important awards, and has taught at Baylor University, the University of Cincinnati, and Ohio State University.*

*At Chancellorsville**

The Battle of the Wilderness

He was an Indiana corporal
shot in the thigh when their line broke
in animal disarray. He'd crawled
into the shade and bled to death.

---

* **Chancellorsville** site of a Confederate victory (May 1–4, 1863) in Virginia.

My uniform was shabby with
continuous wear, worn down to threads
by the inside friction of my flesh on cloth.
The armpit seams were rotted through
and almost half the buttons had dropped off.
My brother said I should remove   10
the Yank's clean shirt: "From now on, Sid,
he'll have no use for it." Imagining
the slack flesh shifting underneath
my hands, the other-person stink
of that man's shirt, so newly his,   15
I cursed Clifford from his eyeballs to
his feet. I'd never talked that way before
and didn't know I could. When we returned,
someone had beat me to the shirt.
So I had compromised my soul   20
for nothing I would want to use—
some knowledge I could do without.
Clifford, thank God, just laughed. It was good
stout wool, unmarked by blood.
By autumn, we wore so much blue   25
we could pass for New York infantry.

[1985]

Topics for Critical Thinking and Writing

1. In an interview published in 2002, Andrew Hudgins states he is "both fascinated and horrified" by violence. Do you find this double attitude expressed in
   his poem?

2. In the same interview, Hudgins says, "Southerners find humor in violence,"
   adding, "I know that things that I routinely think are funny horrify Northerners."
   Is there humor in this poem? Does Hudgins's claim about the difference between Southerners and Northerners strike you as a gross exaggeration, or do
   you think there's something to it?

3. Hudgins also maintains in this interview that there is a kind of "violence" in the
   very act of writing a poem: "Something that's new destroys certain ways of
   looking at the world." Does this comment apply to "At Chancellorsville"?
   Please explain and support your explanation with evidence from the text.

4. One critic has noted that the final lines of the poem are "highly ironic." Do you
   agree?

5. Does our response to Hudgins's poem change when we remember that the
   speaker and his brother fought for a regime that supported slavery? Can you
   imagine fighting on the side of the South? How would you defend such a
   decision?

THE GREAT DEPRESSION

SHORT VIEWS

I have no fears for the future of our country. It is bright with hope.
    Herbert Hoover, president, on March 4, 1929

Like an earthquake, the stock market crash of October 1929 cracked star-tlingly across the United States, the herald of a crisis that was to shake the American way of life to its foundations. The events of the ensuing decade opened a fissure across the landscape of American history no less gaping than that opened by to volley on Lexington Common in April 1775 or by the bombardment of Sumter on another April four score and six years later.
    David M. Kennedy, *Freedom from Fear: The American People in Depression and War, 1929–1945* (1999)

Where once feet stamped over the oily floor,
Dinnerpails clattered, voices rose and fell
In laughter, curses, and songs. Now the guts
Of this mill have ceased their rumbling, now
The fires are banked and red changes to black,
Steam is cold water, silence is rust, and quiet
Spells hunger. Look at these men, now,
Standing before the iron gates, mumbling,
"Who could believe it? Who could believe it?"
    Joseph Kalar, "Papermill" (excerpt), 1931

Men who lost their jobs dropped out of sight. They were quiet; and you had to know just when and where to find them: at night, for instance, on the edge of town huddling for warmth around a bonfire, or even the mu-nicipal incinerator; at dawn, picking over the garbage dump for scraps of food or salvageable clothing.
    Fortune magazine, 1932

If you think the system is working, ask someone who isn't.
    Anonymous

I pledge you, I pledge myself, to a new deal for the American people.
    Franklin Delano Roosevelt, speech accepting the Democratic nomination for president, 1932

Will the New Deal Be a Square Deal for the Negro?
    Jesse O. Thomas, title of an essay in *Opportunity: Journal of Negro Life*, October, 1933

> *With the slow menace of a glacier, depression came on. No one had any measure of its progress; no one had any plan for stopping it. Everyone tried to get out of its way.*
>   Frances Perkins, *People at Work*, 1934

> *At that time hitch-hiking was not so good. People were afraid to trust strangers in their automobiles. The people that would give anyone a ride, did not want their car dirtyed up by bums like us.*
>   Eluard McDaniel, *Bumming in California*, 1937

> *I see one-third of a nation ill-housed, ill-clothed, ill-nourished.*
>   Franklin Delano Roosevelt, president, 1937

> *Buddy, can you spare a dime?*
>   Common saying throughout the 1930s

Topics for Critical Thinking and Writing

1. What do you know about the Great Depression? What about this period would you like to learn more about? What would be the source materials you'd need to consult, and how would you locate them?
2. It is sometimes said that Americans today need the experience of an economic "depression." Isn't this a foolish, even cruel thing to say? Why might someone make such a statement? Do you think there's any truth to it?
3. President Roosevelt said he was working on a "new deal" for the American people. What made his programs and policies "new"? Note: For background, consult the entries on "The New Deal" in *The Reader's Companion to American History*, ed. Eric Foner and John A. Garraty (1991) or *The Oxford Companion to United States History*, ed. Paul S. Boyer (2001).
4. Many people lost their jobs, and many become desperately poor, during the "Depression decade" of the 1930s. Have you, or someone close to you, suddenly lost a job? Why? What happened as a result? Do you know anyone who is poor? How do they live?
5. Has someone ever asked you the equivalent of "Buddy, can you spare a dime?" What was your response? Has this happened often? Do you always respond the same way?

BEN SHAHN

Ben Shahn (1898–1969) came to New York City from Lithuania at the age of 8. As a young man he apprenticed in a lithography shop in Manhattan, then studied drawing and painting, and soon established himself as a significant painter. Shahn was also active as a photographer, devoting much of his time in the 1930s to photographing the plight of unemployed workers during the Depression that began in 1929. The two photographs we reproduce were taken in 1936.

Untitled Photographs
(New York City)

Ben Shahn, Left: *Untitled #1, New York City*, 1931 [1998.135.16-17]. Right: *Untitled #2, New York City*, 1931 [1998.135.16–18]. Harvard University Art Museums, Gift of Bernarda Bryson Shahn Art © The Estate of Ben Shahn/Licensed by VAGA, New York, NY

Topics for Critical Thinking and Writing

1. The chief differences between the two images are (a) the photographer's distance from his subject, and (b) the tilt of the camera, more evident in the picture at the right than in the one at the left? Is one picture better than the other? If so, why?
2. Take one of these pictures and explain why you think it is a good photograph, a so-so photograph, or a poor photograph.
3. How large a part of your evaluation is based on the ironic contrast between the man, who presumably is weary and despondent, and the advertisement, which shows a rather jaunty figure? If you believe the photo is good, is it because of this forceful contrast? If you believe the photo is not so good, it is because the contrast is too obvious?
4. If you were told that Shahn had posed the man, would your evaluation of the photograph change? Explain.
5. If you were told that the man shielded his face from the camera in an effort to preserve his dignity, would your evaluation of the photograph change? Explain.

INTERVIEWS

STUDS TERKEL

Studs Terkel, born Louis Terkel in New York City in 1912, was brought to Chicago at the age of 11. After graduating from the University of Chicago in 1934, where he received a law degree, he acted, produced radio shows, wrote columns, and served as a news commentator and a disc jockey, but he is best known as the man who makes books out of interviews. Among his books are Division Street: America *(1966),* Working *(1974),* Race *(19xx?),* American Dreams Lost and Found *(1999), and (the source of the material that we reprint here)* Hard Times: An Oral History of the Great Depression *(1970).*

Emma Tiller

At the time, she lived and worked in western Texas as a cook.

When tramps and hoboes would come to their door for food, the southern white people would drive them away. But if a Negro come, they will feed him. They'll even give him money. They'll ask them: Do you smoke, do you dip snuff? Yes, ma'am, yes, ma'am. They was always nice in a nasty way to Negroes. But their own color, they wouldn't do *that* for 'em.

They would hire Negroes for these type jobs where they wouldn't hire whites. They wouldn't hire a white woman to do housework, because they were afraid she'd take her husband.

When the Negro woman would say, "Miz So-and-So, we got some cold food in the kitchen left from lunch. Why don't you give it to 'im?" she'll say, "Oh, no, don't give 'im nothin'. He'll be back tomorrow with a gang of 'em. He ought to get a job and work."

The Negro woman who worked for the white woman would take the food and wrap it in newspapers. Sometimes we would hurry down the alley and holler at 'im: "Hey, mister, come here!" And we'd say, "Come back by after a while and I'll put some food in a bag, and I'll sit down aside the garbage can so they won't see it." Then he'd get food, and we'd swipe a bar of soap and a face razor or somethin', stick it in there for 'im. Negroes would always feed these tramps.

5 Sometimes we would see them on the railroad tracks pickin' up stuff, and we would tell 'em: "Come to our house." They would come by and we would give 'em an old shirt or a pair of pants or some old shoes. We would always give 'em food.

Many times I have gone in my house and taken my husband's old shoes— some of 'em he needed hisself, but that other man was in worser shape than he was. Regardless of whether it was Negro or white, we would give to 'em.

We would gather stuff out in the field, pull our corn, roastin' ears, and put 'em in a cloth bag, because a paper bag would tear. When they get hungry, they can stop and build a fire and roast this corn. We did that ourselves, we loved it like that. And given them salt and stuff we figured would last 'em until he gets to the next place.

[1920]

Topic for Critical Thinking and Writing

How do you explain the behavior of whites described in Tiller's first paragraph?

Cesar Chavez

Like so many who have worked from early childhood, particularly in the open country, he appears older than his forty-one years. His manner is diffident, his voice soft.

He is president of the United Farm Workers of America (UFWA). It is, unlike craft and industrial unions, a quite new labor fraternity. In contrast to these others, agricultural workers—those who "follow the crops"—had been excluded from many of the benefits that came along with the New Deal.

[Chavez died in 1993.]

Oh, I remember having to move out of our house. My father had brought in a team of horses and wagons. We had always lived in that house, and we couldn't understand why we were moving out. When we got to the other house, it was a worse house, a poor house. That must have been around 1934. I was about six years old.

It's known as the North Gila Valley, about fifty miles north of Yuma. My dad was being turned out of his small plot of land. He had inherited this from his father, who had homesteaded it. I saw my two, three other uncles also moving out. And for the same reason. The bank had foreclosed on the loan.

If the local bank approved, the Government would guarantee the loan and small farmers like my father would continue in business. It so happened the president of the bank was the guy who most wanted our land. We were surrounded by him: he owned all the land around us. Of course, he wouldn't pass the loan.

One morning a giant tractor came in, like we had never seen before. My daddy used to all his work with horses. So this huge tractor came in and began to knock down this corral, this small corral where my father kept his horses. We didn't understand why. In the matter of a week, the whole face of the land was changed. Ditches were dug, and it was different. I didn't like it as much.

5   We all of us climbed into an old Chevy that my dad had. And then we were in California, and migratory workers. There were five kids—a small family by those standards. It must have been around '36. I was about eight. Well, it was a strange life. We had been poor, but we knew every night there was a bed *there*, and that *this* was our room. There was a kitchen. It was sort of a settled life, and we had chicken and hogs, eggs and all those things. But that all of a sudden changed. When you're small, you can't figure these things out. You know something's not right and you don't like it, but you don't question it and you don't let that get you down. You sort of just continue to move.

But this had quite an impact on my father. He had been used to owning the land and all of a sudden there was no more land. What I heard . . . what I made out of conversations between my mother and my father—things like, we'll work this season and then we'll get enough money and we'll go and buy a piece of land in Arizona. Things like that. Became like a habit. He never gave up hope that some day he would come back and get a little piece of land.

I can understand very, very well this feeling. These conversations were sort of melancholy. I guess my brothers and my sisters could also see this very sad look on my father's face.

That piece of land he wanted . . . ?

No, never. It never happened. He stopped talking about that some years ago. The drive for land, it's a very powerful drive.

When we moved to California, we would work after school. Sometimes we wouldn't go. "Following the crops," we missed much school. Trying to get enough money to stay alive the following winter, the whole family picking apricots, walnuts, prunes. We were pretty new, we had never been migratory workers. We were taken advantage quite a bit by the labor contractor and the crew pusher.[1] In some pretty silly ways. (Laughs.)

10   Sometimes we can't help but laugh about it. We trusted everybody that came around. You're traveling in California with all your belongings in your car: it's obvious. Those days we didn't have a trailer. This is bait for the labor contractor. Anywhere we stopped, there was a labor contractor offering all kinds of jobs and good wages, and we were always deceived by them and we always went. Trust them.

Coming into San Jose, not finding—being lied to, that there was work. We had no money at all, and had to live on the outskirts of town under a bridge and dry creek. That wasn't really unbearable. What was unbearable was so many families living just a quarter of a mile. And you know how kids are. They'd bring in those things that really hurt us quite a bit. Most of those kids were middle-class families.

We got hooked on a real scheme once. We were going by Fresno on our way to Delano. We stopped at some service station and this labor contractor saw the car. He offered a lot of money. We went. We worked the first week: the grapes were pretty bad and we couldn't make much. We all stayed off from school in order to make some money. Saturday we were to be paid and we didn't get paid. He came and said the winery hadn't paid him. We'd have the money next week. He gave us $10. My dad took the $10 and went to the store and bought $10 worth of groceries. So we worked another week and in the middle of the second week, my father was asking him for his last week's pay, and he had the same excuse. This went on and we'd get $5 or $10 or $7 a week for about four weeks. For the whole family.

So one morning my father made the resolution no more work. If he doesn't pay us, we won't work. We got in a car and went over to see him. The house was empty. He had left. The winery said they had paid him and they showed us where they had paid him. This man had taken it. . . .

One of the experiences I had. We went through Indio, California. Along the highway there were signs in most of the small restaurants that said "White Trade Only." My dad read English, but he didn't really know the meaning. He went in to get some coffee—a pot that he had, to get some coffee for my mother. He asked us not to come in, but we followed him anyway. And this young waitress said, "We don't serve Mexicans here. Get out of here." I was there, and I saw it and heard it. She paid no more attention. I'm sure for the rest of her life she never thought of it again. But every time we thought of it, it hurt us. So we got back in the car and we had a difficult time trying—in fact, we never got the coffee. These are sort of unimportant, but they're . . . you remember 'em very well . . .

15   We'd go to school two days sometimes, a week, two weeks, three weeks at most. This is when we were migrating. We'd come back to our winter base, and if we were lucky, we'd get in a good solid all of January, February, March, April, May. So we had five months out of a possible nine months. We started counting how many schools we'd been to and we counted thirty-seven. Elementary schools. From the first to eighth grade. Thirty-seven. We never got a transfer. Friday we didn't tell the teacher or anything. We'd just go home. And they accepted this.

I remember one teacher—I wondered why she was asking so many questions. (In those days anybody asked questions, you became suspicious. Either a cop or a social worker.) She was a young teacher, and she just wanted to know why we were behind. One day she drove into the camp. That was quite an event, because we never had a teacher come over. Never. So it was, you know, a meaningful day for us.

---

[1] "That's a man who specializes in contracting human beings to do cheap labor."

This I remember. Some people put this out of their minds and forget it. I don't. I don't want to forget it. I don't want it to take the best of me, but I want to be there because this is how it happened. This is the truth, you know. History.

[1970]

Topics for Critical Thinking and Writing

1. Why would a businessman post a sign (paragraph 14), "White Trade Only"? Is it legal to post such a sign today? Putting aside the question of whether or not it is legal, should it be legal? Why, or why not?
2. Is it your impression that conditions of migrant workers today have greatly changed since the Depression? Explain.

Diana Morgan

She was a "southern belle" in a small North Carolina town. "I was taught that no prince of royal blood was too good for me." (Laughs.) Her father had been a prosperous cotton merchant and owner of a general store. "It's the kind of town you become familiar with in Thornton Wilder's Our Town. *You knew everybody. We were the only people in town who had a library."*

Her father's recurring illness, together with the oncoming of hard times—the farmers and the townspeople unable to pay their bills—caused the loss of the store. He went into bankruptcy.

The banks failed about the time I was getting ready to go to college. My family thought of my going to Wellesley, Vassar, Smith—but we had so little money, we thought of a school in North Carolina. It wasn't so expensive.

It was in my junior year, and I came home for Christmas . . . I found the telephone disconnected. And this was when I realized that the world was falling apart. Imagine us without a telephone! When I finished school, I couldn't avoid facing the fact that we didn't have a cook any more, we didn't have a cleaning woman any more. I'd see dust under the beds, which is something I'd never seen before. I knew the curtains weren't as clean as they used to be. Things were beginning to look a little shabby . . .

The first thing I noticed about the Depression was that my great-grandfather's house was lost, about to be sold for taxes. Our own house was sold. It was considered the most attractive house in town, about a hundred and fifty years old. We even had a music library. Imagine my shock when it was sold for $5,000 in back taxes. I was born in that house . . .

In the meantime, I would work in the relief office and I began interviewing people . . . and found out how everybody, in order to be eligible for relief, had to have reached absolute bottom. You didn't have to have a lot of brains to realize that once they reached that stage and you put them on an allowance of a dollar a day for food—how could they ever pull out of it?

5   Caroline, who used to cook for us, came in. I was so shocked to see her in a position where she had to go to the agency and ask for food. I was embarrassed for her to see me when she was in that state. She was a wonderful woman, with a big heart. Here she was, elderly by now, and her health wasn't good at all. And she said, "Oh, the Lord's done sent you down from heaven to save me. I've fallen

on hard times. How beautiful you are. You look like an angel to me." In the typical southern Negro way of surviving, she was flattering me. I was humiliated by her putting herself in that position, and by my having to see her go through this. (Weeps softly; continues with difficulty.)

For years, I never questioned the fact that Caroline's house was papered with newspapers. She was our laundress for a while, and I remember going to her house several times. Caroline was out in the yard, just a hard patch of dirt yard. With a big iron pot, with fire under it, stirring, boiling the white clothes . . .

She was always gracious and would invite me in. She never apologized for the way anything looked. I thought to myself at the time: How odd that Caroline uses newspapers to paper walls. I didn't have any brains at eleven or twelve or whatever to think: what kind of country is this that lets people live in houses like this and necessitates their using the Sunday paper for wallpaper. I'm shocked that I can't say to you: "When I was twelve, I was horrified when I first went into this house." I was surprised but I wasn't horrified. . . .

Topic for Critical Thinking and Writing

In the next-to-last paragraph Diana Morgan reports that "it never occurred to her why Caroline used newspaper to paper the walls." Have you had a somewhat comparable revelation about poverty? If so, describe it, and indicate your present response to the experience.

FICTION

TILLIE OLSEN

Tillie Olsen was born in 1913 in Omaha of a family that had fled persecution in czarist Russia. She left school after completing the eleventh grade and at 19 began a novel called Yonnonido, *which was not published until 1947. Her first publications, in the* Partisan Review *in 1934, were some poems and a story (the story was the opening chapter of her novel); in the next twenty years, however, when she was wife, mother of four children, office worker, and political activist, she published nothing. In* Silences *(1978), a collection of essays, she comments on the difficulty of working "fulltime on temporary jobs . . . , wandering from office to office, always hoping to manage two, three writing months ahead."*

Her first published book was Tell Me a Riddle *(1961), a collection of six stories, including "I Stand Here Ironing." (This story, written in 1953–1954), first appeared in a journal in 1956, under the title "Help Her to Believe.") Her stories are marked by their concentration on what the author obviously feels are immensely important emotions and experiences; she is scarcely concerned with seeming to be objective or with the creation of mere versimilitude.*

I Stand Here Ironing

I stand here ironing, and what you asked me moves tormented back and forth with the iron.

"I wish you would manage the time to come in and talk with me about your daughter. I'm sure you can help me understand her. She's a youngster who needs help and whom I'm deeply interested in helping."

"Who needs help." . . . Even if I came, what good would it do? You think because I am her mother I have a key, or that in some way you could use me as a key? She has lived here for nineteen years. There is all that life that has happened outside of me, beyond me.

And when is there time to remember, to sift, to weigh, to estimate, to total? I will start and there will be an interruption and I will have to gather it all together again. Or I will become engulfed with all I did or did not do, with what should have been and what cannot be helped.

5   She was a beautiful baby. The first and only one of our five that was beautiful at birth. You do not guess how new and uneasy her tenancy in her now-loveliness. You did not know her all those years she was thought homely, or see her poring over her baby pictures, making me tell her over and over how beautiful she had been—and would be, I would tell her—and was not, to the seeing eye. But the seeing eyes were few or non-existent. Including mine.

I nursed her. They feel that's important nowadays. I nursed all the children, but with her, with all the fierce rigidity of first motherhood, I did like the books then said. Though her cries battered me to trembling and my breasts ached with swollenness, I waited till the clock decreed.

Why do I put that first? I do not even know if it matters, or if it explains anything.

She was a beautiful baby. She blew shining bubbles of sound. She loved motion, loved light, loved color and music and textures. She would lie on the floor in her blue overalls patting the surface so hard in ecstasy her hands and feet would blur. She was a miracle to me, but when she was eight months old I had to leave her daytimes with the woman downstairs to whom she was no miracle at all, for I worked or looked for work and for Emily's father, who "could no longer endure" (he wrote in his goody-bye note) "sharing want with us."

I was nineteen. It was the pre-relief, pre-WPA world of the depression. I would start running as soon as I got off the streetcar, running up the stairs, the place smelling sour, and awake or asleep to startle awake, when she saw me should would break into a clogged weeping that could not be comforted, a weeping I can hear yet.

10   After a while I found a job hashing at night so I could be with her days, and it was better. But it came to where I had to bring to his family and leave her.

It took a long time to raise the money for her fare back. Then she got chicken pox and I had to wait longer. When she finally came, I hardly knew her, walking quick and nervous like her father, looking like her father, thin, and dressed in a shoddy red that yellowed her skin and glared at the pockmarks. All the baby loveliness gone.

She was two. Old enough for nursery school they said, and I did not know then what I know now—the fatigue of the long day, and the lacerations of group life in the kind of nurseries that are only parking places for children.

Except that it would have made no difference if I had known. It was the only place there was. It was the only way we could be together, the only way I could hold a job.

And even without knowing, I knew. I knew the teacher that was evil because all these years it has curdled into my memory, the little boy hunched in the corner, her rasp, "why aren't you outside, because Alvin hits you? That's no reason, go out, scaredy." I knew Emily hated it even if she did not clutch and implore "don't go Mommy" like the other children, mornings.

15   She always had a reason why we should stay home. Momma, you look sick. Momma, I feel sick. Momma, the teachers aren't there today, they're sick. Momma, we can't go, there was a fire there last night. Momma, it's a holiday today, not school, they told me.

But never a direct protest, never rebellion. I think of our others in their three-four-year-oldness—the explosions, the tempers, the denunciations, the demands—and I feel suddenly ill. I put the iron down. What in me demanded that goodness in her? And what was the cost, the cost to her of such goodness?

The old man living in the back once said in his gentle way: "You should smile at Emily more when you look at her." What *was* in my face when I looked at her? I loved her. There were all the acts of love.

It was only with the others I remembered what he said, and it was the face of joy, and not of care or tightness or worry I turned to them—too late for Emily. She does not smile easily, let along almost always as her brothers and sisters do. Her face is closed and somber, but when she wants, how fluid. You must have seen it in her pantomimes, you spoke of her rare gift for comedy on the stage that rouses a laughter out of the audience so dear they applaud and applaud and do not want to let her go.

Where does it come from, that comedy? There was none of it in her when she came back to me that second time, after I had had to send her away again. She had a new daddy now to learn to love, and I think perhaps it was a better time.

20   Except when we left her alone nights, telling ourselves she was old enough.

"Can't you go some other time, Mommy, like tomorrow?" she would ask. "Will it be just a little while you'll be gone? Do you promise?"

The time we came back, the front door open, the clock on the floor in the hall. She was rigid awake. "It wasn't just a little while. I didn't cry. Three times I called you, just three times, and then I ran downstairs to open the door so you could come faster. The clock talked loud. I threw it away, it scared me what it talked."

She said the clock talked loud again that night I went to the hospital to have Susan. She was delirious with the fever that comes before red measles, but she was fully conscious all the week I was gone and the week after we were home when she could not come near the new baby or me.

She did not get well. She stayed skeleton thin, not wanting to eat, and night after night she had nightmares. She would call for me, and I would rouse from exhaustion to sleepily call back: "You're all right, darling, go to sleep, it's just a dream," and if she still called, in a sterner voice, "now go to sleep, Emily, there's nothing to hurt you." Twice, only twice, when I had to get up for Susan anyhow, I went in to sit with her.

25   Now when it is too late (as if she would let me hold and comfort her like I do the others) I get up and go to her at once at her moan or restless stirring. "Are you awake, Emily? Can I get you something?" And the answer is always the same: "No, I'm all right, go back to sleep, Mother."

They persuaded me at the clinic to send her away to a convalescent home in the country where "she can have the kind of food and care you can't manage for her, and you'll be free to concentrate on the new baby." They still send children to that place. I see pictures on the society page of sleek young women planning affairs to raise money for it, or dancing at the affairs, or decorating Easter eggs or filling Christmas stockings for the children.

They never have a picture of the children so I do not know if the girls still wear those gigantic red bows and the ravaged looks on the every other Sunday when parents can come to visit "unless otherwise notified"—as we were notified the first six weeks.

Oh it is a handsome place, green lawns and tall trees and fluted flower beds. High up on the balconies of each cottage the children stand, the girls in their red bows and white dresses, the boys in white suits and giant red ties. The parents stand below shrieking up to be heard and the children shriek down to be heard, and between them the invisible wall" Not to Be Contaminated by Parental Germs or Physical Affection."

There was a tiny girl who always stood hand in hand with Emily. Her parents never came. One visit she was gone. "They moved her to Rose cottage," Emily shouted in explanation. "They don't like you to love anybody here."

30   She wrote once a week, the labored writing of a seven-year-old. "I am fine. How is the baby. If I write my leter nicly I will have a star. Love." There was never a star. We wrote every other day, letters she could never hold or keep but only hear read—once. "We simply do not have room for children to keep any personal possessions, they patiently explained when we pieced one Sunday's shrieking together to plead how much it would mean to Emily, who loved so to keep things, to be allowed to keep her letters and cards.

Each visit she looked frailer. "She isn't eating," they told us.

(They had runny eggs for breakfast or mush with lumps, Emily said later, I'd hold it in my mouth and not swallow. Nothing ever tasted good, just when they had chicken.)

It took us eight months to get her released home, and only the fact that she gained back so little of her seven lost pounds convinced the social worker.

I used to try to hold and love her after she came back, but her body would stay stiff, and after a while she'd push away. She ate little. Food sickened her, and I think much of life too. Oh she had physical lightness and brightness, twinkling by on skates, bouncing like a ball up and down and up and down over the jump rope, skimming over the hill: but these were momentary.

35   She fretted about her appearance, thin and dark and foreign-looking at a time when every little girl was supposed to look or thought she should look a chubby blonde replica of Shirley Temple. The doorbell sometimes rang for her, but no one seemed to come and play in the house or be a best friend. Maybe because we moved so much.

There was a boy she loved painfully through two school semesters. Months later she told me how she had taken pennies from my purse to buy him candy. "Licorice was his favorite and I brought him some every day, but he still liked Jennifer better'n me. Why, Mommy?" The kind of question for which there is no answer.

School was a worry to her. She was not glib or quick in a world where glibness and quickness were easily confused with ability to learn. To her overworked and exasperated teachers she was an overconscientious "slow lerner" who kept trying to catch up and was absent entirely too often.

I let her be absent, though sometimes the illness was imaginary. How different from my not-strictness about attendance with the others. I wasn't working. We had a new baby, I was home anyhow. Sometimes, after Susan grew old enough, I would keep her home from school, too, to have them all together.

Mostly Emily had asthma, and her breathing, harsh and labored, would fill the house with a curiously tranquil sound. I would bring the two old dresser mirrors and her boxes of collections to her bed. She would select beads and single earrings, bottle tops and shells, dried flowers and pebbles, old postcards and scraps, all sorts of oddments; then she and Susan would play Kingdom, setting up landscapes and furniture, peopleing them with action.

40   Those were the only times of peaceful companionship between her and Susan. I have edged away from it, that poisonous feeling between them, that terrible balancing of hurts and needs I had to do between the two, and did so badly, those earlier years.

Oh there are conflicts between the others too, each one human, needing, demanding, hurting, taking—but only between Emily and Susan, no, Emily toward Susan that corroding resentment. It seems so obvious on the surface, yet it is not obvious. Susan, the second child, Susan, golden- and curly-haired and chubby, quick and articulate and assured, everything in appearance and manner Emily was not; Susan, not able to resist Emily's precious things, losing or sometimes clumsily breaking them; Susan telling jokes and riddles to company for applause while Emily sat silent (to tell me later: that was *my* riddle, Mother, I told it to Susan); Susan, who for all the five years' difference in age was just a year behind Emily in developing physically.

I am glad for that slow physical development that widened the difference between her and her contemporaries, though she suffered over it. She was too vulnerable for that terrible world of youthful competition, of preening and parading, of constant measuring of yourself against every other, of envy, "If I had that copper hair," "If I had that skin . . . ." She tormented herself enough about not looking like the others, there was enough of the unsureness, the having to be conscious of words before you speak, the constant caring—what are they thinking of me? Without having it all magnified by the merciless physical drives.

Ronnie is calling. He is wet and I change him. It is rare there is such a cry now. That time of motherhood is almost behind me when the ear is not one's own but must always be racked and listening for the child cry, the child call. We sit for a while and I hold him, looking out over the city spread in charcoal with its soft aisles of light. *"Shoogily,"* he breathes and curls closer. I carry him back to bed, asleep. *Shoogily.* A funny word, a family word, inherited from Emily, invented by her to say: *comfort.*

In this and other ways she leaves her seal, I say aloud. And startle at my saying it. What do I mean? What did I start to gather together, to try and make coherent? I was at the terrible, growing years. War years. I do not remember them well. I was working, there were four smaller ones now, there was not time for her. She had to help be a mother, and housekeeper, and shopper. She had to set her seal. Mornings of crisis and near hysteria trying to get lunches packed, hair combed, coats and shoes found, everyone to school or Child Care on time, the baby ready for transportation. And always the paper scribbled on by a smaller one, the book looked at by Susan then mislaid, the homework not done. Running out to that huge school where she was one, she was lost, she was a drop; suffering over the unpreparedness, stammering and unsure in her classes.

45   There was so little time left at night after the kids were bedded down. She would struggle over books, always eating (it was in those years she developed her enormous appetite that is legendary in our family) and I would be ironing, or

preparing food for the next day, or writing V-mail to Bill, or tending the baby. Sometimes, to make me laugh, or out of her despair, she would imitate happenings or types at school.

I think I said once: "Why don't you do something like this in the school amateur show?" One morning she phoned me at work, hardly understandable through the weeping; "Mother, I did it. I won, I won; they gave me first prize; they clapped and clapped and wouldn't let me go."

Now suddenly she was Somebody, and as imprisoned in her difference as she had been in anonymity.

She began to be asked to perform at other high schools, even in colleges, then at city and statewide affairs. The first one we went to, I only recognized her that first moment when thin, shy, she almost drowned herself into the curtains. Then: Was this Emily? The control, the command, the convulsing and deadly clowning, the spell, then the roaring, stamping audience, unwilling to let this rare and precious laughter out of their lives.

Afterwards: You ought to do something about her with a gift like that—but without money or knowing how, what does one do? We have left it all to her, and the gift has as often eddied inside, clogged and clotted, as been used and growing.

50   She is coming. She runs up the stairs two at a time with her light graceful step, and I know she is happy tonight. Whatever it was that occasioned your call did not happen today.

"Aren't you ever going to finish the ironing, Mother/ Whistler painted his mother in a rocker. I'd have to paint mine standing over an ironing board." This is one of her communicative nights and she tells me everything and nothing as she fixes herself a plate of food out of the icebox.

She is so lovely. Why did you want me to come in at all? Why were you concerned? She will find her way.

She starts up the stairs to bed. "Don't get me up with the rest in the morning." "But I thought you were having midterms." "Oh, those," she comes back in, kisses me, and says quite lightly, "in a couple of years when we'll all be atom-dead they won't matter a bit."

She has said it before. She *believes* it. But because I have been dredging the past, and all that compounds a human being is so heavy and meaningful in me, I cannot endure it tonight.

55   I will never total it all. I will never come in to say: She was a child seldom smiled at. Her father left me before she was a year old. I had to work her first six years when there was work, or I sent her home and to his relatives. There were years she had care she hated. She was dark and think and foreign-looking in a world where the prestige went to blondeness and curly hair and dimples, she was slow where glibness was prized. She was a child of anxious, not proud, love. We were poor and could not afford for her the soil of easy growth. I was a young mother, I was a distracted mother. There were other children pushing up, demanding. Her younger sister seemed all that she was not. There were years she did not want me to touch her. She kept too much in herself, her life was such she had to keep too much in herself. My wisdom came too late. She has much to her and probably little will come of it. She is a child of her age, of depression, of war, of fear.

Let her be. So al ltha tis in her will not bloom—but in how many does it? There is still enough left to live by. Only help her to know—help make it so there is cause for her to know—that she is more than this dress on the ironing board, helpless before the iron.

[1954]

Topics for Critical Thinking and Writing

1. Who is the "you" whom the mother speaks of? Do you think the mother will visit the "you"? Why, or why not?
2. What do you make of Emily's telling her mother not to awaken her for the midterm examination on the next morning?
3. In what way(s) did your response toward the mother change as you progressed through the story?
4. What, if anything, has the mother learned about life?

POETRY

E. Y. ("YIP") HARBURG

Edgar Harburg (1898–1981), the son of immigrants from Russia who lived in New York, was born Isidore Harburg. He later changed his name to Edgar, but was known as Yip by his friends. Harburg did odd jobs and engaged in various small business ventures until 1929, when he found himself broke. Knowing of Harburg's interest in rhyming, a school friend, Ira Gershwin, introduced him to Jay Gorney, a musician, and the two collaborated on a song, "Brother, Can You Spare a Dime?" Harburg went on to write lyrics for several highly successful musicals, including Gold Diggers *(1936),* The Wizard of Oz *(1939), and* Finian's Rainbow *(1947), but in 1947 he was investigated by the House Un-American Activities Committee for his left-wing views, and he was subsequently blacklisted in Hollywood.*

Among Harburg's other well-known lyrics are "Only a Paper Moon," "April in Paris," and "If This Isn't Love."

Brother, Can You Spare a Dime?

They used to tell me I was building a dream, and so I followed the mob,
When there was earth to plow, or guns to bear, I was always there right on
    the job.
They used to tell me I was building a dream, with peace and glory ahead,
Why should I be standing in line, just waiting for bread?   4

Once I built a railroad, I made it run, made it race against time.
Once I built a railroad; now it's done. Brother, can you spare a dime?
Once I built a tower, up to the sun, brick, and river, and lime;
Once I built a tower, now it's done. Brother, can you spare a dime?   8

                     Once in khaki suits, gee we looked swell,
    Full of that Yankee Doodly Dum,
    Half a million boots went slogging through Hell,
    And I was the kid with the drum!   12

Say, don't you remember, they called me Al; it was Al all the time.
Why don't you remember, I'm your pal? Buddy, can you spare a dime?

Once in khaki suits, gee we looked swell,
Full of that Yankee Doodly Dum,   16
Half a million boots went slogging through Hell,
And I was the kid with the drum!

Say, don't you remember, they called me Al; it was Al all the time.
Why don't you remember, I'm your pal? Buddy, can you spare a dime?   20

[1931]

Topics for Critical Thinking and Writing

1. What kinds of work did the speaker apparently do? Skilled or unskilled? Why would such a worker be especially vulnerable to unemployment?
2. In the first third of the twentieth century the railroad was the symbol of speed, of progress, of American energy and American know-how. What might a comparable symbol be for the America of the last twenty or so years?
3. Is this song just about a man asking for a dime? Would you agree that he is really asking a large question? If you agree, what is the question?
4. The song was immensely popular, and it probably did have a considerable influence on people. Can you think of any song of the last fifty or so years that in your view has been influential? Explain.

ANONYMOUS

The following song, probably composed shortly after 1919 when the Prohibition Amendment was voted, was widely sung in the 1930s, and it seems to have endured. It is sung to the tune of "My Bonnie Lies Over the Ocean."

My God, How the Money Rolls In

My mother she works in the laundry,
My father he bootlegs gin.
My sister makes love for a living,
My God, how the money rolls in.
   Rolls in, rolls in,
   My God how the money rolls in.

Topics for Critical Thinking and Writing

1. As with all songs that are passed down orally, variants have developed. One common version gives the first two lines thus:

   My father makes book on the corner,
   My mother makes secondhand gin.

Which version do you prefer? Why?
2. Why do you suppose this song has endured?

ALFRED HAYES

Alfred Hayes (1911–1985) was born in England but he grew up in New York City, where he worked as a journalist and wrote novels, plays, and film scripts. His most famous work is the song that we reprint below, "Joe Hill."

Joe Hill (1879–1915) was born Joel Emmaneul Hägglund in Sweden, of Lutheran parents. He worked as a laborer, then emigrated in 1902 to the United States, where he again worked at odd jobs, on the docks and in the fields. He seems to have done a good deal of wandering, from New York through Cleveland, Chicago, the Dakotas, and on to Spokane and Portland. Around 1910 he joined the Industrial Workers of the World (IWW, nicknamed the Wobblies), a revolutionary union formed in Chicago in 1905.

Joe Hill became the chief songwriter of the movement ("The Preacher and the Slave," "Casey Jones, the Union Scab"), and his songs were widely distributed in union publications. He was arrested in Utah in 1914, charged with murdering a Salt Lake city grocer, convicted on extremely flimsy evidence—virtually all students of the case agree that he was innocent—and executed by a firing squad in 1915. The day before he was executed he wired the head of the IWW, "Don't waste any time in mourning. Organize!" His ashes, divided into packets and sent to workers in every state except Utah, were scattered on May Day 1916.

The song was immensely popular in the 1930s.

Joe Hill

Music by EARL ROBINSON
Words by ALFRED HAYES

I dreamed I saw Joe Hill last night
Alive as you and me.
Says I, "But Joe, you're ten years dead."
"I never died," says he.
"I never died," says he.   5

"In Salt Lake, Joe, by God," says I,
Him standing by my bed,
"They framed you on a murder charge."
Says Joe, "But I ain't dead."
Says Joe, But I ain't dead."   10

"The copper bosses killed you, Joe,
They shot you, Joe," says I.
"Takes more than guns to kill a man,"
Says Joe, "I didn't die."
Says Joe, "I didn't die."   15

And standing there as big as life
and smiling with his eyes,
Joe says, "What they forgot to kill
Went on to organize.
Went on to organize."   20

"Joe Hill ain't dead," he says to me.
"Joe Hill ain't never died.
Where working men are out on strike
Joe Hill is at their side.
Joe Hill is at their side."   25

"From San Diego up to Maine
In every mine and mill.
Where workers strike and organize,"
Says he, "You'll find Joe Hill."
Says he, "You'll find Joe Hill."   30

I dreamed I saw Joe Hill last night
Alive as you and me.
Says I, "But Joe, you're ten years dead."
"I never died," says he.
"I never died," says he.   35

[1938]

Topics for Critical Thinking and Writing

1. This song is often called a ballad. In what ways does it resemble songs that are called folk ballads, and in what ways does it not resemble them? For a brief comment on folk ballads, see page 1374.
2. Joe Hill's Industrial Workers of the World stood for a classless society, in which everyone was equal and in which everyone worked. It is often said that the United States is classless. Do you think this view is correct? Explain. (You will probably want to define "class.")

LANGSTON HUGHES

Langston Hughes was an accomplished short-story writer, playwright, essayist, autobiographer, editor, and author of children's books. But he is known above all for his poetry, and is now recognized as the premier African American poet of the twentieth century. He was born in Joplin, Missouri, but he was raised in Lawrence, Kansas, though with periods in Illinois, Ohio, and Mexico. He started as a student at Columbia University in 1921, but left in 1922 and worked at a number of low-paying jobs. He traveled to Africa and, later, to France, and he then returned in the mid 1920s to the United States to pursue a literary career.

The pace, structure, and tone of "the blues," mournful and yet resilient, shape many of the poems that Hughes included in his first two books: The Weary Blues *(1926) and* Fine Clothes to the Jew *(1927). He was a major figure in the Harlem or "New Negro" Renaissance of the 1920s and early 1930s, which led to a spirited array of race-conscious new production in literature and the arts. In an essay that became a manifesto for the movement, "The Negro and the Racial Mountain" (1926), Hughes maintained, "We younger Negro artists who create now intend to express our individual dark-skinned selves without fear or shame."*

Out of Work

I walked de streets till
De shoes wore off my feet.
I done walked de streets till
De shoes wore off my feet.
Been lookin' for a job
So's that I could eat.

I couldn't find no job
So I went to de WPA.°
Couldn't find no job
So I went to de WPA.
WPA man told me:
You got to live here a year and a day.

A year and a day, Lawd,
In this great big lonesome town!
A year and a day in this
Great big lonesome town!
I might starve for a year but
That extra day would get me down.

Did you ever try livin'
On two-bits° minus two?
I say did you ever try livin'
On two-bits minus two?
Why don't you try it, folks,
And see what it would do to you?

[1940]

8 WPA Works Progress Administration, a federal program to aid the unemployed, created by Congress in 1935 as part of President Roosevelt's New Deal.   **20 Two-bits** twenty-five cents.

Topics for Critical Thinking and Writing

1. "Out of Work" reflects the impact of the Great Depression on Americans in general and on African Americans in particular. As one scholar has noted, during the 1930s "the real gross national product fell 30 percent, prices declined 23 percent, and unemployment became a fact of life for 25 percent of the labor force." If you wanted to learn more about this period of American history, where would you turn for source materials? What would be the effect of the knowledge you acquired on your response to and understanding of Hughes's poem?

2. Please rewrite this poem, from beginning to end, in "standard" English. Do you think that your version is more or less effective than the poem as Hughes wrote it, in dialect? Please explain.

3. Have you ever looked for a job and had trouble finding one? How did you feel while this was happening? What was the outcome? Was it a good outcome?

4. The speaker of "Out of Work" ends with a question. What would be your response? What question would you in turn ask the speaker? What do you imagine his response to it would be?

DAVID WAGONER

David Wagoner, now a resident in the state of Washington, was born in 1926 in Ohio. The author of numerous books of poetry, he has won many awards from such distinguished institutions as the Guggenheim Foundation and the National Endowment for the Arts.

Hooverville

I wasn't supposed to go where the bums lived,
But I could see their houses made out of crates
And tin cans hammered flat, out of tar paper
And cardboard boxes, the doorways curtained with rags.   4

I watched them wash their clothes and their underwear
And their bodies in cold Lake Michigan for a mile
Between us and South Chicago. Freight engineers
Would whistle and wave at me, but not at them.   8

My mother fed some almost every morning,
So I knew they'd ridden boxcars from somewhere else
And were going somewhere else sooner or later
But meanwhile had to stay here and be hungry.   12

I sneaked out of my bed and bedroom window
Some nights and saw their fires flicker to life
Along the tracks and burn from yellow to red
While a kind of hoedown with banjos and guitars   16

Was creaking and plunking almost as faint and far
And near as the mosquitoes and hoptoads
And crickets. I could hear them singing. Their shadows
Danced in firelight. Nobody danced in our yard.   20

Or in our neighbors' yard. Our short front lawns
Ended in cindery ditches and roadbeds
Where cattails puffed their seeds over the crossties,
Where tumbleweeds, on the loose, were ready to roll.   24

[2004]

Topics for Critical Thinking and Writing

1. What is or was Hooverville? Why was this term invented?
2. To what class of society does the speaker of this poem belong? How would you characterize him?
3. Judging from what the speaker tells us, what sort of people were the bums? Poor, yes, but what else? Do they seem to differ from today's homeless? If so, how?
4. Suppose the poem ended with the next-to-last stanza. Would it be better or worse? Explain.

THE VIETNAM WAR

SHORT VIEWS

We should declare war on North Vietnam. . . . We could pave the whole country and put parking strips on it, and still be home by Christmas.
        Ronald Reagan (1965)

The bombs in Vietnam explode at home; they destroy the hopes and possibilities for a decent America.
        The Rev. Martin Luther King, Jr. (1967)

Television showed us the war. It showed us the war in a way that was—if you chose to watch television, at least—unavoidable. You could not turn the page. You could not even switch channels: all you got was another network showing you the war.
        Nora Ephron (1975)

Television brought the brutality of the war into the comfort of the living room. Vietnam was lost in the living rooms of America—not in the battlefields of Vietnam.
        Marshall McLuhan (1975)

At least there is a light at the end of the tunnel.
        Joseph Alsop, columnist (1965)

I believe there is a light at the end of what has been a long and lonely tunnel.
        President Lyndon B. Johnson (1966)

The light at the end of the tunnel may be an oncoming train.
        Anonymous

The biggest lesson I learned from Vietnam is not to trust [our own] government statements. I had no idea until then that you could not rely on [them].
        Senator J. William Fulbright (1985)

Vietnam presumably taught us that the United States could not serve as the world's policeman; it should also have taught us the dangers of trying to be the world's midwife to democracy when the birth is scheduled to take place under conditions of guerilla warfare.
        Jean Kirkpatrick (1979)

We of the Kennedy and Johnson Administrations who participated in the decision on Vietnam acted according to what we thought to be the principles and traditions of this nation. Yet we were wrong, terribly wrong.
Robert S. McNamara, Secretary of Defense (1995)

American has made no reparation to the Vietnamese, nothing. We are the richest people in the world and they are among the poorest. We savaged them, though they had never hurt us, and we cannot find it in our hearts, our honor, to give them help—because the government of Vietnam is Communist. And perhaps because they won.
Martha Gellhorn (1986)

We call it the Vietnam War, but in Vietnam they call it the American War.
Vietnamese reporter to an American reporter

Topics for Critical Thinking and Writing

1. It is sometimes said that the Vietnam War "never ended." What does this statement mean? Do you agree?
2. Several of the comments here refer to, or imply, the "lessons" that Americans have learned from the Vietnam War. What are these lessons? Does everyone agree about them, or is the nature of the lessons in dispute? Do you think that an event in the past can teach us about how to deal with issues and respond to crises in the present? Or is each crisis new and unique?
3. Have you studied the Vietnam War in school? If you have, what kinds of materials did you examine? If not, do you think that your education is missing something important, perhaps even essential? If you wanted to learn more about the Vietnam War on your own, where would you start?
4. Many people agree that press coverage, especially TV news, strongly influenced Americans' views and opinions about the Vietnam War. Do you think that the media should be allowed to cover a war without any restrictions? Are there some aspects or events of a war that the media should not be allowed to cover and report on?

FICTION

MOLLY IVINS

Molly Ivins, a native of Houston, holds a bachelors' degree from Smith College and a master's degree in journalism from Columbia University. She has worked for the Houston Chronicle, *the* Texas Observer, *and* The New York Times, *and she has published widely in magazines such as* Esquire, The Nation, Ms., *and* Mother Jones. *Her most recent book is* Bushwhacked: Life in George Bush's America *(2003). We reprint a story that originally appeared in the* Dallas Times Herald, *in 1982.*

A Short Story about the Vietnam War Memorial

She had known, ever since she first read about the Vietnam War Memorial, that she would go there someday. Sometime she would be in Washington and would go and see his name and leave again.

So silly, all that fuss about the memorial. Whatever else Vietnam was, it was not the kind of war that calls from some *Raising the Flag at Iwo Jima* kind of statue. She was not prepared, though, for the impact of the memorial. To walk down into it in the pale winter sunshine was like the war itself, like going into a dark valley and damned if there was ever any light at the end of the tunnel. Just death. When you get closer to the two walls, the number of names start to stun you. It is terrible, there in the peace and the pale sunshine.

The names are listed by date of death. There has never been a time, day or night, drunk or sober, for thirteen years that she could not have told you the date. He was killed on August 13, 1969. It is near the middle of the left wall. She went toward it as though she had known beforehand where it would be. His name is near the bottom. She had to kneel to find it. Stupid clichés. His name leaped out at her. It was like being hit.

She stared at it and then reached out and gently ran her fingers over the letters in the cold black marble. The memory of him came back so strong, almost as if he were there on the other side of the stone, she could see his hand reaching out to touch her fingers. It had not hurt for years and suddenly, just for a moment, it hurt again so horribly that it twisted her face and made her gasp and left her with tears running down her face. Then it stopped hurting but she could not stop the tears. Could not stop them running and running down her face.

5   There had been a time, although she had been an otherwise sensible young woman, when she had believed she would never recover from the pain. She did, of course. But she is still determined never to sentimentalize him. He would have hated that. She had thought it was like an amputation, the severing of his life from hers, that you could live on afterward, but it would be like having only one leg and one arm. But it was only a wound. It healed. If there is a scar, it is only faintly visible now at odd intervals.

He was a biologist, a t.a. at the university getting his Ph.D. They lived together for two years. He left the university to finish his thesis but before he lined up a public school job—teachers were safe in those years—the draft board got him. They had friends who had left the country, they had friends who had gone to prison, they had friends who had gone to Nam. There were no good choices in those years. She thinks now he unconsciously wanted to go even though he often said, said in one of his letters, that it was a stupid, f–in' war. He felt some form of guilt about a friend of theirs who was killed during the Tet offensive. Hubert Humphrey called Tet at great victory. His compromise was to refuse officer's training school and go as an enlisted man. She had thought then it was a dumb gesture and they had a half-hearted quarrel about it.

He had been in Nam less than two months when he was killed, without heroics, during a firefight at night by a single bullet in the brain. No one saw it happen. There were some amazing statistics about money and tonnage from that war. Did you know that there were more tons of bombs dropped on Hanoi during the Christmas bombing of 1972 that in all of World War II? Did you know that the war in Vietnam cost the United States $123.3 billion? She has always wanted to know how much that one bullet cost. Sixty-three cents? $1.20? Someone must know.

The other bad part was the brain. Even at this late date, it seems to her that was quite a remarkable mind. Long before she read C. P. Snow[1], the ferociously honest young man who wanted to be a great biologist taught her a great deal about the difference between the way scientists think and the way humanists think. Only once has she been glad he was not with her. It was at one of the bizarre hearings about teaching "creation science." He would have gotten furious and been horribly rude. He had no patience with people who did not understand and respect the process of science.

She used to attribute his fierce honesty to the fact that he was a Yankee. She is still prone to tell "white" lies to make people feel better, to smooth things over, to prevent hard feelings. Surely there have been dumber things for lovers to quarrel over than the social utility of hypocrisy. But not many.

10   She stood up again, still staring at his name, stood for a long time. She said, "There it is," and turned to go. A man to her left was staring at her. She glared at him. The man had done nothing but make the mistake of seeing her weeping. She said, as though daring him to disagree, "It was a stupid, f–in' war," and stalked right past him.

She turned again at the top of the slope to make sure where his name is, so whenever she sees a picture of the memorial she can put her finger where his name is. He never said goodbye, literally. Whenever he left he would say, "Take care, love." He could say it many different ways. He said it when he left for Vietnam. She stood at the top of the slope and found her hand half-raised in some silly gesture of farewell. She brought it down again. She considered thinking to him, "Hey, take care, love" but it seemed remarkably inappropriate. She walked away and was quite entertaining for the rest of the day, because it was expected of her.

She thinks he would have liked the memorial. He would have hated the editorials. He did not sacrifice his life for his country or for a just or noble cause. There just were no good choices in those years and he got killed.

[1982]

[1] **C. P. Snow** Charles Percy Snow (1905–1980), English essayist, novelist, and physicist, best known for a book entitled *The Two Cultures* (1959).

Topics for Critical Thinking and Writing

1. What is your response to the title of the story? Why? If you had written it, what title might you have given to it?
2. In paragraph 7 the narrator reports the death of the man in very simple terms, then gives some statistics, and then briefly enters the mind of the woman. Do you find this paragraph effective? Why, or why not?
3. What is your response to the final paragraph? In your answer, take account of the structures of the sentences "She thinks . . . He would . . . He did not . . . There just were . . . and he. . . ."
4. If you have visited the Vietnam Memorial, report your response to it.

TIM O'BRIEN

Tim O'Brien, born in 1947, in Austin, Minnesota, was drafted into the army in 1968 and served as an infantryman in Vietnam. Drawing on this experience he wrote a memoir, If I Die in a Combat Zone *(1973), in which he explains that he did not believe in the Vietnam War, considered dodging the draft, but, lacking the courage to do so, he served, largely out of fear and embarrassment. A later book, a novel called* Going after Cacciato, *won the National Book Award in 1979.*

"The Things They Carried," first published in 1986, in 1990 was republished as one of a series of interlocking stories in a book entitled The Things They Carried. *In one of the stories, entitled "How To Tell a True War Story," he writes,*

> *A true war story is never moral. It does not instruct, nor encourage virtue, nor suggest models of proper human behavior. . . . If a story seems moral, do not believe it. If at the end of a war story you feel uplifted, or if you feel that some small bit of rectitude has been salvaged from the larger waste, then you have been made the victim of a very old and terrible lie. There is no rectitude whatsoever. There is no virtue. As a first rule of thumb, therefore, you can tell a true war story by its absolute and uncompromising allegiance to obscenity and evil.*

The Things They Carried

First Lieutenant Jimmy Cross carried letters from a girl named Martha, a junior at Mount Sebastian College in New Jersey. They were not love letters, but Lieutenant Cross was hoping, so he kept them folded in plastic at the bottom of his rucksack. In the late afternoon, after a day's march, he would dig his foxhole, wash his hands under a canteen, unwrap the letters, hold them with the tips of his fingers, and spend the last hour of light pretending. He would imagine romantic camping trips into the White Mountains in New Hampshire. He would sometimes taste the envelope flaps, knowing her tongue had been there. More than anything, he wanted Martha to love him as he loved her, but the letters were mostly chatty, elusive on the matter of love. She was a virgin, he was almost sure. She was an English major at Mount Sebastian, and she wrote beautifully about her professors and roommates and midterm exams, about her respect for Chaucer and her great affection for Virginia Woolf. She often quoted lines of poetry; she never mentioned the war, except to say, Jimmy, take care of yourself. The letters weighed ten ounces. They were signed "Love, Martha," but Lieutenant Cross understood that Love was only a way of signing and did not mean what he sometimes pretended it meant. At dusk, he would carefully return the letters to his rucksack. Slowly, a bit distracted, he would get up and move among his men, checking the perimeter, then at full dark he would return to his hole and watch the night and wonder if Martha was a virgin.

The things they carried were largely determined by necessity. Among the necessities or near-necessities were P-38 can openers, pocket knives, heat tabs, wrist watches, dog tags, mosquito repellent, chewing gum, candy, cigarettes, salt tablets, packets of Kool-Aid, lighters, matches, sewing kits, Military Payment Certificates, C rations, and two or three canteens of water. Together, these items weighed between fifteen and twenty pounds, depending upon a man's habits or rate of metabolism. Henry Dobbins, who was a big man, carried extra rations; he was especially fond of canned peaches in heavy syrup over pound cake. Dave

Jensen, who practiced field hygiene, carried a toothbrush, dental floss, and several hotel-size bars of soap he'd stolen on R&R[1] in Sydney, Australia. Ted Lavender, who was scared, carried tranquilizers until he was shot in the head outside the village of Than Khe in mid-April. By necessity, and because it was SOP,[2] they all carried steel helmets that weighed five pounds including the liner and camouflage cover. They carried the standard fatigue jackets and trousers. Very few carried underwear. On their feet they carried jungle boots—2.1 pounds—and Dave Jensen carried three pairs of socks and a can of Dr. Scholl's foot powder as a precaution against trench foot. Until he was shot, Ted Lavender carried six or seven ounces of premium dope, which for him was a necessity. Mitchell Sanders, the RTO,[3] carried condoms. Norman Bowker carried a diary. Rat Kiley carried comic books. Kiowa, a devout Baptist, carried an illustrated New Testament that had been presented to him by his father, who taught Sunday school in Oklahoma City, Okalahoma. As a hedge against bad times, however, Kiowa also carried his grandmother's distrust of the white man, his grandfather's old hunting hatchet. Necessity dictated. Because the land was mined and booby-trapped, it was SOP for each man to carry a steel-centered, nylon-covered flak jacket, which weighed 6.7 pounds, but which on hot days seemed much heavier. Because you could die so quickly, each man carried at least one large compress bandage, usually in the helmet band for easy access. Because the nights were cold, and because the monsoons were wet, each carried a green plastic poncho that could be used as a raincoat or groundsheet or makeshift tent. With its quilted liner, the poncho weighed almost two pounds, but it was worth every ounce. In April, for instance, when Ted Lavender was shot, they used his poncho to wrap him up, then to carry him across the paddy, then to lift him into the chopper that took him away.

They were called legs or grunts.

To carry something was to "hump" it, as when Lieutenant Jimmy Cross humped his love for Martha up the hills and through the swamps. In its intransitive form, "to hump" meant "to walk," or "to march," but it implied burdens far beyond the intransitive.

Almost everyone humped photographs. In his wallet, Lieutenant Cross carried two photographs of Martha. The first was a Kodachrome snapshot signed "Love," though he knew better. She stood against a brick wall. Her eyes were gray and neutral, her lips slightly open as she stared straight-on at the camera. At night, sometimes, Lieutenant Cross wondered who had taken the picture, because he knew she had boyfriends, because he loved her so much, and because he could see the shadow of the picture taker spreading out against the brick wall. The second photograph had been clipped from the 1968 Mount Sebastian yearbook. It was an action shot—women's volleyball—and Martha was bent horizontal to the floor, reaching, the palms of her hands in sharp focus, the tongue taut, the expression frank and competitive. There was no visible sweat. She wore white gym shorts. Her legs, he thought, were almost certainly the legs of a virgin, dry and without hair, the left knee cocked and carrying her entire weight, which was just over one hundred pounds. Lieutenant Cross remembered touching that left knee. A dark theater, he remembered, and the movie was *Bonnie and Clyde*, and Martha wore a tweed skirt, and during the final scene, when he touched her knee, she turned and looked at him in a sad, sober way that made him pull his hand

[1]**R&R** rest and rehabilitation leave.   [2]**SOP** standard operating procedure.   [3]**RTO** radio and telephone operator.

back, but he would always remember the feel of the tweed skirt and the knee beneath it and the sound of the gunfire that killed Bonnie and Clyde, how embarrassing it was, how slow and oppressive. He remembered kissing her goodnight at the dorm door. Right then, he thought, he should've done something brave. He should've carried her up the stairs to her room and tied her to the bed and touched that left knee all night long. He should've risked it. Whenever he looked at the photographs, he thought of new things he should've done.

What they carried was partly a function of rank, partly of field specialty.

As a first lieutenant and platoon leader, Jimmy Cross carried a compass, maps, code books, binoculars, and a .45-caliber pistol that weighed 2.9 pounds fully loaded. He carried a strobe light and the responsibility for the lives of his men.

As an RTO, Mitchell Sanders carried the PRC-25 radio, a killer, twenty-six pounds with its battery.

As a medic, Rat Kiley carried a canvas satchel filled with morphine and plasma and malaria tablets and surgical tape and comic books and all the things a medic must carry, including M&Ms[4] for especially bad wounds, for a total weight of nearly twenty pounds.

As a big man, therefore a machine gunner, Henry Dobbins carried the M-60, which weighed twenty-three pounds unloaded, but which was almost always loaded. In addition, Dobbins carried between ten and fifteen pounds of ammunition draped in belts across his chest and shoulders.

As PFCs or Spec 4s, most of them were common grunts and carried the standard M-16 gas operated assault rifle. The weapon weighed 7.5 pounds unloaded, 8.2 pounds with its full twenty-round magazine. Depending on numerous factors, such as topography and psychology, the riflemen carried anywhere from twelve to twenty magazines, usually in cloth bandoliers, adding on another 8.4 pounds at minimum, fourteen pounds at maximum. When it was available, they also carried M-16 maintenance gear—rods and steel brushes and swabs and tubes of LSA oil—all of which weighed about a pound. Among the grunts, some carried the M-79 grenade launcher, 5.9 pounds unloaded, a reasonably light weapon except for the ammunition, which was heavy. A single round weighed ten ounces. The typical load was twenty-five rounds. But Ted Lavender, who was scared, carried thirty-four rounds when he was shot and killed outside Than Khe, and he went down under an exceptional burden, more than twenty pounds of ammunition, plus the flak jacket and helmet and rations and water and toilet paper and tranquilizers and all the rest, plus the unweighed fear. He was dead weight. There was no twitching or flopping. Kiowa, who saw it happen, said it was like watching a rock fall, or a big sandbag or something—just boom, then down—not like the movies where the dead guy rolls around and does fancy spins and goes ass over teakettle—not like that, Kiowa said, the poor bastard just flat-fuck fell. Boom. Down. Nothing else. It was a bright morning in mid-April. Lieutenant Cross felt the pain. He blamed himself. They stripped off Lavender's canteens and ammo, all the heavy things, and Rat Kiley said the obvious, the guy's dead, and Mitchell Sanders used his radio to report one U.S. KIA[5] and to request a chopper. Then they wrapped Lavender in his poncho. They carried him out to a dry paddy, established security, and sat smoking the dead man's dope until the chopper came. Lieutenant Cross kept to himself. He pictured Martha's smooth young face, thinking he loved her more than anything, more than his men, and now Ted Lavender

---

[4]**M&M** joking term for medical supplies.   [5]**KIA** killed in action.

was dead because he loved her so much and could not stop thinking about her. When the dust-off arrived, they carried Lavender aboard. Afterward they burned Than Khe. They marched until dusk, then dug their holes, and that night Kiowa kept explaining how you had to be there, how fast it was, how the poor guy just dropped like so much concrete. Boom-down, he said. Like cement.

In addition to the three standard weapons—the M-60, M-16, and M-79—they carried whatever presented itself, or whatever seemed appropriate as a means of killing or staying alive. They carried catch-as-catch-can. At various times, in various situations, they carried M-14s and CAR-15s and Swedish Ks and grease guns and captured AK-47s and Chi-Coms and RPGs and Simonov carbines and black-market Uzis and .38-caliber Smith & Wesson handguns and 66 mm LAWs and shotguns and silencers and blackjacks and bayonets and C-4 plastic explosives. Lee Strunk carried a slingshot; a weapon of last resort, he called it. Mitchell Sanders carried brass knuckles. Kiowa carried his grandfather's feathered hatchet. Every third or fourth man carried a Claymore antipersonnel mine—3.5 pounds with its firing device. They all carried fragmentation grenades—fourteen ounces each. They all carried at least one M-18 colored smoke grenade—twenty-four ounces. Some carried CS or tear-gas grenades. Some carried white-phosphorus grenades. They carried all they could bear, and then some, including a silent awe for the terrible power of the things they carried.

In the first week of April, before Lavender died, Lieutenant Jimmy Cross received a goodluck charm from Martha. It was a simple pebble, an ounce at most. Smooth to the touch, it was a milky-white color with flecks of orange and violet, oval-shaped, like a miniature egg. In the accompanying letter, Martha wrote that she had found the pebble on the Jersey shoreline, precisely where the land touched the water at high tide, where things came together but also separated. It was this separate-but-together quality, she wrote, that had inspired her to pick up the pebble and to carry it in her breast pocket for several days, where it seemed weightless, and then to send it through the mail, by air, as a token of her truest feelings for him. Lieutenant Cross found this romantic. But he wondered what her truest feelings were, exactly, and what she meant by separate-but-together. He wondered how the tides and waves had come into play on that afternoon along the Jersey shoreline when Martha saw the pebble and bent down to rescue it from geology. He imagined bare feet. Martha was a poet, with the poet's sensibilities, and her feet would be brown and bare, the toenails unpainted, the eyes chilly and somber like the ocean in March, and though it was painful, he wondered who had been with her that afternoon. He imagined a pair of shadows moving along the strip of sand where things came together but also separated. It was phantom jealousy, he knew, but he couldn't help himself. He loved her so much. On the march, through the hot days of early April, he carried the pebble in his mouth, turning it with his tongue, tasting sea salts and moisture. His mind wandered. He had difficulty keeping his attention on the war. On occasion he would yell at his men to spread out the column, to keep their eyes open, but then he would slip away into daydreams, just pretending, walking barefoot along the Jersey shore, with Martha, carrying nothing. He would feel himself rising. Sun and waves and gentle winds, all love and lightness.

What they carried varied by mission.

When a mission took them to the mountains, they carried mosquito netting, machetes, canvas tarps, and extra bugjuice.

If a mission seemed especially hazardous, or if it involved a place they knew to be bad, they carried everything they could. In certain heavily mined AOs,[6] where the land was dense with Toe Poppers and Bouncing Betties, they took turns humping a twenty-eight-pound mine detector. With its headphones and big sensing plate, the equipment was a stress on the lower back and shoulders, awkward to handle, often useless because of the shrapnel in the earth, but they carried it anyway, partly for safety, partly for the illusion of safety.

On ambush, or other night missions, they carried peculiar little odds and ends. Kiowa always took along his New Testament and a pair of moccasins for silence. Dave Jensen carried night-sight vitamins high in carotin. Lee Strunk carried his slingshot; ammo, he claimed, would never be a problem. Rat Kiley carried brandy and M&Ms. Until he was shot, Ted Lavender carried the starlight scope, which weighed 6.3 pounds with its aluminum carrying case. Henry Dobbins carried his girlfriend's panty hose wrapped around his neck as a comforter. They all carried ghosts. When dark came, they would move out single file across the meadows and paddies to their ambush coordinates, where they would quietly set up the Claymores and lie down and spend the night waiting.

Other missions were more complicated and required special equipment. In mid-April, it was their mission to search out and destroy the elaborate tunnel complexes in the Than Khe area south of Chu Lai. To blow the tunnels, they carried one-pound blocks of pentrite high explosives, four blocks to a man, sixty-eight pounds in all. They carried wiring, detonators, and battery-powered clackers. Dave Jensen carried earplugs. Most often, before blowing the tunnels, they were ordered by higher command to search them, which was considered bad news, but by and large they just shrugged and carried out orders. Because he was a big man, Henry Dobbins was excused from tunnel duty. The others would draw numbers. Before Lavender died there were seventeen men in the platoon, and whoever drew the number seventeen would strip off his gear and crawl in headfirst with a flashlight and Lieutenant Cross's .45-caliber pistol. The rest of them would fan out as security. They would sit down or kneel, not facing the hole, listening to the ground beneath them, imagining cobwebs and ghosts, whatever was down there—the tunnel walls squeezing in—how the flashlight seemed impossibly heavy in the hand and how it was tunnel vision in the very strictest sense, compression in all ways, even time, and how you had to wiggle in—ass and elbows— a swallowed-up feeling—and how you found yourself worrying about odd things—will your flashlight go dead? Do rats carry rabies? If you screamed, how far would the sound carry? Would your buddies hear it? Would they have the courage to drag you out? In some respects, though not many, the waiting was worse than the tunnel itself. Imagination was a killer.

On April 16, when Lee Strunk drew the number seventeen, he laughed and muttered something and went down quickly. The morning was hot and very still. Not good, Kiowa said. He looked at the tunnel opening, then out across a dry paddy toward the village of Than Khe. Nothing moved. No clouds or birds or people. As they waited, the men smoked and drank Kool-Aid, not talking much, feeling sympathy for Lee Strunk but also feeling the luck of the draw. You win some, you lose some, said Mitchell Sanders, and sometimes you settle for a rain check. It was a tired line and no one laughed.

Henry Dobbins ate a tropical chocolate bar. Ted Lavender popped a tranquilizer and went off to pee.

---

[6]**AOs** areas of operation.

After five minutes, Lieutenant Jimmy Cross moved to the tunnel, leaned down, and examined the darkness. Trouble, he thought—a cave-in maybe. And then suddenly, without willing it, he was thinking about Martha. The stresses and fractures, the quick collapse, the two of them buried alive under all that weight. Dense, crushing love. Kneeling, watching the hole, he tried to concentrate on Lee Strunk and the war, all the dangers, but his love was too much for him, he felt paralyzed, he wanted to sleep inside her lungs and breathe her blood and be smothered. He wanted her to be a virgin and not a virgin, all at once. He wanted to know her. Intimate secrets—why poetry? Why so sad? Why that grayness in her eyes? Why so alone? Not lonely, just alone—riding her bike across campus or sitting off by herself in the cafeteria. Even dancing, she danced alone—and it was the aloneness that filled him with love. He remembered telling her that one evening. How she nodded and looked away. And how, later, when he kissed her, she received the kiss without returning it, her eyes wide open, not afraid, not a virgin's eyes, just flat and uninvolved.

Lieutenant Cross gazed at the tunnel. But he was not there. He was buried with Martha under the white sand at the Jersey shore. They were pressed together, and the pebble in his mouth was her tongue. He was smiling. Vaguely, he was aware of how quiet the day was, the sullen paddies, yet he could not bring himself to worry about matters of security. He was beyond that. He was just a kid at war, in love. He was twenty-two years old. He couldn't help it.

A few minutes later Lee Strunk crawled out of the tunnel. He came up grinning, filthy but alive. Lieutenant Cross nodded and closed his eyes while the others clapped Strunk on the back and made jokes about rising from the dead.

Worms, Rat Kiley said. Right out of the grave. Fuckin' zombie.

The men laughed. They all felt great relief.

Spook City, said Mitchell Sanders.

Lee Strunk made a funny ghost sound, a kind of moaning, yet very happy, and right then, when Strunk made that high happy moaning sound, when he went *Ah-hooooo*, right then Ted Lavender was shot in the head on his way back from peeing. He lay with his mouth open. The teeth were broken. There was a swollen black bruise under his left eye. The cheekbone was gone. Oh shit, Rat Kiley said, the guy's dead. The guy's dead, he kept saying, which seemed profound—the guys' dead. I mean really.

The things they carried were determined to some extent by superstition. Lieutenant Cross carried his good-luck pebble. Dave Jensen carried a rabbit's foot. Norman Bowker, otherwise a very gentle person, carried a thumb that had been presented to him as a gift by Mitchell Sanders. The thumb was dark brown, rubbery to the touch, and weighed four ounces at most. It had been cut from a VC corpse, a boy of fifteen or sixteen. They'd found him at the bottom of an irrigation ditch, badly burned, flies in his mouth and eyes. They boy wore black shorts and sandals. At the time of his death he had been carrying a pouch of rice, a rifle, and three magazines of ammunition.

You want my opinion, Mitchell Sanders said, there's a definite moral here.

He put his hand on the dead boy's wrist. He was quiet for a time, as if counting a pulse, then he patted the stomach, almost affectionately, and used Kiowa's hunting hatchet to remove the thumb.

Henry Dobbins asked what the moral was.

Moral?

You know. *Moral.*

Sanders wrapped the thumb in toilet paper and handed it across to Norman Bowker. There was no blood. Smiling, he kicked the boy's head, watched the flies scatter, and said, It's like with that old TV show—Paladin. Have gun, will travel.

Henry Dobbins thought about it.

Yeah, well, he finally said. I don't see no moral.

There it *is,* man.

Fuck off.

They carried USO stationery and pencils and pens. They carried Sterno, safety pins, trip flares, signal flares, spools of wire, razor blades, chewing tobacco, liberated joss sticks and statuettes of the smiling Buddha, candles, grease pencils, *The Stars and Stripes,* fingernail clippers, Psy Ops leaflets, bush hats, bolos, and much more. Twice a week, when the resupply choppers came in, they carried hot chow in green Mermite cans and large canvas bags filled with iced beer and soda pop. They carried plastic water containers, each with a two gallon capacity. Mitchell Sanders carried a set of starched tiger fatigues for special occasions. Henry Dobbins carried Black Flag insecticide. Dave Jensen carried empty sandbags that could be filled at night for added protection. Lee Strunk carried tanning lotion. Some things they carried in common. Taking turns, they carried the big PRC-77 scrambler radio, which weighed thirty pounds with its battery. They shared the weight of memory. They took up what others could no longer bear. Often, they carried each other, the wounded or weak. They carried infections. They carried chess sets, basketballs, Vietnamese-English dictionaries, insignia of rank, Bronze Stars and Purple Hearts, plastic cards imprinted with the Code of Conduct. They carried diseases, among them malaria and dysentery. They carried lice and ringworm and leeches and paddy algae and various rots and molds. They carried the land itself—Vietnam, the place, the soil—a powdery orange-red dust that covered their boots and fatigues and faces. They carried the sky. The whole atmosphere, they carried it, the humidity, the monsoons, the stink of fungus and decay, all of it, they carried gravity. They moved like mules. By daylight they took sniper fire, at night they were mortared, but it was not battle, it was just the endless march, village to village, without purpose, nothing won or lost. They marched for the sake of the march. They plodded along slowly, dumbly, leaning forward against the heat, unthinking, all blood and bone, simple grunts, soldiering with their legs, toiling up the hills and down into the paddies and across the rivers and up again and down, just humping, one step and then the next and then another, but no volition, no will, because it was automatic, it was anatomy, and the war was entirely a matter of posture and carriage, the hump was everything, a kind of inertia, a kind of emptiness, a dullness of desire and intellect and conscience and hope and human sensibility. Their principles were in their feet. Their calculations were biological. They had no sense of strategy or mission. They searched the villages without knowing what to look for, nor caring, kicking over jars of rice, frisking children and old men, blowing tunnels, sometimes setting fires and sometimes not, then forming up and moving on to the next village, then other villages, where it would always be the same. They carried their own lives. The pressures were enormous. In the heat of early afternoon, they would remove their helmets and flak jackets, walking bare, which was dangerous but which helped ease the strain. They would often discard things along the route of march. Purely for comfort, they would throw away rations, blow their Claymores and grenades, no matter, because by nightfall the resupply choppers would arrive with more of the same, then a day or two later still more, fresh watermelons and crates of ammunition and sunglasses and woolen sweaters—the resources were stunning—sparklers for the Fourth of July, colored eggs for Easter. It was the great American war chest—the fruits of sciences, the smokestacks, the canneries, the arsenals at Hartford, the Minnesota forests, the machine shops, the vast fields of corn and wheat—they carried like freight trains; they carried it on their backs and shoulders—and for all the ambiguities of Vietnam, all the mysteries and unknowns, there was at least the single abiding certainty that they would never be at a loss for things to carry.

After the chopper took Lavender away, Lieutenant Jimmy Cross led his men into the village of Than Khe. They burned everything. They shot chickens and dogs, they trashed the village well, they called in artillery and watched the wreckage, then they marched for several hours through the hot afternoon, and then at dusk, while Kiowa explained how Lavender died, Lieutenant Cross found himself trembling.

He tried not to cry. With his entrenching tool, which weighed five pounds, he began digging a hole in the earth.

He felt shame. He hated himself. He had loved Martha more than his men, and as a consequence Lavender was now dead, and this was something he would have to carry like a stone in his stomach for the rest of the war.

All he could do was dig. He used his entrenching tool like an ax, slashing, feeling both love and hate, and then later, when it was full dark, he sat at the bottom of his foxhole and wept. It went on for a long while. In part, he was grieving for Ted Lavender, but mostly it was for Martha, and for himself, because she belonged to another world, which was not quite real, and because she was a junior at Mount Sebastian College in New Jersey, a poet and a virgin and uninvolved, and because he realized she did not love him and never would.

Like cement, Kiowa whispered in the dark. I swear to God—boom-down. Not a word.

I've heard this, said Norman Bowker.

A pisser, you know? Still zipping himself up. Zapped while zipping.

All right, fine. That's enough.

Yeah, but you had to see it, the guy just—

I *heard*, man. Cement. So why not shut the fuck *up?*

Kiowa shook his head sadly and glanced over at the hole where Lieutenant Jimmy Cross sat watching the night. The air was thick and wet. A warm, dense fog had settled over the paddies and there was the stillness that precedes rain.

After a time Kiowa sighed.

One thing for sure, he said. The lieutenant's in some deep hurt. I mean that crying jag—the way he was carrying on—it wasn't fake or anything, it was real heavy-duty hurt. The man cares.

Sure, Norman Bowker said.

Say what you want, the man does care.

We all go problems.

Not Lavender.

No, I guess not, Bowker said. Do me a favor, though.

Shut up?

That's a smart Indian. Shut up.

Shrugging, Kiowa pulled off his boots. He wanted to say more, just to lighten up his sleep, but instead he opened his New Testament and arranged it beneath his head as a pillow. The fog made things seem hollow and unattached. He tried not to think about Ted Lavender, but then he was thinking how fast it was, no drama, down and dead, and how it was hard to feel anything except surprise. It seemed unchristian. He wished he could find some great sadness, or even anger, but the emotion wasn't there and he couldn't make it happen. Mostly he felt pleased to be alive. He liked the smell of the New Testament under his cheek, the leather and ink and paper and glue, whatever the chemicals were. He liked hearing the sounds of night. Even his fatigue, it felt fine, the stiff muscles and the prickly awareness of his own body, a floating feeling. He enjoyed not being dead. Lying there, Kiowa admired Lieutenant Jimmy Cross's capacity for grief. He wanted to share the man's pain, he wanted to care as Jimmy Cross cared. And yet when he closed his eyes, all he could think was Boom-down, and all he could feel was the pleasure of having his boots off and the fog curling in around him and damp soil and the Bible smells and the plush comfort of night.

After a moment Norman Bowker sat up in the dark.

What the hell, he said. You want to talk, *talk*. Tell it to me.

Forget it.

No, man, go on. One thing I hate, it's a silent Indian.

For the most part they carried themselves with poise, a kind of dignity. Now and then, however, there were times of panic, when they squealed or wanted to squeal but couldn't, when they twitched and made moaning sounds and covered their heads and said Dear Jesus and flopped around on the earth and fired their weapons blindly and cringed and sobbed and begged for the noise to stop and went wild and made stupid promises to themselves and to God and to their mothers and fathers, hoping not to die. In different ways, it happened to all of them. Afterward, when the firing ended, they would blink and peek up. They would touch their bodies, feeling shame, then quickly hiding it. They would force themselves to stand. As if in slow motion, frame by frame, the world would take on the old logic—absolute silence, then the wind, then sunlight, then voices. It was the burden of being alive. Awkwardly, the men would reassemble themselves, first in private, then in groups, becoming soldiers again. They would repair the leaks in their eyes. They would check for casualties, call in dust-offs, light cigarettes, try to smile, clear their throats and spit and begin cleaning their weapons. After a time someone would shake his head and say, No lie, I almost shit my pants, and someone else would laugh, which meant it was bad, yes, but the guy had obviously not shit his pants, it wasn't that bad, and in any case nobody would ever do such a thing and then go ahead and talk about it. They would squint into the dense, oppressive sunlight. For a few moments, perhaps, they would fall silent, lighting a joint and tracking its passage from man to man, inhaling, holding in the humiliation. Scary stuff, one of them might say. But then someone else would grin or flick his eyebrows and say, Roger-dodger, almost cut me a new asshole, *almost*.

There were numerous such poses. Some carried themselves with a sort of wistful resignation, others with pride or still soldierly discipline or good humor or macho zeal. They were afraid of dying but they were even more afraid to show it.

They found jokes to tell.

They used a hard vocabulary to contain the terrible softness. *Greased,* they'd say. *Offed, lit up, zapped while zipping*. It wasn't cruelty, just stage presence. They were actors and the war came at them in 3-D. When someone died, it wasn't quite dying, because in a curious way it seemed scripted, and because they had their lines mostly memorized, irony mixed with tragedy, and because they called it by other names, as if to encyst and destroy the reality of death itself. They kicked corpses. They cut off thumbs. They talked grunt lingo. They told stories about Ted Lavender's supply of tranquilizers, how the poor guy didn't feel a thing, how incredibly tranquil he was.

There's a moral here, said Mitchell Sanders.

They were waiting for Lavender's chopper, smoking the dead man's dope.

The moral's pretty obvious, Sanders said, and winked. Stay away from drugs. No joke, they'll ruin your day every time.

Cute, said Henry Dobbins.

Mind-blower, get it? Talk about wiggy—nothing left, just blood and brains.

They made themselves laugh.

There it is, they'd say, over and over, as if the repetition itself were an act of poise, a balance between crazy and almost crazy, knowing without going. There it is, which meant be cool, let it ride, because oh yeah, man, you can't change what can't be changed, there it is, there it absolutely and positively and fucking well *is*.

They were tough.

They carried all the emotional baggage of men who might die. Grief, terror, love, longing—these were intangibles, but the intangibles had their own mass and specific gravity, they had tangible weight. They carried shameful memories. They carried the common secret of cowardice barely restrained, the instinct to run or freeze or hide, and in many respects this was the heaviest burden of all, for it could never be put down, it required perfect balance and perfect posture. They carried their reputations. They carried the soldier's greatest fear, which was the fear of blushing. Men killed, and died, because they were embarrassed not to. It was what had brought them to the war in the first place, nothing positive, no dreams of glory or honor, just to avoid the blush of dishonor. They died so as not to die of embarrassment. They crawled into tunnels and walked point and advanced under fire. Each morning, despite the unknowns, they made their legs move. They endured. They kept humping. They did not submit to the obvious alternative, which was simply to close the eyes and fall. So easy, really. Go limp and tumble to the ground and let the muscles unwind and not speak and not budge until your buddies picked you up and lifted you into the chopper that would roar and dip its nose and carry you off to the world. A mere matter of falling, yet no one ever fell. It was not courage, exactly; the object was not valor. Rather, they were too frightened to be cowards.

By and large they carried these things inside, maintaining the masks of composure. They sneered at sick call. They spoke bitterly about guys who had found release by shooting off their own toes or fingers. Pussies, they'd say. Candyasses. It was fierce, mocking talk, with only a trace of envy or awe, but even so, the image played itself out behind their eyes.

They imagined the muzzle against flesh. They imagined the quick, sweet pain, then the evacuation to Japan, then a hospital with warm beds and cute geisha nurses.

They dreamed of freedom birds.

At night, on guard, staring into the dark, they were carried away by jumbo jets. They felt the rush of takeoff. *Gone!* they yelled. And then velocity, wings and engines, a smiling stewardess—but it was more than a plane, it was a real bird, a big sleek silver bird with feathers and talons and high screeching. They were flying. The weights fell off, there was nothing to bear. They laughed and held on tight, feeling the cold slap of wind and altitude, soaring, thinking *It's over, I'm gone!*—they were naked, they were light and free—it was all lightness, bright and fast and buoyant, light as light, a helium buzz in the brain, a giddy bubbling in the lungs as they were taken up over the clouds and the war, beyond duty, beyond gravity and mortification and global entanglements—*Sin loi!*[7] They yelled, *I'm sorry, motherfuckers, but I'm out of it, I'm goofed, I'm on a space cruise, I'm gone!*—and it was a restful, disencumbered sensation, just riding the light waves, sailing that big silver freedom bird over the mountains and oceans, over America, over the farms and great sleeping cities and cemeteries and highways and the Golden Arches of McDonald's. It was flight, a kind of fleeing, a kind of falling, falling higher and higher, spinning off the edge of the earth and beyond the sun and through the vast, silent vacuum where there were no burdens and where everything weighed exactly nothing. *Gone!* they screamed, *I'm sorry but I'm gone!* And so at night, not quite dreaming, they gave themselves over to lightness, they were carried, they were purely borne.

On the morning after Ted Lavender died, First Lieutenant Jimmy Cross crouched at the bottom of his foxhole and burned Martha's letters. Then he burned the two photographs. There was a steady rain falling, which made it difficult, but he used heat tabs and Sterno to build a small fire, screening it with his body, holding the photographs over the tight blue flame with the tips of his fingers.

He realized it was only a gesture. Stupid, he thought. Sentimental, too, but mostly just stupid.

Lavender was dead. You couldn't burn the blame.

Besides, the letters were in his head. And even now, without photographs, Lieutenant Cross could see Martha playing volleyball in her white gym shorts and yellow T-shirt. He could see her moving in the rain.

When the fire died out, Lieutenant Cross pulled his poncho over his shoulders and ate breakfast from a can.

There was no great mystery, he decided.

In those burned letters Martha had never mentioned the war, except to say, Jimmy, take care of yourself. She wasn't involved. She signed the letters "Love," but it wasn't love, and all the fine lines and technicalities did not matter.

The morning came up wet and blurry. Everything seemed part of everything else, the fog and Martha and the deepening rain.

It was a war, after all.

Half smiling, Lieutenant Jimmy Cross took out his maps. He shook his head hard, as if to clear it, then bent forward and began planning the day's march. In ten minutes, or maybe twenty, he would rouse the men and they would pack up and head west, where the maps showed the country to be green and inviting. They would do what they had always done. The rain might add some weight, but otherwise it would be one more day layered upon all the other days.

He was realistic about it. There was the new hardness in his stomach.

No more fantasies, he told himself.

Henceforth, when he thought about Martha, it would be only to think that she belonged elsewhere. He would shut down the daydreams. This was not Mount Sebastian, it was another world, where there were no pretty poems or midterm exams, a place where men died because of carelessness and gross stupidity. Kiowa was right. Boom-down, and you were dead, never partly dead.

---

[7]*Sin loi* sorry

Briefly, in the rain, Lieutenant Cross saw Martha's gray eyes gazing back at him.

He understood.

It was very sad, he thought. The things men carried inside. The things men did or felt they had to do.

He almost nodded at her, but didn't.

Instead he went back to his maps. He was now determined to perform his duties firmly and without negligence. It wouldn't help Lavender, he knew that, but from this point on he would comport himself as a soldier. He would dispose of his good-luck pebble. Swallow it, maybe, or use Lee Strunk's slingshot, or just drop it along the trail. On the march he would impose strict field discipline. He would be careful to send out flank security, to prevent straggling or bunching up, to keep his troops moving at the proper pace and at the proper interval. He would insist on clean weapons. He would confiscate the remainder of Lavender's dope. Later in the day, perhaps, he would call the men together and speak to them plainly. He would accept the blame for what had happened to Ted Lavender. He would be a man about it. He would look them in the eyes, keeping his chin level, and he would issue the new SOPs in a calm, impersonal tone of voice, an officer's voice, leaving no room for argument or discussion. Commencing immediately, he'd tell them, they would no longer abandon equipment along the route of march. They would police up their acts. They would get their shit together, and keep it together, and maintain it neatly and in good working order.

He would not tolerate laxity. He would show strength, distancing himself.

Among the men there would be grumbling, of course, and maybe worse, because their days would seem longer and their loads heavier, but Lieutenant Cross reminded himself that his obligation was not to be loved but to lead. He would dispense with love; it was not now a factor. And if anyone quarreled or complained, he would simply tighten his lips and arrange his shoulders in the correct command posture. He might give a curt little nod. Or he might not. He might just shrug and say Carry on, then they would saddle up and form into a column and move out toward the villages west of Than Khe.

[1986]

Topics for Critical Thinking and Writing

1. What is the point of the insistent repetition of the words "the things they carried"? What sorts of things does Lieutenant Cross carry?
2. We are told that "Kiowa admired Lieutenant Jimmy Cross's capacity for grief." But we are also told that although Kiowa "wanted to share the man's pain," he could think only of "Boom-down" and of "the pleasure of having his boots off and the fog curling in around him and the damp soil and the Bible smells and the plush comfort of night." What might account for the different responses of the two men?
3. Near the end of the story, Lieutenant Cross "burned the two photographs." Why does he do this?

POETRY

YUSEF KOMUNYAKAA

Yusef Komunyakaa was born in 1947 in Bogalusa, Louisiana. After graduating from high school he entered the army and served in Vietnam, where he was awarded the Bronze Star. On his return to the United States he earned a bachelor's degree at the University of Colorado, and then earned an M.A. at Colorado State University and an M.F.A. in creative writing at the University of California, Irvine. The author of several books of poetry, he has been teaching at Indiana University in Bloomington since 1985. "Facing It" is the last poem in a book of poems about Vietnam, Dien Cai Dau *(1988). The title of the book is a slang word for crazy.*

Facing It

My black face fades,
hiding inside the black granite.
I said I wouldn't,
dammit: No tears.
I'm stone. I'm flesh.   5
My clouded reflection eyes me
like a bird of prey, the profile of night
slanted against morning. I turn
this way—the stone lets me go.
I turn that way—I'm inside   10
the Vietnam Veterans Memorial
again, depending on the light
to make a difference.
I go down the 58,022 names,
half-expecting to find   15
my own in letters like smoke.
I touch the name Andrew Johnson;
I see the booby trap's white flash.
Names shimmer on a woman's blouse
but when she walks away   20
the names stay on the wall.
Brushstrokes flash, a red bird's
wings cutting across my stare.
The sky. A plane in the sky.
A white vet's image floats   25
closer to me, then his pale eyes
look through mine. I'm a window.
He's lost his right arm
inside the stone. In the black mirror
a woman's trying to erase names: 30
No, she's brushing a boy's hair.

[1988]

Vietnam Veterans Memorial, Washington, D.C.

Topics for Critical Thinking and Writing

1. The poem's title is "Facing It." What is the speaker facing? How would you describe his attitude?
2. Three people, whose names we don't know, briefly appear on the wall. How might we describe their actions? Try to paraphrase: "I'm a window. / He's lost his right arm / inside the stone."
3. At the poem's end, has the speaker "faced it"? What is your evidence?
4. If you have seen the Vietnam Veterans Memorial, describe it and your reaction to it in a paragraph or two. If you haven't seen it, try to describe it from "Facing It" and any written or photographic accounts you have seen.

SEPTEMBER 11, 2001

SHORT VIEWS

Who are we now? We are people who know that we never understood what "bad day" meant until that morning that cracked our world cleanly in two, that day that made two days, September 11 and 9-11.
Anna Quindlen

For most of us, airports are the only places where life has really changed since 9/11.
    Michael Kinsley

I have never met an African-American who was surprised by the attack on the world Trade Center. Blacks do not see America as the great liberator of the world. Blacks understand how the rest of the world sees us, because we have also been the victims of American imperialism.
    Walter Mosely (author, in *The New York Times Magazine*,
    8 Feb 2004, p. 17)

The attack made everybody—everybody—remember that finally we're all just the same. We're all Americans. And today we are all New Yorkers.
    Anonymous African American resident in Miami, Florida

Only when the deepest fears of each side are both understood and addressed, and the narratives of all parties become more complex and nuanced, will events such as September 11 become less likely.
    Mark Howard Ross, political scientist

We have the opportunity to tear terrorism out by the roots. . . . The memory of September 11 reminds us all of the need to remain vigilant.
    Donald Rumsfeld, Secretary of Defense

This and each anniversary should not be remembered for the evil act of violence, but for the goodness of these officers and their tremendous spirit that they ran without hesitation into harm's way and laid down their lives for the sake of others.
    Capt. Robert Boyce, New York Police Department

[The memorial] will inspire people. It should not symbolize the loss of our world before Sept. 11 or an America that no longer exists. It should symbolize our survival and our triumph.
    Rudy Giuliani, mayor of New York

Topics for Critical Thinking and Writing

1. Has life in America changed since the events of September 11, 2001? Where do you see the signs of this change? Are the changes as significant as some people claim, or not really that significant after all?
2. Has your own life changed since 9/11? Among people whom you know, who has changed the most? The least?
3. Political leaders and law officers say that despite the threat of terrorist attack in the United States, we should "go about our daily lives as normal." Do you agree? Do you think that this is possible?

4. When interviewed about the impact of 9/11, people frequently comment, "I don't feel safe anymore," or "I'm frightened all the time about what might happen next." Do such comments make sense to you, or do they strike you as an overreaction?

5. What is "terrorism"? What is a terrorist trying to accomplish? Is terrorism always evil, or can you imagine a situation or a context in which it might be defensible?

6. Do you think that the events of 9/11 should be studied in college and university courses? How would you organize such a course? What kinds of materials would you draw upon, and what would be the key issues you would highlight?

ESSAYS

JOHN UPDIKE

John Updike (b. 1932) grew up in Shillington, Pennsylvania, where his father was a teacher and his mother was a writer. After receiving a bachelor of arts degree from Harvard, he studied drawing at Oxford for a year, but an offer from The New Yorker *magazine brought him back to the United States. He at first served as a reporter for the magazine, but soon began contributing poetry, essays, and fiction. Today he is one of America's most prolific and well-known writers.*

The following essay on the destruction of the World Trade Center (September 11, 2001), was published in The New Yorker *about a week after the attack.*

Talk of the Town: September 11, 2001

Suddenly summoned to witness something great and horrendous, we keep fighting not to reduce it to our own smallness. From the viewpoint of a tenth-floor apartment in Brooklyn Heights, where I happened to be visiting some kin, the destruction of the World Trade Center twin towers had the false intimacy of television, on a day of perfect reception. A four-year-old girl and her babysitter called from the library, and pointed out through the window the smoking top of the north tower, not a mile away. It seemed, at that first glance, more curious than horrendous: smoke speckled with bits of paper curled into the cloudless sky, and strange inky rivulets ran down the giant structure's vertically corrugated surface. The W.T.C. had formed a pale background to our Brooklyn view of lower Manhattan, not beloved, like the stony, spired midtown thirties skyscrapers it had displaced as the city's tallest, but, with its pre-postmodern combination of unignorable immensity and architectural reticence, in some lights beautiful. As we watched the second tower burst into ballooning flame (an intervening building had hidden the approach of the second airplane), there persisted the notion that, as on television, this was not quite real; it could be fixed; the technocracy the towers symbolized would find a way to put out the fire and reverse the damage.

And then, within an hour, as my wife and I watched from the Brooklyn building's roof, the south tower dropped from the screen of our viewing; it fell straight down like an elevator, with a tinkling shiver and a groan of concussion distinct across the mile of air. We knew we had just witnessed thousands of

New York, September 11, 2001.

deaths; we clung to each other as if we ourselves were falling. Amid the glittering impassivity of the many buildings across the East River, an empty spot had appeared, as if by electronic command, beneath the sky that, but for the sulfurous cloud streaming south toward the ocean, was pure blue, rendered uncannily pristine by the absence of jet trails. A swiftly expanding burst of smoke and dust hid the rest of lower Manhattan; we saw the collapse of the second tower only on television, where the footage of hellbent airplane, exploding jet fuel, and imploding tower was played and replayed, much rehearsed moments from a nightmare ballet.

The nightmare is still on. The bodies are beneath the rubble, the last-minute cell-phone calls—remarkably calm and loving, many of them—are still being reported, the sound of an airplane overhead still bears an unfamiliar menace, the thought of boarding an airplane with our old blasé blitheness keeps receding into the past. Determined men who have transposed their own lives to a martyr's afterlife can still inflict an amount of destruction that defies belief. War is conducted with a fury that requires abstraction—that turns a planeful of peaceful passengers, children included, into a missile the faceless enemy deserves. The other side has the abstractions; we have only the mundane duties of survivors—to pick up the pieces, to bury the dead, to take more precautions, to go on living.

American freedom of motion, one of our prides, has taken a hit. Can we afford the openness that lets future kamikaze pilots, say, enroll in Florida flying schools? A Florida neighbor of one of the suspects remembers him saying he didn't like the United States: "He said it was too lax. He said, 'I can go anywhere I want to, and they can't stop me.'" It is a weird complaint, a begging perhaps to be stopped. Weird, too, the silence of the heavens these days, as flying has ceased across America. But fly again we must; risk is a price of freedom, and walking around Brooklyn Heights that afternoon, as ash drifted in the air and cars were

A week after September 11, 2001.

few and open-air lunches continued as usual on Montague Street, renewed the impression that, with all its failings, this is a country worth fighting for. Freedom, reflected in the street's diversity and daily ease, felt palpable. It is mankind's elixir, even if a few turn it to poison. The next morning, I went back to the open vantage from which we had watched the tower so dreadfully slip from sight. The fresh sun shone on the eastward façades, a few boats tentatively moved in the river, the ruins were still sending out smoke, but New York looked glorious.

[2001]

Topics for Critical Thinking and Writing

1. Do you think that Updike's first sentence works well? Would the essay be more effective if it began with the second sentence?

2. How would you characterize the style of this essay? In your view, does Updike describe the actual event, or, instead, his own experience of the event? Is it possible to make a distinction between the two—a description of an event, on the one hand, and the description of one's personal experience of it, on the other?

3. Does Updike make a specific point in this piece of writing, or does he have some other intention in mind?
4. This essay was written and published very soon after the events of September 11, 2001. What is its impact when you read it today? How do you imagine that its first readers responded to it?
5. If you were the editor of *The New Yorker* magazine and this essay were submitted to you a few days after September 11 would you accept it for publication or not? What kind of letter would you write to the author, accepting or rejecting his essay, and/or asking for revisions?

MICHAEL KINSLEY

Michael Kinsley, the founding editor of Slate, *is now the editorial and opinions editor of the* Los Angeles Times. *The following essay appeared in* Time, *in September 2002, a year after the destruction of the Twin Towers.*

How to Live a Rational Life

For most of us, airports are the only places where life has really changed since 9/11. The terminal has become a vast theater of the absurd where aspiring passengers line up halfway back to town. The shoes of little old ladies are gravely removed and inspected. Men in suits take their cell phones *out* of the bag and put their laptop computers *into* the bag—no, wait, cell phones *in* and computers *out*. Random passengers stand spread-eagled while strangers say to them softly, "Now I'm going to run my hands around your waist. Is that all right?" Somewhere unseen, a food-service worker is assembling meals headed for first class with cheap plastic knives and short, pointed metal forks. And all the while the public-address system hectors us to "report any suspicious activity."

Many people, understandably skeptical about these quasi-religious rituals, have stopped flying instead. Others are thinking about moving out of New York and other big cities, and some have done so. These are responses more in keeping with the scale and drama of the episode that provoked them, but they may not make any more sense. David G. Meyers of Hope College in Holland, Mich., calculated that terrorists would have to hijack 50 planes a year and kill everyone aboard before flying would be more dangerous than driving an equal distance.

The steps we have taken to protect ourselves from terrorism (not counting the military effort to stop it at the source) seem either farcically trivial or farcically excessive. Is there a middle ground?

Dealing rationally with the risks of terrorism is hard for several reasons. First, human beings are bad at assessing small risks of large catastrophes. And Americans are especially bad at this because we are Americans, and catastrophes are not supposed to happen to us. Our legal culture, our political culture and our media culture all push us toward excessive caution by guaranteeing that any large disaster will produce an orgy of hindsight. Lawyers will sue, politicians will hold hearings, newspapers and newsmagazines will publish overexcited revelations about secret memos that could be interpreted as having warned of this if held up to the light at a certain angle.

5   Second, the actual risk of being a terror victim in not merely small—it is unknown and unknowable. Economists make a distinction between "risk" and "uncertainty." *Risk* refers to hard mathematical odds. *Uncertainty* refers to situations in which the odds are anybody's guess.

"All the News
That's Fit to Print"

The New York Times

VOL. CL . . No. 51,874   Copyright © 2001 The New York Times   NEW YORK, WEDNESDAY, SEPTEMBER 12, 2001 $1 beyond the greater New York metropolitan area.   75 CENTS

Late Edition
New York: Today, sunny, a few afternoon clouds. High 77. Tonight, slightly
more humid. Low 65. Tomorrow, sun
then clouds. High 81. Yesterday, high
81, low 63. Weather map, Page C19.

U.S. ATTACKED

HIJACKED JETS DESTROY TWIN TOWERS AND HIT PENTAGON IN DAY OF TERROR

A CREEPING HORROR

Buildings Burn and Fall as Onlookers Search for Elusive Safety

By N. R. KLEINFIELD

It kept getting worse.

The horror arrived in episodic bursts of chilling disbelief, signified first by trembling floors, sharp eruptions, cracked windows. There was the actual unfathomable realization of a gaping, flaming hole in first one or the tall towers, and then the same thing all over again in its twin. There was the merciless sight of bodies helplessly tumbling out, some of them in flames.

Finally, the mighty towers themselves were reduced to nothing. Dense plumes of smoke raced through the downtown avenues, coursing between the buildings, shaped like tornadoes on their sides.

Every sound was cause for alarm. A plane appeared overhead. Was another one coming? No, it was a fighter jet. But was it friend or enemy? People scrambled for their lives, but they didn't know where to go. Should they go north, south, east, west? Stay outside, go indoors? People hid beneath cars and each other. Some contemplated jumping into the river.

For those trying to flee the very epicenter of the collapsing World Trade Center towers, the most horrid thought of all finally dawned on them: nowhere was safe.

For several panic-stricken hours yesterday morning, people in Lower Manhattan witnessed the inexpressible, the incomprehensible, the unthinkable. "I don't know what the gates of hell look like, but it's got to be like this," said John Maloney, a security director for an Internet firm in the trade center. "I'm a combat veteran, Vietnam, and I never saw anything like this."

The first warnings were small ones. Shocks away, Jim Farmer, a film composer, was having breakfast at a small restaurant on West Broadway. He heard the sound of a jet. An odd sound — too loud, it seemed, to be

Continued on Page A7

A Somber Bush Says Terrorism Cannot Prevail

By ELISABETH BUMILLER
with DAVID E. SANGER

WASHINGTON, Sept. 11 — President Bush vowed tonight to retaliate against those responsible for today's attacks on New York and Washington, declaring that he would "make no distinction between the terrorists who committed these acts and those who harbor them."

"These acts of mass murder were intended to frighten our nation into chaos and retreat, but they have failed," the president said in his first speech to the nation from the Oval Office. "Our country is strong. Terrorist acts can shake the foundation of our biggest buildings, but they cannot touch the foundation of America."

His speech came after a day of trauma used largely to define his presidency. Seeking to at once calm the nation and declare his determination in exact retribution, he told a country numbed by repeated scenes of carnage that "these acts shattered steel, but they cannot dent the steel of American resolve."

Mr. Bush spoke only hours after returning from a zigzag course across the country, as his Secret Service and military security teams moved him from Florida, where he woke up this morning expecting to press for his education bill, to command posts in Louisiana and Nebraska before it was determined the attacks had probably ended and he could safely return to the capital.

It was a sign of the catastrophic

Continued on Page A4

SECOND PLANE United Airlines Flight 175 nearing the trade center's south tower.

President Vows to Exact Punishment for 'Evil'

By SERGE SCHMEMANN

Hijackers rammed jetliners into each of New York's World Trade Center towers yesterday, toppling both in a hellish storm of ash, glass, smoke and leaping victims, while a third jetliner crashed into the Pentagon in Virginia. There was no official count, but President Bush said thousands had perished, and in the immediate aftermath the calamity was already being ranked the worst and most audacious terror attack in American history.

The attacks seemed carefully coordinated. The hijacked planes were all en route to California, and therefore gorged with fuel, and their departures were spaced within an hour and 40 minutes. The first, American Airlines Flight 11, a Boeing 767 out of Boston for Los Angeles, crashed into the north tower at 8:48 a.m. Eighteen minutes later, United Airlines Flight 175, also headed from Boston to Los Angeles, plowed into the south tower.

Then an American Airlines Boeing 757, Flight 77, left Washington's Dulles International Airport bound for Los Angeles, but instead hit the western part of the Pentagon, the military headquarters where 24,000 people work, at 9:40 a.m. Finally, United Airlines Flight 93, a Boeing 757 flying from Newark to San Francisco, crashed near Pittsburgh, raising the possibility that its hijackers had failed in whatever their mission was.

There were indications that the hijackers on at least two of the planes were armed with knives. Attorney General John Ashcroft told reporters in the evening that the suspects on Flight 11 were armed that way. And Barbara Olson, a television commentator who was traveling on American Flight 77, managed to reach her husband, Solicitor General Theodore Olson, by cell phone and to tell him that the hijackers were armed with knives and a box cutter.

In all, 266 people perished in the four planes and several score more were known dead elsewhere. Numerous firefighters, police officers and other rescue workers who responded to the initial disaster in Lower Manhattan were killed or injured when the buildings collapsed. Hundreds were treated for cuts, broken bones, burns and smoke inhalation.

But the real carnage was concealed for now by the twisted, smoking, ash-choked carcasses of the twin towers, in which thousands of people used to work on a weekday. The collapse of the towers caused another World Trade Center building to fall 7 hours later, and several

Continued on Page A14

Awaiting the Aftershocks

Washington and Nation Plunge Into Fight With Enemy Hard to Identify and Punish

By R. W. APPLE Jr.

WASHINGTON, Sept. 11 — Today's devastating and astonishingly well-coordinated attacks on the World Trade Center towers in New York and on the Pentagon outside of Washington plunged the nation into a warlike struggle against an enemy that will be hard to identify with certainty and hard to punish with precision.

The whole nation — to a degree the whole world — shook as hijacked airliners plunged into buildings that symbolize the financial and military might of the United States. The sense of security and self-confidence that Americans take as their birthright suffered a grievous blow, from which recovery will be slow. The aftershocks will be nearly as bad, as hundreds and possibly thousands of people discover that their friends or relatives died awful, fiery deaths.

Scenes of chaos and destruction evocative of the nightmare world of Hieronymus Bosch, with smoke and debris blotting out the sun, were carried by television into homes and workplaces across the nation. Echoing Franklin D. Roosevelt's description of the attack on Pearl Harbor as an event "which will live in infamy," Gov. George E. Pataki of New York, a Republican, spoke of "an incredible outrage" and Senator Charles E. Schumer of New York, a Democrat, spoke of "a dastardly attack."

But mere words were inadequate vessels to contain the sense of shock and horror that people felt.

As Washington struggled to regain

a sense of equilibrium, with warplanes and heavily armed helicopters crossing overhead, past and present national security officials earnestly debated the possibility of a Congressional declaration of war — but against precisely whom, and in what exact circumstances? Warships were maneuvering to protect New York and Washington. The North American Air Defense Command, which had seemed to many a relic of the cold war, adopted a pos-

Continued on Page A24

MORE ON THE ATTACKS

RESCUERS BECOME VICTIMS Firefighters who rushed to the trade center were killed.
PAGE A2

SEARCH FOR SURVIVORS Some people trapped in the rubble for hours were rescued.
PAGE A2

OFFICIALS SUSPECT BIN LADEN Eavesdropping intercepts after the attacks were cited.
PAGE A11

TERRORISTS EXPLOIT WEAKNESS Investigators had criticized precautions against hijacking.
PAGE A11

CASUALTIES IN WASHINGTON An unknown number of people were killed at the Pentagon.
PAGE A8

FOR HOME DELIVERY CALL 1-800-NYTIMES

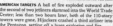

AMERICAN TARGETS A ball of fire exploded outward after the second of two jetliners slammed into the World Trade Center; less than two hours later, both of the 110-story towers were gone. Hijackers crashed a third airliner into the Pentagon, setting off a huge explosion and fire.

Third, even knowing what is theoretically knowable is impossible for most of us. Just attempting to list the fields of knowledge where expertise would be required strains my own ignorance: aeronautical engineering, Middle Eastern politics, nuclear physics, um, microbiology? Clinical psychology? Without a clue about most of these subjects, how can citizens think rationally about them? Walter Lippmann, in his famous 1922 book, *Public Opinion*, said the solution was to turn over most public policy questions to boards of experts.

Fourth, it's hard to be rational about the irrational. Who can guess intelligently what Osama bin Laden might want to try next? How can you discourage a suicide bomber who is looking forward to being dead after killing you? Irrationality holds a treasured place in game theory, the branch of economics dedicated to strategic questions of this sort. Game theory's great insight is that irrationality can be an asset. If you can convince the world that you're nuts—and the surest way to do that is to *be* nuts—your behavior becomes impossible to predict or control. You become, in a way, invulnerable.

What all this adds up to is a strong suspicion that we are not doing too little about terrorism: we are probably doing too much. Our initial instincts are overly risk averse; the danger probably looms larger than it should. A crazed terrorist's next move is going to be a surprise: the burdens we impose on ourselves out of hindsight from the last episode are unlikely to be the ones hindsight will recommend after the next one. We can be skeptical about the warnings of terrorism "experts." They have a psychological or even financial interest in erring on the side of panic.

Before we avoid skyscrapers in case they are hit by hijacked airplanes, we should consider other risks and what we are doing to avoid them. About 4,000 people die by accidental drowning every year. That's more than died on 9/11. Rationality cannot tell us precisely what it's worth to avoid an unknowable risk. But rationality can compare risks and gently suggest that you should not worry about one risk if you are happily oblivious to another. In short, a more rational approach to protecting ourselves from terrorism may not be doing more about it, or doing something different, but actually doing less. We need the courage and good sense to bury our heads in the sand a bit.

[2002]

Topics for Critical Thinking and Writing

1. Kinsley begins by saying that for most of us, "Airports are the only places where life has really changed since 9/11." What was your first response to this assertion? Did you find yourself agreeing (and therefore thinking that this Kinsley fellow is making good sense), disagreeing (and thinking that this Kinsley fellow must be very odd), or wondering whether he may or may not be right? Do you agree with Kinsley? Has your life significantly changed? If so, how?

2. If you were an instructor in a composition course and Kinsley submitted this essay, what grade would you give it? Why?

3. Writing in September, 2002, Kinsley says in his eighth paragraph, "What all this adds up to is a strong suspicion that we are not doing too little about terrorism: we are probably doing too much." Reread Kinsley's earlier paragraphs, and then—whether you agree with him or not—make the best counterargument that you can.

FICTION

CATHARINE R. STIMPSON

Catharine R. Stimpson, a literary critic, teacher, and the founding editor of Signs: Journal of Women in Culture and Society, USA, *has written and edited numerous books. She is now a professor of English and Dean of the Graduate School of Arts and Sciences at New York University.*

Staffing

At church, when I see bishops, I get a little chuckle from their staffs, those sticks they carry, the ones with a crook at the end. They're supposed to remind me that the bishops are my shepherd and I'm a member of their flock. But my position is Administrative Staff, Grade 13, and if I protect anybody, it's my boss, who's nice to me, and whose wife can be pretty nice to me, and who doesn't cheat on his wife, unlike most of the bozos around here, and who takes care of me if one of the bozos hits on me.

Some of the families are going to visit the office today. My boss'll meet with them in his office. After September 11, we put another American flag on his wall, to go with the American flag and the state flag on their stands by his desk. But he'll only meet with them for a minute or two. None of the families live in the district. I checked that out. Believe me, I checked that out. But he has to meet with them, because they are the families, and it would look awful if he didn't. It would be awful if he didn't. We all watched the towers burning on TV, and we all said America will never be the same, and he's a co-sponsor of the bill that says the state is going to crack down on people who cheat on their student visas and ask the state police to make colleges tell us who's really in class on those visas.

I will meet with the families after him. I don't think we're going to get any widows, and I'm glad about that. I don't have trouble talking to people, but meeting the widows, or any of the children, would put me into a meltdown, and I go into enough meltdowns as it is. It's so sad. It's really tragic. I feel so bad for them. I can't begin to describe my feelings. I think we are going to get a brother and two sisters of the victims, and a father if he can manage the trip.

It's going to be hard, very hard. We know what they want. They want September 11 to be declared a state holiday, like Memorial Day or Flag Day. We also put American flags on all the doors of the offices after September 11. But it's turning into a big deal. Yesterday, the boss met for an hour, a lifetime around here, with some constituents and major players. They were very respectful. They didn't want to look as if they were playing politics—god forbid—over the bodies of the victims. So all they said was that they were afraid of a state holiday. But they said it in that tone they use when they mean pay attention. The small business people are afraid of the money. I don't blame them. They lose money on state holidays, because the insurance people and the accountants and the little places have to close, unless they're in retail. And small business—that's mother's milk for us. The Bear himself told us troops that a state holiday would cost $25 million—$25 million—in holiday bonuses for state employees. And I know the staffer who came up with that figure. He doesn't fool around. And then the unions would demand the day off, and that would just mean the usual table-pounding and shouting.

5   The leadership says we should tell the families that we'll guarantee a Day of Remembrance. I have made up a list of Days of Remembrance for them. Pearl Harbor is right there. A Day of Remembrance has dignity, and before September 11, Pearl Harbor was the worst thing any enemy ever did to America. I agree with the boss here. I'm protecting him on this one because I really believe it, and you can believe me, I know the difference between protecting him because I have to because I'm a staffer and because I want to protect him because I believe in him. I'll listen to the families, and remind them of Pearl Harbor. The place where my mouth will stick is having to say that state holidays mostly suck anyway, obviously I'll say it nicer than that, that nobody cares about them except to go shopping and have barbecues. Have you ever seen a supermarket parking lot before a state holiday, before Memorial Day? Nobody's buying books about World War I or World War II. They're buying nachos. But it's going to be hard to say that, because I can't look as if we don't respect Memorial Day or President's Day or Flag Day. And I'll promise the families that my boss will put a provision in the bill, he'll personally see to it, that all the flags on public buildings will fly at half-mast on every September 11 forever and ever. I'll make a Day of Remembrance a great memorial, and a state holiday a joke. But the gentlemen, as they call themselves, in the other chamber say that September 11 was so big and so awful that it has to have a state holiday. We won't remember it unless there's a holiday. Funny, isn't it, to have a holiday so we can think about dead people and debris and the War on Terror. One of them actually saw the towers collapse, and he's impossible to talk to about the issue. His guys say a state holiday would only cost $5 to $8 million. Only $5 to $8 million.

In this job, you've got to learn to count the votes. I often tell my boss I'm going to save all the little pieces of paper where he's scratched down names and how they're going to vote. I tell him they look like betting slips, and he asks me how I know about betting slips. A good question. My Grandad would have to answer it. This is what is going to go down. Our chamber will pass a bill for a Day of Remembrance. The other guys will pass a bill for a state holiday. And if it gets on the news, and if it's more than an inside story in the *Times*, which our constituents don't read, we'll look damn stupid—again. But if it's only an inside story in the *Times*, the leadership will try to strike a deal—although it's hard to make a deal because of the guy who saw the buildings go down, and some of the other guys who actually knew people who were victims. And, I don't want to be crude about it, because evil was done on September 11, but we don't exactly have the same constituencies.

So I'll put on my black suit, with the skirt that goes below my knees, and listen to the families. I'll show them the old copy of the magazine I keep in my desk drawer, with the black cover, where you can just see the outline of the towers in black. I feel for them, I really do, I believe in a Day of Remembrance, for all America. And why not for all the world?

Topics for Critical Thinking and Writing

1. Is this speaker a man or a woman? How can you tell?
2. The speaker says at one point: "It's so sad. It's really tragic. I feel so bad for them. I can't begin to describe my feelings." What is the tone of these sentences? What do they tell us about the speaker?
3. Is this a good story? What leads you to this judgment? Does the story make you want to read more stories by this author? Please explain why, or why not.

POETRY

BILLY COLLINS

"Billy Collins writes lovely poems," the novelist, critic, and poet John Updike has said: "Limpid, gently and consistently startling, more serious than they seem, they describe all the worlds that are and were and some others besides." The recipient of many honors and awards, and a former poet laureate of the United States, Collins was born in New York City in 1941. He has taught at both the City University of New York and Sarah Lawrence College. His Sailing Alone Around the Room: New and Selected Poems *was published in 2002.*

Collins wrote the following poem on the first anniversary of the destruction of the Twin Towers.

The Names

Yesterday, I lay awake in the palm of the night.
A soft rain stole in, unhelped by any breeze,
And when I saw the silver glaze on the windows,
I started with A, with Ackerman, as it happened,
Then Baxter and Calabro,   5
Davis and Eberling, names falling into place
As droplets fell through the dark.
Names printed on the ceiling of the night.
Names slipping around a watery bend.
Twenty-six willows on the banks of a stream.   10
In the morning, I walked out barefoot
Among thousands of flowers
Heavy with dew like the eyes of tears,
And each had a name—
Fiori inscribed on a yellow petal   15
Then Gonzalez and Han, Ishikawa and Jenkins.
Names written in the air
And stitched into the cloth of the day.
A name under a photograph taped to a mailbox.
Monogram on a torn shirt,   20
I see you spelled out on storefront windows
And on the bright unfurled awnings of this city.
I say the syllables as I turn a corner—
Kelly and Lee,
Medina, Nardella, and O'Connor.   25
When I peer in to the woods,
I see a thick tangle where letters are hidden
As in a puzzle concocted for children.
Parker and Quigley in the twigs of an ash,
Rizzo, Schubert, Torres, and Upton,   30
Secrets in the boughs of an ancient maple.
Names written in the pale sky.
Names rising in the updraft amid buildings.
Names silent in stone

Or cried out behind a door.   35
Names blown over the earth and out to sea.
In the evening—weakening light, the last swallows.
A boy on a lake lifts his oars.
A woman by a window puts a match to a candle,
And the names are outlined on the rose clouds—   40
Vanacore and Wallace,
(let X stand, if it can, for the ones unfound)
Then Young and Ziminsky, the final jolt of Z.
Names etched on the head of a pin.
One name spanning a bridge, another undergoing a tunnel.   45
A blue name needled into the skin.
Names of citizens, workers, mothers and fathers,
The bright-eyed daughter, the quick son.
Alphabet of names in a green field.
Names in the small tracks of birds.   50
Names lifted from a hat
Or balanced on the tip of the tongue.
Names wheeled into the dim warehouse of memory.
So many names, there is barely room on the walls of the heart.

[2002]

Topics for Critical Thinking and Writing

1. In an interview that appeared several years before "The Names" was published, Collins says of his intention as a poet: "By the end of the poem, the reader should be in a different place from where he started." When you finished reading "The Names," did you find yourself in a "different place"? How would you describe this place?

2. Collins has also observed, again in an interview before he wrote "The Names": "Poetry is clearly very serious for me, but without heaviness or a glib sense of spirituality." Do you perceive a "spiritual" dimension to this poem—one that is not "glib"? What does it mean to say that a poem is "spiritual," that is creates a spiritual effect? Is this the same thing as saying that a poem is "religious," or is it something different?

3. Many readers have expressed their high regard for "The Names," referring to it as a "great poem." Do you agree? What defines a great poem? Do you think a poet does or does not face a special challenge in trying to write a poem, great or simply good, about the tragedy of September 11, 2001? Please explain.

4. One critic, who otherwise admires Collins's work, has objected to "The Names" for being "too sentimental." How would you define "sentimentality"? (Clarify your definition with an example.) Can you locate evidence in the text that might support the judgment that Collins's poem is sentimental? Are there other passages you could cite and analyze in order to argue against it? And what's the matter with sentimentality? Is sentimentality something that poets should always avoid?

5. How do you feel about your own name? Is it something you give much thought to? Any thought? Why is that? Now that you have read Collins's poem, has your relationship to your own name changed in any way?

DEBORAH GARRISON

The poet Deborah Garrison worked in the 1980s and 1990s as a senior editor for The New Yorker *magazine. She then became the poetry editor at Alfred A. Knopf publisher and a senior editor at Pantheon Books. She is the author of* A Working Girl Can't Win and Other Poems, *published in 1998.*

September Poem

Now can I say?
On that blackest day,

When I learned of
The uncountable, the hellbent obscenity,⠀⠀⠀⠀⠀⠀⠀4

I felt, with shame, a seed in me,
Powerful and inarticulate:

I wanted to be pregnant.
Women in the street flowing toward⠀⠀⠀⠀⠀⠀⠀8

Home, dazed with grief, and my daze
Admixed with jealous awe, I wondered

If they were,
Or wished for it, too,⠀⠀⠀⠀⠀⠀⠀12

To be full, to be forming,
To be giving our blood's food

To the yet to be.
To feel the warp of morning's⠀⠀⠀⠀⠀⠀⠀16

Hormonal chucking, the stutter kiss
Of first movement. At first,

The idea of sex a further horror:
To take pleasure in a collision⠀⠀⠀⠀⠀⠀⠀20

Of bodies was vile, self-centered, too lush.
But the pushy, ennobling pulse

Of the ordinary won't halt
For good taste. Or knows nothing of tragedy.⠀⠀⠀⠀⠀⠀⠀24

Thus. Today I have a boy
A week old. Blessed surplus:

A third child.
Have you heard mothers,⠀⠀⠀⠀⠀⠀⠀28

Matter of fact, call the third
The insurance policy?

That wasn't why.
And not because when so many people   32

Die we want, crudely pining,
To replace them with more people.

But for the wild, heaven-grazing
Pleasure and pain of the arrival.   36

The small head crushed and melony
After a journey

Out. Sheer cliff
Of the first day, flat in bed, gut-empty,   40

Ringed by memories and sharp cries.
Sharp bliss in proximity to the roundness,

The globe already a-spin, particular,
Of a whole new life.   44

Which might in any case
End in towering sorrow.

[2003]

Topics in Critical Thinking and Writing

1. What is your response to "September Poem"? Do you think that it's a good poem?
2. Did this poem give you a new perspective on the events of September 11, 2001? Do you feel you have learned something new from the experience of reading it? Please explain.
3. One poet has stated that he would find it "impossible" to write a poem about 9/11. Why might someone have such a response? Do you agree, or disagree?
4. Deborah Garrison has observed about this poem, that she knew in advance there was a "danger of conflating personal feelings with something so much larger in a way that's offensive." What is she saying? Does her concern make sense to you? In your view, does Garrison avoid this "danger," or does she fall prey to it?
5. Garrison declares, "I wanted to be pregnant." Why does she make such a statement? What is the relationship of this line to the poem as a whole?

24

Identity in America

SHORT VIEWS

America is God's crucible, the great melting pot where all the races of Europe are melting and re-forming.
    Israel Zangwill

We have room for but one language here and that is the English language, for we intend to see that the crucible turns out our people as Americans, of American nationality and not as dwellers in a polyglot boarding house, and we have room for but one loyalty and that is a loyalty to the American people.
    Theodore Roosevelt

No metaphor can capture completely the complexity of ethnic dynamics in the U.S. "Melting pot" ignores the persistence and reconfiguration of ethnicity over the generations. "Mosaic," much more apt for pluralistic societies such as Kenya or India, is too static a metaphor; it fails to take into account the easy penetration of many ethnic boundaries. Nor is "salad bowl" appropriate; the ingredients of a salad bowl are mixed but do not change. "Rainbow" is a tantalizing metaphor, but rainbows disappear. "Symphony," like "rainbow," implies near perfect harmony; both fail to take into account the variety and range of ethnic conflict in the Untied States.

The most accurately descriptive metaphor, the one that best explains the dynamics of ethnicity, is " kaleidoscope." American ethnicity is kaleidoscopic, i.e. "complex and varied, changing form, pattern, color . . . continually shifting from one set of relations to another; rapidly changing" When a kaleidoscope is in motion, the parts give the appearance of rapid change and extensive variety in color and shape and in their interrelationhips. The viewer sees an endless variety of variegated patterns, just as takes place on the American ethnic landscape.
    Lawrence Fuchs

Through our own efforts and concerted good faith in learning to know, thus to respect, the wonderfully rich and diverse subcommunities of America, we can establish a new vision of America: a place where

*"community" may mean many things, yet retains its deeper spiritual sig-
nificance. We may even learn to coincide with the 500th anniversary of
the "discovery" of America by Columbus, that America, in its magnificent
variety, has yet to be discovered.*
   Joyce Carol Oates

*It is impossible for a stranger traveling through the United States to tell
from the appearance of the people or the country whether he is in Toledo,
Ohio, or Portland, Oregon. Ninety million Americans cut their hair in
the same way, eat each morning exactly the same breakfast, tie up the
small girls' curls with precisely the same kind of ribbon fashioned into
bows exactly alike; and in every way all try to look and act as much like
all the others as they can.*
   Alfred Harmsworth, Lord Northcliffe

*I have a dream that my four little children will one day live in a nation
where they will not be judged by the color of their skin but by the content
of their character.*
   Martin Luther King Jr.

*Light came to me when I realized that I did not have to consider any
racial group as a whole. God made them duck by duck and that was the
only way I could see them.*
   Zora Neale Hurston

*Racism is so universal in this country, so wide-spread and deep-seated,
that it is invisible because it is so normal.*
   Shirley Chisholm

Topics for Critical Thinking and Writing

1. If you are an American, are you proud to be an American? Explain why.
2. If you are not an American, are you thinking about becoming one? Why or why not?
3. Do you feel you are more or less of an "American" than other Americans whom you know, or know about? How does one become a "real" American? Is it just a matter of place of birth, or (for someone coming here from abroad) of place of residence? Have you attended an event, or been part of an experience, when you said to yourself, "This is what it feels like to be an American"?
4. If you are an American who has traveled abroad, where, and in what ways, were you conscious of being an American? More so in some places than in others? If you have traveled abroad at different times, have you found yourself more conscious now of your American identity than you were in the past? What sorts of interactions and experiences led you to feel this?
5. Sometimes we hear references to the "heartland of America," or the "true America." Are there some parts of the country that are more "American" than others? If this is the case, is it a bad or a good thing?

6. We see, hear, and read a great deal about racial, ethnic, and religious differences, both within the United States and overseas. But isn't it the case that everyone, finally, is the same?

7. A recent survey concluded that "identity" is now the topic studied the most in college and university courses. Do you agree that it should be? Why is this topic receiving so much attention? Are there other topics that you believe are equally important, and maybe even more important? What are they, and what kinds of courses would you design and develop for studying them?

ESSAYS

THOMAS JEFFERSON

Thomas Jefferson (1743–1826) was a member of a prominent Virginia family; after studying at the College of William and Mary, he practiced law (1767–1774). He was active politically in his home state, and made an important early contribution to the revolutionary movement in "A Summary View of the Rights of British America" (1774). A member of the Continental Congress (1775–1776), Jefferson was the author of the Declaration of Independence, which, it has been said, "encapsulated a cosmology, a political philosophy, and a national creed" in the space of a few brilliantly composed and eloquent paragraphs.

Jefferson later served as governor of Virginia (1779–1781), working to improve education, ensure religious freedom, and advance other social and political reforms. He also was minister to France (1784–1789), the first secretary of state (1789–93), and president of the United States (1801–1809). After his second term as president ended, Jefferson devoted much of his time and energy to the University of Virginia, which he founded, and to his home of Monticello, which he designed himself. He wrote his own epitaph: "Here was buried Thomas Jefferson, Author of the Declaration of Independence, of the Statute of Virginia for Religious Freedom, and Father of the University of Virginia." Well over a century later, at a White House dinner in 1962 honoring forty-nine Nobel Prize winners, President Kennedy observed: "This is the most extraordinary collection of human talent, of human knowledge, that has ever been gathered at the White House—with the possible exception of when Thomas Jefferson dined alone."

An Argument for America

In the spring of 1776, Jefferson was named one of five members of a committee (others included Benjamin Franklin and John Adams) appointed by the Continental Congress to prepare a preamble to a resolution that the colonies were "and of right ought to be, free and Independent States." As the committee member with (in Adam's phrase) the "reputation of a masterly pen," Jefferson was selected to write the text. The committee revised the draft he produced, and it then was presented to the Continental Congress on June 28. After a two-day period of debate, July 2–4, which led to further revisions, the Declaration was adopted on July 4. On the 15th of the month, the Continental Congress added the word unanimous *to the document's title, "Declaration of the Thirteen States of America." An official parchment copy was signed on August 2, and copies were distributed throughout the colonies.*

As the historian Jay Fliegelman noted (New York Times, *July 4, 2001), it is crucial to understand that "the Declaration is an argument." In it Jefferson, the Continental Congress, and the colonies as a whole are making a case against England and on their own behalf in a forthright, focused, and detailed form. The Declaration states principles, gives a list of grievances, and identifies and embraces an alternative to and remedy for the intolerable situation that it describes.*

Jefferson and the others were keenly conscious of the Declaration as an act of writing, a literary as well as a political work. The "object of the Declaration of Independence," Jefferson said in 1825, was

> *not to find out new principles, or new arguments, never before thought of, not merely to say things which had never been said before; but to place before mankind the common sense of the subject, in terms so plain and firm as to command assent, and to justify ourselves in the independent stand we were compelled to take.*

Yet the arguments and principles at the time did seem boldly new, and the Declaration of Independence endures as an astounding piece of writing that was more radical in its implications than even Jefferson realized. Perhaps no one understood this radicalism more profoundly than did Abraham Lincoln, who claimed that American history began not with the settlements in Jamestown and Plymouth, but, rather, with the Declaration of Independence. In 1855, for example, Lincoln said: "As a nation, we began by declaring that all men are created equal." This, to Lincoln, was the essential fact of American life.

Of course in 1776, and afterward, there were terrible contradictions between the ideals of the Declaration and American realities. Jefferson himself, and George Washington, James Madison, and other statesmen of the new nation, owned slaves. Jefferson also sold slaves to pay his debts, and, unlike Washington, he did not provide in his will for his slaves' freedom upon his death.

For Lincoln, however, the manifest contradiction between the words of the Declaration and slavery meant that slavery one day would surely be abolished. The promise of equality gave the United States a special role among nations, making it the "source of hope to all the world, for all future time." To Lincoln it was inconceivable that the United States would remain half-slave and half-free. The words of the Declaration of Independence were too powerful, too incontrovertible in the long run, for that ever to be the case. Indeed, one could propose that it was not only slavery, but also the Declaration of Independence, that caused the Civil War.

In a sense, as Lincoln recognized, all of American history has been an argument—and sometimes a very bloody one—about who does not belong within the terms of the Declaration of Independence, about who is or who is not an authentic American. Women and minorities, African Americans above all, have argued that the Declaration of Independence, with its affirmation that "all men are created equal," in truth applies to them as well. And they have had to overcome arguments, both verbal and violent, from the other side that it does not and must not. As many of the selections that follow indicate, this argument, in various forms, continues today.

The Declaration of Independence

When in the course of human events, it becomes necessary for one people to dissolve the political bands which have connected them with another, and to assume among the Powers of the earth, the separate and equal station to which the

Laws of Nature and of Nature's God entitle them, a decent respect to the opinions of mankind requires that they should declare the causes which impel them to the separation.

We hold these truths to be self-evident, that all men are created equal, that they are endowed by their Creator with certain unalienable Rights, that among these are Life, Liberty and the pursuit of Happiness.

That to secure these rights, Governments are instituted among Men, deriving their just powers from the consent of the governed.

That whenever any Form of Government becomes destructive of these ends, it is the Right of the People to alter or to abolish it, and to institute a new Government, laying its foundation on such principles and organizing its powers in such form, as to them shall seem most likely to effect their Safety and Happiness. Prudence, indeed, will dictate that Governments long established should not be changed for light and transient causes; and accordingly all experience hath shown that mankind are more disposed to suffer, while evils are sufferable, than to right themselves by abolishing the forms to which they are accustomed. But when a long train of abuses and usurpations pursuing invariably the same Object evinces a design to reduce them under absolute Despotism, it is their right, it is their duty, to throw off such government, and to provide new Guards for their future security.

5   Such has been the patient sufferance of these Colonies; and such is now the necessity which constrains them to alter their former Systems of Government. The history of the present King of Great Britain is a history of repeated injuries and usurpations, all having in direct object the establishment of an absolute Tyranny over these States. To prove this, let Facts be submitted to a candid world.

He has refused his Assent to Laws, the most wholesome and necessary for the public good.

He has forbidden his Governors to pass Laws of immediate and pressing importance, unless suspended in their operation till his Assent should be obtained; and when so suspended, he has utterly neglected to attend to them.

He has refused to pass over Laws for the accommodation of large districts of people, unless those people would relinquish the right of Representation in the Legislature, a right inestimable to them and formidable to tyrants only.

He has called together legislative bodies at places unusual, uncomfortable, and distant from the depository of their Public Records, for the sole purpose of fatiguing them into compliance with his measures.

10   He has dissolved Representative Houses repeatedly, for opposing with manly firmness his invasions on the rights of the people.

He has refused for a long time, after such dissolutions, to cause others to be elected; whereby the Legislative Powers, incapable of Annihilation, have returned to the People at large for their exercise; the State remaining in the mean time exposed to all the dangers of invasion from without, and convulsions within.

He has endeavored to prevent the population of these States, for that purpose obstructing the Laws of Naturalization of Foreigners; refusing to pass others to encourage their migration hither, and raising the conditions of new Appropriations of Lands.

He has obstructed the Administration of Justice, by refusing his Assent to Laws for establishing Judiciary Powers.

He has made Judges dependent on his Will alone, for the tenure of their offices, and the amount and payment of their salaries.

15   He has erected a multitude of New Offices, and sent hither swarms of Officers to harass our People, and eat out their substance.

He has kept among us, in time of peace, Standing Armies without the consent of our Legislature.

He has affected to render the Military independent of and superior to the Civil Power.

He has combined with others to subject us to jurisdictions foreign to our constitution, and unacknowledged by our laws; giving his Assent to their acts of pretended Legislation:

For quartering large bodies of armed troops among us:

20   For protecting them, by a mock Trial, from Punishment for any Murders which they should commit on the Inhabitants of these States:

For cutting off our Trade with all parts of the world:

For imposing Taxes on us without our Consent:

For depriving us in many cases, of the benefits of Trial by Jury:

For transporting us beyond Seas to be tried for pretended offenses:

25   For abolishing the free System of English Laws in a Neighbouring Province, establishing therein an Arbitrary government, and enlarging its boundaries so as to render it at once an example and fit instrument for introducing the same absolute rule into these Colonies:

For taking away our Charters, abolishing our most valuable Laws, and altering fundamentally the Forms of our Governments:

For suspending our own Legislatures, and declaring themselves invested with Power to legislate for us in all cases whatsoever.

He has abdicated Government here, by declaring us out of his Protection and waging War against us.

He has plundered our seas, ravaged our Coasts, burnt our towns and destroyed the Lives of our people.

30   He is at this time transporting large Armies of foreign Mercenaries to compleat the works of death, desolation and tyranny, already begun with circumstances of Cruelty & perfidy scarcely paralleled in the most barbarous ages, and totally unworthy the Head of a civilized nation.

He has constrained our fellow Citizens taken Captive on the high Seas to bear Arms against their Country, to become the executioners of their friends and Brethren, or to fall themselves by their Hands.

He has excited domestic insurrections amongst us, and has endeavored to bring on the inhabitants of our frontiers, the merciless Indian Savages, whose known rule of warfare is an undistinguished destruction of all ages, sexes and conditions.

In every stage of these Oppressions We Have Petitioned for Redress in the most humble terms: Our repeated petitions have been answered only by repeated injury. A Prince, whose character is thus marked by every act which may define a Tyrant, is unfit to be the ruler of a free People.

Nor have We been wanting in attention to our British brethren. We have warned them from time to time of attempts by their legislature to extend an unwarrantable jurisdiction over us. We have reminded them of the circumstances of our emigration and settlement here. We have appealed to their native justice and magnanimity and we have conjured them by the ties of our common kindred to disavow these usurpations, which would inevitably interrupt our connections and correspondence. They too have been deaf to the voice of justice and of consanguinity. We must, therefore, acquiesce in the necessity, which denounces our

Separation, and hold them, as we hold the rest of mankind, Enemies in War, in Peace Friends.

35   We, therefore, the Representatives of the United States of America, in General Congress, Assembled, appealing to the Supreme Judge of the world of the rectitude of our intentions, do, in the Name, and by Authority of the good People of these Colonies, solemnly publish and declare, That these United Colonies are, and of Right ought to be, Free and Independent States; that they are Absolved from all Allegiance to the British Crown, and that all political connection between them and the State of Great Britain, is and ought to be totally dissolved; and that as Free and Independent States, they have full power to levy War, conclude Peace, contract Alliances, establish Commerce, and so all the other Acts and Things which Independent States may of right do. And for the support of this Declaration, with a firm reliance on the protection of Divine Providence, we mutually pledge to each other our lives, our Fortunes and our sacred Honor.

[1776]

Topics for Critical Thinking and Writing

1. What audience is being addressed in the Declaration of Independence? Cite passages in the text that support your answer.
2. The Library of Congress has the original manuscript of the rough draft of the Declaration. This manuscript itself includes revisions that are indicated below, but it was later further revised. We print the first part of the second paragraph of the draft and, after it, the corresponding part of the final version. Try to account for the changes within the draft, and from the revised draft to the final version.

   self evident
   We hold these truths to be ~~sacred & undeniable~~, that all men are created
   they are endowed by their creator with
   equal ~~& independent~~, that ~~from that equal creation they derive equal~~
   rights; that   these
   ~~rights some of which are in rights~~ inherent & inalienable among ~~which~~
   are ~~the preservation of~~ life, liberty, & the pursuit of happiness.

   We hold these Truths to be self-evident, that all men are created equal,

   that they are endowed by their Creator with certain unalienable Rights,

   that among these are Life, Liberty and the pursuit of Happiness.

   In a paragraph, evaluate the changes. Try to put yourself into Jefferson's mind and see if you can sense why Jefferson made the changes.
3. In a paragraph, define *happiness;* in a second paragraph, explain why, in your opinion, Jefferson spoke of "the pursuit of happiness" rather than of "happiness."
4. What assumptions lie behind the numerous specific reasons that are given to justify the rebellion? Set forth the gist of the argument of the Declaration using

the form of reasoning known as a *syllogism*, which consists of a major premise (such as "All men are mortal"), a minor premise ("Socrates is a man"), and a conclusion ("Therefore, Socrates is mortal.").

5. In a paragraph, argue that the assertion that "all Men are created equal" is nonsense, or, on the other hand, that it makes sense.

6. If every person has an unalienable right to life, how can capital punishment be reconciled with the Declaration of Independence? You need not in fact be a supporter of capital punishment; simply offer the best defense you can think of, in an effort to make it harmonious with the Declaration.

7. King George III has asked you to reply, on his behalf, to the colonists, in 500–750 words. Write his reply. (Hint: A good reply will probably require you to do some reading about the period.)

8. Write a declaration of your own, setting forth in 500–750 words why some group is entitled to independence. You may want to argue that adolescents should not be compelled to attend school, or that animals should not be confined in zoos, or that persons who use drugs should be able to buy them legally. Begin with a premise, then set forth facts illustrating the unfairness of the present condition, and conclude by stating what the new condition will mean to society.

Anna Lisa Raya

Anna Lisa Raya, daughter of a second-generation Mexican American father and a Puerto Rican mother, grew up in Los Angeles but went to Columbia University in New York. While an undergraduate at Columbia she wrote and published this essay on identity.

It's Hard Enough Being Me

When I entered college, I *discovered* I was Latina. Until then, I had never questioned who I was or where I was from: My father is a second-generation Mexican-American, born and raised in Los Angeles, and my mother was born in Puerto Rico and raised in Compton, Calif. My home is El Sereno, a predominantly Mexican neighborhood in L.A. Every close friend I have back home is Mexican. So I was always just Mexican. Though sometimes I was just Puerto Rican—like when we would visit Mamo (my grandma) or hang out with my Aunt Titi.

Upon arriving in New York as a first-year student, 3000 miles from home, I not only experienced extreme culture shock, but for the first time I had to define myself according to the broad term "Latina." Although culture shock and identity crisis are common for the newly minted collegian who goes away to school, my experience as a newly minted Latina was, and still is, even more complicating. In El Sereno, I felt like I was part of a majority, whereas at the College I am a minority.

I've discovered that many Latinos like myself have undergone similar experiences. We face discrimination for being a minority in this country while also facing criticism for being "whitewashed" or "sellouts" in the countries of our heritage. But as an ethnic group in college, we are forced to define ourselves according to some vague, generalized Latino experience. This requires us to know our history, our language, our music, and our religion. I can't even be a content "Puerto

Mexican" because I have to be a politically-and-socially-aware-Latina-with-a-chip-on-my-shoulder-because-of-how-repressed-I-am-in-this-country.

I am none of the above. I am the quintessential imperfect Latina. I can't dance salsa to save my life, I learned about Montezuma and the Aztecs in sixth grade, and I haven't prayed to the *Virgen de Guadalupe* in years.

5 Apparently I don't even look Latina. I can't count how many times people have just assumed that I'm white or asked me if I'm Asian. True, my friends back home call me *güera* ("whitey") because I have green eyes and pale skin, but that was as bad as it got. I never thought I would wish my skin were a darker shade or my hair a curlier texture, but since I've been in college, I have—many times.

Another thing: my Spanish is terrible. Every time I call home, I berate my mama for not teaching me Spanish when I was a child. In fact, not knowing how to speak the language of my home countries is the biggest problem that I have encountered, as have many Latinos. In Mexico there is a term, *pocha*, which is used by native Mexicans to ridicule Mexican-Americans. It expresses a deep-rooted antagonism and dislike for those of us who were raised on the other side of the border. Our failed attempts to speak pure, Mexican Spanish are largely responsible for the dislike. Other Latin American natives have this same attitude. No matter how well a Latino speaks Spanish, it can never be good enough.

Yet Latinos can't even speak Spanish in the U.S. without running the risk of being called "spic" or "wetback." That is precisely why my mother refused to teach me Spanish when I was a child. The fact that she spoke Spanish was constantly used against her: It prevented her from getting good jobs, and it would have placed me in bilingual education—a construct of the Los Angeles public school system that has proved to be more of a hindrance to intellectual development than a help.

To be fully Latina in college, however, I *must* know Spanish. I must satisfy the equation: Latina [equals] Spanish-speaking.

So I'm stuck in this black hole of an identity crisis, and college isn't making my life any easier, as I thought it would. In high school, I was being prepared for an adulthood in which I would be an individual, in which I wouldn't have to wear a Catholic school uniform anymore. But though I led an anonymous adolescence, I knew who I was. I knew I was different from white, black, or Asian people. I knew there was a language other than English that I could call my own if I only knew how to speak it better. I knew there were historical reasons why I was in this country, distinct reasons that make my existence here easier or more difficult than other people's existence. Ultimately, I was content.

10 Now I feel pushed into a corner, always defining, defending, and proving myself to classmates, professors, or employers. Trying to understand who and why I am, while understanding Plato or Homer, is a lot to ask of myself.

A month ago, I heard three Nuyorican (Puerto Ricans born and raised in New York) writers discuss how New York City has influenced their writing. One problem I have faced as a young writer is finding a voice that is true to my community. I was surprised and reassured to discover that as Latinos, these writers had faced similar pressures and conflicts as myself; some weren't even taught Spanish in childhood. I will never forget the advice that one of them gave me that evening: She said that I need to be true to myself. "Because people will always complain about what you are doing—you're a 'gringa' or a 'spic' no matter what," she explained. "So you might as well do things for yourself and not for them."

12   I don't know why it has taken 20 years to hear this advice, but I'm going to give it a try. *Soy yo* and no one else. *Punto.*[1]

[1994]

Topics for Critical Thinking and Writing

1. In her first paragraph Raya says that although her parents are American citizens, until she went to New York she "was always just Mexican" or "just Puerto Rican." Why do you suppose she thought this way?

2. In her second paragraph Raya says that in New York she "had to" define herself as "Latina," and in her third paragraph she says that many members of "minority" communities "are forced" to define themselves. In paragraph 10 she says, "Now I feel pushed into a corner, always defining, defending, and proving myself to classmates, professors, or employers. Trying to understand who and why I am, while understanding Plato or Homer, is a lot to ask. . . ." Is Raya saying that both the majority culture and the minority culture force her to define herself? Drawing on your own experience, give your views on whether it is a good thing or a bad thing (or some of each) to be forced to define oneself in terms of ethnicity.

3. Today the words *Latino* and *Latina* are common, but until perhaps ten years ago Spanish-speaking people from Mexico, Central America, and South America were called *Hispanics* or *Latin Americans.* Do you think these terms are useful, or do you think that the differences between, say, a poor black woman from Cuba and a rich white man from Argentina are so great that it makes very little sense to put them into the same category, whether the category is called *Latino, Hispanic,* or *Latin American?* Why, incidentally, do you think that *Latino/Latina* is now preferred to *Hispanic?*

4. In paragraph 7 Raya speaks of the Los Angeles bilingual educational program as "a construct of the Los Angeles public school system that has proved to be more of a hindrance to intellectual development than a help." If you have been in a bilingual educational program, evaluate the program. Did it chiefly help you, or chiefly hinder you? Explain.

5. In her last two paragraphs Raya explains that after an acquaintance told her to be true to herself, she concluded, *Soy yo* ("I'm me," or "I'm myself"). You may recall that in *Hamlet* Polonius says to his son Laertes, "This above all: to thine own self be true" (1.3.78). But what does it mean to be true to oneself? Presumably one doesn't behave immorally, but beyond that, what does one do? For instance, if a friend suggested to Raya that she might enjoy (and intellectually profit from) taking a course in Latin American literature, in making a decision, what *self* would she be true to? In your own life, you make many decisions each day. Are many of them based on being true to yourself? Again, putting aside questions concerning immorality, do you think you have a "self" that you are true to? If so, is this self at least in part based on ethnicity?

---

[1]*Soy yo . . . Punto* I'm me . . . Period. (Editors' note.)

ANDREW LAM

Andrew Lam, essayist and short story writer, edits the Pacific News Service. We reprint a PNS essay that originally appeared on May 7, 2003.

Who Will Light Incense When Mother's Gone?

My mother turned 70 recently, and though she remains a vivacious woman—her hair is still mostly black and there is a girlish twang in her laughter—mortality nevertheless weighs heavily on her soul. After the gifts were opened and the cake eaten, mother whispered this confidence to her younger sister: "Who will light incense to the dead when we're gone?"

"Honestly, I don't know," my aunt replied. "None of my children will do it, and we can forget the grandchildren. They don't even understand what we are doing. I guess when we're gone, the ritual ends."

Such is the price of living in America. I can't remember the last time I lit incense sticks and talked to my dead ancestors. Having fled so far from Vietnam, I no longer know to whom I should address my prayers or what promises I could possibly make to the long departed.

My mother, on the other hand, lives in America the way she would in Vietnam. Every morning in my parents' suburban home north of San Jose, she climbs a chair and piously lights a few joss sticks for the ancestral altar that sits on top of the living room bookcase. Every morning she talks to ghosts. She mumbles solemn prayers to the spirits of our dead ancestors, asks them for protection.

5   By contrast, on the shelves below stand my older siblings' engineering and business degrees, my own degree in biochemistry, our combined sports trophies and, last but not least, the latest installments of my own unending quest for self-reinvention—plaques and obelisk-shaped crystals—my journalism awards.

What mother's altar and the shelves beneath it seek ot tell is the narrative of many an Asian immigrant family's journey to America. The collective, agrarian-based ethos in which ancestor worship is central slowly gives way to the glories of individual ambitions.

At that far end of the Asian immigrant trajectory, however, I cannot help but feel a certain twinge of guilt and regret upon hearing my mother's remark. Once when I was still a rebellious teenager and living at home, Mother asked me to speak more Vietnamese inside the house. "No," I answered in English, "what good is it to speak it? It's not as if I'm going to use it after I move out."

Mother, I remember, had a pained look in her eyes and called me the worst thing she could muster. "You've become a little American now, haven't you? A cowboy."

Vietnamese appropriated the word "cowboy" from the movies to imply self-ishness. A cowboy in Vietnamese estimation is a rebel who, as in the spaghetti westerns, leaves town—the communal life—to ride alone into the sunset.

10   America, it had seemed, had stolen my mother's children, especially her youngest and once obedient son. America seduced him with its optimism, twisted his thinking, bent his tongue and dulled his tropic memories. America gave him freeways and fast food and silly cartoons and sitcoms, imbuing him with sappy, happy-ending incitements.

If we have reconciled since then, it does not mean I have become a traditional, incense-lighting Vietnamese son. I visit. I take her to lunch. I come home for important dates—New Year, Thanksgiving, Tet.

But these days in front of the family altar, with all those faded photos of the dead staring down at me, I often feel oddly removed, as if staring at a relic of my distant past. And when, upon my mother's insistence, I light incense, I do not feel as if I am participating in a living tradition so much as pleasing a traditional mother.

We live in two different worlds, Mother and I. Mine is a world of travel and writing and public speaking, of immersing myself in contemporary history. Hers is a world of consulting the Vietnamese horoscope, of attending Buddhist temple on the day of her parents' death anniversaries and of telling and retelling stories of the past.

But on her 70th birthday, having listened to her worries, I have to wonder: What will survive my mother?

15   I wish I could assure my mother that, after she is gone, each morning I would light incense for her and all the ancestor spirits before her, but I can't.

In that odd, contradictory space in which immigrants' children find themselves, I feel strangely comforted when watching my mother's pious gesture each morning in front of the ancestors' altar. She is what connects me and my generation to a traditional past. And essentially, I share her fear that her generation and its memories of the Old World, what preserves us as a community, will fade away like incense smoke. I fear she'll leave me stranded in America, becoming more American than I expected, a lonely cowboy cursed with amnesia.

[2003]

Topics for Critical Thinking and Writing

1. What does Andrew Lam mean when he refers to his mother as "a vivacious woman"? What does he mean when he refers to his own "unending quest for self-reinvention"? And "collective, agrarian-based ethos": what does this phrase mean?

2. How does Lam's mother feel about America? What about Lam himself: What are his feelings about America?

3. Does this essay give you a new perspective on the immigrant experience, or a familiar one? Do you think Lam intends to show the reader something new? Or does he have a different purpose in mind?

4. Imagine that you know the author, and that, before publishing this essay, he sent it to you and asked for your "response and any suggestions" you might have. Compose a letter of 1–2 pages, beginning "Dear Andrew . . . ," in which you reply to him.

FICTION

AMY TAN

Amy Tan was born in Oakland, California, in 1952, of Chinese immigrant parents. When she was 8, she won first prize among elementary students with an essay entitled "What the Library Means to Me." In due time she attended Linfield College in Oregon, then transferred to San Jose State University where, while working two part-time jobs, she became an honors studdent and a President's Scholar. In 1973 she earned an M.A. in linguistics, also at San Jose, and she later enrolled as a doctoral student at the University of California, Berkeley, though she left this program after the murder of a close friend. For the next five years she worked as a language development consultant and a project director, and then she became a freelance business writer. In 1986 she published her first short story, and it was reprinted in Seventeen *where it was noticed by an agent, who encouraged her to continue writing fiction. In 1989* The Joy Luck Club *(a collection of linked short stories, including "Two Kinds") was published. Other books include* The Kitchen God's Wife *(1991),* The Hundred Secret Senses *(1995), and* The Bonesetter's Daughter *(2001). She has also written two books for children,* The Moon Lady *(1992) and* SAGWA The Chinese Siamese Cat *(1994).*

Two Kinds

My mother believed you could be anything you wanted to be in America. You could open a restaurant. You could work for the government and get good retirement. You could buy a house with almost no money down. You could become rich. You could become instantly famous.

"Of course, you can be prodigy, too," my mother told me when I was nine. "You can be best anything. What does Auntie Lindo know? Her daughter, she is only best tricky."

America was where all my mother's hopes lay. She had come here in 1949 after losing everything in China: her mother and father, her family home, her first husband, and two daughters, twin baby girls. But she never looked back with regret. There were so many ways for things to get better.

We didn't immediately pick the right kind of prodigy. At first my mother thought I could be a Chinese Shirley Temple. We'd watch Shirley's old movies on TV as though they were training films. My mother would poke my arm and say, *"Ni kan."* —You watch. And I would see Shirley tapping her feet, or singing a sailor song, or pursing her lips into a very round O while saying "Oh, my goodness."

5   *"Ni kan,"* said my mother as Shirley's eyes flooded with tears. "You already know how. Don't need talent for crying!"

Soon after my mother got this idea about Shirley Temple, she took me to a beauty training school in the Mission district and put me in the hands of a student who could barely hold the scissors without shaking. Instead of getting big fat curls, I emerged with an uneven mass of crinkly black fuzz. My mother dragged me off to the bathroom and tried to wet down my hair.

"You look like Negro Chinese," she lamented, as if I had done this on purpose.

The instructor of the beauty training school had to lop off these soggy clumps to make my hair even again. "Peter Pan is very popular these days," the instructor assured my mother. I now had hair the length of a boy's, with straight-across bangs that hung at a slant two inches above my eyebrows. I liked the haircut and it made me actually look forward to my future fame.

In fact, in the beginning, I was just as excited as my mother, maybe even more so. I pictured this prodigy part of me as many different images, trying each one on for size. I was a dainty ballerina girl standing by the curtains, waiting to hear the music that would send me floating on my tiptoes. I was like the Christ child lifted out of the straw manger, crying with holy indignity. I was Cinderella stepping from her pumpkin carriage with sparkly cartoon music filling the air.

10   In all of my imaginings, I was filled with a sense that I would soon become *perfect*. My mother and father would adore me. I would be beyond reproach. I would never feel the need to sulk for anything.

But sometimes the prodigy in me became impatient. "If you don't hurry up and get me out of here, I'm disappearing for good," it warned. "And then you'll always be nothing."

Every night after dinner, my mother and I would sit at the Formica kitchen table. She would present new tests, taking her examples from stories of amazing children she had read in *Ripley's Believe It or Not,* or *Good Housekeeping, Reader's Digest,* and a dozen other magazines she kept in a pile in our bathroom. My mother got these magazines from people whose houses she cleaned. And since she cleaned many houses each week, we had a great assortment. She would look through them all, searching for stories about remarkable children.

The first night she brought out a story about a three-year-old boy who knew the capitals of all the states and even most of the European countries. A teacher was quoted as saying the little boy could also pronounce the names of the foreign cities correctly.

"What's the capital of Finland?" my mother asked me, looking at the magazine story.

15   All I knew was the capital of California, because Sacramento was the name of the street we lived on in Chinatown. "Nairobi!" I guessed, saying the most foreign word I could think of. She checked to see if that was possibly one way to pronounce "Helsinki" before showing me the answer.

The tests got harder—multiplying numbers in my head, finding the queen of hearts in a deck of cards, trying to stand on my head without using my hands, predicting the daily temperatures in Los Angeles, New York, and London.

One night I had to look at a page from the Bible for three minutes and then report everything I could remember. "Now Jehoshaphat had riches and honor in abundance and . . . that's all I remember, Ma," I said.

And after seeing my mother's disappointed face once again, something inside of me began to die. I hated the tests, the raised hopes and failed expectations. Before going to bed that night, I looked in the mirror above the bathroom sink and when I saw only my face staring back—and that it would always be this ordinary face—I began to cry. Such a sad, ugly girl! I made high-pitched noises like a crazed animal, trying to scratch out the face in the mirror.

And then I saw what seemed to be the prodigy side of me—because I had never seen that face before. I looked at my reflection, blinking so I could see more clearly. The girl staring back at me was angry, powerful. This girl and I were the same. I had new thoughts, willful thoughts, or rather thoughts filled with lots of won'ts. I won't let her change me, I promised myself. I won't be what I'm not.

20   So now on nights when my mother presented her tests, I performed listlessly, my head propped on one arm. I pretended to be bored. And I was. I got so bored I started counting the bellows of the foghorns out on the bay while my mother drilled me in other areas. The sound was comforting and reminded me of the cow jumping over the moon. And the next day, I played a game with myself, seeing if my mother would give up on me before eight bellows. After a while I usually counted only one, maybe two bellows at most. At last she was beginning to give up hope.

Two or three months had gone by without any mention of my being a prodigy again. And then one day my mother was watching *The Ed Sullivan Show* on TV. The TV was old and the sound kept shorting out. Every time my mother got halfway up from the sofa to adjust the set, the sound would go back on and Ed would be talking. As soon as she sat down, Ed would go silent again. She got up, the TV broke into loud piano music. She sat down. Silence. Up and down, back and forth, quiet and loud. It was like a stiff embraceless dance between her and the TV set. Finally she stood by the set with her hand on the sound dial.

She seemed entranced by the music, a little frenzied piano piece with this mesmerizing quality, sort of quick passages and then teasing lilting ones before it returned to the quick playful parts.

"*Ni kan,*" my mother said, calling me over with hurried hand gestures, "Look here."

I could see why my mother was fascinated by the music. It was being pounded out by a little Chinese girl, about nine years old, with a Peter Pan haircut. The girl had the sauciness of a Shirley Temple. She was proudly modest like a proper Chinese child. And she also did this fancy sweep of a curtsy, so that the fluffy skirt of her white dress cascaded slowly to the floor like the petals of a large carnation.

25   In spite of these warning signs, I wasn't worried. Our family had no piano and we couldn't afford to buy one, let alone reams of sheet music and piano lessons. So I could be generous in my comments when my mother bad-mouthed the little girl on TV.

"Play note right, but doesn't sound good! No singing sound," my mother complained.

"What are you picking on her for?" I said carelessly. "She's pretty good. Maybe she's not the best, but she's trying hard." I knew almost immediately I would be sorry I said that.

"Just like you," she said. "Not the best. Because you not trying." She gave a little huff as she let go of the sound dial and sat down on the sofa.

The little Chinese girl sat down also to play an encore of "Anitra's Dance,"[1] by Grieg. I remember the song, because later on I had to learn how to play it.

---

[1]"**Anitra's Tanz**" a section from the incidental musc that Edvard Grieg (1843–1907) wrote for *Peer Gynt,* a play by Henrik Ibsen.

30   Three days after watching *The Ed Sullivan Show,* my mother told me what my schedule would be for piano lessons and piano practice. She had talked to Mr. Chong, who lived on the first floor of our apartment building. Mr. Chong was a retired piano teacher and my mother had traded housecleaning services for weekly lessons and a piano for me to practice on every day, two hours a day, from four until six.

When my mother told me this, I felt as though I had been sent to hell. I whined and then kicked my foot a little when I couldn't stand it anymore.

"Why don't you like me the way I am? I'm *not* a genius! I can't play the piano. And even if I could, I wouldn't go on TV if you paid me a million dollars!" I cried.

My mother slapped me. "Who ask you be genius?" she shouted. "Only ask you be your best. For you sake. You think I want you be genius? Hnnh! What for! Who ask you!"

"So ungrateful," I heard her mutter in Chinese. "If she had as much talent as she has temper, she would be famous now."

35   Mr. Chong, whom I secretly nicknamed Old Chong, was very strange, always tapping his fingers to the silent music of an invisible orchestra. He looked ancient in my eyes. He had lost most of the hair on top of his head and he wore thick glasses and had eyes that always looked tired and sleepy. But he must have been younger than I thought, since he lived with his mother and was not yet married.

I met Old Lady Chong once and that was enough. She had this peculiar smell like a baby that had done something in its pants. And her fingers felt like a dead person's, like an old peach I once found in the back of the refrigerator; the skin just slid off the meat when I picked it up.

I soon found out why Old Chong had retired from teaching piano. He was deaf. "Like Beethoven!" he shouted to me. "We're both listening only in our head!" And he would start to conduct his frantic silent sonatas.

Our lessons went like this. He would open the book and point to different things, explaining their purpose: "Key! Treble! Bass! No sharps or flats! So this is C major! Listen now and play after me!"

And then he would play the C scale a few times, a simple chord, and then, as if inspired by an old, unreachable itch, he gradually added more notes and running trills and a pounding bass until the music was really something quite grand.

40   I would play after him, the simple scale, the simple chord, and then I just played some nonsense that sounded like a cat running up and down on top of garbage cans. Old Chong smiled and applauded and then said, "Very good! But now you must learn to keep time!"

So that's how I discovered that Old Chong's eyes were too slow to keep up with the wrong notes I was playing. He went through the motions in half-time. To help me keep rhythm, he stood behind me, pushing down on my right shoulder for every beat. He balanced pennies on top of my wrists so I would keep them still as I slowly played scales and arpeggios. He had me curve my hand around an apple and keep that shape when playing chords. He marched stiffly to show me how to make each finger dance up and down, staccato like an obedient little soldier.

He taught me all these things, and that was how I also learned I could be lazy and get away with mistakes, lots of mistakes. If I hit the wrong notes because I hadn't practiced enough, I never corrected myself. I just kept playing in rhythm. And Old Chong kept conducting his own private reverie.

So maybe I never really gave myself a fair chance. I did pick up the basics pretty quickly, and I might have become a good pianist at that young age. But I was so determined not to try, not to be anybody different that I learned to play only the most ear-splitting preludes, the most discordant hymns.

Over the next year I practiced like this, dutifully in my own way. And then one day I heard my mother and her friend Lindo Jong both talking in a loud bragging tone of voice so others could hear. It was after church, and I was leaning against the brick wall wearing a dress with stiff white petticoats. Auntie Lindo's daughter, Waverly, who was about my age, was standing farther down the wall about five feet away. We had grown up together and shared all the closeness of two sisters squabbling over crayons and dolls. In other words, for the most part, we hated each other. I thought she was snotty. Waverly Jong had gained a certain amount of fame as "Chinatown's Littlest Chinese Chess Champion."

45   "She bring home too many trophy," lamented Auntie Lindo that Sunday. "All day she play chess. All day I have no time do nothing but dust off her winnings." She threw a scolding look at Waverly, who pretended not to see her.

"You lucky you don't have this problem," said Auntie Lindo with a sigh to my mother.

And my mother squared her shoulders and bragged: "Our problem worser than yours. If we ask Jing-mei wash dish, she hear nothing but music. It's like you can't stop this natural talent."

And right then, I was determined to put a stop to her foolish pride.

A few weeks later, Old Chong and my mother conspired to have me play in a talent show which would be held in the church hall. By then, my parents had saved up enough to buy me a secondhand piano, a black Wurlitzer spinet with a scarred bench. It was the showpiece of our living room.

50   For the talent show, I was to play a piece called "Pleading Child" from Schumann's *Scenes from Childhood*.[2] It was a simple, moody piece that sounded more difficult than it was. I was supposed to memorize the whole thing, playing the repeat parts twice to make the piece sound longer. But I dawdled over it, playing a few bars and then cheating, looking up to see what notes followed. I never really listened to what I was playing. I daydreamed about being somewhere else, about being someone else.

The part I liked to practice best was the fancy curtsy: right foot out, touch the rose on the carpet with a pointed foot, sweep to the side, left leg bends, look up and smile.

My parents invited all the couples from the Joy Luck Club to witness my debut. Auntie Lindo and Uncle Tin were there. Waverly and her two older brothers had also come. The first two rows were filled with children both younger and older than I was. The littlest ones got to go first. They recited simple nursery rhymes, squawked out tunes on miniature violins, twirled Hula Hoops, pranced in pink ballet tutus, and when they bowed or curtsied, the audience would sigh in unison, "Awww," and then clap enthusiastically.

When my turn came, I was very confident. I remember my childish excitement. It was as if I knew, without a doubt, that the prodigy side of me really did exist. I had no fear whatsoever, no nervousness. I remember thinking to myself, This is it! This is it! I looked out over the audience, at my mother's blank face, my father's yawn, Auntie Lindo's stiff-lipped smile, Waverly's sulky expression. I had

[2]***Scenes from Childhood*** a piano work by Robert Shumann (1810–1856) with twelve titled sections and an epilogue.

on a white dress layered with sheets of lace, and a pink bow in my Peter Pan hair-cut. As I sat down I envisioned people jumping to their feet and Ed Sullivan rushing up to introduce me to everyone on TV.

And I started to play. It was so beautiful. I was so caught up in how lovely I looked that at first I didn't worry how I would sound. So it was a surprise to me when I hit the first wrong note and I realized something didn't sound quite right. And then I hit another and another followed that. A chill started at the top of my head and began to trickle down. Yet I couldn't stop playing, as though my hands were bewitched. I kept thinking my fingers would adjust themselves back, like a train switching to the right track. I played this strange jumble through two repeats, the sour notes staying with me all the way to the end.

55   When I stood up, I discovered my legs were shaking. Maybe I had just been nervous and the audience, like Old Chong, had seen me go through the right motions and had not heard anything wrong at all. I swept my right foot out, went down on my knee, looked up and smiled. The room was quiet, except for Old Chong, who was beaming and shouting, "Bravo! Bravo! Well done!" But then I saw my mother's face, her stricken face. The audience clapped weakly, and as I walked back to my chair, with my whole face quivering as I tried not to cry, I heard a little boy whisper loudly to his mother, "That was awful," and the mother whispered back, "Well, she certainly tried."

And now I realized how many people were in the audience, the whole world it seemed. I was aware of eyes burning into my back. I felt the shame of my mother and father as they sat stiffly throughout the rest of the show.

We could have escaped during intermission. Pride and some strange sense of honor must have anchored my parents to their chairs. And so we watched it all: the eighteen-year-old boy with a fake moustache who did a magic show and juggled flaming hoops while riding a unicycle. The breasted girl with white makeup who sang from *Madame Butterfly* and got honorable mention. And the eleven-year-old boy who won first prize playing a tricky violin song that sounded like a busy bee.

After the show, the Hsus, the Jongs, and the St. Clairs from the Joy Luck Club, came up to my mother and father.

"Lots of talented kids," Auntie Lindo said vaguely, smiling broadly.

60   "That was somethin' else," said my father, and I wondered if he was referring to me in a humorous way, or whether he even remembered what I had done.

Waverly looked at me and shrugged her shoulders. "You aren't a genius like me," she said matter-of-factly. And if I hadn't felt so bad, I would have pulled her braids and punched her stomach.

But my mother's expression was what devastated me: a quiet, blank look that said she had lost everything. I felt the same way, and it seemed as if everybody were now coming up, like gawkers at the scene of an accident, to see what parts were actually missing. When we got on the bus to go home, my father was humming the busy-bee tune and my mother was silent. I kept thinking she wanted to wait until we got home before shouting at me. But when my father unlocked the door to our apartment, my mother walked in and then went to the back, into the bedroom. No accusations. No blame. And in a way, I felt disappointed. I had been waiting for her to start shouting, so I could shout back and cry and blame her for all my misery.

I assumed my talent-show fiasco meant I never had to play the piano again. But two days later, after school, my mother came out of the kitchen and saw me watching TV.

"Four clock," she reminded me as if it were any other day. I was stunned, as though she were asking me to go through the talent-show torture again. I wedged myself more tightly in front of the TV.

65 "Turn off TV," she called from the kitchen five minutes later.

I didn't budge. And then I decided. I didn't have to do what my mother said anymore. I wasn't her slave. This wasn't China. I had listened to her before and look what happened. She was the stupid one.

She came out from the kitchen and stood in the arched entryway of the living room. "Four clock," she said once again, louder.

"I'm not going to play anymore," I said nonchalantly. "Why should I? I'm not a genius."

She walked over and stood in front of the TV. I saw her chest was heaving up and down in an angry way.

70 "No!" I said, and I now felt stronger, as if my true self had finally emerged. So this was what had been inside me all along.

"No! I won't!" I screamed.

She yanked me by the arm, pulled me off the floor, snapped off the TV. She was frighteningly strong, half pulling, half carrying me toward the piano as I kicked the throw rugs under my feet. She lifted me up and onto the hard bench. I was sobbing by now, looking at her bitterly. Her chest was heaving even more and her mouth was open, smiling crazily as if she were pleased I was crying.

"You want me to be someone that I'm not!" I sobbed. "I'll never be the kind of daughter you want me to be!"

"Only two kinds of daughters," she shouted in Chinese. "Those who are obedient and those who follow their own mind! Only one kind of daughter can live in this house. Obedient daughter!"

75 "Then I wish I wasn't your daughter. I wish you weren't my mother," I shouted. As I said these things I got scared. It felt like worms and toads and slimy things crawling out of my chest, but it also felt good, as if this awful side of me had surfaced, at last.

"Too late change this," said my mother shrilly.

And I could sense her anger rising to its breaking point. I wanted to see it spill over. And that's when I remembered the babies she had lost in China, the ones we never talked about. "Then I wish I'd never been born!" I shouted. "I wish I were dead! Like them."

It was as if I had said the magic words. Alakazam!—and her face went blank, her mouth closed, her arms went slack, and she backed out of the room, stunned, as if she were blowing away like a small brown leaf, thin, brittle, lifeless.

It was not the only disappointment my mother felt in me. In the years that followed, I failed her so many times, each time asserting my own will, my right to fall short of expectations. I didn't get straight As. I didn't become class president. I didn't get into Stanford. I dropped out of college.

80 For unlike my mother, I did not believe I could be anything I wanted to be. I could only be me.

And for all those years, we never talked about the disaster at the recital or my terrible accusations afterward at the piano bench. All of that remained unchecked, like a betrayal that was now unspeakable. So I never found a way to ask her why she had hoped for something so large that failure was inevitable.

And even worse, I never asked her what frightened me the most: Why had she given up hope?

For after our struggle at the piano, she never mentioned my playing again. The lessons stopped. The lid to the piano was closed, shutting out the dust, my misery, and her dreams.

So she surprised me. A few years ago, she offered to give me the piano, for my thirtieth birthday. I had not played in all those years. I saw the offer as a sign of forgiveness, a tremendous burden removed.

85   "Are you sure?" I asked shyly. "I mean, won't you and Dad miss it?"

"No, this your piano," she said firmly. "Always your piano. You only one can play."

"Well, I probably can't play anymore," I said. "It's been years."

"You pick up fast," said my mother, as if she knew this was certain. "You have natural talent. You could been genius if you want to."

"No I couldn't."

90   "You just not trying," said my mother. And she was neither angry nor sad. She said it as if to announce a fact that could never be disproved. "Take it," she said.

But I didn't at first. It was enough that she had offered it to me. And after that, every time I saw it in my parents' living room, standing in front of the bay windows, it made me feel proud, as if it were a shiny trophy I had won back.

Last week I sent a tuner over to my parents' apartment and had the piano reconditioned, for purely sentimental reasons. My mother had died a few months before and I had been getting things in order for my father, a little bit at a time. I put the jewelry in special silk pouches. The sweaters she had knitted in yellow, pink, bright orange—all the colors I hated—I put those in moth-proof boxes. I found some old Chinese silk dresses, the kind with little slits up the sides. I rubbed the old silk against my skin, then wrapped them in tissue and decided to take them home with me.

After I had the piano tuned, I opened the lid and touched the keys. It sounded even richer than I remembered. Really, it was a very good piano. Inside the bench were the same exercise notes with handwritten scales, the same secondhand music books with their covers held together with yellow tape.

I opened up the Schumann book to the dark little piece I had played at the recital. It was on the left-hand side of the page, "Pleading Child." It looked more difficult than I remembered. I played a few bars, surprised at how easily the notes came back to me.

95   And for the first time, or so it seemed, I noticed the piece on the right-hand side. It was called "Perfectly Contented." I tried to play this one as well. It had a lighter melody but the same flowing rhythm and turned out to be quite easy. "Pleading Child" was shorter but slower; "Perfectly Contented" was longer, but faster. And after I played them both a few times, I realized they were two halves of the same song.

[1989]

Topics for Critical Thinking and Writing

1. Try to recall your responses when you had finished reading the first three paragraphs. At that point, how did the mother strike you? Now that you have read the entire story, is your view of her different? If so, in what way(s)?

2. When the narrator looks in the mirror, she discovers "the prodigy side," a face she had never seen before. What do you think she is discovering?
3. If you enjoyed the story, point out two or three passages that you found particularly engaging, and briefly explain why they appeal to you.
4. Do you think this story is interesting only because it may give a glimpse of life in a Chinese American family? Or do you find it interesting for additional reasons? Explain.
5. Conceivably the story could have ended with the fifth paragraph from the end. What do the last four paragraphs contribute?

ALICE WALKER

Alice Walker was born in 1944 in Eatonton, Georgia, where her parents eked out a living as sharecroppers and dairy farmers; her mother also worked as a domestic. Walker attended Spelman College in Atlanta, and in 1965 she finished her undergraduate work at Sarah Lawrence College near New York City. She then became active in the welfare rights movement in New York and in the voter registration movement in Georgia. Later she taught writing and literature in Mississippi, at Jackson State College and Tougaloo College, and at Wellesley College, the University of Massachusetts, and Yale University.

Walker has written essays, poetry, and fiction. Her best-known novel, The Color Purple *(1982), won a Pulitzer Prize and the National Book Award. She has said that her chief concern is "exploring the oppressions, the insanities, the loyalties, and the triumphs of black women."*

Everyday Use

For your grandmama

I will wait for her in the yard that Maggie and I made so clean and wavy yesterday afternoon. A yard like this is more comfortable than most people know. It is not just a yard. It is like an extended living room. When the hard clay is swept clean as a floor and the fine sand around the edges lined with tiny, irregular grooves, anyone can come and sit and look up into the elm tree and wait for the breezes that never come inside the house.

Maggie will be nervous until after her sister goes: she will stand hopelessly in corners homely and ashamed of the burn scars down her arms and legs, eyeing her sister with a mixture of envy and awe. She thinks her sister had held life always in the palm of one hand, that "no" is a word the world never learned to say to her.

You've no doubt seen those TV shows where the child who has "made it" is confronted, as a surprise, by her own mother and father, tottering in weakly from backstage. (A pleasant surprise, of course: What would they do if parent and child came on the show only to curse out and insult each other?) On TV mother and child embrace and smile into each other's faces. Sometimes the mother and father weep, the child wraps them in her arms and leans across the table to tell how she would not have made it without their help. I have seen these programs.

Sometimes I dream a dream in which Dee and I are suddenly brought together on a TV program of this sort. Out of a dark and soft-seated limousine I am ushered into a bright room filled with many people. There I meet a smiling, gray, sporty man like Johnny Carson who shakes my hand and tells me what a fine girl I have. Then we are on the stage and Dee is embracing me with tears in her eyes. She pins on my dress a large orchid, even though she has told me once that she thinks orchids are tacky flowers.

5   In real life I am a large, big-boned woman with rough, man-working hands. In the winter I wear flannel nightgowns to bed and overalls during the day. I can kill and clean a hog as mercilessly as a man. My fat keeps me hot in zero weather. I can work outside all day, breaking ice to get water for washing. I can eat pork liver cooked over the open fire minutes after it comes steaming from the hog. One winter I knocked a bull calf straight in the brain between the eyes with a sledge hammer and had the meat hung up to chill before nightfall. But of course all this does not show on television. I am the way my daughter would want me to be: a hundred pounds lighter, my skin like an uncooked barley pancake. My hair glistens in the hot bright lights. Johnny Carson has much to do to keep up with my quick and witty tongue.

But that is a mistake. I know even before I wake up. Who ever knew a Johnson with a quick tongue? Who can even imagine me looking a strange white man in the eye? It seems to me I have talked to them always with one foot raised in flight, with my head turned in whichever way is farthest from them. Dee, though. She would always look anyone in the eye. Hesitation was no part of her nature.

"How do I look, Mama?" Maggie says, showing just enough of her thin body enveloped in pink skirt and red blouse for me to know she's there, almost hidden by the door.

"Come out into the yard," I say.

Have you ever seen a lame animal, perhaps a dog run over by some careless person rich enough to own a car, sidle up to someone who is ignorant enough to be kind to him? That is the way my Maggie walks. She has been like this, chin on chest, eyes on ground, feet in shuffle, ever since the fire that burned the other house to the ground.

10   Dee is lighter than Maggie, with nicer hair and a fuller figure. She's a woman now, though sometimes I forget. How long ago was it that the other house burned? Ten, twelve years? Sometimes I can still hear the flames and feel Maggie's arms sticking to me, her hair smoking and her dress falling off her in little black papery flakes. Her eyes seemed stretched open, blazed open by the flames reflected in them. And Dee. I see her standing off under the sweet gum tree she used to dig gum out of; a look of concentration on her face as she watched the last dingy gray board of the house fall in toward the red-hot brick chimney. Why don't you do a dance around the ashes? I'd wanted to ask her. She had hated the house that much.

I used to think she hated Maggie, too. But that was before we raised the money, the church and me, to send her to Augusta to school. She used to read to us without pity; forcing words, lies, other folks' habits, whole lives upon us two, sitting trapped and ignorant underneath her voice. She washed us in a river of make-believe, burned us with a lot of knowledge we didn't necessarily need to know. Pressed us to her with the serious way she read, to shove us away at just the moment, like dimwits, we seemed about to understand.

Dee wanted nice things. A yellow organdy dress to wear to her graduation from high school; black pumps to match a green suit she'd made from an old suit somebody gave me. She was determined to stare down any disaster in her efforts. Her eyelids would not flicker for minutes at a time. Often I fought off the temptation to shake her. At sixteen she had a style of her own: and knew what style was.

I never had an education myself. After second grade the school was closed down. Don't ask me why: in 1927 colored asked fewer questions than they do now. Sometimes Maggie reads to me. She stumbles along goodnaturedly but can't see well. She knows she is not bright. Like good looks and money, quickness passed her by. She will marry John Thomas (who has mossy teeth in an earnest face) and then I'll be free to sit here and I guess just sing church songs to myself. Although I never was a good singer. Never could carry a tune. I was always better at a man's job. I used to love to milk till I was hoofed in the side in '49. Cows are soothing and slow and don't bother you, unless you try to milk them the wrong way.

I have deliberately turned my back on the house. It is three rooms, just like the one that burned, except the roof is tin; they don't make shingle roofs any more. There are no real windows, just some holes cut in the sides, like the portholes in a ship, but not round and not square, with rawhide holding the shutters up on the outside. This house is in a pasture, too, like the other one. No doubt when Dee sees it she will want to tear it down. She wrote me once that no matter where we "choose" to live, she will manage to come see us. But she will never bring her friends. Maggie and I thought about this and Maggie asked me, "Mama, when did Dee ever *have* any friends?"

15 She had a few. Furtive boys in pink shirts hanging about on washday after school. Nervous girls who never laughed. Impressed with her they worshiped the well-turned phrase, the cute shape, the scalding humor that erupted like bubbles in lye. She read to them.

When she was courting Jimmy T she didn't have much time to pay to us, but turned all her faultfinding power on him. He *flew* to marry a cheap gal from a family of ignorant flashy people. She hardly had time to recompose herself.

When she comes I will meet—but there they are!

Maggie attempts to make a dash for the house, in her shuffling way, but I stay her with my hand. "Come back here," I say. And she stops and tries to dig a well in the sand with her toe.

It is hard to see them clearly through the strong sun. But even the first glimpse of leg out of the car tells me it is Dee. Her feet were always neat-looking, as if God himself had shaped them with a certain style. From the other side of the car comes a short, stocky man. Hair is all over his head a foot long and hanging from his chin like a kinky mule tail. I hear Maggie suck in her breath. "Uhnnnh," is what it sounds like. Like when you see the wriggling end of a snake just in front of your foot on the road. "Uhnnnh."

20 Dee next. A dress down to the ground, in this hot weather. A dress so loud it hurts my eyes. There are yellows and oranges enough to throw back the light of the sun. I feel my whole face warming from the heat waves it throws out. Earrings, too, gold and hanging down to her shoulders. Bracelets dangling and making noises when she moves her arm up to shake the folds of the dress out of her armpits. The dress is loose and flows, and as she walks closer, I like it. I hear Maggie go "Uhnnnh" again. It is her sister's hair. It stands straight up like the wool

on a sheep. It is black as night and around the edges are two long pigtails that rope about like small lizards disappearing behind her ears.

"Wa-su-zo-Tean-o!" she says, coming on in that gliding way the dress makes her move. The short stocky fellow with the hair to his navel is all grinning and he follows up with "Asalamalakim, my mother and sister!" He moves to hug Maggie but she falls back, right up against the back of my chair. I feel her trembling there and when I look up I see the perspiration falling off her chin.

"Don't get up," says Dee. Since I am stout it takes something of a push. You can see me trying to move a second or two before I make it. She turns, showing white heels through her sandals, and goes back to the car. Out she peeks next with a Polaroid. She stoops down quickly and lines up picture after picture of me sitting there in front of the house with Maggie cowering behind me. She never takes a shot without making sure the house is included. When a cow comes nibbling around the edge of the yard she snaps it and me and Maggie *and* the house. Then she puts the Polaroid in the back seat of the car, and comes up and kisses me on the forehead.

Meanwhile Asalamalakim is going through the motions with Maggie's hand. Maggie's hand is as limp as a fish, and probably as cold, despite the sweat, and she keeps trying to pull it back. It looks like Asalamalakim wants to shake hands but wants to do it fancy. Or maybe he don't know how people shake hands. Anyhow, he soon gives up on Maggie.

"Well," I say. "Dee."

25 "No, Mama," she says. "Not 'Dee,' Wangero Leewanika Kemanjo!"

"What happened to 'Dee'?" I wanted to know.

"She's dead," Wangero said. "I couldn't bear it any longer being named after the people who oppress me."

"You know as well as me you was named after your aunt Dicie," I said. Dicie is my sister. She named Dee. We called her "Big Dee" after Dee was born.

"But who was *she* named after?" asked Wangero.

30 "I guess after Grandma Dee," I said.

"And who was she named after?" asked Wangero.

"Her mother," I said, and saw Wangero was getting tired. "That's about as far back as I can trace it," I said. Though, in fact, I probably could have carried it back beyond the Civil War through the branches.

"Well," said Asalamalakim, "there you are."

"Uhnnnh," I heard Maggie say.

35 "There I was not," I said, "before 'Dicie' cropped up in our family, so why should I try to trace it that far back?"

He just stood there grinning, looking down on me like somebody inspecting a Model A car. Every once in a while he and Wangero sent eye signals over my head.

"How do you pronounce this name?" I asked.

"You don't have to call me by it if you don't want to," said Wangero.

"Why shouldn't I?" I asked. "If that's what you want us to call you, we'll call you."

40 "I know it might sound awkward at first," said Wangero.

"I'll get used to it," I said. "Ream it out again."

Well, soon we got the name out of the way. Asalamalakim had a name twice as long and three times as hard. After I tripped over it two or three times he told me to just call him Hakim-a-barber. I wanted to ask him was he a barber, but I didn't really think he was, so I didn't ask.

"You must belong to those beef-cattle peoples down the road," I said. They said "Asalamalakim" when they met you, too, but they didn't shake hands. Always too busy: feeding the cattle, fixing the fences, putting up saltlick shelters, throwing down hay. When the white folks poisoned some of the herd the men stayed up all night with rifles in their hands. I walked a mile and a half just to see the sight.

Hakim-a-barber said, "I accept some of their doctrines, but farming and raising cattle is not my style." (They didn't tell me, and I didn't ask, whether Wangero [Dee] had really gone and married him.)

45   We sat down to eat and right away he said he didn't eat collards and pork was unclean. Wangero, though, went on through the chitlins and corn bread, the greens and everything else. She talked a blue streak over the sweet potatoes. Everything delighted her. Even the fact that we still used the benches her daddy made for the table when we couldn't afford to buy chairs.

"Oh, Mama!" she cried. Then turned to Hakim-a-barber. "I never knew how lovely these benches are. You can feel the rump prints," she said, running her hands underneath her and along the bench. Then she gave a sigh and her hand closed over Grandma Dee's butter dish. "That's it!" she said. "I knew there was something I wanted to ask you if I could have." She jumped up from the table and went over in the corner where the churn stood, the milk in it clabber by now. She looked at the churn and looked at it.

"This churn top is what I need," she said. "Didn't Uncle Buddy whittle it out of a tree you all used to have?"

"Yes," I said.

"Uh huh," she said happily. "And I want the dasher, too."

50   "Uncle Buddy whittle that, too?" asked the barber.

Dee (Wangero) looked up at me.

"Aunt Dee's first husband whittled the dash," said Maggie so low you almost couldn't hear her. "His name was Henry, but they called him Stash."

"Maggie's brain is like an elephant's," Wangero said, laughing. "I can use the churn top as a centerpiece for the alcove table," she said, sliding a plate over the churn, "and I'll think of something artistic to do with the dasher."

When she finished wrapping the dasher the handle stuck out. I took it for a moment in my hands. You didn't even have to look close to see where hands pushing the dasher up and down to make butter had left a kind of sink in the wood. In fact, there were a lot of small sinks; you could see where thumbs and fingers had sunk into the wood. It was beautiful light yellow wood, from a tree that grew in the yard where Big Dee and Stash had lived.

55   After dinner Dee (Wangero) went to the trunk at the foot of my bed and started rifling through it. Maggie hung back in the kitchen over the dishpan. Out came Wangero with two quilts. They had been pieced by Grandma Dee and then Big Dee and me had hung them on the quilt frames on the front porch and quilted them. One was in the Lone Star pattern. The other was Walk Around the Mountain. In both of them were scraps of dresses Grandma Dee had worn fifty and more years ago. Bits and pieces of Grandpa Jarrell's paisley shirts. And one teeny faded blue piece, about the size of a penny matchbox, that was from Great Grandpa Ezra's uniform that he wore in the Civil War.

"Mama," Wangero said sweet as a bird. "Can I have these old quilts?"

I heard something fall in the kitchen, and a minute later the kitchen door slammed.

"Why don't you take one or two of the others?" I asked. "These old things was just done by me and Big Dee from some tops your grandma pieced before she died."

Quilt made by a slave in
Mississippi about 1855–1858.
(Courtesy of Michigan State
University Museum)

"No," said Wangero. "I don't want those. They are stitched around the borders
by machine."

60   "That's make them last better," I said.

"That's not the point," said Wangero. "These are all pieces of dresses
Grandma used to wear. She did all this stitching by hand. Imagine!" She held the
quilts securely in her arms, stroking them.

"Some of the pieces, like those lavender ones, come from old clothes her
mother handed down to her," I said, moving up to touch the quilts. Dee
(Wangero) moved back just enough so that I couldn't reach the quilts. They already belonged to her.

"Imagine!" she breathed again, clutching them closely to her bosom.

"The truth is," I said, "I promised to give them quilts to Maggie, for when she
marries John Thomas."

65   She gasped like a bee had stung her.

"Maggie can't appreciate these quilts!" she said. "She'd probably be backward
enough to put them to everyday use."

"I reckon she would," I said. "God knows I been saving 'em for long enough
with nobody using 'em. I hope she will!" I didn't want to bring up how I had offered Dee (Wangero) a quilt when she went away to college. Then she had told
me they were old-fashioned, out of style.

"But they're *priceless!*" she was saying now, furiously; for she has a temper.
"Maggie would put them on the bed and in five years they'd be in rags. Less than
that!"

"She can always make some more," I said. "Maggie knows how to quilt."

70   Dee (Wangero) looked at me with hatred. "You just will not understand. The point is these quilts, *these* quilts!"

"Well," I said, stumped. "What would *you* do with them?"

"Hang them," she said. As if that was the only thing you *could* do with quilts.

Maggie by now was standing in the door. I could almost hear the sound her feet made as they scraped over each other.

"She can have them, Mama," she said, like somebody used to never winning anything, or having anything reserved for her. "I can 'member Grandma Dee without the quilts."

75   I looked at her hard. She had filled her bottom lip with checkerberry snuff and it gave her face a kind of dopey, hangdog look. It was Grandma Dee and Big Dee who taught her how to quilt herself. She stood there with her scarred hands hidden in the folds of her skirt. She looked at her sister with something like fear but she wasn't mad at her. This was Maggie's portion. This was the way she knew God to work.

When I looked at her like that something hit me in the top of my head and ran down to the soles of my feet. Just like when I'm in church and the spirit of God touches me and I get happy and shout. I did something I never had done before: hugged Maggie to me, then dragged her on into the room, snatched the quilts out of Miss Wangero's hands and dumped them into Maggie's lap. Maggie just sat there on my bed with her mouth open.

"Take one or two of the others," I said to Dee.

But she turned without a word and went out to Hakim-a-barber.

"You just don't understand," she said, as Maggie and I came out to the car.

80   "What don't I understand?" I wanted to know.

"Your heritage," she said. And then she turned to Maggie, kissed her, and said, "You ought to try to make something of yourself, too, Maggie. It's really a new day for us. But from the way you and Mama still live you'd never know it."

She put on some sunglasses that hid everything above the tip of her nose and her chin.

Maggie smiled; maybe at the sunglasses. But a real smile, not scared. After we watched the car dust settle I asked Maggie to bring me a dip of snuff. And then the two of us sat there just enjoying, until it was time to go in the house and go to bed.

[1973]

Topics for Critical Thinking and Writing

1. Alice Walker wrote the story, but the story is narrated by one of the characters, Mama. How would you characterize Mama?

2. At the end of the story, Dee tells Maggie, "It's really a new day for us. But from the way you and Mama still live you'd never know it." What does Dee mean? And how do Maggie and Mama respond?

3. In paragraph 76 the narrator says, speaking of Maggie, "When I looked at her like that something hit me in the top of my head and ran down to the soles of my feet." What "hit" Mama? That is, what does she understand at this moment that she had not understood before?

4. In "Everyday Use" why does the family conflict focus on who will possess the quilts? Why are the quilts important? What do they symbolize?

KATHERINE MIN

Katherine Min has published stories in several magazines notable for their excellent fiction, including Tri-Quarterly *and* Ploughshares. *She has received grants from the National Endowment for the Arts and from the New Hampshire State Arts Council, and she has twice been a fellow at the MacDowell Colony.*

Courting a Monk

When I first saw my husband he was sitting cross-legged under a tree on the quad, his hair as short as peach fuzz, large blue eyes staring upward, the smile on his face so wide and undirected as to seem moronic. I went flying by him every minute or two, guarding man-to-man, or chasing down a pass, and out of the corner of my eye I would see him watching and smiling. What I noticed about him most was his tremendous capacity for stillness. His hands were like still-life objects resting on his knees; his posture was impeccable. He looked so rooted there, like some cheerful, exotic mushroom, that I began to feel awkward in my exertion. Sweat funneled into the valley of my back, cooling and sticking when I stopped, hands on knees, to regain my breath. I tried to stop my gape-mouthed panting, refashioned my pony-tail, and wiped my hands on the soft front of my sweatpants.

He was still there two plays later when my team was down by one. Sully stole a pass and flipped to Graham. Graham threw me a long bomb that sailed wide and I leapt for it, sailing with the Frisbee for a moment in a parallel line—floating, flying, reaching—before coming down whap! against the ground. I groaned. I'd taken a tree root in the solar plexus. The wind was knocked out of me. I lay there, the taste of dry leaves in my mouth.

"Sorry, Gina. Lousy pass," Graham said, coming over. "You O.K.?"

"Fine," I gasped, fingering my ribs. "Just let me sit out for a while."

5   I sat down in the leaves, breathing carefully as I watched them play. The day was growing dark and the Frisbee was hard to see. Everyone was tired and played in a sloppy rhythm of errant throws and dropped passes.

Beside me on the grass crept the guy from under the tree. I had forgotten about him. He crouched shyly next to me, leaves cracking under his feet, and, when I looked up, he whispered, "You were magnificent," and walked away smiling.

I spotted him the next day in the vegetarian dining hall. I was passing through with my plate of veal cordon bleu when I saw him sitting by himself next to the window. He took a pair of wooden chopsticks out of the breast pocket of his shirt and poked halfheartedly at his tofu and wilted mung beans. I sat down across from him and demanded his life story.

It turned out he wanted to be a monk. Not the Chaucerian kind, bald-pated and stout, with a hooded robe, ribald humor and penchant for wine. Something even more baffling—a Buddhist. He had just returned from a semester in Nepal, studying in a monastery in the Himalayas. His hair was coming back in soft spikes across his head and he had a watchful manner—not cautious but receptive, waiting.

He was from King of Prussia, off the Philadelphia Main Line, and this made me mistrust the depth of his beliefs. I have discovered that a fascination for the

East is often a prelude to a pass, a romantic overture set in motion by an "I think Oriental girls are so beautiful," and a vise-like grip on the upper thigh. But Micah was different. He understood I was not impressed by his belief, and he did not aim to impress.

10   "My father was raised Buddhist," I told him. "But he's a scientist now."

"Oh," said Micah. "So, he's not spiritual."

"Spirit's insubstantial," I said. "He doesn't hold with intangibility."

"Well, you can't hold atoms in your hand," Micah pointed out.

"Ah," I said, smiling, "but you can count them."

. . .

15   I told Micah my father was a man of science, and this was true. He was a man, also, of silence. Unlike Micah, whose reticence seemed calming, so undisturbed, like a pool of light on still water, my father's silence was like the lid on a pot, sealing off some steaming, inner pressure.

Words were not my father's medium. "Language," my father liked to say, "is an imprecise instrument." (For though he said little, when he hit upon a phrase he liked, he said it many times.) He was fond of Greek letters and numerals set together in intricate equations, symbolizing a certain physical law or experimental hypothesis. He filled yellow legal pads in a strong vertical hand, writing these beauties down in black, indelible felt-tip pen. I think it was a source of tremendous irritation to him that he could not communicate with other people in so ordered a fashion, that he could not simply draw an equals sign after something he'd said, have them solve for x or y.

That my father's English was not fluent was only part of it. He was not a garrulous man, even in Korean, among visiting relatives, or alone with my mother. And with me, his only child—who could speak neither of his preferred languages, Korean or science—my father had conspicuously little to say. "Pick up this mess," he would tell me, returning from work in the evening. "Homework finished?" he would inquire, raising an eyebrow over his rice bowl as I excused myself to go watch television.

He limited himself to the imperative mood, the realm of injunction and command; the kinds of statement that required no answer, that left no opening for discussion or rejoinder. These communications were my father's verbal equivalent to his neat numerical equations. They were hermetically sealed.

When I went away to college, my father's parting words constituted one of the longest speeches I'd heard him make. Surrounded by station wagons packed with suitcases, crates of books and study lamps, amid the excited chattering and calling out of students, among the adults with their nervous parental surveillance of the scene, my father leaned awkwardly forward with his hands in his pockets, looking at me intently. He said, "Study hard. Go to bed early. Do not goof off. And do not let the American boys take advantages."

20   This was the same campus my father had set foot on twenty years before, when he was a young veteran of the Korean War, with fifty dollars in his pocket and about that many words of English. Stories of his college years constituted family legend and, growing up, I had heard them so often they were as vivid and dream-like as my own memories. My father in the dorm bathroom over Christmas, vainly trying to hard-boil an egg in a sock by running it under hot water; his triumph in the physics lab where his ability with the new language did not impede him, and where his maturity and keen scientific mind garnered him highest marks

and the top physics prize in his senior year—these were events I felt I'd witnessed, like some obscure, envious ghost.

In the shadow of my father's achievements then, on the same campus where he had first bowed his head to a microscope, lost in a chalk-dust mathematical dream, I pursued words. English words. I committed myself to expertise. I studied Shakespeare and Eliot, Hardy and Conrad, Joyce and Lawrence and Hemingway and Fitzgerald. It was important to get it right, every word, every nuance, to fill in my father's immigrant silences, the gaps he had left for me.

Other gaps he'd left. Staying up late and studying little, I did things my father would have been too shocked to merely disapprove. As for American boys, I heeded my father's advice and did not let them take advantage. Instead I took advantage of them, of their proximity, their good looks, and the amiable way they would fall into bed with you if you gave them the slightest encouragement. I liked the way they moved in proud possession of their bodies, the rough feel of their unshaven cheeks, their shoulders and smooth, hairless chests, the curve of their backs like burnished wood. I liked the way I could look up at them, or down, feeling their shuddering climax like a distant earthquake; I could make it happen, moving in undulant circles from above or below, watching them, holding them, making them happy. I collected boys like baubles, like objects not particularly valued, which you stash away in the back of some drawer. It was the pleasant interchangeability of their bodies I liked. They were all white boys.

Micah refused to have sex with me. It became a matter of intellectual disagreement with us. "Sex saps the will," he said.

"Not necessarily," I argued. "Just reroutes it."

25   "There are higher forms of union," he said.

"Not with your clothes off," I replied.

"Gina," he said, looking at me with kindness, a concern that made me flush with anger. "What need do you have that sex must fill?"

"Fuck you, Micah," I said. "Be a monk, not a psychologist."

He laughed. His laughter was always a surprise to me, like a small disturbance to the universe. I wanted to seduce him, this was true. I considered Micah the only real challenge among an easy field. But more than seduction, I wanted to rattle him, to get under that sense of peace, that inward contentment. No one my age, I reasoned, had the right to such self-possession.

30   We went for walks in the bird sanctuary, rustling along the paths slowly discussing Emily Dickinson or maple syrup-making, but always I brought the subject around.

"What a waste of life," I said once. "Such indulgence. All that monkly devotion and quest for inner peace. Big deal. It's selfish. Not only is it selfish, it's a cop-out. An escape from this world and its messes."

Micah listened, a narrow smile on his lips, shaking his head regretfully. "You're so wonderfully passionate, Gina, so alive and in the world. I can't make you see. Maybe it is a cop-out as you say, but Buddhism makes no distinction between the world outside or the world within the monastery. And historically, monks have been in the middle of political protest and persecution. Look at Tibet."

"I was thinking about, ahem, something more basic," I said.

Micah laughed. "Of course," he said. "You don't seem to understand, Gina, Buddhism is all about the renunciation of desire."

35   I sniffed. "What's wrong with desire? Without desire, you might as well not be alive."

The truth was that I was fascinated by this idea, the renunciation of desire. My life was fueled by longing, by vast and clamorous desires; a striving toward things I did not have and, perhaps, had no hope of having. I could vaguely imagine an end, some point past desiring, of satiety, but I could not fathom the laying down of desire, walking away in full appetite.

"The desire to renounce desire," I said now, "is still desire, isn't it?"

Micah sunk his hands into his pockets and smiled. "It's not," he said, walking ahead of me. "It's a conscious choice."

We came to a pond, sun-dappled in a clearing, bordered by white birch and maples with the bright leaves of mid-autumn. A fluttering of leaves blew from the trees, landing on the water as gently as if they'd been placed. The color of the pond was a deep canvas green; glints of light snapped like sparks above the surface. There was the lyric coo of a mourning dove, the chitter-chitter of late-second insects. Micah's capacity for appreciation was vast. Whether this had anything to do with Buddhism, I didn't know, but watching him stand on the edge of the pond, his head thrown back, his eyes eagerly taking in the light, I felt his peace and also his sense of wonder. He stood motionless for a long time.

40   I pulled at ferns, weaved their narrow leaves in irregular samplers, braided tendrils together, while Micah sat on a large rock and, taking his chopsticks from his breast pocket, began to tap them lightly against one another in a solemn rhythm.

"Every morning in the monastery," he said, "we woke to the prayer drum. Four o'clock and the sky would be dark and you'd hear the hollow wooden sound—plock, plock, plock—summoning you to meditation." He smiled dreamily. The chopsticks made a somewhat less effectual sound, a sort of ta ta ta. I imagined sunrise across a Himalayan valley—the wisps of pink-tinged cloud on a cold spring morning, the austerity of a monk's chamber.

Micah had his eyes closed, face to the sun. He continued to tap the chopsticks together slowly. He looked singular and new, sitting on that rock, like an advance scout for some new tribe, with his crest of hair and calm, and the attentiveness of his body to his surroundings.

I think it was then I fell in love with him, or, it was in that moment that my longing for him became so great that it was no longer a matter of simple gratification. I needed his response. I understood what desire was then, the disturbance of a perfect moment in anticipation of another.

"Wake-up call," I said. I peeled off my turtleneck and sweater in one clever motion and tossed them at Micah's feet. Micah opened his eyes. I pulled my pants off and my underwear and stood naked. "Plock, plock, who's there?"

45   Micah did not turn away. He looked at me, his chopsticks poised in the air. He raised one toward me and held it, as though he were an artist with a paintbrush raised for a proportion, or a conductor ready to lead an orchestra. He held the chopstick suspended in the space between us, and it was as though I couldn't move for as long as he held it. His eyes were fathomless blue. My nipples constricted with the cold. Around us leaves fell in shimmering lights to the water,

making a soft rustling sound like the rub of stiff fabric. He brought his hand down and I was released. I turned and leapt into the water.

A few nights later I bought a bottle of cheap wine and goaded Micah into drinking it with me. We started out on the steps of the library after it had closed for the night, taking sloppy swigs from a brown paper bag. The lights of the Holyoke range blinked in the distance, across the velvet black of the freshman quad. From there we wandered the campus, sprawling on the tennis courts, bracing a stiff wind from the terrace of the science center, sedately rolling down Memorial Hill like a pair of tumbleweeds.

"J'a know what a koan is?" he asked me, when we were perched at the top of the bleachers behind home plate. We unsteadily contemplated the steep drop off the back side.

"You mean like ice cream?" I said.

"No, a ko-an. In Buddhism."

50   "Nope."

"It's a question that has no answer, sort of like a riddle. You know, like 'What is the sound of one hand clapping?' Or 'What was your face before you were born?'"

"'What was my face before it was born?' That makes no sense."

"Exactly. You're supposed to contemplate the koan until you achieve a greater awareness."

"Of what?"

55   "Of life, of meaning."

"Oh, O.K.," I said, "I've got it." I was facing backwards, the bag with the bottle in both my hands. "How 'bout, 'What's the sound of one cheek farting?'"

He laughed for a long time, then retched off the side of the bleachers. I got him home and put him to bed; his forehead was feverish, his eyes glassy with sickness.

"Sorry," I said. "I'm a bad influence." I kissed him. His lips were hot and slack.

"Don't mind," he murmured, half-asleep.

60   The next night we slept in the same bed together for the first time. He kept his underwear on and his hands pressed firmly to his sides, like Gandhi among his young virgins. I was determined to make it difficult for him. I kept brushing my naked body against him, draping a leg across his waist, stroking his narrow chest with my fingertips. He wiggled and pushed away, feigning sleep. When I woke in the morning, he was gone and the *Ode to Joy* was blasting from my stereo.

Graham said he missed me. We'd slept together a few times before I met Micah, enjoying the warm, healthful feeling we got from running or playing Ultimate, taking a quick sauna and falling into bed. He was good-looking, dark and broad, with sinewy arms and a tight chest. He made love to a woman like he was lifting Nautilus, all grim purpose and timing. It was hard to believe that had ever been appealing. I told him I was seeing someone else.

"Not the guy with the crew cut?" he said. "The one who looks like a baby seal?"

I shrugged.

Graham looked at me skeptically "He doesn't seem like your type," he said.

65   "No," I agreed. "But at least he's not yours."

Meanwhile I stepped up my attack. I asked endless questions about Buddhist teaching. Micah talked about *dukkha*[1]; the four noble truths; the five aggregates of attachment; the noble eightfold path to enlightenment. I listened dutifully, willing to acknowledge that it all sounded nice, that the goal of perfect awareness and peace seemed worth attaining. While he talked, I stretched my feet out until my toes touched his thigh; I slid my hand along his back; or leaned way over so he could see down my loose, barely-buttoned blouse.

"Too bad you aren't Tantric," I said. I'd been doing research.

Micah scoffed. "Hollywood Buddhism," he said. "Heavy breathing and theatrics."

"They believe in physical desire," I said. "They have sex."

70   "Buddha believes in physical desire," Micah said. "It's impermanent, that's all. Something to get beyond."

"To get beyond it," I said petulantly, "you have to do it."

Micah signed. "Gina," he said, "you are beautiful, but I can't. There are a lot of guys who will."

"A lot of them do."

He smiled a bit sadly. "Well, then . . . ."

75   I leaned down to undo his shoelaces. I tied them together in double knots. "But I want you," I said.

My parents lived thirty miles from campus and my mother frequently asked me to come home for dinner. I went only once that year, and that was with Micah. My parents were not the kind of people who enjoyed the company of strangers. They were insular people who did not like to socialize much or go out—or anyway, my father was that way, and my mother accommodated herself to his preferences.

My mother had set the table in the dining room with blue linen. There were crystal wine glasses and silver utensils in floral patterns. She had made some dry baked chicken with overcooked peas and carrots—the meal she reserved for when Americans came to dinner. When it came to Korean cooking, my mother was a master. She made fabulous marinated short ribs and sautéed transparent bean noodles with vegetables and beef, pork dumplings and batter-fried shrimp, and cucumber and turnip kimchis[2] which she made herself and fermented in brown earthenware jars. But American cuisine eluded her; it bored her. I think she thought it was meant to be tasteless.

"Just make Korean," I had urged her on the phone. "He'll like that."

My mother was skeptical. "Too spicy," she said. "I know what Americans like."

80   "Not the chicken dish," I pleaded. "He's a vegetarian."

"We'll see," said my mother, conceding nothing.

Micah stared down at his plate. My mother smiled serenely. Micah nodded. He ate a forkful of vegetables, took a bite of bread. His Adam's apple seemed to be doing a lot of work. My father, too, was busy chewing, his Adam's apple moving up and down his throat like the ratchets of a tire jack. No one had said a thing since my father had uncorked the Chardonnay and read to us the

---

[1]**dukkha** a Pali word meaning "suffering," particularly the suffering that is caused by desire.
[2]**kimchis** pickles.

description from his well-creased paperback edition of *The New York Times Guide to Wine.*

The sound of silverware scraping on ceramic plates seemed amplified. I was aware of my own prolonged chewing. My father cleared his throat. My mother looked at him expectantly. He coughed.

"Micah studied Buddhism in Nepal," I offered into the silence.

85   "Oh!" my mother exclaimed. She giggled.

My father kept eating. He swallowed exaggeratedly and looked up. "That so?" he said, sounding almost interested.

Micah nodded. "I was only there four months," he said. "Gina tells me you were brought up Buddhist."

My father grunted. "Well, of course," he said. "In Korea in those days, our families were all Buddhist. I do not consider myself a Buddhist now."

Micah and I exchanged a look.

90   "It's become quite fashionable, I understand," my father went on. "With you American college kids. Buddhism has become fad."

I saw Micah wince.

"I think it is wonderful, Hi Joon," my mother interceded, "for Americans to learn about Asian religion and philosophy. I was a philosophy major in college, Micah. I studied Whitehead,[3] American pragmatism."

My father leaned back in his chair and watched, frowning, while my mother and Micah talked. It was like he was trying to analyze Micah, not as a psychiatrist analyzes—my father held a dim view of psychology—but as a chemist would, breaking him down to his basic elements, the simple chemical formula that would define his makeup.

Micah was talking about the aggregates of matter, sensation, perception, mental formations, and consciousness that comprise being in Buddhist teaching. "It's a different sense of self than in Christian religions," he explained, looking at my mother.

95   "Nonsense," my father interrupted. "There is no self in Buddhist doctrine. . . ."

My mother and I watched helplessly as they launched into discussion. I was surprised that my father seemed to know so much about it, and by how much he was carrying forth. I was surprised also by Micah's deference. He seemed to have lost all his sureness, the walls of his conviction. He kept nodding and conceding to my father certain points that he had rigorously defended to me before. "I guess I don't know as much about it," he said more than once, and "Yes, I see what you mean" several times, with a sickening air of humility.

I turned from my father's glinting, pitiless intelligence, to Micah's respectfulness, his timid manner, and felt a rising irritation I could not place, anger at my father's belligerence, at Micah's backing down, at my own strange motives for having brought them together. Had I really expected them to get along? And yet, my father was concentrating on Micah with such an intensity—almost as though he were a rival—in a way in which he never focused on me.

When the dialogue lapsed, and after we had consumed as much of the food as we deemed polite, my mother took the dishes away and brought in a bowl of rice with kimchi for my father. Micah's eyes lit up. "May I have some of that, too, Mrs. Kim?"

My mother looked doubtful. "Too spicy," she said.

---

[3]**Whitehead** Alfred North Whitehead (1861–1947), British mathematician and philosopher.

100   "Oh, I love spicy food," Micah assured her. My mother went to get him a bowl.

"You can use chopsticks?" my mother said, as Micah began eating with them.

"Mom, it's no big deal," I said.

My father looked up from his bowl. Together, my parents watched while Micah ate a large piece of cabbage kimchi.

"Hah!" my father said, suddenly smiling. "Gina doesn't like kimchi," he said. He looked at me. "Gina," he said. "This boy more Korean than you."

105   "Doesn't take much," I said.

My father ignored me. "Gina always want to be American," he told Micah. "Since she was little girl, she want blue eyes, yellow hair." He stabbed a chopstick toward Micah's face. "Like yours."

"If I had hair" said Micah, grinning, rubbing a hand across his head.

My father stared into his bowl. "She doesn't want to be Korean girl. She thinks she can be 100 percent American, but she cannot. She has Korean blood—100 percent. Doesn't matter where you grow up—blood is most important. What is in the blood." He gave Micah a severe look. "You think you can become Buddhist. Same way. But it is not in your blood. You cannot know real Buddha's teaching. You should study Bible."

"God, Dad!" I said. "You sound like a Nazi!"

110   "Gina!" my mother warned.

"You're embarrassing me," I said. "Being rude to my guest. Discussing me as if I wasn't here. You can say what you want, Dad, I'm American whether you like it or not. Blood's got nothing to do with it. It's what's up here." I tapped my finger to my temple.

"It's not Nazi," my father said. "Is fact! What you have here," he pointed to his forehead, "is all from blood, from genetics. You got from me!"

"Heaven help me," I said.

"Gina!" my mother implored.

115   "Mr. Kim—" Micah began.

"You just like American girl in one thing," my father shouted. "You have no respect for father. In Korea, daughters do not talk back to their parents, is big shame!"

"In Korea, girls are supposed to be submissive doormats for fathers to wipe their feet on!" I shouted back.

"What do you know about Korea? You went there only once when you were six years old."

"It's in my blood," I said. I stood up. "I'm not going to stay here for this. Come on, Micah."

120   Micah looked at me uncertainly, then turned to my father.

My father was eating again, slowly levering rice to his mouth with his chopsticks. He paused. "She was always this way," he said, seeming to address the table. "So angry. Even as a little girl."

"Mr. Kim," Micah said, "Um, thank you very much. We're . . . I think we're heading out now."

My father chewed ruminatively. "I should never have left Korea," he said quietly, with utter conviction.

125   "Gina," my mother said. "Sit down. Hi Joon, please!"

"Micah," I said. "You coming?"

We left my father alone at the dining-room table.

"I should have sent you to live with Auntie Soo!" he called after me.

My mother followed us out to the driveway with a Tupperware container of chicken Micah hadn't eaten.

On the way home we stopped for ice cream. Koans, I told Micah. "What is the sound of Swiss chocolate almond melting?" I asked him. "What was the vanilla before it was born?"

130   Inside the ice-cream parlor the light was too strong, a ticking fluorescence bleaching everything bone-white. Micah leaned down to survey the cardboard barrels of ice cream in their plastic cases. He looked shrunken, subdued. He ordered a scoop of mint chocolate chip and one of black cherry on a sugar cone and ate it with the long, regretful licks of a child who'd spent the last nickel of his allowance. There was a ruefulness to his movements, a sense of apology. He had lost his monk-like stillness and seemed suddenly adrift.

The cold of the ice cream gave me a headache, all the blood vessels in my temples seemed strung out and tight. I shivered and the cold was like fury, spreading through me with the chill.

Micah rubbed my back.

"You're hard on your father," he said. "He's not a bad guy."

"Forget it," I said. "Let's go."

135   We walked from the dorm parking lot in silence. There were lights going on across the quad and music spilling from the windows out into the cool air. What few stars there were seemed too distant to wage a constant light.

Back in my room, I put on the Rolling Stones at full blast. Mick Jagger's voice was taunting and cruel. I turned out the lights and lit a red candle.

"O.K., this is going to stop," I said. I felt myself trembling. I pushed Micah back on the bed. I was furious. He had ruined it for me, the lightness, the skimming quality of my life. It had seemed easy, with the boys, the glib words and feelings, the simple heat and surface pleasures. It was like the sensation of flying, leaping for the Frisbee and sailing through the air. For a moment you lose a feeling for gravity, for the consciousness of your own skin or species. For a moment you are free.

I started to dance, fast, swinging and swaying in front of the bed. I closed my eyes and twirled wildly, bouncing off the walls like a pinball, stumbling on my own stockings. I danced so hard the stereo skipped, Jagger forced to stutter in throaty monosyllables, gulping repetitions. I whirled and circled, threw my head from side to side until I could feel the baffled blood, brought my hair up off my neck and held it with both hands.

Micah watched me dance. His body made an inverted-S upon my bed, his head propped by the pillar of his own arm. The expression on his face was the same as he'd had talking with my father, that look of deference, of fawn-eyed yielding. But I could see there was something hidden.

140   With white-knuckled fingers, I undid the buttons of my sweater and ripped my shirt lifting it off my head. I danced out of my skirt and underthings, kicking them into the corner, danced until the song was over, until I was soaked with sweat and burning—and then I jumped him.

It was like the taste of food after a day's starvation—unexpectedly strong and substantial. Micah responded to my fury, met it with his own mysterious passion; it was like a brawl, a fight, with something at stake that neither of us wanted to lose. Afterward we sat up in bed and listened to *Ode to Joy* while Micah, who had a surplus supply of chopsticks lying around the room, did his Leonard Bernstein impersonation. Later, we went out for a late-night snack to All-Star Dairy and Micah admitted to me that he was in love.

· · ·

My father refused to attend the wedding. He liked Micah, but he did not want me to marry a Caucasian. It became a joke I would tell people. Korean custom, I said, to give the bride away four months before the ceremony.

Micah became a high-school biology teacher. I am an associate dean of students at the local college. We have two children. When Micah tells the story of our courtship, he tells it with great self-deprecation and humor. He makes it sound as though he were crazy to ever consider becoming a monk. "Think of it," he tells our kids. "Your dad."

Lately I've taken to reading books about Buddhism. Siddhartha Gotama was thirty-five years old when he sat under the Bodhi-tree on the bank of the river Neranjara and gained Enlightenment. Sometimes, when I see my husband looking at me across the breakfast table, or walking toward me from the other side of the room, I catch a look of distress on his face, a blinking confusion, as though he cannot remember who I am. I have happened on him a few times, on a Sunday when he has disappeared from the house, sitting on a bench with the newspaper in his lap staring across the town common, so immersed in his thoughts that he is not roused by my calling of his name.

145   I remember the first time I saw him, the tremendous stillness he carried, the contentment in his face. I remember how he looked on the rocks by that pond, like a pioneer in a new land, and I wonder if he regrets, as I do, the loss of his implausible faith. Does he miss the sound of the prayer drum, the call to an inner life without the configuration of desire? I think of my father, running a sock under heated water thousands of miles from home, as yet unaware of the daughter he will raise with the same hopeful, determined, and ultimately futile, effort. I remember the way I used to play around with koans, and I wonder, "What is the sound of a life not lived?"

[1996]

Topics for Critical Thinking and Writing

1. Halfway through the story, in paragraph 43, the narrator says, "I think it was then I fell in love with him. . . ." Why does she fall in love with Micah at this moment? And how does she describe the feeling of love?

2. When we return to the beginning of the story—first, the Frisbee game, and, second, the scene at the dining hall—what signs do we see of the kind of relationship that will develop between the narrator and Micah? What do we learn about each of these persons and about what might draw them to one another?

3. What is your response to the narrator's father? Why do you think that Min chose to make him a scientist? Is our response to the father meant to be critical? Highly critical? Or, a lot or a little sympathetic?

4. Do you agree with Min's decision to include the brief scene with the narrator's former boyfriend, Graham, paragraphs 61–65? Is this scene important for the meaning of the story as a whole, or would you recommend that it be omitted?

5. Describe what happens during the love-making scene, beginning with paragraph 135. What is the narrator trying to do through her dance, and why? What leads Micah at last to respond to her?

6. Do sexual scenes in literature make you uncomfortable? Is there a right and a wrong way, in your view, to present such scenes?

POETRY

EMMA LAZARUS

Emma Lazarus (1849–1887) was of German-Jewish descent on her mother's side, and of Sephardic descent on her father's side. (Sephardic Jews trace their ancestry back to Spain under Moslem rule, before the Jews were expelled by the Christians in 1492.)

In 1883 a committee was formed to raise funds for a pedestal for the largest statue in the world, Liberty Enlightening the People, to be installed on a small island in New York Harbor. Authors were asked to donate manuscripts that were then auctioned to raise money. Emma Lazarus, keenly aware of ancient persecutions and of contemporary Jewish refugees fleeing Russian persecutions, contributed the following poem. It was read when the statue was unveiled in 1886, and the words of Liberty, spoken in the last five lines, were embossed on a plaque inside the pedestal.

For the ancients, a colossus was a statue larger than life. "The brazen giant of Greek fame," mentioned in Lazarus's first line, was a statue of the sun god, erected in the harbor of the Greek island of Rhodes, celebrating the island's success in resisting the Macedonians in 305–4 B.C. More than 100 feet tall, it stood in the harbor until it toppled during an earthquake in 225 B.C. In later years its size became mythical; it was said to have straddled the harbor (Lazarus speaks of "limbs astride from land to land"), so that ships supposedly entered the harbor by sailing between its legs.

In Lazarus's poem, the "imprisoned lightning" (line 5) in the torch is electricity. The harbor is said to be "air-bridged" because in 1883, the year of the poem, the Brooklyn Bridge was completed, connecting Brooklyn with New York. (These are the "twin cities" of the poem.)

The New Colossus

Not like the brazen giant of Greek fame,
With conquering limbs astride from land to land;
Here at our sea-washed, sunset gates shall stand
A mighty woman with a torch, whose flame
Is the imprisoned lightning, and her name   5
Mother of Exiles. From her beacon-hand
Glows world-wide welcome; her mild eyes command
The air-bridged harbor that twin cities frame.
"Keep, ancient lands, your storied pomp!" cries she
With silent lips. "Give me your tired, your poor,   10
Your huddled masses yearning to breathe free,

Tseng Kwong Chi, "Statue of Liberty, New York City." (Courtesy of Julie Saul Gallery, NY. © 2004 Estate of Tseng Kwong Chi-MTDP/Artists Rights Society [ARS], New York.)

The wretched refuse of your teeming shore.
Send these, the homeless, tempest-tost to me,
I lift my lamp beside the golden door!"

[1883]

THOMAS BAILEY ALDRICH

Thomas Bailey Aldrich (1836–1907) was born in Portsmouth, New Hampshire. He wrote poetry from his youth to his old age, and he also wrote short stories and essays, but his literary career was chiefly that of a journalist and an editor. (One magazine that he edited from 1881 to 1890, Atlantic Monthly, *continues to be important.) As the following poem indicates, Aldrich was deeply conservative. The view that he here expresses is known as Nativism, or the Nativist view.*

The Unguarded Gates

Wide open and unguarded stand our gates,
And through them press a wild, a motley throng—
Men from the Volga and the Tartar steppes,
Featureless figures of the Hoang-Ho,
Malayan, Scythian, Teuton, Kelt, and Slav,   5
Flying the Old World's poverty and scorn;
These bringing with them unknown gods and rites,
Those tiger passions, here to stretch their claws.
In street and alley what strange tongues are these,
Accents of menace alien to our air,   10
Voices that once the tower of Babel knew!

O, Liberty, white goddess, is it well
To leave the gate unguarded? On thy breast
Fold sorrow's children, soothe the hurts of fate,
Lift the downtrodden, but with the hand of steel   15
Stay those who to thy sacred portals come
To waste the fight of freedom. Have a care
Lest from thy brow the clustered stars be torn
And trampled in the dust. For so of old
The thronging Goth and Vandal trampled Rome,   20
And where the temples of the Caesars stood
The lean wolf unmolested made her lair.

[1885]

JOSEPH BRUCHAC III

Joseph Bruchac III (the name is pronounced "Brewshack") was born in Saratoga Springs, New York, in 1942, and educated at Cornell University, Syracuse University, and Union Graduate School. Like many other Americans, he has a multicultural ethnic heritage, and he includes Native Americans as well as Slovaks among his ancestors. Bruchac, who has taught in Ghana and also in the United States, has chiefly worked as an editor.

The Registry Room, Ellis Island, ca. 1912. (William Williams Collection of Photographs. Miriam and Ira D. Wallach Division of Art, Prints and Photographs. New York Public Library.)

Slavic women arrive at Ellis Island in the winter of 1910. (Brown Brothers)

"Much of my writing and my life," Bruchac says, "relates to the problem of being an American. . . . While in college I was active in Civil Rights work and in the antiwar movement. . . . I went to Africa to teach—but more than that to be taught. It showed me many things. How much we have as Americans and take for granted. How much our eyes refuse to see because they are blinded to everything in a man's face except his color."

Ellis Island

Beyond the red brick of Ellis Island
where the two Slovak children
who became my grandparents
waited the long days of quarantine,
after leaving the sickness,   5
the old Empires of Europe,
a Circle Line ship slips easily
on its way to the island
of the tall woman, green
as dreams of forests and meadows   10
waiting for those who'd worked
a thousand years
yet never owned their own.
Like millions of others,
I too come to this island,   15

nine decades the answerer
of dreams.

Yet only one part of my blood loves that memory.
Another voice speaks
of native lands   20
within this nation.
Lands invaded
when the earth became owned.
Lands of those who followed
the changing Moon,   25
knowledge of the seasons
in their veins.

[1978]

EDWIN ARLINGTON ROBINSON

Edwin Arlington Robinson (1869–1935) grew up in Gardiner, Maine, spent two years at Harvard, and then returned to Maine, where he published his first book of poetry in 1896. Though he received encouragement from neighbors, his finances were precarious, even after President Theodore Roosevelt, having been made aware of the book, secured for him an appointment as customs inspector in New York from 1905 to 1909. Additional books won fame for Robinson, and in 1922 he was awarded the first of three Pulitzer Prizes for poetry that he would win.

Richard Cory

Whenever Richard Cory went down town,
We people on the pavement looked at him:
He was a gentleman from sole to crown,
Clean favored, and imperially slim.   4

And he was always quietly arrayed,
And he was always human when he talked;
But still he fluttered pulses when he said,
"Good-morning," and he glittered when he walked.   8

And he was rich—yes, richer than a king—
And admirably schooled in every grace:
In fine,° we thought that he was everything
To make us wish that we were in his place.   12

So on we worked, and waited for the light,
And went without the meat, and cursed the bread;
And Richard Cory, one calm summer night,
Went home and put a bullet through his head.   16

[1896]

---

11 In fine in short.

Topics for Critical Thinking and Writing

1. Consult the entry on irony in the glossary. Then read the pages referred to in the entry. Finally, write an essay of 500 words on irony in "Richard Cory."
2. What do you think were Richard Cory's thoughts shortly before he "put a bullet through his head"? In 500 words, set forth his thoughts and actions (what he sees and does). If you wish, you can write in the first person, from Cory's point of view. Further, if you wish, your essay can be in the form of a suicide note.
3. Write a sketch (250–350 words) setting forth your early impression or understanding of someone whose later actions revealed that you had not understood the person.

AURORA LEVINS MORALES

Aurora Levins Morales, born in Puerto Rico in 1954, came to the United States with her family in 1967. She has lived in Chicago and New Hampshire and now lives in the San Francisco Bay Area. Levins Morales has published stories, essays, prose poems, and poems.

Child of the Americas

I am a child of the Americas,
a light-skinned mestiza of the Caribbean,
a child of many diaspora,° born into this continent at a crossroads.

I am a U.S. Puerto Rican Jew,
a product of the ghettos of New York I have never known.   5
An immigrant and the daughter and granddaughter of immigrants.
I speak English with passion: it's the tongue of my consciousness,
a flashing knife blade of crystal, my tool, my craft.

I am Caribeña,° island grown. Spanish is in my flesh,
ripples from my tongue, lodges in my hips: 10
the language of garlic and mangoes,
the singing in my poetry, the flying gestures of my hands.

I am of Latinoamerica, rooted in the history of my continent:
I speak from that body.

---

3 diaspora literally, "scattering"; the term is used especially to refer to the dispersion of the Jews outside of Israel from the sixth century B.C., when they were exiled to Babylonia, to the present time. **9 Caribeña** Caribbean woman.

I am not african. African is in me, but I cannot return.
I am not taína.° Taíno is in me, but there is no way back.
I am not european. Europe lives in me, but I have no home there.

I am new. History made me. My first language was spanglish.°
I was born at the crossroads
and I am whole.

[1986]

16 **taína** the Taínos were the Indian tribe native to Puerto Rico.   18 **spanglish** a mixture of
Spanish and English.

Topics for Critical Thinking and Writing

1. In the first stanza, Levins Morales speaks of herself as "a child of many diaspora." *Diaspora* often means "a scattering," or "a dispersion of a homogeneous
   people." What does it refer to here?
2. In the second stanza, Levins Morales says that she is "a product of the ghettos
   of New York I have never known." What does she apparently refer to?
3. What attitude does "Child of the Americas" have toward the writer's ethnicity?
   What words or lines particularly communicate it?

Gloria Anzaldúa

*Gloria Anzaldúa, a seventh-generation American, was born in
1942 on a ranch settlement in Texas. When she was 11 her family moved to Hargill, Texas, and in the next few years the family
traveled as migrant workers between Texas and Arkansas. In
1969 she earned a B.A. from Pan American University, and
later she earned an M.A. from the University of Texas at Austin
and did further graduate work at the University of California,
Santa Cruz. Anzaldúa has taught at the University of Texas at
Austin; San Francisco State University; Oakes College at the
University of California, Santa Cruz; and Vermont College.*

   We give a poem from Anzaldúa's Borderlands: La Frontera—The New Mestiza
(1987), *a work that combines seven prose essays with poems. For Anzaldúa—a
woman, a Latina, and a lesbian—the "borderlands" of course are spiritual as well
as geographic.*

To Live in the Borderlands Means You

To live in the Borderlands means you
   are neither *hispana india negra española*
   ni gabacha,° eres mestiza, mulata,° half-breed

2–3 **neither ... *mulata*** neither Spanish indian black Spanish woman, nor white, you are
mixed, a mixed breed.   3 **gabacha** a Chicano term for a white woman.

caught in the crossfire between camps
   while carrying all five races on your back   5
   not knowing which side to turn to, run from;

To live in the Borderlands means knowing
   that the *india* in you, betrayed for 500 years,
   is no longer speaking to you,
   that *mexicanas* call you *rajetas,*°   10
   that denying the Anglo inside you
   is as bad as having denied the Indian or Black;

Cuando vives en la frontera°
   people walk through you, the wind steals your voice,
   you're a *burra, buey,*° scapegoat,   15
   forerunner of a new race,
   half and half—both woman and man, neither—
   a new gender;

To live in the Borderlands means to
   put *chile* in the borscht,   20
   eat whole wheat *tortillas,*
   speak Tex-Mex with a Brooklyn accent;
   be stopped by *la migra*° at the border checkpoints;

Living in the Borderlands means you fight hard to
   resist the gold elixer beckoning from the bottle,   25
   the pull of the gun barrel,
   the rope crushing the hollow of your throat;

In the Borderlands
   you are the battleground
   where enemies are kin to each other;   30
   you are at home, a stranger,
   the border disputes have been settled
   the volley of shots have shattered the truce
   you are wounded, lost in action
   dead, fighting back;   35

To live in the Borderlands means
   the mill with the razor white teeth wants to shred off
   your olive-red skin, crush out the kernel, your heart
   pound you pinch you roll you out
   smelling like white bread but dead;   40

To survive the Borderlands
   you must live *sin fronteras*°
   be a crossroads.

[1987]

---

10 rajetas literally, "split," that is having betrayed your word (author's note). **13 Cuando . . .
frontera** when you live in the borderlands. **15 burra, buey** donkey, oxen (author's note).
23 la migra immigration officials. **42 sin fronteras** without borders.

JIMMY SANTIAGO BACA

Jimmy Santiago Baca, of Chicano and Apache descent, was born in 1952. When he was 2 his parents divorced, and a grandparent brought him up until he was 5, when he was placed in an orphanage in New Mexico. He ran away when he was 11, lived on the streets, took drugs, and at the age of 20 was convicted of drug possession. In prison he taught himself to read and write, and he began to compose poetry. A fellow inmate urged him to send some poems to Mother Jones *magazine, and the work was accepted. In 1979 Louisiana State University Press published a book of his poems,* Immigrants in Our Own Land. *He has since published several other books.*

So Mexicans Are Taking Jobs from Americans

O Yes? Do they come on horses
with rifles, and say,
        Ese gringo,° gimmee your job?
And do you, gringo, take off your ring,
drop your wallet into a blanket   5
spread over the ground, and walk away?

I hear Mexicans are taking your jobs away.
Do they sneak into town at night,
and as you're walking home with a whore,
do they mug you, a knife at your throat,   10
saying, I want your job?
Even on TV, an asthmatic leader
crawls turtle heavy, leaning on an assistant,
and from a nest of wrinkles on his face,
a tongue paddles through flashing waves   15
of lightbulbs, of cameramen, rasping
"They're taking our jobs away."

Well, I've gone about trying to find them,
asking just where the hell are these fighters.

The rifles I hear sound in the night   20
are white farmers shooting blacks and browns
whose ribs I see jutting out
and starving children,
I see the poor marching for a little work,
I see small white farmers selling out   25
to clean-suited farmers living in New York,
who've never been on a farm,
don't know the look of a hoof or the smell
of a woman's body bending all day long in fields.
I see this, and I hear only a few people   30

---

3 Ese gringo Hey, whitey.

got all the money in this world, the rest
count their pennies to buy bread and butter.

Below that cool green sea of money,
millions and millions of people fight to live,
search for pearls in the darkest depths
of their dreams, hold their breath for years   35
trying to cross poverty to just having something.

The children are dead already. We are killing them,
that is what America should be saying;
on TV, in the streets, in offices, should be saying,   40
   "We aren't giving the children a chance to live."

   Mexicans are taking our jobs, they say instead.
   What they really say is, let them die,
   and the children too.

                                                [1979]

LANGSTON HUGHES

*Langston Hughes (1902–1967) was born in Joplin, Missouri. He lived part of his
youth in Mexico, spent a year at Columbia University, served as a merchant seaman, and worked in a Paris nightclub. After returning to the United States, he
showed some of his poems to Dr. Alain Locke, a strong advocate of African
American literature. Hughes went on to publish poetry, fiction, plays, essays, and
biographies.*

Theme for English B

The instructor said,

   *Go home and write
   a page tonight.
   And let that page come out of you—
   Then, it will be true.*   5

I wonder if it's that simple?

I am twenty-two, colored, born in Winston-Salem.
I went to school there, then Durham, then here
to this college on the hill above Harlem.
I am the only colored student in my class.   10
The steps from the hill lead down into Harlem,
through a park, then I cross St. Nicholas,
Eighth Avenue, Seventh, and I come to the Y,
the Harlem Branch Y, where I take the elevator
up to my room, sit down, and write this page: 15

It's not easy to know what is true for you or me
at twenty-two, my age. But I guess I'm what
I feel and see and hear, Harlem, I hear you:
hear you, hear me—we two—you, me, talk on this page.
(I hear New York, too.) Me—who?   20

Well, I like to eat, sleep, drink, and be in love.
I like to work, read, learn, and understand life.
I like a pipe for a Christmas present,
or records—Bessie,° bop, or Bach.
I guess being colored doesn't make me *not* like   25
the same things other folks like who are other races.

So will my page be colored that I write?
Being me, it will not be white.
But it will be
a part of you, instructor.   30

You are white—
yet a part of me, as I am a part of you.
That's American.
Sometimes perhaps you don't want to be a part of me.
Nor do I often want to be a part of you.   35
But we are, that's true!
As I learn from you,
I guess you learn from me—
although you're older—and white—
and somewhat more free.   40

This is my page for English B.

[1949]

24 **Bessie** Bessie Smith (1898?–1937), African American blues singer.

Topics for Critical Thinking and Writing

1. The teacher instructs the students (line 4) to "let that page come out of you," and adds, "Then, it will be true" (6). Does it follow that what we let "come" out of us is "true"? If you were a student, what would be your response to the teacher's instruction?
2. In lines 21–24 Hughes specifies some of the things he likes—things that many people who are not black doubtless also like. Why, then, does he say (line 28) that his page "will not be white"?
3. Pretend that you are the English B instructor who received Hughes's theme. What comment (about 250 words) do you put at the end of the theme?
4. Aside from the statement that he is a "colored" student (10, 27) from Harlem (9, 11, 14, 18), is there anything particularly African American about this poem? Putting aside these references, might the poem have been written by an Asian American, or (say) an American of Middle Eastern descent?
5. In line 10 the speaker says he is "the only colored student in [his] class." If you have ever been the only student of your race or religion or ethnic background or sex in a group, in an essay of 250–500 words set forth the feelings you had, and the feelings you now have about the experience.

PAT PARKER

Pat Parker (1944–1989), author of several books of poems and essays, was a founder of the Black Women's Revolutionary Council in 1980, and a medical co-ordinator at the Oakland Feminist Women's Health Center.

For the white person who wants to know how to be my friend

The first thing you do is to forget that i'm Black.
Second, you must never forget that i'm Black.

You should be able to dig Aretha,°
but don't play her every time i come over.
And if you decide to play Beethoven—don't tell me   5
his life story. They made us take music appreciation too.

Eat soul food if you like it, but don't expect me
to locate your restaurants
or cook it for you.

And if some Black person insults you,
mugs you, rapes your sister, rapes you,
rips your house or is just being an ass—
please, do not apologize to me
for wanting to do them bodily harm.
It makes me wonder if you're foolish.   15

And even if you really believe Blacks are better lovers than
whites—don't tell me. I start thinking of charging stud fees.

In other words—if you really want to be my friend—*don't*
make a labor of it. I'm lazy. Remember.

[1978]

3 **Aretha** Aretha Franklin, African American singer of blues and rock.

Topics for Critical Thinking and Writing

1. The first two lines are contradictory. What sense do you make out of them?
2. Explain lines 4–5.
3. What stereotypes of African Americans does Parker evoke in the last two stanzas? What is her point?
4. If you have ever been involved in an episode of the sort that Parker mentions in her second stanza, in an essay of 500 words narrate the experience and offer a reflection on it.

MITSUYE YAMADA

Mitsuye Yamada, the daughter of Japanese immigrants to the United States, was born in Japan in 1923, during her mother's return visit to her native land. Yamada was raised in Seattle, but in 1942 she and her family were incarcerated and then relocated in a camp in Idaho, when Executive Order 9066 gave military authorities the right to remove any and all persons from "military areas." In 1954 she became an American citizen. Later, she became a member of the Asian American Studies Program at the University at California at Irvine. She is the author of poems and stories.

For another poem by Yamada, see page 1344.

To the Lady

The one in San Francisco who asked:
Why did the Japanese Americans let
the government put them in
those camps without protest?

Come to think of it I   5
    should've run off to Canada
    should've hijacked a plane to Algeria
    should've pulled myself up from my
    bra straps
    and kicked'm in the groin   10
    should've bombed a bank
    should've tried self-immolation
    should've holed myself up in a
    woodframe house
    and let you watch me   15
    burn up on the six o'clock news
    should've run howling down the street
    naked and assaulted you at breakfast
    by AP wirephoto
    should've screamed bloody murder   20
    like Kitty Genovese°

    Then
YOU would've
    come to my aid in shining armor
    laid yourself across the railroad track   25
    marched on Washington

---

21 Kitty Genovese In 1964 Kitty Genovese of Kew Gardens, New York, was stabbed to death when she left her car and walked toward her home. Thirty-eight persons heard her screams, but no one came to her assistance.

Dorothea Lange. "Grandfather and Grandchildren Awaiting
Evacuation Bus." (War Relocation Authority/The National Archives)

tatooed a Star of David on your arm
written six million enraged
letters to Congress

But we didn't draw the line
anywhere
law and order Executive Order 9066°
social order moral order internal order

You let'm
I let'm   35
All are punished.

[1976]

32 **Executive Order 9066** an authorization, signed in 1941 by President Franklin D. Roosevelt,
allowing military authorities to relocate Japanese and Japanese Americans who resided on the
Pacific Coast of the United States.

Topics for Critical Thinking and Writing

1. Has the lady's question (lines 2–4) ever crossed your mind? If so, what answers did you think of?
2. What, in effect, is the speaker really saying in lines 5–21? And in lines 24–29?
3. Explain the last line.

DRAMA

LUIS VALDEZ

Luis Valdez was born into a family of migrant farm workers in Delano, California, in 1940. After completing high school he entered San Jose State College on a scholarship. He wrote his first plays while still an undergraduate, and after receiving his degree (in English and drama) from San Jose in 1964 he joined the San Francisco Mime Troupe, a left-wing group that performed in parks and streets. Revolutionary in technique as well as in political content, the Mime Troupe rejected the traditional forms of drama and instead drew on the traditions of the circus and the carnival.

In 1965 Valdez returned to Delano, where Cesar Chavez had organized a strike of farm workers and a boycott against grape growers. It was here, under the wing of the United Farm Workers, that he established El Teatro Campesino (the Farm Workers' Theater), which at first specialized in doing short, improvised, satirical skits called actos. *When the* teatro *moved to Del Rey, California, it expanded its repertoire beyond farm issues, and it became part of a cultural center that gave workshops (in English and Spanish) in such subjects as history, drama, and politics.*

The actos, *performed by amateurs on college campuses and on flatbed trucks and at the edges of vineyards, were highly political. Making use of stereotypes (the boss, the scab), the* actos *sought not to present the individual thoughts of a gifted playwright but to present the social vision of ordinary people—the* pueblo—*though it was acknowledged that in an oppressive society the playwright might have to help guide the people to see their own best interests.*

Valdez moved from actos *to mitos (myths)—plays that drew on Aztec mythology, Mexican folklore, and Christianity—and then to* Zoot Suit, *a play that ran for many months in California and that became the first Mexican American play to be produced on Broadway. More recently he wrote and directed a hit movie,* La Bamba, *and in 1991 received an award from the AT&T Foundation for his musical,* Bandido, *presented by El Teatro Campesino.*

Los Vendidos *was written in 1967, when Ronald Reagan was governor of California.*

Los Vendidos*

LIST OF CHARACTERS

HONEST SANCHO
SECRETARY
FARM WORKER
JOHNNY
REVOLUCIONARIO
MEXICAN-AMERICAN

SCENE: *Honest Sancho's Used Mexican Lot and Mexican Curio Shop. Three models are on display in Honest* SANCHO's *shop: to the right, there is a* REVOLUCIONARIO, *complete with sombrero, carrilleras,[1] and carabina 30-30. At center, on the floor, there is the* FARM WORKER *under a broad straw sombrero. At stage left is the* PACHUCO,[2] *filero[3] in hand.*

[*Honest* SANCHO *is moving among his models, dusting them off and preparing for another day of business.*]

SANCHO.   Bueno, bueno, mis monos, vamos a ver a quien vendemos ahora, ¿no?[4] [*To audience.*] ¡Quihubo! I'm Honest Sancho and this is my shop. Antes fui contratista pero ahora logré tener mi negocito.[5] All I need now is a customer. [*A bell rings offstage.*] Ay, a customer!

SECRETARY.   [*Entering*] Good morning, I'm Miss Jiménez from—

SANCHO.   ¡Ah, una chicana! Welcome, welcome Señorita Jiménez.

SECRETARY.   [*Anglo pronunciation*] JIM-enez.

SANCHO.   ¿Qué?

SECRETARY.   My name is Miss JIM-enez. Don't you speak English? What's wrong with you?

SANCHO.   Oh, nothing, Señorita JIM-enez. I'm here to help you.

SECRETARY.   That's better. As I was starting to say, I'm a secretary from Governor Reagan's office, and we're looking for a Mexican type for the administration.

SANCHO.   Well, you come to the right place, lady. This is Honest Sancho's Used Mexican lot, and we got all types here. Any particular type you want?

SECRETARY.   Yes, we were looking for somebody suave—

SANCHO.   Suave.

SECRETARY.   Debonair.

SANCHO.   De buen aire.

SECRETARY.   Dark.

SANCHO.   Prieto.

SECRETARY.   But of course not too dark.

SANCHO.   No muy prieto.

SECRETARY.   Perhaps, beige.

SANCHO.   Beige, just the tone. Así como cafecito con leche,[6] ¿no?

---

* **Los Vendidos** the sellouts.   [1]**carrilleras** cartridge belts.   [2]**Pachuco** an urban tough guy.   [3]**filero** blade.   [4]**Bueno . . . no?** Well, well darlings, let's see who we can sell now, O.K.?   [5]**Antes . . . negocito** I used to be a contractor, but now I've succeeded in having my little business.   [6]**Así . . . leche** like coffee with milk.

SECRETARY.   One more thing. He must be hard-working.

SANCHO.   That could only be one model. Step right over here to the center of the shop, lady. [*They cross to the* FARM WORKER.] This is our standard farm worker model. As you can see, in the words of our beloved Senator George Murphy, he is "built close to the ground." Also take special notice of his four-ply Goodyear huaraches, made from the rain tire. This wide-brimmed sombrero is an extra added feature—keeps off the sun, rain, and dust.

SECRETARY.   Yes, it does look durable.

SANCHO.   And our farm worker model is friendly. Muy amable.[7] Watch. [*Snaps his fingers.*]

FARM WORKER   [*Lifts up head*]. Buenos días, señorita. [*His head drops.*]

SECRETARY.   My, he's friendly.

SANCHO.   Didn't I tell you? Loves his patrones! But his most attractive feature is that he's hard working. Let me show you. [*Snaps fingers,* FARM WORKER *stands.*]

FARM WORKER.   ¡El jale![8] [*He begins to work.*]

SANCHO.   As you can see, he is cutting grapes.

SECRETARY.   Oh, I wouldn't know.

SANCHO.   He also picks cotton. [*Snap.* FARM WORKER *begins to pick cotton.*]

SECRETARY.   Versatile isn't he?

SANCHO.   He also picks melons. [*Snap.* FARM WORKER *picks melons.*] That's his slow speed for late in the season. Here's his fast speed. [*Snap.* FARM WORKER *picks faster.*]

SECRETARY.   ¡Chihuahua! . . . I mean, goodness, he sure is a hard worker.

SANCHO   [*Pulls the* FARM WORKER *to his feet*]. And that isn't the half of it. Do you see these little holes on his arms that appear to be pores? During those hot sluggish days in the field, when the vines or the branches get so entangled, it's almost impossible to move; these holes emit a certain grease that allow our model to slip and slide right through the crop with no trouble at all.

SECRETARY.   Wonderful. But is he economical?

SANCHO.   Economical? Señorita, you are looking at the Volkswagen of Mexicans. Pennies a day is all it takes. One plate of beans and tortillas will keep him going all day. That, and chile. Plenty of chile. Chile jalapeños, chile verde, chile colorado. But, of course, if you do give him chile [*Snap.* FARM WORKER *turns left face. Snap.* FARM WORKER *bends over.*] then you have to change his oil filter once a week.

SECRETARY.   What about storage?

SANCHO.   No problem. You know these new farm labor camps our Honorable Governor Reagan has built out by Parlier or Raisin City? They were designed with our model in mind. Five, six, seven, even ten in one of those shacks will give you no trouble at all. You can also put him in old barns, old cars, river banks. You can even leave him out in the field overnight with no worry!

SECRETARY.   Remarkable.

SANCHO.   And here's an added feature: Every year at the end of the season, this model goes back to Mexico and doesn't return, automatically, until next Spring.

SECRETARY.   How about that. But tell me: does he speak English?

SANCHO.   Another outstanding feature is that last year this model was programmed to go out on STRIKE! [*Snap.*]

FARM WORKER.   ¡HUELGA! ¡HUELGA! Hermanos, sálganse de esos files.[9] [*Snap. He stops.*]

---

[7]**Muy amable** very friendly.   [8]**El jale** the job.   [9]**¡Huelga . . . files** Strike! Strike! Brothers, leave those rows.

SECRETARY.   No! Oh no, we can't strike in the State Capitol.

SANCHO.   Well, he also scabs. [*Snap.*]

FARM WORKER.   Me vendo barato, ¿y qué?[10] [*Snap.*]

SECRETARY.   That's much better, but you didn't answer my question. Does he speak English?

SANCHO.   Bueno . . . no, pero[11] he has other—

SECRETARY.   No.

SANCHO.   Other features.

SECRETARY.   NO! He just won't do!

SANCHO.   Okay, okay pues. We have other models.

SECRETARY.   I hope so. What we need is something a little more sophisticated.

SANCHO.   Sophisti—¿qué?

SECRETARY.   An urban model.

SANCHO.   Ah, from the city! Step right back. Over here in this corner of the shop is exactly what you're looking for. Introducing our new 1969 JOHNNY PACHUCO model! This is our fast-back model. Streamlined. Built for speed, low-riding, city life. Take a look at some of these features. Mag shoes, dual exhausts, green chartreuse paint-job, dark-tint windshield, a little poof on top. Let me just turn him on. [*Snap.* JOHNNY *walks to stage center with a pachuco bounce.*]

SECRETARY.   What was that?

SANCHO.   That, señorita, was the Chicano shuffle.

SECRETARY.   Okay, what does he do?

SANCHO.   Anything and everything necessary for city life. For instance, survival: He knife fights. [*Snap.* JOHNNY *pulls out switchblade and swings at* SECRETARY.]

[SECRETARY *screams.*]

SANCHO.   He dances. [*Snap.*]

JOHNNY   [*Singing*]. "Angel Baby, my Angel Baby . . . " [*Snap.*]

SANCHO.   And here's a feature no city model can be without. He gets arrested, but not without resisting, of course. [*Snap.*]

JOHNNY.   ¡En la madre, la placa![12] I didn't do it! I didn't do it! [JOHNNY *turns and stands up against an imaginary wall, legs spread out, arms behind his back.*]

SECRETARY.   Oh no, we can't have arrests! We must maintain law and order.

SANCHO.   But he's bilingual!

SECRETARY.   Bilingual?

SANCHO.   Simón que yes.[13] He speaks English! Johnny, give us some English. [*Snap.*]

JOHNNY.   [*Comes downstage*]. Fuck-you!

SECRETARY   [*Gasps*]. Oh! I've never been so insulted in my whole life!

SANCHO.   Well, he learned it in your school.

SECRETARY.   I don't care where he learned it.

SANCHO.   But he's economical!

SECRETARY.   Economical?

SANCHO.   Nickels and dimes. You can keep Johnny running on hamburgers, Taco Bell tacos, Lucky Lager beer, Thunderbird wine, yesca—

SECRETARY.   Yesca?

SANCHO.   Mota.

SECRETARY.   Mota?

---

[10]**Me . . . qué?** I come cheap. So what?   [11]**Bueno . . . no, pero** Well, no, but.   [12]**¡En . . . la placa!** Wow, the cops!   [13]**Simón que yes** Yea, sure.

SANCHO.   Leños[14] . . . Marijuana. [*Snap;* JOHNNY *inhales on an imaginary joint.*]

SECRETARY.   That's against the law!

JOHNNY   [*Big smile, holding his breath*]. Yeah.

SANCHO.   He also sniffs glue. [*Snap.* JOHNNY *inhales glue, big smile.*]

JOHNNY.   That's too much man, ése.[15]

SECRETARY.   No, Mr. Sancho, I don't think this—

SANCHO.   Wait a minute, he has other qualities I know you'll love. For example, an inferiority complex. [*Snap.*]

JOHNNY.   [*To* SANCHO]. You think you're better than me, huh ése? [*Swings switch-blade.*]

SANCHO.   He can also be beaten and he bruises, cut him and he bleeds; kick him and he—[*He beats, bruises and kicks* PACHUCO.] would you like to try it?

SECRETARY.   Oh, I couldn't.

SANCHO.   Be my guest. He's a great scapegoat.

SECRETARY.   No, really.

SANCHO.   Please.

SECRETARY.   Well, all right. Just once. [*She kicks* PACHUCO.] Oh, he's so soft.

SANCHO.   Wasn't that good? Try again.

SECRETARY   [*Kicks* PACHUCO]. Oh, he's so wonderful! [*She kicks him again.*]

SANCHO.   Okay, that's enough, lady. You ruin the merchandise. Yes, our Johnny Pachuco model can give you many hours of pleasure. Why, the L.A.P.D. just bought twenty of these to train their rookie cops on. And talk about mainte-nance. Señorita, you are looking at an entirely self-supporting machine. You're never going to find our Johnny Pachuco model on the relief rolls. No, sir, this model knows how to liberate.

SECRETARY.   Liberate?

SANCHO.   He steals. [*Snap.* JOHNNY *rushes the* SECRETARY *and steals her purse.*]

JOHNNY.   ¡Dame esa bolsa, vieja![16] [*He grabs the purse and runs. Snap by* SANCHO. *He stops.*]

   [SECRETARY *runs after* JOHNNY *and grabs purse away from him, kicking him as she goes.*]

SECRETARY.   No, no, no! We can't have any *more* thieves in the State Administration. Put him back.

SANCHO.   Okay, we still got other models. Come on, Johnny, we'll sell you to some old lady. [SANCHO *takes* JOHNNY *back to his place.*)

SECRETARY.   Mr. Sancho, I don't think you quite understand what we need. What we need is something that will attract the women voters. Something more tra-ditional, more romantic.

SANCHO.   Ah, a lover. [*He smiles meaningfully.*] Step right over here, señorita. Introducing our standard Revolucionario and/or Early California Bandit type. As you can see he is well-built, sturdy, durable. This is the International Harvester of Mexicans.

SECRETARY.   What does he do?

SANCHO.   You name it, he does it. He rides horses, stays in the mountains, crosses deserts, plains, rivers, leads revolutions, follows revolutions, kills, can be killed, serves as a martyr, hero, movie star—did I say movie star? Did you ever see *Viva Zapata? Viva Villa? Villa Rides? Pancho Villa Returns? Pancho Villa Goes Back? Pancho Villa Meets Abbott and Costello*—

SECRETARY.   I've never seen any of those.

---

[14]**Leños** joints (marijuana).   [15]**ése** fellow.   [16]**¡Dame . . . vieja!** Give me that bag, old lady!

SANCHO.   Well, he was in all of them. Listen to this. [*Snap.*]

REVOLUCIONARIO   [*Scream*]. ¡VIVA VILLAAAAA!

SECRETARY.   That's awfully loud.

SANCHO.   He has a volume control. [*He adjusts volume. Snap.*]

REVOLUCIONARIO   [*Mousey voice*]. ¡Viva Villa!

SECRETARY.   That's better.

SANCHO.   And even if you didn't see him in the movies, perhaps you saw him on TV. He makes commercials. [*Snap.*]

REVOLUCIONARIO.   Is there a Frito Bandito in your house?

SECRETARY.   Oh yes, I've seen that one!

SANCHO.   Another feature about this one is that he is economical. He runs on raw horsemeat and tequila.

SECRETARY.   Isn't that rather savage?

SANCHO.   Al contrario,[17] it makes him a lover. [*Snap.*]

REVOLUCIONARIO   [*To* SECRETARY]. ¡Ay, mamasota, cochota, ven pa'ca![18] [*He grabs* SECRETARY *and folds her back—Latin-Lover style.*]

SANCHO   [*Snap.* REVOLUCIONARIO *goes back upright.*]. Now wasn't that nice?

SECRETARY.   Well, it was rather nice.

SANCHO.   And finally, there is one outstanding feature about this model I KNOW the ladies are going to love: He's a GENUINE antique! He was made in Mexico in 1910!

SECRETARY.   Made in Mexico?

SANCHO.   That's right. Once in Tijuana, twice in Guadalajara, three times in Cuernavaca.

SECRETARY.   Mr. Sancho, I thought he was an American product.

SANCHO.   No, but—

SECRETARY.   No, I'm sorry. We can't buy anything but American-made products. He just won't do.

SANCHO.   But he's an antique!

SECRETARY.   I don't care. You still don't understand what we need. It's true we need Mexican models such as these, but it's more important that he be *American*.

SANCHO.   American?

SECRETARY.   That's right, and judging from what you've shown me, I don't think you have what we want. Well, my lunch hour's almost over: I better—

SANCHO.   Wait a minute! Mexican but American?

SECRETARY.   That's correct.

SANCHO.   Mexican but . . . [*A sudden flash.*] AMERICAN! Yeah, I think we've got exactly what you want. He just came in today! Give me a minute. [*He exits. Talks from backstage.*] Here he is in the shop. Let me just get some papers off. There. Introducing our new 1970 Mexican-American! Ta-ra-ra-ra-ra-ra-RA-RAAA!

   [SANCHO *brings out the* MEXICAN-AMERICAN *model, a clean-shaven middle-class type in a business suit, with glasses.*]

SECRETARY   [*Impressed*]. Where have you been hiding this one?

SANCHO.   He just came in this morning. Ain't he a beauty? Feast your eyes on him! Sturdy US STEEL frame, streamlined, modern. As a matter of fact, he is built exactly like our Anglo models except that he comes in a variety of darker shades: naugahyde, leather, or leatherette.

SECRETARY.   Naugahyde.

---

[17]**Al contrario** on the contrary.   [18]**¡Ay . . . pa'ca!** —, get over here!

SANCHO.   Well, we'll just write that down. Yes, señorita, this model represents the apex of American engineering! He is bilingual, college educated, ambitious! Say the word "acculturate" and he accelerates. He is intelligent, well-mannered, clean—did I say clean? [*Snap.* MEXICAN-AMERICAN *raises his arm.*] Smell.

SECRETARY   [*Smells*]. Old Sobaco, my favorite.

SANCHO   [*Snap.* MEXICAN-AMERICAN *turns toward* SANCHO]. Eric! [*To* SECRETARY.] We call him Eric García. [*To* ERIC.] I want you to meet Miss JIM-enez, Eric.

MEXICAN-AMERICAN.   Miss JIM-enez, I am delighted to make your acquaintance. [*He kisses her hand.*]

SECRETARY.   Oh, my, how charming!

SANCHO.   Did you feel the suction? He has seven especially engineered suction cups right behind his lips. He's a charmer all right!

SECRETARY.   How about boards? Does he function on boards?

SANCHO.   You name them, he is on them. Parole boards, draft boards, school boards, taco quality control boards, surf boards, two-by-fours.

SECRETARY.   Does he function in politics?

SANCHO.   Señorita, you are looking at a political MACHINE. Have you ever heard of the OEO, EOC, COD, WAR ON POVERTY? That's our model! Not only that, he makes political speeches.

SECRETARY.   May I hear one?

SANCHO.   With pleasure. [*Snap.*] Eric, give us a speech.

MEXICAN-AMERICAN.   Mr. Congressman, Mr. Chairman, members of the board, honored guests, ladies and gentlemen. [SANCHO *and* SECRETARY *applaud.*] Please, please. I come before you as a Mexican-American to tell you about the problems of the Mexican. The problems of the Mexican stem from one thing and one thing alone: He's stupid. He's uneducated. He needs to stay in school. He needs to be ambitious, forward-looking, harder-working. He needs to think American, American, American, AMERICAN, AMERICAN, AMERICAN. GOD BLESS AMERICA! GOD BLESS AMERICA! GOD BLESS AMERICA!! [*He goes out of control.*]

[SANCHO *snaps frantically and the* MEXICAN-AMERICAN *finally slumps forward, bending at the waist.*]

SECRETARY.   Oh my, he's patriotic too!

SANCHO.   Sí, señorita, he loves his country. Let me just make a little adjustment here. [*Stands* MEXICAN-AMERICAN *up.*]

SECRETARY.   What about upkeep? Is he economical?

SANCHO.   Well, no, I won't lie to you. The Mexican-American costs a little bit more, but you get what you pay for. He's worth every extra cent. You can keep him running on dry Martinis, Langendorf bread.

SECRETARY.   Apple pie?

SANCHO.   Only Mom's. Of course, he's also programmed to eat Mexican food on ceremonial functions, but I must warn you: an overdose of beans will plug up his exhaust.

SECRETARY.   Fine! There's just one more question: HOW MUCH DO YOU WANT FOR HIM?

SANCHO.   Well, I tell you what I'm gonna do. Today and today only, because you've been so sweet, I'm gonna let you steal this model from me! I'm gonna let you drive him off the lot for the simple price of—let's see taxes and license included—$15,000.

SECRETARY.   Fifteen thousand DOLLARS? For a MEXICAN!

SANCHO.   Mexican? What are you talking, lady? This is a Mexican-AMERICAN! We had to melt down two pachucos, a farm worker and three gabachos[19] to make this model! You want quality, but you gotta pay for it! This is no cheap run-about. He's got class!

SECRETARY.   Okay, I'll take him.

SANCHO.   You will?

SECRETARY.   Here's your money.

SANCHO.   You mind if I count it?

SECRETARY.   Go right ahead.

SANCHO.   Well, you'll get your pink slip in the mail. Oh, do you want me to wrap him up for you? We have a box in the back.

SECRETARY.   No, thank you. The Governor is having a luncheon this afternoon, and we need a brown face in the crowd. How do I drive him?

SANCHO.   Just snap your fingers. He'll do anything you want.

[SECRETARY *snaps.* MEXICAN-AMERICAN *steps forward.*]

MEXICAN-AMERICAN.   RAZA QUERIDA, ¡VAMOS LEVANTANDO ARMAS PARA LIBER-ARNOS DE ESTOS DESGRACIADOS GABACHOS QUE NOS EXPLOTAN! VA-MOS.[20]

SECRETARY.   What did he say?

SANCHO.   Something about lifting arms, killing white people, etc.

SECRETARY.   But he's not supposed to say that!

SANCHO.   Look, lady, don't blame me for bugs from the factory. He's your Mexican-American; you bought him, now drive him off the lot!

SECRETARY.   But he's broken!

SANCHO.   Try snapping another finger.

[SECRETARY *snaps.* MEXICAN-AMERICAN *comes to life again.*]

MEXICAN-AMERICAN.   ¡ESTA GRAN HUMANIDAD HA DICHO BASTA! Y SE HA PUESTO EN MARCHA! ¡BASTA! ¡BASTA! ¡VIVA LA RAZA! ¡VIVA LA CAUSA! ¡VIVA LA HUELGA! ¡VIVAN LOS BROWN BERETS! ¡VIVAN LOS ESTUDI-ANTES![21] ¡CHICANO POWER!

[*The* MEXICAN-AMERICAN *turns toward the* SECRETARY, *who gasps und backs up. He keeps turning toward the* PACHUCO, FARM WORKER, *and* REVOLUCIONARIO *snapping his fingers and turning each of them on, one by one.*]

PACHUCO   [*Snap. To* SECRETARY]. I'm going to get you, baby! ¡Viva La Raza!

FARM WORKER   [*Snap. To* SECRETARY]. ¡Viva la huelga! ¡Viva la Huelga! ¡VIVA LA HUELGA!

REVOLUCIONARIO   [*Snap. To* SECRETARY]. ¡Viva la revolución! ¡VIVA LA REVOLUCIÓN!

[*The three models join together and advance toward the* SECRETARY *who backs up and runs out of the shop screaming.* SANCHO *is at the other end of the shop holding his money in his hand. All freeze. After a few seconds of silence, the* PACHUCO *moves and stretches, shaking his arms and loosening up. The* FARM WORKER *and* REVOLUCIONARIO *do the same.* SANCHO *stays where he is, frozen to his spot.*]

[19]**gabachos** whites.   [20]**Raza . . . Vamos** Beloved Raza [persons of Mexican descent], let's take up arms to liberate ourselves from those damned whites who exploit us. Let's get going.
[21]**¡Esta . . . Estudiantes!** This great mass of humanity has said enough! And it has begun to march. Enough! Enough! Long live La Raza! Long live the Cause! Long live the strike! Long live the Brown Berets! Long live the students!

JOHNNY.   Man, that was a long one, ése.[22] [*Others agree with him.*]

FARM WORKER.   How did we do?

JOHNNY.   Perty good, look at all that lana,[23] man! [*He goes over to* SANCHO *and removes the money from his hand.* SANCHO *stays where he is.*]

REVOLUCIONARIO.   En la madre, look at all the money.

JOHNNY.   We keep this up, we're going to be rich.

FARM WORKER.   They think we're machines.

REVOLUCIONARIO.   Burros.

JOHNNY.   Puppets.

MEXICAN-AMERICAN.   The only thing I don't like is—how come I always got to play the godamn Mexican-American?

JOHNNY.   That's what you get for finishing high school.

FARM WORKER.   How about our wages, ése?

JOHNNY.   Here it comes right now. $3,000 for you, $3,000 for you, $3,000 for you, and $3,000 for me. The rest we put back into the business.

MEXICAN-AMERICAN.   Too much, man. Heh, where you vatos[24] going tonight?

FARM WORKER.   I'm going over to Concha's. There's a party.

JOHNNY.   Wait a minute, vatos. What about our salesman? I think he needs an oil job.

REVOLUCIONARIO.   Leave him to me.

[*The* PACHUCO, FARM WORKER, *and* MEXICAN-AMERICAN *exit, talking loudly about their plans for the night. The* REVOLUCIONARIO *goes over to* SANCHO, *removes his derby hat and cigar, lifts him up and throws him over his shoulder.* SANCHO *hangs loose, lifeless.*]

REVOLUCIONARIO   [*To audience*]. He's the best model we got! ¡Ajua![25]

[*Exit.*]

THE END

[1967]

[22]**ése** man.   [23]**lana** money.   [24]**vatos** guys.   [25]**¡Ajua!** Wow!

Topics for Critical Thinking and Writing

1. If you are an Anglo (shorthand for a Caucasian with traditional northern European values), do you find the play deeply offensive? Why, or why not? If you are a Mexican American, do you find the play entertaining—or do you find parts of it offensive? What might Anglos enjoy in the play, and what might Mexican Americans find offensive?

2. What stereotypes of Mexican Americans are presented here? At the end of the play, what image of the Mexican American is presented? How does it compare with the stereotypes?

3. If you are a member of some other minority group, in a few sentences indicate how *Los Vendidos* might be adapted into a play about that group.

4. Putting aside the politics of the play (and your own politics), what do you think are the strengths of *Los Vendidos?* What do you think are the weaknesses?

5. The play was written in 1967. Putting aside a few specific references, for instance to Governor Reagan, do you find it dated? If not, why not?

6. In 1971 when *Los Vendidos* was produced by El Teatro de la Esperanza, the group altered the ending by having the men decide to use the money to build a community center. Evaluate this ending.

7. When the play was videotaped by KNBC in Los Angeles for broadcast in 1973, Valdez changed the ending. In the revised version we discover that a scientist (played by Valdez) masterminds the operation, placing Mexican American models wherever there are persons of Mexican descent. These models soon will become Chicanos (as opposed to persons with Anglo values) and will aid rather than work against their fellows. Evaluate this ending.

8. In his short essay "The Actos," Valdez says, "Actos: Inspire the audience to social action. Illuminate specific points about social problems. Satirize the opposition. Show or hint at a solution. Express what people are feeling." How many of these do you think *Los Vendidos* does?

9. Many people assume that politics gets in the way of serious art. That is, they assume that artists ought to be concerned with issues that transcend politics. Does this point make any sense to you? Why, or why not?

Case Study: Writing about American Indian Identity

First, a word about nomenclature. When Columbus encountered the Caribs in 1492, he thought he had reached India and therefore he called them *Indios* (Indians). Later, efforts to distinguish the peoples of the Western Hemisphere produced the terms *American Indian, Amerindian,* and *Amerind.* More recently, *Native American* has been used, but of course the people who met the European newcomers were themselves descended from persons who had immigrated from eastern Asia in ancient times, and in any case *American* is a word derived from the name of an Italian. On the other hand, anyone born in America, regardless of ethnicity, is a native American. Further, it appears that most Native Americans (in the new, restricted sense) continue to speak of themselves as Indians (e.g., members of the Navaho Indian Nation), thereby making the use of *Indian* not only acceptable but preferable. Nevertheless, when possible it is advisable to use the name of the specific group, such as Arapaho, Iroquois, or Navaho.

This case study includes three kinds of material:

- writings by Indians,
- writings by whites, and
- pictures.

Although in this abbreviated table of contents we do not list the pictures, they are not only handsome but they also provide opportunities for writing.

The verbal material is as follows:

1. Two anonymous Arapaho Ghost Dance songs
2. Lydia Howard Huntley Sigourney's poem "The Indians' Welcome to the Pilgrim Fathers"
3. Robert Frost's poem "The Vanishing Red"
4. Wendy Rose's poem, "Three Thousand Dollar Death Song"
5. Nila northSun's poem, "Moving Camp Too Far"

ANONYMOUS ARAPAHO

*The Arapaho are North American Plains Indians of Algonquian (or Algonkian)
linguistic stock. Their origins are uncertain, but according to tribal traditions they
migrated from northern Minnesota. During their westward migration they divided
into northern and southern groups, and they now live chiefly in Wyoming and
Oklahoma.*

*The two songs that we reprint are both from the Ghost Dance ritual, part of a
widespread messianic religion that originated in the late nineteenth century, and is
especially associated with a Paiute, Wovoka (c. 1858–1932, known also as Jack
Wilson), the son of a medicine man. Wovoka, influenced by his father as well as by a
Christian family he worked for and by the revivalistic Shaker movement, in 1889
said he had a vision that the earth would soon die and be reborn: All whites would
disappear, and all Indians (living and dead) would be reunited. (The "ghosts" of the
dance are dead Indians.) The songs were sung throughout the night, by singers in
trances. Although Wovoka was a pacifist, the movement became, or seemed to become, warlike, and its adherents wore magic shirts they deemed to be bullet proof. On
December 29, 1890, at Wounded Knee, South Dakota, a group of Sioux were ordered
to disarm; a medicine man threw dust into the air; an Indian with a gun wounded
an officer; U.S. troops opened fire, and almost two hundred Sioux men, women, and
children were killed. The apocalyptic hopes of the Ghost Dance were over.*

*The songs constitute a dialogue between the Sun ("Father") and the Native
Americans ("children"). It is essential to understand that these compositions, like
all Native American poetry of the nineteenth century, are oral, not written, and
like most oral literature they use repetition and parallelism, as well as contrast. We
give two songs in the version of James Mooney, who published his translations in
the last decade of the nineteenth century. Inevitably, translators (from any language into any other) consciously or unconsciously impose some of their own aesthetic criteria on the material that they are translating, and in particular translators of Native American material have often somewhat reduced the amount of
repetition. Further, many contemporary translators believe that oral material must
be presented in such a way as to indicate how it was performed (i.e., with indications of pauses, changes of stress, and so forth). Nevertheless, although Mooney produced his translations about a hundred years ago, and although modern scholars
have tools he never dreamed of, Mooney's translations are still highly regarded.*

My Children, When at First I Liked the Whites

My children, when at first I liked the whites,
My children, when at first I liked the whites,
I gave them fruits,
I gave them fruits.   4

Father, Have Pity on Me

Father, have pity on me,
Father, have pity on me;
I am crying for thirst,
I am crying for thirst;
All is gone—I have nothing to eat.
All is gone—I have nothing to eat.   5

[c. 1889]

James Mooney. *Ghost Dance,* 1893. (National Anthropological Archive, Smithsonian Institution, Washington, DC [Neg# 55, 296].)

LYDIA HOWARD HUNTLEY SIGOURNEY

Lydia Sigourney (1791–1865), born in Norwich, Connecticut, of humble family, was taken up by her father's employer as a child prodigy and was tutored in Latin and Hebrew. She wrote poetry chiefly on public issues, such as historical events and slavery, rather than personal lyric poetry. A fair number of her poems concern the displacement of Native Americans; she did not condemn the settling of the continent, but she did criticize the failure of whites to treat the Native Americans according to Christian ethics.

The Indian's Welcome to the Pilgrim Fathers

"On Friday, March 16th, 1622, while the colonists were busied in their usual labors, they were much surprised to see a savage walk boldly towards them, and salute them with, 'much welcome, English, much welcome, Englishmen.'"

> Above them spread a stranger sky
>   Around, the sterile plain,
> The rock-bound coast rose frowning nigh,
>   Beyond,—the wrathful main:
> Chill remnants of the wintry snow   5
>   Still chok'd the encumber'd soil,
> Yet forth these Pilgrim Fathers go,
>   To mark their future toil.
>
> 'Mid yonder vale their corn must rise
>   In Summer's ripening pride,   10
> And there the church-spire woo the skies
>   Its sister-school beside.

Perchance 'mid England's velvet green
   Some tender thought repos'd,—
Though nought upon their stoic mien   15
   Such soft regret disclos'd.

When sudden from the forest wide
   A red-brow'd chieftain came,
With towering form, and haughty stride,
   And eye like kindling flame: 20
No wrath he breath'd, no conflict sought,
   To no dark ambush drew,
But simply *to the Old World brought,*
   The welcome of the New.

That *welcome* was a blast and ban   25
   Upon thy race unborn.
Was there no seer, thou fated Man!
   Thy lavish zeal to warn?
Thou in thy fearless faith didst hail
   A weak, invading band,   30
But who shall heed thy children's wail,
   Swept from their native land?

Thou gav'st the riches of thy streams,
   The lordship o'er thy waves,
The region of thine infant dreams,   35
   And of thy fathers' graves,
But who to yon proud mansions pil'd
   With wealth of earth and sea,
Poor outcast from thy forest wild,
   Say, who shall welcome thee?   40

                                          [1835]

ROBERT FROST

For a biographical note on Robert Frost (1875–1963), see page 587.

The Vanishing Red

He is said to have been the last Red Man
In Acton.° And the Miller is said to have laughed—
If you like to call such a sound a laugh.
But he gave no one else a laugher's license.
For he turned suddenly grave as if to say,   5
'Whose business—if I take it on myself,
Whose business—but why talk round the barn?—
When it's just that I hold with getting a thing done with.'
You can't get back and see it as he saw it.

---

2 Acton a town in Massachusetts, not far from where Frost spent part of his childhood.

Edward S. Curtis. *The Vanishing Race,* c. 1904. (Platinum print. Christopher Cardozo, Inc.)

It's too long a story to go into now.   10
You'd have to have been there and lived it.
Then you wouldn't have looked on it as just a matter
Of who began it between the two races.

Some guttural exclamation of surprise
The Red Man gave in poking about the mill   15
Over the great big thumping shuffling mill-stone
Disgusted the Miller physically as coming
From one who had no right to be heard from.
'Come, John,' he said, 'you want to see the wheel pit?'°

He took him down below a cramping rafter,   20
And showed him, through a manhole in the floor,
The water in desperate straits like frantic fish,
Salmon and sturgeon, lashing with their tails.
Then he shut down the trap door with a ring in it

That jangled even above the general noise,   25
And came up stairs alone—and gave that laugh,
And said something to a man with a meal-sack
That the man with the meal-sack didn't catch—then.
Oh, yes, he showed John the wheel pit all right.

[1916]

19 **wheel pit** the pit containing the wheel that, agitated by the water, drives the mill.

WENDY ROSE

Wendy Rose, of Hopi and Miwok ancestry, was born in Oakland, California, in 1948. Educated as an anthropologist at the University of California, Berkeley, she has taught at Berkeley and at California State University, and she has edited the American Indian Quarterly. *Rose is the author of several books of poetry. In the course of an interview about the status of American Indian poets, she said, "The usual practice in bookstores upon receiving books of poems by American Indians is to classify them as 'Native Americana' rather than as poetry; the poets are seen as literate fossils more than as living, working artists." In the following poem, the dead are imagined as coming alive.*

Three Thousand Dollar Death Song

Nineteen American Indian Skeletons from Nevada . . . valued at $3000 . . .
—Museum invoice, 1975

Is it in cold hard cash? the kind
that dusts the insides of men's pockets
lying silver-polished surface along the cloth.
Or in bills? papering the wallets of they
who thread the night with dark words. Or   5
checks? paper promises weighing the same
as words spoken once on the other side
of the grown grass and dammed rivers
of history. However it goes, it goes
Through my body it goes assessing each nerve, running its edges   10
along my arteries, planning ahead
for whose hands will rip me
into pieces of dusty red paper,
whose hands will smooth or smatter me
into traces of rubble. Invoiced now,   15
it's official how our bones are valued
that stretch out pointing to sunrise
or are flexed into one last foetal bend,
that are removed and tossed about,
catalogued, numbered with black ink   20
on newly-white foreheads.
As we were formed to the white soldier's voice,
so we explode under white students' hands.
Death is a long trail of days
in our fleshless prison.   25

From this distant point we watch our bones
auctioned with our careful beadwork,
our quilled medicine bundles, even the bridles

of our shot-down horses. You: who have
priced us, you who have removed us: at what cost?   30
What price the pits where our bones share
a single bit of memory, how one century
turns our dead into specimens, our history
into dust, our survivors into clowns.
Our memory might be catching, you know;   35
picture the mortars, the arrowheads, the labrets°
shaking off their labels like bears
suddenly awake to find the seasons have ended
while they slept. Watch them touch each other,
measure reality, march out the museum door!   40
Watch as they lift their faces
and smell about for us; watch our bones rise
to meet them and mount the horses once again!
The cost, then, will be paid
for our sweetgrass-smelling having-been   45
in clam shell beads and steatite,°
dentalia° and woodpecker scalp, turquoise
and copper, blood and oil, coal
and uranium, children, a universe
of stolen things.   50

[1980]

36 **labrets** ornaments worn in pierced lips.   46 **steatite** grayish green or brown soapstone.
47 **dentalia** tooth shells (shells of marine mollusks).

Topics for Critical Thinking and Writing

1. Why would a museum buy Indian skeletons? Would a museum buy the skeletons of whites?
2. What is the real cost of the skeletons?

Nila northSun

Nila northSun was born in 1951 in Schurz, Nevada, of Shoshone-Chippewa stock. She studied at the California State University campuses at Hayward and Humboldt and the University of Montana at Missoula, beginning as a psychology major but switching to art history, specializing in Native American art. She is the author of three books of poetry and is director of an emergency youth shelter in Fallon, Nevada.

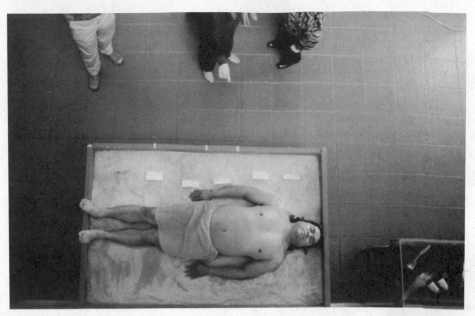

James Luna. *The Artifact Piece,* 1987–1990. Luna (b. 1950), a Luiseño performance artist who lives on the La Jolla Reservation Valley Center, California, exhibited himself in a museum, lying on a bed of sand in an exhibition case (1987–1990). (San Diego Museum of Man [P025909])

Moving Camp Too Far

i can't speak of
   many moons
   moving camp on travois°
i can't tell of
   the last great battle   5
   counting coup° or
   taking scalp
i don't know what it
   was to hunt buffalo
   or do the ghost dance   10
but
i can see an eagle
   almost extinct
   on slurpee plastic cups
i can travel to powwows   15
   in campers & winnebagos
i can eat buffalo meat
   at the tourist burger stand

1 travois a frame slung between trailing poles that are pulled by a horse. Plains Indians used the device to transport their goods.   **6 counting coup** recounting one's exploits in battle.

i can dance to indian music
   rock-n-roll hey-a-hey-o
i can
   & unfortunately
   i do

                                           [1977]

Topic for Critical Thinking and Writing

What is the speaker's attitude toward the world she has lost? What is her attitude toward herself?

25

Law and Disorder

Short Views

The trouble for the thief is not how to steal the bugle, but where to blow it.
African proverb

Whether there was ever a significant increase in crime and when it might have occurred is puzzling, since the phrase, "the land is full of bloody crimes and the city full of violence," did not appear in a recent Chicago newspaper but in a report on a crime wave in the promised land about 600 B.C. as recorded in Ezekiel VII:23. The logical possibility of an ever-increasing crime wave becomes more doubtful when we consider the biblical origin of humankind: Adam, Eve and Cain committed the worst offenses possible and after Abel was killed, all survivors—or 75 percent of the first four human beings—had criminal records. In spite of all righteous claims to the opposite, this crime wave seems to have subsided, never to reach its biblical heights again. It is simpler and more correct to state that crime has always existed but statistics have not.
Kurt Weis and Michael F. Milakovich

Whoever desires to found a state and give it laws, must start with assuming that all men are bad and ever ready to display their vicious nature, whenever they may find occasion for it.
Niccolò Machiavelli

It is questionable whether, when we break a murderer on the wheel, we aren't lapsing into precisely the mistake of the child who hits the chair he bumps into.
G. C. Lichtenberg

If a man were permitted to make all the ballads, he need not care who should make the laws of a nation.
Andrew Fletcher

Nature has given women so much power that the law has very wisely given them very little.
Samuel Johnson

1208

I asked him whether, as a moralist, he did not think that the practice of the law, in some degree, hurt the nice feeling of honesty. JOHNSON. "Why no, Sir, if you act properly. You are not to deceive your clients with false representations of your opinion: you are not to tell lies to a judge." BOSWELL. "But what do you think of supporting a cause which you know to be bad?" JOHNSON. "Sir, you do not know it to be good or bad till the Judge determines it. I have said that you are to state facts fairly; so that your thinking, or what you call knowing, a cause to be bad, must be from reasoning, must be from your supposing your arguments to be weak and inconclusive. But, Sir, that is not enough. An argument which does not convince yourself, may convince the Judge to whom you urge it; and if it does convince him, why, then, Sir, you are wrong, and he is right. It is his business to judge; and you are not to be confident in your own opinion that a cause is bad, but to say all you can for your client, and then hear the Judge's opinion." BOSWELL. "But, Sir, does not affecting a warmth when you have no warmth, and appearing to be clearly of one opinion when you are in reality of another opinion, does not such dissimulation impair one's honesty? Is there not some danger that a lawyer may put on the same mask in common life, in the intercourse with his friends?" JOHNSON. "Why no, Sir. Everybody knows you are paid for affecting warmth for your client; and it is, therefore, properly no dissimulation: the moment you come from the bar you resume your usual behaviour. Sir, a man will no more carry the artifice of the bar into the common intercourse of society, than a man who is paid for tumbling upon his hands will continue to tumble upon his hands when he should walk on his feet."

James Boswell

One law for the ox and the ass is oppression.

William Blake

The law, in its majestic equality, forbids the rich as well as the poor to sleep under bridges, to beg in the streets, and to steal bread.

Anatole France

Decency, security and liberty alike demand that government officials shall be subjected to the same rules of conduct that are commands to the citizen. In a government of laws, existence of the government will be imperilled if it fails to observe the law scrupulously. Our Government is the potent, the omnipresent teacher. For good or for ill, it teaches the whole people by its example. Crime is contagious. If the Government becomes a lawbreaker, it breeds contempt for law; it invites every man to become a law unto himself; it invites anarchy. To declare that in the administration of the criminal law the end justifies the means—to declare that the Government may commit crimes in order to secure the conviction of a private criminal—would bring terrible retribution. Against that pernicious doctrine this Court should resolutely set its face.

Louis D. Brandeis

The trouble about fighting for human freedom is that you have to spend much of your life defending sons of bitches; for oppressive laws are always aimed at them originally, and oppression must be stopped in the beginning if it is to be stopped at all.
   H. L. Mencken

Censorship upholds the dignity of the profession, know what I mean?
   Mae West

Topics for Critical Thinking and Writing

1. Do you agree with the Italian statesman and political philosopher Niccolò Machiavelli when he says that the lawgiver should assume that people are "bad" and inclined toward "vicious" behavior? Isn't this an extreme overstatement? Machiavelli (1469–1527) lived long ago: Do you think his claim held true then, but does not hold true today? Or is it as true today as ever?

2. Identify a law, of some significance, that you believe is unjust. Have you ever been tempted to break this law? If you did, what would your act accomplish?

3. The eighteenth-century poet and essayist Samuel Johnson, quoted above by his friend and biographer James Boswell, says that a lawyer does not know whether a cause is "good or bad" until a judge gives the decision of the court. Is this an insightful point, or merely a clever one? Can you present an argument that would refute Johnson? How might he in turn respond?

4. Should a defense attorney defend a client whose guilt is obvious to everybody? If you were defending a client you believed to be innocent, but then discovered evidence of the client's guilt, would you tell the judge or keep this information to yourself?

5. During the civil rights campaigns of the 1950s and 1960s, Martin Luther King Jr. and many other activists frequently broke the law. What was their aim in doing so? Isn't it always wrong to break the law?

6. Often we say to ourselves or to someone else, "There should be a law against that." Is there an activity or specific form of behavior that you believe should be outlawed? Do you think that most people agree with you about this, or are you clearly in the minority? If your position on this issue became "the law," what would be the consequences?

7. Should a judge strictly abide by the letter of the law all the time? Can you imagine a situation when a judge knew a defendant to be guilty but nonetheless found him or her innocent? Would such a decision make you respect the law more, or less?

8. Does the study of literature affect a person's attitude toward the law? Do you think that it makes a person more respectful of the law, or less? Which literary works have affected your own views about law and order?

9. Has the study of literature made you a better person? How would you prove this to someone?

ESSAYS

HENRY DAVID THOREAU

The essayist, poet, and Transcendental philosopher Henry David Thoreau (1817–1862) was born in Concord and spent most of his life (as he put it) "sojourning" in the town and woods nearby and exploring the nearby ponds and rivers. He was educated at Harvard and then taught with his brother John at a school in Concord, but, inspired by his mentor and friend Ralph Waldo Emerson, he began in the late 1830s to keep a detailed journal and embarked on a career as a writer. Early in 1845, he built a small cabin on the shores of Walden Pond, on property that Emerson owned. Thoreau lived there for two years (though he also spent time at the homes of friends and neighbors, and was away for two months in 1846 on a trip to Maine). The record of his experiment in living is the book Walden, *published in 1854. Thoreau lectured frequently and published a number of essays during his lifetime; other essays, as well as book-length collections, including* The Maine Woods *(1864), appeared after his death from tuberculosis in 1862.*

Thoreau wrote "Civil Disobedience" (see following excerpt) in response to being jailed for a night in July 1846 for failing to pay his poll tax, a tax that Thoreau argued meant giving support to the Mexican War. In his antiwar sentiments he was in the minority, for most Americans endorsed the war, viewing it as a romantic military adventure that would extend America's democratic ideals. Abolitionists, believing that the real goal was the expansion of slavery south and west, criticized the Mexican War and later condemned the peace treaty, signed in 1848, that gave the United States 500,000 square miles of new territory. Thoreau agreed with them from the beginning; he refused to pay his tax, and thought no more about it.

But one day in July, on a trip into Concord to have a shoe repaired, Thoreau was stopped by the town constable Sam Staples, who told him that the tax was overdue. When Thoreau balked at paying it, Staples offered to loan him the money. When Thoreau said no to that too, the constable led him to jail, and he was placed in a cell with another man. Someone, probably Thoreau's Aunt Maria, paid the tax as soon as the family learned what had happened. Thoreau should have been released, but Staples by then was at home and did not want to go back to the jail. He wasn't released until the next morning.

Thoreau did not produce his famous essay right away. It was not until January 26, 1848, that he lectured at the Concord Lyceum on "the relation of the individual to the State." That lecture, with the title "Resistance to Civil Government," was published in 1849 in the volume Aesthetic Papers, *edited by Elizabeth Peabody, an educator, reformer, and Nathaniel Hawthorne's sister-in-law. When it was reprinted after Thoreau's death, it was given the title "Civil Disobedience," by which it is familiarly known.*

"Civil Disobedience" is one of the most influential political essays ever written. The Indian religious and political leader Mohandas K. Gandhi read and translated Thoreau's writings, including "Civil Disobedience," when he campaigned in the 1900s and 1910s for Indian civil rights in South Africa, and he returned to these texts in subsequent decades when he called for Indian independence from the British: "My first introduction to Thoreau's writings was, I think, in 1907, or later, when I was in the thick of the passive resistance struggle. A friend sent me the

essay on 'Civil Disobedience.' It left a deep impression on me." As the literary scholar Perry Miller has observed, "Civil Disobedience" also was a "rallying tract" among resisters of the Nazi occupations in Europe. Martin Luther King Jr. read the essay in college in the 1940s and remembered it in 1955 in the midst of the Montgomery bus boycott: "I became convinced that what we were preparing to do in Montgomery was related to what Thoreau had expressed. We were simply saying to the white community, 'We can no longer lend our cooperation to an evil system.'"

The core of Thoreau's argument is given in the following excerpt. He begins by contending that a person must never support a government with whose policies he or she claims to disagree. Our actions, he insists, should be in accord with our conscience, not at odds with it.

From "Civil Disobedience"

How can a man be satisfied to entertain an opinion merely, and enjoy *it?* Is there any enjoyment in it, if his opinion is that he is aggrieved? If you are cheated out of a single dollar by your neighbor, you do not rest satisfied with knowing that you are cheated, or with saying that you are cheated, or even with petitioning him to pay you your due; but you take effectual steps at once to obtain the full amount, and see that you are never cheated again. Action from principle, the perception and the performance of right, changes things and relations; it is essentially revolutionary, and does not consist wholly with anything which was. It not only divides states and churches, it divides families; ay, it divides the *individual,* separating the diabolical in him from the divine.

Unjust laws exist: shall we be content to obey them, or shall we endeavor to amend them, and obey them until we have succeeded, or shall we transgress them at once? Men generally, under such a government as this, think that they ought to wait until they have persuaded the majority to alter them. They think that, if they should resist, the remedy would be worse than the evil. But it is the fault of the government itself that the remedy *is* worse than the evil. *It* makes it worse. Why is it not more apt to anticipate and provide for reform? Why does it not cherish its wise minority? Why does it cry and resist before it is hurt? Why does it not encourage its citizens to be on the alert to point out its faults, and *do* better than it would have them? Why does it always crucify Christ, and excommunicate Copernicus and Luther, and pronounce Washington and Franklin rebels?

One would think, that a deliberate and practical denial of its authority was the only offence never contemplated by government; else, why has it not assigned its definite, its suitable and proportionate penalty? If a man who has no property refuses but once to earn nine shillings for the State, he is put in prison for a period unlimited by any law that I know, and determined only by the discretion of those who placed him there; but if he should steal ninety times nine shillings from the State, he is soon permitted to go at large again.

If the injustice is part of the necessary friction of the machine of government, let it go, let it go: perchance it will wear smooth,—certainly the machine will wear out. If the injustice has a spring, or a pulley, or a rope, or a crank, exclusively for itself, then perhaps you may consider whether the remedy will not be worse than the evil; but if it is of such a nature that it requires you to be the agent of injustice to another, then, I say, break the law. Let your life be a counter friction to stop the machine. What I have to do is to see, at any rate, that I do not lend myself to the wrong which I condemn.

5   As for adopting the ways which the State has provided for remedying the evil, I know not of such ways. They take too much time, and a man's life will be gone. I have other affairs to attend to. I came into this world, not chiefly to make this a good place to live in, but to live in it, be it good or bad. A man has not everything to do, but something; and because he cannot do *everything*, it is not necessary that he should do *something* wrong. It is not my business to be petitioning the Governor or the Legislature any more than it is theirs to petition me; and, if they should not hear my petition, what should I do then? But in this case the State has provided no way: its very Constitution is the evil. This may seem to be harsh and stubborn and unconciliatory; but it is to treat with the utmost kindness and consideration the only spirit that can appreciate or deserves it. So is all change for the better, like birth and death, which convulse the body.

I do not hesitate to say, that those who call themselves Abolitionists should at once effectually withdraw their support, both in person and property, from the government of Massachusetts, and not wait till they constitute a majority of one, before they suffer the right to prevail through them. I think that it is enough if they have God on their side, without waiting for that other one. Moreover, any man more right than his neighbors constitutes a majority of one already.

I meet this American government, or its representative, the State government, directly, and face to face, once a year—no more—in the person of its tax-gatherer; this is the only mode in which a man situated as I am necessarily meets it; and it then says distinctly, Recognize me; and the simplest, the most effectual, and, in the present posture of affairs, the indispensablest mode of treating with it on this head, of expressing your little satisfaction with and love for it, is to deny it then. My civil neighbor, the tax-gatherer, is the very man I have to deal with,—for it is, after all, with men and not with parchment that I quarrel,—and he has voluntarily chosen to be an agent of the government. How shall he ever know well what he is and does as an officer of the government, or as a man, until he is obliged to consider whether he shall treat me, his neighbor, for whom he has respect, as a neighbor and well-disposed man, or as a maniac and disturber of the peace, and see if he can get over this obstruction to his neighborliness without a ruder and more impetuous thought or speech corresponding with his action. I know this well, that if one thousand, if one hundred, if ten men whom I could name,—if ten *honest* men only,—ay, if *one* HONEST man, in this State of Massachusetts, *ceasing to hold slaves,* were actually to withdraw from this copartnership, and be locked up in the county jail therefor, it would be the abolition of slavery in America. For it matters not how small the beginning may seem to be: what is once well done is done forever. But we love better to talk about it: that we say is our mission. Reform keeps many scores of newspapers in its service, but not one man. If my esteemed neighbor, the State's ambassador, who will devote his days to the settlement of the question of human rights in the Council Chamber, instead of being threatened with the prisons of Carolina, were to sit down the prisoner of Massachusetts, that State which is so anxious to foist the sin of slavery upon her sister,—though at present she can discover only an act of inhospitality to be the ground of a quarrel with her,—the Legislature would not wholly waive the subject the following winter.

Under a government which imprisons any unjustly, the true place for a just man is also a prison. The proper place to-day, the only place which Massachusetts has provided for her freer and less desponding spirits, is in her prisons, to be put out and locked out of the State by her own act, as they have already put themselves out by their principles. It is there that the fugitive slave, and the Mexican prisoner on parole, and the Indian come to plead the wrongs of his race, should find them; on that separate, but more free and honorable ground, where the State places those who are not *with* her, but *against* her,—the only house in a slave State in which a free man can abide with honor. If any think that their influence would be lost there, and their voices no longer afflict the ear of the State, that they would not be as an enemy within its walls, they do not know by how much truth is stronger than error, nor how much more eloquently and effectively he can combat injustice who has experienced a little in his own person. Cast your whole vote, not a strip of paper merely, but your whole influence. A minority is powerless while it conforms to the majority; it is not even a minority then; but it is irresistible when it clogs by its whole weight. If the alternative is to keep all just men in prison, or give up war and slavery, the State will not hesitate which to choose. If a thousand men were not to pay their taxbills this year, that would not be a violent and bloody measure, as it would be to pay them, and enable the State to commit violence and shed innocent blood. This is, in fact, the definition of a peaceable revolution, if any such is possible. If the tax-gatherer, or any other public officer, asks me, as one has done, "But what shall I do?" my answer is, "If you really wish to do anything, resign your office." When the subject has refused allegiance, and the officer has resigned his office, then the revolution is accomplished. But even suppose blood should flow. Is there not a sort of blood shed when the conscience is wounded? Through this wound a man's real manhood and immortality flow out, and he bleeds to an everlasting death. I see this blood flowing now.

[1849]

Topics for Critical Thinking and Writing

1. Do you think that Thoreau really believes, literally, what he says? If you do not, what do you think is the point of the essay?
2. Thoreau emphasizes that each individual must take action—action that bears witness to moral principle. But shouldn't Thoreau also—or instead—stress the importance of individuals joining forces, working together as a morally committed group?
3. In paragraph 7, Thoreau says that if one person alone went to jail, this "would be the abolition of slavery in America." What does Thoreau mean? Does this claim make sense to you?
4. Demonstrators on both sides of the abortion issue, those who support "a woman's right to choose" and those who support "the right to life," have cited Thoreau's essay on "civil disobedience" as a source of inspiration. Can the argument described by Thoreau be applied to opposite positions on a matter of social policy? Would Thoreau find this acceptable, or not?
5. Toward the end of this excerpt, Thoreau refers to the shedding of blood. Is Thoreau conceding that violence might sometimes be the right response to injustice, that an act of moral violence might be needed to counteract immoral violence?

George Orwell

"George Orwell" was the pen name adopted in 1933 by Eric Blair (1903–1950). Orwell was born in India, where his father was serving as a civil servant. The boy was brought up in England and educated at Eton, an exclusive school; but instead of going to a university, he joined the Imperial Indian Police and served for five years in Burma (now Myanmar, but a province of British India from 1886 until 1948). Disenchanted with imperialism, he resigned his post and went to Paris, where he hoped to earn a living as a writer but was forced to support himself with menial jobs. He then returned to England, tramped around, and in 1933 wrote his first book, Down and Out in Paris and London, *using for the first time the pseudonym that he was to use for all of his future writings. Three novels followed, including* Burmese Days *(1934). In 1936 the Spanish civil war broke out, and Orwell joined the Republican (anti-Franco) side as a common soldier, but his book on the experience,* Homage to Catalonia *(1938) did not at all please the Communists. Other books include* Animal Farm *(1945), a fable clearly critical of Stalinism but also implying that any form of government can easily become tyrannical; and* 1984 *(1949), a vision of a totalitarian England. Orwell's last book was* 1984; *he died of tuberculosis in 1950.*

We print an essay based on his days in Burma, but written after he could no longer stomach his duties as a police officer there.

A Hanging

It was in Burma, a sodden morning of the rains. A sickly light, like yellow tinfoil, was slanting over the high walls into the jail yard. We were waiting outside the condemned cells, a row of sheds fronted with double bars, like small animal cages. Each cell measured about ten feet by ten and was quite bare within except for a plank bed and a pot for drinking water. In some of them brown silent men were squatting at the inner bars, with their blankets draped round them. These were the condemned men, due to be hanged within the next week or two.

One prisoner had been brought out of his cell. He was a Hindu, a puny wisp of a man, with a shaven head and vague liquid eyes. He had a thick, sprouting moustache, absurdly too big for his body, rather like the moustache of a comic man on the films. Six tall Indian warders were guarding him and getting him ready for the gallows. Two of them stood by with rifles and fixed bayonets, while the others handcuffed him, passed a chain through his handcuffs and fixed it to their belts, and lashed his arms tight to his sides. They crowded very close about him, with their hands always on him in a careful, caressing grip, as though all the while feeling him to make sure he was there. It was like men handling a fish which is still alive and may jump back into the water. But he stood quite unresisting, yielding his arms limply to the ropes, as though he hardly noticed what was happening.

Eight o'clock struck and a bugle call, desolately thin in the wet air, floated from the distant barracks. The superintendent of the jail, who was standing apart from the rest of us, moodily prodding the gravel with his stick, raised his head at the sound. He was an army doctor, with a gray toothbrush moustache and a gruff voice. "For God's sake hurry up, Francis," he said irritably. "The man ought to have been dead by this time. Aren't you ready yet?"

Francis, the head jailer, a fat Dravidian in a white drill suit and gold spectacles, waved his black hand. "Yes sir, yes sir," he bubbled. "All iss satisfactorily prepared. The hangman iss waiting. We shall proceed."

5   "Well, quick march,[1] then. The prisoners can't get their breakfast till this job's over."

We set out for the gallows. Two warders marched on either side of the prisoner, with their rifles at the slope; two others marched close against him, gripping him by arm and shoulder, as though at once pushing and supporting him. The rest of us, magistrates and the like, followed behind. Suddenly, when we had gone ten yards, the procession stopped short without any order or warning. A dreadful thing had happened—a dog, come goodness knows whence, had appeared in the yard. It came bounding among us with a loud volley of barks, and leapt round us wagging its whole body, wild with glee at finding so many human beings together. It was a large woolly dog, half Airedale, half pariah. For a moment it pranced round us, and then, before anyone could stop it, it had made a dash for the prisoner and, jumping up, tried to lick his face. Everyone stood aghast, too taken aback even to grab at the dog.

"Who let that bloody brute in here?" said the superintendent angrily. "Catch it, someone!"

A warder, detached from the escort, charged clumsily after the dog, but it danced and gamboled just out of his reach, taking everything as part of the game. A young Eurasian jailer picked up a handful of gravel and tried to stone the dog away, but it dodged the stones and came after us again. Its yaps echoed from the jail walls. The prisoner, in the grasp of the two warders, looked on incuriously, as though this was another formality of the hanging. It was several minutes before someone managed to catch the dog. Then we put my handkerchief through its collar and moved off once more, with the dog still straining and whimpering.

It was about forty yards to the gallows. I watched the bare brown back of the prisoner marching in front of me. He walked clumsily with his bound arms, but quite steadily, with that bobbing gait of the Indian who never straightens his knees. At each step his muscles slid neatly into place, the lock of hair on his scalp danced up and down, his feet printed themselves on the wet gravel. And once, in spite of the men who gripped him by each shoulder, he stepped slightly aside to avoid a puddle on the path.

10   It is curious, but till that moment I had never realized what it means to destroy a healthy, conscious man. When I saw the prisoner step aside to avoid the puddle I saw the mystery, the unspeakable wrongness, of cutting a life short when it is in full tide. This man was not dying, he was alive just as we are alive. All the organs of his body were working—bowels digesting food, skin renewing itself, nails growing, tissues forming—all toiling away in solemn foolery. His nails would still be growing when he stood on the drop, when he was falling through the air with a tenth of a second to live. His eyes saw the yellow gravel and the gray walls, and his brain still remembered, foresaw, reasoned—reasoned even about puddles. He and we were a party of men walking together, seeing, hearing, feeling, understanding the same world; and in two minutes, with a sudden snap, one of us would be gone—one mind less, one world less.

The gallows stood in a small yard, separate from the main grounds of the prison, and overgrown with tall prickly weeds. It was a brick erection like three sides of a shed, with planking on top, and above that two beams and a crossbar with the rope dangling. The hangman, a gray-haired convict in the white uniform of the prison, was waiting beside his machine. He greeted us with a servile crouch as we entered. At a word from Francis the two warders, gripping the prisoner

---

[1]**quick march** a marching pace of 120 steps per minute.

more closely than ever, half led half pushed him to the gallows and helped him clumsily up the ladder. Then the hangman climbed up and fixed the rope round the prisoner's neck.

We stood waiting, five yards away. The warders had formed in a rough circle round the gallows. And then, when the noose was fixed, the prisoner began crying out to his god. It was a high, reiterated cry of "Ram! Ram! Ram! Ram!" not urgent and fearful like a prayer or cry for help, but steady, rhythmical, almost like the tolling of a bell. The dog answered the sound with a whine. The hangman, still standing on the gallows, produced a small cotton bag like a flour bag and drew it down over the prisoner's face. But the sound, muffled by the cloth, still persisted, over and over again: "Ram! Ram! Ram! Ram! Ram!"

The hangman climbed down and stood ready, holding the lever. Minutes seemed to pass. The steady, muffled crying from the prisoner went on and on, "Ram! Ram! Ram!" never faltering for an instant. The superintendent, his head on his chest, was slowly poking the ground with his stick; perhaps he was counting the cries, allowing the prisoner a fixed number—fifty, perhaps, or a hundred. Everyone had changed color. The Indians had gone gray like bad coffee, and one or two of the bayonets were wavering. We looked at the lashed, hooded man on the drop, and listened to his cries—each cry another second of life; the same thought was in all our minds: oh, kill him quickly, get it over, stop that abominable noise!

Suddenly the superintendent made up his mind. Throwing up his head he made a swift motion with his stick. "Chalo!"[2] he shouted almost fiercely.

15   There was a clanking noise, and then dead silence. The prisoner had vanished, and the rope was twisting on itself. I let go of the dog, and it galloped immediately to the back of the gallows; but when it got there it stopped short, barked, and then retreated into a corner of the yard, where it stood among the weeds, looking timorously out at us. We went round the gallows to inspect the prisoner's body. He was dangling with his toes pointed straight downward, very slowly revolving, as dead as a stone.

The superintendent reached out with his stick and poked the bare brown body; it oscillated slightly. "*He's* all right," said the superintendent. He backed out from under the gallows, and blew out a deep breath. The moody look had gone out of his face quite suddenly. He glanced at his wrist watch. "Eight minutes past eight. Well, that's all for this morning, thank God."

The warders unfixed bayonets and marched away. The dog, sobered and conscious of having misbehaved itself, slipped after them. We walked out of the gallows yard, past the condemned cells with their waiting prisoners, into the big central yard of the prison. The convicts, under the command of warders armed with lathis,[3] were already receiving their breakfast. They squatted in long rows, each man holding a tin pannikin, while two warders with buckets marched round ladling out rice; it seemed quite a homely, jolly scene, after the hanging. An enormous relief had come upon us now that the job was done. One felt an impulse to sing, to break into a run, to snigger. All at once everyone began chattering gaily.

The Eurasian boy walking beside me nodded toward the way we had come, with a knowing smile: "Do you know, sir, our friend [he meant the dead man] when he heard his appeal had been dismissed, he pissed on the floor of his cell. From fright. Kindly take one of my cigarettes, sir. Do you not admire my new silver case, sir? From the boxwalah, two rupees eight annas. Classy European style."

---

[2]**Chalo!** Proceed!   [3]**lathis** bamboo canes fitted with iron, used as weapons.

Several people laughed—at what, nobody seemed certain.

20   Francis was walking by the superintendent, talking garrulously: "Well, sir, all hass passed off with the utmost satisfactoriness. It was all finished—flick! like that. It iss not always so—oah, no! I have known cases where the doctor wass obliged to go beneath the gallows and pull the prissoner's legs to ensure decease. Most disagreeable!"

"Wriggling about, eh? That's bad," said the superintendent.

"Ach, sir, it iss worse when they become refractory! One man, I recall, clung to the bars of hiss cage when we went to take him out. You will scarcely credit, sir, that it took six warders to dislodge him, three pulling at each leg. We reasoned with him. 'My dear fellow,' we said, 'think of all the pain and trouble you are causing to us!' But no, he would not listen! Ach, he wass very troublesome!"

I found that I was laughing quite loudly. Everyone was laughing. Even the superintendent grinned in a tolerant way. "You'd better all come out and have a drink," he said quite genially. "I've got a bottle of whisky in the car. We could do with it."

We went through the big double gates of the prison into the road. "Pulling at his legs!" exclaimed a Burmese magistrate suddenly, and burst into a loud chuckling. We all began laughing again. At that moment Francis' anecdote seemed extraordinarily funny. We all had a drink together, native and European alike, quite amicably. The dead man was a hundred yards away.

[1931]

Topics for Critical Thinking and Writing

1. The narrative of the hanging is pretty straightforward: The title tells us what we are in for, the first paragraph speaks of "condemned men," and the second paragraph introduces the "one prisoner" who soon will be hanged, and indeed he is soon hanged. But this narrative, brief though it is, is delayed by the intrusion of the dog (paragraphs 6–8), and again slightly delayed by the prisoner's "prayer or cry for help" (12–14). Would anything be gained or lost if Orwell had omitted these delays?

2. The narrative could end with paragraph 15 (when the prisoner is hanged) or paragraph 16 (when the superintendent confirms the death). But Orwell continues the essay, telling us (17) that "an enormous relief had come upon us now that the job was done," and he then continues for seven more paragraphs. Should he have ended after the sixteenth paragraph? Or after the seventeenth? Why?

3. What do you make of the detail in paragraph 9, when Orwell tells us that the condemned man "stepped aside to avoid a puddle" on the path to the gallows?

4. Consider the final two sentences: "We all had a drink together, native and European alike, quite amicably. The dead man was a hundred yards away." Orwell might have written, "We all had a drink together, native and European alike, quite amicably, although the dead man was only a hundred yards away." Or he could have written, "Although the dead man was only a hundred yards away, we all had a drink together, quite amicably, native and European alike." Of these three versions, which is the most effective? Why?

ZORA NEALE HURSTON

Zora Neale Hurston (1891–1960) was brought up in Eatonville, Florida, a town said to be the first all-black self-governing town in the United States. Her early years were spent working at odd jobs (domestic servant, manicurist, waitress), but she managed to attend Howard University and then, with the aid of a scholarship, entered Barnard College, where she was the first black student. At Barnard, influenced by the anthropologists Franz Boas and Ruth Benedict, she set out to study the folklore of Eatonville. Later she published several volumes of folklore, as well as stories, novels, and an autobiography (the source of our selection) called Dust Tracks on a Road *(1942).*

In the 1950s her writing seemed reactionary, almost embarrassing in an age of black protest, and she herself—working as a domestic, a librarian, and a substitute teacher—was almost forgotten. She died in a county welfare home in Florida and was buried in an unmarked grave. In the 1980s Hurston was, so to speak, rediscovered, partly because of the attention given to her by Alice Walker.

A Conflict of Interest

An incident happened that made me realize how theories go by the board when a person's livelihood is threatened. A man, a Negro, came into the shop one afternoon and sank down in Banks's chair. Banks was the manager and had the first chair by the door. It was so surprising that for a minute Banks just looked at him and never said a word. Finally, he found his tongue and asked, "What do you want?"

"Hair-cut and shave," the man said belligerently.

"But you can't get no hair-cut and shave here. Mr. Robinson[1] has a fine shop for Negroes on U Street near Fifteenth," Banks told him.

"I know it, but I want one here. The Constitution of the United States—"

5   But by that time, Banks had him by the arm. Not roughly, but he was helping him out of his chair, nevertheless.

"I don't know how to cut your hair," Banks objected. "I was trained on straight hair. Nobody in here knows how."

"Oh, don't hand me that stuff!" the crusader snarled. "Don't be such an Uncle Tom."

"Run on, fellow. You can't get waited on in here."

"I'll stay right here until I do. I know my rights. Things like this have got to be broken up. I'll get waited on all right, or sue the place."

10   "Go ahead and sue," Banks retorted. "Go on uptown, and get your hair cut, man. Don't be so hard-headed for nothing."

"I'm getting waited on right here!"

"You're next, Mr. Powell," Banks said to a waiting customer. "Sorry, mister, but you better go on uptown."

"But I have a right to be waited on wherever I please," the Negro said, and started towards Updyke's chair which was being emptied. Updyke whirled his chair around so that he could not sit down and stepped in front of it. "Don't you touch *my* chair!" Updyke glared. "Go on about your business."

---

[1]**Robinson** George Robinson, an African American, owned a chain of barber shops. Most of his shops catered to whites in Washington, D.C. (Editors' note).

But instead of going, he made to get into the chair by force.

15   "Don't argue with him! Throw him out of here!" somebody in the back cried. And in a minute, barbers, customers all lathered and hair half cut, and porters, were all helping to throw the Negro out.

The rush carried him way out into the middle of G street and flung him down. He tried to lie there and be a martyr, but the roar of oncoming cars made him jump up and scurry off. We never heard any more about it. I did not participate in the mêlée, but I wanted him thrown out, too. My business was threatened.

It was only that night in bed that I analyzed the whole thing and realized that I was giving sanction to Jim Crow, which theoretically, I was supposed to resist. But here were ten Negro barbers, three porters and two manicurists all stirred up at the threat of our living through loss of patronage. Nobody thought it out at the moment. It was an instinctive thing. That was the first time it was called to my attention that self-interest rides over all sorts of lines. I have seen the same thing happen hundreds of times since, and now I understand it. One sees it breaking over racial, national, religious and class lines. Anglo-Saxon against Anglo-Saxon, Jew against Jew, Negro against Negro, and all sorts of combinations of the three against other combinations of the three. Offhand, you might say that we fifteen Negroes should have felt the racial thing and served him. He was one of us. Perhaps it would have been a beautiful thing if Banks had turned to the shop crowded with customers and announced that this man was going to be served like everybody else even at the risk of losing their patronage, with all of the other employees lined up in the center of the floor shouting, "So say we all!" It would have been a stirring gesture, and made the headlines for a day. Then we could all have gone home to our unpaid rents and bills and things like that. I could leave school and begin my wanderings again. The "militant" Negro who would have been the cause of it all, would have perched on the smuddled-up wreck of things and crowed. Nobody ever found out who or what he was. Perhaps he did what he did on the spur of the moment, not realizing that serving him would have ruined Mr. Robinson, another Negro who had got what he had the hard way. For not only would the G Street shop have been forced to close, but the F Street shop and all of his other six downtown shops. Wrecking George Robinson like that on a "race" angle would have been ironic tragedy. He always helped out any Negro who was trying to do anything progressive as far as he was able. He had no education himself, but he was for it. He would give any Howard University student a job in his shops if they could qualify, even if it was only a few hours a week.

So I do not know what was the ultimate right in this case. I do know how I felt at the time. There is always something fiendish and loathsome about a person who threatens to deprive you of your way of making a living. That is just human-like, I reckon.

[1942]

Topics for Critical Thinking and Writing

1. Hurston published this account in 1942, and she was writing about an event that had taken place a couple of decades earlier. Given the period and given

Hurston's analysis of her action, do you find her behavior understandable and excusable, or do you think that she is rationalizing cowardice? Explain.

2. Words like *outrageous, ironic, pathetic,* and even *tragic* probably can be appropriately applied to this episode. Would you agree, however, that, as Hurston narrates it, it also has comic elements? If so, explain.

3. Hurston argues that self-interest overrides "racial, national, religious, and class lines." Do you agree? Does she persuade you that at least in this incident it was true, or might there have been other reasons for the employees' actions?

MARTIN LUTHER KING JR.

Martin Luther King Jr. (1929–1968) was born in Atlanta and educated at Morehouse College, Crozer Theological Seminary, and Boston University. In 1954 he was called to serve as a Baptist minister in Montgomery, Alabama. During the next two years he achieved national fame when, using a policy of nonviolent resistance, he successfully led the boycott against segregated bus lines in Montgomery. He then organized the Southern Christian Leadership Conference, which furthered civil rights, first in the South and then nationwide. In 1964 he was awarded the Nobel Peace Prize. Four years later he was assassinated in Memphis, Tennessee, while supporting striking garbage workers.

In 1963 Dr. King was arrested in Birmingham, Alabama, for participating in a march for which no parade permit had been issued by the city officials. In jail he wrote a response to a letter that eight local clergymen had published in a newspaper. Their letter, titled "A Call for Unity," is printed here, followed by King's response.

April 12, 1963

We the undersigned clergymen are among those who, in January, issued "An Appeal for Law and Order and Common Sense," in dealing with racial problems in Alabama. We expressed understanding that honest convictions in racial matters could properly be pursued in the courts, but urged that decisions of those courts should in the meantime be peacefully obeyed.

Since that time there had been some evidence of increased forebearance and a willingness to face facts. Responsible citizens have undertaken to work on various problems which cause racial friction and unrest. In Birmingham, recent public events have given indication that we all have opportunity for a new constructive and realistic approach to racial problems.

However, we are now confronted by a series of demonstrations by some of our Negro citizens, directed and led in part by outsiders. We recognize the natural impatience of people who feel that their hopes are slow in being realized. But we are convinced that these demonstrations are unwise and untimely.

We agree rather with certain local Negro leadership which has called for honest and open negotiation of racial issues in our area. And we believe this kind of facing of issues can best be accomplished by citizens of our own metropolitan area, white and Negro, meeting with their knowledge and experience of the local situation. All of us need to face that responsibility and find proper channels for its accomplishment.

Just as we formerly pointed out that "hatred and violence have no sanction in our religious and political traditions," we also point out that such actions as incite to hatred and violence, however technically peaceful those actions may be, have not contributed to the resolution of our local problems. We do not believe that these days of new hope are days when extreme measures are justified in Birmingham.

We commend the community as a whole, and the local news media and law enforcement officials in particular, on the calm manner in which these demonstrations have been handled. We urge the public to continue to show restraint should the demonstrations continue, and the law enforcement officials to remain calm and continue to protect our city from violence.

We further strongly urge our own Negro community to withdraw support from these demonstrations, and to unite locally in working peacefully for a better Birmingham. When rights are consistently denied, a cause should be pressed in the courts and in negotiations among local leaders, and not in the streets. We appeal to both our white and Negro citizenry to observe the principles of law and order and common sense.

C.C.J. Carpenter, D.D., L.L.D., Bishop of Alabama; Joseph A. Durick, D.D., Auxiliary Bishop, Diocese of Mobile-Birmingham; Rabbi Milton L. Grafman, Temple Emanu-El, Birmingham, Alabama; Bishop Paul Hardin, Bishop of the Alabama-West Florida Conference of the Methodist Church; Bishop Nolan B. Harmon, Bishop of the North Alabama Conference of the Methodist Church; George M. Murray, D.D., L.L.D., Bishop Coadjutor, Episcopal Diocese of Alabama; Edward V. Ramage, Moderator, Synod of the Alabama Presbyterian Church in the United States; Earl Stallings, Pastor, First Baptist Church, Birmingham, Alabama.

Letter from Birmingham Jail

April 16, 1963

My Dear Fellow Clergymen:

While confined here in the Birmingham city jail, I came across your recent statement calling my present activities "unwise and untimely."[1] Seldom do I pause to answer criticism of my work and ideas. If I sought to answer all the criticisms that cross my desk, my secretaries would have little time for anything other than such correspondence in the course of the day, and I would have no time for constructive work. But since I feel that you are men of genuine good will and that your criticisms are sincerely set forth, I want to try to answer your statement in what I hope will be patient and reasonable terms.

I think I should indicate why I am here in Birmingham, since you have been influenced by the view which argues against "outsiders coming in." I have the

---

[1]This response to a published statement by eight fellow clergymen from Alabama (Bishop C.C.J. Carpenter, Bishop Joseph A. Durick, Rabbi Milton L. Grafman, Bishop Paul Hardin, Bishop Nolan B. Harmon, the Reverend George M. Murray, the Reverend Edward V. Ramage, and the Reverend Earl Stallings) was composed under somewhat constricting circumstances. Begun on the margins of the newspaper in which the statement appeared while I was in jail, the letter was continued on scraps of writing paper supplied by a friendly Negro trusty, and concluded on a pad my attorneys were eventually permitted to leave me. Although the text remains in substance unaltered, I have indulged in the author's prerogative of polishing it for publication. [King's note.]

honor of serving as president of the Southern Christian Leadership Conference, an organization operating in every southern state, with headquarters in Atlanta, Georgia. We have some eighty-five affiliated organizations across the South, and one of them is the Alabama Christian Movement for Human Rights. Frequently we share staff, educational, and financial resources with our affiliates. Several months ago the affiliate here in Birmingham asked us to be on call to engage in a nonviolent direct-action program if such were deemed necessary. We readily consented, and when the hour came we lived up to our promise. So I, along with several members of my staff, am here because I was invited here. I am here because I have organizational ties here.

But more basically, I am in Birmingham because injustice is here. Just as the prophets of the eighth century B.C. left their villages and carried their "thus saith the Lord" far beyond the boundaries of their home towns, and just as the Apostle Paul left his village of Tarsus and carried the gospel of Jesus Christ to the far corners of the Greco-Roman world, so am I compelled to carry the gospel of freedom beyond my own home town. Like Paul, I must constantly respond to the Macedonian call for aid.

Moreover, I am cognizant of the interrelatedness of all communities and states. I cannot sit idly by in Atlanta and not be concerned about what happens in Birmingham. Injustice anywhere is a threat to justice everywhere. We are caught in an inescapable network of mutuality; tied in a single garment of destiny. Whatever affects one directly, affects all indirectly. Never again can we afford to live with the narrow, provincial "outside agitator" idea. Anyone who lives inside the United States can never be considered an outsider anywhere within its bounds.

5   You deplore the demonstrations taking place in Birmingham. But your statement, I am sorry to say, fails to express a similar concern for the conditions that brought about the demonstrations. I am sure that none of you would want to rest content with the superficial kind of social analysis that deals merely with effects and does not grapple with underlying causes. It is unfortunate that demonstrations are taking place in Birmingham, but it is even more unfortunate that the city's white power structure left the Negro community with no alternative.

In any nonviolent campaign there are four basic steps: collection of the facts to determine whether injustices exist; negotiation; self-purification; and direct action. We have gone through all these steps in Birmingham. There can be no gainsaying the fact that racial injustice engulfs this community. Birmingham is probably the most thoroughly segregated city in the United States. Its ugly record of brutality is widely known. Negroes have experienced grossly unjust treatment in the courts. There have been more unsolved bombings of Negro homes and churches in Birmingham than in any other city in the nation. These are the hard, brutal facts of the case. On the basis of these conditions, Negro leaders sought to negotiate with the city fathers. But the latter consistently refused to engage in good-faith negotiation.

Then, last September, came the opportunity to talk with leaders of Birmingham's economic community. In the course of the negotiations, certain promises were made by the merchants—for example, to remove the stores' humiliating racial signs. On the basis of these promises, the Reverend Fred Shuttleworth and the leaders of the Alabama Christian Movement for Human Rights agreed to a moratorium on all demonstrations. As the weeks and months went by, we realized that we were the victims of a broken promise. A few signs, briefly removed, returned; the others remained.

Martin Luther King Jr.

As in so many past experiences, our hopes had been blasted, and the shadow of deep disappointment settled upon us. We had no alternative except to prepare for direct action, whereby we would present our very bodies as a means of laying our case before the conscience of the local and the national community. Mindful of the difficulties involved, we decided to undertake a process of self-purification. We began a series of workshops on nonviolence, and we repeatedly asked ourselves: "Are you able to accept blows without retaliating?" "Are you able to endure the ordeal of jail?" We decided to schedule our direct-action program for the Easter season, realizing that except for Christmas, this is the main shopping period of the year. Knowing that a strong economic-withdrawal program would be the by-product of direct action, we felt that this would be the best time to bring pressure to bear on the merchants for the needed change.

Then it occurred to us that Birmingham's mayoralty election was coming up in March, and we speedily decided to postpone action until after election day. When we discovered that the Commissioner of Public Safety, Eugene "Bull" Connor, had piled up enough votes to be in the run-off, we decided again to postpone action until the day after the run-off so that the demonstrations could not be used to cloud the issues. Like many others, we waited to see Mr. Connor defeated, and to this end we endured postponement after postponement. Having aided in this community need, we felt that our direct-action program could be delayed no longer.

10   You may well ask: "Why direct action? Why sit-ins, marches, and so forth? Isn't negotiation a better path?" You are quite right in calling for negotiation. Indeed, this is the very purpose of direct action. Nonviolent direct action seeks to create such a crisis and foster such a tension that a community which has constantly refused to negotiate is forced to confront the issue. It seeks so to dramatize the issue that it can no longer be ignored. My citing the creation of tension as part of the work of the nonviolent-resister may sound rather shocking. But I must confess that I am not afraid of the word "tension." I have earnestly opposed violent tension, but there is a type of constructive, nonviolent tension which is necessary for growth. Just as Socrates felt that it was necessary to create a tension in the mind so that individuals could rise from the bondage of myths and half-truths to the unfettered realm of creative analysis and objective appraisal, so must we see the need for nonviolent gadflies to create the kind of tension in society that will help men rise from the dark depths of prejudice and racism to the majestic heights of understanding and brotherhood.

The purpose of our direct-action program is to create a situation so crisis-packed that it will inevitably open the door to negotiation. I therefore concur with you in your call for negotiation. Too long has our beloved Southland been bogged down in a tragic effort to live in monologue rather than dialogue.

One of the basic points in your statement is that the action that I and my associates have taken in Birmingham is untimely. Some have asked: "Why didn't you give the new city administration time to act?" The only answer that I can give to this query is that the new Birmingham administration must be prodded about as much as the outgoing one, before it will act. We are sadly mistaken if we feel that the election of Albert Boutwell as mayor will bring the millennium to Birmingham. While Mr. Boutwell is a much more gentle person than Mr. Connor, they are both segregationists, dedicated to maintenance of the status quo. I have hope that Mr. Boutwell will be reasonable enough to see the futility of massive resistance to desegregation. But he will not see this without pressure from devotees of civil rights. My friends, I must say to you that we have not made a single gain in civil rights without determined legal and nonviolent pressure. Lamentably, it is an historical fact that privileged groups seldom give up their privileges voluntarily. Individuals may see the moral light and voluntarily give up their unjust posture; but as Reinhold Niebuhr[2] has reminded us, groups tend to be more immoral than individuals.

We know through painful experience that freedom is never voluntarily given by the oppressor; it must be demanded by the oppressed. Frankly, I have yet to engage in a direct-action campaign that was "well timed" in the view of those who have not suffered unduly from the disease of segregation. For years now I have heard the word "Wait!" It rings in the ear of every Negro with piercing familiarity. This "Wait" has almost always meant "Never." We must come to see,

[2]**Reinhold Niebuhr** Niebuhr (1892–1971) was a minister, political activist, author, and professor of applied Christianity at Union Theological Seminary. [All notes are the editors' unless otherwise specified.]

with one of our distinguished jurists, that "justice too long delayed is justice denied."[3]

We have waited for more than 340 years for our constitutional and God-given rights. The nations of Asia and Africa are moving with jetlike speed toward gaining political independence, but we still creep at horse-and-buggy pace toward gaining a cup of coffee at a lunch counter. Perhaps it is easy for those who have never felt the stinging darts of segregation to say, "Wait." But when you have seen vicious mobs lynch your mothers and fathers at will and drown your sisters and brothers at whim; when you have seen hate-filled policemen curse, kick, and even kill your black brothers and sisters; when you see the vast majority of your twenty million Negro brothers smothering in an airtight cage of poverty in the midst of an affluent society; when you suddenly find your tongue twisted and your speech stammering as you seek to explain to your six-year-old daughter why she can't go to the public amusement park that has just been advertised on television, and see tears welling up in her eyes when she is told that Funtown is closed to colored children, and see ominous clouds of inferiority beginning to form in her little mental sky, and see her beginning to distort her personality by developing an unconscious bitterness toward white people; when you have to concoct an answer for a five-year-old son who is asking: "Daddy, why do white people treat colored people so mean?"; when you take a cross-country drive and find it necessary to sleep night after night in the uncomfortable corners of your automobile because no motel will accept you; when you are humiliated day in and day out by nagging signs reading "white" and "colored"; when your first name becomes "nigger," your middle name becomes "boy" (however old you are) and your last name becomes "John," and your wife and mother are never given the respected title "Mrs."; when you are harried by day and haunted by night by the fact that you are a Negro, living constantly at tiptoe stance, never quite knowing what to expect next, and are plagued with inner fears and outer resentments; when you are forever fighting a degenerating sense of "nobodiness"—then you will understand why we find it difficult to wait. There comes a time when the cup of endurance runs over, and men are no longer willing to be plunged into the abyss of despair. I hope, sirs, you can understand our legitimate and unavoidable impatience.

15   You express a great deal of anxiety over our willingness to break laws. This is certainly a legitimate concern. Since we so diligently urge people to obey the Supreme Court's decision of 1954 outlawing segregation in the public schools, at first glance it may seem rather paradoxical for us consciously to break laws. One may well ask: "How can you advocate breaking some laws and obeying others?" The answer lies in the fact that there are two types of laws: just and unjust. I would be the first to advocate obeying just laws. One has not only a legal but a moral responsibility to obey just laws. Conversely, one has a moral responsibility to disobey unjust laws. I would agree with St. Augustine that "an unjust law is no law at all."

Now, what is the difference between the two? How does one determine whether a law is just or unjust? A just law is a man-made code that squares with the moral law or the law of God. An unjust law is a code that is out of harmony

---

[3]**Justice . . . denied** A quotation attributed to William E. Gladstone (1809–1898), British statesman and prime minister.

with the moral law. To put it in the terms of St. Thomas Aquinas: An unjust law is a human law that is not rooted in eternal law and natural law. Any law that uplifts human personality is just. Any law that degrades human personality is unjust. All segregation statutes are unjust because segregation distorts the soul and damages the personality. It gives the segregator a false sense of superiority and the segregated a false sense of inferiority. Segregation, to use the terminology of the Jewish philosopher Martin Buber, substitutes an "I-it" relationship for an "I-thou" relationship and ends up relegating persons to the status of things. Hence segregation is not only politically, economically, and sociologically unsound, it is morally wrong and sinful. Paul Tillich[4] has said that sin is separation. Is not segregation an existential expression of man's tragic separation, his awful estrangement, his terrible sinfulness? Thus it is that I can urge men to obey the 1954 decision of the Supreme Court, for it is morally right; and I can urge them to disobey segregation ordinances, for they are morally wrong.

Let us consider a more concrete example of just and unjust laws. An unjust law is a code that a numerical or power majority group compels a minority group to obey but does not make binding on itself. This is *difference* made legal. By the same token, a just law is a code that a majority compels a minority to follow and that it is willing to follow itself. This is *sameness* made legal.

Let me give another explanation. A law is unjust if it is inflicted on a minority that, as a result of being denied the right to vote, had no part in enacting or devising the law. Who can say that the legislature of Alabama which set up that state's segregation laws was democratically elected? Throughout Alabama all sorts of devious methods are used to prevent Negroes from becoming registered voters, and there are some counties in which, even though Negroes constitute a majority of the population, not a single Negro is registered. Can any law enacted under such circumstances be considered democratically structured?

Sometimes a law is just on its face and unjust in its application. For instance, I have been arrested on a charge of parading without a permit. Now, there is nothing wrong in having an ordinance which requires a permit for a parade. But such an ordinance becomes unjust when it is used to maintain segregation and to deny citizens the First Amendment privilege of peaceful assembly and protest.

20   I hope you are able to see the distinction I am trying to point out. In no sense do I advocate evading or defying the law, as would the rabid segregationist. That would lead to anarchy. One who breaks an unjust law must do so openly, lovingly, and with a willingness to accept the penalty. I submit that an individual who breaks a law that conscience tells him is unjust, and who willingly accepts the penalty of imprisonment in order to arouse the conscience of the community over its injustice, is in reality expressing the highest respect for law.

Of course, there is nothing new about this kind of civil disobedience. It was evidenced sublimely in the refusal of Shadrach, Meshach, and Abednego to obey the laws of Nebuchadnezzar, on the ground that a higher moral law was at stake. It was practiced superbly by the early Christians, who were willing to face hungry lions and the excruciating pain of chopping blocks rather than submit to certain unjust laws of the Roman Empire. To a degree, academic freedom is a reality

[4]**Paul Tillich** Tillich (1886–1965), born in Germany, taught theology at several German universities, but in 1933 he was dismissed from his post at the University of Frankfurt because of his opposition to the Nazi regime. At the invitation of Reinhold Niebuhr, he came to the United States and taught at Union Theological Seminary.

today because Socrates practiced civil disobedience. In our own nation, the Boston Tea Party represented a massive act of civil disobedience.

We should never forget that everything Adolf Hitler did in Germany was "legal" and everything the Hungarian freedom fighters did in Hungary was "illegal." It was "illegal" to aid and comfort a Jew in Hitler's Germany. Even so, I am sure that, had I lived in Germany at the time, I would have aided and comforted my Jewish brothers. If today I lived in a Communist country where certain principles dear to the Christian faith are suppressed, I would openly advocate disobeying that country's anti-religious laws.

I must make two honest confessions to you, my Christian and Jewish brothers. First, I must confess that over the past few years I have been gravely disappointed with the white moderate. I have almost reached the regrettable conclusion that the Negro's great stumbling block in his stride toward freedom is not the White Citizen's Counciler or the Ku Klux Klanner, but the white moderate, who is more devoted to "order" than to justice; who prefers a negative peace which is the absence of tension to a positive peace which is the presence of justice; who constantly says: "I agree with you in the goal you seek, but I cannot agree with your methods or direct action"; who paternalistically believes he can set the timetable for another man's freedom; who lives by a mythical concept of time and who constantly advises the Negro to wait for a "more convenient season." Shallow understanding from people of good will is more frustrating than absolute misunderstanding from people of ill will. Lukewarm acceptance is much more bewildering than outright rejection.

I had hoped that the white moderate would understand that law and order exist for the purpose of establishing justice and that when they fail in this purpose they become the dangerously structured dams that block the flow of social progress. I had hoped that the white moderate would understand that the present tension in the South is a necessary phase of the transition from an obnoxious negative peace, in which the Negro passively accepted his unjust plight, to a substantive and positive peace, in which all men will respect the dignity and worth of human personality. Actually, we who engage in nonviolent direct action are not the creators of tension. We merely bring to the surface the hidden tension that is already alive. We bring it out in the open, where it can be seen and dealt with. Like a boil that can never be cured so long as it is covered up but must be opened with all its ugliness to the natural medicines of air and light, injustice must be exposed, with all the tension its exposure creates, to the light of human conscience and the air of national opinion before it can be cured.

25   In your statement you assert that our actions, even though peaceful, must be condemned because they precipitate violence. But is this a logical assertion? Isn't this like condemning a robbed man because his possession of money precipitated the evil act of robbery? Isn't this like condemning Socrates because his unswerving commitment to truth and his philosophical inquiries precipitated the act by the misguided populace in which they made him drink hemlock? Isn't this like condemning Jesus because his unique God-consciousness and never-ceasing devotion to God's will precipitated the evil act of crucifixion? We must come to see that, as the federal courts have consistently affirmed, it is wrong to urge an individual to cease his efforts to gain his basic constitutional rights because the quest may precipitate violence. Society must protect the robbed and punish the robber.

I had also hoped that the white moderate would reject the myth concerning time in relation to the struggle for freedom. I have just received a letter from a white brother in Texas. He writes: "All Christians know that the colored people will receive equal rights eventually, but it is possible that you are in too great a religious hurry. It has taken Christianity almost two thousand years to accomplish what it has. The teachings of Christ take time to come to earth." Such an attitude stems from a tragic misconception of time, from the strangely irrational notion that there is something in the very flow of time that will inevitably cure all ills. Actually, time itself is neutral; it can be used either destructively or constructively. More and more I feel that the people of ill will have used time much more effectively than have the people of good will. We will have to repent in this generation not merely for the hateful words and actions of the bad people but for the appalling silence of the good people. Human progress never rolls in on wheels of inevitability; it comes through the tireless efforts of men willing to be co-workers with God, and without this hard work, time itself becomes an ally of the forces of social stagnation. We must use time creatively, in the knowledge that the time is always ripe to do right. Now is the time to make real the promise of democracy and transform our pending national elegy into a creative psalm of brotherhood. Now is the time to lift our national policy from the quicksand of racial injustice to the solid rock of human dignity.

You speak of our activity in Birmingham as extreme. At first I was rather disappointed that fellow clergymen would see my nonviolent efforts as those of an extremist. I began thinking about the fact that I stand in the middle of two opposing forces in the Negro community. One is a force of complacency, made up in part of Negroes who, as a result of long years of oppression, are so drained of self-respect and a sense of "somebodiness" that they have adjusted to segregation; and in part of a few middle-class Negroes who, because of a degree of academic and economic security and because in some ways they profit by segregation, have become insensitive to the problems of the masses. The other force is one of bitterness and hatred, and it comes perilously close to advocating violence. It is expressed in the various black nationalist groups that are springing up across the nation, the largest and best-known being Elijah Muhammad's Muslim movement. Nourished by the Negro's frustration over the continued existence of racial discrimination, this movement is made up of people who have lost faith in America, who have absolutely repudiated Christianity, and who have concluded that the white man is an incorrigible "devil."

I have tried to stand between these two forces, saying that we need emulate neither the "do-nothingism" of the complacent nor the hatred and despair of the black nationalist. For there is the more excellent way of love and nonviolent protest. I am grateful to God that, through the influence of the Negro church, the way of nonviolence became an integral part of our struggle.

If this philosophy had not emerged, by now many streets of the South should, I am convinced, be flowing with blood. And I am further convinced that if our white brothers dismiss as "rabble-rousers" and "outside agitators" those of us who employ nonviolent direct action, and if they refuse to support our nonviolent efforts, millions of Negroes will, out of frustration and despair, seek solace and security in black-nationalist ideologies—a development that would inevitably lead to a frightening racial nightmare.

30   Oppressed people cannot remain oppressed forever. The yearning for freedom eventually manifests itself, and that is what has happened to the American Negro. Something within has reminded him of his birthright of freedom, and something without has reminded him that it can be gained. Consciously or

unconsciously, he has been caught up by the *Zeitgeist*,[5] and with his black brothers of Africa and his brown and yellow brothers of Asia, South America, and the Caribbean, the United States Negro is moving with a sense of great urgency toward the promised land of racial justice. If one recognizes this vital urge that has engulfed the Negro community, one should readily understand why public demonstrations are taking place. The Negro has many pent-up resentments and latent frustrations, and he must release them. So let him march; let him make prayer pilgrimages to the city hall; let him go on freedom rides—and try to understand why he must do so. If his repressed emotions are not released in nonviolent ways, they will seek expression through violence; this is not a threat but a fact of history. So I have not said to my people: "Get rid of your discontent." Rather, I have tried to say that this normal and healthy discontent can be channeled into the creative outlet of nonviolent direct action. And now this approach is being termed extremist.

But though I was initially disappointed at being categorized as an extremist, as I continued to think about the matter I gradually gained a measure of satisfaction from the label. Was not Jesus an extremist for love: "Love your enemies, bless them that curse you, do good to them that hate you, and pray for them which despitefully use you, and persecute you." Was not Amos an extremist for justice: "Let justice roll down like waters and righteousness like an ever-flowing stream." Was not Paul an extremist for the Christian gospel: "I bear in my body the marks of the Lord Jesus." Was not Martin Luther an extremist: "Here I stand; I cannot do otherwise, so help me God." And John Bunyan: "I will stay in jail to the end of my days before I make a butchery of my conscience." And Abraham Lincoln: "This nation cannot survive half slave and half free." And Thomas Jefferson: "We hold these truths to be self-evident, that all men are created equal. . . ." So the question is not whether we will be extremists, but what kind of extremists we will be. Will we be extremists for hate or for love? Will we be extremists for the preservation of injustice or for the extension of justice? In that dramatic scene on Calvary's hill three men were crucified. We must never forget that all three were crucified for the same crime—the crime of extremism. Two were extremists for immorality, and thus fell below their environment. The other, Jesus Christ, was an extremist for love, truth, and goodness, and thereby rose above his environment. Perhaps the South, the nation, and the world are in dire need of creative extremists.

I had hoped that the white moderate would see this need. Perhaps I was too optimistic; perhaps I expected too much. I suppose I should have realized that few members of the oppressor race can understand the deep groans and passionate yearnings of the oppressed race, and still fewer have the vision to see that injustice must be rooted out by strong, persistent, and determined action. I am thankful, however, that some of our white brothers in the South have grasped the meaning of this social revolution and committed themselves to it. They are still all too few in quantity, but they are big in quality. Some—such as Ralph McGill, Lillian Smith, Harry Golden, James McBride Dabbs, Ann Braden, and Sarah Patton Boyle—have written about our struggle in eloquent and prophetic terms. Others have marched with us down nameless streets of the South. They have languished in filthy, roach-infested jails, suffering the abuse and brutality of policemen who

[5]*Zeitgeist* German for "spirit of the age."

view them as "dirty nigger-lovers." Unlike so many of their moderate brothers and sisters, they have recognized the urgency of the moment and sensed the need for powerful "action" antidotes to combat the disease of segregation.

Let me take note of my other major disappointment. I have been so greatly disappointed with the white church and its leadership. Of course, there are some notable exceptions. I am not unmindful of the fact that each of you has taken some significant stands on this issue. I commend you, Reverend Stallings, for your Christian stand on this past Sunday, in welcoming Negroes to your worship service on a nonsegregated basis. I commend the Catholic leaders of this state for integrating Spring Hill College several years ago.

But despite these notable exceptions, I must honestly reiterate that I have been disappointed with the church. I do not say this as one of those negative critics who can always find something wrong with the church. I say this as a minister of the gospel, who loves the church; who was nurtured in its bosom; who has been sustained by its spiritual blessings and who will remain true to it as long as the cord of life shall lengthen.

35   When I was suddenly catapulted into the leadership of the bus protest in Montgomery, Alabama, a few years ago, I felt we would be supported by the white church. I felt that the white ministers, priests, and rabbis of the South would be among our strongest allies. Instead, some have been outright opponents, refusing to understand the freedom movement and misrepresenting its leaders; all too many others have been more cautious than courageous and have remained silent behind the anesthetizing security of stained-glass windows.

In spite of my shattered dreams, I came to Birmingham with the hope that the white religious leadership of this community would see the justice of our cause and, with deep moral concern, would serve as the channel through which our just grievances could reach the power structure. I had hoped that each of you would understand. But again I have been disappointed.

I have heard numerous southern religious leaders admonish their worshipers to comply with a desegregation decision because it is the law, but I have longed to hear white ministers declare: "Follow this decree because integration is morally right and because the Negro is your brother." In the midst of blatant injustices inflicted upon the Negro, I have watched white churchmen stand on the sideline and mouth pious irrelevancies and sanctimonious trivialities. In the midst of a mighty struggle to rid our nation of racial and economic injustice, I have heard many ministers say: "Those are social issues, with which the gospel has no real concern." And I have watched many churches commit themselves to a completely otherworldly religion which makes a strange, unbiblical distinction between body and soul, between the sacred and the secular.

I have traveled the length and breadth of Alabama, Mississippi, and all the other southern states. On sweltering summer days and crisp autumn mornings I have looked at the South's beautiful churches with their lofty spires pointing heavenward. I have beheld the impressive outlines of her massive religious-education buildings. Over and over I have found myself saying: "What kind of people worship here? Who is their God? Where were their voices when the lips of Governor Barnett dripped with words of interposition and nullification? Where were they when Governor Wallace gave a clarion call for defiance and hatred? Where were their voices of support when bruised and weary Negro men and women decided to rise from the dark dungeons of complacency to the bright hills of creative protest?"

Yes, these questions are still in my mind. In deep disappointment I have wept over the laxity of the church. But be assured that my tears have been tears of love. There can be no deep disappointment where there is not deep love. Yes, I love the church. How could I do otherwise? I am in the rather unique position of being the son, the grandson, and the great-grandson of preachers. Yes, I see the church as the body of Christ. But, Oh! How we have blemished and scarred that body through social neglect and through fear of being nonconformists.

40   There was a time when the church was very powerful—in the time when the early Christians rejoiced at being deemed worthy to suffer for what they believed. In those days the church was not merely a thermometer that recorded the ideas and principles of popular opinion; it was a thermostat that transformed the mores of society. Whenever the early Christians entered a town, the people in power became disturbed and immediately sought to convict the Christians for being "disturbers of the peace" and "outside agitators." But the Christians pressed on, in the conviction that they were "a colony of heaven," called to obey God rather than man. Small in number, they were big in commitment. They were too God-intoxicated to be "astronomically intimidated." By their effort and example they brought an end to such ancient evils as infanticide and gladiatorial contests.

Things are different now. So often the contemporary church is a weak, ineffectual voice with an uncertain sound. So often it is an archdefender of the status quo. Far from being disturbed by the presence of the church, the power structure of the average community is consoled by the church's silent—and often even vocal—sanction of things as they are.

But the judgment of God is upon the church as never before. If today's church does not recapture the sacrificial spirit of the early church, it will lose its authenticity, forfeit the loyalty of millions, and be dismissed as an irrelevant social club with no meaning for the twentieth century. Every day I meet young people whose disappointment with the church has turned into outright disgust.

Perhaps I have once again been too optimistic. Is organized religion too inextricably bound to the status quo to save our nation and the world? Perhaps I must turn my faith to the inner spiritual church, the church within the church, as the true *ekklesia* and the hope of the world. But again I am thankful to God that some noble souls from the ranks of organized religion have broken loose from the paralyzing chains of conformity and joined us as active partners in the struggle for freedom. They have left their secure congregations and walked the streets of Albany, Georgia, with us. They have gone down the highways of the South on tortuous rides for freedom. Yes, they have gone to jail with us. Some have been dismissed from their churches, have lost the support of their bishops and fellow ministers. But they have acted in the faith that right defeated is stronger than evil triumphant. Their witness has been the spiritual salt that has preserved the true meaning of the gospel in these troubled times. They have carved a tunnel of hope through the dark mountain of disappointment.

I hope the church as a whole will meet the challenge of this decisive hour. But even if the church does not come to the aid of justice, I have no despair about the future. I have no fear about the outcome of our struggle in Birmingham, even if our motives are at present misunderstood. We will reach the goal of freedom in Birmingham and all over the nation, because the goal of America is freedom. Abused and scorned though we may be, our destiny is tied up with America's destiny. Before the pilgrims landed at Plymouth, we were here. Before the pen of Jefferson etched the majestic words of the Declaration of Independence across the

pages of history, we were here. For more than two centuries our forebears labored in this country without wages; they made cotton king; they built the homes
of their masters while suffering gross injustice and shameful humiliation—and yet
out of a bottomless vitality they continue to thrive and develop. If the inexpressible cruelties of slavery could not stop us, the opposition we now face will surely
fail. We will win our freedom because the sacred heritage of our nation and the
eternal will of God are embodied in our echoing demands.

45   Before closing I feel impelled to mention one other point in your statement
that has troubled me profoundly. You warmly commended the Birmingham police
force for keeping "order" and "preventing violence." I doubt that you would have
so warmly commended the police force if you had seen its dogs sinking their
teeth into unarmed, nonviolent Negroes. I doubt that you would so quickly commend the policemen if you were to observe their ugly and inhumane treatment of
Negroes here in the city jail; if you were to watch them push and curse old Negro
women and young Negro girls; if you were to see them slap and kick old Negro
men and young boys; if you were to observe them, as they did on two occasions,
refuse to give us food because we wanted to sing our grace together. I cannot join
you in your praise of the Birmingham police department.

It is true that the police have exercised a degree of discipline in handling the
demonstrators. In this sense they have conducted themselves rather "nonvio-
lently" in public. But for what purpose? To preserve the evil system of segregation. Over the past few years I have consistently preached that nonviolence demands that the means we use must be as pure as the ends we seek. I have tried to
make clear that it is wrong to use immoral means to attain moral ends. But now I
must affirm that it is just as wrong, or perhaps even more so, to use moral means
to preserve immoral ends. Perhaps Mr. Connor and his policemen have been
rather nonviolent in public, as was Chief Pritchett in Albany, Georgia, but they
used the moral means of nonviolence to maintain the immoral end of racial injustice. As T. S. Eliot has said: "The last temptation is the greatest treason: To do the
right deed for the wrong reason."

I wish you had commended the Negro sit-inners and demonstrators of
Birmingham for their sublime courage, their willingness to suffer, and their amazing discipline in the midst of great provocation. One day the South will recognize its real heroes. They will be the James Merediths, with the noble sense of
purpose that enables them to face jeering and hostile mobs, and with the agonizing loneliness that characterizes the life of the pioneer. They will be old, oppressed, battered Negro women, symbolized in a seventy-two-year-old woman in
Montgomery, Alabama, who rose up with a sense of dignity and with her people
decided not to ride segregated buses, and who responded with ungrammatical
profundity to one who inquired about her weariness: "My feets is tired, but my
soul is at rest." They will be the young high school and college students, the
young ministers of the gospel and a host of their elders, courageously and non-
violently sitting in at lunch counters and willingly going to jail for conscience'
sake. One day the South will know that when these disinherited children of God
sat down at lunch counters, they were in reality standing up for what is best in
the American dream and for the most sacred values in our Judaeo-Christian heritage, thereby bringing our nation back to those great wells of democracy which
were dug deep by the founding fathers in their formulation of the Constitution
and the Declaration of Independence.

Never before have I written so long a letter. I'm afraid it is much too long to
take your precious time. I can assure you that it would have been much shorter if

I had been writing from a comfortable desk, but what else can one do when he is alone in a narrow jail cell, other than write long letters, think long thoughts, and pray long prayers?

50   If I have said anything in this letter that overstates the truth and indicates an unreasonable impatience, I beg you to forgive me. If I have said anything that understates the truth and indicates my having a patience that allows me to settle for anything less than brotherhood, I beg God to forgive me.

I hope this letter finds you strong in the faith. I also hope that circumstances will soon make it possible for me to meet each of you, not as an integrationist or a civil-rights leader but as a fellow clergyman and a Christian brother. Let us all hope that the dark clouds of racial prejudice will soon pass away and the deep fog of misunderstanding will be lifted from our fear-drenched communities, and in some not too distant tomorrow the radiant stars of love and brotherhood will shine over our great nation with all their scintillating beauty.

Yours for the cause of Peace and Brotherhood,
Martin Luther King Jr.

[1963]

Topics for Critical Thinking and Writing

1. In his first five paragraphs, how does King assure his audience that he is not a meddlesome intruder but a man of good will?

2. In paragraph 3 King refers to Hebrew prophets and to the Apostle Paul, and later (para. 10) to Socrates. What is the point of these references?

3. In paragraph 11 what does King mean when he says that "our beloved Southland" has long tried to "live in monologue rather than dialogue"?

4. King begins paragraph 23 with "I must make two honest confessions to you, my Christian and Jewish brothers." What would have been gained or lost if he had used this paragraph as his opening?

5. King's last three paragraphs do not advance his argument. What do they do?

6. Why does King advocate breaking unjust laws "openly, lovingly" (para. 20)? What does he mean by these words? What other motives or attitudes do these words rule out?

7. Construct two definitions of "civil disobedience," and explain whether and to what extent it is easier (or harder) to justify civil disobedience, depending on how you have defined the expression.

8. If you feel that you wish to respond to King's letter on some point, write a letter nominally addressed to King. You may, if you wish, adopt the persona of one of the eight clergymen whom King initially addressed.

9. King writes (para. 46) that "nonviolence demands that the means we use must be as pure as the ends we seek." How do you think King would evaluate the following acts of civil disobedience: (a) occupying a college administration building in order to protest the administration's unsatisfactory response to a racial incident on campus, or in order to protest the failure of the administration to hire minority persons as staff and faculty; (b) sailing on a collision course with a whaling ship to protest against whaling; (c) trespassing on an abortion clinic to protest abortion? Set down your answer in an essay of 500 words.

FICTION

SEVEN VERY SHORT STORIES

Some stories are extremely short, usually because they deal with few characters and because they report only a single episode. The shortest story that we have encountered is a fable by Aesop, the semilegendary Greek teller of fables. (A **fable** is a brief tale, usually with speaking animals as its characters. Its aim is to point a moral, or to reveal an aspect of human behavior.) Here is Aesop's fable of the Fox and the Lion.

> A fox sneered at a lioness because she never bore more than one cub. "Only one," the lioness replied, "but a lion."

Like the fable, the **parable**—on page 66 we give the Parable of the Prodigal Son— is a short story that invites the hearer or the reader to go beyond the surface. For Westerners, the most famous parables are those told by Jesus; but the Buddha also told parables, and they exist in other cultures too. The story concerning Jesus that we give here, however, is not a parable told by him but rather is a very short story told about him, one that invites the reader to think about the message implicit in his behavior. The **Hasidic tale** (we give three of them in this unit), which originated with Polish Jews, similarly operates on two levels, a story of some immediate interest but also a story with rich implications.

In these forms, as in almost all good stories, the audience is taken forward, so to speak: We hear a sentence, it catches our interest ("A fox sneered at a lioness"), and we wonder, "What happened next?" That is, the teller of the tale reveals something, and makes us long for what is still hidden, what is to come. By the end of the story—if the story is told well—we feel that we have heard it all, there is nothing more to say ("Only one, but a lion"). In addition to this forward movement, this completion of a little invented journey, we are stimulated to look for something else that is still partly hidden—the meaning. We hear the narrative, and we think about its meaning, especially about its relevance to our lives. In other words, the story—however short—has depth as well as length. In the case of Aesop's fables, the depth usually resides in the illumination of human character (the animals commonly stand for human types—the vicious man, the fool, and so on), but when the types are juxtaposed (the hare and the tortoise) we get a moral (something like "overconfidence leads to failure," or "slow but steady wins the race").

AESOP

From the fifth century B.C. and onward, Greek writers refer to Aesop, who is said to have been a witty storyteller of the sixth century B.C. Tradition says that he was a slave, but nothing is really known of him, and presumably all sorts of folkloric stories—especially fables in which animals stand for various kinds of people—were attached to his name. Although for centuries many of the stories have been presented in children's books, the Greeks did not think of him as an entertainer of children, and very few of the stories are sweet or sentimental. For the most part, his animals (by which he represents kinds of human beings) are brutal or cunning or stupid: His society is competitive. Whoever first said that we live in a dog-eat-dog world had an Aesopian view of life.

"Once upon a time, they lived happily ever after."

A Lion and Other Animals Go Hunting

A lion, an ass, a jackal, and a wolf went hunting one day, and every one was to share and share alike in what they took. They plucked down a stag, and cut him up into four parts, but as they were beginning to divide shares, the lion said, "Hands off. *This* quarter is mine, by privilege of my rank, as King of Beasts. *This* quarter is mine because I frightened the stag with my roar. *This* quarter is mine because I delivered the first blow. As for *this* quarter, well, take it who dares." So the mouths of the allies were shut, and they went away, quiet as fishes.

Moral: There is no partnership with those who have the power.

Topics for Critical Thinking and Writing

1. Formulate your own concise, memorable moral for the story, and then argue for its superiority to the printed version. (The version that you have just read is from the middle of the twentieth century.)
2. When the fables were collected into books, the morals were added by various editors. In your view, does the story gain or lose by the explicit moral? Explain.
3. Here is another version (early nineteenth century) of the same story:

   The Lion and other beasts formed an alliance to go out a-hunting. When they had taken a fat stag the Lion proposed himself as commissioner, and dividing it into three parts, thus proceeded: "The first," said he, "I shall take officially, as king; the second I shall take for my own personal share in the hunt; and as for the third part—well, I'd like to see who will dare to lay a paw on it."

> *Moral: You may share the labors of the great, but will not share the spoil.*

If you were compiling a book of stories and were going to include this fable, which of these two versions would you use? Exactly why?

4. Does a moral need a story to be compelling? Does a story add something to the moral, and if so, what is that something?

JOHN (?)

The following story, of the woman taken in adultery, appears in several places in various early manuscripts of the New Testament, for instance in the Gospel according to Luke, after 21.38, and in the Gospel according to John, after 7.36 and, in other manuscripts of John, after 7.53. The most famous English translation of the Bible, the King James Version (1611), gives it at John 8.1–11, and so it is commonly regarded as belonging to John. But most Biblical scholars agree that the language of this short story differs notably from the language of the rest of this Gospel, and that it is not in any manuscript of John before the sixth century is further evidence that it was not originally part of this Gospel.

The Gospel according to John was apparently compiled in the late first century. John 21.20–24 says the author, or "the disciple which testifieth of these things," is "the disciple whom Jesus loved, . . . which also leaned on his breast at supper, and said, Lord, which is he that betrayeth thee?" Since the second century the book has traditionally been ascribed to John, one of the inner circle of twelve disciples.

The Woman Taken in Adultery

Jesus went unto the mount of Olives. And early in the morning he came again into the temple, and all the people came unto him; and he sat down, and taught them.

And the scribes and Pharisees[1] brought unto him a woman taken in adultery; and when they had set her in the midst, they say unto him, "Master, this woman was taken in adultery, in the very act. Now Moses in the law commanded us that such should be stoned: but what sayest thou?" This they said, tempting him, that they might have to accuse him. But Jesus stooped down, and with his finger wrote on the ground, as though he heard them not. So when they continued asking him, he lifted up himself, and said unto them, "He that is without sin among you, let him first cast a stone at her." And again he stooped down, and wrote on the ground. And they which heard it, being convicted by their own conscience, went out one by one, beginning at the eldest, even unto the last: and Jesus was left alone, and the woman standing in the midst.

---

[1]**scribes and Pharisees** the scribes were specialists who copied and interpreted the Hebrew law; the Pharisees were members of a sect that emphasized strict adherence to the Mosaic law.

When Jesus had lifted up himself, and saw none but the woman, he said unto her, "Woman, where are those thine accusers? Hath no man condemned thee?" She said, "No man, Lord." And Jesus said unto her, "Neither do I condemn thee; go, and sin no more."

Topics for Critical Thinking and Writing

1. Do you interpret the episode of the woman taken in adultery to say that crime should go unpunished? Or that adultery is not a crime? Or that a judge cannot punish a crime if he himself is guilty of it? Or what?
2. We read that Jesus wrote with his finger on the ground, but we are not told what Jesus wrote. How relevant to the story do you find this action by Jesus? Explain.
3. This story is widely quoted and alluded to. Why, in your opinion, has the story such broad appeal?

ANONYMOUS

Three Hasidic Tales

Hasidism (or Chasidism), from the Hebrew hasid, *"pietist," is the name given to two religious movements, one in medieval Germany and the other in modern— modern here meaning from the eighteenth century—Eastern Europe, especially Poland. Hitler's genocidal policies seemed to bring this second movement to an end, but the Eastern European tradition survived, and now flourishes in America and in Israel. The tales we reprint are from Eastern Europe, in the eighteenth and nineteenth centuries.*

Hasidism emphasizes the mystical union with God; redemption is found not through the Messiah but in the religious spirit of the individual. In teaching this doctrine, Hasidism makes considerable use of legends and anecdotes, especially concerning the words and deeds of a zaddik *(literally, "righteous"), a Hasidic master who can see from God's perspective rather than from only a human perspective. What is especially impressive about the compressed stories is their presentation of intense spiritual experience—usually joyous—within a simple, homely context. The Jewish philosopher Martin Buber (1878–1965) collected and published many Hasidic stories, and through Buber's writings Hasidism has influenced modern Christian theology.*

Keeping the Law

Disciples asked the maggid[1] of Zlotchov: "In the Talmud we read that our Father Abraham kept all the laws. How could this be, since they had not yet been given to him?"

---

[1]**maggid** teacher.

"All that is needful," he said, "is to love God. If you are about to do something and you think it might lessen your love, then you will know it is sin. If you are about to do something and think it will increase your love, you will know that your will is in keeping with the will of God. That is what Abraham did."

Noting Down

When Rabbi Shmelke was called to Nikolsburg in Moravia, a certain custom prevailed in that congregation. Every new rav was asked to note down in the chronicle some new regulation which was to be followed from that time on. He too was asked to do this, but put it off from day to day. He looked at each and every one and postponed noting anything in the book. He looked at them more and more closely and over and over, and put off writing until they gave him to understand that the delay was becoming unduly long. Then he went to where the chronicle lay and wrote down the ten commandments.

The Recipient

A man who lived in the same town as Rabbi Zusya saw that he was very poor. So each day he put twenty pennies into the little bag in which Zusya kept his phylacteries,[2] so that he and his family might buy the necessaries of life. From that time on, the man grew richer and richer. The more he had, the more he gave Zusya, and the more he gave Zusya, the more he had.

But once he recalled that Zusya was the disciple of a great maggid, and it occurred to him that if what he gave the disciple was so lavishly rewarded, he might become even more prosperous if he made presents to the master himself. So he traveled to Mezritch and induced Rabbi Baer to accept a substantial gift from him. From this time on, his means shrank until he had lost all the profits he had made during the more fortunate period. He took his trouble to Rabbi Zusya, told him the whole story, and asked him what his present predicament was due to. For had not the rabbi himself told him that his master was immeasurably greater than he?

Zusya replied: "Look! As long as you gave and did not bother to whom, whether to Zusya or another, God gave to you and did not bother to whom. But when you began to seek out especially noble and distinguished recipients, God did exactly the same."

[2]**phylacteries** small leather boxes containing strips of parchment inscribed with quotations from the Hebrew Bible.

Topics for Critical Thinking and Writing

"Keeping the Law"

Read the story of Abraham and Isaac (Genesis 22.1–59). How could preparing to sacrifice his son increase Abraham's love for God? If Abraham had hesitated or refused to prepare to sacrifice Isaac, how might this action have lessened his love for God?

"Noting Down"

1. Why, in "Noting Down," do you suppose that Rabbi Shmelke was reluctant to write some new regulation? What does he imply by writing the Ten Commandments?
2. Why are we told that he "looked at each and every one" and again that "he looked at them more and more closely and over and over"? What was he looking at or for?

"The Recipient"

Suppose someone said, of "The Recipient," that Rabbi Zusya's answer is not quite accurate. Zusya begins by saying, "Look! As long as you gave and did not bother to whom . . . " But the rich man, in giving to the poor Zusya, *did* "bother to whom"; that is, he chose a poor but meritorious man. Is this a weakness in the story, or can you justify Zusya's answer? How seriously do we take Zusya's answer?

FRANZ KAFKA

Frank Kafka (1883–1924) was born in Prague, Austria-Hungary, the son of German-speaking middle-class Jewish parents. Trained in law, he worked from 1907 to 1922 in an insurance company sponsored by the government. In 1923 he moved to Berlin to concentrate on becoming a writer, but he suffered from poor health, and during his brief literary career he published only a few stories, including "The Metamorphosis" (1915), which depicts the transformation of its main character into a gigantic insect.

Through the agency of his friend Max Brod, a number of works by Kafka were published posthumously, including The Trial *(1925; trans. 1937),* The Castle *(1926; trans. 1937), and* Amerika *(1927; trans. 1938). Among twentieth-century authors, Kafka's accounts of alienation and anxiety, of bewildered, isolated individuals trapped by law and bureaucracy, are unparalleled in their power and pain. In the words of the poet-critic W. H. Auden, writing in the late 1950s, "Had one to name the author who comes nearest to bearing the same kind of relation to our age as Dante, Shakespeare, and Goethe bore to theirs, Kafka is the first one would think of." "Before the Law" (1914) is among the stories that Kafka published during his lifetime.*

Before the Law

Translated by Willa and Edwin Muir

Before the Law stands a doorkeeper. To this doorkeeper there comes a man from the country and prays for admittance to the Law. But the doorkeeper says that he cannot grant admittance at the moment. The man thinks it over and then asks if he will be allowed in later. "It is possible," says the doorkeeper, "but not at the moment." Since the gate stands open, as usual, and the doorkeeper steps to one side, the man stoops to peer through the gateway into the interior. Observing that, the doorkeeper laughs and says: "If you are so drawn to it, just try to go in despite my veto. But take note: I am powerful. And I am only the least of the doorkeepers. From hall to hall there is one doorkeeper after another, each more powerful than the last. The third doorkeeper is already so terrible that even I cannot bear to look at him." These are difficulties the man from the country has not expected; the Law, he thinks, should surely be accessible at all times and to everyone, but as he now takes a closer look at the doorkeeper in his fur coat, with his big sharp nose and long, thin, black Tartar beard, he decides that it is better to wait until he gets permission to enter. The doorkeeper gives him a stool and lets him sit down at one side of the door. There he sits for days and years. He makes many attempts to be admitted, and wearies the doorkeeper by his importunity. The doorkeeper frequently has little interviews with him, asking him questions about his home and many other things, but the questions are put indifferently, as great lords put them, and always finished with the statement that he cannot be let in yet. The man, who has furnished himself with many things for his journey, sacrifices all he has, however valuable, to bribe the doorkeeper. The doorkeeper accepts everything, but always with the remark: "I am only taking it to keep you from thinking you have omitted anything." During these many years the man fixes his attention almost continuously on the doorkeeper. He forgets the other doorkeepers, and this first one seems to him the sole obstacle preventing access to the Law. He curses his bad luck, in his early years boldly and loudly; later, as he grows old, he only grumbles to himself. He becomes childish, and since in his yearlong contemplation of the doorkeeper he has come to know even the fleas on his fur coat, he begs the fleas as well to help him and to change the doorkeeper's mind. At length his eyesight begins to fail, and he does not know whether the world is really darker or whether his eyes are only deceiving him. Yet in his darkness he is now aware of a radiance that streams inextinguishable from the gateway of the Law. Now he has not very long to live. Before he dies, all his experiences in these long years gather themselves in his head to one point, a question he has not yet asked the doorkeeper. He waves him nearer, since he can no longer raise his stiffening body. The doorkeeper has to bend low towards him, much to the man's disadvantage. "What do you want to know now?" asks the doorkeeper; "you are insatiable." "Everyone strives to reach the Law," says the man, "so how does it happen that for all these many years no one but myself has ever begged for admittance?" The doorkeeper recognizes that the man has reached his end, and, to let his failing senses catch the words, roars in his ears: "No one else could ever be admitted here, since this gate was made only for you. I am now going to shut it."

[1914]

Topics for Critical Thinking and Writing

1. At a glance, we can see that this story consists of a single paragraph. Why would a writer want to do this? Won't such a story inevitably be too short?
2. Why is the first sentence so effective?
3. What is the significance of the man's failing eyesight? Of the imagery of darkness and radiance?
4. At the end of the story, as the man nears death, what at last does he learn? What is it that Kafka wants us as readers to learn?

5. One of the other authors whom we include in this book, Henry David Thoreau (p. 1211), wrote in his *Journal* (1851) that "the man for whom law exists—the man of forms, the conservative—is a tame man." From your reading of "Before the Law," what do you think would be Kafka's response to this claim?

ELIZABETH BISHOP

Elizabeth Bishop (1911–1979) is chiefly known as a poet, and we include several of her poems (as well as a brief biography) earlier in this book. Here, however, we give a prose piece. In a letter (February 3, 1937) Bishop mentions the act that served as the immediate trigger for the piece, but of course far more experience of life is in the work than the trivial act she specifies: "I once hung [my cat's] artificial mouse on a string to a chairback, without thinking what I had done—it looked very sad."

The Hanging of the Mouse

Early, early in the morning, even before five o'clock, the mouse was brought out, but already there were large crowds. Some of the animals had not gone to bed the night before, but had stayed up later and later; at first because of a vague feeling of celebration, and then, after deciding several times that they might as well wander about the town for an hour more, to conclude the night by arriving at the square in time for the hanging became only sensible. These animals hiccupped a little and had an air of cynical lassitude. Those who had got up out of bed to come also appeared weary and silent, but not so bored.

The mouse was led in by two enormous brown beetles in the traditional picturesque armor of an earlier day. They came on to the square through the small black door and marched between the lines of soldiers standing at attention: straight ahead, to the right, around two sides of the hollow square, to the left, and out into the middle where the gallows stood. Before each turn the beetle on the right glanced quickly at the beetle on the left; their traditional long, long antennae swerved sharply in the direction they were to turn and they did it to perfection. The mouse, of course, who had had no military training and who, at the moment, was crying so hard he could scarcely see where he was going, rather spoiled the precision and snap of the beetles. At each corner he fell slightly forward, and when he was jerked in the right direction his feet became tangled together. The beetles, however, without even looking at him, each time lifted him quickly into the air for a second until his feet were untangled.

At that hour in the morning the mouse's gray clothes were almost indistinguishable from the light. But his whimpering could be heard, and the end of his nose was rose-red from crying so much. The crowd of small animals tipped back their heads and sniffed with pleasure.

A raccoon, wearing the traditional black mask, was the executioner. He was very fastidious and did everything just so. One of his young sons, also wearing a black mask, waited on him with a small basin and a pitcher of water. First he washed his hands and rinsed them carefully; then he washed the rope and rinsed it. At the last minute he again washed his hands and drew on a pair of elegant black kid gloves.

5   A large praying mantis was in charge of the religious end of the ceremonies. He hurried up on the stage after the mouse and his escorts, but once there a fit of nerves seemed to seize him. He glided to the left a few steps, to the right a few steps, lifted his arms gracefully, but could not seem to begin; and it was quite apparent that he would have liked nothing better than to have jumped quickly down and left the whole affair. When his arms were stretched to Heaven his large eyes flashed toward the crowd, and when he looked up, his body was twitching and he moved about in a really pathetic way. He seemed to feel ill at ease with the low characters around him: the beetles, the hangmen, and the criminal mouse. At last he made a great effort to pull himself together and, approaching the mouse, said a few words in a high, incomprehensible voice. The mouse jumped from nervousness, and cried harder than ever.

At this point the spectators would all undoubtedly have burst out laughing, but just then the King's messenger appeared on the balcony above the small black door the mouse and his guards had lately come through. He was a very large, overweight bullfrog, also dressed in the traditional costume and carrying the traditional long scroll that dragged for several feet on the ground and had the real speech, on a little slip of paper, pasted inside it. The scroll and the white plume on his hat made him look comically like something in a nursery tale, but his voice was impressive enough to awe the crowd into polite attention. It was a deep bass: "Glug! Glug! Berrr-up!" No one could understand a word of the mouse's death sentence.

With the help of some pushes and pinches from the beetles, the executioner got the mouse into position. The rope was tied exquisitely behind one of his little round ears. The mouse raised a hand and wiped his nose with it, and most of the crowd interpreted this gesture as a farewell wave and spoke of it for weeks afterwards. The hangman's young son, at a signal from his father, sprang the trap.

"Squee-eek! Squee-eek!" went the mouse.

His whiskers rowed hopelessly round and round in the air a few times and his feet flew up and curled into little balls like young fern-plants.

10   The praying mantis, with an hysterical fling of his long limbs, had disappeared in the crowd. It was all so touching that a cat, who had brought her child in her mouth, shed several large tears. They rolled down on to the child's back and he began to squirm and shriek, so that the mother thought that the sight of the hanging had perhaps been too much for him, but an excellent moral lesson, nevertheless.

[1937]

Topics for Critical Thinking and Writing

1. We have several times quoted Robert Frost's observation that a poem (he could have said any work of literature) is "a performance in words." Reread Bishop's first paragraph, and discuss it in terms of "performance." Why, for instance do you think she repeats the word "early" in the first sentence? In this paragraph notice that Bishop says the animals decided "several times that they might as well wander about the town for an hour more." What do you make of deciding "several times"? And then Bishop says that the idea of concluding the night by "arriving at the square in time for the hanging became only sensible." What do

you make of "sensible," especially in the context that immediately follows it: "These animals hiccupped a little and had an air of cynical lassitude." What does "cynical lassitude" mean? How has Bishop juggled her words so as to convey what you assume is her attitude toward the animals?

2. Would you agree that there are humorous touches in the piece? If so, point them out. If you don't think there is anything humorous in it, point to something that someone might conceivably find amusing, and explain why you do not find it so.

3. Describe your response to the sentence, "The rope was tied exquisitely behind one of his little round ears."

4. In the final paragraph Bishop tells us that the cat believed "the sight of the hanging [provided] . . . an excellent moral lesson. . . ." Do you assume that Bishop agrees? By the way, executions used to be public, partly because it was felt that they served to educate the general public. As the proverb puts it, "Who hangs one corrects a thousand." Do you think Bishop would agree or disagree? Why?

THREE LONGER STORIES

URSULA K. LE GUIN

Ursula K. Le Guin was born in 1929 in Berkeley, California, the daughter of a distinguished mother (Theodora Kroeber, a folk-lorist) and father (Alfred L. Kroeber, an anthropologist). After graduating from Radcliffe College, she earned a master's degree at Columbia University; in 1952 she held a Fulbright Fellowship for study in Paris, where she met and married Charles Le Guin, a historian. She began writing in earnest while bringing up three children. Although her work is most widely known to fans of science fiction, because it usually has larger moral or political dimensions it interests many other readers who normally do not care for sci-fi.

Le Guin has said that she was prompted to write the following story by a remark she encountered in William James's "The Moral Philosopher and the Moral Life." James suggests there that if millions of people could be "kept permanently happy on the one simple condition that a certain lost soul on the far-off edge of things should lead a life of lonely torment," our moral sense "would make us immediately feel" it would be "hideous" to accept such a bargain. This story first appeared in New Dimensions 3 *(1973).*

The Ones Who Walk Away from Omelas

With a clamor of bells that set the swallows soaring, the Festival of Summer came to the city Omelas, bright-towered by the sea. The rigging of the boats in harbor sparkled with flags. In the streets between houses with red roofs and painted walls, between old moss-grown gardens and under avenues of trees, past great parks and public buildings, processions moved. Some were decorous: old people in long stiff robes of mauve and gray, grave master workmen, quiet, merry women carrying their babies and chatting as they walked. In other streets the music beat faster, a shimmering of gong and tambourine, and the people went dancing, the procession was a dance. Children dodged in and out, their high calls rising like the swallows' crossing flights over the music and the singing. All the processions wound towards the north side of the city, where on the great water-meadow called the Green Fields boys and girls, naked in the bright air, with mud-stained feet and ankles and long, lithe arms, exercised their restive horses before the race. The horses wore no gear at all but a halter without bit. Their manes were braided with streamers of silver, gold, and green. They flared their nostrils and pranced and boasted to one another; they were vastly excited, the horse being the only animal who has adopted our ceremonies as his own. Far off to the north and west the mountains stood up half encircling Omelas on her bay. The air of morning was so clear that the snow still crowning the Eighteen Peaks burned with white-gold fire across the miles of sunlit air, under the dark blue of the sky. There was just enough wind to make the banners that marked the racecourse snap and flutter now and then. In the silence of the broad green meadows one could hear the music winding through the city streets, farther and nearer and ever approaching, a cheerful faint sweetness of the air that from time to time trembled and gathered together and broke out into the great joyous clanging of the bells.

Joyous! How is one to tell about joy? How describe the citizens of Omelas?

They were not simple folk, you see, though they were happy. But we do not say the words of cheer much any more. All smiles have become archaic. Given a description such as this one tends to make certain assumptions. Given a description such as this one tends to look next for the King, mounted on a splendid stallion and surrounded by his noble knights, or perhaps in a golden litter borne by great-muscled slaves. But there was no king. They did not use swords, or keep slaves. They were not barbarians. I do not know the rules and laws of their society, but I suspect that they were singularly few. As they did without monarchy and slavery, so they also got on without the stock exchange, the advertisement, the secret police, and the bomb. Yet I repeat that these were not simple folk, not dulcet shepherds, noble savages, bland utopians. They were not less complex than us. The trouble is that we have a bad habit, encouraged by pedants and sophisticates, of considering happiness as something rather stupid. Only pain is intellectual, only evil interesting. This is the treason of the artist: a refusal to admit the banality of evil and the terrible boredom of pain. If you can't lick 'em, join 'em. If it hurts, repeat it. But to praise despair is to condemn delight, to embrace violence is to lose hold of everything else. We have almost lost hold, we can no longer describe a happy man, nor make any celebration of joy. How can I tell you about the people of Omelas? They were not naïve and happy children—though their children were, in fact, happy. They were mature, intelligent, passionate adults whose lives were not wretched. O miracle! But I wish I could describe it better. I wish I could convince you. Omelas sounds in my words like a city in a fairy tale, long ago and far away, once upon a time. Perhaps it would be best if you imagined it as your own fancy bids, assuming it will rise to the occasion, for certainly I cannot suit you all. For instance, how about technology? I think that there would be no cars or helicopters in and above the streets; this follows from the fact that the people of Omelas are happy people. Happiness is based on a just discrimination of what is necessary, what is neither necessary nor destructive, and what is destructive. In the middle category, however—that of the unnecessary but undestructive, that of comfort, luxury, exuberance, etc.—they could perfectly well have central heating, subway trains, washing machines, and all kinds of marvelous devices not yet invented here, floating light-sources, fuelless power, a cure for the common cold. Or they could have none of that: it doesn't matter. As you like it. I incline to think that people from towns up and down the coast have been coming in to Omelas during the last days before the Festival on very fast little trains and double-decked trams, and that the train station of Omelas is actually the handsomest building in town, though plainer than the magnificent Farmers' Market. But even granted trains, I fear that Omelas so far strikes some of you as goody-goody. Smiles, bells, parades, horses, bleh. If so, please add an orgy. If an orgy would help, don't hesitate. Let us not, however, have temples from which issue beautiful nude priests and priestesses already half in ecstasy and ready to copulate with any man or woman, lover or stranger, who desires union with the deep godhead of the blood, although that was my first idea. But really it would be better not to have any temples in Omelas—at least, not manned temples. Religion yes, clergy no. Surely the beautiful nudes can just wander about, offering themselves like divine soufflés to the hunger of the needy and the rapture of the flesh. Let them join the processions. Let tambourines be struck above the copulations, and the glory of desire be proclaimed upon the gongs, and (a not unimportant point) let the offspring of these delightful rituals be beloved and looked after by all. One thing I know there is none of in Omelas is guilt. But what else should there be? I thought that first there were no drugs, but that is puritanical. For those who like it, the faint insistent sweetness of *drooz* may perfume the ways of the city, *drooz* which first brings a great lightness and brilliance to the mind and limbs, and then after some hours a dreamy languor, and wonderful visions at last of the very arcana and inmost secrets of the Universe, as well as exciting the pleasure of sex beyond all belief; and it is not habit-forming. For more modest tastes I think there ought to be beer. What else, what else belongs in the joyous city? The sense of victory, surely, the celebration of courage. But as we did without clergy, let us do without soldiers. The joy built upon successful slaughter is not the right kind of joy; it will not do; it is fearful and it is trivial. A boundless and generous contentment, a magnanimous triumph felt not against some outer enemy but in communion with the finest and fairest in the souls of all men everywhere and the splendor of the world's summer: this is what swells the hearts of the people of Omelas, and the victory they celebrate is that of life. I really don't think many of them need to take *drooz*.

Most of the processions have reached the Green Fields by now. A marvelous smell of cooking goes forth from the red and blue tents of the provisioners. The faces of small children are amiably sticky; in the benign grey beard of a man a couple of crumbs of rich pastry are entangled. The youths and girls have mounted their horses and are beginning to group around the starting line of the course. An old woman, small, fat, and laughing, is passing out flowers from a basket, and tall young men wear her flowers in their shining hair. A child of nine or ten sits at the edge of the crowd, alone, playing on a wooden flute. People pause to listen, and they smile, but they do not speak to him, for he never ceases playing and never sees them, his dark eyes wholly rapt in the sweet, thin magic of the tune.

5   He finishes, and slowly lowers his hands holding the wooden flute.

As if that little private silence were the signal, all at once a trumpet sounds from the pavilion near the starting line: imperious, melancholy, piercing. The horses rear on their slender legs, and some of them neigh in answer. Sober-faced, the young riders stroke the horses' necks and soothe them, whispering, "Quiet, quiet, there my beauty, my hope. . . ." They begin to form in rank along the starting line. The crowds along the racecourse are like a field of grass and flowers in the wind. The Festival of Summer has begun.

Do you believe? Do you accept the festival, the city, the joy? No? Then let me describe one more thing.

In a basement under one of the beautiful public buildings of Omelas, or perhaps in the cellar of one of its spacious private homes, there is a room. It has one locked door, and no window. A little light seeps in dustily between cracks in the boards, secondhand from a cobwebbed window somewhere across the cellar. In one corner of the little room a couple of mops, with stiff, clotted, foul-smelling heads, stand near a rusty bucket. The floor is dirt, a little damp to the touch, as cellar dirt usually is. The room is about three paces long and two wide: a mere broom closet or disused tool room. In the room a child is sitting. It could be a boy or a girl. It looks about six, but actually is nearly ten. It is feebleminded. Perhaps it was born defective, or perhaps it has become imbecile through fear, malnutrition, and neglect. It picks its nose and occasionally fumbles vaguely with its toes or genitals, as it sits hunched in the corner farthest from the bucket and the two mops. It is afraid of the mops. It finds them horrible. It shuts its eyes, but it knows the mops are still standing there; and the door is locked; and nobody will come. The door is always locked; and nobody ever comes, except that sometimes—the child has no understanding of time or interval—sometimes the door rattles terribly and opens, and a person, or several people, are there. One of them may come in and kick the child to make it stand up. The others never come close, but peer in at it with frightened, disgusted eyes. The food bowl and the water jug are hastily filled, the door is locked, the eyes disappear. The people at the door never say anything, but the child, who has not always lived in the tool room, and can remember sunlight and its mother's voice, sometimes speaks. "I will be good," it says. "Please let me out. I will be good!" They never answer. The child used to scream for help at night, and cry a good deal, but now it only makes a kind of whining "eh-haa, eh-haa," and it speaks less and less often. It is so thin there are no calves to its legs; its belly protrudes; it lives on a half-bowl of corn meal and grease a day. It is naked. Its buttocks and thighs are a mass of festered sores, as it sits in its own excrement continually.

They all know it is there, all the people of Omelas. Some of them have come to see it, others are content merely to know it is there. They all know that it has to be there. Some of them understand why, and some do not, but they all understand that their happiness, the beauty of their city, the tenderness of their friendships, the health of their children, the wisdom of their scholars, the skill of their makers, even the abundance of their harvest and the kindly weathers of their skies, depend wholly on this child's abominable misery.

10 This is usually explained to children when they are between eight and twelve, whenever they seem capable of understanding; and most of those who come to see the child are young people, though often enough an adult comes, or comes back, to see the child. No matter how well the matter has been explained to them, these young spectators are always shocked and sickened at the sight. They feel disgust, which they had thought themselves superior to. They feel anger, outrage, impotence, despite all the explanations. They would like to do something for the child. But there is nothing they can do. If the child were brought up into the sunlight out of that vile place, if it were cleaned and fed and comforted, that would be a good thing, indeed; but if it were done, in that day and hour all the prosperity and beauty and delight of Omelas would wither and be destroyed. Those are the terms. To exchange all the goodness and grace of every life in Omelas for that single, small improvement: to throw away the happiness of thousands for the chance of the happiness of one: that would be to let guilt within the walls indeed.

The terms are strict and absolute; there may not even be a kind word spoken to the child.

Often the young people go home in tears, or in a tearless rage, when they have seen the child and faced this terrible paradox. They may brood over it for weeks or years. But as time goes on they begin to realize that even if the child could be released, it would not get much good of its freedom: a little vague pleasure of warmth and food, no doubt, but little more. It is too degraded and imbecile to know any real joy. It has been afraid too long ever to be free of fear. Its habits are too uncouth for it to respond to humane treatment. Indeed, after so long it would probably be wretched without walls about it to protect it, and darkness for its eyes, and its own excrement to sit in. Their tears at the bitter injustice dry when they begin to perceive the terrible justice of reality, and to accept it. Yet it is their tears and anger, the trying of their generosity and the acceptance of their helplessness, which are perhaps the true source of the splendor of their lives. Theirs is no vapid, irresponsible happiness. They know that they, like the child, are not free. They know compassion. It is the existence of the child, and their knowledge of its existence, that makes possible the nobility of their architecture, the poignancy of their music, the profundity of their science. It is because of the child that they are so gentle with children. They know that if the wretched one were not there snivelling in the dark, the other one, the flute-player, could make no joyful music as the young riders line up in their beauty for the race in the sunlight of the first morning of summer.

Now do you believe in them? Are they not more credible? But there is one more thing to tell, and this is quite incredible.

At times one of the adolescent girls or boys who go to see the child does not go home to weep or rage, does not, in fact, go home at all. Sometimes also a man or woman much older falls silent for a day or two, and then leaves home. These people go out into the street, and walk down the street alone. They keep walking, and walk straight out of the city of Omelas, through the beautiful gates. They keep walking across the farmlands of Omelas. Each one goes alone, youth or girl, man or woman. Night falls; the traveler must pass down village streets, between the houses with yellow-lit windows, and on out into the darkness of the fields. Each alone, they go west or north, towards the mountains. They go on. They leave Omelas, they walk ahead into the darkness, and they do not come back. The place they go towards is a place even less imaginable to most of us than the city of happiness. I cannot describe it at all. It is possible that it does not exist. But they seem to know where they are going, the ones who walk away from Omelas.

[1973]

Topics for Critical Thinking and Writing

1. Summarize the point of the story—not the plot, but what the story adds up to, what the author is getting at. Next, set forth what you would probably do (and why) if you were born in Omelas.
2. Consider the narrator's assertion (para. 3) that happiness "is based on a just discrimination of what is necessary."
3. Do you think the story implies a criticism of contemporary American society? Explain.

WILLIAM FAULKNER

William Faulkner (1897–1962) was brought up in Oxford, Mississippi. His great-grandfather had been a Civil War hero, and his father was treasurer of the University of Mississippi in Oxford; the family was no longer rich, but it was still respected. In 1918 he enrolled in the Royal Canadian Air Force, though he never saw overseas service. After the war he returned to Mississippi and went to the university for two years. He then moved to New Orleans, where he became friendly with Sherwood Anderson, who was already an established writer. In New Orleans Faulkner worked for the Times-Picayune; *still later, even after he had established himself as a major novelist with* The Sound and the Fury *(1929) he had to do some work in Hollywood in order to make ends meet. In 1950 he was awarded the Nobel Prize in Literature.*

Almost all of Faulkner's writing is concerned with the people of Yoknapatawpha, an imaginary county in Mississippi. "I discovered," he said, "that my own little postage stamp of native soil was worth writing about and that I would never live long enough to exhaust it." Though he lived for brief periods in Canada, New Orleans, New York, Hollywood, and Virginia (where he died), he spent most of his life in his native Mississippi.

Barn Burning

The store in which the Justice of the Peace's court was sitting smelled of cheese. The boy, crouched on his nail keg at the back of the crowded room, knew he smelled cheese, and more: from where he sat he could see the ranked shelves close-packed with the solid, squat, dynamic shapes of tin cans whose labels his stomach read, not from the lettering which mean nothing to his mind but from the scarlet devils and the silver curve of fish—this, the cheese which he knew he smelled and the hermetic meat which his intestines believed he smelled coming in intermittent gusts momentary and brief between the other constant one, the smell and sense just a little of fear because mostly of despair and grief, the old fierce pull of blood. He could not see the table where the Justice sat and before which his father and his father's enemy (*our enemy* he thought in that despair; *ourn! mine and hisn both! He's my father!*) stood, but he could hear them, the two of them that is, because his father had said no word yet:

"But what proof have you, Mr. Harris?"

"I told you. The hog got into my corn. I caught it up and sent it back to him. He had no fence that would hold it. I told him so, warned him. The next time I put the hog in my pen. When he came to get it I gave him enough wire to patch up his pen. The next time I put the hog up and kept it. I rode down to his house and saw the wire I gave him still rolled on to the spool in his yard. I told him he could have the hog when he paid me a dollar pound fee. That evening a nigger came with the dollar and got the hog. He was a strange nigger. he said, 'He say to tell you wood and hay kin burn.' I said, 'What?' 'That whut he say to tell you,' the nigger said. 'Wood and hay kin burn.' That night my barn burned. I got the stock out but I lost the barn."

"Where is the nigger? Have you got him?"

5   "He was a strange nigger, I tell you. I don't know what became of him."

"But that's not proof. Don't you see that's not proof?"

"Get that boy up here. He knows." For a moment the boy thought too that the man meant his older brother until Harris said, "Not him. The little one. The boy," and, crouching, small for his age, small and wiry like his father, in patched and faded jeans even too small for him, with straight, uncombed, brown hair and eyes gray and wild as storm scud, he saw the men between himself and the table part and become a lane of grim faces, at the end of which he saw the Justice, a shabby, collarless, graying man in spectacles, beckoning him. He felt no floor under his bare feet; he seemed to walk beneath the palpable weight of the grim turning faces. His father, stiff in his black Sunday coat donned not for the trial but for the moving, did not even look at him. *He aims for me to lie,* he thought, again with that frantic grief and despair. *And I will have to do hit.*

"What's your name, boy?" the Justice said.

"Colonel Sartoris Snopes," the boy whispered.

10 "Hey?" the Justice said. "Talk louder. Colonel Sartoris? I reckon anybody named for Colonel Sartoris in this country can't help but tell the truth, can they?" The boy said nothing. *Enemy! Enemy!* he thought; for a moment he could not even see, could not see that the Justice's face was kindly nor discern that his voice was troubled when he spoke to the man named Harris: "Do you want me to question this boy?" But he could hear, and during those subsequent long seconds while there was absolutely no sound in the crowded little room save that of quiet and intent breathing it was as if he had swung outward at the end of a grape vine, over a ravine, and at the top of the swing had been caught in a prolonged instant of mesmerized gravity, weightless in time.

"No!" Harris said violently, explosively. "Damnation! Send him out of here!" Now time, the fluid world, rushed beneath him again, the voices coming to him again through the smell of cheese and sealed meat, the fear and despair and the old grief of blood:

"This case is closed. I can't find against you, Snopes, but I can give you advice. Leave this country and don't come back to it."

His father spoke for the first time, his voice cold and harsh, level, without emphasis: "I aim to. I don't figure to stay in a country among people who . . ." he said something unprintable and vile, addressed to no one.

"That'll do," the Justice said. "Take your wagon and get out of this country before dark. Case dismissed."

15 His father turned, and he followed the stiff black coat, the wiry figure walking a little stiffly from where a Confederate provost's man's musket ball had taken him in the heel on a stolen horse thirty years ago, followed the two backs now, since his older brother had appeared from somewhere in the crowd, no taller than the father but thicker, chewing tobacco steadily, between the two lines of grim-faced men and out of the store and across the worn gallery and down the sagging steps and among the dogs and half-grown boys in the mild May dust, where as he passed a voice hissed:

"Barn burner!"

Again he could not see, whirling; there was a face in a red haze, moonlike, bigger than the full moon, the owner of it half again his size, he leaping in the red haze toward the face, feeling no blow, feeling no shock when his head struck the earth, scrabbling up and leaping again, feeling no blow this time either and tasting no blood, scrabbling up to see the other boy in full flight and himself already leaping into pursuit as his father's hand jerked him back, the harsh, cold voice speaking above him: "Go get in the wagon."

It stood in a grove of locusts and mulberries across the road. His two hulking sisters in their Sunday dresses and his mother and her sister in calico and sunbonnets were already in it, sitting on and among the sorry residue of the dozen and more movings which even the boy could remember—the battered stove, the broken beds and chairs, the clock inlaid with mother-of-pearl, which would not run, stopped at some fourteen minutes past two o'clock of a dead and forgotten day and time, which had been his mother's dowry. She was crying, though when she saw him she drew her sleeve across her face and began to descend from the wagon. "Get back," the father said.

"He's hurt. I got to get some water and wash his . . ."

20   "Get back in the wagon," his father said. He got in too, over the tail-gate. His father mounted to the seat where the older brother already sat and struck the gaunt mules two savage blows with the peeled willow, but without heat. It was not even sadistic; it was exactly that same quality which in later years would cause his descendants to over-run the engine before putting a motor car into motion, striking and reining back in the same movement. The wagon went on, the store with its quiet crowd of grimly watching men dropped behind; a curve in the road hid it. *Forever* he thought. *Maybe he's done satisfied now, now that he has . . .* stopping himself, not to say it aloud even to himself. His mother's hand touched his shoulder.

"Does hit hurt?" she said.

"Naw," he said. "Hit don't hurt. Lemme be."

"Can't you wipe some of the blood off before hit dries?"

"I'll wash to-night," he said. "Lemme be, I tell you."

25   The wagon went on. He did not know where they were going. None of them ever did or ever asked, because it was always somewhere, always a house of sorts waiting for them a day or two days or even three days away. Likely his father had already arranged to make a crop on another farm before he . . . Again he had to stop himself. He (the father) always did. There was something about his wolflike independence and even courage when the advantage was at least neutral which impressed strangers, as if they got from his latent ravening ferocity not so much a sense of dependability as a feeling that his ferocious conviction in the rightness of his own actions would be of advantage to all whose interest lay with his.

That night they camped, in a grove of oaks and beeches where a spring ran. The nights were still cool and they had a fire against it, of a rail lifted from a nearby fence and cut into lengths—a small fire, neat, niggard almost, a shrewd fire; such fires were his father's habit and custom always, even in freezing weather. Older, the boy might have remarked this and wondered why not a big one; why should not a man who had not only seen the waste and extravagance of war, but who had in his blood an inherent voracious prodigality with material not his own, have burned everything in sight? Then he might have gone a step farther and thought that that was the reason: that niggard blaze was the living fruit of nights passed during those four years in the woods hiding from all men, blue or gray, with his strings of horses (captured horses, he called them). And older still, he might have divined the true reason: that the element of fire spoke to some deep mainspring of his father's being, as the element of steel or of powder spoke to other men, as the one weapon for the preservation of integrity, else breath were not worth the breathing, and hence to be regarded with respect and used with discretion.

But he did not think this now and he had seen those same niggard blazes all his life. He merely ate his supper beside it and was already half asleep over his iron plate when his father called him, and once more he followed the stiff back, the stiff and ruthless limp, up the slope and on to the starlit road where, turning, he could see his father against the stars but without face or depth—a shape black, flat, and bloodless as though cut from tin in the iron folds of the frockcoat which had not been made for him, the voice harsh like tin and without heat like tin:

"You were fixing to tell them. You would have told him." He didn't answer. his father struck him with the flat of his hand on the side of the head, hard but without heat, exactly as he had struck the two mules at the store, exactly as he would strike either of them with any stick in order to kill a horse fly, his voice still without heat or anger: "You're getting to be a man. You got to learn. You got to learn to stick to your own blood or you ain't going to have any blood to stick to you. Do you think either of them, any man there this morning, would? Don't you know all they wanted was a chance to get at me because they knew I had them beat? Eh?" Later, twenty years later, he was to tell himself, "If I had said they wanted only truth, justice, he would have hit me again." But now he said nothing. He was not crying. He just stood there. "Answer me," his father said.

"Yes," he whispered. His father turned.

30   "Get on to bed. We'll be there to-morrow."

To-morrow they were there. In the early afternoon the wagon stopped before a paintless two-room house identical almost with the dozen others it had stopped before even in the boy's ten years, and again, as on the other dozen occasions, his mother and aunt got down and began to unload the wagon, although his two sisters and his father and brother had not moved.

"Likely hit ain't fitten for hawgs," one of the sisters said.

"Nevertheless, fit it will and you'll hog it and like it," his father said. "Get out of them chairs and help your Ma unload."

The two sisters got down, big, bovine, in a flutter of cheap ribbons; one of them drew from the jumbled wagon bed a battered lantern, the other a worn broom. His father handed the reins to the older son and began to climb stiffly over the wheel. "When they get unloaded, take the team to the barn and feed them." Then he said, and at first the boy thought he was still speaking to his brother: "Come with me."

35   "Me?" he said.

"Yes," his father said. "You."

"Abner," his mother said. His father paused and looked back—the harsh level stare beneath the shaggy, graying, irascible brows.

"I reckon I'll have a word with the man that aims to begin to-morrow owning me body and soul for the next eight months."

They went back up the road. A week ago—or before last night, that is—he would have asked where they were going, but not now. His father had struck him before last night but never before had he paused afterward to explain why; it was as if the blow and the following calm, outrageous voice still rang, repercussed, divulging nothing to him save the terrible handicap of being young, the light weight of his few years, just heavy enough to prevent his soaring free of the world as it seemed to be ordered but not heavy enough to keep him footed solid in it, to resist it and try to change the course of its events.

40   Presently he could see the grove of oaks and cedars and the other flowering trees and shrubs where the house would be, though not the house yet. They walked beside a fence massed with honeysuckle and Cherokee roses and came to a gate swinging open between two brick pillars, and now, beyond a sweep of drive, he saw the house for the first time and at that instant he forgot his father and the terror and despair both, and even when he remembered his father again (who had not stopped) the terror and despair did not return. Because, for all the twelve movings, they had sojourned until now in a poor country, a land of small farms and fields and houses, and he had never seen a house like this before. *Hit's big as a courthouse* he thought quietly, with a surge of peace and joy whose reason he

could not have thought into words, being too young for that: *They are safe from him. People whose lives are a part of this peace and dignity are beyond his touch, he no more to them than a buzzing wasp: capable of stinging for a little moment but that's all; the spell of this peace and dignity rendering even the barns and stable and cribs which belong to it impervious to the puny flames he might contrive . . .* this, the peace and joy, ebbing for an instant as he looked again at the stiff black back, the stiff and implacable limp of the figure which was not dwarfed by the house, for the reason that it had never looked big anywhere and which now, against the serene columned backdrop, had more than ever that impervious quality of something cut ruthlessly from tin, depthless, as though, sidewise to the sun, it would cast no shadow. Watching him, the boy remarked the absolutely undeviating course which his father held and saw the stiff foot come squarely down in a pile of fresh droppings where a horse had stood in the drive and which his father could have avoided by a simple change of stride. But it ebbed only for a moment, though he could not have thought this into words either, walking on in the spell of the house, which he could even want but without envy, without sorrow, certainly never with that ravening and jealous rage which unknown to him walked in the ironlike black coat before him: *Maybe he will feel it too. Maybe it will even change him now from what maybe he couldn't help but be.*

They crossed the portico. Now he could hear his father's stiff foot as it came down on the boards with clocklike finality, a sound out of all proportion to the displacement of the body it bore and which was not dwarfed either by the white door before it, as though it had attained to a sort of vicious and ravening minimum not to be dwarfed by anything—the flat, wide, black hat, the formal coat of broadcloth which had once been black but which had now that friction-glazed greenish cast of the bodies of old house flies, the lifted sleeve which was too large, the lifted hand like a curled claw. The door opened so promptly that the boy knew the Negro must have been watching them all the time, an old man with neat grizzled hair, in a linen jacket, who stood barring the door with his body, saying, "Wipe yo foots, white man, fo you come in here. Major ain't home nohow."

"Get out of my way, nigger," his father said, without heat too, flinging the door back and the Negro also and entering, his hat still on his head. And now the boy saw the prints of the stiff foot on the doorjamb and saw them appear on the pale rug behind the machinelike deliberation of the foot which seemed to bear (or transmit) twice the weight which the body compassed. The Negro was shouting "Miss Lula! Miss Lula!" somewhere behind them, then the boy, deluged as though by a warm wave by a suave turn of carpeted stair and a pendant glitter of chandeliers and a mute gleam of gold frames, heard the swift feet and saw her too, a lady—perhaps he had never seen her like before either—in a gray, smooth gown with lace at the throat and an apron tied at the waist and the sleeves turned back, wiping cake or biscuit dough from her hands with a towel as she came up the hall, looking not at his father at all but at the tracks on the blond rug with an expression of incredulous amazement.

"I tried," the Negro cried. "I tole him to . . ."

"Will you please go away?" she said in a shaking voice. "Major de Spain is not at home. Will you please go away?"

45   His father had not spoken again. He did not speak again. He did not even look at her. He just stood stiff in the center of the rug, in his hat, the shaggy iron-gray brows twitching slightly above the pebble-colored eyes as he appeared to examine the house with brief deliberation. Then with the same deliberation he

turned; the boy watched him pivot on the good leg and saw the stiff foot drag round the arc of the turning, leaving a final long and fading smear. His father never looked at it, he never once looked down at the rug. The Negro held the door. It closed behind them, upon the hysteric and indistinguishable woman-wail. His father stopped at the top of the steps and scraped his boot clean on the edge of it. At the gate he stopped again. He stood for a moment, planted stiffly on the stiff foot, looking back at the house. "Pretty and white, ain't it?" he said. "That's sweat. Nigger sweat. Maybe it ain't white enough yet to suit him. Maybe he wants to mix some white sweat with it."

Two hours later the boy was chopping wood behind the house within which his mother and aunt and the two sisters (the mother and aunt, not the two girls, he knew that; even at this distance and muffled by walls the flat loud voices of the two girls emanated an incorrigible idle inertia) were setting up the stove to prepare a meal, when he heard the hooves and saw the linen-clad man on a fine sorrel mare, whom he recognized even before he saw the rolled rug in front of the Negro youth following on a fat bay carriage horse—a suffused, angry face vanishing, still at full gallop, behind the corner of the house where his father and brother were sitting in the two tilted chairs; and a moment later, almost before he could have put the axe down, he heard the hooves again and watched the sorrel mare go back out of the yard, already galloping again. Then his father began to shout one of the sisters' names, who presently emerged backward from the kitchen door dragging the rolled rug along the ground by one end while the other sister walked behind it.

"If you ain't going to tote, go on and set up the wash pot," the first said.

"You, Sarty!" the second shouted. "Set up the wash pot!" His father appeared at the door, framed against that shabbiness, as he had been against that other bland perfection, impervious to either, the mother's anxious face at his shoulder.

"Go on," the father said. "Pick it up." The two sisters stooped, broad, lethargic; stooping, the presented an incredible expanse of pale cloth and a flutter of tawdry ribbons.

50   "If I thought enough of a rug to have to git hit all the way from France I wouldn't keep hit where folks coming in would have to tromp on hit," the first said. They raised the rug.

"Abner," the mother said. "Let me do it."

"You go back and git dinner," his father said. "I'll tend to this."

From the woodpile through the rest of the afternoon the boy watched them, the rug spread flat in the dust beside the bubbling wash-pot, the two sisters stooping over it with that profound and lethargic reluctance, while the father stood over them in turn, implacable and grim, driving them though never raising his voice again. He could smell the harsh homemade lye they were using; he saw his mother come to the door once and look toward them with an expression not anxious now but very like despair; he saw his father turn, and he fell to with the axe and saw from the corner of his eye his father raise from the ground a flattish fragment of field stone and examine it and return to the pot, and this time his mother actually spoke: "Abner. Abner. Please don't. Please, Abner."

Then he was done too. It was dusk; the whippoorwills had already begun. He could smell coffee from the room where they would presently eat the cold food remaining from the midafternoon meal, though when he entered the house he realized they were having coffee again probably because there was a fire on the hearth, before which the rug now lay spread over the backs of the two chairs. The tracks of his father's foot were gone. Where they had been were now long, water-cloudy scoriations resembling the sporadic course of a liliputian mowing machine.

55   It still hung there while they ate the cold food and then went to bed, scattered without order or claim up and down the two rooms, his mother in one bed, where his father would later lie, the older brother in the other, himself, the aunt, and the two sisters on pallets on the floor. But his father was not in bed yet. The last thing the boy remembered was the depthless, harsh silhouette of the hat and coat bending over the rug and it seemed to him that he had not even closed his eyes when the silhouette was standing over him, the fire almost dead behind it, the stiff foot prodding him awake. "Catch up the mule," his father said.

When he returned with the mule his father was standing in the black door, the rolled rug over his shoulder. "Ain't you going to ride?" he said.

"No. Give me your foot."

He bent his knee into his father's hand, the wiry, surprising power flowed smoothly, rising, he rising with it, on to the mule's bare back (they had owned a saddle once; the boy could remember it though not when or where) and with the same effortlessness his father swung the rug up in front of him. Now in the starlight they retraced the afternoon's path, up the dusty road rife with honeysuckle, through the gate and up the black tunnel of the drive to the lightless house, where he sat on the mule and felt the rough warp of the rug drag across his thighs and vanish.

"Don't you want me to help?" he whispered. His father did not answer and now he heard again that stiff foot striking the hollow portico with that wooden and clocklike deliberation, that outrageous overstatement of the weight it carried. The rug, hunched, not flung (the boy could tell that even in the darkness) from his father's shoulder struck the angle of wall and floor with a sound unbelievably loud, thunderous, then the foot again, unhurried and enormous; a light came on in the house and the boy sat, tense, breathing steadily and quietly and just a little fast, though the foot itself did not increase its beat at all, descending the steps now; now the boy could see him.

60   "Don't you want to ride now?" he whispered. "We kin both ride now," the light within the house altering now, flaring up and sinking. *He's coming down the stairs now*, he thought. He had already ridden the mule up beside the horse block; presently his father was up behind him and he doubled the reins over and slashed the mule across the neck, but before the animal could begin to trot the hard, thin arm came round him, the hard, knotted hand jerking the mule back to a walk.

In the first red rays of the sun they were in the lot, putting plow gear on the mules. This time the sorrel mare was in the lot before he heard it at all, the rider collarless and even bareheaded, trembling, speaking in a shaking voice as the woman in the house had done. His father merely looking up once before stooping again to the hame he was buckling, so that the man on the mare spoke to his stooping back:

"You must realize you have ruined that rug. Wasn't there anybody here, any of your women . . ." he ceased, shaking, the boy watching him, the older brother leaning now in the stable door, chewing, blinking slowly and steadily at nothing apparently. "It cost a hundred dollars. But you never had a hundred dollars. You never will. So I'm going to charge you twenty bushels of corn against your crop. I'll add it in your contract and when you come to the commissary you can sign it. That won't keep Mrs. de Spain quiet but maybe it will teach you to wipe your feet off before you enter her house again."

Then he was gone. The boy looked at his father, who still had not spoken or even looked up again, who was now adjusting the loggerhead in the hame.

"Pap," he said. His father looked at him—the inscrutable face, the shaggy brows beneath which the gray eyes glinted coldly. Suddenly the boy went toward him, fast, stopping as suddenly. "You done the best you could!" he cried. "If he wanted hit done different why didn't he wait and tell you how? He won't git no twenty bushels! He won't git none! We'll gether hit and hide hit! I kin watch . . ."

65   "Did you put the cutter back in that straight stock like I told you?"

"No, sir," he said.

"Then go do it."

That was Wednesday. During the rest of that week he worked steadily, at what was within his scope and some which was beyond it, with an industry that did not need to be driven nor even commanded twice; he had this from his mother, with the difference that some at least of what he did he liked to do, such as splitting wood with the half-size axe which his mother and aunt had earned, or saved money somehow, to present him with at Christmas. In company with the two older women (and on one afternoon, even one of the sisters), he built pens for the shoat and the cow which were a part of his father's contract with the landlord, and one afternoon, his father being absent, gone somewhere on one of the mules, he went to the field.

They were running a middle buster now, his brother holding the plow straight while he handled the reins, and walking beside the straining mule, the rick black soil shearing cool and damp against his bare ankles, he thought *Maybe this is the end of it. Maybe even that twenty bushels that seems hard to have to pay for just a rug will be a cheap price for him to stop forever and always from being what he used to be;* thinking, dreaming now, so that his brother had to speak sharply to him to mind the mule: *Maybe he even won't collect the twenty bushels. Maybe it will all add up and balance and vanish—corn, rug, fire; the terror and grief, the being pulled two ways like between two teams of horses—gone, done with for ever and ever.*

70   Then it was Saturday; he looked up from beneath the mule he was harnessing and saw his father in the black coat and hat. "Not that," his father said. "The wagon gear." And then, two hours later, sitting in the wagon bed behind his father and brother on the seat, the wagon accomplished a final curve, and he saw the weathered paintless store with its tattered tobacco- and patent-medicine posters and the tethered wagons and saddle animals below the gallery. He mounted the gnawed steps behind his father and brother, and there again was the lane of quiet, watching faces for the three of them to walk through. He saw the man in spectacles sitting at the plank table and he did not need to be told this was a Justice of the Peace; he sent one glare of fierce, exultant, partisan defiance at the man in collar and cravat now, whom he had seen but twice before in his life, and that on a galloping horse, who now wore on his face an expression not of rage but of amazed unbelief which the boy could not have known was at the incredible circumstance of being sued by one of his own tenants, and came and stood against his father and cried at the Justice: "He ain't done it! He ain't burnt . . ."

"Go back to the wagon," his father said.

"Burnt?" the Justice said. "Do I understand this rug was burned too?"

"Does anybody here claim it was?" his father said. "Go back to the wagon." But he did not, he merely retreated to the rear of the room, crowded as that other had been, but not to sit down this time, instead, to stand pressing among the motionless bodies, listening to the voices:

"And you claim twenty bushels of corn is too high for the damage you did to the rug?"

75 "He brought the rug to me and said he wanted the tracks washed out of it. I washed the tracks out and took the rug back to him."

"But you didn't carry the rug back to him in the same condition it was in before you made the tracks on it."

His father did not answer, and now for perhaps half a minute there was no sound at all save that of breathing, the faint, steady suspiration of complete and intent listening.

"You decline to answer that, Mr. Snopes?" Again his father did not answer. "I'm going to find against you, Mr. Snopes. I'm going to find that you were responsible for the injury to Major de Spain's rug and hold you liable for it. But twenty bushels of corn seems a little high for a man in your circumstances to have to pay. Major de Spain claims it costs a hundred dollars. October corn will be worth about fifty cents. I figure that if Major de Spain can stand a ninety-five-dollar loss on something he paid cash for, you can stand a five-dollar loss you haven't earned yet. I hold you in damages to Major de Spain to the amount of ten bushels of corn over and above your contract with him, to be paid to him out of your crop at gathering time. Court adjourned."

It had taken no time hardly, the morning was but half begun. He thought they would return home and perhaps back to the field, since they were late, far behind all other farmers. But instead his father passed on behind the wagon, merely indicating with his hand for the older brother to follow with it, and crossed the road toward the blacksmith shop opposite, pressing on after his father, overtaking him, speaking, whispering up at the harsh, calm face beneath the weathered hat: "He won't git no ten bushels neither. He won't git one. We'll . . ." until his father glanced for an instant down at him, the face absolutely calm, the grizzled eyebrows tangled above the cold eyes, the voice almost pleasant, almost gentle:

80 "You think so? Well, we'll wait till October anyway."

The matter of the wagon—the setting of a spoke or two and the tightening of the tires—did not take long either, the business of the tires accomplished by driving the wagon into the spring branch behind the shop and letting it stand there, the mules nuzzling into the water from time to time, and the boy on the seat with the idle reins, looking up the slope and through the sooty tunnel of the shed where the slow hammer rang and where his father sat on an upended cypress bolt, easily, either talking or listening, still sitting there when the boy brought the dripping wagon up out of the branch and halted it before the door.

"Take them on to the shade and hitch," his father said. He did so and returned. His father and the smith and a third man squatting on his heels inside the door were talking, about crops and animals; the boy, squatting too in the ammoniac dust and hoof-parings and scales of rust, heard his father tell a long and unhurried story out of the time before the birth of the older brother even when he had been a professional horsetrader. And then his father came up beside him where he stood before a tattered last year's circus poster on the other side of the store, gazing rapt and quiet at the scarlet horses, the incredible poisings and convolutions of tulle and tights and the painted leers of comedians, and said, "It's time to eat."

But not at home. Squatting beside his brother against the front wall, he watched his father emerge from the store and produce from a paper sack a segment of cheese and divide it carefully and deliberately into three with his pocket knife and produce crackers from the same sack. They all three squatted on the gallery and ate, slowly, without talking; then in the store again, they drank from a tin dipper tepid water smelling of the cedar bucket and of living beech trees. And still they did not go home. It was a horse lot this time, a tall rail fence upon and along which men stood and sat and out of which one by one horses were led, to be talked and trotted and then cantered back and forth along the road while the slow swapping and buying went on and the sun began to slant westward, they— the three of them—watching and listening, the older brother with his muddy eyes and his steady, inevitable tobacco, the father commenting now and then on certain of the animals, to no one in particular.

It was after sundown when they reached home. They ate supper by lamplight, then, sitting on the doorstep, the boy watched the night fully accomplish, listening to the whippoorwills and the frogs, when he heard his mother's voice: "Abner! No! No! Oh, God. Oh, God. Abner!" and he rose, whirled, and saw the altered light through the door where a candle stub now burned in a bottle neck on the table and his father, still in the hat and coat, at once formal and burlesque as though dressed carefully for some shabby and ceremonial violence, emptying the reservoir of the lamp back into the five-gallon kerosene can from which it had been filled, while the mother tugged at his arm until he shifted the lamp to the other hand and flung her back, not savagely or viciously, just hard, into the wall, her hands flung out against the wall for balance, her mouth open and in her face the same quality of hopeless despair as had been in her voice. Then his father saw him standing in the door.

85   "Go to the barn and get that can of oil we were oiling the wagon with," he said. The boy did not move. Then he could speak.

"What . . ." he cried. "What are you . . ."

"Go get that oil," his father said. "Go."

Then he was moving, running, outside the house, toward the stable: this the old habit, the old blood which he had not been permitted to choose for himself, which had been bequeathed him willy nilly and which had run for so long (and who knew where, battening on what of outrage and savagery and lust) before it came to him. *I could keep on,* he thought. *I could run on and on and never look back, never need to see his face again. Only I can't. I can't,* the rusted can in his hand now, the liquid sploshing in it as he ran back to the house and into it, into the sound of his mother's weeping in the next room, and handed the can to his father.

"Ain't you going to even send a nigger?" he cried. "At least you sent a nigger before!"

90   This time his father didn't strike him. The hand came even faster than the blow had, the same hand which had set the can on the table with almost excruciating care flashing from the can to ward him too quick for him to follow it, gripping him by the back of his shirt and on to tiptoe before he had seen it quit the can, the face stooping at him in breathless and frozen ferocity, the cold, dead voice speaking over him to the older brother who leaned against the table, chewing with that steady, curious, sidewise motion of cows:

"Empty the can into the big one and go on. I'll catch up with you."

"Better tie him up to the bedpost," the brother said.

"Do like I told you," the father said. Then the boy was moving, his bunched shirt and the hard, bony hand between his shoulderblades, his toes just touching the floor, across the room and into the other one, past the sisters sitting with spread heavy thighs in the two chairs over the cold hearth, and to where his mother and aunt sat side by side on the bed, the aunt's arms about his mother's shoulders.

"Hold him," the father said. The aunt made a startled movement. "Not you," the father said. "Lennie. Take hold of him. I want to see you do it." His mother took him by the wrist. "You'll hold him better than that. If he gets loose don't you know what he is going to do? He will go up yonder." He jerked his head toward the road. "Maybe I'd better tie him."

95   "I'll hold him," his mother whispered.

"See you do then." Then his father was gone, the stiff foot heavy and mea- sured upon the boards, ceasing at last.

Then he began to struggle. His mother caught him in both arms, he jerking and wrenching at them. He would be stronger in the end, he knew that. But he had no time to wait for it. "Lemme go!" he cried. "I don't want to have to hit you!"

"Let him go!" the aunt said. "If he don't go, before God, I am going up there myself!"

"Don't you see I can't?" his mother cried. "Sarty! Sarty! No! No! Help me, Lizzie!"

100   Then he was free. His aunt grasped at him but it was too late. He whirled, running, his mother stumbled forward on to her knees behind him, crying to the nearer sister: "Catch him, Net! Catch him!" But that was too late too, the sister (the sisters were twins, born at the same time, yet either of them now gave the impression of being, encompassing as much living meat and volume and weight as any other two of the family) not yet having begun to rise from the chair, her head, face, alone merely turned, presenting to him in the flying instant an aston- ishing expanse of young female features untroubled by any surprise even, wear- ing only an expression of bovine interest. Then he was out of the room, out of the house, in the mild dust of the starlit road and the heavy rifeness of honey- suckle, the pale ribbon unspooling with terrific slowness under his running feet, reaching the gate at last and turning in, running, his heart and lungs drumming, on up the drive toward the lighted house, the lighted door. He did not knock, he burst in, sobbing for breath, incapable for the moment of speech; he saw the as- tonished face of the Negro in the linen jacket without knowing when the Negro had appeared.

"De Spain!" he cried, panted. "Where's . . ." then he saw the white man too emerging from a white door down the hall. "Barn!" he cried. "Barn!"

"What?" the white man said. "Barn?"

"Yes!" the boy cried. "Barn!"

105   "Catch him!" the white man shouted.

But it was too late this time too. The Negro grasped his shirt, but the entire sleeve, rotten with washing, carried away, and he was out that door too and in the drive again, and had actually never ceased to run even while he was scream- ing into the white man's face.

Behind him the white man was shouting, "My horse! Fetch my horse!" and he thought for an instant of cutting across the park and climbing the fence into the road, but he did not know the park nor how high the vine-massed fence might be and he dared not risk it. So he ran on down the drive, blood and breath roaring; presently he was in the road again though he could not see it. He could not hear either: the galloping mare was almost upon him before he heard her, and even then he held his course, as if the very urgency of his wild grief and need must in a moment more find him wings, waiting until the ultimate instant to hurl himself aside and into the weed-choked roadside ditch as the horse thundered past and on, for an instant in furious silhouette against the stars, the tranquil early summer night sky which, even before the shape of the horse and rider vanished, stained abruptly and violently upward: a long, swirling roar incredible and soundless, blotting the stars, and he springing up and into the road again, running again, knowing it was too late yet still running even after he heard the shot and, an instant later, two shots, pausing now without knowing he had ceased to run, crying "Pap! Pap!", running again before he knew he had begun to run, stumbling, tripping over something and scrabbling up again without ceasing to run, looking backward over his shoulder at the glares as he got up, running on among the invisible trees, panting, sobbing, "Father! Father!"

At midnight he was sitting on the crest of a hill. He did not know it was midnight and he did not know how far he had come. But there was no glare behind him now and he sat now, his back toward what he had called home for four days anyhow, his face toward the dark woods which he would enter when breath was strong again, small, shaking steadily in the chill darkness, hugging himself into the remainder of his thin, rotten shirt, the grief and despair now no longer terror and fear but just grief and despair. *Father. My father,* he thought. "He was brave!" He cried suddenly, aloud but not loud, no more than a whisper: "He was! He was in the war! He was in Colonel Sartoris' cav'ry!" not knowing that his father had gone to that war a private in the fine old European sense, wearing no uniform, admitting the authority of and giving fidelity to no man or army or flag, going to war as Malbrouck himself did: for booty—it meant nothing and less than nothing to him if it were enemy booty or his own.

The slow constellations wheeled on. It would be dawn and then sun-up after a while and he would be hungry. But that would be to-morrow and now he was only cold, and walking would cure that. His breathing was easier now and he decided to get up and go on, and then he found that he had been asleep because he knew it was almost dawn, the night almost over. He could tell that from the whippoorwills. They were everywhere now among the dark trees below him, constant and inflectioned and ceaseless, so that, as the instant for giving over to the day birds drew nearer and nearer, there was no interval at all between them. He got up. He was a little stiff, but walking would cure that too as it would the cold, and soon there would be the sun. He went on down the hill, toward the dark woods within which the liquid silver voices of the birds called unceasing—the rapid and urgent beating of the urgent and quiring heart of the late spring night. He did not look back.

[1939]

Topics for Critical Thinking and Writing

1. Discuss "point of view" in this story. Identify some passages in the text where we are made aware of the narrator's or a character's point of view.
2. Is Faulkner on Major de Spain's side, or Abner Snopes's, or both, or neither?
3. By the end of the story, how has Sarty changed? Does Faulkner show us this process of change in a convincing way? Do we believe it?
4. While you were reading "Barn Burning," did you feel at any point that you needed "background information" in order to understand and appreciate it? Or do you think that the story itself contains everything you need to know?

5. Many people claim that Faulkner is one of the greatest American writers. Do you think that this story supports such a view? Is this a great story, or a good story?

JAMES ALAN MCPHERSON

Born in a black district in Savannah, Georgia, in 1943, James Alan McPherson attended segregated schools, and then he attended a historically black college in Atlanta, Morris Brown College, from which he received a B.A. in 1965. McPherson next went to Harvard Law School, where he received his law degree in 1968. His first book was a collection of stories, Hue and Cry *(1969), which was followed by* Elbow Room *(1978), a book that was awarded the Pulitzer Prize in fiction. he has taught creative writing and African American literature at the University of Iowa, the University of Santa Cruz, Morgan State University, and the University of Virginia. He has edited special issues of the literary journals* Iowa Review *and* Ploughshares *and has published short stories, book reviews, and essays in other magazines and journals.*

In "On Becoming an American Writer," in the December 1978 issue of The Atlantic, *McPherson describes his goals as a writer and an American in these terms: "I believe that if one can experience diversity, touch a variety of its people, laugh at its craziness, distill wisdom from its tragedies, and attempt to synthesize all this inside oneself without going crazy, one will have earned the right to call oneself a citizen of the United States."*

An Act of Prostitution

When he saw the woman the lawyer put down his pencil and legal pad and took out his pipe.

"Well," he said. "How do you want to play it?"

"I wanna get outta here," the whore said. "Just get me outta here."

"Now get some sense," said the lawyer, puffing on the pipe to draw in the flame from the long wooden match he had taken from his vest pocket. "You ain't got a snowball's chance in hell."

5   "I just want out," she said.

"You'll catch hell in there," he said, pointing with the stem of his pipe to the door which separated them from the main courtroom. "Why don't you just get some sense and take a few days on the city."

"I can't go up there again," she said. "Those dike matrons in Parkville hate my guts because I'm wise to them. They told me last time they'd really give it to me if I came back. I can't do no time up there again."

"Listen," said the lawyer, pointing the stem of his pipe at her this time, "you ain't got a choice. Either you cop a plea or I don't take the case."

"*You* listen, you two-bit Jew shyster." The whore raised her voice, pointing her very chubby finger at the lawyer. "*You* ain't got no choice. The judge told you to be my lawyer and you got to do it. I ain't no dummy, you know that?"

10   "Yeah," said the lawyer. "You're a real smarty. That's why you're out on the streets in all that snow and ice. You're a real smarty all right."

"You chickenshit," she said. "I don't want you on my case anyway, but I ain't got no choice. If you was any good, you wouldn't be working the sweatboxes in this court. I ain't no dummy."

"You're a real smarty," said the lawyer. He looked her up and down: a huge woman, pathetically blonde, big-boned and absurd in a skirt sloppily crafted to be mini. Her knees were ruddy and the flesh below them was thick and white and flabby. There was no indication of age about her. Like most whores, she looked at the same time young but then old, possibly as old as her profession. Sometimes they were very old but seemed to have stopped aging at a certain point so that ranking them chronologically, as the lawyer was trying to do, came hard. He put his pipe on the table, on top of the police affidavit, and stared at her. She sat across the room, near the door in a straight chair, her flesh oozing over its sides. He watched her pull her miniskirt down over the upper part of her thigh, modestly, but with the same hard, cold look she had when she came in the room. "You're a real smarty," he commented, drawing on his pipe and exhaling the smoke into the room.

The fat woman in her miniskirt still glared at him. "Screw you, Yid!" she said through her teeth. "Screw your fat mama and your chubby sister with hair under her arms. Screw your brother and your father and I hope they should go crazy playing with themselves in pay toilets."

The lawyer was about to reply when the door to the consultation room opened and another man came into the small place. "Hell, Jimmy," he said to the lawyer, pretending to ignore the woman, "I got a problem here."

15   "Yeah?" said Jimmy.

The other man walked over to the brown desk, leaned closer to Jimmy so that the woman could not hear and lowered his voice. "I got this kid," he said. "A nice I-talian boy that grabbed this Cadillac outta a parking lot. Now he only done it twice before and I think the Judge might go easy if he got in a good mood before the kid goes on, this being Monday morning and all."

"So?" said Jimmy.

"So I was thinking," the other lawyer said, again lowering his voice and leaning much closer and making a sly motion with his head to indicate the whore on the chair across the room. "So I was thinking. The Judge knows Philomena over there. She's here almost every month and she's always good for a laugh. So I was thinking, this being Monday morning and all and with a cage-load of nigger drunks out there, why not put her on first, give the old man a good laugh and then put my I-talian boy on. I know he'd get a better deal that way."

"What's in it for me?" said Jimmy, rapping the ashes from his pipe into an ashtray.

20   "Look, I done *you* favors before. Remember that Chinaman? Remember the tip I gave you?"

Jimmy considered while he stuffed tobacco from a can into his pipe. He lit the pipe with several matches from his vest pocket and considered some more. "I don't mind, Ralph," he said. "But if she goes first the Judge'll get a good laugh and then he'll throw the book at her."

"*What the hell, Jimmy?*" said Ralph. He glanced over at the whore who was eying them hatefully. "Look, buddy," he went on, "you know who that is? Fatso Philomena Brown. She's up here almost every month. Old Bloom knows her. I tell you, she's good for a laugh. That's all. Besides, she married to a nigger anyway."

"Well," said Jimmy. "So far she ain't done herself much good with me. She's a real smarty. She thinks I'm a Jew."

"There go you," said Ralph. "Come on, Jimmy. I ain't got much time before the Clerk calls my kid up. What you say?"

25 Jimmy looked over at his client, the many pounds of her rolled in great logs of meat under her knees and around her belly. She was still sneering. "O.K." He turned his head back to Ralph. "O.K., I'll do it."

"Now look," said Ralph, "this is how we'll do. When they call me up I'll tell the Clerk I need more time with my kid for consultation. And since you follow me on the docket you'll get on pretty soon, at least before I will. Then after every-body's had a good laugh, I'll bring my I-talian on."

"Isn't *she* Italian?" asked Jimmy, indicating the whore with a slight movement of his pipe.

"Yeah. But she's married to a nigger."

"O.K.," said Jimmy, "we'll do it."

30 "What's that?" said the whore, who had been trying to listen all this time. "What are you two kikes whispering about anyway? What the hell's going on?"

"Shut up," said Jimmy, the stem of his pipe clamped far back in his mouth so that he could not say it as loud as he wanted. Ralph winked at him and left the room. "Now listen," he said to Philomena Brown, getting up from his desk and walking over to where she still sat against the wall. "If you got a story, you better tell me quick because we're going out there soon and I want you to know I ain't telling no lies for you."

"I don't want you on my case anyway, kike," said Philomena Brown.

"It ain't what *you* want. It's what the old man out there says you gotta do. Now if you got a story let's have it *now.*"

"I'm a file clerk. I was just looking for work."

35 "Like *hell!* Don't give *me* that shit. When was the last time you had your shots?"

"I ain't never had none," said Mrs. Brown.

Now they could hear the Clerk, beyond the door, calling the Italian boy into court. They would have to go out in a few minutes. "Forget the story," he told her. "Just pull your dress down some and wipe some of that shit off your eyes. You look like hell."

"I don't want you on the case, Moses," said Mrs. Brown.

"Well you got me," said Jimmy. "You got me whether you want me or not." Jimmy paused, put his pipe in his coat pocket, and then said: "And my name is *Mr. Mulligan!*"

40 The woman did not say anything more. She settled her weight in the chair and make it creak.

"Now let's get in there," said Jimmy.

The Judge was in his Monday morning mood. He was very ready to be angry at almost anyone. He glared at the Court Clerk as the bald, seemingly consumptive man called out the names of six defendants who had defaulted. He glared at the group of drunks and addicts who huddled against the steel net of the prisoners' cage, gazing toward the open courtroom as if expecting mercy from the rows of concerned parties and spectators who sat in the hot place. Judge Bloom looked as though he wanted very badly to spit. There would be no mercy this Monday morning and the prisoners all knew it.

"*Willie Smith!* Willie Smith! Come into Court!" the Clerk barked.

Willie Smith slowly shuffled out of the prisoners' cage and up to the dirty stone wall, which kept all but his head and neck and shoulders concealed from the people in the musty courtroom.

45   From the bench the Judge looked down at the hungover Smith.

"You know, I ain't never seen him sitting down in that chair," Jimmy said to one of the old men who came to court to see the daily procession, filling up the second row of benches, directly behind those reserved for court-appointed lawyers. There were at least twelve of these old men, looking almost semi-professional in faded gray or blue or black suits with shiny knees and elbows. They liked to come and watch the fun. "Watch old Bloom give it to this nigger," the same old man leaned over and said into Jimmy Mulligan's ear. Jimmy nodded without looking back at him. And after a few seconds he wiped his ear with his hand, also without looking back.

The Clerk read the charges: Drunkenness, Loitering, Disorderly Conduct.

"You want a lawyer, Willie?" the Judge asked him. Judge Bloom was now walking back and forth behind his bench, his arms gravely folded behind his back, his belly very close to pregnancy beneath his black robe. "The Supreme Court says I have to give you a lawyer. You want one?"

"No sir," the hung-over Smith said, very obsequiously.

50   "Well, what's your trouble?"

"Nothing."

"You haven't missed a Monday here in months."

"Yes sir."

"All that money you spend on booze, how do you take care of your family?"

55   Smith moved his head and shoulders behind the wall in a gesture that might have been a shuffle.

"When was the last time you gave something to your wife?"

"Last Friday."

"You're a liar. Your wife's been on the City for years."

"I help," said Smith, quickly.

60   "You help, all right. You help her raise her belly and her income every year."

The old men in the second row snickered and the Judge eyed them in a threatening way. They began to stifle their chuckles. Willie Smith smiled.

"If she has one more kid she'll be making more than me," the Judge observed. But he was not saying it to Smith. He was looking at the old men.

Then he looked down at the now bashful, smiling Willie Smith. "You want some time to sleep it off or you want to pay?"

"I'll take the time."

65   "How much you want, Willie?"

"I don't care."

"You want to be out for the weekend, I guess."

Smith smiled again.

"Give him five days," the Judge said to the Clerk. The Clerk wrote in his papers and then said in a hurried voice: "Defendant Willie Smith, you have been found guilty by this court of being drunk in a public place, of loitering while in this condition, and of disorderly conduct. This court sentences you to five days in the House of Correction at Bridgeview and one month's suspended sentence. You have, however, the right to appeal in which case the suspended sentence will not be allowed and the sentence will then be thirty-five days in the House of Correction."

70   "You want to appeal, Willie?"

"Naw sir."

"See you next week," said the Judge.

"Thank you," said Willie Smith.

A black fellow in a very neatly pressed Army uniform came on next. He stood immaculate and proud and clean-shaven with his cap tucked under his left arm while the charges were read. The prosecutor was a hard-faced black police detective, tieless; very long-haired in a short-sleeved white shirt with wet armpits. The detective was tough but very nervous. He looked at his notes while the Clerk read the charges. The Judge, bald and wrinkled and drooping in the face, still paced behind his bench, his nose twitching from time to time, his arms locked behind the back. The soldier was charged with assault and battery with a dangerous weapon on a police officer; he remained standing erect and silent, looking off into the space behind the Judge until his lawyer, a plump, greasy black man in his late fifties, had heard the charge and motioned for him to sit. Then he placed himself beside his lawyer and put his cap squarely in front of him on the table.

75   The big-bellied black detective managed to get the police officer's name, rank and duties from him, occasionally glancing over at the table where the defendant and his lawyer sat, both hard-faced and cold. He shuffled through his notes, paused, and looked up at the Judge, and then said to the white officer: "Now, Officer Bergin, would you tell the Court in your own words what happened?"

The white policeman put his hands together in a prayer-like gesture on the stand. He looked at the defendant whose face was set and whose eyes were fixed on the officer's hands. "We was on duty on the night of July twenty-seventh driving around the Lafayette Street area when we got a call to proceed to the Lafayette Street subway station because there was a crowd gathering there and they thought it might be a riot. We proceeded there, Officer Biglow and me, and when we got there sure enough there was a crowd of colored people running up and down the street and making noise and carrying on. We didn't pull our guns because they been telling us all summer not to do that. We got out of the car and proceeded to join the other officers there in forming a line so's to disperse the crowd. Then we spotted that fellow in the crowd."

"Who do you mean?"

"That fellow over there." Officer Bergin pointed to the defendant at the table. "That soldier, Irving Williams."

"Go on," said the black detective, not turning to look at the defendant.

80   "Well, He had on this red costume and a cape, and he was wearing this big red turban. He was also carrying a big black shield right outta Tarzan and he had that big long cane waving it around in the air."

"Where is that cane now?"

"We took it off him later. That's it over there."

The black detective moved over to his own table and picked up a long brown leather cane. He pressed a small button beneath its handle and then drew out from the interior of the cane a thin, silver-white rapier, three feet long.

"Is this the same cane?"

85   "Yes sir," the white officer said.

"Go on, Officer."

"Well, he was waving it around in the air and he had a whole lot of these colored people behind him and it looked to me that he was gonna charge the police line. So me and Tommy left the line and went in to grab him before he could start something big. That crowd was getting mean. They looked like they was gonna try something big pretty soon."

"Never mind," said the Judge. He had stopped walking now and stood at the edge of his elevated platform, just over the shoulder of the officer in the witness box. "Never mind what you thought, just get on with it."

"Yes sir." The officer pressed his hands together much tighter. "Well, Tommy and me, we tried to grab him and he swung the cane at me. Caught me right in the face here." He pointed his finger to a large red and black mark under his left eye. "So then we hadda use force to subdue him."

90   "What did you do, Officer?" the black detective asked.

"We hadda use the sticks. I hit him over the head once or twice, but not hard. I don't remember. Then Tommy grabbed his arms and we hustled him over to the car before these other colored people with him tried to grab us."

"Did he resist arrest?"

"Yeah. He kicked and fought us and called us lewd and lascivious names. We hadda handcuff him in the car. Then we took him down to the station and booked him for assault and battery."

"Your witness," said the black detective without turning around to face the other lawyer. He sat down at his own table and wiped his forehead and hands with a crumpled white handkerchief. He still looked very nervous but not as tough.

95   "May it please the Court," the defendant's black lawyer said slowly, standing and facing the pacing Judge. "I move . . ." And then he stopped because he saw that the Judge's small eyes were looking over his head, toward the back of the courtroom. The lawyer turned around and looked, and saw that everyone else in the room had also turned their heads to the back of the room. Standing against the back walls and along the left side of the room were twenty-five or so stern-faced, cold-eyed black men, all in African dashikies, all wearing brightly colored hats, and all staring at the Judge and the black detective. Philomena Brown and Jimmy Mulligan, sitting on the first bench, turned to look too, and the whore smiled but the lawyer said, "Oh hell," aloud. The men, all big, all bearded and tight-lipped, now locked hands and formed a solid wall of flesh around almost three-quarters of the courtroom. The Judge looked at the defendant and saw that he was smiling. Then he looked at the defendant's lawyer, who still stood before the Judge's bench, his head down, his shoulders pulled up towards his head. The Judge began to pace again. The courtroom was very quiet. The old men filling the second rows on both sides of the room leaned forward and exchanged glances with each other up and down the row. "Oh hell," Jimmy Mulligan said again.

Then the Judge stopped walking. "Get on with it," he told the defendant's lawyer. "There's justice to be done here."

The lawyer, whose face was now very greasy and wet, looked up at the officer, still standing in the witness box, but with one hand now at his right side, next to his gun.

"Officer Bergin," said the black lawyer. "I'm not clear about something. Did the defendant strike you *before* you asked him for the cane or *after* you attempted to take it from him?"

"Before. It was before. Yes sir."

100   "You *did* ask him for the cane, then?"

"Yes sir. I asked him to turn it over."

"And what did he do?"

"He hit me."

"But if he hit you before you asked for the cane, then it must be true that you asked him for the cane *after* he had hit you. Is that right?"

105   "Yes sir."

"In other words, after he had struck you in the face you were still polite enough to keep your hands off him and ask for the weapon."

"Yes sir. That's what I did."

"In other words, he hit you twice. Once, *before* you requested the cane and once *after* you requested it."

The officer paused. "No sir," he said quickly. "He only hit me once."

110 "And when was that again?"

"I thought it was before I asked for the cane but I don't know now."

"But you did ask for the cane before he hit you?"

"Yeah." The officer's hands were in prayer again.

"Now, Officer Bergin, did he hit you *because* you asked for the cane or did he hit you in the process of giving it to you?"

115 "He just hauled off and hit me with it."

"He made no effort to hand it over?"

"No, no sir. He hit me."

"In other words, he struck you the moment you got close enough for him to swing. He did not hit you as you were taking the cane from him?"

The officer paused again. Then he said: "No sir." He touched his face again, then put his right hand down to the area near his gun again. "I asked him for the cane and he hauled off and hit me in the face."

120 "Officer, are you telling this court that you did not get hit until you tried to take the cane away from this soldier, this Vietnam veteran, or that he saw you coming and immediately began to swing the cane?"

"He swung on me."

"Officer Bergin, did he swing on you, or did the cane accidentally hit you while you were trying to take it from him?"

"All I know is that he *hit me*." The officer was sweating now.

"Then you don't know just when he hit you, before or after you tried to take the cane from him, do you?"

125 The black detective got up and said in a very soft voice: "I object."

The black lawyer for the defendant looked over at him contemptuously. The black detective dropped his eyes and tightened his belt, and sat down again.

"That's all right," the oily lawyer said. Then he looked at the officer again. "One other thing," he said. "Was the knife still inside the cane or drawn when he hit you?"

"We didn't know about the knife till later at the station."

"Do you think that a blow from the cane by itself could kill you?"

130 "Object!" said the detective. But again his voice was low.

"*Jivetime Uncle Tom motherfucker!*" someone said from the back of the room. "Shave that Afro off your head!"

The Judge's eyes moved quickly over the men in the rear, surveying their faces and catching what was in all their eyes. But he did not say anything.

"The prosecution rests," the black detective said. He sounded very tired.

"The defense calls the defendant, Irving Williams," said the black lawyer.

135 Williams took the stand and waited, head high, eyes cool, mouth tight, militarily, for the Clerk to swear him in. He looked always toward the back of the room.

"Now Mr. Williams," his lawyer began, "tell this court in your own words the events of the night of July twenty-seventh of this year."

"I had been to a costume party." Williams voice was slow and deliberate and resonant. The entire courtroom was tense and quiet. The old men stared, stiff and erect, at Irving Williams from their second-row benches. Philomena Brown settled her flesh down next to her lawyer, who tried to edge away from touching her fat arm with his own. The tight-lipped Judge Bloom had reassumed the pacing behind his bench.

"I was on leave from the base," Williams went on, "and I was coming from the party when I saw this group of kids throwing rocks. Being in the military and being just out of Vietnam, I tried to stop them. One of the kids had that cane and I took it from him. The shield belongs to me. I got it in Taiwan last year on R and R. I was trying to break up the crowd with my shield when his honkie cop begins to beat me over the head with his club. Police brutality. I tried to tell . . ."

"That's enough," the Judge said. "That's all I want to hear." He eyed the black men in the back of the room. "This case isn't for my court. Take it upstairs."

140   "If Your Honor pleases," the black lawyer began.

"I don't," said the Judge. "I've heard enough. Mr. Clerk, make out the papers. Send it upstairs to Cabot."

"This court has jurisdiction to hear this case," the lawyer said. He was very close to being angry. "This man is in the service. He has to ship out in a few weeks. We want a hearing today."

"Not in my court you don't get it. Upstairs, and that's *it!*"

Now the blacks in the back of the room began to berate the detective. "Jivetime cat! Handkerchief-head flunky! Uncle Tom motherfucker!" they called. "We'll get *you,* baby!"

145   "Get them out of here," the Judge told the policeman named Bergin. "Get them the hell out!" Bergin did not move. "Get them the hell out!"

At that moment Irving Williams, with his lawyer behind him, walked out of the courtroom. And the twenty-five bearded black men followed them. The black detective remained sitting at the counsel table until the Clerk asked him to make way for counsel on the next case. The detective got up slowly, gathered his few papers, tightened his belt again and moved over, his head held down, to a seat on the right side of the courtroom.

"Philomena Brown!" the Clerk called. "Philomena Brown! Come into Court!"

The fat whore got up from beside Jimmy Mulligan and walked heavily over to the counsel table and lowered herself into one of the chairs. Her lawyer was talking to Ralph, the Italian boy's counsel.

"Do a good job, Jimmy, please," Ralph said. "Old Bloom is gonna be awful mean now."

150   "Yeah," said Jimmy. "I got to really work on him."

One of the old men on the second row leaned over the back of the bench and said to Jimmy: "Ain't that the one that's married to a nigger?"

"That's her," said Jimmy.

"She's gonna catch hell. Make sure they give her hell."

"Yeah," said Jimmy. "I don't see how I'm gonna be able to try this with a straight face."

155   "Do a good job for me, please, Jimmy," said Ralph. "The kid's name is Angelico. Ain't that a beautiful name? He ain't a bad kid."

"Don't you worry, I'll do it." Then Jimmy moved over to the table next to his client.

The defendant and the arresting officer were sworn in. The arresting officer acted for the state as prosecutor and its only witness. He had to refer to his notes from time to time while the Judge paced behind his bench, his head down, ponderous and impatient. Then Philomena Brown got in the witness box and rested her great weight against its sides. She glared at the Judge, at the Clerk, at the officer in the box on the other side, at Jimmy Mulligan, at the old men smiling up and down the second row, at at everyone in the courtroom. Then she rested her eyes on the officer.

"Well," the officer read from his notes. "It was around one-thirty A.M. on the night of July twenty-eight. I was working the night duty around the combat zone. I come across the defendant there soliciting cars. I had seen the defendant there soliciting cars on previous occasions in the same vicinity. I had then on previous occasions warned the defendant there about such activities. But she kept on doing it. On that night I came across the defendant soliciting a car full of colored gentlemen. She was standing on the curb with her arm leaning up against the door of the car and talking with these two colored gentlemen. As I came up they drove off. I then arrested her, after informing her of her rights, for being a common streetwalker and a public nuisance. And that's all I got to say."

Counsel for the whore waived cross-examination of the officer and proceeded to examine her.

160   "What's your name?"

"Mrs. Philomena Brown."

"Speak louder so the Court can hear you, Mrs. Brown."

She narrowed her eyes at the lawyer.

"What is your religion, Mrs. Brown?"

165   "I am a Roman Catholic. Roman Catholic born."

"Are you presently married?"

"Yeah."

"What is your husband's name?"

"Rudolph Leroy Brown, Jr."

170   The old men in the second row were beginning to snicker and the Judge lowered his eyes to them. Jimmy Mulligan smiled.

"Does your husband support you?"

"Yeah. We get along all right."

"Do *you* work, Mrs. Brown?"

175   "Yeah. That's how I make my living."

"What do you do for a living?"

"I'm a file clerk."

"Are you working now?"

"No. I lost my job last month on account of a bad leg I got. I couldn't move outta bed."

The men in the second row were grinning and others in the audience joined them in muffled guffaws and snickerings.

180   "What were you doing on Beaver Avenue on the night of July twenty-eighth?"

"I was looking for a job."

Now the entire court was laughing and the Judge glared out at them from behind his bench as he paced, his arms clasped behind his back.

"Will you please tell this court, Mrs. Brown, how you intended to find a job at that hour?"

"These two guys in a car told me they knew where I could find some work."

185   "As a file clerk?"

"Yeah. What the hell else do you think?"

There was here a roar of laughter from the court, and when the Judge visibly twitched the corners of his usually severe mouth, Philomena Brown saw it and began to laugh too.

"Order! Order!" the Clerk shouted above the roar. But he was laughing.

Jimmy Mulligan bit his lip. "Now, Mrs. Brown, I want you to tell me the truth. Have you ever been arrested before for prostitution?"

190   "Hell no!" she fired back. "They had me here a coupla times but it was all a fluke. They never got nothing on me. I was framed, right from the start."

"How old are you, Mrs. Brown?"

"Nineteen."

Now the Judge stopped pacing and stood next to his chair. His face was dubious: very close and very far away from smiling. The old men in the second row saw this and stopped laughing, awaiting a cue from him.

"That's enough of this," said the Judge. "I know you. You've been up here seven times already this year and it's still summer. I'm going to throw the book at you." He moved over to the left end of the platform and leaned down to where a husky, muscular woman Probation Officer was standing. She had very short hair and looked grim. She had not laughed with the others. "Let me see her record," said the Judge. The manly Probation Officer handed it up to him and then they talked together in whispers for a few minutes.

195   "All right, *Mrs. Brown*," said the Judge, moving over to the right side of the platform near the defendant's box and pointing his finger at her. "You're still on probation from the last time you were up here. I'm tired of this."

"I don't wanna go back up there, Your Honor," the whore said. "They hate me up there."

"You're going back. That's it! You got six months on the State. Maybe while you're there you can learn how to be a file clerk so you can look for work during the day."

Now everyone laughed again.

"Plus you get a one-year suspended sentence on probation."

200   The woman hung her head with the gravity of this punishment.

"Maybe you can even learn a *good* profession while you're up there. Who knows? Maybe you could be a ballerina dancer."

The courtroom roared with laughter. The Judge could not control himself now.

"And another thing," he said. "When you get out, keep off the streets. You're obstructing traffic."

Such was the spontaneity of laughter from the entire courtroom after the remark that the lawyer Jimmy Mulligan had to wipe the tears from his eyes with his finger and the short-haired Probation Officer smiled, and even Philomena Brown had to laugh at this, her final moment of glory. The Judge's teeth showed through his own broad grin, and Ralph, sitting beside his Italian, a very pretty boy with clean, blue eyes, patted him on the back enthusiastically between uncontrollable bursts of laughter.

205   For five minutes after the smiling Probation Officer led the fat whore in a miniskirt out of the courtroom, there was the sound of muffled laughter and occasional sniffles and movements in the seats. Then they settled down again and the Judge resumed his pacings and the Court Clerk, very slyly wiping his eyes with his sleeve, said in a very loud voice: "Angelico Carbone! Angelico Carbone! Come into Court!"

[1969]

Topics for Critical Thinking and Writing

1. Now that you have read the story, explain the meaning and significance of the title.

2. When you began reading the story, did you find the language (the racial and ethnic epithets, for example) offensive? Why is McPherson using language that will offend some readers?

3. What is the function of the scene involving Irving Williams? Would the story be more effective if it focused entirely on Philomena Brown?

4. Is McPherson making a point about the legal system? Explain, and refer to specific passages to support your view.

5. Did you enjoy this story? What did you learn from it?

Case Study: Writing about Ralph Ellison's "Battle Royal"

In this case study, we give a short story by the African American novelist and critic Ralph Ellison, "Battle Royal," first published in 1947 and later included as Chapter One in the novel *Invisible Man* (1952). We also give the following related material:

1. An influential, and controversial, speech delivered in 1895 by the African American educator Booker T. Washington (1856–1915), founder in 1881 and first president of Tuskegee Normal and Industrial Institute. The speech was reprinted in Washington's book, *Up from Slavery* (1901), which was among the most widely read books of the period.

2. Excerpts from *The Souls of Black Folk* (1903), by the African American historian, cultural critic, and man of letters W. E. B. Du Bois (1868–1963), which includes his critique of Washington's policies.

3. A photograph of the statue of Booker T. Washington at Tuskegee, to which Ellison's narrator refers.

4. A commentary on segregation in the South, from *An American Dilemma* (1944), a landmark study of race relations in the United States, written by the Swedish economist and sociologist Gunnar Myrdal (1898–1987).

5. An explanation by Ellison, from an interview published in 1955, of his use of folk material and myth in his fiction.

6. Ellison's reflections (1964) on his youth in Oklahoma and educational experiences at Tuskegee, where he was enrolled as a student in the 1930s.

RALPH ELLISON

Ralph Ellison (1914–1994) was born in Oklahoma City. His father died when Ellison was 3, and his mother supported herself and her child by working as a domestic. A trumpeter since boyhood, after graduating from high school Ellison went to study music at Tuskegee Institute, a black college in Alabama founded by Booker T. Washington. In 1936 he dropped out of Tuskegee and went to Harlem to study music composition and the visual arts; there he met Langston Hughes and Richard Wright, who encouraged him to turn to fiction. Ellison published stories and essays, and in 1942 became the managing editor of Negro Quarterly. *During*

the Second World War he served in the Merchant Marine. After the war he re-
turned to writing and later taught in universities.

"Battle Royal" was first published in 1947 and slightly revised (a transitional
paragraph was added at the end of the story) for the opening chapter of Ellison's
novel, Invisible Man *(1952), a book cited by Book-Week as "the most significant*
work of fiction written by an American" in the years between 1945 and 1965. In
addition to publishing stories and one novel, Ellison published critical essays,
which are brought together in The Collected Essays of Ralph Ellison *(1995).*

Battle Royal

It goes a long way back, some twenty years. All my life I had been looking for
something, and everywhere I turned someone tried to tell me what it was. I accepted their answers too, though they were often in contradiction and even self-
contradictory. I was naïve. I was looking for myself and asking everyone except
myself questions which I, and only I, could answer. It took me a long time and
much painful boomeranging of my expectations to achieve a realization everyone
else appears to have been born with: That I am nobody but myself. But first I had
to discover that I am an invisible man!

And yet I am no freak of nature, nor of history. I was in the cards, other
things having been equal (or unequal) eighty-five years ago. I am not ashamed of
my grandparents for having been slaves. I am only ashamed of myself for having
at one time been ashamed. About eighty-five years ago they were told that they
were free, united with others of our country in everything pertaining to the common good, and, in everything social, separate like the fingers of the hand. And
they believed it. They exulted in it. They stayed in their place, worked hard, and
brought up my father to do the same. But my grandfather is the one. He was an
odd old guy, my grandfather, and I am told I take after him. It was he who caused
the trouble. On his deathbed he called my father to him and said, "Son, after I'm
gone I want you to keep up the good fight. I never told you, but our life is a war
and I have been a traitor all my born days, a spy in the enemy's country ever
since I give up my gun back in the Reconstruction. Live with your head in the
lion's mouth. I want you to overcome 'em with yeses, undermine 'em with grins,
agree 'em to death and destruction, let 'em swoller you till they vomit or bust
wide open." They thought the old man had gone out of his mind. He had been
the meekest of men. The younger children were rushed from the room, the
shades drawn and the flame of the lamp turned so low that it sputtered on the
wick like the old man's breathing. "Learn it to the younguns," he whispered
fiercely; then he died.

But my folks were more alarmed over his last words than over his dying. It
was as though he had not died at all, his words caused so much anxiety. I was
warned emphatically to forget what he had said and, indeed, this is the first time it
has been mentioned outside the family circle. It has a tremendous effect upon me,
however. I could never be sure of what he meant. Grandfather had been a quiet
old man who never made any trouble, yet on his deathbed he had called himself
a traitor and a spy, and he had spoken of his meekness as a dangerous activity. It
became a constant puzzle which lay unanswered in the back of my mind. And
whenever things went well for me I remembered my grandfather and felt guilty
and uncomfortable. It was as though I was carrying out his advice in spite of myself. And to make it worse, everyone loved me for it. I was praised by the most
lily-white men of the town. I was considered an example of desirable conduct—

Gordon Parks, *Ralph Ellison*.
Parks, an African American photographer with an international
reputation, has published many
books of photographs, including
Camera Portraits, where this picture appears.

just as my grandfather had been. And what puzzled me was that the old man had
defined it as *treachery*. When I was praised for my conduct I felt a guilt that in
some way I was doing something that was really against the wishes of the white
folks, that if they had understood they would have desired me to act just the opposite, that I should have been sulky and mean, and that that really would have
been what they wanted, even though they were fooled and thought they wanted
me to act as I did. It made me afraid that some day they would look upon me as
a traitor and I would be lost. Still I was more afraid to act any other way because
they didn't like that at all. The old man's words were like a curse. On my graduation day I delivered an oration in which I showed that humility was the secret, indeed, the very essence of progress. (Not that I believed this—how could I, remembering my grandfather?—I only believed that it worked.) It was a great
success. Everyone praised me and I was invited to give the speech at a gathering
of the town's leading white citizens. It was a triumph for our whole community.

It was in the main ballroom of the leading hotel. When I got there I discovered that it was on the occasion of a smoker, and I was told that since I was to be
there anyway I might as well take part in the battle royal to be fought by some of
my schoolmates as part of the entertainment. The battle royal came first.

5   All of the town's big shots were there in their tuxedoes, wolfing down the
buffet foods, drinking beer and whiskey and smoking black cigars. It was a large
room with a high ceiling. Chairs were arranged in neat rows around three sides of
a portable boxing ring. The fourth side was clear, revealing a gleaming space of
polished floor. I had some misgivings over the battle royal, by the way. Not from
a distaste for fighting, but because I didn't care too much for the other fellows

who were to take part. They were tough guys who seemed to have no grandfather's curse worrying their minds. No one could mistake their toughness. And besides, I suspected that fighting a battle royal might detract from the dignity of my speech. In those pre-invisible days I visualized myself as a potential Booker T. Washington. But the other fellows didn't care too much for me either, and there were nine of them. I felt superior to them in my way, and I didn't like the manner in which we were all crowded together into the servants' elevator. Nor did they like my being there. In fact, as the warmly lighted floors flashed past the elevator we had words over the fact that I, by taking part in the fight, had knocked one of their friends out of a night's work.

We were led out of the elevator through a rococo hall into an anteroom and told to get into our fighting togs. Each of us was issued a pair of boxing gloves and ushered out into the big mirrored hall, which we entered looking cautiously about us and whispering, lest we might accidentally be heard above the noise of the room. It was foggy with cigar smoke. And already the whiskey was taking effect. I was shocked to see some of the most important men of the town quite tipsy. They were all there—bankers, lawyers, judges, doctors, fire chiefs, teachers, merchants. Even one of the more fashionable pastors. Something we could not see was going on up front. A clarinet was vibrating sensuously and the men were standing up and moving eagerly forward. We were a small tight group, clustered together, our bare upper bodies touching and shining with anticipatory sweat; while up front the big shots were becoming increasingly excited over something we still could not see. Suddenly I heard the school superintendent, who had told me to come, yell. "Bring up the shines, gentlemen! Bring up the little shines!"

We were rushed up to the front of the ballroom, where it smelled even more strongly of tobacco and whiskey. Then we were pushed into place. I almost wet my pants. A sea of faces, some hostile, some amused, ringed around us, and in the center, facing us, stood a magnificent blonde—stark naked. There was dead silence. I felt a blast of cold air chill me. I tried to back away, but they were behind me and around me. Some of the boys stood with lowered heads, trembling. I felt a wave of irrational guilt and fear. My teeth chattered, my skin turned to goose flesh, my knees knocked. Yet I was strongly attracted and looked in spite of myself. Had the price of looking been blindness, I would have looked. The hair was yellow like that of a circus kewpie doll, the face heavily powdered and rouged, as though to from an abstract mask, the eyes hollow and smeared a cool blue, the color of a baboon's butt. I felt a desire to spit upon her as my eyes brushed slowly over her body. Her breasts were firm and round as the domes of East Indian temples, and I stood so close as to see the fine skin texture and beads of pearly perspiration glistening like dew around the pink and erected buds of her nipples. I wanted at one and the same time to run from the room, to sink through the floor, or go to her and cover her from my eyes and the eyes of the others with my body; to feel the soft thighs, to caress her and destroy her, to love her and murder her, to hide from her, and yet to stroke where below the small American flag tattooed upon her belly her thighs formed a capital V. I had a notion that of all in the room she saw only me with her impersonal eyes.

And then she began to dance, a slow sensuous movement; the smoke of a hundred cigars clinging to her like the thinnest of veils. She seemed like a fair bird-girl girdled in veils calling to me from the angry surface of some gray and threatening sea. I was transported. Then I became aware of the clarinet playing and the big shots yelling at us. Some threatened us if we looked and others if we did not. On my right I saw one boy faint. And now a man grabbed a silver pitcher from a table and stepped close as he dashed ice water upon him and stood him up and forced two of us to support him as his head hung and moans issued from his thick bluish lips. Another boy began to plead to go home. He was the largest of the group, wearing dark red fighting trunks much too small to conceal the erection which projected from him as though in answer to the insinuating low-registered moans of the clarinet. He tried to hide himself with his boxing gloves.

And all the while the blonde continued dancing, smiling faintly at the big shots who watched her with fascination, and faintly smiling at our fear. I noticed a certain merchant who followed her hungrily, his lips loose and drooling. He was a large man who wore diamond studs in a shirtfront which swelled with the ample paunch underneath, and each time the blonde swayed her undulating hips he ran his hand through the thin hair of his bald head and, with his arms upheld, his posture clumsy like that of an intoxicated panda, wound his belly in a slow and obscene grind. This creature was completely hypnotized. The music had quickened. As the dancer flung herself about with a detached expression on her face, the men began reaching out to touch her. I could see their beefy fingers sink into her soft flesh. Some of the others tried to stop them and she began to move around the floor in graceful circles, as they gave chase, slipping and sliding over the polished floor. It was mad. Chairs went crashing, drinks were spilt, as they ran laughing and howling after her. They caught her just as she reached a door, raised her from the floor, and tossed her as college boys are tossed at a hazing, and above her red, fixed-smiling lips I saw the terror and disgust in her eyes, almost like my own terror and that which I saw in some of the other boys. As I watched, they tossed her twice and her soft breasts seemed to flatten against the air and her legs flung wildly as she spun. Some of the more sober ones helped her to escape. And I started off the floor, heading for the anteroom with the rest of the boys.

10   Some were still crying and in hysteria. But as we tried to leave we were stopped and ordered to get into the ring. There was nothing to do but what we were told. All ten of us climbed under the ropes and allowed ourselves to be blindfolded with broad bands of white cloth. One of the men seemed to feel a bit sympathetic and tried to cheer us up as we stood with our backs against the ropes. Some of us tried to grin. "See that boy over there?" one of the men said. "I want you to run across at the bell and give it to him right in the belly. If you don't get him, I'm going to get you. I don't like his looks." Each of us was told the same. The blindfolds were put on. Yet even then I had been going over my speech. In my mind each word was as bright as flame. I felt the cloth pressed into place, and frowned so that it would be loosened when I relaxed.

But now I felt a sudden fit of blind terror. I was unused to darkness. It was as though I had suddenly found myself in a dark room filled with poisonous cotton-mouths. I could hear the bleary voices yelling insistently for the battle royal to begin.

"Get going in there!"

"Let me at that big nigger!"

I strained to pick up the school superintendent's voice, as though to squeeze some security out of that slightly more familiar sound.

15   "Let me at those black sonsabitches!" someone yelled.

"No, Jackson, no!" another voice yelled. "Here, somebody, help me hold Jack."

"I want to get at that ginger-colored nigger. Tear him limb from limb," the first voice yelled.

I stood against the ropes trembling. For in those days I was what they called ginger-colored, and he sounded as though he might crunch me between his teeth like a crisp ginger cookie.

Quite a struggle was going on. Chairs were being kicked about and I could hear voices grunting as with a terrific effort. I wanted to see, to see more desperately than ever before. But the blindfold was as tight as a thick skin-puckering scab and when I raised my gloved hands to push the layers of white aside a voice yelled, "Oh, no you don't, black bastard! Leave that alone!"

20   "Ring the bell before Jackson kills him a coon!" someone boomed in the sudden silence. And I heard the bell clang and the sound of the feet scuffling forward.

A glove smacked against my head. I pivoted, striking out stiffly as someone went past, and felt the jar ripple along the length of my arm to my shoulder. Then it seemed as though all nine of the boys had turned upon me at once. Blows pounded me from all sides while I struck out as best I could. So many blows landed upon me that I wondered if I were not the only blindfolded fighter in the ring, or if the man called Jackson hadn't succeeded in getting me after all.

Blindfolded, I could no longer control my motions. I had no dignity. I stumbled about like a baby or a drunken man. The smoke had become thicker and with each new blow it seemed to sear and further restrict my lungs. My saliva became like hot bitter glue. A glove connected with my head, filling my mouth with warm blood. It was everywhere. I could not tell if the moisture I felt upon my body was sweat or blood. A blow landed hard against the nape of my neck. I felt myself going over, my head hitting the floor. Streaks of blue light filled the black world behind the blindfold. I lay prone, pretending that I was knocked out, but felt myself seized by hands and yanked to my feet. "Get going, black boy! Mix it up!" My arms were like lead, my head smarting from blows. I managed to feel my way to the ropes and held on, trying to catch my breath. A glove landed in my mid-section and I went over again, feeling as though the smoke had become a knife jabbed into my guts. Pushed this way and that by the legs milling around me, I finally pulled erect and discovered that I could see the black, sweat-washed forms weaving in the smoky-blue atmosphere like drunken dancers weaving to the rapid drum-like thuds of blows.

Everyone fought hysterically. It was complete anarchy. Everybody fought everybody else. No group fought together for long. Two, three, four, fought one, then turned to fight each other, were themselves attacked. Blows landed below the belt and in the kidney, with the gloves open as well as closed, and with my eye partly opened now there was not so much terror. I moved carefully, avoiding blows, although not too many to attract attention, fighting from group to group. The boys groped about like blind, cautious crabs crouching to protect their mid-sections, their heads pulled in short against their shoulders, their arms stretched nervously before them, with their fists testing the smoke-filled air like the knobbed feelers of hypersensitive snails. In one corner I glimpsed a boy violently punching the air and heard him scream in pain as he smashed his hand against a ring post. For a second I saw him bent over holding his hand, then going down as a blow caught his unprotected head. I played one group against the other, slipping and throwing a punch then stepping out of range while pushing the others into the melee to take the blows blindly aimed at me. The smoke was agonizing and there were no rounds, no bells at three minute intervals to relieve our exhaustion. The room spun round me, a swirl of lights, smoke, sweating bodies surrounded by tense white faces. I bled from both nose and mouth, the blood spattering upon my chest.

The men kept yelling, "Slug him, black boy! Knock his guts out!"

25   "Uppercut him! Kill him! Kill that big boy!"

Taking a fake fall, I saw a boy going down heavily beside me as though we were felled by a single blow, saw a sneaker-clad foot shoot into his groin as the two who had knocked him down stumbled upon him. I rolled out of range, feeling a twinge of nausea.

The harder we fought the more threatening the men became. And yet, I had begun to worry about my speech again. How would it go? Would they recognize my ability? What would they give me?

I was fighting automatically and suddenly I noticed that one after another of the boys was leaving the ring. I was surprised, filled with panic, as though I had been left alone with an unknown danger. Then I understood. The boys had arranged it among themselves. It was the custom for the two men left in the ring to slug it out for the winner's prize. I discovered this too late. When the bell sounded two men in tuxedoes leaped into the ring and removed the blindfold. I found myself facing Tatlock, the biggest of the gang. I felt sick at my stomach. Hardly had the bell stopped ringing in my ears than it clanged again and I saw him moving swiftly toward me. Thinking of nothing else to do I hit him smash on the nose. He kept coming, bringing the rank sharp violence of stale sweat. His face was a black blank of a face, only his eyes alive—with hate of me and aglow with a feverish terror from what had happened to us all. I became anxious. I wanted to deliver my speech and he came at me as though he meant to beat it out of me. I smashed him again and again, taking his blows as they came. Then on a sudden impulse I struck him lightly as we clinched, I whispered, "Fake like I knocked you out, you can have the prize."

"I'll break your behind," he whispered hoarsely.

30   "For *them?*"

"For *me*, sonofabitch!"

They were yelling for us to break it up and Tatlock spun me half around with a blow, and as a joggled camera sweeps in a reeling scene, I saw the howling red faces crouching tense beneath the cloud of blue-gray smoke. For a moment the world wavered, unraveled, flowed, then my head cleared and Tatlock bounced before me. That fluttering shadow before my eyes was his jabbing left hand. Then falling forward, my head against his damp shoulder, I whispered,

"I'll make it five dollars more."

"Go to hell!"

35   But his muscles relaxed a trifle beneath my pressure and I breathed, "Seven!"

"Give it to your ma," he said, ripping me beneath the heart.

And while I still held him I butted him and moved away. I felt myself bombarded with punches. I fought back with hopeless desperation. I wanted to deliver my speech more than anything else in the world, because I felt that only these men could judge truly my ability, and now this stupid clown was ruining my chances. I began fighting carefully now, moving in to punch him and out again with my greater speed. A lucky blow to his chin and I had him going too—until I heard a loud voice yell, "I got my money on the big boy."

Hearing this, I almost dropped my guard. I was confused: Should I try to win against the voice out there? Would not this go against my speech, and was not this a moment for humility, for nonresistance? A blow to my head as I danced about sent my right eye popping like a jack-in-the-box and settled my dilemma. The room went red as I fell. It was a dream fall, my body languid and fastidious as to where to land, until the floor became impatient and smashed up to meet me. A moment later I came to. An hypnotic voice said FIVE emphatically. And I lay

there, hazily watching a dark red spot of my own blood shaping itself into a butterfly, glistening and soaking into the soiled gray world of the canvas.

When the voice drawled TEN I was lifted up and dragged to a chair. I sat
dazed. My eye pained and swelled with each throb of my pounding heart and I
wondered if now I would be allowed to speak. I was wringing wet, my mouth
still bleeding. We were grouped along the wall now. The other boys ignored me
as they congratulated Tatlock and speculated as to how much they would be
paid. One boy whimpered over his smashed hand. Looking up front, I saw attendants in white jackets rolling the portable ring away and placing a small square
rug in the vacant space surrounded by chairs. Perhaps, I thought, I will stand on
the rug to deliver my speech.

40   Then the M.C. called to us, "Come on up here boys and get your money."

We ran forward to where the men laughed and talked in their chairs, waiting.
Everyone seemed friendly now.

"There it is on the rug," the man said. I saw the rug covered with coins of all
dimensions and a few crumpled bills. But what excited me, scattered here and
there, were the gold pieces.

"Boys, it's all yours," the man said. "You get all you grab."

"That's right, Sambo," a blond man said, winking at me confidentially.

45   I trembled with excitement, forgetting my pain. I would get the gold and the
bills, I thought. I would use both hands. I would throw my body against the boys
nearest me to block them from the gold.

"Get down around the rug now," the man commanded, "and don't anyone
touch it until I give the signal."

"This ought to be good," I heard.

As told, we got around the square rug on our knees. Slowly the man raised
his freckled hand as we followed it upward with our eyes.

I heard, "These niggers look like they're about to pray!"

50   Then, "Ready," the man said. "Go!"

I lunged for a yellow coin lying on the blue design of the carpet, touching it
and sending a surprised shriek to join those rising around me. I tried frantically to
remove my hand but could not let go. A hot, violent force tore through my body,
shaking me like a wet rat. The rug was electrified. The hair bristled up on my
head as I shook myself free. My muscles jumped, my nerves jangled, writhed. But
I saw that this was not stopping the other boys. Laughing in fear and embarrassment, some were holding back and scooping up the coins knocked off by the
painful contortions of the others. The men roared above us as we struggled.

"Pick it up, goddamnit, pick it up!" someone called like a bass-voiced parrot.
"Go on, get it!"

I crawled rapidly around the floor, picking up the coins, trying to avoid the
coppers and to get greenbacks and the gold. Ignoring the shock by laughing, as I
brushed the coins off quickly, I discovered that I could contain the electricity—a
contradiction, but it works. Then the men began to push us onto the rug. Laughing
embarrassedly, we struggled out of their hands and kept after the coins. We were
all wet and slippery and hard to hold. Suddenly I saw a boy lifted into the air, glistening with sweat like a circus seal, and dropped, his wet back landing flush upon
the charged rug, heard him yell and saw him literally dance upon his back, his elbows beating a frenzied tattoo upon the floor, his muscles twitching like the flesh
of a horse stung by many flies. When he finally rolled off, his face was gray and no
one stopped him when he ran from the floor amid booming laughter.

"Get the money," the M.C. called. "That's good hard American cash!"

55   And we snatched and grabbed, snatched and grabbed. I was careful not to come too close to the rug now, and when I felt the hot whiskey breath descend upon me like a cloud of foul air I reached out and grabbed the leg of a chair. It was occupied and I held on desperately.

"Leggo, nigger! Leggo!"

The huge face wavered down to mine as he tried to push me free. But my body was slippery and he was too drunk. It was Mr. Colcord, who owned a chain of movie houses and "entertainment palaces." Each time he grabbed me I slipped out of his hands. It became a real struggle. I feared the rug more than I did the drunk, so I held on, surprising myself for a moment by trying to topple *him* upon the rug. It was such an enormous idea that I found myself actually carrying it out. I tried not to be obvious, yet when I grabbed his leg, trying to tumble him out of the chair, he raised up roaring with laughter, and, looking at me with soberness dead in the eye, kicked me viciously in the chest. The chair leg flew out of my hand. I felt myself going and rolled. It was as though I had rolled through a bed of hot coals. It seemed a whole century would pass before I would roll free, a century in which I was seared through the deepest levels of my body to the fearful breath within me and the breath seared and heated to the point of explosion. It'll all be over in a flash, I thought as I rolled clear. It'll all be over in a flash.

But not yet, the men on the other side were waiting, red faces swollen as though from apoplexy as they bent forward in their chairs. Seeing their fingers coming toward me I rolled away as a fumbled football rolls off the receiver's fingertips, back into the coals. That time I luckily sent the rug sliding out of place and heard the coins ringing against the floor and the boys scuffling to pick them up and the M.C. calling, "All right, boys, that's all. Go get dressed and get your money."

I was limp as a dish rag. My back felt as though it had been beaten with wires.

60   When we had dressed the M.C. came in and gave us each five dollars, except Tatlock, who got ten for being the last in the ring. Then he told us to leave. I was not to get a chance to deliver my speech, I thought. I was going out into the dim alley in despair when I was stopped and told to go back. I returned to the ballroom, where the men were pushing back their chairs and gathering in groups to talk.

The M.C. knocked on a table for quiet. "Gentlemen," he said, "we almost forgot an important part of the program. A most serious part, gentlemen. This boy was brought here to deliver a speech which he made at his graduation yesterday. . . ."

"Bravo!"

"I'm told that he is the smartest boy we've got out there in Greenwood. I'm told that he knows more big words than a pocket-sized dictionary."

Much applause and laughter.

65   "So now, gentlemen, I want you to give him your attention."

There was still laughter as I faced them, my mouth dry, my eye throbbing. I began slowly, but evidently my throat was tense, because they began shouting, "Louder! Louder!"

"We of the younger generation extol the wisdom of that great leader and educator," I shouted, "who first spoke these flaming words of wisdom: 'A ship lost at sea for many days suddenly sighted a friendly vessel. From the mast of the unfortunate vessel was seen a signal: "Water, water; we die of thirst!" The answer from the friendly vessel came back: "Cast down your bucket where you are." The captain of the distressed vessel, at last heeding the injunction, cast down his bucket, and it came up full of fresh sparkling water from the mouth of the Amazon River.' And like him I say, and in his words. 'To those of my race who depend upon bettering their condition in a foreign land, or who underestimate the importance of cultivating friendly relations with the Southern white man, who is his next-door neighbor. I would say: "Cast down your bucket where you are"—cast it down in making friends in every manly way of the people of all races by whom we are surrounded. . . .'"

I spoke automatically and with such fervor that I did not realize that the men were still talking and laughing until my dry mouth, filling up with blood from the cut, almost strangled me. I coughed, wanting to stop and go to one of the tall brass, sand-filled spittoons to relieve myself, but a few of the men, especially the superintendent, were listening and I was afraid. So I gulped it down, blood, saliva and all, and continued. (What powers of endurance I had during those days! What enthusiasm! What a belief in the rightness of things!) I spoke even louder in spite of the pain. But still they talked and still they laughed, as though deaf with cotton in dirty ears. So I spoke with greater emotional emphasis. I closed my ears and swallowed blood until I was nauseated. The speech seemed a hundred times as long as before, but I could not leave out a single word. All had to be said, each memorized nuance considered, rendered. Nor was that all. Whenever I uttered a word of three or more syllables a group of voices would yell for me to repeat it. I used the phrase "social responsibility" and they yelled:

"What's the word you say, boy?"

70   "Social responsibility," I said.

"What?"

"Social . . ."

"Louder."

". . . responsibility."

75   "More!"

"Respon—"

"Repeat!"

"—sibility."

The room filled with the uproar of laughter until, no doubt, distracted by having to gulp down my blood, I made a mistake and yelled a phrase I had often seen denounced in newspaper editorials, heard debated in private.

80   "Social . . ."

"What?" they yelled.

". . . equality—"

The laughter hung smokelike in the sudden stillness. I opened my eyes, puzzled. Sounds of displeasure filled the room. The M.C. rushed forward. They shouted hostile phrases at me. But I did not understand.

A small dry mustached man in the front row blared out, "Say that slowly, son!"

85   "What sir?"

"What you just said!"

"Social responsibility, sir," I said.

"You weren't being smart, were you, boy?" he said, not unkindly.

"No, sir!"

90   "You sure that about 'equality' was a mistake?"

"Oh, yes, sir," I said. "I was swallowing blood."

"Well, you had better speak more slowly so we can understand. We mean to do right by you, but you've got to know your place at all times. All right, now, go on with your speech."

I was afraid. I wanted to leave but I wanted also to speak and I was afraid they'd snatch me down.

"Thank you, sir," I said, beginning where I had left off, and having them ignore me as before.

Yet when I finished there was a thunderous applause. I was surprised to see the superintendent come forth with a package wrapped in white tissue paper, and gesturing for quiet, address the men.

"Gentlemen, you see that I did not overpraise this boy. He makes a good speech and some day he'll lead his people in the proper paths. And I don't have to tell you that that is important in these days and times. This is a good, smart boy, and so to encourage him in the right direction, in the name of the Board of Education I wish to present him a prize in the form of this . . . ."

He paused, removing the tissue paper and revealing a gleaming calfskin brief case.

". . . in the form of this first-class article from Shad Whitmore's shop."

"Boy," he said, addressing me, "take this prize and keep it well. Consider it a badge of office. Prize it. Keep developing as you are and some day it will be filled with important papers that will help shape the destiny of your people."

I was so moved that I could hardly express my thanks. A rope of bloody saliva forming a shape like an undiscovered continent drooled upon the leather and I wiped it quickly away. I felt an importance that I had never dreamed.

"Open it and see what's inside," I was told.

My fingers a-tremble, I complied, smelling the fresh leather and finding an official-looking document inside. It was a scholarship to the state college for Negroes. My eyes filled with tears and I ran awkwardly off the floor.

I was overjoyed; I did not even mind when I discovered that the gold pieces I had scrambled for were brass pocket tokens advertising a certain make of automobile.

When I reached home everyone was excited. Next day the neighbors came to congratulate me. I even felt safe from grandfather, whose deathbed curse usually spoiled my triumphs. I stood beneath his photograph with my brief case in hand and smiled triumphantly into his stolid black peasant's face. It was a face that fascinated me. The eyes seemed to follow everywhere I went.

That night I dreamed I was at a circus with him and that he refused to laugh at the clowns no matter what they did. Then later he told me to open my brief case and read what was inside and I did, finding an official envelope stamped with the state seal; and inside the envelope I found another and another, endlessly, and I thought I would fall of weariness. "Them's years," he said. "Now open that one." And I did and in it I found an engraved document containing a short message in letters of gold. "Read it," my grandfather said. "Out loud."

"To Whom It May Concern," I intoned, "Keep This Nigger-Boy Running."

I awoke with the old man's laughter ringing in my ears.

(It was a dream I was to remember and dream again for many years after. But at the time I had no insight into its meaning. First I had to attend college.)

[1947]

Topics for Critical Thinking and Writing

1. Now that you have read the entire story, the opening paragraph may be clearer than it was when you first read it. What does the narrator mean when he declares at the end of this paragraph, "I am an invisible man?" Explain how the events described in the story taught him this painful truth.

2. The narrator says of his grandfather's dying speech, "I could never be sure of what he meant." What do you think the grandfather meant by calling himself a traitor and a spy in the enemy's territory?

3. What is the significance of the scene involving the naked blonde woman? How is this scene related to the narrator's discovery that he is invisible?

4. This story is a powerful, indeed shocking study of racism, but in essays and interviews Ellison often noted that he intended his stories and his novel *Invisible Man* to illuminate "universal truths" about human experience as well. In your view, does "Battle Royal" achieve this goal? What insights does it offer about the nature of self-knowledge and human identity?

BOOKER T. WASHINGTON

Atlanta Exposition Address

MR. PRESIDENT AND GENTLEMEN OF THE BOARD OF DIRECTORS AND CITIZENS:

One-third of the population of the South is of the Negro race. No enterprise seeking the material, civil, or moral welfare of this section can disregard this element of our population and reach the highest success. I but convey to you, Mr. President and Directors, the sentiment of the masses of my race when I say that in no way have the value and manhood of the American Negro been more fittingly and generously recognized than by the managers of this magnificent Exposition at every stage of its progress. It is a recognition that will do more to cement the friendship of the two races than any occurrence since the dawn of our freedom.

Not only this, but the opportunity here afforded will awaken among us a new era of industrial progress. Ignorant and inexperienced, it is not strange that in the first years of our new life we began at the top instead of at the bottom; that a seat in Congress or the state legislature was more sought than real estate or industrial skill; that the political convention or stump speaking had more attractions than starting a dairy farm or truck garden.

A ship lost at sea for many days suddenly sighted a friendly vessel. From the mast of the unfortunate vessel was seen a signal, "Water, water; we die of thirst!" The answer from the friendly vessel at once came back, "Cast down your bucket where you are." A second time the signal, "Water, water; send us water!" ran up from the distressed vessel, and was answered, "Cast down your bucket where you are." And a third and fourth signal for water was answered, "Cast down your bucket where you are." The captain of the distressed vessel, at last heeding the injunction, cast down his bucket, and it came up full of fresh, sparkling water from the mouth of the Amazon River. To those of my race who depend on bettering their condition in a foreign land or who underestimate the importance of cultivating friendly relations with the Southern white man, who is their next-door neighbour, I would say: "Cast down your bucket where you are"—cast it down in making friends in every manly way of the people of all races by whom we are surrounded.

Cast it down in agriculture, mechanics, in commerce, in domestic service, and in the professions. And in this connection it is well to bear in mind that whatever other sins the South may be called to bear, when it comes to business, pure and simple, it is in the South that the Negro is given a man's chance in the commercial world, and in nothing is this Exposition more eloquent than in emphasizing this chance. Our greatest danger is that in the great leap from slavery to freedom we may overlook the fact that the masses of us are to live by the productions of our hands, and fail to keep in mind that we shall prosper in proportion as we learn to dignify and glorify common labour and put brains and skill into the common occupations of life; shall prosper in proportion as we learn to draw the line between the superficial and the substantial, the ornamental gewgaws of life and the useful. No race can prosper till it learns that there is as much dignity in tilling a field as in writing a poem. It is at the bottom of life we must begin, and not at the top. Nor should we permit our grievances to overshadow our opportunities.

5   To those of the white race who look to the incoming of those of foreign birth and strange tongue and habits for the prosperity of the South, were I permitted I would repeat what I say to my own race, "Cast down your bucket where you are." Cast it down among the eight millions of Negroes whose habits you know, whose fidelity and love you have tested in days when to have proved treacherous meant the ruin of your firesides. Cast down your bucket among these people who have, without strikes and labour wars, tilled your fields, cleared your forests, builded your railroads and cities, and brought forth treasures from the bowels of the earth, and helped make possible this magnificent representation of the progress of the South. Casting down your bucket among my people, helping and encouraging them as you are doing on these grounds, and to education of head, hand, and heart, you will find that they will buy your surplus land, make blossom the waste places in your fields, and run your factories. While doing this, you can be sure in the future, as in the past, that you and your families will be surrounded by the most patient, faithful, law-abiding, and unresentful people that the world has seen. As we have proved our loyalty to you in the past, in nursing your children, watching by the sick-bed of your mothers and fathers, and often following them with tear-dimmed eyes to their graves, so in the future, in our humble way, we shall stand by you with a devotion that no foreigner can approach, ready to lay down our lives, if need be, in defence of yours, interlacing our industrial, commercial, civil, and religious life with yours in a way that shall make the interests of both races one. In all things that are purely social we can be as separate as the fingers, yet one as the hand in all things essential to mutual progress.

There is no defence or security for any of us except in the highest intelligence and development of all. If anywhere there are efforts tending to curtail the fullest growth of the Negro, let these efforts be turned into stimulating, encouraging, and making him the most useful and intelligent citizen. Effort or means so invested will pay a thousand per cent interest. These efforts will be twice blessed—"blessing him that gives and him that takes."

There is no escape through law of man or God from the inevitable:—

> The laws of changeless justice bind
>   Oppressor with oppressed;
> And close as sin and suffering joined
>   We march to fate abreast.

Nearly sixteen millions of hands will aid you in pulling the load upward, or they will pull against you the load downward. We shall constitute one-third and more of the ignorance and crime of the South, or one-third its intelligence and progress; we shall contribute one-third to the business and industrial prosperity of the South, or we shall prove a veritable body of death, stagnating, depressing, retarding every effort to advance the body politic.

Gentlemen of the Exposition, as we present to you our humble effort at an exhibition of our progress, you must not expect overmuch. Starting thirty years ago with ownership here and there in a few quilts and pumpkins and chickens (gathered from miscellaneous sources), remember the path that has led from these to the inventions and production of agricultural implements, buggies, steam-engines, newspapers, books, statuary, carving, paintings, the management of drug-stores and banks, has not been trodden without contact with thorns and thistles. While we take pride in what we exhibit as a result of our independent efforts, we do not for a moment forget that our part in this exhibition would fall far short of your expectations but for the constant help that has come to our educational life, not only from the Southern states, but especially from Northern philanthropists, who have made their gifts a constant stream of blessing and encouragement.

10   The wisest among my race understand that the agitation of questions of social equality is the extremest folly, and that progress in the enjoyment of all the privileges that will come to us must be the result of severe and constant struggle rather than of artificial forcing. No race that has anything to contribute to the markets of the world is long in any degree ostracized. It is important and right that all privileges of the law be ours, but it is vastly more important that we be prepared for the exercises of these privileges. The opportunity to earn a dollar in a factory just now is worth infinitely more than the opportunity to spend a dollar in an opera-house.

Charles Keck, *The Booker T. Washington Memorial* (1922). The statue shows Washington pulling away the veil of ignorance and revealing to the crouching black man the book of knowledge of life and the implements of industry that will enable African Americans to prosper. On the sides of the pedestal are Washington's words, "We shall prosper in proportion as we learn to dignify and glorify labor and put brains and skill into the common occupations of life." (Courtesy of Tuskegee University. Photograph by Eric J. Sundquist.)

In conclusion, may I repeat that nothing in thirty years has given us more hope and encouragement, and drawn us so near to you of the white race, as this opportunity offered by the Exposition; and here bending, as it were, over the altar that represents the results of the struggles of your race and mine, both starting practically empty-handed three decades ago, I pledge that in your effort to work out the great and intricate problem which God has laid at the doors of the South, you shall have at all times the patient, sympathetic help of my race; only let this be constantly in mind, that, while from representations in these buildings of the product of field, of forest, of mine, of factory, letters, and art, much good will come, yet far above and beyond material benefits will be that higher good, that, let us pray God, will come, in a blotting out of sectional differences and racial animosities and suspicions, in a determination to administer absolute justice, in a willing obedience among all classes to the mandates of law. This, this, coupled with our material prosperity, will bring into our beloved South a new heaven and a new earth.

[1895]

W. E. B. Du Bois
Of Our Spiritual Strivings

Between me and the other world there is ever an unasked question: unasked by some through feelings of delicacy; by others through the difficulty of rightly framing it. All, nevertheless, flutter round it. They approach me in a half-hesitant sort of way, eye me curiously or compassionately, and then, instead of saying directly, How does it feel to be a problem? they say, I know an excellent colored man in my town; or, I fought at Mechanicsville; or, Do not these Southern outrages make your blood boil? At these I smile, or am interested, or reduce the boiling to a simmer, as the occasion may require. To the real question, How does it feel to be a problem? I answer seldom a word.

And yet, being a problem is a strange experience,—peculiar even for one who has never been anything else, save perhaps in babyhood and in Europe. It is in the early days of rollicking boyhood that the revelation first bursts upon one, all in a day, as it were. I remember well when the shadow swept across me. I was a little thing, away up in the hills of New England, where the dark Housatonic winds between Hoosac and Taghkanic to the sea. In a wee wooden schoolhouse, something put it into the boys' and girls' heads to buy gorgeous visiting-cards— ten cents a package—and exchange. The exchange was merry, till one girl, a tall newcomer, refused my card,—refused it peremptorily, with a glance. Then it dawned upon me with a certain suddenness that I was different from the others; or like, mayhap, in heart and life and longing, but shut out from their world by a vast veil. I had thereafter no desire to tear down that veil, to creep through; I held all beyond it in common contempt, and lived above it in a region of blue sky and great wandering shadows. That sky was bluest when I could beat my mates at examination-time, or beat them at a foot-race, or even beat their stringy heads. Alas, with the years all this fine contempt began to fade; for the worlds I longed for, and all their dazzling opportunities, were theirs, not mine. But they should not keep these prizes, I said; some, all, I would wrest from them. Just how I would do it I could never decide: by reading law, by healing the sick, by telling the wonderful tales that swam in my head,—some way. With other black boys the strife was not so fiercely sunny: their youth shrunk into tasteless sycophancy, or into silent hatred of the pale world about them and mocking distrust of everything white; or wasted itself in a bitter cry, Why did God make me an outcast and a stranger in mine own house? The shades of the prison-house closed round about us all: walls strait and stubborn to the whitest; but relentlessly narrow, tall, and unscalable to sons of night who must plod darkly on in resignation, or beat unavailing palms against the stone, or steadily, half hopelessly, watch the streak of blue above.

After the Egyptian and Indian, the Greek and Roman, the Teuton and Mongolian, the Negro is a sort of seventh son, born with a veil, and gifted with second-sight in this American world,—a world which yields him no true self-consciousness, but only lets him see himself through the revelation of the other world. It is a peculiar sensation, this double-consciousness, this sense of always looking at one's self through the eyes of others, of measuring one's soul by the tape of a world that looks on in amused contempt and pity. One ever feels his two-ness,—an American, a Negro; two souls, two thoughts, two unreconciled strivings; two warring ideals in one dark body, whose dogged strength alone keeps it from being torn asunder.

The history of the American Negro is the history of this strife—this longing to attain self-conscious manhood, to merge his double self into a better and truer self. In this merging he wishes neither of the older selves to be lost. He would not Africanize America, for America has too much to teach the world and Africa. He would not bleach his Negro soul in a flood of white Americanism, for he knows that Negro blood has a message for the world. He simply wishes to make it possible for a man to be both a Negro and an American, without being cursed and spit upon by his fellows, without having the doors of Opportunity closed roughly in his face.

[1903]

W. E. B. Du Bois
Of Mr. Booker T. Washington and Others

Mr. Washington represents in Negro thought the old attitude of adjustment and submission; but adjustment at such a peculiar time as to make his programme unique. This is an age of unusual economic development, and Mr. Washington's programme naturally takes an economic cast, becoming a gospel of Work and Money to such an extent as apparently almost completely to overshadow the higher aims of life. Moreover, this is an age when the more advanced races are coming in closer contact with the less developed races, and the race-feeling is therefore intensified; and Mr. Washington's programme practically accepts the alleged inferiority of the Negro races. Again, in our own land, the reaction from the sentiment of war time has given impetus to race-prejudice against Negroes, and Mr. Washington withdraws many of the high demands of Negroes as men and American citizens. In other periods of intensified prejudice all the Negro's tendency to self-assertion has been called forth; at this period a policy of submission is advocated. In the history of nearly all other races and peoples the doctrine preached at such crises has been that manly self-respect is worth more than lands and houses, and that a people who voluntarily surrender such respect, or cease striving for it, are not worth civilizing.

In answer to this, it has been claimed that the Negro can survive only through submission. Mr. Washington distinctly asks that black people give up, at least for the present, three things,—

First, political power,
Second, insistence on civil rights,
Third, higher education of Negro youth,—

and concentrate all their energies on industrial education, the accumulation of wealth, and the conciliation of the South. This policy has been courageously and insistently advocated for over fifteen years, and has been triumphant for perhaps ten years. As a result of this tender of the palm-branch, what has been the return? In these years there have occurred:

1. The disfranchisement of the Negro.
2. The legal creation of a distinct status of civil inferiority for the Negro.
3. The steady withdrawal of aid from institutions for the higher training of the Negro.

These movements are not, to be sure, direct results of Mr. Washington's teachings; but his propaganda has, without a shadow of doubt, helped their speedier accomplishment. The question then comes: Is it possible, and probable, that nine millions of men can make effective progress in economic lines if they are deprived of political rights, made a servile caste, and allowed only the most meagre chance for developing their exceptional men? If history and reason give any distinct answer to these questions, it is an emphatic *No*. And Mr. Washington thus faces the triple paradox of his career:

10

1. He is striving nobly to make Negro artisans business men and property-owners; but it is utterly impossible, under modern competitive methods, for workingmen and property-owners to defend their rights and exist without the right of suffrage.
2. He insists on thrift and self-respect, but at the same time counsels a silent submission to civic inferiority such as is bound to sap the manhood of any race in the long run.
3. He advocates common-school and industrial training, and depreciates institutions of higher learning; but neither the Negro common-schools, nor Tuskegee itself, could remain open a day were it not for teachers trained in Negro colleges, or trained by their graduates.

This triple paradox in Mr. Washington's position is the object of criticism by two classes of colored Americans. One class is spiritually descended from Toussaint the Savior, through Gabriel, Vesey, and Turner, and they represent the attitude of revolt and revenge; they hate the white South blindly and distrust the white race generally, and so far as they agree on definite action, think that the Negro's only hope lies in emigration beyond the borders of the United States. And yet, by the irony of fate, nothing has more effectually made this programme seem hopeless than the recent course of the United States toward weaker and darker peoples in the West Indies, Hawaii, and the Philippines,—for where in the world may we go and be safe from lying and brute force?

The other class of Negroes who cannot agree with Mr. Washington has hitherto said little aloud. They deprecate the sight of scattered counsels, of internal disagreement; and especially they dislike making their just criticism of a useful and earnest man an excuse for a general discharge of venom from small-minded opponents. Nevertheless, the questions involved are so fundamental and serious that it is difficult to see how men like the Grimkes, Kelly Miller, J. W. E. Bowen, and other representatives of this group, can much longer be silent. Such men feel in conscience bound to ask of this nation three things:

15
    1. The right to vote.
    2. Civic equality.
    3. The education of youth according to ability.

They acknowledge Mr. Washington's invaluable service in counselling patience and courtesy in such demands; they do not ask that ignorant black men vote when ignorant whites are debarred, or that any reasonable restrictions in the suffrage should not be applied; they know that the low social level of the mass of the race is responsible for much discrimination against it, but they also know, and the nation knows, that relentless color-prejudice is more often a cause than a result of the Negro's degradation; they seek the abatement of this relic of barbarism, and not its systematic encouragement and pampering by all agencies of social power from the Associated Press to the Church of Christ. They advocate, with Mr. Washington, a broad system of Negro common schools supplemented by thorough industrial training; but they are surprised that a man of Mr. Washington's insight cannot see that no such educational system ever has rested or can rest on any other basis than that of the well-equipped college and university, and they insist that there is a demand for a few such institutions throughout the South to train the best of the Negro youth as teachers, professional men, and leaders.

This group of men honor Mr. Washington for his attitude of conciliation toward the white South; they accept the "Atlanta Compromise" in its broadest interpretation; they recognize, with him, many signs of promise, many men of high purpose and fair judgment, in this section; they know that no easy task has been laid upon a region already tottering under heavy burdens. But, nevertheless, they insist that the way to truth and right lies in straightforward honesty, not in indiscriminate flattery; in praising those of the South who do well and criticising uncompromisingly those who do ill; in taking advantage of the opportunities at hand and urging their fellows to do the same, but at the same time in remembering that only a firm adherence to their higher ideals and aspirations will ever keep those ideals within the realm of possibility. They do not expect that the free right to vote, to enjoy civic rights, and to be educated, will come in a moment; they do not expect to see the bias and prejudices of years disappear at the blast of a trumpet; but they are absolutely certain that the way for a people to gain their reasonable rights is not by voluntarily throwing them away and insisting that they do not want them; that the way for a people to gain respect is not by continually belittling and ridiculing themselves; that, on the contrary, Negroes must insist continually, in season and out of season, that voting is necessary to modern manhood, that color discrimination is barbarism, and that black boys need education as well as white boys.

In failing thus to state plainly and unequivocally the legitimate demands of their people, even at the cost of opposing an honored leader, the thinking classes of American Negroes would shirk a heavy responsibility,—a responsibility to themselves, a responsibility to the struggling masses, a responsibility to the darker races of men whose future depends so largely on this American experiment, but especially a responsibility to this nation,—this common Fatherland. It is wrong to encourage a man or a people in evil-doing; it is wrong to aid and abet a national crime simply because it is unpopular not to do so. The growing spirit of kindliness and reconciliation between the North and South after the frightful differences of a generation ago ought to be a source of deep congratulation to all, and especially to those whose mistreatment caused the war; but if that reconciliation is to be marked by the industrial slavery and civic death of those same black men, with permanent legislation into a position of inferiority, then those black men, if they are really men, are called upon by every consideration of patriotism and loyalty to oppose such a course by all civilized methods, even though such opposition involves disagreement with Mr. Booker T. Washington. We have no right to sit silently by while the inevitable seeds are sown for a harvest of disaster to our children, black and white.

[1903]

GUNNAR MYRDAL
*On Social Equality**

I have heard few comments made so frequently and with so much emphasis and so many illustrations as the one that "Negroes are happiest among themselves" and that "Negroes really don't want white company but prefer to be among their own race." Even sociologists, educators, and interracial experts have informed me that, when the two groups keep apart, the wish for separation is as pronounced among Negroes as among whites. In the South, many liberals are eager to stress this assertion as part of the justification for their unwillingness to give up the Southern doctrine that the Negroes must not be allowed to aspire to "social equality." Southern conservatives will usually give a somewhat different twist to the argument and actually insist that Negroes are perfectly satisfied with their social status in the South. But the conservatives are more likely to contradict themselves bluntly in the next sentence by asserting that in the back of the Negro's mind there is a keen desire to be "like white people" and to "marry white girls."

For the moment, we shall leave it an open question whether the whites understand the Negroes correctly on this point. We shall start from the evident fact that—quite independent of whether or not, to what extent, and how the Negroes have accommodated themselves—*social segregation and discrimination is a system of deprivations forced upon the Negro group by the white group.* This is equally true in the North and in the South, though in this respect, as in all others, there is more segregation and discrimination in the South, and thus the phenomenon is easier to observe.

That segregation and discrimination are forced upon the Negroes by the whites becomes apparent in the *one-sidedness* of their application. Negroes are ordinarily never admitted to white churches in the South, but if a strange white man enters a Negro church the visit is received as a great honor. The guest will be ushered to a front seat or to the platform. The service will often be interrupted, an announcement will be made that there is a "white friend" present, and he will be asked to address the Negro audience, which will loudly testify its high appreciation. Likewise, a white stranger will be received with utmost respect and cordiality in any Negro school, and everything will be done to satisfy his every wish, whereas a Negro under similar circumstances would be pushed off the grounds of a white school. Whenever I have entered a Negro theater in the South, the girl in

* Editors' title.

the ticket office has regularly turned a bewildered face and told me that "it is a colored movie." But she has apparently done this because she thought I was making a mistake and wanted to spare me embarrassment. When I answered that I did not care, the ticket office girls usually sold the ticket and received my visit as a courtesy. I have never been refused service in a Negro restaurant in the South.

When the white conductor in a train has told me occasionally that I was in the wrong car, the underlying assumption has also been the same, that the separation was made in order to save white people from having to tolerate Negro company. Contrary to the laws—which are all written on the fiction of equality— he has, with a shrug of his shoulders, always left me where I was after I told him I had gone there purposely to have a look at the Negroes. A Negro who would disclose a similar desire to observe whites would, of course, be dealt with in quite another way. In the streetcars and buses the separation seems to be enforced fairly well in both directions. When, however, the conductor tells me, a white man, that I have taken the wrong seat, it is done in a spirit of respect and in order to help me preserve my caste status. The assumption is that I have made a mistake with no intention of overstepping the rules. In the case of a Negro the assumption is usually the contrary, that he is trying to intrude. In public buildings or private establishments of the South, I have never encountered any objection to my entering the spaces set aside for the Negroes, nor to my riding in the elevator set apart for Negroes if, for any reason, the white car was not there or was filled.

5   The rules are understood to be for the protection of whites and directed against Negroes. This applies also to social rituals and etiquette. The white man may waive most of the customs, as long as he does not demonstrate such a friendliness that he becomes known as a "nigger lover"; the reaction then comes, however, from the white society. He can recognize the Negro on the street and stop for a chat, or he can ignore him. He can offer his hand to shake, or he can keep it back. Negroes often complain about the uncertainty they experience because of the fact that the initiative in defining the personal situation always belongs to the white man. It is the white man who chooses between the alternatives as to the character of the contact to be established. The Negro, who often does not know how the white man has chosen, receives surprises in one direction or the other, which constantly push him off his balance.

. . .

In his first encounter with the American Negro problem, perhaps nothing perplexes the outside observer more than the popular term and the popular theory of "no social equality." He will be made to feel from the start that it has concrete implications and a central importance for the Negro problem in America. But, nevertheless, the term is kept vague and elusive, and the theory loose and ambiguous. One moment it will be stretched to cover and justify every form of social segregation and discrimination, and, in addition, all the inequalities in justice, politics and breadwinning. The next moment it will be narrowed to express only the denial of close personal intimacies and intermarriage. The very lack of precision allows the notion of "no social equality" to rationalize the rather illogical and wavering system of color caste in America.

The kernel of the popular theory of "no social equality" will, when pursued, be presented as a firm determination on the part of the whites to block amalgamation and preserve "the purity of the white race." The white man identifies himself with "the white race" and feels that he has a stake in resisting the dissipation of its racial identity. Important in this identification is the notion of "the absolute and unchangeable superiority of the white race." From this racial dogma will often be drawn the *direct* inference that the white man shall dominate in all spheres. But when the logic of this inference is inquired about, the inference will be made *indirect* and will be made to lead over to the danger of amalgamation, or, as it is popularly expressed, "intermarriage."

It is further found that the ban on intermarriage is focused on white women. For them it covers both formal marriage and illicit intercourse. In regard to white men it is taken more or less for granted that they would not stoop to marry Negro women, and that illicit intercourse does not fall under the same intense taboo. Their offspring, under the popular doctrine that maternity is more certain than paternity, become Negroes anyway, and the white race easily avoids pollution with Negro blood. To prevent "intermarriage" in this specific sense of sex relations between white women and Negro men, it is not enough to apply legal and social sanctions against . . . it—so the popular theory runs. In using the danger of intermarriage as a defense for the whole caste system, it is assumed both that Negro men have a strong desire for "intermarriage," and that white women would be open to proposals from Negro men, *if* they are not guarded from even meeting them on an equal plane. The latter assumption, of course, is never openly expressed, but is logically implicit in the popular theory. The conclusion follows that the whole system of segregation and discrimination is justified. Every single measure is defended as necessary to block "social equality" which in its turn is held necessary to prevent "intermarriage."

The basic role of the fear of amalgamation in white attitudes to the race problem is indicated by the popular magical concept of "blood." Educated white Southerners, who know everything about modern genetic and biological research, confess readily that they actually feel an irrational or "instinctive" repugnance in thinking of "intermarriage." These measures of segregation and discrimination are often of the type found in the true taboos and in the notion "not to be touched" of primitive religion. The specific taboos are characterized, further, by a different degree of excitement which attends their violation and a different degree of punishment to the violator: the closer the act to sexual association, the more furious is the public reaction. Sexual association itself is punished by death and is accompanied by tremendous public excitement; the other social relations meet decreasing degrees of public fury. Sex becomes in this popular theory the principle around which the whole structure of segregation of the Negroes—down to disfranchisement and denial of equal opportunities on the labor market—is organized. The reasoning is this: "For, say what we will, may not all the equalities be ultimately based on potential social equality, and that in turn on intermarriage? Here we reach the real *crux* of the question." In cruder language, but with the same logic, the Southern man on the street responds to any plea for social equality: "Would you like to have your daughter marry a Negro?"

10   This theory of color caste centering around the aversion to amalgamation determines, as we have just observed, the white man's rather definite rank order of the various measures of segregation and discrimination against Negroes. The relative significance attached to each of those measures is dependent upon their degree of expediency or necessity—in the view of white people—as means of upholding the ban on "intermarriage." In this rank order, (1) the ban on intermarriage and other sex relations involving white women and colored men takes precedence before everything else. It is the end for which the other restrictions are arranged as means. Thereafter follow: (2) all sorts of taboos and etiquettes in personal contacts; (3) segregation in schools and churches; (4) segregation in hotels, restaurants, and theaters, and other public places where people

meet socially; (5) segregation in public conveyances; (6) discrimination in public services; and, finally, inequality in (7) politics, (8) justice and (9) breadwinning and relief.

The degree of liberalism on racial matters in the white South can be designated mainly by the point on this rank order where a man stops because he believes further segregation and discrimination are not necessary to prevent "intermarriage." We have seen that white liberals in the South of the present day, as a matter of principle, rather unanimously stand up against inequality in breadwinning, relief, justice and politics. These fields of discrimination form the chief battleground and considerable changes in them are, as we have seen, on the way. When we ascend to the higher ranks which concern social relations in the narrow sense, we find the Southern liberals less prepared to split off from the majority opinion of the region. Hardly anybody in the South is prepared to go the whole way and argue that even the ban on intermarriage should be lifted. Practically all agree, not only upon the high desirability of preventing "intermarriage," but also that a certain amount of separation between the two groups is expedient and necessary to prevent it. Even the one who has his philosophical doubts on the point must, if he is reasonable, abstain from ever voicing them. The social pressure is so strong that it would be foolish not to conform. Conformity is a political necessity for having any hope of influence; it is, in addition, a personal necessity for not meeting social ostracism.

· · ·

The fixation on the purity of white womanhood, and also part of the intensity of emotion surrounding the whole sphere of segregation and discrimination, are to be understood as the backwashes of the sore conscience on the part of white men for their own or their compeers' relations with, or desires for, Negro women. These psychological effects are greatly magnified because of the puritan *milieu* of America and especially of the South. The upper class men in a less puritanical people could probably have indulged in sex relations with, and sexual daydreams of, lower caste women in a more matter-of-course way and without generating so much pathos about white womanhood. The Negro people have to carry the burden not only of the white men's sins but also of their virtues. The virtues of the honest, democratic, puritan white Americans in the South are great, and the burden upon the Negroes becomes ponderous.

Our practical conclusion is that it would have cleansing effects on race relations in America, and particularly in the South, to have an open and sober discussion in rational terms of this ever present popular theory of "intermarriage" and "social equality," giving matters their factual ground, true proportions and logical relations. Because it is, to a great extent, an opportunistic rationalization, and because it refers directly and indirectly to the most touchy spots in American life and American morals, tremendous inhibitions have been built up against a detached and critical discussion of this theory. But such inhibitions are gradually overcome when, in the course of secularized education, people become rational about their life problems. It must never be forgotten that in our increasingly intellectualized civilization even the plain citizen feels an urge for truth and objectivity, and that this rationalistic urge is increasingly competing with the opportunistic demands for rationalization and escape.

There are reasons to believe that a slow but steady cleansing of the American mind is proceeding as the cultural level is raised. The basic racial inferiority doctrine is being undermined by research and education. For a white man to have illicit relations with Negro women is increasingly meeting disapproval. Negroes themselves are more and more frowning upon such relations. This all must tend to dampen the emotional fires around "social equality." Sex and race fears are, however, even today the main defense for segregation and, in fact, for the whole caste order. The question shot at the interviewer touching any point of this order is still: "Would you like to have your daughter (sister) marry a Negro?"

[1944]

RALPH ELLISON
*On Negro Folklore**

INTERVIEWERS: How representative of the American nation would you say Negro folklore is?

ELLISON: The history of the American Negro is a most intimate part of American history. Through the very process of slavery came the building of the United States. Negro folklore, evolving within a larger culture which regarded it as inferior, was an especially courageous expression. It announced the Negro's willingness to trust his own experience, his own sensibilities as to the definition of reality, rather than allow his masters to define these crucial matters for him. His experience is that of America and the West, and is as rich a body of experience as one would find anywhere. We can view it narrowly as something exotic, folksy or "low-down," or we may identify ourselves with it and recognize it as an important segment of the larger American experience—not lying at the bottom of it, but intertwined, diffused in its very texture. I can't take this lightly or be impressed by those who cannot see its importance; it is important to *me*. One ironic witness to the beauty and the universality of this art is the fact that the descendants of the very men who enslaved us can now sing the spirituals and find in the singing an exaltation of their own humanity. Just take a look at some of the slave songs, blues, folk ballads; their possibilities for the writer are infinitely suggestive. Some of them have named human situations so well that a whole corps of writers could not exhaust their universality. For instance, here's an old slave verse:

Ole Aunt Dinah, she's just like me
She work so hard she want to be free
But old Aunt Dinah's gittin' kinda ole
She's afraid to go to Canada on account of the cold.

Ole Uncle Jack, now he's a mighty "good nigger,"
You tell him that you want to be free for a fac'
Next thing you know they done stripped the skin off your back.

Now old Uncle Ned, he want to be free
He found his way north by the moss on the tree
He cross that river floating in a tub
The patateroller[†] give him a mighty close rub.

* Editors' title.   † Patroller.

It's crude, but in it you have three universal attitudes toward the problem of freedom. You can refine it and sketch in the psychological subtleties and historical and philosophical allusions, action and what not, but I don't think its basic definition can be exhausted. Perhaps some genius could do as much with it as Mann has done with the Joseph story.

INTERVIEWERS: Can you give us an example of the use of folklore in your own novel?

5   ELLISON: Well, there are certain themes, symbols and images which are based on folk material. For example, there is the old saying amongst Negroes: If you're black, stay back; if you're brown, stick around; if you're white, you're right. And there is the joke Negroes tell on themselves about their being so black they can't be seen in the dark. In my book this sort of thing was merged with the meanings which blackness and light have long had in Western mythology: evil and goodness, ignorance and knowledge, and so on. In my novel the narrator's development is one through blackness to light; that is, from ignorance to enlightenment: invisibility to visibility. He leaves the South and goes North; this, as you will notice in reading Negro folktales, is always the road to freedom, the movement upward. You have the same thing again when he leaves his underground cave for the open.

It took me a long time to learn how to adapt such examples of myth into my work—also ritual. The use of ritual is equally a vital part of the creative process. I learned a few things from Eliot, Joyce and Hemingway, but not how to adapt them. When I started writing, I knew that in both *The Waste Land* and *Ulysses* ancient myth and ritual were used to give form and significance to the material, but it took me a few years to realize that the myths and rites which we find functioning in our everyday lives could be used in the same way. In my first attempt at a novel—which I was unable to complete—I began by trying to manipulate the simple structural unities of *beginning, middle* and *end*, but when I attempted to deal with the psychological strata—the images, symbols and emotional configurations—of the experience at hand, I discovered that the unities were simply cool points of stability on which one could suspend the narrative line, but beneath the surface of apparently rational human relationships there seethed a chaos before which I was helpless. People rationalize what they shun or are incapable of dealing with; these superstitions and their rationalizations become ritual as they govern behavior. The rituals become social forms, and it is one of the functions of the artist to recognize them and raise them to the level of art.

I don't know whether I'm getting this over or not. Let's put it this way: take the "Battle Royal" passage in my novel, where the boys are blindfolded and forced to fight each other for the amusement of the white observers. This is a vital part of behavior pattern in the South, which both Negroes and whites thoughtlessly accept. It is a ritual in preservation of caste lines, a keeping of taboo to appease the gods and ward off bad luck. It is also the initiation ritual to which all greenhorns are subjected. This passage which states what Negroes will see I did not have to invent; the patterns were already there in society, so that all I had to do was present them in a broader context of meaning. In any society there are many rituals of situation which, for the most part, go unquestioned. They can be simple or elaborate, but they are the connective tissue between the work of art and the audience.

INTERVIEWERS: Do you think a reader unacquainted with this folklore can properly understand your work?

ELLISON: Yes, I think so. It's like jazz; there's no inherent problem which prohibits understanding but the assumptions brought to it. We don't all dig Shakespeare uniformly, or even Little Red Riding Hood. The understanding of art depends finally upon one's willingness to extend one's humanity and one's knowledge of human life. I noticed, incidentally, that the Germans, having no special caste assumptions concerning American Negroes, dealt with my work simply as a novel. I think the Americans will come to view it that way in twenty years—if it's around that long.

[1955]

RALPH ELLISON
*Life in Oklahoma City**

• • •

In the loosely structured community of that time, knowledge, news of other ways of living, ancient wisdom, the latest literary fads, hate literature—for years I kept a card warning Negroes away from the polls, which had been dropped by the thousands from a plane which circled over the Negro community—information of all kinds found its level, catch-as-catch-can, in the minds of those who were receptive to it. Not that there was no conscious structuring—I read my first Shaw and Maupassant, my first Harvard Classics in the home of a friend whose parents were products of that stream of New England education which had been brought to Negroes by the young and enthusiastic white teachers who staffed the schools set up for the freedmen after the Civil War. These parents were both teachers, and there were others like them in our town.

But the places where a rich oral literature was truly functional were the churches, the schoolyards, the barbershops, the cotton-picking camps—places where folklore and gossip thrived. The drug store where I worked was such a place, where on days of bad weather the older men would sit with their pipes and tell tall tales, hunting yarns and homely versions of the classics. It was here that I heard stories of searching for buried treasure and of headless horsemen, which I was told were my own father's versions told long before. There were even recitals of popular verse, "The Shooting of Dan McGrew," and, along with these, stories of Jesse James, of Negro outlaws and black United States marshals, of slaves who became the chiefs of Indian tribes, and of the exploits of Negro cowboys. There was both truth and fantasy in this, intermingled in the mysterious fashion of literature.

In their formative period, writers absorb into their consciousness much that has no special value until much later, and often much which is of no special value even then, perhaps, beyond the fact that it throbs with affect and mystery and in it "time and pain and royalty in the blood" are suspended in imagery. So, long before I thought of writing, I was claimed by weather, by speech rhythms, by Negro voices and their different idioms, by husky male voices and by the high shrill singing voices of certain Negro women, by music, by tight spaces and by wide spaces in which the eyes could wander, by death, by newly born babies, by

* Editors' title.

manners of various kinds, company manners and street manners, the manners of white society and those of our own high society, and by interracial manners, by street fights, circuses and minstrel shows, by vaudeville and moving pictures, by prize fights and foot races, baseball games and football matches. By spring floods and blizzards, catalpa worms and jack rabbits, honeysuckle and snapdragons (which smelled like old cigar butts), by sunflowers and hollyhocks, raw sugar cane and baked yams, pigs' feet, chili and blue haw ice cream. By parades, public dances and jam sessions, Easter sunrise ceremonies and large funerals. By contests between fire-and-brimstone preachers and by presiding elders who got "laughing-happy" when moved by the spirit of God.

I was impressed by expert players of the "dozens" and certain notorious bootleggers of corn whiskey. By jazz musicians and fortunetellers and by men who did anything well, by strange sicknesses and by interesting brick or razor scars, by expert cursing vocabularies as well as by exalted praying and terrifying shouting, and by transcendent playing or singing of the blues. I was fascinated by old ladies, those who had seen slavery and those who were defiant of white folk and black alike, by the enticing walks of prostitutes and by the limping walks affected by Negro hustlers, especially those who wore Stetson hats, expensive shoes with well-starched overalls, usually with a diamond stickpin (when not in hock) in their tireless collars as their gambling uniforms.

5   And there were the blind men who preached on corners, and the blind men who sang the blues to the accompaniment of washboard and guitar, and the white junkmen who sang mountain music and the famous hucksters of fruit and vegetables.

And there was the Indian-Negro confusion. There were Negroes who were part Indian and who lived on reservations, and Indians who had children who lived in towns as Negroes, and Negroes who were Indians and traveled back and forth between the groups with no trouble. And Indians who were as wild as wild Negroes, and others who were as solid and as steady as bankers. There were the teachers, too: inspiring teachers and villainous teachers who chased after the girl students, and certain female teachers who one wished would chase after young male students. And a handsome old principal of military bearing who had been blemished by his classmates at West Point when they discovered on the eve of graduation that he was a Negro. There were certain Jews, Mexicans, Chinese cooks, a German orchestra conductor and an English grocer who owned a Franklin touring car. And certain Negro mechanics—"Cadillac Slim," "Sticks" Walker, Buddy Bunn and Oscar Pitman—who had so assimilated the automobile that they seemed to be behind a steering wheel even as they walked the streets or danced with girls. And there were the whites who despised us and the others who shared our hardships and our joys.

There is much more, but this is sufficient to indicate some of what was present even in a segregated community to form the background of my work and my sense of life.

And now comes the next step. I went to Tuskegee to study music, hoping to become a composer of symphonies, and there, during my second year, I read *The Waste Land* and that, although I was then unaware of it, was the real transition to writing.

Mrs. L. C. McFarland had taught us much of Negro history in grade school, and from her I'd learned of the New Negro Movement of the twenties, of Langston Hughes, Countee Cullen, Claude McKay, James Weldon Johnson and the others. They had inspired pride and had given me a closer identification with poetry (by now, oddly enough, I seldom thought of my hidden name), but with music so much on my mind it never occurred to me to try to imitate them. Still, I read their work and was excited by the glamour of the Harlem which emerged from their poems, and it was good to know that there were Negro writers. Then came *The Waste Land*.

10   I was much more under the spell of literature than I realized at the time. *Wuthering Heights* had caused me an agony of unexpressible emotion, and the same was true of *Jude the Obscure*, but *The Waste Land* seized my mind. I was intrigued by its power to move me while eluding my understanding. Somehow its rhythms were often closer to those of jazz than were those of the Negro poets, and even though I could not understand then, its range of allusion was as mixed and as varied as that of Louis Armstrong. Yet there were its discontinuities, its changes of pace and its hidden system of organization which escaped me.

     There was nothing to do but look up the references in the footnotes to the poem, and thus began my conscious education in literature. For this, the library at Tuskegee was quite adequate and I used it. Soon I was reading a whole range of subjects drawn upon by the poet, and this led, in turn, to criticism and to Pound, Ford Madox Ford, Sherwood Anderson, Gertrude Stein, Hemingway and Fitzgerald and "round about 'til I was come" back to Melville and Twain—the writers who are taught and doubtless overtaught today. Perhaps it was my good luck that they were not taught at Tuskegee; I wouldn't know. But at the time I was playing, having an intellectually interesting good time.

     Having given so much attention to the techniques of music, the process of learning something of the craft and intention of modern poetry and fiction seemed quite familiar. Besides, it was absolutely painless because it involved no deadlines or credits. Even then, however, a process which I described earlier had begun to operate. The more I learned of literature in this conscious way, the more the details of my background became transformed. I heard undertones in remembered conversations which had escaped me before, local customs took on a more universal meaning, values which I hadn't understood were revealed, some of the people whom I had known were diminished, while others were elevated in stature. More important, I began to see my own possibilities with more objective and in some ways more hopeful eyes.

     The summer of 1936 I went to New York seeking work, which I did not find, and remained there, but the personal transformation continued. Reading had become a conscious process of growth and discovery, a method of reordering the world. And that world had widened considerably.

     At Tuskegee I had handled manuscripts which Prokofiev had given to Hazel Harrison, a Negro concert pianist who taught there and who had known him in Europe, and through Miss Harrison I had become aware of Prokofiev's symphonies. I had also become aware of the radical movement in politics and art, and in New York had begun reading the work of André Malraux, not only the fiction but chapters published from his *Psychology of Art*. And in my search for an expression of modern sensibility in the works of Negro writers I discovered Richard Wright. Shortly thereafter I was to meet Wright, and it was at his suggestion that I wrote both my first book review and my first short story.

15   These were fateful suggestions. For although I had tried my hand at poetry while at Tuskegee, it hadn't occurred to me that I might write fiction, but once he suggested it, it seemed the most natural thing to try. Fortunately for me,

Wright, then on the verge of his first success, was eager to talk with a beginner, and I was able to save valuable time in searching out those works in which writing was discussed as a craft. He guided me to Henry James's prefaces, to Conrad, to Joseph Warren Beach and to the letters of Dostoevsky. There were other advisers and other books involved, of course, but what is important here is that I was consciously concerned with the art of fiction, and that almost from the beginning I was grappling quite consciously with the art through which I wished to realize myself. But this was not done in isolation; the Spanish Civil War was now in progress and the Depression was still on. The world was being shaken up, and through one of those odd instances which occur to young provincials in New York, I was to hear Malraux make an appeal for the Spanish Loyalists at the same party where I first heard the folk singer Leadbelly perform. Wright and I were there seeking money for the magazine which he had come to New York to edit.

Art and politics: a great French novelist and a Negro folk singer, a young writer who was soon to publish *Uncle Tom's Children*, and I who had barely begun to study his craft. It is such accidents, such fortuitous meetings, which count for so much in our lives. I had never dreamed that I would be in the presence of Malraux, of whose work I became aware on my second day in Harlem when Langston Hughes suggested that I read *Man's Fate* and *Days of Wrath* before returning them to a friend of his. And it is this fortuitous circumstance which led to my selecting Malraux as a literary "ancestor," whom, unlike a relative, the artist is permitted to choose. There was in progress at the time all the agitation over the Scottsboro boys and the Herndon Case, and I was aware of both. I had to be; I myself had been taken off a freight train at Decatur, Alabama, only three years before while on my way to Tuskegee. But while I joined in the agitation for their release, my main energies went into learning to write.

I began to publish enough, and not too slowly, to justify my hopes for success, and as I continued, I made a most perplexing discovery—namely, that for all his conscious concern with technique, a writer did not so much create the novel as he was created *by* the novel. That is, one did not make an arbitrary gesture when one sought to write. And when I say that the novelist is created by the novel, I mean to remind you that fictional techniques are not a mere set of objective tools, but something much more intimate: a way of feeling, of seeing and of expressing one's sense of life. And the process of *acquiring* technique is a process of modifying one's responses, of learning to see and feel, to hear and observe, to evoke and evaluate the images of memory and of summoning up and directing the imagination, of learning to conceive of human values in the ways which have been established by the great writers who have developed and extended the art. And perhaps the writer's greatest freedom, as artist, lies precisely in his possession of technique, for it is through technique that he comes to possess and express the meaning of his life.

[1964]

POETRY

ANONYMOUS

Birmingham Jail was famous, not only in the South but throughout the United States, for many decades before Martin Luther King Jr. was arrested and imprisoned there in 1963. A song called "Birmingham Jail" is at least as old as the early twentieth century (a version was published in 1909), and like many popular ballads it draws on older songs, notably "Down in the Valley," which has been sung at least since the late nineteenth century. Like all folk songs, "Birmingham Jail" exists in many versions. Singers make small changes within a line, or sometimes drop or add whole verses. For instance, in what may be the most common version, some lines run thus:

> *Send me a letter, send it by mail,*
> *Send it in care of the Birmingham jail.*

But we have also heard:

> *Send me a letter, send it by mail,*
> *Back it in care of Birmingham jail.*

and in a version sung by Huddie Ledbetter, known as Leadbelly (1888–1949):

> *Send me a letter, send it by mail,*
> *'Dress it all over, that Birmingham jail.*

We print one version as it was actually sung, and then we print some additional stanzas from other versions, that is, from performances by other singers. You can pick and choose and thus create the version that strikes you as most effective. (Inventing new lines and stanzas, or adding lines or stanzas from other ballads, is entirely acceptable.)

Birmingham Jail

Down in the valley, the valley so low,
Put your head out the window, and hear the wind blow.
Hear the wind blow, hear the wind blow,
Put your head out the window, and hear the wind blow.   4

Write me a letter, send it by mail
'Dress it all over, that Birmingham jail.
Birmingham jail, boys, Birmingham jail,
'Dress it all over, that Birmingham jail.   8

Ty Shek [?] will 'rrest you, bound you over in jail,
Can't get nobody, to go your bail.
To go your bail, boys, to go your bail,
Can't get nobody, to go your bail.   12

Send for your lawyer, come down to your cell,
He swear he can clear you, in spite of all hell.
Spite of all hell, boys, spite of all hell,
He swear he can clear you, in spite of all hell.   16

Get the biggest your money, come back for the rest,
Tell you to plead guilty, for he know that is best.
He know that is best, boys, he know that is best,
Tell you plead guilty, he know that is best.   20

Down in the valley, the valley so low,
Put your head out the window, and hear the wind blow.
Hear the wind blow, hear the wind blow,
Put your head out the window, and hear the wind blow.   24

Topics for Critical Thinking and Writing

1. Here are some additional verses, taken from other singers. If you were singing
   "Birmingham Jail," which verses might you include, and which exclude? Why?

   > Writing this letter, containing three lines,
   > Answer my question, will you be mine?
   > Will you be mine, dear, will you be mine,
   > Answer my question, will you be mine?

   > The roses are red, and the vi'lets are blue,
   > Angels in Heaven sing "I love you."
   > Angels in Heaven, Angels in Heaven,
   > Angels in Heaven, sing "I love you."

   > Roses love sunshine, violets love dew,
   > Angels in Heaven know I love you,
   > Know I love you, dear, know I love you,
   > Angels in Heaven know I love you.

   > Go build me a castle, forty feet high,
   > So I can see her, as she goes by.
   > As she goes by, love, as she goes by,
   > So I can see her, as she goes by.

   > Bird in a cage, love, bird in a cage,
   > Dying for freedom, ever a slave.
   > Ever a slave love, ever a slave,
   > Dying for freedom, ever a slave.

2. We have never heard a version of "Birmingham Jail" in which the singer tells
   the hearer *why* he is in jail. Other songs talk about gambling debts or drunkenness or disorderly or criminal behavior, but in "Birmingham Jail" no explanation is offered, not even that the singer is unjustly imprisoned. Would the song
   be better if we were given such information? Why, or why not?

3. How is it that we as readers can feel pleasure in response to a poem that is
   sorrowful in tone and situation? What kind of pleasure is it? Do we share the
   speaker's sorrow, or do we remain somewhat at a distance from it?

A. E. HOUSMAN

Alfred Edward Housman (1859–1936) was born near rural Shropshire, England, and educated in classics and philosophy at Oxford University. Although he was a brilliant student, his final examination was unexpectedly weak—in fact, he failed—and he did not receive the academic appointment that he had anticipated. He began working as a civil servant at the British Patent Office, but in his spare time he wrote scholarly articles on Latin literature. These writings in 1892 won him an appointment as Professor of Latin at the University of London. In 1911 he was appointed to Cambridge University. During his lifetime he published (in addition to his scholarly writings) only two thin books of poetry, A Shropshire Lad *(1896) and* Last Poems *(1922), and a highly readable lecture called* The Name and Nature of Poetry *(1933). After his death a third book of poems,* More Poems *(1936), was published. The best edition of Housman's poems (containing not only the three books of poems already mentioned but also additional poems, fragments, translations, light verse, and Latin verse) is* The Poems of A. E. Housman, *ed. Archie Burnett (1997).*

The usual explanation for Housman's failure at his examination is that he was in a state of shock resulting from his repressed homosexual love for a fellow student. In any case, Housman, like almost all homosexuals of the period, kept his homosexuality a secret from the outside world. This is not surprising; in England, "unnatural acts" between men were punishable by death until 1885, when the penalty was modified to a maximum of two years at hard labor. (Not until 1967 was homosexual behavior between consenting adults legalized in England.) In the poetry published in Housman's lifetime there is nothing explicitly homosexual, but today readers who are aware of his sexual orientation can easily and reasonably perceive the sexual implications in the voice of the man who believes he is doomed to be an outsider.

The first of the four poems that we print here, "The Carpenter's Son," was written in 1895 and published the next year in A Shropshire Lad. *In this poem Housman sets forth, in nineteenth-century rural imagery, the story of a carpenter's son—Jesus was the son of a carpenter—who is carried in a cart to a gallows, where he will be hanged between two thieves. The youth who speaks the poem differs from his two fellow victims, he says, in that he "dies for love."*

The second poem, "Eight O'Clock" (drafted in 1917 and revised in 1922) also deals with a hanging, although nothing is said about who the victim is, or what he did.

The third poem, "Oh who is that young sinner," was written in August 1895, shortly after Oscar Wilde, the most popular British playwright of the period, was convicted of sodomy and given the maximum prison sentence. Although the poem does not mention homosexuality, Wilde's conviction unquestionably inspired it. Housman never published it, but a year after Housman died his brother, Laurence Housman, published it in A. E. H.: Some Poems, Some Letters and a Personal Memoir *(1936).*

The fourth poem, "The laws of God, the laws of man," was drafted in 1894 and revised in 1922. Housman published it in his Last Poems, *so he must have thought it was socially acceptable even though it speaks bitterly of both kinds of laws.*

The Carpenter's Son*

"Here the hangman stops his cart:
Now the best of friends must part.
Fare you well, for ill fare I:
Live, lads, and I will die.   4

"Oh, at home had I but stayed
'Prenticed to my father's trade,
Had I stuck to plane and adze,
I had not been lost, my lads.   8

"Then I might have built perhaps
Gallows-trees for other chaps,
Never dangled on my own,
Had I but left ill alone.   12

"Now, you see, they hang me high,
And the people passing by
Stop to shake their fists and curse;
So 'is come from ill to worse.   16

"Here hang I, and right and left
Two poor fellows hang for theft:
All the same's the luck we prove,
Though the midmost hangs for love.   20

"Comrades all, that stand and gaze,
Walk henceforth in other ways;
See my neck and save your own:
Comrades all, leave ill alone.   24

"Make some day a decent end,
Shrewder fellows than your friend.
Fare you well, for ill fare I:
Live, lads, and I will die."   28

[1895]

Topics for Critical Thinking and Writing

1. We think you will agree that even separated from the context of the other poems in *A Shropshire Lad*—a world in which Housman speaks of lads, barns,
   ploughing, country fairs, and so forth—"The Carpenter's Son" evokes a folksy,
   rural nineteenth-century world. What words make it seem to be set in relatively modern times, rather than the time of the crucifixion of Jesus? Or put it
   this way: Why does the speaker sound like a youth of the modern world (nineteenth century) rather than Jesus?

---

* The Gospels according to Matthew (13.55) and Mark (6.3) identify Jesus as a carpenter's son.
Lines 18–19 in the poem allude to the two thieves between whom Jesus was crucified (Matthew
27.38; Mark 15:27; Luke 23.39–40).

2. The speaker says that he "hangs for love" but he never amplifies what he means. Should he have?

3. Is the poem blasphemous? (If you are not a Christian, try to put yourself into the shoes of a Christian while thinking about this question.)

Eight O'Clock

He stood, and heard the steeple
  Sprinkle the quarters on the morning town.
One, two, three, four, to market-place and people
  It tossed them down.   4

Strapped, noosed, nighing his hour,
  He stood and counted them and cursed his luck;
And then the clock collected in the tower
  Its strength, and struck.   8

[1922]

Topics for Critical Thinking and Writing

1. A manuscript indicates that the poem had an additional stanza, which Housman never published. It ran thus:

> One: it had so much power,—
> If it had more, and if the clock struck two
> Or eight, or twelve, or any other hour—
> He never knew.

Do you think Housman was wise to delete this stanza? Why, or why not?

2. We are never told why the man is being hanged. In this poem, is the absence of this information a virtue or a fault? Explain.

Oh who is that young sinner

Oh who is that young sinner with the handcuffs on his wrists?
And what has he been after that they groan and shake their fists?
And wherefore is he wearing such a conscience-stricken air?
Oh they're taking him to prison for the colour of his hair.   4

'Tis a shame to human nature, such a head of hair as his;
In the good old time 'twas hanging for the colour that it is;
Though hanging isn't bad enough and flaying would be fair
For the nameless and abominable colour of his hair.   8

Oh a deal of pains he's taken and a pretty price he's paid
To hide his poll or dye it of a mentionable shade;
But they've pulled the beggar's hat off for the world to see and stare,
And they're haling him to justice for the colour of his hair.   12

Now 'tis oakum for his fingers° and the treadmill for his feet
And the quarry-gang on Portland in the cold and in the heat,
And between his spells of labour in the time he has to spare
He can curse the God that made him for the colour of his hair.   16

[1895]

13 oakum for his fingers prisoners sentenced to hard labor had to shred jute, a coarse fiber
mixed with tar to make oakum, used for caulking wooden ships. The task bloodied their fingers.

Topics for Critical Thinking and Writing

1. Characterize the tone of the speaker in the first two stanzas. He begins by asking a simple question, but what causes him to change to the tone we hear in the second stanza? What is the tone of the last line of the poem?
2. In a draft of the first line, Housman wrote "fellow" but he then replaced it with "sinner." Why do you suppose he made the change?
3. No one in England, or probably anywhere else, is or was put into prison "for the colour of his hair." What is Housman getting at?

The laws of God, the laws of man

The laws of God, the laws of man,
He may keep that will and can;
Not I: let God and man decree
Laws for themselves and not for me;
And if my ways are not as theirs   5
Let them mind their own affairs.
Their deeds I judge and much condemn,
Yet when did I make laws for them?
Please yourselves, say I, and they
Need only look the other way.   10
But no, they will not; they must still
Wrest their neighbour to their will,
And make me dance as they desire
With jail and gallows and hell-fire.
And how am I to face the odds   15
Of man's bedevilment and God's?
I, a stranger and afraid
In a world I never made.
They will be master, right or wrong;
Though both are foolish, both are strong.   20
And since, my soul, we cannot fly
To Saturn nor to Mercury,
Keep we must, if keep we can,
These foreign laws of God and man.

[1894]

Topics for Critical Thinking and Writing

1. For Housman, born into a Christian English family in the middle of the nineteenth century, what would "the laws of God" be?

2. For a nineteenth-century Christian, one of the laws of God would be Leviticus 18.20 (in the Hebrew Bible), which says: "Thou shalt not lie with mankind, as with womankind." Given the fact that Housman was a closeted homosexual (see headnote), is it reasonable to interpret the poem as in part a defense of his sexual orientation, and perhaps—we know nothing of his sexual activities or inactivities—a defense of his actions?

3. Judging from the entire poem, do you suppose Housman is saying that, ideally, all people should be able to do whatever they wish, which presumably might include rape, torture, and murder? Or does he imply limitations on behavior?

4. The poem begins with quiet rebellion: "The laws of God, the laws of man, / He may keep that will and can. / Not I. . . ." The tone changes as the speaker continues. Trace the steps in the speaker's changing attitudes. At the end is he saying pretty much what he said at the beginning, or has he shifted his position as well as his tone? And while we are talking about tone, taking the poem as a whole, how would you characterize the speaker?

5. Although "the laws of God" do not concern themselves with such things as our traffic regulations, do you agree that it is fair to say that in the United States (as in Housman's England) Judeo-Christian beliefs have shaped our laws so that, in effect, many of "the laws of man" are regarded as derived from "the laws of God"?

6. Does the speaker have a case, and does he make it effectively? And even if you think he does not have a case, does he manage to make you sympathize with him? Explain.

7. If you knew nothing about Housman's sexual orientation, how would you respond to this poem, and to the previous three? Do you think that the poems become more effective, or less, once the reader has some background about Housman and the closeted life he led?

EDGAR LEE MASTERS

Edgar Lee Masters (1869–1950), born in Kansas, raised in western Illinois, and a lawyer by profession, achieved international fame with The Spoon River Anthology *(1915), a collection of poems spoken by the deceased inhabitants of a mythical village called Spoon River. Masters published many other books of poetry, novels, and biographies, including a controversial, highly critical biography of Abraham Lincoln (1931). He titled his autobiography* Across Spoon River *(1936).*

Judge Selah Lively

Suppose you stood just five feet two,
And had worked your way as a grocery clerk,
Studying law by candle light
Until you became an attorney at law?
And then suppose through your diligence,   5
And regular church attendance,

You became attorney for Thomas Rhodes,
Collecting notes and mortgages,
And representing all the widows
In the Probate Court? And through it all   10
They jeered at your size, and laughed at your clothes
And your polished boots? And then suppose
You became the County Judge?
And Jefferson Howard and Kinsey Keene,
And Harmon Whitney, and all the giants   15
Who had sneered at you, were forced to stand
Before the bar and say "Your Honor"—
Well, don't you think it was natural
That I made it hard for them?

[1895]

Topics for Critical Thinking and Writing

1. Like the other poems in *The Spoon River Anthology,* "Judge Selah Lively" is spoken from the grave. Would the poem have a different feel if the speaker were alive?
2. "Selah" appears in several of the psalms in the Hebrew Bible, but the meaning of the word is uncertain. What do you think of Master's choice of a name for this speaker?
3. What is the answer to the question that Judge Lively asks in the last line? "Yes, it was natural"? "Yes, it was natural, but judges should be and can be above such behavior"? "No, it was not natural, and if you think it is natural you are clearly unfit to serve"?
4. Why do you think that Masters uses the pronouns "you" and, at the end, "I," as he does here? Would the poem affect us differently if it were entirely presented in the first person? And what would be the effect if the "I" at the end were a "you" instead?
5. The Judge tells us that he enjoyed a feeling of satisfaction when he was able to hold power over the men who had teased and tormented him. Have you ever been in a situation where you, at last, were in a position superior to others who once had been superior to you—and who might have teased or mocked you? Did you enjoy this experience?

CLAUDE MCKAY

Born in Jamaica, Claude McKay (1890–1948) wrote his first poems there, in dialect that drew upon the island's folk culture. In 1912 he left Jamaica to pursue a literary career in the United States. McKay attended school and worked at a number of jobs in the 1910s, but above all he continued to write poems, which were well received. During the 1920s, he became part of the Harlem literary and cultural renaissance. A political radical, McKay also was active in left-wing groups and causes; in 1922–23, he traveled to the Soviet Union, where he lectured on politics and literature. McKay's books of poems include Songs of Jamaica *(1912) and* Harlem Shadows *(1922). His most notable novel is* Home to Harlem *(1928); it tells the story of an African American soldier who deserts from the army in France and then returns to the United States, and it was the first novel by an African American to become a best-seller. McKay's autobiography is* A Long Way from Home *(1937). "If We Must Die," printed here, is McKay's best-known poem. A response to a horrific outbreak of racial violence in the summer of 1919 in Chicago and other major cities, the poem was first published in July of that year in the radical journal* Liberator.

If We Must Die

If we must die, let it not be like hogs
Hunted and penned in an inglorious spot,
While round us bark the mad and hungry dogs,
Making their mock at our accursed lot.
If we must die, O let us nobly die,   5
So that our precious blood may not be shed
In vain: then even the monsters we defy
Shall be constrained to honor us though dead!
O kinsmen! we must meet the common foe!
Though far outnumbered let us show us brave,   10
And for their thousand blows deal one deathblow!
What though before us lies the open grave?
Like men we'll face the murderous, cowardly pack,
Pressed to the wall, dying, but fighting back!

[1919]

Topics for Critical Thinking and Writing

1. In line 9, the speaker refers to "the common foe." In what other ways in the poem is this "foe" characterized?
2. We know that "If We Must Die" is a poem about racial violence. How would you interpret the poem if you did not know this?
3. Some would argue that violence should never be the response to injustice, no matter how cruel the injustice might be. Do you believe this yourself? Or can you think of instances where violence might be justified?

JIMMY SANTIAGO BACA

Jimmy Santiago Baca (b. 1952), of Chicano and Apache descent, was only 2 years old when his parents divorced. He lived with a grandparent until he was 5, when he was placed in an orphanage in New Mexico. He ran away when he was 11, lived on the streets, took drugs, and at the age of 20 was convicted of drug possession. In prison he taught himself to read and write, and he began to compose poetry. A fellow inmate urged him to send some poems to Mother Jones *magazine, and the work was accepted.* Immigrants in Our Own Land, *published in 1979, was Baca's first book, and it includes the poem printed here. His other books include* Black Mesa Poems *(1989) and* Healing Earthquakes: Poems *(2001). We include another of his poems on page 1184.*

Cloudy Day

It is windy today. A wall of wind crashes against,
windows clunk against, iron frames
as wind swings past broken glass
and seethes, like a frightened cat
in empty spaces of the cellblock.   5

In the exercise yard
we sat huddled in our prison jackets,
on our haunches against the fence,
and the wind carried our words
over the fence,   10
while the vigilant guard on the tower
held his cap at the sudden gust.

I could see the main tower from where I sat,
and the wind in my face
gave me the feeling I could grasp   15
the tower like a cornstalk,
and snap it from its roots of rock.
The wind plays it like a flute,
this hollow shoot of rock.
The brim girded with barbwire   20
with a guard sitting there also,
listening intently to the sounds
as clouds cover the sun.

I thought of the day I was coming to prison,
in the back seat of a police car,   25
hands and ankles chained, the policeman pointed,
    "See that big water tank? The big
    silver one out there, sticking up?
    That's the prison."

And here I am, I cannot believe it.   35
Sometimes it is such a dream, a dream,
where I stand up in the face of the wind,
like now, it blows at my jacket,
and my eyelids flick a little bit.
while I stare disbelieving. . . .   35

The third day of spring,
and four years later, I can tell you,
how a man can endure, how a man
can become so cruel, how he can die
or become so cold. I can tell you this,   40
I have seen it every day, every day,
and still I am strong enough to love you,
love myself and feel good;
even as the earth shakes and trembles,
and I have not a thing to my name,   45
I feel as if I have everything, everything.

[1979]

Topics for Critical Thinking and Writing

1. In an interview in 1997, Baca noted that he wrote "Cloudy Day" in prison. How do the details of the poem's language bear witness to Baca's own experience of imprisonment? Do you think that a person who had never been imprisoned could write such a poem?

2. In the same interview, Baca was asked about this poem: "Was that written for a person?" He replied: "It was written for me." Baca did not say any more than that. What do you think he means? And how, specifically, is this meaning reflected in the poem?

3. In the final stanza, Baca recalls that he has now been in prison for four years. What has he learned about himself, and about the realities of prison, during this period of time?

4. Who is the "you" referred to in the final stanza? How do you interpret the last line? And why does Baca repeat the word "everything"?

DRAMA

SUSAN GLASPELL

Susan Glaspell (1882–1948) was born in Davenport, Iowa, and educated at Drake University in Des Moines. In 1903 she married George Cram Cook and, with Cook and other writers, actors, and artists, in 1915 founded the Provincetown Players, a group that remained vital until 1929. Glaspell wrote Trifles *(1916) for the Provincetown Players, but she also wrote stories, novels, and a biography of her husband. In 1931 she won a Pulitzer Prize for* Alison's House, *a play about the family of a deceased poet who in some ways resembles Emily Dickinson.*

Trifles

SCENE: *The kitchen in the now abandoned farmhouse of* JOHN WRIGHT, *a gloomy kitchen, and left without having been put in order—unwashed pans under the sink, a loaf of bread outside the breadbox, a dish towel on the table—other signs of incompleted work. At the rear the outer door opens, and the* SHERIFF *comes in, followed by the* COUNTY ATTORNEY *and* HALE. *The* SHERIFF *and* HALE *are men in middle life, the* COUNTY ATTORNEY *is a young man; all are much bundled up and go at once to the stove. They are followed by the two women—the* SHERIFF'S WIFE *first; she is a slight wiry woman, a thin nervous face.* MRS. HALE *is larger and would ordinarily be called more comfortable looking, but she is disturbed now and looks fearfully about as she enters. The women have come in slowly and stand close together near the door.*

COUNTY ATTORNEY [*rubbing his hands*].   This feels good. Come up to the fire, ladies.

MRS. PETERS [*after taking a step forward*].   I'm not—cold.

SHERIFF [*unbuttoning his overcoat and stepping away from the stove as if to the beginning of official business*].   Now, Mr. Hale, before we move things about, you explain to Mr. Henderson just what you saw when you came here yesterday morning.

COUNTY ATTORNEY.   By the way, has anything been moved? Are things just as you left them yesterday?

SHERIFF [*looking about*].   It's just the same. When it dropped below zero last night, I thought I'd better send Frank out this morning to make a fire for us—no use getting pneumonia with a big case on; but I told him not to touch anything except the stove—and you know Frank.

COUNTY ATTORNEY.   Somebody should have been left here yesterday.

SHERIFF.   Oh—yesterday. When I had to send Frank to Morris Center for that man who went crazy—I want you to know I had my hands full yesterday. I knew you could get back from Omaha by today, and as long as I went over everything here myself—

COUNTY ATTORNEY.   Well, Mr. Hale, tell just what happened when you came here yesterday morning.

HALE.   Harry and I had started to town with a load of potatoes. We came along the road from my place; and as I got here, I said, "I'm going to see if I can't get John Wright to go in with me on a party telephone." I spoke to Wright about it once before, and he put me off, saying folks talked too much anyway, and all he asked was peace and quiet—I guess you know about how much he talked himself; but I thought maybe if I went to the house and talked about it before his wife, though I said to Harry that I didn't know as what his wife wanted made much difference to John—

COUNTY ATTORNEY.   Let's talk about that later, Mr. Hale. I do want to talk about that, but tell now just what happened when you got to the house.

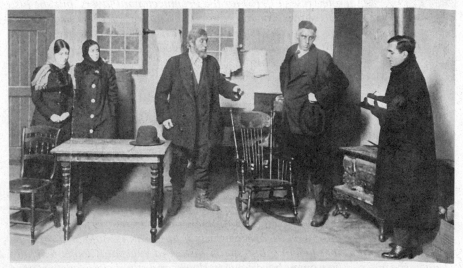

Photo of the original production (1916) of *Trifles*. (New York Public Library/Art Resource)

HALE.   I didn't hear or see anything; I knocked at the door, and still it was all quiet inside. I knew they must be up, it was past eight o'clock. So I knocked again, and I thought I heard somebody say, "Come in." I wasn't sure, I'm not sure yet, but I opened the door—this door [*indicating the door by which the two women are still standing*], and there in that rocker—[*pointing to it*] sat Mrs. Wright. [*They all look at the rocker.*]

COUNTY ATTORNEY.   What—was she doing?

HALE.   She was rockin' back and forth. She had her apron in her hand and was kind of—pleating it.

COUNTY ATTORNEY.   And how did she—look?

HALE.   Well, she looked queer.

COUNTY ATTORNEY.   How do you mean—queer?

HALE.   Well, as if she didn't know what she was going to do next. And kind of done up.

COUNTY ATTORNEY.   How did she seem to feel about your coming?

HALE.   Why, I don't think she minded—one way or other. She didn't pay much attention. I said, "How do, Mrs. Wright, it's cold, ain't it?" And she said, "Is it?"—and went on kind of pleating at her apron. Well, I was surprised; she didn't ask me to come up to the stove, or to set down, but just sat there, not even looking at me, so I said, "I want to see John." And then she—laughed. I guess you would call it a laugh. I thought of Harry and the team outside, so I said a little sharp: "Can't I see John?" "No," she says, kind o' dull like. "Ain't he home?" says I. "Yes," says she, "he's home." "Then why can't I see him?" I asked her, out of patience. "'Cause he's dead," says she. "*Dead?*" says I. She just nodded her head, not getting a bit excited, but rockin' back and forth. "Why—where is he?" says I, not knowing what to say. She just pointed upstairs—like that [*himself pointing to the room above*]. I got up, with the idea of going up there. I walked from there to here—then I says, "Why, what did he die of?" "He died of a rope around his neck," says she, and just went on pleatin' at her apron. Well, I went out and called Harry. I thought I might—need help. We went upstairs, and there he was lyin'—

COUNTY ATTORNEY.   I think I'd rather have you go into that upstairs, where you can point it all out. Just go on now with the rest of the story.

HALE.   Well, my first thought was to get that rope off. I looked . . . [*Stops, his face twitches.*] . . . but Harry, he went up to him, and he said, "No, he's dead all right, and we'd better not touch anything." So we went back downstairs. She was still sitting that same way. "Has anybody been notified?" I asked. "No," says she, unconcerned. "Who did this, Mrs. Wright?" said Harry. He said it businesslike—and she stopped pleatin' of her apron. "I don't know," she says. "You don't *know?*" says Harry. "No," says she. "Weren't you sleepin' in the bed with him?" says Harry. "Yes," says she, "but I was on the inside." "Somebody slipped a rope round his neck and strangled him, and you didn't wake up?" says Harry. "I didn't wake up," she said after him. We must 'a looked as if we didn't see how that could be, for after a minute she said, "I sleep sound." Harry was going to ask her more questions, but I said maybe we ought to let her tell her story first to the coroner, or the sheriff, so Harry went fast as he could to Rivers' place, where there's a telephone.

COUNTY ATTORNEY.   And what did Mrs. Wright do when she knew that you had gone for the coroner?

HALE.   She moved from that chair to this over here . . . [*Pointing to a small chair in the corner.*] . . . and just sat there with her hands held together and looking down. I got a feeling that I ought to make some conversation, so I said I had come in to see if John wanted to put in a telephone, and at that she started to laugh, and then she stopped and looked at me—scared. [*The* COUNTY ATTORNEY, *who has had his notebook out, makes a note.*] I dunno, maybe it wasn't scared. I wouldn't like to say it was. Soon Harry got back, and then Dr. Lloyd came, and you, Mr. Peters, and so I guess that's all I know that you don't.

COUNTY ATTORNEY [*looking around*].   I guess we'll go upstairs first—and then out to the barn and around there. [*To the* SHERIFF.] You're convinced that there was nothing important here—nothing that would point to any motive?

SHERIFF.   Nothing here but kitchen things. [*The* COUNTY ATTORNEY, *after again looking around the kitchen, opens the door of a cupboard closet. He gets up on a chair and looks on a shelf. Pulls his hand away, sticky.*]

COUNTY ATTORNEY.   Here's a nice mess. [*The women draw nearer.*]

MRS. PETERS [*to the other woman*].   Oh, her fruit; it did freeze. [*To the* LAWYER.] She worried about that when it turned so cold. She said the fir'd go out and her jars would break.

SHERIFF.   Well, can you beat the women! Held for murder and worryin' about her preserves.

COUNTY ATTORNEY.   I guess before we're through she may have something more serious than preserves to worry about.

HALE.   Well, women are used to worrying over trifles.

[*The two women move a little closer together.*]

COUNTY ATTORNEY [*with the gallantry of a young politician*].   And yet, for all their worries, what would we do without the ladies? [*The women do not unbend. He goes to the sink, takes a dipperful of water from the pail and, pouring it into a basin, washes his hands. Starts to wipe them on the roller towel, turns it for a cleaner place.*] Dirty towels! [*Kicks his foot against the pans under the sink.*] Not much of a housekeeper, would you say, ladies?

MRS. HALE [*stiffly*].   There's a great deal of work to be done on a farm.

COUNTY ATTORNEY.   To be sure. And yet . . . [*With a little bow to her.*] . . . I know there are some Dickson county farmhouses which do not have such roller towels. [*He gives it a pull to expose its full length again.*]

MRS. HALE.   Those towels get dirty awful quick. Men's hands aren't always as clean as they might be.

COUNTY ATTORNEY.   Ah, loyal to your sex, I see. But you and Mrs. Wright were neighbors. I suppose you were friends, too.

MRS. HALE [*shaking her head*].   I've not seen much of her of late years. I've not been in this house—it's more than a year.

COUNTY ATTORNEY.   And why was that? You didn't like her?

MRS. HALE.   I liked her all well enough. Farmers' wives have their hands full, Mr. Henderson. And then—

COUNTY ATTORNEY.   Yes—?

MRS. HALE [*looking about*].   It never seemed a very cheerful place.

COUNTY ATTORNEY.   No—it's not cheerful. I shouldn't say she had the homemaking instinct.

MRS. HALE.   Well, I don't know as Wright had, either.

COUNTY ATTORNEY.   You mean that they didn't get on very well?

MRS. HALE.   No, I don't mean anything. But I don't think a place'd be any cheerfuler for John Wright's being in it.

COUNTY ATTORNEY.   I'd like to talk more of that a little later. I want to get the lay of things upstairs now. [*He goes to the left, where three steps lead to a stair door.*]

SHERIFF.   I suppose anything Mrs. Peters does'll be all right. She was to take in some clothes for her, you know, and a few little things. We left in such a hurry yesterday.

COUNTY ATTORNEY.   Yes, but I would like to see what you take, Mrs. Peters, and keep an eye out for anything that might be of use to us.

MRS. PETERS.   Yes, Mr. Henderson.

[*The women listen to the men's steps on the stairs, then look about the kitchen.*]

MRS. HALE.   I'd hate to have men coming into my kitchen, snooping around and criticizing. [*She arranges the pans under sink which the* LAWYER *had shoved out of place.*]

MRS. PETERS.   Of course it's no more than their duty.

MRS. HALE.   Duty's all right, but I guess that deputy sheriff that came out to make the fire might have got a little of this on. [*Gives the roller towel a pull.*] Wish I'd thought of that sooner. Seems mean to talk about her for not having things slicked up when she had to come away in such a hurry.

MRS. PETERS [*who has gone to a small table in the left rear corner of the room, and lifted one end of a towel that covers a pan*].   She had bread set. [*Stands still.*]

MRS. HALE [*eyes fixed on a loaf of bread beside the breadbox, which is on a low shelf at the other side of the room. Moves slowly toward it*].   She was going to put this in there. [*Picks up loaf, then abruptly drops it. In a manner of returning to familiar things.*] It's a shame about her fruit. I wonder if it's all gone. [*Gets up on the chair and looks.*] I think there's some here that's all right, Mrs. Peters. Yes—here; [*Holding it toward the window.*] this is cherries, too. [*Looking again.*] I declare I believe that's the only one. [*Gets down, bottle in her hand. Goes to the sink and wipes it off on the outside.*] She'll feel awful bad after all her hard work in the hot weather. I remember the afternoon I put up my cherries last summer. [*She puts the bottle on the big kitchen table, center of the room, front table. With a sigh, is about to sit down in the rocking chair. Before she is seated realizes what chair it is; with a slow look at it, steps back. The chair, which she has touched, rocks back and forth.*]

MRS. PETERS.   Well, I must get those things from the front room closet. [*She goes to the door at the right, but after looking into the other room steps back.*] You coming with me, Mrs. Hale? You could help me carry them. [*They go into the other room; reappear,* MRS. PETERS *carrying a dress and skirt, Mrs. Hale following with a pair of shoes.*]

MRS. PETERS.   My, it's cold in there. [*She puts the cloth on the big table, and hurries to the stove.*]

MRS. HALE [*examining the skirt*].   Wright was close. I think maybe that's why she kept so much to herself. She didn't even belong to the Ladies' Aid. I suppose she felt she couldn't do her part, and then you don't enjoy things when you feel shabby. She used to wear pretty clothes and be lively, when she was Minnie Foster, one of the town girls singing in the choir. But that—oh, that was thirty years ago. This all you was to take in?

MRS. PETERS.   She said she wanted an apron. Funny thing to want, for there isn't much to get you dirty in jail, goodness knows. But I suppose just to make her feel more natural. She said they was in the top drawer in this cupboard. Yes, here. And then her little shawl that always hung behind the door. [*Opens stair door and looks.*] Yes, here it is. [*Quickly shuts door leading upstairs.*]

MRS. HALE [*abruptly moving toward her*].   Mrs. Peters?

MRS. PETERS.   Yes, Mrs. Hale?

MRS. HALE.   Do you think she did it?

MRS. PETERS [*in a frightened voice*].   Oh, I don't know.

MRS. HALE.   Well, I don't think she did. Asking for an apron and her little shawl. Worrying about her fruit.

MRS. PETERS [*starts to speak, glances up, where footsteps are heard in the room above. In a low voice*].   Mr. Peters says it looks bad for her. Mr. Henderson is awful sarcastic in speech, and he'll make fun of her sayin' she didn't wake up.

MRS. HALE.   Well, I guess John Wright didn't wake when they was slipping that rope under his neck.

MRS. PETERS.   No, it's strange. It must have been done awful crafty and still. They say it was such a—funny way to kill a man, rigging it all up like that.

MRS. HALE.   That's just what Mr. Hale said. There was a gun in the house. He says that's what he can't understand.

MRS. PETERS.   Mr. Henderson said coming out that what was needed for the case was a motive; something to show anger, or—sudden feeling.

MRS. HALE [*who is standing by the table*].   Well, I don't see any signs of anger around here. [*She puts her hand on the dish towel which lies on the table, stands looking down at the table, one half of which is clean, the other half messy.*] It's wiped here. [*Makes a move as if to finish work, then turns and looks at loaf of bread outside the breadbox. Drops towel. In that voice of coming back to familiar things.*] Wonder how they are finding things upstairs? I hope she had it a little more red-up there. You know, it seems kind of *sneaking.* Locking her up in town and then coming out here and trying to get her own house to turn against her!

MRS. PETERS.   But, Mrs. Hale, the law is the law.

MRS. HALE.   I s'pose 'is. [*Unbuttoning her coat.*] Better loosen up your things, Mrs. Peters. You won't feel them when you go out.

[MRS. PETERS *takes off her fur tippet, goes to hang it on hook at the back of room, stands looking at the under part of the small corner table.*]

MRS. PETERS.   She was piecing a quilt. [*She brings the large sewing basket, and they look at the bright pieces.*]

MRS. HALE.   It's log cabin pattern. Pretty, isn't it? I wonder if she was goin' to quilt or just knot it?

[*Footsteps have been heard coming down the stairs. The* SHERIFF *enters, followed by* HALE *and the* COUNTY ATTORNEY.]

SHERIFF.   They wonder if she was going to quilt it or just knot it. [*The men laugh, the women look abashed.*]

COUNTY ATTORNEY [*rubbing his hands over the stove*].   Frank's fire didn't do much up there, did it? Well, let's go out to the barn and get that cleared up.

[*The men go outside.*]

MRS. HALE [*resentfully*].   I don't know as there's anything so strange, our takin' up our time with little things while we're waiting for them to get the evidence. [*She sits down at the big table, smoothing out a block with decision.*] I don't see as it's anything to laugh about.

MRS. PETERS [*apologetically*].   Of course they've got awful important things on their minds. [*Pulls up a chair and joins* MRS. HALE *at the table.*]

MRS. HALE [*examining another block*].   Mrs. Peters, look at this one. Here, this is the one she was working on, and look at the sewing! All the rest of it has been so nice and even. And look at this! It's all over the place! Why, it looks as if she didn't know what she was about! [*After she has said this, they look at each other, then started to glance back at the door. After an instant* MRS. HALE *has pulled at a knot and ripped the sewing.*]

MRS. PETERS.   Oh, what are you doing, Mrs. Hale?

MRS. HALE [*mildly*].   Just pulling out a stitch or two that's not sewed very good. [*Threading a needle.*] Bad sewing always made me fidgety.

MRS. PETERS [*nervously*].   I don't think we ought to touch things.

MRS. HALE.   I'll just finish up this end. [*Suddenly stopping and leaning forward.*] Mrs. Peters?

MRS. PETERS.   Yes, Mrs. Hale?

MRS. HALE.   What do you suppose she was so nervous about?

MRS. PETERS.   Oh—I don't know. I don't know as she was nervous. I sometimes sew awful queer when I'm just tired. [MRS. HALE *starts to say something, looks at* MRS. PETERS, *then goes on sewing.*] Well, I must get these things wrapped up. They may be through sooner than we think. [*Putting apron and other things together.*] I wonder where I can find a piece of paper, and string.

MRS. HALE.   In that cupboard, maybe.

MRS. PETERS [*looking in cupboard*].   Why, here's a birdcage. [*Holds it up.*] Did she have a bird, Mrs. Hale?

MRS. HALE.   Why, I don't know whether she did or not—I've not been here for so long. There was a man around last year selling canaries cheap, but I don't know as she took one; maybe she did. She used to sing real pretty herself.

MRS. PETERS [*glancing around*].   Seems funny to think of a bird here. But she must have had one, or why should she have a cage? I wonder what happened to it?

MRS. HALE.   I s'pose maybe the cat got it.

MRS. PETERS.   No, she didn't have a cat. She's got that feeling some people have about cats—being afraid of them. My cat got in her room, and she was real upset and asked me to take it out.

MRS. HALE.   My sister Bessie was like that. Queer, ain't it?

MRS. PETERS [*examining the cage*].   Why, look at this door. It's broke. One hinge is pulled apart.

MRS. HALE [*looking, too*].   Looks as if someone must have been rough with it.

MRS. PETERS.   Why, yes. [*She brings the cage forward and puts it on the table.*]

MRS. HALE.   I wish if they're going to find any evidence they'd be about it. I don't like this place.

MRS. PETERS.   But I'm awful glad you came with me, Mrs. Hale. It would be lonesome for me sitting here alone.

MRS. HALE.   It would, wouldn't it? [*Dropping her sewing.*] But I tell you what I do wish, Mrs. Peters. I wish I had come over sometimes when *she* was here. I—[*Looking around the room.*]—wish I had.

MRS. PETERS.   But of course you were awful busy, Mrs. Hale—your house and your children.

MRS. HALE.   I could've come. I stayed away because it weren't cheerful—and that's why I ought to have come. I—I've never liked this place. Maybe because it's down in a hollow, and you don't see the road. I dunno what it is, but it's a lonesome place and always was. I wish I had come over to see Minnie Foster sometimes. I can see now—[*Shakes her head.*]

MRS. PETERS.   Well, you mustn't reproach yourself, Mrs. Hale. Somehow we just don't see how it is with other folks until—something comes up.

MRS. HALE.   Not having children makes less work—but it makes a quiet house, and Wright out to work all day, and no company when he did come in. Did you know John Wright, Mrs. Peters?

MRS. PETERS.   Not to know him; I've seen him in town. They say he was a good man.

MRS. HALE.   Yes—good; he didn't drink, and kept his word as well as most, I guess, and paid his debts. But he was a hard man, Mrs. Peters. Just to pass the time of day with him. [*Shivers.*] Like a raw wind that gets to the bone. [*Pauses, her eye falling on the cage.*] I should think she would 'a wanted a bird. But what do you suppose went with it?

MRS. PETERS.   I don't know, unless it got sick and died. [*She reaches over and swings the broken door, swings it again; both women watch it.*]

MRS. HALE.   You weren't raised round here, were you? [MRS. PETERS *shakes her head.*] You didn't know—her?

MRS. PETERS.   Not till they brought her yesterday.

MRS. HALE.   She—come to think of it, she was kind of like a bird herself—real sweet and pretty, but kind of timid and—fluttery. How—she—did—change. [*Silence; then as if struck by a happy thought and relieved to get back to everyday things.*] Tell you what, Mrs. Peters; why don't you take the quilt in with you? It might take up her mind.

MRS. PETERS.   Why, I think that's a real nice idea, Mrs. Hale. There couldn't possibly be any objection to it, could there? Now, just what would I take? I wonder if her patches are in here—and her things. [*They look in the sewing basket.*]

MRS. HALE.   Here's some red. I expect this has got sewing things in it [*Brings out a fancy box.*] What a pretty box. Looks like something somebody would give you. Maybe her scissors are in here. [*Opens box. Suddenly puts her hand to her nose.*] Why—[MRS. PETERS *bends nearer, then turns her face away.*] There's something wrapped up in this piece of silk.

MRS. PETERS.   Why, this isn't her scissors.

MRS. HALE [*lifting the silk*].   Oh, Mrs. Peters—it's—[MRS. PETERS *bends closer.*]

MRS. PETERS.   It's the bird.

MRS. HALE [*jumping up*].   But, Mrs. Peters—look at it. Its neck! Look at its neck! It's all—other side *to.*

MRS. PETERS.   Somebody—wrung—its neck.

[*Their eyes meet. A look of growing comprehension of horror. Steps are heard outside.* MRS. HALE *slips box under quilt pieces, and sinks into her chair. Enter* SHERIFF *and* COUNTY ATTORNEY. MRS. PETERS *rises.*]

COUNTY ATTORNEY [*as one turning from serious things to little pleasantries*].   Well, ladies, have you decided whether she was going to quilt it or knot it?

MRS. PETERS.   We think she was going to—knot it.

COUNTY ATTORNEY.   Well, that's interesting, I'm sure. [*Seeing the birdcage.*] Has the bird flown?

MRS. HALE [*putting more quilt pieces over the box*].   We think the—cat got it.

COUNTY ATTORNEY [*preoccupied*].   Is there a cat?

[MRS. HALE *glances in a quick covert way at* MRS. PETERS.]

MRS. PETERS.   Well, not now. They're superstitious, you know. They leave.

COUNTY ATTORNEY [*to* SHERIFF, *continuing an interrupted conversation*].   No sign at all of anyone having come from the outside. Their own rope. Now let's go up again and go over it piece by piece. [*They start upstairs.*] It would have to have been someone who knew just the—[MRS. PETERS *sits down. The two women sit there not looking at one another, but as if peering into something and at the same time holding back. When they talk now, it is the manner of feeling their way over strange ground, as if afraid of what they are saying, but as if they cannot help saying it.*]

MRS. HALE.   She liked the bird. She was going to bury it in that pretty box.

MRS. PETERS [*in a whisper*].   When I was a girl—my kitten—there was a boy took a hatchet, and before my eyes—and before I could get there—[*Covers her face an instant.*] If they hadn't held me back, I would have—[*Catches herself, looks upstairs where steps are heard, falters weakly.*]—hurt him.

MRS. HALE [*with a slow look around her*].   I wonder how it would seem never to have had any children around. [*Pause.*] No, Wright wouldn't like the bird—a thing that sang. She used to sing. He killed that, too.

MRS. PETERS [*moving uneasily*].   We don't know who killed the bird.

MRS. HALE.   I knew John Wright.

MRS. PETERS.   It was an awful thing was done in this house that night, Mrs. Hale. Killing a man while he slept, slipping a rope around his neck that choked the life out of him.

MRS. HALE.   His neck. Choked the life out of him.

[*Her hand goes out and rests on the birdcage.*]

MRS. PETERS [*with a rising voice*].   We don't know who killed him. We don't *know*.

MRS. HALE [*her own feeling not interrupted*].   If there'd been years and years of nothing, then a bird to sing to you, it would be awful—still, after the bird was still.

MRS. PETERS [*something within her speaking*].   I know what stillness is. When we homesteaded in Dakota, and my first baby died—after he was two years old, and me with no other then—

MRS. HALE [*moving*].   How soon do you suppose they'll be through, looking for evidence?

MRS. PETERS.   I know what stillness is. [*Pulling herself back.*] The law has got to punish crime, Mrs. Hale.

MRS. HALE [*not as if answering that*].   I wish you'd seen Minnie Foster when she wore a white dress with blue ribbons and stood up there in the choir and sang. [*A look around the room.*] Oh, I *wish* I'd come over here once in a while! That was a crime! That was a crime! Who's going to punish that?

MRS. PETERS [*looking upstairs*].   We mustn't—take on.

MRS. HALE.   I might have known she needed help! I know how things can be—for women. I tell you, it's queer, Mrs. Peters. We live close together and we live far apart. We all go through the same things—it's all just a different kind of the same thing. [*Brushes her eyes, noticing the bottle of fruit, reaches out for it.*] If I was you, I wouldn't tell her her fruit was gone. Tell her it *ain't*. Tell her it's all right. Take this in to prove it to her. She—she may never know whether it was broke or not.

MRS. PETERS [*takes the bottle, looks about for something to wrap it in; takes petticoat from the clothes brought from the other room, very nervously begins winding this around the bottle. In a false voice*].   My, it's a good thing the men couldn't hear us. Wouldn't they just laugh! Getting all stirred up over a little thing like a—dead canary. As if that could have anything to do with—with—wouldn't they *laugh*!

[*The men are heard coming downstairs.*]

MRS. HALE [*under her breath*]   Maybe they would—maybe they wouldn't.

COUNTY ATTORNEY.   No, Peters, it's all perfectly clear except a reason for doing it. But you know juries when it comes to women. If there was some definite thing. Something to show—something to make a story about—a thing that would connect up with this strange way of doing it.

[*The women's eyes meet for an instant. Enter* HALE *from outer door.*]

HALE.   Well, I've got the team around. Pretty cold out there.

COUNTY ATTORNEY.   I'm going to stay here awhile by myself. [*To the* SHERIFF.] You can send Frank out for me, can't you? I want to go over everything. I'm not satisfied that we can't do better.

SHERIFF.   Do you want to see what Mrs. Peters is going to take in?

[*The* LAWYER *goes to the table, picks up the apron, laughs.*]

COUNTY ATTORNEY.   Oh I guess they're not very dangerous things the ladies have picked up. [*Moves a few things about, disturbing the quilt pieces which cover the box. Steps back.*] No, Mrs. Peters doesn't need supervising. For that matter, a sheriff's wife is married to the law. Ever think of it that way, Mrs. Peters?

MRS. PETERS.   Not—just that way.

SHERIFF [*chuckling*].   Married to the law. [*Moves toward the other room.*] I just want you to come in here a minute, George. We ought to take a look at these windows.

COUNTY ATTORNEY [*scoffingly*].   Oh, windows!

SHERIFF.   We'll be right out, Mr. Hale.

[HALE *goes outside. The* SHERIFF *follows the* COUNTY ATTORNEY *into the other room. Then* MRS. HALE *rises, hands tight together, looking intensely at* MRS. PETERS, *whose eyes take a slow turn, finally meeting,* MRS. HALE*'s. A moment* MRS. HALE *holds her, then her own eyes point the way to where the box is concealed. Suddenly* MRS. PETERS *throws back quilt pieces and tries to put the box in the bag she is wearing. It is too big. She opens box, starts to take the bird out, cannot touch it, goes to pieces, stands there helpless. Sound of a knob turning in the other room.* MRS. HALE *snatches the box and puts it in the pocket of her big coat. Enter* COUNTY ATTORNEY *and* SHERIFF.]

COUNTY ATTORNEY [*facetiously*].   Well, Henry, at least we found out that she was not going to quilt it. She was going to—what is it you call it, ladies?

MRS. HALE [*her hand against her pocket*].   We call it—knot it, Mr. Henderson.

CURTAIN

[1916]

Topics for Critical Thinking and Writing

1. Briefly describe the setting, indicating what it "says" and what atmosphere it evokes.
2. Even before the first word of dialogue is spoken, what do you think the play tells us (in the entrance of the characters) about the distinction between the men and the women?
3. How would you characterize Mr. Henderson, the county attorney?
4. In what way or ways are Mrs. Peters and Mrs. Hale different from each other?
5. Several times the men "laugh" or "chuckle." In their contexts, what do these expressions of amusement convey?
6. At the top of this page, "*the women's eyes meet for an instant.*" What do you think this bit of action "says"? What do you understand by the exchange of glances?

7. On page 1317, when Mrs. Peters tells of the boy who killed her cat, she says, "If they hadn't held me back, I would have—(*Catches herself, looks upstairs where steps are heard, falters weakly.*)—hurt him." What do you think she was about to say before she faltered? Why do you suppose Glaspell included this speech about Mrs. Peters's girlhood?

8. On page 1314, Mrs. Hale, looking at a quilt, wonders whether Mrs. Wright "was goin' to quilt it or just knot it." The men are amused by the women's concern with this topic, and the last line of the play returns to the issue. What do you make of this emphasis on the matter?

9. We never see Mrs. Wright on stage. Nevertheless, by the end of *Trifles* we know a great deal about her. In an essay of 500–750 words explain both what we know about her—physical characteristics, habits, interests, personality, life before her marriage and after—and *how* we know these things.

10. The title of the play is ironic—the "trifles" are important. What other ironics do you find in the play? (On irony, see Glossary.)

11. Do you think the play is immoral? Explain.

12. Assume that the canary has been found, thereby revealing a possible motive, and that Minnie Wright is indicted for murder. You are the defense attorney. In 500 words set forth your defense. (Take any position you wish. For instance, you may want to argue that she committed justifiable homicide or that—on the basis of her behavior as reported by Mr. Hale—she is innocent by reason of insanity.)

13. Assume that the canary had been found and Minnie Wright convicted. Compose the speech you think she might have delivered before the sentence was given.

Appendix A

Remarks about Manuscript Form

BASIC MANUSCRIPT FORM

Much of what follows is nothing more than common sense.

- Use good quality 8½" × 11" paper. Make a photocopy, or, if you have written on a word processor print out a second copy, in case the instructor's copy goes astray.
- If you write on a word processor, **double-space,** and print on one side of the page only; set the printer for professional or best quality. If you submit handwritten copy, use lined paper and write on one side of the page only in black or dark blue ink, on every other line.
- Use **one-inch margins** on all sides.
- Within the top margin, put your last name and then (after hitting the space bar twice) the **page number** (in arabic numerals), so that the number is flush with the right-hand margin.
- On the first page, below the top margin and flush with the left-hand margin, put your **full name,** your **instructor's name,** the **course number** (including the section), and the **date,** one item per line, double-spaced.
- **Center the title** of your essay. Remember that the title is important—it gives the readers their first glimpse of your essay. **Create your own title**—one that reflects your topic or thesis. For example, a paper on Charlotte Perkins Gilman's "The Yellow Wallpaper" should not be called "The Yellow Wallpaper" but might be called

Disguised Tyranny in Gilman's "The Yellow Wallpaper"

or

How to Drive a Woman Mad

These titles do at least a little in the way of rousing a reader's interest.

- **Capitalize the title thus:** Begin the first word of the title with a capital letter, and capitalize each subsequent word except articles (*a, an, the*), conjunctions (*and, but, if, when,* etc.), and prepositions (*in, on, with,* etc.):

A Word on Behalf of Love

Notice that you do *not* enclose your title within quotation marks, and you do *not* underline it—though if it includes the title of a poem or a story, *that* is enclosed within quotation marks, or if it includes the title of a novel or play, *that* is underlined (to indicate italics), thus:

Gilman's "The Yellow Wallpaper" and Medical Practice

and

Gender Stereotypes in <u>Hamlet</u>

1320

- **After writing your title, double-space,** indent five spaces, and begin your first sentence.
- Unless your instructor tells you otherwise, **use a staple** to hold the pages together. (Do not use a stiff binder; it will only add to the bulk of the instructor's stack of papers.)
- Extensive revisions should have been made in your drafts, but minor **last-minute revisions** may be made—neatly—on the finished copy. Proofreading may catch some typographical errors, and you may notice some small weaknesses. You can make corrections using the following proofreader's symbols.

CORRECTIONS IN THE FINAL COPY

Changes in wording may be made by crossing through words and rewriting them:

> The influence of Poe and Hawthorne ~~have~~ *has* greatly diminished.

Additions should be made above the line, with a caret below the line at the appropriate place:

> The influence of Poe and Hawthorne has *greatly* diminished.

Transpositions of letters may be made thus:

> The influence of Poe and Hawthorne has diminished.

Deletions are indicated by a horizontal line through the word or words to be deleted. Delete a single letter by drawing a vertical or diagonal line through it; then indicate whether the letters on either side are to be closed up by drawing a connecting arc:

> The influence of Poe and Hawthorne has greatly diminished.

Separation of words accidentally run together is indicated by a vertical line, closure by a curved line connecting the letters to be closed up:

> The influence/of Poe and Hawthorne has g reatly diminished.

Paragraphing may be indicated by the symbol ¶ before the word that is to begin the new paragraph:

> The influence of Poe and Hawthorne has greatly diminished. ¶ The
>
> influence of Borges has very largely replaced that of earlier writers of
>
> fantasy.

QUOTATIONS AND QUOTATION MARKS

First, a word about the *point* of using quotations. Don't use quotations to pad the length of a paper. Rather, give quotations from the work you are discussing so that your readers will see the material being considered and (especially in a research paper) so that your readers will know what some of the chief interpretations are and what your responses to them are.

Note: The next few paragraphs do *not* discuss how to include citations of sources, a topic taken up in the next appendix under the heading "How to Document: Footnotes, Internal Parenthetical Citations, and a List of Works Cited."

The Golden Rule: If you quote, *comment on* the quotation. Let the reader know what you make of it and why you quote it.

Additional principles:

1. Identify the speaker or writer of the quotation so that the reader is not left with a sense of uncertainty. Usually, in accordance with the principle of letting readers know where they are going, this identification precedes the quoted material, but occasionally it may follow the quotation, especially if it will provide something of a pleasant surprise. For instance, in a discussion of Flannery O'Connor's stories, you might quote a disparaging comment on one of the stories and then reveal that O'Connor herself was the speaker.

2. If the quotation is part of your own sentence, **be sure to fit the quotation grammatically and logically into your sentence.**

> *Incorrect:* Holden Caulfield tells us very little about "what my lousy childhood was like."
>
> *Correct:* Holden Caulfield tells us very little about what his "lousy childhood was like."

3. Indicate any omissions or additions. The quotation must be exact. Any material that you add—even one or two words—must be enclosed within square brackets, thus:

> Hawthorne tells us that "owing doubtless to the depth of the gloom at that
>
> particular spot [in the forest], neither the travellers nor their steeds were
>
> visible."

If you wish to omit material from within a quotation, indicate the ellipsis by three spaced periods. That is, at the point where you are omitting material, type a space, a period, a space, a period, a space, and a third period. If you are omitting material from the end of a sentence, type a space after the last word that you quote, then a period, a space, a period, a space, a third period, and a period to indicate the end of the sentence. The following example is based on a quotation from the sentences immediately above this one:

> The instructions say, "If you . . . omit material from within a quotation, [you
>
> must] indicate the ellipsis. . . . If you are omitting material from the end of a
>
> sentence, type . . . then a period to indicate the end. . . .

Notice that although material preceded "If you," periods are not needed to indicate the omission because "If you" began a sentence in the original. Customarily, initial and terminal omissions are indicated only when they are part of the sentence you are quoting. Even such omissions need not be indicated when the quoted material is obviously incomplete—when, for instance, it is a word or phrase.

4. Distinguish between short and long quotations, and treat each appropriately. **Short quotations** (usually defined as fewer than five lines of typed prose or three lines of poetry) are enclosed within quotation marks and run into the text (rather than being set off, without quotation marks), as in the following example:

> Hawthorne begins the story by telling us that "Young Goodman Brown came forth at sunset into the street at Salem village," thus at the outset connecting the village with daylight. A few paragraphs later, when Hawthorne tells us that the road Brown takes was "darkened by all of the gloomiest trees of the forest," he begins to associate the forest with darkness--and a very little later with evil.

If your short quotation is from a poem, be sure to follow the capitalization of the original, and use a slash mark (with a space before and after it) to indicate separate lines. Give the line numbers, if your source gives them, in parentheses, immediately after the closing quotation marks and before the closing punctuation, thus:

> In "Diving into the Wreck," Adrienne Rich's speaker says that she puts on "body-armor" (5). Obviously the journey is dangerous.

To set off a **long quotation** (more than four typed lines of prose or more than two lines of poetry), indent the entire quotation ten spaces from the left margin. Usually, a long quotation is introduced by a clause ending with a colon—for instance, "The following passage will make this point clear:" or "The closest we come to hearing an editorial voice is a long passage in the middle of the story:" or some such lead-in. After typing your lead-in, double-space, and then type the quotation, indented and double-spaced.

5. Commas and periods go inside the quotation marks.

> Chopin tells us in the first sentence that "Mrs. Mallard was afflicted with heart trouble," and in the last sentence the doctors say that Mrs. Mallard "died of heart disease."

Exception: If the quotation is immediately followed by material in parentheses or in square brackets, close the quotation, then give the parenthetic or bracketed material, and then—after closing the parenthesis or bracket—insert the comma or period.

> Chopin tells us in the first sentence that "Mrs. Mallard was afflicted with heart trouble" (13), and in the last sentence the doctors say that Mrs. Mallard "died of heart disease" (15).

Semicolons, colons, and dashes go outside the closing quotation marks.

Question marks and exclamation points go inside if they are part of the quotation, outside if they are your own.

In the following passage from a student's essay, notice the difference in the position of the question marks. The first question mark is part of the quotation, so it is enclosed within the quotation marks. The second question mark, however, is the student's, so it comes after the closing quotation marks.

> The older man says to Goodman Brown, "Sayest thou so?" Doesn't a reader
>
> become uneasy when the man immediately adds, "We are but a little way in
>
> the forest yet"?

Quotation Marks or Underlining?

Use quotation marks around titles of short stories and other short works—that is, titles of chapters in books, essays, and poems that might not be published by themselves. Underline (to indicate italics) titles of books, periodicals, collections of essays, plays, and long poems such as *The Rime of the Ancient Mariner*. Word processing software will let you use italic type (instead of underlining) if you wish.

A Note on the Possessive

It is awkward to use the possessive case for titles of literary works and secondary sources. Rather than "*The Great Gatsby*'s final chapter," write instead "the final chapter of *The Great Gatsby*." Not "*The Oxford Companion to American Literature*'s entry on Emerson," but, instead, "the entry on Emerson in *The Oxford Companion to American Literature*."

Appendix B

Writing a Research Paper

WHAT RESEARCH IS NOT, AND WHAT RESEARCH IS

Because a research paper requires its writer to collect and interpret evidence—usually including the opinions of earlier investigators—it is sometimes said that a research paper, unlike a critical essay, is not the expression of personal opinion. But such a view is unjust both to criticism and to research. A critical essay is not a mere expression of personal opinions; if it is any good, it offers evidence that supports the opinions and thus persuades the reader of their objective rightness. And a research paper is in the final analysis largely personal, because the author continuously uses his or her own judgment to evaluate the evidence, deciding what is relevant and convincing. A research paper is not the mere presentation of what a dozen scholars have already said about a topic; it is a thoughtful evaluation of the available evidence, and so it is, finally, an expression of what the author thinks the evidence adds up to.

PRIMARY AND SECONDARY MATERIALS

The materials of literary research can be conveniently divided into two sorts, primary and secondary. The *primary materials,* or sources, are the real subject of study; the *secondary materials* are critical and historical accounts already written about these primary materials. For example, Langston Hughes wrote poems, stories, plays, and essays. For a student of Hughes, these works are the primary materials. (We include several of his works in this book.) If you want to study his ways of representing African American speech, or his representations of whites, or his collaboration with Zora Neale Hurston, you will read the primary material—his own writings (and Hurston's, in the case of the collaborative work). But in an effort to reach a thoughtful understanding of some aspect of his work, you will also want to look at later biographical and critical studies of his works and perhaps also at scholarly writing on such topics as Black English. You may even find yourself looking at essays on Black English that do not specifically mention Hughes but that nevertheless may prove helpful.

Similarly, if you are writing about Charlotte Perkins Gilman (we include one of her stories), the primary material includes not only other stories but also her social and political writing. If you are writing about her views of medical treatment of women, you will want to look not only at the story we reprint ("The Yellow Wallpaper") but also at her autobiography. Further, you will also want to look at some secondary material, such as recent scholarly books and articles on medical treatment of women in the late nineteenth and early twentieth centuries.

Locating Materials: First Steps

This appendix is devoted to traditional resources. Consult the next appendix for a detailed introduction to electronic resources.

The easiest way to locate articles and books on literature written in a modern language—that is, on a topic other than literature of the ancient world—is to consult the

> *MLA International Bibliography of Books and Articles in the Modern Languages and Literatures* (1922–),

which until 1969 was published as part of *PMLA* (*Publications of the Modern Language Association*) and since 1969 has been published separately. It is also available on CD-ROM through WilsonDisc, and in fact the disc is preferable since it is updated quarterly, whereas the print version is more than a year behind the times. Many college and university libraries also now offer the *MLA International Bibliography* as part of their package of online resources for research, and it is even more up-to-date.

MLA International Bibliography lists scholarly studies—books as well as articles in academic journals—published in a given year. Because of the great number of items listed, the print version of the bibliography runs to more than one volume, but material on writing in English (including, for instance, South African authors who write in English) is in one volume. To see what has been published on Langston Hughes in a given year, then, in this volume you turn to the section on American literature (as opposed to British, Canadian, Irish, and so forth), and then to the subsection labeled 1900–99, to see if anything that sounds relevant is listed.

Because your time is limited, you probably cannot read everything published on your topic. At least for the moment, therefore, you will use only the last five or ten years of this bibliography. Presumably, any important earlier material will have been incorporated into some of the recent studies listed. When you come to read these recent studies, if you find references to an article of, say, 1975 that sounds essential, of course you will read that article too.

Although *MLA International Bibliography* includes works on American literature, if you are doing research on an aspect of American literature you may want to begin with

> *American Literary Scholarship* (1965–).

This annual publication is noted for its broad coverage of articles and books on major and minor American writers, and is especially valuable for its frank comments on the material that it lists.

On some recent topics—for instance, the arguments for and against dropping *Huckleberry Finn* from high school curricula—there may be few or no books, and there may not even be material in the scholarly journals indexed in *MLA International Bibliography*. Popular magazines, however, such as *Atlantic, Ebony,* and *Newsweek*—unlisted in *MLA*—may include some useful material. These magazines, and about 200 others, are indexed in

> *Readers' Guide to Periodical Literature* (1900–).

If you want to write a research paper on the controversy over *Huckleberry Finn,* or on the popular reception given to Kenneth Branagh's films of Shakespeare's *Henry V, Much Ado about Nothing,* and *Hamlet,* you can locate material (for instance, reviews of Branagh's films) through *Readers' Guide*. For that matter, you can also locate reviews of older films, let's say Olivier's films of Shakespeare's plays, by consulting the volumes for the years in which the films were released.

On many campuses *Readers' Guide* has been supplanted by

InfoTrac (1985–)

on CD-ROM. The disc is preinstalled in a microcomputer that can be accessed from a computer terminal. This index to authors and subjects in popular and scholarly magazines and in newspapers provides access to several database indexes, including

- The *General Periodicals Index,* available in the Academic Library Edition (about 1,100 general and scholarly periodicals) and in the Public Library Edition (about 1,100 popular magazines)
- The *Academic Index* (400 general-interest publications, all of which are also available in the Academic Library Edition of the *General Periodicals Index*)
- The *Magazine Index Plus* (the four most recent years of the *New York Times,* the two most recent months of the *Wall Street Journal,* and 400 popular magazines, all of which are included in the Public Library Edition of the *General Periodicals Index*)
- The *National Newspaper Index* (the four most recent years of the *New York Times,* the *Christian Science Monitor,* the *Washington Post,* and the *Los Angeles Times*)

Once again, many college and university libraries are now making available online versions of these and similar resources for research. Some students (and faculty) prefer to use the books on the shelf, but the electronic editions have significant advantages. Often, it is easier to perform "searches" using them; and in many cases they are updated well before the next print editions are published.

Other Bibliographic Aids

There are hundreds of guides to publications and to reference works. *The Oxford Companion to African American Literature* (1997), edited by William L. Andrews, Frances Smith Foster, and Trudier Harris, provides detailed entries on authors, literary works, and many literary, historical, and cultural topics and terms, as well as suggestions for further reading. *Reader's Guide to Literature in English* (1996), edited by Mark Hawkins-Dady, is a massive work (nearly 1,000 pages) that gives thorough summaries of recent critical and scholarly writing on English and American authors.

How do you find such books? Two invaluable guides to reference works (that is, to bibliographies and to such helpful compilations as handbooks of mythology, place names, and critical terms) are

James L. Harner, *Literary Research Guide: A Guide to Reference Sources for the Study of Literatures in English and Related Topics,* 4th ed. (2004)

and

Michael J. Marcuse, *A Reference Guide for English Studies* (1990).

And there are guides to these guides: reference librarians. If you don't know where to turn to find something, turn to the librarian.

TAKING NOTES

Let's assume now that you have checked some bibliographies and that you have a fair number of references you must read to have a substantial knowledge of the evidence and the common interpretations of the evidence. Most researchers find it convenient, when examining bibliographies and the library catalog, to write down each reference on a 3″ × 5″ index card—one title per card. On the card, put the author's full name (last name first), the exact title of the book or article, and the name of the journal (with dates and pages). Titles of books and periodicals (publications issued periodically—for example, monthly or four times a year) are underlined; titles of articles and of essays in books are enclosed in quotation marks. It's also a good idea to put the library catalog number on the card to save time if you need to get the item for a second look.

Next, start reading or scanning the materials whose titles you have collected. Some of these items will prove irrelevant or silly; others will prove valuable in themselves and also in the leads they give you to further references, which you should duly record on index cards. Notes—aside from these bibliographic notes—are best taken on larger index cards. The 3″ × 5″ cards are too small for summaries of useful materials; we use 4″ × 6″ cards, which allow you to record a moderate amount of information. Using these medium-sized cards rather than larger ones serves as a reminder that you need not take notes on everything. Be selective in taking notes.

Two Mechanical Aids: The Photocopier and the Word Processor

Use the **photocopier** to make copies of material from the library (including material that does not circulate) that you know you need, or that you might want to refer to later. But remember that sometimes it is even more efficient to

- read the material in the library,
- select carefully what pertains to the purpose of your research, and
- take your notes on it.

The **word processor** or **computer** is useful not only in the final stage, to produce a neat copy, but also in the early stages of research, when you are getting ideas and taking notes. With the help of the computer, you can brainstorm ideas, make connections, organize and re-organize material; develop (and change) outlines. This file can be a kind of creative "work space" for your research paper.

A Guide to Note-Taking

Some students use note cards—we have already mentioned that we use 4″ × 6″ cards—for taking notes during the process of research. Others write on separate sheets of a notebook, or on the sheets of a yellow legal pad. Still others take their notes using a computer or word processor, and then organize and rearrange this body of material by copying and pasting, moving the notes into a coherent order. (We advise you not to delete material that, when you reread your notes, strikes you as irrelevant. It *probably* is irrelevant; but on the other hand, it may turn out to be valuable after all. Just put unwanted material into a file called "rejects," or some such thing, until you have completed the paper.)

Whichever method you prefer, keep in mind the following:

- **For everything you consult or read in detail, always specify the source,** so that you know exactly from where you have taken a key point or a quotation.
- **Write summaries (abridgments), not paraphrases (restatements).**
- **Quote sparingly.** Remember that this is *your* paper—it will present your thesis, not the thesis and arguments and analyses of someone else. Quote directly only those passages that are particularly effective, or crucial, or memorable. In your finished paper these quotations will provide authority and emphasis.
- **Quote accurately.** After copying a quotation, check your note against the original, correct any misquotation, and then put a checkmark after your quotation to indicate that it is accurate. Verify the page number also, and then put a checkmark on your note after the page number. If a quotation runs from the bottom of, say, page 306 to the top of 307, on your note put a distinguishing mark (for instance two parallel vertical lines after the last word of the first page), so that if you later use only part of the quotation, you will know the page on which it appeared.

    Use ellipses (three spaced periods) to indicate the omission of any words within a sentence. If the omitted words are at the end of the quoted sentence, put a period where you end the sentence, and then add three spaced periods to indicate the omission:

    If the . . . words were at the end of the quoted sentence, put a period

    where you end. . . .

    Use square brackets to indicate your additions to the quotation. Here is an example:

    Here is an [uninteresting] example.

- **Never copy a passage by changing an occasional word,** under the impression that you are thereby putting it into your own words. Notes of this sort may find their way into your paper, your reader will sense a style other than yours, and suspicions of plagiarism may follow. (For a detailed discussion of plagiarism, see pages 1331–1332.)
- **Comment on your notes** as you do your work, and later as you reflect on what you have jotted down from the sources. Make a special mark—we

recommend using double parentheses ((. . .)) or a different-colored pen to write, for example, "Jones seriously misreads the passage," or "Smith makes a good point but fails to see its implications." As you work, consider it your obligation to *think* about the material, evaluating it and using it as a stimulus to further thought.

- **In the upper corner of each note card, write a brief key**—for example, "Swordplay in *Hamlet*"—so that later you can tell at a glance what is on the note.

DRAFTING THE PAPER

The difficult job of writing up your findings remains, but if you have taken good notes and have put useful headings on each note, you are well on your way.

- Read through the notes and sort them into packets of related material. Remove all notes that you now see are irrelevant to your paper. (Do not destroy them, however; you may want them later.) Go through the notes again and again, sorting and resorting, putting together what belongs together.
- Probably you will find that you have to do a little additional research— somehow you aren't quite clear about this or that—but after you have done this additional research, you should be able to arrange the packets into a reasonable and consistent sequence. You now have a kind of first draft, or at least a tentative organization for your paper.
- Beware of the compulsion to include every note in your essay; that is, beware of telling the reader, "A says . . . ; B says . . . ; C says . . . "
- You must have a point, a thesis. Make sure that you state it early, and that you keep it evident to your readers.
- Make sure that the organization is evident to the reader. When you were doing your research, and even perhaps when you were arranging your notes, you were not entirely sure where you where going; but by now, with your notes arranged into what seems to you to be the right sequence, you think you know what everything adds up to. Doubtless in the process of drafting you will make important changes in your focus, but do not abandon a draft until you think it not only says what you want to say, but says it in what seems to you to be a reasonable order. The final version of the paper should be a finished piece of work, without the inconsistencies, detours, and occasional dead ends of an early draft. Your readers should feel that they are moving toward a conclusion (by means of your thoughtful evaluation of the evidence) rather than merely reading an anthology of commentary on the topic. And so we should get some such structure as "There are three common views on. . . . The first two are represented by A and B; the third, and by far the most reasonable, is C's view that. . . . A argues . . . but. . . . The second view, B's, is based on . . . but. . . . Although the third view, C's, is not conclusive, still. . . . Moreover, C's point can be strengthened when we consider a piece of evidence that she does not make use of. . . ."
- Preface all or almost all quotations with a lead-in, such as "X concisely states the common view" or "Z, without offering any proof, asserts that . . ."

Let the reader know where you are going, or, to put it a little differently, let the reader know how the quotation fits into your argument.

Quotations and summaries, in short, are accompanied by judicious analyses of your own. By the end of the paper, your readers have not only read a neatly typed paper (see page 1320) and gained an idea of what previous writers have said but also are persuaded that under your guidance they have seen the evidence, heard the arguments justly summarized, and reached a sound conclusion.

A bibliography or list of works consulted (see pages 1334–1342) is usually appended to a research paper so that readers may easily look further into the primary and secondary material if they wish; but if you have done your job well, readers will be content to leave the subject where you left it, grateful that you have set matters straight.

FOCUS ON PRIMARY SOURCES

Remember that your paper should highlight *primary* sources, the materials that are your real subject (as opposed to the secondary sources, the critical and historical discussion of these primary materials). It should be, above all, *your* paper, a paper in which you present a thesis that you have developed about the literary work or works that you have chosen to examine. By using secondary sources, you can enrich your analysis, as you place yourself in the midst of the scholarly community interested in this author or authors. But keep a judicious proportion between primary sources, which should receive the greater emphasis, and secondary sources, which should be used selectively.

To help you succeed in this balancing act, when you review your draft, mark with a red pen the quotations from and references to primary sources, and then with a blue pen do the same marking for secondary sources. If, when you scan the pages of your paper-in-progress, you see a lot more blue than red, you should change the emphasis, the proportion, to what it should be. Guard against the tendency to rely heavily on the secondary sources you have compiled. The point of view that really counts is your own.

DOCUMENTATION
What to Document: Avoiding Plagiarism

Honesty requires that you acknowledge your indebtedness for material, not only when you quote directly from a work but also when you appropriate an idea that is not common knowledge. Not to acknowledge such borrowing is plagiarism. If in doubt whether to give credit, give credit.

You ought, however, to develop a sense of what is considered **common knowledge.** Definitions in a dictionary can be considered common knowledge, so there is no need to say, "According to Webster, a novel is . . . " (This is weak in three ways: It's unnecessary, it's uninteresting, and it's unclear, since "Webster" appears in the titles of several dictionaries, some good and some bad.) Similarly, the date of first publication of *The Scarlet Letter* (1850) can be considered common knowledge. Few can give it when asked, but it can be found out from innumerable sources, and no one need get the credit for providing you with the date. The idea that Hamlet delays is also a matter of common knowledge. But if you are impressed by so-and-so's argument that Claudius has been much maligned, you should give credit to so-and-so.

Suppose that in the course of your research for a paper on Langston Hughes you happen to come across Arnold Rampersad's statement, in an essay in *Voices and Visions* (ed. Helen Vendler), that

> Books alone could not save Hughes from loneliness, let alone give him the strength to be a writer. At least one other factor was essential in priming him for creative obsession. In the place in his heart, or psychology, vacated by his parents entered the black masses. (355)

This is an interesting idea, and in the last sentence the shift from heart to psychology is perhaps especially interesting. You certainly *cannot* say—with the implication that the idea and the words are your own—something like

> Hughes let enter into his heart, or his psychology--a place
>
> vacated by his parents--the black masses.

The writer is simply lifting Rampersad's ideas and making only tiny changes in the wording. But even a larger change in the wording is unacceptable unless Rampersad is given credit. Here is a restatement that is an example of plagiarism even though the words differ from Rampersad's:

> Hughes took into himself ordinary black people, thus filling the
>
> gap created by his mother and father.

In this version, the writer presents Rampersad's idea as if it were the writer's own—and presents it less effectively than Rampersad.

What to do? Give Rampersad credit, perhaps along these lines:

> As Arnold Rampersad has said, "in the place in his heart, or his
>
> psychology" where his parents had once been, Hughes now
>
> substituted ordinary black people (355).

You can use another writer's ideas, and even some of the very words, but you must give credit, and you must use quotation marks when you quote. You can

- Give credit and quote directly, or
- Give credit and summarize the writer's point, or
- Give credit and summarize the point but include—within quotation marks —some phrase you think is especially interesting

How to Document: Footnotes, Internal Parenthetical Citations, and a List of Works Cited (MLA Format)

Documentation tells your reader exactly what your sources are. Until fairly recently, the standard form was the footnote, which, for example, told the reader that the source of such and such a quotation was a book by so-and-so. But in 1984 the Modern Language Association, which had established the footnote form used in hundreds of journals, university presses, and classrooms, substituted a new form. It is this newer form—parenthetical citation *within* the text (rather than at the foot of the page or the end of the essay)—that we will discuss at length. Keep in mind, though, that footnotes still have their uses.

FOOTNOTES   If you are using only one source, your instructor may advise you to give the source in a footnote. (Check with your instructors to find out their preferred forms of documentation.)

Let's say that your only source is this textbook. Let's say, too, that all of your quotations will be from a single story—Kate Chopin's "The Story of an Hour"—printed in this book on pages 13–15. If you use a word processor, the software program can probably format the note for you. If, however, you are using a typewriter, type the digit 1 (elevated, and *without* a period after it) after your first reference to (or quotation from) the story, and then put a footnote at the bottom of the page, explaining where the story can be found. After your last line of text on the page, triple-space, indent five spaces from the left-hand margin, and type the arabic number 1, elevated. Do *not* put a period after it. Then type a statement (double-spaced) to the effect that all references are to this book.

Notice that although the footnote begins by being indented five spaces, if the note runs to more than one line the subsequent lines are given flush left.

> [1]Chopin's story appears in Sylvan Barnet et al., eds. Literature
>
> for Composition, 7th ed. (New York: Longman, 2005), 13-15.

(If a book has more than three authors or editors, give the name of only the first author or editor, and follow it with *et al.,* the Latin abbreviation for "and others.")

Even if you are writing a comparison of, say, two stories in this book, you can use a note of this sort. It might run thus:

> [1]All page references given parenthetically within the essay
>
> refer to stories in Sylvan Barnet et al., eds. Literature for
>
> Composition, 7th ed. (New York: Longman, 2005).

If you use such a note, you do not need to use a footnote after each quotation that follows. You can give the citations right in the body of the paper, by putting the page references in parentheses after the quotations.

INTERNAL PARENTHETICAL CITATIONS   On page 1323 we distinguish between embedded quotations (which are short, are run right into your own sentence, and are enclosed in quotation marks) and quotations that are set off on the page and are not enclosed in quotation marks (for example, three or more lines of poetry, five or more lines of typed prose).

For an embedded quotation, put the page reference in parentheses immediately after the closing quotation marks *without* any intervening punctuation. Then, after the parenthesis that follows the number, insert the necessary punctuation (for instance, a comma or a period):

> Woolf says that in the struggling moth there was "something
>
> marvelous as well as pathetic" (605). She goes on to explain . . .

The period comes *after* the parenthetical citation. In the next example *no* punctuation comes after the first citation—because none is needed—and a comma comes *after* (not before or within) the second citation, because a comma is needed in the sentence:

> This is ironic because almost at the start of the story, in
>
> the second paragraph, Richards with the best of motives
>
> "hastened" (14) to bring his sad message; if he had at the start
>
> been "too late" (15), Mallard would have arrived at home first.

For a quotation that is not embedded within the text but is set off (by being indented ten spaces), put the parenthetical citation on the last line of the quotation, one space *after* the period that ends the quoted sentence.

Four additional points:

- The abbreviations *p., pg.,* and *pp.* are *not* used in citing pages.
- If a story is very short, perhaps running for only a page or two, your instructor may tell you there is no need to keep citing the page reference for each quotation. Simply mention in the footnote that the story appears on, say, pages 205–206.
- If you are referring to a poem, your instructor may tell you to use parenthetical citations of line numbers rather than of page numbers. But, again, your footnote will tell the reader that the poem can be found in this book, and on what page.
- If you are referring to a play with numbered lines, your instructor may prefer that in your parenthetical citations you give act, scene, and line, rather than page numbers. Use arabic (not roman) numerals, separating the act from the scene, and the scene from the line, by periods. Here, then, is how a reference to Act 3, Scene 2, line 118 would be given:

> (3.2.118)

PARENTHETICAL CITATIONS AND LIST OF WORKS CITED   Footnotes have fallen into disfavor. Parenthetical citations are now usually clarified not by means of a footnote but by means of a list, headed "Works Cited," given at the end of the essay. In this list you give alphabetically (last name first) the authors and titles that you have quoted or referred to in the essay.

Briefly, the idea is that the reader of your paper encounters an author's name and a parenthetical citation of pages. By checking the author's name in Works

Cited, the reader can find the passage in the book. Suppose you are writing about Kate Chopin's "The Story of an Hour." Let's assume that you have already mentioned the author and the title of the story—that is, you have let the reader know the subject of the essay—and now you introduce a quotation from the story in a sentence such as this. (Notice the parenthetical citation of page numbers immediately after the quotation.)

> True, Mrs. Mallard at first expresses grief when she hears the
>
> news, but soon (unknown to her friends) she finds joy in it. So,
>
> Richards's "sad message" (14), though sad in Richards's eyes, is
>
> in fact a happy message.

Turning to Works Cited, the reader, knowing the quoted words are by Chopin, looks for Chopin and finds the following:

> Chopin, Kate. "The Story of an Hour." Literature for Composition,
>
> 7th ed. Ed. Sylvan Barnet et al. New York: Longman, 2005.

Thus the essayist is informing the reader that the quoted words ("sad message") are to be found on page 15 of this anthology.

If you have not mentioned Chopin's name in some sort of lead-in, you will have to give her name within the parentheses so that the reader will know the author of the quoted words:

> What are we to make out of a story that ends by telling us that
>
> the leading character has died "of joy that kills" (Chopin 15)?

The closing quotation marks come immediately after the last word of the quotation; the citation and the final punctuation—in this case, the essayist's question mark—come *after* the closing quotation marks.

If you are comparing Chopin's story with Gilman's "The Yellow Wallpaper," in Works Cited you will give a similar entry for Gilman—her name, the title of the story, the book in which it is reprinted, and the page numbers that the story occupies.

If you are referring to several works reprinted within one volume, instead of listing each item fully, it is acceptable in Works Cited to list each item simply by giving the author's name, the title of the work, then a period, a space, and the name of the anthologist, followed by the page numbers that the selection spans. Thus a reference to Chopin's "The Story of an Hour" would be followed only by: Barnet 13–15. This form requires that the anthology itself be cited under the name of the first-listed editor, thus:

> Barnet, Sylvan, et al., eds. Literature for Composition, 7th ed.
>
> New York: Longman, 2005.

If you are writing a research paper, you will use many sources. In the essay itself you will mention an author's name, quote or summarize from this author, and follow the quotation or summary with a parenthetical citation of the pages. In Works Cited you will give the full title, place of publication, and other bibliographic material.

Here are a few examples, all referring to an article by Joan Templeton, "The *Doll House* Backlash: Criticism, Feminism, and Ibsen." The article appeared in *PMLA* 104 (1989): 28–40, but this information is given only in Works Cited, not within the text of the student's essay.

If in the text of your essay you mention the author's name, the citation following a quotation (or a summary of a passage) is merely a page number in parentheses, followed by a period, thus:

> In 1989 Joan Templeton argued that many critics, unhappy with
>
> recognizing Ibsen as a feminist, sought "to render Nora
>
> inconsequential" (29).

Or:

> In 1989 Joan Templeton noted that many critics, unhappy with re-
>
> cognizing Ibsen as a feminist, have sought to make Nora trivial (29).

If you don't mention the name of the author in a lead-in, you will have to give the name within the parenthetical citation:

> Many critics, attempting to argue that Ibsen was not a feminist,
>
> have tried to make Nora trivial (Templeton 29).

Notice in all of these examples that the final period comes after the parenthetical citation. *Exception:* If the quotation is longer than four lines and is therefore set off by being indented ten spaces from the left margin, end the quotation with the appropriate punctuation (period, question mark, or exclamation mark), hit the space bar twice, and type (in parentheses) the page number. In this case, do not put a period after the citation.

Another point: If your list of Works Cited includes more than one work by an author, in your essay when you quote or refer to one or the other you'll have to identify *which* work you are drawing on. You can provide the title in a lead-in, thus:

> In "The Doll House Backlash: Criticism, Feminism, and Ibsen,"
>
> Templeton says, "Nora's detractors have often been, from the
>
> first, her husband's defenders" (30).

Or you can provide the information in the parenthetic citation, giving a shortened version of the title. This usually consists of the first word, unless it is *A, An,* or *The,* in which case including the second word is usually enough. Certain titles may require still another word or two, as in this example:

> According to Templeton, "Nora's detractors have often been, from
>
> the first, her husband's defenders" ("Doll House Backlash" 30).

FORMS OF CITATION IN WORKS CITED In looking over the following samples of entries in Works Cited, remember:

- The list of Works Cited appears at the end of the paper. It begins on a new page, and the page continues the numbering of the text.
- The list of Works Cited is arranged alphabetically by author (last name first).
- If a work is anonymous, list it under the first word of the title unless the first word is *A, An,* or *The,* in which case list it under the second word.
- If a work is by two authors, although the book is listed alphabetically under the first author's last name, the second author's name is given in the normal order, first name first.
- If you list two or more works by the same author, the author's name is not repeated but is represented by three hyphens followed by a period and a space.
- Each item begins flush left, but if an entry is longer than one line, subsequent lines in the entry are indented five spaces.

For details about almost every imaginable kind of citation, consult Joseph Gibaldi, *MLA Handbook for Writers of Research Papers,* 6th ed. (New York: Modern Language Association, 2003). We give here, however, information concerning the most common kinds of citations.

For citations of electronic sources, see pages 1364–1369.

Here are samples of the kinds of citations you are most likely to include in your list of Works Cited.

A book by one author:

Douglas, Ann. The Feminization of American Culture. New York:

Knopf, 1977.

Notice that the author's last name is given first, but otherwise the name is given as on the title page. Do not substitute initials for names written out on the title page, but you may shorten the publisher's name—for example, from Little, Brown and Company to Little.

Take the title from the title page, not from the cover or the spine, but disregard unusual typography—for instance, the use of only capital letters or the use of & for *and.* Underline the title and subtitle with one continuous underline, but do not underline the period. The place of publication is indicated by the name of the city. If the city is not well known or if several cities have the same name (for instance, Cambridge, Massachusetts, and Cambridge, England) the name of the state or country is added. If the title page lists several cities, give only the first.

A book by more than one author:

Gilbert, Sandra, and Susan Gubar. The Madwoman in the Attic: The

Woman Writer and the Nineteenth-Century Literary

Imagination. New Haven: Yale UP, 1979.

Notice that the book is listed under the last name of the first author (Gilbert) and that the second author's name is then given with first name (Susan) first. *If the book has more than three authors,* give the name of the first author only (last name first) and follow it with *et al.* (Latin for "and others").

A book in several volumes:

McQuade, Donald, et al., eds. The Harper American Literature.

2nd ed. 2 vols. New York: HarperCollins, 1994.

Pope, Alexander. The Correspondence of Alexander Pope. 5 vols. Ed.

George Sherburn. Oxford: Clarendon, 1955.

The total number of volumes is given after the title, regardless of the number that you have used.

If you have used more than one volume, within your essay you will parenthetically indicate a reference to, for instance, page 30 of volume 3 thus: (3: 30). If you have used only one volume of a multivolume work—let's say you used only volume 2 of McQuade's anthology—in your entry in Works Cited write, after the period following the date, Vol. 2. In your parenthetical citation within the essay you will therefore cite only the page reference (without the volume number), since the reader will (on consulting Works Cited) understand that in this example the reference is in volume 2.

If, instead of using the volumes as a whole, you used only an independent work within one volume—say, an essay in volume 2—in Works Cited omit the abbreviation *Vol.* Instead, give an arabic 2 (indicating volume 2) followed by a colon, a space, and the page numbers that encompass the selection you used:

McPherson, James Alan. "Why I Like Country Music." The Harper

American Literature. Ed. Donald McQuade et al. 2nd ed. 2 vols.

New York: HarperCollins, 1994. 2: 2304-15.

Notice that this entry for McPherson specifies not only that the book consists of two volumes, but also that only one selection ("Why I Like Country Music," occupying pages 2304–2315 in volume 2) was used. If you use this sort of citation in Works Cited, in the body of your essay a documentary reference to this work will be only to the page; the volume number will *not* be added.

A book with a separate title in a set of volumes:

Churchill, Winston. The Age of Revolution. Vol. 3 of A History of the

English-Speaking Peoples. New York: Dodd, 1957.

Jonson, Ben. The Complete Masques. Ed. Stephen Orgel. Vol. 4 of

The Yale Ben Jonson. New Haven: Yale UP, 1969.

A revised edition of a book:

> Chaucer, Geoffrey. The Riverside Chaucer. Ed. Larry Benson. 3rd ed.
>
> Boston: Houghton, 1987.
>
> Ellmann, Richard. James Joyce. Rev. ed. New York: Oxford UP, 1982.

A reprint, such as a paperback version of an older hardcover book:

> Rourke, Constance. American Humor. 1931. Garden City, New York:
>
> Doubleday, 1953.

Notice that the entry cites the original date (1931) but indicates that the writer is using the Doubleday reprint of 1953.

An edited book other than an anthology:

> Keats, John. The Letters of John Keats. Ed. Hyder Edward Rollins.
>
> 2 vols. Cambridge, Mass.: Harvard UP, 1958.

An anthology: You can list an anthology either under the editor's name or under the title.

A work in a volume of works by one author:

> Sontag, Susan. "The Aesthetics of Silence." In Styles of Radical Will.
>
> New York: Farrar, 1969, 3-34.

This entry indicates that Sontag's essay, called "The Aesthetics of Silence," appears in a book of hers entitled *Styles of Radical Will.* Notice that the page numbers of the short work are cited (not page numbers that you may happen to refer to, but the page numbers of the entire piece).

A work in an anthology, that is, in a collection of works by several authors: Begin with the author and the title of the work you are citing, not with the name of the anthologist or the title of the anthology. The entry ends with the pages occupied by the selection you are citing:

> Ng, Fae Myenne. "A Red Sweater." Charlie Chan Is Dead: An
>
> Anthology of Contemporary Asian American Fiction. Ed.
>
> Jessica Hagedorn. New York: Penguin, 1993. 358-68.

Normally, you will give the title of the work you are citing (probably an essay, short story, or poem) in quotation marks. If you are referring to a book-length work (for instance, a novel or a full-length play), underline it to indicate italics. If the work is translated, after the period that follows the title, write *Trans.* and give the name of the translator, followed by a period and the name of the anthology.

If the collection is a multivolume work and you are using only one volume, in Works Cited you will specify the volume, as in the example (p. 1338) of McPherson's essay. Because the list of Works Cited specifies the volume, your parenthetical documentary reference within your essay will specify (as mentioned earlier) only the page numbers, not the volume. Thus, although McPherson's essay appears on pages 2304–2315 in the second volume of a two-volume work, a parenthetical citation will refer only to the page numbers because the citation in Works Cited specifies the volume.

Remember that the pages specified in the entry in your list of Works Cited are to the *entire selection,* not simply to pages you may happen to refer to within your paper.

If you are referring to a *reprint of a scholarly article,* give details of the original publication, as in the following example:

Mack, Maynard. "The World of Hamlet." Yale Review 41 (1952):

502-23. Rpt. in Hamlet. By William Shakespeare. Ed. Sylvan

Barnet. New York: Penguin Putnam, 1998. 265-87.

Two or more works in an anthology: If you are referring to more than one work in an anthology in order to avoid repeating all the information about the anthology in each entry in Works Cited, under each author's name (in the appropriate alphabetical place) give the author and title of the work, then a period, a space, and the name of the anthologist, followed by the page numbers that the selection spans. Thus, a reference to Shakespeare's *Hamlet* would be followed only by

Barnet 883-986

rather than by a full citation of Barnet's anthology. This form requires that the anthology itself also be listed, under Barnet.

Two or more works by the same author: Notice that the works are given in alphabetical order (*Fables* precedes *Fools*) and that the author's name is not repeated but is represented by three hyphens followed by a period and a space. If the author is the translator or editor of a volume, the three hyphens are followed not by a period but by a comma, then a space, then the appropriate abbreviation (*Trans.* or *Ed.*), then the title:

Frye, Northrop. Fables of Identity: Studies in Poetic Mythology.

New York: Harcourt, 1963.

---. Fools of Time: Studies in Shakespearean Tragedy. Toronto: U of

Toronto P, 1967.

A translated book:

Gogol, Nikolai. Dead Souls. Trans. Andrew McAndrew. New York:

New American Library, 1961.

If you are discussing the translation itself, as opposed to the book, list the work under the translator's name. Then put a comma, a space, and "trans." After the period following "trans," skip a space, then give the title of the book, a period, a space, and then "By" and the author's name, first name first. Continue with information about the place of publication, publisher, and date, as in any entry for a book.

An introduction, foreword, or afterword, or other editorial apparatus:

> Fromm, Erich. Afterword. <u>1984</u>. By George Orwell. New American
>
> Library, 1961.

Usually a book with an introduction or some such comparable material is listed under the name of the author of the book rather than the name of the author of the editorial material (see the citation to Pope on page 1338). But if you are referring to the editor's apparatus rather than to the work itself, use the form just given.

Words such as *preface, introduction, afterword,* and *conclusion* are capitalized in the entry but are neither enclosed within quotation marks nor underlined.

A book review: First, here is an example of a review that does not have a title.

> Vendler, Helen. Rev. of <u>Essays on Style</u>. Ed. Roger Fowler. <u>Essays in</u>
>
> <u>Criticism</u> 16 (1966): 457-63.

If the review has a title, give the title after the period following the reviewer's name, before "Rev." If the review is unsigned, list it under the first word of the title, or the second word if the first word is *A, An,* or *The.* If an unsigned review has no title, begin the entry with "Rev. of" and alphabetize it under the title of the work being reviewed.

An encyclopedia: The first example is for a signed article, the second for an unsigned article.

> Lang, Andrew. "Ballads." <u>Encyclopaedia Britannica</u>. 1910 ed.

> "Metaphor." <u>The New Encyclopaedia Britannica: Micropaedia</u>. 1974 ed.

An article in a scholarly journal: Some journals are paginated consecutively; that is, the pagination of the second issue picks up where the first issue left off. Other journals begin each issue with a new page 1. The forms of the citations in Works Cited differ slightly.

First, the citation of a *journal that uses continuous pagination:*

> Burbick, Joan. "Emily Dickinson and the Economics of Desire."
>
> <u>American Literature</u> 58 (1986): 361–78.

This article appeared in volume 58, which was published in 1986. (Notice that the volume number is followed by a space, then by the year in parentheses, and then by a colon, a space, and the page numbers of the entire article.) Although each volume consists of four issues, you do *not* specify the issue number when the journal is paginated continuously.

For a *journal that paginates each issue separately* (a quarterly journal will have four page 1's each year), give the issue number directly after the volume number and a period, with no spaces before or after the period:

> Spillers, Hortense J. "Martin Luther King and the Style of the Black
>
> Sermon." The Black Scholar 3.1 (1971): 14–27.

An article in a weekly, biweekly, or monthly publication:

> McCabe, Bernard. "Taking Dickens Seriously." Commonweal 14 May
>
> 1965: 24.

Notice that the volume number and the issue number are omitted for popular weeklies or monthlies such as *Time* and *Atlantic*.

An article in a newspaper: Because newspapers usually consist of several sections, a section number may precede the page number. The example indicates that an article begins on page 3 of section 2 and is continued on a later page:

> Wu, Jim. "Authors Praise New Forms." New York Times 8 Mar. 1996,
>
> sec. 2: 3+.

You may also have occasion to cite something other than a printed source, for instance, a lecture. Here are the forms for the chief nonprint sources.

An interview:

> Saretta, Howard. Personal interview. 3 Nov. 1998.

A lecture:

> Heaney, Seamus. Lecture. Tufts University. 15 Oct. 1998.

A television or radio program:

> 60 Minutes. CBS. 30 Jan. 1994.

A film or videotape:

> Modern Times. Dir. Charles Chaplin. United Artists, 1936.

A recording:

> Frost, Robert. "The Road Not Taken." Robert Frost Reads His Poetry.
>
> Caedmon, TC 1060, 1956.

A performance:

> The Cherry Orchard. By Anton Chekhov. Dir. Ron Daniels.
>
> American Repertory Theatre, Cambridge, Mass. 3 Feb. 1994.

Reminder: For the form of citations of electronic material, see pages 1364–1368.

Appendix C

New Approaches to the Research Paper: Literature, History, and the World Wide Web

The previous appendix, Appendix B, describes the traditional model and methods for writing a literary research paper. But literary research has recently become more wide-ranging and complicated, and a book like this one needs to devote another section to it, in order to take into account important changes in the field of literary study and developments in technology.

Students in both literature and composition courses are now often asked to work with historical and literary materials and to demonstrate skills in interdisciplinary learning—and this educational change has taken place on the introductory as well as the intermediate and advanced levels. Like other fields, literary study is supplementing printed texts with electronic search tools, databases, and resources; literary analysis, writing, and research increasingly take place as much on the World Wide Web as in the library, and, in some cases, through e-mail and e-mail lists devoted to specific subject areas.

Historical research, enriched by resources on the Internet, can be very rewarding; it opens up new lines of inquiry as it teaches us about the contexts for literary works and enables us to respond to them in more complex ways. But we need the right strategies to perform this research effectively. Students in literature and composition must now possess the insight and understanding to explore, and to make good choices when consulting, ever-multiplying amounts of information.

CASE STUDY ON LITERATURE AND HISTORY: THE INTERNMENT OF JAPANESE AMERICANS

The best means of illustrating the new approach to literature and history, and outlining the process for identifying new kinds of resources, is through a case study. For this purpose we have chosen the literature and history of the internment of Japanese Americans during World War II. This is a subject for research that a student might select or be assigned in a variety of courses—an introduction to literature in which a group of contemporary poems are studied, with some of them related in subject; a first-year writing course in which the subject is the literature of American immigration; a course in American or Asian American literature; a course in multicultural literature or in American literature since World War II; a senior seminar that examines twentieth-century literature and history, types of ethnic and minority literatures, or poetry and politics.

1343

Many books, articles, and conferences have been devoted to the intern-ment—we can hardly do it justice here. This discussion will describe the type of inquiry into the subject that you can undertake, beginning with the analysis of literary texts and moving outward from it into history, and into print and elec-tronic sources.

LITERARY TEXTS

Reprinted here are two poems. The first is Mitsuye Yamada's "The Question of Loyalty," from *Camp Notes and Other Poems* (1992); the second is David Mura's "An Argument: On 1942," from *After We Lost Our Way* (1989).

MITSUYE YAMADA

Mitsuye Yamada, the daughter of Japanese immigrants to the United States, was born in Japan in 1923, during her mother's return visit to her native land. She was raised in Seattle, but in 1942 she and her family were incarcerated and then relo-cated to an internment camp in Idaho. This was the result of Executive Order 9066, signed by President Franklin Roosevelt in February 1942. This order, in the aftermath of the Japanese attack on Pearl Harbor in December 1941, gave military authorities the right to remove any and all persons from "military areas." In 1954 Yamada became an American citizen. In addition to Camp Notes *and Other* Poems, *Yamada has written* Desert Run: Poems and Stories *(1988) and edited* Sowing TI Leaves: Writings by Multicultural Women *(1991).*

Note: *From 1942 to 1945, before leaving an internment camp for eastern sec-tions of the United States, Japanese Americans were expected to sign a statement known as "The Loyalty Oath."*

The Question of Loyalty

I met the deadline
for alien registration
once before
was numbered fingerprinted
and ordered not to travel   5
without permit.

But alien still they said I must
forswear allegiance to the emperor.
for me that was easy
I didn't even know him   10
but my mother who did cried out
    If I sign this
    What will I be?
    I am doubly loyal
    to my American children   15
    also to my own people.
    How can double mean nothing?
    I wish no one to lose this war.
    Everyone does.

I was poor   20
at math.
I signed
my only ticket out.

[1976]

DAVID MURA

David Mura is a sansei, *a third-generation Japanese American. He was born in
1952, seven years after the end of the war. In both poetry and prose, he has examined race, ethnicity, and sexuality, and has described his quest for self-knowledge
and personal and familial identity.* A Male Grief: Notes on Pornography and
Addiction *(1987) was his first book. Two years later he published* After We Lost Our
Way *in the National Poetry Series, and followed it with a second book of verse,* The
Colors of Desire: Poems *(1995). He has also written* Turning Japanese: Memoirs of
a Sansei *(1992) and* Where the Body Meets Memory: An Odyssey of Race,
Sexuality, and Identity *(1996), which tells of his childhood in Chicago, his parents'
recollections of the internment camps, and the impact of internment on several
generations of Japanese Americans.*

An Argument: On 1942

For my mother

*Near Rose's Chop Suey and Jinosuke's grocery,
the temple where incense hovered and inspired
dense evening chants (prayers for Buddha's mercy,
colorless and deep), that day he was fired . . .*

—No, no, no, she tells me. Why bring it back?
The camps are over. (Also overly dramatic.)
Forget *shoyu*-stained *furoshiki,*° *mochi*° on a stick:
You're like a terrier, David, gnawing a bone, an old, old trick . . .   4

Mostly we were bored. Women cooked and sewed,
men played blackjack, dug gardens, a *benjo.*°
Who noticed barbed wire, guards in the towers?
We were children, hunting stones, birds, wild flowers.   8

Yes, Mother hid tins of *tsukemono*° and eel
beneath the bed. And when the last was peeled,
clamped tight her lips, growing thinner and thinner.
But cancer not the camps made her throat blacker   12

. . . And she didn't die then . . . after the war, in St. Paul,
you weren't even born. Oh, I know, I know, it's all

---

3 shoyu-stained furoshiki a soy-stained scarf that is used to carry things; ***mochi*** rice cakes.
6 benjo toilet.   **9 tsukemono** Japanese pickles. [All are author's notes.]

part of your job, your way, but why can't you glean
how far we've come, how much I can't recall—   16

David, it was so long ago—how useless it seems . . .

[1989]

Your goal is eventually to move to historical research, but first you must know the poems well. Reflect upon the movement of each one—how it begins, what occupies its middle sections, and how it ends. Consider the relationship of the structure—the length of the lines, the organization of the stanzas, the diction and imagery—to the dramatic situation and themes.

- For this analysis, reread the discussions of speaker, structure, figurative language, and other key terms presented in Chapter 14 of this book, and refer to the checklist on pages 503–505.

Yamada focuses on the conflict experienced by her mother. The mother expresses her loyalty to her children, to her *American* children, even as she cherishes her loyalty to her own people, the Japanese (though this word, revealingly, is not used). She wants there to be no loser in the war; she hopes for an impossible stalemate, in which neither side loses.

The war manifests itself in her own identity, in the tension between the person she has been and the person, it seems, she must become. If the mother signs the form forswearing allegiance to the Japanese emperor, she will be denying her ancestry, forced to disclaim one-half of herself. She cannot be who she is.

Mura describes the conflict between his mother and himself and delves into the struggle that his mother wages with her memories. Unlike Yamada, Mura was not in the camps himself; he is seeking knowledge about an experience that took place before he was born.

The mother objects to her son's efforts to make her remember: "You're like a terrier, David, gnawing a bone, an old, old trick." But as her own listing of details shows, the mother, if only to herself, has continued to linger over the internment—the men playing blackjack, the barbed wire. She says there is much she cannot recall, but the reader feels that there is much that remains keenly present for her, much that she could recall and has recalled.

The mother portrayed in this poem cannot practice the lesson she gives to her son. Nor will he allow her to. He is curious to know what happened; he wants his mother to tell about her experiences and, one may suspect, to explain why she and the others did not resist then and have not spoken out since.

These are powerful poems even for a reader who knows only a little about the historical facts to which Yamada and Mura bear witness—a reader who knows only in a general way that many Japanese Americans were forced during World War II to leave their West Coast homes and live in internment camps in the California desert, in other western states, and as far east as Arkansas. But the poems become still more effective for a reader who knows in depth and detail about this episode in American history, and who can bring this knowledge to a reading of the texts and present it in an analytical research paper.

One form of *historical* research is to follow a traditional route for *literary* research. The literary resources and methods described in Appendix B can lead to secondary sources on the authors and their writings and to information about their careers, the work they have done, and its major themes. There will be historical information in many of these sources, particularly those of a recent date.

By checking in the *MLA International Bibliography* (see Appendix B, page 1326), you can locate items such as the following:

On Yamada:

Jaskoski, Helen. "Interview with Mitsuye Yamada." *MELUS: The Journal of the Society for the Study of the Multi-Ethnic Literature of the United States.* 15.1 (Spring 1988): 97–108.

Schweik, Susan. "A Needle with Mama's Voice: Mitsuye Yamada's *Camp Notes* and the American Canon of War Poetry." In *Arms and the Woman: War, Gender, and Literary Representation.* Ed. Helen M. Cooper and Adrienne Auslander Munich. Chapel Hill: U of North Carolina P, 1989.

Usui, Masami. "A Language of Her Own in Mitsuye Yamada's Poetry and Stories." *Studies in Culture and the Humanities: Bulletin of the Faculty of Integrated Arts and Sciences,* Hiroshima University: 5.3 (1996): 1–17.

On Mura:

Taylor, Gordon O. "'The Country I Had Thought Was My Home': David Mura's *Turning Japanese* and Japanese-American Narrative since World War II." *Connotations: A Journal for Critical Debate* (Münster, Germany): 6.3 (1996–1997): 283–309.

General studies:

Nakanishi, Don T., ed. *Japanese American Internment: Commemorative Issue.* Special issue of *Amerasia Journal* 19:1 (1993).

Thiesmeyer, Lynn. "The Discourse of Official Violence: Anti-Japanese North American Discourse and the American Internment Camps." *Discourse & Society* 6.3 (July 1995): 319–52.

Yogi, Stan. "Yearning for the Past: The Dynamics of Memory in Sansei Internment Poetry." *Memory and Cultural Politics: New Approaches to American Ethnic Literatures.* Ed. Amritjit Singh, Joseph T. Skerrett, Jr., and Robert E. Hogan. Boston: Northeastern UP, 1996.

Tip: Through electronic access and interlibrary loan, a student can obtain almost any source, even if it is not carried by a library on campus. But sometimes interlibrary loan can take a few days, a week, or more. Remember the importance of starting early on research projects. Request copies of everything while there is still time before the deadline to examine them.

HISTORICAL SOURCES

The sources in the *MLA International Bibliography,* while promising, may take for granted more than at this stage you know; the discussion and analysis presented in them assumes that readers *already* have the background that you are seeking to acquire. How can you begin to acquire a base of historical knowledge?

Start small. Don't overwhelm yourself with more information than you can handle. Keep in mind as well that you are not aiming to become a historian, but instead, intend to enrich your literary explorations with knowledge drawn from another field and set of sources.

Basic Reference Books (Short Paper)

It is best to begin with basic reference books, and you can get to them by consulting the following:

> Balay, Robert. *Guide to Reference Books.* 11th ed. Chicago: American Library Association, 1996.
>
> Blazek, Ron, and Elizabeth Aversa. *The Humanities: A Selective Guide to Information Sources.* 5th ed. Englewood, Colo.: Libraries Unlimited, 2000.
>> This is an annotated guide to research sources in literature, art, and other fields in the humanities.

Or, consult *ARBA Guide to Subject Encyclopedias and Dictionaries* (1986); and *First Stop: The Master Index to Subject Encyclopedias* (1989).

Or, in the online library catalog, check under the subject heading, "History—Dictionaries." (You can do the same thing for literature, for titles of reference works in that field.)

You can also refer to Jules R. Benjamin, *A Student's Guide to History,* 8th ed. (2000); and James R. Bracken, *Reference Works in British and American Literature,* 2nd ed. (1998). See also M. J. Marcuse, *Reference Guide for English Studies* (1992); and James L. Harner, *Literary Research Guide,* 3rd ed. (1998).

Browse in the reference section of your school's library; or better still, talk to a reference librarian—he or she can be a valuable resource and often can direct you quickly to helpful books.

In reply to the question, "Where can I find out about the internment of Japanese Americans during World War II?" the reference librarian recommended to us *The Reader's Companion to American History,* ed. Eric Foner and John A. Garraty (Boston: Houghton Mifflin, 1991), which includes an entry on this subject titled "Japanese-American Relocation."

Here is the entry in full:

Japanese-American Relocation

The relocation of thousands of Japanese-Americans into internment camps during World War II marked an ignoble chapter in American history. In 1941 when the Japanese bombed Pearl Harbor, there were 127,000 persons of Japanese ancestry in America, the majority residing on the West Coast. For years they had been denied the right to vote or own land. After Pearl Harbor, rumors spread that a Japanese plot to sabotage the American war effort was afoot. In early 1942, the Roosevelt administration was pressured to remove Japanese-Americans from the West Coast by agricultural interests seeking to eliminate Japanese competition, a public fearing sabotage, and politicians hoping to gain by aligning against this unpopular group.

In February 1942, the federal government forced all Japanese-Americans regardless of loyalty or citizenship to evacuate the West Coast, which was perceived as a vulnerable military area. To justify this move against Americans only of Japanese—not German or Italian—descent, the government claimed that racial ties inclined the Japanese to disloyalty. When neighboring states resisted the incoming refugees, the government established ten internment camps in California, Idaho, Utah, Arizona, Wyoming, Colorado, and Arkansas to receive them. By

September, 100,000 people had been moved. The camps resembled prisons, with cramped quarters, communal facilities, and poor food. Generational conflict beset the internees: older Issei (immigrants) were deprived of their traditional respect when their children, the Nisei (American-born), were alone permitted authority positions within the camps. Ultimately, 5,766 Nisei renounced their American citzenship. When internees were given the opportunity to leave the camps by joining the U.S. Army, only 1,200 did so.

The U.S. Supreme Court upheld the government's position in two cases challenging the relocation, *Hirabayashi v. United States* and *Korematsu v. United States*. Only after his reelection in 1944 did Franklin D. Roosevelt finally rescind the evacuation order, and by the end of 1945 the camps were closed. In 1968, the Japanese-Americans were reimbursed for property they had lost, and in 1988, Congress enacted legislation awarding resititution payments of twenty thousand dollars each to the 60,000 surviving internees. *See also* World War II. (588–89)

At this point you should remind yourself of the boundaries of the assignment.

- What is the *length* of the essay? Its *due date?*
- *How many* sources did the instructor state that you should use? Did he or she refer to specific kinds of sources that the paper should include—scholarly books and/or articles, other primary sources (literary texts, letters, autobiographies, journals), photographs, and so on?
- The *proportions* of the essay? How much of it should consist of literary analysis, and how much of historical research and context?

For a short paper of three pages that treats one or both of the poems and provides some historical context, the entry from *The Reader's Companion* may be all that you need. It reports what happened, where, and why, emphasizes the outrage done to civil liberties, and highlights an aspect of camp experience that bears on Yamada's and Mura's poems: "Generational conflict beset the internees . . ." (589). You can relate this comment to the differences and struggles between the generations that Yamada and Mura evoke. Here, you have an historical detail that you can develop in your examination of the poems *and,* if the assignment were a longer one calling for extensive research, that you could make the organizing principle for gathering and then sifting through sources.

- It is important, then, to gain basic knowledge of the subject, so that you have a clear, accurate answer to your core question—in this case, What was the internment? But, at the same time, seek to locate in the overview of the subject an idea or issue that is connected to the themes of the specific literary works. *Connect* the literature and the history.

Getting Deeper (Medium Paper)

The entry in *The Reader's Companion to American History* has limitations. It is brief and lacks a bibliography; and the cross-reference leads to an entry on World War II that supplies no further information about the internment. The brief account (under the entry "Asian Americans") in *The Oxford Companion to United States History,* ed. Paul S. Boyer (New York: Oxford University Press, 2001) also may fall short of giving you the range and depth of information that you need.

For a medium-length paper, you will need to search elsewhere for more information—and if you require it, for a bibliography. Here are several good sources we located; we found the first two by browsing in the reference section of the library, and the third resulted from a suggestion by the reference librarian there.

> *Encyclopedia of the United States in the Twentieth Century.* Stanley I. Kutler, general editor. 5 vols. New York: Scribner's, 1996.
>
> *Harvard Encyclopedia of American Ethnic Groups.* Ed. Stephan Thernstrom. Cambridge: Harvard UP, 1980.
>
> *Oxford Companion to World War II.* General editor, I. C. B. Dear; consultant editor, M. R. D. Foot. New York: Oxford UP, 1995.

Like *The Reader's Companion to American History,* the *Oxford Companion to World War II* is recent, prepared by eminent scholars, and published by a reputable press. It is a trustworthy source, and its signed entry on "Japanese-Americans" (632–34) is longer and more detailed than the entry in *The Reader's Companion;* it is cross-referenced to a general entry on "internment" and identifies three books for further reading:

> Daniels, Roger. *Asian America: Chinese and Japanese in the United States since 1850* (Seattle, Wash., 1988).
>
> ———. *Concentration Camps USA* (New York, 1971).
>
> Takaki, Ronald. *Strangers from a Different Shore: A History of Asian Americans* (Boston, 1989).

Now you can start to compile a bibliography of your own, with these three books as its foundation. But—here is a key point—note their dates of publication. No doubt these are good sources, but you should be seeking more recent sources as well to make certain that your knowledge is as up-to-date as possible.

The relevant section in the *Encyclopedia of the United States,* included in the chapter "Ethnicity and Immigration" (see 1.176–77), is about the same length as (and less detailed than) the entry in *The Reader's Companion* from which you started. But the chapter closes with a bibliographic essay that includes this important information:

> On Japanese American internment, the essential work is Roger Daniels, *Prisoners without Trial: Japanese Americans in World War II* (1993).

This tells you that Daniels has written a book on the subject that is more recent than his 1971 book listed in the *Oxford Companion to World War II.* A scholar in the field of ethnic studies has flagged it as "essential" and hence it is a source you should highlight in your notes for special attention.

- Daniels gives a background chapter on the period 1850–1941, four chapters on the internment and its aftermath, an epilogue "Could It Happen Again?", "An Essay in Photographs," "Suggestions for Further Reading," and an appendix of "Documents." This is a first-rate book for your purposes; it is recent, concise (150 pages), written by an accomplished scholar who is in full command of primary and secondary sources and whose bibliography will direct you authoritatively to other materials.

The section on the wartime internment of Japanese Americans in *Harvard Encyclopedia* is part of a long essay devoted to the history of the Japanese in America (561–71). The author, Harry H. L. Kitano, notes at one point:

> In the camps all Japanese, whether highly educated, wealthy, illiterate, or poor, were housed in barracks, ate mess-hall food, and received the same rates of pay for work—$16 a month for manual labor and $19 for professional work. They used communal toilets, took communal showers, waited patiently in line for everything; they wore identical clothes, and the sun, wind, and dust soon endowed them with the same concentration-camp complexion. (566)

Kitano helps you grasp the historical setting for Mura's poem, and the next part of his discussion pertains to it, and to Yamada's poem, even more directly:

> The most difficult problem proved to be the boredom and monotony of camp life; it exacerbated tensions and magnified irritations, resulting in fights, riots, strikes, and even homicides. Inmates complained constantly about the food, their neighbors, living conditions, and camp administrators. Conflicts between the Issei [Japanese-born Americans—the first or immigrant generation] and Nisei [American-born Japanese—the second generation] added to the strain. Ideological arguments between those loyal to Japan and those who stood with the United States grew heated. The derogatory term *inu* [dog] was applied to those suspect of being spies or government collaborators, and some of the inu were the victims of severe beatings. (566)

"Mostly we were bored," recalls Mura's mother, touching on an aspect of life in the camps that Kitano stresses in his historical survey. Kitano makes clear how real and pervasive were the differences between generations, between parents and children. He concludes:

> Family life was disrupted: the authority of the provider-father and the housekeeper-mother was undercut by government supervision; children ate in mess halls rather than in the family circle. They were stifled in an atmosphere of boredom and stagnation. Gambling became a problem, and petty family quarrels often escalated into violence. (567)

Now you can really begin to see the analytical value of historical sources. Details like these make readers wonder if part of the effect of Mura's poem lies in what we sense the mother is trying *not* to remember—the fact, for example, that the men playing blackjack were doing something that not only distracted them but that caused a serious problem in the camps. She acknowledges that life was boring, but possibly the boredom was even graver than she reveals to her son—a boredom that led to arguments among family members and to violence.

Our historical research teaches us about the *contexts* for the Yamada and Mura poems and alerts us to the power and precision of details that the poets include. Sometimes, too, it helps us sense the pressure of feelings and thoughts that a writer or speaker is excluding, is holding back or reacting against. The more we learn about the camps, the more we can perceive what Mura's mother is referring to and what, on some level, she might be struggling to keep from speaking about.

Kitano's chapter ends with a bibliographic essay that includes the following note:

> The internment of the Japanese in relocation camps has received much attention. The most perceptive studies of this painful episode are Leonard Broom

and John I. Kitsuse, *The Managed Casualty: The Japanese American Family in World War II* (Berkeley, 1956); Audrie Girdner and Anne Loftis, *The Great Betrayal* (New York, 1969); Jacobus Ten Broek, Edward N. Barnhart, and Floyd W. Matson, *Prejudice, War, and the Constitution* (Berkeley, 1970); and Michi Weglyn, *Years of Infamy: The Untold Story of America's Concentration Camps* (New York, 1976).

Now you have additional items for your bibliography.

✔ **CHECKLIST:** *Researching a Literary-Historical Paper*

❏ Consult a range of reference books as you are getting launched on a literary-historical paper—it will take less time than you think, and it will be time invested wisely.

❏ Pay attention to *when* the books were published and how up-to-date they are in their suggestions for additional reading.

❏ Even as you acquire familiarity with the subject in general, take special note of where the historical record *makes connections* to the literature that you are studying. The real reward comes when you can perceive the relationship between history and the structure and themes of the literary works.

Question for Consideration

In *Prisoners Without Trial,* Roger Daniels states:

> There were no individual cooking facilities. Everyone ate in the mess hall. Three times a day, prisoners lined up with trays to receive wholesome, starchy, cheap food, not usually prepared in the most appetizing manner. . . . Almost everyone complained about the food, but what the mess halls did to family relationships was worse. Youngsters tended to eat in groups and move around from mess hall to mess hall. The dislocation of the family meal was but another way in which the detention process eroded the dignity and authority of parents. (67)

Write a page or so in which you connect Daniels's description to details that Mura includes in "An Argument: On 1942." Through your commentary show how the historical context enhances the reader's response to and understanding of the poem.

Other Reference Sources (Long Paper)

If your literary-historical research needs to be extended further—say, for a term paper of 15–20 pages, then you will have to make use of other tools for locating historical sources. The items in the *MLA International Bibliography* and the suggestions for further reading given in reference books are excellent, but there are other routes to follow, especially for historical materials.

Humanities Abstracts, an index of articles in the humanities, with their contents summarized, is a good resource. It gives the following item (among others) on the subject of the internment:

> Davidov, Judith Fryer. "'The Color of My Skin, the Shape of My Eyes':
> Photographs of the Japanese-American Internment by Dorothea Lange,
> Ansel Adams, and Toyo Miyatake." *Yale Journal of Criticism* 9 (Fall
> 1996): 223–44, illustrations.
>> A description of the shrouded history of the internment of Japanese-Americans
>> during World War 2 and a discussion of the photographs of these internees
>> taken by Dorothea Lange, Ansel Adams, and Toyo Miyatake. Lange's images are
>> rich in content, demanding an emotional response that seemed to some to be
>> inimical to national security. Adams, whose photographs of the camp at
>> Manzanar, California, were taken with the sanction of the authorities, con-
>> tributed to the official presentation of the internment as humane, orderly, and
>> even beneficial to the internees. Miyatake, who was an internee, took his pho-
>> tographs with smuggled materials, and his images, which are dense in detail, in-
>> sistently show the fallaciousness of demarcating otherness.

The "abstract" or summary of the author's main points is a valuable feature of this reference work. Here you are told about an essay that deals with visual materials—a type of source you have not yet encountered. In the essay the author reproduces some of the photographs (note the reference to "illustrations") and no doubt refers her readers to the collections where the photographs can be found.

Here are several more items from *Humanities Abstracts* (for these, we have cut the abstracts slightly to save space). When you read an abstract, keep in mind that you are seeking sources bearing on the issues in the literary works you have chosen to examine. The abstract may tell you about a source that, while interesting, is not pertinent to your research needs for this particular paper.

For many topics, there is a great deal of material that you could draw upon if your time were limitless; but because you must use your limited time well, you should be focused and selective. Fasten on the best sources for the nature of the research task at hand.

> Yoshino, Ronald W. "Barbed Wire and Beyond: A Sojourn through
> Internment—in Personal Recollection." *Journal of the West* 35 (Jan.
> 1996): 34–43, illustrations.
>> . . . The clash with the federal government and the ensuing incarceration
>> pointed to the importance of the Nisei, the Americanized, second generation
>> Japanese who acted for most internees. With more power as a result of in-
>> creased responsibility, the Nisei led the Japanese Americans into the postwar
>> era, speeding up the process of acculturation. . . .

Now you have another personal story to place alongside the one that Mura's and Yamada's speakers present, and this story, like that in the poems, calls attention to the differences between generations. The reference in the title to "barbed wire" may even remind you of the "barbed wire" in Mura's poem.

> Kuramitsu, Kristine C. "Internment and Identity in Japanese American Art."
> *American Quarterly* 47 (Dec. 1995): 619–58, illustrations.
>> . . . Examines an exhibition of hitherto unseen art from the camps, "The View
>> from Within: Japanese American Art from the Internment Camps 1942–1945,"

and looks at these artworks as aesthetic expressions of personal and cultural identity. She concludes by discussing Japanese American artists who are one or two generations removed from this event and how they deal with the issues surrounding it, with reference to the 1992 exhibition "Relocations and Revisions: The Japanese American Internment Reconsidered." . . .

Works of art, a special exhibition—through this article you can learn about still other perspectives on the subject. Like the article by Davidov cited earlier, this source might be an especially good one if you were asked to give an oral report in class about your research. By making copies for your classmates of some of the illustrations, you could give a visual dimension to the report, making your analysis all the more attention-getting and interesting to the audience.

Greenberg, Cheryl. "Black and Jewish Responses to Japanese Internment." *Journal of American Ethnic History* 14 (Winter 1995): 3–37.
. . . Argues that many of the most prominent and outspoken black and Jewish civil rights organizations did not perceive the injustice of this racially based policy, although they did support fair treatment for individual Japanese Americans not living in militarily sensitive areas. . . .

Now you have a source that places the internment in the context of American ethnic and minority history.

Sundquist, Eric J. "The Japanese-American Internment: A Reappraisal." *The American Scholar* 57 (Autumn 1988): 529–47.

There is no summary given in *Humanities Abstracts* for this item, but you do not need one. The key word "reappraisal" indicates that the author will be discussing the events themselves and the current state of scholarly work.

- Look for key words in titles of books and articles listed in bibliographies; these words offer clues about the author's point of view, approach, or treatment of the subject.

If the paper requires sustained research, a good next step might be to perform a "subject" search in the online card catalogs of your own and other research libraries. It is always tempting to do a search by subject first, before anything else and without bothering to check reference books. While convenient, this method has disadvantages. Your subject search for Japanese American internment might not turn up Daniels's 1993 book at all—maybe your library does not own it. Or, if it does, this book might be in the middle of a long subject list: You would not know that it has been praised as an "essential" source and that—given that you must make choices—you would be better off zeroing in on this source than others on the list.

- When you check the online catalog for one of the books already on your bibliography, you will see on the entry the *subject* category for it. You can then use this category for your more complete *subject* search. The librarian can also assist you in identifying the phrases for the subject you are researching; the *Library of Congress Subject Headings (LCSH)* is another resource.

Too Much Information?

At this point, you may be wondering, "How do I know when to stop?" A good question, but not one with a simple answer. We have known students who have become gripped by a subject and have read everything they can about it. But however excited about a subject you become, in the midst of a busy semester you will need to make choices and budget your time.

- "How do I know when to stop?" Stop when you have acquired the historical knowledge that strengthens your analysis of the literary texts—the knowledge that deepens your understanding of the issues that the authors have treated, and the knowledge that is sufficient for you to meet the terms (that is, the boundaries) of the assignment.

Question for Consideration

As you perform your research, you will often be confronted with lists of sources. It is important to become aware of how you might evaluate these sources and determine which of the items on a list might be most relevant. Review the following items chosen from a lengthy list produced by a subject search for "Japanese Americans—Evacuation and Relocation, 1942–1945." Consider the type of each source and its area of emphasis, the publication date, and the nature of the connection (if any) to the themes in the poem you plan to examine.

Conrat, Maisie. *Executive Order 9066: The Internment of 110,000 Japanese Americans*. With an introd. by Edison Uno and an epilogue by Tom C. Clark. Photographs by Dorothea Lange and others. Cambridge, Mass.: MIT P for the California Historical Society, 1972.

Daniels, Roger, ed. *American Concentration Camps: A Documentary History of the Relocation and Incarceration of Japanese Americans*. 9 vols. New York: Garland, 1989.

Gesensway, Deborah. *Beyond Words: Images from America's Concentration Camps*. Ithaca, N.Y.: Cornell UP, 1987.

Hansen, Arthur A., ed. *Japanese American World War II Evacuation Oral History Project*. 5 vols. Westport, Conn.: Meckler, 1991–93.

Ichihashi, Yamato. *Morning Glory, Evening Shadow: Yamato Ichihashi and His Internment Writings, 1942–1945*. Edited, annotated, and with a biographical essay by Gordon H. Chang. Stanford, Calif.: Stanford UP, 1997.

Mills, Denice Lee. *The Evacuation and Relocation of Japanese Americans During World War II: A Bibliography*. Public Administration Series—Bibliography, P 2788, 1989.

Nagata, Donna K. *Legacy of Injustice: Exploring the Cross-Generational Impact of the Japanese American Internment*. New York: Plenum, 1993.

Smith, Page. *Democracy on Trial: The Japanese American Evacuation and Relocation in World War II*. New York: Simon & Schuster, 1995.

Uchida, Yoshiko. *Desert Exile: The Uprooting of a Japanese American Family*. Seattle: U of Washington P, 1984.

ELECTRONIC SOURCES
Encyclopedias: Print and Electronic Versions

Encyclopedias can give you the basics about a subject, but like all resources, they have limitations. An encyclopedia may not cover the subject that you are researching or not cover it in adequate depth. Knowledge expands rapidly, and because it does, even a fine encyclopedia lags somewhat behind current scholarship. A number of encyclopedias are now in CD-ROM form, preloaded on a personal computer, and the CD makes searches for information easier. Many such encyclopedias can also be connected to the World Wide Web, where updated information and links to reference and research resources are listed. Be sure to check with the librarians at your school—they can tell you about the kinds of resources that are available. And if your library offers a tutorial on the use of electronic and Internet resources, we recommend that you sign up for it. We take such tutorials ourselves with our students every year, and are always pleasantly surprised by the new resources we learn about.

It is helpful to have updated information and links, but only when they are reliable. Remember to be a critical user of reference materials. Not everything is of equal value, and we must make good judgments about the sources we consult—and whether or not we can depend on them for reliable, accurate information. More on this point in a moment.

Perhaps the most popular CD-ROM encyclopedia is the *Grolier Multimedia Encyclopedia*. But when we recently consulted it for information about the internment of Japanese Americans, we found no specific entry; brief discussions are located within other entries, the most comprehensive of which is for Asian Americans. Here is the relevant paragraph:

> The most traumatic blow against Japanese Americans was struck soon after Japan bombed Pearl Harbor. More than 2,000 community leaders along the Pacific Coast and in Hawaii were rounded up by the Federal Bureau of Investigation and imprisoned. On Feb. 19, 1942, President Franklin D. Roosevelt signed Executive Order 9066 authorizing the secretary of war or any military commander designated by him to establish "military areas" and to "exclude any and all persons" from them. In the next few months, 112,000 persons of Japanese ancestry—two-thirds of them American citizens—were forcibly removed from the western half of Washington, Oregon, and California and the southern third of Arizona and incarcerated first in temporary assembly centers and eventually in ten relocation camps. The vast majority of Japanese Americans in Hawaii were not interned, as they made up 40 percent of the islands' labor force and their removal would have crippled Hawaii. Despite the maltreatment they received, some 23,000 Nisei served in the U.S. Army, fighting in both Europe and Asia. The unit in Europe received more decorations than any unit of comparable size during World War II.

> (© Grolier Interactive Inc.)

This is less informative than print sources we have discussed, and the thinness of the entry helps to make clear that electronic sources have not yet done away with the need to go to the library.

The value of *Grolier* and other encyclopedias on CD-ROM often lies less in a specific entry's information than in the fact that through the CD, you can access other sources and links on the World Wide Web. But this can prove frustrating as well as rewarding. When, for example, we tried several times to link to sites listed in one encyclopedia available on CD-ROM, we found that two of the links had expired. In addition, when we attempted to link to another site that was listed, we received the message, "Document contains no data."

There are two things to do when a link does not work:

1. Type in the link, but end with *.edu* or *.com* or *.org* to specify it further. The internal architecture of the site may have changed, but the information you are seeking might still be there, accessible through a different link.
2. Go to a search engine, such as Google <http://www.google.com/>, Yahoo! <http://www.yahoo.com/>, or Infoseek <http://www.infoseek.com/>; type in the exact name of the site and see what you get. Sometimes the link that you tried at first will have expired, but you will manage, via a search engine, to reach the site under a new link.

Note on terms:

- *URL (uniform resource locator).* The URL is the Web address, the location, that your browser points to in order to access a file on an Internet computer.
- *Internet and World Wide Web (WWW):* The Internet is the global network connecting networks of many thousands of computers that communicate with one another; the World Wide Web is a complex system for delivering files of hypertext and multimedia on the Internet. These terms are not identical but are often used as if they were.
- *Web page:* a single screen, whatever its length.
- *Website:* a collection of Web pages, usually includes a main or "home" page for the site.

The best encyclopedia is the *Encyclopaedia Britannica,* and it is available on the library shelves, on CD-ROM, and as part of the electronic resources available through the library at many colleges and universities. (Much of the Britannica is now available free of charge online at <http://www.britannica.com>.) But, like *Grolier,* it does not supply an entry on the internment; the user must first "search" the database and find information among a number of items. For example:

> *Manzanar Relocation Center*—an internment facility for Japanese Americans during World War II. In March 1942 the U.S. War Relocation Authority was set up; it established 10 relocation centres for persons of Japanese ancestry, located in California, Arizona, Idaho, Utah, Wyoming, and Arkansas. The best known of these, and the first to be established, was the Manzanar Relocation Center near Lone Pine, Calif.; it operated from March 1942 to November 1945. During this time more than 11,000 persons were confined there.

Not much here, but from this entry you can link to the WWW site for the Manzanar Relocation Center:

Manzanar National Historic Site

Manzanar War Relocation Center was one of ten camps at which Japanese American citizens and Japanese aliens were interned during World War II. Located at the foot of the imposing Sierra Nevada in eastern California's Owens Valley, Manzanar has been identified as the best preserved of these camps. http://www.nps.gov/manz/

When we first visited this site in 1998, it contained little information about the internment itself; in its current form (August 2001), it is more detailed and much better. We learn, for example:

> The War Relocation Authority took control of Manzanar on June 1, 1942 and operated the camp until it closed in November 1945. A total of 11,400 people were processed through this relocation center. The population reached 10,200 in September 1942; by 1944 it was 6,000.
>
> The camp consisted of 36 blocks of wooden barracks within a confined one-square-mile area. Men, women, and children sought to establish some semblance of normal life while attempting to overcome the trauma of forced evacuation and uncertain future. The camp population, through its strength and resourcefulness, beautified the barracks with gardens and ponds. They built a city—a microcosm of an American society much like what they had to leave behind.
>
> Weather conditions at the camp were often harsh, with high winds and extreme temperatures. Even in late spring, temperatures may drop to below freezing. In the summer, temperatures rise above 100 degrees Fahrenheit. . . .

This kind of detailed background can enrich your discussion of the poems by Yamada and Mura that we quoted and examined earlier. It can help us enter more fully into the historical experiences that the poets are evoking and exploring in their work.

Note: Some WWW sites are updated frequently; some are updated irregularly; and others are never updated. For a short-term project, one visit to the site will either offer you what you need or it won't. But for a long-term project, such as a senior thesis that might span one semester or even two, you might check a particular WWW site a second or a third time in subsequent months. When a WWW site is managed by an academic institution or a museum, it is usually well maintained and will be updated when new information becomes available.

Tip: To find out when a site was last modified (that is, revised, updated, checked), pull down the View menu in Netscape Navigator. Select Page Info, and read the Last Modified line.

The Internet/World Wide Web

Owing to the ease of using the Internet, with its access to electronic mail (e-mail), newsgroups, mailing lists, and, especially, sites and links on the World Wide Web, many students now make it their first—and, unfortunately, too often their *only*—stop for research.

As we noted a moment ago, all of us must be *critical* users of the materials we find on the WWW. The WWW is up-to-date *and* out-of-date, helpful *and* disappointing. It can be a researcher's dream come true—and a source of errors and a time-waster.

Let's work a bit on the literature and history of the internment by means of the WWW and see what we discover.

Start a search using a popular "search engine," such as Yahoo!, with the search phrase *Japanese and internment*.

- Search engines make use of logical operators, such as *and, or, not, near.* *And* searches the field for any uses of both keywords you have specified.

Or searches for either of the keywords. *Not* enables you to restrict the search—e.g., *minority not European*. *Near* looks for the keywords within a certain range (e.g., ten words) of one another.

These operators can help you to tailor a search, and most search engines accept them and offer other refinements. Placing a phrase in quotations, for instance, means that the search will produce items using that specific phrase, such as "internment of Japanese Americans."

When we did such a search on Yahoo! on July 18, 2001, we received a long list of sites. Some of these sites may turn out to be limited or poorly constructed. By the time you do this search and consult the list for yourself, some of the sites and documents may have disappeared. But if you visit and evaluate the sites on this list, just as you carefully consult "print" resources from the library, you will find that some of them are superb.

The description of the Camp Harmony link on Yahoo!'s list, for example, may lead you to conclude it is too specific, not as promising for your needs as the more general categories, and you might bypass it if you proceed too quickly. But be patient; take the time to do some browsing and exploring, and use more than one search engine, since each one may turn up sites that the others do not. Try also to evaluate the merits of the sites based on the brief descriptions given of them. Yahoo! supplies a summary for its list of sites, and Infoseek includes text from the sites themselves. Take note also of whether the URL includes *.edu* since such sites are likely to be more scholarly than others. You should also evaluate the site when you link to it, and later we will offer some guidelines (see page 1363). But first let's consider what the Camp Harmony site contributes to our research project.

Camp Harmony
http://www.lib.washington.edu/exhibits/harmony/exhibit/

Camp Harmony

In the spring of 1942, just months after the bombing of Pearl Harbor, more than 100,000 residents of Japanese ancestry were forcefully evicted by the army from their homes in Washington, Oregon, California, Arizona and Alaska, and sent to nearby temporary assembly centers. From there they were sent by trains to American-style concentration camps at remote inland sites where many people spent the remainder of the war. This exhibit tells the story of Seattle's Japanese American community in the spring and summer of 1942 and their four-month sojourn at the Puyallup Assembly Center known as "Camp Harmony."

Overview
Bainbridge Island
Round-Up to the Camp
The Camp: Administration & Physical Layout
Civil Liberties
Children: Miss Evanson's Class
Students: Mrs. Willis's Class
The Essentials: Housing & Food
The Rhythm of Life: Work, School and Play
The Cycle of Life: Birth, Marriage & Death
The Move to Minidoka

Photograph of Japanese Americans surrendering cameras and radios in 1942, available via World Wide Web (http://www.lib.washington.edu/exhibits/harmony/Photo/m28030.gif). (Photograph from *Seattle Post-Intelligencer* collection, University of Washington Libraries and the Museum of History and Industry.)

The exhibit is based on materials located in the University of Washington Libraries, including newspapers, photographs, correspondence, books, and documents.

> Camp Harmony Newsletter
> Photographs & Drawings
> Documents

The Overview is a well-written page with an informative map of the relocation centers. The page includes lengthy quotations from primary sources, and the sources are identified with complete bibliographic information. The other links take you to cogently written and organized Web pages, filled with primary sources (books, letters, government reports and documents, etc.—and, again, these are fully documented), as well as photographs, drawings, and maps.

The Camp Harmony site, presented and sponsored by a major university and prepared on a high scholarly level, displays the interdisciplinary enrichment that the WWW can provide. The letters from the University of Washington archives, for example, are moving and suggestive—and they bear upon the themes of parents and children, the nature of camp life, and the relationship of the Japanese and Japanese Americans to the United States that Yamada and Mura explore in their poems.

Here is a section of one letter (the site does not include the author's name) to Elizabeth Bayley Willis, a teacher of art, Latin, and English at Garfield High School

Photograph of a family in an apartment in internment camp, available via World Wide Web (http://www.lib.washington.edu/exhibits/harmony/Image/uw526.jpg). (Photograph by Howard Clifford, *Tacoma News Tribune*. Available in Special Collections and Preservation Division of the University of Washington Libraries.)

in Seattle, whose students described their Cape Harmony experiences in letters written between 1942 and 1943.

> . . . Some of the Isseis volunteered in the last war. They were promised their citizenship to this country. They were promised better treatment.
>
> Now these old folks say, what of us now. Have we got our American citizenship? Are we getting better treatment? What of our businesses? Our children are Americans yet they are being kicked around like dogs—by Americans. The American government made a lot of promises in the last war. It is again making the same promises. The promises of today will be as good as the promises of the last war.
>
> Do you wonder why so many of the first generation feel so bitter, Mrs. Willis?
>
> But that is not all. When we moved into this relocation camp, the camp was still being constructed and many, many families had to share rooms with totally strange families while others lived in recreation buildings with a number of others. The days were hot. The wind blew constantly and dust was always fogging up the rooms. It was impossible to keep rooms free of dust. I remember my mother mopping our room about a half dozen times in one day trying to settle some of the dust. We had no hot

water. Our cold water contained chlorine and the smell and taste were repulsive. Our latrines were outdoor affairs. The men had no partitions (we still haven't). It was cold going to the toilets in sub-zero weather. There was a coal shortage. Rain settled the dust but made the ground so muddy people had to wear boots. In general, people suffered so much unnecessary uncomfortable situations that no one can really blame them for being bitter. . . .

> (Letter dated April 11, 1943. Elizabeth Bayley
> Willis Papers. Box 1. Manuscripts and University
> Archives, UW Libraries)

Here, as elsewhere in the process of research, our quest is for particular kinds of historical knowledge that can illuminate the interpretation of the literary works. The details in this letter about the loyalty that the Issei showed toward the U.S. government, and the betrayal of that loyalty, connect it to one of the central themes in Yamada's "The Question of Loyalty." The letter's emphasis on conflict and disagreement between the generations furnishes a point of comparison not only with Yamada's poem but also with Mura's "An Argument: On 1942." And the vivid details about the conditions of life in this camp are described with a bitterness and anger that the mother in Mura's poem, as she recalls the camp, continues on some level to feel but wants to locate at a distance, in the past, long ago.

In this instance, the WWW turns out to be an excellent resource. Wherever he or she might be, a student can in effect undertake research in the University of Washington's holdings on the internment experience, reading primary and secondary materials, viewing photographs and artworks and making copies of (or downloading) them for papers and presentations.

Many universities have well-designed sites like this one, affiliated with a department or the library, and they offer a wide array of visual materials and texts on all sorts of subjects. Because academic institutions maintain these sites, they are very likely to be scholarly, up-to-date, and reliable in the information they assemble.

After completing a search using Yahoo!, you could conduct the same search through another search engine, which gathers sites from its own pool and allows you to narrow from the initial search results. You can find good material this way, but for the AltaVista search <http://www.altavista.digital.com/> *Japanese and internment,* we found 3,130,961 results.

True, the sites are rated or graded, with the "best" presented first. But your own idea about what's best may not match the rating of the list. You will have to do lots of browsing, or else—the better path—you will need to narrow down and/or experiment with other search words and phrases. By refining and altering the words and phrases for the search, you can make the search more specific and exclude sites not relevant to your direct interest.

- Each search engine has its own forms and criteria; and each has its own categories and indexes. Consult the Help pages for each search engine so that you will perform your search as effectively as possible. A handy guide is Randolph Hock, *The Extreme Searcher's Guide to Web Search Engines,* 2nd ed. (2001).

- It is worth noting once again that Websites are a supplement to print sources, not a substitute for them, and the search tools and bibliographical pathways to print sources are often easier to negotiate than are those for the WWW.
- Keeping this point in mind, we recommend to students that for each WWW site they consult (e.g., the Camp Harmony site), they should consult at least two print sources.

EVALUATING SOURCES ON THE WORLD WIDE WEB

The case study we have presented in this chapter proves the value of integrating literary analysis and historical research. It also shows that for sources on the World Wide Web, as with print sources, you must evaluate what you have located and gauge how much or how little it will contribute to your literary analysis and argument. In the words of one reference librarian, Joan Stockard (formerly of Wellesley College), "The most serious mistake students make when they use the Internet for research is to assume everything is of equal (and acceptable) quality. They need to establish who wrote the material, the qualifications of the author to write on the topic, whether any bias is likely, how current the information is, and how other resources compare."

✔ **CHECKLIST:** *Evaluating Sources on the World Wide Web*

❏ *Focus* the topic of your research as precisely as you can before you embark on a WWW search. Lots of surfing and browsing can sometimes turn up good material, but using the WWW without a focus can prove distracting and unproductive. It takes you away from library research (where the results might be better) and from the actual planning and writing of the paper.

❏ Ask the following questions:
  ❏ Does this site or page look like it can help me in my assignment?
  ❏ Whose site or page is this?
  ❏ What is the intended audience?
  ❏ Can you determine the point of view? Are there signs of a specific slant or bias?
  ❏ What is detail, depth, and quality of the material presented?
  ❏ Is the site well constructed and well organized?
  ❏ Is the text well written?
  ❏ Can this WWW information be corroborated or supported by print sources?
  ❏ When was the site or page made available? Has it been recently revised or updated? *Reminder:* Your browser will enable you to get this information; if you are using Netscape 4.7, for example, go to View, and choose Page Info.
  ❏ Can the person or institution, company, or agency responsible for this site or page receive e-mail comments, questions, criticisms?

DOCUMENTATION: CITING SOURCES ON THE WORLD WIDE WEB

Scholars and reference librarians have not reached a consensus about the correct form—what should be included, and in what order—for the citation of WWW sources. But all agree on two principles: (1) Give as much information as you can; (2) Make certain that your readers can retrieve the source themselves—which means that you should check the URL carefully. For accuracy's sake, it is a good idea to copy the URL from the Location line of your browser and paste it into your list of Works Cited.

✔ CHECKLIST: *Citing Sources on the World Wide Web*

Provide the following information:

- ❑ Author
- ❑ Title
- ❑ Publication information
- ❑ Title of archive or database
- ❑ Date (if given) when the site was posted; sometimes termed the "revision" or "modification" date
- ❑ Name of institution or organization that supports or is associated with this site
- ❑ Date that you accessed this source
- ❑ URL

Many Websites and pages, however, are not prepared according to the style and form in which you want to cite them. Sometimes the name of the author is unknown, and other information may be missing or hard to find as well. It is worth repeating that while you should cite the source, including the URL, accurately, you cannot be certain that the site will exist at this URL (or at all) when your readers attempt to access it for themselves. These difficulties aside, perhaps the main point to remember is that a source on the WWW is as much a source as is a book or article that you can track down and read in the library. If you have made use of it, you must acknowledge that you have done so and include the bibliographical information, as fully as you can, in your list of Works Cited for the paper.

Tips:

1. The Wellesley College Library offers a valuable site for searching the Web and evaluating what you find there:

   http://www.wellesley.edu/Internet/subject.html

2. The Modern Language Association provides its own set of guidelines for citing WWW sources, which you can read by following the "Frequently Asked Questions" link at:

   http://www.mla.org

MLA General Conventions

The MLA recommends these general conventions:

PUBLICATION DATES   For sources taken from the Internet, include the date the source was posted to the Internet or last updated or revised; give also the date the source was accessed.

UNIFORM RESOURCE LOCATORS   Include a full and accurate URL for any source taken from the Internet (with access-mode identifier—**http, ftp, gopher,** or **telnet**). Enclose URLs in angle brackets (<>). When a URL continues from one line to the next, break it only after a slash. Do not add a hyphen.

PAGE NUMBERING   Include page or paragraph numbers when given by the source. When citing electronic sources, follow the formatting conventions illustrated by the following models:

An online scholarly project or database:

> The Walt Whitman Hypertext Archive. Eds. Kenneth M. Price and
>
> Ed Folsom. 16 Mar. 1998. College of William and Mary. 3 Apr.
>
> 1998 <http://jefferson.village.Virginia.edu/whitman/>.

1. Title of project or database
2. Name of the editor of project
3. Electronic publication information
4. Date of access and URL

A short work within a scholarly project:

> Whitman, Walt. "Crossing Brooklyn Ferry." The Walt Whitman
>
> Hypertext Archive. Ed. Kenneth M. Price and Ed Folsom. 16 Mar.
>
> 1998. College of William and Mary. 3 Apr. 1998 <http://jefferson.
>
> village.Virginia. edu/whitman/works/leaves/1891/text/index.html>.

A personal or professional site:

> Winter, Mick. How to Talk New Age. 6 Apr. 1998
>
> <http://www.well.com/ user/mick/newagept.html>.

An online book published independently:

> Smith, Adam. The Wealth of Nations. New York: Methuen, 1904.
>
> 3 Mar. 1998 <http://www.mk.net/~dt/Bibliomania/NonFiction/
>
> Smith/Wealth/index.html>.

1. Author's name
2. Title of the work
3. Name of the editor, compiler, or translator
4. Publication information
5. Date of access and URL

An online book within a scholarly project:

Whitman, Walt. Leaves of Grass. Philadelphia: McKay, 1891–92. The

Walt Whitman Hypertext Archive. Ed. Kenneth M. Price and Ed

Folsom. 16 Mar. 1998. College of William and Mary. 3 Apr.

1998 <http://jefferson.village.Virginia.edu/whitman/works/

leaves/1891/text/title.html>.

1. Author's name
2. Title of the work and print publication information
3. Name of the editor, compiler, or translator (if relevant)
4. Electronic publication information
5. Date of access and URL

An article in a scholarly journal:

Jackson, Francis L. "Mexican Freedom: The Ideal of the Indigenous

State." Animus 2.3 (1997). 4 Apr. 1998

<http://www.mun.ca/animus/1997vol2/jackson2.htm>.

1. Author's name
2. Title of the work or material in quotation marks
3. Name of periodical
4. Volume number, issue number, or other identifying number
5. Date of publication
6. Page numbers or number of paragraphs, pages, or other numbered sections (if any)
7. Date of access and URL

An unsigned article in a newspaper or on a newswire:

"Drug Czar Wants to Sharpen Drug War." TopNews 6 Apr. 1998.

6 Apr. 1998 <http://news.lycos.com/stories/TopNews/

19980406_NEWS-DRUGS.asp>.

A signed article in a newspaper or on a newswire:

Davis, Robert. "Drug may prevent breast cancer." USA Today 6 Apr.

1998. 6 Apr. 1998 <http://www.usatoday.com/news/nds14.htm>.

An article in a magazine:

> Pitta, Julie. "Un-Wired?" Forbes 20 Apr. 1998. 6 Apr. 1998
>
> <http://www.forbes.com/Forbes/98/0420/6108045a.htm>.

A review:

> Beer, Francis A. Rev. of Evolutionary Paradigms in the Social
>
> Sciences, Special Issue, International Studies Quarterly 40,
>
> 3 (Sept. 1996). Journal of Memetics 1 (1997). 4 Jan. 1998
>
> <http://www.cpm.mmu. ac.uk/jom-emit/1997/vol1/beer_fa.html>.

An editorial or letter to the editor:

> "The Net Escape Censorship? Ha!" Editorial. Wired 3.09. 1 Apr. 1998
>
> <http://www.wired.com/wired/3.09/departments/baker.if.html>.

An abstract:

> Maia, Ana Couto. "Prospects for United Nations Peacekeeping: Lessons
>
> from the Congo Experience." MAI 36.2 (1998): 400. Abstract. 6
>
> Apr. 1998 <http://wwwlib.umi.com/dissertations/fullcit?289845>.

A periodical source on CD-ROM, diskette, or magnetic tape:

> Ellis, Richard. "Whale Killing Begins Anew." Audubon [GAUD] 94.6
>
> (1992): 20-22. General Periodicals Ondisc-Magazine Express.
>
> CD-ROM. UMI-Proquest. 1992.

1. Author's name
2. Publication information for analogous printed source (title and date)
3. Title of database
4. Publication medium
5. Name of vendor
6. Date of electronic publication

A nonperiodical source on CD-ROM, diskette, or magnetic tape:

> Clements, John. "War of 1812." Chronology of the United States.
>
> CD-ROM. Dallas: Political Research, Inc. 1997.

1. Author's, editor's, compiler's, or translator's name (if given)
2. Part of work being cited
3. Title of the publication

4. Name of the editor, compiler, or translator (if relevant) of entire volume, if work appears in a collection
5. Publication medium
6. Edition, release, or version
7. Place of publication
8. Name of publisher
9. Date of publication

Electronic mail (e-mail):

Mendez, Michael R. "Re: Solar power." E-mail to Edgar V. Atamian.

11 Sept. 1996.

Armstrong, David J. E-mail to the author. 30 Aug. 1996.

AN ONLINE POSTING   For online postings or synchronous communications, try to cite a version stored as a Web file, if one exists, as a courtesy to the reader. Label sources as needed (e.g., *Online posting, Online defense of dissertation,* and so forth, with neither underlining nor quotation marks). Follow these models as appropriate:

Listserv (electronic mailing lists):

Kosten, A. "Major update of the WWWVL Migration and Ethnic

Relations." 7 Apr. 1998. Online posting. ERCOMER News. 7 May

1998 <http://www.ercomer.org/archive/ercomer-news/0002.html>.

Usenet (a worldwide bulletin board system of newsgroups):

Dorsey, Michael. "Environmentalism or Racism." 25 Mar. 1998.

Online posting. 1 Apr. 1998 <news:alt.org.sierra-club>.

Computer Software:

Gamma UniType for Windows 1.5. Vers. 1.1. San Diego: Gamma

Productions, Inc., 1997.

ADDITIONAL PRINT
AND ELECTRONIC SOURCES

We will conclude this appendix by noting additional print and electronic resources that can aid you in a literary and historical project like the one we have undertaken on the Japanese-American internment.

Search Engines and Directories

All-In-One Search Page:

http://www.albany.net/allinone/
> Gathers together search forms for all search engines.

The Argus Clearinghouse:

http://www.clearinghouse.net
> A directory of subject guides to resources; especially useful for scholars.

Galaxy:

http://www.einet.net/
> Directory for resources in many subjects and fields, including Humanities–Literature.

Libweb: Library WWW Servers:

http://sunsite.Berkeley.edu/Libweb/
> List of 2,000+ home pages of libraries in over seventy countries.

Yahoo!

http://www.yahoo.com/
> A guide by subject to the WWW, with links to other sites and an array of search engines.

Print Directories

The following books include listings of Websites on a wide range of topics; as the titles suggest, some also supply tips and suggestions for effective research. Such books can be great time-savers in identifying for you the names and URLs of sites you can consult for your research. Rather than the hundreds, even thousands, of sites that a search engine might turn up, these books will be much more focused and selective in their listings. Their limitation is that however carefully they have been compiled, they always fall behind the ever-changing nature of the WWW.

> Calishain, Tara. *Official Netscape Guide to Internet Research.* Research Triangle Park, N.C.: Ventana, 1997.

> Clark, Michael. *Cultural Treasures of the Internet.* 2nd ed. Upper Saddle River, N.J.: Prentice Hall, 1997.

> Hahn, Harley. *Harley Hahn's Internet & Web Yellow Pages, 2001 Edition.* Berkeley, Calif.: McGraw-Hill, 2000.

> Krol, Ed, and Bruce C. Klopfenstein. *The Whole Internet User's Guide & Catalog.* Wadsworth, 1996.

> Levine, John R., Carol Baroudi, and Margaret Levine Young. *The Internet for Dummies.* 4th ed. IDGB Books Worldwide, 1997.

Morris, Evan. *The Book Lover's Guide to the Internet.* New York: Fawcett, 1998.

Newquist, H. P., ed. *Yahoo! The Ultimate Desk Reference.* Harper Resource, 2000.

Turner, Marcia Layton, et al., eds. *Que's Official International Internet Directory, 2001 Edition.* Que, 2000.

Stout, Rick. *The World Wide Web Complete Reference.* Berkeley, Calif.: Osborne McGraw-Hill, 1996.

The magazine *Yahoo! Internet Life* reviews and compiles lists of sites on a wide range of subjects. This is a mass-circulation magazine, and many of its listings and reviews will not be pertinent to academic work. But the magazine's editors realize that the WWW is now used often for research, and increasingly they are providing advice and commentary on WWW resources in the humanities and other fields. See also <www.yil.com>.

Print Articles on Literature, History, and the WWW

These expert articles give overviews of WWW (and CD-ROM) resources for research, in particular for literature and history. The authors describe the kinds of material now available and supply bibliographies:

Fanning, Jim. "A-level Research on the Net." *History Review* September 1997.

Gates, Joanne E. "Literature in Electronic Format: The Traditional English and American Canon." *Choice* April 1997: 1279–96.

Juhl, Beth. "Red, White, and Boolean: Electronic Resources for American History." *Choice* April 1998: 1313–26.

New Technologies and the Practice of History. Special issue of *Perspectives: American Historical Association Newsletter* 36:2 (February 1998).

O'Malley, Michael, and Roy Rosenzweig. "Brave New World or Blind Alley?: American History on the World Wide Web." *The Journal of American History* 84:1 (June 1997).

The Web Issue. Special supplement of *Choice* 34 (1997).

See also the following helpful article:

Hogan, W. P. "All Academic: The Guide to Free Academic Resources On-line." *Choice* 38 (2001).

For more detailed coverage, we recommend:

Bracken, James K., and Larry G. Hinman. *The Undergraduate's Companion to American Writers and Their Web Sites.* Englewood, Colo.: Libraries Unlimited, 2001.

Browner, Stephanie, et al., eds. *Literature and the Internet: A Guide for Students, Teachers, and Scholars.* New York: Garland, 2000.

Trinkle, Dennis A., and Scott A. Merriman. *The History Highway 2000: A Guide to Internet Resources.* 2nd ed. Armonk, N.Y.: M. E. Sharpe, 2000.

Evaluating Websites and Materials

The following sites, prepared by research librarians, give excellent advice for evaluating WWW sites and materials they contain.

Evaluating Internet Resources (University at Albany Libraries):

> http://www.albany.edu/library/internet/evaluate.html

Thinking Critically about World Wide Web Resources (UCLA College Library):

> http://www.library.ucla.edu/libraries/college/instruct/critical.htm

Thinking Critically about Discipline-Based World Wide Web Resources (UCLA College Library):

> http://www.library.ucla.edu/libraries/college/instruct/discp.htm

Recommended WWW Site for Scholarly Citation and the Internet/WWW

MLA on the Web:

> http://www.mla.org/
>> Includes a link to a site of guidelines for MLA (Modern Language Association) documentation style, for example, Citing Sources from the World Wide Web.

WHAT DOES YOUR OWN INSTITUTION OFFER?

We'll mention again that many colleges and universities now offer as part of their resources for research a wide range of electronic materials and databases. At Wellesley College, for example, the library offers a detailed list of Research Resources, and there is another listing that is arranged according to department and interdisciplinary program. Some of these are open or free sites, available to anyone with a connection to the WWW. But others are by "subscription only," which means that only members of this academic community can access them.

Sign up for a library tutorial at your own school, and browse in and examine both the library's home page and the online catalog's options and directories.

One of the best research sites, to which many libraries subscribe, is the *FirstSearch* commercial database service. It is available through both a telnet connection (which connects two computers on the Internet) and on the WWW.

FirstSearch enables you to find books, articles, theses, films, computer software, and other types of material for just about any field, subject, or topic.

Its categories include

Arts & Humanities	General Science
Business & Economics	Life Sciences
Conferences & Proceedings	Medicine & Health
Consumer Affairs & People	News & Current Events
Education	Public Affairs & Law
Engineering & Technology	Social Sciences
General & Reference	

Within Arts & Humanities, you will find, for example:

WorldCat: Books and other materials in libraries worldwide.
Article 1st: Index of articles from nearly 12,500 journals.
Contents 1st: Table of contents of nearly 12,500 journals.
A&H Search: Arts & Humanities Search. A citation index.
ArtAbstracts: Leading publications in the world of the arts.
HumanitiesAbs: An index of articles in the humanities.
MLA: Literature, languages, linguistics, folklore.
PerContentsIndx: Periodicals Contents Index, 1961–1991.
RILM: RILM Abstracts of Music Literature.

The General & Reference category includes (this is only a partial list):

BookRevDigst: Reviews of fiction and nonfiction books.
BooksInPrint: R. R. Bowker's *Books in Print*.
Diss: Dissertation Abstracts Online.

Your school may also subscribe to more specialized electronic services and WWW sites for literature and the humanities. For example:

Literature On-Line (Chadwyck-Healey Ltd.). <http://lion.chadwyck.com/>.
> This site offers an extraordinary array of literary databases, reference works, and lists of websites for literature. Also included are "featured" databases; recently, one of these was *LionHeart,* a "fully searchable subset of 1,000 love poems extracted from English, American, and African American poetry, featuring Shakespeare, Keats, Donne, Browning, and others."

Appendix D

Glossary of Literary Terms

The terms briefly defined here are for the most part more fully defined earlier in the text. Hence many of the entries are followed by page references to the earlier discussions.

accent   stress given to a syllable

act   a major division of a play

action   (1) the happenings in a narrative or drama, usually physical events (*B* marries *C*, *D* kills *E*), but also mental changes (*F* moves from innocence to experience); in short, the answer to the question, "What happens?" (2) less commonly, the theme or underlying idea of a work (334)

allegory   a work in which concrete elements (for instance, a pilgrim, a road, a splendid city) stand for abstractions (humanity, life, salvation), usually in an unambiguous, one-to-one relationship. The literal items (the pilgrim, and so on) thus convey a meaning, which is usually moral, religious, or political. To take a nonliterary example: The Statue of Liberty holds a torch (enlightenment, showing the rest of the world the way to freedom), and at her feet are broken chains (tyranny overcome). A caution: Not all of the details in an allegorical work are meant to be interpreted. For example, the hollowness of the Statue of Liberty does not stand for the insubstantiality or emptiness of liberty.

alliteration   repetition of consonant sounds, especially at the beginnings of words (*f*ree, *f*orm, *ph*antom) (501)

allusion   an indirect reference; thus when Lincoln spoke of "a nation dedicated to the proposition that all men are created equal," he was making an allusion to the Declaration of Independence.

ambiguity   multiplicity of meaning, often deliberate, that leaves the reader uncertain about the intended significance

anagnorisis   a recognition or discovery, especially in tragedy—for example, when the hero understands the reason for his or her fall (335)

analysis   an examination, which usually proceeds by separating the object of study into parts (29, 46, 61, 190, 624)

anapest   a metrical foot consisting of two unaccented syllables followed by an accented one. Example, showing three anapests: "As I came / to the edge / of the wood" (498)

anecdote   a short narrative, usually reporting an amusing event in the life of an important person

antagonist   a character or force that opposes (literally, "wrestles") the protagonist (the main character). Thus, in *Hamlet* the antagonist is King Claudius, the protagonist is Hamlet; in *Antigonê,* the antagonist is Creon, the protagonist Antigonê.

antecedent action   happenings (especially in a play) that occurred before the present action (336)

apostrophe   address to an absent figure or to a thing as if it were present and could listen. Example: "O rose, thou art sick!" (481)

approximate rhyme   see *half-rhyme*

archetype   a theme, image, motive, or pattern that occurs so often in literary works it seems to be universal. Examples: a dark forest (for mental confusion), the sun (for illumination)

aside   in the theater, words spoken by a character in the presence of other characters, but directed to the spectators—i.e., understood by the audience to be inaudible to the other characters

assonance   repetition of similar vowel sounds in stressed syllables. Example: *light/bride* (501)

atmosphere   the emotional tone (for instance, joy, or horror) in a work, most often established by the setting (230)

ballad   a short narrative poem, especially one that is sung or recited, often in a stanza of four lines, with 8, 6, 8, 6 syllables, with the second and fourth lines rhyming. A **folk** or **popular ballad** is a narrative song that has been transmitted orally by what used to be called "the folk"; a **literary ballad** is a conscious imitation (without music) of such a work, often with complex symbolism.

blank verse   unrhymed iambic pentameter, that is, unrhymed lines of ten syllables, with every second syllable stressed (503)

cacophony   an unpleasant combination of sounds

caesura   a strong pause within a line of verse (499)

canon   a term originally used to refer to those books accepted as Holy Scripture by the Christian Church. The term has come to be applied to literary works thought to have a special merit by a given culture—for instance, the body of literature traditionally taught in colleges and universities. Such works are sometimes called "classics" and their authors are "major authors." As conceived in the United States until recently, the canon consisted chiefly of works by dead white European and American males—partly, of course, because middle-class and upper-class white males were in fact the people who did most of the writing in the Western Hemisphere, but also because white males (for instance, college professors) were the people who chiefly established the canon. Not surprisingly the canon-makers valued (or valorized or "privileged") writings that revealed, asserted, or reinforced the canon-makers' own values. From about the 1960s feminists and Marxists and others argued that these works had been regarded as central not because they were inherently better than other works but because they reflected the interests of the dominant culture, and that other work, such as slave narratives and the diaries of women, had been "marginalized."

In fact, the literary canon has never been static (in contrast to the biblical canon, which has not changed for more than a thousand years), but it is true that certain authors, such as Homer, Chaucer, and Shakespeare have been permanent fixtures. Why? Partly because they do indeed support the values of those who in large measure control the high cultural purse strings, and perhaps partly because these books are rich enough to invite constant reinterpretation from age to age—that is, to allow each generation to find its needs and its values in them.

catastrophe   the concluding action, especially in a tragedy

catharsis   Aristotle's term for the purgation or purification of the pity and terror supposedly experienced while witnessing a tragedy

character (1) a person in a literary work (Romeo); (2) the personality of such a figure (sentimental lover, or whatever). Characters (in the first sense) are sometimes classified as either "flat" (one-dimensional) or "round" (fully realized, complex).

characterization the presentation of a character, whether by direct description, by showing the character in action, or by the presentation of other characters who help to define each other (338)

cliché an expression that through overuse has ceased to be effective. Examples: *acid test; sigh of relief; the proud possessor*

climax the culmination of a conflict; a turning point, often the point of greatest tension in a plot (336)

comedy a literary work, especially a play, characterized by humor and by a happy ending (333)

comparison and contrast to compare is strictly to note similarities; to contrast is to note differences. But *compare* is now often used for both activities. (192)

complication an entanglement in a narrative or dramatic work that causes a conflict

conflict a struggle between a character and some obstacle (for example, another character or fate) or between internal forces, such as divided loyalties (336)

connotation the associations (suggestions, overtones) of a word or expression. Thus *seventy* and *three score and ten* both mean "one more than sixty-nine," but because *three score and ten* is a biblical expression, it has an association of holiness; see also *denotation*. (481)

consistency building the process engaged in during the act of reading, of reevaluating the details that one has just read in order to make them consistent with the new information that the text is providing (6)

consonance repetition of consonant sounds, especially in stressed syllables. Also called *half-rhyme* or slant rhyme. Example: *arouse/doze* (501)

convention a pattern (for instance, the 14-line poem, or sonnet) or motif (for instance, the bumbling police officer in detective fiction) or other device occurring so often that it is taken for granted. Thus it is a convention that actors in a performance of *Julius Caesar* are understood to be speaking Latin, though in fact they are speaking English. Similarly, the soliloquy (a character alone on the stage speaks his or her thoughts aloud) is a convention, for in real life sane people rarely talk aloud to themselves.

couplet a pair of lines of verse, usually rhyming (501)

crisis a high point in the conflict that leads to the turning point (336)

criticism the analysis or evaluation of a literary work (621)

cultural criticism criticism that sets literature in a social context, often of economics or politics or gender. Borrowing some of the methods of anthropology, cultural criticism usually extends the canon to include popular material—for instance, comic books and soap operas.

dactyl a metrical foot consisting of a stressed syllable followed by two unstressed syllables. Example: *underwear* (498)

deconstruction a critical approach that assumes language is unstable and ambiguous and is therefore inherently contradictory. Because authors cannot control their language, texts reveal more than their authors are aware of. For instance, texts (like such institutions as the law, the churches, and the schools) are likely, when closely scrutinized, to reveal connections to a society's economic system, even though the authors may have believed they were outside of the system. (625)

denotation   the dictionary meaning of a word. Thus *soap opera* and *daytime serial* have the same denotation, but the connotations (associations, emotional overtones) of *soap opera* are less favorable. (481)

dénouement   the resolution or the outcome (literally, the "unknotting") of a plot (336)

deus ex machina   literally, "a god out of a machine"; any unexpected and artificial way of resolving the plot—for example, by introducing a rich uncle, thought to be dead, who arrives on the scene and pays the debts that otherwise would overwhelm the young hero

dialogue   exchange of words between characters; speech

diction   the choice of vocabulary and of sentence structure. There is a difference in diction between "One never knows" and "You never can tell."

didactic   pertaining to teaching; having a moral purpose

dimeter   a line of poetry containing two feet (499)

discovery   see *anagnorisis*

drama   (1) a play; (2) conflict or tension, as in "The story lacks drama."

dramatic irony   see *irony*

dramatic monologue   a poem spoken entirely by one character but addressed to one or more other characters whose presence is strongly felt

effaced narrator   a narrator who reports but who does not editorialize or enter into the minds of any of the characters in the story

elegy   a lyric poem, usually a meditation on a death

elision   omission (usually of a vowel or unstressed syllable), as in *o'er* (for *over*) and in "Th' inevitable hour".

end rhyme   identical sounds at the ends of lines of poetry (500)

end-stopped line   a line of poetry that ends with a pause (usually marked by a comma, semicolon, or period) because the grammatical structure and the sense reach (at least to some degree) completion. It is contrasted with a *run-on line*. (499)

English (or Shakespearean) sonnet   a poem of 14 lines (three quatrains and a couplet), rhyming *ababcdcdefefgg* (502)

enjambment   a line of poetry in which the grammatical and logical sense run on, without pause, into the next line or lines (500)

epic   a long narrative, especially in verse, that usually records heroic material in an elevated style

epigram   a brief, witty poem or saying

epigraph   a quotation at the beginning of the work, just after the title, often giving a clue to the theme

epiphany   a "showing forth," as when an action reveals a character with particular clarity

episode   an incident or scene that has unity in itself but is also a part of a larger action

epistle   a letter, in prose or verse

essay   a work, usually in prose and usually fairly short, that purports to be true and that treats its subject tentatively. In most literary essays the reader's interest is as much in the speaker's personality as in any argument that is offered. (207)

euphony   literally, "good sound," a pleasant combination of sounds

explication   a line-by-line unfolding of the meaning of a text (46, 624)

exposition   a setting forth of information. In fiction and drama, introductory material introducing characters and the situation; in an essay, the presentation of information, as opposed to the telling of a story or the setting forth of an argument. (336)

eye rhyme   words that look as though they rhyme, but do not rhyme when pronounced. Example: *come/home* (500)

fable   a short story (often involving speaking animals) with an easily grasped moral (1235)

farce   comedy based not on clever language or on subtleties of characters but on broadly humorous situations (for instance, a man mistakenly enters the women's locker room)

feminine rhyme   a rhyme of two or more syllables, with the stress falling on a syllable other than the last. Examples: *fatter/batter; tenderly/slenderly* (500)

feminist criticism   an approach especially concerned with analyzing the depiction of women in literature—what images do male authors present of female characters?—and also with the reappraisal of work by female authors (630)

fiction   an imaginative work, usually a prose narrative (novel, short story), that reports incidents that did not in fact occur. The term may include all works that invent a world, such as a lyric poem or a play.

figurative language   words intended to be understood in a way that is other than literal. Thus *lemon* used literally refers to a citrus fruit, but *lemon* used figuratively refers to a defective machine, especially a defective automobile. Other examples: "He's a beast." "She's a witch." "A sea of troubles." Literally, such expressions are nonsense, but writers use them to express meanings inexpressible in literal speech. Among the most common kinds of figures of speech are *apostrophe, metaphor,* and *simile* (see the discussions of these words in this glossary).

flashback   an interruption in a narrative that presents an earlier episode

flat character   a one-dimensional character (for instance, the figure who is only and always the jealous husband or the flirtatious wife) as opposed to a round or many-sided character (228)

fly-on-the-wall narrator   a narrator who never editorializes and never enters a character's mind but reports only what is said and done (233)

foil   a character who makes a contrast with another, especially a minor character who helps to set off a major character (339)

foot   a metrical unit, consisting of two or three syllables, with a specified arrangement of the stressed syllable or syllables. Thus the iambic foot consists of an unstressed syllable followed by a stressed syllable. (498)

foreshadowing   suggestions of what is to come (229, 336)

formalist criticism   analysis that assumes a work of art is a constructed object with a stable meaning that can be ascertained by studying the relationships between the elements of the work. Thus a poem is like a chair: a chair *can* of course be stood on, or used for firewood, but it was created with a specific purpose that was evident and remains evident to all viewers. (623)

free verse   poetry in lines of irregular length, usually unrhymed (503)

gap   a term from reader-response criticism, referring to a reader's perception that something is unstated in the text, requiring the reader to fill in the material—for instance, to draw a conclusion as to why a character behaves as she does. Filling in the gaps is a matter of "consistency building." Different readers of course may fill the gaps differently, and readers may even differ as to whether a gap exists at a particular point in the text. (5)

gay criticism   see *gender criticism*

gender criticism   criticism concerned especially with alleged differences in the ways that males and females read and write, and with the representations of gender (straight, bisexual, gay, lesbian) in literature (630)

genre   kind or type, roughly analogous to the biological term *species*. The four chief literary genres are nonfiction, fiction, poetry, and drama; but these can be subdivided into further genres. Thus fiction obviously can be divided into the short story and the novel, and drama obviously can be divided into tragedy and comedy. But these can be still further divided—for instance, tragedy into heroic tragedy and bourgeois tragedy, comedy into romantic comedy and satirical comedy.

gesture   physical movement, especially in a play (337)

haiku   a Japanese form having three unrhymed lines of five, seven, and five syllables (514)

half-rhyme   repetition in accented syllables of the final consonant sound but without identity in the preceding vowel sound; words of similar but not identical sound. Also called near rhyme, slant rhyme, approximate rhyme, and off-rhyme. See also *consonance*. Examples: *light/bet; affirm/perform* (500)

hamartia   a flaw in the tragic hero, or an error made by the tragic hero (334)

heptameter   a metrical line of seven feet (499)

hero, heroine   the main character (not necessarily heroic or even admirable) in a work: cf. *protagonist*

heroic couplet   an end-stopped pair of rhyming lines of iambic pentameter (501)

hexameter   a metrical line of six feet (499)

historical criticism   the attempt to illuminate a literary work by placing it in its historical context (627)

hubris, hybris   a Greek word, usually translated as "overweening pride," "arrogance," "excessive ambition," and often said to be characteristic of tragic figures (333)

hyperbole   figurative language using overstatement, as in "He died a thousand deaths" (487)

iamb, iambic   a poetic foot consisting of an unaccented syllable followed by an accented one. Example: *alone* (498)

image, imagery   imagery is established by language that appeals to the senses, especially sight ("deep blue sea") but also other senses ("tinkling bells," "perfumes of Arabia")

indeterminacy   a passage that careful readers agree is open to more than one interpretation. According to some poststructural critics, because language is unstable and because contexts can never be objectively viewed, all texts are indeterminate. (5)

innocent eye   a naive narrator in whose narration the reader sees more than the narrator sees

internal rhyme   rhyme within a line (501)

interpretation   the assignment of meaning to a text (583)

intertextuality   all works show the influence of other works. If an author writes (say) a short story, no matter how original she thinks she is, she inevitably brings to her own story a knowledge of other stories—for example, a conception of what a short story is; and speaking more generally, an idea of what a story (long or short, written or oral) is. In opposition to formalist critics, who see a literary work as an independent whole containing a fixed meaning, some contemporary critics emphasize the work's *intertextuality*—that is, its connections with a vast context of writings and indeed of all aspects of culture, and in part depending also on what the reader brings to the work. Because different readers bring different things, meaning is thus ever-changing. In this view, then, no text is self-sufficient, and no writer fully controls the meaning of the text. Because we are talking about connections of which the writer is unaware, and because "meaning" is in part the creation of the reader, the author is by no means an authority. Thus the critic should see a novel (for instance) in connection not only with other novels, past and present, but also in connection with other kinds of narratives, such as TV dramas and films, even though the author of the book lived before the age of film and TV. See Jay Clayton and Eric Rothstein, eds., *Influences and Intertextuality in Literary History* (1991).

irony   a contrast of some sort. For instance, in **verbal irony** or **Socratic irony** (487), the contrast is between what is said and what is meant ("You're a great guy," meant bitterly). In **dramatic irony** or **Sophoclean irony**—also called **tragic irony**—(334), the contrast is between what is intended and what is accomplished (Macbeth usurps the throne, thinking he will then be happy, but the action leads him to misery), or between what the audience knows (a murderer waits in the bedroom) and what a character says (the victim enters the bedroom, innocently saying, "I think I'll have a long sleep"). (333)

Italian (or Petrarchan) sonnet   a poem of 14 lines, consisting of an octave (rhyming *abbaabba*) and a sestet (usually *cdecde* or *cdccdc*) (502)

lesbian criticism   see *gender criticism*

litotes   a form of understatement in which an affirmation is made by means of a negation; thus "He was not underweight," meaning "He was grossly overweight."

lyric poem   a short poem, often songlike, with the emphasis not on narrative but on the speaker's emotion or reverie

Marxist criticism   the study of literature in the light of Karl Marx's view that economic forces, controlled by the dominant class, shape the literature (as well as the law, philosophy, religion, etc.) of a society (628)

masculine rhyme   rhyme of one-syllable words (*lies/cries*) or, if more than one syllable, words ending with accented syllables (*behold/foretold*) (500)

mask   a term used to designate the speaker of a poem, equivalent to *persona* or *voice* (473)

meaning   critics seek to interpret "meaning," variously defined as what the writer intended the work to say about the world and human experience, or as what the work says to the reader irrespective of the writer's intention. Both versions imply that a literary work is a nut to be cracked, with a kernel that is to be extracted. Because few critics today hold that meaning is clear and unchanging, the tendency now is to say that a critic offers "an interpretation" or "a reading" rather than a "statement of the meaning of a work." Many critics today would say that an alleged interpretation is really a creation of meaning.

melodrama   a narrative, usually in dramatic form, involving threatening situations but ending happily. The characters are usually stock figures (virtuous heroine, villainous landlord).

metaphor   a kind of figurative language equating one thing with another: "This novel is garbage" (a book is equated with discarded and probably inedible food), "a piercing cry" (a cry is equated with a spear or other sharp instrument) (480)

meter   a pattern of stressed and unstressed syllables (498)

metonymy   a kind of figurative language in which a word or phrase stands not for itself but for something closely related to it: *saber rattling* means "militaristic talk or action" (481)

monologue   a relatively long, uninterrupted speech by a character

monometer   a metrical line consisting of only one foot (499)

montage   in film, quick cutting; in fiction, quick shifts (313)

mood   the atmosphere, usually created by descriptions of the settings and characters

motif   a recurrent theme within a work, or a theme common to many works

motivation   grounds for a character's action (228, 339)

myth   (1) a traditional story reflecting primitive beliefs, especially explaining the mysteries of the natural world (why it rains, or the origin of mountains); (2) a body of belief, not necessarily false, especially as set forth by a writer. Thus one may speak of Yeats and Alice Walker as myth-makers, referring to the visions of reality that they set forth in their works.

myth criticism   see *archetype*

narrative, narrator   a narrative is a story (an anecdote, a novel); a narrator is one who tells a story (not the author, but the invented speaker of the story). On kinds of narrators, see *point of view*. (208)

New Criticism   a mid-twentieth-century movement (also called formalist criticism) that regarded a literary work as an independent, carefully constructed object; hence it made little or no use of the author's biography or of historical context, and it relied chiefly on explication. (624)

New Historicism   a school of criticism holding that the past cannot be known objectively. According to this view, because historians project their own "narrative"—their own invention or "construction"—on the happenings of the past, historical writings are not objective but are, at bottom, political statements. (629)

novel   a long work of prose fiction, especially one that is relatively realistic

novella   a work of prose fiction longer than a short story but shorter than a novel—say, about 40 to 80 pages

objective point of view   a narrator reports but does not editorialize or enter into the minds of any of the characters in the story (233)

octave, octet   an eight-line stanza, or the first eight lines of a sonnet, especially of an Italian sonnet (502)

octosyllabic couplet   a pair of rhyming lines, each line with four iambic feet (501)

ode   a lyric exalting someone (for instance, a hero) or something (for instance, a season)

off-rhyme   see *half-rhyme*

omniscient narrator   a speaker who knows the thoughts of all of the characters in the narrative (233)

onomatopoeia   words (or the use of words) that sound like what they mean. Examples: *buzz; whirr* (501)

open form   poetry whose form seems spontaneous rather than highly patterned

oxymoron   a compact paradox, as in *a mute cry; a pleasing pain; proud humility*

parable   a short narrative that is at least in part allegorical and that illustrates a moral or spiritual lesson (66, 1235)

paradox   an apparent contradiction, as in Jesus's words "Whosoever will save his life shall lose it; but whosoever will lose his life for my sake, the same shall save it." (487)

paraphrase   a restatement that sets forth an idea in diction other than that of the original (43, 131)

parody   a humorous imitation of a literary work, especially of its style (143)

pathos   pity, sadness

pentameter   a line of verse containing five feet (499)

peripeteia   a reversal in the action (334)

persona   literally, a mask; the "I" or speaker of a work, sometimes identified with the author but usually better regarded as the voice or mouthpiece created by the author (473)

personification   a kind of figurative language in which an inanimate object, animal, or other nonhuman is given human traits. Examples: *the creeping tide* (the tide is imagined as having feet); *the cruel sea* (the sea is imagined as having moral qualities) (481)

Petrarchan sonnet   see *Italian sonnet*

plot   the episodes in a narrative or dramatic work—that is, what happens. (But even a lyric poem can be said to have a plot; for instance, the speaker's mood changes from anger to resignation.) Sometimes *plot* is defined as the author's particular arrangement (sequence) of these episodes, and *story* is the episodes in their chronological sequence. Until recently it was widely believed that a good plot had a logical structure: *A* caused *B* (*B* did not simply happen to follow *A*), but in the last few decades some critics have argued that such a concept merely represents the white male's view of experience. (228, 336)

poem   an imaginative work in meter or in free verse, usually employing figurative language

point of view   the perspective from which a story is told—for example, by a major character or a minor character or a fly on the wall; see also *narrative, narrator, omniscient narrator*

postmodernism   the term came into prominence in the 1960s, to distinguish the contemporary experimental writing of such authors as Samuel Beckett and Jorge Luis Borges from such early twentieth-century classics of modernism as James Joyce's *Ulysses* (1922) and T. S. Eliot's *The Waste Land* (1922). Although the classic modernists had been thought to be revolutionary in their day, after World War II they seemed to be conservative, and their works seemed remote from today's society with its new interests in such things as feminism, gay and lesbian rights, and pop culture. Postmodernist literature, though widely varied and not always clearly distinct from modernist literature, usually is more politically concerned, more playful—it is given to parody and pastiche—and more closely related to the art forms of popular culture than is modernist literature.

prosody   the principles of versification (497)

protagonist   the chief actor in any literary work. The term is usually preferable to *hero* and *heroine* because it can include characters—for example, villainous or weak ones—who are not aptly called heroes or heroines.

psychological criticism   a form of analysis especially concerned both with the ways in which authors unconsciously leave traces of their inner lives in their works and with the ways in which readers respond, consciously and unconsciously, to works (629)

pyrrhic foot   in poetry, a foot consisting of two unstressed syllables (499)

quatrain   a stanza of four lines (502)

reader-response criticism   criticism emphasizing the idea that various readers respond in various ways and therefore that readers as well as authors "create" meaning (626)

realism   presentation of plausible characters (usually middle class) in plausible (usually everyday) circumstances, as opposed, for example, to heroic characters engaged in improbable adventures. Realism in literature seeks to give the illusion of reality.

recognition   see *anagnorisis*

refrain   a repeated phrase, line, or group of lines in a poem, especially in a ballad

resolution   the dénouement or untying of the complication of the plot

reversal   a change in fortune, often an ironic twist (334)

rhetorical question   a question to which no answer is expected or to which only one answer is plausible. Example: "Do you think I am unaware of your goings-on?"

rhyme   similarity or identity of accented sounds in corresponding positions, as, for example, at the ends of lines: *love/dove; tender/slender* (500)

rhythm   in poetry, a pattern of stressed and unstressed sounds; in prose, some sort of recurrence (for example, of a motif) at approximately identical intervals (496, 500)

rising action   in a story or play, the events that lead up to the *climax* (336)

rising meter   a foot (for example, iambic or anapestic) ending with a stressed syllable

romance   narrative fiction, usually characterized by improbable adventures and love

round character   a many-sided character, one who does not always act predictably, as opposed to a "flat" or one-dimensional, unchanging character (228)

run-on line   a line of verse whose syntax and meaning require the reader to go on, without a pause, to the next line; an *enjambed* line (499)

sarcasm   crudely mocking or contemptuous language; heavy verbal irony

satire   literature that entertainingly attacks folly or vice; amusingly abusive writing

scansion   description of rhythm in poetry: metrical analysis (499)

scene   (1) a unit of a play, in which the setting is unchanged and the time continuous; (2) the setting (locale, and time of the action); (3) in fiction, a dramatic passage, as opposed to a passage of description or of summary

selective omniscience   a point of view in which the author enters the mind of one character and for the most part sees the other characters only from the outside (233)

sentimentality   excessive emotion, especially excessive pity, treated as appropriate rather than as disproportionate

sestet   a six-line stanza, or the last six lines of an Italian sonnet (502)

sestina   a poem with six stanzas of six lines each and a concluding stanza of three lines. The last word of each line in the first stanza appears as the last word of a line in each of the next five stanzas but in a different order. In the final (three-line) stanza, each line ends with one of these six words, and each line includes in the middle of the line one of the other three words.

setting   the time and place of a story, play, or poem (for instance, a Texas town in winter, about 1900) (230)

Shakespearean sonnet   see *English sonnet*

short story a fictional narrative, usually in prose, rarely longer than 30 pages and often much briefer

simile a kind of figurative language explicitly making a comparison—for example, by using *as, like,* or a verb such as *seems* (480)

soliloquy a speech in a play, in which a character alone on the stage speaks his or her thoughts aloud

sonnet a lyric poem of 14 lines; see *English sonnet, Italian sonnet* (502)

speaker see *persona* (473)

spondee a metrical foot consisting of two stressed syllables (499)

stage direction a playwright's indication to the actors or readers—for example, offering information about how an actor is to speak a line

stanza a group of lines forming a unit that is repeated in a poem (487)

stereotype a simplified conception, especially an oversimplification—for example, a stock character such as the heartless landlord, the kindly old teacher, the prostitute with a heart of gold. Such a character usually has only one personality trait, and this is boldly exaggerated.

stream of consciousness the presentation of a character's unrestricted flow of thought, often with free associations, and often without punctuation (233)

stress relative emphasis on one syllable as compared with another (498)

structuralism a critical theory holding that a literary work consists of conventional elements that, taken together by a reader familiar with the conventions, give the work its meaning. Thus just as a spectator must know the rules of a game (e.g., three strikes and you're out) in order to enjoy the game, so a reader must know the rules of, say, a novel (coherent, realistic, adequately motivated characters, a plausible plot—for instance, *The Color Purple*) or of a satire (caricatures of contemptible figures in amusing situations that need not be at all plausible—for instance, *Gulliver's Travels*). Structuralists normally have no interest in the origins of a work (i.e., in the historical background, or in the author's biography), and no interest in the degree to which a work of art seems to correspond to reality. The interest normally is in the work as a self-sufficient construction. Consult Robert Scholes, *Structuralism in Literature: An Introduction,* and two books by Jonathan Culler, *Structuralist Poetics* (1976) and (for the critical shift from structuralism to poststructuralism) *On Deconstruction* (1982).

structure the organization of a work, the relationship between the chief parts, the large-scale pattern—for instance, a rising action or complication followed by a crisis and then a resolution (487)

style the manner of expression, evident not only in the choice of certain words (for instance, colloquial language) but also in the choice of certain kinds of sentence structure, characters, settings, and themes

subplot a sequence of events often paralleling or in some way resembling the main story

summary a synopsis or condensation

symbol a person, object, action, or situation that, charged with meaning, suggests another thing (for example, a dark forest may suggest confusion, or perhaps evil), though usually with less specificity and more ambiguity than an allegory. A symbol usually differs from a metaphor in that a symbol is expanded or repeated and works by accumulating associations.

synecdoche a kind of figurative language in which the whole stands for a part (*the law,* for a police officer), or a part (*all hands on deck,* for all persons) stands for the whole (481)

tale a short narrative, usually less realistic and more romantic than a short story; a yarn

tercet see *triplet*

tetrameter a verse line of four feet (499)

theme what the work is about; an underlying idea of a work; a conception of human experience suggested by the concrete details. Thus the theme of *Macbeth* is often said to be that "vaulting ambition o'erleaps itself." (234, 334)

thesis the point or argument that a writer announces and develops. A thesis differs from a *topic* by making an assertion. "The fall of Oedipus" is a topic, but "Oedipus falls because he is impetuous" is a thesis, as is "Oedipus is impetuous, but his impetuosity has nothing to do with his fall." (20, 76, 190)

thesis sentence a sentence summarizing, as specifically as possible, the writer's chief point (argument and perhaps purpose) (20, 215)

third-person narrator the teller of a story who does not participate in the happenings (232)

tone the prevailing attitude (for instance, ironic, genial, objective) as perceived by the reader. Notice that a reader may feel that the tone of the persona of the work is genial while the tone of the author of the same work is ironic.

topic a subject, such as "Hamlet's relation to Horatio." A topic becomes a *thesis* when a predicate is added to this subject, thus: "Hamlet's relation to Horatio helps to define Hamlet."

tragedy a serious play showing the protagonist moving from good fortune to bad and ending in death or a deathlike state (333)

tragic flaw a supposed weakness (for example, arrogance) in the tragic protagonist. If the tragedy results from an intellectual error rather than from a moral weakness, it is better to speak of "a tragic error." (334)

tragicomedy a mixture of tragedy and comedy, usually a play with serious happenings that expose the characters to the threat of death but that ends happily

transition a connection between one passage and the next (88, 312)

trimeter a verse line with three feet (499)

triplet a group of three lines of verse, usually rhyming (502)

trochee a metrical foot consisting of a stressed syllable followed by an unstressed syllable. Example: *garden* (498)

understatement a figure of speech in which the speaker says less than what he or she means; an ironic minimizing, as in "You've done fairly well for yourself" said to the winner of a multimillion-dollar lottery (487)

unity harmony and coherence of parts, absence of irrelevance (24)

unreliable narrator a narrator whose report a reader cannot accept at face value, perhaps because the narrator is naive or is too deeply implicated in the action to report it objectively (233)

verbal irony see *irony* (487)

verse (1) a line of poetry; (2) a stanza of a poem (501)

vers libre free verse, unrhymed poetry (503)

villanelle a poem with five stanzas of three lines rhyming *aba,* and a concluding stanza of four lines, rhyming *abaa.* The entire first line is repeated as the third line of the second and fourth stanzas; the entire third line is repeated as the third line of the third and fifth stanzas. These two lines form the final two lines of the last (four-line) stanza.

voice see *persona, style,* and *tone* (208, 473)

Literary Credits

Photo Credits

Index of Authors, Titles, and First Lines of Poems

Index of Terms